*The Works of Robert Browning*

# The Works of
# Robert Browning

With an Introduction and Bibliography by

DR TIM COOK

## Wordsworth Poetry Library

For my husband
**ANTHONY JOHN RANSON**
with love from your wife, the publisher.
Eternally grateful for your unconditional love.

Readers who are interested in other titles from
Wordsworth Editions are invited to visit our website at
www.wordsworth-editions.com

For our latest list and a full mail-order service, contact
Bibliophile Books, 5 Datapoint, South Crescent, London E16 4TL
TEL: +44 (0)20 7474 2474  FAX: +44 (0)20 7474 8589
ORDERS: orders@bibliophilebooks.com
WEBSITE: www.bibliophilebooks.com

First published in 1994 by Wordsworth Editions Limited
8B East Street, Ware, Hertfordshire SG12 9HJ
Reset in 2007

ISBN   978 1 85326 418 4

Text © Wordsworth Editions Limited 1994

Wordsworth® is a registered trade mark of
Wordsworth Editions Limited

Wordsworth Editions
is the company founded in 1987 by
**MICHAEL TRAYLER**

Typeset in Great Britain by Antony Gray
Printed and bound by Clays Ltd, St Ives plc

# INTRODUCTION

From the Renaissance onwards there have been two opposed traditions in English poetry, one ornate and mellifluous, represented by poets such as Spenser, and another, plainer, more colloquial and argumentative, less obviously musical, found in the works of Wyatt and Donne. In the Victorian period the champions of each tradition were Tennyson, whose brooding melancholy and ability to turn out effortlessly melodious verses made him fit everyone's idea of a poet, and Browning, whose verse is often awkward in expression and highly intellectual in content. For him, as he shows us in 'How It Strikes a Contemporary', the poet should be a modest but sharply perceptive observer of his fellow men, someone of whose ultimate value we are left in no doubt, but who may pass through life totally unnoticed.

John Donne's argumentative poems, in which the speaker projects his strong personality as a lover in different dramatic contexts, probably suggested to Browning the poetic form for which he is most famous, the 'dramatic monologue'. In his poems of this kind, he imagines himself into a great variety of characters and situations, designed to reveal individual human beings in all their complexity, often at some important moment in their lives. Through what they say, as well as what they leave unsaid, we are led, in a short space of time, to know them, to understand them and maybe to make a moral judgement on them.

The range of characters portrayed by Browning in his dramatic monologues is huge and often drawn from the world of the Italian Renaissance. They include such creations as the Duke in 'My Last Duchess', whose almost insane possessiveness has led him, we realise as he speaks, to have his deeply lovable and charming wife murdered, and the hedonistic artist Fra Lippo Lippi, who has become a monk through circumstances beyond his control. He has been unable to keep his vows, and yet is, we feel, more admirable both in person and in his art than Andrea del Sarto, the speaker in a companion poem, a temporary commercial success but artistic and moral failure, who has subordinated his art to the demands of an exploitative wife.

In 'Soliloquy in the Spanish Cloister' as in 'My Last Duchess' we see a good-hearted person, an envied fellow monk in this case, through the eyes of an unpleasant one, whereas in 'Caliban upon Setebos' we are given a view of the 'monster' from Shakespeare's *Tempest* very different from that of Prospero or perhaps the play's less discriminating audiences.

These last two poems are good examples of Browning's adventurousness in experimenting with words, since he creates for each speaker a highly individual linguistic personality. This may sometimes produce harsh and contorted effects, dislocations of syntax and odd rhymes, as though the poet is finding words inadequate to express the complexity of the thoughts involved, and it can make him hard to understand. Some of his love poems published in his 1855 collection *Men and Women,* fall into this category.

These poems explore his feelings for his wife, the poet Elizabeth Barrett, after their famous elopement from her tyrannical father. They are unlike any other love poems in the depth of their analysis of a relationship and the way they confront its difficulties. Though he could match his master Donne in exploring the concept of spiritual unity between two people in a love relationship, as in 'By the Fireside', Browning's poems can also deal in a very 'modern' way, sometimes from a woman's point of view, with a sense of 'otherness', the feeling that we can never quite bridge the gap between ourselves and the people we love, especially those of the other sex.

Browning is also a master of mood, and changes of mood. In 'A Toccata of Galuppi's', where the speaker is listening to a piece of early music, we see his feelings gradually change as the thought of the dead Venetians who once enjoyed it brings home to him his own mortality. A mood change of a different kind is apparent in 'Up at a Villa – Down in the City', in which Browning reverses the traditional poetic preference for country over city life. Both these poems are set in the Italy which Browning so loved, where he and Elizabeth lived on a legacy left by a friend after their flight.

In 'By the Fireside' he sees his rescue of Elizabeth from her domestic imprisonment as the action that most of all expressed his character. He was interested in portraying his fictional creations at the moment when they were about to perform, or else to shrink from, such a defining action. In his extraordinary symbolic poem 'Childe Roland to the Dark Tower Came', a work inspired, like 'Caliban upon Setebos', by Shakespeare, he shows a hero at just such a moment standing alone in a hostile and macabre landscape and remembering the failures and disgraces of his predecessors before he sounds a challenge to an unknown and fearful enemy.

Childe Roland rises to his defined task, but in another poem 'The Statue and the Bust' we see a couple who let the moment slip away when they could have ensured their future happiness by eloping, like Browning and Elizabeth

Barrett themselves. Andrea del Sarto's artistic timidity is similarly, we feel, condemned. On the other hand, people who can seem pedantic and unglamorous to the outside world yet dedicate themselves selflessly to their work, like the obscure philologist celebrated in 'A Grammarian's Funeral', are presented as true heroes.

Browning was writing at a time when scientific advances in the work of Darwin and others were calling into question the basis of Christian belief. His contemporary Tennyson responded to this in poems like 'In Memoriam', in which he struggled to retain his faith, but which is infused with pessimistic melancholy and doubt despite its up-beat ending. Browning expresses, through characters such as the worldly Victorian cleric in 'Bishop Blougram's Apology', the doubts that any intellectual had to feel. However, in the end, Blougram comes optimistically if uncertainly down on the side of faith, helped by momentary intuitions of the divine that parallel the brief visions of God experienced, as he extemporises on his organ, by another of Browning's creations, the musician Abt Vogler in the poem of the same name.

In 'The Strange Experience of Karshish … ', Browning takes us back to the time of Christ and adopts the persona of a doctor who, encountering Lazarus long after his restoration to life, hears about Christ and his death as he goes about his work of collecting medicinal herbs and is haunted by the story. One feels that Browning's own personal history as a rescuer made the gospel account of the Redeemer so profoundly attractive to him that it was psychologically impossible for him to reject it. In another poem the philosopher Cleon, who is attracted imaginatively to Christianity but cannot rationally accept it, comes across as a moral failure.

On the other hand Browning was a great admirer of the poetry and the revolutionary rhetoric of the acknowledged atheist Shelley. His reverence for Shelley is powerfully expressed in the short lyric 'Memorabilia', and to the end of his life he remained someone who could not conform to the oppressive mores of Victorian society. His feelings about the once radical Wordsworth who joined the Establishment by accepting the Poet Laureateship are clear in the passionately written 'The Lost Leader'.

To modern readers, Browning's portrayal of women may sometimes seem problematic. His attitude, although he often shows his indignation at men who treat them as objects to possess, rather than as human beings, like the Duke in 'My Last Duchess' and the even more certainly insane stranger in 'Porphyria's Lover', can come across as one of slightly patronising protectiveness. Even though the speaker in 'A Pretty Woman' need not be identified with Browning himself and may be deliberately suspect, its tone can make a reader uneasy.

This feeling could be seen to lie beneath the surface even of his tender love-poems to his wife, despite his admiration for her poetry. However she was, of course, a frail invalid, and one can see Browning's 'robustness', to use the word applied to his work by George Eliot, coming out in his desire to shelter and defend her. His devastating satire on spiritualism, 'Mr Sludge the Medium', is his vigorous verbal revenge for what he saw as confidence tricks performed on her credulity.

Browning's earliest works besides the moderately successful play *Strafford* included the long philosophical poems 'Paracelsus' and 'Sordello', whose tortuous arguments, especially in the case of the second, made them seem alien and impenetrable to nineteenth-century readers. Many of the poems produced after Elizabeth's death in 1861 can also seem inordinately lengthy for their intellectual content, though modern scholars find redeeming features in most of them. Sadly, his psychological masterpiece *The Ring and The Book,* which considers a Renaissance murder from the points of view of many people involved with it, is too vast to be included in this volume, but is well worth making the effort to explore.

Generally, it is through the dramatic monologues in the volumes of his middle period that Browning is most likely to appeal to today's readers. A number of these are in blank verse, of which he was one of the greatest masters since Shakespeare. However, he also experiments a great deal with different stanza forms, both in his dramatic monologues and in a variety of moving or stirring lyrics. Many of these are addressed to Elizabeth, both during her life and posthumously, including several in *Asolando,* his swansong.

Years before the poet's death in 1889 his creation Rabbi Ben Ezra, reflecting on the meaning and value of human lives, had compared a life to a piece of pottery on a wheel controlled by God, which could only be valued once the completing rim had been finished. In the final poems in *Asolando,* one feels that Browning is looking back over his entire life's work and the love that gave it meaning and consciously putting the finishing touches to it as, like Childe Roland, he faces death alone.

*Dr Tim Cook*
*Kingston University*

## SUGGESTED FURTHER READING

W. C. De Vane, *A Browning Handbook*, John Murray, 1955

Robert Langbaum, *The Poetry of Experience*, Chatto, 1957 (new edition, 1972)

Ian Jack, *Browning's Major Poetry*, Oxford University Press, 1973

C. de L. Ryals, *The Life of Robert Browning,* Blackwell, USA, 1993

J. Bristow, *Robert Browning,* Harvester, 1991

## DEDICATION TO THE THREE VOLUMES OF 1863

I dedicate these volumes to my old friend John Forester, glad and grateful that he, who from the first publication of the various poems they include has been their promptest and staunchest helper, should seem even nearer to me now than almost thirty years ago.

*R. B.*
*London, April 21, 1863*

## AUTHOR'S PREFACE TO EDITION OF 1868

The poems that follow are printed in the order of their publication. The first piece in the series I acknowledge and retain with extreme repugnance, indeed purely of necessity; for not long ago I inspected a transcript, and am certified of the existence of others, intended sooner or later to be published abroad: by forestalling these, I can at least correct some misprints (no syllable is changed) and introduce a boyish work by an exculpatory word. The thing was my earliest attempt at 'poetry always dramatic in principle, and so many utterances of so many imaginary persons, not mine', which I have since written according to a scheme less extravagant and scale less impracticable than were ventured upon in this crude preliminary sketch – a sketch that, on reviewal, appears not altogether wide of some hint of the characteristic features of that particular *dramatis persona* it would fain have reproduced: good draughtsmanship, however, and right handling were far beyond the artist at that time.

R. B.
*London, December 25, 1867*

## AUTHOR'S PREFACE TO EDITION OF 1888

I preserve, in order to supplement it, the foregoing preface. I had thought, when compelled to include in my collected works the poem to which it refers, that the honest course would be to reprint, and leave mere literary errors unaltered. Twenty years' endurance of an eyesore seems more than sufficient: my faults remain duly recorded against me, and I claim permission to somewhat diminish these, so far as style is concerned, in the present and final edition where 'Pauline' must needs, first of my performances, confront the reader. I have simply removed solecisms, mended the metre a little, and endeavoured to strengthen the phraseology – experience helping, in some degree, the helplessness of juvenile haste and heat in their untried adventure long ago.

The poems that follow are again, as before, printed in chronological order, but only so far as proves compatible with the prescribed size of each volume, which necessitates an occasional change in the distribution of its contents. Every date is subjoined as before.

R. B.
*London, February 27, 1888*

# CONTENTS

# PAULINE

A Fragment of a Confession

1833

Non dubito, quin titulus libri nostri raritate sua quamplurimos alliciat ad legendum: inter quos nonnulli obliquæ opinionis, mente languidi, multi etiam maligni, et in ingenium, nostrum ingrati accedent, qui temeraria sua ignorantia, vix conspecto titulo clamabunt Nos vetita docere, hæresium semina jacere: piis auribus offendiculo, præclaris ingeniis scandalo esse: ... adeo conscientiæ suæ consulentes, ut nec Apollo, nec Musæ omnes, neque Angelus de cœlo me ab illorum execratione vindicare queant: quibus et ego nunc consulo, ne scripta nostra legant, nec intelligent, nec meminerint: nam noxia sunt, venenosa sunt: Acherontis ostium est in hoc libro, lapides loquitur, caveant, ne cerebrum illis excutiat. Vos autem, qui æqua mente ad legendum venitis, si tantam prudentiæ discretionem adhibueritis, quantam in melle legendo apes, jam securi legite. Puto namque vos et utilitatis haud parum et voluptatis plurimum accepturos. Quod si qua repereritis, quæ vobis non placeant, mittite illa, nec utimini. Nam et ego vobis illa non Probo, sed Narro. Cætera tamen propterea non respuite. ... Ideo, si quid liberius dictum sit, ignoscite adolescentiæ nostræ, qui minor quam adolescens hoc opus composui.

– *Hen. Corn. Agrippa, De Occult. Philosoph. in præfat.*

London: *January* 1833. V.A. XX.

[This introduction would appear less absurdly pretentious did it apply, as was intended, to a completed structure of which the poem was meant for only a beginning and remains a fragment.]

Pauline, mine own, bend o'er me – thy
    soft breast
Shall pant to mine – bend o'er me –
    thy sweet eyes,
And loosened hair and breathing lips,
    and arms
Drawing me to thee – these build up a
    screen
To shut me in with thee, and from all
    fear;
So that I might unlock the sleepless
    brood
Of fancies from my soul, their
    lurkingplace,
Nor doubt that each would pass, ne'er
    to return
To one so watched, so loved and so
    secured.
But what can guard thee but thy naked
    love?

Ah dearest, whoso sucks a poisoned
    wound
Envenoms his own veins! Thou art so
    good,
So calm – if thou shouldst wear a brow
    less light
For some wild thought which but for
    me, were kept
From out thy soul as from a sacred
    star!
Yet till I have unlocked them it were
    vain
To hope to sing; some woe would light
    on me;
Nature would point at one whose
    quivering lip
Was bathed in her enchantments,
    whose brow burned
Beneath the crown to which her secrets
    knelt,

Who learned the spell which can call
   up the dead,
And then departed smiling like a fiend
Who has deceived God, – if such one
   should seek
Again her altars and stand robed and
   crowned
Amid the faithful! Sad confession first,
Remorse and pardon and old claims
   renewed,
Ere I can be – as I shall be no more.

I had been spared this shame if I had
   sat
By thee for ever from the first, in place
Of my wild dreams of beauty and of
   good,
Or with them, as an earnest of their
   truth:
No thought nor hope having been shut
   from thee,
No vague wish unexplained, no
   wandering aim
Sent back to bind on fancy's wings and
   seek
Some strange fair world where it might
   be a law;
But, doubting nothing, had been led
   by thee,
Thro' youth, and saved, as one at
   length awaked
Who has slept through a peril. Ah vain,
   vain!

Thou lovest me; the past is in its grave
Tho' its ghost haunts us; still this
   much is ours,
To cast away restraint, lest a worse
   thing
Wait for us in the dark. Thou lovest
   me;
And thou art to receive not love but
   faith,
For which thou wilt be mine, and
   smile and take
All shapes and shames, and veil
   without a fear

That form which music follows like a
   slave:
And I look to thee and I trust in thee,
As in a Northern night one looks alway
Unto the East for morn and spring and
   joy.
Thou seest then my aimless, hopeless
   state,
And, resting on some few old feelings
   won
Back by thy beauty, wouldst that I essay
The task which was to me what now
   thou art:
And why should I conceal one
   weakness more?

Thou wilt remember one warm morn
   when winter
Crept aged from the earth, and spring's
   first breath
Blew soft from the moist hills; the
   blackthorn boughs,
So dark in the bare wood, when
   glistening
In the sunshine were white with
   coming buds,
Like the bright side of a sorrow, and
   the banks
Had violets opening from sleep like
   eyes.
I walked with thee who knew'st not a
   deep shame
Lurked beneath smiles and careless
   words which sought
To hide it till they wandered and were
   mute,
As we stood listening on a sunny
   mound
To the wind murmuring in the damp
   copse,
Like heavy breathings of some hidden
   thing
Betrayed by sleep; until the feeling
   rushed
That I was low indeed, yet not so low
As to endure the calmness of thine
   eyes.

And so I told thee all, while the cool breast
I leaned on altered not its quiet beating:
And long ere words like a hurt bird's complaint
Bade me look up and be what I had been,
I felt despair could never live by thee:
Thou wilt remember. Thou art not more dear
Than song was once to me; and I ne'er sung
But as one entering bright halls where all
Will rise and shout for him: sure I must own
That I am fallen, having chosen gifts
Distinct from theirs – that I am sad and fain
Would give up all to be but where I was,
Not high as I had been if faithful found,
But low and weak yet full of hope, and sure
Of goodness as of life – that I would lose
All this gay mastery of mind, to sit
Once more with them, trusting in truth and love
And with an aim – not being what I am.

Oh Pauline, I am ruined who believed
That though my soul had floated from its sphere
Of wild dominion into the dim orb
Of self – that it was strong and free as ever.
It has conformed itself to that dim orb,
Reflecting all its shades and shapes, and now
Must stay where it alone can be adored.
I have felt this in dreams – in dreams in which

I seemed the fate from which I fled; I felt
A strange delight in causing my decay.
I was a fiend in darkness chained for ever
Within some ocean cave; and ages rolled,
Till through the cleft rock, like a moon-beam, came
A white swan to remain with me; and ages
Rolled, yet I tired not of my first free joy
In gazing on the peace of its pure wings:
And then I said 'It is most fair to me,
'Yet its soft wings most sure have suffered change
'From the thick darkness, sure its eyes are dim,
'Its silver pinions must be cramped and numbed
'With sleeping ages here; it cannot leave me,
'For it would seem, in light beside its kind,
'Withered, tho' here to me most beautiful.'
And then I was a young witch whose blue eyes,
As she stood naked by the river springs,
Drew down a god: I watched his radiant form
Growing less radiant, and it gladdened me;
Till one morn, as he sat in the sunshine.
Upon my knees, singing to me of heaven,
He turned to look at me, ere I could lose
The grin with which I viewed his perishing:
And he shrieked and departed and sat long
By his deserted throne, but sunk at last
Murmuring, as I kissed his lips and curled

Around him, 'I am still a god – to
    thee.'

Still I can lay my soul bare in its fall,
Since all the wandering and all the
    weakness
Will be a saddest comment on the song:
And if, that done, I can be young
    again,
I will give up all gained, as willingly
As one gives up a charm which shuts
    him out
From hope or part or care in human
    kind.
As life wanes, all its care and strife and
    toil
Seem strangely valueless, while the old
    trees
Which grew by our youth's home, the
    waving mass
Of climbing plants heavy with bloom
    and dew,
The morning swallows with their songs
    like words,
All these seem clear and only worth
    our thoughts:
So, aught connected with my early life,
My rude songs or my wild imaginings,
How I look on them – most distinct
    amid
The fever and the stir of after years!
I ne'er had ventured e'en to hope for
    this,
Had not the glow I felt at His award,
Assured me all was not extinct within:
His whom all honour, whose renown
    springs up
Like sunlight which will visit all the
    world,
So that e'en they who sneered at him
    at first,
Come out to it, as some dark spider
    crawls
From his foul nets which some lit
    torch invades,
Yet spinning still new films for his
    retreat.

Thou didst smile, poet, but can we
    forgive?

Sun-treader,* life and light be thine for
    ever!
Thou art gone from us; years go by and
    spring
Gladdens and the young earth is
    beautiful,
Yet thy songs come not, other bards
    arise,
But none like thee: they stand, thy
    majesties,
Like mighty works which tell some
    spirit there
Hath sat regardless of neglect and
    scorn,
Till, its long task completed, it hath
    risen
And left us, never to return, and all
Rush in to peer and praise when all in
    vain.
The air seems bright with thy past
    presence yet,
But thou art still for me as thou hast
    been
When I have stood with thee as on a
    throne
With all thy dim creations gathered
    round
Like mountains, and I felt of mould
    like them,
And with them creatures of my own
    were mixed,
Like things half-lived, catching and
    giving life.
But thou art still for me who have
    adored
Tho' single, panting but to hear thy
    name
Which I believed a spell to me alone,
Scarce deeming thou wast as a star to
    men!
As one should worship long a sacred
    spring

* Shelley

Scarce worth a moth's flitting, which
    long grasses cross,
And one small tree embowers
    droopingly –
Joying to see some wandering insect
    won
To live in its few rushes, or some locust
To pasture on its boughs, or some wild
    bird
Stoop for its freshness from the trackless
    air:
And then should find it but the fountain-
    head,
Long lost, of some great river washing
    towns
And towers, and seeing old woods
    which will live
But by its banks untrod of human foot,
Which, when the great sun sinks, lie
    quivering
In light as some thing lieth half of life
Before God's foot, waiting a wondrous
    change;
Then girt with rocks which seek to turn
    or stay
Its course in vain, for it does ever spread
Like a sea's arm as it goes rolling on,
Being the pulse of some great country
    – so
Wast thou to me, and art thou to the
    world!
And I, perchance, half feel a strange
    regret
That I am not what I have been to
    thee:
Like a girl one has silently loved long
In her first loneliness in some retreat,
When, late emerged, all gaze and glow
    to view
Her fresh eyes and soft hair and lips
    which bloom
Like a mountain berry: doubtless it is
    sweet
To see her thus adored, but there have
    been
Moments when all the world was in
    our praise,

Sweeter than any pride of after hours.
Yet, sun-treader, all hail! From my
    heart's heart
I bid thee hail! E'en in my wildest
    dreams,
I proudly feel I would have thrown to
    dust
The wreaths of fame which seemed
    o'er-hanging me,
To see thee for a moment as thou art.

And if thou livest, if thou lovest, spirit!
Remember me who set this final seal
To wandering thought – that one so
    pure as thou
Could never die. Remember me who
    flung
All honour from my soul, yet paused
    and said
'There is one spark of love remaining
    yet,
'For I have nought in common with
    him, shapes
'Which followed him avoid me, and
    foul forms
'Seek me, which ne'er could fasten on
    his mind;
'And though I feel how low I am to
    him,
'Yet I aim not even to catch a tone
'Of harmonies he called profusely up;
'So, one gleam still remains, although
    the last.'
Remember me who praise thee e'en
    with tears,
For never more shall I walk calm with
    thee;
Thy sweet imaginings are as an air,
A melody some wondrous singer sings,
Which, though it haunt men oft in the
    still eve,
They dream not to essay; yet it no less
But more is honoured. I was thine in
    shame,
And now when all thy proud renown is
    out,

I am a watcher whose eyes have grown
    dim
With looking for some star which
    breaks on him
Altered and worn and weak and full of
    tears.

Autumn has come like spring returned
    to us,
Won from her girlishness; like one
    returned
A friend that was a lover, nor forgets
The first warm love, but full of sober
    thoughts
Of fading years; whose soft mouth
    quivers yet
With the old smile, but yet so changed
    and still!
And here am I the scoffer, who have
    probed
Life's vanity, won by a word again
Into my own life – by one little word
Of this sweet friend who lives in loving
    me,
Lives strangely on my thoughts and
    looks and words,
As fathoms down some nameless
    ocean thing
Its silent course of quietness and joy.
O dearest, if indeed I tell the past,
May'st thou forget it as a sad sick dream!
Or if it linger – my lost soul too soon
Sinks to itself and whispers we shall be
But closer linked, two creatures whom
    the earth
Bears singly, with strange feelings
    unrevealed
Save to each other; or two lonely things
Created by some power whose reign is
    done,
Having no part in God or his bright
    world.
I am to sing whilst ebbing day dies soft,
As a lean scholar dies worn o'er his
    book,
And in the heaven stars steal out one
    by one

As hunted men steal to their mountain
    watch.
I must not think, lest this new impulse
    die
In which I trust; I have no confidence:
So, I will sing on fast as fancies come;
Rudely, the verse being as the mood it
    paints.

I strip my mind bare, whose first elements
I shall unveil – not as they struggled
    forth
In infancy, nor as they now exist,
When I am grown above them and can
    rule –
But in that middle stage when they
    were full
Yet ere I had disposed them to my will;
And then I shall show how these
    elements
Produced my present state, and what
    it is.
I am made up of an intensest life,
Of a most clear idea of consciousness
Of self, distinct from all its qualities,
From all affections, passions, feelings,
    powers;
And thus far it exists, if tracked, in all:
But linked, in me, to self-supremacy,
Existing as a centre to all things,
Most potent to create and rule and call
Upon all things to minister to it;
And to a principle of restlessness
Which would be all, have, see, know,
    taste, feel, all –
This is myself; and I should thus have
    been
Though gifted lower than the meanest
    soul.
And of my powers, one springs up to
    save
From utter death a soul with such
    desire
Confined to clay – of powers the only
    one
Which marks me – an imagination
    which

Has been a very angel, coming not
In fitful visions but beside me ever
And never failing me; so, though my
    mind
Forgets not, not a shred of life forgets,
Yet I can take a secret pride in calling
The dark past up to quell it regally.

A mind like this must dissipate itself,
But I have always had one lode-star;
    now,
As I look back, I see that I have halted
Or hastened as I looked towards that
    star –
A need, a trust, a yearning after God:
A feeling I have analysed but late,
But it existed, and was reconciled
With a neglect of all I deemed his laws,
Which yet, when seen in others, I
    abhorred.
I felt as one beloved, and so shut in
From fear: and thence I date my trust
    in signs
And omens, for I saw God everywhere;
And I can only lay it to the fruit
Of a sad after-time that I could doubt
Even his being – e'en the while I felt
His presence, never acted from myself,
Still trusted in a hand to lead me
    through
All danger; and this feeling ever fought
Against my weakest reason and resolve.

And I can love nothing – and this dull
    truth
Has come the last: but sense supplies a
    love
Encircling me and mingling with my
    life.
These make myself: I have long sought
    in vain
To trace how they were formed by
    circumstance,
Yet ever found them mould my wildest
    youth
Where they alone displayed themselves,
    converted

All objects to their use: now see their
    course!

They came to me in my first dawn of
    life
Which passed alone with wisest
    ancient books
All halo-girt with fancies of my own;
And I myself went with the tale – a god
Wandering after beauty, or a giant
Standing vast in the sunset – an old
    hunter
Talking with gods, or a high-crested
    chief
Sailing with troops of friends to Tenedos.
I tell you, nought has ever been so
    clear
As the place, the time, the fashion of
    those lives:
I had not seen a work of lofty art,
Nor woman's beauty nor sweet
    nature's face,
Yet, I say, never morn broke clear as
    those
On the dim clustered isles in the blue
    sea,
The deep groves and white temples
    and wet caves:
And nothing ever will surprise me now –
Who stood beside the naked Swift-
    footed,
Who bound my forehead with
    Proserpine's hair.

And strange it is that I who could so
    dream
Should e'er have stooped to aim at
    aught beneath –
Aught low or painful; but I never
    doubted:
So, as I grew, I rudely shaped my life
To my immediate wants; yet strong
    beneath
Was a vague sense of power though
    folded up –
A sense that, though those shades and
    times were past,

Their spirit dwelt in me, with them
    should rule.

Then came a pause, and long restraint
    chained down
My soul till it was changed. I lost myself,
And were it not that I so loathe that
    loss,
I could recall how first I learned to turn
My mind against itself; and the effects
In deeds for which remorse were vain
    as for
The wanderings of delirious dream; yet
    thence
Came cunning, envy, falsehood, all
    world's wrong
That spotted me: at length I cleansed
    my soul.
Yet long world's influence remained;
    and nought
But the still life I led, apart once more,
Which left me free to seek soul's old
    delights,
Could e'er have brought me thus far
    back to peace.

As peace returned, I sought out some
    pursuit;
And song rose, no new impulse but the
    one
With which all others best could be
    combined.
My life has not been that of those whose
    heaven
Was lampless save where poesy shone
    out;
But as a clime where glittering
    mountain-tops
And glancing sea and forests steeped in
    light
Give back reflected the far-flashing sun;
For music (which is earnest of a heaven,
Seeing we know emotions strange by it,
Not else to be revealed,) is like a voice,
A low voice calling fancy, as a friend,
To the green woods in the gay summer
    time:

And she fills all the way with dancing
    shapes
Which have made painters pale, and
    they go on
Till stars look at them and winds call to
    them
As they leave life's path for the twilight
    world
Where the dead gather. This was not at
    first,
For I scarce knew what I would do. I had
An impulse but no yearning – only sang.

And first I sang as I in dream have seen
Music wait on a lyrist for some thought,
Yet singing to herself until it came.
I turned to those old times and scenes
    where all
That's beautiful had birth for me, and
    made
Rude verses on them all; and then I
    paused –
I had done nothing, so I sought to
    know
What other minds achieved. No fear
    outbroke
As on the works of mighty bards I
    gazed,
In the first joy at finding my own
    thoughts
Recorded, my own fancies justified,
And their aspirings but my very own.
With them I first explored passion and
    mind, –
All to begin afresh! I rather sought
To rival what I wondered at than form
Creations of my own; if much was light
Lent by the others, much was yet my
    own.

I paused again: a change was coming –
    came:
I was no more a boy, the past was
    breaking
Before the future and like fever worked.
I thought on my new self, and all my
    powers

Burst out. I dreamed not of restraint,
    but gazed
On all things: schemes and systems
    went and came,
And I was proud (being vainest of the
    weak)
In wandering o'er thought's world to
    seek some one
To be my prize, as if you wandered o'er
The White Way for a star.
                    And my choice fell
Not so much on a system as a man –
On one, whom praise of mine shall not
    offend,
Who was as calm as beauty, being such
Unto mankind as thou to me, Pauline, –
Believing in them and devoting all
His soul's strength to their winning
    back to peace;
Who sent forth hopes and longings for
    their sake,
Clothed in all passion's melodies: such
    first
Caught me and set me, slave of a sweet
    task,
To disentangle, gather sense from song:
Since, song-inwoven, lurked there
    words which seemed
A key to a new world, the muttering
Of angels, something yet unguessed by
    man.
How my heart leapt as still I sought
    and found
Much there, I felt my own soul had
    conceived,
But there living and burning! Soon the
    orb
Of his conceptions dawned on me; its
    praise
Lives in the tongues of men, men's
    brows are high
When his name means a triumph and
    a pride,
So, my weak voice may well forbear to
    shame
What seemed decreed my fate: I threw
    myself

To meet it, I was vowed to liberty,
Men were to be as gods and earth as
    heaven,
And I – ah, what a life was mine to
    prove!
My whole soul rose to meet it. Now,
    Pauline,
I shall go mad, if I recall that time!

    Oh let me look back ere I leave for
        ever
The time which was an hour one fondly
    waits
For a fair girl that comes a withered
    hag!
And I was lonely, far from woods and
    fields,
And amid dullest sights, who should
    be loose
As a stag; yet I was full of bliss, who
    lived
With Plato and who had the key to life;
And I had dimly shaped my first attempt,
And many a thought did I build up on
    thought,
As the wild bee hangs cell to cell; in
    vain,
For I must still advance, no rest for
    mind.

'Twas in my plan to look on real life,
The life all new to me; my theories
Were firm, so them I left, to look and
    learn
Mankind, its cares, hopes, fears, its
    woes and joys;
And, as I pondered on their ways, I
    sought
How best life's end might be attained –
    an end
Comprising every joy. I deeply mused.

And suddenly without heart-wreck I
    awoke
As from a dream: I said ' 'Twas
    beautiful,
'Yet but a dream, and so adieu to it!'

As some world-wanderer sees in a far
  meadow
Strange towers and high-walled
  gardens thick with trees,
Where song takes shelter and delicious
  mirth
From laughing fairy creatures peeping
  over,
And on the morrow when he comes to
  lie
For ever 'neath those garden-trees fruit-
  flushed
Sung round by fairies, all his search is
  vain.
First went my hopes of perfecting man-
  kind,
Next – faith in them, and then in
  freedom's self
And virtue's self, then my own
  motives, ends
And aims and loves, and human love
  went last.
I felt this no decay, because new powers
Rose as old feelings left – wit, mockery,
Light-heartedness; for I had oft been
  sad,
Mistrusting my resolves, but now I cast
Hope joyously away: I laughed and
  said
'No more of this!' I must not think: at
  length
I looked again to see if all went well.

My powers were greater: as some
  temple seemed
My soul, where nought is changed and
  incense rolls
Around the altar, only God is gone
And some dark spirit sitteth in his seat.
So, I passed through the temple and
  to me
Knelt troops of shadows, and they
  cried 'Hail, king!'
'We serve thee now and thou shalt
  serve no more!'
'Call on us, prove us, let us worship
  thee!'

And I said 'Are ye strong? Let fancy
  bear me
'Far from the past!' And I was borne
  away,
As Arab birds float sleeping in the wind,
O'er deserts, towers and forests, I
  being calm.
And I said 'I have nursed up energies,
'They will prey on me.' And a band
  knelt low
And cried 'Lord, we are here and we
  will make
'Safe way for thee in thine appointed
  life!
'But look on us!' And I said 'Ye will
  worship
'Me; should my heart not worship
  too?' They shouted
'Thyself, thou art our king!' So, I stood
  there
Smiling – oh, vanity of vanities!
For buoyant and rejoicing was the
  spirit
With which I looked out how to end
  my course;
I felt once more myself, my powers –
  all mine;
I knew while youth and health so
  lifted me
That, spite of all life's nothingness, no
  grief
Came nigh me, I must ever be light-
  hearted;
And that this knowledge was the only
  veil
Betwixt joy and despair: so, if age came,
I should be left – a wreck linked to a
  soul
Yet fluttering, or mind-broken and
  aware
Of my decay. So a long summer morn
Found me; and ere noon came, I had
  resolved
No age should come on me ere youth
  was spent,
For I would wear myself out, like that
  morn

Which wasted not a sunbeam; every
    hour
I would make mine, and die

                        And thus I sought
To chain my spirit down which erst I
    freed
For flights to fame: I said 'The troubled
    life
'Of genius, seen so gay when working
    forth
'Some trusted end, grows sad when all
    proves vain –
'How sad when men have parted with
    truth's peace
'For falsest fancy's sake, which waited
    first
'As an obedient spirit when delight
'Came without fancy's call: but alters
    soon,
'Comes darkened, seldom, hastens to
    depart,
'Leaving a heavy darkness and warm
    tears.
'But I shall never lose her; she will live
'Dearer for such seclusion. I but catch
'A hue, a glance of what I sing: so, pain
'Is linked with pleasure, for I ne'er may
    tell
'Half the bright sights which dazzle
    me; but now
'Mine shall be all the radiance: let them
    fade
'Untold – others shall rise as fair, as
    fast!
'And when all's done, the few dim
    gleams transferred,' –
(For a new thought sprang up how
    well it were,
Discarding shadowy hope, to weave
    such lays
As straight encircle men with praise
    and love,
So, I should not die utterly, – should
    bring
One branch from the gold forest, like
    the knight

Of old tales, witnessing I had been
    there) –
'And when all's done, how vain seems
    e'en success –
'The vaunted influence poets have o'er
    men!
' 'Tis a fine thing that one weak as
    myself
'Should sit in his lone room, knowing
    the words
'He utters in his solitude shall move
'Men like a swift wind – that tho' dead
    and gone,
'New eyes shall glisten when his
    beauteous dreams
'Of love come true in happier frames
    than his.
'Ay, the still night brings thoughts like
    these, but morn
'Comes and the mockery again laughs
    out
'At hollow praises, smiles allied to sneers;
'And my soul's idol ever whispers me
'To dwell with him and his unhonoured
    song:
And I foreknow my spirit, that would
    press
'First in the struggle, fail again to make
'All bow enslaved, and I again should
    sink.
'And then know that this curse will
    come on us,
'To see our idols perish; we may wither,
'No marvel, we are clay, but our low fate
'Should not extend to those whom
    trustingly
'We sent before into time's yawning gulf
'To face what dread may lurk in
    darkness there.
'To find the painter's glory pass, and
    feel
'Music can move us not as once, or,
    worst,
'To weep decaying wits ere the frail
    body
'Decays! Nought makes me trust some
    love is true,

'But the delight of the contented
      lowness
'With which I gaze on him I keep for
      ever
'Above me; I to rise and rival him?
'Feed his fame rather from my heart's
      best blood,
'Wither unseen that he may flourish
      still.'

Pauline, my soul's friend, thou dost
      pity yet
How this mood swayed me when that
      soul found thine,
When I had set myself to live this life,
Defying all past glory. Ere thou camest
I seemed defiant, sweet, for old
      delights
Had flocked like birds again; music,
      my life,
Nourished me more than ever; then
      the lore
Loved for itself and all it shows – that
      king
Treading the purple calmly to his
      death,*
While round him, like the clouds of
      eve, all dusk,
The giant shades of fate, silently
      flitting,
Pile the dim outline of the coming
      doom;
And him sitting alone in blood while
      friends
Are hunting far in the sunshine; and
      the boy
With his white breast and brow and
      clustering curls
Streaked with his mother's blood, but
      striving hard
To tell his story ere his reason goes.
And when I loved thee as love seemed
      so oft,
Thou lovedst me indeed: I wondering
      searched

* Agamemnon

My heart to find some feeling like such
      love,
Believing I was still much I had been.
Too soon I found all faith had gone
      from me,
And the late glow of life, like change on
      clouds,
Proved not the morn-blush widening
      into day,
But eve faint-coloured by the dying sun
While darkness hastens quickly. I will
      tell
My state as though 'twere none of
      mine – despair
Cannot come near us – this it is, my
      state.

Souls alter not, and mine must still
      advance;
Strange that I knew not, when I flung
      away
My youth's chief aims, their loss might
      lead to loss
Of what few I retained, and no resource
Be left me: for behold how changed is
      all!
I cannot chain my soul: it will not rest
In its clay prison, this most narrow
      sphere:
It has strange impulse, tendency, desire,
Which nowise I account for nor
      explain,
But cannot stifle, being bound to trust
All feelings equally, to hear all sides:
How can my life indulge them? yet
      they live,
Referring to some state of life
      unknown.

My selfishness is satiated not,
It wears me like a flame; my hunger for
All pleasure, howsoe'er minute, grows
      pain;
I envy – how I envy him whose soul
Turns its whole energies to some one
      end,
To elevate an aim, pursue success

However mean! So, my still baffled
    hope
Seeks out abstractions; I would have
    one joy,
But one in life, so it were wholly mine,
One rapture all my soul could fill: and
    this
Wild feeling places me in dream afar
In some vast country where the eye can
    see
No end to the far hills and dales bestrewn
With shining towers and towns, till I
    grow mad
Wellnigh, to know not one a bode but
    holds
Some pleasure, while my soul could
    grasp the world,
But must remain this vile form's slave.
    I look
With hope to age at last, which quenching
    much,
May let me concentrate what sparks it
    spares.

This restlessness of passion meets in
    me
A craving after knowledge: the sole proof
Of yet commanding will is in that
    power
Repressed; for I beheld it in its dawn,
The sleepless harpy with just-budding
    wings,
And I considered whether to forego
All happy ignorant hopes and fears, to
    live,
Finding a recompense in its wild eyes.
And when I found that I should perish
    so,
I bade its wild eyes close from me for
    ever,
And I am left alone with old delights;
See! it lies in me a chained thing, still
    prompt
To serve me if I loose its slightest bond:
I cannot but be proud of my bright
    slave.

How should this earth's life prove my
    only sphere?
Can I so narrow sense but that in life
Soul still exceeds it? In their elements
My love outsoars my reason; but since
    love
Perforce receives its object from this
    earth
While reason wanders chainless, the
    few truths
Caught from its wanderings have
    sufficed to quell
Love chained below; then what were
    love, set free,
Which, with the object it demands,
    would pass
Reason companioning the seraphim?
No, what I feel may pass all human
    love
Yet fall far short of what my love
    should be.
And yet I seem more warped in this
    than aught,
Myself stands out more hideously: of old
I could forget myself in friendship,
    fame,
Liberty, nay, in love of mightier souls;
But I begin to know what thing hate is –
To sicken and to quiver and grow
    white –
And I myself have furnished its first prey.
Hate of the weak and ever-wavering
    will,
The selfishness, the still-decaying
    frame …
But I must never grieve whom wing
    can waft
Far from such thoughts – as now.
    Andromeda!
And she is with me: years roll, I shall
    change,
But change can touch her not – so
    beautiful
With her fixed eyes, earnest and still,
    and hair
Lifted and spread by the salt-sweeping
    breeze,

And one red beam, all the storm leaves
    in heaven,
Resting upon her eyes and hair, such
    hair,
As she awaits the snake on the wet
    beach
By the dark rock and the white wave
    just breaking
At her feet; quite naked and alone; a
    thing
I doubt not, nor fear for, secure some
    god
To save will come in thunder from the
    stars.
Let it pass! Soul requires another
    change.
I will be gifted with a wondrous mind,
Yet sunk by error to men's sympathy,
And in the wane of life, yet only so
As to call up their fears; and there shall
    come
A time requiring youth's best energies;
And lo, I fling age, sorrow, sickness off,
And rise triumphant, triumph through
    decay.

And thus it is that I supply the chasm
'Twixt what I am and all I fain would be:
But then to know nothing, to hope for
    nothing,
To seize on life's dull joys from a strange
    fear
Lest, losing them, all's lost and nought
    remains!

There's some vile juggle with my
    reason here;
I feel I but explain to my own loss
These impulses: they live no less the
    same.
Liberty! what though I despair? my
    blood
Rose never at a slave's name proud as
    now.
Oh sympathies, obscured by
    sophistries! –
Why else have I sought refuge in myself,

But from the woes I saw and could not
    stay?
Love! is not this to love thee, my
    Pauline?
I cherish prejudice, lest I be left
Utterly loveless? witness my belief
In poets, though sad change has come
    there too;
No more I leave myself to follow them –
Unconsciously I measure me by them –
Let me forget it: and I cherish most
My love of England – how her name, a
    word
Of hers in a strange tongue makes my
    heart beat!
Pauline, could I but break the spell!
    Not now –
All's fever – but when calm shall come
    again,
I am prepared: I have made life my own.
I would not be content with all the
    change
One frame should feel, but I have gone
    in thought
Thro' all conjuncture, I have lived all life
When it is most alive, where strangest
    fate
New-shapes it past surmise – the throes
    of men
Bit by some curse or in the grasps of
    doom
Half-visible and still-increasing round,
Or crowning their wide being's general
    aim.

These are wild fancies, but I feel, sweet
    friend,
As one breathing his weakness to the
    ear
Of pitying angel – dear as a winter
    flower,
A slight flower growing alone, and
    offering
Its frail cup of three leaves to the cold
    sun,
Yet joyous and confiding like the
    triumph

Of a child: and why am I not worthy
    thee?
I can live all the life of plants, and gaze
Drowsily on the bees that flit and play,
Or bare my breast for sunbeams which
    will kill,
Or open in the night of sounds, to look
For, the dim stars; I can mount with
    the bird
Leaping airily his pyramid of leaves
And twisted boughs of some tall
    mountain tree,
Or rise cheerfully springing to the
    heavens;
Or like a fish breathe deep the morning
    air
In the misty sun-warm water; or with
    flower
And tree can smile in light at the sinking
    sun
Just as the storm comes, as a girl would
    look
On a departing lover – most serene.

Pauline, come with me, see how I
    could build
A home forus, out of the world, in
    thought!
I am uplifted: fly with me, Pauline!

Night, and one single ridge of narrow
    path
Between the sullen river and the woods
Waving and muttering, for the
    moonless night
Has shaped them into images of life,
Like the uprising of the giant-ghosts,
Looking on earth to know how their
    sons fare:
Thou art so close by me, the roughest
    swell
Of wind in the tree-tops hides not the
    panting
Of thy soft breasts. No, we will pass to
    morning –
Morning, the rocks and valleys and old
    woods.

How the sun brightens in the mist, and
    here,
Half in the air, like creatures of the
    place,
Trusting the element, living on high
    boughs
That swing in the wind – look at the
    silver spray
Flung from the foam-sheet of the cataract
Amid the broken rocks! Shall we stay
    here
With the wild hawks? No, ere the hot
    noon come,
Dive we down – safe! See this our new
    retreat
Walled in with a sloped mound of
    matted shrubs,
Dark, tangled, old and green, still
    sloping down
To a small pool whose waters lie asleep
Amid the trailing boughs turned
    waterplants:
And tall trees overarch to keep us in,
Breaking the sunbeams into emerald
    shafts
And in the dreamy water one small
    group
Of two or three strange trees are got
    together
Wondering at all around, as strange
    beasts herd
Together far from their own land: all
    wildness,
No turf nor moss, for boughs and
    plants pave all,
And tongues of bank go shelving in the
    lymph,
Where the pale-throated snake reclines
    his head,
And old grey stones lie making eddies
    there,
The wild-mice cross them dry-shod.
    Deeper in!
Shut thy soft eyes – now look – still
    deeper in!
This is the very heart of the woods all
    round

Mountain-like heaped above us; yet
    even here
One pond of water gleams; far off the
    river
Sweeps like a sea, barred out from
    land; but one –
One thin clear sheet has overleaped
    and wound
Into this silent depth, which gained, it
    lies
Still, as but let by sufferance; the trees
    bend
O'er it as wild men watch a sleeping
    girl,
And through their roots long creeping
    plants out-stretch
Their twined hair, steeped and
    sparkling; farther on,
Tall rushes and thick flag-knots have
    combined
To narrow it; so, at length, a silver
    thread,
It winds, all noiselessly through the
    deep wood
Till thro' a cleft-way, thro' the moss
    and stone,
It joins its parent-river with a shout.
Up for the glowing day, leave the old
    woods!
See, they part like a ruined arch: the
    sky!
Nothing but sky appears, so close the
    roots
And grass of the hill-top level with the
    air –
Blue sunny air, where a great cloud
    floats laden
With light, like a dead whale that white
    birds pick,
Floating away in the sun in some north
    sea.
Air, air, fresh life-blood, thin and
    searching air,
The clear, dear breath of God that
    loveth us,
Where small birds reel and winds take
    their delight!

Water is beautiful, but not like air:
See, where the solid azure waters lie
Made as of thickened air, and down
    below,
The fern-ranks like a forest spread
    themselves
As though each pore could feel the
    element;
Where the quick glancing serpent
    winds his way,
Float with me there, Pauline! – but not
    like air.

Down the hill! Stop – a clump of trees,
    see, set
On a heap of rock, which look o'er the
    far plain:
So, envious climbing shrubs would
    mount to rest
And peer from their spread boughs;
    wide they wave, looking
At the muleteers who whistle on their
    way,
To the merry chime of morning bells,
    past all
The little smoking cots, mid fields and
    banks
And copses bright in the sun. My spirit
    wanders:
Hedgerows for me – those living
    hedgerows where
The bushes close and clasp above and
    keep
Thought in – I am concentrated – I feel;
But my soul saddens when it looks
    beyond:
I cannot be immortal, taste all joy.

O God, where do they tend – these
    struggling aims?*
What would I have? What is this
    'sleep' which seems
To bound all? can there be a 'waking'
    point

* See note at the end of the poem.

Of crowning life? The soul would never
    rule;
It would be first in all things, it would
    have
Its utmost pleasure filled, but, that
    complete,
Commanding, for commanding,
    sickens it.
The last point I can trace is – rest
    beneath
Some better essence than itself, in
    weakness;
This is 'myself,' not what I think
    should be:
And what is that I hunger for but God?

My God, my God, let me for once look
    on thee
As though nought else existed, we alone!
And as creation crumbles, my soul's
    spark
Expands till I can say, – Even from
    myself
I need thee and I feel thee and I love
    thee.
I do not plead my rapture in thy works
For love of thee, nor that I feel as one
Who cannot die: but there is that in me
Which turns to thee, which loves or
    which should love.

Why have I girt myself with this hell-
    dress?
Why have I laboured to put out my life?
Is it not in my nature to adore,
And e'en for all my reason do I not
Feel him, and thank him, and pray to
    him – now?
Can I forego the trust that he loves me?
Do I not feel a love which only one …
O thou pale form, so dimly seen, deep-
    eyed!
I have denied thee calmly – do I not
Pant when I read of thy consummate
    power,
And burn to see thy calm pure truths
    out-flash

The brightest gleams of earth's philo-
    sophy?
Do I not shake to hear aught question
    thee?
If I am erring save me, madden me,
Take from me powers and pleasures,
    let me die
Ages, so I see thee! I am knit round
As with a charm by sin and lust and
    pride,
Yet though my wandering dreams have
    seen all shapes
Of strange delight, oft have I stood by
    thee –
Have I been keeping lonely watch with
    thee
In the damp night by weeping Olivet,
Or leaning on thy bosom, proudly less,
Or dying with thee on the lonely cross,
Or witnessing thine outburst from the
    tomb.

A mortal, sin's familiar friend, doth here
A vow that he will give all earth's reward,
But to believe and humbly teach the
    faith,
In suffering and poverty and shame,
Only believing he is not unloved.

And now, my Pauline, I am thine for
    ever!
I feel the spirit which has buoyed me up
Desert me, and old shades are gathering
    fast;
Yet while the last light waits, I would
    say much,
This chiefly, it is gain that I have said
Somewhat of love I ever felt for thee
But seldom told; our hearts so beat
    together
That speech seemed mockery; but
    when dark hours come,
And joy departs, and thou, sweet,
    deem'st it strange
A sorrow moves me, thou canst not
    remove,
Look on this lay I dedicate to thee,

Which through thee I began, which
    thus I end,
Collecting the last gleams to strive to
    tell
How I am thine, and more than ever
    now
That I sink fast: yet though I deeplier
    sink,
No less song proves one word has
    brought me bliss,
Another still may win bliss surely back.
Thou knowest, dear, I could not think
    all calm,
For fancies followed thought and bore
    me off,
And left all indistinct; ere one was caught
Another glanced; so, dazzled by my
    wealth,
I knew not which to leave nor which to
    choose,
For all so floated, nought was fixed and
    firm.
And then thou said'st a perfect bard
    was one
Who chronicled the stages of all life,
And so thou bad'st me shadow this
    first stage.
'Tis done, and even now I recognize
The shift, the change from last to past –
    discern
Faintly how life is truth and truth is
    good.
And why thou must be mine is, that
    e'en now
In the dim hush of night, that I have
    done,
Despite the sad forebodings, love looks
    through –
Whispers, – E'en at the last I have her
    still,
With her delicious eyes as clear as heaven
When rain in a quick shower has beat
    down mist,
And clouds float white above like
    broods of swans.
How the blood lies upon her cheek,
    outspread

As thinned by kisses! only in her lips
It wells and pulses like a living thing,
And her neck looks like marble misted
    o'er
With love-breath, – a Pauline from
    heights above,
Stooping beneath me, looking up – one
    look
As I might kill her and be loved the more

So, love me – me, Pauline, and nought
    but me,
Never leave loving! Words are wild and
    weak,
Believe them not, Pauline! I stained myself
But to behold thee purer by my side,
To show thou art my breath, my life, a
    last
Resource, an extreme want: never
    believe
Aught better could so look on thee; nor
    seek
Again the world of good thoughts left
    for mine!
There were bright troops of undiscovered
    suns,
Each equal in their radiant course; there
    were
Clusters of far fair isles which ocean kept
For his own joy, and his waves broke on
    them
Without a choice; and there was a dim
    crowd
Of visions, each a part of some grand
    whole:
And one star left his peers and came
    with peace
Upon a storm, and all eyes pined for
    him;
And one isle harboured a sea-beaten
    ship,
And the crew wandered in its bowers
    and plucked
Its fruits and gave up all their hopes of
    home;
And one dream came to a pale poet's
    sleep,

And he said, 'I am singled out by God,
'No sin must touch me.' Words are
    wild and weak,
But what they would express is, – Leave
    me not,
Still sit by me with beating breast and
    hair
Loosened, be watching earnest by my
    side,
Turning my books or kissing me when I
Look up – like summer wind! Be still
    to me
A help to music's mystery which mind
    fails
To fathom, its solution, no mere clue!
O reason's pedantry, life's rule prescribed!
I hopeless, I the loveless, hope and love.
Wiser and better, know me now, not
    when
You loved me as I was. Smile not! I have
Much yet to dawn on you, to gladden
    you.

No more of the past! I'll look within no
    more.
I have too trusted my own lawless wants,
Too trusted my vain self, vague
    intuition –
Draining soul's wine alone in the still
    night,
And seeing how, as gathering films
    arose,
As by an inspiration life seemed bare
And grinning in its vanity, while ends
Foul to be dreamed of, smiled at me as
    fixed
And fair, while others changed from
    fair to foul
As a young witch turns an old hag at
    night.
No more of this! We will go hand in
    hand,
I with thee, even as a child – love's slave,
Looking no farther than his liege
    commands.
And thou hast chosen where this life
    shall be:

The land which gave me thee shall be
    our home,
Where nature lies all wild amid her
    lakes
And snow-swathed mountains and vast
    pines begirt
With ropes of snow – where nature lies
    all bare,
Suffering none to view her but a race
Or stinted or deformed, like the mute
    dwarfs
Which wait upon a naked Indian
    queen.
And there (the time being when the
    heavens are thick
With storm) I'll sit with thee while
    thou dost sing
Thy native songs, gay as a desert bird
Which crieth as it flies for perfect joy,
Or telling me old stories of dead knights;
Or I will read great lays to thee – how
    she,
The fair pale sister, went to her chill
    grave*
With power to love and to be loved
    and live:
Or we will go together, like twin gods
Of the infernal world, with scented
    lamp
Over the dead, to call and to awake,
Over the unshaped images which lie
Within my mind's cave: only leaving
    all,
That tells of the past doubt. So, when
    spring comes
With sunshine back again like an old
    smile,
And the fresh waters and awakened
    birds
And budding woods await us, I shall
    be
Prepared, and we will question life
    once more,
Till its old sense shall come renewed
    by change,

* Antigone

Like some clear thought which harsh
 words veiled before;
Feeling God loves us, and that all
 which errs
Is but a dream which death will
 dissipate.
And then what need of longer exile?
 Seek
My England, and, again there, calm
 approach
All I once fled from, calmly look on
 those
The works of my past weakness, as one
 views
Some scene where danger met him
 long before.
Ah that such pleasant life should be
 but dreamed!

But whate'er come of it, and though it
 fade,
And though ere the cold morning all be
 gone,
As it may be; – tho' music wait to wile,
And strange eyes and bright wine lure,
 laugh like sin
Which steals back softly on a soul half
 saved,
And I the first deny, decry, despise,
With this avowal, these intents so
 fair, –
Still be it all my own, this moment's
 pride!
No less I make an end in perfect joy.
E'en in my brightest time, a lurking
 fear
Possessed me: I well knew my weak
 resolves,
I felt the witchery that makes mind
 sleep
Over its treasure, as one half afraid
To make his riches definite: but now
These feelings shall not utterly be lost,
I shall not know again that nameless
 care
Lest, leaving all undone in youth, some
 new

And undreamed end reveal itself too
 late:
For this song shall remain to tell for ever
That when I lost all hope of such a
 change,
Suddenly beauty rose on me again.
No less I make an end in perfect joy,
For I, who thus again was visited,
Shall doubt not many another bliss
 awaits,
And, though this weak soul sink and
 darkness whelm,
Some little word shall light it, raise aloft,
To where I clearlier see and better love,
As I again go o'er the tracts of thought
Like one who has a right, and I shall
 live
With poets, calmer, purer still each time,
And beauteous shapes will come for
 me to seize,
And unknown secrets will be trusted me
Which were denied the waverer once;
 but now
I shall be priest and prophet as of old.

Sun-treader, I believe in God and truth
And love; and as one just escaped from
 death
Would bind himself in bands of friends
 to feel
He lives indeed, so, I would lean on
 thee!
Thou must be ever with me, most in
 gloom
If such must come, but chiefly when I
 die,
For I seem, dying, as one going in the
 dark
To fight a giant: but live thou for ever,
And be to all what thou hast been to me!
All in whom this wakes pleasant thoughts
 of me
Know my last state is happy, free from
 doubt
Or touch of fear. Love me and wish me
 well.

*Richmond, October 22, 1832*

## NOTE

Je crains bien que mon pauvre ami ne soit pas toujours parfaitement compris dans ce qui reste à lire de cet étrange fragment, mais il est moins propre que tout autre à éclaircir ce qui de sa nature ne peut jamais être que songe et confusion. D'ailleurs je ne sais trop si en cherchant à mieux co-ordonner certaines parties l'on ne courrait pas le risque de nuire au seul mérite auquel une production si singulière peut prètendre, celui de donner une idée assez précise du genre qu'elle n'a fait qu'ébaucher. Ce début sans prétention, ce remuement des passions qui va d'abord en accroissant et puis s'apaise par degrés, ces élans de l'âme, ce retour soudain sur soi-même, et par-dessus tout, la tournure d'esprit tout particulière de mon ami, rendent les changemens presque impossibles. Les raisons qu'il fait valoir ailleurs, et d'autres encore plus puissantes, ont fait trouver grâce à mes yeux pour cet écrit qu'autrement je lui eusse conseillé de jeter au feu. Je n'en crois pas moins au grand principe de toute composition – à ce principe de Shakespeare, de Rafaelle, de Beethoven, d'où il suit que la concentration des idées est due bien plus à leur conception qu'à leur mise en exécution: j'ai tout lieu de craindre que la première de ces qualités ne soit encore étrangère à mon ami, et je doute fort qu'un redoublement de travail lui fasse acquérir la seconde. Le mieux serait de brûler ceci; mais que faire?

Je crois que dans ce qui suit il fait allusion à un certain examen qu'il fit autrefois de l'âme, ou plutôt de son âme, pour découvrir la suite des objets auxquels il lui serait possible d'atteindre, et dont chacun une fois obtenu devait former une espèce de plateau d'où l'on pouvait apercevoir d'autres buts, d'autres projets, d'autres jouissances qui, à leur tour, devaient être surmontés. Il en résultait que l'oubli et le sommeil devaient tout terminer. Cette idée, que je ne saisis pas parfaitement, lui est peut-être aussi inintelligible qu'à moi.

PAULINE

# PARACELSUS

1835

*Persons*

Aureolus Paracelsus, *a student*. Festus *and* Michal, *his friends*. Aprile, *an Italian poet*.

## 1 – PARACELSUS ASPIRES

*Scene – Würzburg; a garden in the environs. 1512.*

FESTUS, PARACELSUS, MICHAL

*Par.* Come close to me, dear friends; still closer; thus!

Close to the heart which, though long time roll by

Ere it again beat quicker, pressed to yours,

As now it beats – perchance a long, long time –

At least henceforth your memories shall make

Quiet and fragrant as befits their home.

Nor shall my memory want a home in yours –

Alas, that it requires too well such free

Forgiving love as shall embalm it there!

For if you would remember me aright,

As I was born to be, you must forget

All fitful strange and moody way-wardness

Which e'er confused my better spirit, to dwell

Only on moments such as these, dear friends!

– My heart no truer, but my words and ways

More true to it: as Michal, some months hence,

Will say, 'this autumn was a pleasant time,'

For some few sunny days; and overlook

Its bleak wind, hankering after pining leaves.

Autumn would fain be sunny; I would look

Liker my nature's truth: and both are frail,

And both beloved, for all our frailty.

*Mich.*                    Aureole!

*Par.* Drop by drop! she is weeping like a child!

Not so! I am content – more than content;

Nay, autumn wins you best by this its mute

Appeal to sympathy for its decay:

Look up, sweet Michal, nor esteem the less

Your stained and drooping vines their grapes bow down,

Nor blame those creaking trees bent with their fruit.

That apple-tree with a rare after-birth

Of peeping blooms sprinkled its wealth among!

Then for the winds – what wind that ever raved

Shall vex that ash which overlooks you both,

So proud it wears its berries? Ah, at length,

The old smile meet for her, the lady of this

Sequestered nest! – this kingdom, limited

Alone by one old populous green wall

Tenanted by the ever-busy flies,

Grey crickets and shy lizards and quick spiders,

Each family of the silver-threaded moss –

Which, look through near, this way, and it appears

A stubble-field or a cane-brake, a marsh

Of bulrush whitening in the sun: laugh
 now!
Fancy the crickets, each one in his
 house,
Looking out, wondering at the world –
 or best,
Yon painted snail with his gay shell of
 dew,
Travelling to see the glossy balls high
 up
Hung by the caterpillar, like gold lamps.
*Mich.* In truth we have lived carelessly
 and well.
*Par.* And shall, my perfect pair! – each,
 trust me, born
For the other; nay, your very hair,
 when mixed,
Is of one hue. For where save in this
 nook
Shall you two walk, when I am far
 away,
And wish me prosperous fortune? Stay:
 that plant
Shall never wave its tangles lightly and
 softly,
As a queen's languid and imperial arm
Which scatters crowns among her
 lovers, but you
Shall be reminded to predict to me
Some great success! Ah see, the sun
 sinks broad
Behind Saint Saviour's: wholly gone, at
 last!
*Fest.* How, Aureole, stay those
 wandering eyes awhile!
You are ours to-night, at least; and
 while you spoke
Of Michal and her tears, I thought that
 none
Could willing leave what he so seemed
 to love:
But that last look destroys my dream –
 that look
As if, where'er you gazed, there stood a
 star!
How far was Würzburg with its church
 and spire

And garden-walls and all things they
 contain,
From that look's far alighting?
*Par.*                     I but spoke
And looked alike from simple joy to see
The beings I love best, shut in so well
From all rude chances like to be my lot,
That, when afar, my weary spirit, –
 disposed
To lose awhile its care in soothing
 thoughts
Of them, their pleasant features, looks
 and words, –
Needs never hesitate, nor apprehend
Encroaching trouble may have reached
 them too,
Nor have recourse to fancy's busy aid
And fashion even a wish in their behalf
Beyond what they possess already here;
But, unobstructed, may at once forget
Itself in them, assured how well they
 fare.
Beside, this Festus knows he holds me
 one
Whom quiet and its charms arrest in
 vain,
One scarce aware of all the joys I quit,
Too filled with airy hopes to make
 account
Of soft delights his own heart garners
 up:
Whereas beholds how much our sense
 of all
That's beauteous proves alike! When
 Festus learns
That every common pleasure of the
 world
Affects me as himself; that I have just
As varied appetite for joy derived
From common things; a stake in life, in
 short,
Like his; a stake which rash pursuit of
 aims
That life affords not, would as soon
 destroy; –
He may convince himself that, this in
 view,

I shall act well advised. And last, because,
Though heaven and earth and all
    things were at stake,
Sweet Michal must not weep, our parting
    eve.
*Fest.* True: and the eve is deepening,
    and we sit
As little anxious to begin our talk
As though to-morrow I could hint of it
As we paced arm-in-arm the cheerful
    town
At sun-dawn; or could whisper it by fits
(Trithemius busied with his class the
    while)
In that dim chamber where the noon-
    streaks peer
Half-frightened by the awful tomes a-
    round;
Or in some grassy lane unbosom all
From even-blush to midnight: but,
    to-morrow!
Have I full leave to tell my inmost
    mind?
We have been brothers, and henceforth
    the world
Will rise between us: – all my freest
    mind?
'Tis the last night, dear Aureole!
*Par.* Oh, say on!
Devise some test of love, some arduous
    feat
To be performed for you: say on! If
    night
Be spent the while, the better! Recall
    how oft
My wondrous plans and dreams and
    hopes and fears
Have – never wearied you, oh no! – as I
Recall, and never vividly as now,
Your true affection, born when
    Einsiedeln
And its green hills were all the world to
    us;
And still increasing to this night which
    ends
My further stay at Würzburg. Oh, one
    day

You shall be very proud! Say on, dear
    friends!
*Fest.* In truth? 'Tis for my proper peace,
    indeed,
Rather than yours; for vain all projects
    seem
To stay your course: I said my latest
    hope
Is fading even now. A story tells
Of some far embassy despatched to
    win
The favour of an eastern king, and how
The gifts they offered proved but
    dazzling dust
Shed from the ore-beds native to his
    clime.
Just so, the value of repose and love,
I meant should tempt you, better far
    than I
You seem to comprehend; and yet
    desist
No whit from projects where repose
    nor love
Has part.
*Par.*     Once more? Alas! As I foretold.
*Fest.* A solitary brier the bank puts
    forth
To save our swan's nest floating out to
    sea.
*Par.* Dear Festus, hear me. What is it
    you wish?
That I should lay aside my heart's
    pursuit,
Abandon the sole ends for which I live,
Reject God's great commission, and so
    die!
You bid me listen for your true love's
    sake:
Yet how has grown that love? Even in a
    long
And patient cherishing of the self-same
    spirit
It now would quell; as though a
    mother hoped
To stay the lusty manhood of the child
Once weak upon her knees. I was not
    born

Informed and fearless from the first,
    but shrank
From aught which marked me out
    apart from men:
I would have lived their life, and died
    their death,
Lost in their ranks, eluding destiny:
But you first guided me through doubt
    and fear,
Taught me to know mankind and know
    myself;
And now that I am strong and full of
    hope,
That, from my soul, I can reject all aims
Save those your earnest words made
    plain to me,
Now that I touch the brink of my
    design,
When I would have a triumph in their
    eyes,
A glad cheer in their voices – Michal
    weeps,
And Festus ponders gravely!
*Fest.*               When you deign
To hear my purpose . . .
*Par.*            Hear it? I can say
Beforehand all this evening's conference!
'Tis this way, Michal, that he uses: first,
Or he declares, or I, the leading points
Of our best scheme of life, what is man's
    end
And what God's will; no two faiths e'er
    agreed
As his with mine. Next, each of us
    allows
Faith should be acted on as best we
    may;
Accordingly, I venture to submit
My plan, in lack of better, for pursuing
The path which God's will seems to
    authorize.
Well, he discerns much good in it, avows
This motive worthy, that hope plausible,
A danger here to be avoided, there
An oversight to be repaired: in fine
Our two minds go together – all the
    good

Approved by him, I gladly recognize,
All he counts bad, I thankfully discard,
And nought forbids my looking up at
    last
For some stray comfort in bis cautious
    brow.
When, lo! I learn that, spite of all, there
    lurks
Some innate and inexplicable germ
Of failure in my scheme; so that at last
It all amounts to this – the sovereign
    proof
That we devote ourselves to God, is
    seen
In living just as though no God there
    were;
A life which, prompted by the sad and
    blind
Folly of man, Festus abhors the most;
But which these tenets sanctify at once,
Though to less subtle wits it seems the
    same,
Consider it how they may.
*Mich.*            Is it so, Festus?
He speaks so calmly and kindly: is it so?
*Par.* Reject those glorious visions of
    God's love
And man's design; laugh loud that God
    should send
Vast longings to direct us; say how soon
Power satiates these, or lust, or gold; I
    know
The world's cry well, and how to
    answer it.
But this ambiguous warfare . . .
*Fest.*           . . . Wearies so
That you will grant no last leave to your
    friend
To urge it? – for his sake, not yours? I
    wish
To send my soul in good hopes after
    you;
Never to sorrow that uncertain words
Erringly apprehended, a new creed
Ill understood, begot rash trust in you,
Had share in your undoing.
*Par.*           Choose your side,

Hold or renounce: but meanwhile blame
    me not
Because I dare to act on your own
    views,
Nor shrink when they point onward,
    nor espy
A peril where they most ensure success.
*Fest.* Prove that to me – but that! Prove
    you abide
Within their warrant, nor presumptuous
    boast
God's labour laid on you; prove, all you
    covet
A mortal may expect; and, most of all,
Prove the strange course you now
    affect, will lead
To its attainment – and I bid you speed,
Nay, count the minutes till you venture
    forth!
You smile; but I had gathered from
    slow thought –
Much musing on the fortunes of my
    friend –
Matter I deemed could not be urged in
    vain;
But it all leaves me at my need: in shreds
And fragments I must venture what
    remains.
*Mich.* Ask at once, Festus, wherefore he
    should scorn . . .
*Fest.* Stay, Michal: Aureole, I speak
    guardedly
And gravely, knowing well, whate'er
    your error,
This is no ill-considered choice of
    yours,
No sudden fancy of an ardent boy.
Not from your own confiding words
    alone
Am I aware your passionate heart long
    since
Gave birth to, nourished and at length
    matures
This scheme. I will not speak of
    Einsiodeln,
Where I was born your elder by some
    years

Only to watch you fully from the first:
In all beside, our mutual tasks were
    fixed
Even then – 'twas mine to have you in
    my view
As you had your own soul and those
    intents
Which filled it when, to crown your
    dearest wish,
With a tumultuous heart, you left with
    me
Our childhood's home to join the
    favoured few
Whom, here, Trithemius condescends
    to teach
A portion of his lore: and not one youth
Of those so favoured, whom you now
    despise,
Came earnest as you came, resolved,
    like you,
To grasp all, and retain all, and deserve
By patient toil a wide renown like his.
Now, this new ardour which supplants
    the old
I watched, too; 'twas significant and
    strange,
In one matched to his soul's content at
    length
With rivals in the search for wisdom's
    prize,
To see the sudden pause, the total
    change;
From contest, the transition to repose –
From pressing onward as his fellows
    pressed,
To a blank idleness, yet most unlike
The dull stagnation of a soul, content,
Once foiled, to leave betimes a
    thriveless quest.
That careless bearing, free from all
    pretence
Even of contempt for what it ceased to
    seek –
Smiling humility, praising much, yet
    waiving
What it professed to praise – though
    not so well

Maintained but that rare outbreaks,
    fierce and brief,
Revealed the hidden scorn, as quickly
    curbed.
That ostentatious show of past defeat,
That ready acquiescence in contempt,
I deemed no other than the letting go
His shivered sword, of one about to
    spring
Upon his foe's throat; but it was not
    thus:
Not that way looked your brooding
    purpose then.
For after-signs disclosed, what you
    confirmed,
That you prepared to task to the
    uttermost
Your strength, in furtherance of a certain
    aim
Which – while it bore the name your
    rivals gave
Their own most puny efforts – was so
    vast
In scope that it included their best flights,
Combined them, and desired to gain
    one prize
In place of many, – the secret of the
    world,
Of man, and man's true purpose, path
    and fate.
– That you, not nursing as a mere vague
    dream
This purpose, with the sages of the
    past,
Have struck upon a way to this, if all
You trust be true, which following,
    heart and soul,
You, if a man may, dare aspire to know:
And that this aim shall differ from a host
Of aims alike in character and kind,
Mostly in this, – that in itself alone
Shall its reward be, not an alien end
Blending therewith; no hope nor fear
    nor joy
Nor woe, to elsewhere move you, but
    this pure
Devotion to sustain you or betray:

Thus you aspire.
*Par.*         You shall not state it thus:
I should not differ from the dreamy
    crew
You speak of. I profess no other share
In the selection of my lot, than this
My ready answer to the will of God
Who summons me to be his organ. All
Whose innate strength supports them
    shall succeed
No better than the sages.
*Fest.*         Such the aim, then,
God sets before you; and 'tis doubtless
    need
That he appoint no less the way of praise
Than the desire to praise; for, though I
    hold
With you, the setting forth such praise
    to be
The natural end and service of a man,
And hold such praise is best attained
    when man
Attains the general welfare of his kind –
Yet this, the end, is not the instrument.
Presume not to serve God apart from
    such
Appointed channel as he wills shall
    gather
Imperfect tributes, for that sole obedience
Valued perchance! He seeks not that
    his altars
Blaze, careless how, so that they do but
    blaze.
Suppose this, then; that God selected
    you
To know (heed well your answers, for
    my faith
Shall meet implicitly what they affirm)
I cannot think you dare annex to such
Selection aught beyond a steadfast will,
An intense hope; nor let your gifts create
Scorn or neglect of ordinary means
Conducive to success, make destiny
Dispense with man's endeavour. Now,
    dare you search
Your inmost heart, and candidly avow
Whether you have not rather wild desire

For this distinction than security
Of its existence? whether you discern
The path to the fulfilment of your purpose
Clear as that purpose – and again, that
    purpose
Clear as your yearning to be singled out
For its pursuer. Dare you answer this?
*Par.* [*after a pause*]. No, I have nought
    to fear! Who will may know
The secret'st workings of my soul. What
    though
It be so? – if indeed the strong desire
Eclipse the aim in me? – if splendour
    break
Upon the outset of my path alone,
And duskest shade succeed? What
    fairer seal
Shall I require to my authentic mission
Than this fierce energy? – this instinct
    striving
Because its nature is to strive? – enticed
By the security of no broad course.
Without success forever in its eyes!
How know I else such glorious fate my
    own,
But in the restless irresistible force
That works within me? Is it for human
    will
To institute such impulses? – still less,
To disregard their promptings! What
    should I
Do, kept among you all; your loves, your
    cares,
Your life – all to be mine? Be sure that
    God
Ne'er dooms to waste the strength he
    deigns impart!
Ask the geier-eagle why she stoops at
    once
Into the vast and unexplored abyss,
What full-grown power informs her from
    the first,
Why she not marvels, strenuously
    beating
The silent boundless regions of the sky!
Be sure they sleep not whom God needs!
    Nor fear

Their holding light his charge, when
    every hour
That finds that charge delayed, is a new
    death.
This for the faith in which I trust; and
    hence
I can abjure so well the idle arts
These pedants strive to learn and
    teach; Black Arts,
Great Works, the Secret and Sublime,
    forsooth –
Let others prize: too intimate a tie
Connects me with our God! A sullen
    fiend
To do my bidding, fallen and hateful
    sprites
To help me – what are these, at best,
    beside
God helping, God directing everywhere,
So that the earth shall yield her secrets
    up,
And every object there be charged to
    strike,
Teach, gratify her master God appoints?
And I am young, my Festus, happy and
    free!
I can devote myself; I have a life
To give; I, singled out for this, the One!
Think, think! the wide East, where all
    Wisdom sprung;
The bright South, where she dwelt; the
    hopeful North,
All are passed o'er – it lights on me!
    'Tis time
New hopes should animate the world,
    new light
Should dawn from new revealings to a
    race
Weighed down so long, forgotten so
    long; thus shall
The heaven reserved for us at last receive
Creatures whom no unwonted
    splendours blind,
But ardent to confront the unclouded
    blaze
Whose beams not seldom blessed their
    pilgrimage,

Not seldom glorified their life below.

*Fest.* My words have their old fate and
    make faint stand
Against your glowing periods. Call this,
    truth –
Why not pursue it in a fast retreat,
Some one of Learning's many palaces,
After approved example? – seeking there
Calm converse with the great dead, soul
    to soul,
Who laid up treasure with the like
    intent
– So lift yourself into their airy place,
And fill out full their unfulfilled careers,
Unravelling the knots their baffled skill
Pronounced inextricable, true! – but left
Far less confused. A fresh eye, a fresh
    hand,
Might do much at their vigour's waning-
    point;
Succeeding with new-breathed new-
    hearted force,
As at old games the runner snatched
    the torch
From runner still: this way success
    might be.
But you have coupled with your
    enterprise,
An arbitrary self-repugnant scheme
Of seeking it in strange and untried
    paths.
What books are in the desert? Writes
    the sea
The secret of her yearning in vast caves
Where yours will fall the first of human
    feet?
Has wisdom sat there and recorded
    aught
You press to read? Why turn aside from
    her
To visit, where her vesture never glanced,
Now – solitudes consigned to barrenness
By God's decree, which who shall dare
    impugn?
Now – ruins where she paused but
    would not stay,
Old ravaged cities that, renouncing her,

She called an endless curse on, so it
    came:
Or worst of all, now – men you visit,
    men,
Ignoblest troops who never heard her
    voice
Or hate it, men without one gift from
    Rome
Or Athens, – these shall Aureole's
    teachers be!
Rejecting past example, practice, precept,
Aidless 'mid these he thinks to stand
    alone:
Thick like a glory round the Stagirite
Your rivals throng, the sages: here
    stand you!
Whatever you may protest, knowledge
    is not
Paramount in your love; or for her sake
You would collect all help from every
    source –
Rival, assistant, friend, foe, all would
    merge
In the broad class of those who showed
    her haunts,
And those who showed them not.

*Par.*            What shall I say?
Festus, from childhood I have been
    possessed
By a fire – by a true fire, or faint or
    fierce,
As from without some master, so it
    seemed,
Repressed or urged its current: this but
    ill
Expresses what would I convey: but
    rather
I will believe an angel ruled me thus,
Than that my soul's own workings,
    own high nature,
So became manifest. I knew not then
What whispered in the evening, and
    spoke out
At midnight. If some mortal, born too
    soon,
Were laid away in some great trance –
    the ages

Coming and going all the while – till
    dawned
His true time's advent; and could then
    record
The words they spoke who kept watch
    by his bed, –
Then I might tell more of the breath so
    light
Upon my eyelids, and the fingers light
Among my hair. Youth is confused; yet
    never
So dull was I but, when that spirit
    passed,
I turned to him, scarce consciously, as
    turns
A water-snake when fairies cross his
    sleep.
And having this within me and about
    me
While Einsiedeln, its mountains, lakes
    and woods
Confined me – what oppressive joy was
    mine
When life grew plain, and I first viewed
    the thronged,
The everlasting concourse of mankind!
Believe that ere I joined them, ere I knew
The purpose of the pageant, or the place
Consigned me in its ranks – while, just
    awake,
Wonder was freshest and delight most
    pure –
'Twas then that least supportable
    appeared
A station with the brightest of the crowd,
A portion with the proudest of them
    all.
And from the tumult in my breast, this
    only
Could I collect, that I must thenceforth
    die
Or elevate myself far, far above
The gorgeous spectacle. I seemed to long
At once to trample on, yet save mankind,
To make some unexampled sacrifice
In their behalf, to wring some
    wondrous good

From heaven or earth for them, to
    perish, winning
Eternal weal in the act: as who should
    dare
Pluck out the angry thunder from its
    cloud,
That, all its gathered flame discharged
    on him,
No storm might threaten summer's
    azure sleep:
Yet never to be mixed with men so much
As to have part even in my own work,
    share
In my own largess. Once the feat
    achieved,
I would withdraw from their officious
    praise,
Would gently put aside their profuse
    thanks.
Like some knight traversing a wilderness,
Who, on his way, may chance to free a
    tribe
Of desert-people from their dragon-foe;
When all the swarthy race press round
    to kiss
His feet, and choose him for their king,
    and yield
Their poor tents, pitched among the
    sandhills, for
His realm: and he points, smiling, to
    his scarf
Heavy with riveled gold, his burgonet
Gay set with twinkling stones – and to
    the East,
Where these must be displayed!
*Fest.*             Good: let us hear
No more about your nature, 'which
    first shrank
'From all that marked you out apart
    from men!'
*Par.* I touch on that; these words but
    analyse
The first mad impulse: 'twas as brief as
    fond,
For as I gazed again upon the show,
I soon distinguished here and there a
    shape

Palm-wreathed and radiant, forehead
    and full eye.
Well pleased was I their state should
    thus at once
Interpret my own thoughts: – 'Behold
    the clue
'To all,' I rashly said, 'and what I pine
'To do, these have accomplished: we
    are peers.
'They know and therefore rule: I, too,
    will know!'
You were beside me, Festus, as you say;
You saw me plunge in their pursuits
    whom fame
Is lavish to attest the lords of mind,
Not pausing to make sure the prize in
    view
Would satiate my cravings when
    obtained,
But since they strove I strove. Then
    came a slow
And strangling failure. We aspired alike,
Yet not the meanest plodder, Tritheim
    counts
A marvel, but was all-sufficient, strong,
Or staggered only at his own vast wits;
While I was restless, nothing satisfied,
Distrustful, most perplexed. I would
    slur over
That struggle; suffice it, that I loathed
    myself
As weak compared with them, yet felt
    somehow
A mighty power was brooding, taking
    shape
Within me; and this lasted till one night
When, as I sat revolving it and more,
A still voice from without said – 'Seest
    thou not,
'Desponding child, whence spring
    defeat and loss?
'Even from thy strength. Consider: hast
    thou gazed
'Presumptuously on wisdom's
    countenance,
'No veil between; and can thy faltering
    hands,

'Unguided by the brain the sight
    absorbs,
'Pursue their task as earnest blinkers
    do
'Whom radiance ne'er distracted? Live
    their life
'If thou wouldst share their fortune,
    choose their eyes
'Unfed by splendour. Let each task
    present
'Its petty good to thee. Waste not thy
    gifts
'In profitless waiting for the gods'
    descent,
'But have some idol of thine own to
    dress
'With their array. Know, not for
    knowing's sake,
'But to become a star to men for ever;
'Know, for the gain it gets, the praise it
    brings,
'The wonder it inspires, the love it
    breeds:
'Look one step onward, and secure
    that step!'
And I smiled as one never smiles but
    once,
Then first discovering my own aim's
    extent,
Which sought to comprehend the
    works of God,
And God himself, and all God's
    intercourse
With the human mind; I understand,
    no less,
My fellows' studies, whose true worth I
    saw,
But smiled not, well aware who stood
    by me.
And softer came the voice – 'There is a
    way:
' 'Tis hard for flesh to tread therein,
    imbued
'With frailty – hopeless, if indulgence
    first
'Have ripened inborn germs of sin to
    strength:

'Wilt thou adventure for my sake and
  man's,
'Apart from all reward?' And last it
  breathed –
'Be happy, my good soldier: I am by
  thee,
'Be sure, even to the end!' – I answered
  not,
Knowing him. As he spoke, I was endued
With comprehension and a steadfast
  will;
And when he ceased, my brow was
  sealed his own.
If there took place no special change
  in me,
How comes it all things wore a different
  hue
Thenceforward? – pregnant with vast
  consequence,
Teeming with grand result, loaded with
  fate?
So that when, quailing at the mighty
  range
Of secret truths which yearn for birth, I
  haste
To contemplate undazzled some one
  truth,
Its bearings and effects alone – at once
What was a speck expands into a star,
Asking a life to pass exploring thus,
Till I near craze. I go to prove my soul!
I see my way as birds their trackless way.
I shall arrive! what time, what circuit
  first,
I ask not: but unless God send his hail
Or blinding fireballs, sleet or stifling
  snow,
In some time, his good time, I shall
  arrive:
He guides me and the bird. In his good
  time!
*Mich.* Vex him no further, Festus; it is so!
*Fest.* Just thus you help me ever. This
  would hold
Were it the trackless air, and not a path
Inviting you, distinct with footprints
  yet

Of many a mighty marcher gone that
  way.
You may have purer views than theirs,
  perhaps,
But they were famous in their day – the
  proofs
Remain. At least accept the light they
  lend.
*Par.* Their light! the sum of all is briefly
  this:
They laboured and grew famous, and
  the fruits
Are best seen in a dark and groaning
  earth
Given over to a blind and endless strife
With evils, what of all their lore abates?
No; I reject and spurn them utterly
And all they teach. Shall I still sit beside
Their dry wells, with a white lip and
  filmed eye,
While in the distance heaven is blue
  above
Mountains where sleep the unsunned
  tarns?
*Fest.*       And yet
As strong delusions have prevailed ere
  now.
Men have set out as gallantly to seek
Their ruin. I have heard of such:
  yourself
Avow all hitherto have failed and fallen.
*Mich.* Nay, Festus, when but as the
  pilgrims faint
Through the drear way, do you expect
  to see
Their city dawn amid the clouds afar?
*Par.* Ay, sounds it not like some old
  well-known tale?
For me, I estimate their works and them
So rightly, that at times I almost dream
I too have spent a life the sages' way,
And tread once more familiar paths.
  Perchance
I perished in an arrogant self-reliance
Ages ago; and in that act, a prayer
For one more chance went up so
  earnest, so

Instinct with better light let in by death,
That life was blotted out – not so
   completely
But scattered wrecks enough of it
   remain,
Dim memories, as now, when once more
   seems
The goal in sight again. All which,
   indeed,
Is foolish, and only means – the flesh I
   wear,
The earth I tread, are not more clear to
   me
Than my belief, explained to you or no.
*Fest*. And who am I, to challenge and
   dispute
That clear belief? I will divest all fear.
*Mich*. Then Aureole is God's commissary!
   he shall
Be great and grand – and all for us!
*Par*.                         No, sweet!
Not great and grand. If I can serve
   mankind
'Tis well; but there our intercourse
   must end:
I never will be served by those I serve.
*Fest*. Look well to this; here is a plague-
   spot, here,
Disguise it how you may! 'Tis true, you
   utter
This scorn while by our side and
   loving us:
'Tis but a spot as yet: but it will break
Into a hideous blotch if overlooked.
How can that course be safe which
   from the first
Produces carelessness to human love?
It seems you have abjured the helps
   which men
Who overpass their kind, as you would
   do,
Have humbly sought; I dare not
   thoroughly probe
This matter, lest I learn too much. Let be
That popular praise would little
   instigate
Your efforts, nor particular approval

Reward you; put reward aside; alone
You shall go forth upon your arduous
   task,
None shall assist you, none partake
   your toil,
None share your triumph: still you
   must retain
Some one to cast your glory on, to
   share
Your rapture with. Were I elect like
   you,
I would encircle me with love, and
   raise
A rampart of my fellows; it should
   seem
Impossible for me to fail, so watched
By gentle friends who made my cause
   their own.
They should ward off fate's envy – the
   great gift,
Extravagant when claimed by me
   alone,
Being so a gift to them as well as me.
If danger daunted me or ease seduced,
How calmly their sad eyes should gaze
   reproach!
*Mich*. O Aureole, can I sing when all
   alone,
Without first calling, in my fancy, both
To listen by my side – even I! And you?
Do you not feel this? Say that you feel
   this!
*Par*. I feel 'tis pleasant that my aims, at
   length
Allowed their weight, should be supposed
   to need
A further strengthening in these goodly
   helps!
My course allures for its own sake, its
   sole
Intrinsic worth; and ne'er shall boat of
   mine
Adventure forth for gold and apes at
   once.
Your sages say, 'if human, therefore
   weak:'
If weak, more need to give myself entire

To my pursuit; and by its side, all
    else …
No matter! I deny myself but little
In waiving all assistance save its own.
Would there were some real sacrifice to
    make!
Your friends the sages threw their joys
    away,
While I must be content with keeping
    mine.
*Fest.* But do not cut yourself from human
    weal!
You cannot thrive – a man that dares
    affect
To spend his life in service to his kind
For no reward of theirs, unbound to
    them
By any tie; nor do so, Aureole! No –
There are strange punishments for
    such. Give up
(Although no visible good flow thence) some part
Of the glory to another; hiding thus,
Even from yourself, that all is for yourself.
Say, say almost to God – 'I have done all
'For her, not for myself!'
*Par.*                    And who but lately
Was to rejoice in my success like you?
Whom should I love but both of you?
*Fest.*                    I know not:
But know this, you, that 'tis no will of
    mine
You should abjure the lofty claims you
    make;
And this the cause – I can no longer
    seek
To overlook the truth, that there
    would be
A monstrous spectacle upon the earth,
Beneath the pleasant sun, among the
    trees:
– A being knowing not what love is.
    Hear me!
You are endowed with faculties which
    bear
Annexed to them as 'twere a
    dispensation

To summon meaner spirits to do their
    will
And gather round them at their need;
    inspiring
Such with a love themselves can never
    feel,
Passionless 'mid their passionate
    votaries.
I know not if you joy in this or no,
Or ever dream that common men can
    live
On objects you prize lightly, but which
    make
Their heart's sole treasure: the affections
    seem
Beauteous at most to you, which we
    must taste
Or die: and this strange quality accords,
I know not how, with you; sits well
    upon
That luminous brow, though in another
    it scowls
An eating brand, a shame. I dare not
    judge you.
The rules of right and wrong thus set
    aside,
There's no alternative – I own you one
Of higher order, under other laws
Than bind us; therefore, curb not one
    bold glance!
'Tis best aspire. Once mingled with us
    all …
*Mich.* Stay with us, Aureole! cast those
    hopes away,
And stay with us! An angel warns me,
    too,
Man should be humble; you are very
    proud:
And God, dethroned, has doleful
    plagues for such!
– Warns me to have in dread no quick
    repulse,
No slow defeat, but a complete success:
You will find all you seek, and perish so!
*Par. [after a pause].* Are these the
    barren firstfruits of my quest?
Is love like this the natural lot of all?

How many years of pain might one
   such hour
O'erbalance? Dearest Michal, dearest
   Festus,
What shall I say, if not that I desire
To justify your love; and will, dear
   friends,
In swerving nothing from my first
   resolves.
See, the great moon! and ere the mottled
   owls
Were wide awake, I was to go. It seems
You acquiesce at last in all save this –
If I am like to compass what I seek
By the untried career I choose; and then,
If that career, making but small
   account
Of much of life's delight, will yet retain
Sufficient to sustain my soul: for thus
I understand these fond fears just
   expressed.
And first; the lore you praise and I
   neglect,
The labours and the precepts of old
   time,
I have not lightly disesteemed. But,
   friends,
Truth is within ourselves; it takes no
   rise
From outward things, whate'er you may
   believe.
There is an inmost centre in us all,
Where truth abides in fulness; and
   around,
Wall upon wall, the gross flesh hems
   it in,
This perfect, clear perception – which
   is truth.
A baffling and perverting carnal mesh
Binds it, and makes all error: and to
   know
Rather consists in opening out a way
Whence the imprisoned splendour
   may escape,
Than in effecting entry for a light
Supposed to be without. Watch
   narrowly

The demonstration of a truth, its birth,
And you trace back the effluence to its
   spring
And source within us; where broods
   radiance vast,
To be elicited ray by ray, as chance
Shall favour: chance – for hitherto,
   your sage
Even as he knows not how those
   beams are born,
As little knows he what unlocks their
   fount:
And men have oft grown old among
   their books
To die case-hardened in their ignorance,
Whose careless youth had promised
   what long years
Of unremitted labour ne'er performed:
While, contrary, it has chanced some
   idle day,
To autumn loiterers just as fancy-free
As the midges in the sun, gives birth at
   last
To truth – produced mysteriously as
   cape
Of cloud grown out of the invisible air.
Hence, may not truth be lodged alike
   in all,
The lowest as the highest? some slight
   film
The interposing bar which binds a soul
And makes the idiot, just as makes the
   sage
Some film removed, the happy outlet
   whence
Truth issues proudly? See this soul of
   ours!
How it strives weakly in the child, is
   loosed
In manhood, clogged by sickness, back
   compelled
By age and waste, set free at last by
   death:
Why is it, flesh enthrals it or enthrones?
What is this flesh we have to penetrate?
Oh, not alone when life flows still, do
   truth

And power emerge, but also when
    strange chance
Ruffles its current; in unused
    conjuncture,
When sickness breaks the body –
    hunger, watching,
Excess or languor – oftenest death's
    approach,
Peril, deep joy or woe. One man shall
    crawl
Through life surrounded with all stirring
    things,
Unmoved; and he goes mad: and from
    the wreck
Of what he was, by his wild talk alone,
You first collect how great a spirit he hid.
Therefore, set free the soul alike in all,
Discovering the true laws by which the
    flesh
Accloys the spirit! We may not be
    doomed
To cope with seraphs, but at least the
    rest
Shall cope with us. Make no more
    giants, God,
But elevate the race at once! We ask
To put forth just our strength, our
    human strength,
All starting fairly, all equipped alike,
Gifted alike, all eagle-eyed,
    true-hearted –
See if we cannot beat thine angels yet!
Such is my task. I go to gather this
The sacred knowledge, here and there
    dispersed
About the world, long lost or never
    found.
And why should I be sad or lorn of
    hope?
Why ever make man's good distinct
    from God's,
Or, finding they are one, why dare
    mistrust?
Who shall succeed if not one pledged
    like me?
Mine is no mad attempt to build a
    world

Apart from his, like those who set
    themselves
To find the nature of the spirit they
    bore,
And, taught betimes that all their
    gorgeous dreams
Were only born to vanish in this life,
Refused to fit them to its narrow sphere,
But chose to figure forth another world
And other frames meet for their vast
    desires, –
And all a dream! Thus was life scorned;
    but life
Shall yet be crowned: twine amaranth!
    I am priest!
And all for yielding with a lively spirit
A poor existence, parting with a youth
Like those who squander every energy
Convertible to good, on painted toys,
Breath-bubbles, gilded dust! And
    though I spurn
All adventitious aims, from empty praise
To love's award, yet whoso deems such
    helps
Important, and concerns himself for me,
May know even these will follow with
    the rest –
As in the steady rolling Mayne, asleep
Yonder, is mixed its mass of schistous
    ore.
My own affections laid to rest awhile,
Will waken purified, subdued alone
By all I have achieved. Till then – till
    then . . .
Ah, the time-wiling loitering of a page
Through bower and over lawn, till eve
    shall bring
The stately lady's presence whom he
    loves –
The broken sleep of the fisher whose
    rough coat
Enwraps the queenly pearl – these are
    faint types!
See, see, they look on me: I triumph
    now!
But one thing, Festus, Michal! I have
    told

All I shall e'er disclose to mortal: say –
Do you believe I shall accomplish this?
*Fest*. I do believe!
*Mich*.                    I ever did believe!
*Par*. Those words shall never fade from
　　out my brain!
This earnest of the end shall never fade!
Are there not, Festus, are there not,
　　dear Michal,
Two points in the adventure of the diver,
One – when, a beggar, he prepares to
　　plunge,
One – when, a prince, he rises with his
　　pearl?
Festus, I plunge!
*Fest*.          We wait you when you rise!

## 2 – PARACELSUS ATTAINS

*Scene – Constantinople; the house of a
　　Greek Conjurer. 1521.*
### PARACELSUS
Over the waters in the vaporous West
The sun goes down as in a sphere of
　　gold
Behind the arm of the city, which
　　between,
With all that length of domes and
　　minarets,
Athwart the splendour, black and
　　crooked runs
Like a Turk verse along a scimitar.
There lie, sullen memorial, and no more
Possess my aching sight! 'Tis done at
　　last.
Strange – and the juggles of a sallow
　　cheat
Have won me to this act! 'Tis as yon
　　cloud
Should voyage unwrecked o'er many a
　　mountain-top
And break upon a molehill. I have dared
Come to a pause with knowledge; scan
　　for once
The heights already reached, without
　　regard
To the extent above; fairly compute

All I have clearly gained; for once
　　excluding
A brilliant future to supply and perfect
All half-gains and conjectures and
　　crude hopes:
And all because a fortune-teller wills
His credulous seekers should inscribe
　　thus much
Their previous life's attainment, in his
　　roll,
Before his promised secret, as he vaunts,
Make up the sum: and here amid the
　　scrawled
Uncouth recordings of the dupes of this
Old arch-genethliac,* lie my life's results!
A few blurred characters suffice to note
A stranger wandered long through
　　many lands
And reaped the fruit he coveted in a
　　few
Discoveries, as appended here and
　　there,
The fragmentary produce of much toil,
In a dim heap, fact and surmise
　　together
Confusedly massed as when acquired;
　　he was
Intent on gain to come too much to stay
And scrutinise the little gained: the whole
Slipt in the blank space 'twixt an idiot's
　　gibber
And a mad lover's ditty – there it lies.

And yet those blottings chronicle a
　　life –
A whole life, and my life! Nothing to do,
No problem for the fancy, but a life
Spent and decided, wasted past
　　retrieve
Or worthy beyond peer. Stay, what
　　does this
Remembrancer set down concerning
　　'life'?
' "Time fleets, youth fades, life is an
　　empty dream,"

* Birthday-book maker, γενεθλιακός

'It is the echo of time; and he whose
      heart
'Beat first beneath a human heart,
      whose speech
'Was copied from a human tongue,
      can never
'Recall when he was living yet knew
      not this.
'Nevertheless long seasons pass o'er him
'Till some one hour's experience shows
      what nothing,
'It seemed, could clearer show; and
      ever after,
'An altered brow and eye and gait and
      speech
'Attest that now he knows the adage
      true,
' "Time fleets, youth fades, life is an
      empty dream." '

Ay, my brave chronicler, and this same
      hour
As well as any; now, let my time be!

Now! I can go no farther; well or ill,
'Tis done. I must desist and take my
      chance.
I cannot keep on the stretch: 'tis no
      back-shrinking –
For let but some assurance beam,
      some close
To my toil grow visible, and I proceed
At any price, though closing it, I die.
Else, here I pause. The old Greek's
      prophecy
Is like to turn out true: 'I shall not quit
'His chamber till I know what I desire!'
Was it the light wind sang it o'er the sea?

An end, a rest! strange how the notion,
      once
Encountered, gathers strength by
      moments! Rest!
Where has it kept so long? this
      throbbing brow
To cease, this beating heart to cease, all
      cruel

And gnawing thoughts to cease! To dare
      let down
My strung, so high-strung brain, to
      dare unnerve
My harassed o'ertasked frame, to know
      my place,
My portion, my reward, even my failure,
Assigned, made sure for ever! To lose
      myself
Among the common creatures of the
      world,
To draw some gain from having been a
      man,
Neither to hope nor fear, to live at
      length!
Even in failure, rest! But rest in truth
And power and recompense … I hoped
      that once!

What, sunk insensibly so deep? Has all
Been undergone for this? This is the
      request
My labour qualified me to present
With no fear of refusal? Had I gone
Slightingly through my task, and so
      judged fit
To moderate my hopes; nay, were it
      now
My sole concern to exculpate myself,
End things or mend them, – why, I
      could not choose
A humbler mood to wait for the event!
No, no, there needs not this; no, after
      all,
At worst I have performed my share of
      the task:
The rest is God's concern; mine,
      merely this,
To know that I have obstinately held
By my own work. The mortal whose
      brave foot
Has trod, unscathed, the temple-court
      so far
That he descries at length the shrine of
      shrines,
Must let no sneering of the demons'
      eyes,

Whom he could pass unquailing,
     fasten now
Upon him, fairly past their power;
     no, no –
He must not stagger, faint, fall down at
     last,
Having a charm to baffle them; behold,
He bares his front: a mortal ventures
     thus
Serene amid the echoes, beams and
     glooms!
If he be priest henceforth, if he wake up
The god of the place to ban and blast
     him there,
Both well! What's failure or success to
     me?
I have subdued my life to the one
     purpose
Whereto I ordained it; there alone I spy,
No doubt, that way I may be satisfied.

Yes, well have I subdued my life!
     beyond
The obligation of my strictest vow,
The contemplation of my wildest
     bond,
Which gave my nature freely up, in
     truth,
But in its actual state, consenting fully
All passionate impulses its soil was
     formed
To rear, should wither; but foreseeing
     not
The tract, doomed to perpetual
     barrenness,
Would seem one day, remembered as
     it was,
Beside the parched sand-waste which
     now it is,
Already strewn with faint blooms,
     viewless then.
I ne'er engaged to root up loves so frail
I felt them not; yet now, 'tis very plain
Some soft spots had their birth in me
     at first,
If not love, say, like love: there was a
     time

When yet this wolfish hunger after
     knowledge
Set not remorselessly love's claims aside.
This heart was human once, or why
     recall
Einsiedeln, now, and Würzburg which
     the Mayne
Forsakes her course to fold as with an
     arm?

And Festus – my poor Festus, with his
     praise
And counsel and grave fears – where is
     he now
With the sweet maiden, long ago his
     bride?
I surely loved them – that last night, at
     least,
When we … gone! gone! the better. I
     am saved
The sad review of an ambitious youth
Choked by vile lusts, unnoticed in their
     birth,
But let grow up and wind around a will
Till action was destroyed. No, I have
     gone
Purging my path successively of aught
Wearing the distant likeness of such
     lusts.
I have made life consist of one idea:
Ere that was master, up till that was born,
I bear a memory of a pleasant life
Whose small events I treasure; till one
     morn
I ran o'er the seven little grassy fields,
Startling the flocks of nameless birds,
     to tell
Poor Festus, leaping all the while for joy,
To leave all trouble for my future plans,
Since I had just determined to become
The greatest and most glorious man on
     earth.
And since that morn all life has been
     forgotten:
All is one day, one only step between
The outset and the end: one tyrant all –
Absorbing aim fills up the interspace,

One vast unbroken chain of thought,
    kept up
Through a career apparently adverse
To its existence: life, death, light and
    shadow,
The shows of the world, were bare
    receptacles
Or indices of truth to be wrung thence,
Not ministers of sorrow or delight:
A wondrous natural robe in which she
    went.
For some one truth would dimly
    beacon me
From mountains rough with pines, and
    flit and wink
O'er dazzling wastes of frozen snow,
    and tremble
Into assured light in some branching
    mine
Where ripens, swathed in fire, the liquid
    gold –
And all the beauty, all the wonder fell
On either side the truth, as its mere
    robe;
I see the robe now – then I saw the form.
So far, then, I have voyaged with success,
So much is good, then, in this working
    sea
Which parts me from that happy strip
    of land:
But o'er that happy strip a sun shone,
    too!
And fainter gleams it as the waves grow
    rough,
And still more faint as the sea widens;
    last
I sicken on a dead gulf streaked with
    light
From its own putrefying depths alone.
Then, God was pledged to take me by
    the hand;
Now, any miserable juggle can bid
My pride depart. All is alike at length:
God may take pleasure in confounding
    pride
By hiding secrets with the scorned and
    base –

I am here, in short: so little have I
    paused
Throughout! I never glanced behind to
    know
If I had kept my primal light from
    wane,
And thus insensibly am – what I am!

Oh, bitter; very bitter!
                        And more bitter,
To fear a deeper curse, an inner ruin,
Plague beneath plague, the last turning
    the first
To light beside its darkness. Let me
    weep
My youth and its brave hopes, all dead
    and gone,
In tears which burn! Would I were sure
    to win
Some startling secret in their stead, a
    tincture
Of force to flush old age with youth, or
    breed
Gold, or imprison moonbeams till they
    change
To opal shafts! – only that, hurling it
Indignant back, I might convince myself
My aims remained supreme and pure
    as ever!
Even now, why not desire, for mankind's
    sake,
That if I fail, some fault may be the
    cause,
That, though I sink, another may
    succeed?
O God, the despicable heart of us!
Shut out this hideous mockery from
    my heart!
'Twas politic in you, Aureole, to reject
Single rewards, and ask them in the
    lump;
At all events, once launched, to hold
    straight on:
For now 'tis all or nothing. Mighty profit
Your gains will bring if they stop short
    of such
Full consummation! As a man, you had

A certain share of strength; and that is
    gone
Already in the getting these you boast.
Do not they seem to laugh, as who
    should say –
'Great master, we are here indeed,
    dragged forth
'To light; this hast thou done: be glad!
    Now, seek
'The strength to use which thou hast
    spent in getting!'

And yet 'tis much, surely 'tis very
    much,
Thus to have emptied youth of all its
    gifts,
To feed a fire meant to hold out till
    morn
Arrived with inexhaustible light; and lo,
I have heaped up my last, and day
    dawns not!
And I am left with grey hair, faded
    hands,
And furrowed brow. Ha, have I, after
    all,
Mistaken the wild nursling of my breast?
Knowledge it seemed, and power, and
    recompense!
Was she who glided through my room
    of nights,
Who laid my head on her soft knees
    and smoothed
The damp locks, – whose sly soothings
    just began
When my sick spirit craved repose a
    while –
God! was I fighting sleep off for death's
    sake?

God! Thou art mind! Unto the master-
    mind
Mind should be precious. Spare my
    mind alone!
All else I will endure; if, as I stand
Here, with my gains, thy thunder smite
    me down,
I bow me; 'tis thy will, thy righteous will;

I o'erpass life's restrictions, and I die;
And if no trace of my career remain
Save a thin corpse at pleasure of the
    wind
In these bright chambers level with the
    air,
See thou to it! But if my spirit fail,
My once proud spirit forsake me at the
    last,
Hast thou done well by me? So do not
    thou!
Crush not my mind, dear God, though
    I be crushed!
Hold me before the frequence of thy
    seraphs
And say – 'I crushed him, lest he should
    disturb
'My law. Men must not know their
    strength: behold,
'Weak and alone, how he had raised
    himself!'

But if delusions trouble me, and thou,
Not seldom felt with rapture in thy help
Throughout my toils and wanderings,
    dost intend
To work man's welfare through my
    weak endeavour,
To crown my mortal forehead with a
    beam
From thine own blinding crown, to
    smile, and guide
This puny hand and let the work so
    wrought
Be styled my work, – hear me! I covet
    not
An influx of new power, an angel's soul:
It were no marvel then – but I have
    reached
Thus far, a man; let me conclude, a man!
Give but one hour of my first energy,
Of that invincible faith, but only one!
That I may cover with an eagle-glance
The truths I have, and spy some certain
    way
To mould them, and completing them,
    possess!

Yet God is good: I started sure of that,
And why dispute it now? I'll not
    believe
But some undoubted warning long ere
    this
Had reached me: a fire-labarum was
    not deemed
Too much for the old founder of these
    walls.
Then, if my life has not been natural,
It has been monstrous: yet, till late, my
    course
So ardently engrossed me, that delight,
A pausing and reflecting joy, 'tis plain,
Could find no place in it. True, I am
    worn;
But who clothes summer, who is life
    itself?
God, that created all things, can renew!
And then, though after-life to please
    me now
Must have no likeness to the past,
    what hinders
Reward from springing out of toil, as
    changed
As bursts the flower from earth and
    root and stalk?
What use were punishment, unless
    some sin
Be first detected? let me know that first!
No man could ever offend as I have
        done. . .     [*A voice from within.*]

I hear a voice, perchance I heard
Long ago, but all too low,
So that scarce a care it stirred
If the voice were real or no:
I heard it in my youth when first
The waters of my life outburst:
But, now their stream ebbs faint, I
    hear
That voice, still low, but fatal-clear –
As if all poets, God ever meant
Should save the world, and therefore
    lent
Great gifts to, but who, proud, refused
To do his work, or lightly used

Those gifts, or failed through weak
    endeavour,
So, mourn cast off by him for ever, –
As if these leaned in airy ring
To take me; this the song they sing.

'Lost, lost! yet come,
With our wan troop make thy home.
Come, come! for we
Will not breathe, so much as breathe
Reproach to thee,
Knowing what thou sink'st beneath.
So sank we in those old years,
We who bid thee, come! thou last
Who, living yet, hast life o'erpast.
And altogether we, thy peers,
Will pardon crave for thee, the last
Whose trial is done, whose lot is cast
With those who watch but work no
    more,
Who gaze on life but live no more.
Yet we trusted thou shouldst speak
The message which our lips, too
    weak,
Refused to utter, – shouldst redeem
Our fault: such trust, and all a dream!
Yet we chose thee a birthplace
Where the richness ran to flowers:
Couldst not sing one song for grace?
Not make one blossom man's and
    ours?
Must one more recreant to his race
Die with unexerted powers,
And join us, leaving as he found
The world, he was to loosen, bound?
Anguish! ever and for ever;
Still beginning, ending never.
Yet, lost and last one, come!
How couldst understand, alas,
What our pale ghosts strove to say,
As their shades did glance and pass
Before thee night and day?
Thou wast blind as we were dumb:
Once more, therefore, come, O come!
How should we clothe, how arm the
    spirit
Shall next thy post of life inherit –

How guard him from thy speedy ruin?
Tell us of thy sad undoing
Here, where we sit, ever pursuing
Our weary task, ever renewing
Sharp sorrow, far from God who gave
Our powers, and man they could
    not save!'

APRILE *enters.*

Ha, ha! our king that wouldst be, here
    at last?
Art thou the poet who shall save the
    world?
Thy hand to mine! Stay, fix thine eyes
    on mine!
Thou wouldst be king? Still fix thine
    eyes on mine!
*Par.* Ha, ha! why crouchest not? Am I
    not king?
So torture is not wholly unavailing!
Have my fierce spasms compelled thee
    from thy lair?
Art thou the sage I only seemed to be,
Myself of after-time, my very self
With sight a little clearer, strength
    more firm,
Who robes him in my robe and grasps
    my crown
For just a fault, a weakness, a neglect?
I scarcely trusted God with the surmise
That such might come, and thou didst
    hear the while!
*Apr.* Thine eyes are lustreless to mine;
    my hair
Is soft, nay silken soft: to talk with thee
Flushes my cheek, and thou art ashy-
    pale.
Truly, thou hast laboured, hast with-
    stood her lips,
The siren's! Yes, 'tis like thou hast
    attained!
Tell me, dear master, wherefore now
    thou comest?
I thought thy solemn songs would have
    their meed
In after-time; that I should hear the
    earth

Exult in thee and echo with thy praise,
While I was laid forgotten in my grave.
*Par.* Ah fiend, I know thee, I am not
    thy dupe!
Thou art ordained to follow in my
    track,
Reaping my sowing, as I scorned to
    reap
The harvest sown by sages passed
    away.
Thou art the sober searcher, cautious
    striver,
As if, except through me, thou hast
    searched or striven!
Ay, tell the world! Degrade me after all,
To an aspirant after fame, not truth –
To all but envy of thy fate, be sure!
*Apr.* Nay, sing them to me; I shall envy
    not:
Thou shalt be king! Sing thou, and I
    will sit
Beside, and call deep silence for thy
    songs,
And worship thee, as I had ne'er been
    meant
To fill thy throne: but none shall ever
    know!
Sing to me; for already thy wild eyes
Unlock my heart-strings, as some
    crystal-shaft
Reveals by some chance blaze its
    parent fount
After long time: so thou reveal'st my
    soul.
All will flash forth at last, with thee to
    hear!
*Par.* (His secret! I shall get his secret –
    fool!)
I am he that aspired to know: and
    thou?
*Apr.* I would love infinitely, and be loved!
*Par.* Poor slave! I am thy king indeed.
*Apr.*                     Thou deem'st
That – born a spirit, dowered even as
    thou,
Born for thy fate – because I could not
    curb

My yearnings to possess at once the full
Enjoyment, but neglected all the means
Of realizing even the frailest joy,
Gathering no fragments to appease my
    want,
Yet nursing up that want till thus I die –
Thou deem'st I cannot trace thy safe
    sure march
O'er perils that o'erwhelm me,
    triumphing,
Neglecting nought below for aught
    above,
Despising nothing and ensuring all –
Nor that I could (my time to come
    again)
Lead thus my spirit securely as thine
    own.
Listen, and thou shalt see I know thee
    well.
I would love infinitely … Ah, lost! lost!
    Oh ye who armed me at such cost,
    How shall I look on all of ye
    With your gifts even yet on me?
*Par.* (Ah, 'tis some moonstruck
    creature after all!
Such fond fools as are like to haunt
    this den:
They spread contagion, doubtless: yet
    he seemed
To echo one foreboding of my heart
So truly, that … no matter! How he
    stands
With eve's last sunbeam staying on his
    hair
Which turns to it as if they were akin:
And those clear smiling eyes of saddest
    blue
Nearly set free, so far they rise above
The painful fruitless striving of the brow
And enforced knowledge of the lips,
    firmset
In slow despondency's eternal sigh!
Has he, too, missed life's end, and
    learned the cause?)
I charge thee, by thy fealty, be calm!
Tell me what thou wouldst be, and
    what I am.

*Apr.* I would love infinitely, and be
    loved.
First: I would carve in stone, or cast in
    brass,
The forms of earth. No ancient hunter
    lifted
Up to the gods by his renown, no
    nymph
Supposed the sweet soul of a woodland
    tree
Or sapphirine spirit of a twilight star,
Should be too hard for me; no
    shepherd-king
Regal for his white locks; no youth
    who stands
Silent and very calm amid the throng,
His right hand ever hid beneath his
    robe
Until the tyrant pass; no lawgiver,
No swan-soft woman rubbed with
    lucid oils
Given by a god for love of her – too hard!
Every passion sprung from man,
    conceived by man,
Would I express and clothe it in its
    right form,
Or blend with others struggling in one
    form,
Or show repressed by an ungainly form.
Oh, if you marvelled at some mighty
    spirit
With a fit frame to execute its will –
Even unconsciously to work its will –
You should be moved no less beside
    some strong
Rare spirit, fettered to a stubborn body,
Endeavouring to subdue it and inform it
With its own splendour! All this I
    would do:
And I would say, this done, 'His sprites
    created,
'God grants to each a sphere to be its
    world,
'Appointed with the various objects
    needed
'To satisfy its own peculiar want;
'So, I create a world for these my shapes

'Fit to sustain their beauty and their
    strength!'
And, at the word, I would contrive and
    paint
Woods, valleys, rocks and plains, dells,
    sands and wastes,
Lakes which, when morn breaks on
    their quivering bed,
Blaze like a wyvern flying round the sun,
And ocean isles so small, the dog-fish
    tracking
A dead whale, who should find them,
    would swim thrice
Around them, and fare onward – all to
    hold
The offspring of my brain. Nor these
    alone:
Bronze labyrinth, palace, pyramid and
    crypt,
Baths, galleries, courts, temples and
    terraces,
Marts, theatres and wharfs – all filled
    with men,
Men everywhere! And this performed
    in turn,
When those who looked on, pined to
    hear the hopes
And fears and hates and loves which
    moved the crowd,
I would throw down the pencil as the
    chisel,
And I would speak; no thought which
    ever stirred
A human breast should be untold; all
    passions,
All soft emotions, from the turbulent
    stir
Within a heart fed with desires like
    mine,
To the last comfort shutting the tired
    lids
Of him who sleeps the sultry noon
    away
Beneath the tent-tree by the wayside
    well:
And this in language as the need
    should be,

Now poured at once forth in a burning
    flow,
Now piled up in a grand array of words.
This done, to perfect and consummate
    all,
Even as a luminous haze links star to
    star,
I would supply all chasms with music,
    breathing
Mysterious motions of the soul, no way
To be defined save in strange melodies.
Last, having thus revealed all I could
    love,
Having received all love bestowed on it,
I would die: preserving so throughout
    my course
God full on me, as I was full on men:
He would approve my prayer, 'I have
    gone through
'The loveliness of life; create for me
    'If not for men, or take me to thyself,
'Eternal, infinite love!'
                            If thou hast ne'er
Conceived this mighty aim, this full
    desire,
Thou hast not passed my trial, and
    thou art
No king of mine.
*Par.*          Ah me!
*Apr.*                    But thou art here!
Thou didst not gaze like me upon that
    end
Till thine own powers for compassing
    the bliss
Were blind with glory; nor grow mad
    to grasp
At once the prize long patient toil
    should claim,
Nor spurn all granted short of that.
    And I
Would do as thou, a second time: nay,
    listen!
Knowing ourselves, our world, our task
    so great,
Our time so brief, 'tis clear if we refuse
The means so limited, the tools so rude
To execute our purpose, life will fleet,

And we shall fade, and leave our task
   undone.
We will be wise in time: what though
   our work
Be fashioned in despite of their ill-
   service,
Be crippled every way? 'Twere little praise
Did full resources wait on our goodwill
At every turn. Let all be as it is.
Some say the earth is even so contrived
That tree and flower, a vesture gay,
   conceal
A bare and skeleton framework. Had
   we means
Answering to our mind! But now I seem
Wrecked on a savage isle: how rear
   thereon
My palace? Branching palms the props
   shall be,
Fruit glossy mingling; gems are for the
   East;
Who heeds them? I can pass them.
   Serpents' scales,
And painted birds' down, furs and
   fishes' skins
Must help me; and a little here and
   there
Is all I can aspire to: still my art
Shall show its birth was in a gentler
   clime.
'Had I green jars of malachite, this way
'I'd range them: where those sea-shells
   glisten above,
'Cressets should hang, by right: this way
   we set
'The purple carpets, as these mats are
   laid,
'Woven of fern and rush and
   blossoming flag.'
Or if, by fortune, some completer grace
Be spared to me, some fragment, some
   slight sample
Of the prouder workmanship my own
   home boasts,
Some trifle little heeded there, but here
The place's one perfection – with what
   joy

Would I enshrine the relic, cheerfully
Foregoing all the marvels out of reach!
Could I retain one strain of all the psalm
Of the angels, one word of the fiat of
   God,
To let my followers know what such
   things are!
I would adventure nobly for their sakes:
When nights were still, and still the
   moaning sea,
And far away I could descry the land
Whence I departed, whither I return,
I would dispart the waves, and stand
   once more
At home, and load my bark, and
   hasten back,
And fling my gains to them, worthless
   or true.
'Friends,' I would say, 'I went far, far
   for them,
'Past the high rocks the haunt of doves,
   the mounds
'Of red earth from whose sides strange
   trees grow out,
'Past tracks of milk-white minute
   blinding sand,
'Till, by a mighty moon, I tremblingly
'Gathered these magic herbs, berry and
   bud,
'In haste, not pausing to reject the weeds,
'But happy plucking them at any price.
'To me, who have seen them bloom in
   their own soil,
'They are scarce lovely: plait and wear
   them, you!
'And guess, from what they are, the
   springs that fed them,
'The stars that sparkled o'er them,
   night by night,
'The snakes that travelled far to sip
   their dew!'
Thus for my higher loves; and thus
   even weakness
Would win me honour. But not these
   alone
Should claim my care; for common life,
   its wants

And ways, would I set forth in beauteous
    hues:
The lowest hind should not possess a
    hope,
A fear, but I'd be by him, saying better
Than he his own heart's language. I
    would live
For ever in the thoughts I thus explored,
As a discoverer's memory is attached
To all he finds; they should be mine
    henceforth,
Imbued with me, though free to all
    before:
For clay, once cast into my soul's rich
    mine,
Should come up crusted o'er with
    gems. Nor this
Would need a meaner spirit, than the
    first;
Nay, 'twould be but the selfsame spirit,
    clothed
In humbler guise, but still the selfsame
    spirit:
As one spring wind unbinds the
    mountain snow
And comforts violets in their hermitage.

But, master, poet, who hast done all this,
How didst thou 'scape the ruin whelming
    me?
Didst thou, when nerving thee to this
    attempt,
Ne'er range thy mind's extent, as some
    wide hall,
Dazzled by shapes that filled its length
    with light,
Shapes clustered there to rule thee, not
    obey,
That will not wait thy summons, will
    not rise
Singly, nor when thy practised eye and
    hand
Can well transfer their loveliness, but
    crowd
By thee for ever, bright to thy despair?
Didst thou ne'er gaze on each by turns,
    and ne'er

Resolve to single out one, though the rest
Should vanish, and to give that one,
    entire
In beauty, to the world; forgetting, so,
Its peers, whose number baffles mortal
    power?
And, this determined, wast thou ne'er
    seduced
By memories and regrets and passionate
    love,
To glance once more farewell? and did
    their eyes
Fasten thee, brighter and more bright,
    until
Thou couldst but stagger back unto
    their feet,
And laugh that man's applause or
    welfare ever
Could tempt thee to forsake them? Or
    when years
Had passed and still their love possessed
    thee wholly,
When from without some murmur
    startled thee
Of darkling mortals famished for one ray
Of thy so-hoarded luxury of light,
Didst thou ne'er strive even yet to
    break those spells
And prove thou couldst recover and
    fulfil
Thy early mission, long ago renounced,
And to that end, select some shape
    once more?
And did not mist-like influences, thick
    films,
Faint memories of the rest that charmed
    so long
Thine eyes, float fast, confuse thee, bear
    thee off,
As whirling snow-drifts blind a man who
    treads
A mountain ridge, with guiding spear
    through storm?
Say, though I fell, I had excuse to fall;
Say, I was tempted sorely: say but this,
Dear lord, Aprile's lord!
*Par.*              Clasp me not thus,

Aprile! That the truth should reach me
  thus!
We are weak dust. Nay, clasp not or I
  faint!
*Apr.* My king! and envious thoughts
  could outrage thee?
Lo, I forget my ruin, and rejoice
In thy success, as thou! Let our God's
  praise
Go bravely through the world at last!
  What care
Through me or thee? I feel thy breath.
  Why, tears?
Tears in the darkness, and from thee to
  me?
*Par.* Love me henceforth, Aprile, while
  I learn
To love; and, merciful God, forgive us
  both!
We wake at length from weary dreams;
  but both
Have slept in fairy-land: though dark
  and drear
Appears the world before us, we no less
Wake with our wrists and ankles
  jewelled still.
I too have sought to know as thou to
  Love —
Excluding love as thou refusedst
  knowledge.
Still thou hast beauty and I, power. We
  wake:
What penance canst devise for both of
  us?
*Apr.* I hear thee faintly. The thick
  darkness! Even
Thine eyes are hid. 'Tis as I knew: I
  speak,
And now I die. But I have seen thy face!
O poet, think of me, and sing of me!
But to have seen thee and to die so soon!
*Par.* Die not, Aprile! We must never
  part.
Are we not halves of one dissevered
  world,
Whom this strange chance unites once
  more? Part? never!

Till thou the lover, know; and I, the
  knower,
Love — until both are saved. Aprile, hear!
We will accept our gains, and use
  them — now!
God, he will die upon my breast! Aprile!
*Apr.* To speak but once, and die! Yet by
  his side.
Hush! hush!
                    Ha! go you ever girt about
With phantoms, powers? I have
  created such,
But these seem real as I.
*Par.*                    Whom can you see
Through the accursed darkness?
*Apr.*                    Stay; I know,
I know them: who should know them
  well as I?
White brows, lit up with glory; poets
  all!
*Par.* Let him but live, and I have my
  reward!
*Apr.* Yes; I see now. God is the perfect
  poet,
Who in his person acts his own creations.
Had you but told me this at first!
  Hush! hush!
*Par.* Live! for my sake, because of my
  great sin,
To help my brain, oppressed by these
  wild words
And their deep import. Live! 'tis not
  too late.
I have a quiet home for us, and friends.
Michal shall smile on you. Hear you?
  Lean thus,
And breathe my breath. I shall not lose
  one word
Of all your speech, one little word,
  Aprile!
*Apr.* No, no. Crown me? I am not one
  of you!
'Tis he, the king, you seek. I am not one.
*Par.* Thy spirit, at least, Aprile! Let me
  love!

I have attained, and now I may depart.

### 3 – PARACELSUS

*Scene – Basil; a chamber in the house of Paracelsus. 1526.*
PARACELSUS, FESTUS

*Par.* Heap logs and let the blaze laugh out!

*Fest.*      True, true!
'Tis very fit all, time and chance and change
Have wrought since last we sat thus, face to face
And soul to soul – all cares, far-looking fears,
Vague apprehensions, all vain fancies bred
By your long absence, should be cast away,
Forgotten in this glad unhoped renewal
Of our affections.

*Par.*           Oh, omit not aught
Which witnesses your own and Michal's own
Affection: spare not that! Only forget
The honours and the glories and what not,
It pleases you to tell profusely out.

*Fest.* Nay, even your honours, in a sense, I waive:
The wondrous Paracelsus, life's dispenser,
Fate's commissary, idol of the schools
And courts, shall be no more than Aureole still,
Still Aureole and my friend as when we parted
Some twenty years ago, and I restrained
As best I could the promptings of my spirit
Which secretly advanced you, from the first,
To the pre-eminent rank which, since, your own
Adventurous ardour, nobly triumphing,
Has won for you.

*Par.*        Yes, yes. And Michal's face
Still wears that quiet and peculiar light
Like the dim circlet floating round a pearl?

*Fest.*      Just so.

*Par.*           And yet her calm sweet countenance,
Though saintly, was not sad; for she would sing
Alone. Does she still sing alone, bird-like,
Not dreaming you are near? Her carols dropt
In flakes through that old leafy bower built under
The sunny wall at Würzburg, from her lattice
Among the trees above, while I, unseen,
Sat conning some rare scroll from Tritheim's shelves
Much wondering notes so simple could divert
My mind from study. Those were happy days.
Respect all such as sing when all alone!

*Fest.* Scarcely alone: her children, you may guess,
Are wild beside her.

*Par.*           Ah, those children quite
Unsettle the pure picture in my mind:
A girl, she was so perfect, so distinct:
No change, no change! Not but this added grace
May blend and harmonize with its compeers,
And Michal may become her mother-hood;
But 'tis a change, and I detest all change,
And most a change in aught I loved long since.
So, Michal – you have said she thinks of me?

*Fest.* O very proud will Michal be of you!
Imagine how we sat, long winter-nights,
Scheming and wondering, shaping your presumed
Adventure, or devising its reward;

Shutting out fear with all the strength
  of hope.
For it was strange how, even when most
  secure
In our domestic peace, a certain dim
And flitting shade could sadden all; it
  seemed
A restlessness of heart, a silent yearning,
A sense of something wanting,
  incomplete –
Not to be put in words, perhaps avoided
By mute consent – but, said or unsaid,
  felt
To point to one so loved and so long
  lost.
And then the hopes rose and shut out
  the fears –
How you would laugh should I recount
  them now!
I still predicted your return at last
With gifts beyond the greatest of them
  all,
All Tritheim's wondrous troop; did one
  of which
Attain renown by any chance, I smiled,
As well aware of who would prove his
  peer.
Michal was sure some woman, long ere
  this,
As beautiful as you were sage, had
  loved . . .
*Par.* Far-seeing, truly, to discern so much
In the fantastic projects and day-dreams
Of a raw restless boy!
*Fest.*                    Oh, no: the sunrise
Well warranted our faith in this full noon!
Can I forget the anxious voice which
  said
'Festus, have thoughts like these ere
  shaped themselves
'In other brains than mine? have their
  possessors
'Existed in like circumstance? were
  they weak
'As I, or ever constant from the first,
'Despising youth's allurements and
  rejecting

'As spider-films the shackles I endure?
'Is there hope for me?' – and I
  answered gravely
As an acknowledged elder, calmer, wiser,
More gifted mortal. O you must
  remember,
For all your glorious . . .
*Par.*                    Glorious? ay, this hair,
These hands – nay, touch them, they
  are mine! Recall
With all the said recallings, times when
  thus
To lay them by your own ne'er turned
  you pale
As now. Most glorious, are they not?
*Fest.*                    Why – why –
Something must be subtracted from
  success
So wide, no doubt. He would be
  scrupulous, truly,
Who should object such drawbacks.
  Still, still, Aureole,
You are changed, very changed! 'Twere
  losing nothing
To look well to it: you must not be
  stolen
From the enjoyment of your well-won
  meed.
*Par.* My friend! you seek my pleasure,
  past a doubt:
You will best gain your point, by talking,
  not
Of me, but of yourself.
*Fest.*                    Have I not said
All touching Michal and my children?
  Sure
You know, by this, full well how
  Aennchen looks
Gravely, while one disparts her thick
  brown hair;
And Aureole's glee when some stray
  gannet builds
Amid the birch-trees by the lake. Small
  hope
Have I that he will honour (the wild imp)
His namesake. Sigh not! 'tis too much
  to ask

That all we love should reach the same
    proud fate.
But you are very kind to humour me
By showing interest in my quiet life;
You, who of old could never tame your-
    self
To tranquil pleasures, must at heart
    despise . . .
*Par.* Festus, strange secrets are let out
    by death
Who blabs so oft the follies of this
    world:
And I am death's familiar, as you know.
I helped a man to die, some few weeks
    since,
Warped even from his go-cart to one
    end –
The living on princes' smiles, reflected
    from
A mighty herd of favourites. No mean
    trick
He left untried, and truly well-nigh
    wormed
All traces of God's finger out of him:
Then died, grown old. And just an
    hour before,
Having lain long with blank and
    soulless eyes,
He sat up suddenly, and with natural
    voice
Said that in spite of thick air and
    closed doors
God told him it was June; and he knew
    well,
Without such telling, harebells grew in
    June;
And all that kings could ever give or take
Would not be precious as those
    blooms to him.
Just so, allowing I am passing sage,
It seems to me much worthier
    argument
Why pansies,* eyes that laugh, bear
    beauty's prize

* Citrinula (flammula) herba Paracelso multum
   familiaris. – Dorn.

From violets, eyes that dream – (your
    Michal's choice) –
Than all fools find to wonder at in me
Or in my fortunes. And be very sure
I say this from no prurient restlessness,
No self-complaency, itching to turn,
Vary and view its pleasure from all
    points,
And, in this instance, willing other men
May be at pains, demonstrate to itself
The realness of the very joy it tastes.
What should delight me like the news
    of friends
Whose memories were a solace to me oft,
As mountain-baths to wild fowls in
    their flight?
Ofter than you had wasted thought on
    me
Had you been wise, and rightly valued
    bliss.
But there's no taming nor repressing
    hearts:
God knows I need such! – So, you
    heard me speak?
*Fest.*               Speak? when?
*Par.*                      When
    but this morning at my class?
There was noise and crowd enough. I
    saw you not.
Surely you know I am engaged to fill
The chair here? – that 'tis part of my
    proud fate
To lecture to as many thick-skulled
    youths
As please, each day, to throng the theatre,
To my great reputation, and no small
Danger of Basil's benches long unused
To crack beneath such honour?
*Fest.*                 I was there;
I mingled with the throng: shall I avow
Small care was mine to listen? – too
    intent
On gathering from the murmurs of the
    crowd
A full corroboration of my hopes!
What can I learn about your powers?
    but they

Know, care for nought beyond your
        actual state,
Your actual value; yet they worship you,
Those various natures whom you sway
        as one!
But ere I go, be sure I shall attend …
*Par.* Stop, o' God's name: the thing's
        by no means yet
Past remedy! Shall I read this morning's
        labour
– At least in substance? Nought so
        worth the gaining
As an apt scholar! Thus then, with all
        due
Precision and emphasis – you, beside,
        are clearly
Guiltless of understanding more, a
        whit,
The subject than your stool – allowed
        to be
A notable advantage.
*Fest.*                    Surely, Aureole,
You laugh at me!
*Par.*          I laugh? Ha, ha! thank heaven,
I charge you, if't be so! for I forget
Much, and what laughter should be
        like. No less,
However, I forego that luxury
Since it alarms the friend who brings it
        back.
True, laughter like my own must echo
        strangely
To thinking men; a smile were better
        far;
So, make me smile! If the exulting look
You wore but now be smiling, 'tis so
        long
Since I have smiled! Alas, such smiles
        are born
Alone of hearts like yours, or herdsmen's
        souls
Of ancient time, whose eyes, calm as
        their flocks,
Saw in the stars mere garnishry of heaven,
And in the earth a stage for altars only.
Never change, Festus: I say, never
        change!

*Fest.* My God, if he be wretched after
        all!
*Par.* When last we parted, Festus, you
        declared,
– Or Michal, yes, her soft lips whispered
        words
I have preserved. She told me she believed
I should succeed (meaning, that in the
        search
I then engaged in, I should meet success)
And yet be wretched: now, she augured
        false.
*Fest.* Thank heaven! but you spoke
        strangely: could I venture
To think bare apprehension lest your
        friend,
Dazzled by your resplendent course,
        might find
Henceforth less sweetness in his own,
        could move
Such earnest mood in you? Fear not,
        dear friend,
That I shall leave you, inwardly repining
Your lot was not my own!
*Par.*                    And this for ever!
For ever! gull who may, they will be
        gulled!
They will not look nor think; 'tis nothing
        new
In them: but surely he is not of them!
My Festus, do you know, I reckoned,
        you –
Though all beside were sand-blind –
        you, my friend,
Would look at me, once close, with
        piercing eye
Untroubled by the false glare that
        confounds
A weaker vision: would remain serene,
Though singular amid a gaping throng.
I feared you, or I had come, sure, long
        ere this,
To Einsiedeln. Well, error has no end,
And Rhasis is a sage, and Basil boasts
A tribe of wits, and I am wise and blest
Past all dispute! 'Tis vain to fret at it.
I have vowed long ago my worshippers

Shall owe to their own deep sagacity
All further information, good or bad.
Small risk indeed my reputation runs,
Unless perchance the glance now
    searching me
Be fixed much longer; for it seems to
    spell
Dimly the characters a simpler man
Might read distinct enough. Old Eastern
    books
Say, the fallen prince of morning some
    short space
Remained unchanged in semblance;
    nay, his brow
Was hued with triumph: every spirit
    then
Praising, *his* heart on flame the while: –
    a tale!
Well, Festus, what discover you, I pray?
*Fest.* Some foul deed sullies then a life
    which else
Were raised supreme?
*Par.*       Good: I do well, most well!
Why strive to make men hear, feel, fret
    themselves
With what is past their power to
    comprehend?
I should not strive now: only, having
    nursed
The faint surmise that one yet walked
    the earth,
One, at least, not the utter fool of show,
Not absolutely formed to be the dupe
Of shallow plausibilities alone:
One who, in youth, found wise enough
    to choose
The happiness his riper years approve,
Was yet so anxious for another's sake,
That, ere his friend could rush upon a
    mad
And ruinous course, the converse of his
    own,
His gentle spirit essayed, prejudged for
    him
The perilous path, foresaw its destiny,
And warned the weak one in such
    tender words,

Such accents – his whole heart in every
    tone –
That oft their memory comforted that
    friend
When it by right should have increased
    despair:
– Having believed, I say, that this one
    man
Could never lose the light thus from the
    first
His portion – how should I refuse to
    grieve
At even my gain if it disturb our old
Relation, if it make me out more wise?
Therefore, once more reminding him
    how well
He prophesied, I note the single flaw
That spoils his prophet's title. In plain
    words,
You were deceived, and thus were you
    deceived –
I have not been successful, and yet am
Most miserable; 'tis said at last; nor you
Give credit, lest you force me to concede
That common sense yet lives upon the
    world!
*Fest.* You surely do not mean to banter
    me?
*Par.* You know, or – if you have been
    wise enough
To cleanse your memory of such matters
    – knew,
As far as words of mine could make it
    clear,
That 'twas my purpose to find joy or
    grief
Solely in the fulfilment of my plan
Or plot or whatsoe'er it was; rejoicing
Alone as it proceeded prosperously,
Sorrowing then only when mischance
    retarded
Its progress. That was in those Würzburg
    days!
Not to prolong a theme I thoroughly
    hate,
I have pursued this plan with all my
    strength;

And having failed therein most signally,
Cannot object to ruin utter and drear
As all-excelling would have been the
    prize
Had fortune favoured me. I scarce have
    right
To vex your frank good spirit late so
    glad
In my supposed prosperity, I know,
And, were I lucky in a glut of friends,
Would well agree to let your error live,
Nay, strengthen it with fables of success.
But mine is no condition to refuse
The transient solace of so rare a godsend,
My solitary luxury, my one friend:
Accordingly I venture to put off
The wearisome vest of falsehood
    galling me,
Secure when he is by. I lay me bare,
Prone at his mercy – but he is my friend!
Not that he needs retain his aspect
    grave;
That answers not my purpose; for 'tis
    like,
Some sunny morning – Basil being
    drained
Of its wise population, every corner
Of the amphitheatre crammed with
    learned clerks,
Here Oecolampadius, looking worlds of
    wit,
Here Castellanus, as profound as he,
Munsterus here, Frobenius there, all
    squeezed
And staring, – that the zany of the show,
Even Paracelsus, shall put off before them
His trappings with a grace but seldom
    judged
Expedient in such cases: – the grim
    smile
That will go round! Is it not therefore
    best
To venture a rehearsal like the present
In a small way? Where are the signs I
    seek,
The first-fruits and fair sample of the
    scorn

Due to all quacks? Why, this will never
    do!
*Fest.* These are foul vapours, Aureole;
    nought beside!
The effect of watching, study,
    weariness.
Were there a spark of truth in the
    confusion
Of these wild words, you would not
    outrage thus
Your youth's companion. I shall ne'er
    regard
These wanderings, bred of faintness
    and much study.
'Tis not thus you would trust a trouble
    to me,
To Michal's friend.
*Par.*      I have said it, dearest Festus!
For the manner, 'tis ungracious probably;
You may have it told in broken sobs,
    one day,
And scalding tears, ere long: but I
    thought best
To keep that off as long as possible.
Do you wonder still?
*Fest.*      No; it must oft fall out
That one whose labour perfects any work,
Shall rise from it with eye so worn that he
Of all men least can measure the extent
Of what he has accomplished. He alone
Who, nothing tasked, is nothing weary
    too,
May clearly scan the little he effects:
But we, the bystanders, untouched by
    toil,
Estimate each aright.
*Par.*      This worthy Festus
Is one of them, at last! 'Tis so with all!
First, they set down all progress as a
    dream;
And next, when he whose quick
    discomfiture
Was counted on, accomplishes some
    few
And doubtful steps in his career, – behold,
They look for every inch of ground to
    vanish

Beneath his tread, so sure they spy
    success!
*Fest.* Few doubtful steps? when death
    retires before
Your presence – when the noblest of
    mankind,
Broken in body or subdued in soul,
May through your skill renew their vigour,
    raise
The shattered frame to pristine
    stateliness?
When men in racking pain may purchase
    dreams
Of what delights them most, swooning
    at once
Into a sea of bliss or rapt along
As in a flying sphere of turbulent light?
When we may look to you as one
    ordained
To free the flesh from fell disease, as
    frees
Our Luther's burning tongue the
    fettered soul?
When . . .
*Par.*     When and where, the devil,
    did you get
This notable news?
*Fest.*     Even from the common voice;
From those whose envy, daring not
    dispute
The wonders it decries, attributes them
To magic and such folly.
*Par.*         Folly? Why not
To magic, pray? You find a comfort
    doubtless
In holding, God ne'er troubles him about
Us or our doings: once we were judged
    worth
The devil's tempting ... I offend:
    forgive me,
And rest content. Your prophecy on
    the whole
Was fair enough as prophesyings go;
At fault a little in detail, but quite
Precise enough in the main; and
    hereupon
I pay due homage: you guessed long ago

(The prophet!) I should fail – and I
    have failed.
*Fest.* You mean to tell me, then, the
    hopes which fed
Your youth have not been realized as
    yet?
Some obstacle has barred them hitherto?
Or that their innate . . .
*Par.*         As I said but now,
You have a very decent prophet's fame,
So you but shun details here. Little
    matter
Whether those hopes were mad, – the
    aims they sought,
Safe and secure from all ambitious fools;
Or whether my weak wits are overcome
By what a better spirit would scorn: I
    fail.
And now methinks 'twere best to change
    a theme
I am a sad fool to have stumbled on.
I say confusedly what comes uppermost;
But there are times when patience
    proves at fault,
As now: this morning's strange encounter
    – you
Beside me once again! you, whom I
    guessed
Alive, since hitherto (with Luther's
    leave)
No friend have I among the saints at
    peace,
To judge by any good their prayers
    effect.
I knew you would have helped me – why
    not he,
My strange competitor in enterprise,
Bound for the same end by another path,
Arrived, or ill or well, before the time,
At our disastrous journey's doubtful
    close?
How goes it with Aprile? Ah, they miss
Your lone sad sunny idleness of heaven,
Our martyrs for the world's sake;
    heaven shuts fast:
The poor mad poet is howling by this
    time!

Since you are my sole friend then, here
　　or there,
I could not quite repress the varied
　　feelings
This meeting wakens; they have had
　　their vent,
And now forget them. Do the rear-mice
　　still
Hang like a fretwork on the gate (or what
In my time was a gate) fronting the road
From Einsiedeln to Lachen?
*Fest.*　　　　　　　　　　　　Trifle not:
Answer me,for my sake alone! You
　　smiled
Just now, when I supposed some deed,
　　unworthy
Yourself, might blot the else so bright
　　result;
Yet if your motives have continued pure,
Your will unfaltering, and in spite of this,
You have experienced a defeat, why then
I say not you would cheerfully withdraw
From contest – mortal hearts are not
　　so fashioned –
But surely you would ne'ertheless
　　withdraw.
You sought not fame nor gain nor even
　　love,
No end distinct from knowledge, – I
　　repeat
Your very words: once satisfied that
　　knowledge
Is a mere dream, you would announce
　　as much,
Yourself the first. But how is the event?
You are defeated – and I find you here!
*Par.* As though 'here' did not signify
　　defeat!
I spoke not of my little labours here,
But of the break-down of my general
　　aims:
For you, aware of their extent and
　　scope,
To look on these sage lecturings,
　　approved
By beardless boys, and bearded
　　dotards worse,

As a fit consummation of such aims,
Is worthy notice. A professorship
At Basil! Since you see so much in it,
And think my life was reasonably
　　drained
Of life's delights to render me a match
For duties arduous as such post
　　demands, –
Be it far from me to deny my power
To fill the petty circle lotted out
Of infinite space, or justify the host
Of honours thence accruing. So, take
　　notice,
This jewel dangling from my neck
　　preserves
The features of a prince, my skill restored
To plague his people some few years to
　　come:
And all through a pure whim. He had
　　eased the earth
For me, but that the droll despair
　　which seized
The vermin of his household, tickled me.
I came to see. Here, drivelled the
　　physician,
Whose most infallible nostrum was at
　　fault;
There quaked the astrologer, whose
　　horoscope
Had promised him interminable years;
Here a monk fumbled at the sick
　　man's mouth
With some undoubted relic – a sudary
Of the Virgin; while another piebald
　　knave
Of the same brotherhood (he loved them
　　ever)
Was actively preparing 'neath his nose
Such a suffumigation as, once fired,
Had stunk the patient dead ere he could
　　groan.
I cursed the doctor and upset the
　　brother,
Brushed past the conjurer, vowed that
　　the first gust
Of stench from the ingredients just
　　alight

Would raise a cross-grained devil in my
  sword,
Not easily laid: and ere an hour the prince
Slept as he never slept since prince he
  was.
A day – and I was posting for my life,
Placarded through the town as one
  whose spite
Had near availed to stop the blessed
  effects
Of the doctor's nostrum which, well
  seconded
By the sudary, and most by the costly
  smoke –
Not leaving out the strenuous prayers
  sent up
Hard by in the abbey – raised the prince
  to life:
To the great reputation of the seer
Who, confident, expected all along
The glad event – the doctor's
  recompense –
Much largess from his highness to the
  monks –
And the vast solace of his loving people,
Whose general satisfaction to increase,
The prince was pleased no longer to
  defer
The burning of some dozen heretics
Remanded till God's mercy should be
  shown
Touching his sickness: last of all were
  joined
Ample directions to all loyal folk
To swell the complement by seizing me
Who – doubtless some rank sorcerer –
  endeavoured
To thwart these pious offices, obstruct
The prince's cure, and frustrate heaven
  by help
Of certain devils dwelling in his sword.
By luck, the prince in his first fit of
  thanks
Had forced this bauble on me as an
  earnest
Of further favours. This one case may
  serve

To give sufficient taste of many such,
So, let them pass. Those shelves
  support a pile
Of patents, licences, diplomas, titles
From Germany, France, Spain, and
  Italy;
They authorize some honour;
  ne'ertheless,
I set more store by this Erasmus sent;
He trusts me; our Frobenius is his
  friend,
And him 'I raised' (nay, read it) 'from
  the dead.'
I weary you, I see. I merely sought
To show, there's no great wonder after
  all
That, while I fill the class-room and
  attract
A crowd to Basil, I get leave to stay,
And therefore need not scruple to accept
The utmost they can offer, if I please:
For 'tis but right the world should be
  prepared
To treat with favour e'en fantastic wants
Of one like me, used up in serving her.
Just as the mortal, whom the gods in
  part
Devoured, received in place of his lost
  limb
Some virtue or other – cured disease, I
  think;
You mind the fables we have read
  together.
*Fest.* You do not think I comprehend a
  word.
The time was, Aureole, you were apt
  enough
To clothe the airiest thoughts in
  specious breath;
But surely you must feel how vague
  and strange
These speeches sound.
*Par.*   Well, then: you know my hopes;
I am assured, at length, those hopes
  were vain;
That truth is just as far from me as
  ever;

That I have thrown my life away; that
    sorrow
On that account is idle, and further
    effort
To mend and patch what's marred
    beyond repairing,
As useless: and all this was taught your
    friend
By the convincing good old-fashioned
    method
Of force – by sheer compulsion. Is that
    plain?
*Fest.* Dear Aureole, can it be my fears
    were just?
God wills not . . .
*Par.*     Now, 'tis this I most admire –
The constant talk men of your stamp
    keep up
Of God's will, as they style it; one would
    swear
Man had but merely to uplift his eye,
And see the will in question charactered
On the heaven's vault. 'Tis hardly wise
    to moot
Such topics: doubts are many and faith
    is weak.
I know as much of any will of God
As knows some dumb and tortured
    brute what Man,
His stern lord, wills from the perplexing
    blows
That plague him every way; but there,
    of course,
Where least he suffers, longest he
    remains –
My case; and for such reasons I plod on,
Subdued but not convinced. I know as
    little
Why I deserve to fail, as why I hoped
Better things in my youth. I simply
    know
I am no master here, but trained and
    beaten
Into the path I tread; and here I stay,
Until some further intimation reach me,
Like an obedient drudge. Though I
    prefer

To view the whole thing as a task imposed
Which, whether dull or pleasant, must
    be done –
Yet, I deny not, there is made provision
Of joys which tastes less jaded might
    affect;
Nay, some which please me too, for all
    my pride –
Pleasures that once were pains: the iron
    ring
Festering about a slave's neck grows at
    length
Into the flesh it eats. I hate no longer
A host of petty vile delights, undreamed
    of
Or spurned before; such now supply
    the place
Of my dead aims: as in the autumn
    woods
Where tall trees used to flourish, from
    their roots
Springs up a fungous brood sickly and
    pale,
Chill mushrooms coloured like a corpse's
    cheek.
*Fest.* If I interpret well your words, I own
It troubles me but little that your aims,
Vast in their dawning and most likely
    grown
Extravagantly since, have baffled you.
Perchance I am glad; you merit greater
    praise;
Because they are too glorious to be
    gained,
You do not blindly cling to them and
    die;
You fell, but have not sullenly refused
To rise, because an angel worsted you
In wrestling, though the world holds
    not your peer,
And though too harsh and sudden is
    the change
To yield content as yet, still you pursue
The ungracious path as though 'twere
    rosy-strewn.
'Tis well: and your reward, or soon or
    late,

Will come from him whom no man
    serves in vain.
*Par.* Ah, very fine! For my part, I conceive
The very pausing from all futher toil,
Which you find heinous, would
    become a seal
To the sincerity of all my deeds.
To be consistent I should die at once;
I calculated on no after-life;
Yet (how crept in, how fostered, I know
    not)
Here am I with as passionate regret
For youth and health and love so
    vainly lavished,
As if their preservation had been first
And foremost in my thoughts; and this
    strange fact
Humbled me wondrously, and had due
    force
In rendering me the less averse to follow
A certain counsel, a mysterious
    warning –
You will not understand – but 'twas a
    man
With aims not mine and yet pursued
    like mine,
With the same fervour and no more
    success,
Perishing in my sight; who summoned
    me
As I would shun the ghastly fate I saw,
To serve my race at once; to wait no
    longer
That God should interfere in my behalf,
But to distrust myself, put pride away,
And give my gains, imperfect as they
    were,
To men. I have not leisure to explain
How, since, a singular series of events
Has raised me to the station you behold,
Wherein I seem to turn to most account
The mere wreck of the past, – perhaps
    receive
Some feeble glimmering token that God
    views
And may approve my penance: therefore
    here

You find me, doing most good or least
    harm.
And if folks wonder much and profit
    little
'Tis not my fault; only, I shall rejoice
When my part m the farce is shuffled
    through,
And the curtain falls: I must hold out
    till then.
*Fest.* Till when, dear Aureole?
*Par.*                Till I'm fairly thrust
From my proud eminence. Fortune is
    fickle
And even professors fall: should that
    arrive,
I see no sin in ceding to my bent.
You little fancy what rude shocks
    apprise us
We sin; God's intimations rather fail
In clearness than in energy: 'twere well
Did they but indicate the course to
    take
Like that to be forsaken. I would fain
Be spared a further sample. Here I stand,
And here I stay, be sure, till forced to
    flit.
*Fest.* Be you but firm on that head! long
    ere then
All I expect will come to pass, I trust:
The cloud that wraps you will have
    disappeared.
Meantime, I see small chance of such
    event:
They praise you here as one whose lore,
    already
Divulged, eclipses all the past can show,
But whose achievements, marvellous as
    they be,
Are faint anticipations of a glory
About to be revealed. When Basil's
    crowds
Dismiss their teacher, I shall be content
That he depart.
*Par.*         This favour at their hands
I look for earlier than your view of things
Would warrant. Of the crowd you saw
    today,

Remove the full half sheer amazement
    draws,
Mere novelty, nought else; and next,
    the tribe
Whose innate blockish dulness just
    perceives
That unless miracles (as seem my
    works)
Be wrought in their behalf, their chance
    is slight
To puzzle the devil; next, the numerous
    set
Who bitterly hate established schools,
    and help
The teacher that oppugns them, till he
    once
Have planted his own doctrine, when
    the teacher
May reckon on their rancour in his turn;
Take, too, the sprinkling of sagacious
    knaves
Whose cunning runs not counter to the
    vogue
But seeks, by flattery and crafty nursing,
To force my system to a premature
Short-lived development. Why swell the
    list?
Each has his end to serve, and his best
    way
Of serving it: remove all these, remains
A scantling, a poor dozen at the best,
Worthy to look for sympathy and service,
And likely to draw profit from my pains.
*Fest.* 'Tis no encouraging picture: still
    these few
Redeem their fellows. Once the germ
    implanted,
Its growth, if slow, is sure.
*Par.*                    God grant it so!
I would make some amends: but if I
    fail,
The luckless rogues have this excuse to
    urge,
That much is in my method and my
    manner,
My uncouth habits, my impatient spirit,
Which hinders of reception and result

My doctrine: much to say, small skill
    to speak!
These old aims suffered not a looking-
    off
Though for an instant; therefore, only
    when
I thus renounced them and resolved to
    reap
Some present fruit – to teach mankind
    some truth
So dearly purchased – only then I
    found
Such teaching was an art requiring
    cares
And qualities peculiar to itself:
That to possess was one thing – to
    display
Another. With renown first in my
    thoughts,
Or popular praise, I had soon discovered
    it:
One grows but little apt to learn these
    things.
*Fest.* If it be so, which nowise I believe,
There needs no waiting fuller
    dispensation
To leave a labour of so little use.
Why not throw up the irksome
    charge at once?
*Par.*                    A task, a task!
But wherefore hide the whole
Extent of degradation, once engaged
In the confessing vein? Despite of all
My fine talk of obedience and
    repugnance,
Docility and what not, 'tis yet to learn
If when the task shall really be performed,
My inclination free to choose once more,
I shall do aught but slightly modify
The nature of the hated task I quit.
In plain words, I am spoiled; my life
    still tends
As first it tended; I am broken and
    trained
To my old habits: they are part of me.
I know, and none so well, my darling
    ends

Are proved impossible: no less, no less,
Even now what humours me, fond fool,
    as when
Their faint ghosts sit with me and
    flatter me
And send me back content to my dull
    round?
How can I change this soul? – this
    apparatus
Constructed solely for their purposes,
So well adapted to their every want,
To search out and discover, prove and
    perfect;
This intricate machine whose most minute
And meanest motions have their charm
    to me
Though to none else – an aptitude I
    seize,
An object I perceive, a use, a meaning,
A property, a fitness, I explain
And I alone: – how can I change my
    soul?
And this wronged body, worthless save
    when tasked
Under that soul's dominion – used to
    care
For its bright master's cares and quite
    subdue
Its proper cravings – not to ail nor pine
So he but prosper – whither drag this
    poor
Tried patient body? God! how I essayed
To live like that mad poet, for a while,
To love alone; and how I felt too warped
And twisted and deformed! What should
    I do,
Even tho' released from drudgery, but
    return
Faint, as you see, and halting, blind
    and sore,
To my old life and die as I began?
I cannot feed on beauty for the sake
Of beauty only, nor can drink in balm
From lovely objects for their loveliness;
My nature cannot lose her first imprint;
I still must hoard and heap and class
    all truths

With one ulterior purpose: I must
    know!
Would God translate me to his throne,
    believe
That I should only listen to his word
To further my own aim! For other
    men,
Beauty is prodigally strewn around,
And I were happy could I quench as
    they
This mad and thriveless longing, and
    content me
With beauty for itself alone: alas,
I have addressed a frock of heavy mail
Yet may not join the troop of sacred
    knights;
And now the forest-creatures fly from me,
The grass-banks cool, the sunbeams
    warm no more.
Best follow, dreaming that ere night
    arrive,
I shall o'ertake the company and ride
Glittering as they!
*Fest.*                 I think I apprehend
What you would say: if you, in truth,
    design
To enter once more on the life thus left,
Seek not to hide that all this consciousness
Of failure is assumed!
*Par.*                 My friend, my friend,
I toil, you listen; I explain, perhaps
You understand: there our communion
    ends.
Have you learnt nothing from to-day's
    discourse?
When we would thoroughly know the
    sick man's state
We feel awhile the fluttering pulse, press
    soft
The hot brow, look upon the languid
    eye,
And thence divine the rest. Must I lay
    bare
My heart, hideous and beating, or tear
    up
My vitals for your gaze, ere you will
    deem

Enough made known? You! who are
  you, forsooth?
That is the crowning operation claimed
By the arch-demonstrator – heaven the
  hall,
And earth the audience. Let Aprile and
  you
Secure good places: 'twill be worth the
  while.
*Fest.* Are you mad, Aureole? What can I
  have said
To call for this? I judged from your own
  words.
*Par.* Oh, doubtless! A sick wretch
  describes the ape
That mocks him from the bed-foot, and
  all gravely
You thither turn at once: or he recounts
The perilous journey he has late
  performed,
And you are puzzled much how that
  could be!
You find me here, half stupid and half
  mad:
It makes no part of my delight to search
Into these matters, much less undergo
Another's scrutiny; but so it chances
That I am led to trust my state to you:
And the event is, you combine, contrast
And ponder on my foolish words as
  though
They thoroughly conveyed all hidden
  here –
Here, loathsome with despair and hate
  and rage!
Is there no fear, no shrinking and no
  shame?
Will you guess nothing? will you spare
  me nothing?
Must I go deeper? Ay or no?
*Fest.*                     Dear friend . . .
*Par.* True: I am brutal – 'tis a part of it;
The plague's sign – you are not a lazar-
  haunter,
How should you know? Well then, you
  think it strange
I should profess to have failed utterly,

And yet propose an ultimate retur
To courses void of hope: and this,
  because
You know not what temptation is, nor
  how
'Tis like to ply men in the sickliest part.
You are to understand that we who
  make
Sport for the gods, are hunted to the
  end:
There is not one sharp volley shot at us,
Which 'scaped with life, though hurt,
  we slacken pace
And gather by the wayside herbs and
  roots
To staunch our wounds, secure from
  further harm:
We are assailed to life's extremest verge.
It will be well indeed if I return,
A harmless busy fool, to may old ways!
I would forget hints of another fate,
Significant enough, which silent hours
Have lately scared me with.
*Fest.*                     Another! and what?
*Par.* After all, Festus, you say well: I am
A man yet: I need never humble me.
I would have been – something, I know
  not what;
But though I cannot soar, I do not crawl.
There are worse portions than this one
  of mine.
You say well!
*Fest.*     Ah!
*Par.*           And deeper degradation!
If the mean stimulants of vulgar praise,
If vanity should become the chosen
  food
Of a sunk mind, should stifle even the
  wish
To find its early aspirations true,
Should teach it to breathe falsehood
  like life-breath –
An atmosphere of craft and trick and
  lies;
Should make it proud to emulate, surpass
Base natures in the practices which
  woke

Its most indignant loathing once … No, no!
Utter damnation is reserved for hell!
I had immortal feelings; such shall never
Be wholly quenched: no, no!
               My friend, you wear
A melancholy face, and certain 'tis
There's little cheer in all this dismal work.
But was it my desire to set abroach
Such memories and forebodings? I
    foresaw
Where they would drive. 'Twere better
    we discuss
News from Lucerne or Zurich; ask and
    tell
Of Egypt's flaring sky or Spain's cork-
    groves.
*Fest.* I have thought: trust me, this mood
    will pass away!
I know you and the lofty spirit you bear,
And easily ravel out a clue to all.
These are the trials meet for such as you,
Nor must you hope exemption: to be
    mortal
Is to be plied with trials manifold.
Look round! The obstacles which kept
    the rest
From your ambition, have been
    spurned by you;
Their fears, their doubts, the chains
    that bind them all,
Were flax before your resolute soul,
    which nought
Avails to awe save these delusions bred
From its own strength, its selfsame
    strength disguised,
Mocking itself. Be brave, dear Aureole!
    Since
The rabbit has his shade to frighten him,
The fawn a rustling bough, mortals
    their cares,
And higher natures yet would slight
    and laugh
At these entangling fantasies, as you
At trammels of a weaker intellect, –
Measure your mind's height by the
    shade it casts!

I know you.
*Par.* And I know you, dearest Festus!
And how you love unworthily; and how
All admiration renders blind.
*Fest.*              You hold
That admiration blinds?
*Par.*           Ay and alas!
*Fest.* Nought blinds you less than
    admiration, friend!
Whether it be that all love renders wise
In its degree; from love which blends
    with love –
Heart answering heart – to love which
    spends itself
In silent mad idolatry of some
Pre-eminent mortal, some great soul of
    souls,
Which ne'er will know how well it is
    adored.
I say, such love is never blind; but rather
Alive to every the minutest spot
Which mars its object, and which hate
    (supposed
So vigilant and searching) dreams not of.
Love broods on such: what then?
    When first perceived
Is there no sweet strife to forget, to
    change,
To overflush those blemishes with all
The glow of general goodness they
    disturb?
– To make those very defects an endless
    source
Of new affection grown from hopes
    and fears?
And, when all fails, is there no gallant
    stand
Made even for much proved weak? no
    shrinking-back
Lest, since all love assimilates the soul
To what it loves, it should at length
    become
Almost a rival of its idol? Trust me,
If there be fiends who seek to work our
    hurt,
To ruin and drag down earth's
    mightiest spirits

Even at God's foot, 'twill be from such
    as love,
Their zeal will gather most to serve their
    cause;
And least from those who hate, who
    most essay
By contumely and scorn to blot the
    light
Which forces entrance even to their
    hearts:
For thence will our defender tear the veil
And show within each heart, as in a
    shrine,
The giant image of perfection, grown
In hate's despite, whose calumnies
    were spawned
In the untroubled presence of its eyes.
True admiration blinds not; nor am I
So blind. I call your sin exceptional;
It springs from one whose life has
    passed the bounds
Prescribed to life. Compound that fault
    with God!
I speak of men; to common men like me
The weakness you reveal endears you
    more,
Like the far traces of decay in suns.
I bid you have good cheer!
*Par.*                  *Præclare! Optime!*
Think of a quiet mountain-cloistered
    priest
Instructing Paracelsus! yet 'tis so.
Come, I will show you where my merit
    lies.
'Tis in the advance of individual minds
That the slow crowd should ground
    their expectation
Eventually to follow; as the sea
Waits ages in its bed till some one wave
Out of the multitudinous mass, extends
The empire of the whole, some feet
    perhaps,
Over the strip of sand which could
    confine
Its fellows so long time: thenceforth the
    rest,
Even to the meanest, hurry in at once,

And so much is clear gained. I shall be
    glad
If all my labours, failing of aught else,
Suffice to make such inroad and procure
A wider range for thought: nay, they do
    this;
For, whatsoe'er my notions of true
    knowledge
And a legitimate success, may be,
I am not blind to my undoubted rank
When classed with others: I precede my
    age:
And whoso wills is very free to mount
These labours as a platform whence his
    own
May have a prosperous outset. But, alas!
My followers – they are noisy as you
    heard;
But, for intelligence, the best of them
So clumsily wield the weapons I supply
And they extol, that I begin to doubt
Whether their own rude clubs and
    pebblestones
Would not do better service than my
    arms
Thus vilely swayed – if error will not fall
Sooner before the old awkward batterings
Than my more subtle warfare, not half
    learned.
*Fest.* I would supply that art, then, or
    withhold
New arms until you teach their mystery.
*Par.* Content you, 'tis my wish; I have
    recourse
To the simplest training. Day by day I
    seek
To wake the mood, the spirit which
    alone
Can make those arms of any use to men.
Of course they are for swaggering forth
    at once
Graced with Ulysses' bow, Achilles'
    shield –
Flash on us, all in armour, thou Achilles!
Make our hearts dance to thy
    resounding step!
A proper sight to scare the crows away!

*Fest.* Pity you choose not then some
　　other method
Of coming at your point. The marvellous
　　art
At length established in the world bids
　　fair
To remedy all hindrances like these:
Trust to Frobenius' press the precious
　　lore
Obscured by uncouth manner, or unfit
For raw beginners; let his types secure
A deathless monument to after-time;
Meanwhile wait confidently and enjoy
The ultimate effect: sooner or later
You shall be all-revealed.
*Par.* 　　　　　The old dull question
In a new form; no more. Thus: I possess
Two sorts of knowledge; one, – vast,
　　shadowy,
Hints of the unbounded aim I once
　　pursued:
The other consists of many secrets,
　　caught
While bent on nobler prize, – perhaps a
　　few
Prime principles which may conduct to
　　much:
These last I offer to my followers here.
Now, bid me chronicle the first of these,
My ancient study, and in effect you bid
Revert to the wild courses just abjured:
I must go find them scattered through
　　the world.
Then, for the principles, they are so
　　simple
(Being chiefly of the overturning sort),
That one time is as proper to propound
　　them
As any other – to-morrow at my class,
Or half a century hence embalmed in
　　print.
For if mankind intend to learn at all,
They must begin by giving faith to
　　them
And acting on them: and I do not see
But that my lectures serve indifferent
　　well:

No doubt these dogmas fall not to the
　　earth,
For all their novelty and rugged setting.
I think my class will not forget the day
I let them know the gods of Israel,
Aëtius, Oribasius, Galen, Rhasis,
Serapion, Avicenna, Averröes,
Were blocks!
*Fest.* 　　　　And that reminds me,
　　I heard something
About your waywardness: you burned
　　their books,
It seems, instead of answering those
　　sages.
*Par.* And who said that?
*Fest.* 　　　　Some I met yesternight
With Oecolampadius. As you know, the
　　purpose
Of this short stay at Basil was to learn
His pleasure touching certain missives
　　sent
For our Zuinglius and himself. 'Twas he
Apprised me that the famous teacher
　　here
Was my old friend.
*Par.* 　　　Ah, I forgot: you went . . .
*Fest.* From Zurich with advices for the
　　ear
Of Luther, now at Wittenberg – (you
　　know,
I make no doubt, the differences of late
With Carolstadius) – and returning
　　sought
Basil and . . .
*Par.* 　　I remember. Here's a case, now,
Will teach you why I answer not, but
　　burn
The books you mention. Pray, does
　　Luther dream
His arguments convince by their own
　　force
The crowds that own his doctrine? No,
　　indeed!
His plain denial of established points
Ages had sanctified and men supposed
Could never be oppugned while earth
　　was under

And heaven above them – points which
chance or time
Affected not – did more than the array
Of argument which followed. Boldly deny!
There is much breath-stopping, hair-
stiffening
Awhile; then, amazed glances, mute
awaiting
The thunderbolt which does not come:
and next,
Reproachful wonder and inquiry: those
Who else had never stirred, are able
now
To find the rest out for themselves,
perhaps
To outstrip him who set the whole at
work,
– As never will my wise class its
instructor.
And you saw Luther?
*Fest.*                'Tis a wondrous soul!
*Par.* True: the so-heavy chain which
galled mankind
Is shattered, and the noblest of us all
Must bow to the deliverer – nay, the
worker
Of our own project – we who long
before
Had burst our trammels, but forgot the
crowd,
We should have taught, still groaned
beneath their load:
This he has done and nobly. Speed that
may!
Whatever be my chance or my mischance,
What benefits mankind must glad me
too;
And men seem made, though not as I
believed,
For something better than the times
produce.
Witness these gangs of peasants your
new lights
From Suabia have possessed, whom
Münzer leads,
And whom the duke, the landgrave
and the elector

Will calm in blood! Well, well; 'tis not
my world!
*Fest.* Hark!
*Par.*        'Tis the melancholy wind astir
Within the trees; the embers too are
grey:
Morn must be near.
*Fest.*        Best ope the casement: see,
The night, late strewn with clouds and
flying stars,
Is blank and motionless: how peaceful
sleep
The tree-tops altogether! Like an asp,
The wind slips whispering from bough
to bough.
*Par.* Ay; you would gaze on a wind-
shaken tree
By the hour, nor count time lost.
*Fest.*                So you shall gaze:
Those happy times will come again.
*Par.*                Gone, gone,
Those pleasant times! Does not the
moaning wind
Seem to bewail that we have gained
such gains
And bartered sleep for them?
*Fest.*                It is our trust
That there is yet another world to mend
All error and mischance.
*Par.*                Another world!
And why this world, this common
world, to be
A make-shift, a mere foil, how fair soever,
To some fine life to come? Man must
be fed
With angels' food, forsooth; and some
few traces
Of a diviner nature which look out
Through his corporeal baseness, warrant
him
In a supreme contempt of all provision
For his inferior tastes – some straggling
marks
Which constitute his essence, just as
truly
As here and there a gem would
constitute

The rock, their barren bed, one
        diamond.
But were it so – were man all mind –
        he gains
A station little enviable. From God
Down to the lowest spirit ministrant,
Intelligence exists which casts our mind
Into immeasurable shade. No, no:
Love, hope, fear, faith – these make
        humanity;
These are its sign and note and
        character,
And these I have lost! – gone, shut from
        me for ever,
Like a dead friend safe from unkindness
        more!
See, morn at length. The heavy darkness
        seems
Diluted, grey and clear without the stars;
The shrubs bestir and rouse themselves
        as if
Some snake, that weighed them down
        all night, let go
His hold; and from the East, fuller and
        fuller,
Day, like a mighty river, flowing in;
But clouded, wintry, desolate and cold.
Yet see how that broad prickly star-
        shaped plant,
Half-down in the crevice, spreadsits
        woolly leaves
All thick and glistering with diamond
        dew.
And you depart for Einsiedeln this day,
And we have spent all night in talk like
        this!
If you would have me better for your
        love,
Revert no more to these sad themes.
*Fest.*                              One favour,
And I have done. I leave you, deeply
        moved;
Unwilling to have fared so well, the
        while
My friend has changed so sorely. If this
        mood
Shall pass away, if light once more arise

Where all is darkness now, if you see fit
To hope and trust again, and strive
        again,
You will remember – not our love
        alone –
But that my faith in God's desire that
        man
Should trust on his support, (as I must
        think
You trusted) is obscured and dim through
        you:
For you are thus, and this is no reward.
Will you not call me to your side, dear
        Aureole?

## 4 – PARACELSUS ASPIRES

*Scene – Colmar in Alsatia: an Inn. 1528.*
                PARACELSUS, FESTUS
*Par.* [to JOHANNES OPORINUS, *his
        Secretary*]. *Sic itur ad astra!* Dear
        Von Visenburg
Is scandalized, and poor Torinus
        paralysed,
And every honest soul that Basil holds
Aghast; and yet we live, as one may say,
Just as though Liechtenfels had never
        set
So true a value on his sorry carcass,
And learned Pütter had not frowned us
        dumb.
We live; and shall as surely start to-
        morrow
For Nuremberg, as we drink speedy
        scathe
To Basil in this mantling wine, suffused
A delicate blush, no fainter tinge is born
I' the shut heart of a bud. Pledge me,
        good John –
'Basil; a hot plague ravage it, and Pütter
'Oppose the plague!' Even so? Do you
        too share
Their panic, the reptiles? Ha, ha; faint
        through these,
Desist for these! They manage matters so
At Basil, 'tis like: but others may find
        means

To bring the stoutest braggart of the tribe
Once more to crouch in silence – means to breed
A stupid wonder in each fool again,
Now big with admiration at the skill
Which stript a vain pretender of his plumes:
And, that done, – means to brand each slavish brow
So deeply, surely, ineffaceably,
That henceforth flattery shall not pucker it
Out of the furrow; there that stamp shall stay
To show the next they fawn on, what they are,
This Basil with its magnates, – fill my cup, –
Whom I curse soul and limb. And now despatch,
Despatch, my trusty John; and what remains
To do, whate'er arrangements for our trip
Are yet to be completed, see you hasten
This night; we'll weather the storm at least: to-morrow
For Nuremberg! Now leave us; this grave clerk
Has divers weighty matters for my ear:
                    [OPORINUS *goes out*].
And spare my lungs. At last, my gallant Festus,
I am rid of this arch-knave that dogs my heels
As a gaunt crow a gasping sheep; at last
May give a loose to my delight. How kind.
How very kind, my first best only friend!
Why, this looks like fidelity. Embrace me!
Not a hair silvered yet? Right! you shall live
Till I am worth your love; you shall be proud,
And I – but let time show! Did you not wonder?

I sent to you because our compact weighed
Upon my conscience – (you recall the night
At Basil, which the gods confound!) – because
Once more I aspire. I call you to my side:
You come. You thought my message strange?
*Fest.*                    So strange
That I must hope, indeed, your messenger
Has mingled his own fancies with the words
Purporting to be yours.
*Par.*                    He said no more,
'Tis probable, than the precious folk I leave
Said fiftyfold more roughly. Well-a-day,
'Tis true! poor Paracelsus is exposed
At last; a most egregious quack he proves:
And those he overreached must spit their hate
On one who, utterly beneath contempt,
Could yet deceive their topping wits. You heard
Bare truth; and at my bidding you come here
To speed me on my enterprise, as once
Your lavish wishes sped me, my own friend!
*Fest.* What is your purpose, Aureole?
*Par.*                    Oh, for purpose,
There is no lack of precedents in a case
Like mine; at least, if not precisely mine,
The case of men cast off by those they sought
To benefit.
*Fest.*          They really cast you off?
I only heard a vague tale of some priest,
Cured by your skill, who wrangled at your claim,
Knowing his life's worth best; and how the judge
The matter was referred to, saw no cause

To interfere, nor you to hide your full
Contempt of him; nor he, again, to smother
His wrath thereat, which raised so fierce a flame
That Basil soon was made no place for you.
*Par.*　　The affair of Liechtenfels? the shallowest fable,
The last and silliest outrage – mere pretence!
I knew it, I foretold it from the first,
How soon the stupid wonder you mistook
For genuine loyalty – a cheering promise
Of better things to come – would pall and pass;
And every word comes true. Saul is among
The prophets! Just so long as I was pleased
To play off the mere antics of my art,
Fantastic gambols leading to no end,
I got huge praise: but one can ne'er keep down
Our foolish nature's weakness. There they flocked,
Poor devils, jostling, swearing and perspiring,
Till the walls rang again; and all for me!
I had a kindness for them, which was right;
But then I stopped not till I tacked to that
A trust in them and a respect – a sort
Of sympathy for them; I must needs begin
To teach them, not amaze them, 'to impart
'The spirit which should instigate the search
'Of truth,' just what you bade me! I spoke out.
Forthwith a mighty squadron, in disgust,
Filed off – 'the sifted chaff of the sack,' I said,
Redoubling my endeavours to secure
The rest. When lo! one man had tarried so long
Only to ascertain if I supported
This tenet of his, or that; another loved
To hear impartially before he judged,
And having heard, now judged; this bland disciple
Passed for my dupe, but all along, it seems,
Spied error where his neighbours marvelled most;
That fiery doctor who had hailed me friend,
Did it because my by-paths, once proved wrong
And beaconed properly, would commend again
The good old ways our sires jogged safely o'er,
Though not their squeamish sons; the other worthy
Discovered divers verses of St John,
Which, read successively, refreshed the soul,
But, muttered backwards, cured the gout, the stone,
The colic and what not. *Quid multa?* The end
Was a clear class-room, and a quiet leer
From grave folk, and a sour reproachful glance
From those in chief who, cap in hand, installed
The new professor scarce a year before;
And a vast flourish about patient merit
Obscured awhile by flashy tricks, but sure
Sooner or later to emerge in splendour –
Of which the example was some luckless wight
Whom my arrival had discomfited,
But now, it seems, the general voice recalled
To fill my chair and so efface the stain
Basil had long incurred. I sought no better,
Only a quiet dismissal from my post,

And from my heart I wished them better
   suited
And better served. Good night to Basil,
   then!
But fast as I proposed to rid the tribe
Of my obnoxious back, I could not spare
   them
The pleasure of a parting kick.
*Fest.*                     You smile:
Despise them as they merit!
*Par.*                  If I smile,
'Tis with as very contempt as ever turned
Flesh into stone. This courteous
   recompense,
This grateful ... Festus, were your nature
   fit
To be defiled, your eyes the eyes to ache
At gangrene-blotches, eating poison-
   blains,
The ulcerous barky scurf of leprosy
Which finds – a man, and leaves – a
   hideous thing
That cannot but be mended by hell fire,
– I would lay bare to you the human
   heart
Which God cursed long ago, and devils
   make since
Their pet nest and their never-tiring
   home.
Oh, sages have discovered we are born
For various ends – to love, to know: has
   ever
One stumbled, in his search, on any signs
Of a nature in us formed to hate? To
   hate?
If that be our true object which evokes
Our powers in fullest strength, be sure
   'tis hate!
Yet men have doubted if the best and
   bravest
Of spirits can nourish him with hate
   alone.
I had not the monopoly of fools,
It seems, at Basil.
*Fest.*       But your plans, your plans!
I have yet to learn your purpose,
   Aureole!

*Par.* Whether to sink beneath such
   ponderous shame,
To shrink up like a crushed snail,
   undergo
In silence and desist from further toil,
And so subside into a monument
Of one their censure blasted? or to bow
Cheerfully as submissively, to lower
My old pretensions even as Basil
   dictates,
To drop into the rank her wits assign me
And live as they prescribe, and make
   that use
Of my poor knowledge which their
   rules allow,
Proud to be patted now and then, and
   careful
To practise the true posture for receiving
The amplest benefit from their hoofs'
   appliance
When they shall condescend to tutor me?
Then, one may feel resentment like a
   flame
Within, and deck false systems in truth's
   garb,
And tangle and entwine mankind with
   error,
And give them darkness for a dower
   and falsehood
For a possession, ages: or one may mope
Into a shade through thinking, or else
   drowse
Into a dreamless sleep and so die off.
But I, – now Festus shall divine! – but I
Am merely setting out once more,
   embracing
My earliest aims again! What thinks he
   now?
*Fest.* Your aims? the aims? – to Know?
   and where is found
The early trust ...
*Par.*        Nay, not so fast; I say,
The aims – not the old means. You
   know they made me
A laughing-stock; I was a fool; you know
The when and the how: hardly those
   means again!

Not but they had their beauty; who
     should know
Their passing beauty, if not I? Still, dreams
They were, so let them vanish, yet in
     beauty
If that may be. Stay: thus they pass in
     song!                          [*He sings*].

     Heap cassia, sandal-buds and stripes
          Of labdanum, and aloe-balls,
     Smeared with dull nard an Indian
          wipes
             From out her hair: such balsam
                  falls
             Down sea-side mountain pedestals,
     From tree-tops where tired winds
          are fain,
     Spent with the vast and howling
          main,
     To treasure half their island-gain.

     And strew faint sweetness from some
          old
          Egyptian's fine worm-eaten shroud
     Which breaks to dust when once
          unrolled;
             Or shredded perfume, like a cloud
             From closet long to quiet vowed,
     With mothed and dropping arras
          hung,
     Mouldering her lute and books
          among,
     As when a queen, long dead, was
          young.

Mine, every word! And on such pile
     shall die
My lovely fancies, withfair perished
     things,
Themselves fair and forgotten; yes,
     forgotten,
Or why abjure them? So, I made this
     rhyme
That fitting dignity might be preserved;
No little proud was I; though the list of
     drugs
Smacks of my old vocation, and the
     verse

Halts like the best of Luther's psalms.
*Fest.*                        But, Aureole,
Talk not thus wildly and madly. I am
     here –
Did you know all! I have travelled far,
     indeed,
To learn your wishes. Be yourself again!
For in this mood I recognize you less
Than in the horrible despondency
I witnessed last. You may account this,
     joy;
But rather let me gaze on that despair
Than hear these incoherent words and
     see
This flushed cheek and intensely-
     sparkling eye.
*Par.* Why, man, I was light-hearted in
     my prime,
I am light-hearted now; what would you
     have?
Aprile was a poet, I make songs –
'Tis the very augury of success I want!
Why should I not be joyous now as
     then?
*Fest.* Joyous! and how? and what remains
     for joy?
You have declared the ends (which I am
     sick
Of naming) are impracticable.
*Par.*                                   Ay,
Pursued as I pursued them – the arch-
     fool!
Listen: my plan will please you not, 'tis
     like,
But you are little versed in the world's
     ways.
This is my plan – (first drinking its
     good luck) –
I will accept all helps; all I despised
So rashly at the outset, equally
With early impulses, late years have
     quenched:
I have tried each way singly: now for
     both!
All helps! no one sort shall exclude the
     rest.
I seek to know and to enjoy at once,

Not one without the other as before.
Suppose my labour should seem God's
    own cause
Once more, as first I dreamed, – it shall
    not baulk me
Of the meanest earthliest sensualest
    delight
That may be snatched; for every joy is
    gain,
And gain is gain, however small. My
    soul
Can die then, nor be taunted – 'what
    was gained?'
Nor, on the other hand, should pleasure
    follow
As though I had not spurned her hitherto,
Shall she o'ercloud my spirit's rapt
    communion
With the tumultuous past, the teeming
    future,
Glorious with visions of a full success.
*Fest.*                        Success!
*Par.*And wherefore not? Why not prefer
Results obtained in my best state of
    being,
To those derived alone from seasons
    dark
As the thoughts they bred? When I was
    best, my youth
Unwasted, seemed success not surest
    too?
It is the nature of darkness to obscure.
I am a wanderer: I remember well
One journey, how I feared the track
    was missed,
So long the city I desired to reach
Lay hid; when suddenly its spires afar
Flashed through the circling clouds;
    you may conceive
My transport. Soon the vapours closed
    again,
But I had seen the city, and one such
    glance
No darkness could obscure: nor shall
    the present –
A few dull hours, a passing shame or
    two,

Destroy the vivid memories of the past.
I will fight the battle out; a little spent
Perhaps, but still an able combatant.
You look at my grey hair and furrowed
    brow?
But I can turn even weakness to account:
Of many tricks I know, 'tis not the least
To push the ruins of my frame, whereon
The fire of vigour trembles scarce alive,
Into a heap, and send the flame aloft.
What should I do with age? So,
    sickness lends
An aid; it being, I fear, the source of all
We boast of: mind is nothing but disease,
And natural health is ignorance.
*Fest.*                     I see
But one good symptom in this notable
    scheme.
I feared your sudden journey had in
    view
To wreak immediate vengeance on your
    foes.
'Tis not so: I am glad.
*Par.*              And if I please
To spit on them, to trample them,
    what then?
'Tis sorry warfare truly, but the fools
Provoke it. I would spare their self-
    conceit,
But if they must provoke me, cannot
    suffer
Forbearance on my part, if I may keep
No quality in the shade, must needs
    put forth
Power to match power, my strength
    against their strength,
And teach them their own game with
    their own arms –
Why, be it so and let them take their
    chance!
I am above them like a god, there's no
Hiding the fact, what idle scruples,
    then,
Were those that ever bade me soften it,
Communicate it gently to the world,
Instead of proving my supremacy,
Taking my natural station o'er their head,

Then owning all the glory was a man's!
– And in my elevation man's would be.
But live and learn, though life's short,
    learning, hard!
And therefore, though the wreck of my
    past self,
I fear, dear Pütter, that your lecture-
    room
Must wait awhile for its best ornament,
The penitent empiric, who set up
For somebody, but soon was taught his
    place;
Now, but too happy to be let confess
His error, snuff the candles, and illustrate
(*Fiat experientia corpore vili*)
Your medicine's soundness in his person.
    Wait,
Good Pütter!
*Fest.*     He who sneers thus, is a god!
*Par.* Ay, ay, laugh at me! I am very glad
You are not gulled by all this swaggering;
    you
Can see the root of the matter! – how I
    strive
To put a good face on the overthrow
I have experienced, and to bury and hide
My degradation in its length and breadth;
How the mean motives I would make
    you think
Just mingle as is due with nobler aims,
The appetites I modestly allow
May influence me as being mortal still –
Do goad me, drive me on, and fast
    supplant
My youth's desires. You are no stupid
    dupe:
You find me out! Yes, I had sent for you
To palm these childish lies upon you,
    Festus!
Laugh – you shall laugh at me!
*Fest.*         The past, then, Aureole,
Proves nothing? Is our interchange of
    love
Yet to begin? Have I to swear I mean
No flattery in this speech or that? For
    you,
Whate'er you say, there is no degradation;

These low thoughts are no inmates of
    your mind,
Or wherefore this disorder? You are
    vexed
As much by the intrusion of base views,
Familiar to your adversaries, as they
Were troubled should your qualities
    alight
Amid their murky souls; not otherwise,
A stray wolf which the winter forces
    down
From our bleak hills, suffices to affright
A village in the vales – while foresters
Sleep calm, though all night long the
    famished troop
Snuff round and scratch against their
    crazy huts.
These evil thoughts are monsters, and
    will flee.
*Par.* May you be happy, Festus, my own
    friend!
*Fest.* Nay, further; the delights you fain
    would think
The superseders of your nobler aims,
Though ordinary and harmless
    stimulants,
Will ne'er content you . . .
*Par.*         Hush! I once despised them,
But that soon passes. We are high at
    first
In our demand, nor will abate a jot
Of toil's strict value; but time passes
    o'er,
And humbler spirits accept what we
    refuse:
In short, when some such comfort is
    doled out
As these delights, we cannot long retain
Bitter contempt which urges us at first
To hurl it back, but hug it to our breast
And thankfully retire. This life of mine
Must be lived out and a grave
    thoroughly earned:
I am just fit for that and nought beside.
I told you once, I cannot now enjoy,
Unless I deem my knowledge gains
    through joy;

Nor can I know, but straight warm tears
    reveal
My need of liking also joy to knowledge:
So, on I drive, enjoying all I can,
And knowing all I can. I speak, of course,
Confusedly; this will better explain –
    feel here!
Quick beating, is it not? – a fire of the
    heart
To work off some way, this as well as any.
So, Festus sees me fairly launched; his
    calm
Compassionate look might have
    disturbed me once,
But now, far from rejecting, I invite
What bids me press the closer, lay
    myself
Open before him, and be soothed with
    pity;
I hope, if he command hope, and believe
As he directs me – satiating myself
With his enduring love. And Festus
    quits me
To give place to some credulous disciple
Who holds that God is wise, but
    Paracelsus
Has his peculiar merits: I suck in
That homage, chuckle o'er that
    admiration,
And then dismiss the fool; for night is
    come,
And I betake myself to study again,
Till patient searchings after hidden lore
Half wring some bright truth from its
    prison; my frame
Trembles, my forehead's veins swell
    out, my hair
Tingles for triumph. Slow and sure the
    morn
Shall break on my pent room and
    dwindling lamp
And furnace dead, and scattered earths
    and ores;
When, with a failing heart and
    throbbing brow,
I must review my captured truth, sum
    up

Its value, trace what ends to what begins,
Its present power with its eventual
    bearings,
Latent affinities, the views it opens,
And its full length in perfecting my
    scheme.
I view it sternly circumscribed, cast
    down
From the high place my fond hopes
    yielded it,
Proved worthless – which, in getting,
    yet had cost
Another wrench to this fast-falling
    frame.
Then, quick, the cup to quaff, that
    chases sorrow!
I lapse back into youth, and take again
My fluttering pulse for evidence that God
Means good to me, will make my cause
    his own.
See! I have cast off this remorseless care
Which clogged a spirit born to soar so
    free,
And my dim chamber has become a
    tent,
Festus is sitting by me, and his
    Michal . . .
Why do you start? I say, she listening
    here,
(For yonder – Würzburg through the
    orchard-bough!)
Motions as though such ardent words
    should find
No echo in a maiden's quiet soul,
But her pure bosom heaves, her eyes
    fill fast
With tears, her sweet lips tremble all
    the while!
Ha, ha!
*Fest.* It seems, then, you expect to reap
No unreal joy from this your present
    course,
But rather . . .
*Par.* Death! To die! I owe that much
To what, at least, I was. I should be sad
To live contented after such a fall,
To thrive and fatten after such reverse!

The whole plan is a makeshift, but will
    last
My time.
*Fest.*      And you have never mused
    and said,
'I had a noble purpose, and the strength
'To compass it; but I have stopped
    halfway,
'And wrongly given the first-fruits of
    my toil
'To objects little worthy of the gift.
'Why linger round them still? why
    clench my fault?
'Why seek for consolation in defeat,
'In vain endeavours to derive a beauty
'From ugliness? why seek to make the
    most
'Of what no power can change, nor
    strive instead
'With mighty effort to redeem the past
'And, gathering up the treasures thus
    cast down,
'To hold a steadfast course till I arrive
'At their fit destination and my own?'
You have never pondered thus?
*Par.*      Have I, you ask?
Often at midnight, when most fancies
    come,
Would some such airy project visit me:
But ever at the end ... or will you hear
The same thing in a tale, a parable?
You and I, wandering over the world
    wide,
Chance to set foot upon a desert coast.
Just as we cry, 'No human voice before
'Broke the inveterate silence of these
    rocks!'
– Their querulous echo startles us; we
    turn:
What ravaged structure still looks o'er
    the sea?
Some characters remain, too! While we
    read,
The sharp salt wind, impatient for the
    last
Of even this record, wistfully comes
    and goes,

Or sings what we recover, mocking it.
This is the record; and my voice, the
    wind's.        [*He sings.*

    Over the sea our galleys went,
  With cleaving prows in order brave
  To a speeding wind and a bounding
    wave,
    A gallant armament:
Each bark built out of a forest-tree
  Left leafy and rough as first it grew,
And nailed all over the gaping sides,
Within and without, with black
    bullhides,
Seethed in fat and suppled in flame,
To bear the playful billows' game:
So, each good ship was rude to see,
Rude and bare to the outward view,
  But each upbore a stately tent
Where cedar pales in scented row
Kept out the flakes of the dancing
    brine,
And an awning drooped the mast
    below,
In fold on fold of the purple fine,
That neither noontide nor starshine
Nor moonlight cold which maketh
    mad,
    Might pierce the regal tenement.
When the sun dawned, oh, gay and
    glad
We set the sail and plied the oar;
But when the night-wind blew like
    breath,
For joy of one day's voyage more,
We sang together on the wide sea,
Like men at peace on a peaceful
    shore;
Each sail was loosed to the wind so
    free,
Each helm made sure by the twilight
    star,
And in a sleep as calm as death,
We, the voyagers from afar,
    Lay stretched along, each weary
    crew
In a circle round its wondrous tent

Whence gleamed soft light and
　　curled rich scent,
　　And with light and perfume,
　　　music too:
So the stars wheeled round, and the
　　darkness past,
And at morn we started beside the
　　mast,
And still each ship was sailing fast.

Now, one morn, land appeared – a
　　speck
Dim trembling betwixt sea and sky:
'Avoid it,' cried our pilot, 'check
　　The shout, restrain the eager eye!'
But the heaving sea was black behind
For many a night and many a day,
And land, though but a rock, drew
　　nigh;
So, we broke the cedar pales away,
Let the purple awning flap in the
　　wind,
　　And a statue bright was on every
　　　deck!
We shouted, every man of us,
And steered right into the harbour
　　thus,
With pomp and paean glorious.

A hundred shapes of lucid stone!
　　All day we built its shrine for each,
A shrine of rock for every one,
Nor paused till in the westering sun
　　We sat together on the beach
To sing because our task was done.
When lo! what shouts and merry
　　songs!
What laughter all the distance stirs!
A loaded raft with happy throngs
Of gentle islanders!
'Our isles are just at hand,' they
　　cried,
　　'Like cloudlets faint in even
　　　sleeping;
'Our temple-gates are opened wide,
　　'Our olive-groves thick shade are
　　　keeping
'For these majestic forms' – they cried.

Oh, then we awoke with sudden
　　start
From our deep dream, and knew,
　　too late,
How bare the rock, how desolate,
Which had received our precious
　　freight:
　　Yet we called out – 'Depart!
'Our gifts, once given, must here
　　abide.
　　'Our work is done; we have no
　　　heart
'To mar our work,' – we cried.

*Fest.* In truth?
*Par.* 　　　　　Nay, wait: all this in
　　tracings faint
On rugged stones strewn here and
　　there, but piled
In order once: then follows – mark what
　　follows!
'The sad rhyme of the men who
　　proudly clung
'To their first fault, and withered in
　　their pride.'
*Fest.* Come back then, Aureole; as you
　　fear God, come!
This is foul sin; come back! Renounce
　　the past
Forswear the future; look for joy no
　　more,
But wait death's summons amid holy
　　sights,
And trust me for the event – peace, if
　　not joy.
Return with me to Einsiedeln, dear
　　Aureole!
*Par.* No way, no way! it would not turn
　　to good.
A spotless child sleeps on the flowering
　　moss –
'Tis well for him; but when a sinful man,
Envying such slumber, may desire to
　　put
His guilt away, shall he return at once
To rest by lying there? Our sires knew
　　well

(Spite of the grave discoveries of their
    sons)
The fitting course for such: dark cells,
    dim lamps,
A stone floor one may writhe on like a
    worm:
No mossy pillow blue with violets!
*Fest.* I see no symptom of these
    absolute
And tyrannous passions. You are calmer
    now.
This verse-making can purge you well
    enough
Without the terrible penance you
    describe.
You love me still: the lusts you fear will
    never
Outrage your friend. To Einsiedeln, once
    more!
Say but the word!
*Par.*         No, no; those lusts forbid:
They crouch, I know, cowering with
    half-shut eye
Beside you; 'tis their nature. Thrust
    yourself
Between them and their prey; let some
    fool style me
Or king or quack, it matters not – then
    try
Your wisdom, urge them to forego their
    treat!
No, no; learn better and look deeper,
    Festus!
If you knew how a devil sneers within
    me
While you are talking now of this, now
    that,
As though we differed scarcely save in
    trifles!
*Fest.* Do we so differ? True, change
    must proceed,
Whether for good or ill; keep from me,
    which!
Do not confide all secrets: I was born
To hope, and you . . .
*Par.*         To trust: you know
    the fruits!

*Fest.* Listen: I do believe, what you call
    trust
Was self-delusion at the best: for, see!
So long as God would kindly pioneer
A path for you, and screen you from
    the world,
Procure you full exemption from man's
    lot,
Man's common hopes and fears, on
    the mere pretext
Of your engagement in his service –
    yield you
A limitless licence, make you God, in
    fact,
And turn your slave – you were
    content to say
Most courtly praises! What is it, at last,
But selfishness without example? None
Could trace God's will so plain as you,
    while yours
Remained implied in it; but now you
    fail,
And we, who prate about that will, are
    fools!
In short, God's service is established
    here
As he determines fit, and not your way,
And this you cannot brook. Such
    discontent
Is weak. Renounce all creatureship at
    once!
Affirm an absolute right to have and
    use
Your energies; as though the rivers
    should say –
'We rush to the ocean; what have we
    to do
'With feeding streamlets, lingering in
    the vales,
'Sleeping in lazy pools?' Set up that plea,
That will be bold at least!
*Par.*         'Tis like enough.
The serviceable spirits are those, no
    doubt,
The East produces: lo, the master bids, –
They wake, raise terraces and garden-
    grounds

In one night's space; and, this done,
    straight begin
Another century's sleep, to the great
    praise
Of him that framed them wise and
    beautiful,
Till a lamp's rubbing, or some chance
    akin,
Wake them again. I am of different
    mould.
I would have soothed my lord, and
    slaved for him
And done him service past my narrow
    bond,
And thus I get rewarded for my pains!
Beside, 'tis vain to talk of forwarding
God's glory otherwise; this is alone
The sphere of its increase, as far as men
Increase it; why, then, look beyond
    this sphere?
We are his glory; and if we be glorious,
Is not the thing achieved?
*Fest.*          Shall one like me
Judge hearts like yours? Though years
    have changed you much,
And you have left your first love, and
    retain
Its empty shade to veil your crooked
    ways,
Yet I still hold that you have honoured
    God.
And who shall call your course without
    reward?
For, wherefore this repining at defeat
Had triumph ne'er inured you to high
    hopes?
I urge you to forsake the life you curse,
And what success attends me? –
    simply talk
Of passion, weakness and remorse; in
    short,
Anything but the naked truth – you
    choose
This so-despised career, and cheaply hold
My happiness, or rather other men's.
Once more, return!
*Par.*        And quickly. John the thief

Has pilfered half my secrets by this time:
And we depart by daybreak. I am
    weary,
I know not how; not even the wine-
    cup soothes
My brain to-night . . .
Do you not thoroughly despise me,
    Festus?
No flattery! One like you needs not be
    told
We live and breathe deceiving and
    deceived.
Do you not scorn me from your heart
    of hearts,
Me and my cant, each petty subterfuge,
My rhymes and all this frothy shower
    of words,
My glozing self-deceit, my outward
    crust
Of lies which wrap, as tetter, morphew,
    furfair
Wrapt the sound flesh? – so, see you
    flatter not!
Even God flatters: but my friend, at
    least,
Is true. I would depart, secure henceforth
Against all further insult, hate and wrong
From puny foes; my one friend's scorn
    shall brand me:
No fear of sinking deeper!
*Fest.*        No, dear Aureole!
No, no; I came to counsel faithfully.
There are old rules, made long ere we
    were born,
By which I judge you. I, so fallible,
So infinitely low beside your mighty
Majestic spirit! – even I can see
You own some higher law than ours
    which call
Sin, what is no sin – weakness, what is
    strength.
But I have only these, such as they are,
To guide me; and I blame you where
    they bid,
Only so long as blaming promises
To win peace for your soul: the more,
    that sorrow

Has fallen on me of late, and they have
  helped me
So that I faint not under my distress.
But wherefore should I scruple to avow
In spite of all, as brother judging
  brother,
Your fate is most inexplicable to me?
And should you perish without
  recompense
And satisfaction yet – too hastily
I have relied on love: you may have
  sinned,
But you have loved. As a mere human
  matter –
As I would have God deal with fragile
  men
In the end – I say that you will triumph
  yet!
*Par.* Have you felt sorrow, Festus? – 'tis
  because
You love me. Sorrow, and sweet Michal
  yours!
Well thought on: never let her know this
  last
Dull winding-up of all: these miscreants
  dared
Insult me – me she loved: – so, grieve
  her not!
*Fest.* Your ill success can little grieve her
  now.
*Par.* Michal is dead! pray Christ we do
  not craze!
*Fest.* Aureole, dear Aureole, look not on
  me thus!
Fool, fool! this is the heart grown sorrow-
  proof –
I cannot bear those eyes.
*Par.*                          Nay, really dead?
*Fest.* 'Tis scarce a month.
*Par.*                          Stone dead! – then
  you have laid her
Among the flowers ere this. Now, do you
  know,
I can reveal a secret which shall comfort
Even you. I have no julep, as men think,
To cheat the grave; but a far better
  secret.

Know, then, you did not ill to trust
  your love
To the cold earth: I have thought much
  of it:
For I believe we do not wholly die.
*Fest.* Aureole!
*Par.*          Nay, do not laugh; there is a
  reason
For what I say: I think the soul can
  never
Taste death. I am, just now, as you
  may see,
Very unfit to put so strange a thought
In an intelligible dress of words;
But take it as my trust, she is not dead.
*Fest.* But not on this account alone? you
  surely,
– Aureole, you have believed this all
  along?
*Par.* And Michal sleeps among the roots
  and dews,
While I am moved at Basil, and full of
  schemes
For Nuremberg, and hoping and
  despairing,
As though it mattered how the farce
  plays out,
So it be quickly played. Away, away!
Have your will, rabble! while we fight
  the prize,
Troop you in safety to the snug back-
  seats
And leave a clear arena for the brave
About to perish for your sport! –
  Behold!

## 5 – PARACELSUS ATTAINS

*Scene – Salzburg; a cell in the Hospital of
  St Sebastian. 1541.*

FESTUS, PARACELSUS

*Fest.* No change! The weary night is
  well-nigh spent,
The lamp burns low, and through the
  casement-bars
Grey morning glimmers feebly: yet no
  change!

Another night, and still no sigh has
    stirred
That fallen discoloured mouth, no pang
    relit
Those fixed eyes, quenched by the
    decaying body,
Like torch-flame choked in dust. While
    all beside
Was breaking, to the last they held out
    bright,
As a stronghold where life intrenched
    itself;
But they are dead now – very blind and
    dead:
He will drowse into death without a
    groan.

My Aureole – my forgotten, ruined
    Aureole!
The days are gone, are gone! How
    grand thou wast!
And now not one of those who struck
    thee down –
Poor glorious spirit – concerns him
    even to stay
And satisfy himself his little hand
Could turn God's image to a livid
    thing.

Another night, and yet no change! 'Tis
    much
That I should sit by him, and bathe his
    brow,
And chafe his hands; 'tis much: but he
    will sure
Know me, and look on me, and speak
    to me
Once more – but only once! His
    hollow cheek
Looked all night long as though a
    creeping laugh
At his own state were just about to
    break
From the dying man: my brain swam,
    my throat swelled,
And yet I could not turn away. In truth,
They told me how, when first brought
    here, he seemed

Resolved to live, to lose no faculty;
Thus striving to keep up his shattered
    strength,
Until they bore him to this stifling cell:
When straight his features fell, an hour
    made white
The flushed face, and relaxed the
    quivering limb,
Only the eye remained intense awhile
As though it recognized the tomb-like
    place,
And then he lay as here he lies.
                   Ay, here!
Here is earth's noblest, nobly
    garlanded –
Her bravest champion with his well-
    won prize –
Her best achievement, her sublime
    amends
For countless generations fleeting fast
And followed by no trace; – the
    creature-god
She instances when angels would
    dispute
The title of her brood to rank with
    them.
Angels, this is our ange! Those bright
    forms
We clothe with purple, crown and call
    to thrones,
Are human, but not his; those are but
    men
Whom other men press round and
    kneel before;
Those palaces are dwelt in by
    mankind;
Higher provision is for him you seek
Amid our pomps and glories: see it
    here!
Behold earth's paragon! Now, raise
    thee, clay!

God! Thou art love! I build my faith on
    that.
Even as I watch beside thy tortured child
Unconscious whose hot tears fall fast
    by him,

So doth thy right hand guide us through
     the world
Wherein we stumble. God! what shall
     we say?
How has he sinned? How else should
     he have done?
Surely he sought thy praise – thy praise,
     for all
He might be busied by the task so much
As half forget awhile its proper end.
Dost thou well, Lord? Thou canst not
     but prefer
That I should range myself upon his
     side –
How could he stop at every step to set
Thy glory forth? Hadst thou but granted
     him
Success, thy honour would have
     crowned success,
A halo round a star. Or, say he erred, –
Save him, dear God; it will be like thee:
     bathe him
In light and life! Thou are not made like
     us;
We should be wroth in such a case;
     but thou
Forgivest – so, forgive these passionate
     thoughts
Which come unsought and will not pass
     away!
I know thee, who hast kept my path,
     and made
Light for me in the darkness, tempering
     sorrow
So that it reached me like a solemn joy;
It were too strange that I should doubt
     thy love.
But what am I? Thou madest him and
     knowest
How he was fashioned. I could never err
That way: the quiet place beside thy feet,
Reserved for me, was ever in my thoughts:
But he – thou shouldst have favoured
     him as well!

Ah! he wakens! Aureole, I am here! 'tis
     Festus!

I cast away all wishes save one wish –
Let him but know me, only speak to me!
He mutters; louder and louder; any other
Than I, with brain less laden, could
     collect
What he pours forth. Dear Aureole, do
     but look!
Is it talking or singing, this he utters fast?
Misery that he should fix me with his
     eye,
Quick talking to some other all the
     while!
If he would husband this wild vehemence
Which frustrates its intent! – I heard, I
     know
I heard my name amid those rapid words.
Oh, he will know me yet! Could I divert
This current, lead it somehow gently
     back
Into the channels of the past! – His eye
Brighter than ever! It must recognize me!

I am Erasmus: I am here to pray
That Paracelsus use his skill for me.
The schools of Paris and of Padua send
These questions for your learning to
     resolve.
We are your students, noble master:
     leave
This wretched cell, what business have
     you here?
Our class awaits you; come to us once
     more!
(O agony! the utmost I can do
Touches him not; how else arrest his
     ear?)
I am commissioned ... I shall craze like
     him.
Better be mute and see what God shall
     send.
*Par.* Stay, stay with me!
*Fest.*                  I will; I am come here
To stay with you. – Festus, you loved of
     old;
Festus, you know, you must know!
*Par.*                      Festus! Where's
Aprile, then? Has he not chanted softly

The melodies I heard all night? I could
    not
Get to him for a cold hand on my breast,
But I made out his music well enough,
O well enough! If they have filled him
    full
With magical music, as they freight a
    star
With light, and have remitted all his sin,
They will forgive me too, I too shall
    know!
*Fest.* Festus, your Festus!
*Par.*                           Ask him if
Aprile Knows as he Loves – if I shall
    Love and Know?
I try; but that cold hand, like lead – so
    cold!
*Fest.* My hand, see!
*Par.*       Ah, the curse, Aprile, Aprile!
We get so near – so very, very near!
'Tis an old tale: Jove strikes the Titans
    down,
Not when they set about their mountain-
    piling
But when another rock would crown
    the work.
And Phaeton – doubtless his first
    radiant plunge
Astonished mortals, though the gods
    were calm,
And Jove prepared his thunder: all old
    tales!
*Fest.* And what are these to you?
*Par.*                           Ay, fiends must laugh
So cruelly, so well! most like I never
Could tread a single pleasure underfoot,
But they were grinning by my side, were
    chuckling
To see me toil and drop away by flakes!
Hell-spawn! I am glad, most glad, that
    thus I fail!
Your cunning has o'ershot its aim. One
    year,
One month, perhaps, and I had served
    your turn!
You should have curbed your spite
    awhile. But now,

Who will believe 'twas you that held
    me back?
Listen: there's shame and hissing and
    contempt,
And none but laughs who names me,
    none but spits
Measureless scorn upon me, me alone,
The quack, the cheat, the liar, – all
    on me!
And thus your famous plan to sink
    mankind
In silence and despair, by teaching them
One of their race had probed the
    inmost truth,
Had done all man could do, yet failed
    no less –
Your wise plan proves abortive. Men
    despair?
Ha, ha! why, they are hooting the
    empiric,
The ignorant and incapable fool who
    rushed
Madly upon a work beyond his wits;
Nor doubt they but the simplest of
    themselves
Could bring the matter to triumphant
    issue.
So, pick and choose among them all,
    accursed!
Try now, persuade some other to slave
    for you,
To ruin body and soul to work your
    ends!
No, no; I am the first and last, I think.
*Fest.* Dear friend, who are accursed?
    who has done . . .
*Par.* What have I done? Fiends dare ask
    that? or you,
Brave men? Oh, you can chime in boldly,
    backed
By the others! What had you to do,
    sage peers?
Here stands my rivals; Latin, Arab, Jew,
Greek, join dead hands against me: all
    I ask
Is, that the world enrol my name with
    theirs,

And even this poor privilege, it seems,
They range themselves, prepared to
disallow.
Only observe! why, fiends may learn
from them!
How they talk calmly of my throes, my
fierce
Aspirings, terrible watchings, each one
claiming
Its price of blood and brain; how they
dissect
And sneeringly disparage the few truths
Got at a life's cost; they too hanging the
while
About my neck, their lies misleading me
And their dead names browbeating me!
Grey crew,
Yet steeped in fresh malevolence from
hell,
Is there a reason for your hate? My truths
Have shaken a little the palm about each
prince?
Just think, Aprile, all these leering
dotards
Were bent on nothing less than to be
crowned
As we! That yellow blear-eyed wretch
in chief
To whom the rest cringe low with
feigned respect,
Galen of Pergamos and hell – nay speak
The tale, old man! We met there face to
face:
I said the crown should fall from thee.
Once more
We meet as in that ghastly vestibule:
Look to my brow! Have I redeemed my
pledge?
*Fest.* Peace, peace; ah, see!
*Par.*          Oh, emptiness of fame!
Oh Persic Zoroaster, lord of stars!
– Who said these old renowns, dead
long ago,
Could make me overlook the living
world
To gaze through gloom at where they
stood, indeed,

But stand no longer? What a warm light
life
After the shade! In truth, my delicate
witch,
My serpent-queen, you did but well to
hide
The juggles I had else detected. Fire
May well run harmless o'er a breast
like yours!
The cave was not so darkened by the
smoke
But that your white limbs dazzled me:
oh, white,
And panting as they twinkled, wildly
dancing!
I cared not for your passionate gestures
then,
But now I have forgotten the charm of
charms,
The foolish knowledge which I came to
seek,
While I remember that quaint dance;
and thus
I am come back, not for those
mummeries,
But to love you, and to kiss your little
feet
Soft as an ermine's winter coat!
*Fest.*                 A light
Will struggle through these thronging
words at last.
As in the angry and tumultuous West
A soft star trembles through the
drifting clouds.
These are the strivings of a spirit which
hates
So sad a vault should coop it, and calls up
The past to stand between it and its fate.
Were he at Einsiedeln – or Michal here!
*Par.* Cruel! I seek her now – I kneel – I
shriek –
I clasp her vesture – but she fades, still
fades;
And she is gone; sweet human love is
gone!
'Tis only when they spring to heaven
that angels

Reveal themselves to you; they sit all
    day
Beside you, and lie down at night by
    you
Who care not for their presence, muse
    or sleep,
And all at once they leave you, and you
    know them!
We are so fooled, so cheated! Why, even
    now
I am not too secure against foul play;
The shadows deepen and the walls
    contract:
No doubt some treachery is going on.
'Tis very dusk. Where are we put, Aprile?
Have they left us in the lurch? This
    murky loathsome
Death-trap, this slaughter-house, is not
    the hall
In the golden city! Keep by me, Aprile!
There is a hand groping amid the
    blackness
To catch us. Have the spider-fingers got
    you,
Poet? Hold on me for your life! If once
They pull you! – Hold!
'Tis but a dream – no more!
I have you still; the sun comes out again;
Let us be happy: all will yet go well!
Let us confer: is it not like, Aprile,
That spite of trouble, this ordeal passed,
The value of my labours ascertained,
Just as some stream foams long among
    the rocks
But after glideth glassy to the sea,
So, full content shall henceforth be my
    lot?
What think you, poet? Louder! Your
    clear voice
Vibrates too like a harp-string. Do you
    ask
How could I still remain on earth, should
    God
Grant me the great approval which I
    seek?
I, you, and God can comprehend each
    other,

But men would murmur, and with
    cause enough;
For when they saw me, stainless of all sin,
Preserved and sanctified by inward
    light,
They would complain that comfort,
    shut from them,
I drank thus unespied; that they live on.
Nor taste the quiet of a constant joy,
For ache and care and doubt and
    weariness,
While I am calm; help being vouchsafed
    to me,
And hid from them. – 'Twere best
    consider that!
You reason well, Aprile; but at least
Let me know this, and die! Is this too
    much?
I will learn this, if God so please, and die!

If thou shalt please, dear God, if thou
    shalt please!
We are so weak, we know our motives
    least
In their confused beginning. If at first
I sought … but wherefore bare my heart
    to thee?
I know thy mercy; and already thoughts
Flock fast about my soul to comfort it,
And intimate I cannot wholly fail,
For love and praise would clasp me
    willingly
Could I resolve to seek them. Thou art
    good,
And I should be content. Yet – yet first
    show
I have done wrong in daring! Rather give
The supernatural consciousness of
    strength
Which fed my youth! Only one hour of
    that
With thee to help – O what should bar
    me then!

Lost, lost! Thus things are ordered
    here! God's creatures,
And yet he takes no pride in us! –
    none, none!

Truly there needs another life to come!
If this be all – (I must tell Festus that)
And other life await us not – for one,
I say 'tis a poor cheat, a stupid bungle,
A wretched failure. I, for one, protest
Against it, and I hurl it back with
     scorn.

Well, onward though alone! Small time
     remains,
And much to do: I must have fruit, must
     reap
Some profit from my toils. I doubt my
     body
Will hardly serve me through; while I
     have laboured
It has decayed; and now that I demand
Its best assistance, it will crumble fast:
A sad thought, a sad fate! How very full
Of wormwood 'tis, that just at altar-
     service,
The rapt hymn rising with the rolling
     smoke,
When glory dawns and all is at the best,
The sacred fire may flicker and grow faint
And die for want of a wood-piler's help!
Thus fades the flagging body, and the
     soul
Is pulled down in the overthrow. Well,
     well –
Let men catch every word, let them lose
     nought
Of what I say; something may yet be
     done.

They are ruins! Trust me who am one
     of you!
All ruins, glorious once, but lonely now.
It makes my heart sick to behold you
     crouch
Beside your desolate fane: the arches
     dim,
The crumbling columns grand against
     the moon,
Could I but rear them up once more –
     but that
May never be, so leave them! Trust me,
     friends,

Why should you linger here when I
     have built
A far resplendent temple, all your own?
Trust me, they are but ruins! See,
     Aprile,
Men will not heed! Yet were I not
     prepared
With better refuge for them, tongue of
     mine
Should ne'er reveal how blank their
     dwelling is:
I would sit down in silence with the rest.

Ha, what? you spit at me, you grin and
     shriek
Contempt into my ear – my ear which
     drank
God's accents once? you curse me?
     Why men, men,
I am not formed for it! Those hideous
     eyes
Will be before me sleeping, waking,
     praying
They will not let me even die. Spare,
     spare me,
Sinning or no, forget that, only spare me
The horrible scorn! You thought I
     could support it.
But now you see what silly fragile
     creature
Cowers thus. I am not good nor bad
     enough,
Not Christ nor Cain, yet even Cain was
     saved
From Hate like this. Let me but totter
     back!
Perhaps I shall elude those jeers which
     creep
Into my very brain, and shut these
     scorched
Eyelids and keep those mocking faces
     out.

Listen, Aprile! I am very calm:
Be not deceived, there is no passion
     here
Where the blood leaps like an
     imprisoned thing:

I am calm: I will exterminate the race!
Enough of that: 'tis said and it shall be.
And now be merry: safe and sound am I
Who broke through their best ranks to
    get at you.
And such a havoc, such a rout, Aprile!
*Fest.* Have you no thought, no memory
    for me,
Aureole? I am so wretched – my pure
    Michal
Is gone, and you alone are left me now,
And even you forget me. Take my
    hand –
Lean on me thus. Do you not know
    me, Aureole?
*Par.* Festus, my own friend, you are
    come at last?
As you say, 'tis an awful enterprise;
But you believe I shall go through
    with it:
'Tis like you, and I thank you. Thank
    him for me,
Dear Michal! See how bright St
    Saviour's spire
Flames in the sunset; all its figures
    quaint
Gay in the glancing light: you might
    conceive them
A troop of yellow-vested white-haired
    Jews
Bound for their own land where
    redemption dawns.
*Fest.* Not that blest time – not our
    youth's time, dear God!
*Par.* Ha – stay! true, I forget – all is
    done since,
And he is come to judge me. How he
    speaks,
How calm, how well! yes, it is true, all
    true;
All quackery; all deceit; myself can laugh
The first at it, if you desire: but still
You know the obstacles which taught
    me tricks
So foreign to my nature – envy and hate,
Blind opposition, brutal prejudice,
Bald ignorance – what wonder if I sunk

To humour men the way they most
    approved?
My cheats were never palmed on such
    as you,
Dear Festus! I will kneel if you require
    me,
Impart the meagre knowledge I possess,
Explain its bounded nature, and avow
My insufficiency – whate'er you will:
I give the fight up: let there be an end,
A privacy, an obscure nook for me.
I want to be forgotten even by God.
But if that cannot be, dear Festus, lay
    me,
When I shall die, within some narrow
    grave,
Not by itself – for that would be too
    proud –
But where such graves are thickest; let
    it look
Nowise distinguished from the hillocks
    round,
So that the peasant at his brother's bed
May tread upon my own and know it
    not;
And we shall all be equal at the last,
Or classed according to life's natural
    ranks,
Fathers, sons, brothers, friends – not
    rich, nor wise,
Nor gifted: lay me thus, then say, 'He
    lived
'Too much advanced before his brother
    men;
'They kept him still in front: 'twas for
    their good
'But yet a dangerous station. It were
    strange
'That he should tell God he had never
    ranked
'With men: so, here at least he is a man.'
*Fest.* That God shall take thee to his
    breast, dear spirit,
Unto his breast, be sure! and here on
    earth
Shall spendour sit upon thy name for
    ever.

Sun! all the heaven is glad for thee: what
    care
If lower mountains light their snowy
    phares
At thine effulgence, yet acknowledge not
The source of day? Their theft shall be
    their bale:
For after-ages shall retrack thy beams,
And put aside the crowd of busy ones
And worship thee alone – the master-
    mind,
The thinker, the explorer, the creator!
Then, who should sneer at the convulsive
    throes
With which thy deeds were born, would
    scorn as well
The sheet of winding subterraneous fire
Which, pent and writhing, sends no less
    at last
Huge islands up amid the simmering
    sea.
Behold thy might in me! thou hast
    infused
Thy soul in mine; and I am grand as
    thou,
Seeing I comprehend thee – I so simple,
Thou so august. I recognize thee first;
I saw thee rise, I watched thee early and
    late,
And though no glance reveal thou dost
    accept
My homage – thus no less I proffer it,
And bid thee enter gloriously thy rest.
*Par.* Festus!
*Fest.*     I am for noble Aureole, God!
I am upon his side, come weal or woe.
His portion shall be mine. He has done
    well.
I would have sinned, had I been strong
    enough,
As he has sinned. Reward him or I waive
Reward! If thou canst find no place for
    him,
He shall be king elsewhere, and I will be
His slave for ever. There are two of us.
*Par.* Dear Festus!
*Fest.*   Here, dear Aureole! ever by you!

*Par.* Nay, speak on, or I dream again.
    Speak on!
Some story, anything – only your voice.
I shall dream else. Speak on! ay, leaning
    so!
*Fest.* Thus the Mayne glideth
    Where my Love abideth.
    Sleep's no softer: it proceeds
    On through lawns, on through meads,
    On and on, whate'er befall,
    Meandering and musical,
    Though the niggard pasturage
    Bears not on its shaven ledge
    Aught but weeds and waving grasses
    To view the river as it passes,
    Save here and there a scanty patch
    Of primroses too faint to catch
    A weary bee.
*Par.* More, more; say on!
*Fest.*             And scarce it pushes
    Its gentle way through strangling rushes
    Where the glossy kingfisher
    Flutters when noon-heats are near,
    Glad the shelving banks to shun,
    Red and steaming in the sun,
    Where the shrew-mouse with pale
        throat
    Burrows, and the speckled stoat;
    Where the quick sandpipers flit
    In and out the marl and grit
    That seems to breed them, brown as
        they:
    Nought disturbs its quiet way,
    Save some lazy stork that springs,
    Trailing it with legs and wings,
    Whom the shy fox from the hill
    Rouses, creep he ne'er so still.
*Par.* My heart! they loose my heart,
    those simple words;
Its darkness passes, which nought else
    could touch:
Like some dark snake that force may not
    expel,
Which glideth out to music sweet and
    low.
What were you doing when your voice
    broke through

A chaos of ugly images? You, indeed!
Are you alone here?
*Fest.*          All alone: you know me?
This cell?
*Par.*          An unexceptionable vault:
Good brick and stone: the bats kept
     out, the rats
Kept in: a snug nook: how should I
     mistake it?
*Fest.* But wherefore am I here?
*Par.*               Ah, well remembered!
Why, for a purpose – for a purpose,
     Festus!
'Tis like me: here I trifle while time
     fleets,
And this occasion, lost, will ne'er return.
You are here to be instructed. I will tell
God's message; but I have so much to
     say,
I fear to leave half out. All is confused
No doubt; but doubtless you will learn
     in time.
He would not else have brought you
     here: no doubt
I shall see clearer soon.
*Fest.*               Tell me but this –
You are not in despair?
*Par.*               I? and for what?
*Fest.* Alas, alas! he knows not, as I feared!
*Par.* What is it you would ask me with
     that earnest
Dear searching face?
*Fest.*          How feel you, Aureole?
*Par.*               Well:
Well. 'Tis a strange thing: I am dying,
     Festus,
And now that fast the storm of life
     subsides,
I first perceive how great the whirl has
     been.
I was calm then, who am so dizzy now –
Calm in the thick of the tempest, but
     no less
A partner of its motion and mixed up
With its career. The hurricane is spent,
And the good boat speeds through the
     brightening weather;

But is it earth or sea that heaves below?
The gulf rolls like a meadow-swell,
     o'erstrewn
With ravaged boughs and remnants of
     the shore;
And now some islet, loosened from the
     land,
Swims past with all its trees, sailing to
     ocean;
And now the air is full of uptorn canes,
Light strippings from the fan-trees,
     tamarisks
Unrooted, with their birds still clinging
     to them,
All high in the wind. Even so my varied
     life
Drifts by me; I am young, old, happy,
     sad,
Hoping, desponding, acting, taking
     rest,
And all at once: that is, those past
     conditions
Float back at once on me. If I select
Some special epoch from the crowd,
     'tis but
To will, and straight the rest dissolve
     away,
And only that particular state is present
With all its long-forgotten circumstance
Distinct and vivid as at first – myself
A careless looker-on and nothing more,
Indifferent and amused, but nothing
     more.
And this is death: I understand it all.
New being waits me; new perceptions
     must
Be born in me before I plunge therein;
Which last is Death's affair; and while I
     speak,
Minute by minute he is filling me
With power; and while my foot is on
     the threshold
Of boundless life – the doors unopened
     yet,
All preparations not complete within –
I turn new knowledge upon old events,
And the effect is … but I must not tell;

It is not lawful. Your own turn will come
One day. Wait, Festus! You will die like
    me.
*Fest.* 'Tis of that past life that I burn to
    hear.
*Par.* You wonder it engages me just now?
In truth, I wonder too. What's life to
    me?
Where'er I look is fire, where'er I listen
Music, and where I tend bliss evermore.
Yet how can I refrain? 'Tis a refined
Delight to view those chances, – one last
    view.
I am so near the perils I escape,
That I must play with them and turn
    them over,
To feel how fully they are past and gone.
Still, it is like, some further cause exists
For this peculiar mood – some hidden
    purpose;
Did I not tell you something of it, Festus?
I had it fast, but it has somehow slipt
Away from me; it will return anon.
*Fest.* (Indeed his cheek seems young
    again, his voice
Complete with its old tones: that little
    laugh
Concluding every phrase, with upturned
    eye,
As though one stooped above his head
    to whom
He looked for confirmation and approval,
Where was it gone so long, so well
    preserved?
Then, the fore-finger pointing as he
    speaks,
Like one who traces in an open book
The matter he declares; 'tis many a year
Since I remarked it last: and this in him,
But now a ghastly wreck!)
And can it be,
Dear Aureole, you have then found out
    at last
That worldly things are utter vanity?
That man is made for weakness, and
    should wait
In patient ignorance, till God appoint . . .

*Par.* Ha, the purpose: the true purpose:
    that is it!
How could I fail to apprehend! You
    here,
I thus! But no more trifling: I see all,
I know all: my last mission shall be
    done
If strength suffice. No trifling! Stay; this
    posture
Hardly befits one thus about to speak:
I will arise.
*Fest.*         Nay, Aureole, are you wild?
You cannot leave your couch.
*Par.*            No help; no help;
Not even your hand. So! there, I stand
    once more!
Speak from a couch? I never lectured
    thus.
My gown – the scarlet lined with fur;
    now put
The chain about my neck: my signet-ring
Is still upon my hand, I think – even
    so;
Last, my good sword; ah, trusty Azoth,
    leapest
Beneath thy master's grasp for the last
    time?
This couch shall be my throne: I bid
    these walls
Be consecrate, this wretched cell become
A shrine, for here God speaks to men
    through me.
Now, Festus, I am ready to begin.
*Fest.* I am dumb with wonder.
*Par.*         Listen, therefore, Festus!
There will be time enough, but none to
    spare.
I must content myself with telling only
The most important points. You
    doubtless feel
That I am happy, Festus; very happy.
*Fest.* 'Tis no delusion which uplifts him
    thus!
Then you are pardoned, Aureole, all
    your sin?
*Par.* Ay, pardoned: yet why pardoned?
*Fest.*           'Tis God's praise

That man is bound to seek, and you . . .
*Par.*                              Have lived!
We have to live alone to set forth well
God's praise. 'Tis true, I sinned much,
     as I thought,
And in effect need mercy, for I strove
To do that very thing; but, do your best
Or worst, praise rises, and will rise for
     ever.
Pardon from him, because of praise
     denied –
Who calls me to himself to exalt himself?
He might laugh as I laugh!
*Fest.*                        But all comes
To the same thing. 'Tis fruitless for
     mankind
To fret themselves with what concerns
     them not;
They are no use that way: they should
     lie down
Content as God has made them, nor
     go mad
In thriveless cares to better what is ill.
*Par.* No, no; mistake me not; let me
     not work
More harm than I have worked! This is
     my case:
If I go joyous back to God, yet bring
No offering, if I render up my soul
Without the fruits it was ordained to
     bear,
If I appear the better to love God
For sin, as one who has no claim on
     him, –
Be not deceived! It may be surely thus
With me, while higher prizes still await
The mortal persevering to the end.
Beside I am not all so valueless:
I have been something, though too
     soon I left
Following the instincts of that happy
     time.
*Fest.* What happy time? For God's
     sake, for man's sake,
What time was happy? All I hope to know
That answer will decide. What happy
     time?

*Par.* When but the time I vowed myself
     to man?
*Fest.* Great God, thy judgments are
     inscrutable!
*Par.* Yes, it was in me; I was born for it –
I, Paracelsus: it was mine by right.
Doubtless a searching and impetuous
     soul
Might learn from its own motions that
     some task
Like this awaited it about the world;
Might seek somewhere in this blank
     life of ours
For fit delights to stay its longings vast;
And, grappling Nature, so prevail on her
To fill the creature full she dared thus
     frame
Hungry for joy; and, bravely tyrannous,
Grow in demand, still craving more and
     more,
And make each joy conceded prove a
     pledge
Of other joy to follow – bating nought
Of its desires, still seizing fresh pretence
To turn the knowledge and the rapture
     wrung
As an extreme, last boon, from destiny,
Into occasion for new covetings,
New strifes, new triumphs: – doubtless
     a strong soul,
Alone, unaided might attain to this,
So glorious is our nature, so august
Man's inborn uninstructed impulses,
His naked spirit so majestical!
But this was born in me; I was made so;
Thus much time saved: the feverish
     appetites,
The tumult of unproved desire, the
     unaimed
Uncertain yearnings, aspirations blind,
Distrust, mistake, and all that ends in
     tears
Were saved me; thus I entered on my
     course.
You may be sure I was not all exempt
From human trouble; just so much of
     doubt

As bade me plant a surer foot upon
The sun-road, kept my eye unruined
'mid
The fierce and flashing splendour, set
my heart
Trembling so much as warned me I
stood there
On sufferance – not to idly gaze, but
cast
Light on a darkling race; save for that
doubt,
I stood at first where all aspire at last
To stand: the secret of the world was
mine.
I knew, I felt, (perception unexpressed,
Uncomprehended by our narrow
thought,
But somehow felt and known in every
shift
And change in the spirit, – nay, in every
pore
Of the body, even,) – what God is, what
we are,
What life is – how God tastes an infinite
joy
In infinite ways – one everlasting bliss,
From whom all being emanates, all
power
Proceeds; in whom is life for evermore,
Yet whom existence in its lowest form
Includes; where dwells enjoyment there
is he:
With still a flying point of bliss remote,
A happiness in store afar, a sphere
Of distant glory in full view; thus climbs
Pleasure its heights for ever and for ever.
The centre-fire heaves underneath the
earth,
And the earth changes like a human
face;
The molten ore bursts up among the
rocks,
Winds into the stone's heart, outbranches
bright
In hidden mines, spots barren river-beds,
Crumbles into fine sand where
sunbeams bask –

God joys therein. The wroth sea's
waves are edged
With foam, white as the bitten lip of
hate,
When, in the solitary waste, strange
groups
Of young volcanos come up, cyclops-
like,
Staring together with their eyes on
flame –
God tastes a pleasure in their uncouth
pride.
Then all is still; earth is a wintry clod:
But spring-wind, like a dancing psaltress,
passes
Over its breast to waken it, rare verdure
Buds tenderly upon rough banks,
between
The withered tree-roots and the cracks
of frost,
Like a smile striving with a wrinkled
face;
The grass grows bright, the boughs are
swoln with blooms
Like chrysalids impatient for the air,
The shining dorrs are busy, beetles run
Along the furrows, ants make their
ado;
Above, birds fly in merry flocks, the lark
Soars up and up, shivering for very joy;
Afar the ocean sleeps; white fishing-
gulls
Flit where the strand is purple with its
tribe
Of nested limpets; savage creatures seek
Their loves in wood and plain – and
God renews
His ancient rapture. Thus he dwells in
all,
From life's minute beginnings, up at last
To man – the consummation of this
scheme
Of being, the completion of this sphere
Of life: whose attributes had here and
there
Been scattered o'er the visible world
before,

Asking to be combined, dim fragments
    meant
To be united in some wondrous whole,
Imperfect qualities throughout creation,
Suggesting some one creature yet to
    make,
Some point where all those scattered
    rays should meet
Convergent in the faculties of man.
Power – neither put forth blindly, nor
    controlled
Calmly by perfect knowledge; to be
    used
At risk, inspired or checked by hope
    and fear:
Knowledge – not intuition, but the slow
Uncertain fruit of an enhancing toil,
Strengthened by love: love – not
    serenely pure,
But strong from weakness, like a
    chance-sown plant
Which, cast on stubborn soil, puts
    forth changed buds
And softer stains, unknown in happier
    climes;
Love which endures and doubts and is
    oppressed
And cherished, suffering much and
    much sustained,
And blind, oft-failing, yet believing
    love.
A half-enlightened, often-chequered
    trust: –
Hints and previsions of which faculties,
Are strewn confusedly everywhere about
The inferior natures, and all lead up
    higher,
All shape out dimly the superior race,
The heir of hopes too fair to turn out
    false,
And man appears at last. So far the seal
Is put on life; one stage of being complete,
One scheme wound up: and from the
    grand result
A supplementary reflux of light,
Illustrates all the inferior grades, explains
Each back step in the circle. Not alone

For their possessor dawn those qualities,
But the new glory mixes with the heaven
And earth; man, once descried,
    imprints for ever
His presence on all lifeless things: the
    winds
Are henceforth voices, wailing or a shout,
A querulous mutter or a quick gay laugh,
Never a senseless gust now man is born.
The herded pines commune and have
    deep thoughts,
A secret they assemble to discuss
When the sun drops behind their trunks
    which glare
Like grates of hell: the peerless cup
    afloat
Of the lake-lily is an urn, some nymph
Swims bearing high above her head: no
    bird
Whistles unseen, but through the gaps
    above
That let light in upon the gloomy woods,
A shape peeps from the breezy forest-
    top,
Arch with small puckered mouth and
    mocking eye.
The morn has enterprise, deep quiet
    droops
With evening, triumph takes the sunset
    hour,
Voluptuous transport ripens with the
    corn
Beneath a warm moon like a happy face:
– And this to fill us with regard for man.
With apprehension of his passing worth,
Desire to work his proper nature out,
And ascertain his rank and final place,
For these things tend still upward,
    progress is
The law of life, man is not Man as yet.
Nor shall I deem his object served, his
    end
Attained, his genuine strength put fairly
    forth,
While only here and there a star dispels
The darkness, here and there a
    towering mind

O'erlooks its prostrate fellows: when the
    host
Is out at once to the despair of night,
When all mankind alike is perfected,
Equal in full-blown powers – then, not
    till then,
I say, begins man's general infancy.
For wherefore make account of feverish
    starts
Of restless members of a dormant whole,
Impatient nerves which quiver while the
    body
Slumbers as in a grave? Oh long ago
The brow was twitched, the tremulous
    lids astir,
The peaceful mouth disturbed; half-
    uttered speech
Ruffled the lip, and then the teeth were
    set,
The breath drawn sharp, the strong
    righthand clenched stronger,
As it would pluck a lion by the jaw;
The glorious creature laughed out even
    in sleep!
But when full roused, each giant-limb
    awake,
Each sinew strung, the great heart
    pulsing fast,
He shall start up and stand on his own
    earth,
Then shall his long triumphant march
    begin,
Thence shall his being date, – thus
    wholly roused,
What he achieves shall be set down to
    him.
When all the race is perfected alike
As man, that is; all tended to mankind,
And, man produced, all has its end
    thus far:
But in completed man begins anew
A tendency to God. Prognostics told
Man's near approach; so in man's self
    arise
August anticipations, symbols, types
Of a dim splendour ever on before
In that eternal circle life pursues.

For men begin to pass their nature's
    bound,
And find new hopes and cares which
    fast supplant
Their proper joys and griefs; they grow
    too great
For narrow creeds of right and wrong,
    which fade
Before the unmeasured thirst for good:
    while peace
Rises within them ever more and more.
Such men are even now upon the
    earth,
Serene amid the half-formed creatures
    round
Who should be saved by them and
    joined with them.
Such was my task, and I was born to it –
Free, as I said but now, from much that
    chains
Spirits, high-dowered but limited and
    vexed
By a divided and delusive aim,
A shadow mocking a reality
Whose truth avails not wholly to disperse
The flitting mimic called up by itself,
And so remains perplexed and nigh
    put out
By its fantastic fellow's wavering gleam.
I, from the first, was never cheated thus;
I never fashioned out a fancied good
Distinct from man's; a service to be
    done,
A glory to be ministered unto
With powers put forth at man's expense,
    withdrawn
From labouring in his behalf; a strength
Denied that might avail him. I cared not
Lest his success ran counter to success
Elsewhere: for God is glorified in man,
And to man's glory vowed I soul and
    limb.
Yet, constituted thus, and thus endowed,
I failed: I gazed on power till I grew
    blind.
Power; I could not take my eyes from
    that:

That only, I thought, should be preserved,
    increased
At any risk, displayed, struck out at
    once –
The sign and note and character of man.
I saw no use in the past: only a scene
Of degradation, ugliness and tears,
The record of disgraces best forgotten,
A sullen page in human chronicles
Fit to erase. I saw no cause why man
Should not stand all-sufficient even now,
Or why his annals should be forced to
    tell
That once the tide of light, about to
    break
Upon the world, was sealed within its
    spring:
I would have had one day, one
    moment's space,
Change man's condition, push each
    slumbering claim
Of mastery o'er the elemental world
At once to full maturity, then roll
Oblivion o'er the work, and hide from
    man
What night had ushered morn. Not so,
    dear child
Of after-days, wilt thou reject the past
Big with deep warnings of the proper
    tenure
By which thou hast the earth: for thee
    the present
Shall have distinct and trembling beauty,
    seen
Beside that past's own shade when, in
    relief,
Its brightness shall stand out: nor yet
    · on thee
Shall burst the future, as successive
    zones
Of several wonder open on some spirit
Flying secure and glad from heaven to
    heaven:
But thou shalt painfully attain to joy,
While hope and fear and love shall
    keep thee man!
All this was hid from me: as one by one

My dreams grew dim, my wide aims
    circumscribed,
As actual good within my reach decreased,
While obstacles sprung up this way
    and that
To keep me from effecting half the sum,
Small as it proved; as objects, mean
    within
The primal aggregate, seemed, even the
    least,
Itself a match for my concentred
    strength –
What wonder if I saw no way to shun
Despair? The power I sought for man,
    seemed God's.
In this conjuncture, as I prayed to die,
A strange adventure made me know,
    one sin
Had spotted my career from its uprise;
I saw Aprile – my Aprile there!
And as the poor melodious wretch
    disburthened
His heart, and moaned his weakness in
    my ear,
I learned my own deep error; love's
    undoing
Taught me the worth of love in man's
    estate,
And what proportion love should hold
    with power
In his right constitution; love preceding
Power, and with much power, always
    much more love;
Love still too straitened in his present
    means,
And earnest for new power to set love
    free.
I learned this, and supposed the whole
    was learned:
And thus, when men received with
    stupid wonder
My first revealings, would have
    worshipped me,
And I despised and loathed their
    proffered praise –
When, with awakened eyes, they took
    revenge

For past credulity in casting shame
On my real knowledge, and I hated
    them –
It was not strange I saw no good in man,
To overbalance all the wear and waste
Of faculties, displayed in vain, but born
To prosper in some better sphere: and
    why?
In my own heart love had not been
    made wise
To trace love's faint beginnings in
    mankind,
To know even hate is but a mask of
    love's,
To see a good in evil, and a hope
In ill-success; to sympathize, be proud
Of their half-reasons, faint aspirings, dim
Struggles for truth, their poorest fallacies,
Their prejudice and fears and cares and
    doubts;
All with a touch of nobleness, despite
Their error, upward tending all though
    weak,
Like plants in mines which never saw
    the sun,
But dream of him, and guess where he
    may be,
And do their best to climb and get to
    him.
All this I knew not, and I failed. Let men
Regard me, and the poet dead long ago
Who loved too rashly; and shape forth
    a third

And better-tempered spirit, warned by
    both:
As from the over-radiant star too mad
To drink the life-springs, beamless thence
    itself –
And the dark orb which borders the
    abyss,
Ingulfed in icy night, – might have its
    course
A temperate and equidistant world.
Meanwhile, I have done well, though
    not all well.
As yet men cannot do without contempt;
'Tis for their good, and therefore fit
    awhile
That they reject the weak, and scorn
    the false,
Rather than praise the strong and true,
    in me:
But after, they will know me. If I stoop
Into a dark tremendous sea of cloud,
It is but for a time; I press God's lamp
Close to my breast; its splendour, soon
    or late,
Will pierce the gloom: I shall emerge
    one day.
You understand me? I have said enough?
*Fest.* Now die, dear Aureole!
*Par.*                    Festus, let my hand –
This hand, lie in your own, my own
    true friend!
Aprile! Hand in hand with you, Aprile!
*Fest.* And this was Paracelsus!

NOTES ON 'PARACELSUS

The liberties I have taken with my subject are very trifling; and the reader may slip the foregoing scenes between the leaves of any memoir of Paracelsus he pleases, by way of commentary. To prove this, I subjoin a popular account, translated from the *Biographie Universelle*, Paris, 1822, which I select, not as the best, certainly, but as being at hand, and sufficiently concise for my purpose. I also append a few notes, in order to correct those parts which do not bear out my own view of the character of Paracelsus; and have incorporated with them a notice or two, illustrative of the poem itself.

Paracelsus (Philippus Aureolus Theophrastus Bombastus ab Hohenheim) was born in 1493 at Einsiedeln (I), a little town in the canton of Schwyz, some leagues distant from Zurich. His father, who exercised the profession of medicine at Villach in Carinthia, was nearly related to George Bombast de Hohenheim, who became afterward Grand Prior of the Order of Malta: consequently Paracelsus could not spring from the dregs of the people, as Thomas Erastus, his sworn enemy, pretends.*
It appears that his elementary

education was much neglected, and that he spent part of his youth in pursuing the life common to the travelling *literati* of the age; that is to say, in wandering from country to country, predicting the future by astrology and cheiromancy, evoking apparitions, and practising the different operations of magic and alchemy, in which he had been initiated whether by his father or by various ecclesiastics, among the number of whom he particularizes the Abbot Tritheim (2), and many German bishops.

As Paracelsus displays everywhere an ignorance of the rudiments of the most ordinary knowledge, it is not probable that he ever studied seriously in the schools: he contented himself with visiting the Universities of Germany, France, and Italy; and in spite of his boasting himself to have been the ornament of those institutions, there is no proof of his having legally acquired the title of Doctor, which he assumes. It is only known that he applied himself long, under the direction of the wealthy Sigismond Fugger of Schwatz, to the discovery of the Magnum Opus.

Paracelsus travelled among the mountains of Bohemia, in the East, and in Sweden, in order to inspect the labours of the miners, to be initiated in the mysteries of the oriental adepts, and to observe the secrets of nature and the famous mountain of loadstone (3). He professes also to have visited Spain, Portugal, Prussia, Poland, and Transylvania; everywhere communicating freely, not merely with the physicians, but the old women, charlatans and conjurers of these several lands. It is even believed that he extended his journeyings as far as Egypt and Tartary, and that he

---

* I shall disguise M. Renauldin's next sentence a little. 'Hic (Erastus sc.) Paracelsum trimum a milite quodam, alii a sue exectum ferunt: constat imberbem illum, mulierumque osorem fuisse.' A standing High-Dutch joke in those days at the expense of a number of learned men, as may be seen by referring to such rubbish as Melander's *Jocoseria*, etc. In the prints from his portrait by Tintoretto, painted a year before his death, Paracelsus is *barbatulus*, at all events. But Erastus was never without a good reason for his faith – e.g. 'Helvetium fuisse (Paracelsum) vix credo, vix enim ea regio tale monstrum ediderit.' (*De Medicina Nova*.)

accompanied the son of the Khan of the Tartars to Constantinople, for the purpose of obtaining the secret of the tincture of Trismegistus from a Greek who inhabited that capital.

The period of his return to Germany is unknown: it is only certain that, at about the age of thirty-three, many astonishing cures which he wrought on eminent personages procured him such a celebrity, that he was called in 1526, on the recommendation of Oecolampadius (4), to fill a chair of physic and surgery at the University of Basil. There Paracelsus began by burning publicly in the amphitheatre the works of Avicenna and Galen, assuring his auditors that the latchets of his shoes were more instructed than those two physicians; that all Universities, all writers put together, were less gifted than the hairs of his beard and of the crown of his head; and that, in a word, he was to be regarded as the legitimate monarch of medicine. 'You shall follow me,' cried he, 'you, Avicenna, Galen, Rhasis, Montagnana, Mesues, you, gentlemen of Paris, Montpellier, Germany, Cologne, Vienna,† and whomsoever the Rhine and Danube nourish; you who inhabit the isles of the sea; you, likewise, Dalmatians, Athenians; thou, Arab; thou, Greek; thou, Jew: all shall follow me, and the monarchy shall be mine."‡

But at Basil it was speedily perceived that the new Professor was no better than an egregious quack. Scarcely a year elapsed before his lectures had fairly driven away an audience incapable of comprehending their emphatic jargon. That which above all contributed to sully his reputation was the debauched life he led. According to the testimony of Oporinus, who lived two years in his intimacy, Paracelsus scarcely ever ascended the lecture-desk unless half drunk, and only dictated to his secretaries when in a state of intoxication: if summoned to attend the sick, he rarely proceeded thither without previously drenching himself with wine. He was accustomed to retire to bed without changing his clothes; sometimes he spent the night in pot-houses with peasants, and in the morning knew no longer what he was about; and, nevertheless, up to the age of twenty-five his only drink had been water (5).

At length, fearful of being punished for a serious outrage on a magistrate (6), he fled from Basil towards the end of the year 1527, and took refuge in Alsatia, whither he caused Oporinus to follow with his chemical apparatus.

He then entered once more upon the career of ambulatory theosophist.§ Accordingly we find him at Colmar

---

† Erastus, who relates this, here oddly remarks, 'mirum quod non et Garamantos, Indos et *Anglos* adjunxit.' Not so wonderful neither, if we believe what another adversary 'had heard somewhere' – that all Paracelsus' system came of his pillaging 'Anglum quendam, Rogerium Bacchonem.'

‡ See his works *passim*. I must give one specimen: – Somebody had been styling him 'Luther alter.' 'And why not?' (he asks, as he well might). 'Luther is abundantly learned, therefore you hate him and me; but we are at least a match for you. – Nam et contra vos et vestros universos principes Avicennam, Galenum, Aristotelem, etc. me satis superque munitum esse novi. Et vertex iste meus calvus ac depilis multo plura et sublimiora novit quam vester vel Avicenna vel universæ academiæ. Prodite, et signum date, qui viri sitis, quid roboris habeatis? quid autem sitis? Doctores et magistri, pediculos pectentes et fricantes podicem.' (Frag. Med.)

§ 'So migratory a life could afford Paracelsus

in 1528; at Nuremberg in 1529; at St Gall in 1531; at Pfeffers in 1535; and at Augsburg in 1536: he next made some stay in Moravia, where he still further compromised his reputation by the loss of many distinguished patients, which compelled him to betake himself to Vienna; from thence he passed into Hungary; and in 1538 was at Villach, where he dedicated his *Chronicle* to the States of Carinthia, in gratitude for the many kindnesses with which they had honoured his father. Finally, from Mindelheim, which he visited in 1540, Paracelsus proceeded to Salzburg, where he died in the Hospital of St Stephen (*Sebastian* is meant), Sept. 24, 1541.' – (Here follows a criticism on his writings, which I omit.)

(1) *Paracelsus* would seem to be a fantastic version of *Von Hohenheim*; Einsiedeln is the Latinized Eremus, whence Paracelsus is sometimes called, as in the correspondence of Erasmus, Eremita; Bombast, his proper name, probably acquired, from the characteristic phraseology of his lectures, that unlucky signification which it has ever since retained.

(2) Then Bishop of Spanheim, and residing at Würzburg in Franconia; a town situated in a grassy fertile country, whence its name, Herbipolis. He was much visited there by learned men, as

---

but little leisure for application to books, and accordingly he informs us that for the space of ten years he never opened a single volume, and that his whole medical library was not composed of six sheets: in effect, the inventory drawn up after his death states that the only books which he left were the Bible, the New Testament, the Commentaries of St Jerome on the Gospels, a printed volume on Medicine, and seven manuscripts.'

may be seen by his *Epistolæ Familiares*, Hag. 1536: among others, by his staunch friend Cornelius Agrippa, to whom he dates thence, in 1510, a letter in answer to the dedicatory epistle prefixed to the treatise *De Occult. Philosoph.*, which last contains the following ominous allusion to Agrippa's sojourn: 'Quum nuper tecum, R. P. in cœnobio tuo apud Herbipolim aliquamdiu conversatus, multa de chymicis, multa de magicis, multa de cabalisticis, cæterisque quæ adhuc in occulto delitescunt, arcanis scientiis atque artibus una contulissemus,' etc.

(3) 'Inexplebilis illa aviditas naturæ perscrutandi secreta et reconditarum supellectile scientiarum animum locupletandi, uno eodemque loco diu persistere non patiebatur, sed Mercurii instar, omnes terras, nationes et urbes perlustrandi igniculos supponebat, ut cum viris naturæ scrutatoribus, chymicis præsertim, ore tenus conferret, et quæ: diuturnis laboribus nocturnisque vigiliis invenerant una vel altera communic-atione obtineret.' (Bitiskius in *Præfat.*) 'Patris auxilio primum, deinde propria industria doctissimos viros in Germania, Italia, Gallia, Hispania, aliisque Europæ regionibus, nactus est præceptores; quorum liberali doctrina, et potissimum propria inquisitione ut qui esset ingenio acutissimo ac fere divino, tantum profecit, ut multi testati sint, in universa philosophia, tam ardua, tam arcana et abdita eruisse mortalium neminem.' (Melch. Adam. in *Vit. Germ. Medic.*) 'Paracelsus qui in intima naturæ viscera sic penitus introierit, metallorum stirpiaumque vires et facultates tam incredibili ingenii acumine exploraverit ac perviderit, ad morbos omnes vel desperatos et opinione hominum insanabiles percurandum; ut cum Theophrasto nata primum medicina

perfectaque videtur.' (*Petri Rami Orat. de Basilea.*) His passion for wandering is best described in his own words: 'Ecce amatorem adolescentem difficillimi itineris haud piget, ut venustam saltem puellam vel fœminam aspiciat: quanto minus nobilissimarum artium amore laboris ac cujuslibet tædii pigebit?' etc. (*Defensiones Septem adversus Æmulos suos.* 1573. Def. 4ta. *De peregrinationibus et exilio.*)

(4) The reader may remember that it was in conjunction with Œcolampadius, then Divinity Professor at Basil, that Zuinglius published in 1528 an answer to Luther's Confession of Faith; and that both proceeded in company to the subsequent conference with Luther and Melanchthon at Marpurg. Their letters fill a large volume. – *D.D. Johannis Œcolampadii et Huldrichi Zuinglii Epistolarum*, lib. quatuor, Bas. 1536. It must be also observed that Zuinglius began to preach in 1516, and at Zurich in 1519, and that in 1525 the Mass was abolished in the cantons. The tenets of Œcolampadius were supposed to be more evangelical than those up to that period maintained by the glorious German, and our brave Bishop Fisher attacked them as the fouler heresy: – 'About this time arose out of Luther's school one Œcolampadius, like a mighty and fierce giant; who, as his master had gone beyond the Church, went beyond his master (or else it had been impossible he could have been reputed the better scholar), who denied the real presence; him, this worthy champion (the Bishop) sets upon, and with five books (like so many smooth stones taken out of the river that doth always run with living water) slays the Philistine; which five books were written in the year of our Lord 1526, at which time he had governed the see of Rochester twenty

years.' (*Life of Bishop Fisher*, 1655.) Now, there is no doubt of the Protestantism of Paracelsus, Erasmus, Agrippa, etc., but the nonconformity of Paracelsus was always scandalous. L. Crasso (*Elogj d'Huomini Letterati*, Ven. 1666) informs us that his books were excommunicated by the Church. Quenstedt (*de Patr. Doct.*) affirms 'nec tantum novæ medicinæ, verum etiam novæ theologiæ autor est.' Delrio, in his *Disquisit. Magicar.*, classes him among those 'partim atheos, partim hæreticos' (lib. i, cap. 3). 'Omnino tamen multa theologica in ejusdem scriptis plane atheismum olent, ac duriuscule sonant in auribus vere Christiani.' D. *Gabrielis Clauderi Schediasma de Tinct.Univ. Norimb.*, 1736.) I shall only add one more authority: – 'Oporinus dicit se (Paracelsum) aliquando Lutherum et Papam, non minus quam nunc Galenum et Hippocratem redacturum in ordinem minabatur, neque enim eorum qui hactenus in scripturam sacram scripsissent, sive veteres, sive recentiores, quenquam scripturæ nucleum recte eruisse, sed circa corticem et quasi membranam tantum hærére.' (*Th. Erastus, Disputat. de Med. Nova.*) These and similar notions had their due effect on Oporinus, who, says Zuingerus, in his *Theatrum*, 'longum vale dixit ei (Paracelso), ne ob præceptoris, alioqui amicissimi, horrendas blasphemias ipse quoque aliquando pœnas Deo Opt. Max. lueret.'

(5) His defenders allow the drunkenness. Take a sample of their excuses: 'Gentis hoc, non viri vitiolum est, a Taciti seculo ad nostrum usque non interrupto filo devolutum, sinceritati forte Germanæ coævum, et nescio an aliquo censanguinitatis vinculo junctum.' (Bitiskius.) The other charges were chiefly trumped up by Oporinus: 'Domi, quod Oporinus amanuensis ejus sæpe narravit,

nunquam nisi potus ad explicanda sua accessit, atque in medio conclavi ad columnam τετυφωμένος adsistens, apprehenso manibus capulo ensis, cujus κοίλωμα hospitium præbuit, ut aiunt, spiritui familiari, imaginationes aut concepta sua protulit: – alii illud quod in capulo habuit, ab ipso Azoth appellatum, medicinam fuisse præstantissimam aut lapidem Philosophicum putant.' (Melch. Adam.) This famous sword was no laughing-matter in those days, and it is now a material feature in the popular idea of Paracelsus. I recollect a couple of allusions to it in our own literature, at the moment.

Ne had been known the Danish Gonswart, Or Paracelsus with his long sword.
                    *Volpone*, Act ii, Scene 2

Bumbastus kept a devil's bird
Shut in the pummel of his sword,
That taught him all the cunning pranks
Of past and future mountebanks.
                    *Hudibras*, Part ii, Canto 3

This Azoth was simply '*laudanum suum.*' But in his time he was commonly believed to possess the double tincture – the power of curing diseases and transmuting metals. Oporinus often witnessed, as he declares, both these effects, as did also Franciscus, the servant of Paracelsus, who describes, in a letter to Neander, a successful projection at which he was present, and the results of which, good golden ingots, were confided to his keeping. For the other quality, let the following notice vouch among many others: – 'Degebat Theophrastus Norimbergæ procitus a medentibus illius urbie et vaniloquus deceptorque proclamatus, qui, ut laboranti famæ subveniat, viros quosdam authoritatis summae in Republica illa adit, et infamiæ amoliendæ, artique suæ asserendæ, specimen ejus pollicetur editurum, nullo

stipendio vel accepto pretio, horum faciles præbentium aures jussu elephantiacos aliquot, a communione hominum cæterorum segregatos, et in valetudinarium detrusos, qui alieno arbitrio eliguntur, quos virtute singulari remediorum suorum Theophrastus a fœda Græcorum lepra mundat, pristinæque sanitati restituit; conservat illustre harum curationum urbs in archivis suis testimonium.' (Bitiskius.)* It is to be remarked that Oporinus afterwards repented of hit treachery: 'Sed resipuit tandem, et quem vivum convitiis insectatus fuerat defunctum veneratione prosequutus, infames famæ præceptoris morsus in remorsus conscientiæ conversi pœnitentia, heu nimis tarda, vulnera clausere exanimi quæ spiranti inflixerant.' For these 'bites' of Oporinus, see *Disputat. Erasti*, and Andreæ Jocisci *Oratio de Vit. ob. Opor*[i]; for the 'remorse', Mic. Toxita *in pref. Testamenti*, and Conringius (otherwise an enemy of Paracelsus), who says it was contained in a letter from Oporinus to Doctor Vegerus.[†]

Whatever the moderns may think of

---

* The premature death of Paracelsus casts no manner of doubt on the fact of his having possessed the Llixir Vitæ: the alchemists have abundant reasons to adduce, from which I select the following, as explanatory of a property of the Tincture not calculated on by its votaries: – 'Objectionem illam, quod Paracelsus non fuerit longævus, nonnulli quoque solvunt per rationes physicas: vitæ; nimirum aboreviationem fortasse talibus accidere posse, ob Tincturam frequentiore ac largiore dosi sumtam, dum a summe efficaci et penetrabili hujus virtute calor innatus quasi suffocatur.' (Gabrielis Clauderi Schediasma.)

† For a good defence of Paracelsus I refer the reader to Olaus Borrichius' treatise – *Hermetis*, *etc. Sapientia vindicata*, 1674. Or, if he is no more learned than myself in such matters, I mention simply that Paracelsus introduced the use of Mercury and Laudanum.

these marvellous attributes, the title of Paracelsus to be considered the father of modern chemistry is indisputable. Gerardus Vossius, *De Philos^a et Philos^um sectis*, thus prefaces the ninth section of cap. 9, 'De Chymia' – 'Nobilem hanc medicinæ; partem, diu sepultam avorum ætate, quasi ab orco revocavit Th. Paracelsus.' I suppose many hints lie scattered in his neglected books, which clever appropriators have since developed with applause. Thus, it appears from his treatise *De Phlebotomia*, and elsewhere, that he had discovered the circulation of the blood and the sanguification of the heart; as did after him Realdo Colombo, and still more perfectly Andrea Cesalpino of Arezzo, as Bayle and Bartoli observe. Even Lavater quotes a passage from his work, *De Natura Rerum*, on practical Physiognomy, in which the definitions and axioms are precise enough: he adds, 'though an astrological enthusiast, a man of prodigious genius.' See Holcroft's translation, vol. iii, p. 179 – 'The Eyes.' While on the subject of the writings of Paracelsus, I may explain a passage in the third part of the Poem. He was, as I have said, unwilling to publish his works, but in effect did publish a vast number. Valentius (in *Præfat. in Paramyr.*) declares 'quod ad librorum Paracelsi copiam attinet, audio, a Germanis prope trecentos recenseri.' 'O fœcunditas ingenii!' adds, he, appositely. Many of these were, however, spurious; and Fred. Bitiskius gives his good edition (3 vols. fol. Gen. 1658) 'rejectis suppositis solo ipsius nomine superbientibus quorum ingens circumfertur numerus.' The rest were 'charissimum et pretiosissimum authoris pignus, extorsum potius ab illo quam obtentum.' 'Jam minime eo volente atque jubente hæc ipsius scripta in lucem prodisse videntur; quippe quæ muro inclusa ipso absente, servi cujusdam indicio, furto surrepta atque sublata sunt,' says Valentius. These have been the study of a host of commentators, amongst whose labours are most notable, Petri Severini, *Idea Medicinæ Philosophiæ*, Bas. 1571; Mic. Toxetis, *Onomastica*, Arg. 1574; Dornei, *Dict. Parac.*, Franc. 1584; and P^i *Philos^æ Compendium cum scholiis auctore Leone Suavio*. Paris. (This last, a good book.)

(6) A disgraceful affair. One Liechtenfels, a canon, having been rescued *in extremis* by the '*laudanum*' of Paracelsus, refused the stipulated fee, and was supported in his meanness by the authorities, whose interference Paracelsus would not brook. His own liberality was allowed by his bitterest foes, who found a ready solution of his indifference to profit in the aforesaid sword-handle and its guest. His freedom from the besetting sin of a profession he abhorred – (as he curiously says somewhere, 'Quis quæso deinceps honorem deferat professioni tali, quæ a tam facinorosis nebulonibus obitur et administratur?') – is recorded in his epitaph, which affirms – 'Bona sua in pauperes distribuenda collocandaque erogavit,' *honoravit*, or *ordinavit* – for accounts differ.

# STRAFFORD

A Tragedy

1837

Dedicated, in all affectionate admiration to
William C. Macready
London: *April* 23, 1837.

## Persons

Charles I. Earl of Holland. Lord Savile. Sir Henry Vane. Wentworth, *Viscount Wentworth*, Earl of Strafford. John Pym. John Hampden. *The younger* Vane. Denzil Hollis. Benjamin Rudyard. Nathaniel Fiennes. Earl of Loudon. Maxwell, *Usher of the Black Rod.* Balfour, *Constable of the Tower.* A Puritan. Queen Henrietta. Lucy Percy, *Countess of Carlisle. Presbyterians, Scots Commissioners, Adherents of Strafford, Secretaries, Officers of the Court, etc. Two of Strafford's children.*

## ACT 1

*Scene 1 – A House near Whitehall.*

HAMPDEN, HOLLIS, THE YOUNGER VANE, RUDYARD, FIENNES and MANY OF THE PRESBYTERIAN PARTY: LOUDON and OTHER SCOTS COMMISSIONERS.

*Vane.* I say, if he be here –

*Rud.*  (And he is here!) –

*Hol.* For England's sake let every man be still
Nor speak of him, so much as say his name,
Till Pym rejoin us! Rudyard! Henry Vane!
One rash conclusion may decide our course
And with it England's fate – think – England's fate!
Hampden, for England's sake they should be still!

*Vane.* You say so, Hollis? Well, I must be still.
It is indeed too bitter that one man,
Any one man's mere presence, should suspend
England's combined endeavour: little need
To name him!

*Rud.*  For you are his brother, Hollis!

*Hamp.* Shame on you, Rudyard! time to tell him that
When he forgets the Mother of us all.

*Rud.* Do I forget her?

*Hamp.*  You talk idle hate
Against her foe: is that so strange a thing?
Is hating Wentworth all the help she needs?

*A Puritan.* The Philistine strode, cursing as he went:
But David – five smooth pebbles from the brook
Within his scrip . . .

*Rud.*  Be you as still as David

*Fien.* Here's Rudyard not ashamed to wag a tongue
Stiff with ten years' disuse of Parliaments;
Why, when the last sat, Wentworth sat with us!

*Rud.* Let's hope for news of them now he returns –
He that was safe in Ireland, as we thought!
– But I'll abide Pym's coming.

*Vane.*  Now, by Heaven,
They may be cool who can, silent who will –
Some have a gift that way! Wentworth is here,
Here, and the King's safe closeted with him
Ere this. And when I think on all that's past

Since that man left us, how his single
      arm
Rolled the advancing good of England
      back
And set the woeful past up in its place,
Exalting Dagon where the Ark should
      be, –
How that man has made firm the fickle
      King
(Hampden, I will speak out!) – in aught
      he feared
To venture on before; taught tyranny
Her dismal trade, the use of all her tools,
To ply the scourge yet screw the gag so
      close
That strangled agony bleeds mute to
      death;
How he turns Ireland to a private stage
For training infant villanies, new ways
Of wringing treasure out of tears and
      blood,
Unheard oppressions nourished in the
      dark
To try how much man's nature can
      endure
– If he dies under it, what harm? if not,
Why, one more trick is added to the rest
Worth a king's knowing, and what
      Ireland bears
England may learn to bear: – how all
      this while
That man has set himself to one dear
      task,
The bringing Charles to relish more
      and more
Power, power without law, power and
      blood too
– Can I be still?
*Hamp.*       For that you should be still.
*Vane.* Oh Hampden, then and now!
      The year he left us,
The People in full Parliament could wrest
The Bill of Rights from the reluctant
      King;
And now, he'll find in an obscure small
      room
A stealthy gathering of great-hearted men

That take up England's cause: England
      is here!
*Hamp.* And who despairs of England?
*Rud.*                              That do I,
If Wentworth comes to rule her. I am
      sick
To think her wretched masters, Hamilton,
The muckworm Cottington, the maniac
      Laud,
May yet be longed-for back again. I say,
I do despair.
*Vane.*        And, Rudyard, I'll say this –
Which all true men say after me, not
      loud
But solemnly and as you'd say a prayer!
This King, who treads our England
      underfoot,
Has just so much … it may be fear or
      craft,
As bids him pause at each fresh outrage;
      friends,
He needs some sterner hand to grasp
      his own,
Some voice to ask, 'Why shrink? Am I
      not by?'
Now, one whom England loved for
      serving her,
Found in his heart to say, 'I know
      where best
'The iron heel shall bruise her, for she
      leans
'Upon me when you trample.' Witness,
      you!
So Wentworth heartened Charles, so
      England fell.
But inasmuch as life is hard to take
From England …
*Many Voices.* Go on, Vane! 'Tis well
      said, Vane!
*Vane.*        – Who has not so forgotten
      Runnymead! –
*Voices.* 'Tis well and bravely spoken,
      Vane! Go on!
*Vane.* – There are some little signs of
      late she knows
The ground no place for her. She glances
      round,

Wentworth has dropped the hand, is
    gone his way
On other service: what if she arise?
No! the King beckons, and beside him
    stands
The same bad man once more, with the
    same smile
And the game gesture. Now shall England
    crouch,
Or catch at us and rise?
*Voices.*                   The Renegade!
Haman! Ahithophel!
*Hamp.*         Gentlemen of the North,
It was not thus the night your claims
    were urged,
And we pronounced the League and
    Covenant,
The cause of Scotland, England's cause
    as well:
Vane there, sat motionless the whole
    night through.
*Vane.* Hampden!
*Fien.*     Stay, Vane!
*Lou.*         Be just and patient, Vane!
*Vane.* Mind how you counsel patience,
    Loudon! you
Have still a Parliament, and this your
    League
To back it; you are free in Scotland still:
While we are brothers, hope's for England
    yet.
But know you wherefore Wentworth
    comes? to quench
This last of hopes? that he brings war
    with him?
Know you the man's self? what he dares?
*Lou.*               We know,
All know – 'tis nothing new.
*Vane.*          And what's new, then,
In calling for his life? Why, Pym
    himself –
You must have heard – ere Wentworth
    dropped our cause
He would see Pym first; there were many
    more
Strong on the people's side and friends
    of his,

Eliot that's dead, Rudyard and Hampden
    here,
But for these Wentworth cared not; only,
    Pym
He would see – Pym and he were sworn,
    'tis said,
To live and die together; so, they met
At Greenwich. Wentworth, you are sure,
    was long,
Specious enough, the devil's argument
Lost nothing on his lips; he'd have
    Pym own
A patriot could not play a purer part
Than follow in his track; they two
    combined
Might put down England. Well, Pym
    heard him out;
One glance – you know Pym's eye –
    one word was all:
'You leave us, Wentworth! while your
    head is on.
'I'll not leave you.'
*Hamp.*     Has he left Wentworth, then?
Has England lost him? Will you let him
    speak,
Or put your crude surmises in his mouth?
Away with this! Will you have Pym or
    Vane?
*Voices.* Wait Pym's arrival! Pym shall
    speak.
*Hamp.*     Meanwhile
Let Loudon read the Parliament's report
From Edinburgh: our last hope, as Vane
    says,
Is in the stand it makes. Loudon!
*Vane.*               No, no!
Silent I can be: not indifferent!
*Hamp.* Then each keep silence, praying
    God to spare
His anger, cast not England quite away
In this her visitation!
    *A Puritan.*     Seven years long
The Midianite drove Israel into dens
And caves. Till God sent forth a mighty
    man,
              PYM *enters.*
Even Gideon!

*Pym.* Wentworth's come: nor sickness, care,
The ravaged body nor the ruined soul,
More than the winds and waves that beat his ship,
Could keep him from the King. He has not reached
Whitehall: they've hurried up a Council there
To lose no time and find him work enough.
Where's Loudon? your Scots' Parliament …
*Lou.*                    Holds firm:
We were about to read reports.
*Pym.*                    The King
Has just dissolved your Parliament.
*Lou. and other Scots.*        Great God!
An oath-breaker! Stand by us, England, then!
*Pym.* The King's too sanguine; doubtless Wentworth's here;
But still some little form might be kept up.
*Hamp.* Now speak, Vane! Rudyard, you had much to say!
*Hol.* The rumour's false, then …
*Pym.*            Ay, the Court gives out
His own concerns have brought him back: I know
'Tis the King calls him. Wentworth super-sedes
The tribe of Cottingtons and Hamiltons
Whose part is played; there's talk enough, by this, –
Merciful talk, the King thinks: time is now
To turn the record's last and bloody leaf
Which, chronicling a nation's great despair,
Tells they were long rebellious, and their lord
Indulgent, till, all kind expedients tried,
He drew the sword on them and reigned in peace.
Laud's laying his religion on the Scots

Was the last gentle entry: the new page
Shall run, the King thinks, 'Wentworth thrust it down
'At the sword's point.'
*A Puritan.*        I'll do your bidding, Pym,
England's and God's – one blow!
*Pym.*                A goodly thing –
We all say, friends, it is a goodly thing
To right that England. Heaven grows dark above:
Let's snatch one moment ere the thunder fall,
To say how well the English spirit comes out
Beneath it! All have done their best, indeed,
From lion Eliot, that grand Englishman,
To the least here: and who, the least one here,
When she is saved (for her redemption dawns
Dimly, most dimly, but it dawns – it dawns)
Who'd give at any price his hope away
Of being named along with the Great Men?
We would not – no, we would not give that up!
*Hamp.* And one name shall be dearer than all names.
When children, yet unborn, are taught that name
After their fathers', – taught what matchless man …
*Pym.* … Saved England? What if Wentworth's should be still
That name?
*Rud. and others.* We have just said it, Pym! His death
Saves her! We said it – there's no way beside!
I'll do God's bidding, Pym! They struck down Joab
And purged the land.
*Vane.*        No villanous striking-down!
*Rud.* No, a calm vengeance: let the whole land rise

And shout for it. No Feltons!

*Pym.*                              Rudyard, no!
England rejects all Feltons; most of all
Since Wentworth … Hampden, say the
    trust again
Of England in her servants – but I'll
    think
You know me, all of you. Then, I believe,
Spite of the past, Wentworth rejoins
    you, friends!

*Vane and others.* Wentworth? Apostate!
    Judas! Double-dyed
A traitor! Is it Pym, indeed …

*Pym.*                       ….Who says
Vane never knew that Wentworth,
    loved that man,
Was used to stroll with him, arm locked
    in arm,
Along the streets to see the people pass,
And read in every island-countenance
Fresh argument for God against the
    King, –
Never sat down, say, in the very house
Where Eliot's brow grew broad with
    noble thoughts,
(You've joined us, Hampden – Hollis,
    you as well,)
And then left talking over Gracchus'
    death …

*Vane.* To frame, we know it well, the
    choicest clause
In the Petition of Right: he framed such
    clause
One month before he took at the King's
    hand
His Northern Presidency, which that Bill
Denounced.

*Pym.* Too true! Never more, never more
Walked we together! Most alone I went.
I have had friends – all here are fast my
    friends –
But I shall never quite forget that friend.
And yet it could not but be real in him!
You, Vane, – you, Rudyard, have no
    right to trust
To Wentworth: but can no one hope
    with me?

Hampden, will Wentworth dare shed
    English blood
Like water?

*Hamp.*          Ireland is Aceldama.

*Pym.* Will he turn Scotland to a hunting-
    ground
To please the King, now that he knows
    the King?
The People or the King? and that King,
    Charles!

*Hamp.* Pym, all here know you: you'll
    not set your heart
On any baseless dream. But say one
    deed
Of Wentworth's since he left us …
                    [*Shouting without.*

*Vane.*               There! he comes,
And they shout for him! Wentworth's
    at Whitehall,
The King embracing him, now, as we
    speak,
And he, to be his match in courtesies,
Taking the whole war's risk upon himself,
Now, while you tell us here how changed
    he is!
Hear you?

*Pym.* And yet if 'tis a dream, no more,
That Wentworth chose their side, and
    brought the King
To love it as though Laud had loved it
    first,
And the Queen after; – that he led their
    cause
Calm to success, and kept it spotless
    through,
So that our very eyes could look upon
The travail of our souls, and close content
That violence, which something mars
    even right
Which sanctions it, had taken off no
    grace
From its serene regard. Only a dream!

*Hamp.* We meet here to accomplish
    certain good
By obvious means, and keep tradition
    up
Of free assemblages, else obsolete,

In this poor chamber: nor without effect
Has friend met friend to counsel and
    confirm,
As, listening to the beats of England's
    heart,
We spoke its wants to Scotland's prompt
    reply
By these her delegates. Remains alone
That word grow deed, as with God's
    help it shall –
But with the devil's hindrance, who
    doubts too?
Looked we or no that tyranny should
    turn
Her engines of oppression to their use?
Whereof, suppose the worst be
    Wentworth here –
Shall we break off the tactics which
    succeed
In drawing out our formidablest foe,
Let bickering and disunion take their
    place?
Or count his presence as our conquest's
    proof,
And keep the old arms at their steady
    play?
Proceed to England's work! Fiennes,
    read the list!

*Fien.* Ship-money is refused or fiercely
    paid
In every county, save the northern parts
Where Wentworth's influence ...
                              [*Shouting.*
*Vane.*              I, in England's name,
Declare her work, this way, at end! Till
    now,
Up to this moment, peaceful strife was
    best.
We English had free leave to think; till
    now,
We had a shadow of a Parliament
In Scotland. But all's changed: they
    change the first,
They try brute-force for law, they, first
    of all ...
*Voices.* Good! Talk enough! The old
    true hearts with Vane!

*Vane.* Till we crush Wentworth for her,
    there's no act
Serves England!
*Voices.*        Vane for England!
*Pym.*                        Pym should be
Something to England. I seek Wentworth,
    friends.

*Scene 2 – Whitehall*
    LADY CARLISLE and WENTWORTH
*Went.* And the King?
*Lady Car.*              Wentworth, lean
    on me! Sit then!
I'll tell you all; this horrible fatigue
Will kill you.
*Went.* No; – or, Lucy, just your arm;
I'll not sit till I've cleared this up with
    him:
After that, rest. The King?
*Lady Car.*        Confides in you.
*Went.* Why? or, why now? – They have
    kind throats, the knaves!
Shout for me – they!
*Lady Car.* You come so strangely soon:
Yet we took measures to keep off the
    crowd –
Did they shout for you?
*Went.*        Wherefore should they not?
Does the King take such measures for
    himself?
Beside, there's such a dearth of
    malcontents,
You say!
*Lady Car.* I said but few dared carp at
    you.
*Went.* At me? at us, I hope! The King
    and I!
He's surely not disposed to let me bear
The fame away from him of these late
    deeds
In Ireland? I am yet his instrument
Be it for well or ill? He trusts me, too!
*Lady Car.* The King, dear Wentworth,
    purposes, I said,
To grant you, in the face of all the
    Court ...

*Went.* All the Court! Evermore the Court
    about us!
Savile and Holland, Hamilton and Vane
About us, – then the King will grant me
    – what?
That he for once put these aside and say –
'Tell me your whole mind, Wentworth!'
*Lady Car.*            You professed
You would be calm.
*Went.*         Lucy, and I am calm!
How else shall I do all I come to do,
Broken, as you may see, body and mind,
How shall I serve the King? Time wastes
    meanwhile,
You have not told me half. His footstep!
    No.
Quick, then, before I meet him, – I am
    calm –
Why does the King distrust me?
*Lady Car.*          He does not
Distrust you.
*Went.*    Lucy, you can help me; you
Have even seemed to care for me: one
    word!
Is it the Queen?
 *Lady Car.* No, not the Queen: the party
That poisons the Queen's ear, Savile and
    Holland.
*Went.* I know, I know: old Vane, too,
    he's one too?
Go on – and he's made Secretary. Well?
Or leave them out and go straight to
    the charge –
The charge!
*Lady Car.*    Oh, there's no charge, no
    precise charge;
Only they sneer, make light of – one
    may say,
Nibble at what you do.
*Went.*        I know! but, Lucy,
I reckoned on you from the first ! Go on!
– Was sure could I once see this gentle
    friend
When I arrived, she'd throw an hour
    away
To help her … what am I?
*Lady Car.*      You thought of me,

Dear Wentworth?
*Went.*      But go on! The party here!
*Lady Car.* They do not think your Irish
    government
Of that surpassing value …
*Went.*          The one thing
Of value! The one service that the crown
May count on! All that keeps these very
    Vanes
In power, to vex me – not that they do
    vex,
Only it might vex some to hear that
    service
Decried, the sole support that's left the
    King!
*Lady Car.* So the Archbishop says.
*Went.*         Ah? well, perhaps
The only hand held up in my defence
May be old Laud's! These Hollands
    then, these Saviles
Nibble? They nibble? – that's the very
    word!
*Lady Car.* Your profit in the Customs,
    Bristol says,
Exceeds the due proportion: while the
    tax …
*Went.* Enough! 'tis too unworthy, – I am
    not
So patient as I thought. What's Pym
    about?
*Lady Car.* Pym?
*Went.*        Pym and the People.
*Lady Car.*         Oh, the Faction!
Extinct – of no account: there'll never be
Another Parliament.
*Went.*       Tell Savile that!
You may know – (ay, you do – the
    creatures here
Never forget!) that in my earliest life
I was not … much that I am now! The
    King
May take my word on points concerning
    Pym
Before Lord Savile's, Lucy, or if not,
I bid them ruin their wise selves, not me,
These Vanes and Hollands! I'll not be
    their tool

Who might be Pym's friend yet.
                    But there's the King!
Where is he?
*Lady Car.* Just apprised that you arrive.
*Went.* And why not here to meet me? I
    was told
He sent for me, nay, longed for me.
*Lady Car.*                    Because, –
He is now ... I think a Council's sitting
    now
About this Scots affair.
*Went.*                    A Council sits?
They have not taken a decided course
Without me in the matter?
*Lady Car.*            I should say ...
*Went.*                    The war?
They cannot have agreed to that?
Not the Scots' war? – without consulting
    me –
Me, that am here to show how rash it is,
How easy to dispense with? – Ah, you
    too
Against me! well, – the King may take
    his time.
– Forget it, Lucy! Cares make peevish:
    mine
Weigh me (but 'tis a secret) to my grave.
*Lady Car.* For life or death I am your
    own, dear friend!            [*Goes out.*
*Went.* Heartless! but all are heartless
    here. Go now,
Forsake the People!
                    I did not forsake
The People: they shall know it, when
    the King
Will trust me! – who trusts all beside at
    once,
While I have not spoke Vane and Savile
    fair,
And am not trusted: have but saved the
    throne:
Have not picked up the Queen's glove
    prettily,
And am not trusted. But he'll see me
    now.
Weston is dead: the Queen's half
    English now –

More English: one decisive word will
    brush
These insects from ... the step I know
    so well!
The King! But now, to tell him ... no –
    to ask
What's in me he distrusts: – or, best
    begin
By proving that this frightful Scots affair
Is just what I foretold. So much to say,
And the flesh fails, now, and the time is
    come,
And one false step no way to be repaired.
You were avenged, Pym, could you
    look on me.

PYM *enters*

*Went.* I little thought of you just then.
*Pym.*                    No? I
Think always of you, Wentworth.
*Went.*                    The old voice!
I wait the King, sir.
*Pym.*        True – you look so pale!
A Council sits within; when that breaks
    up
He'll see you.
*Went.*        Sir, I thank you.
*Pym.*                O, thank Laud!
You know when Laud once gets on
    Church affairs
The case is desperate: he'll not be long
To-day: he only means to prove, to-day,
We English all are mad to have a hand
In butchering the Scots for serving God
After their fathers' fashion: only that!
*Went.* Sir, keep your jests for those who
    relish them!
(Does he enjoy their confidence?) 'Tis
    kind
To tell me what the Council does.
*Pym.*                You grudge
That I should know it had resolved on
    war
Before you came? no need: you shall
    have all
The credit, trust me!
*Went.*        Have the Council dared –

They have not dared ... that is – I know
   you not.
Farewell, sir: times are changed.
*Pym.*                    – Since we two met
At Greenwich? Yes: poor patriots
   though we be,
You cut a figure, makes some slight
   return
For your exploits in Ireland! Changed
   indeed,
Could our friend Eliot look from out his
   grave!
Ah, Wentworth, one thing for
   acquaintance' sake,
Just to decide a question; have you,
   now,
Felt your old self since you forsook us?
*Went.*                              Sir!
*Pym.* Spare me the gesture! you
   misapprehend.
Think not I mean the advantage is with
   me.
I was about to say that, for my part,
I never quite held up my head since
   then –
Was quite myself since then: for first,
   you see,
I lost all credit after that event
With those who recollect how sure I was
Wentworth would outdo Eliot on our
   side.
Forgive me: Savile, old Vane, Holland
   here,
Eschew plain-speaking: 'tis a trick I keep.
*Went.* How, when, where, Savile, Vane,
   and Holland speak,
Plainly or otherwise, would have my
   scorn,
All of my scorn, sir ...
*Pym.*       ... Did not my poor thoughts
   Claim somewhat?
*Went.*  Keep your thoughts! believe the
   King
Mistrusts me for their prattle, all these
   Vanes
And Saviles! make your mind up, o'
   God's love,

That I am discontented with the King!
*Pym.* Why, you may be: I should be,
   that I know,
Were I like you.
*Went.*        Like me?
*Pym.*                 I care not much
For titles: our friend Eliot died no lord,
Hampden's no lord, and Savile is a
   lord;
But you care, since you sold your soul
   for one.
I can't think, therefore, your soul's
   purchaser
Did well to laugh you to such utter scorn
When you twice prayed so humbly for
   its price,
The thirty silver pieces ... I should say,
The Earldom you expected, still expect,
And may. Your letters were the movingest!
Console yourself: I've borne him prayers
   just now
From Scotland not to be oppressed by
   Laud,
Words moving in their way: he'll pay,
   be sure,
As much attention as to those you sent.
*Went.* False, sir! Who showed them you?
   Suppose it so,
The King did very well ... nay, I was
   glad
When it was shown me: I refused, the
   first!
John Pym, you were my friend – forbear
   me once!
*Pym.* Oh, Wentworth, ancient brother
   of my soul,
That all should come to this!
*Went.*                 Leave me!
*Pym.*                          My friend,
Why should I leave you?
*Went.*              To tell Rudyard this,
And Hampden this!
*Pym.*        Whose faces once were bright
At my approach, now sad with doubt
   and fear,
Because I hope in you – yes, Wentworth,
   you

Who never mean to ruin England – you
Who shake off, with God's help, an
   obscene dream
In this Ezekiel chamber, where it crept
Upon you first, and wake, yourself, your
   true
And proper self, our Leader, England's
   Chief,
And Hampden's friend!
               This is the proudest day!
Come, Wentworth! Do not even see the
   King!
The rough old room will seem itself
   again!
We'll both go in together: you've not
   seen
Hampden so long: come: and there's
   Fiennes: you'll have
To know young Vane. This is the
   proudest day!

   *The* KING *enters.* WENTWORTH
       *lets fall* PYM'S *hand.*
*Cha.* Arrived, my lord? – This gentleman,
   we know
Was your old friend.
               The Scots shall be informed
What we determine for their happiness.
                     [PYM *goes out.*
You have made haste, my lord.
*Went.*               Sir, I am come …
*Cha.* To see an old familiar – nay 'tis
   well;
Aid us with his experience: this Scots'
   League
And Covenant spreads too far, and we
   have proofs
That they intrigue with France: the
   Faction too,
Whereof your friend there is the head
   and front,
Abets them, – as he boasted, very like.
*Went.* Sir, trust me! but for this once,
   trust me, sir!
*Cha.* What can you mean?
*Went.*     That you should trust me, sir!
Oh – not for my sake! but 'tis sad, so sad

That for distrusting me, you suffer – you
Whom I would die to serve: sir, do you
   think
That I would die to serve you?
*Cha.*               But rise, Wentworth!
*Went.* What shall convince you? What
   does Savile do
To prove him … Ah, one can't tear out
   one's heart
And show it, how sincere a thing it is!
*Cha.* Have I not trusted you?
*Went.*               Say aught but that!
There is my comfort, mark you; all will
   be
So different when you trust me – as you
   shall!
It has not been your fault, – I was away,
Mistook, maligned, how was the King
   to know?
I am here, now – he means to trust me,
   now –
All will go on so well!
*Cha.*               Be sure I do –
I've heard that I should trust you: as
   you came,
Your friend, the Countess, told me …
*Went.*               No, – hear nothing –
Be told nothing about me! – you're not
   told
Your right-hand serves you, or your
   children love you!
*Cha.* You love me, Wentworth: rise!
*Went.*               I can speak now.
I have no right to hide the truth. 'Tis I
Can save you: only I. Sir, what must be?
*Cha.* Since Laud's assured (the minutes
   are within)
– Loath as I am to spill my subjects'
   blood …
*Went.* That is, he'll have a war: what's
   done is done!
*Cha.* They have intrigued with France;
   that's clear to Laud.
*Went.* Has Laud suggested any way to
   meet
The war's expense?
*Cha.*               He'd not decide so far

Until you joined us.
*Went.*                    Most considerate!
He's certain they intrigue with France,
    these Scots?
The People would be with us.
*Cha.*                    Pym should know.
*Went.* The People for us – were the
    People for us!
Sir, a great thought comes to reward
    your trust:
Summon a Parliament! in Ireland first,
Then, here.
*Cha.*        In truth?
*Went.*            That saves us! that puts off
The war, gives time to right their
    grievances –
To talk with Pym. I know the Faction,
    – Laud
So styles it, – tutors Scotland: all their
    plans
Suppose no Parliament: in calling one
You take them by surprise. Produce the
    proofs
Of Scotland's treason; then bid England
    help:
Even Pym will not refuse.
*Cha.*                    You would begin
With Ireland?
*Went.* Take no care for that: that's sure
To prosper.
*Cha.*    You shall rule me. You were best
Return at once: but take this ere you go!
Now, do I trust you? You're an Earl: my
    Friend
Of Friends: yes, while … You hear me
    not!
*Went.* Say it all o'er again – but once
    again:
The first was for the music: once again!
*Cha.* Strafford, my friend, there may
    have been reports,
Vain rumours. Henceforth touching
    Strafford is
To touch the apple of my sight: why
    gaze
So earnestly?
*Went.*            I am grown young again,

And foolish. What was it we spoke of?
*Cha.*                    Ireland,
The Parliament, –
*Went.*            I may go when I will?
– Now?
*Cha.* Are you tired so soon of us?
*Went.*                    My King!
But you will not so utterly abhor
A Parliament? I'd serve you any way.
*Cha.* You said just now this was the only
    way.
*Went.*    Sir, I will serve you.
*Cha.*                Strafford, spare yourself:
You are so sick, they tell me.
*Went.*                    'Tis my soul
That's well and prospers now.
                    This Parliament –
We'll summon it, the English one – I'll
    care
For everything. You shall not need them
    much.
*Cha.*            If they prove restive …
*Went.*            I shall be with you.
*Cha.* Ere they assemble?
*Went.*            I will come, or else
Deposit this infirm humanity
I' the dust. My whole heart stays with
    you, my King!
                [*As* WENTWORTH *goes out,*
                    *the* QUEEN *enters.*
*Cha.* That man must love me.
*Queen.*                It is over then?
Why, he looks yellower than ever! Well,
At least we shall not hear eternally
Of services – services: he's paid at least.
*Cha.* Not done with: he engages to
    surpass
All yet performed in Ireland.
*Queen.*                I had thought
Nothing beyond was ever to be done.
The war, Charles – will he raise supplies
    enough?
*Cha.* We've hit on an expedient; he …
    that is,
I have advised … we have decided on
The calling – in Ireland – of a Parliament.
*Queen.* O truly! You agree to that? Is that

The first fruit of his counsel? But I guessed
As much.
*Cha.*      This is too idle, Henriette!
I should know best. He will strain every
     nerve,
And once a precedent established …
*Queen.*                Notice
How sure he is of a long term of favour!
He'll see the next, and the next after
     that;
No end to Parliaments!
*Cha.*            Well, it is done.
He talks it smoothly, doubtless. If, indeed.
The Commons here …
*Queen.*    Here! you will summon them
Here? Would I were in France again to
     see A King!
*Cha.*        But, Henriette …
*Queen.*        Oh, the Scots see clear!
Why should they bear your rule?
*Cha.*           But listen, sweet!
*Queen.* Let Wentworth listen – you
     confide in him!
*Cha.* I do not, love, – I do not so confide!
The Parliament shall never trouble us
… Nay, hear me! I have schemes, such
     schemes: we'll buy
The leaders off: without that, Went-
     worth's counsel
Had ne'er prevailed on me. Perhaps I
     call it
To have excuse for breaking it for ever,
And whose will then the blame be? See
     you not?
Come, dearest! – look, the little fairy,
     now,
That cannot reach my shoulder!
     Dearest, come!

### ACT 2

*Scene 1 – (As in Act 1, Scene 1) The Same
     Party enters.*

*Rud.* Twelve subsidies!
*Vane.*      Oh, Rudyard, do not laugh
At least!
*Rud.*      True: Strafford called the
     Parliament –

'Tis he should laugh!
*A Puritan.*      Out of the serpent's root
Comes forth a cockatrice.
*Fien.*          – A stinging one,
If that's the Parliament: twelve subsidies!
A stinging one! but, brother, where's
     your word
For Strafford's other nest-egg, the Scots'
     war?
*The Puritan.* His fruit shall be a fiery
     flying serpent.
*Fien.* Shall be? It chips the shell, man;
     peeps abroad.
Twelve subsidies! – Why, how now,
     Vane?
*Rud.*        Peace, Fiennes!
*Fien.* Ah? – But he was not more a
     dupe than I,
Or you, or any here, the day that Pym
Returned with the good news. Look
     up, friend Vane!
We all believed that Strafford meant us
     well
In summoning the Parliament.

HAMPDEN *enters.*
*Vane.*            Now, Hampden,
Clear me! I would have leave to sleep
     again:
I'd look the People in the face again:
Clear me from having, from the first,
     hoped, dreamed
Better of Strafford!
*Hamp.*      You may grow one day
A steadfast light to England, Henry Vane!
*Rud.* Meantime, by flashes I make shift
     to see
Strafford revived our Parliaments; before,
War was but talked of; there's an army,
     now:
Still, we've a Parliament! Poor Ireland
     bears
Another wrench (she dies the hardest
     death!) –
Why, speak of it in Parliament! and lo,
'Tis spoken, so console yourselves!
*Fien.*           The jest!

We clamoured, I suppose, thus long,
 to win
The privilege of laying on our backs
A sorer burden than the King dares lay!
*Rud.* Mark now: we meet at length,
 complaints pour in
From every county, all the land cries
 out
On loans and levies, curses ship-money,
Calls vengeance on the Star Chamber;
 we lend
An ear. 'Ay, lend them all the ears you
 have!'
Puts in the King; 'my subjects, as you
 find,
'Are fretful, and conceive great things
 of you.
'Just listen to them, friends; you'll
 sanction me
'The measures they most wince at, make
 them yours,
'Instead of mine, I know: and, to begin,
'They say my levies pinch them, – raise
 me straight
'Twelve subsidies!'
*Fien.*    All England cannot furnish
Twelve subsidies!
*Hol.*   But Strafford, just returned
From Ireland – what has he to do with
 that?
How could he speak his mind? He left
 before
The Parliament assembled. Pym, who
 knows
Strafford …
*Rud.*  Would I were sure we know
 ourselves!
What is for good, what, bad – who
 friend, who foe!
*Hol.* Do you count Parliaments no gain?
*Rud.*      A gain?
While the King's creatures overbalance
 us?
– There's going on, beside, among
 ouselves
A quiet, slow, but most effectual course
Of buying over, sapping, leavening

The lump till all is leaven. Glanville's
 gone.
I'll put a case; had not the Court
 declared
That no sum short of just twelve
 subsidies
Will be accepted by the King – our
 House,
I say, would have consented to that
 offer
To let us buy off ship-money!
*Hol.*      Most like,
If, say, six subsidies will buy it off,
The House …
*Rud.*   Will grant them! Hampden,
 do you hear?
Congratulate with me! the King's the
 king,
And gains his point at last – our own
 assent
To that detested tax? All's over, then!
There's no more taking refuge in this
 room,
Protesting, 'Let the King do what he
 will,
'We, England, are no party to our shame:
'Our day will come!' Congratulate with
 me!

PYM *enters*

*Vane.* Pym, Strafford called this Parlia-
 ment, you say,
But we'll not have our Parliaments like
 those
In Ireland, Pym!
*Rud.*  Let him stand forth, your friend!
One doubtful act hides far too many
 sins;
It can be stretched no more, and, to my
 mind,
Begins to drop from those it covered.
*Other Voices.*     Good!
Let him avow himself! No fitter time!
We wait thus long for you.
*Rud.*    Perhaps, too long!
Since nothing but the madness of the
 Court,

In thus unmasking its designs at once,
Has saved us from betraying England.
       Stay –
This Parliament is Strafford's: let us vote
Our list of grievances too black by far
To suffer talk of subsidies: or best,
That ship-money's disposed of long ago
By England: any vote that's broad
       enough:
And then let Strafford, for the love of it,
Support his Parliament!
*Vane.*                And vote as well
No war to be with Scotland! Hear you,
       Pym?
We'll vote, no war! No part nor lot in it
For England!
*Many Voices.*    Vote, no war! Stop the
       new levies!
No Bishops' war! At once! When next
       we meet!
*Pym.* Much more when next we meet!
       Friends, which of you
Since first the course of Strafford was in
       doubt,
Has fallen the most away in soul from
       me?
*Vane.* I sat apart, even now under God's
       eye,
Pondering the words that should
       denounce you, Pym,
In presence of us all, as one at league
With England's enemy.
*Pym.*                You are a good
And gallant spirit, Henry. Take my hand
And say you pardon me for all the pain
Till now! Strafford is wholly ours.
*Many Voices.*                Sure? sure?
*Pym.* Most sure: for Charles dissolves
       the Parliament
While I speak here.
– And I must speak, friends, now!
Strafford is ours. The King detects the
       change,
Casts Strafford off for ever, and resumes
His ancient path: no Parliament for us,
No Strafford for the King!
Come, all of you,

To bid the King farewell, predict success
To his Scots' expedition, and receive
Strafford, our comrade now. The next
       will be
Indeed a Parliament!
*Vane.*                Forgive me, Pym!
*Voices.* This looks like truth: Strafford
       can have, indeed,
No choice.
*Pym.*    Friends, follow me! He's with
       the King.
Come, Hampden, and come, Rudyard,
       and come, Vane!
This is no sullen day for England, sirs!
Strafford shall tell you!
*Voices.*        To Whitehall then! Come!

*Scene 2 – Whitehall*
       CHARLES *and* STRAFFORD
*Cha.* Strafford!
*Straf.*  Is it a dream? my papers, here –
Thus, as I left them, all the plans you
       found
So happy – (look! the track you pressed
       my hand
For pointing out) – and in this very
       room,
Over these very plans, you tell me, sir,
With the same face, too – tell me just
       one thing
That ruins them! How's this? What
       may this mean?
Sir, who has done this?
*Cha.*                Strafford, who but I?
You bade me put the rest away: indeed
You are alone.
*Straf.*        Alone, and like to be!
No fear, when some unworthy scheme
       grows ripe,
Of those, who hatched it, leaving me to
       loose
The mischief on the world! Laud
       hatches war,
Falls to his prayers, and leaves the rest
       to me,
And I'm alone.
*Cha.*        At least, you knew as much

When first you undertook the war.
*Straf.*                                  My liege,
Was this the way? I said, since Laud
     would lap
A little blood, 'twere best to hurry over
The loathsome business, not to be
     whole months
At slaughter – one blow, only one,
     then, peace,
Save for the dreams. I said, to please
     you both
I'd lead an Irish army to the West,
While in the South an English ... but
     you look
As though you had not told me fifty
     times
'Twas a brave plan! My army is all
     raised,
I am prepared to join it ...
*Cha.*                          Hear me, Strafford!
*Straf.* ... When, for some little thing,
     my whole design
Is set aside – (where is the wretched
     paper?)
I am to lead – (ay, here it is) – to lead
The English army: why? Northumberland
That I appointed, chooses to be sick –
Is frightened: and, meanwhile, who
     answers for
The Irish Parliament? or army, either?
Is this my plan?
*Cha.*              So disrespectful, sir?
*Straf.* My liege, do not believe it! I am
     yours,
Yours ever: 'tis too late to think about:
To the death, yours. Elsewhere, this
     untoward step
Shall pass for mine; the world shall
     think it mine.
But here! But here! I am so seldom here,
Seldom with you, my King! I, soon to
     rush
Alone upon a giant in the dark!
*Cha.* My Strafford!
*Straf.* [*examines papers awhile*]. 'Seize
     the passes of the Tyne!'
But, sir, you see – see all I say is true?

My plan was sure to prosper, so, no
     cause
To ask the Parliament for help; whereas
We need them frightfully.
*Cha.*                    Need the Parliament?
*Straf.* Now, for God's sake, sir, not one
     error more!
We can afford no error; we draw, now,
Upon our last resource: the Parliament
Must help us!
*Cha.*           I've undone you, Strafford!
*Straf.*                                    Nay –
Nay – why despond, sir, 'tis not come
     to that!
I have not hurt you? Sir, what have I said
To hurt you? I unsay it! Don't despond!
Sir, do you turn from me?
*Cha.*                    My friend of friends!
*Straf.* We'll make a shift. Leave me the
     Parliament!
Help they us ne'er so little and I'll make
Sufficient out of it. We'll speak them
     fair.
They're sitting, that's one great thing;
     that half gives
Their sanction to us; that's much:
     don't despond!
Why, let them keep their money, at the
     worst!
The reputation of the People's help
Is all we want: we'll make shift yet!
*Cha.*                          Good Strafford!
*Straf.* But meantime, let the sum be
     ne'er so small
They offer, we'll accept it: any sum –
For the look of it: the least grant tells
     the Scots
The Parliament is ours – their staunch
     ally
Turned ours: that told, there's half the
     blow to strike!
What will the grant be? What does
     Glanville think?
*Cha.* Alas!
*Straf.*    My liege?
*Cha.*              Strafford!
*Straf.*                        But answer me!

Have they ... O surely not refused us
    half?
Half the twelve subsidies? We never
    looked
For all of them. How many do they give?
*Cha.* You have not heard ...
*Straf.*     (What has he done?) – Heard
    what?
But speak at once, sir, this grows terrible!
        [*The* KING *continuing silent.*
You have dissolved them! – I'll not leave
    this man.
*Cha.* 'Twas old Vane's ill-judged
    vehemence.
*Straf.*         Old Vane?
*Cha.* He told them, just about to vote
    the half,
That nothing short of all twelve subsidies
Would serve our turn, or be accepted.
*Straf.*         Vane!
Vane! Who, sir, promised me, that very
    Vane ...
O God, to have it gone, quite gone from
    me,
The one last hope – I that despair, my
    hope –
That I should reach his heart one day,
    and cure
All bitterness one day, be proud again
And young again, care for the sunshine
    too,
And never think of Eliot any more, –
God, and to toil for this, go far for this,
Get nearer, and still nearer, reach this
    heart
And find Vane there!
        [*Suddenly taking up a paper, and*
        *continuing with a forced calmness.*
        Northumberland is sick:
Well, then, I take the army: Wilmot
    leads
The horse, and he, with Conway, must
    secure
The passes of the Tyne: Ormond supplies
My place in Ireland. Here, we'll try the
    City:
If they refuse a loan – debase the coin

And seize the bullion! we've no other
    choice.
Herbert ...
    And this while I am here! with you!
And there are hosts such, hosts like
    Vane! I go,
And, I once gone, they'll close around
    you, sir,
When the least pique, pettiest mistrust,
    is sure
To ruin me – and you along with me!
Do you see that? And you along with
    me!
– Sir, you'll not ever listen to these men,
And I away, fighting your battle? Sir,
If they – if She – charge me, no matter
    how –
Say you, 'At any time when he returns
'His head is mine!' Don't stop me
    there! You know
My head is yours, but never stop me
    there!
*Cha.* Too shameful, Strafford! You advised
    the war,
And ...
*Straf.* I! I! that was never spoken with
Till it was entered on! That loathe the
    war!
That say it is the maddest, wickedest ...
Do you know, sir, I think within my
    heart,
That you would say I did advise the
    war;
And if, through your own weakness, or
    what's worse,
These Scots, with God to help them,
    drive me back,
You will not step between the raging
    People
And me, to say ...
        I knew it! from the first
I knew it! Never was so cold a heart!
Remember that I said it – that I never
Believed you for a moment!
        – And, you loved me?
You thought your perfidy profoundly hid
Because I could not share the whisperings

With Vane, with Savile? What, the face
    was masked?
I had the heart to see, sir! Face of flesh,
But heart of stone – of smooth cold
    frightful stone!
Ay, call them! Shall I call for you? The
    Scots
Goaded to madness? Or the English –
    Pym –
Shall I call Pym, your subject? Oh, you
    think
I'll leave them in the dark about it all?
They shall not know you? Hampden,
    Pym shall not?
    PYM, HAMPDEN, VANE, *etc., enter.*
[*Dropping on his knee.*] Thus favoured
    with your gracious countenance
What shall a rebel League avail against
Your servant, utterly and ever yours?
So, gentlemen, the King's not even left
The privilege of bidding me farewell
Who haste to save the People – that
    you style
Your People – from the mercies of the
    Scots
And France their friend?
[*To* CHARLES.]      Pym's grave
    grey eyes are fixed
Upon you, sir!
            Your pleasure, gentlemen?
*Hamp.* The King dissolved us – 'tis the
    King we seek
And not Lord Strafford.
*Straf.*        – Strafford, guilty too
Of counselling the measure. [*To*
    CHARLES.] (Hush … you know –
You have forgotten – sir, I counselled it)
A heinous matter, truly! But the King
Will yet see cause to thank me for a
    course
Which now, perchance … (Sir, tell
    them so!) – he blames.
Well, choose some fitter time to make
    your charge:
I shall be with the Scots, you understand?
Then yelp at me!
            Meanwhile, your Majesty

Binds me, by this fresh token of your
    trust …
    [*Under the pretence of an earnest
    farewell,* STRAFFORD *conducts*
    CHARLES *to the door, in such a
    manner as to hide his agitation from
    the rest: as the* KING *disappears,
    they turn as by one impulse to* PYM,
    who has not changed his original
    posture of surprise.*
*Hamp.* Leave we this arrogant strong
    wicked man!
*Vane and others.* Hence, Pym! Come
    out of this unworthy place
To our old room again! He's gone.
    [STRAFFORD, *just about to follow the
            KING, looks back.*
*Pym.*                Not gone:
[*To* Strafford.] Keep tryst! the old
    appointment's made anew:
Forget not we shall meet again!
*Straf.*           So be it!
And if an army follows me?
*Vane.*           His friends
Will entertain your army!
*Pym.*           I'll not say
You have misreckoned, Strafford: time
    shows.
            Perish
Body and spirit! Fool to feign a doubt,
Pretend the scrupulous and nice reserve
Of one whose prowess shall achieve the
    feat!
What share have I in it? Do I affect
To see no dismal sign above your head
When God suspends his ruinous
    thunder there?
Strafford is doomed. Touch him no one
of you!    [PYM, HAMPDEN, *etc., go out.*
*Straf.* Pym, we shall meet again!

        LADY CARLISLE *enters*
           You here, child?
*Lady Car.*          Hush –
I know it all: hush, Strafford!
*Straf.*          Ah? you know?
Well. I shall make a sorry soldier, Lucy!

All knights begin their enterprise, we
read,
Under the best of auspices; 'tis morn,
The Lady girds his sword upon the Youth
(He's always very young) – the trumpets
    sound,
Cups pledge him, and, why, the King
    blesses him –
You need not turn a page of the romance
To learn the Dreadful Giant's fate. Indeed,
We've the fair Lady here; but she
    apart, –
A poor man, rarely having handled lance,
And rather old, weary, and far from sure
His Squires are not the Giant's friends.
All's one:
Let us go forth!
*Lady Car.*    Go forth?
*Straf.*         What matters it?
We shall die gloriously – as the book says.
*Lady Car.* To Scotland? Not to Scotland?
*Straf.*           Am I sick
Like your good brother, brave
    Northumberland?
Beside, these walls seem falling on me.
*Lady Car.*         Strafford,
The wind that saps these walls can
    undermine
Your camp in Scotland, too. Whence
    creeps the wind?
Have you no eyes except for Pym? Look
    here!
A breed of silken creatures lurk and
    thrive
In your contempt. You'll vanquish Pym?
    Old Vane
Can vanquish you. And Vane you
    think to fly?
Rush on the Scots! Do nobly! Vane's
    slight sneer
Shall test success, adjust the praise,
    suggest
The faint result: Vane's sneer shall reach
    you there.
– You do not listen!
*Straf.*         Oh, – I give that up!
There's fate in it: I give all here quite up.

Care not what old Vane does or Holland
    does
Against me! 'Tis so idle to withstand!
In no case tell me what they do!
*Lady Car.*         But, Strafford ...
*Straf.* I want a little strife, beside; real
    strife;
This petty palace-warfare does me harm:
I shall feel better, fairly out of it.
*Lady Car.* Why do you smile?
*Straf.*        I got to fear them, child!
I could have torn his throat at first, old
    Vane's,
As he leered at me on his stealthy way
To the Queen's closet. Lord, one loses
    heart!
I often found it on my lips to say
'Do not traduce me to her!'
*Lady Car.*        But the King ...
*Straf.* The King stood there, 'tis not so
    long ago,
– There; and the whisper, Lucy, 'Be my
    friend
'Of friends!' – My King! I would have ...
*Lady Car.*        ... Died for him?
*Straf.* Sworn him true, Lucy: I can die
    for him.
*Lady Car.* But go not, Strafford! But
    you must renounce
This project on the Scots! Die, wherefore
    die?
Charles never loved you.
*Straf.*        And he never will.
He's not of those who care the more for
    men
That they're unfortunate.
*Lady Car.*       Then wherefore die
For such a master?
*Straf.*       You that told me first
How good he was – when I must leave
    true friends
To find a truer friend! – that drew me
    here
From Ireland, – 'I had but to show
    myself
'And Charles would spurn Vane,
    Savile, and the rest' –

You, child, to ask me this?
*Lady Car.*                    (If he have set
His heart abidingly on Charles!)
                    Then, friend,
I shall not see you any more.
*Straf.*                    Yes, Lucy.
There's one man here I have to meet.
*Lady Car.*                    (The King!
What way to save him from the King?
                    My soul —
That lent from its own store the charmed
    disguise
Which clothes the King — he shall behold
    my soul!)
Strafford, — I shall speak best if you'll not
    gaze
Upon me: I had never thought, indeed,
To speak, but you would perish too, so
    sure!
Could you but know what 'tis to bear,
    my friend,
One image stamped within you, turning
    blank
The else imperial brilliance of your
    mind, —
A weakness, but most precious, — like a
    flaw
I' the diamond, which should shape
    forth some sweet face
Yet to create, and meanwhile treasured
    there
Lest nature lose her gracious thought for
    ever!
*Straf.* When could it be? no! Yet … was
    it the day
We waited in the anteroom, till Holland
Should leave the presence-chamber?
*Lady Car.*                    What?
*Straf.*                    — That I
Described to you my love for Charles?
*Lady Car.*                    (Ah, no —
One must not lure him from a love like
    that!
Oh, let him love the King and die! 'Tis
    past.
I shall not serve him worse for that one
    brief

And passionate hope, silent for ever now!)
And you are really bound for Scotland
    then?
I wish you well: you must be very sure
Of the King's faith, for Pym and all his
    crew
Will not be idle — setting Vane aside!
*Straf.* If Pym is busy, — you may write of
    Pym.
*Lady Car.* What need, since there's your
    King to take your part?
He may endure Vane's counsel; but for
    Pym —
Think you he'll suffer Pym to …
*Straf.*                    Child, your hair
Is glossier than the Queen's!
*Lady Car.*                    Is that to ask
A curl of me?
*Starf.*          Scotland — the weary way!
*Lady Car.* Stay, let me fasten it.
                    — A rival's, Strafford?
*Straf.* [*showing the George*]. He hung it
    there: twine yours around it, child!
*Lady Car.*    No — no — another time — I
    trifle so!
And there's a masque on foot. Farewell.
    The Court
Is dull; do something to enliven us
In Scotland: we expect it at your hands.
*Straf.* I shall not fail in Scotland.
*Lady Car.*                    Prosper — if
You'll think of me sometimes!
*Straf.*                    How think of him
And not of you? of you, the lingering
    streak
(A golden one) in my good fortune's eve.
*Lady Car.* Strafford … Well, when the
    eve has its last streak
The night has its first star. [*She goes out.*
*Straf.*                    That voice of hers —
You'd think she had a heart sometimes!
    His voice
Is soft too.
          Only God can save him now.
Be Thou about his bed, about his path!
His path! Where's England's path?
          Diverging wide,

And not to join again the track my foot
Must follow – whither? All that forlorn
   way
Among the tombs! Far – far – till …
   What, they do
Then join again, these paths? For, huge
   in the dusk,
There's – Pym to face!
          Why then, I have a foe
To close with, and a fight to fight at last
Worthy my soul! What, do they beard
   the king,
And shall the King want Strafford at his
   need?
Am I not here?
        Not in the market-place,
Pressed on by the rough artisans, so
   proud
To catch a glance from Wentworth! They
   lie down
Hungry yet smile 'Why, it must end
   some day:
'Is he not watching for our sake?' Not
   there!
But in Whitehall, the whited sepulchre,
The …
       Curse nothing to-night! Only
   one name
They'll curse in all those streets to-night.
   Whose fault?
Did I make kings? set up, the first, a man
To represent the multitude, receive
All love in right of them – supplant
   them so.
Until you love the man and not the
   king –
The man with the mild voice and
   mournful eyes
Which send me forth.
        – To breast the bloody sea
That sweeps before me: with one star for
   guide.
Night has its first, supreme, forsaken
   star.

## ACT 3

*Scene 1 – Opposite Westminster Hall*

SIR HENRY VANE, LORD SAVILE, LORD
   HOLLAND *and others of the Court.*

*Sir H. Vane.* The Commons thrust you
   out?

*Sav.*       And what kept you
From sharing their civility?

*Sir H. Vane.*          Kept me?
Fresh news from Scotland, sir! worse
   than the last,
If that may be. All's up with Strafford
   there:
Nothing to bar the mad Scots marching
   hither
Next Lord's-day morning. That detained
   me, sir!
Well now, before they thrust you out,
   – go on, –
Their Speaker – did the fellow Lenthal
   say
All we set down for him?

*Holland.*        Not a word missed.
Ere he began, we entered, Savile, I
And Bristol and some more, with hope
   to breed
A wholesome awe in the new Parliament.
But such a gang of graceless ruffians,
   Vane,
As glared at us!

*Vane.*      So many?

*Sav.*          Not a bench
Without its complement of burly knaves;
Your hopeful son among them: Hampden
   leant
Upon his shoulder – think of that!

*Vane.*          I'd think
On Lenthal's speech, if I could get at it.
Urged he, I ask, how grateful they
   should prove
For this unlooked-for summons from
   the King?

*Holland.* Just as we drilled him.

*Vane.*      That the Scots will march
On London?

*Holland.*  All, and made so much of it,
A dozen subsidies at least seemed sure

To follow, when …
*Vane.* Well?
*Holland.* 'Tis a strange thing, now!
I've a vague memory of a sort of sound,
A voice, a kind of vast unnatural voice –
Pym, sir, was speaking! Savile, help me
        out:
What was it all?
*Sav.* Something about 'a matter' –
No, – 'work for England.'
*Holland.* 'England's great revenge'
He talked of.
*Sav.* How should I get used to Pym
More than yourselves?
*Holland.* However that be,
'Twas something with which we had
        nought to do,
For we were 'strangers' and 'twas
        'England's work' –
(All this while looking us straight in the
        face)
In other words, our presence might be
        spared.
So, in the twinkling of an eye, before
I settled to my mind what ugly brute
Was likest Pym just then, they yelled us
        out,
Locked the doors after us, and here
        are we.
*Vane.* Eliot's old method …
*Sav.* Prithee, Vane, a truce
To Eliot and his times, and t'great Duke,
And how to manage Parliaments! 'Twas
        you
Advised the Queen to summon this:
        why, Strafford
(To do him justice) would not hear of it.
*Vane.* Say rather, you have done the best
        of turns
To Strafford: he's at York, we all know
        why.
I would you had not set the Scots on
        Strafford
Till Strafford put down Pym for us, my
        lord!
*Sav.* Was it I altered Strafford's plans?
        did I …

*A* MESSENGER *enters.*

*Mes.* The Queen, my lords – she sends
        me: follow me
At once; 'tis very urgent! she requires
Your counsel: something perilous and
        strange
Occasions her command.
*Sav.* We follow, friend!
Now, Vane; – your Parliament will plague
        us all!
*Vane.* No Strafford here beside!
*Sav.* If you dare hint
I had a hand in his betrayal, sir …
*Holland.* Nay, find a fitter time for
        quarrels – Pym
Will overmatch the best of you; and,
        think,
The Queen!
*Vane.* Come on, then: understand,
        I loathe
Strafford as much as any – but his use!
To keep off Pym, to screen a friend or
        two,
I would we had reserved him yet awhile.

*Scene 2 – Whitehall*
        *The* QUEEN *and* LADY CARLISLE.
*Queen.* It cannot be.
*Lady Car.* It is so.
*Queen.* Why, the House
Have hardly met.
*Lady Car.* They met for that.
*Queen.* No, no!
Meet to impeach Lord Strafford? 'Tis a
        jest.
*Lady Car.* A bitter one.
*Queen.* Consider! 'Tis the House
We summoned so reluctantly, which
        nothing
But the disastrous issue of the war
Persuaded us to summon. They'll wreak
        all
Their spite on us, no doubt; but the old
        way
Is to begin by talk of grievances:
They have their grievances to busy them.
*Lady Car.* Pym has begun his speech.

*Queen.*               Where's Vane? – That is,
Pym will impeach Lord Strafford if he
    leaves
His Presidency; he's at York, we know,
Since the Scots beat him: why should he
    leave York?
*Lady Car.* Because the King sent for him.
*Queen.*                          Ah – but if
The King did send for him, he let him
    know
We had been forced to call a Parliament
A step which Strafford, now I come to
    think,
Was vehement against.
*Lady Car.*                The policy
Escaped him, of first striking Parliaments
To earth, then setting them upon their
    feet
And giving them a sword: but this is
    idle.
Did the King send for Strafford? He will
    come.
*Queen.* And what am I to do?
*Lady Car.*        What do? Fail, madam!
Be ruined for his sake! what matters
    how,
So it but stand on record that you made
An effort, only one?
*Queen.*               The King away
At Theobald's!
*Lady Car.*        Send for him at once: he
    must
Dissolve the House.
*Queen.*     Wait till Vane finds the truth
Of the report: then …
*Lady Car.*            – It will matter little
What the King does. Strafford that lends
    his arm
And breaks his heart for you!
           SIR H. VANE *enters.*
*Vane.*           The Commons, madam,
Are sitting with closed doors. A huge
    debate,
No lack of noise; but nothing, I should
    guess,
Concerning Strafford: Pym has certainly
Not spoken yet.

*Queen [to* LADY CARLISLE]. You hear?
*Lady Car.*                    I do not hear
That the King's sent for!
*Vane.*              Savile will be able
To tell you more.
           HOLLAND *enters*
*Queen.*       The last news, Holland?
*Holland.*                          Pym
Is raging like a fire. The whole House
    means
To follow him together to Whitehall
And force the King to give up Strafford.
*Queen.*                          Strafford?
*Holland.* If they content themselves
    with Strafford! Laud
Is talked of, Cottington and Windebank
    too.
Pym has not left out one of them – I
    would
You heard Pym raging!
*Queen.*             Vane, go find the King!
Tell the King, Vane, the People follow
    Pym
To brave us at Whitehall!
           SAVILE *enters*
*Sav.*                Not to Whitehall –
'Tis to the Lords they go: they seek
    redress
On Strafford from his peers – the legal
    way,
They call it.
*Queen.*    (Wait, Vane!)
*Sav.*                But the adage gives
Long life to threatened men. Strafford
    can save
Himself so readily: at York, remember,
In his own county: what has he to fear?
The Commons only mean to frighten
    him
From leaving York. Surely, he will not
    come.
*Queen.* Lucy, he will not come!
*Lady Car.*        Once more, the King
Has sent for Strafford. He will come.
*Vane.*                Oh doubtless!
And bring destruction with him: that's
    his way.

What but his coming spoilt all Conway's
    plan?
The King must take his counsel, choose
    his friends,
Be wholly ruled by him! What's the result?
The North that was to rise, Ireland to
    help –
What came of it? In my poor mind, a
    fright
Is no prodigious punishment.
*Lady Car.*               A fright?
Pym will fail worse than Strafford if he
    thinks
To frighten him. [*To the* QUEEN.] You
    will not save him then?
*Sav.* When something like a charge is
    made, the King
Will best know how to save him: and
    'tis clear,
While Strafford suffers nothing by the
    matter,
The King may reap advantage: this in
    question,
No dinning you with ship-money
    complaints!
*Queen* [*to* Lady Carlisle]. If we dissolve
    them, who will pay the army?
Protect us from the insolent Scots?
*Lady Car.*             In truth,
I know not, madam. Strafford's fate
    concerns
Me little: you desired to learn what
    course
Would save him: I obey you.
*Vane.*             Notice, too,
There can't be fairer ground for taking
    full
Revenge – (Strafford's revengeful) – than
    he'll have
Against his old friend Pym.
*Queen.*         Why, he shall claim
Vengeance on Pym!
*Vane.*        And Strafford, who is he
To 'scape unscathed amid the accidents
That harass all beside? I, for my part,
Should look for something of
    discomfiture

Had the King trusted me so thoroughly
And been so paid for it.
*Holland.*         He'll keep at York:
All will blow over: he'll return no worse,
Humbled a little, thankful for a place
Under as good a man. Oh, we'll dispense
With seeing Strafford for a month or
    two!

STRAFFORD *enters*

*Queen.* You here!
*Straf.* The King sends for me, madam.
*Queen.*                  Sir,
The King …
*Straf.*    An urgent matter that imports
    the King!
[*To* LADY CARLISLE.] Why, Lucy, what's
    in agitation now,
That all this muttering and shrugging,
    see,
Begins at me? They do not speak!
*Lady Car.*          'Tis welcome!
For we are proud of you – happy and
    proud
To have you with us, Strafford! You
    were staunch
At Durham: you did well there! Had
    you not
Been stayed, you might have … we
    said, even now,
Our hope's in you!
*Vane.* [*to* LADY CARLISLE] The Queen
    would speak with you.
*Straf.* Will one of you, his servants
    here, vouchsafe
To signify my presence to the King?
*Sav.* An urgent matter?
*Straf.*        None that touches you,
Lord Savile! Say, it were some treacherous
Sly pitiful intriguing with the Scots –
You would go free, at least! (They half
    divine
My purpose!) Madam, shall I see the
    King?
The service I would render, much
    concerns
His welfare.
*Queen.*    But his Majesty, my lord,

May not be here, may …
*Straf.* Its importance, then,
Must plead excuse for this withdrawal,
    madam,
And for the grief it gives Lord Savile here.
*Queen* [*who has been conversing with*
    VANE *and* HOLLAND].
The King will see you, sir!
        [*To* LADY CARLISLE.] Mark me:
    Pym's worst
Is done by now: he has impeached the
    Earl,
Or found the Earl too strong for him, by
    now.
Let us not seem instructed! We should
    work
No good to Strafford, but deform
    ourselves
With shame in the world's eye. [*To*
    STRAFFORD.] His Majesty
Has much to say with you.
*Straf.* Time fleeting, too!
[*To* LADY CARLISLE.] No means of
    getting them away? And She –
What does she whisper? Does she know
    my purpose?
What does she think of it? Get them
    away!
*Queen* [*to* LADY CARLISLE]. He comes to
    baffle Pym – he thinks the danger
Far off: tell him no word of it! a time
For help will come; we'll not be wanting
    then.
Keep him in play, Lucy – you, self-
    possessed
And calm! [*To* STRAFFORD.] To spare
    your lordship some delay
I will myself acquaint the King. [*To*
    LADY CARLISLE.] Beware!
        [*The* QUEEN, VANE, HOLLAND,
            *and* SAVILE *go out.*
*Straf.* She knows it?
*Lady Car.* Tell me, Strafford!
*Straf.* Afterward!
This moment's the great moment of all
    time.
She knows my purpose?

*Lady Car.* Thoroughly: just now
She bade me hide it from you.
*Straf.* Quick, dear child,
The whole o' the scheme?
*Lady Car.* (Ah, he would learn if they
Connive at Pym's procedure! Could
    they but
Have once apprised the King! But
    there's no time
For falsehood, now.) Strafford, the
    whole is known.
*Straf.* Known and approved?
*Lady Car.* Hardly discountenanced.
*Straf.* And the King – say, the King
    consents as well?
*Lady Car.* The King's not yet informed,
    but will not dare
To interpose.
*Straf.* What need to wait him, then?
He'll sanction it! I stayed, child, tell
    him, long!
It vexed me to the soul – this waiting
    here.
You know him, there's no counting on
    the King.
Tell him I waited long!
*Lady Car.* (What can he mean?
Rejoice at the King's hollowness?)
*Straf.* I knew
They would be glad of it, – all over once,
I knew they would be glad: but he'd
    contrive,
The Queen and he, to mar, by helping it,
An angel's making.
*Lady Car.* (Is he mad?) Dear Strafford,
You were not wont to look so happy.
*Straf.* Sweet,
I tried obedience thoroughly. I took
The King's wild plan: of course, ere I
    could reach
My army, Conway ruined it. I drew
The wrecks together, raised all heaven
    and earth,
And would have fought the Scots: the
    King at once
Made truce with them. Then, Lucy,
    then, dear child,

God put it in my mind to love, serve, die
For Charles, but never to obey him
    more!
While he endured their insolence at
    Ripon
I fell on them at Durham. But you'll tell
The King I waited? All the anteroom
Is filled with my adherents.

*Lady Car.*        Strafford – Strafford,
What daring act is this you hint?

*Straf.*           No, no!
'Tis here, not daring if you knew? all here!
    [*Drawing papers from his breast.*
Full proof, see, ample proof – does the
    Queen know
I have such damning proof? Bedford
    and Essex,
Brooke, Warwick, Savile (did you notice
    Savile?
The simper that I spoilt?), Saye, Mande-
    ville –
Sold to the Scots, body and soul, by
    Pym!

*Lady Car.* Great heaven!

*Straf.*          From Savile and
    his lords, to Pym
And his losels, crushed! – Pym shall not
    ward the blow
Nor Savile creep aside from it! The Crew
And the Cabal – I crush them!

*Lady Car.*        And you go –
Strafford, – and now you go? –

*Straf.*         – About no work
In the background, I promise you! I go
Straight to the House of Lords to claim
    these knaves.
Mainwaring!

*Lady Car.* Stay – stay, Strafford!

*Straf.*         She'll return,
The Queen – some little project of her
    own!
No time to lose: the King takes fright
    perhaps.

*Lady Car.* Pym's strong, remember!

*Straf.*        Very strong, as fits
The Faction's head – with no offence to
    Hampden,

Vane, Rudyard and my loving Hollis:
    one
And all they lodge within the Tower
    tonight
In just equality. Bryan! Mainwaring!
    [*Many of his* ADHERENTS *enter.*
The Peers debate just now (a lucky
    chance)
On the Scots' war; my visit's opportune.
When all is over, Bryan, you proceed
To Ireland: these dispatches, mark me,
    Bryan,
Are for the Deputy, and these for
    Ormond:
We want the army here – my army,
    raised
At such a cost, that should have done
    such good.
And was inactive all the time! no matter,
We'll find a use for it. Willis … or, no
    – you!
You, friend, make haste to York: bear
    this at once …
Or, – better stay for form's sake, see
    yourself
The news you carry. You remain with me
To execute the Parliament's command,
Mainwaring! Help to seize these lesser
    knaves,
Take care there's no escaping at
    backdoors;
I'll not have one escape, mind me – not
    one!
I seem revengeful, Lucy? Did you know
What these men dare!

*Lady Car.*    It is so much they dare!

*Straf.* I proved that long ago; my turn is
    now.
Keep sharp watch, Goring, on the
    citizens!
Observe who harbours any of the brood
That scramble off: be sure they smart
    for it!
Our coffers are but lean.
           And you, child, too,
Shall have your task; deliver this to
    Laud.

Laud will not be the slowest in my
    praise:
'Thorough' he'll cry! – Foolish, to be so
    glad!
This life is gay and glowing, after all:
'Tis worth while, Lucy, having foes like
    mine
Just for the bliss of crushing them.
    To-day
Is worth the living for.
*Lady Car.*        That reddening brow!
You seem …
*Straf.*        Well – do I not? I would
    be well –
I could not but be well on such a day!
And, this day ended, 'tis of slight import
How long the ravaged frame subjects
    the soul
In Strafford.
*Lady Car.*   Noble Strafford!
*Straf.*         No farewell!
I'll see you anon, to-morrow – the first
    thing.
– If She should come to stay me!
*Lady Car.*      Go – 'tis nothing –
Only my heart that swells: it has been
    thus
Ere now: go, Strafford!
*Straf.*       To-night, then, let it be.
I must see Him: you, the next after Him.
I'll tell you how Pym looked. Follow me,
    friends!
You, gentlemen, shall see a sight this
    hour
To talk of all your lives. Close after me!
'My friend of friends!'
       [STRAFFORD *and the rest go out.*
*Lady Car.*   The King – ever the King!
No thought of one beside, whose little
    word
Unveils the King to him – one word
    from me,
Which yet I do not breathe!
          Ah, have I spared
Strafford a pang, and shall I seek reward
Beyond that memory? Surely too, some
    way

He is the better for my love. No, no –
He would not look so joyous – I'll
    believe
His very eye would never sparkle thus,
Had I not prayed for him this long,
    long while.

*Scene 3 – The Antechamber of the House
    of Lords.*
    *Many of the Presbyterian Party. The*
    ADHERENTS *of* STRAFFORD, *etc.*
*A Group of Presbyterians.* – 1. I tell you
    he struck Maxwell: Maxwell sought
To stay the Earl: he struck him and
    passed on.
2. Fear as you may, keep a good
    countenance
Before these rufflers.
3.           Strafford here the first,
With the great army at his back!
4.               No doubt.
I would Pym had made haste: that's
    Bryan, hush –
The gallant pointing.
*Strafford's Followers.* – 1. Mark these
    worthies, now!
2. A goodly gathering! 'Where the
    carcass is
'There shall the eagles' – what's the rest?
3.            For eagles
Say crows.
*A Presbyterian.* Stand back, sirs!
*One of Strafford's Followers.*   Are we in
    Geneva?
*A Presbyterian.* No, nor in Ireland; we
    have leave to breathe.
*One of Strafford's Followers.*    Truly?
    Behold how privileged we be
That serve 'King Pym'! There's
    Someone at Whitehall
Who skulks obscure; but Pym struts …
*The Presbyterian.*      Nearer.
*A Follower of Strafford.*     Higher,
We look to see him. [*To his* COMPANIONS.]
    I'm to have St John
In charge; was he among the knaves
    just now

That followed Pym within there?

*Another.*                    The gaunt man
Talking with Rudyard. Did the Earl expect
Pym at his heels so fast? I like it not.

MAXWELL *enters*

*Another.* Why, man, they rush into the
    net! Here's Maxwell –

Ha, Maxwell? How the brethren flock
    around
The fellow! Do you feel the Earl's hand
    yet
Upon your shoulder, Maxwell?

*Max.*                            Gentlemen,
Stand back! a great thing passes here.

*A Follower of Strafford.* [*To another.*] The
    Earl
Is at his work! [*To M.*] Say, Maxwell,
    what great thing!
Speak out! [*To a* PRESBYTERIAN.] Friend,
    I've a kindness for you! Friend,
I've seen you with St John: O
    stockishness!
Wear such a ruff, and never call to mind
St John's head in a charger? How, the
    plague,
Not laugh?

*Another.*      Say, Maxwell, what great
    thing!

*Another.*      Nay, wait:
The jest will be to wait.

*First.*                   And who's to bear
These demure hypocrites? You'd swear
    they came …
Came … just as we come!

    [*A* PURITAN *enters hastily and without
    observing* STRAFFORD'S FOLLOWERS.

*The Puritan.*      How goes on the work?
    Has Pym …

*A Follower of Strafford.* The secret's out
    at last. Aha,
The carrion's scented! Welcome, crow
    the first!
Gorge merrily, you with the blinking eye!
'King Pym has fallen!'

*The Puritan.*           Pym?

*A Strafford.*                  Pym!

*A Presbyterian.*                    Only Pym?

*Many of Strafford's Followers.* No, brother,
    not Pym only; Vane as well,
Rudyard as well, Hampden, St John as
    well!

*A Presbyterian.* My mind misgives: can
    it be true?

*Another.*           Lost! Lost!

*A Strafford.* Say we true, Maxwell? jam]

*The Puritan.* Pride before destruction,
A haughty spirit goeth before a fall.

*Many of Strafford's Followers.* Ah now!
The very thing! A word in season!
A golden apple in a silver picture,
To greet Pym as he passes!

      [*The doors at the back begin to
      open, noise and light issuing.*

*Max.*                    Stand back, all!

*Many of the Presbyterians.* I hold with
    Pym! And I!

*Strafford's Followers.* Now for the text!
He comes! Quick!

*The Puritan.* How hath the oppressor
    ceased!
The Lord hath broken the staff of the
    wicked!
The sceptre of the rulers, he who smote
The people in wrath with a continual
    stroke,
That ruled the nations in his anger – he
Is persecuted and none hindereth!

    [*The doors open, and* STRAFFORD *issues
    in the greatest disorder, and amid cries
    from within of* 'Void the House!'

*Straf.* Impeach me! Pym! I never struck,
    I think,
The felon on that calm insulting mouth
When it proclaimed – Pym's mouth
    proclaimed me … God!
Was it a word, only a word that held
The outrageous blood back on my heart
    – which beats!
Which beats! Some one word – 'Traitor,'
    did he say,
Bending that eye, brimful of bitter fire,
Upon me?

*Max.*      In the Commons' name, their
    servant

Demands Lord Strafford's sword.

*Straf.*                    What did you say?

*Max.* The Commons bid me ask your
   lordship's sword.

*Straf.* Let us go forth: follow me, gentle-
   men!

Draw your swords too: cut any down
   that bar us.

On the King's service! Maxwell, clear
   the way!

            [*The* PRESBYTERIANS *prepare
                to dispute his passage.*

*Straf.* I stay: the King himself shall see
   me here.

Your tablets, fellow!

[*To* MAINWARING.]   Give that to the
   King!

Yes, Maxwell, for the next half-hour, let
   be!

Nay, you shall take my sword!

            [MAXWELL *advances to take it.*
                Or, no – not that!

Their blood, perhaps, may wipe out all
   thus far,

All up to that – not that! Why, friend,
   you see

When the King lays your head beneath
   my foot

It will not pay for that. Go, all of you!

*Max.* I dare, my lord, to disobey: none
   stir!

*Straf.* This gentle Maxwell! – Do not
   touch him, Bryan!

[*To the* PRESBYTERIANS.] Whichever cur
   of you will carry this

Escapes his fellow's fate. None saves his
   life?

None?

[*Cries from within of* 'Strafford!'
        Slingsby, I've loved you at least:
   make haste!

Stab me! I have not time to tell you why.

You then, my Bryan! Mainwaring, you
   then!

Is it because I spoke so hastily

At Allerton? The King had vexed me.

[*To the* PRESBYTERIANS.]            You!

– Not even you? If I live over this,

The King is sure to have your heads,
   you know!

But what if I can't live this minute
   through?

Pym, who is there with his pursuing
   smile!

            [*Louder cries of* 'Strafford!'

The King! I troubled him, stood in the
   way

Of his negotiations, was the one

Great obstacle to peace, the Enemy

Of Scotland: and he sent for me, from
   York,

My safety guaranteed – having prepared

A Parliament – I see! And at Whitehall

The Queen was whispering with Vane
   – I see

The trap!            [*Tearing off the George.*
            I tread a gewgaw underfoot,

And cast a memory from me. One stroke,
   now!

        [*His own* ADHERENTS *disarm him.*
            *Renewed cries of* 'Strafford!'

England! I see thy arm in this and yield.

Pray you now – Pym awaits me – pray
   you now!

        [STRAFFORD *reaches the doors:
            they open wide.* HAMPDEN
            *and a crowd discovered, and,
            at the bar,* PYM *standing apart. As*
            STRAFFORD *kneels, the scene shuts.*

ACT 4

*Scene 1 – Whitehall.*

   The KING, *the* QUEEN, HOLLIS, LADY
   CARLISLE. (VANE, HOLLAND, SAVILE,
            *in the background.*)

*Lady Car.* Answer them, Hollis, for his
   sake! One word!

*Cha.* [*To* HOLLIS.] You stand, silent and
   cold, as though I meant

Deceiving you – my friend, my playfellow

Of other times. What wonder after all?

Just so, I dreamed my People loved me.

*Hol.*                                    Sir,

It is yourself that you deceive, not me.

You'll quit me comforted, your mind
    made up
That, since you've talked thus much
    and grieved thus much,
All you can do for Strafford has been
    done.
*Queen.* If you kill Strafford – (come, we
    grant you leave,
Suppose) –
*Hol.*       I may withdraw, sir?
*Lady Car.*          Hear them out!
'Tis the last chance for Strafford! Hear
    them out!
*Hol.* 'If we kill Strafford' – on the
    eighteenth day
Of Strafford's trial – 'We!'
*Cha.*         Pym, my good Hollis –
Pym, I should say!
*Hol.*        Ah, true – sir, pardon me!
You witness our proceedings every day;
But the screened gallery, I might have
    guessed,
Admits of such a partial glimpse at us,
Pym takes up all the room, shuts out
    the view.
Still, on my honour, sir, the rest of the
    place
Is not unoccupied. The Commons sit
– That's England; Ireland sends, and
    Scotland too,
Their representatives; the Peers that
    judge
Are easily distinguished; one remarks
The People here and there: but the close
    curtain
Must hide so much!
*Queen.*    Acquaint your insolent crew,
This day the curtain shall be dashed
    aside!
It served a purpose.
*Hol.*        Think! This very day?
Ere Strafford rises to defend himself?
*Cha.* I will defend him, sir! – sanction
    the past
This day: it ever was my purpose. Rage
At me, not Strafford!
*Lady Car.*      Nobly! – will he not

Do nobly?
*Hol.*    Sir, you will do honestly;
And, for that deed, I too would be a
    king.
*Cha.* Only, to do this now! – 'deaf' (in
    your style)
'To subjects' prayers,' – I must oppose
    them now!
It seems their will the trial should
    proceed, –
So palpably their will!
*Hol.*          You peril much,
But it were no bright moment save for
    that.
Strafford, your prime support, the sole
    roof-tree
Which props this quaking House of
    Privilege,
(Floods come, winds beat, and see –
    the treacherous sand!)
Doubtless, if the mere putting forth an
    arm
Could save him, you'd save Strafford.
*Cha.*         And they dare
Consummate calmly this great wrong!
    No hope?
This ineffaceable wrong! No pity then?
*Hol.* No plague in store for perfidy? –
    Farewell!
You called me, sir – [*To* LADY CARLISLE.]
    you, lady, bade me come
To save the Earl: I came, thank God for
    it,
To learn how far such perfidy can go!
You, sir, concert with me on saving him
Who have just ruined Strafford!
*Cha.*         I? – and how?
*Hol.* Eighteen days long he throws, one
    after one,
Pym's charges back: a blind moth-eaten
    law!
– He'll break from it at last: and whom
    to thank?
The mouse that gnawed the lion's net
    for him
Got a good friend, – but he, the other
    mouse,

That looked on while the lion freed
    himself –
Fared he so well, does any fable say?
*Cha.* What can you mean?
*Hol.*      Pym never could have proved
Strafford's design of bringing up the
    troops
To force this kingdom to obedience:
    Vane –
Your servant, not our friend, has
    proved it
*Cha.*        Vane?
*Hol.* This day. Did Vane deliver up or no
Those notes which, furnished by his son
    to Pym,
Seal Strafford's fate?
*Cha.*          Sir, as I live, I know
Nothing that Vane has done! What
    treason next?
I wash my hands of it. Vane, speak the
    truth!
Ask Vane himself!
*Hol.*         I will not speak to Vane,
Who speak to Pym and Hampden every
    day.
*Queen.* Speak to Vane's master then!
    What gain to him
Were Strafford's death?
*Hol.*        Ha? Strafford cannot turn
As you, sir, sit there – bid you forth,
    demand
If every hateful act were not set down
In his commission? – whether you
    contrived
Or no, that all the violence should seem
His work, the gentle ways – your own,
    – his part,
To counteract the King's kind
    impulses –
While … but you know what he could
    say! And then
He might produce, – mark, sir! – a
    certain charge
To set the King's express command
    aside,
If need were, and be blameless. He
    might add …

*Cha.* Enough!
*Hol.*        – Who bade him break the
    Parliament,
Find some pretence for setting up sword-
    law!
*Queen.* Retire!
*Cha.*        Once more, whatever Vane
    dared do,
I know not: he is rash, a fool – I know
Nothing of Vane!
*Hol.*        Well – I believe you. Sir,
Believe me, in return, that …
[*Turning to* LADY CARLISLE.] Gentle lady,
The few words I would say, the stones
    might hear
Sooner than these, – I rather speak to
    you,
You, with the heart! The question, trust
    me, takes
Another shape, to-day: not, if the King
Or England shall succumb, – but, who
    shall pay
The forfeit, Strafford or his master. Sir,
You loved me once: think on my warning
    now!          [*Goes out.*
*Cha.* On you and on your warning both!
    – Carlisle!
That paper!
*Queen.*      But consider!
*Cha.*              Give it me!
There, signed – will that content you?
    Do not speak!
You have betrayed me, Vane! See! any
    day,
According to the tenor of that paper,
He bids your brother bring the army up,
Strafford shall head it and take full
    revenge.
Seek Strafford! Let him have the same,
    before
He rises to defend himself!
*Queen.*          In truth?
That your shrewd Hollis should have
    worked a change
Like this! You, late reluctant …
*Cha.*        Say, Carlisle,
Your brother Percy brings the army up,

Falls on the Parliament – (I'll think of
  you,
My Hollis!) say, we plotted long – 'tis
  mine,
The scheme is mine, remember! Say, I
  cursed
Vane's folly in your hearing! If the Earl
Does-rise to do us shame, the fault shall
  lie
With you, Carlisle!
*Lady Car.*      Nay, fear not me! but still
That's a bright moment, sir, you throw
  away.
Tear down the veil and save him!
*Queen.*                     Go, Carlisle!
*Lady Car.* (I shall see Strafford – speak to
  him: my heart
Must never beat so, then! And if I tell
The truth? What's gained by falsehood?
  There they stand
Whose trade it is, whose life it is! How
  vain
To gild such rottenness! Strafford shall
  know,
Thoroughly know them!)
*Queen.*                     Trust to me!
  [*To* CARLISLE.] Carlisle,
You seem inclined, alone of all the Court,
To serve poor Strafford: this bold plan
  of yours
Merits much praise, and yet …
*Lady Car.*      Time presses, madam.
*Queen.* Yet – may it not be something
  premature?
Strafford defends himself to-day –
  reserves
Some woundrous effort, one may well
  suppose!
*Lady Car.* Ay, Hollis hints as much.
*Cha.*                 Why linger then?
Haste with the scheme – my scheme: I
  shall be there
To watch his look. Tell him I watch his
  look!
*Queen.* Stay, we'll precede you!
*Lady Car.*              At your pleasure.
*Cha.*                             Say –

Say, Vane is hardly ever at Whitehall!
I shall be there, remember!
*Lady Car.*              Doubt me not.
*Cha.* On our return, Carlisle, we wait
  you here!
*Lady Car.* I'll bring his answer. Sir, I
  follow you.
(Prove the King faithless, and I take
  away
All Strafford cares to live for: let it be –
'Tis the King's scheme!
                My Strafford, I can save,
Nay, I have saved you, yet am scarce
  content,
Because my poor name will not cross
  your mind.
Strafford, how much I am unworthy
  you!)

*Scene 2 – A Passage adjoining
    Westminster Hall.*
  *Many Groups of* SPECTATORS *of the
    Trial.* OFFICERS *of the Court, etc.*
*1st Spec.* More crowd than ever! Not
  know Hampden, man?
That's he, by Pym, Pym that is speaking
  now.
No, truly, if you look so high you'll see
Little enough of either!
*2nd Spec.*              Stay: Pym's arm
Points like a prophet's rod.
*3rd Spec.*              Ay, ay, we've heard
Some pretty speaking: yet the Earl
  escapes.
*4th Spec.* I fear it: just a foolish word or
  two
About his children – and we see, forsooth,
Not England's foe in Strafford, but the
  man
Who, sick, half-blind …
*2nd Spec.* What's that Pym's saying now
Which makes the curtains flutter? look!
  A hand
Clutches them. Ah! The King's hand!
*5th Spec.*              I had thought
Pym was not near so tall. What said
  he, friend?

2nd Spec. 'Nor is this way a novel way
    of blood,'
And the Earl turns as if to ... look! look!
Many Spectators.                    There!
What ails him? no – he rallies, see – goes
    on,
And Strafford smiles. Strange!
An Officer.                        Haselrig!
Many Spectators.            Friend? Friend?
The Officer. Lost, utterly lost: just when
    we looked for Pym
To make a stand against the ill effects
Of the Earl's speech! Is Haselrig
    without?
Pym's message is to him.
3rd Spec.                Now, said I true?
Will the Earl leave them yet at fault or
    no?
1st Spec. Never believe it, man! These
    notes of Vane's
Ruin the Earl.
5th Spec.        A brave end; not a whit
Less firm, less Pym all over. Then, the
    trial
Is closed. No – Strafford means to speak
    again?
An Officer. Stand back, there!
5th Spec.                        Why, the
    Earl is coming hither!
Before the court breaks up! His brother,
    look, –
You'd say he'd deprecated some fierce
    act
In Strafford's mind just now.
An Officer.            Stand back, I say!
2nd Spec. Who's the veiled woman that
    he talks with?
Many Spectators.                    Hush –
The Earl! the Earl!
  Enter STRAFFORD, SLINGSBY, and other
SECRETARIES, HOLLIS, LADY CARLISLE,
  MAXWELL, BALFOUR, etc. STRAFFORD
  converses with LADY CARLISLE.
Hol.            So near the end! Be
    patient – Return!
Straf. [to his SECRETARIES]. Here –
    anywhere – or, 'tis freshest here!

To spend one's April here, the
    blossom-month:
Set it down here!
        [They arrange a table, papers, etc.
        So, Pym can quail, can cower
Because I glance at him, yet more's to
    do?
What's to be answered, Slingsby? Let us
    end!
[To Lady Carlisle.] Child, I refuse his
    offer; whatsoe'er
It be! Too late! Tell me no word of him!
'Tis something, Hollis, I assure you
    that –
To stand, sick as you are, some eighteen
    days
Fighting for life and fame against a pack
Of very curs, that lie through thick and
    thin,
Eat flesh and bread by wholesale, and
    can' say
'Strafford' if it would take my life!
Lady Car.                    Be moved!
Glance at the paper!
Straf.            Already at my heels!
Pym's faulting bloodhounds scent the
    track again.
Peace, child! Now, Slingsby!
    [MESSENGERS from LANE and other of
    STRAFFORD'S COUNSEL within the Hall
    are coming and going during the Scene.
Straf. [setting himself to write and dictate].
    I shall beat you, Hollis!
Do you know that? In spite of St John's
    tricks,
In spite or Pym – your Pym who shrank
    from me!
Eliot would have contrived it otherwise.
[To a Messenger.] In truth? This slip,
    tell Lane, contains as much
As I can call to mind about the matter.
Eliot would have disdained ...
[Calling after the MESSENGER.] And
    Radcliffe, say,
The only person who could answer Pym,
Is safe in prison, just for that.
                        Well, well!

It had not been recorded in that case,
I baffled you.
[*To* LADY CARLISLE.] Nay, child, why
    look so grieved?
All's gained without the King! You saw
    Pym quail?
What shall I do when they acquit me,
    think; you,
But tranquilly resume my task as though
Nothing had intervened since I proposed
To call that traitor to account! Such
    tricks,
Trust me, shall not be played a second
    time,
Not even against Laud, with his grey
    hair –
Your good work, Hollis! Peace! To make
    amends,
You, Lucy, shall be here when I impeach
Pym and his fellows.
*Hol.*              Wherefore not protest
Against our whole proceeding, long ago?
Why feel indignant now? Why stand
    this while
Enduring patiently?
*Straf.*              Child, I'll tell you –
You, and not Pym – you, the slight
    graceful girl
Tall for a flowering lily, and not Hollis –
Why I stood patient! I was fool enough
To see the will of England in Pym's will;
To fear, myself had wronged her, and to
    wait
Her judgment: when, behold, in place
    of it ...
[*To a* MESSENGER *who whispers.*] Tell Lane
    to answer no such question! Law, –
I grapple with their law! I'm here to try
My actions by their standard, not my
    own!
Their- law allowed that levy: what's the
    rest
To Pym, or Lane, any but God and me?
*Lady Car.* The King's so weak! Secure
    this chance! 'Twas Vane,
Never forget, who furnished Pym the
    notes ...

*Straf.* Fit, – very fit, those precious notes
    of Vane,
To close the Trial worthily! I feared
Some spice of nobleness might linger yet
And spoil the character of all the past.
Vane eased me ... and I will go back
    and say
As much – to Pym, to England! Follow
    me!
I have a word to say! There, my defence
Is done!
          Stay! why be proud? Why care
    to own
My gladness, my surprise? – Nay, not
    surprise!
Wherefore insist upon the little pride
Of doing all myself, and sparing him
The pain? Child, say the triumph is my
    King's!
When Pym grew pale, and trembled,
    and sank down,
One image was before me: could I fail?
Child, care not for the past, so indistinct,
Obscure – there's nothing to forgive in it
'Tis so forgotten! From this day begins
A new life, founded on a new belief
In Charles.
*Hol.*       In Charles? Rather believe
    in Pym!
And here he comes in proof! Appeal to
    Pym!
Say how unfair ...
*Straf.*   To Pym? I would say nothing!
I would not look upon Pym's face again.
*Lady Car.* Stay, let me have to think
I pressed your hand!
          [STRAFFORD *and his friends go out.*
          *Enter* HAMPDEN *and* VANE.
*Vane.* O Hampden, save the great
    misguided man!
Plead Strafford's cause with Pym! I
    have remarked
He moved no muscle when we all
    declaimed
Against him: you had but to breathe –
    he turned
Those kind calm eyes upon you.

*Enter* PYM, *the* SOLICITOR-GENERAL ST
  JOHN, *the* MANAGERS *of the Trial*,
    FIENNES, RUDYARD, *etc.*

*Rud.*                                   Horrible!
Till now all hearts were with you: I
    withdraw
For one. Too horrible! But we mistake
Your purpose, Pym: you cannot snatch
    away
The last spar from the drowning man.
*Fien.*                                  He talks
With St John of it – see, how quietly!
[*To other* Presbyterians.] You'll join us?
Strafford may deserve the worst:
But this new course is monstrous. Vane,
    take heart!
This Bill of his Attainder shall not have
One true man's hand to it.
*Vane.*                          Consider, Pym!
Confront your Bill, your own Bill: what
    is it?
You cannot catch the Earl on any
    charge, –
No man will say the law has hold of him
On any charge; and therefore you resolve
To take the general sense on his desert,
As though no law existed, and we met
To found one. You refer to Parliament
To speak its thought upon the abortive
    mass
Of half-borne-out assertions, dubious
    hints
Hereafter to be cleared, distortions – ay,
And wild inventions. Every man is saved
The task of fixing any single charge
On Strafford: he has but to see in him
The enemy of England.
*Pym.*                         A right scruple!
I have heard some called England's enemy
With less consideration.
*Vane.*                          Pity me!
Indeed you made me think I was your
    friend!
I who have murdered Strafford, how
    remove
That memory from me?
*Pym.*              I absolve you, Vane.

Take you no care for aught that you
    have done!
*Vane.* John Hampden, not this Bill!
    Reject this Bill!
He staggers through the ordeal: let him
    go,
Strew no fresh fire before him! Plead for
    us!
When Strafford spoke, your eyes were
    thick with tears!
*Hamp.* England speaks louder: who are
    we, to play
The generous pardoner at her expense,
Magnanimously waive advantages,
And, if he conquer us, applaud his skill?
*Vane.* He was your friend.
*Pym.*            I have heard that before.
*Fien.* And England trusts you.
*Hamp.*             Shame be his, who turns
The opportunity of serving her
She trusts him with, to his own mean
    account –
Who would look nobly frank at her
    expense!
*Fien.* I never thought it could have come
    to this.
*Pym.* But I have made myself familiar,
    Fiennes,
With this one thought – have walked,
    and sat, and slept,
This thought before me. I have done
    such things,
Being the chosen man that should
    destroy
The traitor. You have taken up this
    thought
To play with, for a gentle stimulant,
To give a dignity to idler life
By the dim prospect of emprise to come,
But ever with the softening, sure belief,
That all would end some strange way
    right at last.
*Fien.* Had we made out some weightier
    charge!
*Pym.*            You say
That these are petty charges: can we
    come

To the real charge at all? There he is safe
In tyranny's stronghold. Apostasy
Is not a crime, treachery not a crime:
The cheek burns, the blood tingles,
    when you speak
The words, but where's the power to
    take revenge
Upon them? We must make occasion
    serve, –
The oversight shall pay for the main sin
That mocks us.
*Rud.*          But this unexampled course,
This Bill!
*Pym.*    By this, we roll the clouds away
Of precedent and custom, and at once
Bid the great beacon-light God sets in
    all,
The conscience of each bosom, shine
    upon
The guilt of Strafford: each man lay his
    hand
Upon his breast, and judge!
*Vane.*                    I only see
Strafford, nor pass his corpse for all
    beyond!
*Rud. and others.* Forgive him! He would
    join us, now he finds
What the King counts reward! The
    pardon, too,
Should be your own. Yourself should
    bear to Strafford
The pardon of the Commons.
*Pym.*              Meet him? Strafford?
Have we to meet once more, then? Be
    it so!
And yet – the prophecy seemed half
    fulfilled
When, at the Trial, as he gazed, my
    youth,
Our friendship, divers thoughts came
    back at once
And left me, for a time … 'Tis very sad!
To-morrow we discuss the points of law
With Lane – to-morrow?
*Vane.*              Not before to-morrow –
So, time enough! I knew you would
    relent!

*Pym.* The next day, Haselig, your
    introduce
The Bill of his Attainder. Pray for me!

*Scene 3 – Whitehall.*
                    The KING.
*Cha.* My loyal servant! To defend himself
Thus irresistibly, – withholding aught
That seemed to implicate us!
                        We have done
Less gallantly by Strafford. Well, the
    future
Must recompense the past.
                        She tarries long.
I understand you, Strafford, now!
                        The scheme –
Carlisle's mad scheme – he'll sanction
    it, I fear,
For love of me. 'Twas too precipitate:
Before the army's fairly on its march,
He'll be a large: no matter
                        Well, Carlisle?
            *Enter* PYM.
*Pym.* Fear me not, sir: – my mission is
    to save,
This time.
*Cha.*      To break thus on me!
            Unannounced!
*Pym.* It is of Strafford I would speak.
*Cha.*                    No more
Of Strafford! I have heard too much
    from you.
*Pym.* I spoke, sir, for the People; will
    you hear
A word upon my own account?
*Cha.*                    Of Strafford?
(So turns the tide already? Have we
    tamed
The insolent brawler? – Stafford's
    eloquence
Is gwift in its effect.) Lord Strafford, sir,
Has spoken for himself.
*Pym.*                Sufficiently.
I would apprise you of the novel course
The People take: the Trial fails.
*Cha.*                    Yes, yes:
We are aware, sir: for your part in it

Means shall be found to thank you.
*Pym.*                                   Pray you, read
This schedule! I would learn from your
    own mouth
– (It is a matter much concerning me) –
Whether, if two Estates of us concede
The death of Strafford, on the grounds
    set forth
Within that parchment, you, sir, can
    resolve
To grant your own consent to it. This
    Bill
Is framed by me. If you determine, sir,
That England's manifested will should
    guide
Your judgment, ere another week such
    will
Shall manifest itself. If not, – I cast Aside
    the measure.
*Cha.*                   You can hinder, then,
The introduction of this Bill?
*Pym.*                                        I can.
*Cha.* He is my friend, sir: I have wronged
    him: mark you,
Had I not wronged him, this might be.
    You think
Because you hate the Earl … (turn not
    away,
We know you hate him) – no one else
    could love
Stafford: but he has saved me, some
    affirm.
Think of his pride! And do you know
    one strange,
One frightful thing? We all have used
    the man
As though a drudge of ours, with not a
    source
Of happy thoughts except in us; and yet
Strafford has wife and children, house-
    hold cares,
Just as if we had never been. Ah sir,
You are moved, even you, a solitary man
Wed to your cause – to England if you
    will!
*Pym.* Yes – think, my soul – to England!
    Draw not back!

*Cha.* Prevent that Bill, sir! All your course
    seems fair
Till now. Why, in the end, 'tis I should
    sign
The warrant for his death! You have said
    much
I ponder on; I never meant, indeed,
Strafford should serve me any more. I
    take
The Commons' counsel; but this Bill is
    yours –
Nor worthy of its leader: care not, sir,
For that, however! I will quite forget
You named it to me. You are satisfied?
*Pym.* Listen to me, sir! Eliot laid his hand,
Wasted and white, upon my forehead
    once;
Wentworth – he's gone now! – has
    talked on, whole nights,
And I beside him; Hampden loves me:
    sir,
How can I breathe and not wish England
    well,
And her King well?
*Cha.*              I thank you, sir, who leave
That King his servant. Thanks, sir!
*Pym.*                              Let me speak!
– Who may not speak again; whose
    spirit yearns
For a cool night after this weary day:
– Who would not have my soul turn
    sicker yet
In a new task, more fatal, more august,
More full of England's utter weal or woe.
I thought, sir, could I find myself with
    you,
After this trial, alone, as man to man –
I might say something, warn you, pray
    you, save –
Mark me, King Charles, save – – you!
But God must do it. Yet I warn you, sir –
(With Stafford's faded eyes yet full on
    me)
As you would have no deeper question
    moved
– 'How long the Many must endure
    the One,'

Assure me, sir, if England give assent
To Strafford's death, you will not interfere!
Or –
*Cha.* God forsakes me. I am in a net
And cannot move. Let all be as you
    say!

    *Enter* LADY CARLISLE.

*Lady Car.* He loves you – looking
    beautiful with joy
Because you sent me! he would spare
    you all
The pain! he never dreamed you would
    forsake
Your servant in the evil day – nay, see
Your scheme returned! That generous
    heart of his!
He needs it not – or, needing it, disdains
A course that might endanger you – you,
    sir,
Whom Strafford from his inmost
    soul ...
            [*Seeing* Pym.] Well met!
No fear for Strafford! All that's true and
    brave
On your own side shall help us: we are
    now
Stronger than ever.
                    Ha – what, sir, is this?
All is not well! What parchment have
    you there?
*Pym.* Sir, much is saved us both.
*Lady Car.*              This Bill! Your lip
Whitens – you could not read one line
    to me
Your voice would falter so!
*Pym.*                  No recreant yet!
The great word went from England to
    my soul,
And I arose. The end is very near.
*Lady Car.* I am to save him! All have
    shrunk beside;
'Tis only I ám left. Heaven will make
    strong
The hand now as the heart. Then let
    both die!

ACT 5

*Scene 1 – Whitehall.*

    HOLLIS, LADY CARLISLE.

*Hol.* Tell the King then! Come in
    with me!
*Lady Car.*        Not so
He must not hear till it succeeds.
*Hol.*                      Succeed?
No dream was half so vain – you'd
    rescue Strafford
And outwit Pym! I cannot tell you ...
    lady,
The block pursues me, and the hideous
    show.
To-day ... is it to-day? And all the while
He's sure of the King's pardon. Think, I
    have
To tell this man he is to die. The King
May rend his hair, for me! I'll not see
    Strafford!
*Lady Car.* Only, if I succeed, remember
    – Charles
Has saved him. He would hardly value
    life
Unless his gift. My staunch friends wait.
    Go in –
You must go in to Charles!
*Hol.*                    And all beside
Left Strafford long ago. The King has
    signed
The warrant for his death! the Queen
    was sick
Of the eternal subject. For the Court, –
The Trial was amusing in its way,
Only too much of it: the Earl withdrew
In time. But you, fragile, alone, so young
Amid rude mercenaries – you devise
A plan to save him! Even though it fails,
What shall reward you?
*Lady Car.*              I may go, you think,
To France with him? And you reward
    me, friend,
Who lived with Strafford even from his
    youth
Before he set his heart on state-affairs
And they bent down that noble brow
    of his.

I have learned somewhat of his latter
    life,
And all the future I shall know: but,
    Hollis,
I ought to make his youth my own as
    well.
Tell me, – when he is saved!
*Hol.*                          My gentle friend,
He should know all and love you, but
    'tis vain!
*Lady Car.* Love? no – too late now! Let
    him love the King!
'Tis the King's scheme! I have your
    word, remember!
We'll keep the old delusion up. But,
    quick!
Quick! Each of us has work to do, beside!
Go to the King! I hope – Hollis – I hope!
Say nothing of my scheme! Hush, while
    we speak
Think where he is! Now for my gallant
    friends!
*Hol.* Where he is? Calling wildly upon
    Charles,
Guessing his fate, pacing the prison-
    floor.
Let the King tell him! I'll not look on
    Strafford.

*Scene 2 – The Tower.*
    STRAFFORD *sitting with his* CHILDREN.
*They sing.*
            O bell' andare
            Per barca in mare,
            Verso la sera
            Di Primavera!
*William.* The boat's in the broad moon-
        light all this while –
            Verso la sera
            Di Primavera!
And the boat shoots from underneath
    the moon
Into the shadowy distance; only still
You hear the dipping oar –
            Verso la sera,
And faint, and fainter, and then all's
    quite gone,

Music and light and all, like a lost star.
*Anne.* But you should sleep, father: you
    were to sleep.
*Straf.* I do sleep, Anne; or if not – you
    must know
There's such a thing as …
*Wil.*                You're too tired to sleep?
*Straf.* It will come by-and-by and all day
    long,
In that old quiet house I told you of:
We sleep safe there
*Anne.*                Why not in Ireland?
*Straf.*                                No!
Too many dreams! – That song's for
    Venice, William:
You know how Venice looks upon the
    map –
Isles that the mainland hardly can let go?
*Wil.* You've been to Venice, father?
*Straf.*                I was young, then.
*Wil.* A city with no King; that's why I like
Even a song that comes from Venice.
*Straf.*                        William!
*Wil.* Oh, I know why! Anne, do you
    love the King?
But I'll see Venice for myself one day.
*Straf.* See many lands, boy – England
    last of all, –
That way you'll love her best.
*Wil.* Why do men say
You sought to ruin her then?
*Straf.*        Ah, – they say that.
*Wil.*                            Why?
*Straf.* I suppose they must have words
    to say,
As you to sing.
*Anne.*        But they make songs beside:
Last night I heard one, in the street
    beneath,
That called you … Oh, the names!
*Wil.*            Don't mind her, father!
They soon left off when I cried out to
    them.
*Straf.* We shall so soon be out of it, my
    boy!
'Tis not worth while: who heeds a
    foolish song?

*Wil.*Why, not the King.

*Straf.*          Well: it has been the fate
Of better; and yet, – wherefore not feel
     sure
That Time, who in the twilight comes
     to mend
All the fantastic day's caprice, consign
To the low ground once more the
     ignoble Term,
And raise the Genius on his orb again, –
That Time will do me right?

*Anne.*          (Shall we sing, William?
He does not look thus when we sing.)

*Straf.*                    For Ireland,
Something is done: too little, but enough
To show what might have been.

*Wil.*                    (I have no heart
To sing now! Anne, how very sad he
     looks!
Oh, I so hate the King for all he says!)

*Straf.*          Forsook them! What, the
     common songs will run
That I forsook the People? Nothing
     more?
Ay, Fame, the busy scribe, will pause,
     no doubt,
Turning a deaf ear to her thousand
     slaves
Noisy to be enrolled, – will register
The curious glosses, subtle notices,
Ingenious clearings-up one fain would
     see
Beside that plain inscription of The
     Name –
The Patriot Pym, or the Apostate
     Strafford!

          [*The* CHILDREN *resume their song
               timidly, but break off.*
     *Enter* HOLLIS *and an* ATTENDANT.

*Straf.* No, – Hollis? in good time! –
     Who is he?

*Hol.*          One
That must be present.

*Straf.*          Ah – I understand.
They will not let me see poor Laud
     alone.
How politic! They'd use me by degrees

To solitude: and, just as you came in,
I was solicitous what life to lead
When Stafford's 'not so much as
     Constable
'In the King's service.' Is there any means
To keep oneself awake? What would
     you do
After this bustle, Hollis, in my place?

*Hol.*                    Strafford!

*Straf.* Observe, not but that Pym and
     you
Will find me news enough – news I shall
     hear
Under a quince tree by a fish-pond side
At Wentworth. Garrard must be re-
     engaged
My newsman. Or, a better project now –
What if when all's consummated, and
     the Saints
Reign, and the Senate's work goes
     swimmingly, –
What if I venture up, some day, unseen,
To saunter through the Town, notice
     how, Pym,
Your Tribune, likes Whitehall, drop
     quietly
Into a tavern, hear a point discussed,
As, whether Stafford's name were John
     or James –
And be myself appealed to – I, who shall
Myself have near forgotten!

*Hol.*                    I would speak …

*Straf.* Then you shall speak, – not now.
     I want, just now,
To hear the sound of my own tongue.
     This place
Is full of ghosts.

*Hol.*               Nay, you must hear me,
     Strafford!

*Straf.* Oh, readily! Only, one rare thing
     more, –
The minister! Who will advise the King,
Turn his Sejanus, Richelieu and what not,
And yet have health – children, for aught
     I know –
My patient pair of traitors! Ah, – but,
     William –

Does not his cheek grow thin?
*Wil.*                    'Tis you look thin, Father!
*Straf.* A scamper o'er the breezy wolds
Sets all to-rights.
*Hol.*                    You cannot sure forget
A prison-roof is o'er you, Strafford?
*Straf.*                            No,
Why, no. I would not touch on that,
    the first.
I left you that. Well, Hollis? Say at once,
The King can find no time to set me free!
A mask at Theobald's?*
*Hol.*                    Hold: no such affair
Detains him.
*Straf.*        True: what needs so great a
    matter?
The Queen's lip may be sore. Well:
    when he pleases, –
Only, I want the air: it vexes flesh To
    be pent up so long.
*Hol.*                    The King – I bear
His message, Strafford: pray you, let
    me speak!
*Straf.* Go, William! Anne, try o'er your
    song again! [*The* CHILDREN *retire.*
They shall be loyal, friend, at all events.
I know your message: you have nothing
    new
To tell me: from the first I guessed as
    much.
I know, instead of coming here himself,
Leading me forth in public by the hand,
The King prefers to leave the door ajar
As though I were escaping – bids me
    trudge
While the mob gapes upon some show
    prepared
On the other side of the river! Give at
    once
His order of release! I've heard, as well
Of certain poor manoeuvres to avoid
The granting pardon at his proper risk;
First, he must prattle somewhat to the
    Lords,

Must talk a trifle with the Commons first,
Be grieved I should abuse his confidence,
And far from blaming them, and …
    Where's the order?
*Hol.* Spare me!
*Straf.*                Why, he'd not have me
    steal away?
With an old doublet and a steeple hat
Like Prynne's? Be smuggled into
    France, perhaps?
Hollis,'tis for my children! 'Twas for
    them
I first consented to stand day by day
And give your Puritans the best of words,
Be patient, speak when called upon,
    observe
Their rules, and not return them prompt
    their lie!
What's in that boy of mine that he
    should prove
Son to a prison-breaker? I shall stay
And he'll stay with me. Charles should
    know as much,
He too has children! [*Turning to* HOLLIS'S
    COMPANION.] Sir, you feel for me!
No need to hide that face! Though it
    have looked
Upon me from the judgment-seat … I
    know
Strangely, that somewhere it has looked
    on me …
Your coming has my pardon, nay, my
    thanks:
For there is one who conies not.
*Hol.*                    Whom forgive,
As one to die!
*Straf.*        True, all die, and all need
Forgiveness: I forgive him from my soul
*Hol.* 'Tis a world's wonder: Strafford, you
    must die!
*Straf.* Sir, if your errand is to set me free
This heartless jest mars much. Ha! Tears
    in truth?
We'll end this! See this paper, warm –
    feel – warm
With lying next my heart! Whose hand
    is there?

---

* A house near Cheshunt in Hertfordshire

Whose promise? Read, and loud for God
   to hear!
'Strafford shall take no hurt' – read it, I
   say!
'In person, honour, nor estate' –
*Hol.*                 The King ...
*Straf.* I could unking him by a breath!
   You sit
Where Loudon sat, who came to
   prophesy
The certain end, and offer me Pym's
   grace
If I'd renounce the King: and I stood
   firm
On the King's faith. The King who
   lives ...
*Hol.*        To sign
The warrant for your death.
*Straf.*            'Put not your trust
'In princes, neither in the sons of men,
'In whom is no salvation!'
*Hol.*              Trust in God!
The scaffold is prepared: they wait for
   you:
He has consented. Cast the earth behind!
*Charles.* You would not see me, Strafford,
   at your foot!
It was wrung from me! Only, curse me
   not!
*Hol.* [*to* STRAFFORD]. As you hope grace
   and pardon in your need.
Be merciful to this most wretched man.
              [*Voices from within.*
      Verso la sera
      Di Primavera.
*Straf.* You'll be good to those children,
   sir? I know
You'll not believe her, even should the
   Queen
Think they take after one they rarely saw.
I had intended that my son should live
A stranger to these matters: but you are
So utterly deprived of friends! He too
Must serve you – will you not be good
   to him?
Or, stay, sir, do not promise – do not
   swear!

You, Hollis – do the best you can for me!
I've not a soul to trust to: Wandesford's
   dead,
And you've got Radcliffe safe, Laud's
   turn comes next:
I've found small time of late for my
   affairs,
But I trust any of you, Pym himself –
No one could hurt them: there's an
   infant, too.
These tedious cares! Your Majesty
   could spare them.
Nay – pardon me, my King! I had
   forgotten
Your education, trials, much temptation,
Some weakness: there escaped a
   peevish word –
'Tis gone: I bless you at the last. You
   know
All's between you and me: what has
   the world
To do with it? Farewell!
*Cha.* [*at the door*]. Balfour! Balfour!
            *Enter* BALFOUR.
The Parliament! – go to them: I grant all
Demands. Their sittings shall be
   permanent:
Tell them to keep their money if they
   will:
I'll come to them for every coat I wear
And every crust I eat: only I choose
To pardon Strafford. As the Queen
   shall choose!
– You never heard the People howl for
   blood,
Beside!
*Dal.* Your Majesty may hear them now:
The walls can hardly keep their
   murmurs out:
Please you retire!
*Cha.*       Take all the troops, Balfour!
*Bal.* There are some hundred thousand
   of the crowd.
*Cha.* Come with me, Strafford! You'll
   not fear, at least!
*Straf.* Balfour, say nothing to the world
   of this!

I charge you, as a dying man, forget
You gazed upon this agony of one …
Of one … or if … why you may say,
    Balfour,
The King was sorry: 'tis no shame in
    him:
Yes, you may say he even wept, Balfour,
And that I walked the lighter to the
    block
Because of it. I shall walk lightly, sir!
Earth fades, heaven breaks on me: I
    shall stand next
Before God's throne: the moment's
    close at hand
When man the first, last time, has leave
    to lay
His whole heart bare before its Maker,
    leave
To clear up the long error of a life
And choose one happiness for evermore.
With all mortality about me, Charles,
The sudden wreck, the dregs of violent
    death –
What if, despite the opening angel-song,
There penetrate one prayer for you? Be
    saved
Through me! Bear witness, no one
    could prevent
My death! Lead on! ere he awake – best,
    now!
All must be ready: did you say, Balfour,
The crowd began to murmur? They'll be
    kept
Too late for sermon at St Antholin's!
Now! But tread softly – children are at
    play
In the next room. Precede! I follow –
    *Enter* LADY CARLISLE, *with many*
        ATTENDANTS.
*Lady Car.*                            Me!
Follow me, Strafford, and be saved! The
    King?
[*To the* KING.] Well – as you ordered,
    they are ranged without,
The convoy … [*seeing the* KING's *state.*]
[*To* STRAFFORD.] You know all, then!
    Why, I thought

It looked best that the King should
    save you, – Charles
Alone; 'tis a shame that you should
    owe me aught.
Or no, not shame! Strafford, you'll not
    feel shame
At being saved by me?
*Hol.*                    All true! Oh Strafford,
She saves you! all her deed! this lady's
    deed!
And is the boat in readiness? You, friend,
Are Billingsley, no doubt. Speak to her,
    Strafford!
See how she trembles, waiting for your
    voice!
The world's to learn its bravest story yet.
*Lady Car.* Talk afterward! Long nights
    in France enough,
To sit beneath the vines and talk of home.
*Straf.* You love me, child? Ah, Strafford
    can be loved
As well as Vane! I could escape, then?
*Lady Car.*                            Haste!
Advance the torches, Bryan!
*Straf.*                    I will die.
They call me proud: but England had
    no right,
When she encountered me – her strength
    to mine –
To find the chosen foe a craven. Girl,
I fought her to the utterance, I fell,
I am hers now, and I will die. Beside,
The lookers-on! Eliot is all about
This place, with his most uncomplaining
    brow.
*Lady Car.*    Strafford!
*Straf.*                    I think if you
    could know how much
I love you, you would be repaid, my
    friend!
*Lady Car.* Then, for my sake!
*Straf.*                Even for your sweet sake,
I stay.
*Hol.* For *their* sake!
*Straf.*                To bequeath a stain?
Leave me! Girl, humour me and let me
    die!

*Lady Car.* Bid him escape – wake, King! Bid him escape!

*Straf.* True, I will go! Die, and forsake the King?
I'll not draw back from the last service.

*Lady Car.*                                                Strafford!

*Straf.* And, after all, what is disgrace to me?
Let us come, child! That it should end this way!
Lead then! but I feel strangely: it was not
To end this way.

*Lady Car.*          Lean – lean on me!

*Straf.*                                        My King!
Oh, had he trusted me – his friend of friends!

*Lady Car.* I can support him, Hollis!

*Straf.*                                Not this way!
This gate – I dreamed of it, this very gate.

*Lady Car.* It opens on the river: our good boat
Is moored below, our friends are there.

*Straf.*                                        The same:
Only with something ominous and dark,
Fatal, inevitable.

*Lady Car.*          Strafford! Strafford!

*Straf.* Not by this gate! I feel what will be there!
I dreamed of it, I tell you: touch it not!

*Lady Car.* To save the King, – Strafford, to save the King!

[*As* STRAFFORD *opens the door,* PYM *is discovered with* HAMPDEN, VANE, *etc.*
STRAFFORD *falls back;* PYM *follows slowly and confronts him.*

*Pym.* Have I done well? Speak, England! Whose sole sake
I still have laboured for, with disregard
To my own heart, – for whom my youth was made
Barren, my manhood waste, to offer up
Her sacrifice – this friend, this Wentworth here –
Who walked in youth with me, loved me, it may be,
And whom, for his forsaking England's cause,

I hunted by all means (trusting that she
Would sanctify all means) even to the block
Which waits for him. And saying this, I feel
No bitterer pang than first I felt, the hour
I swore that Wentworth might leave us, but I
Would never leave him: I do leave him now.
I render up my charge (be witness, God!)
To England who imposed it. I have done
Her bidding – poorly, wrongly, – it may be,
With ill effects – for I am weak, a man:
Still, I have done my best, my human best,
Not faltering for a moment. It is done.
And this said, if I say … yes, I will say
I never loved but one man – David not
More Jonathan! Even thus, I love him now:
And look for my chief portion in that world
Where great hearts led astray are turned again,
(Soon it may be, and, certes, will be soon:
My mission over, I shall not live long,) –
Ay, here I know I talk – I dare and must,
Of England, and her great reward, as all
I look for there; but in my inmost heart,
Believe, I think of stealing quite away
To walk once more with Wentworth – my youth's friend
Purged from all error, gloriously renewed,
And Eliot shall not blame us. Then indeed …
This is no meeting, Wentworth! Tears increase
Too hot. A thin mist – is it blood? – enwraps
The face I loved once. Then, the meeting be!

*Straf.* I have loved England too; we'll
    meet then, Pym.
As well die now! Youth is the only time
To think and to decide on a great course:
Manhood with action follows; but 'tis
    dreary,
To have to alter our whole life in age –
The time past, the strength gone! As well
    die now.
When we meet, Pym, I'd be set right –
    not now!
Best die. Then if there's any fault, fault
    too
Dies, smothered up. Poor grey old little
    Laud
May dream his dream out, of a perfect
    Church,
In some blind corner. And there's no
    one left.
I trust the King now wholly to you, Pym!
And yet, I know not: I shall not be there:
Friends fail – if he have any. And he's
    weak,
And loves the Queen, and … Oh, my
    fate is nothing –
Nothing! But not that awful head – not
    that!
*Pym.* If England shall declare such will
    to me …
*Straf.* Pym, you help England! I, that am
    to die,
What I must see! 'tis here – all here! My
    God,
Let me but gasp out, in one word of fire,
How thou wilt plague him, satiating
    hell!
What? England that you help, become
    through you
A green and putrefying charnel, left
Our children … some of us have
    children, Pym –

Some who, without that, still must ever
    wear
A darkened brow, an over-serious look,
And never properly be young! No word?
What if I curse you? Send a strong
    curse forth
Clothed from my heart, lapped round
    with horror till
She's fit with her white face to walk the
    world
Scaring kind natures from your cause
    and you –
Then to sit down with you at the
    board-head,
The gathering for prayer … O speak,
    but speak!
… Creep up, and quietly follow each
    one home,
You, you, you, be a nestling care for each
To sleep with, – hardly moaning in his
    dreams,
She gnaws so quietly, – till, lo he starts,
Gets off with half a heart eaten away!
Oh, shall you 'scape with less if she's
    my child?
You will not say a word – to me – to
    Him?
*Pym.* If England shall declare such will
    to me …
*Straf.* No, not for England now, not for
    Heaven now, –
See, Pym, for my sake, mine who kneel
    to you!
There, I will thank you for the death, my
    friend!
This is the meeting: let me love you well!
*Pym.* England, – I am thine own! Dost
    thou exact
That service? I obey thee to the end.
*Straf.* O God, I shall die first – I shall
    die first!

# SORDELLO

1840

To J. Milsand, of Dijon

Dear Friend, – Let the next poem be introduced by your name, therefore remembered along with one of the deepest of my affections, and so repay all trouble it ever cost me. I wrote it twenty-five years ago for only a few, counting even in these on somewhat more care about its subject than they really had. My own faults of expression were many; but with care for a man or book such would be surmounted, and without it what avails the faultlessness of either? I blame nobody, least of all myself,who did my best then and since; for I lately gave time and pains to turn my work into what the many might, – instead of what the few must, – like: but after all, I imagined another thing at first, and therefore leave as I find it. The historical decoration was purposely of no more importance than a background requires; and my stress lay on the incidents in the development of a soul: little else is worth study. I, at least, always thought so – you, with many known and unknown to me, think so – others may one day think so; and whether my attempt remain for them or not, I trust, though away and past it, to continue ever yours.

London: *June* 9, 1863. R. B.

## BOOK THE FIRST

Who will, may hear Sordello's story told:
His story? Who believes me shall behold
The man, pursue his fortunes to the end,
Like me: for as the friendless-people's
    friend
Spied from his hill-top once, despite the
    din
And dust of multitudes, Pentapolin
Named o' the Naked Arm,* I single out
Sordello, compassed murkily about
With ravage of six long sad hundred
    years.
Only believe me. Ye believe?

                Appears
Verona … Never, – I should warn you
    first, –
Of my own choice had this, if not the
    worst
Yet not the best expedient, served to tell
A story I could body forth so well
By making speak, myself kept out of
    view,
The very man as he was wont to do,
And leaving you to say the rest for him.

* See *Don Quixote*, Part 1, ch. 18.

Since, though I might be proud to see
    the dim
Abysmal past divide its hateful surge,
Letting of all men this one man emerge
Because it pleased me, yet, that moment
    past,
I should delight in watching first to last
His progress as you watch it, not a whit
More in the secret than yourselves who
    sit
Fresh-chapleted to listen. But it seems
Your setters-forth of unexampled themes,
Makers of quite new men, producing
    them,
Would best chalk broadly on each
    vesture's hem
The wearer's quality; or take their stand,
Motley on back and pointing-pole in
    hand,
Beside him. So, for once I face ye, friends,
Summoned together from the world's
    four ends,
Dropped down from heaven or cast up
    from hell,
To hear the story I propose to tell.
Confess now, poets know the dragnet's
    trick,

Catching the dead, if fate denies the
  quick,
And shaming her; 'tis not for fate to
  choose
Silence or song because she can refuse
Real eyes to glisten more, real hearts to
  ache
Less oft, real brows turn smoother for
  our sake:
I have experienced something of her
  spite;
But there's a realm wherein she has no
  right
And I have many lovers. Say, but few
Friends fate accords me? Here they are:
  now view
The host I muster! Many a lighted face
Foul with no vestige of the grave's
  disgrace;
What else should tempt them back to
  taste our air
Except to see how their successors fare?
My audience! and they sit, each ghostly
  man
Striving to look as living as he can,
Brother by breathing brother; thou art
  set,
Clear-witted critic, by … but I'll not fret
A wondrous soul of them, nor move
  death's spleen
Who loves not to unlock them. Friends!
  I mean
The living in good earnest – ye elect
Chiefly for love – suppose not I reject
Judicious praise, who contrary shall
  peep,
Some fit occasion, forth, for fear ye sleep,
To glean your bland approvals. Then,
  appear,
Verona! stay – thou, spirit, come not
  near
Now – not this time desert thy cloudy
  place
To scare me, thus employed, with that
  pure face!
I need not fear this audience, I make
  free

With them, but then this is no place
  for thee!
The thunder-phrase of the Athenian,*
  grown
Up out of memories of Marathon,
Would echo like his own sword's
  griding screech
Braying a Persian shield, – the silver
  speech
Of Sidney's self, the starry paladin,
Turn intense as a trumpet sounding in
The knights to tilt, – wert thou to hear!
  What heart
Have I to play my puppets, bear my part
Before these worthies?
                            Lo, the past is hurled
In twain: up-thrust, out-staggering on
  the world,
Subsiding into shape, a darkness rears
Its outline, kindles at the core, appears
Verona. 'Tis six hundred years and more
Since an event. The Second Friedrich
  wore
The purple, and the Third Honorius
  filled
The holy chair. That autumn eve was
  stilled:
A last remains of sunset dimly burned
O'er the far forests, like a torch-flame
  turned
By the wind back upon its bearer's hand
In one long flare of crimson; as a brand,
The woods beneath lay black. A single
  eye
From all Verona cared for the soft sky.
But, gathering in its ancient market-
  place,
Talked group with restless group; and
  not a face
But wrath made livid, for among them
  were
Death's staunch purveyors, such as have
  in care
To feast him. Fear had long since taken
  root

---

* Aeschylus

In every breast, and now these crushed
    its fruit,
The ripe hate, like a wine: to note the
    way
It worked while each grew drunk! Men
    grave and grey
Stood, with shut eyelids, rocking to and
    fro,
Letting the silent luxury trickle slow
About the hollows where a heart should
    be;
But the young gulped with a delirious
    glee
Some foretaste of their first debauch in
    blood
At the fierce news: for, be it understood,
Envoys apprised Verona that her prince
Count Richard of Saint Boniface, joined
    since
A year with Azzo, Este's Lord, to thrust
Taurello Salinguerra, prime in trust
With Ecelin Romano, from his seat
Ferrara, – over zealous in the feat
And stumbling on a peril unaware,
Was captive, trammelled in his proper
    snare,
They phrase it, taken by his own intrigue.
Immediate succour from the Lombard
    League
Of fifteen cities that affect the Pope,
For Azzo, therefore, and his fellow-hope
Of the Guelf cause, a glory overcast!
Men's faces, late agape, are now aghast.
'Prone is the purple pavis;* Este makes
'Mirth for the devil when he ùndertakes
'To play the Ecelin; as if it cost
'Merely your pushing-by to gain a post
'Like his! The patron tells ye, once for
    all,
'There be sound reasons that preferment
    fall
'On our beloved' …
        'Duke o' the Rood, why not?'
Shouted an Estian, 'grudge ye such a lot?

\* Shield

'The hill-cat boasts some cunning of
    her own,
'Some stealthy trick to better beasts
    unknown,
'That quick with prey enough her
    hunger blunts,
'And feeds her fat while gaunt the lion
    hunts.'
    'Taurello,' quoth an envoy, 'as in wane
'Dwelt at Ferrara. Like an osprey fain
'To fly but forced the earth his couch
    to make
'Far inland, till his friend the tempest
    wake,
'Waits he the Kaiser's coming; and as yet
'That fast friend sleeps, and he too sleeps:
    but let
'Only the billow freshen, and he snuffs
'The aroused hurricane ere it enroughs
'The sea it means to cross because of
    him.
'Sinketh the breeze? His hope-sick eye
    grows dim;
'Creep closer on the creature! Every day
'Strengthens the Pontiff; Ecelin, they say,
'Dozes now at Oliero, with dry lips
'Telling upon his perished finger-tips
'How many ancestors are to depose
'Ere he be Satan's Viceroy when the doze
'Deposits him in hell. So, Guelfs rebuilt
'Their houses; not a drop of blood was
    spilt
'When Cino Bocchimpane chanced to
    meet
'Buccio Virtù – God's wafer, and the
    street
'Is narrow! Tutti Santi, think, a-swarm
'With Ghibellins, and yet he took no
    harm!
'This could not last. Off Salinguerra went
'To Padua, Podestà, "with pure intent,"
'Said he, "my presence, judged the single
    bar
' "To permanent tranquillity, may jar
' "No longer". – so! his back is fairly
    turned?
'The pair of goodly palaces are burned,

'The gardens ravaged, and our Guelfs
    laugh, drunk
'A week with joy. The next, their laughter
    sunk
'In sobs of blood, for they found, some
    strange way,
'Old Salinguerra back again – I say,
'Old Salinguerra in the town once more
'Uprooting, overturning, flame before,
'Blood fetlock-high beneath him. Azzo
    fled;
'Who 'scaped the carnage followed; then
    the dead
'Were pushed aside from Salinguerra's
    throne,
'He ruled once more Ferrara, all alone,
'Till Azzo, stunned awhile, revived,
    would pounce
'Coupled with Boniface, like lynx and
    ounce,
'On the gorged bird. The burghers ground
    their teeth
'To see troop after troop encamp beneath
'I' the standing corn thick o'er the scanty
    patch
'It took so many patient months to
    snatch
'Out of the marsh; while just within
    their walls
'Men fed on men. At length Taurello
    calls
'A parley: "let the Count wind up the
    war!"
'Richard, light-hearted as a plunging star,
'Agrees to enter for the kindest ends
'Ferrara, flanked with fifty chosen friends,
'No horse-boy more, for fear your timid
    sort
'Should fly Ferrara at the bare report.
'Quietly through the town they rode,
    jog-jog;
' "Ten, twenty, thirty, – curse the
    catalogue
' "Of burnt Guelf houses! Strange,
    Taurello shows
' "Not the least sign of life" – whereat
    arose

'A general growl: "How? With his victors
    by?
' "I and my Veronese? My troops and I?
' "Receive us, was your word?" So jogged
    they on,
'Nor laughed their host too openly: once
    gone
'Into the trap! – '
                    Six hundred years ago!
Such the time's aspect and peculiar
    woe
(Yourselves may spell it yet in chronicles,
Albeit the worm, our busy brother, drills
His sprawling path through letters
    anciently
Made fine and large to suit some abbot's
    eye)
When the new Hohenstauffen dropped
    the mask,
Flung John of Brienne's favour from his
    casque,
Forswore crusading, had no mind to
    leave
Saint Peter's proxy leisure to retrieve
Losses to Otho and to Barbaross,
Or make the Alps less easy to recross;
And, thus confirming Pope Honorius'
    fear,
Was excommunicate that very year.
'The triple-bearded Teuton come to life!'
Groaned the Great League; and, arming
    for the strife,
Wide Lombardy, on tiptoe to begin,
Took up, as it was Guelf or Ghibellin,
Its cry: what cry?
                    'The Emperor to come!'
His crowd of feudatories, all and some,
That leapt down with a crash of swords,
    spears, shields,
One fighter on his fellow, to our fields,
Scattered anon, took station here and
    there,
And carried it, till now, with little care –
Cannot but cry for him; how else rebut
Us longer? – cliffs, an earthquake suffered
    jut
In the mid-sea, each domineering crest

Which nought save such another throe
    can wrest
From out (conceive) a certain chokeweed
    grown
Since o'er the waters, twine and tangle
    thrown
Too thick, too fast accumulating round,
Too sure to over-riot and confound
Ere long each brilliant islet with itself,
Unless a second shock save shoal and
    shelf,
Whirling the sea-drift wide: alas, the
    bruised
And sullen wreck! Sunlight to be diffused
For that! – sunlight, 'neath which, a
    scum at first,
The million fibres of our chokeweed
    nurst
Dispread themselves, mantling the
    troubled main,
And, shattered by those rocks, took hold
    again,
So kindly blazed it – that same blaze to
    brood
O'er every cluster of the multitude
Still hazarding new clasps, ties, filaments,
An emulous exchange of pulses, vents
Of nature into nature; till some growth
Unfancied yet, exuberantly clothe
A surface solid now, continuous, one:
'The Pope, for us the People, who begun
'The People, carries on the People thus,
'To keep that Kaiser off and dwell with
    us!'
See you?
        Or say, Two Principles that live
Each fitly by its Representative.
'Hill-cat' – who called him so? – the
    gracefullest
Adventurer, the ambiguous stranger-
    guest
Of Lombardy (sleek but that ruffling fur,
Those talons to their sheath!) whose
    velvet purr
Soothes jealous neighbours when a
    Saxon scout
– Arpo or Yoland, is it? – one without

A country or a name, presumes to couch
Beside their noblest; until men avouch
That, of all Houses in the Trevisan,
Conrad descries no fitter, rear or van,
Than Ecelo! They laughed as they
    enrolled
That name at Milan on the page of gold,
Godego's lord, – Ramon, Marostica,
Cartiglion, Bassano, Loria,
And every sheep-cote on the Suabian's
    fief!
No laughter when his son, 'the Lombard
    Chief'
Forsooth, as Barbarossa's path was bent
To Italy along the Vale of Trent,
Welcomed him at Roncaglia! Sadness
    now –
The hamlets nested on the Tyrol's brow,
The Asolan and Euganean hills,
The Rhetian and the Julian, sadness fills
Them all, for Ecelin vouchsafes to stay
Among and care about them; day by day
Choosing this pinnacle, the other spot,
A castle building to defend a cot,
A cot built for a castle to defend,
Nothing but castles, castles, nor an end
To boasts how mountain ridge may
    join with ridge
By sunken gallery and soaring bridge.
He takes, in brief, a figure that beseems
The griesliest nightmare of the Church's
    dreams,
– A Signory firm-rooted, unestranged
From its old interests, and nowise
    changed
By its new neighbourhood: perchance
    the vaunt
Of Otho, 'my own Este shall supplant
'Your Este,' come to pass. The sire led in
A son as cruel; and this Ecelin
Had sons, in turn, and daughters sly
    and tall
And curling and compliant; but for all
Romano (so they styled him) throve,
    that neck
Of his so pinched and white, that hungry
    cheek

Proved 'twas some fiend, not him, the
      man's-flesh went
To feed: whereas Romano's instrument,
Famous Taurello Salinguerra, sole
I' the world, a tree whose boughs were
      slipt the bole
Successively, why should not he shed
      blood
To further a design? Men understood
Living was pleasant to him as he wore
His careless surcoat, glanced some
      missive o'er,
Propped on his truncheon in the public
      way,
While his lord lifted writhen hands to
      pray,
Lost at Oliero's convent.
                              Hill-cats, face
Our Azzo, our Guelf Lion! Why disgrace
A worthiness conspicuous near and far
(Atii at Rome while free and consular,
Este at Padua who repulsed the Hun)
By trumpeting the Church's princely
      son?
– Styled Patron of Rovigo's Polesine,
Ancona's march, Ferrara's … ask, in
      fine,
Our chronicles, commenced when some
      old monk
Found it intolerable to be sunk
(Vexed to the quick by his revolting cell)
Quite out of summer while alive and
      well:
Ended when by his mat the Prior stood,
'Mid busy promptings of the brother-
      hood,
Striving to coax from his decrepit brains
The reason Father Porphyry took pains
To blot those ten lines out which used
      to stand
First on their charter drawn by Hilde-
      brand.
      The same night wears. Verona's rule
      of yore
Was vested in a certain Twenty-four;
And while within his palace these
      debate

Concerning Richard and Ferrara's fate,
Glide we by clapping doors, with sudden
      glare
Of cressets vented on the dark, nor care
For aught that's seen or heard until we
      shut
The smother in, the lights, all noises but
The carroch's booming: safe at last! Why
      strange
Such a recess should lurk behind a range
Of banquet rooms? Your finger – thus –
      you push
A spring, and the wall opens, would you
      rush
Upon the banqueters, select your prey,
Waiting (the slaughter-weapons in the
      way
Strewing this very bench) with sharpened
      ear
A preconcerted signal to appear;
Or if you simply crouch with beating
      heart,
Bearing in some voluptuous pageant
      part
To startle them. Nor mutes nor masquers
      now;
Nor any … does that one man sleep
      whose brow
The dying lamp-flame sinks and rises
      o'er?
What woman stood beside him? not the
      more
Is he unfastened from the earnest eyes
Because that arras fell between! Her wise
And lulling words are yet about the
      room,
Her presence wholly poured upon the
      gloom
Down even to her vesture's creeping
      stir.
And so reclines he, saturate with her,
Until an outcry from the square beneath
Pierces the charm: he springs up, glad to
      breathe,
Above the cunning element, and shakes
The stupor off as (look you) morning
      breaks

On the gay dress, and, near concealed
    by it,
The lean frame like a half-burnt taper, lit
Erst at some marriage-feast, then laid
    away
Till the Armenian bridegroom's dying
    day,
In his wool wedding-robe.
                     For he – for he,
Gate-vein of this hearts' blood of
    Lombardy,
(If I should falter now) – for he is thine!
Sordello, thy forerunner, Florentine!
A herald-star I know thou didst absorb
Relentless into the consummate orb
That scared it from its right to roll along
A sempiternal path with dance and song
Fulfilling its allotted period,
Serenest of the progeny of God –
Who yet resigns it not! His darling stoops
With no quenched lights, desponds
    with no blank troops
Of disenfranchised brilliances, for, blent
Utterly with thee, its shy element
Like thine upburneth prosperous and
    clear.
Still, what if I approach the august sphere
Named now with only one name,
    disentwine
That under-current soft and argentine
From its fierce mate in the majestic mass
Leavened as the sea whose fire was mixt
    with glass
In John's transcendent vision, – launch
    once more
That lustre? Dante, pacer of the shore
Where glutted hell disgorgeth filthiest
    gloom,
Unbitten by its whirring sulphur-
    spume –
Or whence the grieved and obscure
    waters slope
Into a darkness quieted by hope;
Plucker of amaranths grown beneath
    God's eye
In gracious twilights where his chosen
    lie, –

I would do this! If I should falter now!
    In Mantua territory half is slough,
Half pine-tree forest; maples, scarlet
    oaks
Breed o'er the river-beds; even Mincio
    chokes
With sand the summer through: but 'tis
    morass
In winter up to Mantua walls. There was,
Some thirty years before this evening's
    coil,
One spot reclaimed from the surrounding
    spoil,
Goito; just a castle built amid
A few low mountains; firs and larches
    hid
Their main defiles, and rings of vineyard
    bound
The rest. Some captured creature in a
    pound,
Whose artless wonder quite precludes
    distress,
Secure beside in its own loveliness,
So peered with airy head, below, above,
The castle at its toils, the lapwings love
To glean among at grape-time. Pass
    within.
A maze of corridors contrived for sin,
Dusk winding-stairs, dim galleries got
    past,
You gain the inmost chambers, gain at
    last
A maple-panelled room: that haze which
    seems
Floating about the panel, if there gleams
A sunbeam over it, will turn to gold
And in light-graven characters unfold
The Arab's wisdom everywhere; what
    shade
Marred them a moment, those slim
    pillars made,
Cut like a company of palms to prop
The roof, each kissing top entwined
    with top,
Leaning together; in the carver's mind
Some knot of bacchanals, flushed
    cheek combined

With straining forehead, shoulders
    purpled, hair
Diffused between, who in a goat-skin
    bear
A vintage; graceful sister-palms! But quick
To the main wonder, now. A vault, see;
    thick
Black shade about the ceiling, though
    fine slits
Across the buttress suffer light by fits
Upon a marvel in the midst. Nay,
    stoop –
A dullish grey-streaked cumbrous font,
    a group
Round it, – each side of it, where'er one
    sees, –
Upholds it; shrinking Caryatides
Of just-tinged marble like Eve's lilied
    flesh
Beneath her maker's finger when the
    fresh
First pulse of life shot brightening the
    snow.
The font's edge burthens every shoulder,
    so
They muse upon the ground, eyelids
    half closed;
Some, with meek arms behind their
    . backs disposed,
Some, crossed above their bosoms,
    some, to veil
Their eyes, some, propping chin and
    cheek so pale,
Some, hanging slack an utter helpless
    length
Dead as a buried vestal whose whole
    strength
Goes when the grate above shuts heavily.
So dwell these noiseless girls, patient to
    see,
Like priestesses because of sin impure
Penanced for ever, who resigned endure,
Having that once drunk sweetness to the
    dregs.
And every eve, Sordello's visit begs
Pardon for them: constant as eve he
    came

To sit beside each in her turn, the same
As one of them, a certain space: and awe
Made a great indistinctness till he saw
Sunset slant cheerful through the
    buttress-chinks,
Gold seven times globed; surely our
    maiden shrinks
And a smile stirs her as if one faint
    grain
Her load were lightened, one shade
    less the stain
Obscured her forehead, yet one more
    bead slipt
From off the rosary whereby the crypt
Keeps count of the contritions of its
    charge?
Then with a step more light, a heart
    more large,
He may depart, leave her and every one
To linger out the penance in mute stone.
Ah, but Sordello? 'Tis the tale I mean
To tell you.
                    In this castle may be seen,
On the hill-tops, or underneath the vines,
Or eastward by the mound of firs and
    pines
That shuts out Mantua, still in loneliness,
A slender boy in a loose page's dress,
Sordello: do but look on him awhile
Watching ('tis autumn) with an earnest
    smile
The noisy flock of thievish birds at work
Among the yellowing vineyards; see him
    lurk
('Tis winter with its sullenest of storms)
Beside that arras length of broidered
    forms,
On tiptoe, lifting in both hands a light
Which makes yon warrior's visage
    flutter bright
– Ecelo, dismal father of the brood,
And Ecelin, close to the girl he wooed,
Auria, and their Child, with all his wives
From Agnes to the Tuscan that survives,
Lady of the castle, Adelaide. His face
– Look, now he turns away! Yourselves
    shall trace

(The delicate nostril swerving wide and
    fine,
A sharp and restless lip, so well combine
With that calm brow) a soul fit to receive
Delight at every sense; you can believe
Sordello foremost in the regal class
Nature has broadly severed from her mass
Of men, and framed for pleasure, as she
    frames
Some happy lands, that have luxurious
    names,
For loose fertility; a footfall there
Suffices to upturn to the warm air
Half-germinating spices; mere decay
Produces richer life; and day by day
New pollen on the lily-petal grows,
And still more labyrinthine buds the
    rose.
You recognize at once the finer dress
Of flesh that amply lets in loveliness
At eye and ear, while round the rest is
    furled
(As though she would not trust them
    with her world)
A veil that shows a sky not near so blue,
And lets but half the sun look fervid
    through.
How can such love? – like souls on each
    full-fraught
Discovery brooding, blind at first to aught
Beyond its beauty, till exceeding love
Becomes an aching weight; and, to
    remove
A curse that haunts such natures – to
    preclude
Their finding out themselves can work
    no good
To what they love nor make it very blest
By their endeavour, – they are fain invest
The lifeless thing with life from their
    own soul,
Availing it to purpose, to control,
To dwell distinct and have peculiar joy
And separate interests that may employ
That beauty fitly, for its proper sake.
Nor rest they here; fresh births of
    beauty wake

Fresh homage, every grade of love is
    past,
With every mode of loveliness: then cast
Inferior idols off their borrowed crown
Before a coming glory. Up and down
Runs arrowy fire, while earthly forms
    combine
To throb the secret forth; a touch
    divine –
And the scaled eyeball owns the mystic
    rod;
Visibly through his garden walketh God.
So fare they. Now revert. One character
Denotes them through the progress and
    the stir, –
A need to blend with each external
    charm,
Bury themselves, the whole heart wide
    and warm, –
In something not themselves; they
    would belong
To what they worship – stronger and
    more strong
Thus prodigally fed – which gathers
    shape
And feature, soon imprisons past escape
The votary framed to love and to submit
Nor ask, as passionate he kneels to it,
Whence grew the idol's empery. So runs
A legend; light had birth ere moons and
    suns,
Flowing through space a river and alone,
Till chaos burst and blank the spheres
    were strown
Hither and thither, foundering and blind:
When into each of them rushed light –
    to find
Itself no place, foiled of its radiant chance.
Let such forego their just inheritance!
For there's a class that eagerly looks, too,
On beauty, but, unlike the gentler crew,
Proclaims each new revealment born a
    twin
With a distinctest consciousness within,
Referring still the quality, now first
Revealed, to their own soul – its instinct
    nursed

In silence, now remembered better,
    shown
More thoroughly, but not the less their
    own;
A dream come true; the special exercise
Of any special function that implies
The being fair, or good, or wise, or
    strong,
Dormant within their nature all along –
Whose fault? So, homage, other souls
    direct
Without, turns inward. 'How should
    this deject
'Thee, soul?' they murmur; 'wherefore
    strength be quelled
'Because, its trivial accidents withheld,
'Organs are missed that clog the world,
    inert,
'Wanting a will, to quicken and exert,
'Like thine – existence cannot satiate,
'Cannot surprise? Laugh thou at envious
    fate,
'Who, from earth's simplest combination
    stampt
'With individuality – uncrampt
'By living its faint elemental life,
'Dost soar to heaven's complexest
    essence, rife
'With grandeurs, unaffronted to the last,
'Equal to being all!'
                    In truth? Thou hast
Life, then – wilt challenge life for us. Our
    race
Is vindicated so, obtains its place
In thy ascent, the first of us; whom we
May follow, to the meanest, finally,
With our more bounded wills?
                            Ah, but to find
A certain mood enervate such a mind,
Counsel it slumber in the solitude
Thus reached nor, stooping, task for
    mankind's good
Its nature just as life and time accord
' – Too narrow an arena to reward
'Emprize – the world's occasion
    worthless since
'Not absolutely fitted to evince

'Its mastery!' Or if yet worse befall,
And a desire possess it to put all
That nature forth, forcing our straitened
    sphere
Contain it, – to display completely here
The mastery another life should learn,
Thrusting in time eternity's concern, –
So that Sordello …
                    Fool, who spied the mark
Of leprosy upon him, violet-dark
Already as he loiters? Born just now,
With the new century, beside the glow
And efflorescence out of barbarism;
Witness a Greek or two from the abysm
That stray through Florence-town with
    studious air,
Calming the chisel of that Pisan pair:
If Nicolo should carve a Christus yet!
While at Siena is Guidone set,
Forehead on hand; a painful birth must
    be
Matured ere Saint Eufemia's sacristy
Or transept gather fruits of one great
    gaze
At the moon: look you! The same orange
    haze, –
The same blue stripe round that – and,
    in the midst,
Thy spectral whiteness, Mother-maid,
    who didst
Pursue the dizzy painter!
                        Woe, then, worth
Any officious babble letting forth
The leprosy confirmed and ruinous
To spirit lodged in a contracted house!
Go back to the beginning, rather; blend
It gently with Sordello's life; the end
Is piteous, you may see, but much
    between
Pleasant enough. Meantime, some pyx
    to screen
The full-grown pest, some lid to shut
    upon
The goblin! So they found at Babylon,
(Colleagues, mad Lucius and sage
    Antonine)
Sacking the city, by Apollo's shrine,

In rummaging among the rarities,
A certain coffer; he who made the prize
Opened it greedily; and out there
    curled
Just such another plague, for half the
    world
Was stung. Crawl in then, hag, and
    couch asquat,
Keeping that blotchy bosom thick in
    spot
Until your time is ripe! The coffer-lid
Is fastened, and the coffer safely hid
Under the Loxian's* choicest gifts of
    gold.
    Who will may hear Sordello's story
    told,
And how he never could remember when
He dwelt not at Goito. Calmly, then,
About this secret lodge of Adelaide's
Glided his youth away; beyond the
    glades
On the fir-forest border, and the rim
Of the low range of mountain, was for
    him
No other world: but this appeared his
    own
To wander through at pleasure and alone.
The castle too seemed empty; far and
    wide
Might he disport; only the northern side
Lay under a mysterious interdict –
Slight, just enough remembered to
    restrict
His roaming to the corridors, the vault
Where those font-bearers expiate their
    fault,
The maple-chamber, and the little nooks
And nests, and breezy parapet that looks
Over the woods to Mantua: there he
    strolled.
Some foreign women-servants, very old,
Tended and crept about him – all his
    clue
To the world's business and embroiled
    ado

* Apollo (the bowman)

Distant a dozen hill-tops at the most.
And first a simple sense of life engrossed
Sordello in his drowsy Paradise;
The day's adventures for the day
    suffice –
Its constant tribute of perceptions strange,
With sleep and stir in healthy
    interchange,
Suffice, and leave him for the next at
    ease
Like the great palmer-worm that strips
    the trees,
Eats the life out of every luscious plant,
And, when September finds them sere
    or scant,
Puts forth two wondrous winglets, alters
    quite,
And hies him after unforeseen delight.
So fed Sordello, not a shard dissheathed;
As ever, round each new discovery,
    wreathed
Luxuriantly the fancies infantine
His admiration, bent on making fine
Its novel friend at any risk, would fling
In gay profusion forth: a ficklest king,
Confessed those minions! – eager to
    dispense
So much from his own stock of thought
    and sense
As might enable each to stand alone
And serve him for a fellow; with his own,
Joining the qualities that just before
Had graced some older favourite. Thus
    they wore
A fluctuating halo, yesterday
Set flicker and to-morrow filched away, –
Those upland objects each of separate
    name,
Each with an aspect never twice the
    same,
Waxing and waning as the new-born
    host
Of fancies, like a single night's hoar-
    frost,
Gave to familiar things a face grotesque;
Only, preserving through the mad
    burlesque

A grave regard. Conceive! the orpine
    patch
Blossoming earliest on the log-house
    thatch
The day those archers wound along the
    vines –
Related to the Chief that left their lines
To climb with clinking step the northern
    stair
Up to the solitary chambers where
Sordello never came. Thus thrall
    reached thrall:
He o'er-festooning every interval,
As the adventurous spider, making
    light
Of distance, shoots her threads from
    depth to height,
From barbican to battlement: so flung
Fantasies forth and in their centre swung
Our architect, – the breezy morning
    fresh
Above, and merry, – all his waving mesh
Laughing with lucid dew-drops
    rainbow-edged.
This world of ours by tacit pact is pledged
To laying such a spangled fabric low
Whether by gradual brush or galiant
    blow.
But its abundant will was baulked here:
    doubt
Rose tardily in one so fenced about
From most that nurtures judgment, –
    care and pain:
Judgment, that dull expedient we are
    fain,
Less favoured, to adopt betimes and
    force
Stead us, diverted from our natural course
Of joys – contrive some yet amid the
    dearth,
Vary and render them, it may be, Worth
Most we forego. Suppose Sordello hence
Selfish enough, without a moral sense
However feeble; what informed the boy
Others desired a portion in his joy?
Or say a ruthful chance broke woof and
    warp –

A heron's nest beat down by March
    winds sharp,
A fawn breathless beneath the precipice,
A bird with unsoiled breast and unfilmed
    eyes
Warm in the brake – could these undo
    the trance
Lapping Sordello? Not a circumstance
That makes for you, friend Naddo! Eat
    fern-seed
And peer beside us and report indeed
If (your word) 'genius'dawned with
    throes and stings
And the whole fiery catalogue, while
    springs,
Summers, and winters quietly came
    and went.
  Time put at length that period to
    content,
By right the world should have imposed:
    bereft
Of its good offices, Sordello, left
To study his companions, managed rip
Their fringe off, learn the true
    relationship,
Core with its crust, their nature with his
    own:
Amid his wild-wood sights he lived alone.
As if the poppy felt with him! Though he
Partook the poppy's red effrontery
Till Autumn spoiled their fleering quite
    with rain,
And, turbanless, a coarse brown rattling
    crane
Lay bare. That's gone: yet why renounce,
    for that,
His disenchanted tributaries – fiat
Perhaps, but scarce so utterly forlorn,
Their simple presence might not well be
    borne
Whose parley was a transport once:
    recall
The poppy's gifts, it flaunts you, after
    all,
A poppy: – why distrust the evidence
Of each soon satisfied and healthy
    sense?

The new-born judgment answered, 'little
    boots
'Beholding other creatures' attributes
'And having none!' or, say that it sufficed,
'Yet, could one but possess, oneself,'
    (enticed
Judgment) 'some special office!' Nought
    beside
Serves you? 'Well then, be somehow
    justified
'For this ignoble wish to circumscribe
'And concentrate, rather than swell, the
    tribe
'Of actual pleasures: what, now, from
    without
'Effects it? – proves, despite a lurking
    doubt,
'Mere sympathy sufficient, trouble spared?
'That, tasting joys by proxy thus, you
    fared
'The better for them?'Thus much craved
    his soul.
Alas, from the beginning love is whole
And true; if sure of nought beside, most
    sure
Of its own truth at least; nor may endure
A crowd to see its face, that cannot
    know
How hot the pulses throb its heart below:
While its own helplessness and utter
    want
Of means to worthily be ministrant
To what it worships, do but fan the more
Its flame, exalt the idol far before
Itself as it would have it ever be.
Souls like Sordello, on the contrary,
Coerced and put to shame, retaining
    will,
Care little, take mysterious comfort still,
But look forth tremblingly to ascertain
If others judge their claims not urged in
    vain,
And say for them their stifled thoughts
    aloud.
So, they must ever live before a crowd:
– 'Vanity,' Naddo tells you.
                  Whence contrive

A crowd, now? From these women just
    alive,
That archer-troop? Forth glided – not
    alone
Each painted warrior, every girl of stone,
Nor Adelaide (bent double o'er a scroll,
One maiden at her knees, that eve, his
    soul
Shook as he stumbled through the
    arras'd glooms
On them, for, 'mid quaint robes and
    weird perfumes,
Started the meagre Tuscan up, – her
    eyes,
The maiden's, also, bluer with surprise)
– But the entire out-world: whatever,
    scraps
And snatches, song and story, dreams
    perhaps,
Conceited the world's offices, and he
Had hitherto transferred to flower or
    tree,
Not counted a befitting heritage
Each, of its own right, singly to engage
Some man, no other, – such now dared
    to stand
Alone. Strength, wisdom, grace on every
    hand
Soon disengaged themselves, and he
    discerned
A sort of human life: at least, was turned
A stream of lifelike figures through his
    brain.
Lord, liegeman, valvassor and suzerain,
Ere he could choose, surrounded him;
    a stuff
To work his pleasure on; there, sure
    enough:
But as for gazing, what shall fix that
    gaze?
Are they to simply testify the ways
He who convoked them sends his soul
    along
With the cloud's thunder or a dove's
    brood-song?
– While they live each his life, boast
    each his own

Peculiar dower of bliss, stand each alone
In some one point where something
    dearest loved
Is easiest gained – far worthier to be
    proved
Than aught he envies in the forest-
    wights!
No simple and self-evident delights,
But mixed desires of unimagined range,
Contrasts or combinations, new and
    strange,
Irksome perhaps, yet plainly recognized
By this, the sudden company – loves
    prized
By those who are to prize his own amount
Of loves. Once care because such make
    account,
Allow that foreign recognitions stamp
The current value, and his crowd shall
    vamp
Him counterfeits enough; and so their
    print
Be on the piece, 'tis gold, attests the
    mint,
And 'good,' pronounce they whom his
    new appeal
Is made to: if their casual print conceal –
This arbitrary good of theirs o'ergloss
What he has lived without, nor felt the
    loss –
Qualities strange, ungainly, wearisome,
– What matter? So must speech expand
    the dumb
Part-sigh, part-smile with which Sordello,
    late
Whom no poor woodland-sights could
    satiate,
Betakes himself to study hungrily
Just what the puppets his crude phantasy
Supposes notablest, – popes, kings,
    priests, knights, –
May please to promulgate for appetites;
Accepting all their artificial joys
Not as he views them, but as he employs
Each shape to estimate the other's stock
Of attributes, whereon – a marshaled
    flock

Of authorized enjoyments – he may
    spend
Himself, be men, now, as he used to
    blend
With tree and flower – nay more
    entirely, else
'Twere mockery: for instance, 'How
    excels
'My life that chieftain's?'(who apprised
    the youth
Ecelin, here, becomes this month, in
    truth,
Imperial Vicar?) 'Turns he in his tent
'Remissly? Be it so – my head is bent
'Deliciously amid my girls to sleep.
'What if he stalks the Trentine-pass?
    Yon steep
'I climbed an hour ago with little toil:
'We are alike there. But can I, too, foil
'The Guelf's paid stabber, carelessly
    afford
'Saint Mark's a spectacle, the sleight o'
    the sword
'Baffling the treason in a moment?' Here
No rescue! Poppy he is none, but peer
To Ecelin, assuredly: his hand,
Fashioned no otherwise, should wield
    a brand
With Ecelin's success – try, now! He
    soon
Was satisfied, returned as to the moon
From earth; left each abortive boy's-
    attempt
For feats, from failure happily exempt,
In fancy at his beck. 'One day I will
'Accomplish it! Are they not older still
' – Not grown-up men and women? 'Tis
    beside
'Only a dream; and though I must abide
'With dreams now, I may find a thorough
    vent
'For all myself, acquire an instrument
'For acting what these people act; my
    soul
'Hunting a body out may gain its whole
'Desire some day!'How else express
    chagrin

And resignation, show the hope steal in
With which he let sink from an aching
    wrist
The rough-hewn ash-bow? Straight, a
    gold shaft hissed
Into the Syrian air, struck Malek down
Superbly! 'Crosses to the breach! God's
    Town
'Is gained him back!' Why bend rough
    ash-bows more?
    Thus lives he: if not careless as before,
Comforted: for one may anticipate,
Rehearse the future, be prepared when
    fate
Shall have prepared in turn real men
    whose names
Startle, real places of enormous fames,
Este abroad and Ecelin at home
To worship him, – Mantua, Verona,
    Rome
To witness it. Who grudges time so
    spent?
Rather test qualities to heart's content –
Summon them, thrice selected, near and
    far –
Compress the starriest into one star,
And grasp the whole at once!
                The pageant thinned
Accordingly; from rank to rank, like
    wind
His spirit passed to winnow and divide;
Back fell the simpler phantasms; every
    side
The strong clave to the wise; with either
    classed
The beauteous; so, till two or three
    amassed
Mankind's beseemingnesses, and reduced
Themselves eventually, – graces loosed,
Strengths lavished, – all to heighten up
    One Shape
Whose potency no creature should
    escape.
Can it be Friedrich of the bowmen's
    talk?
Surely that grape-juice, bubbling at the
    stalk,

Is some grey scorching Saracenic wine
The Kaiser quaffs with the Miramoline* –
Those swarthy hazel-clusters, seamed
    and chapped,
Or filberts russet-sheathed and velvet-
    capped,
Are dates plucked from the bough John
    Brienne sent
To keep in mind his sluggish armament
Of Canaan: – Friedrich's, all the pomp
    and fierce
Demeanour! But harsh sounds and
    sights transpierce
So rarely the serene cloud where he
    dwells
Whose looks enjoin, whose lightest
    words are spells
On the obdurate! That right arm indeed
Has thunder for its slave; but where's
    the need
Of thunder if the stricken multitude
Hearkens, arrested in its angriest mood,
While songs go up exulting, then
    dispread,
Dispart, disperse, lingering overhead
Like an escape of angels? 'Tis the tune,
Nor much unlike the words his women
    croon
Smilingly, colourless and faint-designed
Each, as a worn-out queen's face some
    remind
Of her extreme youth's love-tales.
        'Eglamor
'Made that!' Half minstrel and half
    emperor,
What but ill objects vexed him? Such
    he slew.
The kinder sort were easy to subdue
By those ambrosial glances, dulcet tones;
And these a gracious hand advanced to
    thrones
Beneath him. Wherefore twist and
    torture this,
Striving to name afresh the antique
    bliss,

---

* *Emir al Maromenim*, Prince of the Faithful

Instead of saying, neither less nor more,
He had discovered, as our world before,
Apollo? That shall be the name; nor bid
Me rag by rag expose how patchwork
    hid
The youth – what thefts of every clime
    and day
Contributed to purfle the array
He climbed with (June at deep) some
    close ravine
Mid clatter of its million pebbles sheen,
Over which, singing soft, the runnel
    slipped
Elate with rains: into whose streamlet
    dipped
He foot, yet trod, you thought, with
    unwet sock –
Though really on the stubs of living rock
Ages ago it crenelled; vines for roof,
Lindens for wall; before him, aye aloof,
Flittered in the cool some azure damselfly,
Born of the simmering quiet, there to
    die.
Emerging whence, Apollo still, he spied
Mighty descents of forest; multiplied
Tuft on tuft, here, the frolic myrtle-trees,
There gendered the grave maple stocks
    at ease.
And, proud of its observer, straight the
    wood
Tried old surprises on him; black it
    stood
A sudden barrier ('twas a cloud passed
    o'er)
So dead and dense, the tiniest brute no
    more
Must pass; yet presently (the cloud
    dispatched)
Each clump, behold, was glistering
    detached
A shrub, oak-boles shrunk into ilex
    stems!
Yet could not he denounce the stratagems
He saw thro', till, hours thence, aloft
    would hang
White summer-lightnings; as it sank
    and sprang

To measure, that whole palpitating breast
Of heaven, 'twas Apollo, nature prest
At eve to worship.
                    Time stole: by degrees
The Pythons perish off; his votaries
Sink to respectful distance; songs redeem
Their pains, but briefer; their dismissals
    seem
Emphatic; only girls are very slow
To disappear – his Delians! Some that
    glow
O'the instant, more with earlier loves to
    wrench
Away, reserves to quell, disdains to
    quench;
Alike in one material circumstance –
All soon or late adore Apollo! Glance
The bevy through, divine Apollo's choice,
His Daphne! 'We secure Count Richard's
    voice
'In Este's counsels, good for Este's ends
'As our Taurello,'say his faded friends,
'By granting him our Palma!' – the sole
    child
They mean, of Agnes Este who beguiled
Ecelin, years before this Adelaide
Wedded and turned him wicked: 'but
    the maid
'Rejects his suit,' those sleepy women
    boast.
She, scorning all beside, deserves the
    most
Sordello: so, conspicuous in his world
Of dreams sat Palma. How the tresses
    curled
Into a sumptuous swell of gold and
    wound
About her like a glory! even the ground
Was bright as with spilt sunbeams;
    breathe not, breathe
Not! – poised, see, one leg doubled
    underneath,
Its small foot buried in the dimpling
    snow,
Rests, but the other, listlessly below,
O'er the couch-side swings feeling for
    cool air.

The vein-streaks swollen a richer violet
     where
The languid blood lies heavily; yet calm
On her slight prop, each flat and out-
     spread palm,
As but suspended in the act to rise
By consciousness of beauty, whence her
     eyes
Turn with so frank a triumph, for she
     meets
Apollo's gaze in the pine glooms.
                              Time fleets:
That's worst! Because the pre-appointed
     age
Approaches. Fate is tardy with the stage
And crowd she promised. Lean he grows
     and pale,
Though restlessly at rest. Hardly avail
Fancies to soothe him. Time steals, yet
     alone
He tarries here! The earnest smile is
     gone.
How long this might continue matters
     not;
– For ever, possibly; since to the spot
None come: our lingering Taurello
     quits
Mantua at last, and light our lady flits
Back to her place disburthened of a care.
Strange – to be constant here if he is
     there!
Is it distrust? Oh, never! for they both
Goad Ecelin alike, Romano's growth
Is daily manifest, with Azzo dumb
And Richard wavering: let but
     Friedrich come,
Find matter for the minstrelsy's report
– Lured from the Isle and its young
     Kaiser's court
To sing us a Messina morning up,
And, double rillet of a drinking cup,
Sparkle along to ease the land of drouth,
Northward to Provence that, and thus
     far south
The other! What a method to apprise
Neighbours of births, espousals,
     obsequies,

Which in their very tongue the
     Troubadour
Records! and his performance makes a
     tour,
For Trouveres bear the miracle about,
Explain its cunning to the vulgar rout,
Until the Formidable House is famed
Over the country – as Taurello aimed,
Who introduced, although the rest
     adopt,
The novelty. Such games, her absence
     stopped,
Begin afresh now Adelaide, recluse
No longer, in the light of day pursues
Her plans at Mantua: whence an accident
Which, breaking on Sordello's mixed
     content
Opened, like any flash that cures the
     blind,
The veritable business of mankind.

### BOOK THE SECOND

The woods were long austere with snow:
     at last
Pink leaflets budded on the beech, and
     fast
Larches, scattered through pine-tree
     solitudes,
Brightened, 'as in the slumbrous heart
     o' the woods
'Our buried year, a witch, grew young
     again
'To placid incantations, and that stain
'About were from her cauldron, green
     smoke blent
'With those black pines' – so Eglamor
     gave vent
To a chance fancy. Whence a just rebuke
From his companion; brother Naddo
     shook
The solemnest of brows: 'Beware,'he
     said,
'Of setting up conceits in nature's stead!'
Forth wandered our Sordello. Nought so
     sure
As that to-day's adventure will secure

Palma, the visioned lady – only pass
O'er yon damp mound and its exhausted
    grass,
Under that brake where sundawn feeds
    the stalks
Of withered fern with gold, into those
    walks
Of pine and take her! Buoyantly he
    went.
Again his stooping forehead was besprent
With dew-drops from the skirting ferns.
    Then wide
Opened the great morass, shot every
    side
With flashing water through and through;
    a-shine,
Thick-steaming, all-alive. Whose shape
    divine,
Quivered i' the farthest rainbow-vapour,
    glanced
Athwart the flying herons? He advanced,
But warily; though Mincio leaped no
    more,
Each foot-fall burst up in the marish-
    floor
A diamond jet: and if he stopped to pick
Rose-lichen, or molest the leeches quick,
And circling blood-worms, minnow,
    newt or loach,
A sudden pond would silently encroach
This way and that. On Palma passed.
    The verge
Of a new wood was gained. She will
    emerge
Flushed, now, and panting, – crowds
    to see, – will own
She loves him – Boniface to hear, to
    groan,
To leave his suit! One screen of pine
    trees still
Opposes: but – the startling spectacle –
Mantua, this time! Under the walls – a
    crowd
Indeed, real men and women, gay and
    loud
Round a pavilion. How he stood!
              In truth

No prophecy had come to pass: his
    youth
In its prime now – and where was
    homage poured
Upon Sordello? – born to be adored,
And suddenly discovered weak, scarce
    made
To cope with any, cast into the shade
By this and this. Yet something seemed
    to prick
And tingle in his blood; a sleight – a
    trick –
And much would be explained. It went
    for nought –
The best of their endowments were ill
    bought
With his identity: nay, the conceit,
That this day's roving led to Palma's
    feet
Was not so vain – list! The word, 'Palma!'
    Steal
Aside, and die, Sordello; this is real,
And this – abjure!
What next? The curtains see
Dividing! She is there; and presently
He will be there – the proper You, at
    length –
In your own cherished dress of grace
    and strength:
Most like, the very Boniface!.
                  Not so.
It was a showy man advanced; but though
A glad cry welcomed him, then every
    sound
Sank and the crowd disposed themselves
    around,
– 'This is not he,' Sordello felt; while,
    'Place
'For the best Troubadour of Boniface!'
Hollaed the Jongleurs, – 'Eglamor, whose
    lay
'Concludes his patron's Court of Love
    today!'
Obsequious Naddo strung the master's
    lute
With the new lute-string, 'Elys,' named
    to suit

The song: he stealthily at watch, the
    while,
Biting his lip to keep down a great smile
Of pride: then up he struck. Sordello's
    brain
Swam; for he knew a sometime deed
    again;
So, could supply each foolish gap and
    chasm
The minstrel left in his enthusiasm,
Mistaking its true version – was the tale
Not of Apollo? Only, what avail
Luring her down, that Elys an he pleased,
If the man dared no further? Has he
    ceased?
And, lo, the people's frank applause
    half done,
Sordello was beside him, had begun
(Spite of indignant twitchings from his
    friend
The Trouvere) the true lay with the true
    end,
Taking the other's names and time and
    place
For his. On flew the song, a giddy race,
After the flying story; word made leap
Out word, rhyme – rhyme; the lay could
    barely keep
Pace with the action visibly rushing past:
Both ended. Back fell Naddo more aghast
Than some Egyptian from the harassed
    bull
That wheeled abrupt and, bellowing,
    fronted full
His plague, who spied a scarab 'neath
    the tongue,
And found 'twas Apis' flank his hasty
    prong
Insulted. But the people – but the cries,
The crowding round, and proffering
    the prize!
– For he had gained some prize. He
    seemed to shrink
Into a sleepy cloud, just at whose brink
One sight withheld him. There sat
    Adelaide,
Silent; but at her knees the very maid

Of the North Chamber, her red lips as
    rich,
The same pure fleecy hair; one weft of
    which,
Golden and great, quite touched his
    cheek as o'er
She leant, speaking some six words and
    no more.
He answered something, anything; and
    she
Unbound a scarf and laid it heavily
Upon him, her neck's warmth and all.
    Again
Moved the arrested magic; in his brain
Noises grew, and a light that turned to
    glare,
And greater glare, until the intense flare
Engulfed him, shut the whole scene
    from his sense.
And when he woke 'twas many a
    furlong thence,
At home; the sun shining his ruddy
    wont;
The customary birds'-chirp; but his
    front
Was crowned – was crowned! Her
    scented scarf around
His neck! Whose gorgeous vesture
    heaps the ground?
A prize? He turned, and peeringly on
    him
Brooded the women-faces, kind and dim,
Ready to talk – 'The Jongleurs in a troop
'Had brought him back, Naddo and
    Squarcialupe
'And Tagliafer; how strange! a childhood
    spent
'In taking, well for him, so brave a bent!
'Since Eglamor,'they heard, 'was dead
    with spite,
'And Palma chose him for her minstrel.'
                                        Light
Sordello rose – to think, now; hitherto
He had perceived. Sure, a discovery grew
Out of it all! Best live from first to last
The transport o'er again. A week he
    passed,

Sucking the sweet out of each circum-
    stance,
From the bard's outbreak to the luscious
    trance
Bounding his own achievement. Strange!
    A man
Recounted an adventure, but began
Imperfectly; his own task was to fill
The frame-work up, sing well what he
    sung ill,
Supply the necessary points, set loose
As many incidents of little use
– More imbecile the other, not to see
Their relative importance clear as he!
But, for a special pleasure in the act
Of singing – had he ever turned, in fact,
From Elys, to sing Elys? – from each fit
Of rapture to contrive a song of it?
True, this snatch or the other seemed
    to wind
Into a treasure, helped himself to find
A beauty in himself; for, see, he soared
By means of that mere snatch, to many
    a hoard
Of fancies; as some falling cone bears soft
The eye along the fir-tree-spire, aloft
To a dove's nest. Then, how divine the
    cause
Why such performance should exact
    applause
From men, if they had fancies too? Did
    fate
Decree they found a beauty separate
In the poor snatch itself? – 'Take Elys,
    there,
' – "Her head that's sharp and perfect
    like a pear,
' "So close and smooth are laid the few
    fine locks
' "Coloured like honey oozed from
    topmost rocks
' "Sun-blanched the livelong summer"
    – if they heard
'Just those two rhymes, assented at my
    word,
'And loved them as I love them who
    have run

'These fingers through those pale locks,
    let the sun
'Into the white cool skin – who first
    could clutch,
'Then praise – I needs must be a god to
    such.
'Or what if some, above themselves, and
    yet
'Beneath me, like their Eglamor, have
    set
'An impress on our gift? So, men believe
'And worship what they know not, nor
    receive
'Delight from. Have they fancies – slow,
    perchance,
'Not at their beck, which indistinctly
    glance
'Until, by song, each floating part be
    linked
'To each, and all grow palpable, distinct!'
He pondered this.
Meanwhile, sounds low and drear
Stole on him, and a noise of footsteps,
    near
And nearer, while the underwood was
    pushed
Aside, the larches grazed, the dead
    leaves crushed
At the approach of men. The wind
    seemed laid;
Only, the trees shrunk slightly and a
    shade
Came o'er the sky although 'twas midday
    yet:
You saw each half-shut downcast floweret
Flutter – 'a Roman bride, when they'd
    dispart
'Her unbound tresses with the Sabine
    dart,
'Holding that famous rape in memory
    still,
'Felt creep into her curls the iron chill,
'And looked thus,' Eglamor would say
    – indeed
'Tis Eglamor, no other, these precede
Home hither in the woods. ' 'Twere
    surely sweet

'Far from the scene of one's forlorn
    defeat
'To sleep!' judged Naddo, who in person
    led
Jongleurs and Trouveres, chanting at
    their head,
A scanty company; for, sooth to say,
Our beaten Troubadour had seen his
    day.
Old worshippers were something
    shamed, old friends
Nigh weary; still the death proposed
    amends.
'Let us but get them safely through my
    song
'And home again!'quoth Naddo.
                              All along,
This man (they rest the bier upon the
    sand)
– This calm corpse with the loose flowers
    in his hand,
Eglamor, lived Sordello's opposite.
For him indeed was Naddo's notion
    right,
And verse a temple-worship vague and
    vast,
A ceremony that withdrew the last
Opposing bolt, looped back the lingering
    veil
Which hid the holy place: should one
    so frail
Stand there without such effort? or
    repine
If much was blank, uncertain at the
    shrine
He knelt before, till, soothed by many a
    rite,
The power responded, and some sound
    or sight
Grew up, his own forever, to be fixed,
In rhyme, the beautiful, forever! – mixed
With his own life, unloosed when he
    should please,
Having it safe at hand, ready to ease
All pain, remove all trouble; every time
He loosed that fancy from its bonds of
    rhyme

(Like Perseus when he loosed his naked
    love)
Faltering; so distinct and far above
Himself, these fancies! He, no genius
    rare,
Transfiguring in fire or wave or air
At will, but a poor gnome that, cloistered
    up
In some rock-chamber with his agate
    cup,
His topaz rod, his seed-pearl, in these
    few
And their arrangement finds enough to
    do
For his best art. Then, how he loved
    that art!
The calling marking him a man apart
From men – one not to care, take
    counsel for
Cold hearts, comfortless faces –
    (Eglamor
Was neediest of his tribe) – since verse,
    the gift,
Was his, and men, the whole of them,
    must shift
Without it, e'en content themselves
    with wealth
And pomp and power, snatching a life
    by stealth.
So, Eglamor was not without his pride!
The sorriest bat which cowers through-
    out noontide
While other birds are jocund, has one
    time
When moon and stars are blinded, and
    the prime
Of earth is his to claim, nor find a peer;
And Eglamor was noblest poet here –
He well knew, 'mid those April woods
    he cast
Conceits upon in plenty as he passed,
That Naddo might suppose him not to
    think
Entirely on the coming triumph: wink
At the one weakness! 'Twas a fervid
    child,
That song of his; no brother of the guild

Had e'er conceived its like. The rest you
    know,
The exaltation and the overthrow:
Our poet lost his purpose, lost his rank,
His life – to that it came. Yet envy sank
Within him, as he heard Sordello out,
And, for the first time, shouted – tried
    to shout
Like others, not from any zeal to show
Pleasure that way: the common sort did
    so,
What else was Eglamor? who, bending
    down
As they, placed his beneath Sordello's
    crown,
Printed a kiss on his successor's hand,
Left one great tear on it, then joined his
    band
– In time; for some were watching at the
    door:
Who knows what envy may effect? 'Give
    o'er,
'Nor charm his lips, nor craze him!'(here
    one spied
And disengaged the withered crown) –
    'Beside
'His crown? How prompt and clear
    those verses rang
'To answer yours! nay, sing them!' And
    he sang
Them calmly. Home he went; friends
    used to wait
His coming, zealous to congratulate;
But, to a man – so quickly runs report –
Could do no less than leave him, and
    escort
His rival. That eve, then, bred many a
    thought:
What must his future life be? was he
    brought
So low, who stood so lofty this Spring
    morn?
At length he said, 'Best sleep now with
    my scorn,
'And by to-morrow I devise some plain
'Expedient!' So, he slept, nor woke
    again.

They found as much, those friends,
    when they returned
O'erflowing with the marvels they had
    learned
About Sordello's paradise, his roves
Among the hills and vales and plains
    and groves,
Wherein, no doubt, this lay was
    roughly cast,
Polished by slow degrees, completed
    last
To Eglamor's discomfiture and death.
    Such form the chanters now, and,
    out of breath,
They lay the beaten man in his abode,
Naddo reciting that same luckless ode,
Doleful to hear. Sordello could explore
By means of it, however, one step more
In joy; and, mastering the round at
    length,
Learnt how to live in weakness as in
    strength,
When from his covert forth he stood,
    addressed
Eglamor, bade the tender ferns invest,
Primæval pines o'ercanopy his couch,
And, most of all, his fame – (shall I
    avouch
Eglamor heard it, dead though he
    might look,
And laughed as from his brow Sordello
    took
The crown, and laid on the bard's
    breast, and said
It was a crown, now, fit for poet's
    head?)
– Continue. Nor the prayer quite
    fruitless fell.
A plant they have, yielding a three-
    leaved bell*
Which whitens at the heart ere noon,
    and ails
Till evening; evening gives it to her
    gales
To clear away with such forgotten things

---

* St Bruno's lily, the *Anthericum Liliastrum*.

As are an eyesore to the morn: this
   brings
Him to their mind, and bears his very
   name.
   So much for Eglamor. My own month
   came;
'Twas a sunrise of blossoming and May.
Beneath a flowering laurel thicket lay
Sordello; each new sprinkle of white
   stars
That smell fainter of wine than Massic
   jars
Dug up at Baiæ, when the south wind
   shed
The ripest, made him happier; filleted
And robed the same, only a lute beside
Lay on the turf. Before him far and wide
The country stretched: Goito slept behind
– The castle and its covert, which
   confined
Him with his hopes and fears; so fain of
   old
To leave the story of his birth untold.
At intervals, 'spite the fantastic glow
Of his Apollo-life, a certain low
And wretched whisper, winding
   through the bliss,
Admonished, no such fortune could be
   his,
All was quite false and sure to fade one
   day:
The closelier drew he round him his
   array
Of brilliance to expel the truth. But
   when
A reason for his difference from men
Surprised him at the grave, he took no
   rest
While aught of that old life, superbly
   dressed
Down to its meanest incident, remained
A mystery: alas, they soon explained
Away Apollo! and the tale amounts
To this: when at Vicenza both her
   counts
Banished the Vivaresi kith and kin,
Those Maltraversi hung on Ecelin,

Reviled him as he followed; he for spite
Must fire their quarter, though that
   self-same night
Among the flames young Ecelin was
   born
Of Adelaide, there too, and barely torn
From the roused populace hard on the
   rear,
By a poor archer when his chieftain's
   fear
Grew high; into the thick Elcorte leapt,
Saved her, and died; no creature left
   except
His child to thank. And when the full
   escape
Was known – how men impaled from
   chine to nape
Unlucky Prata, all to pieces spurned
Bishop Pistore's concubines, and burned
Taurello's entire household, flesh and
   fell,
Missing the sweeter prey – such courage
   well
Might claim reward. The orphan, ever
   since,
Sordello, had been nurtured by his prince
Within a blind retreat where Adelaide –
(For, once this notable discovery made,
The past at every point was understood)
– Might harbour easily when times were
   rude,
When Azzo schemed for Palma, to
   retrieve
That pledge of Agnes Este – loth to leave
Mantua unguarded with a vigilant eye,
While there Taurello bode
   ambiguously –
He who could have no motive now to
   moil
For his own fortunes since their utter
   spoil –
As it were worth while yet (went the
   report)
To disengage himself from her. In short,
Apollo vanished; a mean youth, just
   named
His lady's minstrel, was to be proclaimed

– How shall I phrase it? – Monarch of
    the World!
For, on the day when that array was
    furled
Forever, and in place of one a slave
To longings, wild indeed, but longings
    save
In dreams as wild, suppressed – one
    daring not
Assume the mastery such dreams allot,
Until a magical equipment, strength,
Grace, wisdom, decked him too, – he
    chose at length,
Content with unproved wits and failing
    frame,
In virtue of his simple will, to claim
That mastery, no less – to do his best
With means so limited, and let the rest
Go by, – the seal was set: never again
Sordello could in his own sight remain
One of the many, one with hopes and
    cares
And interests nowise distinct from
    theirs,
Only peculiar in a thriveless store
Of fancies, which were fancies and no
    more;
Never again for him and for the crowd
A common law was challenged and
    allowed
If calmly reasoned of, howe'er denied
By a mad impulse nothing justified
Short of Apollo's presence. The divorce
Is clear: why needs Sordello square his
    course
By any known example? Men no more
Compete with him than tree and flower
    before.
Himself, inactive, yet is greater far
Than such as act, each stooping to his
    star,
Acquiring thence his function; he has
    gained
The same result with meaner mortals
    trained
To strength or beauty, moulded to
    express

Each the idea that rules him; since no
    less
He comprehends that function, but
    can still
Embrace the others, take of might his
    fill
With Richard as of grace with Palma, mix
Their qualities, or for a moment fix
On one; abiding free meantime,
    uncramped
By any partial organ, never stamped
Strong, and to strength turning all
    energies –
Wise, and restricted to becoming wise –
That is, he loves not, nor possesses One
Idea that, star-like over, lures him on
To its exclusive purpose. 'Fortunate!
'This flesh of mine ne'er strove to
    emulate
'A soul so various – took no casual
    mould
'Of the first fancy and, contracted, cold,
'Clogged her forever – soul averse to
    change
'As flesh: whereas flesh leaves soul free
    to range,
'Remains itself a blank, cast into shade,
'Encumbers little, if it cannot aid.
'So, range, free soul! – who, by self-
    consciousness,
'The last drop of all beauty dost
    express –
'The grace of seeing grace, a quintessence
'For thee: while for the world, that can
    dispense
'Wonder on men who, themselves,
    wonder – make
'A shift to love at second-hand, and
    take
'For idols those who do but idolize,
'Themselves, – the world that counts
    men strong or wise,
'Who, themselves, court strength,
    wisdom, – it shall bow
'Surely in unexampled worship now,
'Discerning me!' –
             (Dear monarch, I beseech,

Notice how lamentably wide a breach
Is here: discovering this, discover too
What our poor world has possibly to do
With it! As pigmy natures as you
        please –
So much the better for you; take your
        ease,
Look on, and laugh; style yourself God
        alone;
Strangle some day with a cross olive-
        stone!
All that is right enough: but why want
        us
To know that you yourself know thus
        and thus?)
'The world shall bow to me conceiving
        all
'Man's life, who see its blisses, great and
        small,
'Afar – not tasting any; no machine
'To exercise my utmost will is mine:
'Be mine mere consciousness! Let men
        perceive
'What I could do, a mastery believe,
'Asserted and established to the throng
'By their selected evidence of song
'Which now shall prove, whate'er they
        are, or seek
'To be, I am – whose words, not actions
        speak,
'Who change no standards of perfection,
        vex
'With no strange forms created to perplex
'But just perform their bidding and no
        more,
'At their own satiating-point give o'er,
'While each shall love in me the love
        that leads
'His soul to power's perfection.' Song,
        not deeds,
(For we get tired) was chosen. Fate
        would brook
Mankind no other organ; he would look
For not another channel to dispense
His own volition by, receive men's
        sense
Of its supremacy – would live content,

Obstructed else, with merely verse for
        vent.
Nor should, for instance, strength an
        outlet seek
And, striving, be admired: nor grace
        be-speak
Wonder, displayed in gracious
        attitudes:
Nor wisdom, poured forth, change
        unseemly moods;
But he would give and take on song's
        one point.
Like some huge throbbing stone that,
        poised a-joint,
Sounds, to affect on its basaltic bed,
Must sue in just one accent; tempests
        shed
Thunder, and raves the windstorm: only
        let
That key by any little noise be set –
The far benighted hunter's halloo pitch
On that, the hungry curlew chance to
        scritch
Or serpent hiss it, rustling through the
        rift,
However loud, however low – all lift
The groaning monster, stricken to the
        heart.
    Lo ye, the world's concernment, for
        its part,
And this, for his, will hardly interfere!
Its businesses in blood and blaze this
        year
But wile the hour away – a pastime
        slight
Till he shall step upon the platform:
        right!
And, now thus much is settled, cast in
        rough,
Proved feasible, he counselled! thought
        enough, –
Slumber, Sordello! any day will serve:
Were it a less digested plan! how swerve
To-morrow? Meanwhile eat these sun-
        dried grapes,
And watch the soaring hawk there! Life
        escapes

Merrily thus.
           He thoroughly read o'er
His truchman Naddo's missive six
    times more,
Praying him visit Mantua and supply
A famished world.
       The evening star was high
When he reached Mantua, but his fame
    arrived
Before him: friends applauded, foes
    connived,
And Naddo looked an angel, and the
    rest
Angels, and all these angels would be
    blest
Supremely by a song – the thrice-
    renowned
Goito-manufacture. Then he found
(Casting about to satisfy the crowd)
That happy vehicle, so late allowed,
A sore annoyance; 'twas the song's
    effect
He cared for, scarce the song itself:
    reflect!
In the past life, what might be singing's
    use?
Just to delight his Delians, whose profuse
Praise, not the toilsome process which
    procured
That praise, enticed Apollo: dreams
    abjured,
No overleaping means for ends – take
    both
For granted or take neither! I am loth
To say the rhymes at last were Eglamor's;
But Naddo, chuckling, bade competitors
Go pine; 'the master certes meant to
    waste
'No effort, cautiously had probed the
    taste
'He'd please anon: true bard, in short, –
    disturb
'His title if they could; nor spur nor
    curb,
'Fancy nor reason, wanting in him;
    whence
'The staple of his verses, common sense:

'He built on man's broad nature – gift
    of gifts,
'That power to build! The world
    contented shifts
'With counterfeits enough, a dreary
    sort
'Of warriors, statesmen, ere it can extort
'Its poet-soul – that's, after all, a freak
'(The having eyes to see and tongue to
    speak)
'With our herd's stupid sterling happiness
'So plainly incompatible that – yes –
'Yes – should a son of his improve the
    breed
'And turn out poet, he were cursed
    indeed!'
'Well, there's Goito and its woods anon,
'If the worst happen; best go stoutly on
'Now!' thought Sordello.
          Ay, and goes on yet!
You pother with your glossaries to get
A notion of the Troubadour's intent
In rondel, tenzon, virlai or sirvent –
Much as you study arras how to twirl
His angelot, plaything of page and girl
Once; but you surely reach, at last, –
    or, no!
Never quite reach what struck the people
    so,
As from the welter of their time he drew
Its elements successively to view,
Followed all actions backward on their
    course,
And catching up, unmingled at the
    source,
Such a strength, such a weakness, added
    then
A touch or two, and turned them into
    men.
Virtue took form, nor vice refused a
    shape;
Here heaven opened, there was hell
    agape,
As Saint this simpered past in sanctity,
Sinner the other flared portentous by
A greedy people. Then why stop,
    surprised

At his success? The scheme was realized
Too suddenly in one respect: a crowd
Praising, eyes quick to see, and lips as
    loud
To speak, delicious homage to receive,
The woman's breath to feel upon his
    sleeve,
Who said, 'But Anafest – why asks he
    less
'Than Lucio, in your verses? how confess,
'It seemed too much but yestereve!' –
    the youth,
Who bade him earnestly, 'Avow the
    truth!
'You love Bianca, surely, from your song;
'I knew I was unworthy!' – soft or strong,
In poured such tributes ere he had
    arranged
Ethereal ways to take them, sorted,
    changed,
Digested. Courted thus at unawares,
In spite of his pretensions and his cares,
He caught himself shamefully hankering
After the obvious petty joys that spring
From true life, fain relinquish pedestal
And condescend with pleasures – one
    and all
To be renounced, no doubt; for, thus
    to chain
Himself to single joys and so refrain
From tasting their quintessence,
    frustrates, sure,
His prime design; each joy must he
    abjure
Even for love of it.
                    He laughed: what sage
But perishes if from his magic page
He look because, at the first line, a proof
'Twas heard salutes him from the cavern
    roof?
'On! Give yourself, excluding aught
    beside,
'To the day's task; compel your slave
    provide
'Its utmost at the soonest; turn the leaf
'Thoroughly conned. These lays of
    yours, in brief –

'Cannot men bear, now, something
    better? – fly
'A pitch beyond this unreal pageantry
'Of essences? the period sure has ceased
'For such: present us with ourselves, at
    least,
'Not portions of ourselves, mere loves
    and hates
'Made flesh: wait not!'
                    Awhile the poet waits
However. The first trial was enough:
He left imagining, to try the stuff
That held the imaged thing, and, let it
    writhe
Never so fiercely, scarce allowed a tithe
To reach the light – his Language. How
    he sought
The cause, conceived a cure, and slow
    re-wrought
That Language, – welding words into
    the crude
Mass from the new speech round him,
    till a rude
Armour was hammered out, in time
    to be
Approved beyond the Roman panoply
Melted to make it, – boots not. This
    obtained
With some ado, no obstacle remained
To using it; accordingly he took
An action with its actors, quite forsook
Himself to live in each, returned anon
With the result – a creature, and, by one
And one, proceeded leisurely to equip
Its limbs in harness of his workmanship.
'Accomplished! Listen, Mantuans!' Fond
    essay!
Piece after piece that armour broke away,
Because perceptions whole, like that he
    sought
To clothe, reject so pure a work of
    thought
As language: thought may take
    perception's place
But hardly co-exist in any case,
Being its mere presentment – of the
    whole

By parts, the simultaneous and the sole
By the successive and the many. Lacks
The crowd perception? painfully it tacks
Thought to thought, which Sordello,
        needing such,
Has rent perception into: it's to clutch
And reconstruct – his office to diffuse,
Destroy: as hard, then, to obtain a Muse
As to become Apollo. 'For the rest,
'E'en if some wondrous vehicle
        expressed
'The whole dream, what impertinence
        in me
'So to express it, who myself can be
'The dream! nor, on the other hand,
        are those
'I sing to, over-likely to suppose
'A higher than the highest I present
'Now, which they praise already: be
        content
'Both parties, rather – they with the old
        verse,
'And I with the old praise – far go, fare
        worse!'
A few adhering rivets loosed, upsprings
The angel, sparkles off his mail, which
        rings
Whirled from each delicatest limb it
        warps;
So might Apollo from the sudden corpse
Of Hyacinth have cast his luckless quoits.
He set to celebrating the exploits
Of Montfort o'er the Mountaineers.
                        Then came
The world's revenge: their pleasure, now
        his aim
Merely, – what was it? 'Not to play the
        fool
'So much as learn our lesson in your
        school!'
Replied the world. He found that, every
        time
He gained applause by any ballad-rhyme,
His auditory recognized no jot
As he intended, and, mistaking not
Him for his meanest hero, ne'er was
        dunce

Sufficient to believe him – all, at once.
His will … conceive it caring for his
        will!
– Mantuans, the main of them, admiring
        still
How a mere singer, ugly, stunted, weak,
Had Montfort at completely (so to speak)
His fingers'ends; while past the praise-
        tide swept
To Montfort, either's share distinctly
        kept:
The true meed for true merit! – his
        abates
Into a sort he most repudiates,
And on them angrily he turns. Who
        were
The Mantuans, after all, that he should
        care
About their recognition, ay or no?
In spite of the convention months ago,
(Why blink the truth?) was not he
        forced to help
This same ungrateful audience, every
        whelp
Of Naddo's litter, make them pass for
        peers
With the bright band of old Goito years,
As erst he toiled for flower or tree? Why,
        there
Sat Palma! Adelaide's funereal hair
Ennobled the next corner. Ay, he strewed
A fairy dust upon that multitude,
Although he feigned to take them by
        themselves;
His giants dignified those puny elves,
Sublimed their faint applause. In short,
        he found
Himself still footing a delusive round,
Remote as ever from the self-display
He meant to compass, hampered every
        way
By what he hoped assistance. Wherefore
        then
Continue, make believe to find in men
A use he found not?
                        Weeks, months, years went by,
And lo, Sordello vanished utterly,

Sundered in twain; each spectral part at
   strife
With each; one jarred against another
   life;
The Poet thwarting hopelessly the Man –
Who, fooled no longer, free in fancy ran
Here, there: let slip no opportunities
As pitiful, forsooth, beside the prize
To drop on him some no-time and acquit
His constant faith (the Poet-half's to
   wit –
That waiving any compromise between
No joy and all joy kept the hunger keen
Beyond most methods) – of incurring
   scoff
From the Man-portion – not to be put off
With self-reflectings by the Poet's scheme,
Though ne'er so bright. Who sauntered
   forth in dream,
Dressed any how, nor waited mystic
   frames,
Immeasurable gifts, astounding claims,
But just his sorry self? – who yet might
   be
Sorrier for aught he in reality
Achieved, so pinioned Man's the Poet-
   part,
Fondling, in turn of fancy, verse; the Art
Developing his soul a thousand ways –
Potent, by its assistance, to amaze
The multitude with majesties, convince
Each sort of nature that the nature's
   prince
Accosted it. Language, the makeshift,
   grew
Into a bravest of expedients, too;
Apollo, seemed it now, perverse had
   thrown
Quiver and bow away, the lyre alone
Sufficed. While, out of dream, his day's
   work went
To tune a crazy tenzon* or sirvent† –

So hampered him the Man-part, thrust
   to judge
Between the bard and the bard's
   audience, grudge
A minute's toil that missed its due
   reward!
But the complete Sordello, Man and
   Bard,
John's cloud-girt angel, this foot on the
   land,
That on the sea, with, open in his
   hand,
A bitter-sweetling of a book – was gone.
   Then, if internal struggles to be one,
Which frittered him incessantly
   piecemeal,
Referred, ne'er so obliquely, to the real
Intruding Mantuans! ever with some call
To action while he pondered, once for
   all,
Which looked the easier effort – to
   pursue
This course, still leap o'er paltry joys,
   yearn through
The present ill-appreciated stage
Of self-revealment, and compel the age
Know him – or else, forswearing
   bardcraft, wake
From out his lethargy and nobly shake
Off timid habits of denial, mix
With men, enjoy like men. Ere he
   could fix
On aught, in rushed the Mantuans;
   much they cared
For his perplexity! Thus unprepared,
The obvious if not only shelter lay
In deeds, the dull conventions of his day
Prescribed the like of him: why not be
   glad
'Tis settled Palma's minstrel, good or
   bad,
Submits to this and that established
   rule?
Let Vidal change, or any other fool,
His murrey-coloured robe for filamot,
And crop his hair; too skin-deep, is it
   not,

---

* *Tenzon.* A dramatic skirmish in verse before
the Court of Lover
† *Sirvent.* Martial, political, and satirical songs.
Both Provencal terms.

Such vigour? Then, a sorrow to the
    heart,
His talk! Whatever topics they might
    start
Had to be groped for in his consciousness
Straight, and as straight delivered them
    by guess.
Only obliged to ask himself, 'What was,'
A speedy answer followed; but, alas,
One of God's large ones, tardy to
    condense
Itself into a period; answers whence
A tangle of conclusions must be stripped
At any risk ere, trim to pattern clipped,
They matched rare specimens the
    Mantuan flock
Regaled him with, each talker from his
    stock
Of sorted-o'er opinions, every stage,
Juicy in youth or desiccate with age,
Fruits like the fig-tree's, rathe-ripe,
    rotten-rich,
Sweet-sour, all tastes to take: a practice
    which
He too had not impossibly attained,
Once either of those fancy-flights
    restrained;
(For, at conjecture how might words
    appear
To others, playing there what
    happened here,
And occupied abroad by what he
    spurned
At home, 'twas slipped, the occasion
    he returned
To seize:) he'd strike that lyre adroitly
    – speech,
Would but a twenty-cubit plectre reach;
A clever hand, consummate instrument,
Were both brought close; each
    excellency went
For nothing, else. The question Naddo
    asked,
Had just a lifetime moderately tasked
To answer, Naddo's fashion. More disgust
And more: why move his soul, since
    move it must

At minute's notice or as good it failed
To move at all? The end was, he retailed
Some ready-made opinion, put to use
This quip, that maxim, ventured
    reproduce
Gestures and tones – at any folly caught
Serving to finish with, nor too much
    sought
It false or true 'twas spoken; praise and
    blame
Of what he said grew pretty nigh the
    same
– Meantime awards to meantime acts:
    his soul,
Unequal to the compassing a whole,
Saw, in a tenth part, less and less to
    strive
About. And as for men in turn …
    contrive
Who could to take eternal interest
In them, so hate the worst, so love the
    best!
Though, in pursuance of his passive
    plan,
He hailed, decried, the proper way.
                    As Man
So figured he; and how as Poet? Verse
Came only not to a stand-still. The
    worse,
That his poor piece of daily work to do
Was – not sink under any rivals; who
Loudly and long enough, without these
    qualms,
Turned, from Bocafoli's stark-naked
    psalms,
To Plara's sonnets spoilt by toying with,
'As knops that stud some almug to the
    pith
'Prickèd for gum, wry thence, and
    crinklèd worse
'Than pursèd eyelids of a river-horse
'Sunning himself o' the slime when
    whirrs the breese' –
*Gad-fly*, that is. He might compete with
    these!
But – but –
       'Observe a pompion-twine afloat;

'Pluck me one cup from off the castle-
     moat!
'Along with cup you raise leaf, stalk
     and root,
'The entire surface of the pool to boot.
'So could I pluck a cup, put in one song
'A single sight, did not my hand, too
     strong,
'Twitch in the least the root-strings of
     the whole.
'How should externals satisfy my soul?'
'Why that's precise the error Squarcialupe'
(Hazarded Naddo) 'finds; "the man can't
     stoop
' "To sing us out," quoth he, "a mere
     romance;
' "He'd fain do better than the best,
     enhance
' "The subjects' rarity, work problems
     out
' "Therewith." Now, you're a bard, a
     bard past doubt,
'And no philosopher; why introduce
'Crotchets like these? fine, surely, but
     no use
'In poetry – which still must be, to
     strike,
'Based upon common sense; there's
     nothing like
'Appealing to our nature! what beside
'Was your first poetry? No tricks were
     tried
'In that, no hollow thrills, affected throes!
' "The man," said we, "tells his own
     joys and woes:
' "We'll trust him." Would you have
     your songs endure?
'Build on the human heart! – why, to be
     sure
'Yours is one sort of heart – but I mean
     theirs,
'Ours, every one's, the healthy heart
     one cares
'To build on! Central peace, mother of
     strength,
'That's father of … nay, go yourself
     that length,

'Ask those calm-hearted doers what they
     do
'When they have got their calm! And is
     it true,
'Fire rankles at the heart of every globe?
'Perhaps. But these are matters one may
     probe
'Too deeply for poetic purposes:
'Rather select a theory that … yes,
'Laugh! what does that prove? –
     stations you midway
'And saves some little o'er-refining. Nay,
'That's rank injustice done me! I restrict
'The poet? Don't I hold the poet picked
'Out of a host of warriors, statesmen …
     did
'I tell you? Very like! As well you hid
'That sense of power, you have! True
     bards believe
'All able to achieve what they achieve –
'That is, just nothing – in one point
     abide
'Profounder simpletons than all beside.
'Oh, ay! The knowledge that you are a
     bard
'Must constitute your prime, nay sole,
     reward!'
So prattled Naddo, busiest of the tribe
Of genius-haunters – how shall I describe
What grubs or nips or rubs or rips –
     your louse
For love, your flea for hate, magnanimous,
Malignant, Pappacoda, Tagliafer,
Picking a sustenance from wear and
     tear
By implements it sedulous employs
To undertake, lay down, mete out,
     o'er-toise
Sordello? Fifty creepers to elude
At once! They settled staunchly; shame
     ensued:
Behold the monarch of mankind
     succumb
To the last fool who turned him round
     his thumb,
As Naddo styled it! 'Twas not worth
     oppose

The matter of a moment, gainsay those
He aimed at getting rid of; better think
Their thoughts and speak their speech,
    secure to slink
Back expeditiously to his safe place,
And chew the cud – what he and what
    his race
Were really, each of them. Yet even this
Conformity was partial. He would miss
Some point, brought into contact with
    them ere
Assured in what small segment of the
    sphere
Of his existence they attended him;
Whence blunders, falsehoods rectified –
    a grim
List – slur it over! How? If dreams were
    tried,
His will swayed sicklily from side to side,
Nor merely neutralized his waking act
But tended e'en in fancy to distract
The intermediate will, the choice of
    means.

He lost the art of dreaming: Mantuan
    scenes
Supplied a baron, say, he sang before,
Handsomely reckless, full to running-
    o'er
Of gallantries; 'abjure the soul, content
'With body, therefore!' Scarcely had he
    bent
Himself in dream thus low, when matter
    fast
Cried out, he found, for spirit to contrast
And task it duly; by advances slight,
The simple stuff becoming composite,
Count Lori grew Apollo: best recall
His fancy! Then would some rough
    peasant-Paul,
Like those old Ecelin confers with, glance
His gay apparel o'er; that countenance
Gathered his shattered fancies into one,
And, body clean abolished, soul alone
Sufficed the grey Paulician; by and by,
To balance the ethereality,
Passions were needed; foiled he sank
    again.

Meanwhile the world rejoiced ('tis
    time explain)
Because a sudden sickness set it free
From Adelaide. Missing the mother-bee,
Her mountain-hive Romano swarmed;
    at once
A rustle-forth of daughters and of sons
Blackened the valley. 'I am sick too, old,
'Half-crazed I think; what good's the
    Kaiser's gold
'To such an one? God help me! for I
    catch
'My children's greedy sparkling eyes at
    watch –
' "He bears that double breastplate
    on," they say,
' "So many minutes less than yesterday!"
'Beside, Monk Hilary is on his knees
'Now, sworn to kneel and pray till God
    shall please
'Exact a punishment for many things
'You know, and some you never knew;
    which brings
'To memory, Azzo's sister Beatrix
'And Richard's Giglia are my Alberic's
'And Ecelin's betrothed; the Count
    himself
'Must get my Palma: Ghibellin and Guelf
'Mean to embrace each other.' So began
Romano's missive to his fighting man
Taurello – on the Tuscan's death, away
With Friedrich sworn to sail from Naples'
    bay
Next month for Syria. Never thunderclap
Out of Vesuvius' throat, like this mishap
Startled him. 'That accursed Vicenza! I
'Absent, and she selects this time to
    die!
'Ho, fellows, for Vicenza!' Half a score
Of horses ridden dead, he stood before
Romano in his reeking spurs: too late –
'Boniface urged me, Este could not wait,'
The chieftain stammered; 'let me die in
    peace –
'Forget me! Was it I who craved increase
'Of rule? Do you and Friedrich plot
    your worst

'Against the Father: as you found me
  first
'So leave me now. Forgive me! Palma,
  sure,
'Is at Goito still. Retain that lure –
'Only be pacified!'
                      The country rung
With such a piece of news: on every
  tongue,
How Ecelin's great servant, congeed off,
Had done a long day's service, so, might
  doff
The green and yellow, and recover breath
At Mantua, whither, – since Retrude's
  death,
(The girlish slip of a Sicilian bride
From Otho's house, he carried to reside
At Mantua till the Ferrarese should pile
A structure worthy her imperial style,
The gardens raise, the statues there
  enshrine,
She never lived to see) – although his
  line
Was ancient in her archives and she took
A pride in him, that city, nor forsook
Her child when he forsook himself and
  spent
A prowess on Romano surely meant
For his own growth – whither he ne'er
  resorts
If wholly satisfied (to trust reports)
With Ecelin. So, forward in a trice
Were shows to greet him. 'Take a friend's
  advice,'
Quoth Naddo to Sordello, 'nor be rash
'Because your rivals (nothing can abash
'Some folks) demur that we pronounced
  you best
'To sound the great man's welcome; 'tis
  a test,
'Remember! Strojavacca looks asquint,
'The rough fat sloven; and there's plenty
  hint
'Your pinions have received of late a
  shock –
'Outsoar them, cobswan of the silver
  flock!

'Sing well!'A signal wonder, song's no
  whit
Facilitated.
                Fast the minutes flit;
Another day, Sordello finds, will bring
The soldier, and he cannot choose but
  sing;
So, a last shift, quits Mantua – slow,
  alone:
Out of that aching brain, a very stone,
Song must be struck. What occupies
  that front?
Just how he was more awkward than
  his wont
The night before, when Naddo, who
  had seen
Taurello on his progress, praised the
  mien
For dignity no crosses could affect –
Such was a joy, and might not he detect
A satisfaction if established joys
Were proved imposture? Poetry annoys
Its utmost: wherefore fret? Verses may
  come
Or keep away! And thus he wandered,
  dumb
Till evening, when he paused, thoroughly
  spent,
On a blind hill-top: down the gorge he
  went,
Yielding himself up as to an embrace.
The moon came out; like features of a
  face,
A querulous fraternity of pines,
Sad blackthorn clumps, leafless and
  grovelling vines
Also came out, made gradually up
The picture; 'twas Goito's mountain-
  cup
And castle. He had dropped through
  one defile
He never dared explore, the Chief
  erewhile
Had vanished by. Back rushed the
  dream, enwrapped
Him wholly. 'Twas Apollo now they
  lapped,

Those mountains, not a pettish minstrel
    meant
To wear his soul away in discontent,
Brooding on fortune's malice. Heart and
    brain
Swelled; he expanded to himself again,
As some thin seedling spice-tree starved
    and frail,
Pushing between cat's head and ibis'
    tail
Crusted into the porphyry pavement
    smooth,
– Suffered remain just as it sprung, to
    soothe
The Soldan's pining daughter, never yet
Well in her chilly green-glazed
    minaret, –
When rooted up, the sunny day she
    died,
And flung into the common court beside
Its parent tree. Come home, Sordello!
    Soon
Was he low muttering, beneath the moon,
Of sorrow saved, of quiet evermore, –
Since from the purpose, he maintained
    before,
Only resulted wailing and hot tears.
Ah, the slim castle! dwindled of late
    years,
But more mysterious; gone to ruin –
    trails
Of vine through every loop-hole.
        Nought avails
The night as, torch in hand, he must
    explore
The maple chamber: did I say, its floor
Was made of intersecting cedar beams?
Worn now with gaps so large, there
    blew cold streams
Of air quite from the dungeon; lay your
    ear
Close and 'tis like, one after one, you
    hear
In the blind darkness water drop. The
    nests
And nooks retain their long ranged
    vesture-chests

Empty and smelling of the iris root
The Tuscan grated o'er them to recruit
Her wasted wits. Palma was gone that
    day,
Said the remaining women. Last, he lay
Beside the Carian group reserved and
    still.
    The Body, the Machine for Acting
        Will,
Had been at the commencement proved
    unfit;
That for Demonstrating, Reflecting it,
Mankind – no fitter: was the Will Itself
In fault?
        His forehead pressed the moonlit
            shelf
Beside the youngest marble maid awhile;
Then, raising it, he thought, with a long
    smile,
'I shall be king again!' as he withdrew
The envied scarf; into the font he threw
His crown.
            Next day, no poet! 'Wherefore?'
                asked
Taurello, when the dance of Jongleurs,
    masked
As devils, ended; 'don't a song come
    next?'
The master of the pageant looked
    perplexed
Till Naddo's whisper came to his relief.
'His Highness knew what poets were:
    in brief,
'Had not the tetchy race prescriptive
    right
'To peevishness, caprice? or, call it spite,
'One must receive their nature in its
    length
'And breadth, expect the weakness
    with the strength!'
– So phrasing, till, his stock of phrases
    spent,
The easy-natured soldier smiled assent,
Settled his portly person, smoothed his
    chin,
And nodded that the bull-bait might
    begin.

### BOOK THE THIRD

And the font took them: let our laurels
    lie!
Braid moonfern now with mystic trifoly
Because once more Goito gets, once
    more,
Sordello to itself! A dream is o'er,
And the suspended life begins anew;
Quiet those throbbing temples, then,
    subdue
That cheek's distortion! Nature's strict
    embrace,
Putting aside the past, shall soon efface
Its print as well – factitious humours
    grown
Over the true – loves, hatreds not his
    own –
And turn him pure as some forgotten
    vest
Woven of painted byssus, silkiest
Tufting the Tyrrhene whelk's pearl-
    sheeted lip,
Left welter where a trireme let it slip
I' the sea, and vexed a satrap; so the
    stain
O' the world forsakes Sordello, with its
    pain,
Its pleasure: how the tinct loosening
    escapes,
Cloud after cloud! Mantua's familiar
    shapes
Die, fair and foul die, fading as they flit,
Men, women, and the pathos and the
    wit,
Wise speech and foolish, deeds to
    smile or sigh
For, good, bad, seemly or ignoble, die.
The last face glances through the
    eglantines,
The last voice murmurs, 'twixt the
    biossomed vines,
Of Men, of that machine supplied by
    thought
To compass self-perception with, he
    sought
By forcing half himself – an insane pulse

Of a god's blood, on clay it could
    convulse, .
Never transmute – on human sights
    and sounds,
To watch the other half with; irksome
    bounds
It ebbs from to its source, a fountain
    sealed
Forever. Better sure be unrevealed
Than part revealed: Sordello well or ill
Is finished: then what further use of
    Will,
Point in the prime idea not realized,
An oversight? inordinately prized,
No less, and pampered with enough of
    each
Delight to prove the whole above its
    reach.
'To need become all natures, yet retain
'The law of my own nature – to remain
'Myself, yet yearn … as if that
    chestnut, think,
'Should yearn for this first larch-bloom
    crisp and pink,
'Or those pale fragrant tears where
    zephyrs stanch
'March wounds along the fretted pine-
    tree branch!
'Will and the means to show will, great
    and small,
'Material, spiritual, – abjure them all
'Save any so distinct, they may be left
'To amuse, not tempt become! and,
    thus bereft,
'Just as I first was fashioned would I be!
'Nor, moon, is it Apollo now, but me
'Thou visitest to comfort and befriend!
'Swim thou into my heart, and there an
    end,
'Since I possess thee! – nay, thus shut
    mine eyes
'And know, quite know, by this heart's
    fall and rise,
'When thou dost bury thee in clouds,
    and when
'Out-standest: wherefore practise upon
    men

'To make that plainer to myself?'
                              Slide here
Over a sweet and solitary year
Wasted; or simply notice change in
    him –
How eyes, once with exploring bright,
    grew dim
And satiate with receiving. Some distress
Was caused, too, by a sort of
    consciousness
Under the imbecility, – nought kept
That down; he slept, but was aware he
    slept,
So, frustrated: as who brainsick made
    pact
Erst with the overhanging cataract
To deafen him, yet still distinguished
    plain
His own blood's measured clicking at
    his brain.
   To finish. One declining Autumn
    day –
Few birds about the heaven chill and
    grey,
No wind that cared trouble the tacit
    woods –
He sauntered home complacently, their
    moods
According, his and nature's. Every spark
Of Mantua life was trodden out; so dark
The embers, that the Troubadour, who
    sung
Hundreds of songs, forgot, its trick his
    tongue,
Its craft his brain, how either brought to
    pass
Singing at all; that faculty might class
Wife any of Apollo's now. The year
Began to find its early promise sere
As well. Thus beauty vanishes; thus stone
Outlingers flesh: nature's and his youth
    gone,
They left the world to you, and wished
    you joy.
When, stopping his benevolent employ,
A presage shuddered through the
    welkin; harsh

The earth's remonstrance followed. 'Twas
    the marsh
Gone of a sudden. Mincio, in its place,
Laughed, a broad water, in next
    morning's face,
And, where the mists broke up immense
    and white
I' the steady wind, burned like a spilth
    of light
Out of the crashing of a myriad stars.
And here was nature, bound by the
    same bars
Of fate with him!
                     'No! youth once gone is gone:
'Deeds, let escape, are never to be done.
'Leaf-fall and grass-spring for the year;
    for us –
'Oh forfeit I unalterably thus
'My chance? nor two lives wait me, this
    to spend,
'Learning save that? Nature has time,
    may mend
'Mistake, she knows occasion will recur;
'Landslip or seabreach, how affects it her
'With her magnificent resources? – I
'Must perish once and perish utterly.
'Not any strollings now at even-close
'Down the field-path, Sordello! by thorn
    rows
'Alive with lamp-flies, swimming spots
    of fire
'And dew, outlining the black cypress'
    spire
'She waits you at, Elys, who heard you
    first
'Woo her, the snow-month through, but
    ere she durst
'Answer 'twas April. Linden-flower-time-
    long
'Her eyes were on the ground; 'tis July,
    strong
'Now; and because white dust-clouds
    overwhelm
'The woodside, here or by the village
    elm
'That holds the moon, she meets you,
    somewhat pale,

'But letting you lift up her coarse flax
veil
'And whisper (the damp little hand in
yours)
'Of love, heart's love, your heart's love
that endures
'Till death. Tush! No mad mixing with
the rout
'Of haggard ribalds wandering about
'The hot torchlit wine-scented island-
house
'Where Friedrich holds his wickedest
carouse,
'Parading, – to the gay Palermitans,
'Soft Messinese, dusk Saracenic clans
'Nuocera holds, – those tall grave
dazzling Norse,
'High-cheeked, lank-haired, toothed
whiter than the morse,
'Queens of the caves of jet stalactites,
'He sent his barks to fetch through icy
seas,
'The blind night seas without a saving
star,
'And here in snowy birdskin robes they
are,
'Sordello! – here, mollitious alcoves gilt
'Superb as Byzant domes that devils
built!
' – Ah, Byzant, there again! no chance
to go
'Ever like august cheery Dandolo,
'Worshipping hearts about him for a
wall,
'Conducted, blind eyes, hundred years
and all,
'Through vanquished Byzant where
friends note for him
'What pillar, marble massive, sardius
slim,
' 'Twere fittest he transport to Venice'
Square –
'Flattered and promised life to touch
them there
'Soon, by those fervid sons of senators!
'No more lifes, deaths, loves, hatreds,
peaces, wars!

'Ah, fragments of a whole ordained to be,
'Points in the life I waited! what are ye
'But roundels of a ladder which
appeared
'Awhile the very platform it was reared
'To lift me on? – that happiness I find
'Proofs of my faith in, even in the blind
'Instinct which bade forego you all unless
'Ye led me past yourselves. Ay, happiness
'Awaited me; the way life should be
used
'Was to acquire, and deeds like you
conduced
'To teach it by a self-revealment, deemed
'Life's very use, so long! Whatever seemed
'Progress to that, was pleasure; aught
that stayed
'My reaching it – no pleasure. I have laid
'The ladder down; I climb not; still, aloft
'The platform stretches! Blisses strong
and soft,
'I dared not entertain, elude me; yet
'Never of what they promised could I get
'A glimpse till now! The common sort,
the crowd,
'Exist, perceive; with Being are endowed,
'However slight, distinct from what they
See,
'However bounded; Happiness must be,
'To feed the first by gleanings from the
last,
'Attain its qualities, and slow or fast
'Become what they behold; such peace-
in-strife,
'By transmutation, is the Use of Life,
'The Alien turning Native to the soul
'Or body – which instructs me; I am
whole
'There and demand a Palma; had the
world
'Been from my soul to a like distance
hurled,
' 'Twere Happiness to make it one with
me:
'Whereas I must, ere I begin to Be,
'Include a world, in flesh, I
comprehend

'In spirit now; and this done, what's to
     blend
'With? Nought is Alien in the world –
     my Will
'Owns all already; yet can turn it – still
'Less – Native, since my Means to
     correspond
'With Will are so unworthy, 'twas my
     bond
'To tread the very joys that tantalize
'Most now, into a grave, never to rise.
'I die then! Will the rest agree to die?
'Next Age or no? Shall its Sordello try
'Clue after clue, and catch at last the
     clue
'I miss? – that's underneath my finger
     too,
'Twice, thrice a day, perhaps, – some
     yearning traced
'Deeper, some petty consequence
     embraced
'Closer! Why fled I Mantua, then? –
     complained
'So much my Will was fettered, yet
     remained
'Content within a tether half the range
'I could assign it? – able to exchange
'My ignorance (I felt) for knowledge, and
'Idle because I could thus understand –
'Could e'en have penetrated to its core
'Our mortal mystery, yet – fool – forbore,
'Preferred elaborating in the dark
'My casual stuff, by any wretched spark
'Born of my predecessors, though one
     stroke
'Of mine had brought the flame forth!
     Mantua's yoke,
'My minstrel's-trade, was to behold
     mankind, –
'My own concern was just to bring my
     mind
'Behold, just extricate, for my acquist,
'Each object suffered stifle in the mist
'Which hazard, custom, blindness
     interpose
'Betwixt things and myself.'
                              Whereat he rose.

The level wind carried above the firs
Clouds, the irrevocable travellers,
Onward.
          'Pushed thus into a drowsy copse,
'Arms twine about my neck, each
     eyelid drops
'Under a humid finger; while there
     fleets,
'Outside the screen, a pageant time
     repeats
'Never again! To be deposed, immured
'Clandestinely – still petted, still assured
'To govern were fatiguing work – the
     Sight
'Fleeting meanwhile! 'Tis noontide:
     wreak ere night
'Somehow my will upon it, rather! Slake
'This thirst somehow, the poorest
     impress take
'That serves! A blasted bud displays you,
     torn,
'Faint rudiments of the full flower
     unborn;
'But who divines what glory coats o'er-
     clasp
'Of the bulb dormant in the mummy's
     grasp
'Taurello sent?' …
                         'Taurello? Palma sent
'Your Trouvere,' (Naddo interposing
     leant
Over the lost bard's shoulder) – 'and,
     believe,
'You cannot more reluctantly receive
'Than I pronounce her message: we
     depart
'Together. What avail a poet's heart
'Verona's pomps and gauds? five
     blades of grass
'Suffice him. News? Why, where your
     marish was,
'On its mud-banks smoke rises after
     smoke
'I'the valley, like a spout of hell new-
     broke.
'Oh, the world's tidings! small your
     thanks, I guess,

'For them. The father of our Patroness,
'Has played Taurello an astounding
trick,
'Parts between Ecelin and Alberic
'His wealth and goes into a convent:
both
'Wed Guelfs: the Count and Palma
plighted troth
'A week since at Verona: and they want
'You doubtless to contrive the marriage-
chant
'Ere Richard storms Ferrara.' Then was
told
The tale from the beginning – how,
made bold
By Salinguerra's absence, Guelfs had
burned
And pillaged till he unawares returned
To take revenge: how Azzo and his
friend
Were doing their endeavour, how the end
O' the siege was nigh, and how the
Count, released
From further care, would with his
marriage-feast
Inaugurate a new and better rule,
Absorbing thus Romano.
                              'Shall I school
'My master,' added Naddo, 'and suggest
'How you may clothe in a poetic vest
'These doings, at Verona? Your response
'To Palma! Wherefore jest? "Depart at
once?"
'A good resolve! In truth, I hardly hoped
'So prompt an acquiescence. Have you
groped
'Out wisdom in the wilds here? –
thoughts may be
'Over-poetical for poetry.
'Pearl-white, you poets liken Palma's
neck;
'And yet what spoils an orient like some
speck
'Of genuine white, turning its own white
grey?
'You take me? Curse the cicala!'
                              One more day,

One eve – appears Verona! Many a
group,
(You mind) instructed of the osprey's
swoop
On lynx and ounce, was gathering –
Christendom
Sure to receive, whate'er the end was,
from
The evening's purpose cheer or detriment,
Since Friedrich only waited some event
Like this, of Ghibellins establishing
Themselves within Ferrara, ere, as King
Of Lombardy, he'd glad descend there,
wage
Old warfare with the Pontiff, disengage
His barons from the burghers, and
restore
The rule of Charlemagne, broken of yore
By Hildebrand.
                    I' the palace, each by each,
Sordello sat and Palma: little speech
At first in that dim closet, face with face
(Despite the tumult in the market-place)
Exchanging quick low laughters: now
would rush
Word upon word to meet a sudden
flush,
A look left off, a shifting lips' surmise –
But for the most part their two histories
Ran best thro' the locked fingers and
linked arms.
And so the night flew on with its alarms
Till in burst one of Palma's retinue;
'Now, Lady! gasped he. Then arose the
two
And leaned into Verona's air, dead-still.
A balcony lay black beneath until
Out, 'mid a gush of torchfire, grey-
haired men
Came on it and harangued the people:
then
Sea-like that people surging to and fro
Shouted, 'Hale forth the carroch –
trumpets, ho,
'A flourish! Run it in the ancient grooves!
'Back from the bell! Hammer – that
whom behoves

'May hear the League is up! Peal – learn
    who list,
'Verona means not first of towns break
    tryst
'To-morrow with the League!'
               Enough. Now turn –
Over the eastern cypresses: discern!
Is any beacon set a-glimmer?
                       Rang
The air with shouts that overpowered
    the clang
Of the incessant carroch, even: 'Haste –
'The candle's at the gateway! ere it waste,
'Each soldier stand beside it, armed to
    march
'With Tiso Sampier through the eastern
    arch!'
Ferrara's succoured, Palma!
                 Once again
They sat together; some strange thing
    in train
To say, so difficult was Palma's place
In taking, with a coy fastidious grace
Like the bird's flutter ere it fix and feed.
But when she felt she held her friend
    indeed
Safe, she threw back her curls, began
    implant
Her lessons; telling of another want
Goito's quiet nourished than his own;
Palma – to serve him – to be served,
    alone
Importing; Agnes' milk so neutralized
The blood of Ecelin. Nor be surprised
If, while Sordello fain had captive led
Nature, in dream was Palma subjected
To some out-soul, which dawned not
    though she pined
Delaying, till its advent, heart and mind
Their life. 'How dared I let expand the
    force
'Within me, till some out-soul, whose
    resource
'It grew for, should direct it? Every law
'Of life, its every fitness, every flaw,
'Must One determine whose corporeal
    shape

'Would be no other than the prime
    escape
'And revelation to me of a Will
'Orb-like o'ershrouded and inscrutable
'Above, save at the point which, I should
    know,
'Shone that myself, my powers, might
    overflow
'So far, so much; as now it signified
'Which earthly shape it henceforth
    chose my guide,
'Whose mortal lip selected to declare
'Its oracles, what fleshly garb would wear
' – The first of intimations, whom to
    love;
'The next, how love him. Seemed that
    orb, above
'The castle-covert and the mountain-
    close,
'Slow in appearing? – if beneath it rose
'Cravings, aversions, – did our green
    precinct
'Take pride in me, at unawares distinct
'With this or that endowment, – how,
    repressed
'At once, such jetting power shrank to
    the rest!
'Was I to have a chance touch spoil me,
    leave
'My spirit thence unfitted to receive
'The consummating spell? – that spell
    so near
'Moreover! "Waits he not the waking
    year?
' "His almond-blossoms must be honey-
    ripe
' "By this; to welcome him, fresh runnels
    stripe
' "The thawed ravines; because of him,
    the wind
' "Walks like a herald. I shall surely find
' "Him now!"
          'And chief, that earnest April morn
'Of Richard's Love-court, was it time, so
    worn
'And white my cheek, so idly my blood
    beat,

'Sitting that morn beside the Lady's feet
'And saying as she prompted; till outburst
'One face from all the faces. Not then
    first
'I knew it; where in maple chamber
    glooms,
'Crowned with what sanguine-heart
    pomegranate blooms,
'Advanced it ever? Men's
    acknowledgment
'Sanctioned my own: 'twas taken,
    Palma's bent, –
'Sordello, – recognized, accepted.
                                'Dumb
'Sat she still scheming. Ecelin would
    come
'Gaunt, scared, "Cesano baffles me,"
    he'd say:
' "Better I fought it out, my father's
    way!
' "Strangle Ferrara in its drowning flats,
' "And you and your Taurello yonder! –
    what's
' "Romano's business there?"An hour's
    concern
'To cure the froward Chief! – induce
    return
'As heartened from those overmeaning
    eyes,
'Wound up to persevere, – his enterprise
'Marked out a new, its exigent of wit
'Apportioned, – she at liberty to sit
'And scheme against the next
    emergence, I –
'To covet her Taurello-sprite, made fly
'Or fold the wing – to con your horoscope
'For leave command those steely shafts
    shoot ope,
'Or straight assuage their blinding
    eagerness
'In blank smooth snow. What
    semblance of success
'To any of my plans for making you
'Mine and Romano's? Break the first
    wall through,
'Tread o'er the ruins of the Chief,
    supplant

'His sons beside, still, vainest were the
    vaunt:
'There, Salinguerra would obstruct me
    sheer,
'And the insuperable Tuscan, here,
'Stay me! But one wild eve that Lady
    died
'In her lone chamber: only I beside:
'Taurello far at Naples, and my sire
'At Padua, Ecelin away in ire
'With Alberic. She held me thus – a
    clutch
'To make our spirits as our bodies
    touch –
'And so began flinging the past up,
    heaps
'Of uncouth treasure from their sunless
    sleeps
'Within her soul; deeds rose along with
    dreams,
'Fragments of many miserable schemes,
'Secrets, more secrets, then – no, not
    the last –
' 'Mongst others, like a casual trick o'
    the past,
'How … ay, she told me, gathering up
    her face,
'All left of it, into one arch-grimace
'To die with …
                    'Friend, 'tis gone! but not the fear
'Of that fell laughing, heard as now I
    hear.
'Nor faltered voice, nor seemed her
    heart grow weak
'When i' the midst abrupt she ceased
    to speak
' – Dead, as to serve a purpose, mark!
    – for in
'Rushed o' the very instant Ecelin
'(How summoned, who divines?) –
    looking as if
'He understood why Adelaide lay stiff
'Already in my arms; for "Girl, how
    must
' "I manage Este in the matter thrust
' "Upon me, how unravel your bad
    coil? –

' "Since" (he declared) "'tis on your brow
    – a soil
' "Like hers there!" then in the same
    breath, "he lacked
' "No counsel after all, had signed no
    pact
' "With devils, nor was treason here or
    there,
' "Goito or Vicenza, his affair:
' "He buried it in Adelaide's deep
    grave,
' "Would begin life afresh, now, – would
    not slave
' "For any Friedrich's nor Taurello's sake!
' "What booted him to meddle or to
    make
' "In Lombardy?" And afterward I knew
'The meaning of his promise to undo
'All she had done – why marriages were
    made,
'New friendships entered on, old
    followers paid
'With curses for their pains, – new
    friends' amaze
'At height, when, passing out by Gate
    Saint Blaise,
'He stopped short in Vicenza, bent his
    head
'Over a friar's neck, – "had vowed," he
    said,
' "Long since, nigh thirty years, because
    his wife
' "And child were saved there, to bestow
    his life
' "On God, his gettings on the Church."
                                    'Exiled
'Within Goito, still one dream beguiled
'My days and nights; 'twas found, the
    orb I sought
'To serve, those glimpses came of Fomal-
    haut,
'No other: but how serve it? – authorize
'You and Romano mingle destinies?
'And straight Romano's angel stood
    beside
'Me who had else been Boniface's
    bride,

'For Salinguerra 'twas, with neck low
    bent,
'And voice lightened to music, (as he
    meant
'To learn, not teach me,) who withdrew
    the pall
'From the dead past and straight revived
    it all,
'Making me see how first Romano waxed,
'Wherefore he waned now, why, if I
    relaxed
'My grasp (even I!) would drop a thing
    effete,
'Frayed by itself, unequal to complete
'Its course, and counting every step
    astray
'A gain so much. Romano, every way
'Stable, a Lombard House now – why
    start back
'Into the very outset of its track?
'This patching principle which late allied
'Our House with other Houses – what
    beside
'Concerned the apparition, the first
    Knight
'Who followed Conrad hither in such
    plight
'His utmost wealth was summed in his
    one steed?
'For Ecelo, that prowler, was decreed
'A task, in the beginning hazardous
'To him as ever task can be to us;
'But did the weather-beaten thief despair
'When first our crystal cincture of warm
    air
'That binds the Trevisan, – as its spice-
    belt
'(Crusaders say) the tract where Jesus
    dwelt, –
'Furtive he pierced, and Este was to
    face –
'Despaired Saponian strength of
    Lombard grace?
'Tried he at making surer aught made
    sure,
'Maturing what already was mature?
'No; his heart prompted Ecelo, "Confront

' "Este, inspect yourself. What's nature?
          Wont.
' "Discard three-parts your nature, and
          adopt
' "The rest as an advantage!" Old strength
          propped
'The man who first grew Podestà among
'The Vicentines, no less than, while there
          sprung
'His palace up in Padua like a threat,
'Their noblest spied a grace, unnoticed
          yet
'In Conrad's crew. Thus far the object
          gained,
'Romano was established – has
          remained –
' "For are you not Italian, truly peers
' "With Este? *Azzo* better soothes our
          ears
' "Than *Alberic*? or is this lion's-crine
' "From over-mounts" (this yellow hair
          of mine)
' "So weak a graft on Agnes Este's
          stock?"
'(Thus went he on with something of a
          mock)
' "Wherefore recoil, then, from the very
          fate
' "Conceded you, refuse to imitate
' "Your model farther? Este long since
          left
' "Being mere Este: as a blade its heft,
' "Este required the Pope to further him:
' "And you, the Kaiser – whom your
          father's whim
' "Foregoes or, better, never shall forego
' "If Palma dare pursue what Ecelo
' "Commenced, but Ecelin desists from:
          just
' "As Adelaide of Susa could intrust
' "Her donative, – her Piedmont given
          the Pope,
' "Her Alpine-pass for him to shut or ope
' " 'Twixt France and Italy, – to the
          superb
' "Matilda's perfecting, – so, lest aught
          curb

' "Our Adelaide's great counter-project
          for
' "Giving her Trentine to the Emperor
' "With passage here from Germany, –
          shall you
' "Take it, – my slender plodding
          talent, too!"
' – Urged me Taurello with his half-smile.
                                        'He
'As Patron of the scattered family
'Conveyed me to his Mantua, kept in
          bruit
'Azzo's alliances and Richard's suit
'Until, the Kaiser excommunicate,
' "Nothing remains," Taurello said, "but
          wait
' "Some rash procedure: Palma was the
          link,
' "As Agnes' child, between us, and they
          shrink
' "From losing Palma: judge if we
          advance,
' "Your father's method, your
          inheritance!"
'The day I was betrothed to Boniface
'At Padua by Taurello's self, took place
'The outrage of the Ferrarese: again,
'The day I sought Verona with the train
'Agreed for, – by Taurello's policy
'Convicting Richard of the fault, since
          we
'Were present to annul or to confirm, –
'Richard, whose patience had outstayed
          its term,
'Quitted Verona for the siege.
                                  'And now
'What glory may engird Sordello's brow
'Through this? A month since at Oliero
          clunk
'All that was Ecelin into a monk;
'But how could Salinguerra so forget
'His liege of thirty years as grudge even
          yet
'One effort to recover him? He sent
'Forthwith the tidings of this last event
'To Ecelin – declared that he, despite
"The recent folly, recognized his right

'To order Salinguerra: "Should he wring
' "Its uttermost advantage out, or fling
' "This chance away? Or were his sons
    now Head
' "O'the House?" Through me Taurello's
    missive sped;
'My father's answer will by me return.
'Behold! "For him," he writes, "no more
    concern
' "With strife than, for his children, with
    fresh plots
' "Of Friedrich. Old engagements out
    he blots
' "For aye: Taurello shall no more subserve,
' "Nor Ecelin impose." Lest this unnerve
'Taurello at this juncture, slack his grip
'Of Richard, suffer the occasion slip, –
'I, in his sons' default (who, mating with
'Este, forsake Romano as the frith
'Its mainsea for that firmland, sea makes
    head
'Against) I stand, Romano, – in their
    stead
'Assume the station they desert, and
    give
'Still, as the Kaiser's representative,
'Taurello licence he demands.
        Midnight –
'Morning – by noon to-morrow, making
    light
'Of the League's issue, we, in some gay
    weed
'Like yours, disguised together, may
    precede
'The arbitrators to Ferrara: reach
'Him, let Taurello's noble accents teach
'The rest! Then say if I have misconceived
'Your destiny, too readily believed
'The Kaiser's cause your own!'
             And Palma's fled.
Though no affirmative disturbs the head,
A dying lamp-flame sinks and rises o'er,
Like the alighted planet Pollux wore,
Until, morn breaking, he resolves to be
Gate-vein of this heart's blood of
    Lormbardy,
Soul of this body – to wield this aggregate

Of souls and bodies, and so conquer
    fate
Though he should live – a centre of
    disgust
Even – apart, core of the outward crust
He vivifies, assimilates. For thus
I bring Sordello to the rapturous
Exclaim at the crowd's cry, because one
    round
Of life was quite accomplished; and he
    found
Not only that a soul, whate'er its might,
Is insufficient to its own delight,
Both in corporeal organs and in skill
By means of such to body forth its
    Will –
And, after, insufficient to apprise
Men of that Will, oblige them recognize
The Hid by the Revealed – but that, –
    the last
Nor lightest of the struggles overpast, –
Will, he bade abdicate, which would
    not void
The throne, might sit there, suffer be
    enjoyed
Mankind, a varied and divine array
Incapable of homage, the first way,
Nor fit to render incidentally
Tribute connived at, taken by the by,
In joys. If thus with warrant to rescind
The ignominious exile of mankind –
Whose proper service, ascertained intact
As yet, (to be by him themselves made
    act,
Not watch Sordello acting each of them)
Was to secure – if the true diadem
Seemed imminent while our Sordello
    drank
The wisdom of that golden Palma, –
    thank
Verona's Lady in her citadel
Founded by Gaulish Brennus, legends
    tell:
And truly when she left him, the sun
    reared
A head like the first clamberer's who
    peered

A-top the Capitol, his face on flame
With triumph, triumphing till Manlius
    came.
Nor slight too much my rhymes – that
    spring, dispread,
Dispart, disperse, lingering overhead
Like an escape of angels! Rather say,
My transcendental platan! mounting
    gay
(An archimage so courts a novice-queen)
With tremulous silvered trunk, whence
    branches sheen
Laugh out, thick-foliaged next, a-shiver
    soon
With coloured buds, then glowing like
    the moon
One mild flame, – last a pause, a burst,
    and all
Her ivory limbs are smothered by a fall,
Bloom-flinders and fruit-sparkles and
    leaf-dust,
Ending the weird work prosecuted just
For her amusement; he decrepit, stark,
Dozes; her uncontrolled delight may mark
Apart –
        Yet not so, surely never so
Only, as good my soul were suffered go
O'er the lagune: forth fare thee, put
    aside –
Entrance thy synod, as a god may glide
Out of the world he fills, and leave it
    mute
For myriad ages as we men compute,
Returning into it without a break
O' the consciousness! They sleep, and
    I awake
O'er the lagune, being at Venice.
                                Note,
In just such songs as Eglamor (say)
    wrote
With heart and soul and strength, for
    he believed
Himself achieving all to be achieved
By singer – in such songs you find alone
Completeness, judge the song and
    singer one,
And either purpose answered, his in it

Or its in him: while from true works
    (to wit
Sordello's dream-performances that will
Never be more than dreamed) escapes
    there still
Some proof, the singer's proper life was
    'neath
The life his song exhibits, this a sheath
To that; a passion and a knowledge far
Transcending these, majestic as they are,
Smouldered; his lay was but an episode
In the bard's life: which evidence you
    owed
To some slight weariness, some looking-
    off
Or start-away. The childish skit or scoff
In 'Charlemagne', (his poem, dreamed
    divine
In every point except one silly line
About the restiff daughters) – what may
    lurk
In that? 'My life commenced before this
    work,'
(So I interpret the significance
Of the bard's start aside and look
    askance)
'My life continues after: on I fare
'With no more stopping, possibly, no
    care
'To note the undercurrent, the why and
    how,
'Where, when, o' the deeper life, as thus
    just now.
'But, silent, shall I cease to live? Alas
'For you! who sigh, "When shall it come
    to pass
' "We read that story? How will he
    compress
' "The future gains, his life's true business,
' "Into the better lay which – that one
    flout,
' "Howe'er inopportune it be, lets out –
' "Engrosses him already, though
    professed
' "To meditate with us eternal rest,
' "And partnership in all his life has
    found?" '

'Tis but a sailor's promise, weather-
   bound:
'Strike sail, slip cable, here the bark be
   moored
'For once, the awning stretched, the
   poles assured!
'Noontide above; except the wave's
   crisp dash,
'Or buzz of colibri, or tortoise' splash,
'The margin's silent: out with every
   spoil
'Made in our tracking, coil by mighty
   coil,
'This serpent of a river to his head
'I' the midst! Admire each treasure, as
   we spread
'The bank, to help us tell our history
'Aright: give ear, endeavour to descry
'The groves of giant rushes, how they
   grew
'Like demons' endlong tresses we sailed
   through,
'What mountains yawned, forests to give
   us vent
'Opened, each doleful side, yet on we
   went
'Till … may that beetle (shake your cap)
   attest
'The springing of a land-wind from the
   West!'
  – Wherefore? Ah yes, you frolic it
   today!
To-morrow, and, the pageant moved
   away
Down to the poorest tent-pole, we and
   you
Part company: no other may pursue
Eastward your voyage, be informed
   what fate
Intends, if triumph or decline await
The tempter of the everlasting steppe.
  I muse this on a ruined palace-step
At Venice: why should I break off, nor
   sit
Longer upon my step, exhaust the fit
England gave birth to? Who's adorable
Enough reclaim a – no Sordello's Will

Alack! – be queen to me? That Bassanese
Busied among her smoking fruit-boats?
   These
Perhaps from our delicious Asolo
Who twinkle, pigeons o'er the portico
Not prettier, bind June lilies into sheaves
To deck the bridge-side chapel, dropping
   leaves
Soiled by their own loose gold-meal? Ah,
   beneath
The cool arch stoops she, brownest
   check! Her wreath
Endures a month – a half-month – if I
   make
A queen of her, continue for her sake
Sordello's story? Nay, that Paduan girl
Splashes with barer legs where a live
   whirl
In the dead black Giudecca proves sea-
   weed
Drifting has sucked down three, four,
   all indeed
Save one pale-red striped, pale-blue
   turbaned post
For gondolas.
          You sad dishevelled ghost
That pluck at me and point, are you
   advised
I breathe? Let stay those girls (e'en her
   disguised
– Jewels i' the locks that love no crownet
   like
Their nativefield-buds and the green
   wheat-spike,
So fair! – who left this end of June's
   turmoil,
Shook off, as might a lily its gold soil,
Pomp, save a foolish gem or two, and
   free
In dream, came join the peasants o'er
   the sea.)
Look they too happy, too tricked out?
   Confess
There is such niggard stock of happiness
To share, that, do one's uttermost,
   dear wretch,
One labours ineffectually to stretch

It o'er you so that mother and children,
　　both
May equitably flaunt the sumpter-cloth!
Divide the robe yet farther: be content
With seeing just a score pre-eminent
Through shreds of it, acknowledged
　　happy wights,
Engrossing what should furnish all, by
　　rights!
For, these in evidence, you clearlier
　　claim
A like garb for the rest, – grace all, the
　　same
As these my peasants. I ask youth and
　　strength
And health for each of you, not more –
　　at length
Grown wise, who asked at home that
　　the whole race
Might add the spirit's to the body's
　　grace,
And all be dizened out as chiefs and
　　bards.
But in this magic weather one discards
Much old requirement. Venice seems a
　　type
Of Life – 'twixt blue and blue extends,
　　a stripe,
As Life, the somewhat, hangs 'twixt
　　nought and nought:
'Tis Venice, and 'tis Life – as good you
　　sought
To spare me the Piazza's slippery stone
Or keep me to the unchoked canals
　　alone,
As hinder Life the evil with the good
Which make up Living, rightly
　　understood.
Only, do finish something! Peasants,
　　queens,
Take them, made happy by whatever
　　means,
Parade them for the common credit,
　　vouch
That a luckless residue, we sent to crouch
In corners out of sight, was just as
　　framed

For happiness, its portion might have
　　claimed
As well, and so, obtaining joy, had stalked
Fastuous as any! – such my project,
　　baulked
Already; I hardly venture to adjust
The first rags, when you find me. To
　　mistrust
Me! – nor unreasonably. You, no doubt,
Have the true knack of tiring suitors out
With those thin lips on tremble, lashless
　　eyes
Inveterately tear-shot: there, be wise,
Mistress of mine, there, there, as if I
　　meant
You insult! – shall your friend (not slave)
　　be shent
For speaking home? Beside, care-bit
　　erased
Broken-up beauties ever took my taste
Supremely; and I love you more, far
　　more
Than her I looked should foot Life's
　　temple-floor.
Years ago, leagues at distance, when and
　　where
A whisper came, 'Let others seek! – thy
　　care
'Is found, thy life's provision; if thy race
'Should be thy mistress, and into one
　　face
'The many faces crowd?' Ah, had I,
　　judge,
Or no, your secret? Rough apparel –
　　grudge
All ornaments save tag or tassel worn
To hint we are not thoroughly forlorn –
Slouch bonnet, unloop mantle, careless
　　go
Alone (that's saddest, but it must be so)
Through Venice, sing now and now
　　glance aside,
Aught desultory or undignified, –
Then, ravishingest lady, will you pass
Or not each formidable group, the mass
Before the Basilic (that feast gone by,
God's great day of the Corpus Domini)

And, wistfully foregoing proper men,
Come timid up to me for alms? And then
The luxury to hesitate, feign do
Some unexampled grace! – when, whom
    but you
Dare I bestow your own upon? And hear
Further before you say, it is to sneer
I call you ravishing; for I regret
Little that she, whose early foot was set
Forth as she'd plant it on a pedestal,
Now, i' the silent city, seems to fall
Toward me – no wreath, only a lip's
    unrest
To quiet, surcharged eyelids to be pressed
Dry of their tears upon my bosom.
    Strange
Such sad chance should produce in thee
    such change,
My love! Warped souls and bodies! yet
    God spoke
Of right-hand, foot and eye – selects our
    yoke,
Sordello, as your poetship may find!
So, sleep upon my shoulder, child, nor
    mind
Their foolish talk; we'll manage reinstate
Your old worth; ask moreover, when
    they prate
Of evil men past hope, 'Don't each
    contrive,
'Despite the evil you abuse, to live? –
'Keeping, each losel, through a maze of
    lies,
'His own conceit of truth? to which he
    hies
'By obscure windings, tortuous, if you
    will,
'But to himself not inaccessible;
'He sees truth, and his lies are for the
    crowd
'Who cannot see; some fancied right
    allowed
'His vilest wrong empowered the losel
    clutch
'One pleasure from a multitude of such
'Denied him.' Then assert, 'All men
    appear

'To think all better than themselves, by
    here
'Trusting a crowd they wrong; but really,'
    say,
'All men think all men stupider than
    they,
'Since, save themselves, no other
    comprehends
'The complicated scheme to make
    amends
' – Evil, the scheme by which, thro'
    Ignorance.
'Good labours to exist.' A slight
    advance, …
Merely to find the sickness you die
    through,
And nought beside! but if one can't
    eschew
One's portion in the common lot, at
    least
One can avoid an ignorance increased
Tenfold by dealing out hint after hint
How nought were like dispensing
    without stint
The water of life – so easy to dispense
Beside, when one has probed the centre
    whence
Commotion's born – could tell you of it
    all!
' – Meantime, just meditate my madrigal
'O' the mugwort that conceals a dewdrop
    safe!'
What, dullard? we and you in smothery
    chafe,
Babes, baldheads, stumbled thus far
    into Zin
The Horrid,* getting neither out nor in,
A hungry sun above us, sands that
    bung
Our throats, – each dromedary lolls a
    tongue,
Each camel churns a sick and frothy
    chap,
And you, 'twixt tales of Potiphar's
    mishap,

* Isaiah 13:21, 22

And sonnets on the earliest ass that
  spoke,
– Remark, you wonder any one needs
  choke
With founts about! Potsherd him,
  Gibeonites!
While awkwardly enough your Moses
  smites
The rock, though he forego his Promised
  Land
Thereby, have Satan claim his carcass,
  and
Figure as Metaphysic Poet … ah,
Mark ye the dim first oozings? Meribah!*
Then, quaffing at the fount my courage
  gained,
Recall – not that I prompt ye – who
  explained …
'Presumptuous!'interrupts one. You,
  not I
'Tis, brother, marvel at and magnify
Such office: 'office,' quotha? can we get
To the beginning of the office yet?
What do we here? simply experiment
Each on the other's power and its
  intent
When elsewhere tasked, – if this of
  mine were trucked
For yours to either's good, – we watch
  construct,
In short, an engine: with a finished
  one,
What it can do, is all, – nought, how
  'tis done.
But this of ours yet in probation, dusk
A kernel of strange wheelwork through
  its husk
Grows into shape by quarters and by
  halves;
Remark this tooth's spring, wonder
  what that valve's
Fall bodes, presume each faculty's
  device,
Make out each other more or less
  precise –
The scope of the whole engine's to be
  proved;

We die: which means to say, the whole's
  removed,
Dismounted wheel by wheel, this
  complex gin, –
To be set up anew elsewhere, begin
A task indeed, but with a clearer clime
Than the murk lodgment of our building-
  time.
And then, I grant you, it behoves forget
How 'tis done – all that must amuse us
  yet
So long: and, while you turn upon your
  heel,
Pray that I be not busy slitting steel
Or shredding brass, camped on some
  virgin shore
Under a cluster of fresh stars, before
I name a tithe o' the wheels I trust
  to do!
  So occupied, then, are we: hitherto,
At present, and a weary while to come,
The office of ourselves, – nor blind nor
  dumb,
And seeing somewhat of man's state, –
  has been,
For the worst of us, to say they so have
  seen;
For the better, what it was they saw; the
  best
Impart the gift of seeing to the rest:
'So that I glance,' says such an one,
  'around,
'And there's no face but I can read
  profound
'Disclosures in; this stands for hope,
  that – fear,
'And for a speech, a deed in proof,
  look here!
' "Stoop, else the strings of blossom,
  where the nuts
O'erarch, will blind thee! Said I not? She
  shuts
' "Both eyes this time, so close the hazels
  meet!

* Waters of Meribah, that is, of Strife. See
  Exodus 17:7.

' "Thus, prisoned in the Piombi, I
  repeat
' "Events one rove occasioned, o'er and
  o'er,
' "Putting 'twixt me and madness
  evermore
' "Thy sweet shape, Zanze! Therefore
  stoop!"
                              ' "That's truth!"
'(Adjudge you) "the incarcerated youth
' "Would say that!"
'Youth? Plara the bard? Set down
'That Plara spent his youth in a grim
  town
'Whose cramped ill-featured streets
  huddled about
'The minster for protection, never out
'Of its black belfry's shade and its bells'
  roar.
'The brighter shone the suburb, – all the
  more
'Ugly and absolute that shade's reproof
'Of any chance escape of joy, – some
  roof,
'Taller than they, allowed the rest
  detect, –
'Before the sole permitted laugh (suspect
'Who could, 'twas meant for laughter,
  that ploughed cheek's
'Repulsive gleam!) when the sun
  stopped both peaks
'Of the cleft belfry like a fiery wedge,
'Then sank, a huge flame on its socket
  edge,
'With leavings on the grey glass oriel-
  pane
'Ghastly some minutes more. No fear
  of rain –
'The minster minded that! in heaps the
  dust
'Lay everywhere. This town, the minster's
  trust,
'Held Plara; who, its denizen, bade hail
'In twice twelve sonnets, Tempe's dewy
  vale.'
    ' "Exact the town, the minster and
      the street!" '

'As all mirth triumphs, sadness
  mean defeat:
'Lust triumphs and is gay, Love's
  triumphed o'er
'And sad: but Lucio's sad. I said before,
'Love's sad, not Lucio; one who loves
  may be
'As gay his love has leave to hope, as he
'Downcast that lusts' desire escapes the
  springe:
'Tis of the mood itself I speak, what
  tinge
Determines it, else colourless, – or mirth,
'Or melancholy, as from heaven or earth.
   ' "Ay, that's the variation's gist!"
                                      'Indeed
'Thus far advanced in safety then,
  proceed!
'And having seen too what I saw, be
  bold
'And next encounter what I do behold
'(That's sure) but bid you take on trust!'
                                      Attack
The use and purpose of such sights!
    Alack,
Not so unwisely does the crowd dispense
On Salinguerras praise in preference
To the Sordellos: men of action, these!
Who, seeing just as little as you please,
Yet turn that little to account, – engage
With, do not gaze at, – carry on, a stage,
The work o' the world, not merely make
  report
The work existed ere their day! In short,
When at some future no-time a brave
  band
Sees, using what it sees, then shake my
  hand
In heaven, my brother! Meanwhile
  where's the hurt
Of keeping the Makers-see on the alert,
At whose defection mortals stare aghast
As though heaven's bounteous
  windows were slammed fast
Incontinent? Whereas all you, beneath,
Should scowl at, bruise their lips and
  break their teeth

Who ply the pullies, for neglecting
    you:
And therefore have I moulded, made
    anew
A Man, and give him to be turned and
    tried,
Be angry with or pleased at. On your
    side,
Have ye times, places, actors of your
    own?
Try them upon Sordello when full-
    grown,
And then – ah then! If Hercules first
    parched
His foot in Egypt only to be marched
A sacrifice for Jove with pomp to suit,
What chance have I? The demigod was
    mute
Till, at the altar, where time out of mind
Such guests became oblations, chaplets
    twined
His forehead long enough, and he
    began
Slaying the slayers, nor escaped a man.
Take not affront, my gentle audience!
    whom
No Hercules shall make his hecatomb,
Believe, nor from his brows your
    chaplet rend –
That's your kind suffrage, yours, my
    patron-friend,
Whose great verse blares unintermittent
    on
Like your own trumpeter at Marathon, –
You who, Platæa and Salamis being
    scant,
Put up with Aetna for a stimulant –
And did well, I acknowledged, as he
    loomed
Over the midland sea last month,
    presumed
Long, lay demolished in the blazing
    West
At eve, while towards him tilting
    cloudlets pressed
Like Persian ships at Salamis. Friend,
    wear

A crest proud as desert while I declare
Had I a flawless ruby fit to wring
Tears of its colour from that painted
    king*
Who lost it, I would, for that smile
    which went
To my heart, fling it in the sea, content,
Wearing your verse in place, an amulet
Sovereign against all passion, wear and
    fret!
My English Eyebright, if you are not glad
That, as I stopped my task awhile, the
    sad
Dishevelled form, wherein I put mankind
To come at times and keep my pact in
    mind,
Renewed me, – hear no crickets in the
    hedge,
Nor let a glowworm spot the river's edge
At home, and may the summer
    showers gush
Without a warning from the missel
    thrush!
So, to our business, now – the fate of
    such
As find our common nature – overmuch
Despised because restricted and unfit
To bear the burthen they impose on it –
Cling when they would discard it;
    craving strength
To leap from the allotted world, at length
They do leap, – flounder on without a
    term,
Each a god's germ, doomed to remain a
    germ
In unexpanded infancy, unless …
But that's the story – dull enough,
    confess!
There might be fitter subjects to allure;
Still, neither misconceive my portraiture
Nor undervalue its adornments quaint:
What seems a fiend perchance may
    prove a saint.
Ponder a story ancient pens transmit,
Then say if you condemn me or acquit.

* Polycrates of Samos

John the Beloved, banished Antioch
For Patmos, bade collectively his flock
Farewell, but set apart the closing eve
To comfort those his exile most would
    grieve,
He knew: a touching spectacle, that
    house
In motion to receive him! Xanthus'
    spouse
You missed, made panther's meat a
    month since; but
Xanthus himself (his nephew 'twas,
    they shut
'Twixt boards and sawed asunder)
    Polycarp,
Soft Charicle, next year no wheel could
    warp
To swear by Caesar's fortune, with the
    rest
Were ranged; thro' whom the grey
    disciple pressed.
Busily blessing right and left, just
    stopped
To pat one infant's curls, the hangman
    cropped
Soon after, reached the portal. On its
    hinge
The door turns and he enters: what
    quick twinge
Ruins the smiling mouth, those wide
    eyes fix
Whereon, why like some spectral
    candlestick's
Branch the disciple's arms? Dead
    swooned he, woke
Anon, heaved sigh, made shift to gasp,
    heart-broke,
'Get thee behind me, Satan! Have I
    toiled
'To no more purpose? Is the gospel
    foiled
'Here too, and o'er my son's, my Xanthus'
    hearth,
'Portrayed with sooty garb and features
    swarth –
'Ah, Xanthus, am I to thy roof beguiled
'To see the – the – the Devil domiciled?'

Whereto sobbed Xanthus, 'Father, 'tis
    yourself
'Installed, a limning which our utmost
    pelf
'Went to procure against to-morrow's
    loss;
'And that's no twy-prong, but a pastoral
    cross,
'You're painted with!'
           His puckered brows unfold –
And you shall hear Sordello's story told.

## BOOK THE FOURTH

Meantime Ferrara lay in rueful case;
The lady-city, for whose sole embrace
Her pair of suitors struggled, felt their
    arms
A brawny mischief to the fragile charms
They tugged for – one discovering that
    to twist
Her tresses twice or thrice about his
    wrist
Secured a point of vantage – one, how
    best
He'd parry that by planting in her breast
His elbow spike – each party too intent
For noticing, howe'er the battle went,
The conqueror would but have a corpse
    to kiss.
'May Boniface be duly damned for this!'
– Howled some old Ghibellin, as up he
    turned,
From the wet heap of rubbish where
    they burned
His house, a little skull with dazzling
    teeth:
'A boon, sweet Christ – let Salinguerra
    seethe
'In hell for ever, Christ, and let myself
'Be there to laugh at him!' – moaned
    some young Guelf
Stumbling upon a shrivelled hand nailed
    fast
To the charred lintel of the doorway, last
His father stood within to bid him
    speed.

The thoroughfares were overrun with
    weed
– Docks, quitchgrass, loathly mallows
    no man plants.
  The stranger, none of its inhabitants
Crept out of doors to taste fresh air
    again,
And ask the purpose of a splendid train
Admitted on a morning; every town
Of the East League was come by envoy
    down
To treat for Richard's ransom: here you
    saw
The Vicentine, here snowy oxen draw
The Paduan carroch, its vermilion cross
On its white field. A-tiptoe o'er the fosse
Looked Legate Montelungo wistfully
After the flock of steeples he might spy
In Este's time, gone (doubts he) long
    ago
To mend the ramparts: sure the laggards
    know
The Pope's as good as here! They paced
    the streets
More soberly. At least, 'Taurello greets
'The League,' announced a pursuivant,
    – 'will match
'Its courtesy, and labours to dispatch
'At earliest Tito, Friedrich's Pretor, sent
'On pressing matters from his post at
    Trent,
'With Mainard Count of Tyrol, – simply
    waits
'Their going to receive the delegates.'
'Tito !' Our delegates exchanged a glance,
And, keeping the main way, admired
    askance
The lazy engines of outlandish birth,
Couched like a king each on its bank
    of earth –
Arbalist, manganel and catapult;
While stationed by, as waiting a result,
Lean silent gangs of mercenaries ceased
Working to watch the strangers. 'This,
    at least,
'Were better spared; he scarce presumes
    gainsay

'The League's decision! Get our friend
    away
'And profit for the future: how else
    teach
'Fools 'tis not safe to stray within claw's
    reach
'Ere Salinguerra's final gasp be blown?'
'Those mere convulsive scratches find
    the bone.
'Who bade him bloody the spent osprey's
    nare?'
    The carrochs halted in the public
    square.
Pennons of every blazon once a-flaunt,
Men prattled, freelier that the crested
    gaunt
White ostrich with a horse-shoe in her
    beak
Was missing, and whoever chose might
    speak
'Ecelin' boldly out: so, – 'Ecelin
'Needed his wife to swallow half the sin
'And sickens by himself: the devil's
    whelp,
'He styles his son, dwindles away, no
    help
'From conserves, your fine triple-curded
    froth
'Of virgin's blood, your Venice viper
    broth –
'Eh? Jubilate!' – 'Peace! no little word
'You utter here that's not distinctly
    heard
'Up at Oliero: he was absent sick
'When we besieged Bassano – who, i'
    the thick
'O' the work, perceived the progress
    Azzo made,
'Like Ecelin, through his witch Adelaide?
'She managed it so well that, night by
    night
'At their bed-foot stood up a soldier-
    sprite,
'First fresh, pale by-and-by without a
    wound,
'And, when it came with eyes filmed as
    in swound,

'They knew the place was taken.' –
    'Ominous
'That Ghibellins should get what
    cautelous
'Old Redbeard sought from Azzo's sire
    to wrench
'Vainly; Saint George contrived his town
    a trench
'O' the marshes, an impermeable bar.'
' – Young Ecelin is meant the tutelar
'Of Padua, rather; veins embrace upon
'His hand like Brenta and Bacchiglion.'
What now? – 'The founts! God's bread,
    touch not a plank!
'A crawling hell of carrion – every tank
'Choke-full! – found out just now to
    Cino's cost –
'The same who gave Taurello up for lost,
'And, making no account of fortune's
    freaks,
'Refused to budge from Padua then, but
    sneaks
'Back now with Concorezzi:' faith! they
    drag
'Their carroch to San Vitale, plant the
    flag
'On his own palace, so adroitly razed
'He knew it not; a sort of Guelf folk
    gazed
'And laughed apart; Cino disliked then
    air –
'Must pluck up spirit, show he does not
    care –
'Seats himself on the tank's edge – will
    begin
'To hum, za za, *Cavaler Ecelin* –
'A silence; he gets warmer, clinks to
    chime,
'Now both feet plough the ground,
    deeper each time,
'At last, za, za and up with a fierce kick
'Comes his own mother's face caught
    by the thick
'Grey hair about his spur!'
                    Which means, they lift
The covering, Salinguerra made a shift
To stretch upon the truth; as well avoid

Further disclosures; leave them thus
    employed.
Our dropping Autumn morning clears
    apace,
And poor Ferrara puts a softened face
On her misfortunes. Let us scale this
    tall
Huge foursquare line of red brick garden-
    wall
Bastioned within by trees of every sort
On three sides, slender, spreading, long
    and short;
Each grew as it contrived, the poplar
    ramped,
The fig-tree reared itself, – but stark and
    cramped,
Made fools of, like tamed lions: whence,
    on the edge,
Running 'twixt trunk and trunk to
    smooth one ledge
Of shade, were shrubs inserted, warp
    and woof,
Which smothered up that variance.
    Scale the roof
Of solid tops, and o'er the slope you
    slide
Down to a grassy space level and wide,
Here and there dotted with a tree, but
    trees
Of rarer leaf, each foreigner at ease,
Set by itself: and in the centre spreads,
Borne upon three uneasy leopards' heads,
A laver, broad and shallow, one bright
    spirt
Of water bubbles in. The walls begirt
With trees leave off on either hand;
    pursue
Your path along a wondrous avenue
Those walls abut on, heaped of gleamy
    stone,
With aloes leering everywhere, grey-grown
From many a Moorish summer: how
    they wind
Out of the fissures! likelier to bind
The building than those rusted cramps
    which drop
Already in the eating sunshine. Stop,

You fleeting shapes above there! Ah,
    the pride
Or else despair of the whole countryside!
A range of statues, swarming o'er with
    wasps,
God, goddess, woman, man, the Greek
    rough-rasps
In crumbling Naples marble – meant to
    look
Like those Messina marbles Constance
    took
Delight in, or Taurello's self conveyed
To Mantua for his mistress, Adelaide, –
A certain font with caryatides
Since cloistered at Goito; only, these
Are up and doing, not abashed, a troop
Able to right themselves – who see you,
    stoop
Their arms o' the instant after you!
    Unplucked
By this or that, you pass; for they conduct
To terrace raised on terrace, and, between,
Creatures of brighter mould and braver
    mien
Than any yet, the choicest of the Isle
No doubt. Here, left a sullen breathing-
    while,
Up-gathered on himself the Fighter
    stood
For his last fight, and, wiping treacherous
    blood
Out of the eyelids just held ope beneath
Those shading fingers in their iron
    sheath,
Steadied his strengths amid the buzz
    and stir
Of the dusk hideous amphitheatre
At the announcement of his over-match
To wind the day's diversion up, dispatch
The pertinacious Gaul: while, limbs
    one heap,
The Slave, no breath in her round
    mouth, watched leap
Dart after dart forth, as her hero's car
Clove dizzily the solid of the war
– Let coil about his knees for pride in
    him.

We reach the farthest terrace, and the
    grim
San Pietro Palace stops us.
                              Such the state
Of Salinguerra's plan to emulate
Sicilian marvels, that his girlish wife
Retrude still might lead her ancient life
In her new home: whereat enlarged so
    much
Neighbours upon the novel princely
    touch
He took, – who hare imprisons Boniface.
Here must the Envoys come to sue for
    grace;
And here, emerging from the labyrinth
Below, Sordello paused beside the
    plinth
Of the door-pillar.
                        He had really left
Verona for the cornfields (a poor theft
From the morass) where Este's camp
    was made;
The Envoys' march, the Legate's
    cavalcade –
All had been seen by him, but scarce as
    when, –
Eager for cause to stand aloof from men
At every point save the fantastic tie
Acknowledged in his boyish sophistry, –
He made account of such. A crowd, – he
    meant
To task the whole of it; each part's intent
Concerned him therefore: and, the more
    he pried,
The less became Sordello satisfied
With his own figure at the moment.
                                        Sought
He respite from his task? Descried he
    aught
Novel in the anticipated sight
Of all these livers upon all delight?
This phalanx, as of myriad points
    combined,
Whereby he still had imaged the
    mankind
His youth was passed in dreams of
    rivalling,

His age – in plans to prove at least
     such thing
Had been so dreamed, – which now he
     must impress
With his own will, effect a happiness
By theirs, – supply a body to his soul
Thence, and become eventually whole
With them as he had hoped to be
     without –
Made these the mankind he once raved
     about?
Because a few of them were notable,
Should all be figured worthy note? As
     well
Expect to find Taurello's triple line
Of trees a single and prodigious pine.
Real pines rose here and there; but,
     close among,
Thrust into and mixed up with pines, a
     throng
Of shrubs, he saw – a nameless common
     sort
O'erpast in dreams, left out of the report
And hurried into corners, or at best
Admitted to be fancied like the rest.
Reckon that morning's proper chiefs –
     how few!
And yet the people grew, die people
     grew,
Grew ever, as if the many there indeed,
More left behind and most who should
     succeed, –
Simply in virtue of their mouths and eyes,
Petty enjoyments and huge miseries, –
Mingled with, and made veritably great
Those chiefs: he overlooked not
     Mainard's state
Nor Concorezzi's station, but instead
Of stopping there, each dwindled to be
     head
Of infinite and absent Tyrolese
Or Paduans; startling all the more, that
     these
Seemed passive and disposed of, uncared
     for,
Yet doubtless on the whole (like Eglamor)
Smiling; for if a wealthy man decays

And out of store of robes must wear,
     all days,
One tattered suit, alike in sun and shade,
'Tis commonly some tarnished gay
     brocade
Fit for a feast-night's flourish and no
     more:
Nor otherwise poor Misery from her
     store
Of looks is fain upgather, keep unfurled
For common wear as she goes through
     the world,
The faint remainder of some worn-out
     smile
Meant for a feast-night's service merely.
     While
Crowd upon crowd rose on Sordello
     thus, –
(Crowds no way interfering to discuss,
Much less dispute, life's joys with one
     employed
In envying them, – or, if they aught
     enjoyed,
Where lingered something indefinable
In every look and tone, the mirth as well
As woe, that fixed at once his estimate
Of the result, their good or bad estate) –
Old memories returned with new effect:
And the new body, ere he could suspect,
Cohered, mankind and he were really
     fused,
The new self seemed impatient to be
     used
By him, but utterly another way
Than that anticipated: strange to say,
They were too much below him, more
     in thrall
Than he, the adjunct than the principal.
What booted scattered units? – here a
     mind
And there, which might repay his own
     to find,
And stamp, and use? – a few, howe'er
     august,
If all the rest were grovelling in the dust?
No: first a mighty equilibrium, sure,
Should he establish, privilege procure

For all, the few had long possessed! He
    felt
An error, an exceeding error melt:
While he was occupied with Mantuan
    chants,
Behoved him think of men, and take
    their wants,
Such as he now distinguished every
    side,
As his own want which might be
    satisfied, –
And, after that, think of rare qualities
Of his own soul demanding exercise.
It followed naturally, through no claim
On their part, which made virtue of the
    aim
At serving them, on his, – that, past
    retrieve,
He felt now in their toils, theirs – nor
    could leave
Wonder how, in the eagerness to rule,
Impress his will on mankind, he (the
    fool!)
Had never even entertained the thought
That this his last arrangement might be
    fraught
With incidental good to them as well,
And that mankind's delight would help
    to swell
His own. So, if he sighed, as formerly
Because the merry time of life must
    fleet,
'Twas deeplier now, – for could the
    crowds repeat
Their poor experiences? His hand that
    shook
Was twice to be deplored. 'The Legate,
    look!
'With eyes, like fresh-blown thrush-
    eggs on a thread,
'Faint-blue and loosely floating in his
    head,
'Large tongue, moist open mouth; and
    this long while
'That owner of the idiotic smile
'Serves them!'
            He fortunately saw in time

His fault, however, and since the office
    prime
Includes the secondary – best accept
Both offices; Taurello, its adept,
Could teach him the preparatory one,
And how to do what he had fancied
    done
Long previously, ere take the greater
    task.
How render first these people happy?
    Ask
The people's friends: for there must be
    one good,
One way to it – the Cause! He understood
The meaning now of Falma; why the jar
Else, the ado, the trouble wide and far
Of Guelfs and Ghibellins, the Lombard
    hope
And Rome's despair? – 'twixt Emperor
    and Pope
The confused shifting sort of Eden tale –
Hardihood still recurring, still to fail –
That foreign interloping fiend, this free
And native overbrooding deity:
Yet a dire fascination o'er the palms
The Kaiser ruined, troubling even the
    calms
Of paradise; or, on the other hand,
The Pontiff, as the Kaisers understand,
One snake-like cursed of God to love
    the ground,
Whose heavy length breaks in the
    noon profound
Some saving tree – which needs the
    Kaiser, dressed
As the dislodging angel of that pest:
Yet flames that pest bedropped, flat
    head, full fold,
With coruscating dower of dyes. 'Behold
'The secret, so to speak, and master-
    spring
'O' the contest! – which of the two
    Powers shall bring
'Men good, perchance the most good:
    ay, it may
'Be that! – the question, which best
    knows the way.'

And hereupon Count Mainard strutted past
Out of San Pietro; never seemed the last
Of archers, slingers: and our friend began
To recollect strange modes of serving man –
Arbalist, catapult, brake, manganel,
And more. 'This way of theirs may, – who can tell? –
'Need perfecting,' said he: 'let all be solved
'At once! Taurello 'tis, the task devolved
'On late: confront Taurello!'
                                              And at last
He did confront him. Scarce an hour had past
When forth Sordello came, older by years
Than at his entry. Unexampled fears
Oppressed him, and he staggered off, blind, mute
And deaf, like some fresh-mutilated brute,
Into Ferrara – not the empty town
That morning witnessed: he went up and down
Streets whence the veil had been stript shred by shred,
So that, in place of huddling with their dead
Indoors, to answer Salinguerra's ends,
Townsfolk make shift to crawl forth, sit like friends
With any one. A woman gave him choice
Of her two daughters, the infantile voice
Or the dimpled knee, for half a half, his throat
Was clasped with; but an archer knew the coat –
Its blue cross and eight lilies, – bade beware
One dogging him in concert with the pair
Though thrumming on the sleeve that hid his knife.

Night set in early, autumn dews were rife,
They kindled great fires while the Leaguers' mass
Began at every carroch: he must pass
Between the kneeling people. Presently
The carroch of Verona caught his eye
With purple trappings; silently he bent
Over its fire, when voices violent
Began, 'Affirm not whom the youth was like
'That struck me from the porch: I did not strike
'Again: I too have chestnut hair; my kin
'Hate Azzo and stand up for Ecelin.
'Here, minstrel, drive bad thoughts away! Sing! Take
'My glove for guerdon!' And for that man's sake
He turned: 'A song of Eglamor's!' – scarce named,
When, 'Our Sordello's rather!' – all exclaimed;
'Is not Sordello famousest for rhyme?'
He had been happy to deny, this time, –
Profess as heretofore the aching head
And failing heart, – suspect that in his stead.
Some true Apollo had the charge of them,
Was champion to reward or to condemn,
So his intolerable risk might shift
Or share itself; but Naddo's precious gift
Of gifts, he owned, be certain! At the close –
'I made that,' said he to a youth who rose
As if to hear: 'twas Palma through the band
Conducted him in silence by her hand.
  Back now for Salinguerra. Tito of Trent
Gave place to Palma and her friend, who went
In turn at Montelungo's visit: one
After the other were they come and gone, –

These spokesmen for the Kaiser and
    the Pope,
This incarnation of the People's hope,
Sordello, – all the say of each was said;
And Salinguerra sat, – himself instead
Of these to talk with, lingered musing
    yet.
'Twas a drear vast presence-chamber
    roughly set
In order for the morning's use; full
    face,
The Kaiser's ominous sign-mark had
    first place,
The crowned grim twy-necked eagle,
    coarsely-blacked
With ochre on the naked wall; nor lacked
Romano's green and yellow either side;
But the new token Tito brought had
    tried
The Legate's patience – nay, if Palma
    knew
What Salinguerra almost meant to do
Until the sight of her restored his lip
A certain half-smile, three months'
    chieftainship
Had banished! Afterward, the Legate
    found
No change in him, nor asked what
    badge he wound
And unwound carelessly. Now sat the
    Chief
Silent as when our couple left, whose
    brief
Encounter wrought so opportune effect
In thoughts he summoned not, nor
    would reject,
Though time 'twas now if ever, to pause
    – fix
On any sort of ending: wiles and tricks
Exhausted, judge! his charge, the crazy
    town,
Just managed to be hindered crashing
    down –
His last sound troops ranged – care
    observed to post
His best of the maimed soldiers inner-
    most –

So much was plain enough, but
    somehow struck
Him not before. And now with this
    strange luck
Of Tito's news, rewarding his address
So well, what thought he of ? – how
    success
With Friedrich's rescript there, would
    either hush
Old Ecelin's scruples, bring the manly
    flush
To his young son's white cheek, or, last
    exempt
Himself from telling what there was to
    tempt?
No: that this minstrel was Romano's last
Servant – himself the first! Could he
    contrast
The whole! – that minstrel's thirty
    years just spent
In doing nought, their notablest event
This morning's journey hither, as I
    told –
Who yet was lean, outworn and really
    old,
A stammering awkward man that scarce
    dared raise
His eye before the magisterial gaze –
And Salinguerra with his fears and hopes
Of sixty years, his Emperors and Popes,
Cares and contrivances, yet, you would
    say,
'Twas a youth nonchalantly looked away
Through the embrasure northward o'er
    the sick
Expostulating trees – so agile, quick
And graceful turned the head on the
    broad chest
Encased in pliant steel, his constant vest,
Whence split the sun off in a spray of
    fire
Across the room; and, loosened of its
    tire
Of steel, that head let breathe the comely
    brown
Large massive locks discoloured as if
    crown

Encircled them, so frayed the basnet
    where
A sharp white line divided clean the
    hair;
Glossy above, glossy below, it swept
Curling and fine about a brow thus kept
Calm, laid coat upon coat, marble and
    sound:
This was the mystic mark the Tuscan
    found,
Mused oft turned over books about.
    Square-faced,
No lion more; two vivid eyes, enchased
In hollows filled with many a shade
    and streak
Settling from the bold nose and bearded
    cheek.
Nor might the half-smile reach them
    that deformed
A lip supremely perfect else – unwarmed,
Unwidened, less or more; indifferent
Whether on trees or men his thoughts
    were bent,
Thoughts rarely, after all, in trim and
    train
As now a period was fulfilled again:
Of such, a series made his life,
    compressed
In each, one story serving for the rest –
How his life-streams rolling arrived at
    last
At the barrier, whence, were it once
    overpast,
They would emerge, a river to the end, –
Gathered themselves up, paused, bade
    fate befriend,
Took the leap, hung a minute at the
    height,
Then fell back to oblivion infinite:
Therefore he smiled. Beyond stretched
    garden-grounds
Where the late adversary, breaking
    bounds,
Had gained him an occasion, That
    above,
That eagle, testified he could improve
Effectually. The Kaiser's symbol lay

Beside his rescript, a new badge by way
Of baldric; while, – another thing that
    marred
Alike emprise, achievement and
    reward, –
Ecelin's missive was conspicuous too.
What past life did those flying
    thoughts pursue?
As his, few names in Mantua half so old;
But at Ferrara, where his sires enrolled
It latterly, the Adelardi spared
No pains to rival them: both factions
    shared
Ferrara, so that, counted out, 'twould
    yield
A product very like the city's shield,
Half black and white, or Ghibellin and
    Guelf
As after Salinguerra styled himself
And Este who, till Marchesalla died,
(Last of the Adelardi) – never tried
His fortune there: with Marchesalla's
    child
Would pass, – could Blacks and Whites
    be reconciled
And young Taurello wed Linguetta, –
    wealth
And sway to a sole grasp. Each treats by
    stealth
Already: when the Guelfs, the Ravennese
Arrive, assault the Pietro quarter, seize
Linguetta, and are gone! Men's first
    dismay
Abated somewhat, hurries down, to lay
The after indignation, Boniface,
This Richard's father. 'Learn the full
    disgrace
'Averted, ere you blame us Guelfs, who
    rate
'Your Salinguerra, your sole potentate
'That might have been, 'mongst Este's
    valvassors –
'Ay, Azzo's – who, not privy to, abhors
'Our step: but we were zealous.' Azzo
    then
To do with! Straight a meeting of old
    men:

'Old Salinguerra dead, his heir a boy,
'What if we change our ruler and decoy
'The Lombard Eagle of the azure sphere
'With Italy to build in, fix him here,
'Settle the city's troubles in a trice?
'For private wrong, let public good
          suffice!'
In fine, young Salinguerra's staunchest
          friends
Talked of the townsmen making him
          amends,
Gave him a goshawk, and affirmed there
          was
Rare sport, one morning, over the green
          grass
A mile or so. He sauntered through the
          plain,
Was restless, fell to thinking, turned
          again
In time for Azzo's entry with the bride;
Count Boniface rode smirking at their
          side;
'She brings him half Ferrara,' whispers
          flew,
'And all Ancona! If the stripling knew!'
     Anon the stripling was in Sicily
Where Heinrich ruled in right of
          Constance; he
Was gracious nor his guest incapable;
Each understood the other. So it fell,
One Spring, when Azzo, thoroughly at
          ease,
Had near forgotten by what precise
          degrees
He crept at first to such a downy seat,
The Count trudged over in a special
          heat
To bid him of God's love dislodge from
          each
Of Salinguerra's palaces, – a breach
Might yawn else, not so readily to shut,
For who was just arrived at Mantua but
The youngster, sword on thigh and tuft
          on chin,
With tokens for Celano, Ecelin,
Pistore, and the like! Next news, – no
          whit

Do any of Ferrara's domes befit
His wife of Heinrich's very blood: a band
Of foreigners assemble, understand
Garden-constructing, level and surround,
Build up and bury in. A last news
          crowned
The consternation: since his infant's
          birth,
He only waits they end his wondrous
          girth
Of trees that link San Pietro with Tomà,
To visit Mantua. When the Podestà
Ecelin, at Vicenza, called his friend
Taurello thither, what could be their end
But to restore the Ghibellins' late Head,
The Kaiser helping? He with most to
          dread
From vengeance and reprisal, Azzo, there
With Boniface beforehand, as aware
Of plots in progress, gave alarm, expelled
Both plotters: but the Guelfs in triumph
          yelled
Too hastily. The burning and the flight,
And how Taurello, occupied that night
With Ecelin, lost wife and son, I told:
– Not how he bore the blow, retained
          his hold,
Got friends safe through, left enemies
          the worst
O' the fray, and hardly seemed to care at
          first:
But afterward men heard not constantly
Of Salinguerra's House so sure to be!
Though Azzo simply gained by the event
A shifting of his plagues – the first,
          content
To fall behind the second and estrange
So far his nature, suffer such a change
That in Romano sought he wife and
          child,
And for Romano's sake seemed
          reconciled
To losing individual life, which shrunk
As the other prospered – mortised in
          his trunk;
Like a dwarf palm which wanton Arabs
          foil

Of bearing its own proper wine and oil,
By grafting into it the stranger-vine,
Which sucks its heart out, sly and
  serpentine,
Till forth one vine-palm feathers to the
  root,
And red drops moisten the insipid fruit.
Once Adelaide set on, – the subtle mate
Of the weak soldier, urged to emulate
The Church's valiant women deed for
  deed,
And paragon her namesake, win the
  meed
O' the great Matilda, – soon they overbore
The rest of Lombardy, – not as before
By an instinctive truculence, but patched
The Kaiser's strategy until it matched
The Pontiff's, sought old ends by novel
  means.
'Only, why is it Salinguerra screens
'Himself behind Romano? – him we
  bade
'Enjoy our shine i' the front, not seek
  the shade!'
– Asked Heinrich, somewhat of the
  tardiest
To comprehend. Nor Philip acquiesced
At once in the arrangement; reasoned,
  plied
His friend with offers of another bride,
A statelier function – fruitlessly: 'twas
  plain
Taurello through some weakness must
  remain
Obscure. And Otho, free to judge of
  both
– Ecelin the unready, harsh and loth,
And this more plausible and facile wight
With every point a-sparkle – chose the
  right,
Admiring how his predecessors harped
On the wrong man: 'thus,' quoth he,
  'wits are warped
'By outsides!' Carelessly, meanwhile,
  his life
Suffered its many turns of peace and
  strife

In many lands – you hardly could
  surprise
The man; who shamed Sordello
  (recognize!)
In this as much beside, that, unconcerned
What qualities were natural or earned,
With no ideal of graces, as they came
He took them, singularly well the same –
Speaking the Greek's own language,
  just because
Your Greek eludes you, leave the least
  of flaws
In contracts with him; while, since Arab
  lore
Holds the stars' secret – take one trouble
  more
And master it! 'Tis done, and now deter
Who may the Tuscan, once Jove trined
  for her,
From Friedrich's path! – Friedrich,
  whose pilgrimage
The same man puts aside, whom he'll
  engage
To leave next year John Brienne in the
  lurch,
Come to Bassano, see Saint Francis'
  church
And judge of Guido the Bolognian's
  piece
Which, – lend Taurello credit, – rivals
  Greece –
Angels, with aureoles like golden quoits
Pitched home, applauding Ecelin's
  exploits.
For elegance, he strung the angelot,
Made rhymes thereto; for prowess,
  clove he not
Tiso, last siege, from crest to crupper?
  Why
Detail you thus a varied mastery
But to show how Taurello, on the watch
For men, to read their hearts and
  thereby catch
Their capabilities and purposes,
Displayed himself so far as displayed
  these:
While our Sordello only cared to know

About men as a means whereby he'd
   show
Himself, and men had much or little
   worth
According as they kept in or drew forth
That self; the other's choicest instruments
Surmised him shallow.
                    Meantime, malcontents
Dropped off, town after town grew
   wiser. 'How
'Change the world's face?' asked
   people; 'as 'tis now
'It has been, will be ever: very fine
'Subjecting things profane to things
   divine,
'In talk! This contumacy will fatigue
'The vigilance of Este and the League!
'The Ghibellins gain on us!' – as it
   happed.
Old Azzo and old Boniface, entrapped
By Ponte Alto, both in one month's
   space
Slept at Verona: either left a brace
Of sons – but, three years after, either's
   pair
Lost Guglielm and Aldobrand its heir:
Azzo remained and Richard – all the
   stay
Of Este and Saint Boniface, at bay
As 'twere. Then, either Ecelin grew old
Or his brain altered – not o' the proper
   mould
For new appliances – his old palm-stock
Endured no influx of strange strengths.
   He'd rock
As in a drunkenness, or chuckle low
As proud of the completeness of his
   woe,
Then weep real tears; – now make
   some mad onslaught
On Este, heedless of the lesson taught
So painfully, – now cringe for peace,
   sue peace
At price of past gain, bar of fresh
   increase
To the fortunes of Romano. Up at last
Rose Este, down Romano sank as fast.

And men remarked these freaks of
   peace and war
Happened while Salinguerra was afar:
Whence every friend besought him, all
   in vain,
To use his old adherent's wits again.
Not he! – 'who had advisers in his sons,
'Could plot himself, nor needed any
   one's
'Advice.' 'Twas Adelaide's remaining
   staunch
Prevented his destruction root and
   branch
Forthwith; but when she died, doom
   fell, for gay
He made alliances, gave lands away
To whom it pleased accept them, and
   withdrew
For ever from the world. Taurello, who
Was summoned to the convent, then
   refused
A word at the wicket, patience thus
   abused,
Promptly threw off alike his imbecile
Ally's yoke, and his own frank, foolish
   smile.
Soon a few movements of the happier
   sort
Changed matters, put himself in men's
   report
As heretofore; he had to fight, beside,
And that became him ever. So, in pride
And flushing of this kind of second
   youth,
He dealt a good-will blow. Este in truth
Lay prone – and men remembered,
   somewhat late,
A laughing old outrageous stifled hate
He bore to Este – how it would
   outbreak
At times spite of disguise, like an
   earthquake
In sunny weather – as that noted day
When with his hundred friends he
   tried to slay
Azzo before the Kaiser's face: and how,
On Azzo's calm refusal to allow

A liegeman's challenge, straight he too
    was calmed:
As if his hate could bear to lie
    embalmed,
Bricked up, the moody Pharaoh, and
    survive
All intermediate crumblings, to arrive
At earth's catastrophe – 'twas Este's
    crash
Not Azzo's he demanded, so, no rash
Procedure! Este's true antagonist
Rose out of Ecelin: all voices whist,
All eyes were sharpened, wits predicted.
    He
'Twas, leaned in the embrasure absently,
Amused with his own efforts, now, to
    trace
With his steel-sheathed forefinger
    Friedrich's face
I' the dust: but as the trees waved sere,
    his smile
Deepened, and words expressed its
    thought erewhile.
    'Ay, fairly housed at last, my old
    compeer?
'That we should stick together, all the
    year
'I kept Vicenza! – How old Boniface,
'Old Azzo caught us in its market-place,
'He by that pillar, I at this, – caught
    each
'In mid swing, more than fury of his
    speech,
'Egging the rabble on to disavow
'Allegiance to their Marquis – Bacchus,
    how
'They boasted! Ecelin must turn their
    drudge,
'Nor, if released, will Salinguerra grudge
'Paying arrears of tribute due long
    since –
'Bacchus! My man could promise then,
    nor wince:
'The bones-and-muscles! Sound of
    wind and limb,
'Spoke he the set excuse I framed for
    him:

'And now he sits me, slavering and
    mute,
'Intent on chafing each starved purple
    foot
'Benumbed past aching with the altar
    slab:
'Will no vein throb there when some
    monk shall blab
'Spitefully to the circle of bald scalps,
' "Friedrich's affirmed to be our side
    the Alps"
' – Eh, brother Lactance, brother
    Anaclet?
'Sworn to abjure the world, its fume
    and fret,
'God's own now? Drop the dormitory
    bar,
'Enfold the scanty grey serge scapular
'Twice o'er the cowl to muffle memories
    out!
'So! But the midnight whisper turns a
    shout,
'Eyes wink, mouths open, pulses
    circulate
'In the stone walls: the past, the world
    you hate
'Is with you, ambush, open field – or
    see
'The surging flame – we fire Vicenza –
    glee!
'Follow, let Pilio and Bernardo chafe!
'Bring up the Mantuans – through San
    Biagio – safe!
'Ah, the mad people waken? Ah, they
    writhe
'And reach us? If they block the gate?
    No tithe
'Can pass – keep back, you Bassanese!
    The edge,
'Use the edge – shear, thrust, hew,
    melt down the wedge,
'Let out the black of those black
    upturned eyes!
'Hell – are they sprinkling fire too? The
    blood fries
'And hisses on your brass gloves as
    they tear

'Those upturned faces choking with
    despair.
'Brave! Slidder through the reeking
    gate! "How now?
' "You six had charge of her?" And
    then the vow
'Comes, and the foam spirts, hair's
    plucked, till one shriek
'(I hear it) and you fling – you cannot
    speak –
'Your gold-flowered basnet to a man
    who haled
'The Adelaide he dared scarce view
    unveiled
'This morn, naked across the fire: how
    crown
'The archer that exhausted lays you
    down
'Your infant, smiling at the flame, and
    dies?
'While one, while mine …
            'Bacchus! I think there lies
'More than one corpse there' (and he
    paced the room)
' – Another cinder somewhere: 'twas
    my doom!
'Beside, my doom! If Adelaide is dead,
'I live the same, this Azzo lives instead
'Of that to me, and we pull, any how,
'Este into a heap: the matter's now
'At the true juncture slipping us so oft.
'Ay, Heinrich died and Otho, please
    you, doffed
'His crown at such a juncture! Still, if
    holds
'Our Friedrich's purpose, if this chain
    enfolds
'The neck of … who but this same
    Ecelin
'That must recoil when the best days
    begin!
'Recoil? that's nought; if the recoiler
    leaves
'His name for me to fight with, no one
    grieves:
'But he must interfere, forsooth,
    unlock

'His cloister to become my stumbling-
    block
'Just as of old! Ay, ay, there 'tis again –
'The land's inevitable Head – explain
'The reverences that subject us! Count
'These Ecelins now! Not to say as fount,
'Originating power of thought, – from
    twelve
'That drop i' the trenches they joined
    hands to delve,
'Six shall surpass him, but … why men
    must twine
'Somehow with something! Ecelin's a
    fine
'Clear name! 'Twere simpler, doubtless,
    twine with me
'At once: our cloistered friend's capacity
'Was of a sort! I had to share myself
'In fifty portions, like an o'ertasked elf
'That's forced illume in fifty points the
    vast
'Rare vapour he's environed by. At last
'My strengths, though sorely frittered,
    e'en converge
'And crown … no, Bacchus, they have
    yet to urge
'The man be crowned!
            'That aloe, an he durst,
'Would climb! Just such a bloated
    sprawler first
'I noted in Messina's castle-court
'The day I came, when Heinrich asked
    in sport
'If I would pledge my faith to win him
    back
'His right in Lombardy: "for, once bid
    pack
' "Marauders," he continued, "in my
    stead
' "You rule, Taurello!" and upon this
    head
'Laid the silk glove of Constance – I see
    her
'Too, mantled head to foot in miniver,
'Retrude following!
            'I am absolved
'From further toil: the empery devolved

'On me, 'twas Tito's word: I have to lay
'For once my plan, pursue my plan my way,
'Prompt nobody, and render an account
'Taurello to Taurello! Nay, I mount
'To Friedrich: he conceives the post I kept,
' – Who did true service, able or inept,
'Who's worthy guerdon, Ecelin or I.
'Me guerdoned, counsel follows: would he vie
'With the Pope really? Azzo, Boniface
'Compose a right-arm Hohenstauffen's race
'Must break ere govern Lombardy. I point
'How easy 'twere to twist, once out of joint,
'The socket from the bone: my Azzo's stare
'Meanwhile! for I, this idle strap to wear.
'Shall – fret myself abundantly, what end
'To serve? There's left me twenty years to spend
' – How better than my old way? Had I one
'Who laboured to o'erthrow my work – a son
'Hatching with Azzo superb treachery,
'To root my pines up and then poison me,
'Suppose – 'twere worth while frustrate that! Beside
'Another life's ordained me: the world's tide
'Rolls, and what hope of parting from the press
'Of waves, a single wave through weariness
'Gently lifted aside, laid upon shore?
'My life must be lived out in foam and roar,
'No question. Fifty years the province held
'Taurello; troubles raised, and troubles quelled,

'He in the midst – who leaves this quaint stone place,
'These trees a year or two, then not a trace 'Of him! How obtain hold, fetter men's tongues
'Like this poor minstrel with the foolish songs –
'To which, despite our bustle, he is linked?
' – Flowers one may teaze, that never grow extinct.
'Ay, that patch, surely, green as ever, where
'I set Her Moorish lentisk, by the stair,
'To overawe the aloes; and we trod
'Those flowers, how call you such? – into the sod;
'A stately foreigner – a world of pain
'To make it thrive, arrest rough winds – all vain!
'It would decline; these would not be destroyed:
'And now, where is it? where can you avoid
'The flowers? I frighten children twenty years
'Longer! – which way, too, Ecelin appears
'To thwart me, for his son's besotted youth
'Gives promise of the proper tiger-tooth:
'They feel it at Vicenza! Fate, fate, fate,
'My fine Taurello! Go you, promulgate
'Friedrich's decree, and here's shall aggrandize
'Young Ecelin – your Prefect's badge! A prize
'Too precious, certainly.
                              'How now? Compete
With my old comrade? shuffle from their seat
'His children? Paltry dealing! Don't I know
Ecelin? now, I think, and years ago!
'What's changed – the weakness? did not I compound
'For that, and undertake to keep him sound

'Despite it? Here's Taurello hankering
'After a boy's preferment – this plaything
'To carry, Bacchus!' And he laughed.
                    Remark
Why schemes wherein cold-blooded
          men embark
Prosper, when your enthusiastic sort
Fail: while these last are ever stopping
          short –
(So much they should – so little they
          can do!)
The careless tribe see nothing to pursue
If they desist; meantime their scheme
          succeeds.
     Thoughts were caprices in the course
          of deeds
Methodic with Taurello; so, he turned, –
Enough amused by fancies fairly
          earned
Of Este's horror-struck submitted
          neck,
And Richard, the cowed braggart, at his
          beck, –
To his own petty but immediate doubt
If he could pacify the League without
Conceding Richard; just to this was
          brought
That interval of vain discursive thought!
As, shall I say, some Ethiop, past pursuit
Of all enslavers, dips a shackled foot
Burnt to the blood, into the drowsy
          black
Enormous watercourse which guides
          him back
To his own tribe again, where he is king;
And laughs because he guesses,
          numbering
The yellower poison-wattles on the
          pouch
Of the first lizard wrested from its
          couch
Under the slime (whose skin, the
          while, he strips
To cure his nostril with, and festered
          lips,
And eyeballs bloodshot through the
          desert-blast)

That he has reached its boundary, at
          last
May breathe; – thinks o'er enchantments
          of the South
Sovereign to plague his enemies, their
          mouth,
Eyes, nails, and hair; but, these
          enchantments tried
In fancy, puts them soberly aside
For truth, projects a cool return with
          friends,
The likelihood of winning mere amends
Ere long; thinks that, takes comfort
          silently,
Then, from the river's brink, his
          wrongs and he,
Hugging revenge close to their hearts,
          are soon
Off-striding for the Mountains of the
          Moon.
     Midnight: the watcher nodded on
          his spear,
Since clouds dispersing left a passage
          clear
For any meagre and discoloured moon
To venture forth; and such was peering
          soon
Above the harassed city – her close lanes
Closer, not half so tapering her fanes,
As though she shrunk into herself to
          keep
What little life was saved, more safely.
          Heap
By heap the watch-fires mouldered, and
          beside
The blackest spoke Sordello and replied
Palma with none to listen. ' 'Tis your
          cause:
'What makes a Ghibellin? There should
          be laws –
'(Remember how my youth escaped! I
          trust
'To you for manhood, Palma! tell me just
'As any child) – there must be laws at
          work
'Explaining this. Assure me, good may
          lurk

'Under the bad, – my multitude has
      part
'In your designs, their welfare is at
      heart
'With Salinguerra, to their interest
'Refer the deeds he dwelt on, – so
      divest
'Our conference of much that scared
      me. Why
'Affect that heartless tone to Tito? I
'Esteemed myself, yes, in my inmost
      mind
'This morn, a recreant to my race –
      mankind
'O'erlooked till now: why boast my
      spirit's force,
' – Such force denied its object? Why
      divorce
'These, then admire my spirit's flight
      the same
'As though it bore up, helped some
      half-orbed flame
'Else quenched in the dead void, to
      living space?
'That orb cast off to chaos and disgrace,
'Why vaunt so much my unencumbered
      dance,
'Making a feat's facilities enhance
'Its marvel? But I front Taurello, one
'Of happier fate, and all I should have
      done,
'He does; the people's good being
      paramount
'With him, their progress may perhaps
      account
'For his abiding still; whereas you heard
'The talk with Tito – the excuse preferred
'For burning those five hostages, – and
      broached
'By way of blind, as you and I
      approached,
'I do believe.'
            She spoke: then he, 'My thought
'Plainlier expressed! All to your profit –
      nought
'Meantime of these, of conquests to
      achieve

'For them, of wretchedness he might
      relieve
'While profiting your party. Azzo, too,
'Supports a cause: what cause? Do
      Guelfs pursue
'Their ends by means like yours, or
      better?'
            When
The Guelfs were proved alike, men
      weighed with men,
And deed with deed, blaze, blood, with
      blood and blaze,
Morn broke: 'Once more, Sordello,
      meet its gaze
'Proudly – the people's charge against
      thee fails
'In every point, while either party quails!
'These are the busy ones: be silent thou!
'Two parties take the world up, and
      allow
'No third, yet have one principle, subsist
'By the same injustice; whoso shall
      enlist
'With either, ranks with man's inveterate
      foes.
'So there is one less quarrel to compose:
'The Guelf, the Ghibellin may be to
      curse –
'I have done nothing, but both sides do
      worse
'Than nothing. Nay, to me, forgotten,
      reft
'Of insight, lapped by trees and flowers,
      was left
'The notion of a service – ha? What
      lured
'Me here, what mighty aim was I
      assured
'Must move Taurello? What if there
      mained
'A cause, intact, distinct from these,
      ordained
'For me, its true discoverer?'
                              Some one pressed
Before them here, a watcher, to suggest
The subject for a ballad: 'They must
      know

'The tale of the dead worthy, long ago
'Consul of Rome – that's long ago for
    us,
'Minstrels and bowmen, idly squabbling
    thus
'In the world's corner – but too late no
    doubt,
'For the brave time he sought to bring
    about.
' – Not know Crescentius Nomentanus?'
    Then
He cast about for terms to tell him,
    when
Sordello disavowed it, how they used
Whenever their Superior introduced
A novice to the Brotherhood – ('for I
'Was just a brown-sleeve brother,
    merrily
'Appointed too,' quoth he, 'till Innocent
'Bade me relinquish, to my small
    content,
'My wife or my brown sleeves') – some
    brother spoke
Ere nocturns of Crescentius, to revoke
The edict issued, after his demise,
Which blotted fame alike and effigies,
All out except a floating power, a name
Including, tending to produce the same
Great act. Rome, dead, forgotten, lived
    at least
Within that brain, though to a vulgar
    priest
And a vile stranger, – two not worth a
    slave
Of Rome's, Pope John, King Otho, –
    fortune gave
The rule there: so, Crescentius, haply
    dressed
In white, called Roman Consul for a
    jest,
Taking the people at their word, forth
    stepped
As upon Brutus' heel, nor ever kept
Rome waiting, – stood erect, and from
    his brain
Gave Rome out on its ancient place
    again,

Ay, bade proceed with Brutus' Rome,
    Kings styled
Themselves mere citizens of, and,
    beguiled
Into great thoughts thereby, would
    choose the gem
Out of a lapfull, spoil their diadem
– The Senate's cypher was so hard to
    scratch!
He flashes like a phanal, all men catch
The flame, Rome's just accomplished!
    when returned
Otho, with John, the Consul's step had
    spurned,
And Hugo Lord of Este, to redress
The wrongs of each. Crescentius in the
    stress
Of adverse fortune bent. 'They crucified
'Their Consul in the Forum; and abide
'E'er since such slaves at Rome, that I –
    (for I
'Was once a brown-sleeve brother,
    merrily
'Appointed) – I had option to keep wife
'Or keep brown sleeves, and managed
    in the strife
'Lose both. A song of Rome!'
                    And Rome, indeed,
Robed at Goito in fantastic weed,
The Mother-City of his Mantuan days,
Looked an established point of light
    whence rays
Traversed the world; for, all the
    clustered homes
Beside of men, seemed bent on being
    Romes
In their degree; the question was, how
    each
Should most resemble Rome, clean out
    of reach.
Nor, of the Two, did either principle
Struggle to change, but to possess
    Rome, – still
Guelf Rome or Ghibellin Rome.
Let Rome advance!
Rome, as she struck Sordello's
    ignorance –

How could he doubt one moment?
   Rome's the Cause!
Rome of the Pandects, all the world's
   new laws –
Of the Capitol, of Castle Angelo;
New structures, that inordinately glow,
Subdued, brought back to harmony,
   made ripe
By many a relic of the archetype
Extant for wonder; every upstart church
That hoped to leave old temples in the
   lurch,
Corrected by the Theatre forlorn
That, – as a mundane shell, its world
   late born, –
Lay and o'ershadowed it. These hints
   combined
Rome typifies the scheme to put
   mankind
Once more in full possession of their
   rights.
'Let us have Rome again! On me it
   lights
'To build up Rome – on me, the first
   and last:
'For such a future was endured the
   past!'
And thus, in the grey twilight, forth he
   sprung
To give his thought consistency among
The very People – let their facts avail
Finish the dream grown from the
   archer's tale.

### BOOK THE FIFTH

Is it the same Sordello in the dusk
As at the dawn? – merely a perished
   husk
Now, that arose a power fit to build
Up Rome again? The proud conception
   chilled
So soon? Ay, watch that latest dream of
   thine
– A Rome indebted to no Palatine –
Drop arch by arch, Sordello! Art
   possessed

Of thy wish now, rewarded for thy
   quest
To-day among Ferrara's squalid sons?
Are this and this and this the shining
   ones
Meet for the Shining City? Sooth to say,
Your favoured tenantry pursue their way
After a fashion! This companion slips
On the smooth causey, t'other blinkard
   trips
At his mooned sandal. 'Leave to lead
   the brawls
'Here i' the atria?' No, friend! He that
   sprawls
On aught but a stibadium … what his
   dues
Who puts the lustral vase to such an
   use?
Oh, huddle up the day's disasters!
   March,
Ye runagates, and drop thou, arch by
   arch, Rome!
Yet before they quite disband – a
   whim –
Study mere shelter, now, for him, and
   him,
Nay, even the worst, – just house them!
   Any cave
Suffices: throw out earth! A loophole?
   Brave!
They ask to feel the sun shine, see the
   grass
Grow, hear the larks sing? Dead art
   thou, alas,
And I am dead! But here's our son
   excels
At hurdle-weaving any Scythian, fells
Oak and devises rafters, dreams and
   shapes
His dream into a door-post, just escapes
The mystery of hinges. Lie we both
Perdue another age. The goodly growth
Of brick and stone! Our building-pelt
   was rough,
But that descendant's garb suits well
   enough
A portico-contriver. Speed the years –

What's time to us? At last, a city rears
Itself! nay, enter – what's the grave to
  us?
Lo, our forlorn acquaintance carry thus
The head! Successively sewer, forum,
  cirque –
Last age, an aqueduct was counted
  work,
But now they tire the artificer upon
Blank alabaster, black obsidian,
– Careful, Jove's face be duly fulgurant,
And mother Venus' kiss-creased nipples
  pant
Back into pristine pulpiness, ere fixed
Above the baths. What difference
  betwixt
This Rome and ours – resemblance
  what, between
That scurvy dumb-show and this
  pageant sheen –
These Romans and our rabble? Use thy
  wit!
The work marched: step by step, – a
  workman fit
Took each, nor too fit, – to one task,
  one time, –
No leaping o'er the petty to the prime,
When just the substituting osier lithe
For brittle bulrush, sound wood for
  soft withe,
To further loam-and-roughcast-work a
  stage, –
Exacts an architect, exacts an age:
No tables of the Mauritanian tree
For men whose maple log's their luxury!
That way was Rome built. 'Better' (say
  you) 'merge
'At once all workmen in the demiurge,
'All epochs in a lifetime, every task
'In one!' So should the sudden city
  bask
I' the day – while those we'd feast
  there, want the knack
Of keeping fresh-chalked gowns from
  speck and brack,
Distinguish not rare peacock from vile
  swan,

Nor Mareotic juice from Cæcuban.
'Enough of Rome! 'Twas happy to
  conceive
'Rome on a sudden, nor shall fate bereave
'Me of that credit: for the rest, her spite
'Is an old story – serves my folly right
'By adding yet another to the dull
'List of abortions – things proved
  beautiful
'Could they be done, Sordello cannot
  do.'
   He sat upon the terrace, plucked and
     threw
The powdery aloe-cusps away, saw shift
Rome's walls, and drop arch after arch,
  and drift
Mist-like afar those pillars of all stripe,
Mounds of all majesty. ' Thou archetype,
'Last of my dreams and loveliest, depart!
   And then a low voice wound into his
     heart:
'Sordello!' (low as some old Pythoness
Conceding to a Lydian King's distress
The cause of his long error – one mistake
Of her past oracle) 'Sordello, wake!
'God has conceded two sights to a
  man –
'One, of men's whole work, time's
  completed plan,
'The other, of the minute's work, man's
  first
'Step to the plan's completeness: what's
  dispersed
'Save hope of that supreme step which,
  descried
'Earliest, was meant still to remain
  untried
'Only to give you heart to take your
  own
'Step, and there stay, leaving the rest
  alone?
'Where is the vanity? Why count as one
'The first step, with the last step? What
  is gone
'Except Rome's aëry magnificence,
'That last step you'd take first? – an
  evidence

'You were God: be man now! Let those
        glances fall!
'The basis, the beginning step of all,
'Which proves you just a man – is that
        gone too?
'Pity to discontent one versed as you
'In fate's ill-nature! but its full extent
'Eludes Sordello, even: the veil rent,
'Read the black writing – that collective
        man
'Outstrips the individual. Who began
'The acknowledged greatnesses? Ay,
        your own art
'Shall serve us: put the poet's mimes
        apart –
'Close with the poet's self, and lo, a dim
'Yet too plain form divides itself from
        him!
'Alcamo's song enmeshes the lulled
        Isle,
'Woven into the echoes left erewhile
'By Nina, one soft web of song: no more
'Turning his name, then, flower-like
        o'er and o'er!
'An elder poet in the younger's place;
'Nina's the strength, but Alcamo's the
        grace:
'Each neutralizes each then! Search your
        fill;
'You get no whole and perfect Poet –
        still
'New Ninas, Alcamos, till time's
        midnight
'Shrouds all – or better say, the
        shutting light
'Of a forgotten yesterday. Dissect
'Every ideal workman – (to reject
'In favour of your fearful ignorance
'The thousand phantasms eager to
        advance,
'And point you but to those within
        your reach) –
'Were you the first who brought – (in
        modern speech)
'The Multitude to be materialized?
'That loose eternal unrest – who devised
'An apparition i' the midst? The rout

'Was checked, a breathless ring was
        formed about
'That sudden flower: get round at any
        risk
'The gold-rough pointel, silver-blazing
        disk
'O' the lily! Swords across it! Reign thy
        reign
'And serve thy frolic service,
        Charlemagne!
' – The very child of over-joyousness,
'Unfeeling thence, strong therefore:
        Strength by stress
'Of Strength comes of that forehead
        confident,
'Those widened eyes expecting heart's
        content,
'A calm as out of just-quelled noise;
        nor swerves
'For doubt, the ample cheek in gracious
        curves
'Abutting on the upthrust nether lip:
'He wills, how should he doubt then?
        Ages slip:
'Was it Sordello pried into the work
'So far accomplished, and discovered
        lurk
'A company amid the other clans,
'Only distinct in priests for castellans
'And popes for suzerains (their rule
        confessed
'Its rule, their interest its interest,
'Living for sake of living – there an end –
'Wrapt in itself, no energy to spend
'In making adversaries or allies) –
'Dived you into its capabilities
'And dared create, out of that sect, a soul
'Should turn a multitude, already whole,
'Into its body? Speak plainer! Is't so
        sure
'God's church lives by a King's
        investiture?
'Look to last step! A staggering – a
        shock –
'What's mere sand is demolished,
        while the rock
Endures: a column of black fiery dust

Blots heaven – that help was
    prematurely thrust
'Aside, perchance! – but air clears,
    nought's erased
'Of the true outline.Thus much being
    firm based,
'The other was a scaffold. See him stand
'Buttressed upon his mattock,
    Hildebrand
'Of the huge brain-mask welded ply
    o'er ply
'As in a forge; it buries either eye
'White and extinct, that stupid brow;
    teeth clenched,
'The neck tight-corded, too, the chin
    deep-trenched,
'As if a cloud enveloped him while
    fought
'Under its shade, grim prizers, thought
    with thought
'At dead-lock, agonizing he, until
'The victor thought leap radiant up,
    and Will,
'The slave with folded arms and drooping
    lids
'They fought for, lean forth flame-like
    as it bids.
'Call him no flower – a mandrake of
    the earth,
'Thwarted and dwarfed and blasted in
    its birth,
'Rather, – a fruit of suffering's excess,
'Thence feeling, therefore stronger: still
    by stress
'Of Strength, work Knowledge! Full
    three hundred years
'Have men to wear away in smiles and
    tears
'Between the two that nearly seemed to
    touch,
'Observe you! quit one workman and
    you clutch
'Another, letting both their: trains go
    by –
'The actors-out of either's policy,
'Heinrich, on this hand, Otho,
    Barbaross,

'Carry the three Imperial crowns across,
'Aix' Iron, Milan's Silver, and Rome's
    Gold –
'While Alexander, Innocent uphold
'On that, each Papal key – but, link on
    link,
'Why is it neither chain betrays a chink?
'How coalesce the small and great?
    Alack,
'For one thrust forward, fifty such fall
    back!
'Do the popes coupled there help
    Gregory
'Alone? Hark – from the hermit Peter's
    cry
'At Claremont, down to the first serf
    that says
'Friedrich's no liege of his while he
    delays
'Getting the Pope's curse off him! The
    Crusade –
'Or trick of breeding Strength by other
    aid
'Than Strength, is safe. Hark – from the
    wild harangue
'Of Vimmercato, to the carroch's clang
'Yonder! The League – or trick of turning
    Strength
'Against Pernicious Strength, is safe at
    length.
'Yet hark – from Mantuan Albert making
    cease
'The fierce ones, to Saint Francis
    preaching peace
'Yonder! God's Truce – or trick to
    supersede
'The very Use of Strength, is safe. Indeed
'We trench upon the future. Who is
    found
'To take next step, next age – trail o'er
    the ground –
'Shall I say, gourd-like? – not the
    flower's display
'Nor the root's prowess, but the
    plenteous way
'O' the plant – produced by joy and
    sorrow, whence

'Unfeeling and yet feeling, strongest
      thence?
'Knowledge by stress of merely Know-
      ledge? No –
'E'en were Sordello ready to forego
'His life for this, 'twere overleaping
      work
'Some one has first to do, howe'er it irk,
'Nor stray a foot's breadth from the
      beaten road.
'Who means to help must still support
      the load
'Hildebrand lifted – "why hast Thou,"
      he groaned,.
' "Imposed on me a burthen, Paul had
      moaned,
' "And Moses dropped beneath?" Much
      done – and yet
'Doubtless that grandest task God ever
      set
'One man, left much to do: at his arm's
      wrench,
'Charlemagne's scaffold fell; but pillars
      blench
'Merely, start back again – perchance
      have been
'Taken for buttresses: crash every screen,
'Hammer the tenons better, and engage
'A gang about your work, for the next
      age
'Or two, of Knowledge, part by Strength
      and part
'By Knowledge! Then, indeed, perchance
      may start
'Sordello on his race – would time
      divulge
'Such secrets! If one step's awry, one
      bulge
'Calls for correction by a step we thought
'Got over long since, why, till that is
      wrought,
'No progress! And the scaffold in its
      turn
'Becomes, its service o'er, a thing to
      spurn.
'Meanwhile, if your half-dozen years of
      life

'In store dispose you to forego the strife,
'Who takes exception? Only bear in
      mind
'Ferrara's reached, Goito's left behind:
'As you then were, as half yourself,
      desist!
' – The warrior-part of you may, an it
      list,
'Finding real faulchions difficult to poise,
'Fling them afar and taste the cream of
      joys
'By wielding such in fancy, – what is
      bard
'Of you may spurn the vehicle that
      marred
'Elys so much, and in free fancy glut
'His sense, yet write no verses – you
      have but
'To please yourself for law, and once
      could please
'What once appeared yourself, by
      dreaming these
'Rather than doing these, in days gone
      by.
'But all is changed the moment you
      descry
'Mankind as half yourself, – then,
      fancy's trade
'Ends once and always: how may half
      evade
'The other half? men are found half of
      you.
'Out of a thousand helps, just one or
      two
'Can be accomplished presently: but
      flinch
'From these (as from the faulchion,
      raised an inch,
'Elys, described a couplet) and make
      proof
'Of fancy, – then, while one half lolls
      aloof
'I' the vines, completing Rome to the
      tiptop –
'See if, for that, your other half will stop
'A tear, begin a smile! The rabble's
      woes,

'Ludicrous in their patience as they
       chose
'To sit about their town and quietly
'Be slaughtered, – the poor reckless
       soldiery.
'With their ignoble rhymes on Richard,
       how
' "Polt-foot," sang they, "was in a pitfall
       now,"
'Cheering each other from the engine-
       mounts, –
'That crippled spawling idiot who
       recounts
'How, lopped of limbs, he lay, stupid
       as stone,
'Till the pains crept from out him one
       by one,
'And wriggles round the archers on his
       head
'To earn a morsel of their chestnut
       bread, –
'And Cino, always in the self-same place
'Weeping; beside that other wretch's
       case,
'Eyepits to ear, one gangrene since he
       plied
'The engine in his coat of raw sheep's
       hide
'A double watch in the noon sun; and
       see
'Lucchino, beauty, with the favours free,
'Trim hacqueton, spruce beard and
       scented hair,
'Campaigning it for the first time – cut
       there
'In two already, boy enough to crawl
'For latter orpine round the southern
       wall,
'Tomà, where Richard's kept, because
       that whore
'Marfisa, the fool never saw before,
'Sickened for flowers this wearisomest
       siege:
'And Tiso's wife – man like their pretty
       liege,
'Cared for her least fo whims once, –
       Berta, wed

'A twelvemonth gone, and, now poor
       Tiso's dead,
'Delivering herself of his first child
'On that chance heap of wet filth,
       reconciled
'To fifty gazers!' – (Here a wind below
Made moody music augural of woe
From the pine barrier) – 'What if, now
       the scene
'Draws to a close, yourself have really
       been
' – You, plucking purples in Goito's
       moss
'Like edges of a trabea (not to cross
'Your consul-humour) or dry aloe-shafts
'For fasces, at Ferrara – he, fate wafts,
'This very age, her whole inheritance
'Of opportunities? Yet you advance
'Upon the last! Since talking is your
       trade,
'There's Salinguerra left you to persuade:
'Fail! then' –
              'No – no – which latest
       chance secure!'
Leaped up and cried Sordello: 'this
       made sure,
'The past were yet redeemable; its work
'Was – help the Guelfs, whom I,
       howe'er it irk,
'Thus help!' He shook the foolish aloe-
       haulm
Out of his doublet, paused, proceeded
       calm
To the appointed presence. The large
       head
Turned on its socket; 'And your
       spokesman,' said
The large voice, 'is Elcorte's happy
       sprout?
'Few such' – (so finishing a speech no
       doubt
Addressed to Palma, silent at his side)
' – My sober councils have diversified.
'Elcorte's son! good: forward as you
       may,
'Our lady's minstrel with so much to
       say!'

The hesitating sunset floated back,
Rosily traversed in the wonted track
The chamber, from the lattice o'er the
     girth
Of pines, to the huge eagle blacked in
     earth
Opposite, – outlined sudden, spur to
     crest,
That solid Salinguerra, and caressed
Palma's contour; 'twas day looped
     back night's pall;
Sordello had a chance left spite of all.
     And much he made of the convincing
     speech
Meant to compensate for the past and
     reach
Through his youth's daybreak of unprofit,
     quite
To his noon's labour, so proceed till
     night
Leisurely! The great argument to bind
Taurello with the Guelf Cause, body
     and mind,
– Came the consummate rhetoric to
     that?
Yet most Sordello's argument dropped
     flat
Through his accustomed fault of
     breaking Yoke
Disjoining him who felt from him who
     spoke.
Was't not a touching incident – so
     prompt
A rendering the world its just accompt,
Once proved its debtor? Who'd suppose,
     before
This proof, that he, Goito's god of yore,
At duty's instance could demean himself
So memorably, dwindle to a Guelf?
Be sure, in such delicious flattery
     steeped,
His inmost self at the out-portion peeped,
Thus occupied; then stole a glance at
     those
Appealed to, curious if her colour rose
Or his lip moved, while he discreetly
     urged

The need of Lombardy becoming purged
At soonest of her barons; the poor part
Abandoned thus, missing the blood at
     heart
And spirit in brain, unseasonably off
Elsewhere! But, though his speech was
     worthy scoff,
Good-humoured Salinguerra, famed for
     tact
And tongue, who, careless of his phrase,
     ne'er lacked
The right phrase, and harangued
     Honorius dumb
At his accession, – looked as all fell
     plumb
To purpose and himself found interest
In every point his new instructor
     pressed
– Left playing with the rescript's white
     wax seal
To scrutinize Sordello head and heel.
He means to yield assent sure? No, alas!
All he replied was, 'What, it comes to
     pass
'That poesy, sooner than politics,
'Makes fade those young hair?' To think such
     speech could fix
Taurello!
               Then a flash of bitter truth:
So fantasies could break and fritter youth
That he had long ago lost earnestness,
Lost will to work, lost power to even
     express
The need of working! Earth was turned
     a grave:
No more occasions now, though he
     should crave
Just one, in right of superhuman toil,
To do what was undone, repair such
     spoil,
Alter the past – nothing would give the
     chance!
Not that he was to die; he saw askance
Protract the ignominious years beyond
To dream in – time to hope and time
     despond,
Remember and forget, be sad, rejoice

As saved a trouble; he might, at his
          choice,
One way or other, idle life out, drop
No few smooth verses by the way – for
          prop,
A thyrsus, these sad people, all the
          same,
Should pick up, and set store by, – far
          from blame,
Plant o'er his hearse, convinced his
          better part
Survived him. 'Rather tear men out the
          heart
'O' the truth!' – Sordello muttered, and
          renewed
His propositions for the Multitude.
    But Salinguerra, who at this attack
Had thrown great breast and ruffling
          corslet back
To hear the better, smilingly resumed
His task; beneath, the carroch's
          warning boomed;
He must decide with Tito; courteously
He turned then, even seeming to agree
With his admonisher – 'Assist the Pope,
'Extend Guelf domination, fill the scope
'O' the Church, thus based on All, by
          All, for All –
'Change Secular to Evangelical' –
Echoing his very sentence: all seemed
          lost,
When suddenly he looked up, laughingly
          almost,
To Palma: 'This opinion of your
          friend's –
'For instance, would it answer Palma's
          ends?
'Best, were it not, turn Guelf, submit
          our Strength' –
(Here he drew out his baldric to its
          length)
– 'To the Pope's Knowledge – let our
          captive slip,
'Wide to the walls throw ope our gates,
          equip
'Azzo with … what I hold here! Who'll
          subscribe

'To a trite censure of the minstrel tribe
'Henceforward? or pronounce, as
          Heinrich used,
' "Spear-heads for battle, burr-heads for
          the joust!"
' – When Constance, for his couplets,
          would promote
'Alcamo, from a parti-coloured coat,
'To holding her lord's stirrup in the
          wars.
'Not that I see where couplet-making
          jars
'With common sense: at Mantua I had
          borne
'This chanted, better than their most
          forlorn
'Of bull-baits, – that's indisputable!'
                              Brave!
Whom vanity nigh slew, contempt
          shall save!
All's at an end: a Troubadour suppose
Mankind will class him with their
          friends or foes?
A puny uncouth ailing vassal think
The world and him bound in some
          special link?
Abrupt the visionary tether burst.
What were rewarded here, or what
          amerced
If a poor drudge, solicitous to dream
Deservingly, got tangled by his theme
So far as to conceit the knack or gift
Or whatsoe'er it be, of verse, might lift
The globe, a lever like the hand and
          head
Of – 'Men of Action,' as the Jongleurs
          said,
– 'The Great Men,' in the people's
          dialect?
And not a moment did this scorn affect
Sordello: scorn the poet? They, for once,
Asking 'what was,' obtained a full
          response.
Bid Naddo think at Mantua – he had
          but
To look into his promptuary, put
Finger on a set thought in a set speech:

But was Sordello fitted thus for each
Conjecture? Nowise: since within his
    soul,
Perception brooded unexpressed and
    whole.
A healthy spirit like a healthy frame
Craves aliment in plenty – all the same,
Changes, assimilates its aliment.
Perceived Sordello, on a truth intent?
Next day no formularies more you saw
Than figs or oli'ves in a sated maw.
'Tis Knowledge, whither such
    perceptions tend;
They lose themselves in that, means to
    an end,
The many old producing some one new,
A last unlike the first. If lies are true,
The Caliph's wheel-work man of brass
    receives
A meal, munched millet grains and
    lettuce leaves
Together in his stomach rattle loose;
You find them perfect next day to
    produce:
But ne'er expect the man, on strength
    of that,
Can roll an iron camel-collar flat
Like Haroun's self! I tell you, what was
    stored
Bit by bit through Sordello's life,
    outpoured
That eve, was, for that age, a novel
    thing:
And round those three the People
    formed a ring,
Of visionary judges whose award
He recognized in full – faces that barred
Henceforth return to the old careless
    life,
In whose great presence, therefore, his
    first strife
For their sake must not be ignobly
    fought;
All these, for once, approved of him, he
    thought,
Suspended their own vengeance, chose
    await

The issue of this strife to reinstate
Them in the right of taking it – in fact
He must be proved king ere they could
    exact
Vengeance for such king's defalcation.
    Last,
A reason why the phrases flowed so fast
Was in his quite forgetting for a time
Himself in his amazement that the
    rhyme
Disguised the royalty so much: he
    there –
And Salinguerra yet all-unaware
Who was the lord, who liegeman!
                              'Thus I lay
'On thine my spirit and compel obey
'His lord, – my liegeman, – impotent
    to build
'Another Rome, but hardly so unskilled
'In what such builder should have been,
    as brook
'One shame beyond the charge that I
    forsook
'His function! Free me from that shame,
    I bend
'A brow before, suppose new years to
    spend, –
'Allow each chance, nor fruitlessly,
    recur –
'Measure thee with the Minstrel, then,
    demur
'At any crown he claims! That I must
    cede
'Shamed now, my right to my especial
    meed –
'Confess thee fitter help the world than I
'Ordained its champion from eternity,
'Is much: but to behold thee scorn the
    post
'I quit in thy behalf – to hear thee boast
'What makes my own despair!' And
    while he rung
The changes on this theme, the roof up-
    sprung,
The sad walls of the presence-chamber
    died
Into the distance, or embowering vied

With far-away Goito's vine-frontier;
And crowds of faces – (only keeping
     clear
The rose-light in the midst, his vantage-
     ground
To fight their battle from) – deep
     clustered round
Sordello, with good wishes no mere
     breath,
Kind prayers for him no vapour, since,
     come death,
Come life, he was fresh-sinewed every
     joint,
Each bone new-marrowed as whom gods
     anoint
Though mortal to their rescue. Now let
     sprawl
The snaky volumes hither! Is Typhon all
For Hercules to trample – good report
From Salinguerra only to extort?
'So was I' (closed he his inculcating
A poet must be earth's essential king)
'So was I, royal so, and if I fail,
' 'Tis not the royalty, ye witness quail,
'But one deposed who, caring not exert
'Its proper essence, trifled malapert
'With accidents instead – good things
     assigned
'As heralds of a better thing behind –
'And, worthy through display of these,
     put forth
'Never the inmost all-surpassing worth
'That constitutes him king precisely
     since
'As yet no other spirit may evince
'Its like: the power he took most pride
     to test,
'Whereby all forms of life had been
     professed
'At pleasure, forms already on the earth,
'Was but a means to power beyond,
     whose birth
'Should, in its novelty, be kingship's
     proof.
'Now, whether he came near or kept
     aloof
'The several forms he longed to imitate,

'Not there the kingship lay, he sees too
     late.
'Those forms, unalterable first as last,
'Proved him her copier, not the protoplast
'Of nature: what would come of being
     free,
'By action to exhibit tree for tree,
'Bird, beast, for beast and bird, or prove
     earth bore
'One veritable man or woman more?
'Means to an end, such proofs are: what
     the end?
'Let essence, whatsoe'er it be, extend –
'Never contract.Already you include
'The multitude; then let the multitude
'Include yourself; and the result were
     new:
'Themselves before, the multitude turn
     you.
'This were to live and move and have, in
     them,
'Your being, and secure a diadem
'You should transmit (because no cycle
     yearns
'Beyond itself, but on itself returns)
'When, the full sphere in wane, the
     world o'erlaid
'Long since with you, shall have in turn
     obeyed
'Some orb still prouder, some displayer,
     still
'More potent than the last, of human
     will,
'And some new king depose the old. Of
     such
'Am I – whom pride of this elates too
     much?
'Safe, rather say, 'mid troops of peers
     again;
'I, with my words, hailed brother of the
     train
'Deeds once sufficed: for, let the world
     roll back,
'Who fails, through deeds howe'er
     diverse, retrack
'My purpose still, my task? A teeming
     crust –

'Air, flame, earth, wave at conflict! Then,
     needs must
'Emerge some Calm embodied, these
     refer
'The brawl to – yellow-bearded Jupiter?
'No! Saturn; some existence like a pact
'And protest against Chaos, some first
     fact
'I' the faint of time. My deep of life, I
     know,
'Is unavailing e'en to poorly show' …
(For here the Chief immeasurably
     yawned)
… 'Deeds in their due gradation till
     Song dawned –
'The fullest effluence of the finest mind,
'All in degree, no way diverse in kind
'From minds about it, minds which,
     more or less,
'Lofty or low, move seeking to impress
'Themselves on somewhat; but one mind
     has climbed
'Step after step, by just ascent sublimed.
'Thought is the soul of act, and, stage
     by stage,
'Soul is from body still to disengage
'As tending to a freedom which rejects
'Such help and incorporeally affects
'The world, producing deeds but not
     by deeds,
'Swaying, in others, frames itself exceeds,
'Assigning them the simpler tasks it
     used
'To patiently perform till Song produced
'Acts, by thoughts only, for the mind:
     divest
'Mind of e'en Thought, and, lo, God's
     unexpressed
'Will draws above us! All then is to win
'Save that How much for me, then?
     where begin
'My work? About me, faces! and they
     flock,
'The earnest faces. What shall I unlock
'By song? behold me prompt, whate'er
     it be,
'To minister: how much can mortals see

'Of Life? No more than so? I take the
     task
'And marshal you Life's elemental
     masque,
'Show Men, on evil or on good lay
     stress,
'This light, this shade make prominent,
     suppress
'All ordinary hues that softening blend
'Such natures with the level. Apprehend
'Which sinner is, which saint, if I allot
'Hell, Purgatory, Heaven, a blaze or
     blot,
'To those you doubt concerning! I
     en-womb
'Some wretched Friedrich with his red-
     hot tomb;
'Some dubious spirit, Lombard Agilulph
'With the black chastening river I
     engulph!
'Some unapproached Matilda I enshrine
'With languors of the planet of decline –
'These, fail to recognize, to arbitrate
'Between henceforth, to rightly estimate
'Thus marshalled in the masque! Myself,
     the while,
'As one of you, am witness, shrink or
     smile
'At my own showing! Next age – what's
     to do?
'The men and women stationed hitherto
'Will I unstation, good and bad, conduct
'Each nature to its farthest, or obstruct
'At soonest, in the world: light, thwarted,
     breaks
'A limpid purity to rainbow flakes,
'Or shadow, massed, freezes to gloom:
     behold
'How such, with fit assistance to unfold,
'Or obstacles to crush them, disengage
'Their forms, love, hate, hope, fear,
     peace make, war wage,
'In presence of you all! Myself, implied
'Superior now, as, by the platform's
     side,
'I bade them do and suffer, – would
     last content

'The world ... no – that's too far! I
      circumvent
' A few, my masque contented, and to
      these
'Offer unveil the last of mysteries –
'Man's inmost life shall have yet freer
      play:
'Once more I cast external things away,
'And natures composite, so decompose
'That' ... Why, he writes *Sordello!*
                          'How I rose,
'And how have you advanced! since
      evermore
'Yourselves effect what I was fain before
'Effect, what I supplied yourselves
      suggest,
'What I leave bare yourselves can now
      invest.
'How we attain to talk as brothers talk,
'In half-words, call things by half-names,
      no balk
'From discontinuing old aids. To-day
'Takes in account the work of Yesterday:
'Has not the world a Past now, its adept
'Consults ere he dispense with or accept
'New aids? a single touch more may
      enhance,
'A touch less turn to insignificance
'Those structures' symmetry the past
      has strewed
'The world with, once so bare. Leave
      the mere rude
'Explicit details! 'tis but brother's speech
'We need, speech where an accent's
      change gives each
'The other's soul – no speech to under-
      stand
'By former audience: need was then to
      expand,
'Expatiate – hardly were we brothers!
      true –
'Nor I lament my small remove from
      you,
'Nor reconstruct what stands already.
      Ends
'Accomplished turn to means: my art
      intends

'New structure from the ancient: as
      they changed
'The spoils of every clime at Venice,
      ranged
'The horned and snouted Libyan god,
      upright
'As in his desert, by some simple bright
'Clay cinerary pitcher – Thebes as Rome,
'Athens as Byzant rifled, till their Dome
'From earth's reputed consummations
      razed
'A seal, the all-transmuting Triad blazed
'Above. Ah, whose that fortune? Ne'er-
      theless
'E'en he must stoop contented to
      express
'No tithe of what's to say – the vehicle
'Never sufficient: but his work is still
'For faces like the faces that select
'The single service I am bound effect, –
'That bid me cast aside such fancies,
      bow
'Taurello to the Guelf cause, disallow
'The Kaiser's coming – which with
      heart, soul, strength,
'I labour for, this eve, who feel at length
'My past career's outrageous vanity,
'And would, as it amends, die, even die
'Now I first estimate the boon of life,
'If death might win compliance – sure,
      this strife
'Is right for once – the People my
      support.'
My poor Sordello! what may we extort
By this, I wonder? Palma's lighted eyes
Turned to Taurello who, long past
      surprise,
Began, 'You love him – what you'd say
      at large
'Let me say briefly. First, your father's
      charge
'To me, his friend, peruse: I guessed
      indeed
'You were no stranger to the course
      decreed.
'He bids me leave his children to the
      saints:

'As for a certain project, he acquaints
'The Pope with that, and offers him the best
'Of your possessions to permit the rest
'Go peaceably – to Ecelin, a stripe
'Of soil the cursed Vicentines will gripe,
' – To Alberic, a patch the Trevisan
'Clutches already; extricate, who can,
'Treville, Villarazzi, Puissolo,
'Loria and Cartiglione! – all must go,
'And with them go my hopes. 'Tis lost, then! Lost
'This eve, our crisis, and some pains it cost
'Procuring; thirty years – as good I'd spent
'Like our admonisher! But each his bent
'Pursues: no question, one might live absurd
'Oneself this while, by deed as he by word
'Persisting to obtrude an influence where
' 'Tis made account of, much as ... nay, you fare
'With twice the fortune, youngster! – I submit,
'Happy to parallel my waste of wit
'With the renowned Sordello's: you decide
'A course for me. Romano may abide
'Romano, – Bacchus! After all, what dearth
'Of Ecelins and Alberics on earth?
'Say there's a prize in prospect, must disgrace
'Betide competitors, unless they style
'Themselves Romano? Were it worth my while
'To try my own luck! But an obscure place
'Suits me – there wants a youth to bustle, stalk
'And attitudinize – some fight, more talk,
'Most flaunting badges – how, I might make clear
'Since Friedrich's very purposes lie here

' – Here, pity they are like to lie! For me,
'With station fixed unceremoniously
'Long since, small use contesting; I am but
'The liegeman – you are born the lieges: shut
'That gentle mouth now! or resume your kin
'In your sweet self; were Palma Ecelin
'For me to work with! Could that neck endure
'This bauble for a cumbrous garniture,
'She should ... or might one bear it for her? Stay –
'I have not been so flattered many a day
'As by your pale friend – Bacchus! The least help
'Would lick the hind's fawn to a lion's whelp:
'His neck is broad enough – a ready tongue
'Beside: too writhled – but, the main thing, young –
'I could ... why, look ye!'
                                    And the badge was thrown
Across Sordello's neck: 'This badge alone
'Makes you Romano's Head – becomes superb
'On your bare neck, which would, on mine, disturb
'The pauldron,' said Taurello. A mad act,
Nor dreamed about before – in fact,
Not when his sportive arm rose for the nonce –
But he had dallied overmuch, this once,
With power: the thing was done, and he, aware
The thing was done, proceeded to declare –
(So like a nature made to serve, excel
In serving, only feel by service well!)
– That he would make Sordello that and more.
'As good a scheme as any. What's to pore

'At in my face?' he asked – 'ponder
        instead
'This piece of news; you are Romano's
        Head!
'One cannot slacken pace so near the
        goal,
'Suffer my Azzo to escape heart-whole
'This time! For you there's Palma to
        espouse –
'For me, one crowning trouble ere I
        house
'Like my compeer.'
                On which ensued a strange
And solemn visitation; there came
        change
O'er every one of them; each looked on
        each:
Up in the midst a truth grew, without
        speech.
And when the giddiness sank and the
        haze
Subsided, they were sitting, no amaze,
Sordello with the baldric on, his sire
Silent, though his proportions seemed
        aspire
Momently; and, interpreting the thrill, –
Night at its ebb, – Palma was found
        there still
Relating somewhat Adelaide confessed
A year ago, while dying on her breast, –
Of a contrivance, that Vicenza night
When Ecelin had birth. 'Their convoy's
        flight,
'Cut off a moment, coiled inside the
        flame
'That wallowed like a dragon at his
        game
'The toppling city through – San Biagio
        rocks!
'And wounded lies in her delicious
        locks
'Retrude, the frail mother, on her face,
'None of her wasted, just in one
        embrace
'Covering her child: when, as they lifted
        her,
'Cleaving the tumult, mighty, mightier

'And mightiest Taurello's cry outbroke,
'Leapt like a tongue of fire that cleaves
        the smoke,
'Midmost to cheer his Mantuans onward
        – drown
'His colleague Ecelin's clamour, up and
        down
'The disarray: failed Adelaide see then
'Who was the natural chief, the man of
        men?
'Outstripping time, her infant there
        burst swathe,
'Stood up with eyes haggard beyond the
        scathe
'From wandering after his heritage
'Lost once and lost for aye: and why
        that rage,
'That deprecating glance? A new shape
        leant
'On a familiar shape – gloatingly bent
'O'er his discomfiture; 'mid wreaths it
        wore,
'Still one outflamed the rest – her child's
        before
' 'Twas Salinguerra's for his child: scorn,
        hate,
'Rage now might startle her when all
        too late!
'Then was the moment! – rival's foot
        had spurned
'Never that House to earth else! Sense
        returned –
'The act conceived, adventured and
        complete,
'They bore away to an obscure retreat
'Mother and child – Retrude's self not
        slain'
(Nor even here Taurello moved)
        'though pain
'Was fled; and what assured them
        most 'twas fled,
'All pain, was, if they raised the pale
        hushed head
' 'Twould turn this way and that, waver
        awhile,
'And only settle into its old smile –
'(Graceful as the disquieted water-flag

'Steadying itself, remarked they, in the
  quag
'On either side their path) – when
  suffered look
'Down on her child. They marched: no
  sign once shook
'The company's close litter of crossed
  spears
'Till, as they reached Goito, a few tears
'Slipped in the sunset from her long
  black lash,
'And she was gone. So far the action
  rash;
'No crime. They laid Retrude in the
  font,
'Taurello's very gift, her child was wont
'To sit beneath – constant as eve he
  came
'To sit by its attendant girls the same
'As one of them. For Palma, she would
  blend
'With this magnific spirit to the end,
'That ruled her first; but scarcely had
  she dared
'To disobey the Adelaide who scared
'Her into vowing never to disclose
'A secret to her husband, which so
  froze
'His blood at half-recital, she contrived
'To hide from him Taurello's infant
  lived,
'Lest, by revealing that, himself should
  mar
'Romano's fortunes. And, a crime so
  far,
'Palma received that action: she was
  told
'Of Salinguerra's nature, of his cold
'Calm acquiescence in his lot! But free
'To impart the secret to Romano, she
'Engaged to repossess Sordello of
'His heritage, and hers, and that way
  doff
'Their mask, but after years, long years:
  while now,
'Was not Romano's sign-mark on that
  brow?'

Across Taurello's heart his arms were
  locked:
And when he did speak 'twas as if he
  mocked
The minstrel, 'who had not to move,'
  he said,
'Nor stir – should fate defraud him of a
  shred
'Of his son's infancy? much less his
  youth!'
(Laughingly all this) – 'which to aid, in
  truth,
'Himself, reserved on purpose, had not
  grown
'Old, not too old – 'twas best they kept
  alone
'Till now, and never idly met till now;'
– Then, in the same breath, told Sordello
  bow
All intimations of this eve's event
Were lies, for Friedrich must advance
  to Trent,
Thence to Verona, then to Rome, there
  stop,
Tumble the Church down, institute
  a-top
The Alps a Prefecture of Lombardy:
– 'That's now! – no prophesying what
  may be
'Anon, with a new monarch of the clime,
'Native of Gesi, passing his youth's
  prime
'At Naples. Tito bids my choice decide
'On whom … '
                'Embrace him, madman!'
  Palma cried,
Who through the laugh saw sweat-drops
  burst apace,
And his lips blanching: he did not
  embrace
Sordello, but he laid Sordello's hand
On his own eyes, mouth, forehead.
                          Understand,
This while Sordello was becoming
  flushed
Out of his whiteness; thoughts rushed,
  fancies rushed;

He pressed his hand upon his head
　　and signed
Both should forbear him. 'Nay, the
　　best's behind!'
Taurello laughed – not quite with the
　　same laugh:
'The truth is, thus we scatter, ay, like
　　chaff
'These Guelfs, a despicable monk recoils
'From: nor expect a fickle Kaiser spoils
'Our triumph! – Friedrich? Think you, I
　　intend
'Friedrich shall reap the fruits of blood
　　I spend
'And brain I waste? Think you, the
　　people clap
'Their hands at my out-hewing this
　　wild gap
'For any Friedrich to fill up? 'Tis mine –
'That's yours: I tell you, towards some
　　such design
'Have I worked blindly, yes, and idly,
　　yes,
'And for another, yes – but worked no
　　less
'With instinct at my heart; I else had
　　swerved,
'While now – look round! My cunning
　　has preserved
'Samminiato – that's a central place
'Secures us Florence, boy, – in Pisa's
　　case.
'By land as she by sea; with Pisa ours,
'And Florence, and Pistoia, one devours
'The land at leisure! Gloriously
　　dispersed –
'Brescia, observe, Milan, Piacenza first
'That flanked us (ah, you know not!) in
　　the March;
'On these we pile, as keystone of our
　　arch,
'Romagna and Bologna, whose first span
'Covered the Trentine and the Valsugan;
'Sofia's Egna by Bolgiano's sure!' …
So he proceeded: half of all this, pure
Delusion, doubtless, nor the rest too
　　true,

But what was undone he felt sure to do,
As ring by ring he wrung off, flung away
The pauldron-rings to give his sword-
　　arm play –
Need of the sword now! That would
　　soon adjust
Aught wrong at present; to the sword
　　intrust
Sordello's whiteness, undersize: 'twas
　　plain
He hardly rendered right to his own
　　brain –
Like a brave hound, men educate to
　　pride
Himself on speed or scent nor aught
　　beside,
As though he could not, gift by gift,
　　match men!
Palma had listened patiently: but when
'Twas time expostulate, attempt
　　withdraw
Taurello from his child, she, without
　　awe
Took off his iron arms from, one by
　　one,
Sordello's shrinking shoulders, and,
　　that done,
Made him avert his visage and relieve
Sordello (you might see his corslet
　　heave
The while) who, loose, rose – tried to
　　speak, then sank:
They left him in the chamber. All was
　　blank.
And even reeling down the narrow stair
Taurello kept up, as though unaware
Palma was by to guide him, the old
　　device
– Something of Milan – 'how we muster
　　thrice
'The Torriani's strength there; all along
'Our own Visconti cowed them' – thus
　　the song
Continued even while she bade him
　　stoop,
Thrid somehow, by some glimpse of
　　arrow-loop,

The turnings to the gallery below,
Where he stopped short as Palma let
    him go.
When he had sat in silence long
    enough
Splintering the stone bench, braving a
    rebuff
She stopped the truncheon; only to
    commence
One of Sordello's poems, a pretence
For speaking, some poor rhyme of 'Elys'
    hair
'And head that's sharp and perfect like
    a pear,
'So smooth and close are laid the few
    fine locks
'Stained like pale honey oozed from
    top-most rocks
'Sun-blanched the livelong summer' –
    from his worst
Performance, the Goito, as his first:
And that at end, conceiving from the
    brow
And open mouth no silence would
    serve now,
Went on to say the whole world loved
    that man
And, for that matter, thought his face,
    tho' wan,
Eclipsed the Count's – he sucking in
    each phrase
As if an angel spoke. The foolish praise
Ended, he drew her on his mailed
    knees, made
Her face a framework with his hands, a
    shade,
A crown, an aureole: there must she
    remain
(Her little mouth compressed with
    smiling pain
As in his gloves she felt her tresses
    twitch)
To get the best look at, in fittest niche
Dispose his saint. That done, he kissed
    her brow,
– 'Lauded her father for his treason
    now,'

He told her, 'only, how could one
    suspect
'The wit in him? – whose clansman,
    recollect,
'Was ever Salinguerra – she, the same,
'Romano and his lady – so, might claim
'To know all, as she should' – and thus
    begun
Schemes with a vengeance, schemes on
    schemes, 'not one
'Fit to be told that foolish boy,' he said,
'But only let Sordello Palma wed,
' – Then!'
                'Twas a dim long narrow place
    at best:
Midway a sole grate showed the fiery
    West,
As shows its corpse the world's end
    some split tomb –
A gloom, a rift of fire, another gloom,
Faced Palma – but at length Taurello
    set
Her free; the grating held one ragged
    jet
Of fierce gold fire: he lifted her within
The hollow underneath – how else begin
Fate's second marvellous cycle, else
    renew
The ages than with Palma plain in view?
Then paced the passage, hands clenched,
    head erect,
Pursuing his discourse: a grand
    unchecked
Monotony made out from his quick
    talk
And the recurring noises of his walk;
– Somewhat too much like the o'er-
    charged assent
Of two resolved friends in one danger
    blent,
Who hearten each the other against
    heart;
Boasting there's nought to care for,
    when, apart
The boaster, all's to care for. He, beside
Some shape not visible, in power and
    pride

Approached, out of the dark, ginglingly
    near,
Nearer, passed close in the broad light,
    his ear
Crimson, eyeballs suffused, temples
    full-fraught,
Just a snatch of the rapid speech you
    caught,
And on he strode into the opposite
    dark
Till presently the harsh heel's turn, a
    spark
I' the stone, and whirl of some loose
    embossed thong
That crashed against the angle aye so
    long
After the last, punctual to an amount
Of mailed great paces you could not
    but count, –
Prepared you for the pacing back again.
And by the snatches you might ascertain
That, Friedrich's Prefecture surmounted,
    left
By this alone in Italy, they cleft
Asunder, crushed together, at command
Of none, were free to break up Hilde-
    brand,
Rebuild, he and Sordello, Charle-
    magne –
But garnished, Strength with Knowledge,
    'if we deign
'Accept that compromise and stoop to
    give
'Rome law, the Cæsar's Representative.'
Enough, that the illimitable flood
Of triumphs after triumphs, understood
In its faint reflux (you shall hear) sufficed
Young Ecelin for appanage, enticed
Him on till, these long quiet in their
    graves,
He found 'twas looked for that a whole
    life's braves
Should somehow be made good; so,
    weak and worn,
Must stagger up at Milan, one grey
    morn
Of the to-come, and fight his latest fight.

But, Salinguerra's prophecy at height –
He voluble with a raised arm and stiff,
A blaring voice, a blazing eye, as if
He had our very Italy to keep
Or cast away, or gather in a heap
To garrison the better – ay, his word
Was, 'run the cucumber into a gourd,
'Drive Trent upon Apulia' – at their
    pitch
Who spied the continents and islands
    which
Grew mulberry leaves and sickles, in
    the map –
(Strange that three such confessions so
    should hap
To Palma, Dante spoke with in the clear
Amorous silence of the Swooning-
    sphere, –
*Cunizza*, as he called her! Never ask
Of Palma more! She sat, knowing her
    task
Was done, the labour of it, – for, success
Concerned not Palma, passion's
    votaress.)
Triumph at height, and thus Sordello
    crowned –
Above the passage suddenly a sound
Stops speech, stops walk: back shrinks
    Taurello, bids
With large involuntary asking lids,
Palma interpret. ' 'Tis his own foot-
    stamp –
'Your hand! His summons! Nay, this
    idle damp
'Befits not!' Out they two reeled dizzily.
'Visconti's strong at Milan,' resumed he,
In the old, somewhat insignificant way –
(Was Palma wont, years afterward, to
    say)
As though the spirit's flight, sustained
    thus far,
Dropped at that very instant.
                    Gone they are –
Palma, Taurello; Eglamor anon,
Ecelin, – only Naddo's never gone!
– Labours, this moonrise, what the
    Master meant:

'Is Squarcialupo speckled? – purulent,
'I'd say, but when was Providence put
        out?
'He carries somehow handily about
'His spite nor fouls himself!' Goito's
        vines
Stand like a cheat detected – stark
        rough lines,
The moon breaks through, a grey mean
        scale against
The vault where, this eve's Maiden,
        thou remain'st
Like some fresh martyr, eyes fixed –
        who can tell?
As Heaven, now all's at end, did not so
        well,
Spite of the faith and victory, to leave
Its virgin quite to death in the lone eve.
While the persisting hermit-bee … ha!
        wait
No longer: these in compass, forward
        fate!

BOOK THE SIXTH

The thought of Eglamor's least like a
        thought,
And yet a false one, was, 'Man shrinks
        to nought
'If matched with symbols of immensity;
'Must quail, forsooth, before a quiet sky
'Or sea, too little for their quietude:'
And, truly, somewhat in Sordello's mood
Confirmed its speciousness, while eve
        slow sank
Down the near terrace to the farther
        bank,
And only one spot left from out the
        night
Glimmered upon the river opposite –
A breadth of watery heaven like a bay,
A sky-like space of water, ray for ray,
And star for star, one richness where
        they mixed
As this and that wing of an angel,
        fixed,
Tumultuary splendours folded in

To die. Nor turned he till Ferrara's din
(Say, the monotonous speech from a
        man's lip
Who lets some first and eager purpose
        slip
In a new fancy's birth – the speech
        keeps on
Though elsewhere its informing soul be
        gone)
– Aroused him, surely offered succour.
        Fate
Paused with this eve; ere she precipitate
Herself, – best put off new strange
        thoughts awhile,
That voice, those large hands, that
        portentous smile, –
What help to pierce the future as the
        past
Lay in the plaining city?
                        And at last
The main discovery and prime concern,
All that just now imported him to learn,
Truth's self, like yonder slow moon to
        complete
Heaven, rose again, and, naked at his
        feet,
Lighted his old life's every shift and
        change,
Effort with counter-effort; nor the range
Of each looked wrong except wherein
        it checked,
Some other – which of these could he
        suspect,
Prying into them by the sudden blaze?
The real way seemed made up of all the
        ways –
Mood alter mood of the one mind in
        him;
Tokens of the existence, bright or dim,
Of a transcendent all-embracing sense
Demanding only outward influence,
A soul, in Palma's phrase, above his
        soul,
Power to uplift his power, – such moon's
        control
Over such sea-depths, – and their mass
        had swept

Onward from the beginning and still
  kept
Its course: but years and years the sky
  above
Held none, and so, untasked of any
  love,
His sensitiveness idled, now amort,
Alive now, and, to sullenness or sport
Given wholly up, disposed itself anew
At every passing instigation, grew
And dwindled at caprice, in foam-
  showers spilt,
Wedge-like insisting, quivered now a
  gilt
Shield in the sunshine, now a blinding
  race
Of whitest ripples o'er the reef – found
  place
For much display; not gathered up and,
  hurled
Right from its heart, encompassing the
  world.
So had Sordello been, by consequence,
Without a function: others made
  pretence
To strength not half his own, yet had
  some core
Within, submitted to some moon, before
Them still, superior still whate'er their
  force, –
Were able therefore to fulfil a course,
Nor missed life's crown, authentic
  attribute.
To each who lives must be a certain fruit
Of having lived in his degree, – a stage,
Earlier or later in men's pilgrimage,
To stop at: and to this the spirits tend
Who, still discovering beauty without
  end,
Amass the scintillations, make one star
– Something unlike them, self-sustained,
  afar, –
And meanwhile nurse the dream of
  being blest
By winning it to notice and invest
Their souls with alien glory, some one
  day

Whene'er the nucleus, gathering shape
  alway,
Round to the perfect circle – soon or
  late,
According as themselves are formed to
  wait,
Whether mere human beauty will
  suffice
– The yellow hair and the luxurious
  eyes,
Or human intellect seem best, or each
Combine in some ideal form past reach
On earth, or else some shade of these,
  some aim,
Some love, hate even, take their place,
  the same,
So to be served – all this they do not
  lose,
Waiting for death to live, nor idly choose
What must be Hell – a progress thus
  pursued
Through all existence, still above the
  food
That's offered them, still fain to reach
  beyond
The widened range, in virtue of their
  bond
Of sovereignty. Not that a Palma's Love,
A Salinguerra's Hate, would equal prove
To swaying all Sordello: but why doubt
Some love meet for such strength, some
  moon without
Would match his sea? – or fear, Good
  manifest,
Only the Best breaks faith? – Ah but the
  Best
Somehow eludes us ever, still might be
And is not! Crave we gems? No penury
Of their material round us! Pliant earth
And plastic flame – what balks the
  mage his birth
– Jacinth in balls or lodestone by the
  block?
Flinders enrich the strand, veins swell
  the rock;
Nought more! Seek creatures? Life's i'
  the tempest, thought

Clothes the keen hill-top, mid-day woods
    are fraught
With fervours: human forms are well
    enough!
But we had hoped, encouraged by the
    stuff
Profuse at nature's pleasure, men
    beyond
These actual men! – and thus are over-
    fond
In arguing, from Good – the Best, from
    force
Divided – force combined, an ocean's
    course
From this our sea whose mere intestine
    pants
Might seem at times sufficient to our
    wants.
    External power! If none be adequate,
And he stand forth ordained (a prouder
    fate)
Himself a law to his own sphere?
    'Remove
'All incompleteness!' for that law, that
    love?
Nay, if all other laws be feints, – truth
    veiled
Helpfully to weak vision that had failed
To grasp aught but its special want, –
    for lure,
Embodied? Stronger vision could endure
The unbodied want: no part – the
    whole of truth!
The People were himself; nor, by the
    ruth
At their condition, was he less impelled
To alter the discrepancy beheld,
Than if, from the sound whole, a sickly
    part
Subtracted were transformed, decked
    out with art,
Then palmed on him as alien woe – the
    Guelf
To succour, proud that he forsook
    himself.
All is himself; all service, therefore,
    rates

Alike, nor serving one part, immolates
The rest: but all in time! 'That lance of
    yours
'Makes havoc soon with Malek and his
    Moors,
'That buckler's lined with many a giant's
    beard
'Ere long, our champion, be the lance
    up-reared,
'The buckler wielded handsomely as
    now!
'But view your escort, bear in mind
    your vow.
'Count the pale tracts of sand to pass
    ere that,
'And, if you hope we struggle through
    the flat,
'Put lance and buckler by! Next half-
    month lacks
'Mere sturdy exercise of mace and axe
'To cleave this dismal brake of prickly-
    pear
'Which bristling holds Cydippe by the
    hair.
'Lames barefoot Agathon: this felled,
    we'll try
'The picturesque achievements by and
    by –
'Next life!'
        Ay, rally, mock, O People, urge
Your claims! – for thus he ventured, to
    the verge,
Push a vain mummery which perchance
    distrust
Of his fast-slipping resolution thrust
Likewise: accordingly the Crowd – (as
    yet
He had unconsciously contrived forget
I' the whole, to dwell o' the points …
    one might assuage
The signal horrors easier than engage
With a dim vulgar vast unobvious grief
Not to be fancied off, nor gained relief
In brilliant fits, cured by a happy quirk,
But by dim vulgar vast unobvious work
To correspond … ) this Crowd then,
    forth they stood.

'And now content thy stronger vision,
     brood
'On thy bare want; uncovered, turf by
     turf,
'Study the corpse-face thro' the taint-
     worms' scurf!'
    Down sank the People's Then; uprose
     their Now.
These sad ones render service to! And
     how
Piteously little must that service prove
– Had surely proved in any case! for,
     move
Each other obstacle away, let youth
Become aware it had surprised a truth
'Twere service to impart – can truth be
     seized,
Settled forthwith, and, of the captive
     eased,
Its captor find fresh prey, since this alit
So happily, no gesture luring it,
The earnest of a flock to follow? Vain,
Most vain! a life to spend ere this he
     chain
To the poor crowd's complacence: ere
     the crowd
Pronounce it captured, he descries a
     cloud
Its kin of twice the plume; which he, in
     turn,
If he shall live as many lives, may learn
How to secure: not else. Then Mantua
     called
Back to his mind how certain bards
     were thralled
– Buds blasted, but of breath more like
     perfume
Than Naddo's staring nosegay's carrion
     bloom;
Some insane rose that burnt heart out
     in sweets,
A spendthrift in the spring, no summer
     greets;
Some Dularete, drunk with truths and
     wine,
Grown bestial, dreaming how become
     divine.

Yet to surmount this obstacle,
     commence
With the commencement, merits
     crowning! Hence
Must truth be casual truth, elicited
In sparks so mean, at intervals dispread
So rarely, that 'tis like at no one time
Of the world's story has not truth, the
     prime
Of truth, the very truth which, loosed,
     had hurled
The world's course right, been really in
     the world
– Content the while with some mean
     spark by dint
Of some chance-blow, the solitary hint
Of buried fire, which, rip earth's breast,
     would stream
Sky-ward!
                    Sordello's miserable gleam
Was looked for at the moment: he
     would dash
This badge, and all it brought, to earth,
     – abash
Taurello thus, perhaps persuade him
     wrest
The Kaiser from his purpose, – would
     attest
His own belief, in any case. Before
He dashes it however, think once more!
For, were that little, truly service? 'Ay,
'I' the end, no doubt; but meantime?
     Plain you spy
'Its ultimate effect, but many flaws
'Of vision blur each intervening cause.
'Were the day's fraction clear as the
     life's sum
'Of service, Now as filled as teems
     To-come
'With evidence of good – nor too minute
'A share to vie with evil! No dispute,
' 'Twere fitliest maintain the Guelfs in
     rule:
'That makes your life's work: but you
     have to school
'Your day's work on these natures ·
     circumstanced

'Thus variously, which yet, as each
    advanced
'Or might impede the Guelf rule, must
    be moved
'Now, for the Then's sake, – hating what
    you loved,
'Loving old hatreds! Nor if one man
    bore
'Brand upon temples while his fellow
    wore
'The aureole, would it task you to decide:
'But, portioned duly out, the future vied
'Never with the unparcelled present!
    Smite
'Or spare so much on warrant all so
    slight?
'The present's complete sympathies to
    break,
'Aversions bear with, for a future's sake
'So feeble? Tito ruined through one
    speck,
'The Legate saved by his sole lightish
    fleck?
'This were work, true, but work
    performed at cost
'Of other work; aught gained here, else-
    where lost.
'For a new segment spoil an orb half-
    done?
'Rise with the People one step, and sink
    – one?
'Were it but one step, less than the
    whole face
'Of things, your novel duty bids erase!
'Harms to abolish! What, the prophet
    saith,
'The minstrel singeth vainly then? Old
    faith,
'Old courage, only born because of
    harms,
'Were not, from highest to the lowest,
    charms?
'Flame may persist; but is not glare as
    staunch?
'Where the salt marshes stagnate, crystals
    branch;
'Blood dries to crimson; Evil's beautified

'In every shape. Thrust Beauty then
    aside
'And banish Evil! Wherefore? After all,
'Is Evil a result less natural
'Than Good? For overlook the seasons'
    strife
'With tree and flower, – the hideous
    animal life,
'(Of which who seeks shall find a
    grinning taunt
'For his solution, and endure the vaunt
'Of nature's angel, as a child that
    knows
'Himself befooled, unable to propose
'Aught better than the fooling) – and
    but care
'For men, for the mere People then and
    there, –
'In these, could you but see that Good
    and Ill
'Claimed you alike! Whence rose their
    claim but still
'From Ill, as fruit of Ill? What else could
    knit
'You theirs but Sorrow? Any free from it
'Were also free from you! Whose
    happiness
'Could be distinguished in this
    morning's press
'Of miseries? – the fool's who passed a
    gibe
' "On thee," jeered he, "so wedded to
    thy tribe,
' "Thou carriest green and yellow tokens
    in
' "Thy very face that thou art Ghibellin!"
'Much hold on you that fool obtained!
    Nay mount
'Yet higher – and upon men's own
    account
'Must Evil stay: for, what is joy? – to
    heave
'Up one obstruction more, and common
    leave
'What was peculiar, by such act destroy
'Itself; a partial death is every joy;
'The sensible escape, enfranchisement

'Of a sphere's essence: once the vexed
  – content,
'The cramped – at large, the growing
  circle – round,
'All's to begin again – some novel
  bound
'To break, some new enlargement to
  entreat;
'The sphere though larger is not more
  complete.
'Now for Mankind's experience: who
  alone
'Might style the unobstructed world his
  own?
'Whom palled Goito with its perfect
  things?
'Sordello's self: whereas for Mankind
  springs
'Salvation by each hindrance interposed.
'They climb; life's view is not at once
  disclosed
'To creatures caught up, on the summit
  left,
'Heaven plain above them, yet of wings
  bereft:
'But lower laid, as at the mountain's
  foot.
'So, range on range, the girdling forests
  shoot
' 'Twixt your plain prospect and the
  throngs who scale
'Height after height, and pierce mists,
  veil by veil,
'Heartened with each discovery; in
  their soul,
'The Whole they seek by Parts – but,
  found that Whole,
'Could they revert, enjoy past gains?
  The space
'Of time you judge so meagre to
  embrace
'The Parts were more than plenty, once
  attained
'The Whole, to quite exhaust it: nought
  were gained
'But leave to look – not leave to do:
  Beneath

'Soon sates the looker – look Above,
  and Death
'Tempts ere a tithe of Life be tasted.
  Live
'First, and die soon enough, Sordello!
  Give
'Body and spirit the first right they
  claim,
'And pasture soul on a voluptuous
  shame
'That you, a pageant-city's denizen,
'Are neither vilely lodged midst
  Lombard men –
'Can force joy out of sorrow, seem to
  truck
'Bright attributes away for sordid muck,
'Yet manage from that very muck educe
'Gold; then subject, nor scruple, to
  your cruce
'The world's discardings! Though real
  ingots pay
'Your pains, the clods that yielded
  them are clay
'To all beside, – would clay remain,
  though quenched
'Your purging-fire; who's robbed then?
  Had you wrenched
'An ampler treasure forth! – As 'tis,
  they crave
'A share that ruins you and will not save
'Them. Why should sympathy
  command you quit
'The course that makes your joy, nor
  will remit
'Their woe? Would all arrive at joy?
  Reverse
'The order (time instructs you) nor
  coerce
'Each unit till, some predetermined
  mode,
'The total be emancipate; men's road
'Is one, men's times of travel many;
  thwart
'No enterprising soul's precocious start
'Before the general march! If slow or fast
'All struggle up to the same point at
  last,

'Why grudge your having gained, a
     month ago,
'The brakes at balm-shed, asphodels in
     blow,
'While they were landlocked? Speed
     their Then, but how
'This badge would suffer you improve
     your Now!'
   His time of action for, against, or with
Our world (I labour to extract the pith
Of this his problem) grew, that even-
     tide,
Gigantic with its power of joy, beside
The world's eternity of impotence
To profit though at his whole joy's
     expense.
'Make nothing of my day because so
     brief?
'Rather make more: instead of joy, use
     grief
'Before its novelty have time subside!
'Wait not for the late savour, leave
     untried
'Virtue, the creaming honey-wine,
     quick squeeze
'Vice like a biting spirit from the lees
'Of life! Together let wrath, hatred, lust,
'All tyrannies in every shape, be thrust
'Upon this Now, which time may reason
     out
'As mischiefs, far from benefits, no
     doubt;
'But long ere then Sordello will have
     slipt
'Away; you teach him at Goito's crypt,
'There's a blank issue to that fiery thrill.
'Stirring, the few cope with the many,
     still:
'So much of sand as, quiet, makes a
     mass
'Unable to produce three tufts of grass,
'Shall, troubled by the whirlwind, render
     void
'The whole calm glebe's endeavour: be
     employed!
'And e'en though somewhat smart the
     Crowd for this,

'Contribute each his pang to make your
     bliss,
' 'Tis but one pang – one blood-drop to
     the bowl
'Which brimful tempts the sluggish asp
     uncowl
'At last, stains ruddily the dull red cape,
'And, kindling orbs grey as the unripe
     grape
'Before, avails forthwith to disentrance
'The portent, soon to lead a mystic
     dance
'Among you! For, who sits alone in
     Rome?
'Have those great hands indeed hewn
     out a home,
'And set me there to live? Oh life, life-
     breath,
'Life-blood, – ere sleep, come travail,
     life ere death!
'This life stream on my soul, direct,
     oblique,
'But always streaming! Hindrances?
     They pique:
'Helps? Such … but why repeat, my
     soul o'ertops
'Each height, then every depth
     profound-lier drops?
'Enough that I can live, and would live!
     Wait
'For some transcendent life reserved by
     Fate
'To follow this? Oh, never! Fate, I trust
'The same, my soul to; for, as who
     flings dust,
'Perchance (so facile was the deed) she
     chequed
'The void with these materials to affect
'My soul diversely: these consigned
     anew
'To nought by death, what marvel if she
     threw
'A second and superber spectacle
'Before me? What may serve for sun,
     what still
'Wander a moon above me? What else
     wind

'About me like the pleasures left behind,
'And how shall some new flesh that is
    not flesh
'Cling to me? What's new laughter?
    Soothes the fresh
'Sleep like sleep? Fate's exhaustless for
    my sake
'In brave resource: but whether bids
    she slake
'My thirst at this first rivulet, or count
'No draught worth lip save from some
    rocky fount
'Above i' the clouds, while here she's
    provident
'Of pure loquacious pearl, the soft tree-
    tent
'Guards, with its face of reate and sedge,
    nor fail
'The silver globules and gold-sparkling
    grail
'At bottom? Oh, 'twere too absurd to
    slight
'For the hereafter the to-day's delight!
'Quench thirst at this, then seek next
    well-spring: wear
'Home-lilies ere strange lotus in my
    hair!
'Here is the Crowd, whom I with freest
    heart
'Offer to serve, contented for my part
'To give life up in service, – only grant
'That I do serve; if otherwise, why want
'Aught further of me? If men cannot
    choose
'But set aside life, why should I refuse
'The gift? I take it – I, for one, engage
'Never to falter through my pilgrimage –
'Nor end it howling that the stock or
    stone
'Were enviable, truly: I, for one,
'Will praise the world, you style mere
    ante-room
'To palace – be it so! shall I assume
' – My foot the courtly gait, my tongue
    the trope,
'My mouth the smirk, before the doors
    fly ope

'One moment? What? with guarders
    row on row,
'Gay swarms of varletry that come and
    go,
'Pages to dice with, waiting-girls unlace
'The plackets of, pert claimants help
    displace,
'Heart-heavy suitors get a rank for, –
    laugh
'At yon sleek parasite, break his own
    staff
' 'Cross Beetle-brows the Usher's
    shoulder, – why
'Admitted to the presence by and by,
'Should thought of having lost these
    make me grieve
'Among new joys I reach, for joys I
    leave?
'Cool citrine-crystals, fierce pyropus-
    stone,
'Are floor-work there! But do I let alone
'That black-eyed peasant in the vestibule
'Once and for ever? – Floor-work? No
    such fool!
'Rather, were heaven to forestall earth,
    I'd say
'I, is it, must be blest? Then, my own
    way
'Bless me! Give firmer arm and fleeter
    foot,
'I'll thank you: but to no mad wings
    transmute
'These limbs of mine – our greensward
    was so soft!
'Nor camp I on the thunder-cloud aloft:
'We feel the bliss distinctlier, having
    thus
'Engines subservient, not mixed up with
    us.
'Better move palpably through heaven:
    nor, freed
'Of flesh forsooth, from space to space
    proceed
' 'Mid flying synods of worlds! No: in
    heaven's marge
'Show Titan still, recumbent o'er his
    targe

'Solid with stars – the Centaur at his
  game,
'Made tremulously out in hoary flame!
  'Life! Yet the very cup whose
    extreme dull
'Dregs, even, I would quaff, was dashed,
  at full,
'Aside so oft; the death I fly, revealed
'So oft a better life this life concealed,
'And which sage, champion, martyr,
    through each path
'Have hunted fearlessly – the horrid
  bath,
'The crippling-irons and the fiery chair.
'Twas well for them; let me become
  aware
'As they, and I relinquish life, too! Let
'What masters life disclose itself! Forget
'Vain ordinances, I have one appeal –
'I feel, am what I feel, know what I feel;
'So much is truth to me. What Is, then?
    Since
'One object, viewed diversely, may evince
'Beauty and ugliness – this way attract,
'That way repel, – why gloze upon the
  fact?
'Why must a single of the sides be right?
'What bids choose this and leave the
  opposite?
'Where's abstract Right for me? – in
  youth endued
'With Right still present, still to be
  pursued,
'Thro' all the interchange of circles, rife
'Each with its proper law and mode of
  life,
'Each to be dwelt at ease in: where, to
  sway
'Absolute with the Kaiser, or obey
'Implicit with his serf of fluttering
  heart,
'Or, like a sudden thought of God's, to
  start
'Up, Brutus in the presence, then go
  shout
'That some should pick the unstrung
  jewels out –

'Each, well!'
    And, as in moments when the past
Gave partially enfranchisement, he cast
Himself quite through mere secondary
    states
Of his soul's essence, little loves and
  hates,
Into the mid deep yearnings overlaid
By these; as who should pierce hill,
    plain, grove, glade,
And on into the very nucleus probe
That first determined there exist a
    globe.
As that were easiest, half the globe
    dissolved,
So seemed Sordello's closing-truth
    evolved
By his flesh-half's break-up; the sudden
    swell
Of his expanding soul showed Ill and
    Well,
Sorrow and Joy, Beauty and Ugliness,
Virtue and Vice, the Larger and the
    Less,
All qualities, in fine, recorded here,
Might be but modes of Time and this
    one sphere,
Urgent on these, but not of force to
    bind
Eternity, as Time – as Matter – Mind,
If Mind, Eternity, should choose assert
Their attributes within a Life: thus girt
With circumstance, next change beholds
    them cinct
Quite otherwise – with Good and Ill
    distinct,
Joys, sorrows, tending to a like result –
Contrived to render easy, difficult,
This or the other course of … what
    new bond
In place of flesh may stop their flight
    beyond
Its new sphere, as that course does
    harm or good
To its arrangements. Once this under-
    stood,
As suddenly he felt himself alone,

Quite out of Time and this world: all
    was known.
What made the secret of his past despair?
– Most imminent when he seemed most
    aware
Of his own self-sufficiency: made mad
By craving to expand the power he had,
And not new power to be expanded? –
    just
This made it; Soul on Matter being
    thrust,
Joy comes when so much Soul is
    wreaked in Time
On Matter: let the Soul's attempt
    sublime
Matter beyond the scheme and so
    prevent
By more or less that deed's
    accomplishment,
And Sorrow follows: Sorrow how avoid?
Let the employer match the thing
    employed,
Fit to the finite his infinity,
And thus proceed for ever, in degree
Changed but in kind the same, still
    limited
To the appointed circumstance and
    dead
To all beyond. A sphere is but a sphere;
Small, Great, are merely terms we bandy
    here;
Since to the spirit's absoluteness all
Are like. Now, of the present sphere we
    call
Life, are conditions; take but this among
Many; the body was to be so long
Youthful, no longer: but, since no control
Tied to that body's purposes his soul,
She chose to understand the body's
    trade
More than the body's self – had fain
    conveyed
Her boundless to the body's bounded
    lot.
Hence, the soul permanent, the body
    not, –
Scarcely its minute for enjoying here, –

The soul must needs instruct her weak
    compeer,
Run o'er its capabilities and wring
A joy thence, she held worth
    experiencing:
Which, far from half discovered even, –
    lo,
The minute gone, the body's power let
    go
Apportioned to that joy's acquirement!
    Broke
Morning o'er earth, he yearned for all it
    woke –
From the volcano's vapour-flag, winds
    hoist
Black o'er the spread of sea, – down to
    the moist
Dale's silken barley-spikes sullied with
    rain,
Swayed earthwards, heavily to rise
    again –
The Small, a sphere as perfect as the
    Great
To the soul's absoluteness. Meditate
Too long on such a morning's cluster-
    chord
And the whole music it was framed
    afford, –
The chord's might half discovered,
    what should pluck
One string, his finger, was found palsy-
    struck.
And then no marvel if the spirit, shown
A saddest sight – the body lost alone
Through her officious proffered help,
    deprived
Of this and that enjoyment Fate
    contrived, –
Virtue, Good, Beauty, each allowed slip
    hence, –
Vain-gloriously were fain, for recompense,
To stem the ruin even yet, protract
The body's term, supply the power it
    lacked
From her infinity, compel it learn
These qualities were only Time's
    concern,

And body may, with spirit helping,
   barred –
Advance the same, vanquished – obtain
   reward,
Reap joy where sorrow was intended
   grow,
Of Wrong make Right, and turn Ill
   Good below.
And the result is, the poor body soon
Sinks under what was meant a
   wondrous boon,
Leaving its bright accomplice all aghast.
   So much was plain then, proper in
   the past;
To be complete for, satisfy the whole
Series of spheres – Eternity, his soul
Needs must exceed, prove incomplete
   for, each
Single sphere – Time. But does our
   knowledge reach
No farther? Is the cloud of hindrance
   broke
But by the failing of the fleshly yoke,
Its loves and hates, as now when death
   lets soar
Sordello, self-sufficient as before,
Though during the mere space that
   shall elapse
'Twixt his enthralment in new bonds
   perhaps?
Must life be ever just escaped, which
   should
Have been enjoyed? – nay, might have
   been and would,
Each purpose ordered right – the soul's
   no whit
Beyond the body's purpose under it.
Like yonder breadth of watery heaven,
   a bay,
And that sky-space of water, ray for ray
And star for star, one richness where
   they mixed
As this and that wing of an angel, fixed,
Tumultuary splendours folded in
To die – would soul, proportioned
   thus, begin
Exciting discontent, or surelier quell

The body if, aspiring, it rebel?
But how so order life? Still brutalize
The soul, the sad world's way, with
   muffled eyes
To all that was before, all that shall be
After this sphere – all and each quality
Save some sole and immutable Great,
   Good
And Beauteous whither fate has loosed
   its hood
To follow? Never may some soul see All
– The Great Before and After, and the
   Small
Now, yet be saved by this the simplest
   lore,
And take the single course prescribed
   before,
As the king-bird with ages on his plumes
Travels to die in his ancestral glooms?
But where descry the Love that shall
   select
That course? Here is a soul whom, to
   affect,
Nature has plied with all her means,
   from trees
And flowers e'en to the Multitude! –
   and these,
Decides he save or no? One word to end!
Ah my Sordello, I this once befriend
And speak for you. Of a Power above
   you still
Which, utterly incomprehensible,
Is out of rivalry, which thus you can
Love, tho'unloving all conceived by
   man –
What need! And of – none the minutest
   duct
To that out-nature, nought that would
   instruct
And so let rivalry begin to live –
But of a Power its representative
Who, being for authority the same,
Communication different, should claim
A course, the first chose but this last
   revealed –
This Human clear, as that Divine
   concealed –

What utter need!
            What has Sordello found?
Or can his spirit go the mighty round,
End where poor Eglamor begun? So,
    says
Old fable, the two eagles went two ways
About the world: where, in the midst,
    they met,
Though on a shifting waste of sand,
    men set
Jove's temple. Quick, what has Sordello
    found?
For they approach – approach – that
    foot's rebound …
Palma? No, Salinguerra though in mail;
They mount, have reached the
    threshold, dash the veil
Aside – and you divine who sat there
    dead,
Under his foot the badge: still, Palma
    said,
A triumph lingering in the wide eyes,
Wider than some spent swimmer's if he
    spies
Help from above in his extreme despair,
And, head far back on shoulder thrust,
    turns there
With short quick passionate cry: as
    Palma pressed
In one great kiss, her lips upon his
    breast,
It beat.
    By this, the hermit-bee has stopped
His day's toil at Goito: the new-cropped
Dead vine-leaf answers, now 'tis eve, he
    bit,
Twirled so, and filed all day: the
    mansion's fit,
God counselled for. As easy guess the
    word
That passed betwixt them, and become
    the third
To the soft small unfrighted bee, as tax
Him with one fault – so, no
    remembrance racks
Of the stone maidens and the font of
    stone

He, creeping through the crevice,
    leaves alone.
Alas, my friend, alas Sordello, whom
Anon they laid within that old font-
    tomb,
And, yet again, alas!
            And now is't worth
Our while bring back to mind, much
    less set forth
How Salinguerra extricates himself
Without Sordello? Ghibellin and Guelf
May fight their fiercest out? If Richard
    sulked
In durance or the Marquis paid his
    mulct,
Who cares, Sordello gone? The upshot,
    sure,
Was peace; our chief made some frank
    overture
That prospered; compliment fell thick
    and fast
On its disposer, and Taurello passed
With foe and friend for an outstripping
    soul,
Nine days at least. Then, – fairly reached
    the goal, –
He, by one effort, blotted the great hope
Out of his mind, nor further tried to
    cope
With Este, that mad evening's style,
    but sent
Away the Legate and the League,
    content
No blame at least the brothers had
    incurred,
– Dispatched a message to the Monk,
    he heard
Patiently first to last, scarce shivered at,
Then curled his limbs up on his
    wolfskin mat
And ne'er spoke more, – informed the
    Ferrarese
He but retained their rule so long as
    these
Lingered in pupilage, – and last, no
    mode
Apparent else of keeping safe the road

From Germany direct to Lombardy
For Friedrich, – none, that is, to
    guarantee
The faith and promptitude of who
    should next
Obtain Sofia's dowry, – sore perplexed –
(Sofia being youngest of the tribe
Of daughters, Ecelin was wont to bribe
The envious magnates with – nor, since
    he sent
Henry of Egna this fair child, had Trent
Once failed the Kaiser's purposes – 'we
    lost
'Egna last year, and who takes Egna's
    post –
'Opens the Lombard gate if Friedrich
    knock?')
Himself espoused the Lady of the Rock
In pure necessity, and, so destroyed
His slender last of chances, quite made
    void
Old prophecy, and spite of all the
    schemes
Overt and covert, youth's deeds, age's
    dreams,
Was sucked into Romano. And so
    hushed
He up this evening's work that, when
    'twas brushed
Somehow against by a blind chronicle
Which, chronicling whatever woe befell
Ferrara, noted this the obscure woe
Of 'Salinguerra's sole son Giacomo
'Deceased, fatuous and doting, ere his
    sire,'
The townsfolk rubbed their eyes, could
    but admire
Which of Sofia's five was meant.
                    The chaps
Of earth's dead hope were tardy to
    collapse,
Obliterated not the beautiful
Distinctive features at a crash: but dull
And duller these, next year, as Guelfs
    withdrew
Each to his stronghold. Then (securely
    too

Ecelin at Campese slept; close by,
Who likes may see him in Solagna lie,
With cushioned head and gloved hand
    to denote
The cavalier he was) – then his heart
    smote
Young Ecelin at last; long since adult.
And, save Vicenza's business, what
    result
In blood and blaze? (So hard to intercept
Sordello till his plain withdrawal!)
    Stepped
Then its new lord on Lombardy. I' the
    nick
Of time when Ecelin and Alberic
Closed with Taurello, come precisely
    news
That in Verona half the souls refuse
Allegiance to the Marquis and the
    Count –
Have cast them from a throne they bid
    him mount,
Their Podestà, thro' his ancestral worth.
Ecelin flew there, and the town
    henceforth
Was wholly his – Taurello sinking back
From temporary station to a track
That suited. News received of this
    acquist,
Friedrich did come to Lombardy: who
    missed
Taurello then? Another year: they took
Vicenza, left the Marquis scarce a nook
For refuge, and, when hundreds two or
    three
Of Guelfs conspired to call themselves
    'The Free,'
Opposing Alberic, – vile Bassanese, –
(Without Sordello!) – Ecelin at ease
Slaughtered them so observably, that
    oft
A little Salinguerra looked with soft
Blue eyes up, asked his sire the proper
    age
To get appointed his proud uncle's page.
More years passed, and that sire had
    dwindled down

To a mere showy turbulent soldier,
    grown
Better through age, his parts still in
    repute,
Subtle – how else? – but hardly so astute
As his contemporaneous friends
    professed;
Undoubtedly a brawler: for the rest,
Known by each neighbour, and
    allowed for, let
Keep his incorrigible ways, nor fret
Men who would miss their boyhood's
    bugbear: 'trap
'The ostrich, suffer our bald osprey flap
'A battered pinion!' – was the word. In
    fine,
One flap too much and Venice's marine
Was meddled with; no overlooking that!
She captured him in his Ferrara, fat
And florid at a banquet, more by fraud
Than force, to speak the truth; there's
    slender laud
Ascribed you for assisting eighty years
To pull his death on such a man; fate
    shears
The life-cord prompt enough whose
    last fine thread
You fritter: so, presiding his board-
    head,
The old smile, your assurance all went
    well
With Friedrich (as if he were like to
    tell!)
In rushed (a plan contrived before) our
    friends,
Made some pretence at fighting, some
    amends
For the shame done his eighty years –
    (apart
The principle, none found it in his heart
To be much angry with Taurello) –
    gained
Their galleys with the prize, and what
    remained
But carry him to Venice for a show?
– Set him, as 'twere, down gently – free
    to go

His gait, inspect our square, pretend
    observe
The swallows soaring their eternal
    curve
'Twixt Theodore and Mark, if citizens
Gathered importunately, fives and tens,
To point their children the Magnifico,
All but a monarch once in firm-land, go
His gait among them now – 'it took,
    indeed,
'Fully this Ecelin to supersede
'That man,' remarked the seniors.
    Singular!
Sordello's inability to bar
Rivals the stage, that evening, mainly
    brought
About by his strange disbelief that
    aught
Was ever to be done, – this thrust the
    Twain
Under Taurello's tutelage, – whom,
    brain
And heart and hand, he forthwith in
    one rod
Indissolubly bound to baffle God
Who loves the world – and thus
    allowed the thin
Grey wizened dwarfish devil Ecelin,
And massy-muscled big-boned Alberic
(Mere man, alas!) to put his problem
    quick
To demonstration – prove wherever's
    will
To do, there's plenty to be done, or ill
Or good. Anointed, then, to rend and
    rip –
Kings of the gag and flesh-hook, screw
    and whip,
They plagued the world: a touch of
    Hildebrand
(So far from obsolete!) made Lombards
    band
Together, cross their coats as for Christ's
    cause,
And saving Milan win the world's
    applause.
Ecelin perished: and I think grass grew

Never so pleasant as in Valley Rù
By San Zenon where Alberic in turn
Saw his exasperated captors burn
Seven children and their mother; then,
　　regaled
So far, tied on to a wild horse, was
　　trailed
To death through raunce and bramble-
　　bush. I take
God's part and testify that 'mid the
　　brake
Wild o'er his castle on the pleasant
　　knoll,
You hear its one tower left, a belfry, toll –
The earthquake spared it last year, laying
　　flat
The modern church beneath, – no harm
　　in that!
Chirrups the contumacious grasshopper,
Rustles the lizard and the cushats chirre
Above the ravage: there, at deep of day
A week since, heard I the old Canon say
He saw with his own eyes a barrow
　　burst
And Alberic's huge skeleton unhearsed
Only five years ago. He added, 'June's
'The month for carding off our first
　　cocoons
'The silkworms fabricate' – a double
　　news,
Nor he nor I could tell the worthier.
　　Choose!
　　And Naddo gone, all's gone; not
　　Eglamor!
Believe, I knew the face I waited for,
A guest my spirit of the golden courts!
Oh strange to see how, despite ill-
　　reports,
Disuse, some wear of years, that face
　　retained
Its joyous look of love! Suns waxed and
　　waned,
And still my spirit held an upward
　　flight,
Spiral on spiral, gyres of life and light
More and more gorgeous – ever that
　　face there

The last admitted! crossed, too, with
　　some care
As perfect triumph were not sure for
　　all,
But, on a few, enduring damp must
　　fall,
– A transient struggle, haply a painful
　　sense
Of the inferior nature's clinging – whence
Slight starting tears easily wiped away,
Fine jealousies soon stifled in the play
Of irrepressible admiration – not
Aspiring, all considered, to their lot
Who ever, just as they prepare ascend
Spiral on spiral, wish thee well, impend
Thy frank delight at their exclusive track,
That upturned fervid face and hair put
　　back!
　　Is there no more to say? He of the
　　rhymes –
Many a tale, of this retreat betimes,
Was born: Sordello die at once for
　　men?
The Chroniclers of Mantua tired their
　　pen
Telling how *Sordello Prince Visconti* saved
Mantua, and elsewhere notably
　　behaved –
Who thus, by fortune ordering events,
Passed with posterity, to all intents,
For just the god he never could become.
As Knight, Bard, Gallant, men were
　　never dumb
In praise of him: while what he should
　　have been,
Could be, and was not – the one step
　　too mean
For him to take, – we suffer at this day
Because of: Ecelin had pushed away
Its chance ere Dante could arrive and
　　take
That step Sordello spurned, for the
　　world's sake:
He did much – but Sordello's chance
　　was gone.
Thus, had Sordello dared that step
　　alone,

Apollo had been compassed: 'twas a fit
He wished should go to him, not he to it
– As one content to merely be supposed
Singing or fighting elsewhere, while he
  dozed
Really at home – one who was chiefly
  glad
To have achieved the few real deeds he
  had,
Because that way assured they were not
  worth
Doing, so spared from doing them
  henceforth –
A tree that covets fruitage and yet tastes
Never itself, itself. Had he embraced
Their cause then, men had plucked
  Hesperian fruit
And, praising that, just thrown him in
  to boot
All he was anxious to appear, but scarce
Solicitous to be. A sorry farce
Such life is, after all! Cannot I say
He lived for some one better thing? this
  way. –
Lo, on a heathy brown and nameless
  hill
By sparkling Asolo, in mist and chill,
Morning just up, higher and higher
  runs
A child barefoot and rosy. See! the sun's
On the square castle's inner-court's low
  wall
Like the chine of some extinct animal
Half turned to earth and flowers; and
  through the haze
(Save where some slender patches of
  grey maize

Are to be overleaped) that boy has
  crossed
The whole hill-side of dew and powder-
  frost
Matting the balm and mountain
  camomile.
Up and up goes he, singing all the
  while
Some unintelligible words to beat
The lark, God's poet, swooning at his
  feet,
So worsted is he at 'the few fine locks
'Stained like pale honey oozed from
  topmost rocks
'Sun-blanched the livelong summer,' –
  all that's left
Of the Goito lay! And thus bereft,
Sleep and forget, Sordello! In effect
He sleeps, the feverish poet – I suspect
Not utterly companionless; but, friends,
Wake up! The ghost's gone, and the
  story ends
I'd fain hope, sweetly; seeing, peri or
  ghoul,
That spirits are conjectured fair or foul,
Evil or good, judicious authors think,
According as they vanish in a stink
Or in a perfume. Friends, be frank! ye
  snuff
Civet, I warrant. Really? Like enough!
Merely the savour's rareness; any nose
May ravage with impunity a rose:
Rifle a musk-pod and 'twill ache like
  yours!
I'd tell you that some pungency ensures
An after-gust, but that were overbold.
Who would has heard Sordello's story
  told.

# PIPPA PASSES

A Drama

1841

I dedicate My best intentions, in this poem, admiringly to the author of 'Ion',
affectionately to Mr Sergeant Talfourd. London, 1841 R. B.

## Persons

Pippa. Ottima. Sebald. Foreign Students. Gottlieb. Schramm. Jules. Phene.
Austrian Police. Bluphocks. Luigi *and his* Mother. Poor Girls.
Monsignor *and his* Attendants.

## INTRODUCTION

### NEW YEAR'S DAY AT ASOLO IN THE TREVISAN

*Scene – A large mean airy chamber. A girl, PIPPA, from the Silk-mills, springing out of bed.*

Day!
Faster and more fast,
O'er night's brim, day boils at last:
Boils, pure gold, o'er the cloud-cup's
     brim
Where spurting and suppressed it lay,
For not a froth-flake touched the rim
Of yonder gap in the solid gray
Of the eastern cloud, an hour away;
But forth one wavelet, then another,
     curled,
Till the whole sunrise, not to be
     suppressed,
Rose, reddened, and its seething breast
Flickered in bounds, grew gold, then
     overflowed the world.
Oh, Day, if I squander a wavelet of
     thee,
A mite of my twelve hours' treasure,
The least of thy gazes or glances,
(Be they grants thou art bound to or
     gifts above measure)
One of thy choices or one of thy
     chances,
(Be they tasks God imposed thee or
     freaks at thy pleasure)
– My Day, if I squander such labour or
     leisure,

Then shame fall on Asolo, mischief on
     me!

Thy long blue solemn hours serenely
     flowing,
Whence earth, we feel, gets steady help
     and good –
Thy fitful sunshine-minutes, coming,
     going,
As if earth turned from work in
     gamesome mood –
All shall be mine! But thou must treat
     me not
As prosperous ones are treated, those
     who live
At hand here, and enjoy the higher lot,
In readiness to take what thou wilt
     give,
And free to let alone what thou
     refusest;
For, Day, my holiday, if thou ill-usest
Me, who am only Pippa, – old-year's
     sorrow,
Cast off last night, will come again
     tomorrow:
Whereas, if thou prove gentle, I shall
     borrow
Sufficient strength of thee for new-
     year's sorrow.
All other men and women that this
     earth
Belongs to, who all days alike possess,
Make general plenty cure particular
     dearth,
Get more joy one way, if another, less:

Thou art my single day, God lends to
 leaven
What were all earth else, with a feel of
 heaven, –
Sole light that helps me through the
 year, thy sun's!
Try now! Take Asolo's Four Happiest
 Ones –
And let thy morning rain on that superb
Great haughty Ottima; can rain disturb
Her Sebald's homage? All the while thy
 rain
Beats fiercest on her shrub-house
 window-pane,
He will but press the closer, breathe
 more warm
Against her cheek; how should she
 mind the storm?
And, morning past, if mid-day shed a
 gloom
O'er Jules and Phene, – what care bride
 and groom
Save for their dear selves? 'Tis their
 marriage-day;
And while they leave church and go
 home their way,
Hand clasping hand, within each
 breast would be
Sunbeams and pleasant weather spite
 of thee.
Then, for another trial, obscure thy eve
With mist, – will Luigi and his mother
 grieve –
The lady and her child, unmatched,
 forsooth,
She in her age, as Luigi in bis youth,
For true content? The cheerful town,
 warm, close
And safe, the sooner that thou art morose,
Receives them. And yet once again,
 outbreak
In storm at night on Monsignor, they
 make
Such stir about, – whom they expect
 from Rome
To visit Asolo, his brother's home,
And say here masses proper to release

A soul from pain, – what storm dares
 hurt his peace?
Calm would he pray, with his own
 thoughts to ward
Thy thunder off, nor want the angels'
 guard.
But Pippa – just one such mischance
 would spoil
Her day that lightens the next twelve-
 month's toil
At wearisome silk-winding, coil on coil!
 And here I let time slip for nought!
Aha, you foolhardy sunbeam, caught
With a single splash from my ewer!
You that would mock the best pursuer,
Was my basin over-deep?
One splash of water ruins you asleep,
And up, up, fleet your brilliant bits
Wheeling and counterwheeling,
Reeling, broken beyond healing:
Now grow together on the ceiling!
That will task your wits.
Whoever it was quenched fire first,
 hoped to see
Morsel after morsel flee
As merrily, as giddily …
Meantime, what lights my sunbeam on,
Where settles by degrees the radiant
 cripple?
Oh, is it surely blown, my martagon?
New-blown and ruddy as St Agnes'
 nipple,
Plump as the flesh-bunch on some
 Turk bird's poll!
Be sure if corals, branching 'neath the
 ripple
Of ocean, bud there, – fairies watch
 unroll
Such turban-flowers; I say, such lamps
 disperse
Thick red flame through that dusk
 green universe!
I am queen of thee, floweret!
And each fleshy blossom
Preserve I not – (safer
Than leaves that embower it,
Or shells that embosom)

– From weevil and chafer?
Laugh through my pane then; solicit the
   bee;
Gibe him, be sure; and, in midst of thy
   glee
Love thy queen, worship me!

– Worship whom else? For am I not,
   this day,
Whate'er I please? What shall I please
   today?
My morn, noon, eve and night – how
   spend my day?
To-morrow I must be Pippa who winds
   silk,
The whole year round, to earn just
   bread and milk:
But, this one day, I have leave to go,
And play out my fancy's fullest games;
I may fancy all day – and it shall be so –
That I taste of the pleasures, am called
   by the names
Of the Happiest Four in our Asolo!

See! Up the hill-side yonder, through
   the morning,
Some one shall love me, as the world
   calls love:
I am no less than Ottima, take warning!
The gardens, and the great stone house
   above,
And other house for shrubs, all glass in
   front,
Are mine; where Sebald steals, as he is
   wont,
To court me, while old Luca yet reposes:
And therefore, till the shrub-house door
   uncloses,
I ... what now? – give abundant cause
   for prate
About me – Ottima, I mean – of late,
Too bold, too confident she'll still face
   down
The spitefullest of talkers in our town.
How we talk in the little town below!
   But love, love, love – there's better
   love, I know!

This foolish love was only day's first
   offer;
I choose my next love to defy the
   scoffer:
For do not our Bride and Bridegroom
   sally
Out of Possagno church at noon?
Their house looks over Orcana valley:
Why should not I be the bride as soon
As Ottima? For I saw, beside,
Arrive last night that little bride –
Saw, if you call it seeing her, one flash
Of the pale snow-pure cheek and black
   bright tresses,
Blacker than all except the black eyelash;
I wonder she contrives those lids no
   dresses!
– So strict was she, the veil
Should cover close her pale
Pure cheeks – a bride to look at and
   scarce touch,
Scarce touch, remember, Jules! For are
   not such
Used to be tended, flower-like, every
   feature,
As if one's breath would fray the lily of
   a creature?
A soft and easy life these ladies lead:
Whiteness in us were wonderful indeed.
Oh, save that brow its virgin dimness,
Keep that foot its lady primness,
Let those ankles never swerve
From their exquisite reserve,
Yet have to trip along the streets like
   me,
All but naked to the knee!
How will she ever grant her Jules a bliss
So startling as her real first infant kiss?
Oh, no – not envy, this!

– Not envy, sure! – for if you gave me
Leave to take or to refuse,
In earnest, do you think I'd choose
That sort of new love to enslave me?
Mine should have lapped me round
   from the beginning;
As little fear of losing it as winning:

Lovers grow cold, men learn to hate
  their wives,
And only parents' love can last our lives.
At eve the Son and Mother, gentle pair,
Commune inside our turret: what
  prevents
My being Luigi? While that mossy lair
Of lizards through the winter-time is
  stirred
With each to each imparting sweet
  intents
For this new-year, as brooding bird to
  bird –
(For I observe of late, the evening walk
Of Luigi and his mother, always ends
Inside our ruined turret, where they
  talk,
Calmer than lovers, yet more kind than
  friends)
– Let me be cared about, kept out of
  harm,
And schemed for, safe in love as with a
  charm;
Let me be Luigi! If I only knew
What was my mother's face – my father,
  too!
  Nay, if you come to that, best love of
  all
Is God's; then why not have God's love
  befall
Myself as, in the palace by the Dome,
Monsignor? – who to-night will bless
  the home
Of his dead brother; and God bless in
  turn
That heart which beats, those eyes which
  mildly burn
With love for all men! I, to-night at
  least,
Would be that holy and beloved priest.
Now wait! – even I already seem to
  share
In God's love: what does New-year's
  hymn declare?
What other meaning do these verses
  bear?

*All service ranks the same with God:*
*If now, as formerly he trod*
*Paradise, his presence fills*
*Our earth, each only as God wills*
*Can work – God's puppets, best and*
  *worst,*
*Are we; there is no last nor first.*
*Say not 'a small event!' Why 'small'?*
*Costs it more pain that this, ye call*
*A 'great event', should come to pass,*
*Than that? Untwine me from the mass*
*Of deeds which make up life, one deed*
*Power shall fall short in or exceed!*

And more of it, and more of it! – oh
  yes –
I will pass each, and see their
  happiness,
And envy none – being just as great, no
  doubt,
Useful to men, and dear to God, as
  they!
A pretty thing to care about
So mightily, this single holiday!
But let the sun shine! Wherefore
  repine?
– With thee to lead me, O Day of mine,
Down the grass path grey with dew,
Under the pine-wood, blind with
  boughs,
Where the swallow never flew
Nor yet cicala dared carouse –
No, dared carouse!
                    [*She enters the street.*

1 – MORNING

*Scene – Up the Hill-side, inside the Shrub-*
  *house. Luca's wife, Ottima, and her*
  *paramour, the German Sebald.*
*Seb.* [*sings*].
  *Let the watching lids wink!*
  *Day's a-blaze with eyes, think!*
  *Deep into the night, drink !*
*Otti.* Night? Such may be your
  Rhineland nights perhaps;
But this blood-red beam through the
  shutter's chink

– We call such light, the morning: let us see!
Mind how you grope your way, though! How these tall
Naked geraniums straggle! Push the lattice
Behind that frame! – Nay, do I bid you? – Sebald,
It shakes the dust down on me! Why, of course
The slide-bolt catches. Well, are you content,
Or must I find you something else to spoil?
Kiss and be friends, my Sebald! Is't full morning?
Oh, don't speak then!
*Seb.*                    Ay, thus it used to be.
Ever your house was, I remember, shut
Till mid-day; I observed that, as I strolled
On mornings through the vale here; country girls
Were noisy, washing garments in the brook,
Hinds drove the slow white oxen up the hills:
But no, your house was mute, would ope no eye.
And wisely: you were plotting one thing there,
Nature, another outside. I looked up –
Rough white wood shutters, rusty iron bars,
Silent as death, blind in a flood of light.
Oh, I remember! – and the peasants laughed
And said, 'The old man sleeps with the young wife.'
This house was his, this chair, this window – his.
*Otti.* Ah, the clear morning! I can see St Mark's;
That black streak is the belfry. Stop: Vicenza
Should lie … there's Padua, plain enough, that blue!
Look o'er my shoulder, follow my ringer!

*Seb.*                              Morning?
It seems to me a night with a sun added.
Where's dew, where's freshness? That bruised plant, I bruised
In getting through the lattice yestereve,
Droops as it did. See, here's my elbow's mark
I' the dust o' the sill.
*Otti.*          Oh, shut the lattice, pray!
*Seb.* Let me lean out. I cannot scent blood here,
Foul as the morn may be.
There, shut the world out!
How do you feel now, Ottima? There, curse
The world and all outside! Let us throw off
This mask: how do you bear yourself? Let's out
With all of it.
*Otti.*          Best never speak of it.
*Seb.* Best speak again and yet again of it..
Till words cease to be more than words. 'His blood,'
For instance – let those two words mean 'His blood'
And nothing more. Notice, I'll say them now,
'His blood.'
*Otti.*          Assuredly if I repented
The deed –
*Seb.* Repent? Who should repent, or why?
What puts that in your head? Did I once say
That I repented?
*Otti.*          No, I said the deed …
*Seb.* 'The deed' and 'the event' – just now it was
'Our passion's fruit' – the devil take such cant!
Say, once and always, Luca was a wittol,
I am his cut-throat, you are …
*Otti.*                    Here's the wine;
I brought it when we left the house above,

And glasses too – wine of both sorts.
Black? White then?

*Seb.* But am not I his cut-throat? What
are you?

*Otti.* There trudges on his business
from the Duomo

Benet the Capuchin, with his brown
hood

And bare feet; always in one place at
church,

Close under the stone wall by the south
entry

I used to take him for a brown cold piece
Of the wall's self, as out of it he rose
To let me pass – at first, I say, I used:
Now, so has that dumb figure fastened
on me,

I rather should account the plastered
wall

A piece of him, so chilly does it strike.
This, Sebald?

*Seb.*            No, the white wine – the
white wine!

Well, Ottima, I promised no new year
Should rise on us the ancient shameful
way;

Nor does it rise. Pour on! To your black
eyes!

Do you remember last damned New
Year's day?

*Otti.* You brought those foreign prints.
We looked at them

Over the wine and fruit. I had to scheme
To get him from the fire. Nothing but
saying

His own set wants the proof-mark,
roused him up

To hunt them out.

*Seb.*            'Faith, he is not alive
To fondle you before my face.

*Otti.*                        Do you
Fondle me then! Who means to take
your life

For that, my Sebald?

*Seb.*            Hark you, Ottima!
One thing to guard against. We'll not
make much

One of the other – that is, not make
more

Parade of warmth, childish officious
coil,

Than yesterday: as if, sweet, I supposed
Proof upon proof were needed now,
now first,

To show I love you – yes, still love you
– love you

In spite of Luca and what's come to him
– Sure sign we had him ever in our
thoughts,

White sneering old reproachful face
and all!

We'll even quarrel, love, at times, as if
We still could lose each other, were not
tied

By this: conceive you?

*Otti.*                Love!

*Seb.*                        Not tied so sure.
Because though I was wrought upon,
have struck

His insolence back into him – am I
So surely yours? – therefore forever
yours?

*Otti.* Love, to be wise, (one counsel
pays another)

Should we have – months ago, when
first we loved,

For instance that May morning we two
stole

Under the green ascent of sycamores –
If we had come upon a thing like that
Suddenly …

*Seb.* 'A thing' – there again – 'a thing!'

*Otti.* Then, Venus' body, had we
comeupon

My husband Luca Gaddi's murdered
corpse

Within there, at his couch-foot, covered
close –

Would you have pored upon it? Why
persist

In poring now upon it? For 'tis here
As much as there in the deserted
house:

You cannot rid your eyes of it. For me,

Now he is dead I hate him worse: I
    hate ...
Dare you stay here? I would go back
    and hold
His two dead hands, and say, 'I hate
    you worse,
'Luca, than ... '
*Seb.*          Off, off – take your hands
    off mine,
'Tis the hot evening – off! oh, morning
    is it?
*Otti.* There's one thing must be done;
    you know what thing.
Come in and help to carry. We may
    sleep
Anywhere in the whole wide house to-
    night.
*Seb.* What would come, think you, if
    we let him lie
Just as he is? Let him lie there until
The angels take him! He is turned by
    this
Off from his face beside, as you will see.
*Otti.* This dusty pane might serve for
    looking glass.
Three, four – four grey hairs! Is it so you
    said
A plait of hair should wave across my
    neck?
No – this way.
*Seb.*    Ottima, I would give your neck,
Each splendid shoulder, both those
    breasts of yours,
That this were undone! Killing! Kill the
    world
So Luca lives again! – ay, lives to sputter
His fulsome dotage on you – yes, and
    feign
Surprise that I return at eve to sup,
When all the morning I was loitering
    here –
Bid me despatch my business and
    begone.
I would ...
*Otti.*    See!
*Seb.*       No, I'll finish. Do you think
I fear to speak the bare truth once for all?

All we have talked of, is, at bottom, fine
To suffer; there's a recompense in guilt;
One must be venturous and fortunate:
What is one young for, else? In age we'll
    sigh
O'er the wild reckless wicked days flown
    over;
Still, we have lived: the vice was in its
    place.
But to have eaten Luca's bread, have
    worn
His clothes, have felt his money swell
    my purse –
Do lovers in romances sin that way?
Why, I was starving when I used to call
And teach you music, starving while
    you plucked me
These flowers to smell!
*Otti.*       My poor lost friend!
*Seb.*               He gave me
Life, nothing less: what if he did reproach
My perfidy, and threaten, and do more –
Had he no right? What was to wonder
    at?
He sat by us at table quietly:
Why must you lean across till our
    cheeks touched?
Could he do less than make pretence
    to strike?
'Tis not the crime's sake – I'd commit
    ten crimes
Greater, to have this crime wiped out,
    undone!
And you – O how feel you? Feel you
    for me?
*Otti.* Well then, I love you better now
    than ever,
And best (look at me while I speak to
    you) –
Best for the crime; nor do I grieve, in
    truth,
This mask, this simulated ignorance,
This affectation of simplicity,
Falls off our crime; this naked crime of
    ours
May not now be looked over: look it
    down!

Great? let it be great; but the joys it
  brought,
Pay they or no its price? Come: they or
  it!
Speak not! The past, would you give up
  the past
Such as it is, pleasure and crime together?
Give up that noon I owned my love for
  you?
The garden's silence: even the single bee
Persisting in his toil, suddenly stopped,
And where he hid you only could
  surmise
By some campanula chalice set a-swing.
Who stammered – 'Yes, I love you'?
*Seb.*                          And I drew
Back; put far back your face with both
  my hands
Lest you should grow too full of me –
  your face
So seemed athirst for my whole soul
  and body!
*Otti.* And when I ventured to receive
  you here,
Made you steal hither in the mornings –
*Seb.*                               When
I used to look up 'neath the shrub-
  house here,
Till the red fire on its glazed windows
  spread
To a yellow haze?
*Otti.*        Ah – my sign was, the sun
Inflamed the sere side of yon chestnut-
  tree
Nipped by the first frost.
*Seb.*            You would always laugh
At my wet boots: I had to stride thro'
  grass
Over my ankles.
*Otti.*      Then our crowning night!
*Seb.* The July night?
*Otti.*        The day of it too. Sebald!
When heaven's pillars seemed
  o'erbowed with heat,
Its black-blue canopy suffered descend
Close on us both, to weigh down each
  to each,

And smother up all life except our life.
So lay we till the storm came.
*Seb.*                    How it came!
*Otti.* Buried in woods we lay, you
  recollect;
Swift ran the searching tempest
  overhead;
And ever and anon some bright white
  shaft
Burned thro' the pine-tree roof, here
  burned and there,
As if God's messenger thro' the close
  wood screen
Plunged and replunged his weapon at
  a venture,
Feeling for guilty thee and me: then
  broke
The thunder like a whole sea overhead –
*Seb.*                                Yes!
*Otti.* – While I stretched myself upon
  you, hands
To hands, my mouth to your hot
  mouth, and shook
All my locks loose, and covered you
  with them –
You, Sebald, the same you!
*Seb.*                  Slower, Ottima!
*Otti.* And as we lay –
*Seb.*        Less vehemently! Love me!
Forgive me! Take not words, mere words,
  to heart!
Your breath is worse than wine! Breathe
  slow, speak slow!
Do not lean on me!
*Otti.*              Sebald, as we lay,
Rising and falling only with our pants,
Who said, 'Let death come now! 'Tis
  right to die!
'Right to be punished! Nought completes
  such bliss
'But woe!' Who said that?
*Seb.*            How did we ever rise?
Was't that we slept? Why did it end?
*Otti.*                        I felt you
Taper into a point the ruffled ends
Of my loose locks 'twixt both your
  humid lips.

My hair is fallen now: knot it again!

*Seb.* I kiss you now, dear Ottima, now
    and now!
This way? Will you forgive me – be once
    more
My great queen?

*Otti.*      Bind it thrice about my brow;
Crown me your queen, your spirit's
    arbitress,
Magnificent in sin. Say that!

*Seb.*              I crown you
My great white queen, my spirit's
    arbitress,
Magnificent …

> [*From without is heard the
> voice of* PIPPA, *singing* –

> The year's at the spring
> And day's at the morn;
> Morning's at seven;
> The hill-side's dew-pearled;
> The lark's on the wing;
> The snail's on the thorn:
> God's in his heaven –
> All's right with the world!

> [PIPPA *passes.*

*Seb.* God's in his heaven! Do you hear
    that? Who spoke?
You, you spoke!

*Otti.*      Oh – that little ragged girl!
She must have rested on the step: we
    give them
But this one holiday the whole year
    round.
Did you ever see our silk-mills – their
    inside?
There are ten silk-mills now belong to
    you.
She stoops to pick my double heartsease
    … Sh!
She does not hear: call you out louder!

*Seb.*           Leave me!
Go, get your clothes on – dress those
    shoulders!

*Otti.*      Sebald?

*Seb.* Wipe off that paint! I hate you.

*Otti.*           Miserable!

*Seb.* My God, and she is emptied of it
    now!
Outright now! – how miraculously
    gone
All of the grace – had she not strange
    grace once?
Why, the blank cheek hangs listless as
    it likes,
No purpose holds the features up
    together,
Only the cloven brow and puckered
    chin
Stay in their places: and the very hair,
That seemed to have a sort of life in it,
Drops, a dead web!

*Otti.*      Speak to me – not of me!

*Seb.* – That round great full-orbed face,
    where not an angle
Broke the delicious indolence – all
    broken!

*Otti.* To me – not of me! Ungrateful,
    perjured cheat!
A coward too: but ingrate's worse than
    all.
Beggar – my slave – a fawning, cringing
    lie!
Leave me! Betray me! I can see your
    drift!
A lie that walks and eats and drinks!

*Seb.*               My God!
Those morbid olive faultless shoulder-
    blades –
I should have known there was no
    blood beneath!

*Otti.* You hate me then? You hate me
    then?

*Seb.*      To think
She would succeed in her absurd
    attempt,
And fascinate by sinning, show herself
Superior – guilt from its excess superior
To innocence! That little peasant's voice
Has righted all again. Though I be lost,
I know which is the better, never fear,
Of vice or virtue, purity or lust,
Nature or trick! I see what I have done,
Entirely now! Oh I am proud to feel

Such torments – let the world take
    credit thence –
I, having done my deed, pay too its
    price!
I hate, hate – curse you! God's in his
    heaven!
*Otti.*              – Me!
Me! no, no, Sebald, not yourself – kill
    me!
Mine is the whole crime. Do but kill me
    – then
Yourself – then – presently – first hear
    me speak!
I always meant to kill myself – wait, you!
Lean on my breast – not as a breast;
    don't love me
The more because you lean on me, my
    own
Heart's Sebald! There, there, both
    deaths presently!
*Seb.* My brain is drowned now – quite
    drowned: all I feel
Is … is, at swift-recurring intervals,
A hurry-down within me, as of waters
Loosened to smother up some ghastly
    pit:
There they go – whirls from a black
    fiery sea!
*Otti.* Not me – to him, O God, be
    merciful!

*Talk by the way, while* PIPPA *is passing
    from the hill-side to Orcana. Foreign
    STUDENTS of painting and sculpture,
    from Venice, assembled opposite the
    house of* JULES, *a young French
    statuary, at Possagno.*

*1st Stud.* Attention! My own post is
beneath this window, but the pome-
granate clump yonder will hide three or
four of you with a little squeezing, and
Schramm and his pipe must lie flat in
the balcony. Four, five – who's a
defaulter? We want every-body, for Jules
must not be suffered to hurt his bride
when the jest's found out.
*2nd Stud.* All here! Only our poet's
away – never having much meant to be

present, moonstrike him! The airs of
that fellow, that Giovacchino! He was
in violent love with himself, and had a
fair prospect of thriving in his suit, so
unmolested was it, – when suddenly a
woman falls in love with him, too; and
out of pure jealousy he takes himself off
to Trieste, immortal poem and all:
whereto is this prophetical epitaph
appended already, as Bluphocks assures
me, – '*Here a mammoth-poem lies, Fouled
to death by butterflies.*' His own fault, the
simpleton! Instead of cramp couplets,
each like a knife in your entrails, he
should write, says Bluphocks, both
classically and intelligibly. – *Æsculapius,
an Epic. Catalogue of the drugs: Hebe's
plaister – One strip Cools your lip. Phœbus'
emulsions – One bottle Clears your throttle.
Mercury's bolus – One box Cures …*
*3rd Stud.* Subside, my fine fellow! If the
marriage was over by ten o'clock, Jules
will certainly be here in a minute with
his bride.
*2nd Stud.* Good! – only, so should the
poet's muse have been universally
acceptable, says Bluphocks, *et canibus
nostris* … and Delia not better known
to our literary dogs than the boy
Giovacchino!
*1st Stud.* To the point, now. Where's
Gottlieb, the new-comer? Oh, – listen,
Gottlieb, to what has called down this
piece of friendly vengeance on Jules, of
which we now assemble to witness the
winding-up. We are all agreed, all in a
tale, observe, when Jules shall burst out
on us in a fury by and by: I am
spokesman – the verses that are to
undeceive Jules bear my name of
Lutwyche – but each professes himself
alike insulted by this strutting stone-
squarer, who came alone from Paris to
Munich, and thence with a crowd of us
to Venice and Possagno here, but
proceeds in a day or two alone again –
oh, alone indubitably! – to Rome and

Florence. He, forsooth, take up his portion with these dissolute, brutalized, heartless bunglers! – so he was heard to call us all: now, is Schramm brutalized, I should like to know? Am I heartless?

*Gott.* Why, somewhat heartless; for, suppose Jules a coxcomb as much as you choose, still, for this mere coxcombry, you will have brushed off – what do folks style it? – the bloom of his life. Is it too late to alter? These love-letters now, you call his – I can't laugh at them.

*4th Stud.* Because you never read the sham letters of our inditing which drew forth these.

*Gott.* His discovery of the truth will be frightful.

*4th Stud.* That's the joke. But you should have joined us at the beginning: there's no doubt he loves the girl – loves a model he might hire by the hour!

*Gott.* See here! 'He has been accus-'tomed,' he writes, 'to have Canova's 'women about him, in stone, and the 'world's women beside him, in flesh; these 'being as much below, as those above, his 'soul's aspiration: but now he is to have 'the reality.' There you laugh again! I say, you wipe off the very dew of his youth.

*1st Stud.* Schramm! (Take the pipe out of his mouth, somebody!) Will Jules lose the bloom of his youth?

*Schramm.* Nothing worth keeping is ever lost in this world: look at a blossom – it drops presently, having done its service and lasted its time; but fruits succeed, and where would be the blossom's place could it continue? As well affirm that your eye is no longer in your body, because its earliest favourite, whatever it may have first loved to look on, is dead and done with – as that any affection is lost to the soul when its first object, whatever happened first to satisfy it, is superseded in due course. Keep

but ever looking, whether with the body's eye or the mind's, and you will soon find something to look on! Has a man done wondering at women? – there follow men, dead and alive, to wonder at. Has he done wondering at men? – there's God to wonder at: and the faculty of wonder may be, at the same time, old and tired enough with respect to its first object, and yet young and fresh sufficiently, so far as concerns its novel one. Thus …

*1st Stud.* Put Schramm's pipe into his mouth again! There, you see! Well, this Jules … a wretched fribble – oh, I watched his disportings at Possagno, the other day! Canova's gallery – you know: there he marches first resolvedly past great works by the dozen without vouchsafing an eye: all at once he stops full at the *Psiche-fanciulla* – cannot pass that old acquaintance without a nod of encouragement – 'In your new place, beauty? Then behave yourself as well here as at Munich – I see you!' Next he posts himself deliberately before the unfinished *Pietà* for half an hour without moving, till up he starts of a sudden, and thrusts his very nose into – I say, into – the group; by which gesture you are informed that precisely the sole point he had not fully mastered in Canova's practice was a certain method of using the drill in the articulation of the knee-joint – and that, likewise, has he mastered at length! Good-bye, therefore, to poor Canova – whose gallery no longer needs detain his successor Jules, the predestinated novel thinker in marble!

*5th Stud.* Tell him about the women: go on to the women!

*1st Stud.* Why, on that matter he could never be supercilious enough. How should we be other (he said) than the poor devils you see, with those debasing habits we cherish? He was not to wallow in that mire, at least: he would wait, and love only at the proper time, and meanwhile put up with the *Psiche-fanciulla*. Now, I happened to hear of a young Greek – real Greek girl at Malamocco; a true Islander, do you see, with Alciphron's 'hair like sea-moss' – Schramm knows! – white and quiet as an apparition, and fourteen years old at farthest, – a daughter of Natalia, so she swears – that hag Natalia, who helps us to models at three *lire* an hour. We selected this girl for the heroine of our jest. So first, Jules received a scented letter – somebody had seen his Tydeus at the Academy, and my picture was nothing to it: a profound admirer bade him persevere – would make herself known to him ere long. (Paolina, my little friend of the *Fenice*, transcribes divinely.) And in due time, the mysterious correspondent gave certain hints of her peculiar charms – the pale cheeks, the black hair – whatever, in short, had struck us in our Malamocco model: we retained her name, too – Phene, which is, by interpretation, seaeagle. Now, think of Jules finding himself distinguished from the herd of us by such a creature! In his very first answer he proposed marrying his monitress: and fancy us over these letters, two, three times a day, to receive and despatch! I concocted the main of it: relations were in the way – secrecy must be observed – in fine, would he wed her on trust, and only speak to her when they were indissolubly united? St – st – . Here they come!

*6th Stud.* Both of them! Heaven's love, speak softly, speak within yourselves!

*5th Stud.* Look at the bridegroom! Half his hair in storm and half in calm, – patted down over the left temple, – like a frothy cup one blows on to cool it: and the same old blouse that he murders the marble in.

*2nd Stud.* Not a rich vest like yours, Hannibal Scratchy! – rich, that your face may the better set it off.

*6th Stud.* And the bride! Yes, sure enough, our Phene! Should you have known her in her clothes? How magnificently pale!

*Gott.* She does not also take it for earnest, I hope?

*1st Stud.* Oh, Natalia's concern, that is! We settle with Natalia.

*6th Stud.* She does not speak – has evidently let out no word. The only thing is, will she equally remember the rest of her lesson, and repeat correctly all those verses which are to break the secret to Jules?

*Gott.* How he gazes on her! Pity – pity!

*1st Stud.* They go in: now, silence! You three, – not nearer the window, mind, than that pomegranate: just where the little girl, who a few minutes ago passed us singing, is seated!


2 – NOON

*Scene – Over Orcana. The House of* JULES,
  *who crosses its threshold with* PHENE:
  *she is silent, on which* JULES *begins* –


Do not die, Phene! I am yours now, you
Are mine now; let fate reach me how
    she likes,
If you'll not die: so, never die! Sit here –
My work-room's single seat. I over-lean
This length of hair and lustrous front;
    they turn
Like an entire flower upward: eyes, lips,
    last
Your chin – no, last your throat turns:
    'tis their scent
Pulls down my face upon you. Nay,
    look ever
This one way till I change, grow you – I
    could
Change into you, beloved!
                          You by me,

And I by you; this is your hand in mine,
And side by side we sit: all's true. Thank
    God!
I have spoken: speak you!
                    O my life to come!
My Tydeus must be carved that's there
    in clay;
Yet how be carved, with you about the
    room?
Where must I place you? When I think
    that once
This room-full of rough block-work
    seemed my heaven
Without you! Shall I ever work again,
Get fairly into my old ways again,
Bid each conception stand while, trait
    by trait,
My hand transfers its lineaments to stone?
Will my mere fancies live near you,
    their truth –
The live truth, passing and repassing me,
Sitting beside me?
                    Now speak!
                            Only first,
See, all your letters! Was't not well
    contrived?
Their hiding-place is Psyche's robe; she
    keeps
Your letters next her skin: which drops
    out foremost?
Ah, – this that swam down like a first
    moonbeam
Into my world!
                    Again those eyes complete
Their melancholy survey, sweet and
    slow,
Of all my room holds; to return and
    rest
On me, with pity, yet some wonder too:
As if God bade some spirit plague a
    world,
And this were the one moment of
    surprise
And sorrow while she took her station,
    pausing
O'er what she sees, finds good, and
    must destroy!

What gaze you at? Those? Books, I told
    you of;
Let your first word to me rejoice them,
    too:
This minion, a Coluthus, writ in red
Bistre and azure by Bessarion's scribe –
Read this line … no, shame – Homer's
    be the Greek
First breathed me from the lips of my
    Greek girl!
This Odyssey in coarse black vivid type
With faded yellow blossoms 'twixt page
    and page,
To mark great places with due gratitude;
'He said, and on Antinous directed
'A bitter shaft' … a flower blots out the
    rest
Again upon your search? My statues,
    then!
– Ah, do not mind that – better that
    will look
When cast in bronze – an Almaign
    Kaiser, that,
Swart-green and gold, with truncheon
    based on hip.
This, rather, turn to! What, unrecognized?
I thought you would have seen that
    here you sit
As I imagined you, – Hippolyta,
Naked upon her bright Numidian
    horse.
Recall you this then? 'Carve in bold
    relief' –
So you commanded – 'carve, against I
    come,
'A Greek, in Athens, as our fashion was,
'Feasting, bay-filleted and thunder-free,
'Who rises 'neath the lifted myrtle-
    branch.
' "Praise those who slew Hipparchus!"
    cry the guests,
' "While o'er thy head the singer's
    myrtle waves
' "As erst above our champion: stand
    up, all!" '
See, I have laboured to express your
    thought.

Quite round, a cluster of mere hands
    and arms,
(Thrust in all senses, all ways, from all
    sides,
Only consenting at the branch's end
They strain toward) serves for frame to
    a sole face,
The Praiser's, in the centre: who with
    eyes
Sightless, so bend they back to light
    inside
His brain where visionary forms throng
    up,
Sings, minding not that palpitating arch
Of hands and arms, nor the quick drip
    of wine
From the drenched leaves o'erhead, nor
    crowns cast off,
Violet and parsley crowns to trample
    on –
Sings, pausing as the patron-ghosts
    approve,
Devoutly their unconquerable hymn.
But you must say a 'well' to that – say
    'well!'
Because you gaze – am I fantastic,
    sweet?
Gaze like my very life's-stuff, marble –
    marbly
Even to the silence! Why, before I found
The real flesh Phene, I inured myself
To see, throughout all nature, varied
    stuff
For better nature's birth by means of
    art:
With me, each substance tended to
    one form
Of beauty – to the human archetype.
On every side occurred suggestive
    germs
Of that – the tree, the flower – or take
    the fruit, –
Some rosy shape, continuing the peach,
Curved beewise o'er its bough; as rosy
    limbs,
Depending, nestled in the leaves; and
    just

From a cleft rose-peach the whole
    Dryad sprang.
But of the stuffs one can be master of,
How I divined their capabilities!
From the soft-rinded smoothening
    facile chalk
That yields your outline to the air's
    embrace,
Half-softened by a halo's pearly gloom;
Down to the crisp imperious steel, so
    sure
To cut its one confided thought clean
    out
Of all the world. But marble! – 'neath
    my tools
More pliable than jelly – as it were
Some clear primordial creature dug
    from depths
In the earth's heart, where itself breeds
    itself,
And whence all baser substance may
    be worked;
Refine it off to air, you may, – condense
    it
Down to the diamond; – is not metal
    there,
When o'er the sudden speck my chisel
    trips?
– Not flesh, as flake off flake I scale,
    approach,
Lay bare those bluish veins of blood
    asleep?
Lurks flame in no strange windings
    where, surprised
By the swift implement sent home at
    once,
Flushes and glowings radiate and hover
About its track?
        Phene? what – why is this?
That whitening cheek, those still dilating
    eyes!
Ah, you will die – I knew that you
    would die!
    PHENE *begins, on his having long*
        *remained silent.*
Now the end's coming; to be sure, it
    must

Have ended sometime! Tush, why need
   I speak
Their foolish speech? I cannot bring to
   mind
One half of it, beside; and do not care
For old Natalia now, nor any of them.
Oh, you – what are you? – if I do not
   try
To say the words Natalia made me
   learn,
To please your friends, – it is to keep
   myself
Where your voice lifted me, by letting
   that
Proceed: but can it? Even you, perhaps,
Cannot take up, now you have once let
   fall,
The music's life, and me along with
   that –
No, or you would! We'll stay, then, as
   we are:
Above the world.
         You creature with the eyes!
If I could look for ever up to them,
As now you let me, – I believe, all sin,
All memory of wrong done, suffering
   borne,
Would drop down, low and lower, to
   the earth
Whence all that's low comes, and there
   touch and stay
– Never to overtake the rest of me,
All that, unspotted, reaches up to you,
Drawn by those eyes! What rises is
   myself,
Not me the shame and suffering; but
   they sink,
Are left, I rise above them. Keep me so,
Above the world!
         But you sink, for your eyes
Are altering – altered! Stay – 'I love you,
   love' …
I could prevent it if I understood:
More of your words to me: was't in the
   tone
Or the words, your power?
         Or stay – I will repeat

Their speech, if that contents you! Only
   change
No more, and I shall find it presently
Far back here, in the brain yourself
   filled up.
Natalia threatened me that harm
   should follow
Unless I spoke their lesson to the end,
But harm to me, I thought she meant,
   not you.
Your friends, – Natalia said they were
   your friends
And meant you well, – because, I
   doubted it,
Observing (what was very strange to
   see)
On every face, so different in all else,
The same smile girls like me are used
   to bear,
But never men, men cannot stoop so
   low;
Yet your friends, speaking of you, used
   that smile,
That hateful smirk of boundless self-
   conceit
Which seems to take possession of the
   world
And make of God a tame confederate,
Purveyor to their appetites … you
   know!
But still Natalia said they were your
   friends,
And they assented though they smiled
   the more,
And all came round me, – that thin
   Englishman
With light lank hair seemed leader of
   the rest;
He held a paper – 'What we want,' said
   he,
Ending some explanation to his
   friends –
'Is something slow, involved and
   mystical,
'To hold Jules long in doubt, yet take
   his taste
'And lure him on until, at innermost

'Where he seeks sweetness' soul, he
    may find – this!
' – As in the apple's core, the noisome
    fly:
'For insects on the rind are seen at once,
'And brushed aside as soon, but this is
    found
'Only when on the lips or loathing
    tongue.'
And so he read what I have got by
    heart:
I'll speak it, – 'Do not die, love! I am
    yours.'
No – is not that, or like that, part of
    words
Yourself began by speaking? Strange to
    lose
What cost such pains to learn! Is this
    more right?

    *I am a painter who cannot paint;*
    *In my life, a devil rather than saint;*
    *In my brain, as poor a creature too:*
    *No end to all I cannot do!*
    *Yet do one thing at least I can –*
    *Love a man or hate a man*
    *Supremely: thus my lore began.*
    *Through the Valley of Love I went,*
    *In the lovingest spot to abide,*
    *And just on the verge where I pitched*
      *my tent,*
    *I found Hate dwelling beside.*
    *(Let the Bridegroom ask what the*
      *painter meant,*
    *Of his Bride, of the peerless Bride!)*
    *And further, I traversed Hate's grove,*
    *In the hatefullest nook to dwell;*
    *But lo, where I flung myself prone,*
      *couched Love*
    *Where the shadow threefold fell.*
    *(The meaning – those black bride's-*
      *eyes above,*
    *Not a painter's lip should tell!)*

'And here,' said he, 'Jules probably will
    ask,
' "You have black eyes, Love, – you are,
    sure enough,

' "My peerless bride, – then do you tell
    indeed
' "What needs some explanation! What
    means this?" '
– And I am to go on, without a word-

    *So, I grew wise in Love and Hate,*
    *From simple that I was of late.*
    *Once, when I loved, I would enlace*
    *Breast, eyelids, hands, feet, form and*
      *face*
    *Of her I loved, in one embrace –*
    *As if by mere love I could love immensely!*
    *Once, when I hated, I would plunge*
    *My sword, and wipe with the first lunge*
    *My foe's whole life out like a sponge –*
    *As if by mere hate I could hate intensely!*
    *But now I am wiser, know better the*
      *fashion*
    *How passion seeks aid from its opposite*
      *passion:*
    *And if I see cause to love more, hate more*
    *Than ever man loved, ever hated*
      *before –*
    *And seek in the Valley of Love,*
    *The nest, or the nook in Hate's Grove,*
    *Where my soul may surely reach*
    *The essence, nought less, of each,*
    *The Hate of all Hates, the Love*
    *Of all Loves, in the Valley or Grove, –*
    *I find them the very warders*
    *Each of the other's borders.*
    *When I love most, Love is disguised*
    *In Hate; and when Hate is surprised*
    *In Love, then I hate most: ask*
    *How Love smiles through Hate's iron*
      *casque,*
    *Hate grins through Love's rose-braided*
      *mask, –*
    *And how, having hated thee,*
    *I sought long and painfully*
    *To reach thy heart, nor prick*
    *The skin but pierce to the quick –*
    *Ask this, my Jules, and be answered*
      *straight*
    *By thy bride – how the painter Lutwyche*
    *can hate!*

JULES *interposes.*

Lutwyche! Who else? But all of them,
    no doubt,
Hated me: they at Venice – presently
Their turn, however! You I shall not
    meet:
If I dreamed, saying this would wake me. Keep
What's here, the gold – we cannot meet
    again,
Consider! and the money was but meant
For two years' travel, which is over now,
All chance or hope or care or need of it.
This – and what comes from selling
    these, my casts
And books and medals, except … let
    them go
Together, so the produce keeps you safe
Out of Natalia's clutches! If by chance
(For all's chance here) I should survive
    the gang
At Venice, root out all fifteen of them,
We might meet some where, since the
    world is wide.

> [*From without is heard the
> voice of* PIPPA, *singing –*

Give her but a least excuse to love me!
When – where –
How – can this arm establish her above
    me,
If fortune fixed her as my lady there,
There already, to eternally reprove me?
    ('Hist!' – said Kate the Queen;
    But 'Oh!' – cried the maiden, binding
        her tresses,
    ' 'Tis only a page that carols unseen,
    'Crumbling your hounds their messes!')
Is she wronged? – To the rescue of her
    honour,
My heart!
Is she poor? – What costs it to be styled
    a donor?
Merely an earth to cleave, a sea to part.
But that fortune should have thrust all
    this upon her!
    ('Nay, list!' – bade Kate the Queen;

And still cried the maiden, binding
    her tresses
    ' 'Tis only a page that carols unseen,
    'Fitting your hawks their jesses!')

> [PIPPA *passes.*

JULES *resumes.*

What name was that the little girl sang
    forth?
Kate? The Cornaro, doubtless, who
    renounced
The crown of Cyprus to be lady here
At Asolo, where still her memory stays,
And peasants sing how once a certain
    page
Pined for the grace of her so far above
His power of doing good to, 'Kate the
    Queen –
'She never could be wronged, be poor,'
    he sighed,
'Need him to help her!'
                    Yes, a bitter thing
To see our lady above all need of us;
Yet so we look ere we will love; not I,
But the world looks so. If whoever loves
Must be, in some sort, god or
    worshipper,
The blessing or the blest one, queen or
    page,
Why should we always choose the page's
    part?
Here is a woman with utter need of
    me, –
I find myself queen here, it seems!
                    How strange!
Look at the woman here with the new
    soul,
Like my own Psyche, – fresh upon her
    lips
Alit, the visionary butterfly,
Waiting my word to enter and make
    bright,
Or flutter off and leave all blank as
    first.
This body had no soul before, but slept
Or stirred, was beauteous or ungainly,
    free

From taint or foul with stain, as outward
    things
Fastened their image on its passiveness:
Now, it will wake, feel, live – or die
    again!
Shall to produce form out of unshaped
    stuff
Be Art – and further, to evoke a soul
From form be nothing? This new soul
    is mine!

Now, to kill Lutwyche, what would
    that do? – save
A wretched dauber, men will hoot to
    death
Without me, from their hooting. Oh,
    to hear
God's voice plain as I heard it first,
    before
They broke in with their laughter! I
    heard them
Henceforth, not God.
            To Ancona – Greece – some isle!
I wanted silence only; there is clay
Everywhere. One may do whate'er one
    likes
In Art: the only thing is, to make sure
That one does like it – which takes
    pains to know.
    Scatter all this, my Phene – this mad
    dream!
Who, what is Lutwyche, what Natalia's
    friends,
What the whole world except our love
    – my own,
Own Phene? But I told you, did I not,
Ere night we travel for your land –
    some isle
With the sea's silence on it? Stand
    aside –
I do but break these paltry models up
To begin Art afresh. Meet Lutwyche, I –
And save him from my statue meeting
    him?
Some unsuspected isle in the far seas!
Like a god going through his world,
    there stands

One mountain for a moment in the
    dusk,
Whole brotherhoods of cedars on its
    brow:
And you are ever by me while I gaze
– Are in my arms as now – as now – as
    now!
Some unsuspected isle in the far seas!
Some unsuspected isle in far-off seas!

*Talk by the way, while* PIPPA *is passing
    from Orcana to the Turret. Two or
    three of the Austrian Police loitering
    with* BLUPHOCKS, *an English
    vagabond, just in view of the Turret.*

Bluph.* So, that is your Pippa, the little
girl who passed us singing? Well, your
Bishop's Intendant's money shall be
honestly earned: – now, don't make me
that sour face because I bring the
Bishop's name into the business; we
know he can have nothing to do with
such horrors: we know that he is a saint
and all that a bishop should be, who is
a great man beside. *Oh were but every
worm a maggot, Every fly a grig, Every
bough a Christmas faggot, Every tune a
jig!* In fact, I have abjured all religions;
but the last I inclined to, was the
Armenian: for I have travelled, do you
see, and at Koenigsberg, Prussia
Improper (so styled because there's a
sort of bleak hungry sun there), you
might remark over a venerable house-
porch, a certain Chaldee inscription;
and brief as it is, a mere glance at it
used absolutely to change the mood of
every bearded passenger. In they turned,
one and all; the young and lightsome,
with no irreverent pause, the aged and
decrepit, with a sensible alacrity: 'twas
the Grand Rabbi's abode, in short.
Struck with curiosity, I lost no time in

* 'He maketh his sun to rise on the evil and
on the good, and sendeth rain on the just and
on the unjust.'

learning Syriac – (these are vowels, you dogs, – follow my stick's end in the mud – *Celarent, Darii, Ferio!*) and one morning presented myself, spelling-book in hand, a, b, c, – I picked it out letter by letter, and what was the purport of this miraculous posy? Some cherished legend of the past, you'll say – '*How Moses hocus-pocussed Egypt's land with fly and locust,*' – or, '*How to Jonah sounded harshish, Get thee up and go to Tarshish,*' – or, '*How the angel meeting Balaam, Straight his ass returned a salaam.*' In no wise! '*Shackabrack – Boach – somebody or other – Isaach, Recei-ver, Pur–cha–ser and Ex–chan–ger of – Stolen Goods!*' So, talk to me of the religion of a bishop! I have renounced all bishops save Bishop Beveridge – mean to live so – and die – *As some Greek dog-sage, dead and merry, Hellward bound in Charon's wherry, With food for both worlds, under and upper, Lu-pine-seed and Hecate's supper, And never an obolus* … (Though thanks to you, or this Intendant through you, or this Bishop through his Intendant – I possess a burning pocketful of *zwanzigers*) … *To pay the Stygian Ferry!*

1st Pol. There is the girl, then; go and deserve them the moment you have pointed out to us Signor Luigi and his mother. [*To the rest.*] I have been noticing a house yonder, this long while: not a shutter unclosed since morning!

2nd Pol. Old Luca Gaddi's, that owns the silk-mills here: he dozes by the hour, wakes up, sighs deeply, says he should like to be Prince Metternich, and then dozes again, after having bidden young Sebald, the foreigner, set his wife to playing draughts. Never molest such a household, they mean well.

Bluph. Only, cannot you tell me something of this little Pippa, I must have to do with? One could make

something of that name. Pippa – that is, short for Felippa – rhyming to *Panurge consults Hertrippa – Believest thou, King Agrippa?* Something might be done with that name.

2nd Pol. Put into rhyme that your head and a ripe musk-melon would not be dear at half a *zwanziger!* Leave this fooling, and look out; the afternoon's over or nearly so.

3rd Pol. Where in this passport of Signor Luigi does our Principal instruct you to watch him so narrowly? There? What's there beside a simple signature? (That English fool's busy watching.)

2nd Pol. Flourish all round – 'Put all possible obstacles in his way;' oblong dot at the end – 'Detain him till further advices reach you;' scratch at bottom – 'Send him back on pretence of some informality in the above;' ink-spirt on right-hand side (which is the case here) – 'Arrest him at once.' Why and wherefore, I don't concern myself, but my instructions amount to this: if Signor Luigi leaves home to-night for Vienna – well and good, the passport deposed with us for our *visa* is really for his own use, they have misinformed the Office, and he means well; but let him stay over to-night – there has been the pretence we suspect, the accounts of his corresponding and holding intelligence with the Carbonari are correct, we arrest him at once, to-morrow comes Venice, and presently Spielberg. Bluphocks makes the signal, sure enough! That is he, entering the turret with his mother, no doubt.

### 3 – EVENING

*Scene – Inside the Turret on the Hill
    above Asolo.* LUIGI *and his* MOTHER
    *entering.*

*Mother.* If there blew wind, you'd hear
    a long sigh, easing
The utmost heaviness of music's heart.
*Luigi.* Here in the archway?
*Mother.*           Oh no, no – in farther,
Where the echo is made, on the ridge.
*Luigi.*           Here surely, then.
How plain the tap of my heel as I
    leaped up!
Hark – 'Lucius Junius!' The very ghost
    of a voice
Whose body is caught and kept by …
    what are those?
Mere withered wallflowers, waving
    overhead?
They seem an elvish group with thin
    bleached hair
That lean out of their topmost fortress
    – look
And listen, mountain men, to what we
    say,
Hand under chin of each grave earthy
    face.
Up and show faces all of you! – 'All of
    you!'
That's the king dwarf with the scarlet
    comb; old Franz,
Come down and meet your fate? Hark
    – 'Meet your fate!'
*Mother.* Let him not meet it, my Luigi –
    do not
Go to his City! Putting crime aside,
Half of these ills of Italy are feigned:
Your Pellicos and writers for effect,
Write for effect.
*Luigi.*      Hush! Say A. writes, and B.
*Mother.* These A.s and B.s write for
    effect, I say.
Then, evil is in its nature loud, while
    good
Is silent; you hear each petty injury,
None of his virtues; he is old beside,

Quiet and kind, and densely stupid.
    Why
Do A. and B. not kill him themselves?
*Luigi.*           They teach
Others to kill him – me – and, if I fail,
Others to succeed; now, if A. tried and
    failed,
I could not teach that: mine's the lesser
    task.
Mother, they visit night by night …
*Mother.*           – You, Luigi?
Ah, will you let me tell you what you
    are?
*Luigi.* Why not? Oh, the one thing you
    fear to hint,
You may assure yourself I say and say
Ever to myself! At times – nay, even a
    snow
We sit – I think my mind is touched,
    suspect
All is not sound: but is not knowing
    that,
What constitutes one sane or otherwise?
I know I am thus – so, all is right again.
I laugh at myself as through the town I
    walk,
And see men merry as if no Italy
Were suffering; then I ponder – 'I am
    rich,
'Young, healthy; why should this fact
    trouble me,
'More than it troubles these?' But it
    does trouble.
No, trouble's a bad word: for as I walk
There's springing and melody and
    giddiness,
And old quaint turns and passages of
    my youth,
Dreams long forgotten, little in
    themselves,
Return to me – whatever may amuse me:
And earth seems in a truce with me,
    and heaven
Accords with me, all things suspend
    their strife,
The very cicala laughs 'There goes he,
    and there!'

'Feast him, the time is short; he is on
    his way
'For the world's sake: feast him this
    once, our friend!'
And in return for all this, I can trip
Cheerfully up the scaffold-steps. I go
This evening, mother!
*Mother.*            But mistrust yourself –
Mistrust the judgment you pronounce
    on him!
*Luigi.* Oh, there I feel – am sure that I
    am right!
*Mother.* Mistrust your judgment then,
    of the mere means
To this wild enterprise. Say, you are
    right, –
How should one in your state e'er bring
    to pass
What would require a cool head, a cold
    heart,
And a calm hand? You never will escape.
*Luigi.* Escape? To even wish that, would
    spoil all.
The dying *is* best part of it. Too much
Have I enjoyed these fifteen years of
    mine,
To leave myself excuse for longer life:
Was not life pressed down, running
    o'er with joy,
That I might finish with it ere my
    fellows
Who, sparelier feasted, make a longer
    stay?
I was put at the board-head, helped to
    all
At first; I rise up happy and content.
God must be glad one loves his world
    so much.
I can give news of earth to all the dead
Who ask me: – last year's sunsets, and
    great stars
Which had a right to come first and see
    ebb
The crimson wave that drifts the sun
    away –
Those crescent moons with notched
    and burning rims

That strengthened into sharp fire, and
    there stood,
Impatient of the azure – and that day
In March, a double rainbow stopped
    the storm –
May's warm slow yellow moonlit
    summer nights –
Gone are they, but I have them in my
    soul!
*Mother.* (He will not go!)
*Luigi.*        You smile at me? 'Tis true, –
Voluptuousness, grotesqueness,
    ghastliness,
Environ my devotedness as quaintly
As round about some antique altar
    wreathe
The rose festoons, goats' horns, and
    oxen's skulls.
*Mother.* See now: you reach the city,
    you must cross
His threshold – how?
*Luigi.*         Oh, that's if we conspired!
Then would come pains in plenty, as
    you guess –
But guess not how the qualities most fit
For such an office, qualities I have,
Would little stead me, otherwise
    employed,
Yet prove of rarest merit only here.
Every one knows for what his excellence
Will serve, but no one ever will consider
For what his worst defect might serve:
    and yet
Have you not seen me range our coppice
    yonder
In search of a distorted ash? – I find
The wry spoilt branch a natural perfect
    bow.
Fancy the thrice-sage, thrice-pre-
    cautioned man
Arriving at the palace on my errand!
No, no! I have a handsome dress
    packed up –
White satin here, to set off my black
    hair;
In I shall march – for you may watch
    your life out

Behind thick walls, make friends there
    to betray you;
More than one man spoils everything.
    March straight –
Only, no clumsy knife to fumble for.
Take the great gate and walk (not
    saunter) on
Thro' guards and guards – I have
    rehearsed it all
Inside the turret here a hundred times.
Don't ask the way of whom you meet,
    observe!
But where they cluster thickliest is the
    door
Of doors; they'll let you pass – they'll
    never blab
Each to the other, he knows not the
    favourite,
Whence he is bound and what's his
    business now.
Walk in – straight up to him; you have
    no knife:
Be prompt, how should he scream?
    Then, out with you!
Italy, Italy, my Italy!
You're free, you're free! Oh mother, I
    could dream
They got about me – Andrea from his
    exile,
Pier from his dungeon, Gualtier from
    his grave!
*Mother.* Well, you shall go. Yet seems
    this patriotism
The easiest virtue for a selfish man
To acquire: he loves himself – and next,
    the world –
If he must love beyond, – but nought
    between:
As a short-sighted man sees nought
    midway
His body and the sun above. But you
Are my adored Luigi, ever obedient
To my least wish, and running o'er
    with love:
I could not call you cruel or unkind.
Once more, your ground for killing
    him! – then go!

*Luigi.* Now do you try me, or make
    sport of me?
How first the Austrians got these
    provinces …
(If that is all, I'll satisfy you soon)
– Never by conquest but by cunning, for
That treaty whereby …
*Mother.*         Well?
*Luigi.*         (Sure, he's arrived,
The tell-tale cuckoo: spring's his
    confidant,
And he lets out her April purposes!)
Or … better go at once to modern
    time,
He has … they have … in fact, I
    understand
But can't restate the matter; that's my
    boast:
Others could reason it out to you, and
    prove
Things they have made me feel.
*Mother.*         Why go to-night?
Morn's for adventure. Jupiter is now
A morning-star. I cannot hear you, Luigi!
*Luigi.* 'I am the bright and morning-
    star,' saith God –
And, 'to such an one I give the morning-
    star.'
The gift of the morning-star! Have I
    God's gift
Of the morning-star?
*Mother.*         Chiara will love to see
That Jupiter an evening-star next June.
*Luigi.* True, mother. Well for those
    who live through June!
Great noontides, thunder-storms, all
    glaring pomps
That triumph at the heels of June the
    god
Leading his revel through our leafy
    world.
Yes, Chiara will be here.
*Mother.*         In June: remember,
Yourself appointed that month for her
    coming.
*Luigi.* Was that low noise the echo?
*Mother.*         The night-wind.

She must be grown – with her blue eyes
  upturned
As if life were one long and sweet
  surprise:
In June she comes.
Luigi.          We were to see together
The Titian at Treviso. There, again!

> [*From without is heard the*
> *voice of* PIPPA, *singing –*

> *A king lived long ago,*
> *In the morning of the world,*
> *When earth was nigher heaven than*
>   *now:*
> *And the king's locks curled,*
> *Disparting o'er a forehead ful*
> *As the milk-white space 'twixt horn and*
>   *horn*
> *Of some sacrificial bull –*
> *Only calm as a babe new-born:*
> *For he was got to a sleepy mood,*
> *So safe from all decrepitude,*
> *Age with its bane, so sure gone by,*
> *(The gods so loved him while he*
>   *dreamed)*
> *That, having lived thus long, there*
>   *seemed*
> *No need the king should ever die.*

Luigi. No need that sort of king should
  ever die!

> *Among the rocks his city was:*
> *Before his palace, in the sun,*
> *He sat to see his people pass,*
> *And judge them every one*
> *From its threshold of smooth stone.*
> *They haled him many a valley-thief*
> *Caught in the sheep-pens, robber-chief*
> *Swarthy and shameless, beggar-cheat,*
> *Spy-prowler, or rough pirate found*
> *On the sea-sand left aground;*
> *And sometimes clung about his feet,*
> *With bleeding lip and burning cheek,*
> *A woman, bitterest wrong to speak*
> *Of one with sullen thickset brows:*
> *And sometimes from the prison-house*
> *The angry priests a pale wretch brought,*

> *Who through some chink had pushed*
>   *and Dressed*
> *On knees and elbows, belly and breast,*
> *Worm-like into the temple, – caught*
> *He was by the very god,*
> *Who ever in the darkness strode*
> *Backward and forward, keeping watch*
> *O'er his brazen bowls, such rogues to*
>   *catch!*
> *These, all and every one,*
> *The king judged, sitting in the sun.*

Luigi. That king should still judge
  sitting in the sun!

> *His councillors, on left and right,*
> *Looked anxious up, – but no surprise*
> *Disturbed the king's old smiling eyes*
> *Where the very blue had turned to*
>   *white.*
> *'Tis said, a Python scared one day*
> *The breathless city, till he came,*
> *With forky tongue and eyes on flame,*
> *Where the old king sat to judge alway;*
> *But when he saw the sweepy hair*
> *Girt with a crown of berries rare*
> *Which the god will hardly give to wear*
> *To the maiden who singeth, dancing*
>   *bare*
> *In the altar-smoke by the pine-torch*
>   *lights,*
> *At his wondrous forest rites, –*
> *Seeing this, he did not dare*
> *Approach that threshold in the sun,*
> *Assault the old king smiling there.*
> *Such grace had kings when the world*
>   *begun!*

> [PIPPA *passes.*

Luigi. And such grace have they, now
  that the world ends!
The Python at the city, on the throne,
And brave men, God would crown for
  slaying him,
Lurk in bye-corners lest they fall his
  prey.
Are crowns yet to be won in this late
  time,

Which weakness makes me hesitate to
    reach?
'Tis God's voice calls: how could I
    stay? Farewell!

*Talk by the way, while* PIPPA *is passing
from the Turret to the Bishop's
Brother's House, close to the Duomo
S. Maria. Poor* GIRLS *sitting on the
steps.*

*1st Girl.* There goes a swallow to Venice
    – the stout seafarer!
Seeing those birds fly, makes one wish
    for wings.
Let us all wish; you wish first!
*2nd Girl.*               I? This sunset
To finish.
*3rd Girl.* That old – somebody I know,
Greyer and older than my grandfather,
To give me the same treat he gave last
    week –
Feeding me on his knee with fig-peckers,
Lampreys and red Breganze-wine, and
    mumbling
The while some folly about how well I
    fare,
Let sit and eat my supper quietly:
Since had he not himself been late this
    morning
Detained at – never mind where, – had
    he not ...
'Eh, baggage, had I not!' –
*2nd Girl.*           How she can lie!
*3rd Girl.* Look there – by the nails!
*2nd Girl.*             What
    makes your fingers red!
*3rd Girl.* Dipping them into wine to
    write bad words with
On the bright table: how he laughed!
*1st Girl.*             My turn.
Spring's come and summer's coming. I
    would wear
A long loose gown, down to the feet
    and hands,
With plaits here, close about the
    throat, all day;
And all night lie, the cool long nights,
    in bed;

And have new milk to drink, apples to
    eat,
Deuzans and junetings, leather-coats
    ... ah, I should say,
This is away in the fields – miles!
*3rd Girl.*           Say at once
You'd be at home: she'd always be at
    home!
Now comes the story of the farm among
The cherry orchards, and how April
    snowed
White blossoms on her as she ran.
    Why, fool,
They've rubbed the chalk-mark out,
    how tall you were,
Twisted your starling's neck, broken
    his cage,
Made a dung-hill of your garden!
*1st Girl.*           They, destroy
My garden since I left them well? –
    perhaps!
I would have done so: so I hope they
    have!
A fig-tree curled out of our cottage wall;
They called it mine, I have forgotten
    why,
It must have been there long ere I was
    born:
*Cric – cric –* I think I hear the wasps
    o'er-head
Pricking the papers strung to flutter
    there
And keep off birds in fruit-time –
    coarse long papers,
And the wasps eat them, prick them
    through and through.
*3rd Girl.* How her mouth twitches!
    Where was I? – before
She broke in with her wishes and long
    gowns
And wasps – would I be such a fool! –
    Oh, here!
This is my way: I answer every one
Who asks me why I make so much of
    him –
(If you say, 'you love him' – straight
    'he'll not be gulled!')

'He that seduced me when I was a girl
'Thus high – had eyes like yours, or
    hair like yours,
'Brown, red, white,' – as the case may
    be: that pleases!
See how that beetle burnishes in the
    path!
There sparkles he along the dust: and,
    there –
Your journey to that maize-tuft spoiled
    at least!
*1st Girl.* When I was young, they said if
    you killed one
Of those sunshiny beetles, that his
    friend
Up there, would shine no more that
    day nor next.
*2nd Girl.* When you were young? Nor
    are you young, that's true.
How your plump arms, that were, have
    dropped away!
Why, I can span them. Cecco beats you
    still?
No matter, so you keep your curious
    hair.
I wish they'd find a way to dye our hair
Your colour – any lighter tint, indeed,
Than black: the men say they are sick
    of black,
Black eyes, black hair!
*4th Girl.*        Sick of yours, like enough.
Do you pretend you ever tasted lampreys
And ortolans? Giovita, of the palace,
Engaged (but there's no trusting him)
    to slice me
Polenta with a knife that had cut up
An ortolan.
*2nd Girl.* Why, there! Is not that Pippa
We are to talk to, under the window, –
    quick, –
Where the lights are?
*1st Girl.*            That she? No, or
    she would sing,
For the Intendant said ...
*3rd Girl.*            Oh, you sing first!
Then, if she listens and comes close
    ... I'll tell you, –

Sing that song the young English noble
    made,
Who took you for the purest of the
    pure,
And meant to leave the world for you –
    what fun!
*2nd Girl* [*sings*].

   *You'll love me yet! – and I can tarry
      Your love's protracted growing:
   June reared that bunch of flowers you
      carry,
      From seeds of April's sowing.*

   *I plant a heartful now: some seed
      At least is sure to strike,
   And yield – what you'll not pluck
      indeed,
      Not love, but, may be, like.*

   *You'll look at least on love's remains,
      A grave's one violet:
   Your look? – that pays a thousand
      pains.
      What's death? You'll love me yet!*

*3rd Girl* [*to* PIPPA *who approaches*]. Oh,
you may come closer – we shall not eat
you! Why, you seem the very person
that the great rich handsome English-
man has fallen so violently in love with.
I'll tell you all about it.


4 – NIGHT
*Scene – Inside the Palace by the Duomo.*
MONSIGNOR, *dismissing his*
ATTENDANTS.

*Mon.* Thanks, friends, many thanks! I
chiefly desire life now, that I may
recompense every one of you. Most I
know something of already. What, a
repast prepared? *Benedicto benedicatur*
... ugh, ugh! Where was I? Oh, as you
were remarking, Ugo, the weather is
mild, very unlike winter-weather: but I
am a Sicilian, you know, and shiver in
your Julys here. To be sure, when 'twas
full summer at Messina, as we priests

used to cross in procession the great square on Assumption Day, you might see our thickest yellow tapers twist suddenly in two, each like a falling star, or sink down on themselves in a gore of wax. But go, my friends, but go! [*To the* Intendant.] Not you, Ugo! [*The others leave the apartment.*] I have long wanted to converse with you, Ugo.

*Inten.* Uguccio –

*Mon.* … 'guccio Stefani, man! of Ascoli, Fermo and Fossombruno; – what I do need instructing about, are these accounts of your administration of my poor brother's affairs. Ugh! I shall never get through a third part of your accounts: take some of these dainties before we attempt it, however. Are you bashful to that degree? For me, a crust and water suffice.

*Inten.* Do you choose this especial night to question me?

*Mon.* This night, Ugo. You have managed my late brother's affairs since the death of our elder brother: fourteen years and a month, all but three days. On the Third of December, I find him …

*Inten.* If you have so intimate an acquaintance with your brother's affairs, you will be tender of turning so far back: they will hardly bear looking into, so far back.

*Mon.* Ay, ay, ugh, ugh, – nothing but disappointments here below! I remark a considerable payment made to yourself on this Third of December. Talk of disappointments! There was a young fellow here, Jules, a foreign sculptor I did my utmost to advance, that the Church might be a gainer by us both: he was going on hopefully enough, and of a sudden he notifies to me some marvellous change that has happened in his notions of Art. Here's his letter, – 'He never had a clearly conceived Ideal within his brain till to-day. Yet since his hand could manage a chisel, he has practised expressing other men's Ideals; and, in the very perfection he has attained to, he foresees an ultimate failure: his unconscious hand will pursue its prescribed course of old years, and will reproduce with a fatal expertness the ancient types, let the novel one appear never so palpably to his spirit. There is but one method of escape: confiding the virgin type to as chaste a hand, he will turn painter instead of sculptor, and paint, not carve, its characteristics,' – strike out, I dare say, a school like Correggio: how think you, Ugo?

*Inten.* Is Correggio a painter?

*Mon.* Foolish Jules! and yet, after all, why foolish? He may – probably will – fail egregiously; but if there should arise a new painter, will it not be in some such way, by a poet now, or a musician (spirits who have conceived and perfected an Ideal through some other channel), transferring it to this, and escaping our conventional roads by pure ignorance of them; eh, Ugo? If you have no appetite, talk at least, Ugo!

*Inten.* Sir, I can submit no longer to this course of yours. First, you select the group of which I formed one, – next you thin it gradually, – always retaining me with your smile, – and so do you proceed till you have fairly got me alone with you between four stone walls. And now then? Let this farce, this chatter end now: what is it you want with me?

*Mon.* Ugo!

*Inten.* From the instant you arrived, I felt your smile on me as you questioned me about this and the other article in those papers – why your brother should have given me this villa, that *podere*, – and your nod at the end meant, – what?

*Mon.* Possibly that I wished for no loud talk here. If once you set me coughing, Ugo! –

*Inten.* I have your brother's hand and seal to all I possess: now ask me what for! what service I did him – ask me!

*Mon.* I would better not: I should rip up old disgraces, let out my poor brother's weaknesses. By the way, Maffeo of Forli (which, I forgot to observe, is your true name), was the interdict ever taken off you, for robbing that church at Cesena?

*Inten.* No, nor needs be: for when I murdered your brother's friend, Pasquale, for him …

*Mon.* Ah, he employed you in that business, did he? Well, I must let you keep, as you say, this villa and that *podere*, for fear the world should find out my relations were of so indifferent a stamp? Maffeo, my family is the oldest in Messina, and century after century have my progenitors gone on polluting themselves with every wickedness under heaven: my own father … rest his soul! – I have, I know, a chapel to support that it may rest: my dear two dead brothers were, – what you know tolerably well; I, the youngest, might have rivalled them in vice, if not in wealth: but from my boyhood I came out from among them, and so am not partaker of their plagues. My glory springs from another source; or if from this, by contrast only, – for I, the bishop, am the brother of your employers, Ugo. I hope to repair some of their wrong, however; so far as my brother's ill-gotten treasure reverts to me, I can stop the consequences of his crime: and not one *soldo* shall escape me. Maffeo, the sword we quiet men spurn away, you shrewd knaves pick up and commit murders with; what opportunities the virtuous forego, the villanous seize. Because, to pleasure myself apart from other considerations, my food would be millet-cake, my dress sackcloth, and my couch straw, – am I

therefore to let you, the offscouring of the earth, seduce the poor and ignorant by appropriating a pomp these will be sure to think lessens the abominations so unaccountably and exclusively associated with it? Must I let villas and *poderi* go to you, a murderer and thief, that you may beget by means of them other murderers and thieves? No – if my cough would but allow me to speak!

*Inten.* What am I to expect? You are going to punish me?

*Mon.* – Must punish you, Maffeo. I cannot afford to cast away a chance. I have whole centuries of sin to redeem, and only a month or two of life to do it in. How should I dare to say …

*Inten.* 'Forgive us our trespasses'?

*Mon.* My friend, it is because I avow myself a very worm, sinful beyond measure, that I reject a line of conduct you would applaud perhaps. Shall I proceed, as it were, a-pardoning? – I? – who have no symptom of reason to assume that aught less than my strenuousest efforts will keep myself out of mortal sin, much less keep others out. No: I do trespass, but will not double that by allowing you to trespass.

*Inten.* And suppose the villas are not your brother's to give, nor yours to take? Oh, you are hasty enough just now!

*Mon.* 1, 2 – N° 3! – ay, can you read the substance of a letter, N° 3, I have received from Rome? It is precisely on the ground there mentioned, of the suspicion I have that a certain child of my late elder brother, who would have succeeded to his estates, was murdered in infancy by you, Maffeo, at the instigation of my late younger brother – that the Pontiff enjoins on me not merely the bringing that Maffeo to condign punishment, but the taking all pains, as guardian of the infant's heritage for the Church, to recover it parcel by parcel, howsoever, whensoever, and wheresoever. While you are now gnawing those fingers, the police are engaged in sealing up your papers, Maffeo, and the mere raising my voice brings my people from the next room to dispose of yourself. But I want you to confess quietly, and save me raising my voice. Why, man, do I not know the old story? The heir between the succeeding heir, and this heir's ruffianly instrument, and their complot's effect, and the life of fear and bribes and ominous smiling silence? Did you throttle or stab my brother's infant? Come now!

*Inten.* So old a story, and tell it no better? When did such an instrument ever produce such an effect? Either the child smiles in his face; or, most likely, he is not fool enough to put himself in the employer's power so thoroughly: the child is always ready to produce – as you say – howsoever, wheresoever, and whensoever.

*Mon.* Liar!

*Inten.* Strike me? Ah, so might a father chastise! I shall sleep soundly to-night at least, though the gallows await me to-morrow; for what a life did I lead! Carlo of Cesena reminds me of his connivance, every time I pay his annuity; which happens commonly thrice a year. If I remonstrate, he will confess all to the good bishop – you!

*Mon.* I see through the trick, caitiff! I would you spoke truth for once. All shall be sifted, however – seven times sifted.

*Inten.* And how my absurd riches encumbered me! I dared not lay claim to above half my possessions. Let me but once unbosom myself, glorify Heaven, and die!

Sir, you are no brutal dastardly idiot like your brother I frightened to death: let us understand one another. Sir, I will make away with her for you – the girl – here close at hand; not the stupid obvious kind of killing; do not speak – know nothing of her nor of me! I see her every day – saw her this morning: of course there is to be no killing; but at Rome the courtesans perish off every three years, and I can entice her thither – have indeed begun operations already. There's a certain lusty blue-eyed florid-complexioned English knave, I and the Police employ occasionally. You assent, I perceive – no, that's not it – assent I do not say – but you will let me convert my present havings and holdings into cash, and give me time to cross the Alps? 'Tis but a little black-eyed pretty singing Felippa, gay silk-winding girl. I have kept her out of harm's way up to this present; for I always intended to make your life a plague to you with her. 'Tis as well settled once and for ever. Some women I have procured will pass Bluphocks, my handsome scoundrel, off for somebody; and once Pippa entangled! – you conceive? Through her singing? Is it a bargain?

[*From without is heard the voice of* PIPPA, *singing –*

*Overhead the tree-tops meet,*
*Flowers and grass spring 'neath one's feet;*
*There was nought above me, nought below,*
*My childhood had not learned to know:*
*For, what are the voices of birds*
*– Ay, and of beasts, – but words, our words,*
*Only so much more sweet?*
*The knowledge of that with my life begun.*
*But I had so near made out the sun,*
*And counted your stars, the seven and one,*
*Like the fingers of my hand:*
*Nay, I could all but understand*
*Wherefore through heaven the white moon ranges;*

*And just when out of her soft fifty*
   *changes*
*No unfamiliar face might overlook me –*
*Suddenly God took me.*

                  [PIPPA *passes.*

Mon. [*springing up*]. My people – one
and all – all – within there! Gag this
villain – tie him hand and foot! He
dares … I know not half he dares – but
remove him – quick! *Miserere mei,
Domine!* Quick, I say!


Scene – Pippa's chamber again. *She
    enters it.*
The bee with his comb,
The mouse at her dray,
The grub in his tomb,
Wile winter away;
But the fire-fly and hedge-shrew and
    lob-worm, I pray,
How fare they?
Ha, ha, thanks for your counsel, my
    Zanze!
'Feast upon lampreys, quaff Breganze' –
The summer of life so easy to spend,
And care for to-morrow so soon put
    away!
But winter hastens at summer's end,
And fire-fly, hedge-shrew, lob-worm,
    pray,
How fare they?
No bidding me then to … what did
    Zanze say?
'Pare your nails pearlwise, get your small
    feet shoes
'More like' … (what said she?) – 'and
    less like canoes!'
How pert that girl was! – would I be
    those pert
Impudent staring women! It had done
    me,
However, surely no such mighty hurt
To learn his name who passed that jest
    upon me:
No foreigner, that I can recollect,

Came, as she says, a month since, to
    inspect
Our silk-mills – none with blue eyes
    and thick rings
Of raw-silk-coloured hair, at all events.
Well, if old Luca keep his good intents,
We shall do better, see what next year
    brings.
I may buy shoes, my Zanze, not appear
More destitute than you perhaps next
    year!
Bluph … something! I had caught the
    uncouth name
But for Monsignor's people's sudden
    clatter
Above us – bound to spoil such idle
    chatter
As ours: it were indeed a serious matter
If silly talk like ours should put to
    shame
The pious man, the man devoid of
    blame,
The … ah but – ah but, all the same,
No mere mortal has a right
To carry that exalted air;
Best people are not angels quite:
While – not the worst of people's
    doings scare
The devil; so there's that proud look to
    spare!
    Which is mere counsel to myself,
      mind! For
I have just been the holy Monsignor:
And I was you too, Luigi's gentle
    mother,
And you too, Luigi! – how that Luigi
    started
Out of the turret – doubtlessly departed
On some good errand or another,
For he passed just now in a traveller's
    trim,
And the sullen company that prowled
About his path, I noticed, scowled
As if they had lost a prey in him.
And I was Jules the sculptor's bride,
And I was Ottima beside,
And now what am I? – tired of fooling.

Day for folly, night for schooling!
New Year's day is over and spent,
Ill or well, I must be content.
　　Even my lily's asleep, I vow:
Wake up – here's a friend I've plucked
　　you:
Call this flower a heart's-ease now!
Something rare, let me instruct you,
Is this, with petals triply swollen,
Three times spotted, thrice the pollen;
While the leaves and parts that witness
Old proportions and their fitness,
Here remain unchanged, unmoved now;
Call this pampered thing improved now!
Suppose there's a king of the flowers
And a girl-show held in his bowers –
'Look ye, buds, this growth of ours,'
Says he, 'Zanze from the Brenta,
'I have made her gorge polenta
'Till both cheeks are near as bouncing
'As her ... name there's no pronouncing!
'See this heightened colour too,
'For she swilled Breganze wine
'Till her nose turned deep carmine;
' 'Twas but white when wild she grew.
'And only by this Zanze's eyes
'Of which we could not change the size,
'The magnitude of all achieved
'Otherwise, may be perceived.'

Oh what a drear dark close to my poor
　　day!
How could that red sun drop in that
　　black cloud?
Ah Pippa, morning's rule is moved
　　away,
Dispensed with, never more to be
　　allowed!
Day's turn is over, now arrives the
　　night's.
Oh lark, be day's apostle
To mavis, merle and throstle,
Bid them their betters jostle
From day and its delights!
But at night, brother howlet, over the
　　woods,
Toll the world to thy chantry;
Sing to the bats' sleek sisterhoods
Full complines with gallantry:
Then, owls and bats,
Cowls and twats,
Monks and nuns, in a cloister's moods,
Adjourn to the oak-stump pantry!
　　　　　　　　[*After she has begun to
　　　　　　　　undress herself.*
Now, one thing I should like to really
　　know:
How near I ever might approach all
　　these
I only fancied being, this long day:
– Approach, I mean, so as to touch
　　them, so
As to ... in some way ... move them –
　　if you please,
Do good or evil to them some slight
　　way.
For instance, if I wind
Silk to-morrow, my silk may bind
　　　　　　　　[*Sitting on the bedside.*
And border Ottima's cloak's hem.
Ah me, and my important part with
　　them,
This morning's hymn half promised
　　when I rose!
True in some sense or other, I suppose.
　　　　　　　　[*As she lies down.*
God bless me! I can pray no more to-
　　night.
No doubt, some way or other, hymns
　　say right.

　　*All service ranks the same with God –*
　　*With God, whose puppets, best and*
　　　　*worst,*
　　*Are we: there is no last nor first.*
　　　　　　　　[*She sleeps.*

# KING VICTOR AND KING CHARLES

A Tragedy

1842

Note: So far as I know, this Tragedy is the first artistic consequence of what Voltaire termed 'a terrible event without consequences;' and although it professes to be historical, I have taken more pains to arrive at the history than most readers would thank me for particularizing: since acquainted, as I will hope them to be, with the chief circumstances of Victor's remarkable European career – nor quite ignorant of the sad and surprising facts I am about to reproduce (a tolerable account of which is to be found, for instance, in Abbé Roman's *Récit*, or even the fifth of Lord Orrery's *Letters from Italy*) – I cannot expect them to be versed, nor desirous of becoming so, in all the detail of the memoirs, correspondence, and relations of the time. From these only may be obtained a knowledge of the fiery and audacious temper, unscrupulous selfishness, profound dissimulation, and singular fertility in resources, of Victor – the extreme and painful sensibility, prolonged immaturity of powers, earnest good purpose and vacillating will of Charles – the noble and right woman's manliness of his wife – and the ill-considered rascality and subsequent better-advised rectitude of D'Ormea. When I say, therefore, that I cannot but believe my statement (combining as it does what appears correct in Voltaire and plausible in Condorcet) more true to person and thing than any it has hitherto been my fortune to meet with, no doubt my word will be taken, and my evidence spared as readily.                   London, 1842. R. B.

## *Persons*

Victor Amadeus, *first King of Sardinia*. Charles Emmanuel, *his son*, *Prince of Piedmont*. Polyxena, *wife of Charles*. D'Ormea, *minister*.

*Scene – The Council Chambers of Rivoli Palace, near Turin, communicating with a Hall at the back, an Apartment to the left, and another to the right of the stage. Time, 1730–1731.*

### FIRST YEAR, 1730 – KING VICTOR

#### PART 1

#### CHARLES, POLYXENA

*Cha.* You think so? Well, I do not.
*Pol.*                   My beloved,
All must clear up; we shall be happy yet:
This cannot last for ever – oh, may change
To-day or any day!
*Cha.*         – May change? Ah yes –
May change!
*Pol.*     Endure it, then.
*Cha.*               No doubt, a life
Like this drags on, now better and now worse.

My father may ... may take to loving me;
And he may take D'Ormea closer yet
To counsel him; – may even cast off her
– That bad Sebastian; but he also may
... Or no, Polyxena, my only friend,
He may not force you from me?
*Pol.*                 Now, force me
From you! – me, close by you as if there gloomed
No Sebastians, no D'Ormeas on our path –
At Rivoli or Turin, still at hand,
Arch-counsellor, prime confidant ... force me!
*Cha.* Because I felt as sure, as I feel sure
We clasp hands now, of being happy once.
Young was I, quite neglected, nor concerned
By the world's business that engrossed so much

My father and my brother: if I peered
From out my privacy, – amid the crash
And blaze of nations, domineered
   those two.
'Twas war, peace – France our foe,
   now – England, friend –
In love with Spain – at feud with
   Austria! Well –
I wondered, laughed a moment's laugh
   for pride
In the chivalrous couple, then let drop
My curtain – 'I am out of it,' I said –
When …
*Pol.*    You have told me, Charles.
*Cha.*                  Polyxena –
When suddenly, – a warm March day,
   just that!
Just so much sunshine as the cottage
   child
Basks in delighted, while the cottager
Takes off his bonnet, as he ceases work,
To catch the more of it – and it must
   fall
Heavily on my brother! Had you seen
Philip – the lion-featured! not like me!
*Pol.* I know –
*Cha.*        And Philip's mouth yet fast
   to mine,
His dead cheek on my cheek, his arm
   still round
My neck, – they bade me rise, 'for I was
   heir
'To the Duke,' they said, 'the right hand
   of the Duke:'
Till then he was my father, not the
   Duke.
So … let me finish … the whole
   intricate
World's-business their dead boy was
   born to, I
Must conquer, – ay, the brilliant thing
   he was,
I, of a sudden must be: my faults, my
   follies,
– All bitter truths were told me, all at
   once,
To end the sooner. What I simply styled

Their over looking me, had been
   contempt:
How should the Duke employ himself,
   for-sooth,
With such an one, while lordly Philip
   rode
By him their Turin through? But he was
   punished,
And must put up with – me! 'Twas sad
   enough
To learn my future portion and submit.
And then the wear and worry, blame on
   blame!
For, spring-sounds in my ears, spring-
   smells about,
How could I but grow dizzy in their
   pent
Dim palace-rooms at first? My mother's
   look
As they discussed my insignificance,
She and my father, and I sitting by, –
I bore; I knew how brave a son they
   missed:
Philip had gaily run state-papers through,
While Charles was spelling at them
   painfully!
But Victor was my father spite of that.
'Duke Victor's entire life has been,' I
   said,
'Innumerable efforts to one end;
'And on the point now of that end's
   success,
'Our Ducal turning to a Kingly crown,
'Where's time to be reminded 'tis his
   child
'He spurns?' And so I suffered –
   scarcely suffered,
Since I had you at length!
*Pol.*             – To serve in place
Of monarch, minister, and mistress,
   Charles.
*Cha.* But, once that crown obtained,
   then was't not like
Our lot would alter? 'When he rests,
   takes breath,
'Glances around, sees who there's left
   to love –

'Now that my mother's dead, sees I am
    left –
'Is it not like he'll love me at the last?'
Well, Savoy turns Sardinia; the Duke's
    King:
Could I – precisely then – could you
    expect
His harshness to redouble? These few
    months
Have been … have been … Polyxena,
    do you
And God conduct me, or I lose myself!
What would he have? What is't they
    want with me?
Him with this mistress and this minister,
– You see me and you hear him; judge
    us both!
Pronounce what I should do, Polyxena!
*Pol.* Endure, endure, beloved! Say you
    not
He is your father? All's so incident
To novel sway! Beside, our life must
    change:
Or you'll acquire his kingcraft, or he'll
    find
Harshness a sorry way of teaching it.
I bear this – not that there's so much
    to bear.
*Cha.* You bear? Do not I know that you,
    tho' bound
To silence for my sake, are perishing
piecemeal beside me? And how other-
    wise
When every creephole from the hideous
    Court
Is stopped: the Minister to dog me,
    here –
The Mistress posted to entrap you,
    there!
And thus shall we grow old in such a
    life;
Not careless, never estranged, – but old:
    to alter
Our life, there is so much to alter!
*Pol.*                Come –
Is it agreed that we forego complaint
Even at Turin, yet complain we here

At Rivoli? 'Twere wiser you announced
Our presence to the King. What's now
    afoot,
I wonder? Not that any more's to dread
Than every day's embarrassment: but
    guess
For me, why train so fast succeeded
    train
On the high-road, each gayer still than
    each!
I noticed your Archbishop's pursuivant,
The sable cloak and silver cross; such
    pomp
Bodes … what now, Charles? Can
    you conceive?
*Cha.*           Not I.
*Pol.* A matter of some moment.
*Cha.*             There's our life!
Which of the group of loiterers that
    stare
From the lime-avenue, divines that I –
About to figure presently, he thinks,
In face of all assembled – am the one
Who knows precisely least about it?
*Pol.*               Tush!
D'Ormea's contrivance!
*Cha.*           Ay, how otherwise
Should the young Prince serve for the
    old King's foil?
– So that the simplest courtier may
    remark
'Twere idle raising parties for a Prince
Content to linger the Court's laughing-
    stock.
Something, 'tis like, about that weary
    business
    [*Pointing to papers he has laid down,
        and which* POLYXENA *examines.*
– Not that I comprehend three words,
    of course,
After all last night's study.
*Pol.*            The faint heart!
Why, as we rode and you rehearsed
    just now
Its substance … (that's the folded
    speech I mean,
Concerning the Reduction of the Fiefs)

– What would you have? – I fancied
    while you spoke,
Some tones were just your father's.
*Cha.*                       Flattery!
*Pol.* I fancied so: – and here lurks, sure
    enough,
My note upon the Spanish Claims!
    You've mastered
The fief-speech thoroughly: this other,
    mind,
Is an opinion you deliver, – stay,
Best read it slowly over once to me;
Read – there's bare time; you read it
    firmly – loud
– Rather loud, looking in his face, –
    don't sink
Your eye once – ay, thus! 'If Spain
    claims … ' begin
– Just as you look at me!
*Cha.*              At you! Oh truly,
You have I seen, say, marshalling your
    troops,
Dismissing councils, or, through doors
    ajar,
Head sunk on hand, devoured by slow
    chagrins
– Then radiant, for a crown had all at
    once
Seemed possible again! I can behold
Him, whose least whisper ties my spirit
    fast,
In this sweet brow, nought could divert
    me from
Save objects like Sebastian's shameless
    lip,
Or worse, the clipped grey hair and
    dead white face
And dwindling eye as if it ached with
    guile,
D'Ormea wears … ·
              [*As he kisses her, enter from t
    he* KING'S *apartment* D'ORMEA.
               I said he would divert
My kisses from your brow!
*D'O.* [*aside*].     Here! So, King Victor
Spoke truth for once: and who's
    ordained, but I

To make that memorable? Both in call,
As he declared. Were't better gnash the
    teeth,
Or laugh outright now?
*Cha.* [*to* POLYXENA]. What's his visit for?
*D'O.* [*aside*]. I question if they even
    speak to me.
*Pol.* [*to* CHARLES]. Face the man! He'll
    suppose you fear him, else.
[*Aloud.*] The Marquis bears the King's
    command, no doubt?
*D'O.* [*aside*]. Precisely! – If I threatened
    him, perhaps?
Well, this at least is punishment enough!
Men used to promise punishment
    would come.
*Cha.* Deliver the King's message,
    Marquis!
*D'O.* [*aside*].    Ah –
So anxious for his fate? [*Aloud.*] A word,
    my Prince,
Before you see your father – just one
    word
Of counsel!
*Cha.*        Oh, your counsel certainly!
Polyxena, the Marquis counsels us!
Well, sir? Be brief, however!
*D'O.*             What? You know
As much as I? – preceded me, most like,
In knowledge! So! ('Tis in his eye,
    beside –
His voice: he knows it, and his heart's
    on flame
Already.) You surmise why you, myself,
Del Borgo, Spava, fifty nobles more,
Are summoned thus?
*Cha.*        Is the Prince used to know,
At any time, the pleasure of the King,
Before his minister? – Polyxena,
Stay here till I conclude my task: I feel
Your presence (smile not) through the
    walls, and take
Fresh heart. The King's within that
    chamber?
*D'O.* [*passing the table whereon a paper
    lies, exclaims, as he glances at it*].
                       'Spain!'

*Pol.* [*aside to* Charles]. Tarry awhile:
what ails the minister?

*D'O.* Madam, I do not often trouble
you.
The Prince loathes, and you scorn me
– let that pass!
But since it touches him and you, not
me,
Bid the Prince listen!

*Pol.* [*to* CHARLES]. Surely you will listen!
– Deceit? – those fingers crumpling up
his vest?

*Cha.* Deceitful to the very fingers' ends!

*D'O.* [*who has approached them, over-
looks the other paper* CHARLES
*continues to hold*]. My project for
the Fiefs! As I supposed!
Sir, I must give you light upon those
measures
– For this is mine, and that I spied of
Spain,
Mine too!

*Cha.* Release me! Do you gloze on me
Who bear in the world's face (that is,
the world
You make for me at Turin) your
contempt?
– Your measures? – When was not a
hateful task
D'Ormea's imposition? Leave my robe!
What post can I bestow, what grant
concede?
Or do you take me for the King?

*D'O.* Not I!
Not yet for King, – not for, as yet, thank
God,
One who in ... shall I say a year, a
month?
Ay! – shall be wretcheder than e'er was
slave
In his Sardinia. – Europe's spectacle
And the world's bye-word! What? The
Prince aggrieved
That I excluded him our counsels? Here
[*Touching the paper in*
CHARLES's *hand.*
Accept a method of extorting gold

From Savoy's nobles, who must wring
its worth
In silver first from tillers of the soil,
Whose hinds again have to contribute
brass
To make up the amount: there's
counsel, sir,
My counsel, one year old; and the fruit,
this –
Savoy's become a mass of misery
And wrath, which one man has to
meet – the King:
You're not the King! Another counsel,
sir!
Spain entertains a project (here it lies)
Which, guessed, makes Austria offer
that same King
Thus much to baffle Spain; he
promises;
Then comes Spain, breathless lest she
be forestalled,
Her offer follows; and he promises ...

*Cha.* – Promises, sir, when he has just
agreed
To Austria's offer?

*D'O.* That's a counsel, Prince!
But past our foresight, Spain and Austria
(choosing
To make their quarrel up between them-
selves
Without the intervention of a friend)
Produce both treaties, and both
promises ...

*Cha.* How?

*D'O.* Prince, a counsel! And the
fruit of that?
Both parties covenant afresh, to fall
Together on their friend, blot out his
name,
Abolish him from Europe. So, take note,
Here's Austria and here's Spain to fight
against:
And what sustains the King but Savoy
here,
A miserable people mad with wrongs?
You're not the King!

*Cha.* Polyxena, you said

All would clear up: all does clear up to
     me.
D'O. Clear up! 'Tis no such thing to
     envy, then?
You see the King's state in its length
     and breadth?
You blame me now for keeping you
     aloof
From counsels and the fruit of counsels?
     Wait
Till I explain this morning's business!
Cha. [aside].                    No –
Stoop to my father, yes, – D'Ormea, no:
– The King's son, not to the King's
     counsellor!
I will do something, but at least retain
The credit of my deed. [Aloud.] Then it
     is this
You now expressly come to tell me?
D'O.                              This
To tell! You apprehend me?
Cha.                    Perfectly.
Further, D'Ormea, you have shown
     yourself,
For the first time these many weeks
     and months,
Disposed to do my bidding?
D'O.                    From the heart!
Cha. Acquaint my father, first, I wait
     his pleasure:
Next ... or, I'll tell you at a fitter time.
Acquaint the King!
D'O. [aside].     If I 'scape Victor yet!
First, to prevent this stroke at me: if
     not, –
Then, to avenge it! [To CHARLES.]
     Gracious sir, I go.          [Goes.
Cha. God, I forbore! Which more
     offends, that man
Or that man's master? Is it come to
     this?
Have they supposed (the sharpest
     insult yet)
I needed e'en his intervention? No!
No – dull am I, conceded, – but so dull,
Scarcely! Their step decides me.
Pol.                    How decides?

Cha. You would be freed D'Ormea's
     eye and hers?
– Could fly the court with me and live
     content?
So, this it is for which the knights
     assemble!
The whispers and the closeting of late,
The savageness and insolence of old,
– For this!
Pol.     What mean you?
Cha.                    How? You fail to catch
Their clever plot? I missed it, but could
     you?
These last two months of care to
     inculcate
How dull I am, – D'Ormea's present
     visit
To prove that, being dull, I might be
     worse
Were I a King – as wretched as now
     dull –
You recognize in it no winding up
Of a long plot?
Pol.          Why should there be a plot?
Cha. The crown's secure now; I should
     shame the crown –
An old complaint; the point is, how to
     gain
My place for one, more fit in Victor's
     eyes,
His mistress the Sebastian's child.
Pol.                              In truth?
Cha. They dare not quite dethrone
     Sardinia's Prince:
But they may descant on my dulness
     till
They sting me into even praying them
Grant leave to hide my head, resign my
     state,
And end the coil. Not see now? In a
     word,
They'd have me tender them myself my
     rights
As one incapable; – some cause for
     that,
Since I delayed thus long to see their
     drift!

I shall apprise the King he may resume
My rights this moment.
*Pol.*                    Pause! I dare not think
So ill of Victor.
*Cha.*                    Think no ill of him!
*Pol.* – Nor think him, then, so shallow
    as to suffer
His purpose be divined thus easily.
And yet – you are the last of a great line;
There's a great heritage at stake; new
    days
Seemed to await this newest of the
    realms
Of Europe: – Charles, you must with-
    stand this!
*Cha.*                    Ah –
You dare not then renounce the
    splendid Court
For one whom all the world despises?
    Speak!
*Pol.* My gentle husband, speak I will,
    and truth.
Were this as you believe, and I once
    sure
Your duty lay in so renouncing rule,
I could … could? Oh what happiness
    it were –
To live, my Charles, and die, alone with
    you!
*Cha.* I grieve I asked you. To the
    presence, then!
By this, D'Ormea acquaints the King,
    no doubt,
He fears I am too simple for mere hints,
And that no less will serve than
    Victor's mouth
Demonstrating in council what I am.
I have not breathed, I think, these
    many years!
*Pol.* Why, it may be! – if he desire to
    wed
The woman, call legitimate her child.
*Cha.* You see as much? Oh, let his will
    have way!
You'll not repent confiding in me, love?
There's many a brighter spot in
    Piedmont, far,

Than Rivoli. I'll seek him: or, suppose
You hear first how I mean to speak my
    mind?
– Loudly and firmly both, this time, be
    sure!
I yet may see your Rhine-land, who can
    tell?
Once away, even then away! I breathe.
*Pol.* And I too breathe.
*Cha.*                    Come, my Polyxena!

## KING VICTOR

### PART 2

*Enter* KING VICTOR, *bearing the Regalia
    on a cushion, from his apartment.
    He calls loudly.*
*Vic.* D'Ormea! – for patience fails me,
    treading thus
Among the obscure trains I have laid, –
    my knights
Safe in the hall here – in that anteroom,
My son, – D'Ormea, where? Of this,
    one touch –
                    [*Laying down the crown.*
This fireball to these mute black cold
    trains – then
Outbreak enough!
[*Contemplating it.*] To lose all, after all!
This, glancing o'er my house for ages –
    shaped,
Brave meteor, like the crown of Cyprus
    now,
Jerusalem, Spain, England, every change
The braver, – and when I have clutched
    a prize
My ancestry died wan with watching
    for,
To lose it! – by a slip, a fault, a trick
Learnt to advantage once and not
    unlearned
When past the use, – 'just this once
    more' (I thought)
'Use it with Spain and Austria happily,
'And then away with trick!' An
    oversight
I'd have repaired thrice over, any time

These fifty years, must happen now!
     There's peace
At length; and I, to make the most of
     peace,
Ventured my project on our people
     here,
As needing not their help: which
     Europe knows,
And means, cold-blooded, to dispose
     herself
(Apart from plausibilities of war)
To crush the new-made King – who
     ne'er till now
Feared her. As Duke, I lost each foot of
     earth
And laughed at her: my name was left,
     my sword
Left, all was left! But she can take, she
     knows,
This crown, herself conceded … That's
     to try,
Kind Europe! My career's not closed as
     yet!
This boy was ever subject to my will,
Timid and tame – the fitter! D'Ormea,
     too –
What if the sovereign also rid himself
Of thee, his prime of parasites? – I
     delay!
D'Ormea! [As D'ORMEA enters, the KING
     seats himself.
My son, the Prince – attends he?
*D'O.*                              Sir,
He does attend. The crown prepared! –
     it seems
That you persist in your resolve.
*Vic.*                        Who's come?
The chancellor and the chamberlain?
     My knights?
*D'O.* The whole Annunziata. If, my liege,
Your fortune had not tottered worse
     than now …
*Vic.* Del Borgo has drawn up the
     schedules? mine –
My son's, too? Excellent! Only, beware
Of the least blunder, or we look but
     fools.

First, you read the Annulment of the
     Oaths;
Del Borgo follows … no, the Prince
     shall sign;
Then let Del Borgo read the Instrument:
On which, I enter.
*D'O.*            Sir, this may be truth;
You, sir, may do as you affect – may
     break
Your engine, me, to pieces: try at least
If not a spring remain worth saving!
     Take
My counsel as I've counselled many
     times!
What if the Spaniard and the Austrian
     threat?
There's England, Holland, Venice –
     which ally
Select you?
*Vic.*   Aha! Come, D'Ormea, – 'truth'
Was on your lip a minute since. Allies?
I've broken faith with Venice, Holland,
     England
– As who knows if not you?
*D'O.*                  But why with me
Break faith – with one ally, your best,
     break faith?
*Vic.* When first I stumbled on you,
     Marquis – 'twas
At Mondovi – a little lawyer's clerk …
*D'O.* Therefore your soul's ally! – who
     brought you through
Your quarrel with the Pope, at pains
     enough –
Who simply echoed you in these
     affairs –
On whom you cannot therefore visit
     these
Affairs' ill-fortune – whom you trust to
     guide
You safe (yes, on my soul) through
     these affairs!
*Vic.* I was about to notice, had you not
Prevented me, that since that great
     town kept
With its chicane D'Ormea's satchel
     stuffed

And D'Ormea's self sufficiently recluse,
He missed a sight, – my naval armament
When I burned Toulon. How the skiff
    exults
Upon the galliot's wave! – rises its
    height,
O'ertops it even; but the great wave
    bursts,
And hell-deep in the horrible profound
Buries itself the galliot: shall the skiff
Think to escape the sea's black trough
    in turn?
Apply this: you have been my minister
– Next me, above me possibly; – sad
    post,
Huge care, abundant lack of peace of
    mind;
Who would desiderate the eminence?
Who gave your soul to get it; you'd yet
    give
Your soul to keep it, as I mean you
    shall,
D'Ormea! What if the wave ebbed with
    me?
Whereas it cants you to another crest;
I toss you to my son; ride out your ride!
*D'O.* Ah, you so much despise me?
*Vic.*            You, D'Ormea?
Nowise: and I'll inform you why. A king
Must in his time have many ministers,
And I've been rash enough to part with
    mine
When I thought proper. Of the tribe,
    not one
( … Or wait, did Pianezze? – ah, just
    the same!)
Not one of them, ere his remonstrance
    reached
The length of yours, but has assured
    me (commonly
Standing much as you stand, – or
    nearer, say,
The door to make his exit on his speech)
– I should repent of what I did.
            D'Ormea,
Be candid, you approached it when I
    bade you

Prepare the schedules! But you
    stopped in time,
You have not so assured me: how
    should I
Despise you then?
            *Enter* CHARLES.
*Vic.* [*changing his tone*]. Are you
    instructed? Do
My order, point by point! About it, sir!
*D'O.* You so despise me! [*Aside.*] One
    last stay remains –
The boy's discretion there.
    [*To* CHARLES.] For your sake, Prince,
I pleaded, wholly in your interest,
To save you from this fate!
*Cha.* [*aside*].            Must I be told
The Prince was supplicated for – by
    him?
*Vic.* [*to* D'ORMEA]. Apprise Del Borgo,
    Spava, and the rest,
Our son attends them; then return.
*D'O.*                One word!
*Cha.* [*aside*]. A moment's pause and
    they would drive me hence,
I do believe!
*D'O.* [*aside*]. Let but the boy be firm!
*Vic.* You disobey?
*Cha.* [*to* D'ORMEA]. You do not disobey
Me, at least? Did you promise that or no?
*D'O.* Sir, I am yours: what would you?
    Yours am I!
*Cha.* When I have said what I shall say,
    'tis like
Your face will ne'er again disgust me.
    Go!
Through you, as through a breast of
    glass, I see.
And for your conduct, from my youth
    till now,
Take my contempt! You might have
    spared me much,
Secured me somewhat, nor so harmed
    yourself:
That's over now. Go, ne'er to come
    again!
*D'O.* As son, the father – father as, the
    son!

My wits! My wits!                    [*Goes.*
*Vic.* [*seated*].    And you, what meant
    you, pray,
Speaking thus to D'Ormea?
*Cha.*                    Let us not
Waste words upon D'Ormea! Those I
    spent
Have half unsettled what I came to say.
His presence vexes to my very soul.
*Vic.* One called to manage a kingdom,
    Charles, needs heart
To bear up under worse annoyances
Than seems D'Ormea – to me, at least.
*Cha.* [*aside*].                    Ah, good!
He keeps me to the point. Then be it so.
[*Aloud.*] Last night, sir, brought me
    certain papers – these –
To be reported on, – your way of late.
Is it last night's result that you demand?
*Vic.* For God's sake, what has night
    brought forth? Pronounce
The ... what's your word? – result!
*Cha.*                    Sir, that had proved
Quite worthy of your sneer, no doubt:
    – a few
Lame thoughts, regard for you alone
    could wring,
Lame as they are, from brains like mine,
    believe!
As 'tis, sir, I am spared both toil and
    sneer.
These are the papers.
*Vic.*                    Well, sir? I suppose
You hardly burned them. Now for your
    result!
*Cha.* I never should have done great
    things of course,
But ... oh my father, had you loved me
    more!
*Vic.* Loved? [*Aside.*] Has D'Ormea
    played me false, I wonder?
[*Aloud.*] Why, Charles, a king's love is
    diffused – yourself
May overlook, perchance, your part in it.
Our monarchy is absolutest now
In Europe, or my trouble's thrown
    away.

I love, my mode, that subjects each
    and all
May have the power of loving, all and
    each,
Their mode: I doubt not, many have
    their sons
To trifle with, talk soft to, all day long:
I have that crown, this chair, D'Ormea,
    Charles!
*Cha.* 'Tis well I am a subject then, not
    you.
*Vic.* [*aside*]. D'Ormea has told him
    everything.
        [*Aloud.*] Aha!
I apprehend you: when all's said, you
    take
Your private station to be prized beyond
My own, for instance?
*Cha.*                    – Do and ever did
So take it: 'tis the method you pursue
That grieves ...
*Vic.*    These words! Let me express, my
    friend,
Your thoughts. You penetrate what I
    supposed
Secret. D'Ormea plies his trade
    betimes!
I purpose to resign my crown to you.
*Cha.* To me?
*Vic.*        Now, – in that chamber.
*Cha.*                    You resign
The crown to me?
*Vic.*            And time enough, Charles,
    sure?
Confess with me, at four-and-sixty
    years
A crown's a load. I covet quiet once
Before I die, and summoned you for
    that.
*Cha.* 'Tis I will speak: you ever hated me.
I bore it, – have insulted me, borne
    too –
Now you insult yourself; and I remember
What I believed you, what you really
    are,
And cannot bear it. What! My life has
    passed

Under your eye, tormented as you
    know, –
Your whole sagacities, one after one,
At leisure brought to play on me – to
    prove me
A fool, I thought and I submitted; now
You'd prove ... what would you prove
    me?
*Vic.*        This to me?
I hardly know you!
*Cha.*                Know me? Oh indeed
You do not! Wait till I complain next
    time
Of my simplicity! – for here's a sage
Knows the world well, is not to be
    deceived,
And his experience and his Macchiavels,
D'Ormeas, teach him – what? – that I
    this while
Have envied him his crown! He has not
    smiled,
I warrant, – has not eaten, drunk, nor
    slept,
For I was plotting with my Princess
    yonder!
Who knows what we might do or might
    not do?
Go now, be politic, astound the world!
That sentry in the antechamber – nay,
The varlet who disposed this precious
    trap        [*Pointing to the crown.*
That was to take me – ask them if they
    think
Their own sons envy them their posts!
    – Know me!
*Vic.* But you know me, it seems: so,
    learn in brief,
My pleasure. This assembly is
    convened ...
*Cha.* Tell me, that woman put it in
    your head!
You were not sole contriver of the
    scheme,
My father!
*Vic.*        Now observe me, sir! I jest
Seldom – on these points, never. Here,
    I say,

The knights assemble to see me
    concede,
And you accept, Sardinia's crown.
*Cha.*                                Farewell!
'Twere vain to hope to change this: I
    can end it.
Not that I cease from being yours, when
    sunk
Into obscurity: I'll die for you,
But not annoy you with my presence.
    Sir,
Farewell! Farewell!
                *Enter* D'ORMEA.
*D'O.* [*aside*].        Ha, sure he's changed
    again –
Means not to fall into the cunning trap!
Then Victor, I shall yet escape you,
    Victor!
*Vic.* [*suddenly placing the crown upon the
    head of* CHARLES]. D'Ormea, your
    King! [*To* CHARLES.] My son, obey
    me! Charles,
Your father, clearer-sighted than yourself,
Decides it must be so. 'Faith, this looks
    real!
My reasons after; reason upon reason
After: but now, obey me! Trust in me!
Be this, you save Sardinia, you save me!
Why, the boy swoons! [*To* D'ORMEA.]
    Come this side!
*D'O.* [*as* CHARLES *turns from him to*
    VICTOR]        You persist?
*Vic.* Yes, I conceive the gesture's
    meaning. 'Faith,
He almost seems to hate you: how is
    that?
Be re-assured, my Charles! Is't over
    now?
Then, Marquis, tell the new King what
    remains
To do! A moment's work. Del Borgo
    reads
The Act of Abdication out, you sign it,
Then I sign; after that, come back to me.
*D'O.* Sir, for the last time, pause!
*Vic.*                        Five minutes longer
I am your sovereign, Marquis. Hesitate –

And I'll so turn those minutes to account
That … Ay, you recollect me! [*Aside.*]
    Could I bring
My foolish mind to undergo the reading
That Act of Abdication!
               [*As* CHARLES *motions*
               D'ORMEA *to precede him.*
        Thanks, dear Charles!
      [CHARLES *and* D'ORMEA *retire.*

*Vic.* A novel feature in the boy, – indeed
Just what I feared he wanted most.
    Quite right,
This earnest tone: your truth, now, for
    effect!
It answers every purpose: with that
    look,
That voice, – I hear him: 'I began no
    treaty,'
(He speaks to Spain), 'nor ever
    dreamed of this
'You show me; this I from my soul
    regret;
'But if my father signed it, bid not me
'Dishonour him – who gave me all,
    beside:'
And, 'True,' says Spain, ' 'twere harsh
    to visit that
'Upon the Prince.' Then come the
    nobles trooping:
'I grieve at these exactions – I had cut
'This hand off ere impose them; but
    shall I
'Undo my father's deed?' – and they
    confer:
'Doubtless he was no party, after all;
'Give the Prince time!'
Ay, give us time, but time!
Only, he must not, when the dark day
    comes,
Refer our friends to me and frustrate
    all.
We'll have no child's play, no
    desponding fits,
No Charles at each cross turn
    entreating Victor
To take his crown again. Guard against
    that!

             *Enter* D'ORMEA.
Long live King Charles!
         No – Charles's counsellor!
Well, is it over, Marquis? Did I jest?
*D'O.* 'King Charles!' What then may
    you be?
*Vic.*        Anything!
A country gentleman that, cured of
    bustle,
Now beats a quick retreat toward
    Chambery,
Would hunt and hawk and leave you
    noisy folk
To drive your trade without him. I'm
    Count Remont –
Count Tende – any little place's Count!
*D'O.* Then Victor, Captain against Catinat
At Staffarde, where the French beat you;
    and Duke
At Turin, where you beat the French;
    King late
Of Savoy, Piedmont, Montferrat,
    Sardinia,
– Now, 'any little place's Count' –
*Vic.*                  Proceed!
*D'O.* Breaker of vows to God, who
    crowned you first;
Breaker of vows to man, who kept you
    since;
Most profligate to me who outraged
    God
And man to serve you, and am made
    pay crimes
I was but privy to, by passing thus
To your imbecile son – who, well you
    know,
Must – (when the people here, and
    nations there,
Clamour for you the main delinquent,
    slipped
From King to – 'Count of any little
    place')
Must needs surrender me, all in his
    reach, –
I, sir, forgive you: for I see the end –
See you on your return – (you will
    return) –

To him you trust, a moment …
*Vic.*                    Trust him? How?
My poor man, merely a prime-minister,
Make me know where my trust errs!
*D'O.*                    In his fear,
His love, his – but discover for yourself
What you are weakest, trusting in!
*Vic.*                    Aha,
D'Ormea, not a shrewder scheme than
     this
In your repertory? You know old
     Victor –
Vain, choleric, inconstant, rash – (I've
     heard
Talkers who little thought the King so
     close)
Felicitous now, were't not, to provoke
     him
To clean forget, one minute afterward,
His solemn act, and call the nobles back
And pray them give again the very
     power
He has abjured? – for the dear sake of
     what?
Vengeance on you, D'Ormea! No: such
     am I,
Count Tende or Count anything you
     please,
– Only, the same that did the things
     you say,
And, among other things you say not,
     used
Your finest fibre, meanest muscle, – you
I used, and now, since you will have
     it so,
Leave to your fate – mere lumber in the
     midst,
You and your works. Why, what on
     earth beside
Are you made for, you sort of ministers?
*D'O.* Not left, though, to my fate! Your
     witless son
Has more wit than to load himself with
     lumber:
He foils you that way, and I follow you.
*Vic.* Stay with my son – protect the
     weaker side!

*D'O.* Ay, to be tossed the people like a
     rag,
And flung by them for Spain and
     Austria's sport,
Abolishing the record of your part
In all this perfidy!
*Vic.*                    Prevent, beside,
My own return!
*D'O.*          That's half prevented now!
'Twill go hard but you find a wondrous
     charm
In exile, to discredit me. The Alps,
Silk-mills to watch, vines asking
     vigilance –
Hounds open for the stag, your hawk's
     a-wing –
Brave days that wait the Louis of the
     South,
Italy's Janus!
*Vic.*          So, the lawyer's clerk
Won't tell me that I shall repent!
*D'O.*                    You give me
Full leave to ask if you repent?
*Vic.*                    Whene'er
Sufficient time's elapsed for that, you
     judge!
               [*Shouts inside* 'King Charles!'
*D'O.* Do you repent?
*Vic.* [*after a slight pause*] … I've kept
     them waiting? Yes!
Come in, complete the Abdication, sir!
                         [*They go out.*
               *Enter* POLYXENA.
*Pol.* A shout! The sycophants are free of
     Charles!
Oh is not this like Italy? No fruit
Of his or my distempered fancy, this,
But just an ordinary fact! Beside,
Here they've set forms for such
     proceedings; Victor
Imprisoned his own mother: he should
     know,
If any, how a son's to be deprived
Of a son's right. Our duty's palpable.
Ne'er was my husband for the wily
     king
And the unworthy subjects: be it so!

Come you safe out of them, my Charles!
 Our life
Grows not the broad and dazzling life,
 I dreamed
Might prove your lot; for strength was
 shut in you
None guessed but I – strength which,
 untramelled once,
Had little shamed your vaunted
 ancestry –
Patience and self-devotion, fortitude,
Simplicity and utter truthfulness
– All which, they shout to lose!
    So, now my work
Begins – to save him from regret. Save
 Charles
Regret? – the noble nature! He's not
 made
Like these Italians: 'tis a German soul.
  CHARLES *enters crowned.*
Oh, where's the King's heir? Gone! –
 the Crown Prince? Gone! –
Where's Savoy? Gone! – Sardinia?
 Gone! But Charles
Is left! And when my Rhine-land bowers
 arrive,
If he looked almost handsome yester-
 twilight
As his grey eyes seemed widening into
 black
Because I praised him, then how will
 he look?
Farewell, you stripped and whited
 mulberry-trees
Bound each to each by lazy ropes of
 vine!
Now I'll teach you my language: I'm
 not forced
To speak Italian now, Charles?
  [*She sees the crown.*] What is this?
Answer me – who has done this?
 Answer!
*Cha.*    He!
I am King now.
*Pol.*  Oh worst, worst, worst of all!
Tell me! What, Victor? He has made
 you King?

What's he then? What's to follow this?
 You, King?
*Cha.* Have I done wrong? Yes, for you
 were not by!
*Pol.* Tell me from first to last.
*Cha.*    Hush – a new world
Brightens before me; he is moved away
– The dark form that eclipsed it, he
 subsides
Into a shape supporting me like you,
And I, alone, tend upward, more and
 more
Tend upward: I am grown Sardinia's
 King.
*Pol.* Now stop: was not this Victor, Duke
 of Savoy
At ten years old?
*Cha.*  He was.
*Pol.*    And the Duke spent
Since then, just four-and-fifty years in
 toil
To be – what?
*Cha.*  King.
*Pol.*   Then why unking himself?
*Cha.* Those years are cause enough.
*Pol.*    The only cause?
*Cha.* Some new perplexities.
*Pol.*   Which you can solve
Although he cannot?
*Cha.*   He assures me so.
*Pol.* And this he means shall last – how
 long?
*Cha.*  How long?
Think you I fear the perils I confront?
He's praising me before the people's
 face –
My people!
*Pol.*  Then he's changed – grown
 kind, the King?
Where can the trap be?
*Cha.*  Heart and soul I pledge!
My father, could I guard the crown you
 gained,
Transmit as I received it, – all good else
Would I surrender!
*Pol.*   Ah, it opens then
Before you, all you dreaded formerly?

You are rejoiced to be a king, my
    Charles?
*Cha.* So much to dare? The better; –
    much to dread?
The better. I'll adventure though alone.
Triumph or die, there's Victor still to
    witness
Who dies or triumphs – either way,
    alone!
*Pol.* Once I had found my share in
    triumph, Charles,
Or death.
*Cha.*       But you are I! But you I call
To take, Heaven's proxy, vows I
    tendered Heaven
A moment since. I will deserve the crown!
*Pol.* You will. [*Aside.*] No doubt it were
    a glorious thing
For any people, if a heart like his
Ruled over it. I would I saw the trap.
        *Enter* VICTOR.
'Tis he must show me.
*Vic.*         So, the mask falls off
An old man's foolish love at last. Spare
    thanks!
I know you, and Polyxena I know.
Here's Charles – I am his guest now –
    does he bid me
Be seated? And my light-haired blue-
    eyed child
Must not forget the old man far away
At Chambery, who dozes while she
    reigns.
*Pol.* Most grateful shall we now be,
    talking least
Of gratitude – indeed of anything
That hinders what yourself must need
    to say
To Charles.
*Cha.*     Pray speak, sir!
*Vic.*         'Faith, not much to say:
Only what shows itself, you once i' the
    point
Of sight. You're now the King: you'll
    comprehend
Much you may oft have wondered at –
    the shifts,

Dissimulation, wiliness I showed.
For what's our post? Here's Savoy and
    here's Piedmont,
Here's Montferrat – a breadth here, a
    space there –
To o'ersweep all these, what's one
    weapon worth?
I often think of how they fought in
    Greece:
(Or Rome, which was it? You're the
    scholar, Charles!)
You made a front-thrust? But if your
    shield too
Were not adroitly planted, some shrewd
    knave
Reached you behind; and him foiled,
    straight if thong
And handle of that shield were not cast
    loose,
And you enabled to outstrip the wind,
Fresh foes assailed you, either side;
    'scape these,
And reach your place of refuge – e'en
    then, odds
If the gate opened unless breath enough
Were left in you to make its lord a
    speech.
Oh, you will see!
*Cha.*       No: straight on shall I go,
Truth helping; win with it or die with it.
*Vic.* 'Faith, Charles, you're not made
    Europe's fighting-man!
The barrier-guarder, if you please. You
    clutch
Hold and consolidate, with envious
    France
This side, with Austria that, the territory
I held – ay, and will hold … which *you*
    shall hold
Despite the couple! But I've surely
    earned
Exemption from these weary politics,
– The privilege to prattle with my son
And daughter here, though Europe
    wait the while.
*Pol.* Nay, sir, – at Chambery, away for
    ever,

As soon you will be, 'tis farewell we bid
   you:
Turn these few fleeting moments to
   account!
'Tis just as though it were a death.
*Vic.*                  Indeed!
*Pol.* [*aside*]. Is the trap there?
*Cha.*     Ay, call this parting – death!
The sacreder your memory becomes.
If I misrule Sardinia, how bring back
My father?
*Vic.*     I mean ...
*Pol.* [*who watches* Victor *narrowly this*
   *while*]. Your father does not mean
You should be ruling for your father's
   sake:
It is your people must concern you
   wholly
Instead of him. You mean this, sir? (He
   drops
My hand!)
*Cha.*     That people is now part of me.
*Vic.* About the people! I took certain
   measures
Some short time since ... Oh, I know
   well, you know
But little of my measures! These affect
The nobles; we've resumed some
   grants, imposed
A tax or two: prepare yourself, in short,
For clamour on that score. Mark me:
   you yield
No jot of aught entrusted you!
*Pol.*                No jot
You yield!
*Cha.*    My father, when I took the oath,
Although my eye might stray in search
   of yours,
I heard it, understood it, promised God
What you require. Till from this
   eminence
He move me, here I keep, nor shall
   concede
The meanest of my rights.
*Vic.* [*aside*].       The boy's a fool!
– Or rather, I'm a fool: for, what's
   wrong here?

To-day the sweets of reigning: let
   to-morrow
Be ready with its bitters.
            *Enter* D'ORMEA.
                   There's beside
Somewhat to press upon your notice
   first.
*Cha.* Then why delay it for an instant,
   sir?
That Spanish claim perchance? And,
   now you speak,
– This morning, my opinion was mature,
Which, boy-like, I was bashful in
   producing
To one I ne'er am like to fear in future!
My thought is formed upon that Spanish
   claim.
*Vic.* Betimes indeed. Not now, Charles!
   You require
A host of papers on it.
*D'O.* [*coming forward*]. Here they are.
[*To* Charles.] I, sir, was minister and
   much beside
Of the late monarch; to say little, him
I served: on you I have, to say e'en less,
No claim. This case contains those
   papers: with them
I tender you my office.
*Vic.* [*hastily*].       Keep him, Charles!
There's reason for it – many reasons:
   you
Distrust him, nor are so far wrong
   there, – but
He's mixed up in this matter – he'll
   desire
To quit you, for occasions known to me:
Do not accept those reasons: have him
   stay!
*Pol.* [*aside*]. His minister thrust on us!
*Cha.* [*to* D'ORMEA].       Sir, believe,
In justice to myself, you do not need
E'en this commending: howsoe'er
   might seem
My feelings toward you, as a private
   man,
They quit me in the vast and untried
   field

Of action. Though I shall myself (as late
In your own hearing I engaged to do)
Preside o'er my Sardinia, yet your help
Is necessary. Think the past forgotten
And serve me now!

*D'O.*                    I did not offer you
My service – would that I could serve
        you, sir!
As for the Spanish matter …

*Vic.*                    But despatch
At least the dead, in my good daughter's
        phrase,
Before the living! Help to house me safe
Ere with D'Ormea you set the world
        a-gape!
Here is a paper – will you overlook
What I propose reserving for my needs?
I get as far from you as possible:
Here's what I reckon my expenditure.

*Cha.* [*reading*]. A miserable fifty thousand
        crowns –

*Vic.* Oh, quite enough for country
        gentlemen!
Beside the exchequer happens … but
        find out
All that, yourself!

*Cha.* [*still reading*]. 'Count Tende' –
        what means this?

*Vic.* Me: you were but an infant when I
        burst
Through the defile of Tende upon
        France.
Had only my allies kept true to me!
No matter. Tende's, then, a name I take
Just as …

*D'O.* – The Marchioness Sebastian takes
The name of Spigno.

*Cha.*                    How, sir?

*Vic.* [*to* D'ORMEA].          Fool! All that
Was for my own detailing. [*To* CHARLES.]
        That anon!

*Cha.* [*to* D'Ormea]. Explain what you
        have said, sir!

*D'O.*                    I supposed
The marriage of the King to her I named,
Profoundly kept a secret these few
        weeks,

Was not to be one, now he's Count.

*Pol.* [*aside*].                    With us
The minister – with him the mistress!

*Cha.* [*to* Victor].               No –
Tell me you have not taken her – that
        woman
To live with, past recall!

*Vic.*          And where's the crime …

*Pol.* [*to* Charles]. True, sir, this is a
        matter past recall
And past your cognizance. A day before,
And you had been compelled to note
        this: now, –
Why note it? The King saved his House
        from shame:
What the Count did, is no concern of
        yours.

*Cha.* [*after a pause*]. The Spanish claim,
        D'Ormea!

*Vic.*                    Why, my son,
I took some ill-advised … one's age, in
        fact,
Spoils everything: though I was over-
        reached,
A younger brain, we'll trust, may
        extricate
Sardinia readily. To-morrow, D'Ormea,
Inform the King!

*D'O.* [*without regarding* Victor, *and
        leisurely*].          Thus stands the case
        with Spain:
When first the Infant Carlos claimed
        his proper
Succession to the throne of Tuscany …

*Vic.* I tell you, that stands over! Let that
        rest!
There is the policy!

*Cha.* [*to* D'ORMEA]. Thus much I know,
And more – too much: the remedy?

*D'O.*                    Of course!
No glimpse of one.

*Vic.*               No remedy at all!
It makes the remedy itself – time makes
        it.

*D'O.* [*to* CHARLES]. But if …

*Vic.* [*still more hastily*].    In fine, I shall
        take care of that:

And, with another project that I have …
*D'O.* [*turning on him.*] Oh, since Count
    Tende means to take again
King Victor's crown! –
*Pol.* [*throwing herself at* VICTOR's *feet*].
            E'en now retake it, sir!
Oh speak! We are your subjects both,
    once more!
Say it – a word effects it! You meant not,
Nor do mean now, to take it: but you
    must!
'Tis in you – in your nature – and the
    shame's
Not half the shame 'twould grow to
    afterwards!
*Cha.* Polyxena!
*Pol.*      A word recalls the knights –
Say it! What's promising and what's
    the past?
Say you are still King Victor!
*D'O.*              Better say
The Count repents, in brief! [VICTOR
    *rises.*
*Cha.*          With such a crime
I have not charged you, sir!
*Pol.*      (Charles turns from me!)

## SECOND YEAR, 1731 – KING CHARLES

### PART 1

*Enter* QUEEN POLYXENA *and* D'ORMEA. –
    *A pause.*
*Pol.* And now, sir, what have you to
    say?
*D'O.*    Count Tende …
*Pol.* Affirm not I betrayed you; you
    resolve
On uttering this strange intelligence
– Nay, post yourself to find me ere I
    reach
The capital, because you know King
    Charles
Tarries a day or two at Evian baths
Behind me: – but take warning, – here
    and thus
        [*Seating herself in the royal seat.*

I listen, if I listen – not your friend.
Explicitly the statement, if you still
Persist to urge it on me, must proceed:
I am not made for aught else.
*D'O.*         Good! Count Tende …
*Pol.* I, who mistrust you, shall acquaint
    King Charles
Who even more mistrusts you.
*D'O.*              Does he so?
*Pol.* Why should he not?
*D'O.*      Ay, why not? Motives, seek
You virtuous people, motives! Say, I
    serve
God at the devil's bidding – will that
    do?
I'm proud: our people have been
    pacified,
Really I know not how –
*Pol.*            By truthfulness.
*D'O.* Exactly; that shows I had nought
    to do
With pacifying them. Our foreign perils
Also exceed my means to stay: but here
'Tis otherwise, and my pride's piqued.
    Count Tende
Completes a full year's absence: would
    you, madam,
Have the old monarch back, his mistress
    back,
His measures back? I pray you, act
    upon
My counsel, or they will be.
*Pol.*           When?
*D'O.*              Let's think.
Home-matters settled – Victor's coming
    now;
Let foreign matters settle – Victor's here
Unless I stop him; as I will, this way.
*Pol.* [*reading the papers he presents*].
    If this should prove a plot 'twixt
    you and Victor?
You seek annoyances to give the pretext
For what you say you fear.
*D'O.*         Oh, possibly!
I go for nothing. Only show King
    Charles
That thus Count Tende purposes return,

And style me his inviter, if you please!

*Pol.* Half of your tale is true; most like,
the Count

Seeks to return: but why stay you with
us?

To aid in such emergencies.

*D'O.*                                              Keep safe

Those papers: or, to serve me, leave no
proof

I thus have counselled! When the Count
returns,

And the King abdicates, 'twill stead me
little

To have thus counselled.

*Pol.*                          The King abdicate!

*D'O.* He's good, we knew long since –
wise, we discover –

Firm, let us hope: – but I'd have gone
to work

With him away. Well!

[*Charles without*].        In the Council
Chamber?

*D'O.* All's lost!

*Pol.* Oh, surely not King Charles! He's
changed –

That's not this year's care-burthened
voice and step:

'Tis last year's step, the Prince's voice!

*D'O.*                                              I know.

            [*Enter* CHARLES: – D'ORMEA
                            *retiring a little.*

*Cha.* Now wish me joy, Polyxena! Wish
it me

The old way!        [*She embraces him.*
There was too much cause for that!

But I have found myself again. What
news

At Turin? Oh, if you but felt the load

I'm free of – free! I said this year would
end

Or it, or me – but I am free,
thank God!

*Pol.*                          How, Charles?

*Cha.*You do not guess? The day I found

Sardinia's hideous coil, at home,
abroad,

And how my father was involved in it, –

Of course, I vowed to rest and smile no
more

Until I cleared his name from obloquy.

We did the people right – 'twas much
to gain

That point, redress our nobles'
grievance, too –

But that took place here, was no crying
shame:

All must be done abroad, – if I abroad

Appeased the justly-angered Powers,
destroyed

The scandal, took down Victor's name
at last

From a bad eminence, I then might
breathe

And rest! No moment was to lose.
Behold

The proud result – a Treaty, Austria,
Spain

Agree to –

*D'O.* [*aside*]. I shall merely stipulate

For an experienced headsman.

*Cha.*                                      Not a soul

Is compromised: the blotted past's a
blank:

Even D'Ormea escapes unquestioned.
See!

It reached me from Vienna; I remained

At Evian to despatch the Count his
news;

'Tis gone to Chambery a week ago –

And here am I: do I deserve to feel

Your warm white arms around me?

*D'O.* [*coming forward*]. He knows that?

*Cha.* What, in Heaven's name, means
this?

*D'O.*        He knows that matters

Are settled at Vienna? Not too late!

Plainly, unless you post this very hour

Some man you trust (say, me) to
Chambery

And take precautions I acquaint you
with,

Your father will return here.

*Cha.*                                Are you crazed,

D'Ormea? Here? For what? As well return

To take his crown!

*D'O.* He will return for that.

*Cha.* [*to* POLYXENA]. You have not
   listened to this man?

*Pol.* He spoke
About your safety – and I listened.
   [*He disengages himself from her arms.*

*Cha.* [*to* D'ORMEA]. What
Apprised you of the Count's intentions?

*D'O.* Me?
His heart, sir; you may not be used to
   read
Such evidence however; therefore read
   [*Pointing to* POLYXENA'S *papers.*
My evidence.

*Cha.* [*to* POLYXENA]. Oh, worthy this of
   you!
And of your speech I never have forgotten,
Though I professed forgetfulness;
   which haunts me
As if I did not know how false it was;
Which made me toil unconsciously
   thus long
That there might be no least occasion
   left
For aught of its prediction coming true!
And now, when there is left no least
   occasion
To instigate my father to such crime –
When I might venture to forget (I hoped)
That speech and recognize Polyxena –
Oh worthy, to revive, and tenfold
   worse,
That plague! D'Ormea at your ear, his
   slanders
Still in your hand! Silent?

*Pol.* As the wronged are.

*Cha.* And you, D'Ormea, since when
   have you presumed
To spy upon my father? I conceive
What that wise paper shows, and easily.
Since when?

*D'O.* The when and where and
   how belong
To me. 'Tis sad work, but I deal in such.
You ofttimes serve yourself; I'd serve
   you here:

Use makes me not so squeamish. In a
   word,
Since the first hour he went to Chambery,
Of his seven servants, five have I
   suborned.

*Cha.* You hate my father?

*D'O.* Oh, just as you will!
   [*Looking at* POLYXENA.
A minute since, I loved him – hate him,
   now!
What matter? – if you ponder just one
   thing:
Has he that treaty? – he is setting forward
Already. Are your guards here?

*Cha.* Well for you
They are not! [*To* POLYXENA]. Him I
   knew of old, but you –
To hear that pickthank, further his
   designs! [*To* D'ORMEA.
Guards? – were they here, I'd bid them,
   for your trouble,
Arrest you.

*D'O.* Guards you shall not want.
   I lived
The servant of your choice, not of your
   need.
You never greatly needed me till now
That you discard me. This is my arrest.
Again I tender you my charge – its duty
Would bid me press you read those
   documents.
Here, sir! [*Offering his badge of office.*

*Cha.* [*taking it*]. The papers also! Do you
   think
I dare not read them?

*Pol.* Read them, sir!

*Cha.* They prove,
My father, still a month within the year
Since he so solemnly consigned it me,
Means to resume his crown? They shall
   prove that,
Or my best dungeon …

*D'O.* Even say, Chambery!
'Tis vacant, I surmise, by this.

*Cha.* You prove
Your words or pay their forfeit, sir. Go
   there!

Polyxena, one chance to rend the veil
Thickening and blackening 'twixt us
    two! Do say,
You'll see the falsehood of the charges
    proved!
Do say, at least, you wish to see them
    proved
False charges – my heart's love of other
    times!
*Pol.* Ah, Charles!
*Cha.* [*to* D'ORMEA]. Precede me, sir!
*D'O.*                    And I'm at length
A martyr for the truth! No end, they
    say,
Of miracles. My conscious innocence!
    [*As they go out, enter – by the middle
    door, at which he pauses –* VICTOR.
*Vic.* Sure I heard voices? No. Well, I do
    best
To make at once for this, the heart o'
    the place.
The old room! Nothing changed! So
    near my seat,
D'Ormea? [*Pushing away the stool which
    is by the* KING's *chair.*
            I want that meeting over first,
I know not why. Tush, he, D'Ormea,
    slow
To hearten me, the supple knave? That
    burst
Of spite so eased him! He'll inform
    me …
            What?
Why come I hither? All's in rough: let
    all
Remain rough. There's full time to draw
    back – nay,
There's nought to draw back from, as
    yet; whereas,
If reason should be, to arrest a course
Of error – reason good, to interpose
And save, as I have saved so many
    times,
Our House, admonish my son's giddy
    youth,
Relieve him of a weight that proves too
    much –

Now is the time, – or now, or never.
                            'Faith,
This kind of step is pitiful, not due
To Charles, this stealing back – hither,
    because
He's from his capital! Oh Victor! Victor!
But thus it is. The age of crafty men
Is loathsome; youth contrives to carry
    off
Dissimulation; we may intersperse
Extenuating passages of strength,
Ardour, vivacity, and wit – may turn
E'en guile into a voluntary grace:
But one's old age, when graces drop
    away
And leave guile the pure staple of our
    lives –
Ah, loathsome!
            Not so – or why pause I? Turin
Is mine to have, were I so minded, for
The asking; all the army's mine – I've
    witnessed
Each private fight beneath me; all the
    Court's
Mine too; and, best of all, D'Ormea's
    still
D'Ormea and mine. There's some grace
    clinging yet.
Had I decided on this step, ere midnight
I'd take the crown.
                        No. Just this step to rise
Exhausts me. Here am I arrived: the
    rest
Must be done for me. Would I could
    sit here
And let things right themselves, the
    masque unmasque
Of the old King, crownless, grey hair
    and hot blood, –
The young King, crowned, but calm
    before his time,
They say, – the eager mistress with her
    taunts, –
And the sad earnest wife who motions
    me
Away – ay, there she knelt to me! E'en
    yet

I can return and sleep at Chambery
A dream out.
          Rather shake it off at Turin,
King Victor! Say: to Turin – yes, or no?
  'Tis this relentless noonday-lighted
    chamber,
Lighted like life but silent as the grave,
That disconcerts me. That's the change
    must strike.
No silence last year! Some one flung
    doors wide
(Those two great doors which scrutinize
    me now)
And out I went 'mid crowds of men –
    men talking,
Men watching if my lip fell or brow
    knit,
Men saw me safe forth, put me on my
    road:
That makes the misery of this return.
Oh had a battle done it! Had I dropped,
Haling some battle, three entire days
    old,
Hither and thither by the forehead –
    dropped
In Spain, in Austria, best of all, in
    Frances –
Spurned on its horns or underneath its
    hooves,
When the spent monster went upon its
    knees
To pad and pash the prostrate wretch –
    I, Victor,
Sole to have stood up against France,
    beat down
By inches, brayed to pieces finally
In some vast unimaginable charge,
A flying hell of horse and foot and guns
Over me, and all's lost, for ever lost,
There's no more Victor when the world
    wakes up!
Then silence, as of a raw battle-field,
Throughout the world. Then after (as
    whole days
After, you catch at intervals faint noise
Through the stiff crust of frozen blood)
  – there creeps

A rumour forth, so faint, no noise at all,
That a strange old man, with face
    outworn for wounds,
Is stumbling on from frontier town to
    town,
Begging a pittance that may help him
    find
His Turin out; what scorn and laughter
    follow
The coin you fling into his cap! And
    last,
Some bright morn, how men crowd
    about the midst
O' the market-place, where takes the
    old king breath
Ere with his crutch he strike the palace-
    gate
Wide ope!
        To Turin, yes or no – or no?
    *Re-enter* CHARLES *with papers.*
*Cha.* Just as I thought! A miserable
    falsehood
Of hirelings discontented with their pay
And longing for enfranchisement! A few
Testy expressions of old age that thinks
To keep alive its dignity o'er slaves
By means that suit their natures!
       [*Tearing them.*] Thus they shake
My faith in Victor!
        [*Turning, he discovers* VICTOR.
*Vic.* [*after a pause*]. Not at Evian, Charles?
What's this? Why do you run to close
    the doors?
No welcome for your father?
*Cha.* [*aside*].         Not his voice!
What would I give for one imperious
    tone
Of the old sort! That's gone for ever.
*Vic.*                   Must
I ask once more …
*Cha.*      No – I concede it, sir!
You are returned for … true, your
    health declines;
True, Chambery's a bleak unkindly
    spot;
You'd choose one fitter for your final
    lodge –

Veneria, or Moncaglier – ay, that's close
And I concede it.
*Vic.*                    I received advices
Of the conclusion of the Spanish
     matter,
Dated from Evian Baths …
*Cha.*                    And you forbore
To visit me at Evian, satisfied
The work I had to do would fully task
The little wit I have, and that your
     presence
Would only disconcert me –
*Vic.*                    Charles?
*Cha.*                    – Me, set
For ever in a foreign course to yours,
And …
          Sir, this way of wile were good
     to catch,
But I have not the sleight of it. The truth!
Though I sink under it! What brings
     you here?
*Vic.* Not hope of this reception, certainly,
From one who'd scarce assume a
     stranger mode
Of speech, did I return to bring about
Some awfulest calamity!
*Cha.*                    – You mean,
Did you require your crown again! Oh
     yes,
I should speak otherwise! But turn not
     that
To jesting! Sir, the truth! Your health
     declines?
Is aught deficient in your equipage?
Wisely you seek myself to make
     complaint,
And foil the malice of the world which
     laughs
At petty discontents; but I shall care
That not a soul knows of this visit.
     Speak!
*Vic.* [*aside*]. Here is the grateful much-
     professing son
Prepared to worship me, for whose
     sole sake
I think to waive my plans of public
     good!

[*Aloud.*] Nay, Charles, if I did seek to
     take once more
My crown, were so disposed to plague
     myself,
What would be warrant for this
     bitterness?
I gave it – grant I would resume it –
     well?
*Cha.* I should say simply – leaving out
     the why
And how – you made me swear to keep
     that crown:
And as you then intended …
*Vic.*                    Fool! What way
Could I intend or not intend? As man,
With a man's will, when I say 'I intend,'
I can intend up to a certain point,
No farther. I intended to preserve
The crown of Savoy and Sardinia whole:
And if events arise demonstrating
The way, I hoped should guard it,
     rather like
To lose it …
*Cha.*          Keep within your sphere
     and mine!
It is God's province we usurp on, else.
Here, blindfold through the maze of
     things we walk
By a slight clue of false, true, right and
     wrong;
All else is rambling and presumption. I
Have sworn to keep this kingdom:
     there's my truth.
*Vic.* Truth, boy, is here, within my
     breast; and in
Your recognition of it, truth is, too;
And in the effect of all this tortuous
     dealing
With falsehood, used to carry out the
     truth,
– In its success, this falsehood turns,
     again,
Truth for the world. But you are right:
     these themes
Are over-subtle. I should rather say
In such a case, frankly, – it fails, my
     scheme:

I hoped to see you bring about, yourself,
What I must bring about. I interpose
On your behalf – with my son's good in sight –
To hold what he is nearly letting go,
Confirm his title, add a grace perhaps.
There's Sicily, for instance, – granted me
And taken back, some years since: till I give
That island with the rest, my work's half done.
For his sake, therefore, as of those he rules …

*Cha.* Our sakes are one; and that, you could not say,
Because my answer would present itself
Forthwith: – a year has wrought an age's change.
This people's not the people now, you once
Could benefit; nor is my policy
Your policy.

*Vic.* [*with an outburst*]. I know it! You undo
All I have done – my life of toil and care!
I left you this the absolutest rule
In Europe: do you think I sit and smile,
Bid you throw power to the populace –
See my Sardinia, that has kept apart,
Join in the mad and democratic whirl
Whereto I see all Europe haste full tide?
England casts off her kings; France mimics England:
This realm I hoped was safe. Yet here I talk,
When I can save it, not by force alone,
But bidding plagues, which follow sons like you,
Fasten upon my disobedient …
                         [*Recollecting himself.*] Surely
I could say this – if minded so – my son?

*Cha.* You could not. Bitterer curses than your curse

Have I long since denounced upon myself
If I misused my power. In fear of these
I entered on those measures – will abide
By them: so, I should say, Count Tende …

*Vic.*                No!
But no! But if, my Charles, your – more than old –
Half-foolish father urged these arguments,
And then confessed them futile, but said Plainly
That he forgot his promise, found his strength
Fail him, had thought at savage Chambery
Too much of brilliant Turin, Rivoli here,
And Susa, and Veneria, and Superga –
Pined for the pleasant places he had built
When he was fortunate and young –

*Cha.*                My father!

*Vic.* Stay yet! – and if he said he could not die
Deprived of baubles he had put aside.
He deemed, for ever – of the Crown that binds
Your brain up, whole, sound and impregnable,
Creating kingliness – the Sceptre too,
Whose mere wind, should you wave it, back would beat
Invaders – and the golden Ball which throbs
As if you grasped the palpitating heart
Indeed o' the realm, to mould as choose you may!
– If I must totter up and down the streets
My sires built, where myself have introduced
And fostered laws and letters, sciences,
The civil and the military arts!
Stay, Charles! I see you letting me pretend

To live my former self once more – King
     Victor,
The venturous yet politic: they style me
Again, the Father of the Prince: friends
     wink
Good-humouredly at the delusion you
So sedulously guard from all rough
     truths
That else would break upon my dotage!
     – You –
Whom now I see preventing my old
     shame –
I tell not, point by cruel point, my tale –
For is't not in your breast my brow is
     hid?
Is not your hand extended? Say you
     not …

*Enter* D'ORMEA, *leading in* POLYXENA.

*Pol.* [*advancing and withdrawing* CHARLES
     – *to* VICTOR]. In this conjuncture
     even, he would say
(Though with a moistened eye and
     quivering lip)
The suppliant is my father. I must save
A great man from himself, nor see him
     fling
His well-earned fame away: there must
     not follow
Ruin so utter, a break-down of worth
So absolute: no enemy shall learn,
He thrust his child 'twixt danger and
     himself,
And, when that child somehow stood
     danger out,
Stole back with serpent wiles to ruin
     Charles
– Body, that's much, – and soul, that's
     more – and realm,
That's most of all! No enemy shall
     say …

*D'O.* Do you repent, sir?
*Vic.* [*resuming himself*]. D'Ormea? This
     is well!
Worthily done, King Charles, craftily
     done!
Judiciously you post these, to o'erhear
The little your importunate father thrusts

Himself on you to say! – Ah, they'll
     correct
The amiable blind facility
You show in answering his peevish suit.
What can he need to sue for? Thanks,
     D'Ormea!
You have fulfilled your office: but for
     you,
The old Count might have drawn some
     few more livres
To swell his income! Had you, lady,
     missed
The moment, a permission might be
     granted
To buttress up my ruinous old pile!
But you remember properly the list
Of wise precautions I took when I gave
Nearly as much away – to reap the
     fruits
I should have looked for!
*Cha.*                    Thanks, sir: degrade me,
So you remain yourself! Adieu!
*Vic.*                                   I'll not
Forget it for the future, nor presume
Next time to slight such mediators!
     Nay –
Had I first moved them both to
     intercede,
I might secure a chamber in
     Moncaglier –
Who knows?
*Cha.*          Adieu!
*Vic.*                    You bid me this adieu
With the old spirit?
*Cha.*              Adieu!
*Vic.*                        Charles – Charles!
*Cha.*                                        Adieu!
                                        [VICTOR *goes.*
*Cha.* You were mistaken, Marquis, as
     you hear.
'Twas for another purpose the Count
     came.
The Count desires Moncaglier. Give
     the order!
*D'O.* [*leisurely*]. Your minister has lost
     your confidence,
Asserting late, for his own purposes,

Count Tende would …
*Cha.* [*flinging his badge back*]. Be still the
   minister!
And give a loose to your insulting joy;
It irks me more thus stifled than
   expressed:
Loose it!
*D'O.*   There's none to loose, alas! I see
I never am to die a martyr.
*Pol.*                    Charles!
*Cha.* No praise, at least, Polyxena – no
   praise!


## KING CHARLES

### PART 2

D'ORMEA, *seated, folding papers he has*
*been examining.*

This at the last effects it: now, King
   Charles
Or else King Victor – that's a balance:
   but now,
D'Ormea the arch-culprit, either turn
O' the scale, – that's sure enough. A
   point to solve,
My masters, moralists, whate'er your
   style!
When you discover why I push myself
Into a pitfall you'd pass safely by,
Impart to me among the rese! No
   matter.
Prompt are the righteous ever with
   their rede
To us the wrongful; lesson them this
   once!
For safe among the wicked are you set,
D'Ormea! We lament life's brevity,
Yet quarter e'en the threescore years
   and ten,
Nor stick to call the quarter roundly
   'life.'
D'Ormea was wicked, say, some twenty
   years;
A tree so long was stunted; afterward,
What if it grew, continued growing, till
No fellow of the forest equalled it?

'Twas a stump then; a stump it still
   must be:
While forward saplings, at the outset
   checked,
In virtue of that first sprout keep their
   style
Amid the forest's green fraternity.
Thus I shoot up to surely get lopped
   down
And bound up for the burning. Now
   for it!

   *Enter* CHARLES *and* POLYXENA
      *with* ATTENDANTS.

*D'O.* [*rises*]. Sir, in the due discharge of
   this my office –
This enforced summons of yourself
   from Turin,
And the disclosure I am bound to make
To-night, – there must already be, I feel,
So much that wounds …
*Cha.*              Well, sir?
*D'O.*                  – That I, perchance,
May utter also what, another time,
Would irk much, – it may prove less
   irk-some now.
*Cha.* What would you utter?
*D'O.*                  That I from my soul
Grieve at to-night's event: for you I
   grieve,
E'en grieve for …
*Cha.*        Tush, another time for talk!
My kingdom is in imminent danger?
*D'O.*                          Let
The Count communicate with France –
   its King,
His grandson, will have Fleury's aid for
   this,
Though for no other war.
*Cha.*                First for the levies:
What forces can I muster presently?
               [D'ORMEA *delivers papers*
                 *which* CHARLES *inspects.*
*Cha.* Good – very good. Montorio …
   how is this?
– Equips me double the old complement
Of soldiers?
*D'O.*   Since his land has been relieved

From double imposts, this he manages:
But under the late monarch …
*Cha*.                          Peace! I know.
Count Spava has omitted mentioning
What proxy is to head these troops of
    his.
*D'O.* Count Spava means to head his
    troops himself.
Something to fight for now; 'Whereas'
    says he,
'Under the sovereign's father' …
*Cha*.                    It would seem
That all my people love me.
*D'O.*                    Yes.
            [*To* POLYXENA *while* CHARLES
            *continues to inspect the papers.*
                              A temper
Like Victor's may avail to keep a state;
He terrifies men and they fall not off;
Good to restrain: best, if restraint were
    all.
But, with the silent circle round him,
    ends
Such sway: our King's begins precisely
    there.
For to suggest, impel and set at work,
Is quite another function. Men may
    slight,
In time of peace, the King who brought
    them peace:
In war, – his voice, his eyes, help more
    than fear.
They love you, sir!
*Cha*. [*to* ATTENDANTS]. Bring the regalia
    forth!
Quit the room! And now, Marquis,
    answer me!
Why should the King of France invade
    my realm?
*D'O.* Why? Did I not acquaint your
    Majesty
An hour ago?
*Cha*.          I choose to hear again
What then I heard.
*D'O.*              Because, sir, as I said,
Your father is resolved to have his crown
At any risk; and, as I judge, calls in

The foreigner to aid him.
*Cha*.                And your reason
For saying this?
*D'O.* [*aside*].   Ay, just his father's way!
[*To* Charles.] The Count wrote yesterday
    to your forces' Chief,
Rhebinder – made demand of help –
*Cha*.                        To try
Rhebinder – he's of alien blood: aught
    else?
*D'O.* Receiving a refusal, – some hours
    after,
The Count called on Del Borgo to deliver
The Act of Abdication: he refusing,
Or hesitating, rather –
*Cha*.                What ensued?
*D'O.* At midnight, only two hours since,
    at Turin,
He rode in person to the citadel
With one attendant, to Soccorso gate,
And bade the governor, San Remi,
    open –
Admit him.
*Cha*.      For a purpose I divine.
These three were faithful, then?
*D'O.*                  They told it me.
And I –
*Cha*.  Most faithful –
*D'O.*              Tell it you – with this
Moreover of my own: if, an hour hence,
You have not interposed, the Count
    will be
O' the road to France for succour.
*Cha*.                        Very good!
You do your duty now to me your
    monarch
Fully, I warrant? – have, that is, your
    project
For saving both of us disgrace, no doubt?
*D'O.* I give my counsel, – and the only
    one.
A month since, I besought you to employ
Restraints which had prevented many a
    pang:
But now the harsher course must be
    pursued.
These papers, made for the emergency,

Will pain you to subscribe: this is a list
Of those suspected merely – men to
    watch;
This – of the few of the Count's very
    house-hold
You must, however reluctantly, arrest;
While here's a method of remonstrance
    – sure
Not stronger than the case demands –
    to take
With the Count's self.
*Cha.*      Deliver those three papers.
*Pol.* [*while* CHARLES *inspects them – to*
    D'Ormea].Your measures are not
    over-harsh, sir: France
Will hardly be deterred from her intents
By these.
*D'O.*     If who proposes might dispose,
I could soon satisfy you. Even these,
Hear what he'll say at my presenting!
*Cha.* [*who has signed them*].     There!
About the warrants! You've my signature.
What turns you pale? I do my duty by
    you
In acting boldly thus on your advice.
*D'O.* [*reading them separately*].     Arrest
    the people I suspected merely?
*Cha.* Did you suspect them?
*D'O.*      Doubtless: but – but – sir,
This Forquieri's governor of Turin,
And Rivarol and he have influence over
Half of the capital! Rabella, too?
Why, sir –
*Cha.*      Oh, leave the fear to me!
*D'O.* [*still reading*].      You bid me
Incarcerate the people on this list?
Sir –
*Cha.* But you never bade arrest those
    men,
So close related to my father too,
On trifling grounds?
*D'O.*      Oh, as for that, St George,
President of Chambery's senators,
Is hatching treason! still –
    [*More troubled.*] Sir, Count Cumiane
Is brother to your father's wife! What's
    here?

Arrest the wife herself?
*Cha.*      You seem to think
A venial crime this plot against me.
    Well?
*D'O.* [*who has read the last paper*].
    Wherefore am I thus ruined? Why
    not take
My life at once? This poor formality
Is, let me say, unworthy you! Prevent it
You, madam! I have served you, am
    prepared
For all disgraces: only, let disgrace
Be plain, be proper – proper for the
    world
To pass its judgment on 'twixt you and
    me!
Take back your warrant, I will none of it!
*Cha.* Here is a man to talk of fickleness!
He stakes his life upon my father's
    falsehood;
I bid him …
*D'O.*      Not you! Were he trebly false,
You do not bid me …
*Cha.*      Is't not written there?
I thought so: give – I'll set it right.
*D'O.*      Is it there?
Oh yes, and plain – arrest him now –
    drag here
Your father! And were all six times as
    plain,
Do you suppose I trust it?
*Cha.*      Just one word!
You bring him, taken in the act of flight,
Or else your life is forfeit.
*D'O.*      Ay, to Turin
I bring him, and to-morrow?
*Cha.*      Here and now!
The whole thing is a lie, a hateful lie,
As I believed and as my father said.
I knew it from the first, but was
    compelled
To circumvent you; and the great
    D'Ormea,
That baffled Alberoni and tricked Coscia,
The miserable sower of such discord
'Twixt sire and son, is in the toils at
    last.

Oh I see! you arrive – this plan of yours,
Weak as it is, torments sufficiently
A sick old peevish man – wrings hasty
    speech,
An ill-considered threat from him; that's
    noted;
Then out you ferret papers, his
    amusement
In lonely hours of lassitude – examine
The day-by-day report of your paid
    spies –
And back you come: all was not ripe,
    you find,
And, as you hope, may keep from
    ripening yet,
But you were in bare time! Only, 'twere
    best
I never saw my father – these old men
Are potent in excuses: and meanwhile,
D'Ormea's the man I cannot do without!
*Pol.* Charles –
*Cha.*        Ah, no question! You against
    me too!
You'd have me eat and drink and sleep,
    live, die
With this lie coiled about me, choking
    me!
No, no, D'Ormea! You venture life, you
    say,
Upon my father's perfidy: and I
Have, on the whole, no right to disregard
The chains of testimony you thus wind
About me; though I do – do from my
    soul
Discredit them: still I must authorize
These measures, and I will. Perugia!
[*Many* OFFICERS *enter.*]        Count –
You and Solar, with all the force you
    have,
Stand at the Marquis' orders: what he
    bids
Implicitly perform! You are to bring
A traitor here; the man that's likest one
At present, fronts me; you are at his
    beck
For a full hour! he undertakes to show
A fouler than himself, – but, failing that,

Return with him, and, as my father lives,
He dies this night! The clemency you
    blame
So oft, shall be revoked – rights exercised,
Too long abjured.
[*To* D'ORMEA.] Now sir, about the work!
To save your king and country! Take
    the warrant!
*D'O.* You hear the sovereign's man
    date, Count Perugia?
Obey me! As your diligence, expect
Reward! All follow to Moncaglier!
*Cha.* [*in great anguish*].        D'Ormea!
                    [D'ORMEA *goes.*
He goes, lit up with that appalling
    smile! [*To* POLYXENA, *after a pause.*
At least you understand all this?
*Pol.*                    These means
Of our defence – these measures of
    precaution?
*Cha.* It must be the best way; I should
    have else
Withered beneath his scorn.
*Pol.*            What would you say?
*Cha.* Why, do you think I mean to keep
    the crown,
Polyxena?
*Pol.*    You then believe the story
In spite of all – that Victor comes?
*Cha.*                    Believe it?
I know that he is coming – feel the
    strength
That has upheld me leave me at his
    coming!
'Twas mine, and now he takes his own
    again.
Some kinds of strength are well enough
    to have;
But who's to have that strength? Let
    my crown go!
I meant to keep it; but I cannot –
    cannot!
Only, he shall not taunt me – he, the
    first ...
See if he would not be the first to taunt
    me
With having left his kingdom at a word.

With letting it be conquered without
  stroke,
With ... no – no – 'tis no worse than
  when he left!
I've just to bid him take it, and, that
  over,
We'll fly away – fly, for I loathe this
  Turin,
This Rivoli, all titles loathe, all state.
We'd best go to your country – unless
  God
Send I die now!
*Pol.*          Charles, hear me!
*Cha.*                     And again
Shall you be my Polyxena – you'll take
  me
Out of this woe! Yes, do speak, and
  keep speaking!
I would not let you speak just now, for
  fear
You'd counsel me against him: but talk,
  now,
As we two used to talk in blessed times:
Bid me endure all his caprices; take me
From this mad post above him!
*Pol.*                     I believe
We are undone, but from a different
  cause.
All your resources, down to the least
  guard,
Are at D'Ormea's beck. What if, the
  while,
He act in concert with your father? We
Indeed were lost. This lonely Rivoli –
Where find a better place for them?
*Cha.* [*pacing the room*].          And why
Does Victor come? To undo all that's
  done,
Restore the past, prevent the future!
  Seat
His mistress in your seat, and place in
  mine
... Oh, my own people, whom will you
  find there,
To ask of, to consult with, to care for,
To hold up with your hands? Whom?
  One that's false –

False – from the head's crown to the
  foot's sole, false!
The best is, that I knew it in my heart
From the beginning, and expected this,
And hated you, Polyxena, because
You saw thro' him, though I too saw
  thro' him,
Saw that he meant this while he crowned
  me, while
He prayed for me, – nay, while he kissed
  my brow,
I saw –
*Pol.*     But if your measures take effect,
D'Ormea true to you?
*Cha.*                     Then worst of all!
I shall have loosed that callous wretch
  on him!
Well may the woman taunt him with
  his child –
I, eating here his bread, clothed in his
  clothes,
Seated upon his seat, let slip D'Ormea
To outrage him! We talk – perchance
  he tears
My father from his bed; the old hands
  feel
For one who is not, but who should be
  there,
He finds D'Ormea! D'Ormea too finds
  him!
The crowded chamber when the lights
  go out –
Closed doors – the horrid scuffle in the
  dark –
The accursed prompting of the minute!
  My guards!
To horse – and after, with me – and
  prevent!
*Pol.* [*seizing his hand*]. King Charles!
  Pause here upon this strip of time
Allotted you out of eternity!
Crowns are from God: you in his name
  hold yours.
Your life's no least thing, were it fit your
  life
Should be abjured along with rule; but
  now,

Keep both! Your duty is to live and
    rule –
You, who would vulgarly look fine
    enough
In the world's eye, deserting your soul's
    charge, –
Ay, you would have men's praise, this
    Rivoli
Would be illumined! While, as 'tis, no
    doubt,
Something of stain will ever rest on you;
No one will rightly know why you refused
To abdicate; they'll talk of deeds you
    could
Have done, no doubt, – nor do I much
    expect
Future achievement will blot out the
    past,
Envelope it in haze – nor shall we two
Live happy any more. 'Twill be, I feel,
Only in moments that the duty's seen
As palpably as now: the months, the
    years
Of painful indistinctness are to come,
While daily must we tread these palace-
    rooms
Pregnant with memories of the past:
    your eye
May turn to mine and find no comfort
    there,
Through fancies that beset me, as
    yourself,
Of other courses, with far other issues,
We might have taken this great night:
    such bear,
As I will bear! What matters happiness?
Duty! There's man's one moment: this
    is yours!
    [*Putting the crown on his head, and the
        sceptre in his hand, she places him
        on his seat: a long pause and silence.*]
*Enter* D'ORMEA *and* VICTOR, *with* GUARDS.
*Vic.* At last I speak; but once – that
    once, to you!
'Tis you I ask, not these your varletry,
Who's King of us?
*Cha.* [*from his seat*]. Count Tende …

*Vic.*                 What your spies
Assert I ponder in my soul, I say –
Here to your face, amid your guards! I
    choose
To take again the crown whose shadow
    I gave –
For still its potency surrounds the weak
White locks their felon hands have
    discomposed.
Or I'll not ask who's King, but simply,
    who
Withholds the crown I claim? Deliver it!
I have no friend in the wide world: nor
    France
Nor England cares for me: you see the
    sum
Of what I can avail. Deliver it!
*Cha.* Take it, my father!
                And now say in turn,
Was it done well, my father – sure not
    well,
To try me thus! I might have seen much
    cause
For keeping it – too easily seen cause!
But, from that moment, e'en more
    woefully
My life had pined away, than pine it will.
Already you have much to answer for.
My life to pine is nothing, – her sunk
    eyes
Were happy once! No doubt, my
    people think
I am their King still … but I cannot
    strive!
Take it!
*Vic.* [*one hand on the crown* CHARLES
    *offers, the other on his neck*]. So few
    years give it quietly,
My son! It will drop from me. See you
    not?
A crown's unlike a sword to give away –
That, let a strong hand to a weak hand
    give!
But crowns should slip from palsied
    brows to heads
Young as this head: yet mine is weak
    enough,

E'en weaker than I knew. I seek for
    phrases
To vindicate my right. 'Tis of a piece!
All is alike gone by with me – who beat
Once D'Orleans in his lines – his very
    _ lines!
To have been Eugene's comrade, Louis's
    rival,
And now ...
*Cha.* [*putting the crown on him, to the
    rest*]. The King speaks, yet none
    kneels, I think!
*Vic.* I am then King! As I became a King
Despite the nations, kept myself a King,
So I die King, with Kingship dying too
Around me. I have lasted Europe's time.
What wants my story of completion?
    Where
Must needs the damning break show?
    Who mistrusts
My children here – tell they of any break
'Twixt my day's sunrise and its fiery fall?
And who were by me when I died but
    they?
D'Ormea there!
*Cha.*        What means he?
*Vic.*                        Ever there!
Charles – how to save your story! Mine
    must go.
Say – say that you refused the crown to
    me!
Charles, yours shall be my story! You
    immured
Me, say, at Rivoli. A single year
I spend without a sight of you, then die.
That will serve every purpose – tell that
    tale
The world!
*Cha.*    Mistrust me? Help!
*Vic.*            Past help, past reach!
'Tis in the heart – you cannot reach the
    heart:
This broke mine, that I did believe, you,
    Charles,
Would have denied me and disgraced
    me.
*Pol.*    Charles

Has never ceased to be your subject, sir!
He reigned at first through setting up
    yourself
As pattern: if he e'er seemed harsh to
    you,
'Twas from a too intense appreciation
Of your own character: he acted you –
Ne'er for an instant did I think it real,
Nor look for any other than this end.
I hold him worlds the worse on that
    account;
But so it was.
*Cha.* [*to* POLYXENA]. I love you now
    indeed.
[*To* VICTOR.] You never knew me.
*Vic.*                Hardly till this moment,
When I seem learning many other things
Because the time for using them is past.
If 'twere to do again! That's idly wished.
Truthfulness might prove policy as good
As guile. Is this my daughter's forehead?
    Yes:
I've made it fitter now to be a queen's
Than formerly: I've ploughed the deep
    lines there
Which keep too well a crown from
    slipping off.
No matter. Guile has made me King
    again.
*Louis – 'twas in King Victor's time: –
    long since,*
*When Louis reigned and, also, Victor
    reigned.*
How the world talks already of us two!
God of eclipse and each discoloured
    star,
Why do I linger then?
                    Ha! Where lurks he?
D'Ormea! Nearer to your King! Now
    stand!
                [*Collecting his strength
                as* D'ORMEA *approaches*.
You lied, D'Ormea! I do not repent.
                                    [*Dies.*

# DRAMATIC LYRICS

## Cavalier Tunes

### 1

#### MARCHING ALONG

**1**

Kentish Sir Byng stood for his King,
Bidding the crop-headed Parliament
    swing:
And, pressing a troop unable to stoop
And see the rogues flourish and honest
    folk droop,
Marched them along, fifty-score strong,
Great-hearted gentlemen, singing this
    song.

**2**

God for King Charles! Pym and such
    carles
To the Devil that prompts 'em their
    treasonous parles!
Cavaliers, up! Lips from the cup,
Hands from the pasty, nor bite take nor
    sup
Till you're –
CHORUS
*Marching along, fifty-score strong,*
*Great-hearted gentlemen, singing this*
    *song.*

**3**

Hampden to hell, and his obsequies'
    knell
Serve Hazelrig, Fiennes, and young
    Harry as well!
England, good cheer! Rupert is near!
Kentish and loyalists, keep we not here
CHORUS
*Marching along, fifty-score strong,*
*Great-hearted gentlemen, singing this*
    *song?*

**4**

Then, God for King Charles! Pym and
    his snarls
To the Devil that pricks on such
    pestilent carles!
Hold by the right, you double your
    might;

So, onward to Nottingham, fresh for
    the fight,
CHORUS
*March we along, fifty-score strong,*
*Great-hearted gentlemen, singing this*
    *song!*

### 2

#### GIVE A ROUSE

**1**

King Charles, and who'll do him right
    now?
King Charles, and who's ripe for fight
    now?
Give a rouse: here's, in hell's despite
    now,
King Charles!

**2**

Who gave me the goods that went since?
Who raised me the house that sank
    once?
Who helped me to gold I spent since?
Who found me in wine you drank once?
CHORUS
*King Charles, and who'll do him right*
    *now?*
*King Charles, and who's ripe for fight*
    *now?*
*Give a rouse: here's, in hell's despite*
    *now,*
*King Charles!*

**3**

To whom used my boy George quaff
    else,
By the old fool's side that begot him?
For whom did he cheer and laugh else,
While Noll's damned troopers shot him?
CHORUS
*King Charles, and who'll do him right*
    *now?*
*King Charles, and who's ripe for fight*
    *now?*
*Give a rouse: here's, in hell's despite*
    *now.*
*King Charles!*

## 3

### BOOT AND SADDLE

#### 1

Boot, saddle, to horse, and away!
Rescue my castle before the hot day
Brightens to blue from its silvery grey,
CHORUS
*Boot, saddle, to horse, and away!*

#### 2

Ride past the suburbs, asleep as you'd
    say;
Many's the friend there, will listen and
    pray
'God's luck to gallants that strike up
    the lay –
CHORUS
*'Boot, saddle, to horse, and away!'*

#### 3

Forty miles off, like a roebuck at bay,
Flouts Castle Brancepeth the
    Roundheads' array:
Who laughs, 'Good fellows ere this, by
    my fay,
CHORUS
*'Boot, saddle, to horse, and away!'*

#### 4

Who? My wife Gertrude; that, honest
    and gay,
Laughs when you talk of surrendering,
    'Nay!
I've better counsellors; whatcounsel
    they?
CHORUS
*'Boot, saddle, to horse, and away!'*

## *The Lost Leader*

#### 1

Just for a handful of silver he left us,
    Just for a riband to stick in his coat –
Found the one gift of which fortune
    bereft us,
    Lost all the others she lets us devote;
They, with the gold to give, doled him
    out silver,
    So much was theirs who so little
    allowed:

How all our copper had gone for his
    service!
    Rags – were they purple, his heart
    had been proud!
We that had loved him so, followed
    him, honoured him,
    Lived in his mild and magnificent eye,
Learned his great language, caught his
    clear accents,
    Made him our pattern to live and to
    die!
Shakespeare was of us, Milton was for
    us,
    Burns, Shelley, were with us, – they
    watch from their graves!
He alone breaks from the van and the
    freemen,
    – He alone sinks to the rear and the
    slaves!

#### 2

We shall march prospering, – not thro'
    his presence;
    Songs may inspirit us, – not from his
    lyre;
Deeds will be done, – while he boasts
    his quiescence,
    Still bidding crouch whom the rest
    bade aspire:
Blot out his name, then, record one lost
    soul more,
    One task more declined, one more
    footpath untrod,
One more devils'-triumph and sorrow
    for angels,
    One wrong more to man, one more
    insult to God!
Life's night begins: let him never come
    back to us!
    There would be doubt, hesitation and
    pain,
Forced praise on our part – the glimmer
    of twilight,
    Never glad confident morning again!
Best fight on well, for we taught him –
    strike gallantly,
    Menace our heart ere we master his
    own;

Then let him receive the new knowledge
and wait us,
Pardoned in heaven, the first by the
throne!

## 'How They Brought the Good News from Ghent to Aix'

### 1

I sprang to the stirrup, and Joris, and
he;
I galloped, Dirck galloped, we galloped
all three;
'Good speed!' cried the watch, as the
gate bolts undrew;
'Speed!' echoed the wall to us
galloping through;
Behind shut the postern, the lights
sank to rest,
And into the midnight we galloped
abreast.

### 2

Not a word to each other; we kept the
great pace
Neck by neck, stride by stride, never
changing our place;
I turned in my saddle and made its
girths tight,
Then shortened each stirrup, and set
the pique right,
Rebuckled the cheek-strap, chained
slacker the bit,
Nor galloped less steadily Roland a
whit.

### 3

'Twas moonset at starting; but while
we drew near
Lokeren, the cocks crew and twilight
dawned clear;
At Boom, a great yellow star came out
to see;
At Düffeld, 'twas morning as plain as
could be;
And from Mecheln church-steeple we
heard the half-chime,
So, Joris broke silence with, 'Yet there
is time!'

### 4

At Aershot, up leaped of a sudden the
sun,
And against him the cattle stood black
every one,
To stare thro' the mist at us galloping
past,
And I saw my stout galloper Roland at
last,
With resolute shoulders, each butting
away
The haze, as some bluff river headland
its spray:

### 5

And his low head and crest, just one
sharp ear bent back
For my voice, and the other pricked out
on his track,
And one eye's black intelligence, – ever
that glance
O'er its white edge at me, his own
master, askance!
And the thick heavy spume-flakes
which aye and anon
His fierce lips shook upwards in
galloping on.

### 6

By Hasselt, Dirck groaned; and cried
Joris, 'Stay spur!
'Your Roos galloped bravely' the fault's
not in her,
'We'll remember at Aix' – for one
heard the quick wheeze
Of her chest, saw the stretched neck
and staggering knees,
And sunk tail, and horrible heave of
the flank,
As down on her haunches she
shuddered and sank.

### 7

So, we were left galloping, Joris and I,
Past Looz and past Tongres, no cloud
in the sky;
The broad sun above laughed a pitiless
laugh,
'Neath our feet broke the brittle bright
stubble like chaff;

Till over by Dalhem a dome-spire sprang
    white,
And 'Gallop,' gasped Joris, 'for Aix is in
    sight!'

8

'How they'll greet us!' – and all in a
    moment his roan
Rolled neck and croup over, lay dead
    as a stone;
And there was my Roland to bear the
    whole weight
Of the news which alone could save
    Aix from her fate,
With his nostrils like pits full of blood
    to the brim,
And with circles of red for his eye-
    sockets' rim.

9

Then I cast loose my buffcoat, each
    holster let fall,
Shook off both my jack-boots, let go
    belt and all,
Stood up in the stirrup, leaned, patted
    his ear,
Called my Roland his pet-name, my
    horse without peer;
Clapped my hands, laughed and sang,
    any noise, bad or good,
Till at length into Aix Roland galloped
    and stood.

10

And all I remember is – friends flocking
    round
As I sat with his head 'twixt my knees
    on the ground;
And no voice but was praising this
    Roland of mine,
As I poured down his throat our last
    measure of wine,
Which (the burgesses voted by
    common consent)
Was no more than his due who
    brought good news from Ghent.

## Through the Metidja to Abd-el-Kadr

1

As I ride, as I ride,
With a full heart for my guide,
So its tide rocks my side,
As I ride, as I ride,
That, as I were double-eyed,
He, in whom our Tribes confide,
Is descried, ways untried
As I ride, as I ride.

2

As I ride, as I ride
To our Chief and his Allied,
Who dares chide my heart's pride
As I ride, as I ride?
Or are witnesses denied –
Through the desert waste and wide
Do I glide unespied
As I ride, as I ride?

3

As I ride, as I ride,
When an inner voice has cried,
The sands slide, nor abide
(As I ride, as I ride)
O'er each visioned homicide
That came vaunting (has he lied?)
To reside – where he died,
As I ride, as I ride.

4

As I ride, as I ride,
Ne'er has spur my swift horse plied,
Yet his hide, streaked and pied,
As I ride, as I ride,
Shows where sweat has sprung and dried,
– Zebra-footed, ostrich-thighed –
How has vied stride with stride
As I ride, as I ride!

5

As I ride, as I ride,
Could I loose what Fate has tied,
Ere I pried, she should hide
(As I ride, as I ride)
All that's meant me – satisfied
When the Prophet and the Bride
Stops veins I'd have subside
As I ride, as I ride!

## Nationality in Drinks

### 1

My heart sank with our Claret-flask,
  Just now, beneath the heavy sedges
That serve this pond's black face for
    mask;
  And still at yonder broken edges
O' the hole, where up the bubbles
    glisten,
After my heart I look and listen.

### 2

Our laughing little flask, compelled
  Thro' depth to depth more bleak
    and shady;
As when, both arms beside her held,
  Feet straightened out, some gay
    French lady
Is caught up from life's light and motion,
And dropped into death's silent ocean!

\*    \*    \*

Up jumped Tokay on our table,
Like a pygmy castle-warder,
Dwarfish to see, but stout and able,
Arms and accoutrements all in order;
And fierce he looked North, then,
    wheeling South,
Blew with his bugle a challenge to
    Drouth,
Cocked his flap-hat with the tosspot-
    feather,
Twisted his thumb in his red moustache,
Jingled his huge brass spurs together,
Tightened his waist with its Buda sash,
And then, with an impudence nought
    could abash,
Shrugged his hump-shoulder, to tell the
    beholder,
For twenty such knaves he should laugh
    but the bolder:
And so, with his sword-hilt gallantly
    jutting,
And dexter-hand on his haunch
    abutting,
Went the little man, Sir Ausbruch,
    strutting!

\*    \*    \*

Here's to Nelson's memory!
'Tis the second time that I, at sea,
Right off Cape Trafalgar here,
Have drunk it deep in British Beer.
Nelson for ever – any time
Am I his to command in prose or
    rhyme!
Give me of Nelson only a touch,
And I save it, be it little or much:
Here's one our Captain gives, and so
Down at the word, by George, shall it
    go!
He says that at Greenwich they point
    the beholder
To Nelson's coat, 'still with tar on the
    shoulder:
'For he used to lean with one shoulder
    digging,
'Jigging, as it were, and zig-zag-zigging
'Up against the mizen-rigging!'

## Garden Fancies

### 1

#### THE FLOWER'S NAME

##### 1

Here's the garden she walked across,
  Arm in my arm, such a short while
    since:
Hark, now I push its wicket, the moss
  Hinders the hinges and makes them
    wince!
She must have reached this shrub ere
    she turned,
  As back with that murmur the wicket
    swung;
For she laid the poor snail, my chance
    foot spurned,
  To feed and forget it the leaves among.

##### 2

Down this side of the gravel-walk
  She went while her robe's edge
    brushed the box:
And here she paused in her gracious
    talk

To point me a moth on the milk-
    white phlox.
Roses, ranged in valiant row,
    I will never think that she passed
      you by!
She loves you noble roses, I know;
    But yonder, see, where the rock-
      plants lie!

3

This flower she stopped at, finger on
    lip,
    Stooped over, in doubt, as settling
      its claim;
Till she gave me, with pride to make no
    slip,
    Its soft meandering Spanish name:
What a name! Was it love or praise?
    Speech half-asleep or song half-
      awake?
I must learn Spanish, one of these days,
    Only for that slow sweet name's sake.

4

Roses, if I live and do well,
    I may bring her, one of these days,
To fix you fast with as fine a spell,
    Fit you each with his Spanish phrase;
But do not detain me now; for she
      fingers
    There, like sunshine over the ground,
And ever I see her soft white ringers
    Searching after the bud she found.

5

Flower, you Spaniard, look that you
    grow not,
    Stay as you are and be loved for ever!
Bud, if I kiss you 'tis that you blow
    not:
    Mind, the snut pink mouth opens
      never!
For while it pouts, her fingers wrestle,
    Twinkling the audacious leaves
      between,
Till round they turn and down they
    nestle –
    Is not the dear mark still to be seen?

6

Where I find her not, beauties vanish;
    Whither I follow her, beauties flee;
Is there no method to tell her in Spanish
    June's twice June since she breathed
      it with me?
Come, bud, show me the least of her
    traces,
    Treasure my lady's lightest footfall!
– Ah, you may flout and turn up your
    faces –
    Roses, you are not so fair after all!

2

SIBRANDUS SCHAFNABURGENSIS

1

Plague take all your pedants, say I!
    He who wrote what I hold in my
      hand,
Centuries back was so good as to die,
    Leaving this rubbish to cumber the
      land;
This, that was a book in its time,
    Printed on paper and bound in
      leather,
Last month in the white of a matin-
    prime
    Just when the birds sang all together.

2

Into the garden I brought it to read,
    And under the arbute and laurustine
Read it, so help me grace in my need,
    From title-page to closing line.
Chapter on chapter did I count,
    As a curious traveller counts Stone-
      henge;
Added up the mortal amount;
    And then proceeded to my revenge

3

Yonder's a plum-tree with a crevice
    An owl would build in, were he but
      sage;
For a lap of moss, like a fine pont-levis
    In a castle of the Middle Age,
Joins to a lip of gum, pure amber;
    When he'd be private, there might
      he spend

Hours alone in his lady's chamber:
    Into this crevice I dropped our friend.

4

Splash, went he, as under he ducked,
    – At the bottom, I knew, rain-
        drippings stagnate:
Next, a handful of blossoms I plucked
    To bury him with, my bookshelf's
        magnate;
Then I went in-doors, brought out a
        loaf,
  Half a cheese, and a bottle of Chablis;
Lay on the grass and forgot the oaf
    Over a jolly chapter of Rabelais.

5

Now, this morning, betwixt the moss
    And gum that locked our friend in
        limbo,
A spider had spun his web across,
    And sat in the midst with arms
        akimbo:
So, I took pity, for learning's sake,
    And, *de profundis, accentibus lætis,*
*Cantate!* quoth I, as I got a rake;
    And up I fished his delectable
       treatise.

6

Here you have it, dry in the sun,
    With all the binding all of a blister,
And great blue spots where the ink has
       run,
    And reddish streaks that wink and
       glister
O'er the page so beautifully yellow:
    Oh, well have the droppings played
       their tricks!
Did he guess how toadstools grow, this
       fellow?
    Here's one stuck in his chapter six!

7

How did he tike it when the live
       creatures
    Tickled and toused and browsed
       him all over,
And worm, slug, eft, with serious
       features,

    Came in, each one, for his right of
       trover?
– When the water-beetle with great
       blind deaf face
Made of her eggs the stately deposit,
And the newt borrowed just so much
       of the preface
    As tiled in the top of his black wife's
       closet?

8

All that life and fun and romping,
    All that frisking and twisting and
       coupling,
While slowly our poor friend's leaves
       were swamping
    And clasps were cracking and covers
       suppling!
As if you had carried sour John Knox
    To the play-house at Paris, Vienna or
       Munich,
Fastened him into a front-row box,
    And danced off the ballet with
       trousers and tunic.

9

Come, old martyr! What, torment
    enough is it?
    Back to my room shall you take your
       sweet self.
Good-bye, mother-beetle; husband-eft,
    *sufficit!*
    See the snug niche I have made on
       my shelf!
A.'s book shall prop you up, B.'s shall
    cover you,
    Here's C. to be grave with, or D. to
       be gay,
And with E. on each side, and F. right
    over you,
Dry-rot at ease till the Judgment-day!

## Soliloquy of the Spanish Cloister

### 1

Gr–r–r – there go, my heart's abhorrence!
  Water your damned flower-pots, do!
If hate killed men, Brother Lawrence,
  God's blood, would not mine kill
    you!
What? your myrtle-bush wants trimming?
  Oh, that rose has prior claims –
Needs its leaden vase filled brimming?
  Hell dry you up with its flames!

### 2

At the meal we sit together:
  *Salve tibi!* I must hear
Wise talk of the kind of weather,
  Sort of season, time of year:
*Not a plenteous cork-crop: scarcely*
  *Dare we hope oak-galls, I doubt:*
*What's the Latin name for 'parsley'?*
What's the Greek name for Swine's
    Snout?

### 3

Whew! We'll have our platter burnished,
  Laid with care on our own shelf!
With a fire-new spoon we're furnished,
  And a goblet for ourself,
Rinsed like something sacrificial
  Ere 'tis fit to touch our chaps –
Marked with L. for our initial!
  (He–he! There his lily snaps!)

### 4

*Saint,* forsooth! While brown Dolores
  Squats outside the Convent bank
With Sanchicha, telling stories,
  Steeping tresses in the tank,
Blue-black, lustrous, thick like horsehairs,
  – Can't I see his dead eye glow,
Bright as 'twere a Barbary corsair's?
  (That is, if he'd let it show!)

### 5

When he finishes refection,
  Knife and fork he never lays
Cross-wise, to my recollection,
  As do I, in Jesu's praise.

I the Trinity illustrate,
  Drinking watered orange-pulp –
In three sips the Arian frustrate;
  While he drains his at one gulp.

### 6

Oh, those melons? If he's able
  We're to have a feast! so nice!
One goes to the Abbot's table,
  All of us get each a slice.
How go on your flowers? None double?
  Not one fruit-sort can you spy?
Strange! – And I, too, at such trouble,
  Keep them close-nipped on the sly!

### 7

There's a great text in Galatians,
  Once you trip on it, entails
Twenty-nine distinct damnations,
  One sure, if another fails:
If I trip him just a-dying,
  Sure of heaven as sure can be,
Spin him round and send him flying
  Off to hell, a Manichee?

### 8

Or, my scrofulous French novel
  On grey paper with blunt type!
Simply glance at it, you grovel
  Hand and foot in Belial's gripe:
If I double down its pages
  At the woeful sixteenth print,
When he gathers his greengages,
  Ope a sieve and slip it in't?

### 9

Or, there's Satan! – one might venture
  Pledge one's soul to him, yet leave
Such a flaw in the indenture
  As he'd miss till, past retrieve,
Blasted lay that rose-acacia
  We're so proud of! *Hy, Zy, Hine …*
'St, there's Vespers! *Plena gratiâ*
  *Ave, Virgo!* Gr–r–r – you swine!

## The Laboratory

### ANCIEN RÉGIME

**1**

Now that I, tying thy glass mask tightly,
May gaze thro' these faint smokes curling whitely,
As thou pliest thy trade in this devil's-smithy –
Which is the poison to poison her, prithee?

**2**

He is with her, and they know that I know
Where they are, what they do: they believe my tears flow
While they laugh, laugh at me, at me fled to the drear
Empty church, to pray God in, for them! – I am here.

**3**

Grind away, moisten and mash up thy paste,
Pound at thy powder, – I am not in haste!
Better sit thus, and observe thy strange things,
Than go where men wait me and dance at the King's.

**4**

That in the mortar – you call it a gum?
Ah, the brave tree whence such gold oozings come!
And yonder soft phial, the exquisite blue,
Sure to taste sweetly, – is that poison too?

**5**

Had I but all of them, thee and thy treasures,
What a wild crowd of invisible pleasures!
To carry pure death in an earring, a casket,
A signet, a fan-mount, a filigree basket!

**6**

Soon, at the King's, a mere lozenge to give,
And Pauline should have just thirty minutes to live!
But to light a pastile, and Elise, with her head
And her breast and her arms and her hands, should drop dead!

**7**

Quick – is it finished? The colour's too grim!
Why not soft like the phial's, enticing and dim?
Let it brighten her drink, let her turn it and stir,
And try it and taste, ere she fix and prefer!

**8**

What a drop! She's not little, no minion like me!
That's why she ensnared him: this never will free
The soul from those masculine eyes, – say, 'no!'
To that pulse's magnificent come-and-go.

**9**

For only last night, as they whispered, I brought
My own eyes to bear on her so, that I thought
Could I keep them one half minute fixed, she would fall
Shrivelled; she fell not; yet this does it all!

**10**

Not that I bid you spare her the pain;
Let death be felt and the proof remain:
Brand, burn up, bite into its grace –
He is sure to remember her dying face!

**11**

Is it done? Take my mask off! Nay, be not morose;
It kills her, and this prevents seeing it close;
The delicate droplet, my whole fortune's fee!
If it hurts her, beside, can it ever hurt me?

### 12

Now, take all my jewels, gorge gold to
      your fill,
You may kiss me, old man, on my
      mouth if you will!
But brush this dust off me, lest horror
      it brings
Ere I know it – next moment I dance at
      the King's!

## The Confessional

### [SPAIN]

### 1

It is a lie – their Priests, their Pope,
Their Saints, their … all they fear or
      hope
Are lies, and lies – there! through my
      door
And ceiling, there! and walls and floor,
There, lies, they lie – shall still be
      hurled
Till spite of them I reach the world!

### 2

You think Priests just and holy men!
Before they put me in this den
I was a human creature too,
With flesh and blood like one of you,
A girl that laughed in beauty's pride
Like lilies in your world outside.

### 3

I had a lover – shame avaunt!
This poor wrenched body, grim and
      gaunt,
Was kissed all over till it burned,
By lips the truest, love e'er turned
His heart's own tint: one night they
      kissed
My soul out in a burning mist.

### 4

So, next day when the accustomed
      train
Of things grew round my sense again,
'That is a sin,' I said: and slow
With downcast eyes to church I go,
And pass to the confession-chair,
And tell the old mild father there.

### 5

But when I falter Beltran's name,
'Ha?' quoth the father; 'much I blame
'The sin; yet wherefore idly grieve?
'Despair not – strenuously retrieve!
'Nay, I will turn this love of thine
'To lawful love, almost divine;

### 6

'For he is young, and led astray,
'This Beltran, and he schemes, men say,
'To change the laws of church and state;
'So, thine shall be an angel's fate,
'Who, ere the thunder breaks, should
      roll
'Its cloud away and save his soul.

### 7

'For, when he lies upon thy breast,
'Thou mayst demand and be possessed
'Of all his plans, and next day steal
'To me, and all those plans reveal,
'That I and every priest, to purge
'His soul, may fast and use the scourge.'

### 8

That father's beard was long and white,
With love and truth his brow seemed
      bright;
I went back, all on fire with joy,
And, that same evening, bade the boy
Tell me, as lovers should, heart-free,
Something to prove his love of me.

### 9

He told me what he would not tell
For hope of heaven or fear of hell;
And I lay listening in such pride!
And, soon as he had left my side,
Tripped to the church by morning-light
To save his soul in his despite.

### 10

I told the father all his schemes,
Who were his comrades, what their
      dreams;
'And now make haste,' I said, 'to pray
'The one spot from his soul away;
'To-night he comes, but not the same
'Will look!' At night he never came.

11

Nor next night: on the after-morn,
I went forth with a strength new-born.
The church was empty; something drew
My steps into the street; I knew
It led me to the market-place:
Where, lo, on high, the father's face!

12

That horrible black scaffold dressed,
That stapled block ... God sink the
    rest!
That head strapped back, that blinding
    vest,
Those knotted hands and naked breast,
Till near one busy hangman pressed,
And, on the neck these arms
    caressed ...

13

No part in aught they hope or fear!
No heaven with them, no hell! – and
    here,
No earth, not so much space as pens
My body in their worst of dens
But shall bear God and man my cry,
Lies – lies, again – and still, they lie!

## Cristina

1

She should never have looked at me
    If she meant I should not love her!
There are plenty ... men, you call such,
    I suppose ... she may discover
All her soul to, if she pleases,
    And yet leave much as she found
    them:
But I'm not so, and she knew it
    When she fixed me, glancing round
    them.

2

What? To fix me thus meant nothing!
    But I can't tell (there's my weakness)
What her look said! – no vile cant, sure,
    About 'need to strew the bleakness
'Of some lone shore with its pearl-seed.
    'That the sea feels' – no 'strange
    yearning

'That such souls have, most to lavish
    'Where there's chance of least
    returning.'

3

Oh, we're sunk enough here, God
    knows!
    But not quite so sunk that moments,
Sure tho' seldom, are denied us,
    When the spirit's true endowments
Stand out plainly from its false ones,
    And apprise it if pursuing
Or the right way or the wrong way,
    To its triumph or undoing.

4

There are flashes struck from midnights,
    There are fire-flames noondays
    kindle,!
Whereby piled-up honours perish,
    Whereby swollen ambitions dwindle,
While just this or that poor impulse,
    Which for once had play unstifled,
Seems the sole work of a life-time
    That away the rest have trifled.

5

Doubt you if, in some such moment,
    As she fixed me, she felt clearly,
Ages past the soul existed,
    Here an age 'tis resting merely,
And hence fleets again for ages,
    While the true end, sole and single,
It stops here for is, this love-way,
    With some other soul to mingle?

6

Else it loses what it lived for,
    And eternally must lose it;
Better ends may be in prospect,
    Deeper blisses (if you choose it),
But this life's end and this love-bliss
    Have been lost here. Doubt you
    whether
This she felt as, looking at me,
    Mine and her souls rushed together?

7

Oh, observe! Of course, next moment,
    The world's honours, in derision,
Trampled out the light for ever:
    Never fear but there's provision

Of the devil's to quench knowledge
  Lest we walk the earth in rapture!
– Making those who catch God's secret
  Just so much more prize their
    capture!

8

Such am I: the secret's mine now!
  She has lost me, I have gained her;
Her soul's mine: and thus, grown
    perfect,
  I shall pass my life's remainder.
Life will just hold out the proving
  Both our powers, alone and
    blended:
And then, come next life quickly!
  This world's use will have been
    ended.

## The Lost Mistress

1

All's over, then: does truth sound
    bitter
  As one at first believes?
Hark, 'tis the sparrows' good-night
    twitter
  About your cottage eaves!

2

And the leaf-buds on the vine are woolly,
  I noticed that, to-day;
One day more bursts them open fully
  – You know the red turns grey.

3

To-morrow we meet the same then,
    dearest?
  May I take your hand in mine?
Mere friends are we, – well, friends the
    merest
  Keep much that I resign:

4

For each glance of the eye so bright
    and black,
  Though I keep with heart's
    endeavour, –
Your voice, when you wish the
    snowdrops back,
  Though it stay in my soul for ever! –

5

Yet I will but say what mere friends say,
  Or only a thought stronger;
I will hold your hand but as long as all
    may,
  Or so very little longer!

## Earth's Immortalities

### FAME

See, as the prettiest graves will do in
    time,
Our poet's wants the freshness of its
    prime;
Spite of the sexton's browsing horse,
    the sods
Have struggled through its binding
    osier rods;
Headstone and half-sunk footstone
    lean awry,
Wanting the brick-work promised by-
    and-by;
How the minute grey lichens, plate o'er
    plate,
Have softened down the crisp-cut
    name and date!

### LOVE

So, the year's done with!
    (*Love me for ever!*)
All March begun with,
    April's endeavour;
May-wreaths that bound me
    June needs must sever;
Now snows fall round me,
    Quenching June's fever –
    (*Love me for ever!*)

## Meeting at Night

1

The grey sea and the long black land;
And the yellow half-moon large and low;
And the startled little waves that leap
In fiery ringlets from their sleep,
As I gain the cove with pushing prow,
And quench its speed i' the slushy sand.

### 2

Then a mile of warm sea-scented beach;
Three fields to cross till a farm appears;
A tap at the pane, the quick sharp
    scratch
And blue spurt of a lighted match,
And a voice less loud, thro' its joys and
    fears,
Than the two hearts beating each to
    each!

## Parting at Morning

Round the cape of a sudden came the
    sea,
And the sun looked over the mountain's
    rim:
And straight was a path of gold for him,
And the need of a world of men for me.

## Song

### 1

Nay but you, who do not love her,
    Is she not pure gold, my mistress?
Holds earth aught – speak truth – above
    her?
    Aught like this tress, see, and this
    tress,
And this last fairest tress of all,
    So fair, see, ere I let it fall?

### 2

Because, you spend your lives in
    praising;
    To praise, you search the wide world
    over:
Then why not witness, calmly gazing,
    If earth holds aught – speak truth –
    above her?
Above this tress, and this, I touch
But cannot praise, I love so much!

## A Woman's Last Word

### 1

Let's contend no more, Love,
    Strive nor weep:
All be as before, Love,
    – Only sleep!

### 2

What so wild as words are?
    I and thou
In debate, as birds are,
    Hawk on bough!

### 3

See the creature stalking
    While we speak!
Hush and hide the talking,
    Cheek on cheek!

### 4

What so false as truth is,
    False to thee?
Where the serpent's tooth is
    Shun the tree –

### 5

Where the apple reddens
    Never pry –
Lest we lose our Edens,
    Eve and I.

### 6

Be a god and hold me
    With a charm!
Be a man and fold me
    With thine arm!

### 7

Teach me, only teach, Love!
    As I ought
I will speak thy speech, Love,
    Think thy thought –

### 8

Meet, if thou require it,
    Both demands,
Laying flesh and spirit
    In thy hands.

### 9

That shall be to-morrow
    Not to-night:
I must bury sorrow
    Out of sight:

10

– Must a little weep, Love,
    (Foolish me!)
And so fall asleep, Love,
    Loved by thee.

## Evelyn Hope

1

Beautiful Evelyn Hope is dead!
    Sit and watch by her side an hour.
That is her book-shelf, this her bed;
    She plucked that piece of geranium-
        flower,
Beginning to die too, in the glass;
    Little has yet been changed, I think:
The shutters are shut, no light may pass
    Save two long rays thro' the hinge's
        chink.

2

Sixteen years old when she died!
    Perhaps she had scarcely heard my
        name;
It was not her time to love; beside,
    Her life had many a hope and aim,
Duties enough and little cares,
    And how was quiet, now astir,
Till God's hand beckoned unawares, –
    And the sweet white brow is all of her.

3

Is it too late then, Evelyn Hope?
    What, your soul was pure and true,
The good stars met in your horoscope,
    Made you of spirit, fire and dew –
And, just because I was thrice as old
    And our paths in the world diverged
        so wide,
Each was nought to each, must I be
        told?
    We were fellow mortals, nought
        beside?

4

No, indeed! for God above
    Is great to grant, as mighty to make,
And creates the love to reward the love:
    I claim you still, for my own love's
        sake!

Delayed it may be for more lives yet,
    Through worlds I shall traverse, not
        a few:
Much is to learn, much to forget
    Ere the time be come for taking you.

5

But the time will come, – at last it will,
    When, Evelyn Hope, what meant (I
        shall say)
In the lower earth, in the years long
        still,
    That body and soul so pure and gay?
Why your hair was amber, I shall
        divine,
    And your mouth of your own
        geranium's red –
And what you would do with me, in
        fine,
    In the new life come in the old one's
        stead.

6

I have lived (I shall say) so much since
        then,
    Given up myself so many times,
Gained me the gains of various men,
    Ransacked the ages, spoiled the
        climes;
Yet one thing, one, in my soul's full
        scope,
    Either I missed or itself missed me:
And I want and find you, Evelyn Hope!
    What is the issue? let us see!

7

I loved you, Evelyn, all the while.
    My heart seemed full as it could
        hold?
There was place and to spare for the
        frank young smile,
    And the red young mouth, and the
        hair's young gold.
So, hush, – I will give you this leaf to
        keep:
    See, I shut it inside the sweet cold
        hand!
There, that is our secret: go to sleep!
    You will wake, and remember, and
        understand.

## Love Among the Ruins

### 1

Where the quiet-coloured end of
    evening smiles,
        Miles and miles
On the solitary pastures where our sheep
    Half-asleep
Tinkle homeward thro' the twilight,
    stray or stop
        As they crop –
Was the site of a city great and gay,
        (So they say)
Of our country's very capital, its prince
        Ages since
Held his court in, gathered councils,
    wielding far
        Peace or war.

### 2

Now, – the country does not even boast
    a tree,
        As you see,
To distinguish slopes of verdure, certain
    rills
        From the hills
Intersect and give a name to, (else they
    run Into one)
Where the domed and daring palace
    shot its spires
        Up like fires
O'er the hundred-gated circuit of a wall
        Bounding all,
Made of marble, men might march on
    nor be pressed,
        Twelve abreast.

### 3

And such plenty and perfection, see, of
    grass
        Never was!
Such a carpet as, this summer-time,
    o'er-spreads
        And embeds
Every vestige of the city, guessed alone,
        Stock or stone –
Where a multitude of men breathed
    joy and woe
        Long ago;

Lust of glory pricked their hearts up,
    dread of shame
        Struck them tame;
And that glory and that shame alike, the
    gold
        Bought and sold.

### 4

Now, – the single little turret that remains
        On the plains,
By the caper overrooted, by the gourd
        Overscored,
While the patching houseleek's head of
    blossom winks
        Through the chinks –
Marks the basement whence a tower in
    ancient time
        Sprang sublime,
And a burning ring, all round, the
    chariots traced
        As they raced,
And the monarch and his minions and
    his dames
        Viewed the games.

### 5

And I know, while thus the quiet-
    coloured eve
        Smiles to leave
To their folding, all our many-tinkling
    fleece
        In such peace,
And the slopes and rills in undistin-
    guished grey
        Melt away –
That a girl with eager eyes and yellow
    hair
        Waits me there
In the turret whence the charioteers
    caught soul
        For the goal,
When the king looked, where she
    looks now, breathless, dumb
        Till I come.

### 6

But he looked upon the city, every side,
        Far and wide,

All the mountains topped with
　　　temples, all the glades'
　　　　　Colonnades,
All the causeys, bridges, aqueducts, –
　　and then,
　　　　　All the men!
When I do come, she will speak not,
　　she will stand,
　　　　　Either hand
On my shoulder, give her eyes the first
　　embrace
　　　　　Of my face,
Ere we rush, ere we extinguish sight
　　and speech
　　　　　Each on each.

### 7

In one year they sent a million fighters
　　forth
　　　　　South and North,
And they built their gods a brazen
　　pillar high
　　　　　As the sky,
Yet reserved a thousand chariots in full
　　force –
　　　　　Gold, of course.
Oh heart! oh blood that freezes, blood
　　that burns!
　　　　　Earth's returns
For whole centuries of folly, noise and
　　sin!
　　　　　Shut them in,
With their triumphs and their glories
　　and the rest!
　　　　　Love is best.

## A Lovers' Quarrel

### 1

Oh, what a dawn of day!
How the March sun feels like May!
　　　All is blue again
　　　After last night's rain,
And the South dries the hawthorn-spray.
　　　Only, my Love's away!
I'd as lief that the blue were grey.

### 2

Runnels, which rillets swell,
Must be dancing down the dell,
　　　With a foaming head
　　　On the beryl bed
Paven smooth as a hermit's cell;
　　　Each with a tale to tell,
Could my Love but attend as well.

### 3

Dearest, three months ago!
When we lived blocked-up with snow,
　　　When the wind would edge
　　　In and in his wedge,
In, as far as the point could go –
　　　Not to our ingle, though,
Where we loved each the other so!

### 4

Laughs with so little cause!
We devised games out of straws.
　　　We would try and trace
　　　One another's face
In the ash, as an artist draws;
　　　Free on each other's flaws,
How we chattered like two church daws!

### 5

What's in the 'Times'? – a scold
At the Emperor deep and cold;
　　　He has taken a bride
　　　To his gruesome side,
That's as fair as himself is bold:
　　　There they sit ermine-stokd,
And she powders her hair with gold.

### 6

Fancy the Pampas' sheen!
Miles and miles of gold and green
　　　Where the sunflowers blow
　　　In a solid glow,

And – to break now and then the
 screen –
  Black neck and eyeballs keen,
Up a wild horse leaps between!

7

Try, will our table turn?
Lay your hands there light, and yearn
  Till the yearning slips
  Thro' the finger-tips
In a fire which a few discern,
  And a very few feel burn,
And the rest, they may live and learn!

8

Then we would up and pace,
For a change, about the place,
  Each with arm o'er neck:
  'Tis our quarter-deck,
We are seamen in woeful case.
  Help in the ocean-space!
Or, if no help, we'll embrace.

9

See, how she looks now, dressed
In a sledging-cap and vest!
  'Tis a huge fur cloak –
  Like a reindeer's yoke
Falls the lappet along the breast:
  Sleeves for her arms to rest,
Or to hang, as my Love likes best.

10

Teach me to flirt a fan
As the Spanish ladies can,
  Or I tint your lip
  With a burnt stick's tip
And you turn into such a man!
  Just the two spots that span
Half the bill of the young male swan.

11

Dearest, three months ago
When the mesmerizer Snow
  With his hand's first sweep
  Put the earth to sleep:
'Twas a time when the heart could show
  All – how was earth to know,
'Neath the mute hand's to-and-fro?

12

Dearest, three months ago
When we loved each other so,
  Lived and loved the same
  Till an evening came
When a shaft from the devil's bow
  Pierced to our ingle-glow,
And the friends were friend and foe!

13

Not from the heart beneath –
'Twas a bubble born of breath,
  Neither sneer nor vaunt,
  Nor reproach nor taunt.
See a word, how it severeth!
  Oh, power of life and death
In the tongue, as the Preacher saith!

14

Woman, and will you cast
For a word, quite off at last
  Me, your own, your You, –
  Since, as truth is true,
I was You all the happy past –
  Me do you leave aghast
With the memories We amassed?

15

Love, if you knew the light
That your soul casts in my sight,
  How I look to you
  For the pure and true
And the beauteous and the right, –
  Bear with a moment's spite
When a mere mote threats the white!

16

What of a hasty word?
Is the fleshly heart not stirred
  By a worm's pin-prick
  Where its roots are quick?
See the eye, by a fly's foot blurred –
  Ear, when a straw is heard
Scratch the brain's coat of curd!

17

Foul be the world or fair
More or less, how can I care?
  'Tis the world the same
  For my praise or blame,

And endurance is easy there.
    Wrong in the one thing rare –
Oh, it is hard to bear!

18

Here's the spring back or close,
When the almond-blossom blows:
    We shall have the word
    In a minor third
There is none but the cuckoo knows:
    Heaps of the guelder-rose!
I must bear with it, I suppose.

19

Could but November come,
Were the noisy birds struck dumb
    At the warning slash
    Of his driver's-lash –
I would laugh like the valiant Thumb
    Facing the castle glum
And the giant's fee-faw-fum!

20

Then, were the world well stripped
Of the gear wherein equipped
    We can stand apart,
    Heart dispense with heart
In the sun, with the flowers unnipped, –
    Oh, the world's hangings ripped,
We were both in a bare-walled crypt!

21

Each in the crypt would cry
'But one freezes here! and why?
    'When a heart, as chill,
    'At my own would thrill
'Back to life, and its fires out-fly?
    'Heart, shall we live or die?
'The rest, … settle by-and-by!'

22

So, she'd efface the score,
And forgive me as before.
    It is twelve o'clock:
    I shall hear her knock
In the worst of a storm's uproar,
    I shall pull her through the door,
I shall have her for evermore!

## *Up at a Villa – Down in the City*

(As distinguished by an Italian person of quality)

1

Had I but plenty of money, money
    enough and to spare,
The house for me, no doubt, were a
    house in the city-square;
Ah, such a life, such a life, as one leads
    at the window there!

2

Something to see, by Bacchus,
    something to hear, at least!
There, the whole day long, one's life is
    a perfect feast;
While up at a villa one lives, I maintain
    it, no more than a beast.

3

Well now, look at our villa! stuck like
    the horn of a bull
Just on a mountain-edge as bare as the
    creature's skull,
Save a mere shag or a bush with hardly
    a leaf to pull!
– I scratch my own, sometimes, to see
    if the hair's turned wool.

4

But the dry, oh the city – the square
    with the houses! Why?
They are stone-faced, white as a curd,
    there's something to take the eye!
Houses in four straight lines, not a
    single front awry;
You watch who crosses and gossips,
    who saunters, who hurries by;
Green blinds, as a matter of course, to
    draw when the sun gets high;
And the shops with fanciful signs
    which are painted properly.

5

What of a villa? Though winter be over
    in March by rights,
'Tis May perhaps ere the snow shall
    have withered well off the heights:
You've the brown ploughed land
    before, where the oxen steam and
    wheeze,

And the hills over-smoked behind by
    the faint grey olive-trees.

6

Is it better in May, I ask you? You've
    summer all at once;
In a day he leaps complete with a few
    strong April suns.
'Mid the sharp short emerald wheat,
    scarce risen three fingers well,
The wild tulip, at end of its tube, blows
    out its great red bell
Like a thin clear bubble of blood, for
    the children to pick and sell.

7

Is it ever hot in the square? There's a
    fountain to spout and splash!
In the shade it sings and springs; in the
    shine such foam-bows flash
On the horses with curling fish-tails,
    that prance and paddle and pash
Round the lady atop in her conch –
    fifty gazers do not abash,
Though all that she wears is some weeds
    round her waist in a sort of sash.

8

All the year long at the villa, nothing to
    see though you linger,
Except yon cypress that points like
    death's lean lifted forefinger.
Some think fireflies pretty, when they
    mix i' the corn and mingle,
Or thrid the stinking hemp till the
    stalks of it seem a-tingle.
Late August or early September, the
    stunning cicala is shrill,
And the bees keep their tiresome whine
    round the resinous firs on the hill.
Enough of the seasons, – I spare you
    the months of the fever and chill.

9

Ere you open your eyes in the city, the
    blessed church-bells begin:
No sooner the bells leave off than the
    diligence rattles in:
You get the pick of the news, and it
    costs you never a pin.

By-and-by there's the travelling doctor
    gives pills, lets blood, draws teeth;
Or the Pulcinello-trumpet breaks up
    the market beneath.
At the post-office such a scene-picture
    – the new play, piping hot!
And a notice how, only this morning,
    three Liberal thieves were shot.
Above it, behold the Archbishop's
    most fatherly of rebukes,
And beneath, with his crown and his
    lion, some little new law of the
    Duke's!
Or a sonnet with flowery marge, to the
    Reverend Don So-and-so
Who is Dante, Boccaccio, Petrarca,
    Saint Jerome and Cicero,
'And moreover,' (the sonnet goes
    rhyming,) 'the skirts of Saint Paul
    has reached,
'Having preached us those six Lent-
    lectures more unctuous than ever
    he preached.'
Noon strikes, – here sweeps the
    procession! our Lady borne
    smiling and smart
With a pink gauze gown all spangles,
    and seven swords stuck in her
    heart!
*Bang-whang-whang* goes the drum,
    *tootte-te-tootle* the fife;
No keeping one's haunches still: it's
    the greatest pleasure in life.

10

But bless you, it's dear – it's dear!
    fowls, wine, at double the rate.
They have clapped a new tax upon salt,
    and what oil pays passing the gate
It's a horror to think of. And so, the
    villa for me, not the city!
Beggars can scarcely be choosers: but
    still – ah, the pity, the pity!
Look, two and two go the priests, then
    the monks with cowls and sandals,
And the penitents dressed in white
    shirts, a-holding the yellow candles;

One, he carries a flag up straight, and
    another a cross with handles,
And the Duke's guard brings up the rear,
    for the better prevention of scandals:
*Bang-whang-whang* goes the drum,
    *tootle-te-tootle* the fife.
Oh, a day in the city-square, there is no
    such pleasure in life!

## A Toccata of Galuppi's

1

Oh Galuppi, Baldassaro, this is very
    sad to find!
I can hardly misconceive you; it would
    prove me deaf and blind;
But although I take your meaning, 'tis
    with such a heavy mind!

2

Here you come with your old music,
    and here's all the good it brings.
What, they lived once thus at Venice
    where the merchants were the
    kings,
Where Saint Mark's is, where the Doges
    used to wed the sea with rings?

3

Ay, because the sea's the street there;
    and 'tis arched by … what you
    call
… Shylock's bridge with houses on it,
    where they kept the carnival:
I was never out of England – it's as if I
    saw it all.

4

Did young people take their pleasure
    when the sea was warm in May?
Balls and masks begun at midnight,
    burning ever to mid-day,
When they made up fresh adventures
    for the morrow, do you say?

5

Was a lady such a lady, cheeks so
    round and lips so red, –
On her neck the small face buoyant,
    like a bell-flower on its bed,

O'er the breast's superb abundance
    where a man might base his head?

6

Well, and it was graceful of them –
    they'd break talk off and afford –
– She, to bite her mask's black velvet –
    he, to finger on his sword,
While you sat and played Toccatas,
    stately at the clavichord?

7

What? Those lesser thirds so plaintive,
    sixths diminished, sigh on sigh,
Told them something? Those
    suspensions, those solutions –
    'Must we die?'
Those commiserating sevenths – 'Life
    might last! we can but try!'

8

'Were you happy?' – 'Yes.' – 'And are
    you still as happy?' – 'Yes. And
    you?'
– 'Then, more kisses!' – 'Did /stop them,
    when a million seemed so few?'
Hark, the dominant's persistence till it
    must be answered to!

9

So, an octave struck the answer. Oh,
    they praised you, I dare say!
'Brave Galuppi! that was music! good
    alike at grave and gay!
'I can always leave off talking when I
    hear a master play!'

10

Then they left you for their pleasure:
    till in due time, one by one,
Some with lives that came to nothing,
    some with deeds as well undone,
Death stepped tacitly and took them
    where they never see the sun.

11

But when I sit down to reason, think to
    take my stand nor swerve,
While I triumph o'er a secret wrung
    from nature's close reserve,
In you come with your cold music till I
    creep thro' every nerve.

12

Yes, you, like a ghostly cricket, creaking
　　where a house was burned:
'Dust and ashes, dead and done with,
　　Venice spent what Venice earned.
'The soul, doubtless, is immortal –
　　where a soul can be discerned.

13

'Yours for instance: you know physics,
　　something of geology,
'Mathematics are your pastime; souls
　　shall rise in their degree;
'Butterflies may dread extinction, –
　　you'll not die, it cannot be!

14

'As for Venice and her people, merely
　　born to bloom and drop,
'Here on earth they bore their fruitage,
　　mirth and folly were the crop:
'What of soul was left, I wonder, when
　　the kissing had to stop?

15

'Dust and ashes!' So you creak it, and I
　　want the heart to scold.
Dear dead women, with such hair, too
　　– what's become of all the gold
Used to hang and brush their bosoms?
　　I feel chilly and grown old.

## Old Pictures in Florence

1

The morn when first it thunders in
　　March,
　　The eel in the pond gives a leap,
　　　they say:
As I leaned and looked over the aloed
　　arch
　　Of the villa-gate this warm March
　　　day.
No flash snapped, no dumb thunder
　　rolled
　　In the valley beneath where, white
　　　and wide
And washed by the morning water-gold,
　　Florence lay out on the mountain-
　　　side.

2

River and bridge and street and square
　　Lay mine, as much at my beck and
　　　call,
Through the live translucent bath of air,
　　As the sights in a magic crystal ball.
And of all I saw and of all I praised,
　　The most to praise and the best to see
Was the startling bell-tower Giotto raised:
　　But why did it more than startle me?

3

Giotto, how, with that soul of yours,
　　Could you play me false who loved
　　　you so?
Some slights if a certain heart endures
　　Yet it feels, I would have your fellows
　　　know!
I' faith, I perceive not why I should care
　　To break a silence that suits them
　　　best,
But the thing grows somewhat hard to
　　bear
　　When I find a Giotto join the rest.

4

On the arch where olives overhead
　　Print the blue sky with twig and leaf,
(That sharp-curled leaf which they never
　　shed)
　　'Twixt the aloes, I used to lean in
　　　chief,
And mark through the winter afternoons,
　　By a gift God grants me now and
　　　then,
In the mild decline of those suns like
　　moons,
　　Who walked in Florence, besides her
　　　men.

5

They might chirp and chaffer, come and
　　go
　　For pleasure or profit, her men alive –
My business was hardly with them, I
　　trow.
　　But with empty cells of the human
　　　hive;
– With the chapter-room, the cloister-
　　porch,

The church's apsis, aisle or nave,
Its crypt, one fingers along with a torch,
　Its face set full for the sun to shave.

### 6

Wherever a fresco peels and drops,
　Wherever an outline weakens and
　　wanes
Till the latest life in the painting stops,
　Stands One whom each fainter pulse-
　　tick pains:
One, wishful each scrap should clutch
　the brick,
　Each tinge not wholly escape the
　　plaster,
– A lion who dies of an ass's kick,
　The wronged great soul of an ancient
　　Master.

### 7

For oh, this world and the wrong it
　does!
　They are safe in heaven with their
　　backs to it,
The Michaels and Rafaels, you hum
　and buzz
　Round the works of, you of the little
　　wit!
Do their eyes contract to the earth's
　old scope,
　Now that they see God face to face,
And have all attained to be poets, I
　hope?
　'Tis their holiday now, in any case.

### 8

Much they reck of your praise and you!
　But the wronged great souls – can
　　they be quit
Of a world where their work is all to do,
　Where you style them, you of little
　　wit,
Old Master This and Early the Other,
　Not dreaming that Old and New are
　　fellows:
A younger succeeds to an elder brother,
　Da Vincis derive in good time from
　　Dellos.

### 9

And here where your praise might yield
　returns,
　And a handsome word or two give
　　help,
Here, after your kind, the mastiff girns
　And the puppy pack of poodles yelp.
What, not a word for Stefano there,
　Of brow once prominent and starry,
Called Nature's Ape and the world's
　despair
　For his peerless painting? (See Vasari.)

### 10

There stands the Master. Study, my
　friends,
　What a man's work comes to! So he
　　plans it,
Performs it, perfects it, makes amends
　For the tolling and moiling, and
　　then, *sic transit!*
Happier the thrifty blind-folk labour,
　With upturned eye while the hand is
　　busy,
Not sidling a glance at the coin of their
　neighbour!
　'Tis looking downward that makes
　　one dizzy.

### 11

'If you knew their work you would deal
　your dole.'
　May I take upon me to instruct you?
When Greek Art ran and reached the
　goal,
　Thus much had the world to boast
　　*in fructu* –
The Truth of Man, as by God first
　spoken,
　Which the actual generations garble,
Was re-uttered, and Soul (which Limbs
　betoken)
　And Limbs (Soul informs) made new
　　in marble.

12

So, you saw yourself as you wished you
    were,
    As you might have been, as you
        cannot be;
Earth here, rebuked by Olympus there:
    And grew content in your poor degree
With your little power, by those statues'
        godhead,
    And your little scope, by their eyes'
        full sway,
And your little grace, by their grace
        embodied,
    And your little date, by their forms
        that stay.

13

You would fain be kinglier, say, than I
    am?
    Even so, you will not sit like Theseus.
You would prove a model? The Son of
    Priam
    Has yet the advantage in arms' and
        knees' use.
You're wroth – can you slay your snake
    like Apollo?
    You're grieved – still Niobe's the
        grander!
You live – there's the Racers' frieze to
    follow:
    You die – there's the dying Alexander.

14

So, testing your weakness by their
    strength,
    Your meagre charms by their rounded
        beauty.
Measured by Art in your breadth and
    length,
    You learned – to submit is a mortal's
        duty.
– When I say 'you' 'tis the common
    soul,
    The collective, I mean: the race of
        Man
That receives life in parts to live in a
    whole,
    And grow here according to God's
        clear plan.

15

Growth came when, looking your last
    on them all,
    You turned your eyes inwardly one
        fine day
And cried with a start – What if we so
    small
    Be greater and grander the while
        than they?
Are they perfect of lineament, perfect of
    stature?
    In both, of such lower types are we
Precisely because of our wider nature;
    For time, theirs – ours, for eternity.

16

To-day's brief passion limits their range;
    It seethes with the morrow for us
        and more.
They are perfect – how else? they shall
    never change:
    We are faulty – why not? we have
        time in store.
The Artificer's hand is not arrested
    With us; we are rough-hewn, nowise
        polished:
They stand for our copy, and, once in
        vested
    With all they can teach, we shall see
        them abolished.

17

'Tis a life-long toil till our lump be
    leaven –
    The better! What's come to perfection
        perishes.
Things learned on earth, we shall
    practice in heaven:
    Works done least rapidly, Art most
        cherishes.
Thyself shalt afford the example, Giotto!
    Thy one work, not to decrease or
        diminish,
Done at a stroke, was just (was it not?)
    'O!'
    Thy great Campanile is still to finish.

### 18

Is it true that we are now, and shall be
    hereafter,
    But what and where depend on life's
        minute?
Hails heavenly cheer or infernal laughter
    Our first step out of the gulf or in it?
Shall Man, such step within his
    endeavour,
    Man's face, have no more play and
        action
Than joy which is crystallized for ever,
    Or grief, an eternal petrifaction?

### 19

On which I conclude, that the early
    painters,
    To cries of 'Greek Art and what more
        wish you?' –
Replied, 'To become now self-
    acquainters,
    'And paint man man, whatever the
        issue!
'Make new hopes shine through the
    flesh they fray,
    'New fears aggrandize the rags and
        tatters:
'To bring the invisible full into play!
    'Let the visible go to the dogs – what
        matters?'

### 20

Give these, I exhort you, their guerdon
    and glory
    For daring so much, before they well
        did it.
The first of the new, in our race's story,
    Beats the last of the old; 'tis no idle
        quiddit.
The worthies began a revolution,
    Which if on earth you intend to
        acknowledge,
Why, honour them now! (ends my
    allocution)
    Nor confer your degree when the
    folk leave college.

### 21

There's a fancy some lean to and
    others hate –
    That, when this life is ended, begins
New work for the soul in another state,
    Where it strives and gets weary,
    loses and wins:
Where the strong and the weak, this
    world's congeries,
    Repeat in large what they practised
    in small,
Through life after life in unlimited series;
    Only the scale's to be changed,
    that's all.

### 22

Yet I hardly know. When a soul has
    seen
    By the means of Evil that Good is
    best,
And, through earth and its noise, what
    is heaven's serene, –
    When our faith in the same has
    stood the test –
Why, the child grown man, you burn
    the rod,
    The uses of labour are surely done;
There remaineth a rest for the people
    of God:
    And I have had troubles enough, for
    one.

### 23

But at any rate I have loved the season
    Of Art's spring-birth so dim and dewy;
My sculptor is Nicolo the Pisan,
    My painter – who but Cimabue?
Nor ever was man of them all indeed,
    From these to Ghiberti and Ghirlan-
    dajo,
Could say that he missed my critic-
    meed.
    So, now to my special grievance –
    heigh ho!

### 24

Their ghosts still stand, as I said before,
    Watching each fresco flaked and
    rasped,

Blocked up, knocked out, or white-
washed o'er:
– No getting again what the church
has grasped!
The works on the wall must take their
chance;
'Works never conceded to England's
thick clime!'
(I hope they prefer their inheritance
Of a bucketful of Italian quick-lime.)

25

When they go at length, with such a
shaking
Of heads o'er the old delusion, sadly
Each master his way through the black
streets taking,
Where many a lost work breathes
though badly –
Why don't they bethink them of who
has merited?
Why not reveal, while their pictures
dree
Such doom, how a captive might be
out-ferreted?
Why is it they never remember me?

26

Not that I expect the great Bigordi,
Nor Sandro to hear me, chivalric,
bellicose;
Nor the wronged Lippino; and not a
word I
Say of a scrap of Frà Angelico's:
But are you too fine, Taddeo Gaddi,
To grant me a taste of your intonaco,
Some Jerome that seeks the heaven
with a sad eye?
Not a churlish saint, Lorenzo Monaco?

27

Could not the ghost with the close red
cap,
My Pollajolo, the twice a craftsman,
Save me a sample, give me the hap
Of a muscular Christ that shows the
draughtsman?
No Virgin by him the somewhat petty,
Of finical touch and tempera
crumbly –

Could not Alesso Baldovinetti
Contribute so much, I ask him
humbly?

28

Margheritone of Arezzo,
With the grave-clothes garb and
swaddling barret
(Why purse up mouth and beak in a
pet so,
You bald old saturnine poll-clawed
parrot?)
Not a poor glimmering Crucifixion,
Where in the foreground kneels the
donor?
If such remain, as is my conviction,
The hoarding it does you but little
honour.

29

They pass; for them the panels may
thrill,
The tempera grow alive and tinglish;
Their pictures are left to the mercies still
Of dealers and stealers, Jews and the
English,
Who, seeing mere money's worth in
their prize,
Will sell it to somebody calm as Zeno
At naked High Art, and in ecstasies
Before some clay-cold vile Carlino!

30

No matter for these! But Giotto, you,
Have you allowed, as the town-
tongues babble it, –
Oh, never! it shall not be counted true –
That a certain precious little tablet
Which Buonarroti eyed like a lover, –
Was buried so long in oblivion's
womb
And, left for another than I to discover,
Turns up at last! and to whom? – to
whom?

31

I, that have haunted the dim San Spirito,
(Or was it rather the Ognissanti?)
Patient on altar-step planting a weary
toe!

Nay, I shall have it yet! *Detur amanti!*
My Koh-i-noor – or (if that's a platitude)
    Jewel of Giamschid, the Persian Sofi's
      eye;
So, in anticipative gratitude,
    What if I take up my hope and
      prophesy?

32

When the hour grows ripe, and a certain
    dotard
    Is pitched, no parcel that needs
      invoicing,
To the worse side of the Mont Saint
    Gothard,
    We shall begin by way of rejoicing;
None of that shooting the sky (blank
    cartridge),
    Nor a civic guard, all plumes and
      lacquer,
Hunting Radetzky's soul like a partridge
    Over Morello with squib and cracker.

33

This time we'll shoot better game and
    bag 'em hot –
    No mere display at the stone of
      Dante,
But a kind of sober Witanagemot
    (Ex: 'Casa Guidi' *quod videos ante*)
Shall ponder, once Freedom restored
    to Florence,
    How Art may return that departed
    with her.
Go, hated house, go each trace of the
    Loraine's,
    And bring us the days of Orgagna
    hither!

34

How we shall prologize, how we shall
    perorate,
    Utter fit things upon art and history,
Feel truth at blood-heat and falsehood
    at zero rate,
    Make of the want of the age no
    mystery;
Contrast the fructuous and sterile eras,
    Show – monarchy ever its uncouth
    cub licks

Out of the bear's shape into Chimaera's,
    While Pure Art's birth is still the
    republic's.

35

Then one shall propose in a speech
    (curt Tuscan,
    Expurgate and sober, with scarcely
    an '*issimo*,')
To end now our half-told tale of
    Cambuscan,
    And turn the bell-tower's *alt* to
    *altissimo*:
And fine as the beak of a young beccaccia
    The Campanile, the Duomo's fit ally,
Shall soar up in gold full fifty braccia,
    Completing Florence, as Florence
    Italy.

36

Shall I be alive that morning the scaffold
    Is broken away, and the long-pent
    fire,
Like the golden hope of the world,
    unbaffled
    Springs from its sleep, and up goes
    the spire
While 'God and the People' plain for
    its motto,
    Thence the new tricolour flaps at the
    sky?
At least to foresee that glory of Giotto
    And Florence together, the first am I!

## 'De Gustibus – '

1

Your ghost will walk, you lover of trees,
    (If our loves remain)
      In an English lane,
By a cornfield-side a-flutter with poppies.
Hark, those two in the hazel coppice –
A boy and a girl, if the good fates please,
    Making love, say, –
      The happier they!
Draw yourself up from the light of the
    moon,
And let them pass, as they will too
    soon,

With the bean-flowers' boon,
And the blackbird's tune,
And May, and June!

2

What I love best in all the world
Is a castle, precipice-encurled,
In a gash of the wind-grieved Apennine.
Or look for me, old fellow of mine,
(If I get my head from out the mouth
O' the grave, and loose my spirit's bands,
And come again to the land of lands) –
In a sea-side house to the farther South,
Where the baked cicala dies of drouth,
And one sharp tree – 'tis a cypress –
    stands,
By the many hundred years red-rusted,
Rough iron-spiked, ripe fruit-o'ercrusted,
My sentinel to guard the sands
To the water's edge. For, what expands
Before the house, but the great opaque
Blue-breadth of sea without a break?
While, in the house, for ever crumbles
Some fragment of the frescoed walls,
From blisters where a scorpion sprawls.
A girl bare-footed brings, and tumbles
Down on the pavement, green-flesh
    melons,
And says there's news to-day – the king
Was shot at, touched in the liver-wing,
Goes with his Bourbon arm in a sling:
– She hopes they have not caught the
    felons.
Italy, my Italy!
Queen Mary's saying serves for me –
        When fortune's malice
        Lost her – Calais) –
Open my heart and you will see
Graved inside of it, 'Italy.'
Such lovers old are I and she:
So it always was, so shall ever be!

## Home-Thoughts, from Abroad

1

Oh, to be in England
Now that April's there,
And whoever wakes in England
Sees, some morning, unaware,
That the lowest boughs and the brush-
    wood sheaf
Round the elm-tree bole are in tiny leaf,
While the chaffinch sings on the orchard
    bough
In England – now!

2

And after April, when May follows,
And the whitethroat builds, and all the
    swallows!
Hark, where my blossomed pear-tree in
    the hedge
Leans to the field and scatters on the
    clover
Blossoms and dewdrops – at the bent
    spray's edge –
That's the wise thrush; he sings each
    song twice over,
Lest you should think he never could
    recapture
The first fine careless rapture!
And though the fields look rough with
    hoary dew,
All will be gay when noontide wakes
    anew
The buttercups, the little children's
    dower
– Far brighter than this gaudy melon-
    flower!

## Home-Thoughts, from the Sea

Nobly, nobly Cape Saint Vincent to the
    North-west died away;
Sunset ran, one glorious blood-red,
    reeking into Cadiz Bay;
Bluish 'mid the burning water, full in
    face Trafalgar lay;
In the dimmest North-east distance
    dawned Gibraltar grand and grey:

'Here and here did England help me:
    how can I help England?' – say,
Whoso turns as I, this evening, turn to
    God to praise and pray,
While Jove's planet rises yonder, silent
    over Africa.

## Saul

1

Said Abner, 'At last thou art come! Ere
    I tell, ere thou speak,
'Kiss my cheek, wish me well!' Then I
    wished it, and did kiss his cheek.
And he, 'Since the King, O my friend,
    for thy countenance sent,
'Neither drunken nor eaten have we;
    nor until from his tent
'Thou return with the joyful assurance
    the King liveth yet,
'Shall our lip with the honey be bright,
    with the water be wet.
'For out of the black mid-tent's silence,
    a space of three days,
'Not a sound hath escaped to thy
    servants, of prayer nor of praise,
'To betoken that Saul and the Spirit
    have ended their strife,
'And that, faint in his triumph, the
    monarch sinks back upon life.

2

'Yet now my heart leaps, O beloved!
    God's child with his dew
'On thy gracious gold hair, and those
    lilies still living and blue
'Just broken to twine round thy harp-
    strings, as if no wild heat
'Were now raging to torture the desert!'

3

            Then I, as was meet,
Knelt down to the God of my fathers,
    and rose on my feet,
And ran o'er the sand burnt to powder.
    The tent was unlooped;
I pulled up the spear that obstructed,
    and under I stooped;

Hands and knees on the slippery grass-
    patch, all withered and gone,
That extends to the second enclosure, I
    groped my way on
Till I felt where the foldskirts fly open.
    Then once more I prayed,
And opened the foldskirts and entered,
    and was not afraid
But spoke, 'Here is David, thy servant!'
    And no voice replied.
At the first I saw nought but the
    blackness; but soon I descried
A something more black than the
    blackness – the vast, the upright
Main prop which sustains the pavilion:
    and slow into sight
Grew a figure against it, gigantic and
    blackest of all.
Then a sunbeam, that burst thro' the
    tent-roof, showed Saul.

4

He stood as erect as that tent-prop,
    both arms stretched out wide
On the great cross-support in the
    centre, that goes to each side;
He relaxed not a muscle, but hung
    there as, caught in his pangs,
And waiting his change, the king-
    serpent all heavily hangs.
Far away from his land, in the pine, till
    deliverance come
With the spring-time, – so agonized
    Saul, drear and stark, blind and
    dumb.

5

Then I tuned my harp, – took off the
    lilies we twine round its chords
Lest they snap 'neath the stress of the
    noontide – those sunbeams like
    swords!
And I first played the tune all our
    sheep know, as, one after one,
So docile they come to the pen-door till
    folding be done.
They are white and untorn by the
    bushes, for lo, they have fed

Where the long grasses stifle the water
　　within the stream's bed;
And now one after one seeks its
　　lodging, as star follows star
Into eve and the blue far above us, – so
　　blue and so far!

6

– Then the tune, for which quails on the
　　cornland win each leave his mate
To fly after the player; then, what
　　makes the crickets elate
Till for boldness they fight one another:
　　and then, what has weight
To set the quick jerboa a-musing
　　outside his sand house –
There are none such as he for a
　　wonder, half bird and half mouse!
God made all the creatures and gave
　　them our love and our fear,
To give sign, we and they are his
　　children, one family here.

7

Then I played the help-tune of our
　　reapers, their wine-song, when
　　hand
Grasps at hand, eye lights eye in good
　　friendship, and great hearts expand
And grow one in the sense of this
　　world's life. – And then, the last
　　song
When the dead man is praised on his
　　journey – 'Bear, bear him along
'With his few faults shut up like dead
　　flowerets! Are balm-seeds not here
'To console us? The land has none left
　　such as he on the bier.
'Oh, would we might keep thee, my
　　brother!' – And then, the glad
　　chaunt
Of the marriage, – first go the young
　　maidens, next, she whom we vaunt
As the beauty, the pride of our
　　dwelling. – And then, the great
　　march
Wherein man runs to man to assist
　　him and buttress an arch

Nought can break; who shall harm
　　them, our friends? – Then, the
　　chorus in toned
As the Levites go up to the altar in
　　glory enthroned.
But I stopped here: for here in the
　　darkness Saul groaned.

8

And I paused, held my breath in such
　　silence, and listened apart;
And the tent shook, for mighty Saul
　　shuddered: and sparkles 'gandart
From the jewels that woke in his
　　turban, at once with a start,
All its lordly male-sapphires, and
　　rubies courageous at heart.
So the head: but the body still moved
　　not, still hung there erect.
And I bent once again to my playing,
　　pursued it unchecked,
As I sang, –

9

　'Oh, our manhood's prime vigour!
　　No spirit feels waste,
'Not a muscle is stopped in its playing
　　nor sinew unbraced.
'Oh, the wild joys of living! the leaping
　　from rock up to rock,
'The strong rending of boughs from the
　　fir-tree, the cool silver shock
'Of the plunge in a pool's living water,
　　the hunt of the bear,
'And the sultriness showing the Lion is
　　couched in his lair.
'And the meal, the rich dates yellowed
　　over with gold dust divine,
'And the locust-flesh steeped in the
　　pitcher, the full draught of wine,
'And the sleep in the dried river-
　　channel where bulrushes tell
'That the water was wont to go
　　warbling so softly and well.
'How good is man's life, the mere
　　living! how fit to employ
'All the heart and the soul and the
　　senses for ever in joy!

'Hast thou loved the white locks of thy
    father, whose sword thou didst
    guard
'When he trusted thee forth with the
    armies, for glorious reward?
'Didst thou see the thin hands of thy
    mother, held up as men sung
'The low song of the nearly-departed,
    and hear her faint tongue
'Joining in while it could to the
    witness, "Let one more attest,
' "I have lived, seen God's hand thro' a
    lifetime, and all was for best"?
'Then they sung thro' their tears in
    strong triumph, not much, but
    the rest.
'And thy brothers, the help and the
    contest, the working whence grew
'Such result as, from seething grape-
    bundles, the spirit strained true:
'And the friends of thy boyhood – that
    boyhood of wonder and hope,
'Present promise and wealth of the
    future beyond the eye's scope, –
'Till lo, thou art grown to a monarch; a
    people is thine;
'And all gifts, which the world offers
    singly, on one head combine!
'On one head, all the beauty and
    strength, love and rage (like the
    throe
'That, a-work in the rock, helps its
    labour and lets the gold go)
'High ambition and deeds which surpass
    it, fame crowning them, – all
'Brought to blaze on the head of one
    creature, – King Saul!'
            10
And lo, with that leap of my spirit, –
    heart, hand, harp and voice,
Each lifting Saul's name out of sorrow,
    each bidding rejoice
Saul's fame in the light it was made for
    – as when, dare I say,
The Lord's army, in rapture of service,
    strains through its array,

And upsoareth the cherubim-chariot –
    'Saul!' cried I, and stopped,
And waited the thing that should follow.
    Then Saul, who hung propped
By the tent's cross-support in the
    centre, was struck by his name.
Have ye seen when Spring's arrowy
    summons goes right to the aim,
And some mountain, the last to
    withstand her. that held (he alone,
While the vale laughed in freedom and
    flowers) on a broad bust of stone
A year's snow bound about for a breast
    plate, – leaves grasp of the sheet?
Fold on fold all at once it crowds
    thunderously down to his feet,
And there fronts you, stark, black, but
    alive yet, your mountain of old,
With his rents, the successive
    bequeathings of ages untold –
Yea, each harm got in fighting your
    battles, each furrow and scar
Of his head thrust 'twixt you and the
    tempest – all hail, there they are!
– Now again to be softened with
    verdure, again hold the nest
Of the dove, tempt the goat and its
    young to the green on his crest
For their food in the ardours of summer.
    One long shudder thrilled
All the tent till the very air tingled, then
    sank and was stilled
At the King's self left standing before
    me, released and aware.
What was gone, what remained? All to
    traverse, 'twixt hope and despair;
Death was past, life not come: so he
    waited. Awhile his right hand
Held the brow, helped the eyes left too
    vacant forthwith to remand
To their place what new objects should
    enter: 'twas Saul as before.
I looked up and dared gaze at those
    eyes, nor was hurt any more
Than by slow pallid sunsets in
    autumn, ye watch from the shore,

At their sad level gaze o'er the ocean –
    a sun's slow decline
Over hills which, resolved in stern
    silence, o'erlap and entwine
Base with base to knit strength more in
    tensely: so, arm folded arm
O'er the chest whose slow heavings
    subsided.

11

    What spell or what charm,
(For, awhile there was trouble within
    me) what next should I urge
To sustain him where song had
    restored him? – Song filled to the
    verge
His cup with the wine of this life,
    pressing all that it yields
Of mere fruitage, the strength and the
    beauty: beyond, on what fields,
Glean a vintage more potent and
    perfect to brighten the eye
And bring blood to the lip, and commend
    them the cup they put by?
He saith, 'It is good;' still he drinks
    not: he lets me praise life,
Gives assent, yet would die for his own
    part.

12

    Then fancies grew rife
Which had come long ago on the
    pasture, when round me the sheep
Fed in silence – above, the one eagle
    wheeled slow as in sleep;
And I lay in my hollow and mused on
    the world that might lie
'Neath his ken, though I saw but the
    strip 'twixt the hill and the sky:
And I laughed – 'Since my days are
    ordained to be passed with my
    flocks,
'Let me people at least, with my
    fancies, the plains and the rocks,
'Dream the life I am never to mix with,
    and image the show
'Of mankind as they live in those
    fashions I hardly shall know!

'Schemes of life, its best rules and right
    uses, the courage that gains,
'And the prudence that keeps what men
    strive for.' And now these old trains
Of vague thought came again; I grew
    surer; so, once more the string
Of my harp made response to my
    spirit, as thus –

13

    'Yea, my King,'
I began – 'thou dost well in rejecting
    mere comforts that spring
'From the mere mortal life held in
    common by man and by brute:
'In our flesh grows the branch of this
    life, in our soul it bears fruit.
'Thou hast marked the slow rise of the
    tree, – how its stem trembled first
'Till it passed the kid's lip, the stag's
    antler; then safely outburst
'The fan-branches all round; and thou
    mindest when these too, in turn
'Broke a-bloom and the palm-tree
    seemed perfect: yet more was to
    learn,
'E'en the good that comes in with the
    palm-fruit. Our dates shall we
    slight,
'When their juice brings a cure for all
    sorrow? or care for the plight
'Of the palm's self whose slow growth
    produced them? Not so! stem and
    branch
'Shall decay, nor be known in their
    place, while the palm-wine shall
    staunch
'Every wound of man's spirit in winter.
    I pour thee such wine.
'Leave the flesh to the fate it was fit for!
    the spirit be thine!
'By the spirit, when age shall o'ercome
    thee, thou still shaft enjoy
'More indeed, than at first when
    inconscious, the life of a boy.
'Crush that life, and behold its wine
    running! Each deed thou hast
    done

'Dies, revives, goes to work in the
    world; until e'en as the sun
'Looking down on the earth, though
    clouds spoil him, though
    tempests efface,
'Can find nothing his own deed pro-
    duced not, must everywhere trace
'The results of his past summer-prime,
    – so, each ray of thy will,
'Every flash of thy passion and
    prowess, long over, shall thrill
'Thy whole people, the countless, with
    ardour, till they too give forth
'A like cheer to their sons, who in turn,
    fill the South and the North
'With the radiance thy deed was the
    germ of. Carouse in the past!
'But the license of age has its limit;
    thou diest at last:
'As the lion when age dims his eyeball,
    the rose at her height,
'So with man – so his power and his
    beauty for ever take flight.
'No! Again a long draught of my soul-
    wine! Look forth o'er the years!
'Thou hast done now with eyes for the
    actual; begin with the seer's!
'Is Saul dead? In the depth of the vale
    make his tomb – bid arise
'A grey mountain of marble heaped
    four-square, till, built to the skies,
'Let it mark where the great First King
    slumbers: whose fame would ye
    know?
'Up above see the rock's naked face,
    where the record shall go
'In great characters cut by the scribe, –
    Such was Saul, so he did;
'With the sages directing the work, by
    the populace chid, –
'For not half, they'll affirm, is comprised
    there! Which fault to amend,
'In the grove with his kind grows the
    cedar, whereon they shall spend
'(See, in tablets 'tis level before them)
    their praise, and record

'With the gold of the graver, Saul's
    story, – the statesman's great
    word
'Side by side with the poet's sweet
    comment. The river's a-wave
'With smooth paper-reeds grazing each
    other when prophet-winds rave:
'So the pen gives unborn generations
    their due and their part
'In thy being! Then, first of the mighty,
    thank God that thou art!'

14

And behold while I sang … but O
    Thou who didst grant me that day,
And before it not seldom hast granted
    thy help to essay,
Carry on and complete an adventure, –
    my shield and my sword
In that act where my soul was thy
    servant, thy word was my word, –
Still be with me, who then at the
    summit of human endeavour
And scaling the highest, man's thought
    could, gawd hopeless as ever
On the new stretch of heaven above
    me – till, mighty to save,
Just one lift of thy hand cleared that
    distance – God's throne from
    man's grave!
Let me tell out my tale to its ending –
    my voice to my heart
Which can scarce dare believe in what
    marvels last night I took part,
As this morning I gather the fragments,
    alone with my sheep,
And still fear lest the terrible glory
    evanish like sleep!
For I wake in the grey dewy covert,
    while Hebron upheaves
The dawn struggling with night on his
    shoulder, and Kidron retrieves
Slow the damage of yesterday's sunshine.

15

  I say then, – my song
While I sang thus, assuring the monarch,
    and ever more strong

Made a proffer of good to console him
  – he slowly resumed
His old motions and habitudes kingly.
  The right-hand replumed
His black locks to their wonted
  composure, adjusted the swathes
Of his turban, and see – the huge sweat
  that his countenance bathes,
He wipes off with the robe; and he
  girds now his loins as of yore,
And feels slow for the armlets of price,
  with the clasp set before.
He is Saul, ye remember in glory, – ere
  error had bent
The broad brow from the daily
  communion; and still, though
  much spent
Be the life and the bearing that front
  you, the same, God did choose,
To receive what a man may waste,
  desecrate, never quite lose.
So sank he along by the tent-prop till,
  stayed by the pile
Of his armour and war-cloak and
  garments, he leaned there awhile,
And sat out my singing, – one arm
  round the tent-prop, to raise
His bent head, and the other hung
  slack – till I touched on the praise
I foresaw from all men in all time, to
  the man patient there;
And thus ended, the harp falling
  forward. Then first I was 'ware
That he sat, as I say, with my head just
  above his vast knees
Which were thrust out on each side
  around me, like oak-roots which
  please
To encircle a lamb when it slumbers. I
  looked up to know
If the best I could do had brought
  solace: he spoke not, but slow
Lifted up the hand slack at his side, till
  he laid it with care
Soft and grave, but in mild settled will,
  on my brow: thro' my hair

The large fingers were pushed, and he
  bent back my head, with kind
  power –
All my face back, intent to peruse it, as
  men do a flower.
Thus held he me there with his great
  eyes that scrutinized mine –
And oh, all my heart how it loved him!
  but where was the sign?
I yearned – 'Could I help thee, my
  father, inventing a bliss,
'I would add, to that life of the past,
  both the future and this;
'I would give thee new life altogether,
  as good, ages hence,
'As this moment, – had love but the
  warrant, love's heart to dispense!'

16

Then the truth came upon me. No harp
  more – no song more! outbroke –

17

'I have gone the whole round of creation:
  I saw and I spoke:
'I, a work of God's hand for that
  purpose, received in my brain
'And pronounced on the rest of his
  hand work – returned him again
'His creation's approval or censure: I
  spoke as I saw:
'I report, as a man may of God's work
  – all's love, yet all's law.
'Now I lay down the judgeship he lent
  me. Each faculty tasked
'To perceive him, has gained an abyss,
  where a dewdrop was asked.
'Have! knowledge? confounded it
  shrivels at Wisdom laid bare.
'Have I forethought? how purblind,
  how blank, to the Infinite Care!
'Do I task any faculty highest, to image
  success?
'I but open my eyes, – and perfection,
  no more and no less,
'In the kind I imagined, full-fronts me,
  and God is seen God
'In the star, in the stone, in the flesh,
  in the soul and the clod.

'And thus looking within and around
    me, I ever renew
'(With that stoop of the soul which in
    bending upraises it too)
'The submission of man's nothing-
    perfect to God's all-complete,
'As by each new obeisance in spirit, I
    climb to his feet.
'Yet with all this abounding experience,
    this deity known,
'I shall dare to discover some province,
    some gift of my own.
'There's a faculty pleasant to exercise,
    hard to hoodwink,
'I am fain to keep still in abeyance, (I
    laugh as I think)
'Lest, insisting to claim and parade in
    it, wot ye, I worst
'E'en the Giver in one gift. – Behold, I
    could love if I durst!
'But I sink the pretension as fearing a
    man may o'ertake
'God's own speed in the one way of
    love: I abstain for love's sake.
'  – What, my soul? see thus far and no
    farther? when doors great and small,
'Nine-and-ninety flew ope at our touch,
    should the hundredth appal?
'In the least things have faith, yet
    distrust in the greatest of all?
'Do I find love so full in my nature,
    God's ultimate gift,
'That I doubt his own love can compete
    with it? Here, the parts shift?
'Here, the creature surpass the Creator,
    – the end, what Began?
'Would I fain in my impotent yearning
    do all for this man,
And dare doubt he alone shall not help
    him, who yet alone can?
'Would it ever have entered my mind,
    the bare will, much less power,
'To bestow on this Saul what I sang of,
    the marvellous dower
'Of the life he was gifted and filled
    with? to make such a soul,

'Such a body, and then such an earth
    for insphering the whole?
'And doth it not enter my mind (as my
    warm tears attest)
'These good things being given, to go
    on, and give one more, the best?
'Ay, to save and redeem and restore
    him, maintain at the height
'This perfection, – succeed with life's
    day-spring, death's minute of night?
'Interpose at the difficult minute,
    snatch Saul the mistake,
'Saul the failure, the ruin he seems
    now, – and bid him awake
'From the dream, the probation, the
    prelude, to find himself set
'Clear and safe in new light and new
    life, – a new harmony yet
'To be run, and continued, and ended
    – who knows? – or endure!
'The man taught enough, by life's
    dream, of the rest to make sure;
'By the pain-throb, triumphantly
    winning intensified bliss,
'And the next world's reward and
    repose, by the struggles in this.

### 18

'I believe it! 'Tis thou, God, that givest,
    'tis I who receive:
'In the first is the last, in thy will is my
    power to believe.
'All's one gift: thou canst grant it
    moreover, as prompt to my prayer
'As I breathe out this breath, as I open
    these arms to the air.
'From thy will, stream the worlds, life
    and nature, thy dread Sabaoth:
'I will? – the mere atoms despise me!
    Why am I not loth
'To look that, even that in the face too?
    Why is it I dare
'Think but lightly of such impuissance?
    What stops my despair?
'This; – 'tis not what man Does which
    exalts him, but what man Would
    do!

'See the King – I would help him but
    cannot, the wishes fall through.
'Could I wrestle to raise him from
    sorrow, grow poor to enrich,
'To fill up his life, starve my own out, I
    would – knowing which,
'I know that my service is perfect. Oh,
    speak through me now!
'Would I suffer for him that I love? So
    wouldst thou – so wilt thou!
'So shall crown thee the topmost,
    ineffablest, uttermost crown –
'And thy love fill infinitude wholly, nor
    leave up nor down
'One spot for the creature to stand in!
    It is by no breath,
'Turn of eye, wave of hand, that
    salvation joins issue with death!
'As thy Love is discovered almighty,
    almighty be proved
'Thy power, that exists with and for it,
    of being Beloved!
'He who did most, shall bear most; the
    strongest shall stand the most weak.
' 'Tis the weakness in strength, that I
    cry for! my flesh, that I seek
'In the Godhead! I seek and I find it. O
    Saul, it shall be
'A Face like my face that receives thee;
    a Man like to me,
'Thou shalt love and be loved by, for
    ever: a Hand like this hand
'Shall throw open the gates of new life
    to thee! See the Christ stand!'

19

I know not too well how I found my
    way home in the night.
There were witnesses, cohorts about
    me, to left and to right,
Angels, powers, the unuttered, unseen,
    the alive, the aware:
I repressed, I got through them as
    hardly, as strugglingly there,
As a runner beset by the populace
    famished for news –

Life or death. The whole earth was
    awakened, hell loosed with her
    crews;
And the stars of night beat with
    emotion, and tingled and shot
Out in fire the strong pain of pent
    knowledge: but I fainted not,
For the Hand still impelled me at once
    and supported, suppressed
All the tumult, and quenched it with
    quiet, and holy behest,
Till the rapture was shut in itself, and
    the earth sank to rest.
Anon at the dawn, all that trouble had
    withered from earth –
Not so much, but I saw it die out in
    the day's tender birth:
In the gathered intensity brought to the
    grey of the hills;
In the shuddering forests' held breath;
    in the sudden wind-thrills;
In the startled wild beasts that bore off,
    each with eye sidling still
Though averted with wonder and
    dread; in the birds stiff and chill
That rose heavily, as I approached
    them, made stupid with awe:
E'en the serpent that slid away silent, –
    he felt the new law.
The same stared in the white humid
    faces upturned by the flowers;
The same worked in the heart of the
    cedar and moved the vine-bowers:
And the little brooks witnessing
    murmured, persistent and low,
With their obstinate, all but hushed
    voices – 'E'en so, it is so!'

## My Star

All that I know
    Of a certain star
Is, it can throw
    (Like the angled spar)
Now a dart of red,
    Now a dart of blue;
Till my friends have said
    They would fain see, too,
My star that dartles the red and the blue!
Then it stops like a bird; like a flower,
    hangs furled:
  They must solace themselves with
    the Saturn above it.
What matter to me if their star is a
    world?
  Mine has opened its soul to me;
    therefore I love it.

## By the Fireside

### 1

How well I know what I mean to do
  When the long dark autumn-evenings
    come:
And where, my soul, is thy pleasant hue?
  With the music or all thy voices,
    dumb
In life's November too!

### 2

I shall be found by the fire, suppose,
  O'er a great wise book as beseemeth
    age,
While the shutters flap as the cross-
    wind blows
  And I turn the page, and I turn the
    page,
Not verse now, only prose!

### 3

Till the young ones whisper, finger on
    lip,
  'There he is at it, deep in Greek:
'Now then, or never, out we slip
  'To cut from the hazels by the creek
'A mainmast for our Ship!'

### 4

I shall be at it indeed, my friends:
  Greek puts already on either side
Such a branch-work forth as soon
    extend
  To a vista opening far and wide,
And I pass out where it ends.

### 5

The outside-frame, like your hazel-trees:
  But the inside-archway widens fast,
And a rarer sort succeeds to these,
  And we slope to Italy at last
And youth, by green degrees.

### 6

I follow wherever I am led,
  Knowing so well the leader's hand:
Oh woman-country, wooed not wed,
  Loved all the more by earth's male-
    lands,
Laid to their hearts instead!

### 7

Look at the ruined chapel again
  Half-way up in the Alpine gorge!
Is that a tower, I point you plain,
  Or is it a mill, or an iron-forge
Breaks solitude in vain?

### 8

A turn, and we stand in the heart of
    things:
  The woods are round us, heaped
    and dim;
From slab to slab how it slips and
    springs,
  The thread of water single and slim,
Through the ravage some torrent brings!

### 9

Does it feed the little lake below?
  That speck of white just on its marge
Is Pella; see, in the evening-glow,
  How sharp the silver spear-heads
    charge
When Alp meets heaven in snow!

### 10

On our other side is the straight-up
    rock;
  And a path is kept 'twixt the gorge
    and it

By boulder-stones where lichens mock
  The marks on a moth, and small
    ferns fit
Their teeth to the polished block.

11

Oh the sense of the yellow mountain-
    flowers,
  And thorny balls, each three in one,
The chestnuts throw on our path in
    showers!
    For the drop of the woodland fruit's
      begun,
These early November hours,

12

That crimson the creeper's leaf across
  Like a splash of blood, intense, abrupt,
O'er a shield else gold from rim to boss,
  And lay it for show on the fairy-
    cupped
Elf-needled mat of moss,

13

By the rose-flesh mushrooms, undivulged
  Last evening – nay, in to-day's first
    dew
Yon sudden coral nipple bulged,
  Where a freaked fawn-coloured flaky
    crew
Of toadstools peep indulged.

14

And yonder, at foot of the fronting
    ridge
  That takes the turn to a range beyond,
Is the chapel reached by the one-arched
    bridge
  Where the water is stopped in a
    stagnant pond
Danced over by the midge.

15

The chapel and bridge are of stone
    alike,
  Blackish-grey and mostly wet;
Cut hemp-stalks steep in the narrow
    dyke.
  See here again, how the lichens fret
And the roots of the ivy strike!

16

Poor little place, where its one priest
    comes
  On a festa-day, if he comes at all,
To the dozen folk from their scattered
    homes,
  Gathered within that precinct small
By the dozen ways one roams –

17

To drop from the charcoal-burners' huts,
  Or climb from the hemp-dressers'
    low shed,
Leave the grange where the woodman
    stores his nuts,
  Or the wattled cote where the fowlers
    spread
Their gear on the rock's bare juts.

18

It has some pretension too, this front,
  With its bit of fresco half-moon-wise
Set over the porch, Art's early wont:
  'Tis John in the Desert, I surmise,
But has borne the weather's brunt –

19

Not from the fault of the builder, though,
  For a pent-house properly projects
Where three carved beams make a
    certain show,
  Dating – good thought of our
    architect's –
'Five, six, nine, he lets you know.

20

And all day long a bird sings there,
  And a stray sheep drinks at the pond
    at times;
The place is silent and aware;
  It has had its scenes, its joys and
    crimes,
But that is its own affair.

21

My perfect wife, my Leonor,
  Oh heart, my own, oh eyes, mine too,
Whom else could I dare look backward
    for,
  With whom beside should I dare
    pursue
The path grey heads abhor?

### 22

For it leads to a crag's sheer edge with
     them;
     Youth, flowery all the way, there
          stops –
Not they; age threatens and they
     contemn,
     Till they reach the gulf wherein
          youth drops,
One inch from life's safe hem!

### 23

With me, youth led ... I will speak now,
     No longer watch you as you sit
Reading by fires-light, that great brow
     And the spirit-small hand propping it,
Mutely, my heart knows how –

### 24

When, if I think but deep enough,
     You are wont to answer, prompt as
          rhyme;
And you, too, find without rebuff
     Response your soul seeks many a time
Piercing its fine flesh-stuff.

### 25

My own, confirm me! If I tread
     This path back, is it not in pride
To think how little I dreamed it led
     To an age so blest that, by its side,
Youth seems the waste instead?

### 26

My own, see where the years conduct!
     At first, 'twas something our two souls
Should mix as mists do; each is sucked
     In each now: on, the new stream
          rolls,
Whatever rocks obstruct.

### 27

Think, when our one soul understands
     The great Word which makes all
          things new,
When earth breaks up and heaven
     expands,
     How will the change strike me and
          you
In the house not made with hands?

### 28

Oh I must feel your brain prompt mine,
     Your heart anticipate my heart,
You must be just before, in fine,
     See and make me see, for your part,
New depths of the divine!

### 29

But who could have expected this
     When we two drew together first
Just for the obvious human bliss,
     To satisfy life's daily thirst
With a thing men seldom miss?

### 30

Come back with me to the first of all,
     Let us lean and love it over again,
Let us now forget and now recall,
     Break the rosary in a pearly rain,
And gather what we let fall!

### 31

What did I say? – that a small bird sings
     All day long, save when a brown pair
Of hawks from the wood float with
     wide wings
     Strained to a bell: 'gainst noon-day
          glare
You count the streaks and rings.

### 32

But at afternoon or almost eve
     'Tis better; then the silence grows
To that degree, you half believe
     It must get rid of what it knows,
Its bosom does so heave.

### 33

Hither we walked then, side by side,
     Arm in arm and cheek to cheek,
And still I questioned or replied,
     While my heart, convulsed to really
          speak,
Lay choking in its pride.

### 34

Silent the crumbling bridge we cross,
     And pity and praise the chapel sweet,
And care about the fresco's loss,
     And wish for our souls a like retreat,
And wonder at the moss.

### 35

Stoop and kneel on the settle under,
  Look through the window's grated
    square:
Nothing to see! For fear of plunder,
  The cross is down and the altar bare,
As if thieves don't fear thunder.

### 36

We stoop and look in through the grate,
  See the little porch and rustic door,
Read duly the dead builder's date;
  Then cross the bridge that we crossed
    before,
Take the path again – but wait!

### 37

Oh moment, one and infinite!
  The water slips o'er stock and stone;
The West is tender, hardly bright:
  How grey at once is the evening
    grown –
One star, its chrysolite!

### 38

We two stood there with never a third,
  But each by each, as each knew well:
The sights we saw and the sounds we
    heard,
  The lights and the shades made up a
    spell
Till the trouble grew and stirred.

### 39

Oh, the little more, and how much it is!
  And the little less, and what worlds
    away!
How a sound shall quicken content to
    bliss,
  Or a breath suspend the blood's best
    play,
And life be a proof of this!

### 40

Had she willed it, still had stood the
    screen
  So slight, so sure, 'twixt my love and
    her:
I could fix her face with a guard between,
  And find her soul as when friends
    confer,
Friends – lovers that might have been.

### 41

For my heart had a touch of the wood-
    land-time,
  Wanting to sleep now over its best.
Shake the whole tree in the summer-
    prime,
  But bring to the last leaf no such test!
'Hold the last fast!' runs the rhyme.

### 42

For a chance to make your little much,
  To gain a lover and lose a friend,
Venture the tree and a myriad such,
  When nothing you mar but the year
    can mend:
But a last leaf – fear to touch!

### 43

Yet should it unfasten itself and fall
  Eddying down till it find your face
At some slight wind – best chance of all!
  Be your heart henceforth its dwelling-
    place
You trembled to forestall!

### 44

Worth how well, those dark grey eyes,
  That hair so dark and dear, how
    worth
That a man should strive and agonize,
  And taste a veriest hell on earth
For the hope of such a prize!

### 45

You might have turned and tried a man,
  Set him a space to weary and wear,
And prove which suited more your plan,
  His best of hope or his worst despair,
Yet end as he began.

### 46

But you spared me this, like the heart
    you are,
  And filled my empty heart at a word.
If two lives join, there is oft a scar,
  They are one and one, with a
    shadowy third;
One near one is too far.

#### 47

A moment after, and hands unseen
   Were hanging the night around us
     fast;
But we knew that a bar was broken
    between
   Life and life: we were mixed at last
In spite of the mortal screen.

#### 48

The forests had done it; there they
    stood;
   We caught for a moment the powers
    at play:
They had mingled us so, for once and
    good,
   Their work was done – we might go
    or stay,
They relapsed to their ancient mood.

#### 49

How the world is made for each of us!
   How all we perceive and know in it
Tends to some moment's product thus,
   When a soul declares itself – to wit,
By its fruit, the thing it does!

#### 50

Be hate that fruit or love that fruit,
   It forwards the general deed of man,
And each of the Many helps to recruit
   The life of the race by a general plan;
Each living his own, to boot.

#### 51

I am named and known by that
    moment's feat;
   There took my station and degree;
So grew my own small life complete,
   As nature obtained her best of me –
One born to love you, sweet!

#### 52

And to watch you sink by the fire-side
    now
   Back again, as you mutely sit
Musing by fire-light, that great brow
   And the spirit-small hand propping it,
Yonder, my heart knows how!

#### 53

So, earth has gained by one man the
    more,
   And the gain of earth must be
    heaven's gain too;
And the whole is well worth thinking
    o'er
   When autumn comes: which I mean
    to do
One day, as I said before.


### Any Wife to Any Husband

#### 1

My love, this is the bitterest, that thou
Who art all truth, and who dost love me
    now
   As thine eyes say, as thy voice breaks
    to say –
Shouldst love so truly, and couldst love
    me still
A whole long life through, had but love
    its will,
   Would death that leads me from thee
    brook delay.

#### 2

I have but to be by thee, and thy hand
Will never let mine go, nor heart with-
    stand
   The beating of my heart to reach its
    place.
When shall I look for thee and feel thee
    gone?
When cry for the old comfort and find
    none?
   Never, I know! Thy soul is in thy face.

#### 3

Oh, I should fade – 'tis willed so! Might
    I save,
Gladly I would, whatever beauty gave
   Joy to thy sense, for that was precious
    too.
It is not to be granted. But the soul
Whence the love comes, all ravage
    leaves that whole;
   Vainly the flesh fades; soul makes all
    things new.

#### 4

It would not be because my eye grew
dim
Thou couldst not find the love there,
thanks to Him
Who never is dishonoured in the
spark
He gave us from his fire of fires, and
bade
Remember whence it sprang, nor be
afraid
While that burns on, though all the
rest grow dark.

#### 5

So, how thou wouldst be perfect, white
and clean
Outside as inside, soul and soul's
demesne
Alike, this body given to show it by!
Oh, three-parts through the worst of
life's abyss,
What plaudits from the next world after
this,
Couldst thou repeat a stroke and
gain the sky!

#### 6

And is it not the bitterer to think
That, disengage our hands and thou
wilt sink
Although thy love was love in very
deed?
I know that nature! Pass a festive day,
Thou dost not throw its relic-flower
away
Nor bid its music's loitering echo
speed.

#### 7

Thou let'st the stranger's glove lie where
it fell;
If old things remain old things all is
well,
For thou art grateful as becomes man
best:
And hadst thou only heard me play one
tune,
Or viewed me from a window, not so
soon

With thee would such things fade as,
with the rest.

#### 8

I seem to see! We meet and part; 'tis
brief;
The book I opened keeps a folded leaf,
The very chair I sat on, breaks the
rank;
That is a portrait of me on the wall –
Three lines, my face comes at so slight
a call:
And for all this, one little hour to
thank!

#### 9

But now, because the hour through
years was fixed,
Because our inmost beings met and
mixed,
Because thou once hast loved me –
wilt thou dare
Say to thy soul and Who may list
beside,
'Therefore she is immortally my bride;
'Chance cannot change my love, nor
time impair.

#### 10

'So, what if in the dusk of life that's
left,
'I, a tired traveller of my sun bereft,
'Look from my path when, mimicking
the same,
'The fire-fly glimpses past me, come
and gone?
' – Where was it till the sunset? Where
anon
'It will be at the sunrise! What's to
blame?'

#### 11

Is it so helpful to thee? Canst thou take
The mimic up, nor, for the true thing's
sake,
Put gently by such efforts at a beam?
Is the remainder of the way so long,
Thou need'st the little solace, thou the
strong?
Watch out thy watch, let weak ones
doze and dream!

12

– Ah, but the fresher faces! 'Is it true,'
'Thou It ask, 'some eyes are beautiful
   and new?
   'Some hair, – how can one choose
   but grasp such wealth?
'And if a man would press his lips to
   lips
'Fresh as the wilding hedge-rose-cup
   there slips
   'The dew-drop out of, must it be by
   stealth?

13

'It cannot change the love still kept for
   Her,
'More than if such a picture I prefer
   'Passing a day with, to a room's bare
   side:
The painted form takes nothing she
   possessed,
Yet, while 'the Titian's Venus lies at rest,
   A man looks. Once more, what is
   there to chide?'

14

So must I see, from where I sit and
   watch,
My own self sell myself, my hand attach
   Its warrant to the very thefts from
   me –
Thy singleness of soul that made me
   proud,
Thy purity of heart I loved aloud,
   Thy man's-truth I was bold to bid
   God see!

15

Love so, then, if thou wilt! Give all
   thou canst
Away to the new faces – disentranced,
   (Say it and think it) obdurate no
   more:
Re-issue looks and words from the old
   mint,
Pass them afresh, no matter whose the
   print
   Image and superscription once they
   bore!

16

Re-coin thyself and give it them to
   spend, –
It all comes to the same thing at the
   end,
   Since mine thou wast, mine art and
   mine shalt be,
Faithful or faithless, sealing up the sum
Or lavish of my treasure, thou must
   come
   Back to the heart's place here I keep
   for thee!

17

Only, why should it be with stain at all?
Why must I, 'twixt the leaves of coronal,
   Put any kiss of pardon on thy brow?
Why need the other women know so
   much,
And talk together, 'Such the look and
   such
   'The smile he used to love with, then
   as now!'

18

Might I die last and show thee! Should
   I find
Such hardship in the few years left
   behind,
   If free to take and light my lamp, and
   go
Into thy tomb, and shut the door and
   sit,
Seeing thy face on those four sides of it
   The better that they are so blank, I
   know!

19

Why, time was what I wanted, to turn
   o'er
Within my mind each look, get more
   and more
   By heart each word, too much to
   learn at first;
And join thee all the fitter for the pause
'Neath the low doorway's lintel. That
   were cause
   For lingering, though thou calledst,
   if I durst!

20

And yet thou art the nobler of us two:
What dare I dream of, that thou canst
      not do,
   Outstripping my ten small steps
      with one stride?
I'll say then, here's a trial and a task –
Is it to bear? – if easy, I'll not ask:
   Though love fail, I can trust on in
      thy pride.

21

Pride? – when those eyes forestall the
      life behind
The death I have to go through! – when
      I find,
   Now that I want thy help most, all of
      thee!
What did I fear? Thy love shall hold me
      fast
Until the little minute's sleep is past
   And I wake saved. – And yet it will
      not be!

## Two in the Campagna

1

I wonder do you feel to-day
   As I have felt since, hand in hand,
We sat down on the grass, to stray
   In spirit better through the land,
This morn of Rome and May?

2

For me, I touched a thought, I know,
   Has tantalized me many times,
(Like turns of thread the spiders throw
   Mocking across our path) for rhymes
To catch at and let go.

3

Help me to hold it! First it left
   The yellowing fennel, run to seed
There, branching from the brickwork's
      cleft,
   Some old tomb's ruin: yonder weed
Took up the floating weft,

4

Where one small orange cup amassed
   Five beetles, – blind and green they
      grope
Among the honey-meal: and last,
   Everywhere on the grassy slope
I traced it. Hold it fast!

5

The champain with its endless fleece
   Of feathery grasses everywhere!
Silence and passion, joy and peace,
   An everlasting wash of air –
Rome's ghost since her decease.

6

Such life here, through such lengths of
      hours,
   Such miracles performed in play,
Such primal naked forms of flowers,
   Such letting nature have her way
While heaven looks from its towers!

7

How say you? Let us, O my dove,
   Let us be unashamed of soul,
As earth lies bare to heaven above!
   How is it under our control
To love or not to love?

8

I would that you were all to me,
   You that are just so much, no more.
Nor yours nor mine, nor slave nor free!
   Where does the fault lie? What the
      core
O' the wound, since wound must be?

9

I would I could adopt your will,
   See with your eyes, and set my heart
Beating by yours, and drink my fill
   At your soul's springs, – your part my
      part
In life, for good and ill.

10

No. I yearn upward, touch you close,
   Then stand away. I kiss your cheek,
Catch your soul's warmth, – I pluck
      the rose

And love it more than tongue can
    speak –
Then the good minute goes.

11

Already how am I so far
    Out of that minute? Must I go
Still like the thistle-ball, no bar,
    Onward, whenever light winds blow,
Fixed by no friendly star?

12

Just when I seemed about to learn!
    Where is the thread now? Off again!
The old trick! Only I discern –
    Infinite passion, and the pain
Of finite hearts that yearn.

## Misconceptions

1

This is a spray the Bird clung to,
    Making it blossom with pleasure,
Ere the high tree-top she sprung to,
    Fit for her nest and her treasure.
    Oh, what a hope beyond measure
Was the poor spray's, which the flying
    feet hung to, –
So to be singled out, built in, and sung
    to!

2

This is a heart the Queen leant on,
    Thrilled in a minute erratic,
Ere the true bosom she bent on,
    Meet for love's regal dalmatic.
    Oh, what a fancy ecstatic
Was the poor heart's, ere the wanderer
    went on –
Love to be saved for it, proffered to,
    spent on!

## A Serenade at the Villa

1

That was I, you heard last night,
    When there rose no moon at all,
Nor, to pierce the strained and tight
    Tent of heaven, a planet small:
Life was dead and so was light.

2

Not a twinkle from the fly,
    Not a glimmer from the worm;
When the crickets stopped their cry,
    When the owls forbore a term,
You heard music; that was I.

3

Earth turned in her sleep with pain,
    Sultrily suspired for proof:
In at heaven and out again,
    Lightning! – where it broke the roof,
Bloodlike, some few drops of rain.

4

What they could my words expressed,
    O my love, my all, my one!
Singing helped the verses best,
    And when singing's best was done,
To my lute I left the rest.

5

So wore the night; the East was gray,
    White the broad-faced hemlock-
        flowers:
There would be another day;
    Ere its first of heavy hours
Found me, I had passed away.

6

What became of all the hopes,
    Words and song and lute as well?
Say, this struck you – 'When life
        gropes
    'Feebly for the path where fell
'Light last on the evening slopes,

7

'One friend in that path shall be,
    'To secure my step from wrong;
'One to count night day for me,
    'Patient through the watches long,
'Serving most with none to see,'

8

Never say – as something bodes –
　'So, the worst has yet a worse!
'When life halts 'neath double loads,
　'Better the taskmaster's curse
'Than such music on the roads!

9

'When no moon succeeds the sun,
　'Nor can pierce the midnight's tent
'Any star, the smallest one,
　'While some drops, where lightning
　　rent,
'Show the final storm begun –

10

'When the fire-fly hides its spot,
　'When the garden-voices fail
'In the darkness thick and hot, –
　'Shall another voice avail,
'That shape be where these are not?

11

'Has some plague a longer lease,
　'Proffering its help uncouth?
'Can't one even die in peace?
　'As one shuts one's eyes on youth,
'Is that face the last one sees?'

12

Oh how dark your villa was,
　Windows fast and obdurate!
How the garden grudged me grass
　Where I stood – the iron gate
Ground its teeth to let me pass!

## One Way of Love

1

All June I bound the rose in sheaves.
Now, rose by rose, I strip the leaves
And strew them where Pauline may
　　pass.
She will not turn aside? Alas!
Let them lie. Suppose they die?
The chance was they might take her eye.

2

How many a month I strove to suit
These stubborn fingers to the lute!

To-day I venture all I know.
She will not hear my music? So!
Break the string; fold music's wing:
Suppose Pauline had bade me sing!

3

My whole life long I learned to love.
This hour my utmost art I prove
And speak my passion – heaven or hell?
She will not give me heaven? 'Tis well!
Lose who may – I still can say,
Those who win heaven, blest are they!

## Another Way of Love

1

June was not over
　　Though past the full,
And the best of her roses
　　Had yet to blow,
　　When a man I know
(But shall not discover,
　　Since ears are dull,
And time discloses)
Turned him and said with a man's true
　air,
Half sighing a smile in a yawn, as
　'twere, –
'If I tire of your June, will she greatly
　care?'

2

　　Well, dear, in-doors with you!
　　　True! serene deadness
Tries a man's temper.
　　What's in the blossom
　　June wears on her bosom?
Can it clear scores with you?
　　Sweetness and redness.
　　*Eadem semper!*
Go, let me care for it greatly or slightly!
If June mend her bower now, your hand
　left unsightly
By plucking the roses, – my June will
　do rightly.

3

And after, for pastime,
    If June be refulgent
With flowers in completeness,
    All petals, no prickles,
    Delicious as trickles
Of wine poured at mass-time, –
    And choose One indulgent
To redness and sweetness:
Or if, with experience of man and of
    spider,
June use my June-lightning, the strong
    insect-ridder,
And stop the fresh film-work, – why,
    June will consider.


## A Pretty Woman

1

That fawn-skin-dappled hair of hers,
    And the blue eye
    Dear and dewy,
And that infantine fresh air of hers!

2

To think men cannot take you, Sweet,
    And enfold you,
    Ay, and hold you,
And so keep you what they make you,
    Sweet!

3

You like us for a glance, you know –
    For a word's sake
    Or a sword's sake,
All's the same, whate'er the chance,
    you know.

4

And in turn we make you ours, we say –
    You and youth too,
    Eyes and mouth too,
All the face composed of flowers, we say.

5

All's our own, to make the most of,
    Sweet –
    Sing and say for,
    Watch and pray for,
Keep a secret or go boast of, Sweet!

6

But for loving, why, you would not,
    Sweet,
    Though we prayed you,
    Paid you, brayed you
In a mortar – for you could not, Sweet!

7

So, we leave the sweet face fondly
    there:
    Be its beauty
    Its sole duty!
Let all hope of grace beyond, lie there!

8

And while the face lies quiet there,
    Who shall wonder
    That I ponder
A conclusion? I will try it there.

9

As, – why must one, for the love
    foregone,
    Scout mere liking?
    Thunder-striking
Earth, – the heaven, we looked above
    for, gone!

10

Why, with beauty, needs there money
    be,
    Love with liking?
    Crush the fly-king
In his gauze, because no honey-bee?

11

May not liking be so simple-sweet,
    If love grew there
    'Twould undo there
All that breaks the cheek to dimples
    sweet?

12

Is the creature too imperfect, say?
    Would you mend it
    And so end it?
Since not all addition perfects aye!

13

Or is it of its kind, perhaps,
    Just perfection –
    Whence, rejection
Of a grace not to its mind, perhaps?

14

Shall we burn up, tread that face at
    once
        Into tinder,
        And so hinder
Sparks from kindling all the place at
    once?

15

Or else kiss away one's soul on her?
        Your love-fancies!
        – A sick man sees
Truer, when his hot eyes roll on her!

16

Thus the craftsman thinks to grace the
    rose, –
        Plucks a mould-flower
        For his gold flower,
Uses fine things that efface the rose:

17

Rosy rubies make its cup more rose,
        Precious metals
        Ape the petals, –
Last, some old king locks it up, morose!

18

Then how grace a rose? I know a way!
        Leave it, rather.
        Must you gather?
Smell, kiss, wear it – at last, throw away!


## Respectability

1

Dear, had the world in its caprice
    Deigned to proclaim 'I know you
        both,
    'Have recognized your plighted troth,
'Am sponsor for you: live in peace!' –
How many precious months and years
    Of youth had passed, that speed so
        fast,
    Before we found it out at last,
The world, and what it fears?

2

How much of priceless life were spent
    With men that every virtue decks,
    And women models of their sex,
Society's true ornament, –
Ere we dared wander, nights like this,
    Thro' wind and rain, and watch the
        Seine,
    And feel the Boulevart break again
To warmth and light and bliss?

3

I know! the world proscribes not love;
    Allows my finger to caress
    Your lips' contour and downiness,
Provided it supply a glove.
The world's good word! – the Institute!
    Guizot receives Montalembert!
    Eh? Down the court three lampions
        flare:
Put forward your best foot!


## Love in a Life

1

Room after room,
I hunt the house through
We inhabit together.
Heart, fear nothing, for, heart, thou
    shalt find her –
Next time, herself! – not the trouble
    behind her
Left in the curtain, the couch's perfume!
As she brushed it, the cornice-wreath
    blossomed anew:
Yon looking-glass gleamed at the wave
    of her feather.

2

Yet the day wears,
And door succeeds door;
I try the fresh fortune –
Range the wide house from the wing to
    the centre.
Still the same chance! she goes out as I
    enter.
Spend my whole day in the quest, –
    who cares?
But 'tis twilight, you see, – with such
    suites to explore,
Such closets to search, such alcoves to
    importune!

## Life in a Love

Escape me?
Never –
Beloved!
While I am I, and you are you,
  So long as the world contains us both,
  Me the loving and you the loth,
While the one eludes, must the other
    pursue.
My life is a fault at last, I fear:
  It seems too much like a fate, indeed!
  Though I do my best I shall scarce
    succeed.
But what if I fail of my purpose here?
It is but to keep the nerves at strain,
  To dry one's eyes and laugh at a fall,
And, baffled, get up and begin again, –
  So the chace takes up one's life,
    that's all.
While, look but once from your farthest
    bound
  At me so deep in the dust and dark,
No sooner the old hope goes to ground
  Than a new one, straight to the self-
    same mark,
I shape me –
Ever
Removed!

## In Three Days

1

So, I shall see her in three days
And just one night, but nights are short,
Then two long hours, and that is morn.
See how I come, unchanged, unworn!
Feel, where my life broke off from thine,
How fresh the splinters keep and fine, –
Only a touch and we combine!

2

Too long, this time of year, the days!
But nights, at least the nights are short.
As night shows where her one moon is,
A hand's-breadth of pure light and
    bliss,
So life's night gives my lady birth
And my eyes hold her! What is worth
The rest of heaven, the rest of earth?

3

O loaded curls, release your store
Of warmth and scent, as once before
The tingling hair did, lights and darks
Outbreaking into fairy sparks,
When under curl and curl I pried
After the warmth and scent inside,
Thro' lights and darks how manifold –
The dark inspired, the light controlled!
As early Art embrowns the gold.

4

What great fear, should one say, 'Three
    days                    ↲
'That change the world might change
    as well
'Your fortune; and if joy delays,
'Be happy that no worse befell!'
What small fear, if another says,
'Three days and one short night beside
'May throw no shadow on your ways;
'But years must teem with change
    untried,
'With chance not easily defied,
'With an end somewhere undescried.'
No fear! – or if a fear be born
This minute, it dies out in scorn.
Fear? I shall see her in three days
And one night, now the nights are short,
Then just two hours, and that is morn.

## In a Year

1

Never any more,
  While I live,
Need I hope to see his face
  As before.
Once his love grown chill,
  Mine may strive:
Bitterly we re-embrace,
  Single still.

2

Was it something said,
    Something done,
Vexed him? was it touch of hand,
    Turn of head?
Strange! that very way
    Love begun:
I as little understand
    Love's decay.

3

When I sewed or drew,
    I recall
How he looked as if I sung,
    – Sweetly too.
If I spoke a word,
    First of all
Up his cheek the colour sprung,
    Then he heard.

4

Sitting by my side,
    At my feet,
So he breathed but air I breathed,
    Satisfied!
I, too, at love's brim
    Touched the sweet:
I would die if death bequeathed
    Sweet to him.

5

'Speak, I love thee best!'
    He exclaimed:
'Let thy love my own foretell!'
    I confessed:
'Clasp my heart on thine
    'Now unblamed,
'Since upon thy soul as well
    'Hangeth mine!'

6

Was it wrong to own,
    Being truth?
Why should all the giving prove
    His alone?
I had wealth and ease,
    Beauty, youth:
Since my lover gave me love,
I gave these.

7

That was all I meant,
    – To be just,
And the passion I had raised,
    To content.
Since he chose to change
    Gold for dust,
If I gave him what he praised
    Was it strange?

8

Would he loved me yet,
    On and on,
While I found some way
undreamed
    – Paid my debt!
Gave more life and more,
    Till, all gone,
He should smile 'She never seemed
    'Mine before.

9

'What, she felt the while,
    'Must I think?
'Love's so different with us men!'
    He should smile:
'Dying for my sake –
    'White and pink!
'Can't we touch these bubbles then
    'But they break?'

10

Dear, the pang is brief,
    Do thy part,
Have thy pleasure! How perplexed
    Grows belief!
Well, this cold clay clod
    Was man's heart:
Crumble it, and what comes next?
    Is it God?

## Women and Roses

### 1

I dream of a red-rose tree.
And which of its roses three
Is the dearest rose to me?

### 2

Round and round, like a dance of snow
In a dazzling drift, as its guardians, go
Floating the women faded for ages,
Sculptured in stone, on the poet's pages.
Then follow women fresh and gay,
Living and loving and loved to-day.
Last, in the rear, flee the multitude of
    maidens,
Beauties yet unborn. And all, to one
    cadence,
They circle their rose on my rose tree.

### 3

Dear rose, thy term is reached,
Thy leaf hangs loose and bleached:
Bees pass it unimpeached.

### 4

Stay then, stoop, since I cannot climb,
You, great shapes of the antique time!
How shall I fix you, fire you, freeze you,
Break my heart at your feet to please
    you?
Oh, to possess and be possessed!
Hearts that beat 'neath each pallid
    breast!
Once but of love, the poesy, the passion,
Drink but once and die! – In vain, the
    same fashion,
They circle their rose on my rose tree.

### 5

Dear rose, thy joy's undimmed,
Thy cup is ruby-rimmed,
Thy cup's heart nectar-brimmed.

### 6

Deep, as drops from a statue's plinth
The bee sucked in by the hyacinth,
So will I bury me while burning,
Quench like him at a plunge my
    yearning,
Eyes in your eyes, lips on your lips!

Fold me fast where the cincture slips,
Prison all my soul in eternities of
    pleasure,
Girdle me for once! But no – the old
    measure,
They circle their rose on my rose tree.

### 7

Dear rose without a thorn,
Thy bud's the babe unborn:
First streak of a new morn.

### 8

Wings, lend wings for the cold, the
    clear!
What is far conquers what is near.
Roses will bloom nor want beholders,
Sprung from the dust where our flesh
    moulders.
What shall arrive with the cycle's change?
A novel grace and a beauty strange.
I will make an Eve, be the artist that
    began her,
Shaped her to his mind! – Alas! in like
    manner
They circle their rose on my rose tree.

## Before

### 1

Let them fight it out, friend! things have
    gone too far.
God must judge the couple: leave them
    as they are
– Whichever one's the guiltless, to his
    glory,
And whichever one the guilt's with, to
    my story!

### 2

Why, you would not bid men, sunk in
    such a slough,
Strike no arm out further, stick and
    stink as now,
Leaving right and wrong to settle the
    embroilment,
Heaven with snaky hell, in torture and
    entoilment?

3

Who's the culprit of them? How must
   he conceive
God – the queen he caps to, laughing
   in his sleeve,
' 'Tis but decent to profess oneself
   beneath her:
'Still, one must not be too much in
   earnest, either!'

4

Better sin the whole sin, sure that God
   observes;
Then go live his life out! Life will try his
   nerves,
When the sky, which noticed all,
   makes no disclosure,
And the earth keeps up her terrible
   composure.

5

Let him pace at pleasure, past the walls
   of rose,
Pluck their fruits when grape-trees
   graze him as he goes!
For he 'gins to guess the purpose of
   the garden,
With the sly mute thing, beside there,
   for a warden.

6

What's the leopard-dog-thing, constant
   at his side,
A leer and lie in every eye of its
   obsequious hide?
When will come an end to all the
   mock obeisance,
And the price appear that pays for the
   misfeasance?

7

So much for the culprit. Who's the
   martyred man?
Let him bear one stroke more, for be
   sure he can!
He that strove thus evil's lump with
   good to leaven,
Let him give his blood at last and get
   his heaven!

8

All or nothing, stake it! Trusts he God
   or no?
Thus far and no farther? farther? be
   it so!
Now, enough of your chicane of
   prudent pauses,
Sage provisos, sub-intents and saving-
   clauses!

9

Ah, 'forgive' you bid him? While God's
   champion lives,
Wrong shall be resisted: dead, why, he
   forgives.
But you must not end my friend ere
   you begin him;
Evil stands not crowned on earth,
   while breath is in him.

10

Once more – Will the wronger, at this
   last of all,
Dare to say, 'I did wrong,' rising in his
   fall?
No? – Let go, then! Both the fighters to
   their places!
While I count three, step you back as
   many paces!

*After*

Take the cloak from his face, and at first
   Let the corpse do its worst!
How he lies in his rights of a man!
   Death has done all death can.
And, absorbed in the new life he leads,
   He recks not, he heeds
Nor his wrong nor my vengeance; both
   strike
   On his senses alike,
And are lost in the solemn and strange
   Surprise of the change.
Ha, what avails death to erase
   His offence, my disgrace?
I would we were boys as of old
   In the field, by the fold:

His outrage, God's patience, man's scorn
    Were so easily borne!
I stand here now, he lies in his place:
    Cover the face!


## The Guardian-Angel

### A PICTURE AT FANO

1

Dear and great Angel, wouldst thou
        only leave
    That child, when thou hast done
        with him, for me!
Let me sit all the day here, that when eve
    Shall find performed thy special
        ministry,
And time come for departure, thou,
        suspending
Thy flight, mayst see another child for
        tending,
    Another still, to quiet and retrieve.
Then I shall feel thee step one step, no
        more,
From where thou standest now, to
        where I gaze,
– And suddenly my head is covered o'er
With those wings, white above the
        child who prays
Now on that tomb – and I shall feel
        thee guarding
Me, out of all the world; for me,
        discarding
    Yon heaven thy home, that waits
        and opes its door.

3

I would not look up thither past thy
        head
    Because the door opes, like that
        child, I know,
For I should have thy gracious face
        instead,
    Thou bird of God! And wilt thou
        bend me low
Like him, and lay, like his, my hands
        together,

And lift them up to pray, and gently
        tether
    Me, as thy lamb there, with thy
        garment's spread?

4

If this was ever granted, I would rest
    My head beneath thine, while thy
        healing hands
Close-covered both my eyes beside thy
        breast,
    Pressing the brain, which too much
        thought expands,
Back to its proper size again, and
        smoothing
Distortion down till every nerve had
        soothing,
    And all lay quiet, happy and
        suppressed.

5

How soon all worldly wrong would be
        repaired!
    I think how I should view the earth
        and skies
And sea, when once again my brow was
        bared
    After thy healing, with such different
        eyes.
O world, as God has made it! All is
        beauty:
And knowing this, is love, and love is
        duty.
    What further may be sought for or
        declared?

6

Guercino drew this angel I saw teach
    (Alfred, dear friend!) – that little
        child to pray,
Holding the little hands up, each to
        each
    Pressed gently, – with his own head
        turned away
Over the earth where so much lay
        before him
Of work to do, though heaven was
        opening o'er him,
    And he was left at Fano by the beach.

#### 7

We were at Fano, and three times we
went
   To sit and see him in his chapel there,
And drink his beauty to our soul's
content
   – My angel with me too: and since I
care
For dear Guercino's fame (to which in
power
And glory comes this picture for a dower,
   Fraught with a pathos so
magnificent) –

#### 8

And since he did not work thus
earnestly
   At all times, and has else endured
some wrong –
I took one thought his picture struck
from me,
   And spread it out, translating it to
song.
My love is here. Where are you, dear
old friend?
How rolls the Wairoa at your world's
far end?
   This is Ancona, yonder is the sea.

### Memorabilia

#### 1

Ah, did you once see Shelley plain,
   And did he stop and speak to you,
And did you speak to him again?
   How strange it seems and new!

#### 2

But you were living before that,
   And also you are living after;
And the memory I started at –
   My starting moves your laughter.

#### 3

I crossed a moor, with a name of its own
   And a certain use in the world no
doubt,
Yet a hand's-breadth of it shines alone
   'Mid the blank miles round about:

#### 4

For there I picked up on the heather
   And there I put inside my breast
A moulted feather, an eagle-feather!
   Well, I forget the rest.

### Popularity

#### 1

Stand still, true poet that you are!
   I know you; let me try and draw
you.
Some night you'll fail us: when afar
   You rise, remember one man saw
you,
Knew you, and named a star!

#### 2

My star, God's glow-worm! Why extend
   That loving hand of his which leads
you
Yet locks you safe from end to end
   Of this dark world, unless he needs
you,
Just saves your light to spend?

#### 3

His clenched hand shall unclose at
last,
   I know, and let out all the beauty:
My poet holds the future fast,
   Accepts the coming ages' duty,
Their present for this past.

#### 4

That day, the earth's feast-master's
brow
   Shall clear, to God the chalice
raising;
'Others give best at first, but thou
   'Forever set'st our table praising,
'Keep'st the good wine till now!'

#### 5

Meantime, I'll draw you as you stand,
   With few or none to watch and
wonder:
I'll say – a fisher, on the sand
   By Tyre the old, with ocean-plunder,
A netful, brought to land.

6

Who has not heard how Tyrian shells
    Enclosed the blue, that dye of dyes
Whereof one drop worked miracles,
    And coloured like Astarte's eyes
Raw silk the merchant sells?

7

And each bystander of them all
    Could criticize, and quote tradition
How depths of blue sublimed some pall
    – To get which, pricked a king's
        ambition;
Worth sceptre, crown and ball.

8

Yet there's the dye, in that rough mesh,
    The sea has only just o'erwhispered!
Live whelks, each lip's beard dripping
        fresh,
    As if they still the water's lisp heard
Through foam the rock-weeds thresh.

9

Enough to furnish Solomon
    Such hangings for his cedar-house,
That, when gold-robed he took the
        throne
    In that abyss of blue, the Spouse
Might swear his presence shone

10

Most like the centre-spike of gold
    Which burns deep in the blue-bell's
        womb,
What time, with ardours manifold,
    The bee goes singing to her groom,
Drunken and overbold.

11

Mere conchs! not fit for warp or woof!
    Till cunning come to pound and
        squeeze
And clarify, – refine to proof
    The liquor filtered by degrees,
While the world stands aloof.

12

And there's the extract, flasked and
        fine,
    And priced and saleable at last!

And Hobbs, Nobbs, Stokes and Nokes
        combine
    To paint the future from the past,
Put blue into their line.

13

Hobbs hints blue, – straight he turtle
        eats:
    Nobbs prints blue, – claret crowns
        his cup:
Nokes outdares Stokes in azure feats, –
    Both gorge. Who fished the murex
        up?
What porridge had John Keats?


## Master Hugues of Saxe-Gotha

1

Hist, but a word, fair and soft!
    Forth and be judged, Master Hugues!
Answer the question I've put you so oft:
    What do you mean by your
        mountainous fugues?
See, we're alone in the loft, –

2

I, the poor organist here,
    Hugues, the composer of note,
Dead though, and done with, this many
        a year:
    Let's have a colloquy, something to
        quote,
Make the world prick up its ear!

3

See, the church empties apace:
    Fast they extinguish the lights.
Hallo there, sacristan! Five minutes'
        grace!
    Here's a crank pedal wants setting to
        rights,
Baulks one of holding the base.

4

See, our huge house of the sounds,
    Hushing its hundreds at once,
Bids the last loiterer back to his bounds!
    – O you may challenge them, not a
        response
Get the church-saints on their rounds!

5

(Saints go their rounds, who shall doubt?
  – March, with the moon to admire,
Up nave, down chancel, turn transept
    about,
    Supervise all betwixt pavement and
    spire,
Put rats and mice to the rout –

6

Aloys and Jurien and Just –
  Order things back to their place,
Have a sharp eye lest the candlesticks
    rust,
    Rub the church-plate, darn the
    sacrament-lace,
Clear the desk-velvet of dust.)

7

Here's your book, younger folks shelve!
  Played I not off-hand and runningly,
Just now, your masterpiece, hard
    number twelve?
    Here's what should strike, could one
    handle it cunningly:
Help the axe, give it a helve!

8

Page after page as I played,
  Every bar's rest, where one wipes
Sweat from one's brow, I looked up and
    surveyed,
    O'er my three claviers, yon forest of
    pipes
Whence you still peeped in the shade.

9

Sure you were wishful to speak?
  You, with brow ruled like a score,
Yes, and eyes buried in pits on each
    cheek,
    Like two great breves, as they wrote
    them of yore,
Each side that bar, your straight beak!

10

Sure you said – 'Good, the mere notes!
  'Still, couldst thou take my intent,
'Know what procured me our Company's
    votes –

'A master were lauded and sciolists
    shent,
'Parted the sheep from the goats!'

11

Well then, speak up, never flinch!
  Quick, ere my candle's a snuff
– Burnt, do you see? to its uttermost
    inch –
    I believe in you, but that's not
    enough:
Give my conviction a clinch!

12

First you deliver your phrase
  – Nothing propound, that I see,
Fit in itself for much blame or much
    praise –
    Answered no less, where no answer
    needs be:
Off start the Two on their ways.

13

Straight must a Third interpose,
  Volunteer needlessly help;
In strikes a Fourth, a Fifth thrusts in
    his nose,
    So the cry's open, the kennel's a-
    yelp,
Argument's hot to the close.

14

One dissertates, he is candid;
  Two must discept, – has
    distinguished;
Three helps the couple, if ever yet man
    did;
    Four protests; Five makes a dart at
    the thing wished:
Back to One, goes the case bandied.

15

One says his say with a difference;
  More of expounding, explaining!
All now is wrangle, abuse, and
    vociferance;
    Now there's a truce, all's subdued,
    self-restraining:
Five, though, stands out all the stiffer
    hence.

16

One is incisive, corrosive;
  Two retorts, nettled, curt, crepitant;
Three makes rejoinder, expansive,
    explosive;
    Four overbears them all, strident
    and strepitant:
Five ... O Danaides, O Sieve!

17

Now, they ply axes and crowbars;
  Now, they prick pins at a tissue
Fine as a skein of the casuist Escobar's
    Worked on the bone of a lie. To
    what issue?
Where is our gain at the Two-bars?

18

*Est fuga, volvitur rota.*
    On we drift: where looms the dim
    port?
One, Two, Three, Four, Five,
    contribute their quota;
    Something is gained, if one caught
    but the import –
Show it us, Hugues of Saxe-Gotha!

19

What with affirming, denying,
  Holding, risposting, subjoining,
All's like ... it's like ... for an instance
    I'm trying ...
    There! See our roof, its gilt moulding
    and groining
Under those spider-webs lying!

20

So your fugue broadens and thickens,
    Greatens and deepens and
    lengthens,
Till we exclaim – 'But where's music,
    the dickens?
    'Blot ye the gold, while your spider-
    web strengthens
' – Blacked to the stoutest of tickens?'

21

I for man's effort am zealous:
    Prove me such censure unfounded!

Seems it surprising a lover grows
    jealous –
    Hopes 'twas for something, his
    organ-pipes sounded,
Tiring three boys at the bellows?

22

Is it your moral of life?
    Such a web, simple and subtle,
Weave we on earth here in impotert
    strife,
    Backward and forward each
    throwing his shuttle,
Death ending all with a knife?

23

Over our heads truth and nature –
    Still our life's zigzags and dodges,
Ins and outs, weaving a new
    legislature –
    God's gold just shining its last
    where that lodges,
Palled beneath man's usurpature.

24

So we o'ershroud stars and roses,
    Cherub and trophy and garland;
Nothings grow something which
    quietly closes
    Heaven's earnest eye: not a glimpse
    of the far land
Gets through our comments and
    glozes.

25

Ah but traditions, inventions,
    (Say we and make up a visage)
So many men with such various
    intentions,
    Down the past ages, must know
    more than this age!
Leave we the web its dimensions!

26

Who thinks Hugues wrote for the deaf,
    Proved a mere mountain in labour?
Better submit; try again; what's the clef?
    'Faith, 'tis no trifle tor pipe and for
    tabor –
Four flats, the minor in F.

27

Friend, your fugue taxes the finger:
    Learning it once, who would lose it?
Yet all the while a misgiving will linger,
    Truth's golden o'er us although we
        refuse it –
Nature, thro' cobwebs we string her.

28

Hugues! I advise *meâ pœnâ*
    (Counterpoint glares like a Gorgon)
Bid One, Two, Three, Four, Five, clear
    the arena!
    Say the word, straight I unstop the
        full-organ,
Blare out the *mode Palestrina*.

29

While in the roof, if I'm right there,
    ... Lo you, the wick in the socket!
Hallo, you sacristan, show us a light
    there!
    Down it dips, gone like a rocket.
What, you want, do you, to come
    unawares,
Sweeping the church up for first
    morning-prayers,
And find a poor devil has ended his
    cares
At the foot of your rotten-runged rat-
    riddled stairs?
    Do I carry the moon in my pocket?

# THE RETURN OF THE DRUSES

A Tragedy

1843

*Persons*

*The Grand-Master's* Prefect. *The Patriarch's* Nuncio. *The Republic's* Admiral.
Loys De Dreux, *Knight-Novice. Initiated Druses* – Djabal, Khalil, Anael, Maani,
Karshook, Raghib, Ayoob, *and others. Uninitiated Druses. Prefect's Guard.
Nuncio's Attendants. Admiral's Force.*

*Time, 14—. Place – An Islet of the Southern Sporades, colonized by
Druses of Lebanon, and garrisoned by the Knights-Hospitallers of Rhodes.
Scene – A Hall in the Prefect's Palace.*

## ACT 1

*Enter stealthily* KARSHOOK, RAGHIB,
AYOOB *and other initiated* DRUSES,
*each as he enters casting off a robe
that conceals his distinctive black
vest and white turban; then, as
giving a loose to exultation, –*

*Kar.* The moon is carried off in purple
fire:
Day breaks at last! Break glory, with the
day,
On Djabal's dread incarnate mystery
Now ready to resume its pristine shape
Of Hakeem, as the Khalif vanished erst
In what seemed death to uninstructed
eyes,
On red Mokattam's verge – our
Founder's flesh,
As he resumes our Founder's function!
*Ragh.*                              – Death
Sweep to the Christian Prefect that
enslaved
So long us sad Druse exiles o'er the sea!
*Ay.* Most joy be thine, O Mother-mount!
Thy brood
Returns to thee, no outcasts as we left,
But thus – but thus! Behind, our
Prefect's corse;
Before, a presence like the morning –
thine,
Absolute Djabal late, – God Hakeem
now
That day breaks!
*Kar.*     Off then, with disguise at last!

As from our forms this hateful garb we
strip,
Lose every tongue its glozing accent
too,
Discard each limb the ignoble gesture!
Cry,
'Tis the Druse Nation, warders on our
Mount
Of the world's secret, since the birth of
time,
– No kindred slips, no offsets from thy
stock,
No spawn of Christians are we, Prefect,
we
Who rise …
*Ay.*     Who shout …
*Ragh.*          Who seize, a first-fruits, ha –
Spoil of the spoiler! Brave!
     [*They begin to tear down, and to dispute
          for, the decorations of the hall.*
*Kar.*               Hold!
*Ay.*               – Mine, I say;
And mine shall it continue!
*Kar.*               Just this fringe!
Take anything beside! Lo, spire on spire,
Curl serpentwise wreathed columns to
the top
O' the roof, and hide themselves
mysteriously
Among the twinkling lights and darks
that haunt
Yon cornice! Where the huge veil, they
suspend

Before the Prefect's chamber of delight,
Floats wide, then falls again as if its
     slave,
The scented air, took heart now, and
     anon
Lost hearts to buoy its breadths of
     gorgeousness
Above the gloom they droop in – all
     the porch
Is jewelled o'er with frostwork charactery;
And, see, yon eight-point cross of
     white flame, winking
Hoar-silvery like some fresh-broke
     marble stone:
Raze out the Rhodian cross there, so
     thou leav'st me
This single fringe!
*Ay.*     Ha, wouldst thou, dog-fox? Help!
– Three hand-breadths of gold fringe,
     my son was set
To twist, the night he died!
*Kar.*               Nay, hear the knave!
And I could witness my one daughter
     borne,
A week since, to the Prefect's couch,
     yet fold
These arms, be mute, lest word of
     mine should mar
Our Master's work, delay the Prefect
     here
A day, prevent his sailing hence for
     Rhodes –
How know I else? – Hear me denied
     my right
By such a knave!
*Ragh.* [*interposing*]. Each ravage for
     himself!
Booty enough! On, Druses! Be there
     found
Blood and a heap behind us; with us,
     Djabal
Turned Hakeem; and before us,
     Lebanon!
Yields the porch? Spare not! There his
     minions dragged
Thy daughter, Karshook, to the
     Prefect's couch!

Ayoob! Thy son, to soothe the Prefect's
     pride,
Bent o'er that task, the death-sweat on
     his brow,
Carving the spice-tree's heart in scroll-
     work there!
Onward in Djabal's name!
  *As the tumult is at height, enter* KHALIL.
A pause and silence.
*Kha.*               Was it for this,
Djabal hath summoned you? Deserve
     you thus
A portion in to-day's event? What,
     here –
When most behoves your feet fall soft,
     your eyes
Sink low, your tongues lie still, – at
     Djabal's side,
Close in his very hearing, who, perchance,
Assumes e'en now God Hakeem's
     dreaded shape, –
Dispute you for these gauds?
*Ay.*               How say'st thou, Khalil?
Doubtless our Master prompts thee!
     Take the fringe,
Old Karshook! I supposed it was a
     day …
*Kha.* For pillage?
*Kar.*     Hearken, Khalil! Never spoke
A boy so like a song-bird; we avouch
     thee
Prettiest of all our Master's instruments
Except thy bright twin-sister; thou and
     Anael
Challenge his prime regard: but we may
     crave
(Such nothings as we be) a portion too
Of Djabal's favour; in him we believed,
His bound ourselves, him moon by
     moon obeyed,
Kept silence till this daybreak – so, may
     claim
Reward: who grudges me my claim?
*Ay.*                         To-day
Is not as yesterday!
*Ragh.*          Stand off!
*Kha.*                    Rebel you?

Must I, the delegate of Djabal, draw
His wrath on you, the day of our
    Return?
*Other Druses.* Wrench from their grasp
    the fringe! Hounds! must the
    earth
Vomit her plagues on us thro' thee? –
    and thee?
Plague me not, Khalil, for their fault!
*Kha.*                  Oh, shame!
Thus breaks to-day on you, the mystic
    tribe
Who, flying the approach of Osman,
    bore
Our faith, a merest spark, from Syria's
    ridge
Its birthplace, hither! 'Let the sea
    divide
'These hunters from their prey,' you
    said; 'and safe
'In this dim islet's virgin solitude
'Tend we our faith, the spark, till
    happier time
'Fan it to fire; till Hakeem rise again,
'According to his word that, in the flesh
'Which faded on Mokattam ages since,
'He, at our extreme need, would
    interpose
'And, reinstating all in power and bliss,
'Lead us himself to Lebanon once more.'
Was't not thus you departed years ago.
Ere I was born?
*Druses.*     'Twas even thus, years ago.
*Kha.* And did you call – (according to
    old laws
Which bid us, lest the sacred grow
    profane,
Assimilate ourselves in outward rites
With strangers fortune makes our
    lords, and live
As Christian with the Christian, Jew
    with Jew,
Druse only with the Druses) – did you
    call
Or no, to stand 'twixt you and Osman's
    rage
(Mad to pursue e'en hither thro' the sea

The remnant of our tribe), a race self-
    vowed
To endless warfare with his hordes and
    him,
The White-cross Knights of the
    adjacent Isle?
*Kar.* And why else rend we down,
    wrench up, rase out?
These Knights of Rhodes we thus
    solicited
For help, bestowed on us a fiercer pest
Than aught we fled – their Prefect; who
    began
His promised mere paternal governance
By a prompt massacre of all our Sheikhs
Able to thwart the Order in its scheme
Of crushing, with our nation's memory,
Each chance of our return, and taming
    us
Bondslaves to Rhodes for ever – all, he
    thinks
To end by this day's treason.
*Kha.*              Say I not?
You, fitted to the Order's purposes,
Your Sheikhs cut off, your rites, your
    garb proscribed,
Must yet receive one degradation more;
The Knights at last throw off the mask
    – transfer,
As tributary now and appanage,
This islet they are but protectors of,
To their own ever-craving liege, the
    Church,
Who licenses all crimes that pay her
    thus.
You, from their Prefect, were to be
    consigned
(Pursuant of I know not what vile pact)
To the Knights' Patriarch, ardent to
    out-vie
His predecessor in all wickedness.
When suddenly rose Djabal in the
    midst,
Djabal, the man in semblance, but our
    God
Confessed by signs and portents. Ye
    saw fire

Bicker round Djabal, heard strange
    music flit
Bird-like about his brow?
*Druses.*         We saw – we heard!
Djabal is Hakeem, the incarnate Dread,
The phantasm Khalif, King of Prodigies!
*Kha.* And as he said has not our Khalif
    done,
And so disposed events (from land to
    land
Passing invisibly) that when, this morn,
The pact of villany complete, there comes
This Patriarch's Nuncio with this
    Master's Prefect
Their treason to consummate, – each
    will face
For a crouching handful, an uplifted
    nation:
For simulated Christians, confessed
    Druses:
And, for slaves past hope of the Mother-
    mount,
Freedmen returning there 'neath Venice'
    flag;
That Venice which, the Hospitallers'
    foe,
Grants us from Candia escort home at
    price
Of our relinquished isle, Rhodes counts
    her own –
Venice, whose promised argosies should
    stand
Toward harbour: is it now that you, and
    you,
And you, selected from the rest to bear
The burthen of the Khalif's secret, furt
    her
To-day's event, entitled by your wrongs,
And witness in the Prefect's hall his
    fate –
That you dare clutch these gauds? Ay,
    drop them!
*Kar.*       True,
Most true, all this; and yet, may one
    dare hint,
Thou art the youngest of us? – though
    employed

Abundantly as Djabal's confidant,
Transmitter of his mandates, even now.
Much less, whene'er beside him Anael
    graces
The cedar throne, his queen-bride, art
    thou like
To occupy its lowest step that day!
Now, Khalil, wert thou checked as
    thou aspirest,
Forbidden such or such an honour, –
    say,
Would silence serve so amply?
*Kha.*         Karshook thinks
I covet honours? Well, nor idly thinks.
Honours? I have demanded of them all
The greatest.
*Kar.*    I supposed so.
*Kha.*         Judge, yourselve
Turn, thus: 'tis in the alcove at the back
Of yonder columned porch, whose
    entrance now
The veil hides, that our Prefect holds
    his state,
Receives the Nuncio, when the one,
    from Rhodes,
The other lands from Syria; there they
    meet.
Now, I have sued with earnest
    prayers …
*Kar.*      For what
Shall the Bride's brother vainly sue?
*Kha.*         That mine –
Avenging in one blow a myriad wrongs
– Might be the hand to slay the Prefect
    there!
Djabal reserves that office for himself.
                [*A silence.*
Thus far, as youngest of you all, I speak
– Scarce more enlightened than
    yourselves; since, near
As I approach him, nearer as I trust
Soon to approach our Master, he
    reveals
Only the God's power, not the glory
    yet.
Therefore I reasoned with you: now, as
    servant

To Djabal, bearing his authority,
Hear me appoint your several posts!
    Till noon
None see him save myself and Anael:
    once
The deed achieved, our Khalif, casting
    off
The embodied Awe's tremendous
    mystery,
The weakness of the flesh disguise,
    resumes
His proper glory, ne'er to fade again.
            *Enter a* DRUSE.
*The Druse.* Our Prefect lands from
    Rhodes! – without a sign
That he suspects aught since he left
    our Isle;
Nor in his train a single guard beyond
The few he sailed with hence: so have
    we learned
From Loys.
*Kar.*            Loys? Is not Loys gone
For ever?
*Ay.* Loys, the Frank Knight, returned?
*The Druse.* Loys, the boy, stood on the
    leading prow
Conspicuous in his gay attire, and leapt
Into the surf the foremost. Since day-
    dawn
I kept watch to the Northward; take
    but note
Of my poor vigilance to Djabal!
*Kha.*                    Peace!
Thou, Karshook, with thy company,
    receive
The Prefect as appointed: see, all keep
The wonted show of servitude: announce
His entry here by the accustomed peal
Of trumpets, then await the further
    pleasure
Of Djabal! (Loys back, whom Djabal
    sent
To Rhodes that we might spare the
    single Knight
Worth sparing!)
            *Enter a second* DRUSE.
*The Druse.*        I espied it first! Say, I

First spied the Nuncio's galley from the
    South!
Said'st thou a Crossed-keys' flag would
    flap the mast?
It nears apace! One galley and no more.
If Djabal chance to ask who spied the
    flag,
Forget not, I it was!
*Kha.*                Thou, Ayoob, bring
The Nuncio and his followers hither!
    Break
One rule prescribed, ye wither in your
    blood,
Die at your fault!
            *Enter a third* DRUSE.
*The Druse.* I shall see home, see home!
– Shall banquet in the sombre groves
    again!
Hail to thee, Khalil! Venice looms afar;
The argosies of Venice, like a cloud,
Bear up from Candia in the distance!
*Kha.*                        Joy!
Summon our people, Raghib! Bid all
    forth!
Tell them the long-kept secret, old and
    young!
Set free the captive, let the trampled
    raise
Their faces from the dust, because at
    length
The cycle is complete, God Hakeem's
    reign
Begins anew! Say, Venice for our guard,
Ere night we steer for Syria! Hear you,
    Druses?
Hear you this crowning witness to the
    claims
Of Djabal? Oh, I spoke of hope and fear,
Reward and punishment, because he
    bade
Who has the right; for me, what should
    I say
But, mar not those imperial lineaments,
No majesty of all that rapt regard
Vex by the least omission! Let him rise
Without a check from you!
*Druses.*                Let Djabal rise!

*Enter* LOYS. – *The* DRUSES *are silent.*

*Loys.* Who speaks of Djabal? – for I
    seek him, friends!
[*Aside.*] *Tu Dieu!* 'Tis as our Isle broke
    out in song
For joy, its Prefect-incubus drops off
To-day, and I succeed him in his rule!
But no – they cannot dream of their
    good fortune!
[*Aloud.*] Peace to you, Druses! I have
    tidings for you,
But first for Djabal: where's your tall
    bewitcher,
With that small Arab thin-lipped silver-
    mouth?
*Kha.* [*aside to* KARSHOOK]. Loys, in
    truth! Yet Djabal cannot err!
*Kar.* [*to* KHALIL]. And who takes charge
    of Loys? That's forgotten,
Despite thy wariness! Will Loys stand
And see his comrades slaughtered?
*Loys* [*aside*].           How they shrink
And whisper, with those rapid faces!
    What?
The sight of me in their oppressors' garb
Strikes terror to the simple tribe? God's
    shame
On those that bring our Order ill repute!
But all's at end now; better days begin
For these mild mountaineers from
    oversea:
The timidest shall have in me no Prefect
To cower at thus! [*Aloud.*] I asked for
    Djabal –
*Kar.* [*aside*]. Better
One lured him, ere he can suspect,
    inside
The corridor; 'twere easy to dispatch
A youngster. [*To* Loys.] Djabal passed
    some minutes since
Thro' yonder porch, and …
*Kha.* [*aside*].         Hold! What,
    him despatch?
The only Christian of them all we charge
No tyranny upon? Who, – noblest Knight
Of all that learned from time to time
    their trade

Of lust and cruelty among us, – heir
To Europe's pomp, a truest child of
    pride, –
Yet stood between the Prefect and
    ourselves
From the beginning? Loys, Djabal
    makes
Account of, and precisely sent to Rhodes
For safety? I take charge of him!
             [*To* LOYS.] Sir Loys, –
*Loys.* There, cousins! Does Sir Loys
    strike you dead?
*Kha.* [*advancing*]. Djabal has intercourse
    with few or none
Till noontide: but, your pleasure?
*Loys.*            'Intercourse
'With few or none?' – (Ah, Khalil, when
    you spoke
I saw not your smooth face! All health!
    – and health
To Anael! How fares Anael?) – 'Inter
    course
'With few or none?' Forget you, I've
    been friendly
With Djabal long ere you or any Druse?
– Enough of him at Rennes, I think,
    beneath
The Duke my father's roof! He'd tell by
    the hour,
With fixed white eyes beneath his
    swarthy brow,
Plausiblest stories …
*Kha.*         Stories, say you? – Ah,
The quaint attire!
*Loys.*         My dress for the last time!
How sad I cannot make you understand,
This ermine, o'er a shield, betokens me
Of Bretagne, ancientest of provinces
And noblest; and, what's best and oldest
    there,
See, Dreux', our house's blazon, which
    the Nuncio
Tacks to an Hospitaller's vest to-day!
*Kha.* The Nuncio we await? What
    brings you back
From Rhodes, Sir Loys?
*Loys.*         How you island-tribe

Forget the world's awake while here
    you drowse!
What brings me back? What should
    not bring me, rather!
Our Patriarch's Nuncio visits you
    to-day –
Is not my year's probation out? I come
To take the knightly vows.
*Kha.*             What's that you wear?
*Loys.* This Rhodian cross? The cross
    your Prefect wore.
You should have seen, as I saw, the full
    Chapter
Rise, to a man, while they transferred
    this cross
From that unworthy Prefect's neck
    to ... (fool –
My secret will escape me!) In a word,
My year's probation passed, a Knight
    ere eve
Am I; bound like the rest, to yield my
    wealth
To the common stock, to live in chastity,
(We Knights espouse alone our Order's
    fame)
– Change this gay weed for the black
    white-crossed gown,
And fight to death against the Infidel
– Not, therefore, against you, you
    Christians with
Such partial difference only as befits
The peacefullest of tribes. But Khalil,
    prithee,
Is not the Isle brighter than wont
    to-day?
*Kha.* Ah, the new sword!
*Loys.*     See now! You handle sword
As 'twere a camel-staff. Pull! That's my
    motto,
Annealed '*Pro fide,*' on the blade in blue.
*Kha.* No curve in it? Surely a blade
    should curve.
*Loys.* Straight from the wrist! Loose – it
    should poise itself!
*Kha.* [*waving with irrepressible exultation
the sword*].We are a nation, Loys,
    of old fame

Among the mountains! Rights have we
    to keep
With the sword too!
[*Remembering himself.*] But I forget – you
    bid me
Seek Djabal?
*Loys.*     What! A sword's sight scares
    you not?
(The People I will make of him and
    them!
Oh let my Prefect-sway begin at once!)
Bring Djabal – say, indeed, that come
    he must!
*Kha.* At noon seek Djabal in the
    Prefect's Chamber,
And find ... [*Aside.*] Nay, 'tis thy
    cursed race's token,
Frank pride, no special insolence of
    thine!
[*Aloud.*] Tarry, and I will do your
    bidding, Loys!
[*To the rest aside.*] Now, forth you! I
    proceed to Djabal straight.
Leave this poor boy, who knows not
    what he says!
Oh will it not add joy to even thy joy,
Djabal, that I report all friends were
    true?
    [KHALIL *goes, followed by the* DRUSES.
*Loys. Tu Dieu!* How happy I shall make
    these Druses!
Was't not surpassingly contrived of me
To get the long list of their wrongs by
    heart,
Then take the first pretence for stealing
    off
From these poor islanders, present
    myself
Sudden at Rhodes before the noble
    Chapter,
And (as best proof of ardour in its cause
Which ere to-night will have become,
    too, mine)
Acquaint it with this plague-sore in its
    body,
This Prefect and his villanous career?
The princely Synod! All I dared request

Was his dismissal; and they graciously
Consigned his very office to myself –
Myself may cure the Isle diseased!
                                    And well
For them, they did so! Since I never felt
How lone a lot, tho' brilliant, I embrace,
Till now that, past retrieval, it is mine.
To live thus, and thus die! Yet, as I leapt
On shore, so home a feeling greeted me
That I could half believe in Djabal's
        story,
He used to tempt my father with, at
        Rennes –
And me, too, since the story brought
        me here –
Of some Count Dreux and ancestor of
        our
Who, sick of wandering from Bouillon's
        war,
Left his old name in Lebanon.
                                    Long days
At least to spend in the Isle! and, my
        news known
An hour hence, what if Anael turn
        on me
The great black eyes I must forget?
                                    Why, fool,
Recall them, then? My business is with
        Djabal,
Not Anael! Djabal tarries: if I seek
        him? –
The Isle is brighter than its wont to-day.

## ACT 2
### Enter DJABAL.

*Dja.* That a strong man should think
        himself a God!
I – Hakeem? To have wandered through
        the world,
Sown falsehood, and thence reaped now
        scorn, now faith,
For my one chant with many a change,
        my tale
Of outrage, and my prayer for vengeance
        – this
Required, forsooth, no mere man's
        faculty,

Nought less than Hakeem's? The
        persuading Loys
To pass probation here; the getting
        access
By Loys to the Prefect; worst of all,
The gaining my tribe's confidence by
        fraud
That would disgrace the very Frank, – a
        few
Of Europe's secrets which subdue the
        flame,
The wave, – to ply a simple tribe with
        these,
Took Hakeem?
                And I feel this first to-day!
Does the day break, is the hour imminent
When one deed, when my whole life's
        deed, my deed
Must be accomplished? Hakeem? Why
        the God?
Shout, rather, 'Djabal, Youssof's child,
        thought slain
'With his whole race, the Druses'
        Sheikhs, this Prefect
'Endeavoured to extirpate – saved, a
        child,
'Returns from traversing the world, a
        man,
'Able to take revenge, lead back the
        march
'To Lebanon' – so shout, and who
        gainsays?
But now, because delusion mixed itself
Insensibly with this career, all's changed!
Have I brought Venice to afford us
        convoy?
'True – but my jugglings wrought that!'
        Put I heart
Into our people where no heart lurked?
        – Ah,
'What cannot an impostor do!'
                                    Not this!
Not do this which I do! Not bid avaunt
Falsehood! Thou shalt not keep thy
        hold on me!
– Nor even get a hold on me! 'Tis
        now –

This day – hour – minute – 'tis as here
    I stand
On the accursed threshold of the Prefect,
That I am found deceiving and deceived!
And now what do I? – hasten to the few
Deceived, ere they deceive the many –
    shout,
'As I professed, I did believe myself!
'Say, Druses, had you seen a butchery –
'If Ayoob, Karshook saw — Maani there
'Must tell you how I saw my father sink;
'My mother's arms twine still about my
    neck;
'I hear my brother shriek, here's yet the
    scar
'Of what was meant for my own death-
    blow – say,
'If you had woke like me, grown year
    by year
'Out of the tumult in a far-off clime,
'Would it be wondrous such delusion
    grew?
'I walked the world, asked help at every
    hand;
'Came help or no? Not this and this?
    Which helps
'When I returned with, found the Prefect
    here,
'The Druses here, all here but Hakeem's
    self,
'The Khalif of the thousand prophecies,
'Reserved for such a juncture, – could I
    call
'My mission aught but Hakeem's?
    Promised Hakeem
'More than performs the Djabal – you
    absolve?
' – Me, you will never shame before the
    crowd
'Yet happily ignorant? – Me, both throngs
    surround,
'The few deceived, the many unabused,
' – Who, thus surrounded, slay for you
    and them
'The Prefect, lead to Lebanon? No Khalif,
'But Sheikh once more! Mere Djabal –
    not ...

*Enter* KHALIL *hastily.*

Kha.              – God Hakeem!
'Tis told! The whole Druse nation
    knows thee, Hakeem,
As we! and mothers lift on high their
    babes
Who seem aware, so glisten their great
    eyes,
Thou hast not failed us; ancient brows
    are proud;
Our elders could not earlier die, it seems,
Than at thy coming! The Druse heart is
    thine!
Take it! my lord and theirs, be thou
    adored!
Dja. [*aside*]. Adored! – but I renounce
    it utterly!
Kha. Already are they instituting choirs
And Dances to the Khalif, as of old
'Tis chronicled thou bad'st them.
Dja. [*aside*].         I abjure it!
'Tis not mine – not for me!
Kha.        Why pour they wine
Flavoured like honey and bruised
    mountain-herbs,
Or wear those strings of sun-dried cedar-
    fruit?
Oh, let me tell thee – Esaad, we supposed
Doting, is carried forth, eager to see
The last sun rise on the Isle: he can see
    now!
The shamed Druse women never wep
    before:
They can look up when we reach home,
    they say.
Smell! – sweet cane, saved in Lilith's
    breast thus long –
Sweet! – it grows wild in Lebanon. And I
Alone do nothing for thee! 'Tis my
    office
Just to announce what well thou
    know'st – but thus
Thou bidst me. At this self-same
    moment tend
The Prefect, Nuncio and the Admiral
Hither by their three sea-paths: nor
    forget

Who were the trusty watchers! – thou
    forget?
Like me, who do forget that Anael
    bade …
*Dja*. [*aside*]. Ay, Anael, Anael – is that
    said at last?
Louder than all, that would be said, I
    knew!
What does abjuring mean, confessing
    mean,
To the people? Till that woman crossed
    my path,
On went I, solely for my people's sake:
I saw her, and I then first saw myself,
And slackened pace: 'if I should prove
    indeed
'Hakeem – with Anael by!'
*Kha*. [*aside*].              Ah, he is rapt!
Dare I at such a moment break on him
Even to do my sister's bidding? Yes:
The eyes are Djabal's and not Hakeem's
    yet,
Though but till I have spoken this,
    perchance.
*Dja*. [*aside*]. To yearn to tell her, and
    yet have no one
Great heart's word that will tell her! I
    could gasp
Doubtless one such word out, and die.
[*Aloud*.] You said
That Anael …
*Kha*.              … Fain would see thee,
    speak with thee,
Before you change, discard this Djabal's
    shape
She knows, for Hakeem's shape she is
    to know.
Something to say that will not from her
    mind!
I know not what – 'Let him but come!'
    she said.
*Dja*. [*half-apart*]. My nation – all my
    Druses – how fare they?
Those I must save, and suffer thus to
    save,
Hold they their posts? Wait they their
    Khalif too?

*Kha*. All at the signal pant to flock
    around
That banner of a brow!
*Dja*. [*aside*].              And when they flock,
Confess them this: and after, for reward,
Be chased with howlings to her feet
    perchance!
– Have the poor outraged Druses, deaf
    and blind,
Precede me there, forestall my story
    there,
Tell it in mocks and jeers!
                              I lose myself.
Who needs a Hakeem to direct him
    now?
I need the veriest child – why not this
    child?
              [*Turning abruptly to* KHALIL.
You are a Druse too, Khalil; you were
    nourished
Like Anael with our mysteries: if she
Could vow, so nourished, to love only
    one
Who should avenge the Druses, whence
    proceeds
Your silence? Wherefore made you no
    essay,
Who thus implicitly can execute
My bidding? What have I done, you
    could not?
Who, knowing more than Anael the
    prostration
Of our once lofty tribe, the daily life
Of this detested …
                    Does he come, you say,
This Prefect? All's in readiness?
*Kha*.                          The sword,
The sacred robe, the Khalif's mystic tiar,
Laid up so long, are all disposed beside
The Prefect's chamber.
*Dja*.            – Why did you despair?
*Kha*. I know our nation's state? Too
    surely know,
As thou who speak'st to prove me!
    Wrongs like ours
Should wake revenge: but when I sought
    the wronged

And spoke, – 'The Prefect stabbed your
    son – arise!
'Your daughter, while you starve, eats
    shameless bread
'In his pavilion – then arise!' – my
    speech
Fell idly: 'twas, 'Be silent, or worse fare!
'Endure till time's slow cycle prove
    complete!
'Who mayst thou be that takest on thee
    to thrust
'Into this peril – art thou Hakeem?' No!
Only a mission like thy mission renders
All these obedient at a breath, subdues
Their private passions, brings their wills
    to one.
*Dja.* You think so?
*Kha.*      Even now – when they have
    witnessed
Thy miracles – had I not threatened all
With Hakeem's vengeance, they would
    mar the work,
And couch ere this, each with his
    special prize,
Safe in his dwelling, leaving our main
    hope
To perish. No! When these have kissed
    thy feet
At Lebanon, the past purged off, the
    present
Clear, – for the future, even Hakeem's
    mission
May end, and I perchance, or any youth,
Shall rule them thus renewed. – I tutor
    thee!
*Dja.* And wisely. (He is Anael's brother,
    pure
As Anael's self.) Go say, I come to her.
Haste! I will follow you.    [KHALIL *goes.*
               Oh, not confess
To these, the blinded multitude –
    confess,
Before at least the fortune of my deed
Half-authorize its means! Only to her
Let me confess my fault, who in my path
Curled up like incense from a Mage-
    king's tomb

When he would have the wayfarer
    descend
Through the earth's rift and bear hid
    treasure forth!
How should child's-carelessness prove
    manhood's crime
Till now that I, whose lone youth
    hurried past,
Letting each joy 'scape for the Druses'
    sake,
At length recover in one Druse all joy?
Were her brow brighter, her eyes richer,
    still
Would I confess. On the gulf's verge I
    pause.
How could I slay the Prefect, thus and
    thus?
Anael, be mine to guard me, not destroy!
                      [*Goes.*
*Enter* ANAEL, *and* MAANI *who is assisting
    to array her in the ancient dress of the
    Druses.*
*An.* Those saffron vestures of the tabret-
    ghis!
Comes Djabal, think you?
*Maa.*          Doubtless Djabal comes.
*An.* Dost thou snow-swathe thee kinglier,
    Lebanon,
Than in my dreams? – Nay all the
    tresses off
My forehead! Look I lovely so? He says
That I am lovely.
*Maa.*         Lovely! nay, that hangs
Awry.
*An.*    You tell me how a khandjar hangs?
The sharp side, thus, along the heart,
    see, marks
The maiden of our class. Are you
    content
For Djabal as for me?
*Maa.*          Content, my child.
*An.* Oh mother, tell me more of him!
    He comes
Even now – tell more, fill up my soul
    with him!
*Maa.* And did I not ... yes, surely ...
    tell you all?

*An.* What will be changed in Djabal
 when the Change
Arrives? Which feature? Not his eyes!
*Maa.*       'Tis writ
Our Hakeem's eyes rolled fire and clove
 the dark
Superbly.
*An.* Not his eyes! His voice perhaps?
Yet that's no change; for a grave current
 lived
– Grandly beneath the surface ever lived,
That, scattering, broke as in live silver
 spray
While … ah, the bliss … he would
 discourse to me
In that enforced still fashion, word on
 word!
'Tis the old current which must swell
 thro' that,
For what least tone, Maani, could I lose?
'Tis surely not his voice will change!
      – If Hakeem
Only stood by! If Djabal, somehow,
 passed
Out of the radiance as from out a robe;
Possessed, but was not it!
      He lived with you?
Well – and that morning Djabal saw me
 first
And heard me vow never to wed but one
Who saved my People – on that day …
 proceed!
*Maa.* Once more, then: from the time of
 his return
In secret, changed so since he left the
 Isle
That I, who screened our Emir's last of
 sons.
This Djabal, from the Prefect's massacre
– Who bade him ne'er forget the child
 he was,
– Who dreamed so long the youth he
 might become –
I knew not in the man that child; the
 man
Who spoke alone of hope to save our
 tribe,

How he had gone from land to land to
 save
Our tribe – allies were sure, nor foes to
 dread.
And much he mused, days, nights, alone
 he mused:
But never till that day when, pale and
 worn
As by a persevering woe, he cried
'Is there not one Druse left me?' – and
 I showed
The way to Khalil's and your hiding-
 place
From the abhorred eye of the Prefect
 here,
So that he saw you, heard you speak –
 till then,
Never did he announce – (how the
 moon seemed
To ope and shut, the while, above us
 both!)
– His mission was the mission promised
 us;
The cycle had revolved; all things
 renewing,
He was lost Hakeem clothed in flesh to
 lead
His children home anon, now veiled to
 work
Great purposes: the Druses now would
 change!
*An.* And they have changed! And
 obstacles did sink,
And furtherances rose! And round his
 form
Played fire, and music beat her angel
 wings!
My people, let me more rejoice, oh more
For you than for myself! Did I but
 watch
Afar the pageant, feel our Khalif pass,
One of the throng, how proud were I –
 tho' ne'er
Singled by Djabal's glance! But to be
 chosen
His own from all, the most his own of
 all,

To be exalted with him, side by side,
Lead the exulting Druses, meet ... ah,
     how
Worthily meet the maidens who await
Ever beneath the cedars – how deserve
This honour, in their eyes? So bright
     are they
Who saffron-vested sound the tabret
     there,
The girls who throng there in my dream!
     One hour
And all is over: how shall I do aught
That may deserve next hour's
     exalting? – How? –
                    [*Suddenly to* MAANI.
Mother, I am not worthy him! I read it
Still in his eyes! He stands as if to tell me
I am not, yet forbears. Why else revert
To one theme ever? – how mere human
     gifts
Suffice him in myself – whose worship
     fades,
Whose awe goes ever off at his approach,
As now, who when he comes ...
                    [DJABAL *enters.*] Oh why is it
I cannot kneel to you?
*Dja.*                    Rather, 'tis I
Should kneel to you, my Anael!
*An.*                    Even so!
For never seem you – shall I speak the
     truth? –
Never a God to me! 'Tis the Man's
     hand,
Eye, voice! Oh do you veil these to our
     people,
Or but to me? To them, I think, to
     them!
And brightness is their veil, shadow –
     my truth!
You mean that I should never kneel to
     you
– So, thus I kneel!
*Dja.* [*preventing her*]. No – no!
     [*Feeling the khandjar as he raises her.*
               Ha, have you chosen ...
*An.* The khandjar with our ancient garb.
     But, Djabal,

Change not, be not exalted yet! Give
     time
That I may plan more, perfect more!
     My blood
Beats, beats!
     [*Aside.*] Oh must I then – since Loys
     leaves us
Never to come again, renew in me
These doubts so near effaced already –
     must
I needs confess them now to Djabal? –
     own
That when I saw that stranger, heard
     his voice,
My faith fell, and the woeful thought
     flashed first
That each effect of Djabal's presence,
     taken
For proof of more than human attributes
In him, by me whose heart at his
     approach
Beat fast, whose brain while he was by
     swam round,
Whose soul at his departure died away,
– That every such effect might have
     been wrought
In other frames, tho' not in mine, by
     Loys
Or any merely mortal presence? Doubt
Is fading fast; shall I reveal it now?
How shall I meet the rapture presently,
With doubt unexpiated, undisclosed?
*Dja.* [*aside*]. Avow the truth? I cannot!
     In what words
Avow that all she loved in me was
     false?
– Which yet has served that flower-like
     love of hers
To climb by, like the clinging gourd,
     and clasp
With its divinest wealth of leaf and
     bloom.
Could I take down the prop-work, in
     itself
So vile, yet interlaced and overlaid
With painted cups and fruitage –
     might these still

Bask in the sun, unconscious their own
    strength
Of matted stalk and tendril had replaced
The old support thus silently withdrawn!
But no; the beauteous fabric crushes
    too.
'Tis not for my sake but for Anael's sake
I leave her soul this Hakeem where it
    leans.
Oh could I vanish from her, quit the
    Isle!
And yet – a thought comes: here my
    work is done
At every point; the Druses must return –
Have convoy to their birth-place back,
    whoe'er
The leader be, myself or any Druse –
Venice is pledged to that: 'tis for myself,
For my own vengeance in the Prefect's
    death,
I stay now, not for them: to slay or spare
The Prefect, whom imports it save
    myself?
He cannot bar their passage from the
    Isle;
What would his death be but my own
    reward?
Then, mine I will forego. It is foregone!
Let him escape with all my House's
    blood!
Ere he can reach land, Djabal disappears,
And Hakeem, Anael loved, shall, fresh
    as first,
Live in her memory, keeping her sublime
Above the world. She cannot touch
    that world
By ever knowing what I truly am,
Since Loys, – of mankind the only one
Able to link my present with my past,
My life in Europe with my Island life,
Thence, able to unmask me, – I've
    disposed
Safely at last at Rhodes, and
        *Enter* KHALIL.
*Kha.*          Loys greets thee!
*Dja.* Loys? To drag me back? It cannot
    be!

*An.* [*aside*]. Loys! Ah, doubt may not
    be stifled so!
*Kha.* Can I have erred that thou so
    gazest? Yes,
I told thee not in the glad press of
    tidings
Of higher import, Loys is returned
Before the Prefect, with, if possible,
Twice the light-heartedness of old. As
    though
On some inauguration he expects,
To-day, the world's fate hung!
*Dja.*            – And asks for me?
*Kha.* Thou knowest all things. Thee in
    chief he greets,
But every Druse of us is to be happy
At his arrival, he declares: were Loys
Thou, Master, he could have no wider
    soul
To take us in with. How I love that Loys!
*Dja.* [*aside*]. Shame winds me with her
    tether round and round.
*An.* [*aside*]. Loys? I take the trial! it is
    meet,
The little I can do, be done; that faith,
All I can offer, want no perfecting
Which my own act may compass. Ay,
    this way
All may go well, nor that ignoble doubt
Be chased by other aid than mine.
        Advance
Close to my fear, weigh Loys with my
    Lord,
The mortal with the more than mortal
    gifts!
*Dja.* [*aside*]. Before, there were so few
    deceived! and now
There's doubtless not one least Druse
    in the Isle
But, having learned my superhuman
    claims,
And calling me his Khalif-God, will
    clash
The whole truth out from Loys at first
    word!
While Loys, for his part, will hold me
    up,

With a Frank's unimaginable scorn
Of such imposture, to my people's
    eyes!
Could I but keep him longer yet awhile
From them, amuse him here until I plan
How he and I at once may leave the
    Isle!
Khalil I cannot part with from my side –
My only help in this emergency:
There's Anael!
*An.*　　　Please you?
*Dja.*　　　　Anael – none but she
[*To* Anael.] I pass some minutes in the
    chamber there,
Ere I see Loys: you shall speak with him
Until I join you. Khalil follows me.
*An.* [*aside*]. As I divined: he bids me
    save myself,
Offers me a probation – I accept.
Let me see Loys!
*Loys* [*without*].　　Djabal!
*An.* [*aside*].　　　　'Tis his voice.
The smooth Frank trifler with our
    people's wrongs,
The self-complacent boy-inquirer, loud
On this and that inflicted tyranny.
– Aught serving to parade an ignorance
Of how wrong feels, inflicted! Let me
    close
With what I viewed at distance: let
    myself
Probe this delusion to the core!
*Dja.*　　　　　　He comes.
Khalil, along with me! while Anael waits
Till I return once more – and but once
    more.

### ACT 3
#### ANAEL *and* LOYS.

*An.* Here leave me! Here I wait another.
    'Twas
For no mad protestation of a love
Like this you say possesses you, I came.
*Loys.* Love? how protest a love I dare
    not feel?
Mad words may doubtless have escaped
    me: you

Are here – I only feel you here!
*An.*　　　　　　　　No more!
*Loys.* But once again, whom could you
    love? I dare,
Alas, say nothing of myself, who am
A Knight now, for when Knighthood
    we embrace,
Love we abjure: so, speak on safely:
    speak,
Lest I speak, and betray my faith! And
    yet
To say your breathing passes through
    me, changes
My blood to spirit, and my spirit to
    you,
As Heaven the sacrificer's wine to it –
This is not to protest my love! You said
You could love one ...
*An.*　　　　One only! We are bent
To earth – who raises up my tribe, I
    love;
The Prefect bows us – who removes
    him; we
Have ancient rights – who gives them
    back to us,
I love. Forbear me! Let my hand go!
*Loys.*　　　　　　　　　Him
You could love only? Where is Djabal?
    Stay!
[*Aside.*] Yet wherefore stay? Who does
    this but myself?
Had I apprised her that I come to do
Just this, what more could she
    acknowledge? No,
She sees into my heart's core! What is
    it
Feeds either cheek with red, as June
    some rose?
Why turns she from me? Ah fool, over-
    fond
To dream I could call up ...
　　　　　　　... what never dream
Yet feigned! 'Tis love! Oh Anael, speak
    to me!
Djabal –
*An.*　　Seek Djabal by the Prefect's
    chamber

At noon!            [*She paces the room.*
*Loys* [*aside*]. And am I not the Prefect
    now?
Is it my fate to be the only one
Able to win her love, the only one
Unable to accept her love? The past
Breaks up beneath my footing: came I
    here
This morn as to a slave, to set her free
And take her thanks, and then spend
    day by day
Content beside her in the Isle? What
    works
This knowledge in me now? Her eye
    has broken
The faint disguise away: for Anael's sake
I left the Isle, for her espoused the cause
Of the Druses, all for her I thought, till
    now,
To live without!
        – As I must live! To-day
Ordains me Knight, forbids me ...
    never shall
Forbid me to profess myself, heart,
    arm,
Thy soldier!
*An.*      Djabal you demanded, comes.
*Loys* [*aside*]. What wouldst thou, Loys?
    See him? Nought beside
Is wanting: I have felt his voice a spell
From first to last. He brought me here,
    made known
The Druses to me, drove me hence to
    seek
Redress for them; and shall I meet him
    now,
When nought is wanting but a word of
    his,
To – what? – induce me to spurn hope,
    faith, pride,
Honour away, – to cast my lot among
His tribe, become a proverb in men's
    mouths,
Breaking my high pact of companionship
With those who graciously bestowed
    on me
The very opportunities I turn

Against them! Let me not see Djabal
    now!
*An.* The Prefect also comes.
*Loys* [*aside*].            Him let me see,
Not Djabal! Him, degraded at a word,
To soothe me, – to attest belief in me –
And after, Djabal! Yes, ere I return
To her, the Nuncio's vow shall have
    destroyed
This heart's rebellion, and coerced this
    will
For ever.
            Anael, not before the vows
Irrecoverably fix me ...
            Let me fly!
The Prefect, or I lose myself for ever!
                    [*Goes.*
*An.* Yes, I am calm now; just one way
    remains –
One, to attest my faith in him: for, see,
I were quite lost else: Loys, Djabal,
    stand
On either side – two men! I balance
    looks
And words, give Djabal a man's
    preference,
No more. In Djabal, Hakeem is
    absorbed!
And for a love like this, the God who
    saves
My race, selects me for his bride?
    Oneway!
            *Enter* DJABAL.
*Dja.* [*to himself*]. No moment is to waste
    then; 'tis resolved.
If Khalil may be trusted to lead back
My Druses, and if Loys can be lured
Out of the Isle – if I procure his silence,
Or promise never to return at least, –
All's over. Even now my bark awaits:
I reach the next wild islet and the next,
And lose myself beneatn the sun for
    ever.
And now, to Anael!
*An.*                  Djabal, I am thine!
*Dja.* Mine? Djabal's? – As if Hakeem
    had not been?

*An.* Not Djabal's? Say first, do you read
    my thought?
Why need I speak, if you can read my
    thought?
*Dja.* I do not, I have said a thousand
    times.
*An.* (My secret's safe, I shall surprise
    him yet!)
Djabal, I knew your secret from the
    first:
Djabal, when first I saw you … (by our
    porch
You leant, and pressed the tinkling veil
    away,
And one fringe fell behind your neck –
    I see!)
. . . I knew you were not human, for I
    said
'This dim secluded house where the
    sea beats
'Is heaven to me – my people's huts
    are hell
'To them; this august form will follow
    me,
'Mix with the waves his voice will, – I
    have him;
'And they, the Prefect! Oh, my happiness
'Rounds to the full whether I choose or
    no!
'His eyes met mine, he was about to
    speak,
'His hand grew damp – surely he meant
    to say
'He let me love him: in that moment's
    bliss
'I shall forget my people pine for home –
'They pass and they repass with pallid
    eyes!'
I vowed at once a certain vow; this
    vow –
Not to embrace you till my tribe was
    saved.
Embrace me!
*Dja.* [*apart*]. And she loved me! Nought
    remained
But that! Nay, Anael, is the Prefect
    dead?

*An.* Ah, you reproach me! True, his
    death crowns all,
I know – or should know: and I would
    do much,
Believe! but, death! Oh, you, who have
    known death,
Would never doom the Prefect, were
    death fearful
As we report!
        Death! – a fire curls within us
From the foot's palm, and fills up to
    the brain,
Up, out, then shatters the whole
    bubble-shell
Of flesh, perchance!
        Death! – witness, I would die,
Whate'er death be, would venture now
    to die
For Khalil, for Maani – what for thee?
Nay but embrace me, Djabal, in
    assurance
My vow will not be broken, for I must
Do something to attest my faith in you,
Be worthy you!
*Dja.* [*avoiding her*]. I come for that – to
    say
Such an occasion is at hand: 'tis like
I leave you – that we part, my Anael, –
    part
For ever!
*An.* We part? Just so! I have
    succumbed, –
I am, he thinks, unworthy – and nought
    less
Will serve than such approval of my
    faith.
Then, we part not! Remains there no
    way short
Of that? Oh not that!
        Death! – yet a hurt bird
Died in my hands; its eyes filmed –
    'Nay, it sleeps',
I said, 'will wake to-morrow well:'
    'twas dead.
*Dja.* I stand here and time fleets. Anael
    – I come
To bid a last farewell to you: perhaps

We never meet again. But, ere the
    Prefect
Arrive …
      *Enter* KHALIL, *breathlessly.*
*Kha.*    He's here! The Prefect! Twenty
    guards,
No more: no sign he dreams of danger.
    All
Awaits thee only. Ayoob, Karshook, keep
Their posts – wait but the deed's
    accomplishment
To join us with thy Druses to a man.
Still holds his course the Nuncio – near
    and near
The fleet from Candia steering.
*Dja.* [*aside*].         · All is lost!
– Or won?
*Kha.*    And I have laid the sacred robe,
The sword, the head-tiar, at the porch
    – the place
Commanded. Thou wilt hear the
    Prefect's trumpet.
*Dja.* Then I keep Anael, – him then,
    past recall,
I slay – 'tis forced on me. As I began
I must conclude – so be it!
*Kha.*           For the rest,
Save Loys, our foe's solitary sword,
All is so safe that … I will ne'er entreat
Thy post again of thee: tho' danger
    none,
There must be glory only meet for thee
In slaying the Prefect.
*An.* [*aside*]. And 'tis now that Djabal
Would leave me! – in the glory meet
    for him!
*Dja.* As glory, I would yield the deed to
    you
Or any Druse; what peril there may be,
I keep. [*Aside.*] All things conspire to
    hound me on.
Not now, my soul, draw back, at least!
    Not now!
The course is plain, howe'er obscure all
    else.
Once offer this tremendous sacrifice,
Prevent what else will be irreparable,

Secure these transcendental helps,
    regain
The Cedars – then let all dark clear itself!
I slay him!
*Kha.*      Anael, and no part for us!
[*To Djabal.*] Hast thou possessed he
    with …
*Dja.* [*to* Anael]. Whom speak you to?
What is it you behold there? Nay, this
    smile
Turns stranger. Shudder you? The man
    must die,
As thousands of our race have died
    thro' him.
One blow, and I discharge his weary
    soul
From the flesh that pollutes it! Let him
    fill
Straight some new expiatory form, on
    earth
Or sea, the reptile or some aëry thing:
What is there in his death?
*An.* ·         My brother said,
Is there no part in it for us?
*Dja.*          For Khalil, –
The trumpet will announce the
    Nuncio's entry;
Here, I shall find the Prefect hastening
In the Pavilion to receive him – here
I slay the Prefect; meanwhile Ayoob
    leads
The Nuncio with his guards within:
    once these
Secured in the outer hall, bid Ayoob bar
Entry or egress till I give the sign
Which waits the landing of the argosies
You will announce to me: this double
    sign
That justice is performed and help
    arrived,
When Ayoob shall receive, but not before,
Let him throw ope the palace doors,
    admit
The Druses to behold their tyrant, ere
We leave for ever this detested spot.
Go, Khalil, hurry all! No pause, no
    pause!

Whirl on the dream, secure to wake
    anon!
*Kha*. What sign? and who the bearer?
*Dja*.               Who shall show
My ring, admit to Ayoob. How she
    stands!
Have I not … I must have some task
    for her.
Anael, not that way! 'Tis the Prefect's
    chamber!
Anael, keep you the ring – give you the
    sign!
(It holds her safe amid the stir.) You will
Be faithful?
*An*. [*taking the ring*]. I would fain be
    worthy. Hark! [*Trumpet without*.
*Khal*. He comes.
*Dja*.     And I too come.
*An*.          One word, but one!
Say, shall you be exalted at the deed?
Then? On the instant?
*Dja*.          I exalted? What?
He, there – we, thus – our wrongs
    revenged, our tribe
Set free? Oh, then shall I, assure yourself,
Shall you, shall each of us, be in his
    death
Exalted!
*Kha*.   He is here.
*Dja*.         Away – away! [*They go*.
    *Enter the* PREFECT *with* GUARDS,
        *and* LOYS.
*The Prefect* [*to* GUARDS]. Back, I say, to
    the galley every guard!
That's my sole care now; see each
    bench retains
Its complement of rowers; I embark
O' the instant, since this Knight will
    have it so.
Alas me! Could you have the heart, my
    Loys!
[*To a* GUARD *who whispers*.] Oh, bring
    the holy Nuncio here forthwith!
               [*The* GUARDS *go*.
Loys, a rueful sight, confess, to see
The grey discarded Prefect leave his
    post,

With tears i' the eye! So, you are
    Prefect now?
You depose me – you succeed me? Ha,
    ha!
*Loys*. And dare you laugh, whom
    laughter less becomes
Than yesterday's forced meekness we
    beheld …
*Pref*. – When you so eloquently pleaded,
    Loys,
For my dismissal from the post? Ah,
    meek
With cause enough, consult the
    Nuncio else!
And wish him the like meekness: for so
    staunch
A servant of the Church can scarce
    have bought
His share in the Isle, and paid for it,
    hard pieces!
You've my successor to condole with,
    Nuncio!
I shall be safe by then i' the galley,
    Loys!
*Loys*. You make as you would tell me
    you rejoice
To leave your scene of …
*Pref*.        Trade in the dear Druses?
Blood and sweat traffic? Spare what
    yesterday
We heard enough of! Drove I in the Isle
A profitable game? Learn wit, my son,
Which you'll need shortly! Did it never
    breed
Suspicion in you, all was not pure profit,
When I, the insatiate … and so forth –
    was bent
On having a partaker in my rule?
Why did I yield this Nuncio half the
    gain,
If not that I might also shift – what on
    him?
Half of the peril, Loys!
*Loys*.        Peril?
*Pref*.          Hark you!
I'd love you if you'd let me – this for
    reason,

You save my life at price of … well, say
    risk
At least, of yours. I came a long time
    since
To the Isle; our Hospitallers bade me
    tame
These savage wizards, and reward
    myself –
*Loys*. The Knights who so repudiate
    your crime?
*Pref*. Loys, the Knights! we doubtless
    understood
Each other; as for trusting to reward
From any friend beside myself … no,
    no!
I clutched mine on the spot, when it
    was sweet,
And I had taste for it. I felt these
    wizards
Alive – was sure they were not on me,
    only
When I was on them: but with age
    comes caution:
And stinging pleasures please less and
    sting more.
Year by year, fear by fear! The girls were
    brighter
Than ever ('faith, there's yet one Anael
    left,
I set my heart upon – Oh, prithee, let
That brave new sword lie still!) – These
    joys looked brighter,
But silenter the town, too, as I passed.
With this alcove's delicious memories
Began to mingle visions of gaunt fathers,
Quick-eyed sons, fugitives from the
    mine, the oar,
Stealing to catch me. Brief, when I
    began
To quake with fear – (I think I hear the
    Chapter
Solicited to let me leave, now all
Worth staying for was gained and
    gone!) – I say,
Just when, for the remainder of my life,
All methods of escape seemed lost –
    that then

Up should a young hot-headed Loys
    spring,
Talk very long and loud, – in fine,
    compel
The Knights to break their whole
    arrangement, have me
Home for pure shame – from this safe-
    hold of mine
Where but ten thousand Druses seek
    my life,
To my wild place of banishment, San
    Gines
By Murcia, where my three fat manors
    lying
Purchased by gains here and the
    Nuncio's gold,
Are all I have to guard me, – that such
    fortune
Should fall to me, I hardly could expect.
Therefore I say, I'd love you.
*Loys*.              Can it be?
I play into your hands then? Oh no, no!
The Venerable Chapter, the Great Order
Sunk o' the sudden into fiends of the
    pit?
But I will back – will yet unveil you!
*Pref*.                Me?
To whom? – perhaps Sir Galeas, who
    in Chapter
Shook his white head thrice – and
    some dozen times
My hand next morning shook, for
    value paid!
To that Italian saint, Sir Cosimo? –
Indignant at my wringing year by year
A thousand bezants from the coral-
    divers,
As you recounted; felt the saint
    aggrieved?
Well might he – I allowed for his half-
    share
Merely one hundred. To Sir …
*Loys*.          See! you dare
Inculpate the whole Order; yet should I,
A youth, a sole voice, have the power
    to change
Their evil way, had they been firm in it?

Answer me!

*Pref.* Oh, the son of Bretagne's Duke,
And that son's wealth, the father's
    influence, too,
And the young arm, we'll even say, my
    Loys,
– The fear of losing or diverting these
Into another channel, by gainsaying
A novice too abruptly, could not
    influence
The Order! You might join, for aught
    they cared,
Their red-cross rivals of the Temple!
    Well,
I thank you for my part, at all events.
Stay here till they withdraw you! You'll
    inhabit
My palace – sleep, perchance, in the
    alcove
Whither I go to meet our holy friend.
Good! and now disbelieve me if you
    can, –
This is the first time for long years I
    enter
Thus [*lifts the arras*] without feeling
    just as if I lifted
The lid up of my tomb.

*Loys.*               They share his crime!
God's punishment will overtake you
    yet.

*Pref.* Thank you it does not! Pardon
    this last flash:
I bear a sober visage presently
With the disinherited Nuncio here –
His purchase-money safe at Murcia, too!
Let me repeat – for the first time, no
    draught
Coming as from a sepulchre salutes me.
When we next meet, this folly may
    have passed,
We'll hope. Ha, ha!
                [*Goes through the arras.*

*Loys.*               Assure me but …
    he's gone!
He could not lie. Then what have I
    escaped,
I, who had so nigh given up happiness

For ever, to be linked with him and
    them!
Oh, opportunest of discoveries! I
Their Knight? I utterly renounce them
    all!
Hark! What, he meets by this the
    Nuncio? Yes,
The same hyæna groan-like laughter!
    Quick –
To Djabal! I am one of them at last,
These simple-hearted Druses – Anael's
    tribe!
Djabal! She's mine at last. Djabal, I say!
                        [*Goes.*

## ACT 4

*Enter* DJABAL.

*Dja.* Let me but slay the Prefect. The
    end now!
To-morrow will be time enough to pry
Into the means I took: suffice, they
    served,
Ignoble as they were, to hurl revenge
True to its object.
        [*Seeing the robe, etc. disposed.*
Mine should never so
Have hurried to accomplishment!
    Thee, Djabal,
Far other mood befitted! Calm the
    Robe
Should clothe this doom's awarder!
[*Taking the robe.*] Shall I dare
Assume my nation's Robe? I am at
    least
A Druse again, chill Europe's policy
Drops from me: I dare take the Robe.
    Why not
The Tiar? I rule the Druses, and what
    more
Betokens it than rule? – yet – yet –
                [*Lays down the tiar.*
[*Footsteps in the alcove.*]       He comes!
                [*Taking the sword.*
If the Sword serve, let the Tiar lie! So,
    feet
Clogged with the blood of twenty years
    can fall

Thus lightly! Round me, all ye ghosts!
    He'll lift …
Which arm to push the arras wide? –
    or both?
Stab from the neck down to the heart –
    there stay!
Near he comes – nearer – the next
    footstep! Now!
            [*As he dashes aside the arras,*
                ANAEL *is discovered.*
Ha! Anael! Nay, my Anael, can it be?
Heard you the trumpet? I must slay
    him here,
And here you ruin all. Why speak you
    not?
Anael, the Prefect comes! [ANAEL
    *screams.*]          So slow to feel
'Tis not a sight for you to look upon?
A moment's work – but such work! Till
    you go,
I must be idle – idle, I risk all!
            [*Pointing to her hair.*
Those locks are well, and you are
    beauteous thus,
But with the dagger 'tis, I have to do!
*An.* With mine!
*Dja.*          Blood – Anael?
*An.*                    Djabal, 'tis thy deed!
It must be! I had hoped to claim it
    mine –
Be worthy thee – but I must needs
    confess
'Twas not I, but thyself … not I have
    . . . Djabal!
Speak to me!
*Dja.*          Oh, my punishment!
*An.*                    Speak to me
While I can speak! touch me, despite
    the blood!
When the command passed from thy
    soul to mine,
I went, fire leading me, muttering of
    thee,
And the approaching exaltation, –
    'make
'One sacrifice!' I said, – and he sat
    there,

Bade me approach; and, as I did
    approach,
Thy fire with music burst into my
    brain.
'Twas but a moment's work, thou
    saidst – perchance
It may have been so! Well, it is thy
    deed.
*Dja.* It is my deed.
*An.*          His blood all this! – this! and …
And more! Sustain me, Djabal! Wait
    not – now
Let flash thy glory! Change thyself and
    me!
It must be! Ere the Druses flock to us!
At least confirm me! Djabal, blood
    gushed forth –
He was our tyrant – but I looked he'd
    fall
Prone as asleep – why else is death
    called sleep?
Sleep? He bent o'er his breast! 'Tis sin,
    I know, –
Punish me, Djabal, but wilt thou let
    him?
Be it thou that punishest, not he – who
    creeps
On his red breast – is here! 'Tis the
    small groan
Of a child – no worse! Bestow the new
    life, then!
Too swift it cannot be, too strange,
    surpassing!
            [*Following him as he retreats.*
Now! Change us both! Change me
    and change thou!
*Dja.* [*sinks on his knees*]. Thus!
Behold my change! You have done nobly.
    I! –
*An.* Can Hakeem kneel?
*Dja.*          No Hakeem, and scarce Djabal!
I have dealt falsely, and this woe is
    come.
No – hear me ere scorn blast me! Once
    and ever,
The deed is mine. Oh think upon the
    past!

*An.* [*to herself*]. Did I strike once, or
     twice, or many times?
*Dja.* I came to lead my tribe where,
     bathed in glooms,
Doth Bahumid the Renovator sleep:
Anael, I saw my tribe: I said, 'Without
'A miracle this cannot be' – I said
'Be there a miracle!' – for I saw you.
*An.* His head lies south the portal.
*Dja.*                    – Weighed with this
The general good, how could I choose
   · my own?
What matter was my purity of soul?
Little by little I engaged myself –
Heaven would accept me for its
     instrument,
I hoped: I said Heaven had accepted me.
*An.* Is it this blood breeds dreams in
     me? Who said
You were not Hakeem? And your
     miracles –
The fire that plays innocuous round
     your form?
     [*Again changing her whole manner.*
Ah, thou wouldst try me – thou art
     Hakeem still!
*Dja.* Woe – woe! As if the Druses of the
     Mount
(Scarce Arabs, even there, but here, in
     the Isle,
Beneath their former selves) should
     comprehend
The subtle lore of Europe! A few secrets
That would not easily affect the
     meanest
Of the crowd there, could wholly sub-
     jugate
The best of our poor tribe. Again that
     eye?
*An.* [*after a pause springs to his neck*].
Djabal, in this there can be no deceit!
Why, Djabal, were you human only, –
     think,
Maani is but human, Khalil human,
Loys is human even – did their words
Haunt me, their looks pursue me?
     Shame on you

So to have tried me! Rather, shame on
     me
So to need trying! Could I, with the
     Prefect
And the blood, there – could I see only
     you?
– Hang by your neck over this gulf of
     blood?
Speak, I am saved! Speak, Djabal! Am I
     saved?
     [*As* Djabal *slowly unclasps her arms,*
          *and puts her silently from him.*
Hakeem would save me. Thou art Djabal.
     Crouch!
Bow to the dust, thou basest of our
     kind!
The pile of thee, I reared up to the
     cloud –
Full, midway, of our fathers' trophied
     tombs,
Based on the living rock, devoured not
     by
The unstable desert's jaws of sand, –
     falls prone.
Fire, music, quenched: and now thou
     liest there
A ruin, obscene creatures will moan
     through.
– Let us come, Djabal!
*Dja.*              Whither come?
*An.*                        At once –
Lest so it grow intolerable. Come!
Will I not share it with thee? Best at
     once!
So, feel less pain! Let them deride, – thy
     tribe
Now trusting in thee, – Loys shall deride!
Come to them, hand in hand, with me!
*Dja.*                    Where come?
*An.* Where? – to the Druses thou hast
     wronged! Confess,
Now that the end is gained – (I love
     thee now – )
That thou hast so deceived them –
     (perchance love thee
Better than ever.) Come, receive their
     doom

Of infamy! O, best of all I love thee!
Shame with the man, no triumph with
    the God,
Be mine! Come!
*Dja.*           Never! More shame yet?
    and why?
Why? You have called this deed mine –
    it is mine!
And with it I accept its circumstance.
How can I longer strive with fate? The
    past
Is past: my false life shall henceforth
    show true.
Hear me! The argosies touch land by
    this;
They bear us to fresh scenes and
    happier skies.
What if we reign together? – if we keep
Our secret for the Druses' good? – by
    means
Of even their superstition, plant in them
New life? I learn from Europe: all who
    seek
Man's good must awe man, by such
    means as these.
We two will be divine to them – we are!
All great works in this world spring
    from the ruins
Of greater projects – ever, on our earth,
Babels men block out, Babylons they
    build.
I wrest the weapon from your hand! I
    claim
The deed! Retire! You have my ring –
    you bar
All access to the Nuncio till the forces
From Venice land.
*An.*     Thou wilt feign Hakeem then?
*Dja.* [*putting the Tiara of Hakeem on his
    head*]. And from this moment that
    I dare ope wide
Eyes that till now refused to see, begins
My true dominion: for I know myself,
And what am I to personate. No word?
               [ANAEL *goes.*
'Tis come on me at last! His blood on
    her

What memories will follow that! Her
    eye,
Her fierce distorted lip and ploughed
    black brow!
Ah, fool! Has Europe then so poorly
    tamed
The Syrian blood from out thee? Thou,
    presume
To work in this foul earth by means
    not foul?
Scheme, as for heaven, – but, on the
    earth be glad
If a least ray like heaven's be left thee!
                       Thus
I shall be calm – in readiness – no way
Surprised.           [*A noise without.*
This should be Khalil and my Druses.
Venice is come then! Thus I grasp thee,
    sword!
Druses, 'tis Hakeem saves you! In! Behold
Your Prefect!
        *Enter* LOYS. DJABAL *hides
        the khandjar in his robe.*
*Loys.* Oh, well found, Djabal! – but no
    time for words.
You know who waits there?
            [*Pointing to the alcove.*
          Well! – and that 'tis there
He meets the Nuncio? Well? Now, a
    surprise –
He there –
*Dja.*     I know –
*Loys.*         – is now no mortal's lord,
Is absolutely powerless – call him,
    dead –
He is no longer Prefect – you are Prefect!
Oh, shrink not! I do nothing in the
    dark,
Nothing unworthy Breton blood,
    believe!
I understand at once your urgency
That I should leave this isle for Rhodes;
    I felt
What you were loath to speak – your
    need of help.
I have fulfilled the task, that
    earnestness

Imposed on me: have, face to face,
    confronted
The Prefect in full Chapter, charged on
    him
The enormities of his long rule; he
    stood
Mute, offered no defence, no crime
    denied.
On which, I spoke of you, and of your
    tribe,
Your faith so like our own, and all you
    urged
Of old to me: I spoke, too, of your
    goodness,
Your patience – brief, I hold henceforth
    the Isle
In charge, am nominally lord, – but you,
You are associated in my rule –
Are the true Prefect! Ay, such faith had
    they
In my assurance of your loyalty
(For who insults an imbecile old man?)
That we assume the Prefecture this
    hour.
You gaze at me? Hear greater wonders
    yet –
I cast down all the fabric I have built.
These Knights, I was prepared to
    worship … but
Of that another time; what's now to say,
Is – I shall never be a Knight! Oh,
    Djabal,
Here first I throw all prejudice aside,
And call you brother! I am Druse like
    you:
My wealth, my friends, my power, are
    wholly yours,
Your people's, which is now my people:
    for
There is a maiden of your tribe, I love –
She loves me – Khalil's sister –
*Dja.*                              Anael?
*Loys.*                         Start you?
Seems what I say, unknightly? Thus it
    chanced:
When first I came, a novice, to the
    isle …

*Enter one of the* NUNCIO'S GUARDS *from
    the alcove.*
*Guard.* Oh horrible! Sir Loys! Here is
    Loys!
And here – [*Others enter from the alcove.*
[*Pointing to* DJABAL.] Secure him, bind
    him – this is he!
                    [*They surround* DJABAL.
*Loys.* Madmen – what is't you do?
    Stand from my friend,
And tell me!
*Guard.* Thou canst have no part in this –
Surely no part! But slay him not! The
    Nuncio
Commanded, slay him not!
*Loys.*                    Speak, or …
*Guard.*                    The Prefect
Lies murdered there by him thou dost
    embrace.
*Loys.* By Djabal? Miserable fools! How
    Djabal?
        [*A* GUARD *lifts* DJABAL's *robe;*
        DJABAL *flings down the khandjar.*
*Loys* [*after a pause*]. Thou hast received
    some insult worse than all,
Some outrage not to be endured –
        [*To the* Guards.] Stand back!
He is my friend – more than my friend.
                        Thou hast
Slain him upon that provocation.
*Guard.*                        No!
No provocation! 'Tis a long devised
Conspiracy: the whole tribe is involved.
He is their Khalif – 'tis on that
    pretence –
Their mighty Khalif who died long ago,
And now comes back to life and light
    again!
All is just now revealed, I know not how,
By one of his confederates – who, struck
With horror at this murder, first apprised
The Nuncio. As 'twas said, we find this
    Djabal
Here where we take him.
*Dja.* [*aside*]. Who broke faith with me?
*Loys* [*to Djabal*]. Hear'st thou? Speak!
    Till thou speak, I keep off these,

Or die with thee. Deny this story! Thou
A Khalif, an impostor? Thou, my friend,
Whose tale was of an inoffensive tribe,
With … but thou know'st – on that
    tale's truth I pledged
My faith before the Chapter: what art
    thou?
*Dja.* Loys, I am as thou hast heard. All's
    true.
No more concealment! As these tell
    thee, all
Was long since planned. Our Druses
    are enough
To crush this handful: the Venetians
    land
Even now in our behalf. Loys, we part.
Thou, serving much, wouldst fain have
    served me more;
It might not be. I thank thee. As thou
    hearest,
We are a separated tribe: farewell!
*Loys.* Oh where will truth be found
    now? Canst thou so
Belie the Druses? Do they share thy
    crime?
Those thou professest of our Breton
    stock,
Are partners with thee? Why, I saw but
    now
Khalil, my friend: he spoke with me –
    no word
Of this! and Anael – whom I love, and
    who
Loves me – she spoke no word of this.
*Dja.*                Poor boy!
Anael, who loves thee? Khalil, fast thy
    friend?
We, offsets from a wandering Count of
    Dreux?
No: older than the oldest, princelier
Than Europe's princeliest race, our
    tribe: enough
For thee, that on our simple faith we
    found
A monarchy to shame your monarchies
At their own trick and secret of
    success.

The child of this our tribe shall laugh
    upon
The palace-step of him whose life ere
    night
Is forfeit, as that child shall know, and
    yet
Shall laugh there! What, we Druses
    wait forsooth
The kind interposition of a boy
– Can only save ourselves if thou
    concede:
– Khalil admire thee? He is my right-
    hand,
My delegate! – Anael accept thy love?
She is my bride!
*Loys.*       Thy bride? She one of them?
*Dja.* My bride!
*Loys.* And she retains her glorious eyes!
She, with those eyes, has shared this
    miscreant's guilt!
Ah – who but she directed me to find
Djabal within the Prefect's chamber?
    Khalil
Bade me seek Djabal there, too. All is
    truth.
What spoke the Prefect worse of them
    than this?
Did the Church ill to institute long since
Perpetual warfare with such serpentry?
And I – have I desired to shift my part,
Evade my share in her design? 'Tis well.
*Dja.* Loys, I wronged thee – but
    unwittingly:
I never thought there was in thee a
    virtue
That could attach itself to what thou
    deemest
A race below thine own. I wronged
    thee, Loys,
But that is over: all is over now,
Save the protection I ensure against
My people's anger. By their Khalif's
    side,
Thou art secure and mayst depart: so,
    come!
*Loys.* Thy side? I take protection at thy
    hand?

*Enter other* GUARDS.

*Guards.* Fly with him! Fly, Sir Loys! 'Tis
    too true:
And only by his side thou mayst
    escape.
The whole tribe is in full revolt: they
    flock
About the palace – will be here – on
    thee –
And there are twenty of us, we the
    Guards
O' the Nuncio, to withstand them!
    Even we
Had stayed to meet our death in
    ignorance,
But that one Druse, a single faithful
    Druse,
Made known the horror to the Nuncio.
    Fly!
The Nuncio stands aghast. At least
    let us
Escape thy wrath, O Hakeem! We are
    nought
In thy tribe's persecution! [*To* LOYS.]
    Keep by him!
They hail him Hakeem, their dead
    Prince returned:
He is their God, they shout, and at his
    beck
Are life and death!
*Loys* [*springing at the khandjar* DJABAL
    *had thrown down, seizes him by the
    throat*].          Thus by his side am I!
Thus I resume my knighthood and its
    warfare,
Thus end thee, miscreant, in thy pride
    of place!
Thus art thou caught. Without, thy
    dupes may cluster:
Friends aid thee, foes avoid thee, – thou
    art Hakeem,
How say they? – God art thou! but also
    here
Is the least, youngest, meanest the
    Church calls
Her servant, and his single arm avails
To aid her as she lists. I rise, and thou

Art crushed. Hordes of thy Druses
    flock without:
Here thou hast me, who represent the
    Cross,
Honour and Faith, 'gainst Hell,
    Mahound and thee.
Die! [Djabal *remains calm.*] Implore my
    mercy, Hakeem, that my scorn
May help me! Nay, I cannot ply thy
    trade;
I am no Druse, no stabber: and thine
    eye,
Thy form, are too much as they were –
    my friend
Had such. Speak! Beg for mercy at my
    foot!          [DJABAL *still silent.*
Heaven could not ask so much of me –
    not, sure,
So much. I cannot kill him so.
                    [*After a pause.*] Thou art
Strong in thy cause, then – dost outbrave
    us, then.
Heardst thou that one of thine
    accomplices,
Thy very people, has accused thee? Meet
His charge! Thou hast not even slain
    the Prefect
As thy own vile creed warrants. Meet
    that Druse!
Come with me and disprove him – be
    thou tried
By him, nor seek appeal! Promise me
    this,
Or I will do God's office. What, shalt
    thou
Boast of assassins at thy beck, yet truth
Want even an executioner? Consent,
Or I will strike – look in my face – I will!
*Dja.* Give me again my khandjar, if thou
    darest!
                              [LOY *gives it.*
Let but one Druse accuse me, and I
    plunge
This home. A Druse betray me? Let us
    go!
[*Aside.*] Who has betrayed me?
    [*Shouts without.*] Hearest thou? I hear

No plainer than long years ago I heard
That shout – but in no dream now.
   They return!
Wilt thou be leader with me, Loys?
   Well.

### ACT 5

*The Uninitiated* DRUSES, *filling the hall
tumultuously, and speaking together.*
Here flock we, obeying the summons.
Lo, Hakeem hath appeared, and the
Prefect is dead, and we return to Lebanon!
My manufacture of goats' fleece must, I
doubt, soon fall away there. Come, old
Nasif – link thine arm in mine – we
fight, if needs be. Come, what is a great
fight-word? – 'Lebanon?' (My daughter –
my daughter!) – But is Khalil to have the
office of Hamza? – Nay, rather, if he be
wise, the monopoly of henna and cloves.
Where is Hakeem? – The only prophet I
ever saw, prophesied at Cairo once, in
my youth: a little black Copht, dressed
all in black too, with a great stripe of
yellow cloth flapping down behind him
like the back-fin of a water-serpent. Is
this he? Biamrallah! Biamreh! Hakeem!

*Enter the* NUNCIO, *with* GUARDS.
*Nuncio* [*to his* ATTENDANTS]. Hold both,
   the sorcerer and this accomplice
Ye talk of, that accuseth him! And tell
Sir Loys he is mine, the Church's hope:
Bid him approve himself our Knight
   indeed!
Lo, this black disemboguing of the Isle!
[*To the* Druses.] Ah children, what a
   sight for these old eyes
That kept themselves alive this voyage
   through
To smile their very last on you! I came
To gather one and all you wandering
   sheep
Into my fold, as though a father
   came …
As though, in coming, a father
   should …

[*To his* GUARDS.] (Ten, twelve,
– Twelve guards of you, and not an
   outlet? None?
The wizards stop each avenue? Keep
   close!)
[*To the* DRUSES.] As if one came to a
   son's house, I say,
So did I come – no guard with me – to
   find …
Alas – alas!
*A Druse.* Who is the old man?
*Another.*          Oh, ye are to shout!
Children, he styles you.
*Druses.*        Ay, the Prefect's slain!
Glory to the Khalif, our Father!
*Nuncio.*            Even so
I find, (ye prompt aright) your father
   slain.
While most he plotted for your good,
   that father
(Alas, how kind, ye never knew) – lies
   slain.
[*Aside.*] (And hell's worm gnaw the
   glozing knave – with me,
For being duped by his cajoleries!
Are these the Christians? These the
   docile crew
My bezants went to make me Bishop
   o'er?)
[*To his* ATTENDANTS, *who whisper.*] What
   say ye does this wizard style himself?
Hakeem? Biamrallah? The third
   Fatemite?
What is this jargon? He – the insane
   Khalif,
Dead near three hundred years ago,
   come back
In flesh and blood again?
*Druses.*       He mutters! Hear ye?
He is blaspheming Hakeem. The old
   man
Is our dead Prefect's friend. Tear him!
*Nuncio.*          Ye dare not.
I stand here with my five-and-seventy
   years,
The Patriarch's power behind me,
   God's above.

Those years have witnessed sin
    enough; ere now
Misguided men arose against their
    lords,
And found excuse; but ye, to be enslaved
By sorceries, cheats – alas! the same
    tricks, tried
On my poor children in this nook o'
    the earth,
Could triumph, that have been
    successively
Exploded, laughed to scorn, all nations
    through:
'*Romaioi, Ioudaioite kai proselutoi,*
'Cretes and Arabians' – you are duped
    the last.
Said I, refrain from tearing me? I pray ye
Tear me! Shall I return to tell the Patriarch
That so much love was wasted – every
    gift
Rejected, from his benison I brought,
Down to the galley-full of bezants, sunk
An hour since at the harbour's mouth,
    by that …
That … never will I speak his hated
    name!
[*To his* SERVANTS.] What was the name
    his fellow slip-fetter
Called their arch-wizard by? [*They
    whisper.*] Oh, Djabal was't?
*Druses.* But how a sorcerer? false wherein?
*Nuncio.*      (Ay, Djabal!)
How false? Ye know not, Djabal has
    confessed …
Nay, that by tokens found on him we
    learn …
What I sailed hither solely to divulge –
How by his spells the demons were
    allured
To seize you: not that these be aught
    save lies
And mere illusions. Is this clear? I say,
By measures such as these, he would
    have led you
Into a monstrous ruin: follow ye?
Say, shall ye perish for his sake, my
    sons?

*Druses.* Hark ye!
*Nuncio* – Be of one privilege amerced?
No! Infinite the Patriarch's mercies are!
No! With the Patriarch's licence, still I
    bid
Tear him to pieces who misled you!
    Haste!
*Druses.* The old man's beard shakes,
and his eyes are white fire! After all, I
know nothing of Djabal beyond what
Karshook says; he knows but what
Khalil says, who knows just what Djabal
says himself. Now, the little Copht
Prophet, I saw at Cairo in my youth,
began by promising each bystander three
full measures of wheat …
*Enter* KHALIL *and the initiated* DRUSES.
*Kha.* Venice and her deliverance are at
    hand:
Their fleet stands through the harbour.
    Hath he slain
The Prefect yet? Is Djabal's change come
    yet?
*Nuncio* [*to* ATTENDANTS]. What's this
of Venice? Who's this boy?
[*Attendants whisper.*]      One Khalil?
Djabal's accomplice, Loys called, but
    now,
The only Druse, save Djabal's self, to
    fear?
[*To the Druses.*] I cannot hear ye with
    these aged ears:
Is it so? Ye would have my troops
    assist?
Doth he abet him in his sorceries?
Down with the cheat, guards, as my
    children bid!
            [*They spring at* KHALIL;
            *as he beats them back,*
Stay! No more bloodshed! Spare
    deluded youth!
Whom seek'st thou? (I will teach him)
    – whom, my child?
Thou know'st not what these know,
    what these declare.
I am an old man as thou seest – have
    don

With life; and what should move me
    but the truth?
Art thou the only fond one of thy tribe?
'Tis I interpret for thy tribe.
*Kha.*                 Oh, this
Is the expected Nuncio! Druses, hear –
Endure ye this? Unworthy to partake
The glory Hakeem gains you! While I
    speak,
The ships touch land: who makes for
    Lebanon?
They plant the winged lion in these
    halls!
*Nuncio* [*aside*]. If it be true! Venice? Oh,
    never true!
Yet Venice would so gladly thwart our
    Knights,
So fain get footing here, stand close by
    Rhodes!
Oh, to be duped this way!
*Kha.*             Ere he appear
And lead you gloriously, repent, I say!
*Nuncio* [*aside*]. Nor any way to stretch
    the arch-wizard stark
Ere the Venetians come? Cut off the
    head,
The trunk were easily stilled. [*To the*
    DRUSES.] He? Bring him forth!
Since so you needs will have it, I
    assent.
You'd judge him, say you, on the spot
    – confound
The sorcerer in his very circle? Where's
Our short black-bearded sallow friend
    who swore
He'd earn the Patriarch's guerdon by
    one stab?
Bring Djabal forth at once!
*Druses.*           Ay, bring him forth!
The Patriarch drives a trade in oil and
    silk,
And we're the Patriarch's children –
    true men, we!
Where is the glory? Show us all the
    glory!
*Kha.* You dare not so insult him! What,
    not see ...

(I tell thee, Nuncio, these are
    uninstructed,
Untrusted: they know nothing of our
    Khalif!)
– Not see that if he lets a doubt arise
'Tis but to give yourselves the chance
    of seeming
To have some influence in your own
    Return!
That all may say ye would have trusted
    him
Without the all-convincing glory – ay,
And did! Embrace the occasion,
    friends! For, think –
What wonder when his change takes
    place? But now
For your sakes, he should not reveal
    himself.
No: could I ask and have, I would not
    ask
The change yet!
        *Enter* DJABAL *and* LOYS.
            Spite of all, reveal thyself!
I had said, pardon them for me – for
    Anael –
For our sakes pardon these besotted
    men –
Ay, for thine own – they hurt not thee!
    Yet now
One thought swells in me and keeps
    down all else.
This Nuncio couples shame with thee,
    has called
Imposture thy whole course, all bitter
    things
Has said: he is but an old fretful man!
Hakeem – nay, I must call thee
    Hakeem now –
Reveal thyself! See! Where is Anael?
    See!
*Loys* [*to* Djabal]. Here are thy people.
    Keep thy word to me!
*Dja.* Who of my people hath accused
    me?
*Nuncio.* So!
So this is Djabal, Hakeem, and what
    not?

A fit deed, Loys, for thy first Knight's
    day!
May it be augury of thy after-life!
Ever prove truncheon of the Church as
    now
That, Nuncio of the Patriarch, having
    charge
Of the Isle here, I claim thee [*turning to*
    DJABAL] as these bid me,
Forfeit for murder done thy lawful
    prince,
Thou conjurer that peep'st and
    mutterest!
Why should I hold thee from their
    hands? (Spells, children?
But hear how I dispose of all his
    spells!)
Thou art a prophet? – wouldst entice
    thy tribe
From me? – thou workest miracles?
    (Attend!
Let him but move me with his spells!)
    I, Nuncio ...
*Dja.* ... Which how thou camest to be,
    I say not now,
Though I have also been at Stamboul,
    Luke!
Ply thee with spells, forsooth! What
    need of spells?
If Venice, in her Admiral's person,
    stoop
To ratify thy compact with her foe,
The Hospitallers, for this Isle –
    withdraw
Her warrant of the deed which reinstates
My people in their freedom, tricked
    away
By him I slew, – refuse to convoy us
To Lebanon and keep the Isle we leave –
Then will be time to try what spells can
    do!
Dost thou dispute the Republic's power?
*Nuncio.*                            Lo ye!
He tempts me too, the wily exorcist!
No! The renowned Republic was and is
The Patriarch's friend: 'tis not for
    courting Venice

That I – that these implore thy blood of
    me.
Lo ye, the subtle miscreant! Ha, so
    subtle?
Ye, Druses, hear him. Will ye be
    deceived?
How he evades me! Where's the
    miracle
He works? I bid him to the proof – fish
    up
Your galley-full of bezants that he sank!
That were a miracle! One miracle!
Enough of trifling, for it chafes my years.
I am the Nuncio, Druses! I stand forth
To save you from the good Republic's
    rage
When she shall find her fleet was
    summoned here
To aid the mummeries of a knave like
    this.
                    [*As the* DRUSES *hesitate,*
                    *his* ATTENDANTS *whisper.*
Ah, well suggested! Why, we hold the
    while
One who, his close confederate till now,
Confesses Djabal at the last a cheat,
And every miracle a cheat. Who throws
    me
His head? I make three offers, once I
    offer, –
And twice ...
*Dja.*  Let who moves perish at my foot!
*Kha.* Thanks, Hakeem, thanks! Oh,
    Anael, Maani,
Why tarry they?
*Druses* [*to each other*]. He can! He can!
    Live fire –
[*To the* Nuncio.] I say he can, old man!
    Thou know'st him not.
Live fire like that thou seest now in his
    eyes,
Plays fawning round him. See! The
    change begins.
All the brow lightens as he lifts his
    arm.
Look not at me! It was not I!
*Dja.*                        What Druse

Accused me, as he saith? I bid each
    bone
Crumble within that Druse! None,
    Loys, none
Of my own people, as thou said'st,
    have raised
A voice against me.
*Nuncio* [*aside*]. Venice to come! Death!
*Dja.* [*continuing*].       Confess and go
    unscathed, however false!
Seest thou my Druses, Luke? I would
    submit
To thy pure malice did one Druse
    confess!
How said I, Loys?
*Nuncio* [*to his* ATTENDANTS *who whisper*].
            Ah, ye counsel so?
[*Aloud.*] Bring in the witness, then, who,
    first of all,
Disclosed the treason! Now I have thee
    wizard!
Ye hear that? If one speaks, he bids you
    tear him
Joint after joint: well then, one does
    speak! One,
Befooled by Djabal, even as yourselves,
But who hath voluntarily proposed
To expiate, by confessing thus, the fault
Of having trusted him.
            [*They bring in a veiled* Druse.
*Loys.*            Now, Djabal, now!
*Nuncio.* Friend, Djabal fronts thee!
    Make a ring, sons. Speak!
Expose this Djabal – what he was, and
    how:
The wiles he used, the aims he
    cherished: all,
Explicitly as late 'twas spoken to these
My servants: I absolve and pardon
    thee.
*Loys.* Thou hast the dagger ready, Djabal?
*Dja.*            Speak,
Recreant!
*Druses.*    Stand back, fool! farther!
    Suddenly
You shall see some huge serpent glide
    from under

The empty vest, or down will thunder
    crash!
Back, Khalil!
*Kha.*            I go back? Thus go I back!
[*To* ANAEL.] Unveil! Nay, thou shalt
    face the Khalif! Thus!
            [*He tears away* ANAEL's *veil;*
            DJABAL *folds his arms and bows his*
            *head; the* DRUSES *fall back;* Loys
            *springs from the side of* DJABAL
            *and the* NUNCIO.
*Loys.* Then she was true – she only of
    them all!
True to her eyes – may keep those
    glorious eyes,
And now be mine, once again mine!
    Oh, Anael!
Dared I think thee a partner in his
    crime –
That blood could soil that hand? nay,
    'tis mine – Anael,
– Not mine? – who offer thee before all
    these
My heart, my sword, my name – so
    thou wilt say
That Djabal, who affirms thou art his
    bride,
Lies – say but that he lies!
*Dja.*            Thou, Anael?
*Loys.* Nay, Djabal, nay, one chance for
    me – the last!
Thou hast had every other; thou hast
    spoken
Days, nights, what falsehood listed
    thee – let me
Speak first now; I will speak now!
*Nuncio.*            Loys,
    pause!
Thou art the Duke's son, Bretagne's
    choicest stock,
Loys of Dreux, God's sepulchre's first
    sword:
This wilt thou spit on, this de
grade, this trample
To earth?
*Loys* [*to* Anael]. Who had foreseen that
    one day Loys

Would stoke these gifts against some
    other good
In the whole world? I give them thee!
    would
My strong will might bestow real shape
    on them,
That I might see, with my own eyes,
    thy foot
Tread on their very neck! 'Tis not by
    gifts
I put aside this Djabal: we will stand –
We do stand, see, two men! Djabal,
    stand forth!
Who's worth her, I or thou? I – who
    for Anael
Uprightly, purely kept my way, the long
True way – left thee each by-path,
    boldly lived
Without the lies and blood, – or thou,
    or thou?
Me! love me, Anael! Leave the blood
    and him!
[*To* DJABAL.] Now speak – now, quick
    on this that I have said, –
Thou with the blood, speak if thou art
    a man!
*Dja*. [*to* ANAEL]. And was it thou
    betrayedst me? 'Tis well!
I have deserved this of thee, and submit.
Nor 'tis much evil thou inflictest: life
Ends here. The cedars shall not wave
    for us:
For there was crime, and must be
    punishment.
See fate! By thee I was seduced, by thee
I perish: yet do I – can I repent?
I with my Arab instinct, thwarted ever
By my Frank policy, – and with, in
    turn,
My Frank brain, thwarted by my Arab
    heart –
While these remained in equipoise, I
    lived
– Nothing; had either been predominant,
As a Frank schemer or an Arab mystic,
I had been something; – now, each has
    destroyed

The other – and behold, from out their
    crash,
A third and better nature rises up –
My mere man's-nature! And I yield to it:
I love thee, I who did not love before!
*An*. Djabal!
*Dja.* It seemed love, but it was not love:
How could I love while thou adoredst
    me?
Now thou despisest, art above me so
Immeasurably! Thou, no other, doomest
My death now; this my steel shall
    execute
Thy judgment; I shall feel thy hand in it.
Oh luxury to worship, to submit,
Transcended, doomed to death by thee!
*An*.              My Djabal!
*Dja*. Dost hesitate? I force thee then.
    Approach,
Druses! for I am out of reach of fate;
No further evil waits me. Speak the
    doom!
Hear, Druses, and hear, Nuncio, and
    hear, Loys!
*An*. Hakeem!         [*She falls dead.*
                [*The* DRUSES *scream,*
                *grovelling before him.*
*Druses*.      Ah Hakeem! – not on me
    thy wrath!
Biamrallah, pardon! never doubted I!
Ha, dog, how sayest thou?
    [*They surround and seize the* NUNCIO
           *and his* GUARDS. LOYS *flings*
           *himself upon the body of* ANAEL, *on*
           *which* DJABAL *continues to*
           *gaze as stupefied.*
*Nuncio*.        Caitiffs! Have ye eyes?
Whips, racks should teach you! What,
    his fools? his dupes?
Leave me! Unhand me!
*Kha*. [*approaching* Djabal *timidly*].
              Save her for my sake!
She was already thine; she would have
    shared
To-day thine exaltation: think, this day
Her hair was plaited thus because of
    thee!

Yes, feel the soft bright hair – feel!
*Nuncio [struggling with those who have
    seized him].*
                        What, because
His leman dies for him? You think it
    hard
To die? Oh, would you were at Rhodes,
    and choice
Of deaths should suit you!
*Kha. [bending over* ANAEL's *body].*
                        Just restore her life!
So little does it! there – the eyelids
    tremble!
'Twas not my breath that made them:
    and the lips
Move of themselves. I could restore her
    life!
Hakeem, we have forgotten – have
    presumed
On our free converse: we are better
    taught.
See, I kiss – how I kiss thy garment's
    hem
For her! She kisses it – Oh, take her
    deed
In mine! Thou dost believe now,
    Anael? – See,
She smiles! Were her lips open o'er the
    teeth
Thus, when I spoke first? She believes
    in thee!
Go not without her to the cedars, lord!
Or leave us both – I cannot go alone!
I have obeyed thee, if I dare so speak:
Hath Hakeem thus forgot all Djabal
    knew?
Thou feelest then my tears fall hot and
    fast
Upon thy hand, and yet thou speakest
    not?
Ere the Venetian trumpet sound – ere
    thou
Exalt thyself, O Hakeem! save thou her!
*Nuncio.* And the accursed Republic will
    arrive
And find me in their toils – dead, very
    like,

Under their feet!
                    What way – not one way yet
To foil them? None?
*[Observing* DJABAL's *face.* What ails the
    Khalif? Ah,
That ghastly face! A way to foil them
    yet!
*[To the* DRUSES.] Look to your Khalif,
    Druses! Is that face
God Hakeem's? Where is triumph, –
    where is … what
Said he of exaltation – hath he promised
So much to-day? Why then, exalt thyself!
Cast off that husk, thy form, set free thy
    soul
In splendour! Now, bear witness! here I
    stand –
I challenge him exalt himself, and I
Become, for that, a Druse like all of you!
*The Druses.* Exalt thyself! Exalt thyself,
    O Hakeem!
*Dja. [advances].* I can confess now all
    from first to last.
There is no longer shame for me.
            I am …
    *[Here the Venetian trumpet sounds: the*
        DRUSES *shout,* DJABAL's *eye catches
        the expression of those about him,
        and , as the old dream comes back,
        he is again confident and inspired.*
– Am I not Hakeem? And ye would
    have crawled
But yesterday within these impure
    courts
Where now ye stand erect! Not grand
    enough?
– What more could be conceded to
    such beasts
As all of you, so sunk and base as you,
Than a mere man? A man among such
    beasts
Was miracle enough: yet him you
    doubt,
Him you forsake, him fain would you
    destroy –
With the Venetians at your gate, the
    Nuncio

Thus – (see the baffled hypocrite!) and,
    best,
The Prefect there!
*Druses.*          No, Hakeem, ever thine!
*Nuncio.* He lies – and twice he lies –
    and thrice he lies!
Exalt thyself, Mahound! Exalt thyself!
*Dja.* Druses! we shall henceforth be far
    away –
Out of mere mortal ken – above the
    cedars –
But we shall see ye go, hear ye return,
Repeopling the old solitudes, –
    through thee,
My Khalil! Thou art full of me: I fill
Thee full – my hands thus fill thee!
    Yester-eve,
– Nay, but this morn, I deemed thee
    ignorant
Of all to do, requiring word of mine
To teach it: now, thou hast all gifts in
    one,
With truth and purity go other gifts,
All gifts come clustering to that. Go,
    lead
My people home whate'er betide!
[*Turning to the* DRUSES.] Ye take
This Khalil for my delegate? To him
Bow as to me? He leads to Lebanon –
Ye follow?
*Druses.*   We follow! Now exalt thyself!
*Dja.* [*raises* Loys]. Then to thee, Loys!
    How I wronged thee, Loys!
Yet, wronged, no less thou shalt have
    full revenge,
Fit for thy noble self, revenge – and
    thus.
Thou, loaded with such wrongs, the
    princely soul,
The first sword of Christ's sepulchre –
    thou shalt
Guard Khalil and my Druses home again!
Justice no less, God's justice and no
    more,

For those I leave! To seeking this, devote
Some few days out of thy Knight's
    brilliant life:
And, this obtained them, leave their
    Lebanon,
My Druses' blessing in thine ears –
    (they shall
Bless thee with blessing sure to have its
    way)
– One cedar-blossom in thy ducal cap,
One thought of Anael in thy heart, –
    perchance,
One thought of him who thus, to bid
    thee speed,
His last word to the living speaks! This
    done,
Resume thy course, and, first amidst
    the first
In Europe, take my heart along with
    thee!
Go boldly, go serenely, go augustly –
What shall withstand thee then?
[*He bends over* ANAEL.]          And last
    to thee!
Ah, did I dream I was to have, this day,
Exalted thee? A vain dream: hast thou
    not
Won greater exaltation? What remains
But press to thee, exalt myself to thee?
Thus I exalt myself, set free my soul!
    [*He stabs himself. As he falls, supported
        by* KHALIL *and* LOYS, *the* Venetians
            *enter; the* ADMIRAL *advances.*
*Admiral.* God and St Mark for Venice!
    Plant the Lion!
    [*At the clash of the planted standard,
        the* DRUSES *shout and move
            tumultuously forward,* LOYS
                *drawing his sword.*
*Dja.* [*leading them a few steps between
    KHALIL and* LOYS ]. On to the
    Mountain! At the Mountain,
    Druses!                    [*Dies.*

# A BLOT IN THE 'SCUTCHEON

A Tragedy

1843

*Persons*

Mildred Tresham. Guendolen Tresham. Thorold, Earl Tresham. Austin Tresham.
Henry, Earl Mertoun. Gerard, *and other retainers of* Lord Tresham.

Time, 17—

## ACT 1

*Scene 1 – The Interior of a Lodge in*
LORD TRESHAM'S *Park.*

*Many* RETAINERS *crowded at the window,
supposed to command a view of the
entrance to his mansion.* GERARD, *the
warrener, his back to a table on
which are flagons, etc.*

*1st Ret.* Ay, do! push, friends, and then
    you'll push down me!
– What for? Does any hear a runner's
    foot
Or a steed's trample or a coach-wheel's
    cry?
Is the Earl come or his least poursuivant?
But there's no breeding in a man of you
Save Gerard yonder: here's a half-place
    yet,
Old Gerard!
*Ger.*     Save your courtesies, my friend.
Here is my place.
*2nd Ret.*     Now, Gerard, out with it!
What makes you sullen, this of all the
    days
I' the year? To-day that young rich
    bountiful
Handsome Earl Mertoun, whom alone
    they match
With our Lord Tresham through the
    country-side,
Is coming here in utmost bravery
To ask our master's sister's hand?
*Ger.*     What then?
*2nd Ret.* What then? Why, you, she
    speaks to, if she meets
Your worship, smiles on as you hold
    apart

The boughs to let her through her
    forest walks,
You, always favourite for your no-deserts,
You've heard, these three days, how
    Earl Mertoun sues
To lay his heart and house and broad
    lands too
At Lady Mildred's feet: and while we
    squeeze
Ourselves into a mousehole lest we miss
One congee of the least page in his
    train,
You sit o' one side – 'there's the Earl,
    say I –
'What then?' say you!
*3rd Ret.*     I'll wager he has let
Both swans he tamed for Lady Mildred
    swim
Over the falls and gain the river!
*Ger.*     Ralph,
Is not to-morrow my inspecting-day
For you and for your hawks?
*4th Ret.*     Let Gerard be!
He's coarse-grained, like his carved
    black cross-bow stock.
Ha, look now, while we squabble with
    him, look!
Well done, now – is not this beginning,
    now,
To purpose?
*1st Ret.* Our retainers look as fine –
That's comfort. Lord, how Richard
    holds himself
With his white staff! Will not a knave
    behind
Prick him upright?
*4th Ret.*     He's only bówing, fool!

The Earl's man bent us lower by this
   much.
1st *Ret.* That's comfort. Here's a very
   cavalcade!
3rd *Ret.* I don't see wherefore Richard,
   and his troop
Of silk and silver varlets there, should
   find
Their perfumed selves so indispensable
On high days, holidays! Would it so
   disgrace
Our family, if I, for instance, stood –
In my right hand a cast of Swedish
   hawks,
A leash of greyhounds in my left? –
*Ger.*             – With Hugh
The logman for supporter, in his right
The bill-hook, in his left the brushwood-
   shears!
3rd *Ret.* Out on you, crab! What next,
   what next? The Earl!
1st *Ret.* Oh Walter, groom, our horses,
   do they match
The Earl's? Alas, that first pair of the
   six –
They paw the ground – Ah Walter! and
   that brute
Just on his haunches by the wheel!
6th *Ret.*            Ay – ay!
You, Philip, are a special hand, I hear,
At soups and sauces: what's a horse to
   you?
D'ye mark that beast they've slid into
   the midst
So cunningly? – then, Philip, mark this
   further;
No leg has he to stand on!
1st *Ret.*        No? That's comfort.
2nd *Ret.* Peace, Cook! The Earl
   descends. Well, Gerard, see
The Earl at least! Come, there's a proper
   man,
I hope! Why, Ralph, no falcon, Pole or
   Swede,
Has got a starrier eye.
3rd *Ret.*          His eyes are blue:
But leave my hawks alone!

4th *Ret.*        So young, and yet
So tall and shapely!
5th *Ret.*   Here's Lord Tresham's self!
There now – there's what a nobleman
   should be!
He's older, graver, loftier, he's more like
A House's head.
2nd *Ret.* But you'd not have a boy
– And what's the Earl beside? – possess
   too soon
That stateliness?
1st *Ret.*   Our master takes his hand –
Richard and his white staff are on the
   move –
Back fall our people – (tsh! – there's
   Timothy
Sure to get tangled in his ribbon-ties,
And Peter's cursed rosette's a-coming
   off!)
– At last I see our lord's back and his
   friend's;
And the whole beautiful bright company
Close round them – in they go!
   *[Jumping down from the window-*
   *bench, and making for the table and*
   *its jugs.*
Good health, long life,
Great joy to our Lord Tresham and his
   House!
6th *Ret.* My father drove his father first
   to court,
After his marriage-day – ay, did he!
2nd *Ret.*            God bless
Lord Tresham, Lady Mildred, and the
   Earl!
Here, Gerard, reach your beaker!
*Ger.*           Drink, my boys!
Don't mind me – all's not right about
   me – drink!
2nd *Ret.* [*aside*]. He's vexed, now, that
   he let the show escape!
[*To* Gerard.] Remember that the Earl
   returns this way.
*Ger.* That way?
2nd *Ret.*   Just so.
*Ger.*          Then my way's here.
                     [*Goes.*

*2nd Ret.*                                    Old Gerard
Will die soon – mind, I said it! He was
    used
To care about the pitifullest thing
That touched the House's honour, not
    an eye
But his could see wherein: and on a
    cause
Of scarce a quarter this importance,
    Gerard
Fairly had fretted flesh and bone away
In cares that this was right, nor that
    was wrong,
Such point decorous, and such square
    by rule –
He knew such niceties, no herald more:
And now – you see his humour: die he
    will!
*2nd Ret.* God help him! Who's for the
    great servants'-hall
To hear what's going on inside? They'd
    follow
Lord Tresham into the saloon.
*3rd Ret.*                                    I! –
*4th Ret.*                                    I! –
Leave Frank alone for catching, at the
    door,
Some hint of how the parley goes inside!
Prosperity to the great House once more!
Here's the last drop!
*1st Ret.*       Have at you! Boys, hurrah!

*Scene 2 – A Saloon in the Mansion.*
*Enter* LORD TRESHAM, LORD MERTOUN,
    AUSTIN, *and* GUENDOLEN.
*Tresh.* I welcome you, Lord Mertoun,
    yet once more,
To this ancestral roof of mine. Your
    name
– Noble among the noblest in itself,
Yet taking in your person, fame avers,
New price and lustre, – (as that gem
    you wear,
Transmitted from a hundred knightly
    breasts,
Fresh chased and set and fixed by its
    last lord,

Seems to re-kindle at the core) – your
    name
Would win you welcome! –
*Mer.*                    Thanks!
*Tresh.*              – But add to that,
The worthiness and grace and dignity
Of your proposal for uniting both
Our Houses even closer than respect
Unites them now – add these, and you
    must grant
One favour more, nor that the least, –
    to think
The welcome I should give; – 'tis given!
    My lord,
My only brother, Austin: he's the king's.
Our cousin, Lady Guendolen – betrothed
To Austin: all are yours.
*Mer.*                    I thank you – less
For the expressed commendings which
    your seal,
And only that, authenticates – forbids
My putting from me … to my heart I
    take
Your praise … but praise less claims
    my gratitude,
Than the indulgent insight it implies
Of what must needs be uppermost
    with one
Who comes, like me, with the bare
    leave to ask,
In weighed and measured
    unimpassioned words,
A gift, which, if as calmly 'tis denied,
He must withdraw, content upon his
    cheek,
Despair within his soul. That I dare ask
Firmly, near boldly, near with confidence
That gift, I have to thank you. Yes, Lord
    Tresham,
I love your sister – as you'd have one
    love
That lady … oh more, more I love her!
    Wealth,
Rank, all the world thinks me, they're
    yours, you know,
To hold or part with, at your choice –
    but grant

My true self, me without a rood of
    land,
A piece of gold, a name of yesterday,
Grant me that lady, and you … Death
    or life?
*Guen.* [*apart to* AUSTIN]. Why, this is
    loving, Austin!
*Aus.*                          He's so young!
*Guen.* Young? Old enough, I think, to
    half surmise
He never had obtained an entrance
    here
Were all this fear and trembling needed.
*Aus.*                          Hush!
He reddens.
*Guen.*      Mark him, Austin; that's true
    love!
Ours must begin again.
*Tresh.*              We'll sit, my lord.
Ever with best desert goes diffidence.
I may speak plainly nor be misconceived.
That I am wholly satisfied with you
On this occasion, when a falcon's eye
Were dull compared with mine to
    search out faults,
Is somewhat. Mildred's hand is hers to
    give
Or to refuse.
*Mer.*        But you, you grant my suit?
I have your word if hers?
*Tresh.*                My best of words
If hers encourage you. I trust it will.
Have you seen Lady Mildred, by the
    way?
*Mer.* I … I … our two demesnes,
    remember, touch;
I have been used to wander carelessly
After my stricken game: the heron
    roused
Deep in my woods, has trailed its
    broken wing
Thro' thicks and glades a mile in yours,
    – or else
Some eyass ill-reclaimed has taken
    flight
And lured me after her from tree to
    tree,

I marked not whither. I have come
    upon
The lady's wondrous beauty unaware,
And – and then … I have seen her.
*Guen.* [*aside to* AUSTIN]. Note that mode
Of faltering out that, when a lady
    passed,
He, having eyes, did see her! You had
    said –
'On such a day I scanned her, head to
    foot;
'Observed a red, where red should not
    have been,
'Outside her elbow; but was pleased
    enough
'Upon the whole.' Let such irreverent
    talk
Be lessoned for the future!
*Tresh.*                ⌐ What's to say
May be said briefly. She has never
    known
A mother's care; I stand for father too.
Her beauty is not strange to you, it
    seems –
You cannot know the good and tender
    heart,
Its girl's trust and its woman's
    constancy,
How pure yet passionate, how calm yet
    kind,
How grave yet joyous, how reserved yet
    free
As light where friends are – how imbued
    with lore
The world most prizes, yet the simplest,
    yet
The … one might know I talked of
    Mildred – thus
We brothers talk!
*Mer.*              I thank you.
*Tresh.*                        In a word,
Control's not for this lady; but her wish
To please me outstrips in its subtlety
My power of being pleased: herself
    creates
The want she means to satisfy. My
    heart

Prefers your suit to her as 'twere its own.
Can I say more?
*Mer.*                No more – thanks, thanks –
     no more!
*Tresh.* This matter then discussed ...
*Mer.*                    – We'll waste no breath
On aught less precious. I'm beneath
     the roof
Which holds her: while I thought of
     that, my speech
To you would wander – as it must not
     do,
Since as you favour me I stand or fall.
I pray you suffer that I take my leave!
*Tresh.* With less regret 'tis suffered,
     that again
We meet, I hope, so shortly.
*Mer.*                        We? again? –
Ah yes, forgive me – when shall ... you
     will crown
Your goodness by forthwith apprising
     me
When ... if ... the lady will appoint a
     day
For me to wait on you – and her.
*Tresh.*                        So soon
As I am made acquainted with her
     thoughts
On your proposal – howsoe'er they
     lean –
A messenger shall bring you the result.
*Mer.* You cannot bind me more to you,
     my lord.
Farewell till we renew ... I trust, renew
A converse ne'er to disunite again.
*Tresh.* So may it prove!
*Mer.*                You, lady, you, sir, take
My humble salutation!
*Guen. and Aus.*        Thanks!
*Tresh.*                        Within there!
     [SERVANTS *enter.* TRESHAM *conducts*
          MERTOUN *to the door. Meantime*
                    AUSTIN *remarks,*
                              Well,
Here I have an advantage of the Earl,
Confess now! I'd not think that all was
     safe

Because my lady's brother stood my
     friend!
Why, he makes sure of her – 'do you
     say, yes –
'She'll not say, no,' – what comes it to
     beside?
I should have prayed the brother,
     'speak this speech,
'For Heaven's sake urge this on her –
     put in this –
'Forget not, as you'd save me, t'other
     thing, –
'Then set down what she says, and
     how she looks,
'And if she smiles, and' (in an under
     breath)
'Only let her accept me, and do you
'And all the world refuse me, if you
     dare!'
*Guen.* That way you'd take, friend
     Austin? What a shame
I was your cousin, tamely from the first
Your bride, and all this fervour's run to
     waste!
Do you know you speak sensibly to-day?
The Earl's a fool.
*Aus.*        Here's Thorold. Tell him so!
*Tresh.* [*returning*]. Now, voices, voices!
     'St! the lady's first!
How seems he? – seems he not ...
     come, faith give fraud
The mercy-stroke whenever they engage!
Down with fraud, up with faith! How
     seems the Earl?
A name! a blazon! if you knew their
     worth,
As you will never! come – the Earl?
*Guen.*                        He's young.
*Tresh.* What's she? an infant save in
     heart and brain.
Young! Mildred is fourteen, remark!
     And you ...
Austin, how old is she?
*Guen.*                There's tact for you!
I meant that being young was good
     excuse
If one should tax him ...

*Tresh.* Well?

*Guen.* – With lacking wit.

*Tresh.* He lacked wit? Where might he lack wit, so please you?

*Guen.* In standing straighter than the steward's rod

And making you the tiresomest harangue,

Instead of slipping over to my side

And softly whispering in my ear, 'Sweet lady,

'Your cousin there will do me detriment

'He little dreams of: he's absorbed, I see,

'In my old name and fame – be sure he'll leave

'My Mildred, when his best account of me

'Is ended, in full confidence I wear

'My grandsire's periwig down either cheek.

'I'm lost unless your gentleness vouchsafes' …

*Tresh.* … 'To give a best of best accounts, yourself,

'Of me and my demerits.' You are right!

He should have said what now I say for him.

Yon golden creature, will you help us all?

Here's Austin means to vouch for much, but you

– You are … what Austin only knows! Come up,

All three of us: she's in the library

No doubt, for the day's wearing fast. Precede!

*Guen.* Austin, how we must – !

*Tresh.* Must what? Must speak truth,

Malignant tongue! Detect one fault in him!

I challenge you!

*Guen.* Witchcraft's a fault in him,

For you're bewitched.

*Tresh.* What's urgent we obtain

Is, that she soon receive him – say, tomorrow,

Next day at furthest.

*Guen.* Ne'er instruct me!

*Tresh.* Come!

– He's out of your good graces, since forsooth,

He stood not as he'd carry us by storm

With his perfections! You're for the composed

Manly assured becoming confidence!

– Get her to say, 'to-morrow,' and I'll give you …

I'll give you black Urganda, to be spoiled

With petting and snail-paces. Will you? Come!

*Scene 3* – MILDRED's *chamber. A painted window overlooks the park.*
   MILDRED *and* GUENDOLEN.

*Guen.* Now, Mildred, spare those pains. I have not left

Our talkers in the library, and climbed

The wearisome ascent to this your bower

In company with you, – I have not dared …

Nay, worked such prodigies as sparing you

Lord Mertoun's pedigree before the flood,

Which Thorold seemed in very act to tell

– Or bringing Austin to pluck up that most

Firm-rooted heresy – your suitor's eyes,

He would maintain, were grey instead of blue –

I think I brought him to contrition! – Well,

I have not done such things, (all to deserve

A minute's quiet cousin's talk with you,)

To be dismissed so coolly.

*Mil.* Guendolen!

What have I done? what could suggest …

*Guen.* There, there!

Do I not comprehend you'd be alone

To throw those testimonies in a heap,

Thorold's enlargings, Austin's brevities,

With that poor silly heartless Guendolen's

Ill-timed misplaced attempted
　　smartnesses –
And sift their sense out? now, I come to
　　spare you
Nearly a whole night's labour. Ask and
　　have!
Demand, be answered! Lack I ears and
　　eyes?
Am I perplexed which side of the rock-
　　table
The Conqueror dined on when he
　　landed first,
Lord Mertoun's ancestor was bidden
　　take –
The bow-hand or the arrow-hand's
　　great meed?
Mildred, the Earl has soft blue eyes!
*Mil.*　　　　　　　　My brother –
Did he ... you said that he received
　　him well?
*Guen*. If I said only 'well' I said not
　　much.
Oh, stay – which brother?
*Mil.*　　　　Thorold! who – who else?
*Guen*. Thorold (a secret) is too proud
　　by half, –
Nay, hear me out – with us he's even
　　gentler
Than we are with our birds. Of this
　　great House
The least retainer that e'er caught his
　　glance
Would die for him, real dying – no
　　mere talk:
And in the world, the court, if men
　　would cite
The perfect spirit of honour, Thorold's
　　name
Rises of its clear nature to their lips.
But he should take men's homage,
　　trust in it,
And care no more about what drew it
　　down.
He has desert, and that, acknow-
　　ledgment;
Is he content?
*Mil.*　　　You wrong him, Guendolen.

*Guen*. He's proud, confess; so proud
　　with brooding o'er
The light of his interminable line,
An ancestry with men all paladins,
And women all ...
*Mil.*　　　　　Dear Guendolen, 'tis late!
When yonder purple pane the climbing
　　moon
Pierces, I know 'tis midnight.
*Guen*.　　　　　　Well, that Thorold
Should rise up from such musings and
　　receive
One come audaciously to graft himself
Into this peerless stock, yet find no flaw,
No slightest spot in such an one ...
*Mil.*　　　　　　　　　Who finds
A spot in Mertoun?
*Guen*.　　Not your brother; therefore,
Not the whole world.
*Mil.*　　　　I am weary, Guendolen.
Bear with me!
*Guen*.　　　I am foolish.
*Mil.*　　　　　　　Oh no, kind!
But I would rest.
*Guen*.　　Good night and rest to you!
I said how gracefully his mantle lay
Beneath the rings of his light hair?
*Mil.*　　　　　　　　　Brown hair.
*Guen*. Brown? why, it *is* brown: how
　　could you know that?
*Mil*. How? did not you – Oh, Austin
　　'twas, declared
His hair was light, not brown – my
　　head! – and look,
The moon-beam purpling the dark
　　chamber! Sweet,
Good night!
*Guen*. Forgive me – sleep the soundlier
　　for me!
　　　　　　　[*Going, she turns suddenly.*
　　　　　　　　　　　　　　Mildred!
Perdition! all's discovered! Thorold
　　finds
– That the Earl's greatest of all grand-
　　mothers
Was grander daughter still – to that fair
　　dame

Whose garter slipped down at the famous
dance!                    [*Goes.*

*Mil.* Is she – can she be really gone at
last?

My heart! I shall not reach the window.
Needs

Must I have sinned much, so to suffer.
        [*She lifts the small lamp which is
            suspended before the Virgin's
            image in the window, and places
                it by the purple pane.
                            There!*
        [*She returns to the seat in front.*

Mildred and Mertoun! Mildred, with
consent

Of all the world and Thorold, Mertoun's
bride!

Too late! 'Tis sweet to think of, sweeter
still

To hope for, that this blessed end soothes
up

The curse of the beginning; but I know

It comes too late: 'twill sweetest be of
all

To dream my soul away and die upon.
                    [*A noise without.*

The voice! Oh why, why glided sin the
snake

Into the paradise Heaven meant us
both?

            [*The window opens softly.
                A low voice sings.*

There's a woman like a dew-drop, she's
    so purer than the purest;
And her noble heart's the noblest, yes,
    and her sure faith's the surest:
And her eyes are dark and humid, like
    the depth on depth of lustre
Hid i' the harebell, while her tresses,
    sunnier than the wild-grape cluster,
Gush in golden-tinted plenty down her
    neck's rose-misted marble:
Then her voice's music ... call it the
    well's bubbling, the bird's warble!

            [*A figure wrapped in a mantle
                appears at the window.*

*And this woman says, 'My days were
    sunless and my nights were
    moonless,*
*'Parched the pleasant April herbage,
    and the lark's heart's outbreak
    tuneless,*
*'If you loved me not!' And! who – (all,
    for words of flame!) adore her,*
*Who am mad to lay my spirit prostrate
    palpably before her –*

            [*He enters, approaches her seat,
                and bends over her.*

*I may enter at her portal soon, as now
    her lattice takes me,*
*And by noontide as by midnight make
    her mine, as hers she makes me!*

            [*The EARL throws off his
                slouched hat and long cloak.*

My very heart sings, so I sing, Beloved!

*Mil.* Sit, Henry – do not take my hand!

*Mer.*                    'Tis mine.

The meeting that appalled us both so
much

Is ended.

*Mil.*        What begins now?

*Mer.*                    Happiness

Such as the world contains not.

*Mil.*    -                That is it.

Our happiness would, as you say, exceed

The whole world's best of blisses: we –
do we

Deserve that? Utter to your soul, what
mine

Long since, Beloved, has grown used to
hear,

Like a death-knell, so much regarded
once, once,

And so familiar now; this will not be!

*Mer.* Oh, Mildred, have I met your
brother's face?

Compelled myself – if not to speak
untruth,

Yet to disguise, to shun, to put aside

The truth, as – what had e'er prevailed
on me

Save you, to venture? Have I gained at
    last
Your brother, the one scarer of your
    dreams,
And waking thoughts' sole apprehension
    too?
Does a new life, like a young sunrise,
    break
On the strange unrest of our night,
    confused
With rain and stormy flaw – and will
    you see
No dripping blossoms, no fire-tinted
    drops
On each live spray, no vapour steaming
    up,
And no expressless glory in the East?
When I am by you, to be ever by you,
When I have won you and may
    worship you,
Oh, Mildred, can you say 'this will not
    be'?
*Mil.* Sin has surprised us, so will
    punishment.
*Mer.* No – me alone, who sinned alone!
*Mil.*                                    The night
You likened our past life to – was it
    storm
Throughout to you then, Henry?
*Mer.*                                    Of your life
I spoke – what am I, what my life, to
    waste
A thought about when you are by me?
    – you
It was, I said my folly called the storm
And pulled the night upon. 'Twas day
    with me –
Perpetual dawn with me.
*Mil.*                      Come what, come will,
You have been happy: take my hand!
*Mer.* [*after a pause*].           How good
Your brother is! I figured him a cold –
Shall I say, haughty man?
*Mil.*                                    They told me all.
I know all.
*Mer.*           It will soon be over.
*Mil.*                                    Over?

Oh, what is over? what must I live
    through
And say, ' 'tis over'? Is our meeting
    over?
Have I received in presence of them all
The partner of my guilty love – with
    brow
Trying to seem a maiden's brow – with
    lips
Which make believe that when they
    strive to form
Replies to you and tremble as they
    strive,
It is the nearest ever they approached
A stranger's … Henry, yours that
    stranger's … lip –
With cheek that looks a virgin's, and
    that is …
Ah God, some prodigy of thine will
    stop
This planned piece of deliberate
    wickedness
In its birth even! some fierce leprous
    spot
Will mar the brow's dissimulating! I
Shall murmur no smooth speeches got
    by heart,
But, frenzied, pour forth all our woeful
    story,
The love, the shame, and the despair –
    with them
Round me aghast as round some cursed
    fount
That should spirt water, and spouts
    blood. I'll not
… Henry, you do not wish that I
    should draw
This vengeance down? I'll not affect a
    grace
That's gone from me – gone once, and
    gone for ever!
*Mer.* Mildred, my honour is your own.
    I'll share
Disgrace I cannot suffer by myself.
A word informs your brother I retract
This morning's offer; time will yet
    bring forth

Some better way of saving both of us.
*Mil.* I'll meet their faces, Henry!
*Mer.*                    When? to-morrow!
Get done with it!
*Mil.*          Oh, Henry, not to-morrow!
Next day! I never shall prepare my words
And looks and gestures sooner. – How
     you must
Despise me!
*Mer*.    Mildred, break it if you choose,
A heart the love of you uplifted – still
Uplifts, thro' this protracted agony,
To heaven! but Mildred, answer me, –
     first pace
The chamber with me – once again –
     now, say
Calmly the part, the … what it is of me
You see contempt (for you did say
     contempt)
– Contempt for you in! I would pluck
     it off
And cast it from me! – but no – no,
     you'll not
Repeat that? – will you, Mildred, repeat
     that?
*Mil.* Dear Henry!
*Mer*.      I was scarce a boy – e'en now
What am I more? And you were infantine
When first I met you; why, your hair
     fell loose
On either side! My fool's-cheek reddens
     now
Only in the recalling how it burned
That morn to see the shape of many a
     dream
– You know we boys are prodigal of
     charms
To her we dream of – I had heard of one,
Had dreamed of her, and I was close to
     her,
Might speak to her, might live and die
     her own,
Who knew? I spoke. Oh, Mildred, feel
     you not
That now, while I remember every glance
Of yours, each word of yours, with
     power to test

And weigh them in the diamond scales
     of pride,
Resolved the treasure of a first and last
Heart's love shall have been bartered at
     its worth,
– That now I think upon your purity
And utter ignorance of guilt – your own
Or other's guilt – the girlish undisguised
Delight at a strange novel prize – (I talk
A silly language, but interpret, you!)
If I, with fancy at its full, and reason
Scarce in its germ, enjoined you secrecy,
If you had pity on my passion, pity
On my protested sickness of the soul
To sit beside you, hear you breathe,
     and watch
Your eyelids and the eyes beneath – if
     you
Accorded gifts and knew not they were
     gifts –
If I grew mad at last with enterprise
And must behold my beauty in her
     bower
Or perish – (I was ignorant of even
My own desires – what then were you?)
     if sorrow –
Sin – if the end came – must I now
     renounce
My reason, blind myself to light, say
     truth
Is false and lie to God and my own
     soul?
Contempt were all of this!
*Mil.*                    Do you believe …
Or, Henry, I'll not wrong you – you
     believe
That I was ignorant. I scarce grieve o'er
The past. We'll love on; you will love
     me still.
*Mer*. Oh, to love less what one has
     injured! Dove,
Whose pinion I have rashly hurt, my
     breast –
Shall my heart's warmth not nurse thee
     into strength?
Flower I have crushed, shall I not care
     for thee?

Bloom o'er my crest, my fight-mark
    and device!
Mildred, I love you and you love me.
*Mil.*                    Go!
Be that your last word. I shall sleep
    tonight.
*Mer.* This is not our last meeting?
*Mil.*          One night more.
*Mer.* And then – think, then!
*Mil.*    Then, no sweet courtship-days,
No dawning consciousness of love for
    us,
No strange and palpitating births of
    sense
From words and looks, no innocent
    fears and hopes,
Reserves and confidences: morning's
    over!
*Mer.* How else should love's perfected
    noontide follow?
All the dawn promised shall the day
    perform.
*Mil.* So may it be! but –
          You are cautious, Love?
Are sure that unobserved you scaled
    the walls?
*Mer.* Oh, trust me! Then our final
    meeting's fixed
To-morrow night?
*Mil.*       Farewell! Stay, Henry …
    wherefore?
His foot is on the yew-tree bough; the
    turf
Receives him: now the moonlight as he
    runs
Embraces him – but he must go – is
    gone.
Ah, once again he turns – thanks,
    thanks, my Love!
He's gone. Oh, I'll believe him every
    word!
I was so young, I loved him so, I had
No mother, God forgot me, and I fell.
There may be pardon yet: all's doubt
    beyond.
Surely the bitterness of death is past.

### ACT 2
*Scene – The Library.*

    *Enter* LORD TRESHAM, *hastily.*
*Tresh.* This way! In, Gerard, quick!
             [*As* GERARD *enters,*
      TRESHAM *secures the door.*
         Now speak! or, wait –
I'll bid you speak directly. [*Seats*
    *himself.*         Now repeat
Firmly and circumstantially the tale
You just now told me; it eludes me;
    either
I did not listen, or the half is gone
Away from me. How long have you
    lived here?
Here in my house, your father kept our
    woods
Before you?
*Ger.*      – As his father did, my lord.
I have been eating, sixty years almost,
Your bread.
*Tres.* Yes, yes. You ever were of all
The servants in my father's house. I
    know,
The trusted one. You'll speak the truth.
*Ger.*               I'll speak
God's truth. Night after night …
*Tresh.*         Since when?
*Ger.*                At least
A month – each midnight has some
    man access
To Lady Mildred's chamber.
*Tresh.*         Tush, 'access' –
No wide words like 'access' to me!
*Ger.*               He runs
Along the woodside, crosses to the South,
Takes the left tree that ends the
    avenue …
*Tresh.* The last great yew tree?
*Ger.*        You might stand upon
The main boughs like a platform. Then
    he …
*Tresh.*   Quick!
*Ger.* Climbs up, and, where they lessen
    at the top,
– I cannot see distinctly, but he throws,

I think – for this I do not vouch – a
  line
That reaches to the lady's casement –
*Tresh.*                               – Which
He enters not! Gerard, some wretched
  fool
Dares pry into my sister's privacy!
When such are young, it seems a
  precious thing
To have approached, – to merely have
  approached,
Got sight of, the abode of her they set
Their frantic thoughts upon. He does
  not enter?
Gerard?
*Ger.*     There is a lamp that's full i' the
  midst,
Under a red square in the painted glass
Of Lady Mildred's ...
*Tresh.*         Leave that name out! Well?
That lamp?
*Ger.*  – Is moved at midnight higher up
To one pane – a small dark-blue pane;
  he waits
For that among the boughs: at sight of
  that,
I see him, plain as I see you, my lord,
Open the lady's casement, enter
  there ...
*Tresh.* – And stay?
*Ger.*        An hour, two hours.
*Tresh.*                        And this you saw
Once? – twice? – quick!
*Ger.*        Twenty times.
*Tresh.*                And what brings you
Under the yew trees?
*Ger.*              The first night I left
My range so far, to track the stranger
  stag
That broke the pale, I saw the man.
*Tresh.*                         Yet sent
No cross-bow shaft through the
  marauder?
*Ger.*         But
He came, my lord, the first time he was
  seen,
In a great moonlight, light as any day,

*From* Lady Mildred's chamber.
*Tresh.* [*after a pause*].You have no cause
– Who could have cause to do my sister
  wrong?
*Ger.* Oh, my lord, only once – let me
  this once
Speak what is on my mind! Since first I
  noted
All this, I've groaned as if a fiery net
Plucked me this way and that – fire if I
  turned
To her, fire if I turned to you, and fire
If down I flung myself and strove to die.
The lady could not have been seven
  years old
When I was trusted to conduct her safe
Through the deer-herd to stroke the
  snow-white fawn
I brought to eat bread from her tiny
  hand
Within a month. She ever had a smile
To greet me with – she ... if it could
  undo
What's done, to lop each limb from off
  this trunk ...
All that is foolish talk, not fit for you –
I mean, I could not speak and bring her
  hurt
For Heaven's compelling. But when I
  was fixed
To hold my peace, each morsel of your
  food
Eaten beneath your roof, my birth-place
  too,
Choked me. I wish I had grown mad
  doubts
What it behoved me do. This morn it
  seemed
Either I must confess to you, or die:
Now it is done, I seem the vilest worm
That crawls, to have betrayed my lady.
*Tresh.*                             No –
No, Gerard!
*Ger.*      Let me go!
*Tresh.*              A man you say:
What man? Young? Not a vulgar hind?
  What dress?

*Ger*. A slouched hat and a large dark
    foreign cloak
Wraps his whole form; even his face is
    hid;
But I should judge him young: no hind,
    be sure!
*Tresh*. Why?
*Ger*.         He is ever armed: his sword
    projects
Beneath the cloak.
*Tresh*.         Gerard, – I will not say
No word, no breath of this!
*Ger*.         Thanks, thanks, my lord!
                        *[Goes.*
*Tresh*. *[paces the room. After a pause]*.
Oh, thought's absurd! – as with some
    monstrous fact
Which, when ill thoughts beset us,
    seems to give
Merciful God that made the sun and
    stars,
The waters and the green delights of
    earth,
The lie! I apprehend the monstrous
    fact –
Yet know the maker of all worlds is
    good,
And yield my reason up, inadequate
To reconcile what yet I do behold –
Blasting my sense! There's cheerful day
    outside:
This is my library, and this the chair
My father used to sit in carelessly
After his soldier-fashion, while I stood
Between his knees to question him:
    and here
Gerard our grey retainer, – as he says,
Fed with our food, from sire to son, an
    age, –
Has told a story – I am to believe!
That Mildred … oh, no, no! both tales
    are true,
Her pure cheek's story and the forester's!
Would she, or could she, err – much
    less, confound
All guilts of treachery, of craft, of …
    Heaven

Keep me within its hand! – I will sit
    here
Until thought settle and I see my
    course.
Avert, oh God, only this woe from me!
        *[As he sinks his head between his*
        *arms on the table,* GUENDOLEN's
        *voice is heard at the door.*
Lord Tresham! *[She knocks.]* Is Lord
    Tresham there?
        *[*TRESHAM, *hastily turning, pulls*
        *down the first book above*
        *him and opens it.*
*Tresh*.         Come in! *[She enters.*
Ha, Guendolen! – good morning.
*Guen*.         Nothing more?
*Tresh*. What should I say more?
*Guen*.         Pleasant question! more?
This more. Did I besiege poor Mildred's
    brain
Last night till close on morning with
    'the Earl,'
'The Earl' – whose worth did I asseverate
Till I am very fain to hope that …
    Thorold,
What is all this? You are not well!
*Tresh*.         Who, I?
You laugh at me.
*Guen*.         Has what I'm fain to hope,
Arrived then? Does that huge tome show
    some blot
In the Earl's 'scutcheon come no
    longer back
Than Arthur's time?
*Tresh*.         When left you Mildred's
    chamber?
*Guen*. Oh, late enough, I told you! The
    main thing
To ask is, how I left her chamber, –
    sure,
Content yourself, she'll grant this
    paragon
Of Earls no such ungracious …
*Tresh*.         Send her here!
*Guen*. Thorold?
*Tresh*.         I mean – acquaint her,
    Guendolen,

– But mildly!
*Guen.*          Mildly?
*Tresh.*          Ah, you guessed aright!
I am not well: there is no hiding it.
But tell her I would see her at her
          leisure –
That is, at once! here in the library!
The passage in that old Italian book
We hunted for so long is found, say,
          found –
And if I let it slip again … you see,
That she must come – and instantly!
*Guen.*                    I'll die
Piecemeal, record that, if there have not
          gloomed
Some blot i' the 'scutcheon!
*Tresh.*          Go! or, Guendolen,
Be you at call, – with Austin, if you
          choose, –
In the adjoining gallery! There, go!
                    [GUENDOLEN *goes.*
Another lesson to me! You might bid
A child disguise his heart's sore, and
          conduct
Some sly investigation point by point
With a smooth brow, as well as bid me
          catch
The inquisitorial cleverness some praise.
If you had told me yesterday, 'There's
          one
'You needs must circumvent and
          practise with,
'Entrap by policies, if you would worm
'The truth out: and that one is – Mildred!'
          There,
There – reasoning is thrown away on it!
Prove she's unchaste … why, you may
          after prove
That she's a poisoner, traitress, what
          you will!
Where I can comprehend nought,
          nought's to say.
Or do, or think. Force on me but the
          first
Abomination, – then outpour all plagues,
And I shall ne'er make count of them.
                    *Enter* MILDRED.

*Mil.*                    What book
Is it I wanted, Thorold? Guendolen
Thought you were pale; you are not
          pale. That book?
That's Latin surely.
*Tresh.*          Mildred, here's a line,
(Don't lean on me: I'll English it for
          you)
'Love conquers all things.' What love
          conquers them?
What love should you esteem – best
          love?
*Mil.*          True love.
*Tresh.* I mean, and should have said,
          whose love is best
Of all that love or that profess to love?
*Mil.* The list's so long: there's father's,
          mother's, husband's …
*Tresh.* Mildred, I do believe a brother's
          love
For a sole sister must exceed them all.
For see now, only see! there's no alloy
Of earth that creeps into the perfect'st
          gold
Of other loves – no gratitude to claim;
You never gave her life, not even aught
That keeps life – never tended her,
          instructed,
Enriched her – so, your love can claim
          no right
O'er her save pure love's claim: that's
          what I call
Freedom from earthliness. You'll never
          hope
To be such friends, for instance, she
          and you,
As when you hunted cowslips in the
          woods
Or played together in the meadow hay.
Oh yes – with age, respect comes, and
          your worth
Is felt, there's growing sympathy of
          tastes,
There's ripened friendship, there's
          confirmed esteem:
– Much head these make against the
          new-comer!

The startling apparition, the strange
    youth –
Whom one half-hour's conversing
    with, or, say,
Mere gazing at, shall change (beyond
    all change
This Ovid ever sang about) your soul
. . . Her soul, that is, – the sister's soul!
    With her
'Twas winter yesterday; now, all is
    warmth,
The green leaf's springing and the
    turtle's voice,
'Arise and come away!' Come whither?
    – far
Enough from the esteem, respect, and
    all
The brother's somewhat insignificant
Array of lights! All which he knows
    before,
Has calculated on so long ago!
I think such love, (apart from yours
    and mine,)
Contented with its little term of life,
Intending to retire betimes, aware
How soon the background must be
    place for it,
– I think, am sure, a brother's love
    exceeds
All the world's love in its unworldliness.
*Mil.* What is this for?
*Tresh.*        This, Mildred, is it for!
Or, no, I cannot go to it so soon!
That's one of many points my haste left
    out –
Each day, each hour throws forth its
    silk-slight film
Between the being tied to you by birth,
And you, until those slender threads
    compose
A web that shrouds her daily life of
    hopes
And fears and fancies, all her life, from
    yours:
So close you live and yet so far apart!
And must I rend this web, tear up,
    break down

The sweet and palpitating mystery
That makes her sacred? You – for you I
    mean,
Shall I speak, shall I not speak?
*Mil.*                Speak!
*Tresh.*                I will.
Is there a story men could – any man
Could tell of you, you would conceal
    from me?
I'll never think there's falsehood on that
    lip.
Say 'There is no such story men could
    tell,'
And I'll believe you, though I disbelieve
The world – the world of better men
    than I,
And women such as I suppose you.
    Speak!
[*After a pause.*] Not speak? Explain
    then! Clear it up then! Move
Some of the miserable weight away
That presses lower than the grave! Not
    speak?
Some of the dead weight, Mildred! Ah,
    if I
Could bring myself to plainly make
    their charge
Against you! Must I, Mildred? Silent
    still?
[*After a pause.*] Is there a gallant that
    has night by night
Admittance to your chamber?
[*After a pause.*]       Then, his name!
Till now, I only had a thought for you:
But now, – his name!
*Mil.*          Thorold, do you devise
Fit expiation for my guilt, if fit
There be! 'Tis nought to say that I'll
    endure
And bless you, – that my spirit yearns
    to purge
Her stains off in the fierce renewing
    fire:
But do not plunge me into other guilt!
Oh, guilt enough! I cannot tell his name.
*Tresh.* Then judge yourself! How
    should I act? Pronounce!

*Mil.* Oh, Thorold, you must never
 tempt me thus!
To die here in this chamber by that
 sword
Would seem like punishment: so should
 I glide,
Like an arch-cheat, into extremest bliss!
'Twere easily arranged for me: but you –
What would become of you?
*Tresh.*     And what will now
Become of me? I'll hide your shame
 and mine
From every eye; the dead must heave
 their hearts
Under the marble of our chapel-floor;
They cannot rise and blast you. You may
 wed
Your paramour above our mother's
 tomb;
Our mother cannot move from 'neath
 your foot.
We too will somehow wear this one day
 out:
But with to-morrow hastens here – the
 Earl!
The youth without suspicion face can
 come
From Heaven, and heart from … 
 whence proceed such hearts?
I have despatched last night at your
 command
A missive bidding him present himself
To-morrow – here – thus much is said;
 the rest
Is understood as if 'twere written
 down –
'His suit finds favour in your eyes.' Now
 dictate
This morning's letter that shall counter-
 mand
Last night's – do dictate that!
*Mil.*     But, Thorold – if
I will receive him as I said?
*Tresh.*     The Earl?
*Mil.* I will receive him.
*Tresh.* [*starting up*]. Ho there!
 Guendolen!

GUENDOLEN *and* AUSTIN *enter.*
And, Austin, you are welcome, too!
 Look there!
The woman there!
*Aus. and Guen.* How? Mildred?
*Tresh.*     Mildred once!
Now the receiver night by night, when
 sleep
Blesses the inmates of her father's house,
– I say, the soft sly wanton that receives
Her guilt's accomplice 'neath this roof
 which holds
You, Guendolen, you, Austin, and has
 held
A thousand Treshams – never one like
 her!
No lighter of the signal-lamp her quick
Foul breath near quenches in hot
 eagerness
To mix with breath as foul! no loosener
O' the lattice, practised in the stealthy
 tread,
The low voice and the noiseless come-
 and-go!
Not one composer of the bacchant's
 mien
Into – what you thought Mildred's, in
 a word!
Know her!
*Guen.*Oh, Mildred, look to me, at least!
Thorold – she's dead, I'd say, but that
 she stands
Rigid as stone and whiter!
*Tresh.*     You have heard …
*Guen.* Too much! You must proceed
 no further.
*Mil.*    Yes –
Proceed! All's truth. Go from me!
*Tresh.*     All is truth,
She tells you! Well, you know, or ought
 to know,
All this I would forgive in her. I'd con
Each precept the harsh world enjoins,
 I'd take
Our ancestors' stern verdicts one by
 one,
I'd bind myself before them to exact

The prescribed vengeance – and one
    word of hers,
The sight of her, the bare least memory
Of Mildred, my one sister, my heart's
    pride
Above all prides, my all in all so long,
Would scatter every trace of my
    resolve.
What were it silently to waste away
And see her waste away from this day
    forth,
Two scathed things with leisure to
    repent,
And grow acquainted with the grave,
    and die
Tired out if not at peace, and be
    forgotten?
It were not so impossible to bear.
But this – that, fresh from last night's
    pledge renewed
Of love with the successful gallant there,
She calmly bids me help her to entice,
Inveigle an unconscious trusting youth
Who thinks her all that's chaste and
    good and pure,
– Invites me to betray him … who so
    fit
As honour's self to cover shame's arch-
    deed?
– That she'll receive Lord Mertoun –
    (her own phrase) –
This, who could bear? Why, you have
    heard of thieves,
Stabbers, the earth's disgrace, who yet
    have laughed,
'Talk not to me of torture – I'll betray
'No comrade I've pledged faith to!' –
    you have heard
Of wretched women – all but Mildreds
    – tied
By wild illicit ties to losels vile
You'd tempt them to forsake; and they'll
    reply
'Gold, friends, repute, I left for him, I
    find
'In him, why should I leave him then
    for gold,

'Repute or friends?' – and you have felt
    your heart
Respond to such poor outcasts of the
    world
As to so many friends; bad as you
    please,
You've felt they were God's men and
    women still,
So, not to be disowned by you. But she
That stands there, calmly gives her
    lover up
As means to wed the Earl that she may
    hide
Their intercourse the surelier: and, for
    this,
I curse her to her face before you all.
Shame hunt her from the earth! Then
    Heaven do right
To both! It hears me now – shall judge
    her then!
       [As MILDRED *faints and falls*,
           TRESHAM *rushes out.*

*Aus.* Stay, Tresham, we'll accompany
    you!
*Guen.*    We?
What, and leave Mildred? We? Why,
    where's my place
But by her side, and where yours but
    by mine?
Mildred – one word! Only look at me,
    then!
*Aus.* No, Guendolen! I echoThorold's
    voice.
She is unworthy to behold …
*Guen.*            Us two?
If you spoke on reflection, and if I
Approved your speech – if you (to put
    the thing
At lowest) you the soldier, bound to
    make
The king's cause yours and fight for it,
    and throw
Regard to others of its right or wrong,
– If with a death-white woman you can
    help,
Let alone sister, let alone a Mildred,
You left her – or if I, her cousin, friend

This morning, playfellow but yesterday,
Who said, or thought at least a thousand
    times,
'I'd serve you if I could,' should now
    face round
And say, 'Ah, that's to only signify
'I'd serve you while you're fit to serve
    yourself:
'So long as fifty eyes await the turn
'Of yours to forestall its yet half-formed
    wish,
'I'll proffer my assistance you'll not
    need –
'When every tongue is praising you, I'll
    join
'The praisers' chorus – when you're
    hemmed about
'With lives between you and detraction
    – lives
'To be laid down if a rude voice, rash
    eye,
'Rough hand should violate the sacred
    ring
'Their worship throws about you, –
    then indeed,
'Who'll stand up for you stout as I?'
    If so
We said, and so we did, – not Mildred
    there
Would be unworthy to behold us both,
But we should be unworthy, both of us,
To be beheld by – by – your meanest
    dog,
Which, if that sword were broken in
    your face
Before a crowd, that badge torn off
    your breast,
And you cast out with hooting and
    contempt,
– Would push his way thro' all the
    hooters, gain
Your side, go off with you and all your
    shame
To the next ditch you choose to die in!
    Austin,
Do you love me? Here's Austin, Mildred,
    – here's

Your brother says he does not believe
    half –
No, nor half that – of all he heard! He
    says,
Look up and take his hand!
*Aus.*            Look up and take
My hand, dear Mildred!
*Mil.*            I – I was so young!
Beside, I loved him, Thorold – and I had
No mother; God forgot me: so, I fell.
*Guen.* Mildred!
*Mil.*    Require no further! Did I dream
That I could palliate what is done? All's
    true.
Now, punish me! A woman takes my
    hand?
Let go my hand! You do not know, I
    see.
I thought that Thorold told you.
*Guen.*                What is this?
Where start you to?
*Mil.*            Oh, Austin, loosen me!
You heard the whole of it – your eyes
    were worse,
In their surprise, than Thorold's! Oh,
    unless
You stay to execute his sentence, loose
My hand! Has Thorold gone, and are
    you here?
*Guen.* Here, Mildred, we two friends of
    yours will wait
Your bidding; be you silent, sleep or
    muse!
Only, when you shall want your
    bidding done,
How can we do it if we are not by?
Here's Austin waiting patiently your
    will!
One spirit to command, and one to
    love
And to believe in it and do its best,
Poor as that is, to help it – why, the
    world
Has been won many a time, its length
    and breadth,
By just such a beginning!
*Mil.*            I believe

If once I threw my arms about your
    neck
And sunk my head upon your breast,
    that I
Should weep again.

*Guen.*     Let go her hand now, Austin!
Wait for me. Pace the gallery and think
On the world's seemings and realities,
Until I call you.     [AUSTIN *goes.*

*Mil.*     No – I cannot weep.
No more tears from this brain – no
    sleep – no tears!
O Guendolen, I love you!

*Guen.*     Yes: and 'love'
Is a short word that says so very much!
It says that you confide in me.

*Mil.*     Confide!

*Guen.* Your lover's name, then! I've so
    much to learn,
Ere I can work in your behalf!

*Mil.*     My friend,
You know I cannot tell his name.

*Guen.*     At least
He is your lover? and you love him too?

*Mil.* Ah, do you ask me that? – but I am
    fallen
So low!

*Guen.* You love him still, then?

*Mil.*     My sole prop
Against the guilt that crushes me! I say,
Each night ere I lie down, 'I was so
    young –
'I had no mother, and I loved him so!'
And then God seems indulgent, and I
    dare
Trust him my soul in sleep.

*Guen.*     How could you let us
E'en talk to you about Lord Mertoun
    then?

*Mil.* There is a cloud around me.

*Guen.*     But you said
You would receive his suit in spite of
    this?

*Mil.* I say there is a cloud ...

*Guen.*     No cloud to me!
Lord Mertoun and your lover are the
    same!

*Mil.* What maddest fancy ...

*Guen.* [*calling aloud*].     Austin! (spare
    your pains –
When I have got a truth, that truth I
    keep) –

*Mil.* By all you love, sweet Guendolen,
    forbear!
Have I confided in you ...

*Guen.*     Just for this!
Austin! – Oh, not to guess it at the first!
But I did guess it – that is, I divined,
Felt by an instinct how it was: why else
Should I pronounce you free from all
    that heap
Of sins which had been irredeemable?
I felt they were not yours – what other
    way
Than this, not yours? The secret's wholly
    mine!

*Mil.* If you would see me die before his
    face ...

*Guen.* I'd hold my peace! And if the Earl
    returns
To-night?

*Mil.* Ah Heaven, he's lost!

*Guen.*     I thought so. Austin!
    *Enter* AUSTIN.
Oh, where have you been hiding?

*Aus.*     Thorold's gone,
I know not how, across the meadow-
    land.
I watched him till I lost him in the skirts
O' the beech-wood.

*Guen.*     Gone? All thwarts us.

*Mil.*     Thorold too?

*Guen.* I have thought. First lead this
    Mildred to her room.
Go on the other side; and then we'll
    seek
Your brother: and I'll tell you, by the
    way,
The greatest comfort in the world. You
    said
There was a clue to all. Remember,
    Sweet,
He said there was a clue! I hold it.
    Come!

ACT 3

*Scene 1 – The end of the Yew Tree Avenue under* MILDRED's *window. A light seen through a central red pane.*

*Enter* TRESHAM *through the trees.*

Again here! But I cannot lose myself.
The heath – the orchard – I have traversed glades
And dells and bosky paths which used to lead
Into green wild-wood depths, bewildering
My boy's adventurous step. And now they tend
Hither or soon or late; the blackest shade
Breaks up, the thronged trunks of the trees ope wide,
And the dim turret I have fled from, fronts
Again my step; the very river put
Its arm about me and conducted me
To this detested spot. Why then, I'll shun
Their will no longer: do your will with me!
Oh, bitter! To have reared a towering scheme
Of happiness, and to behold it razed.
Were nothing: all men hope, and see their hopes
Frustrate, and grieve awhile, and hope anew.
But I ... to hope that from a line like ours
No horrid prodigy like this would spring,
Were just as though I hoped that from these old
Confederates against the sovereign day,
Children of older and yet older sires,
Whose living coral berries dropped, as now
On me, on many a baron's surcoat once,
On many a beauty's wimple – would proceed
No poison-tree, to thrust, from hell its root,

Hither and thither its strange snaky arms.
Why came I here? What must I do? [*A bell strikes.*] A bell?
Midnight! and 'tis at midnight ... Ah, I catch
– Woods, river, plains, I catch your meaning now,
And I obey you! Hist! This tree will serve.
        [*He retires behind one of the trees.
        After a pause, enter* MERTOUN
                *cloaked as before.*

*Mer.* Not time! Beat out thy last voluptuous beat
Of hope and fear, my heart! I thought the clock
I' the chapel struck as I was pushing through
The ferns. And so I shall no more see rise
My love-star! Oh, no matter for the past!
So much the more delicious task to watch
Mildred revive: to pluck out, thorn by thorn,
All traces of the rough forbidden path
My rash love lured her to! Each day must see
Some fear of hers effaced, some hope renewed:
Then there will be surprises, unforeseen
Delights in store. I'll not regret the past.
        [*The light is placed above
                in the purple pane.*
And see, my signal rises, Mildred's star!
I never saw it lovelier than now
It rises for the last time. If it sets,
'Tis that the re-assuring sun may dawn.
        [*As he prepares to ascend the last
                tree of the avenue,* TRESHAM
                        *arrests his arm.*
Unhand me – peasant, by your grasp! Here's gold.
'Twas a mad freak of mine. I said I'd pluck
A branch from the white-blossomed shrub beneath

The casement there. Take this, and
    hold your peace.
*Tresh*. Into the moonlight yonder, come
    with me!
Out of the shadow!
*Mer*.         I am armed, fool!
*Tresh*.                Yes,
Or no? You'll come into the light, or no?
My hand is on your throat – refuse! –
*Mer*.            That voice!
Where have I heard … no – that was
    mild and slow.
I'll come with you.     [*They advance.*
*Tresh*. You're armed: that's well. Declare
Your name: who are you?
*Mer*.       (Tresham! – she is lost!)
*Tresh*. Oh, silent? Do you know, you
    bear yourself
Exactly as, in curious dreams I've had
How felons, this wild earth is full of,
    look
When they're detected, still your kind
    has looked!
The bravo holds an assured countenance,
The thief is voluble and plausible,
But silently the slave of lust has crouched
When I have fancied it before a man.
Your name!
*Mer*.   I do conjure Lord Tresham – ay,
Kissing his foot, if so I might prevail –
That he for his own sake forbear to ask
My name! As heaven's above, his future
    weal
Or woe depends upon my silence! Vain!
I read your white inexorable face.
Know me, Lord Tresham!
[*He throws off his disguises.*
*Tresh*.         Mertoun!
[*After a pause.*]      Draw now!
*Mer*.            Hear me
But speak first!
*Tresh*.     Not one least word on
    your life!
Be sure that I will strangle in your
    throat
The least word that informs me how
    you live

And yet seem what you seem! No
    doubt 'twas you
Taught Mildred still to keep that face
    and sin.
We should join hands in frantic
    sympathy
If you once taught me the unteachable,
Explained how you can live so, and so
    lie.
With God's help I retain, despite my
    sense,
The old belief – a life like yours is still
Impossible. Now draw!
*Mer*.         Not for my sake,
Do I entreat a hearing – for your sake,
And most, for her sake!
*Tresh*.       Ha ha, what should I
Know of your ways? A miscreant like
    yourself,
How must one rouse his ire? A blow? –
    that's pride
No doubt, to him! One spurns him,
    does one not?
Or sets the foot upon his mouth, or
    spits
Into his face! Come! Which, or all of
    these?
*Mer*. 'Twixt him and me and Mildred,
    Heaven be judge!
Can I avoid this? Have your will, my
    lord!
[*He draws and, after a few passes, falls.*
*Tresh*. You are not hurt?
*Mer*.      You'll hear me now!
*Tresh*.            But rise!
*Mer*. Ah, Tresham, say I not 'you'll
    hear me now!'
And what procures a man the right to
    speak
In his defence before his fellow man,
But – I suppose – the thought that
    presently
He may have leave to speak before his
    God
His whole defence?
*Tresh*.     Not hurt? It cannot be!
You made no effort to resist me. Where

Did my sword reach you? Why not
    have returned
My thrusts? Hurt where?
*Mer.*              My lord —
*Tresh.*           How young he is!
*Mer.* Lord Tresham, I am very young,
    and yet
I have entangled other lives with mine.
Do let me speak, and do believe my
    speech!
That when I die before you presently, —
*Tresh.* Can you stay here till I return
    with help?
*Mer.* Oh, stay by me! When I was less
    than boy
I did you grievous wrong and knew it
    not —
Upon my honour, knew it not! Once
    known,
I could not find what seemed a better
    way
To right you than I took: my life — you
    feel
How less than nothing were the giving
    you
The life you've taken! But I thought my
    way
The better — only for your sake and
    hers:
And as you have decided otherwise,
Would I had an infinity of lives
To offer you! Now say — instruct me —
    think!
Can you, from the brief minutes I have
    left,
Eke out my reparation? Oh think —
    think!
For I must wring a partial — dare I say,
Forgiveness from you, ere I die?
*Tresh.*              I do
Forgive you.
*Mer.* Wait and ponder that great word!
Because, if you forgive me, I shall hope
To speak to you of — Mildred!
*Tresh.*         Mertoun, haste
And anger have undone us. 'Tis not
    you

Should tell me for a novelty you're
    young,
Thoughtless, unable to recall the past.
Be but your pardon ample as my own!
*Mer.* Ah, Tresham, that a sword-stroke
    and a drop
Of blood or two, should bring all this
    about!
Why, 'twas my very fear of you, my love
Of you — (what passion like a boy's for
    one
Like you?) — that ruined me! I dreamed
    of you —
You, all accomplished, courted every-
    where,
The scholar and the gentleman. I burned
To knit myself to you: but I was young,
And your surpassing reputation kept me
So far aloof! Oh, wherefore all that love?
With less of love, my glorious yesterday
Of praise and gentlest words and
    kindest looks,
Had taken place perchance six months
    ago.
Even now, how happy we had been!
    And yet
I know the thought of this escaped
    you, Tresham!
Let me look up into your face; I feel
'Tis changed above me: yet my eyes are
    glazed.
Where? where?
        [*As he endeavours to raise himself,*
           *his eye catches the lamp.*
    Ah, Mildred! What will Mildred do?
Tresham, her life is bound up in the life
That's bleeding fast away! I'll live — must
    live,
There, if you'll only turn me I shall live
And save her! Tresham — oh, had you
    but heard!
Had you but heard! What right was
    yours to set
The thoughtless foot upon her life and
    mine,
And then say, as we perish, 'Had I
    thought,

'All had gone otherwise'? We've sinned
    and die:
Never you sin, Lord Tresham! for you'll
    die,
And God will judge you.
*Tresh*.             Yes, be satisfied!
That process is begun.
*Mer*.          And she sits there
Waiting for me! Now, say you this to
    her –
You, not another – say, I saw him die
As he breathed this, 'I love her' – you
    don't know
What those three small words mean!
    Say, loving her
Lowers me down the bloody slope to
    death
With memories … I speak to her, not
    you,
Who had no pity, will have no remorse,
Perchance intend her … Die along
    with me,
Dear Mildred! 'tis so easy, and you'll
    'scape
So much unkindness! Can I lie at rest,
With rude speech spoken to you, ruder
    deeds
Done to you? – heartless men shall
    have my heart,
And I tied down with grave-clothes and
    the worm,
Aware, perhaps, of every blow – oh
    God! –
Upon those lips – yet of no power to
    tear
The felon stripe by stripe! Die, Mildred!
    Leave
Their honourable world to them! For
    God
We're good enough, though the world
    casts us out.    [*A whistle is heard*.
*Tresh*. Ho, Gerard!
      Enter GERARD, AUSTIN *and*
      GUENDOLEN, *with lights*.
  No one speak! You see what's done.
I cannot bear another voice.
*Mer*.            There's light –

Light all about me, and I move to it.
Tresham, did I not tell you – did you
    not
Just promise to deliver words of mine
To Mildred?
*Tresh*.    I will bear those words to her.
*Mer*. Now?
*Tresh*.     Now. Lift you the body, and
    leave me
The head.
     [*As they have half raised* MERTOUN,
               *he turns suddenly*.
*Mer*. I knew they turned me: turn me
    not from her!
There! stay you! there!         [*Dies*.
*Guen*. [*after a pause*]. Austin, remain
    you here
With Thorold until Gerard comes with
    help:
Then lead him to his chamber. I must
    go
To Mildred.
*Tresh*.    Guendolen, I hear each word
You utter. Did you hear him bid me give
His message? Did you hear my
    promise? I,
And only I, see Mildred.
*Guen*.           She will die.
*Tresh*. Oh no, she will not die! I dare
    not hope
She'll die. What ground have you to
    think she'll die?
Why, Austin's with you!
*Aus*.         Had we but arrived
Before you fought!
*Tresh*.     There was no fight atall.
He let me slaughter him – the boy! I'll
    trust
The body there to you and Gerard –
    thus!
Now bear him on before me.
*Aus*.         Whither bear him?
*Tresh*. Oh, to my chamber! When we
    meet there next,
We shall be friends.
     [*They bear out the body of* MERTOUN.
Will she die, Guendolen?

*Guen.* Where are you taking me?
*Tresh.*                     He fell just here.
Now answer me. Shall you in your
　　whole life
– You who have nought to do with
　　Mertoun's fate,
Now you have seen his breast upon the
　　turf,
Shall you e'er walk this way if you can
　　help?
When you and Austin wander arm-in-
　　arm
Through our ancestral grounds, will
　　not a shade
Be ever on the meadow and the waste –
Another kind of shade than when the
　　night
Shuts the woodside with all its whispers
　　up?
But will you ever so forget his breast
As carelessly to cross this bloody turf
Under the black yew avenue? That's
　　well!
You turn your head: and I then? –
*Guen.*                     What is done
Is done. My care is for the living. Thorold,
Bear up against this burden: more
　　remains
To set the neck to!
*Tresh.*               Dear and ancient trees
My fathers planted, and I loved so well!
What have I done that, like some
　　fabled crime
Of yore, lets loose a Fury leading thus
Her miserable dance amidst you all?
Oh, never more for me shall winds
　　intone
With all your tops a vast antiphony,
Demanding and responding in God's
　　praise!
Hers ye are now, not mine! Farewell –
　　farewell!

*Scene 2* – MILDRED's *chamber.* MILDRED
　　*alone.*

He comes not! I have heard of those
　　who seemed
Resourceless in prosperity, – you
　　thought
Sorrow might slay them when she
　　listed; yet
Did they so gather up their diffused
　　strength
At her first menace, that they bade her
　　strike,
And stood and laughed her subtlest
　　skill to scorn.
Oh, 'tis not so with me! The first woe
　　fell,
And the rest fall upon it, not on me:
Else should I bear that Henry comes
　　not? – fails
Just this first night out of so many
　　nights?
Loving is done with. Were he sitting
　　now,
As so few hours since, on that seat,
　　we'd love
No more – contrive no thousand
　　happy ways
To hide love from the loveless, any
　　more.
I think I might have urged some little
　　point
In my defence, to Thorold; he was
　　breathless
For the least hint of a defence: but no,
The first shame over, all that would
　　might fall.
No Henry! Yet I merely sit and think
The morn's deed o'er and o'er. I must
　　have crept
Out of myself. A Mildred that has lost
Her lover – oh, I dare not look upon
Such woe! I crouch away from it! 'Tis
　　she,
Mildred, will break her heart, not I!
　　The world
Forsakes me: only Henry's left me –
　　left?

When I have lost him, for he does not
    come,
And I sit stupidly ... Oh Heaven, break
    up
This worse than anguish, this mad
    apathy,
By any means or any messenger!
*Tresh.* [*without*]. Mildred!
*Mil.*              Come in! Heaven
    hears me!
[*Enter* Tresham.] You? alone?
Oh, no more cursing!
*Tresh.*           Mildred, I must sit.
There – you sit!
*Mil.*    Say it, Thorold – do not look
The curse! deliver all you come to say!
What must become of me? Oh, speak
    that thought
Which makes your brow and cheeks so
    pale!
*Tresh.*    My thought?
*Mil.* All of it!
*Tresh.*    How we waded – years ago –
After those water-lilies, till the plash,
I know not how, surprised us; and you
    dared
Neither advance nor turn back: so, we
    stood
Laughing and crying until Gerard
    came –
Once safe upon the turf, the loudest too,
For once more reaching the relinquished
    prize!
How idle thoughts are, some men's,
    dying men's!
Mildred, –
*Mil.*   You call me kindlier by my name
Than even yesterday: what is in that?
*Tresh.* It weighs so much upon my
    mind that I
This morning took an office not my
    own!
I might ... of course, I must be glad or
    grieved,
Content or not, at every little thing
That touches you. I may with a wrung
    heart

Even reprove you, Mildred; I did more:
Will you forgive me?
*Mil.*          Thorold? do you mock!
Or no ... and yet you bid me ... say
    that word!
*Tresh.* Forgive me, Mildred! – are you
    silent, Sweet?
*Mil.* [*starting up*]. Why does not Henry
    Mertoun come to-night?
Are you, too, silent?
    [*Dashing his mantle aside, and pointing
        to his scabbard, which is empty.*
           Ah, this speaks for you!
You've murdered Henry Mertoun! Now
    proceed!
What is it I must pardon? This and all?
Well, I do pardon you – I think I do.
Thorold, how very wretched you must
    be!
*Tresh.* He bade me tell you ...
*Mil.*           What I do forbid
Your utterance of! So much that you
    may tell
And will not – how you murdered him
    ... but, no!
You'll tell me that he loved me, never
    more
Than bleeding out his life there: must I
    say
'Indeed' to that? Enough! I pardon you.
*Tresh.* You cannot, Mildred! for the
    harsh words, yes:
Of this last deed Another's judge: whose
    doom
I wait in doubt, despondency and fear.
*Mil.* Oh, true! There's nought for me to
    pardon! True!
You loose my soul of all its cares at
    once.
Death makes me sure of him for ever!
    You
Tell me his last words? He shall tell me
    them,
And take my answer – not in words,
    but reading
Himself the heart I had to read him
    late,

Which death …
*Tresh.*        Death? You are dying too?
    Well said
Of Guendolen! I dared not hope you'd
    die:
But she was sure of it.
*Mil.*              Tell Guendolen
I loved her, and tell Austin …
*Tresh.*              Him you loved:
And me?
*Mil.*      Ah, Thorold! Was't not rashly
    done
To quench that blood, on fire with
    youth and hope
And love of me – whom you loved too,
    and yet
Suffered to sit here waiting his approach
While you were slaying him? Oh,
    doubtlessly
You let him speak his poor confused
    boy's-speech
– Do this poor utmost to disarm your
    wrath
And respite me! – you let him try to give
The story of our love and ignorance,
And the brief madness and the long
    despair –
You let him plead all this, because your
    code
Of honour bids you hear before you
    strike:
But at the end, as he looked up for life
Into your eyes – you struck him down!
*Tresh.*              No! No!
Had I but heard him – had I let him
    speak
Half the truth – less – had I looked
    long on him
I had desisted! Why, as he lay there,
The moon on his flushed cheek, I
    gathered all
The story ere he told it: I saw through
The troubled surface of his crime and
    yours
A depth of purity immovable,
Had I but glanced, where all seemed
    turbidest

Had gleamed some inlet to the calm
    beneath;
I would not glance: my punishment's
    at hand.
There, Mildred, is the truth! and you –
    say on –
You curse me?
*Mil.*      As I dare approach that Heaven
Which has not bade a living thing
    despair,
Which needs no code to keep its grace
    from stain,
But bids the vilest worm that turns on it
Desist and be forgiven, – I – forgive not,
But bless you, Thorold, from my soul
    of souls!        [*Falls on his neck.*
There! Do not think too much upon
    the past!
The cloud that's broke was all the
    same a cloud
While it stood up between my friend
    and you;
You hurt him 'neath its shadow: but is
    that
So past retrieve? I have his heart, you
    know;
I may dispose of it: I give it you!
It loves you as mine loves! Confirm
    me, Henry!        [*Dies.*
*Tresh.* I wish thee joy, Beloved! I am
    glad
In thy full gladness!
*Guen.* [*without*].  Mildred! Tresham!
[*Entering with* AUSTIN.]        Thorold,
I could desist no longer. Ah, she swoons!
That's well.
*Tresh.*    Oh, better far than that!
*Guen.*              She's dead!
Let me unlock her arms!
*Tresh.*              She threw them thus
About my neck, and blessed me, and
    then died:
You'll let them stay now, Guendolen!
*Aus.*              Leave her
And look to him! What ails you,
    Thorold?
*Guen.*        White

As she, and whiter! Austin! quick – this
    side!
*Aus*. A froth is oozing through his
    clenched teeth;
Both lips, where they're not bitten
    through, are black:
Speak, dearest Thorold!
*Tresh*.     Something does weigh down
My neck beside her weight: thanks: I
    should fall
But for you, Austin, I believe! – there,
    there,
'Twill pass away soon! – ah, – I had
    forgotten:
I am dying.
*Guen*.     Thorold – Thorold – why
    was this?
*Tresh*. I said, just as I drank the poison
    off,
The earth would be no longer earth to
    me,
The life out of all life was gone from me.
There are blind ways provided, the
    fore-done
Heart-weary player in this pageant-
    world
Drops out by, letting the main masque
    defile
By the conspicuous portal: I am
    through –

Just through!
*Guen*.     Don't leave him, Austin!
    Death is close.
*Tresh*. Already Mildred's face is
    peacefuller.
I see you, Austin – feel you: here's my
    hand,
Put yours in it – you, Guendolen,
    yours too!
You're lord and lady now – you're
    Treshams; name
And fame are yours: you hold our
    'scutcheon up.
Austin, no blot on it! You see how
    blood
Must wash one blot away: the first blot
    came
And the first blood came. To the vain
    world's eye
All's gules again: no care to the vain
    world,
From whence the red was drawn!
*Aus*.     No blot shall come!
*Tresh*. I said that: yet it did come.
    Should it come,
Vengeance is God's, not man's.
    Remember me!     [*Dies*.
*Guen*. [*letting fall the pulseless arm*]. Ah,
    Thorold, we can but – remember
    you!

# COLOMBE'S BIRTHDAY

A Play

1844

No one loves and honours Barry Cornwall more than does Robert Browning;
Who, having nothing better than this play to give him in proof of it, must say so.

London, 1844

Ivy and violet, what do ye here
With blossom and shoot in the warm spring-weather.
Hiding the arms of Monchenci and Vere? – *Hanmer*

## Persons

Colombe of Ravestein, Duchess of Juliers and Cleves. Sabyne, Adolf, *her attendants.*
Guibert, Gaucelme, Maufroy. Clugnet, *courtiers.* Valence, *advocate of Cleves.*
Prince Berthold, *claimant of the Duchy.* Melchior, *his confidant.*
*Place. – The Palace at Juliers. Time, 16—.*

## ACT 1

*Scene – Morning. A corridor leading to
the Audience-chamber.* GAUCELME,
CLUGNET, MAUFROY *and other*
COURTIERS, *round* GUIBERT, *who is
silently reading a paper: as he drops
it at the end –*

*Gui.* That this should be her birthday;
and the day
We all invested her, twelve months
ago,
As the late Duke's true heiress and our
liege;
And that this also must become the
day …
Oh, miserable lady!
*1st Court.*                                   Ay, indeed?
*2nd Court.* Well, Guibert?
*3rd Court.*         But your news, my friend,
your news!
The sooner, friend, one learns Prince
Berthold's pleasure,
The better for us all: how writes the
Prince?
Give me! I'll read it for the common
good.
*Gui.* In time, sir, – but till time comes,
pardon me!
Our old Duke just disclosed his child's
retreat,

Declared her true succession to his
rule,
And died: this birthday was the day,
last year,
We convoyed her from Castle
Ravestein –
That sleeps out trustfully its extreme
age
On the Meuse' quiet bank, where she
lived queen
Over the water-buds, – to Juliers' court
With joy and bustle. Here again we
stand;
Sir Gaucelme's buckle's constant to his
cap:
To-day's much such another sunny day!
*Gau.* Come, Guibert, this outgrows a
jest, I think!
You're hardly such a novice as to need
The lesson, you pretend.
*Gui.*                             What lesson, sir?
That everybody, if he'd thrive at court,
Should, first and last of all, look to
himself?
Why, no: and therefore with your good
example,
( – Ho, Master Adolf!) – to myself I'll
look.

*Enter* ADOLF.

*Gui.* The Prince's letter; why, of all
men else,

Comes it to me?
*Adolf.* By virtue of your place,
Sir Guibert! 'Twas the Prince's express charge,
His envoy told us, that the missive there
Should only reach our lady by the hand
Of whosoever held your place.
*Gui.* Enough!
[ADOLF *retires.*
Then, gentles, who'll accept a certain poor
Indifferently honourable place,
My friends, I make no doubt, have gnashed their teeth
At leisure minutes these half-dozen years,
To find me never in the mood to quit?
Who asks may have it, with my blessing, and –
This to present our lady. Who'll accept?
You, – you, – you? There it lies, and may, for me!
*Mau.* [*a youth, picking up the paper, reads aloud*]. 'Prince Berthold, proved by titles following
'Undoubted Lord of Juliers, comes this day
'To claim his own, with licence from the Pope,
'The Emperor, the Kings of Spain and France' ...
*Gau.* Sufficient 'titles following,' I judge!
Don't read another! Well, – 'to claim his own?'
*Mau.* ' – And take possession. of the Duchy held
'Since twelve months, to the true heir's prejudice,
'By' ... Colombe, Juliers' mistress, so she thinks,
And Ravestein's mere lady, as we find.
Who wants the place and paper? Guibert's right.
I hope to climb a little in the world, –
I'd push my fortunes, – but, no more than he,

Could tell her on this happy day of days,
That, save the nosegay in her hand, perhaps,
There's nothing left to call her own. Sir Clugnet,
You famish for promotion; what say you?
*Clug.* [*an old man*]. To give this letter were a sort, I take it,
Of service: services ask recompense:
What kind of corner may be Ravestein?
*Gui.* The castle? Oh, you'd share her fortunes? Good!
Three walls stand upright, full as good as four,
With no such bad remainder of a roof.
*Clug.* Oh, – but the town?
*Gui.* Five houses, fifteen huts;
A church whereto was once a spire, 'tis judged;
And half a dyke, except in time of thaw.
*Clug.* Still, there's some revenue?
*Gui.* Else Heaven forfend!
You hang a beacon out, should fogs increase;
So, when the Autumn floats of pine-wood steer
Safe 'mid the white confusion, thanks to you,
Their grateful raftsman flings a guilder in;
– That's if he mean to pass your way next time.
*Clug.* If not?
*Gui.* Hang guilders, then! He blesses you.
*Clug.* What man do you suppose me? Keep your paper!
And, let me say, it shows no handsome spirit
To dally with misfortune: keep your: place!
*Gau.* Some one must tell her.
*Gui.* Some one may: you may!
*Gau.* Sir Guibert, 'tis no trifle turns me sick
Of court-hypocrisy at years like mine,

But this goes near it. Where's there
        news at all?
Who'll have the face, for instance, to
        affirm
He never heard, e'en while we crowned
        the girl,
That Juliers' tenure was by Salic law;
That one, confessed her father's cousin'
        child,
And, she away, indisputable heir,
Against our choice protesting and the
        Duke's,
Claimed Juliers? – nor, as he preferred
        his claim,
That first this, then another potentate,
Inclined to its allowance? – I or you,
Or any one except the lady's self?
Oh, it had been the direst cruelty
To break the business to her! Things
        might change:
At all events, we'd see next masque at
        end,
Next mummery over first: and so the
        edge
Was taken off sharp tidings as they
        came,
Till here's the Prince upon us, and
        there's she
– Wreathing her hair, a song between
        her lips,
With just the faintest notion possible
That some such claimant earns a
        livelihood
About the world, by feigning
        grievances –
Few pay the story of, but grudge its
        price,
And fewer listen to, a second time.
Your method proves a failure; now try
        mine!
And, since this must be carried …
*Gui.* [*snatching the paper from him*]. By
        your leave!
Your zeal transports you! 'Twill not
        serve the Prince
So much as you expect, this course
        you'd take.

If she leaves quietly her palace, – well;
But if she died upon its threshold, – no:
He'd have the trouble of removing her.
Come, gentles, we're all – what the
        devil knows!
You, Gaucelme, won't lose character,
        beside:
You broke your father's heart superiorly
To gather his succession – never blush!
You're from my province, and, be
        comforted,
They tell of it with wonder to this day.
You can afford to let your talent sleep.
We'll take the very worst supposed, as
        true:
There, the old Duke knew, when he
        hid his child
Among the river-flowers at Ravestein,
With whom the right lay! Call the
        Prince our Duke!
There, she's no Duchess, she's no
        anything
More than a young maid with the
        bluest eyes:
And now, sirs, we'll not break this
        young maid's heart
Coolly as Gaucelme could and would!
        No haste!
His talent's full-blown, ours but in the
        bud:
We'll not advance to his perfection
        yet –
Will we, Sir Maufroy? See, I've ruined
        Maufroy
For ever as a courtier!
*Gau.*                    Here's a coil!
And, count us, will you? Count its
        residue,
This boasted convoy, this day last
        year's crowd!
A birthday, too, a gratulation day!
I'm dumb: bid that keep silence!
*Mau. and others.* Eh, Sir Guibert?
He's right: that does say something:
        that's bare truth.
Ten – twelve, I make: a perilous
        dropping off!

*Gui.* Pooh – is it audience hour? The vestibule
Swarms too, I wager, with the common sort
That want our privilege of entry here.
*Gau.* Adolf! [*Re-enter* ADOLF.] Who's outside?
*Gui.*          Oh, your looks suffice!
Nobody waiting?
*Mau.* [*looking through the door-folds*].
          Scarce our number!
*Gui.*                    'Sdeath!
Nothing to beg for, to complain about?
It can't be! Ill news spreads, but not so fast
As thus to frighten all the world!
*Gau.*                    The world
Lives out of doors, sir – not with you and me
By presence-chamber porches, state-room stairs,
Wherever warmth's perpetual: outside's free
To every wind from every compass-point,
And who may get nipped needs be weather-wise.
The Prince comes and the lady's People go;
The snow-goose settles down, the swallows flee –
Why should they wait for winter-time? 'Tis instinct.
Don't you feel somewhat chilly?
*Gui.*                    That's their craft:
And last year's crowders-round and criers-forth
That strewed the garlands, overarched the roads,
Lighted the bonfires, sang the loyal songs!
Well 'tis my comfort, you could never call me
The People's Friend! The People keep their word –
I keep my place: don't doubt I'll entertain

The People when the Prince comes, and the People
Are talked of! Then, their speeches – no one tongue
Found respite, not a pen had holiday
– For they wrote, too, as well as spoke, these knaves!
Now see: we tax and tithe them, pill and poll,
They wince and fret enough, but pay they must
– We manage that, – so, pay with a good grace
They might as well, it costs so little more.
But when we've done with taxes, meet folk next
Outside the toll-booth and the rating-place,
In public – there they have us if they will,
We're at their mercy after that, you see!
For one tax not ten devils could extort –
Over and above necessity, a grace;
This prompt disbosoming of love, to wit –
Their vine-leaf wrappage of our tribute penny,
And crowding attestation, all works well.
Yet this precisely do they thrust on us!
These cappings quick, these crook-and-cringings low,
Hand to the heart, and forehead to the knee,
With grin that shuts the eyes and opes the mouth –
So tender they their love; and, tender made,
Go home to curse us, the first doit we ask.
As if their souls were any longer theirs!
As if they had not given ample warrant
To who should clap a collar on their neck,
Rings in their nose, a goad to either flank,

And take them for the brute they boast
     themselves!
Stay – there's a bustle at the outer door –
And somebody entreating … that's my
     name!
Adolf, – I heard my name!
*Adolf.*                     'Twas probably
The suitor.
*Gui.*        Oh, there is one?
*Adolf.*                     With a suit
He'd fain enforce in person.
*Gui.*                     The good heart
– And the great fool! Just ope the mid-
     door's fold!
Is that a lappet of his cloak, I see?
*Adolf.* If it bear plenteous sign of travel
     … ay,
The very cloak my comrades tore!
*Gui.*                     Why tore?
*Adolf.* He seeks the Duchess' presence
     in that trim:
Since daybreak, was he posted hereabouts
Lest he should miss the moment.
*Gui.*                     Where's he now?
*Adolf.* Gone for a minute possibly, not
     more:
They have ado enough to thrust him
     back.
*Gui.* Ay – but my name, I caught?
*Adolf.*                     Oh, sir – he said
– What was it? – You had known him
     formerly,
And, he believed, would help him did
     you guess
He waited now; you promised him as
     much:
The old plea! 'Faith, he's back, –
     renews the charge!
[*Speaking at the door.*] So long as the
     man parleys, peace outside –
Nor be too ready with your halberts,
     there!
*Gau.* My horse bespartered, as he
     blocked the path
A thin sour man, not unlike somebody.
*Adolf.* He holds a paper in his breast,
     whereon

He glances when his cheeks flush and
     his brow
At each repulse –
*Gau.*                     I noticed he'd a brow.
*Adolf.* So glancing, he grows calmer,
     leans awhile
Over the balustrade, adjusts his dress,
And presently turns round, quiet again,
With some new pretext for admittance.
     – Back!
[*To* GUIBERT.] – Sir, he has seen you!
     Now cross halberts! Ha –
Pascal is prostrate – there lies Fabian
     too!
No passage! Whither would the madman
     press?
Close the doors quick on me!
*Gui.*                     Too late! He's here.
     *Enter, hastily and with discomposed
          dress,* VALENCE.
*Val.* Sir Guibert, will you help me? –
     me, that come
Charged by your townsmen, all who
     starve at Cleves,
To represent their heights and depths
     of woe
Before our Duchess and obtain relief!
Such errands barricade such doors, it
     seems:
But not a common hindrance drives me
     back
On all the sad yet hopeful faces, lit
With hope for the first time, which
     sent me forth.
Cleves, speak for me! Cleves' men and
     women, speak!
Who followed me – your strongest –
     many a mile
That I might go the fresher from their
     ranks,
– Who sit – your weakest – by the city
     gates,
To take me fuller of what news I bring
As I return – for I must needs return!
– Can I? 'Twere hard, no listener for
     their wrongs,
To turn them back upon the old despair

Harder, Sir Guibert, than imploring
thus –
So, I do – any way you please –
implore!
If you … but how should you
remember Cleves?
Yet they of Cleves remember you so
well!
Ay, comment on each trait of you they
keep,
Your words and deeds caught up at
second hand, –
Proud, I believe, at bottom of their
hearts,
O' the very levity and recklessness
Which only prove that you forget their
wrongs.
Cleves, the grand town, whose men
and women starve,
Is Cleves forgotten? Then, remember
me!
You promised me that you would help
me once,
For other purpose: will you keep your
word?
*Gui.* And who may you be, friend?
*Val.*                    Valence of Cleves.
*Gui.* Valence of … not the advocate of
Cleves,
I owed my whole estate to, three years
back?
Ay, well may you keep silence! Why,
my lords,
You've heard, I'm sure, how, Pentecost
three years,
I was so nearly ousted of my land
By some knave's-pretext – (eh? when
you refused me
Your ugly daughter, Clugnet!) – and
you've heard
How I recovered it by miracle
– (When I refused her!) Here's the very
friend,
– Valence of Cleves, all parties have to
thank!
Nay, Valence, this procedure's vile in
you!

I'm no more grateful than a courtier
should,
But politic am I – I bear a brain,
Can cast about a little, might require
Your services a second time. I tried
To tempt you with advancement here
to court
– 'No!' – well, for curiosity at least
To view our life here – 'No!' – our
Duchess, then, –
A pretty woman's worth some pains to
see,
Nor is she spoiled, I take it, if a crown
Complete the forehead pale and tresses
pure …
*Val.* Our city trusted me its miseries,
And I am come.
*Gui.*    So much for taste! But 'come,' –
So may you be, for anything I know,
To beg the Pope's cross, or Sir
Clugnet's daughter,
And with an equal chance you get all
three.
If it was ever worth your while to
come,
Was not the proper way worth finding
too?
*Val.* Straight to the palace-portal, sir, I
came –
*Gui.* – And said? –
*Val.*                    – That I had brought
the miseries
Of a whole city to relieve.
*Gui.*                    – Which saying
Won your admittance? You saw me,
indeed,
And here, no doubt, you stand: as
certainly,
My intervention, I shall not dispute,
Procures you audience; which, if I
procure, –
That paper's closely written – by Saint
Paul,
Here flock the Wrongs, follow the
Remedies,
Chapter and verse, One, Two, A, B and
C!

Perhaps you'd enter, make a reverence,
And launch these 'miseries' from first
    to last?
*Val.* How should they let me pause or
    turn aside?
*Gau.* [*to* VALENCE]. My worthy sir, one
    question! You've come straight
From Cleves, you tell us: heard you
    any talk
At Cleves about our lady?
*Val.*                Much.
*Gau.*               And what?
*Val.* Her wish was to redress all wrongs
    she knew.
*Gau.* That, you believed?
*Val.*         You see me, sir!
*Gau.*            – Nor stopped
Upon the road from Cleves to Juliers
    here,
For any – rumours you might find afloat:
*Val.* I had my townsmen's wrongs to
    busy me.
*Gau.* This is the lady's birthday, do you
    know?
– Her day of pleasure?
*Val.*      – That the great, I know,
For pleasure born, should still be on
    the watch
To exclude pleasure when a duty offers:
Even as, for duty born, the lowly too
May ever snatch a pleasure if in reach:
Both will have plenty of their birthright,
    sir!
*Gau.* [*aside to* GUIBERT]. Sir Guibert,
    here's your man! No scruples
    now –
You'll never find his like! Time presses
    hard.
I've seen your drift and Adolf's too, this
    while,
But you can't keep the hour of audience
    back
Much longer, and at noon the Prince
    arrives.
[*Pointing to* VALENCE.] Entrust him
    with it – fool no chance away!
*Gui.* Him?

*Gau.*    – With the missive! What's the
    man to her?
*Gui.* No bad thought! Yet, 'tis yours,
    who ever played
The tempting serpent: else 'twere no
    bad thought!
I should – and do – mistrust it for your
    sake,
Or else …
      *Enter an* OFFICIAL *who*
      *communicates with* ADOLF.
*Adolf.* The Duchess will receive the
    court.
*Gui.* Give us a moment, Adolf!
    Valence, friend,
I'll help you. We of the service, you're
    to mark,
Have special entry, while the herd …
    the folk
Outside, get access through our help
    alone;
– Well, it is so, was so, and I suppose
So ever will be: your natural lot is,
    therefore,
To wait your turn and opportunity,
And probably miss both. Now, I
    engage
To set you, here and in a minute's
    space,
Before the lady, with full leave to plead
Chapter and verse, and A, and B, and
    C,
To heart's content.
*Val.*         I grieve that I must ask, –
This being, yourself admit, the custom
    here, –
To what the price of such a favour
    mounts?
*Gui.* Just so! You're not without a
    courtier's tact.
Little at court, as your quick instinct
    prompts,
Do such as we without a recompense.
*Val.* Yours is? –
*Gui.*        A trifle: here's a document
'Tis some one's duty to present her
    Grace –

I say, not mine – these say, not theirs –
        such points
Have weight at court. Will you relieve
        us all
And take it? Just say, 'I am bidden lay
'This paper at the Duchess' feet!'
*Val.*                           No more?
I thank you, sir!
*Adolf.*        Her Grace receives the court.
*Gui.* [*aside*]. Now, *sursum corda*, quoth
        the mass-priest! Do –
Whoever's my kind saint, do let alone
These pushings to and fro, and pullings
        back;
Peaceably let me hang o' the devil's arm
The downward path, if you can't pluck
        me off
Completely! Let me live quite his, or
        yours!
        [*The* COURTIERS *begin to range them-*
            *selves, and move toward the door.*
After me, Valence! So, our famous
        Cleves
Lacks bread? Yet don't we gallants buy
        their lace?
And dear enough – it beggars me, I
        know,
To keep my very gloves fringed properly.
This, Valence, is our Great State Hall
        you cross;
Yon grey urn's veritable marcasite,
The Pope's gift: and those salvers
        testify
The Emperor. Presently you'll set your
        foot
. . . But you don't speak, friend Valence!
*Val.*                      I shall speak.
*Gau.* [*aside to* GUIBERT]. Guibert – it
        were no such ungraceful thing
If you and I, at first, seemed horror-
        struck
With the bad news. Look here, what
        you shall do.
Suppose you, first, clap hand to sword
        and cry
'Yield strangers our allegiance? First I'll
        perish

'Beside your Grace!' – and so give me
        the cue
To …
*Gui.*        – Clap your hand to note-book
        and jot down
That to regale the Prince with? I
        conceive.
[*To* Valence.] Do, Valence, speak, or I
        shall half suspect
You're plotting to supplant us, me the
        first,
I' the lady's favour! Is't the grand
        harangue
You mean to make, that thus engrosses
        you?
– Which of her virtues you'll
        apostrophize?
Or is't the fashion you aspire to start,
Of that close-curled, not unbecoming
        hair?
Or what else ponder you?
*Val.*              My townsmen's wrongs.

### ACT 2

*Scene – Noon. The Presence-chamber.*
        *The* DUCHESS *and* SABYNE.
*The D.* Announce that I am ready for
        the court!
*Sab.* 'Tis scarcely audience-hour, I think;
        your Grace
May best consult your own relief, no
        doubt,
And shun the crowd: but few can have
        arrived.
*The D.* Let those not yet arrived, then,
        keep away!
'Twas me, this day last year at
        Ravestein,
You hurried. It has been full time,
        beside,
This half-hour. Do you hesitate?
*Sab.*                        Forgive me!
*The D.* Stay, Sabyne; let me hasten to
        make sure
Of one true thanker: here with you
        begins

My audience, claim you first its
    privilege!
It is my birth's event they celebrate:
You need not wish me more such
    happy days.
But – ask some favour! Have you none
    to ask?
Has Adolf none, then? this was far
    from least
Of much I waited for impatiently,
Assure yourself! It seemed so natural
Your gift, beside this bunch of river-
    bells,
Should be the power and leave of
    doing good
To you, and greater pleasure to myself.
You ask my leave to-day to marry
    Adolf?
The rest is my concern.
*Sab.*          Your Grace is ever
Our lady of dear Ravestein, – but, for
    Adolf …
*The D.* 'But'? You have not, sure,
    changed in your regard
And purpose towards him?
*Sab.*        We change?
*The D.*        Well then? Well?
*Sab.* How could we two be happy, and,
    most like,
Leave Juliers, when – when … but 'tis
    audience-time!
*The D.* 'When, if you left me, I were left
    indeed!'
Would you subjoin that? – Bid the
    court approach!
– Why should we play thus with each
    other, Sabyne?
Do I not know, if courtiers prove remiss,
If friends detain me, and get blame
    for it,
There is a cause? Of last year's fervid
    throng
Scarce one half comes now.
*Sab.* [*aside*].    One half? No, alas!
*The D.* So can the mere suspicion of a
    cloud
Over my fortunes, strike each loyal heart.

They've heard of this Prince Berthold;
    and, forsooth,
Some foolish arrogant pretence he
    makes,
May grow more foolish and more
    arrogant,
They please to apprehend! I thank
    their love.
Admit them!
*Sab.* [*aside*]. How much has she really
    learned?
*The D.* Surely, whoever's absent,
    Tristan waits?
– Or at least Romuald, whom my
    father raised
From nothing – come, he's faithful to
    me, come!
(Sabyne, I should but be the prouder –
    yes,
The fitter to comport myself aright)
Not Romuald? Xavier – what said he to
    that?
For Xavier hates a parasite, I know!
               [SABYNE *goes out.*
*The D.* Well, sunshine's everywhere,
    and summer too.
Next year 'tis the old place again,
    perhaps –
The water-breeze again, the birds
    again.
– It cannot be! It is too late to be!
What part had I, or choice in all of it?
Hither they brought me; I had not to
    think
Nor care, concern myself with doing
    good
Or ill, my task was just – to live, – to
    live,
And, answering ends there was no
    need explain,
To render Juliers happy – so they said.
All could not have been falsehood:
    some was love,
And wonder and obedience. I did all
They looked for: why then cease to do
    it now?
Yet this is to be calmly set aside,

And – ere next birthday's dawn, for
    aught I know,
Things change, a claimant may arrive,
    and I …
It cannot nor it shall not be! His right?
Well then, he has the right, and I have
    not,
– But who bade all of you surround my
    life
And close its growth up with your ducal
    crown
Which, plucked off rudely, leaves me
    perishing?
I could have been like one of you, –
    loved, hoped,
Feared, lived and died like one of you –
    but you
Would take that life away and give me
    this,
And I will keep this! I will face you!
    Come!
    *Enter the* COURTIERS *and* VALENCE.
*The Courtiers.* Many such happy
    mornings to your Grace!
*The D.* [*aside, as they pay their devoir*].
    The same words, the same faces, –
    the same love!
I have been overfearful. These are few;
But these, at least, stand firmly: these
    are mine.
As many come as may; and if no more,
'Tis that these few suffice – they do
    suffice!
What succour may not next year bring
    me? Plainly,
I feared too soon. [*To the* COURTIERS.] I
    thank you, sirs: all thanks!
*Val.* [*aside, as the* DUCHESS *passes from
    one group to another, conversing*].
    'Tis she – the vision this day last
    year brought,
When, for a golden moment at our
    Cleves,
She tarried in her progress hither.
    Cleves
Chose me to speak its welcome, and I
    spoke

– Not that she could have noted the
    recluse
– Ungainly, old before his time – who
    gazed.
Well, Heaven's gifts are not wasted,
    and that gaze
Kept, and shall keep me to the end,
    her own!
She was above it – but so would not
    sink
My gaze to earth! The People caught it,
    hers –
Thenceforward, mine; but thus entirely
    mine,
Who shall affirm, had she not raised
    my soul
Ere she retired and left me – them? She
    turns –
There's all her wondrous face at once!
    The ground
Reels and … [*suddenly occupying
    himself with his paper*]
These wrongs of theirs I have to plead!
*The D.* [*to the* COURTIERS]. Nay,
    compliment enough! and
    kindness' self
Should pause before it wish me more
    such years.
'Twas fortunate that thus, ere youth
    escaped,
I tasted life's pure pleasure – one such,
    pure,
Is worth a thousand, mixed – and
    youth's for pleasure:
Mine is received; let my age pay for it.
*Gau.* So, pay, and pleasure paid for,
    thinks your Grace,
Should never go together?
*Gui.*             How, Sir Gaucelme?
Hurry one's feast down unenjoyingly
At the snatched breathing-intervals of
    work?
As good you saved it till the dull day's-
    end
When, stiff and sleepy, appetite is gone.
Eat first, then work upon the strength
    of food!

*The D.* True: you enable me to risk my future,
By giving me a past beyond recall.
I lived, a girl, one happy leisure year:
Let me endeavour to be the Duchess now!
And so, – what news, Sir Guibert, spoke you of?

        *[As they advance a little, and*
               *GUIBERT speaks –*

– That gentleman?
*Val.* [*aside*].        I feel her eyes on me.
*Gui.* [*to* VALENCE]. The Duchess, sir, inclines to hear your suit.
Advance! He is from Cleves.
*Val.* [*coming forward. Aside*]. Their wrongs – their wrongs!
*The D.* And you, sir, are from Cleves? How fresh in mind,
The hour or two I passed at queenly Cleves!
She entertained me bravely, but the best
Of her good pageant seemed its standers-by
With insuppressive joy on every face!
What says my ancient famous happy Cleves?
*Val.* Take the truth, lady – you are made for truth!
So think my friends: nor do they less deserve
The having you to take it, you shall think,
When you know all – nay, when you only know
How, on that day you recollect at Cleves,
When the poor acquiescing multitude
Who thrust themselves with all their woes apart
Into unnoticed corners, that the few,
Their means sufficed to muster trappings for,
Might fill the foreground, occupy your sight
With joyous faces fit to bear away
And boast of as a sample of all Cleves

– How, when to daylight these crept out once more,
Clutching, unconscious, each his empty rags
Whence the scant coin, which had not half bought bread,
That morn he shook forth, counted piece by piece,
And, well-advisedly, on perfumes spent them
To burn, or flowers to strew, before your path
– How, when the golden flood of music and bliss
Ebbed, as their moon retreated, and again
Left the sharp black-point rocks of misery bare
– Then I, their friend, had only to suggest
'Saw she the horror as she saw the pomp!'
And as one man they cried 'He speaks the truth:
'Show her the horror! Take from our own mouths
'Our wrongs and show them, she will see them too!'
This they cried, lady! I have brought the wrongs.
*The D.* Wrongs? Cleves has wrongs – apparent now and thus?
I thank you! In that paper? Give it me!
*Val.* (There, Cleves!) In this! (What did I promise, Cleves?)
Our weavers, clothiers, spinners are reduced
Since ... Oh, I crave your pardon! I forget
I buy the privilege of this approach, .
And promptly would discharge my debt. I lay
This paper humbly at the Duchess' feet.
        *[Presenting GUIBERT's paper.*
*Gui.* Stay! for the present ...
*The D.*          Stay, sir? I take aught

That teaches me their wrongs with
    greater pride
Than this your ducal circlet. Thank
    you, sir!
           [*The* DUCHESS *reads hastily;*
    *then, turning to the* COURTIERS *–*
What have I done to you? Your deed or
    mine
Was it, this crowning me? I gave myself
No more a title to your homage, no,
Than church-flowers, born this season,
    wrote the words
In the saint's-book that sanctified them
    first.
For such a flower, you plucked me;
    well, you erred –
Well, 'twas a weed; remove the eye-
    sore quick!
But should you not remember it has
    lain
Steeped in the candles' glory, palely
    shrined,
Nearer God's Mother than most earthly
    things?
– That if't be faded 'tis with prayer's
    sole breath –
That the one day it boasted was God's
    day?
Still, I do thank you! Had you used
    respect,
Here might I dwindle to my last white
    leaf,
Here lose life's latest freshness, which
    even yet
May yield some wandering insect rest
    and food:
So, fling me forth, and – all is best for
    all!
[*After a pause.*] Prince Berthold, who
    art Juliers' Duke it seems –
The King's choice, and the Emperor's,
    and the Pope's –
Be mine, too! Take this People! Tell not
    me
Of rescripts, precedents, authorities,
– But take them, from a heart that
    yearns to give!

Find out their love, – I could not; find
    their fear, –
I would not; find their like, – I never
    shall,
Among the flowers!
           [*Taking off her coronet.*
           Colombe of Ravestein
Thanks God she is no longer Duchess
    here!
*Val.* [*advancing to* GUIBERT]. Sir Guibert,
    knight, they call you – this of mine
Is the first step I ever set at court.
You dared make me your instrument, I
    find;
For that, so sure as you and I are men,
We reckon to the utmost presently:
But as you are a courtier and I none,
Your knowledge may instruct me. I,
    already,
Have too far outraged, by my ignorance
Of courtier-ways, this lady, to proceed
A second step and risk addressing her:
– I am degraded – you let me address!
Out of her presence, all is plain enough
What I shall do – but in her presence,
    too,
Surely there's something proper to be
    done.
[*To the others.*] You, gentles, tell me if I
    guess aright –
May I not strike this man to earth?
*The Courtiers* [*as* GUIBERT *springs*
    *forward, withholding him*]. Let go!
– The clothiers' spokesman, Guibert?
    Grace a churl?
*The D.* [*to* VALENCE]. Oh, be
    acquainted with your party, sir!
He's of the oldest lineage Juliers boasts;
A lion crests him for a cognizance;
'Scorning to waver' – that's his
    'scutcheon's word;
His office with the new Duke – probably
The same in honour as with me; or
    more,
By so much as this gallant turn deserves.
He's now, I dare say, of a thousand
    times

The rank and influence that remain
　　with her
Whose part you take! So, lest for taking
　　it
You suffer ...
*Val.* 　　　I may strike him then to earth
*Gui.* [*falling on his knee*]. Great and
　　dear lady, pardon me! Hear once!
Believe me and be merciful – be just!
I could not bring myself to give that
　　paper
Without a keener pang than I dared
　　meet
– And so felt Clugnet here, and Maufroy
　　here
– No one dared meet it. Protestation's
　　cheap, –
But, if to die for you did any good,
[*To* GAUCELME.] Would not I die, sir?
　　Say your worst of me!
But it does no good, that's the mournful
　　truth.
And since the hint of a resistance, even,
Would just precipitate, on you the first,
A speedier ruin – I shall not deny,
Saving myself indubitable pain,
I thought to give you pleasure (who
　　might say?)
By showing that your only subject
　　found
To carry the sad notice, was the man
Precisely ignorant of its contents;
A nameless, mere provincial advocate;
One whom 'twas like you never saw
　　before,
Never would see again. All has gone
　　wrong;
But I meant right, God knows, and you,
　　I trust!
*The D.* A nameless advocate, this
　　gentleman?
– (I pardon you, Sir Guibert!)
*Gui.* [*rising, to* VALENCE]. Sir, and you?
*Val.* – Rejoice that you are lightened of
　　a load.
Now, you have only me to reckon
　　with.

*The D.* One I have never seen, much
　　less obliged?
*Val.* Dare I speak, lady?
*The D.* 　　　Dare you! Heard you not
I rule no longer?
*Val.* 　　　　　　　　Lady, if your rule
Were based alone on such a ground as
　　these 　[*Pointing to the* COURTIERS.
Could furnish you, – abjure it! They
　　have hidden
A source of true dominion from your
　　sight.
*The D.* You hear them – no such
　　source is left ...
*Val.* 　　　　　　　　　Hear Cleves!
Whose haggard craftsmen rose to
　　starve this day,
Starve now, and will lie down at night
　　to starve,
Sure of a like to-morrow – but as sure
Of a most unlike morrow-after-that,
Since end things must, end howsoe'er
　　things may.
What curbs the brute-force instinct in
　　its hour?
What makes – instead of rising, all as
　　one,
And teaching fingers, so expert to
　　wield
Their tool, the broadsword's play or
　　carbine's trick,
– What makes that there's an easier
　　help, they think,
For you, whose name so few of them
　　can spell,
Whose face scarce one in every
　　hundred saw, –
You simply have to understand their
　　wrongs,
And wrongs will vanish – so, still
　　trades are plied,
And swords lie rusting, and myself
　　stand here?
There is a vision in the heart of each
Of justice, mercy, wisdom, tenderness
To wrong and pain, and knowledge of
　　its cure:

And these embodied in a woman's
   form
That best transmits them, pure as first
   received,
From God above her, to mankind
   below.
Will you derive your rule from such a
   ground,
Or rather hold it by the suffrage, say,
Of this man – this – and this?
*The D.* [*after a pause*]. You come from
   Cleves:
How many are at Cleves of such a
   mind?
*Val.* [*front his paper*]. 'We, all the
   manufacturers of Cleves – '
*The D.* Or stay, sir – lest I seem too
   covetous –
Are you my subject? such as you describe,
Am I to you, though to no other man?
*Val.* [*from his paper*]. – 'Valence, ordained
   your Advocate at Cleves' –
*The D.* [*replacing the coronet*]. Then I
   remain Cleves' Duchess! Take you
   note,
While Cleves but yields one subject of
   this stamp,
I stand her lady till she waves me off!
For her sake, all the Prince claims I
   withhold;
Laugh at each menace; and, his power
   defying,
Return his missive with its due contempt!
              [*Casting it away.*
*Gui.* [*picking it up*]. – Which to the
   Prince I will deliver, lady,
(Note it down, Gaucelme) – with your
   message too!
*The D.* I think the office is a subject's,
   sir!
– Either … how style you him? – my
   special guarder
The Marshal's – for who knows but
   violence
May follow the delivery? – Or, perhaps,
My Chancellor's – for law may be to
   urge

On its receipt! – Or, even my
   Chamberlain's –
For I may violate established form!
[*To* Valence.] Sir, – for the half-hour till
   this service ends,
Will you become all these to me?
*Val.* [*falling on his knee*]. My liege!
*The D.* Give me!
[*The* COURTIERS *present their badges of*
   *office.*
[*Putting them by.*] Whatever was their
   virtue once,
They need new consecration. [*Raising*
   VALENCE.] Are you mine?
I will be Duchess yet!       [*She retires.*
*The Courtiers.*      Our Duchess yet!
A glorious lady! Worthy love and dread!
I'll stand by her, – And I, whate'er
   betide!
*Gui.* [*to* VALENCE]. Well done, well
   done, sir! I care not who knows,
You have done nobly and I envy you –
Tho' I am but unfairly used, I think:
For when one gets a place like this I
   hold,
One gets too the remark that its mere
   wages,
The pay and the preferment, make our
   prize.
Talk about zeal and faith apart from
   these,
We're laughed at – much would zeal
   and faith subsist
Without these also! Yet, let these be
   stopped,
Our wages discontinue, – then, indeed,
Our Zeal and faith, (we hear on every
   side,)
Are not released – having been pledged
   away
I wonder, for what zeal and faith in
   turn?
Hard money purchased me my place!
   No, no –
I'm right, sir – but your wrong is better
   still,
If I had time and skill to argue it.

Therefore, I say, I'll serve you, how you
please –
If you like, – fight you, as you seem to
wish –
(The kinder of me that, in sober truth,
I never dreamed I did you any harm) …
*Gau.* – Or, kinder still, you'll introduce,
no doubt,
His merits to the Prince who's just at
hand,
And let no hint drop he's made
Chancellor
And Chamberlain and Heaven knows
what beside!
*Clug.* [to VALENCE]. You stare, young
sir, and threaten! Let me say,
That at your age, when first I came to
court,
I was not much above a gentleman;
While now …
*Val.*          – You are Head-Lackey?
With your office
I have not yet been graced, sir!
*Other Courtiers* [to CLUGNET]. Let him
talk!
Fidelity, disinterestedness,
Excuse so much! Men claim my
worship ever
Who staunchly and steadfastly …
            Enter ADOLF.
*Adolf.*               The Prince arrives.
*Courtiers.* Ha? How?
*Adolf.* He leaves his guard a stage behind
At Aix, and enters almost by himself.
*1st Court.* The Prince! This foolish
business puts all out.
*2nd Court.* Let Gaucelme speak first!
*3rd Court.*               Better I began
About the state of Juliers: should one
say
All's prosperous and inviting him?
*4th Court.*               – Or rather,
All's prostrate and imploring him?
*5th Court.*               That's best!
Where's the Cleves' paper, by the way?
*4th Court.* [to Valence].      Sir – sir –
If you'll but lend that paper – trust it me,

I'll warrant …
*5th Court.*      Softly, sir – the Marshal's
duty!
*Clug.* Has not the Chamberlain a
hearing first
By virtue of his patent?
*Gau.*               Patents? – Duties?
All that, my masters, must begin again!
One word composes the whole
controversy:
We're simply now – the Prince's!
*The Others.*               Ay – the Prince's!
            *Enter* SABYNE.
*Sab.* Adolf! Bid … Oh, no time for
ceremony!
Where's whom our lady calls her only
subject?
She needs him. Who is here the
Duchess's?
*Val.* [*starting from his reverie*]. Most
gratefully I follow to her feet.


ACT 3

*Scene – Afternoon. The Vestibule.*
*Enter* PRINCE BERTHOLD *and* MELCHIOR.
*Berth.* A thriving little burgh this Juliers
looks.
[*Half-apart.*] Keep Juliers, and as good
you kept Cologne:
Better try Aix, though! –
*Mel.*               Please't your Highness
speak?
*Berth.* [*as before*]. Aix, Cologne,
Frankfort, – Milan; – Rome! –
*Mel.*                    The Grave.
More weary seems your Highness, I
remark,
Than sundry conquerors whose path
I've watched
Through fire and blood to any prize
they gain.
I could well wish you, for your proper
sake,
Had met some shade of opposition
here
– Found a blunt seneschal refuse unlock,

Or a scared usher lead your steps
    astray.
You must not look for next achievement's
    palm
So easily: this will hurt your conquering.
*Berth.* My next? Ay, as you say, my next
    and next!
Well, I am tired, that's truth, and moody
    too,
This quiet entrance-morning: listen why!
Our little burgh, now, Juliers – 'tis
    indeed
One link, however insignificant,
Of the great chain by which I reach my
    hope,
– A link I must secure; but otherwise,
You'd wonder I esteem it worth my
    grasp.
Just see what life is, with its shifts and
    turns!
It happens now – this very nook – to be
A place that once … not a long while
    since, neither –
When I lived an ambiguous hanger-on
Of foreign courts, and bore my claims
    about,
Discarded by one kinsman, and the
    other
A poor priest merely, – then, I say, this
    place
Shone my ambition's object; to be
    Duke –
Seemed then, what to be Emperor
    seems now.
My rights were far from judged as plain
    and sure
In those days as of late, I promise you:
And 'twas my day-dream, Lady
    Colombe here
Might e'en compound the matter, pity
    me,
Be struck, say, with my chivalry and
    grace
(I was a boy!) – bestow her hand at
    length,
And make me Duke, in her right if not
    mine.

Here am I, Duke confessed, at Juliers
    now.
Hearken: if ever I be Emperor,
Remind me what I felt and said to-day!
*Mel.* All this consoles a bookish man
    like me.
– And so will weariness cling to you.
    Wrong,
Wrong! Had you sought the lady's
    court yourself, –
Faced the redoubtables composing it,
Flattered this, threatened that man,
    bribed the other, –
Pleaded by writ and word and deed,
    your cause, –
Conquered a footing inch by painful
    inch, –
And, after long years' struggle, pounced
    at last
On her for prize, – the right life had
    been lived,
And justice done to divers faculties
Shut in that brow. Yourself were visible
As you stood victor, then; whom now
    – (your pardon!)
I am forced narrowly to search and see,
So are you hid by helps – this Pope,
    your uncle –
Your cousin, the other King! You are a
    mind, –
They, body: too much of mere legs-
    and-arms
Obstructs the mind so! Match these
    with their like:
Match mind with mind!
*Berth.*               And where's your
    mind to match?
They show me legs-and-arms to cope
    withal!
I'd subjugate this city – where's its
    mind?
            [*The* COURTIERS *enter slowly.*
*Mel.* Got out of sight when you came
    troops and all!
And in its stead, here greets you flesh-
    and-blood:
A smug œconomy of both, this first!

[*As* CLUGNET *bows obsequiously.*
Well done, gout, all considered! – I may
    go?
*Berth*. Help me receive them!
*Mel*.          Oh, they just will say
What yesterday at Aix their fellows
    said –
At Treves, the day before! Sir Prince,
    my friend,
Why do you let your life slip thus? –
    Meantime,
I have my little Juliers to achieve –
The understanding this tough
    Platonist,
Your holy uncle disinterred, Amelius:
Lend me a company of horse and foot,
To help me through his tractate – gain
    my Duchy!
*Berth*. And Empire, after that is gained,
    will be – ?
*Mel*. To help me through your uncle's
    comment, Prince!     [*Goes.*
*Berth*. Ah? Well: he o'er-refines – the
    scholar's fault!
How do I let my life slip? Say, this life,
I lead now, differs from the common
    life
Of other men in mere degree, not kind,
Of joys and griefs, – still there is such
    degree
Mere largeness in a life is something,
    sure, –
Enough to care about and struggle for,
In this world: for this world, the size of
    things;
The sort of things, for that to come, no
    doubt.
A great is better than a little aim:
And when I wooed Priscilla's rosy mouth
And failed so, under that grey convent-
    wall,
Was I more happy than I should be now
        [*By this time, the* COURTIERS
        *are ranged before him.*
If failing of my Empire? Not a whit.
– Here comes the mind, it once had
    tasked me sore

To baffle, but for my advantages!
All's best as 'tis: these scholars talk and
    talk.     [*Seats himself.*
*The Courtiers*. Welcome our Prince to
    Juliers! – to his heritage!
Our dutifullest service proffer we!
*Clug*. I, please your Highness, having
    exercised
The function of Grand Chamberlain at
    court,
With much acceptance, as men
    testify …
*Berth*. I cannot greatly thank you,
    gentlemen!
The Pope declares my claim to the
    Duchy founded
On strictest justice – you concede it,
    therefore,
I do not wonder: and the kings my
    friends
Protest they mean to see such claim
    enforced, –
You easily may offer to assist.
But there's a slight discretionary power
To serve me in the matter, you've had
    long,
Though late you use it. This is well to
    say –
But could you not have said it months
    ago?
I'm not denied my own Duke's
    truncheon, true –
'Tis flung me – I stoop down, and from
    the ground
Pick it, with all you placid standers-by:
And now I have it, gems and mire at
    once,
Grace go with it to my soiled hands,
    you say!
*Gui*. (By Paul, the advocate our doughty
    friend
Cuts the best figure!)
*Gau*.          If our ignorance
May have offended, sure our loyalty …
*Berth*. Loyalty? Yours? Oh – of
    yourselves you speak!
I mean the Duchess all this time, I hope!

And since I have been forced repeat my
    claims
As if they never had been urged before,
As I began, so must I end, it seems.
The formal answer to the grave
    demand!
What says the lady?
*Courtiers* [*one to another*]. 1*st Court.*
    Marshal! 2*nd Court.* Orator!
*Gui.* A variation of our mistress' way!
Wipe off his boots' dust, Clugnet! –
    that, he waits!
1*st Court.* Your place!
2*nd Court.*    Just now it was your own!
*Gui.*              The devil's!
*Berth.* [*to* Guibert]. Come forward,
    friend – you with the paper, there!
Is Juliers the first city I've obtained?
By this time, I may boast proficiency
In each decorum of the circumstance.
Give it me as she gave it – the petition,
Demand, you style it! What's required,
    in brief?
What title's reservation, appanage's
Allowance? I heard all at Treves, last
    week.
*Gau.* [*to* GUIBERT]. 'Give it him as she
    gave it!'
*Gui.*        And why not?
[*To* BERTHOLD.] The lady crushed your
    summons thus together,
And bade me, with the very greatest
    scorn
So fair a frame could hold, inform
    you …
*Courtiers.*    Stop – Idiot!
*Gui.* – Inform you she denied your
    claim,
Defied yourself! (I tread upon his heel,
The blustering advocate!)
*Berth.*         By heaven and earth!
Dare you jest, sir?
*Gui.*      Did they at Treves, last week?
*Berth.* [*starting up*]. Why then, I look
    much bolder than I knew,
And you prove better actors than I
    thought:

Since, as I live, I took you as you
    entered
For just so many dearest friends of
    mine,
Fled from the sinking to the rising
    power
– The sneaking'st crew, in short, I e'er
    despised!
Whereas, I am alone here for the
    moment,
With every soldier left behind at Aix!
Silence? That means the worst? I
    thought as much!
What follows next then?
*Courtiers.* Gracious Prince, he raves!
*Gui.* He asked the truth and why not
    get the truth?
*Berth.* Am I a prisoner? Speak, will
    somebody?
– But why stand paltering with imbeciles?
Let me see her, or …
*Gui.* Her, without her leave,
Shall no one see: she's Duchess yet!
*Courtiers* [*footsteps without, as they are*
    *disputing*].    Good chance!
She's here – the Lady Colombe's self!
*Berth.*             'Tis well!
[*Aside.*] Array a handful thus against
    my world?
Not ill done, truly! Were not this a
    mind
To match one's mind with? Colombe!
    Let us wait!
I failed so, under that grey convent
    wall!
She comes.
*Gui.*    The Duchess! Strangers, range
    yourselves!
    [*As the* DUCHESS *enters in conversation*
      *with* VALENCE, BERTHOLD *and the*
        COURTIERS *fall back a little.*
*The D.* Presagefully it beats, presagefully,
My heart: the right is Berthold's and
    not mine.
*Val.* Grant that he has the right, dare I
    mistrust
Your power to acquiesce so patiently

As you believe, in such a dream-like
  change
Of fortune – change abrupt, profound,
  complete?
*The D.* Ah, the first bitterness is over
  now!
Bitter I may have felt it to confront
The truth, and ascertain those natures'
  value
I had so counted on; that was a pang:
But I did bear it, and the worst is over.
Let the Prince take them!
*Val.*                And take Juliers too?
– Your people without crosses, wands
  and chains –
Only with hearts?
*The D.*            There I feel guilty, sir!
I cannot give up what I never had:
For I ruled these, not them – these
  stood between.
Shall I confess, sir? I have heard by
  stealth
Of Berthold from the first; more news
  and more:
Closer and closer swam the thunder-
  cloud,
But I was safely housed with these, I
  knew.
At times when to the casement I would
  turn,
At a bird's passage or a flower-trail's
  play,
I caught the storm's red glimpses on its
  edge –
Yet I was sure some one of all these
  friends
Would interpose: I followed the bird's
  flight
Or plucked the flower: some one
  would interpose!
*Val.* Not one thought on the People –
  and Cleves there!
*The D.* Now, sadly conscious my real
  sway was missed,
Its shadow goes without so much regret:
Else could I not again thus calmly bid
  you,

Answer Prince Berthold!
*Val.*                Then you acquiesce?
*The D.* Remember over whom it was I
  ruled!
*Gui.* [*stepping forward*]. Prince Berthold,
  yonder, craves an audience, lady!
*The D.* [*to* VALENCE]. I only have to
  turn, and I shall face
Prince Berthold! Oh, my very heart is
  sick!
It is the daughter of a line of Dukes
This scornful insolent adventurer
Will bid depart from my dead father's
  halls!
I shall not answer him – dispute with
  him –
But, as he bids, depart! Prevent it, sir!
Sir – but a mere day's respite! Urge for
  me
– What I shall call to mind I should
  have urged
When time's gone by: 'twill all be
  mine, you urge!
A day – an hour – that I myself may lay
My rule down! 'Tis too sudden – must
  not be!
The world's to hear of it! Once done –
  for ever!
How will it read, sir? How be sung
  about?
Prevent it!
*Berth.* [*approaching*]. Your frank
  indignation, lady,
Cannot escape me. Overbold I seem;
But somewhat should be pardoned my
  surprise
At this reception, – this defiance, rather.
And if, for their and your sake, I rejoice
Your virtues could inspire a trusty few
To make such gallant stand in your
  behalf,
I cannot but be sorry, for my own,
Your friends should force me to retrace
  my steps:
Since I no longer am permitted speak
After the pleasant peaceful course
  prescribed

No less by courtesy than relationship –
Which I remember, if you once forgot.
But never must attack pass unrepelled.
Suffer that, through you, I demand of
    these,
Who controverts my claim to Juliers?
*The D.*                            – Me
You say, you do not speak to –
*Berth.*                    Of your subjects
I ask, then: whom do you accredit?
    Where
Stand those should answer?
*Val.* [*advancing*].      The lady is alone.
*Berth.* Alone, and thus? So weak and
    yet so bold?
*Val.* I said she was alone –
*Berth.*                    And weak, I said.
*Val.* When is man strong until he feels
    alone?
It was some lonely strength at first, be
    sure,
Created organs, such as those you
    seek,
By which to give its varied purpose
    shape:
And, naming the selected ministrants,
Took sword, and shield, and sceptre, –
    each, a man!
That strength performed its work and
    passed its way:
You see our lady: there, the old shapes
    stand!
– A Marshal, Chamberlain, and
    Chancellor –
'Be helped their way, into their death
    put life
'And find advantage!' – so you counsel
    us.
But let strength feel alone, seek help
    itself, –
And, as the inland-hatched sea-
    creature hunts
The sea's breast out, – as, littered 'mid
    the waves
The desert-brute makes for the desert's
    joy,
So turns our lady to her true resource,

Passing o'er hollow fictions, worn-out
    types,
– And I am first her instinct fastens on.
And prompt I say, as clear as heart can
    speak,
The People will not have you; nor shall
    have!
It is not merely I shall go bring Cleves
And fight you to the last, – though that
    does much,
And men and children, – ay, and
    women too,
Fighting for home, are rather to be
    feared
Than mercenaries fighting for their pay
    –
But, say you beat us, since such things
    have been,
And, where this Juliers laughed, you
    set your foot
Upon a steaming bloody plash – what
    then?
Stand you the more our lord that there
    you stand?
Lord it o'er troops whose force you
    concentrate,
A pillared flame whereto all ardours
    tend –
Lord it 'mid priests whose schemes
    you amplify,
A cloud of smoke 'neath which all
    shadows brood –
But never, in this gentle spot of earth,
Can you become our Colombe, our
    play-queen,
For whom, to furnish lilies for her hair,
We'd pour our veins forth to enrich the
    soil.
– Our conqueror? Yes! – Our despot?
    Yes! – Our Duke?
Know yourself, know us!
*Berth.* [*who has been in thought*]. Know
    your lady, also!
[*Very deferentially.*] – To whom I needs
    must exculpate myself
For having made a rash demand, at
    least.

Wherefore to you, sir, who appear to be
Her chief adviser, I submit my claims,
                              [*Giving papers.*
But, this step taken, take no further step,
Until the Duchess shall pronounce their worth.
Here be our meeting-place; at night, its time:
Till when I humbly take the lady's leave!
              [*He withdraws. As the* DUCHESS
                    *turns to* VALENCE,
                *the* COURTIERS *interchange
              glances and come forward a little.*
*1st Court.* So, this was their device!
*2nd Court.*                No bad device!
*3rd Court.* You'd say they love each other, Guibert's friend
From Cleves, and she, the Duchess!
*4th Court.*              – And moreover,
That all Prince Berthold comes for, is to help
Their loves!
*5th Court.*  Pray, Guibert, what is next to do?
*Gui.* [*advancing*]. I laid my office at the Duchess' foot –
*Others.* And I – and I – and I!
*The D.*              I took them, sirs.
*Gui.* [*apart to* Valence. And now, sir, I am simple knight again –
Guibert, of the great ancient house, as yet
That never bore affront; whate'er your birth, –
As things stand now, I recognize yourself
(If you'll accept experience of some date)
As like to be the leading man o' the time,
Therefore as much above me now, as I
Seemed above you this morning. Then, I offered
To fight you: will you be as generous
And now fight me?
*Val.*        Ask when my life is mine!

*Gui.* ('Tis hers now!)
*Clug.* [*apart* to VALENCE, *as* GUIBERT
       *turns from him*]. You, sir, have insulted me
Grossly, – will grant me, too, the selfsame favour
You've granted him, just now, I make no question?
*Val.* I promise you, as him, sir.
*Clug.*                  Do you so?
Handsomely said! I hold you to it, sir.
You'll get me reinstated in my office
As you will Guibert!
*The D.*              I would be alone!
              [*They begin to retire slowly;
              as* VALENCE *is about to follow –*
Alone, sir – only with my heart: you stay!
*Gau.* You hear that? Ah, light breaks upon me! Cleves –
It was at Cleves some man harangued us all –
With great effect, – so those who listened said,
My thoughts being busy elsewhere: was this he?
Guibert, – your strange, disinterested man!
Your uncorrupted, if uncourtly friend!
The modest worth you mean to patronize!
He cares about no Duchesses, not he –
His sole concern is with the wrongs of Cleves!
What, Guibert? What, it breaks on you at last?
*Gui.* Would this hall's floor were a mine's roof! I'd back
And in her very face …
*Gau.*                Apply the match
That fired the train, – and where would you be, pray?
*Gui.* With him!
*Gau.* Stand, rather, safe outside with me!
The mine's charged: shall I furnish you the match

And place you properly? To the ante-
    chamber!

*Gui.* Can you?

*Gau.*   Try me! Your friend's in fortune!

*Gui.*                     Quick –
To the antechamber! He is pale with
    bliss!

*Gau.* No wonder! Mark her eyes!

*Gui.*              To the antechamber!
                    [*The* COURTIERS *retire.*

*The D.* Sir, could you know all you
    have done for me
You were content! You spoke, and I am
    saved.

*Val.* Be not too sanguine, lady! Ere you
    dream,
That transient flush of generosity
Fades off, perchance. The man, beside,
    is gone, –
Him we might bend; but see, the
    papers here –
Inalterably his requirement stays,
And cold hard words have we to deal
    with now.
In that large eye there seemed a latent
    pride,
To self-denial not incompetent,
But very like to hold itself dispensed
From such a grace: however, let us
    hope!
He is a noble spirit in noble form.
I wish he less had bent that brow to
    smile
As with the fancy how he could subject
Himself upon occasion to – himself!
From rudeness, violence, you rest
    secure;
But do not think your Duchy rescued
    yet!

*The D.* You, – who have opened a new
    world to me,
Will never take the faded language up
Of that I leave? My Duchy – keeping it,
Or losing it – is that my sole world
    now?

*Val.* Ill have I spoken if you thence
    despise

Juliers; although the lowest, on true
    grounds,
Be worth more than the highest rule,
    on false:
Aspire to rule, on the true grounds!

*The D.*                Nay, hear –
False, I will never – rash, I would not be!
This is indeed my birthday – soul and
    body,
Its hours have done on me the work of
    years.
You hold the requisition: ponder it!
If I have right, my duty's plain: if he –
Say so, nor ever change a tone of voice!
At night you meet the Prince; meet me
    at eve!
Till when, farewell! This discomposes
    you?
Believe in your own nature, and its
    force
Of renovating mine! I take my stand
Only as under me the earth is firm:
So, prove the first step stable, all will
    prove.
That first, I choose: [*Laying her hand on
    his.*] – the next to take, choose you!
                    [*She withdraws.*

*Val.* [*after a pause*]. What drew down
    this on me? – on me, dead once,
She thus bids live, – since all I hitherto
Thought dead in me, youth's ardours
    and emprise,
Burst into life before her, as she bids
Who needs them. Whither will this
    reach, where end?
Her hand's print burns on mine ... Yet
    she's above –
So very far above me! All's too plain:
I served her when the others sank away,
And she rewards me as such souls
    reward –
The changed voice, the suffusion of the
    cheek,
The eye's acceptance, the expressive
    hand,
– Reward, that's little, in her generous
    thought,

Though all to me …
                    I cannot so disclaim
Heaven's gift, nor call it other than it is!
She loves me!
[*Looking at the Prince's papers.*] –
                    Which love, these,
    perchance, forbid.
Can I decide against myself – pronounce
She is the Duchess and no mate for me?
– Cleves, help me! Teach me, – every
    haggard face, –
To sorrow and endure! I will do right
Whatever be the issue. Help me, Cleves!

### ACT 4

*Scene – Evening. An Antechamber.*
        *Enter the* COURTIERS.
*Mau.* Now, then, that we may speak –
    how spring this mine?
*Gau.* Is Guibert ready for its match? He
    cools!
Not so friend Valence with the Duchess
    there!
'Stay, Valence! Are not you my better
    self?'
And her cheek mantled –
*Gui.*            Well, she loves him, sir:
And more, – since you will have it I
    grow cool, –
She's right: he's worth it.
*Gau.*            For his deeds today?
Say so!
*Gui.*   What should I say beside?
*Gau.*                    Not this –
For friendship's sake leave this for me
    to say –
That we're the dupes of an egregious
    cheat!
This plain unpractised suitor, who found
    way
To the Duchess through the merest
    die's turn-up
A year ago, had seen her and been seen,
Loved and been loved.
*Gui.*            Impossible!
*Gau.*                – Nor say,

How sly and exquisite a trick, moreover,
Was this which – taking not their
    stand on facts
Boldly, for that had been endurable,
But worming on their way by craft,
    they choose
Resort to, rather, – and which you and
    we,
Sheep-like, assist them in the playing-off.
The Duchess thus parades him as
    preferred,
Not on the honest ground of preference,
Seeing first, liking more, and there an
    end –
But as we all had started equally,
And at the close of a fair race he proved
The only valiant, sage and loyal man.
Herself, too, with the pretty fits and
    starts, –
The careless, winning, candid ignorance
Of what the Prince might challenge or
    forego –
She had a hero in reserve! What risk
Ran she? This deferential easy Prince
Who brings his claims for her to ratify
– He's just her puppet for the nonce!
        You'll see, –
Valence pronounces, as is equitable,
Against him: off goes the confederate:
As equitably, Valence takes her hand!
*The Chancellor.* You run too fast: her
    hand, no subject takes.
Do not our archives hold her father's
    will?
That will provides against such accident,
And gives next heir, Prince Berthold,
    the reversion
Of Juliers, which she forfeits, wedding
    so.
*Gau.* I know that, well as you, – but
    does the Prince?
Knows Berthold, think you, that this
    plan, he helps,
For Valence's ennoblement, – would
    end,
If crowned with the success which
    seems its due,

In making him the very thing he plays,
The actual Duke of Juliers? All agree
That Colombe's title waived or set aside,
He is next heir.

*The Chan.*          Incontrovertibly

*Gau.* Guibert, your match, now, to the train!

*Gui.*          Enough!
I'm with you: selfishness is best again.
I thought of turning honest – what a dream!
Let's wake now!

*Gau.*          Selfish, friend, you never were:
'Twas but a series of revenges taken
On your unselfishness for prospering ill.
But now that you're grown wiser, what's our course?

*Gui.* – Wait, I suppose, till Valence weds our lady,
And then, if we must needs revenge ourselves,
Apprise the Prince.

*Gau.* – The Prince, ere then dismissed
With thanks for playing his mock part so well?
Tell the Prince now, sir! Ay, this very night,
Ere he accepts his dole and goes his way,
Explain how such a marriage makes him Duke,
Then trust his gratitude for the surprise!

*Gui.* – Our lady wedding Valence all the same
As if the penalty were undisclosed?
Good! If she loves, she'll not disown her love,
Throw Valence up. I wonder you see that.

*Gau.* The shame of it – the suddenness and shame!
Within her, the inclining heart – without,
A terrible array of witnesses –
And Valence by, to keep her to her word,
With Berthold's indignation or disgust!

We'll try it! – Not that we can venture much.
Her confidence we've lost for ever: Berthold's
Is all to gain.

*Gui.*          To-night, then, venture we!
Yet – if lost confidence might be renewed?

*Gau.* Never in noble natures! With the base ones, –
Twist off the crab's claw, wait a smarting-while,
And something grows and grows and gets to be
A mimic of the lost joint, just so like
As keeps in mind it never, never will
Replace its predecessor! Crabs do that:
But lop the lion's foot – and …

*Gui.*          To the Prince!

*Gau.* [*aside*]. And come what will to the lion's foot, I pay you,
My cat's-paw, as I long have yearned to pay.
[*Aloud.*] Footsteps! Himself! 'Tis Valence breaks on us,
Exulting that their scheme succeeds. We'll hence –
And perfect ours! Consult the archives, first –
Then, fortified with knowledge, seek the Hall!

*Cug.* [*to* GAUCELME *as they retire*]. You have not smiled so since your father died!

> *As they retire, enter* VALENCE *with papers*.

*Val.* So must it be! I have examined these
With scarce a palpitating heart – so calm,
Keeping her image almost wholly off,
Setting upon myself determined watch,
Repelling to the uttermost his claims:
And the result is – all men would pronounce
And not I, only, the result to be –
Berthold is heir; she has no shade of right

To the distinction which divided us,
But, suffered to rule first, I know not
    why,
Her rule connived at by those Kings
    and Popes,
To serve some devil's-purpose, – now
    'tis gained,
Whate'er it was, the rule expires as
    well.
– Valence, this rapture ... selfish can it
    be?
Eject it from your heart, her home! – It
    stays!
Ah, the brave world that opens on us
    both!
– Do my poor townsmen so esteem it?
    Cleves, –
I need not your pale faces! This, reward
For service done to you? Too horrible!
I never served you: 'twas myself I
    served –
Nay, served not – rather saved from
    punishment
Which, had I failed you then, would
    plague me now.
My life continues yours, and your life,
    mine.
But if, to take God's gift, I swerve no
    step –
Cleves! If I breathe no prayer for it – if
    she,       [*Footsteps without*.
Colombe, that comes now, freely gives
    herself –
Will Cleves require, that, turning thus
    to her,
I ...
      Enter PRINCE BERTHOLD.
    Pardon, sir! I did not look for you
Till night, i' the Hall; nor have as yet
    declared
My judgment to the lady.
*Berth*.           So I hoped.
*Val*. And yet I scarcely know why that
    should check
The frank disclosure of it first to you –
What her right seems, and what, in
    consequence,

She will decide on.
*Berth*.         That I need not ask.
*Val*. You need not: I have proved the
    lady's mind:
And, justice being to do, dare act for her.
*Berth*. Doubtless she has a very noble
    mind,
*Val*. Oh, never fear but she'll in each
    conjuncture
Bear herself bravely! She no whit depends
On circumstance; as she adorns a
    throne,
She had adorned ...
*Berth*.       A cottage – in what book
Have I read that, of every queen that
    lived?
A throne! You have not been instructed,
    sure,
To forestall my request?
*Val*.           'Tis granted, sir!
My heart instructs me. I have scrutinized
Your claims ...
*Berth*.       Ah – claims, you mean,
    at first preferred?
I come, before the hour appointed me,
To pray you let those claims at present
    rest,
In favour of a new and stronger one.
*Val*. You shall not need a stronger: on
    the part
O' the lady, all you offer I accept,
Since one clear right suffices: yours is
    clear.
Propose!
*Berth*.   I offer her my hand.
*Val*.           Your hand?
*Berth*. A Duke's, yourself say; and, at
    no far time,
Something here whispers me – an
    Emperor's.
The lady's mind is noble: which
    induced
This seizure of occasion ere my claims
Were – settled, let us amicably say!
*Val*. Your hand!
*Berth*.    (He will fall down and kiss it
    next!)

Sir, this astonishment's too flattering,
Nor must you hold your mistress'
　　worth so cheap.
Enhance it, rather, – urge that blood is
　　blood –
The daughter of the Burgraves,
　　Landgraves, Markgraves,
Remains their daughter! I shall scarce
　　gainsay.
Elsewhere or here, the lady needs must
　　rule;
Like the imperial crown's great
　　chrysoprase,
They talk of – somewhat out of
　　keeping there,
And yet no jewel for a meaner cap.
*Val.* You wed the Duchess?
*Berth.*　　　　　Cry you mercy, friend!
Will the match also influence fortunes
　　here?
A natural solicitude enough.
Be certain, no bad chance it proves for
　　you!
However high you take your present
　　stand,
There's prospect of a higher still
　　remove –
For Juliers will not be my resting-place,
And, when I have to choose a
　　substitute
To rule the little burgh, I'll think of you
Who need not give your mates a
　　character.
And yet I doubt your fitness to supplant
The grey smooth Chamberlain: he'd
　　hesitate
A doubt his lady could demean herself
So low as to accept me. Courage, sir!
I like your method better: feeling's play
Is franker much, and flatters me beside.
*Val.* I am to say, you love her?
*Berth.*　　　　　　Say that too!
Love has no great concernment, thinks
　　the world,
With a Duke's marriage. How go
　　precedents
In Juliers' story – how use Juliers' Dukes?

I see you have them here in goodly row;
Yon must be Luitpold – ay, a stalwart
　　sire!
Say, I have been arrested suddenly
In my ambition's course, its rocky
　　course,
By this sweet flower: I fain would
　　gather it
And then proceed: so say and speedily
– (Nor stand there like Duke
　　Luitpold's brazen self!)
Enough, sir: you possess my mind, I
　　think.
This is my claim, the others being
　　withdrawn,
And to this be it that, i' the Hall to-night,
Your lady's answer comes; till when,
　　farewell!
　　　　　　　　　[*He retires.*
*Val.* [*after a pause*]. The heavens and
　　earth stay as they were; my heart
Beats as it beat: the truth remains the
　　truth.
What falls away, then, if not faith in her?
Was it my faith, that she could
　　estimate
Love's value, and, such faith still
　　guiding me,
Dare I now test her? Or grew faith so
　　strong
Solely because no power of test was
　　mine?
　　　　　*Enter the* DUCHESS.
*The D.* My fate, sir! Ah, you turn away.
　　All's over.
But you are sorry for me? Be not so!
What I might have become, and never
　　was,
Regret with me! What I have merely
　　been,
Rejoice I am no longer! What I seem
Beginning now, in my new state, to be,
Hope that I am! – for, once my rights
　　proved void,
This heavy roof seems easy to exchange
For the blue sky outside – my lot
　　henceforth.

*Val*. And what a lot is Berthold's!
*The D*.                    How of him?
*Val*. He gathers earth's whole good into
      his arms;
Standing, as man now, stately, strong
      and wise,
Marching to fortune, not surprised by
      her.
One great aim, like a guiding-star,
      above –
Which tasks strength, wisdom,
      stateliness, to lift
His manhood to the height that takes
      the prize;
A prize not near – lest overlooking
      earth
He rashly spring to seize it – nor remote,
So that he rest upon his path content:
But day by day, while shimmering
      grows shine,
And the faint circlet prophesies the
      orb,
He sees so much as, just evolving
      these,
The stateliness, the wisdom and the
      strength,
To due completion, will suffice this
      life,
And lead him at his grandest to the
      grave.
After this star, out of a night he springs;
A beggar's cradle for the throne of thrones
He quits; so, mounting, feels each step
      he mounts,
Nor, as from each to each exultingly
He passes, overleaps one grade of joy.
This, for his own good: – with the
      world, each gift
Of God and man, – reality, tradition,
Fancy and fact – so well environ him,
That as a mystic panoply they serve –
Of force, untenanted, to awe mankind,
And work his purpose out with half the
      world,
While he, their master, dexterously slipt
From such encumbrance, is meantime
      employed

With his own prowess on the other half.
Thus shall he prosper, every day's
      success
Adding, to what is he, a solid strength –
An aëry might to what encircles him,
Till at the last, so life's routine lends
      help,
That as the Emperor only breathes and
      moves,
His shadow shall be watched, his step
      or stalk
Become a comfort or a portent, how
He trails his ermine take significance, –
Till even his power shall cease to be
      most power,
And men shall dread his weakness
      more, nor dare
Peril their earth its bravest, first and
      best,
Its typified invincibility.
Thus shall he go on, greatening, till he
      ends –
The man of men, the spirit of all flesh,
The fiery centre of an earthly world!
*The D*. Some such a fortune I had
      dreamed should rise
Out of my own – that is, above my
      power
Seemed other, greater potencies to
      stretch –
*Val*. For you?
*The D*.        It was not I moved there, I
      think:
But one I could, – though constantly
      beside,
And aye approaching, – still keep
      distant from,
And so adore. 'Twas a man moved
      there.
*Val*.        Who?
*The D*. I felt the spirit, never saw the
      face.
*Val*. See it! 'Tis Berthold's! He enables
      you
To realize your vision.
*The D*.                Berthold?
*Val*.                            Duke –

*Emperor* to be: he proffers you his
    hand.
*The D.* Generous and princely!
*Val.*                 He is all of this.
*The D.* Thanks, Berthold, for my
    father's sake! No hand
Degrades me.
*Val.* You accept the proffered hand?
*The D.* That he should love me!
*Val.*           'Loved' I did not say.
Had that been – love might so incline
    the Prince
To the world's good, the world that's
    at his foot, –
I do not know, this moment, I should
    dare
Desire that you refused the world –
    and Cleves –
The sacrifice he asks.
*The D.*          Not love me, sir?
*Val.* He scarce affirmed it.
*The D.*       May not deeds affirm?
*Val.* What does he? … Yes, yes, very
    much he does!
All the shame saved, he thinks, and
    sorrow saved –
Immitigable sorrow, so he thinks, –
Sorrow that's deeper than we dream,
    perchance.
*The D.* Is not this love?
*Val.*        So very much he does!
For look, you can descend now
    gracefully:
All doubts are banished, that the world
    might have,
Or worst, the doubts yourself, in
    aftertime,
May call up of your heart's sincereness
    now.
To such, reply, 'I could have kept my
    rule –
'Increased it to the utmost of my
    dreams –
'Yet I abjured it.' This, he does for you:
It is munificently much.
*The D.*         Still 'much!'
But why is it not love, sir? Answer me!

*Val.* Because not one of Berthold's
    words and looks
Had gone with love's presentment of a
    flower
To the beloved: because bold confidence,
Open superiority, free pride –
Love owns not, yet were all that
    Berthold owned:
Because where reason, even, finds no
    flaw,
Unerringly a lover's instinct may.
*The D.* You reason, then, and doubt?
*Val.*          I love, and know.
*The D.* You love? How strange! I never
    cast a thought
On that. Just see our selfishness! You
    seemed
So much my own … I had no ground
    – and yet,
I never dreamed another might divide
My power with you, much less exceed it.
*Val.*               Lady,
I am yours wholly.
*The D.*       Oh, no, no, not mine!
'Tis not the same now, never more can
    be.
– Your first love, doubtless. Well, what's
    gone from me?
What have I lost in you?
*Val.*          My heart replies –
No loss there! So, to Berthold back
    again:
This offer of his hand, he bids me
    make –
Its obvious magnitude is well to weigh.
*The D.* She's … yes, she must be very
    fair for you!
*Val.* I am a simple advocate of Cleves.
*The D.* You! With the heart and brain
    that so helped me,
I fancied them exclusively my own,
Yet find are subject to a stronger sway!
She must be … tell me, is she very fair?
*Val.* Most fair, beyond conception or
    belief.
*The D.* Black eyes? – no matter!
    Colombe, the world leads

Its life without you, whom your friends
    professed
The only woman: see how true they
    spoke!
One lived this while, who never saw
    your face,
Nor heard your voice – unless … Is she
    from Cleves?
Vol. Cleves knows her well.
*The D.*          Ah – just a fancy, now!
When you poured forth the wrongs of
    Cleves, – I said,
– Thought, that is, afterward …
*Val.*          You thought of me?
*The D.* Of whom else? Only such great
    cause, I thought,
For such effect: see what true love can
    do!
Cleves is his love. I almost fear to ask
… And will not. This is idling: to our
    work!
Admit before the Prince, without reserve,
My claims misgrounded; then may
    follow better
… When you poured out Cleves'
    wrongs impetuously,
Was she in your mind?
*Val.*          All done was done for her
– To humble me!
*The D.*          She will be proud at least.
*Val.* She?
*The D.*   When you tell her.
*Val.*                    That will never be.
*The D.* How – are there sweeter things
    you hope to tell?
No, sir! You counselled me, – I counsel
    you
In the one point I – any woman – can.
Your worth, the first thing; let her own
    come next –
Say what you did through her, and she
    through you –
The praises of her beauty afterward!
Will you?
*Val.*      I dare not.
*The D.*          Dare not?
*Val.*                    She I love

Suspects not such a love in me.
*The D.*                    You jest.
*Val.* The lady is above me and away.
Not only the brave form, and the bright
    mind,
And the great heart, combine to press
    me low –
But all the world calls rank divides us.
*The D.*                    Rank!
Now grant me patience! Here's a man
    declares
Oracularly in another's case –
Sees the true value and the false, for
    them –
Nay, bids them see it, and they straight
    do see.
You called my court's love worthless –
    so it turned:
I threw away as dross my heap of wealth,
And here you stickle for a piece or two!
First – has she seen you?
*Val.*          Yes.
*The D.*          She loves you, then.
*Val.* One flash of hope burst; then
    succeeded night:
And all's at darkest now. Impossible!
*The D.* We'll try: you are – so to speak
    – my subject yet?
*Val.* As ever – to the death.
*The D.*                    Obey me, then!
*Val.* I must.
*The D.*          Approach her, and … no!
    first of all
Get more assurance. 'My instructress,'
    say,
'Was great, descended from a line of
    kings,
'And even fair' – (wait why I say this
    folly) –
'She said, of all men, none for
    eloquence,
'Courage, and (what cast even these to
    shade)
'The heart they sprung from, – none
    deserved like him
'Who saved her at her need: if she said
    this,

'What should not one I love, say?'
*Val.*                    Heaven – this hope –
Oh, lady, you are filling me with fire!
*The D.* Say this! – nor think I bid you
     cast aside
One touch of all the awe and reverence;
Nay, make her proud for once to
     heart's content
That all this wealth of heart and soul's
     her own!
Think you are all of this, – and,
     thinking it,
. . . (Obey!)
*Val.*     I cannot choose.
*The Duchess.*          Then, kneel to her
          [VALENCE *sinks on his knee.*
I dream!
*Val.*     Have mercy! Yours, unto the
     death, –
I have obeyed. Despise, and let me die!
*The D.* Alas, sir, is it to be ever thus?
Even with you as with the world? I
     know
This morning's service was no vulgar
     deed
Whose motive, once it dares avow
     itself,
Explains all done and infinitely more,
So, takes the shelter of a nobler cause.
Your service named its true source, –
     loyalty!
The rest's unsaid again. The Duchess
     bids you,
Rise, sir! The Prince's words were in
     debate.
*Val.* [*rising*]. Rise? Truth, as ever, lady,
     comes from you!
I should rise – I who spoke for Cleves,
     can speak
For Man – yet tremble now, who stood
     firm then.
I laughed – for 'twas past tears – that
     Cleves should starve
With all hearts beating loud the
     infamy,
And no tongue daring trust as much to
     air:

Yet here, where all hearts speak, shall I
     be mute?
Oh, lady, for your own sake look on me!
On all I am, and have, and do – heart,
     brain,
Body and soul, – this Valence and his
     gifts!
I was proud once: I saw you, and they
     sank,
So that each, magnified a thousand
     times,
Were nothing to you – but such
     nothingness,
Would a crown gild it, or a sceptre
     prop,
A treasure speed, a laurel-wreath
     enhance?
What is my own desert? But should
     your love
Have … there's no language helps here
     … singled me, –
Then – oh, that wild word 'then!' – be
     just to love,
In generosity its attribute!
Love, since you pleased to love! All's
     cleared – a stage
For trial of the question kept so long:
Judge you – Is love or vanity the best?
You, solve it for the world's sake – you,
     speak first
What all will shout one day – you,
     vindicate
Our earth and be its angel! All is said.
Lady, I offer nothing – I am yours:
But, for the cause' sake, look on me
     and him,
And speak!
*The D.*     I have received the Prince's
     message:
Say, I prepare my answer!
*Val.*               Take me, Cleves!
          [*He withdraws.*
*The D.* Mournful – that nothing's what
     it calls itself!
Devotion, zeal, faith, loyalty – mere love!
And, love in question, what may
     Berthold's be?

I did ill to mistrust the world so soon:
Already was this Berthold at my side.
The valley-level has its hawks no
  doubt:
May not the rock-top have its eagles,
  too?
Yet Valence … let me see his rival then!

### ACT 5

*Scene – Night. The Hall.*
  Enter BERTHOLD and MELCHIOR.
*Mel*. And here you wait the matter's
  issue?
*Berth*.    Here.
*Mel*. I don't regret I shut Amelius, then.
But tell me, on this grand disclosure, –
  how
Behaved our spokesman with the
  forehead?
*Berth*.    Oh,
Turned out no better than the fore-
  headless –
Was dazzled not so very soon, that's all!
For my part, this is scarce the hasty
  showy
Chivalrous measure you give me credit
  of.
Perhaps I had a fancy, – but 'tis gone.
– Let her commence the unfriended
  innocent
And carry wrongs about from court to
  court?
No, truly! The least shake of fortune's
  sand,
– My uncle-Pope chokes in a coughing
  fit,
King-cousin takes a fancy to blue eyes, –
And wondrously her claims would
  brighten up;
Forth comes a new gloss on the ancient
  law,
O'er-looked provisoes, o'er-past
  premises,
Follow in plenty. No: 'tis the safe step.
The hour beneath the convent-wall is
  lost:

Juliers and she, once mine, are ever
  mine.
*Mel*. Which is to say, you, losing heart
  already,
Elude the adventure.
*Berth*.    Not so – or, if so –
Why not confess at once that I advise
None of our kingly craft and guild just
  now
To lay, one moment, down their privilege
With the notion they can any time at
  pleasure
Retake it: that may turn out hazardous.
We seem, in Europe, pretty well at end
O' the night, with our great masque:
  those favoured few
Who keep the chamber's top, and
  honour's chance
Of the early evening, may retain their
  place
And figure as they list till out of breath.
But it is growing late: and I observe
A dim grim kind of tipstaves at the
  doorway
Not only bar new-comers entering now,
But caution those who left, for any
  cause,
And would return, that morning draws
  too near;
The ball must die off, shut itself up.
  We –
I think, may dance lights out and
  sunshine in,
And sleep off headache on our frippery:
But friend the other, who cunningly
  stole out,
And, after breathing the fresh air outside,
Means to re-enter with a new costume,
Will be advised go back to bed, I fear.
I stick to privilege, on second thoughts.
*Mel*. Yes – you evade the adventure:
  and, beside,
Give yourself out for colder than you
  are.
King Philip, only, notes the lady's eyes?
Don't they come in for somewhat of
  the motive

With you too?

*Berth*.      Yes – no: I am past that now.

Gone 'tis: I cannot shut my soul to fact.

Of course, I might by forethought and
    contrivance

Reason myself into a rapture. Gone:

And something better come instead,
    no doubt.

*Mel*. So be it! Yet, all the same, proceed
    my way,

Though to your ends; so shall you
    prosper best!

The lady, – to be won for selfish ends, –

Will be won easier my unselfish … call
    it,

Romantic way.

*Berth*.          Won easier?

*Mel*.                    Will not she?

*Berth*. There I profess humility without
    bound:

Ill cannot speed – not I – the Emperor.

*Mel*. And I should think the Emperor
    best waived,

From your description of her mood
    and way.

You could look, if it pleased you, into
    hearts;

But are too indolent and fond of
    watching

Your own – you know that, for you
    study it.

*Berth*. Had you but seen the orator her
    friend,

So bold and vobuble an hour before,

Abashed to earth at aspect of the
    change!

Make her an Empress? Ah, that
    changed the case!

Oh, I read hearts! 'Tis for my own
    behoof,

I court her with my true worth: wait
    the event!

I learned my final lesson on that head

When years ago, – my first and last
    essay –

Before the priest my uncle could by help

Of his superior, raise me from the dirt –

Priscilla left me for a Brabant lord

Whose cheek was like the topaz on his
    thumb.

I am past illusion on that score.

*Mel*.                    Here comes

The lady –

*Berth*.      – And there you go. But do
    not! Give me

Another chance to please you! Hear me
    plead!

*Mel*. You'll keep, then, to the lover, to
    the man?

*Enter the* DUCHESS – *followed by* ADOLF
    *and* SABYNE *and, after an interval,*
    *by the* COURTIERS.

*Berth*. Good auspice to our meeting!

*The D.*                    May it prove!

– And you, sir, will be Emperor one
    day?

*Berth*. (Ay, that's the point!) I may be
    Emperor.

*The D.* 'Tis not for my sake only, I am
    proud

Of this you offer: I am prouder far

That from the highest state should duly
    spring

The highest, since most generous, of
    deeds.

*Berth*. (Generous – still that!) You
    underrate yourself.

You are, what I, to be complete, must
    gain –

Find now, and may not find, another
    time.

While I career on all the world for
    stage,

There needs at home my representative.

*The D.* – Such, rather, would some
    warrior-woman be –

One dowered with lands and gold, or
    rich in friends –

One like yourself.

*Berth*.          Lady, I am myself,

And have all these: I want what's not
    myself,

Nor has all these. Why give one hand
    two swords?

Here's one already: be a friend's next
        gift
A silk glove, if you will – I have a sword.
*The D*. You love me, then?
*Berth*.                     Your lineage I revere,
Honour your virtue, in your truth
        believe,
Do homage to your intellect, and bow
Before your peerless beauty.
*The D*.                     But, for love –
*Berth*. A further love I do not understand.
Our best course is to say these hideous
        truths,
And see them, once said, grow
        endurable:
Like waters shuddering from their
        central bed,
Black with the midnight bowels of the
        earth,
That, once up-spouted by an earth-
        quake's throe,
A portent and a terror – soon subside,
Freshen apace, take gold and rainbow
        hues
In sunshine, sleep in shadow, and at
        last
Grow common to the earth as hills or
        trees –
Accepted by all things they came to
        scare.
*The D*. You cannot love, then?
*Berth*.           – Charlemagne, perhaps!
Are you not over-curious in love-lore?
*The D*. I have become so, very recently.
It seems, then, I shall best deserve
        esteem,
Respect, and all your candour promises,
By putting on a calculating mood –
Asking the terms of my becoming
        yours?
*Berth*. Let me not do myself injustice,
        neither.
Because I will not condescend to fictions
That promise what my soul can ne'er
        acquit,
It does not follow that my guarded
        phrase

May not include far more of what you
        seek,
Than wide profession of less scrupulous
        men.
You will be Empress, once for all: with
        me
The Pope disputes supremacy – you
        stand,
And none gainsays, the earth's first
        woman.
*The D*.     That –
Or simple Lady of Ravestein again?
*Berth*. The matter's not in my
        arbitrament:
Now I have made my claims – which I
        regret –
Cede one, cede all.
*The D*. This claim then, you enforce?
*Berth*. The world looks on.
*The D*.           And when must I decide?
*Berth*. When, lady? Have I said thus
        much so promptly
For nothing? – Poured out, with such
        pains, at once
What I might else have suffered to ooze
        forth
Droplet by droplet in a lifetime long –
For aught less than as prompt an
        answer, too?
All's fairly told now: who can teach you
        more?
*The D*. I do not see him.
*Berth*.               I shall ne'er deceive.
This offer should be made befittingly
Did time allow the better setting forth
The good of it, with what is not so
        good,
Advantage, and disparagement as well:
But as it is, the sum of both must serve.
I am already weary of this place;
My thoughts are next stage on to Rome.
        Decide!
The Empire – or, – not even Juliers now!
Hail to the Empress – farewell to the
        Duchess!
[*The* COURTIERS, *who have been drawing
        nearer and nearer, interpose.*

*Gau.* – 'Farewell,' Prince? when we
       break in at our risk –
*Clug.* Almost upon court-licence
       trespassing –
*Gau.* – To point out how your claims
       are valid yet!
You know not, by the Duke her
       father's will,
The lady, if she weds beneath her rank,
Forfeits her Duchy in the next heir's
       favour –
So 'tis expressly stipulate. And if
It can be shown 'tis her intent to wed
A subject, then yourself, next heir, by
       right
Succeed to Juliers.
*Berth.*                What insanity? –
*Gui.* Sir, there's one Valence, the pale
       fiery man
You saw and heard this morning –
       thought, no doubt,
Was of considerable standing here:
I put it to your penetration, Prince,
If aught save love, the truest love for her
Could make him serve the lady as he
       did!
He's simply a poor advocate of Cleves
– Creeps here with difficulty, finds a
       place
With danger, gets in by a miracle,
And for the first time meets the lady's
       face –
So runs the story: is that credible?
For, first – no sooner in, than he's
       apprised
Fortunes have changed; you are all-
       powerful here,
The lady as powerless: he stands fast
       by her!
*The D. [aside].* And do such deeds
       spring up from love alone?
*Gui.* But here occurs the question,
       does the lady
Love him again? I say, how else can
       she?
Can she forget how he stood singly
       forth

In her defence, dared outrage all of us,
Insult yourself – for what, save love's
       reward?
*The D. [aside].* And is love then the sole
       reward of love?
*Gui.* But, love him as she may and
       must – you ask,
Means she to wed him? 'Yes,' both
       natures answer!
Both, in their pride, point out the sole
       result;
Nought less would he accept nor she
       propose.
For each conjuncture was she great
       enough
– Will be, for this.
*Clug.*           Though, now that this
       is known,
Policy, doubtless, urges she deny …
*The D.* – What, sir, and wherefore? –
       since I am not sure
That all is any other than you say!
You take this Valence, hold him close
       to me,
Him with his actions: can I choose but
       look?
I am not sure, love trulier shows itself
Than in this man, you hate and would
       degrade,
Yet, with your worst abatement, show
       me thus.
Nor am I – (thus made look within
       myself,
Ere I had dared) – now that the look is
       dared –
Sure that I do not love him!
*Gui.*                Hear you, Prince?
*Berth.* And what, sirs, please you, may
       this prattle mean
Unless to prove with what alacrity
You give your lady's secrets to the
       world?
How much indebted, for discovering
That quality, you make me, will be
       found
When there's a keeper for my own to
       seek.

*Courtiers*. 'Our lady?'
*Berth*.                          – She assuredly remains,
*The D*. Ah, Prince – and you too can be
     generous?
You could renounce your power, if this
     were so,
And let me, as these phrase it, wed my
     love
Yet keep my Duchy? You perhaps exceed
Him, even, in disinterestedness!
*Berth*. How, lady, should all this affect
     my purpose?
Your will and choice are still as ever,
     free.
Say, you have known a worthier than
     myself
In mind and heart, of happier form and
     face –
Others must have their birthright: I have
     gifts,
To balance theirs, not blot them out of
     sight.
Against a hundred alien qualities,
I lay the prize I offer. I am nothing:
Wed you the Empire?
*The D*.                    And my heart away?
*Berth*. When have I made pretension to
     your heart?
I give none. I shall keep your honour
     safe;
With mine I trust you, as the sculptor
     trusts
Yon marble woman with the marble
     rose,
Loose on her hand, she never will let
     fall,
In graceful, slight, silent security.
You will be proud of my world-wide
     career,
And I content in you the fair and good.
What were the use of planting a few
     seeds
The thankless climate never would
     mature –
Affections all repelled by circumstance?
Enough: to these no credit I attach, –
To what you own, find nothing to object.

Write simply on my requisition's face
What shall content my friends – that
     you admit,
As Colombe of Ravestein, the claims
     therein,
Or never need admit them, as my wife –
And either way, all's ended!
*The D*.                         Let all end!
*Berth*. The requisition!
*Gui*.              – Valence holds, of course!
*Berth*. Desire his presence!
                         [ADOLF goes out.
*Courtiers* [*to each other*]. Out it all comes
     yet;
He'll have his word against the bargain
     yet;
He's not the man to tamely acquiesce.
One passionate appeal – upbraiding
     even,
May turn the tide again. Despair not
     yet!
                         [*They retire a little*.
*Berth*. [*to* MELCHIOR]. The Empire has
     its old success, my friend!
*Mel*. You've had your way: before the
     spokesman speaks,
Let me, but this once, work a problem
     out,
And ever more be dumb! The Empire
     wins?
To better purpose have I read my books!
                         Enter VALENCE.
*Mel*. [*to the* COURTIERS]. Apart, my
     masters!
[*To* Valence.] Sir, one word with you!
I am a poor dependant of the Prince's –
Pitched on to speak, as of slight
     consequence.
You are no higher, I find: in other
     words,
We two, as probably the wisest here,
Need not hold diplomatic talk like
     fools.
Suppose I speak, divesting the plain
     fact
Of all their tortuous phrases, fit for
     them?

Do you reply so, and what trouble
    saved!
The Prince, then – an embroiled
    strange heap of news
This moment reaches him – if true or
    false,
All dignity forbids he should inquire
In person, or by worthier deputy;
Yet somehow must inquire, lest slander
    come:
And so, 'tis I am pitched on. You have
    heard
His offer to your lady?
*Val.*           Yes.
*Mel.*          – Conceive
Her joy thereat?
*Val.*       I cannot.
*Mel.*          No one can.
All draws to a conclusion, therefore.
*Val.* [*aside*].        So!
No after-judgment – no first thought
    revised –
Her first and last decision! – me, she
    leaves,
Takes him; a simple heart is flung
    aside,
The ermine o'er a heartless breast
    embraced.
Oh Heaven, this mockery has been
    played too oft!
Once, to surprise the angels – twice,
    that fiends
Recording, might be proud they chose
    not so –
Thrice, many thousand times, to teach
    the world
All men should pause, misdoubt their
    strength, since men
Can have such chance yet fail so signally,
– But ever, ever this farewell to Heaven,
Welcome to earth – this taking death
    for life –
This spurning love and kneeling to the
    world –
Oh Heaven, it is too often and too old!
*Mel.* Well, on this point, what but an
    absurd rumour

Arises – these, its source – its subject,
    you!
Your faith and loyalty misconstruing,
They say, your service claims the lady's
    hand!
Of course, nor Prince nor lady can
    respond:
Yet something must be said: for, were
    it true
You made such claim, the Prince
    would …
*Val.*        Well, sir, – would?
*Mel.* – Not only probably withdraw his
    suit,
But, very like, the lady might be forced
Accept your own. Oh, there are reasons
    why!
But you'll excuse at present all save
    one, –
I think so. What we want is, your own
    witness,
For, or against – her good, or yours:
    decide!
*Val.* [*aside*]. Be it her good if she
    accounts it so!
[*After a contest.*] For what am I but
    hers, to choose as she?
Who knows how far, beside, the light
    from her
May reach, and dwell with, what she
    looks upon?
*Mel.* [*to the* Prince]. Now to him, you!
*Berth.* [*to* Valence]. My friend acquaints
    you, sir,
The noise runs …
*Val.*   – Prince, how fortunate you are,
Wedding her as you will, in spite of
    noise,
To show belief in love! Let her but love
    you,
All else you disregard! What else can be?
You know how love is incompatible
With falsehood – purifies, assimilates
All other passions to itself.
*Mel.*          Ay, sir:
But softly! Where, in the object we
    select,

Such love is, perchance, wanting?
*Val.*                              Then indeed,
What is it you can take?
*Mel.*                    Nay, ask the world!
Youth, beauty, virtue, an illustrious
      name,
An influence o'er mankind.
*Val.*              When man perceives …
– Ah, I can only speak as for myself!
*The D.* Speak for yourself!
*Val.*          May I? – no, I have spoken,
And time's gone by. Had I seen such
      an one,
As I loved her – weighing thoroughly
      that word –
So should my task be to evolve her love:
If for myself! – if for another – well.
*Berth.* Heroic truly! And your sole
      reward, –
The secret pride in yielding up love's
      right?
*Val.* Who thought upon reward? And
      yet how much
Comes after – oh, what amplest
      recompense!
Is the knowledge of her, nought? the
      memory, nought?
– Lady, should such an one have
      looked on you,
Ne'er wrong yourself so far as quote
      the world
And say, love can go unrequited here!
You will have blessed him to his whole
      life's end –
Low passions hindered, baser cares
      kept back,
All goodness cherished where you
      dwelt – and dwell.
What would he have? He holds you –
      you, both form
And mind, in his, – where self-love
      makes such room
For love of you, he would not serve
      you now
The vulgar way, – repulse your enemies,
Win you new realms, or best, to save
      the old

Die blissfully – that's past so long ago!
He wishes you no need, thought, care
      of him –
Your good, by any means, himself
      unseen,
Away, forgotten! – He gives that life's
      task up,
As it were … but this charge which I
      return –
      [*Offers the requisition, which she takes.*
Wishing your good.
*The D.* [*having subscribed it*]. And
      opportunely, sir –
Since at a birthday's close, like this of
      mine,
Good wishes gentle deeds reciprocate.
Most on a wedding-day, as mine is too,
Should gifts be thought of: yours
      comes first by right.
Ask of me!
*Berth.*   He shall have whate'er he asks,
For your sake and his own.
*Val.* [*aside*].              If I should ask –
The withered bunch of flowers she
      wears – perhaps,
One last touch of her hand, I never
      more
Shall see! [*After a pause, presenting his
      paper to the* PRINCE.
            Cleves' Prince, redress the
      wrongs of Cleves!
*Berth.* I will, sir!
*The D.* [*as* VALENCE *prepares to retire*].
            – Nay, do out your duty, first!
You bore this paper; I have registered
My answer to it: read it and have done!
                  [VALENCE *reads it.*
I take him – give up Juliers and the
      world.
This is my Birthday.
*Mel.*              Berthold, my one hero
Of the world she gives up, one friend
      worth my books,
Sole man I think it pays the pains to
      watch, –
Speak, for I know you through your
      Popes and Kings!

*Berth.* [*after a pause*]. Lady, well
    rewarded! Sir, as well deserved!
I could not imitate – I hardly envy –
I do admire you. All is for the best.
Too costly a flower were this, I see it
    now,
To pluck and set upon my barren helm
To wither – any garish plume will do.
I'll not insult you and refuse your
    Duchy –
You can so well afford to yield it me,
And I were left, without it, sadly lorn.
As it is – for me – if that will flatter you,
A somewhat wearier life seems to
    remain
Than I thought possible where …
    'faith, their life
Begins already! They're too occupied
To listen: and few words content me
    best.
[*Abruptly to the* COURTIERS.] I am your
    Duke, though! Who obey me here?
*The D.* Adolf and Sabyne follow us –
*Gui.* [*starting from the* COURTIERS].
                    – And I?

Do I not follow them, if I mayn't you?
Shall not I get some little duties up
At Ravestein and emulate the rest?
God save you, Gaucelme! 'Tis my
    Birthday, too!
*Berth.* You happy handful that remain
    with me
. . . That is, with Dietrich the black
    Barnabite
I shall leave over you – will earn your
    wages
Or Dietrich has forgot to ply his trade!
Meantime, – go copy me the precedents
Of every installation, proper styles
And pedigrees of all your Juliers'
    Dukes –
While I prepare to plod on my old way,
And somewhat wearily, I must confess!
*The D.* [*with a light joyous laugh as she
    turns from them*]. Come, Valence,
    to our friends, God's earth …
*Val.* [*as she falls into his arms*].
                  – And thee!

## Incident of the French Camp

### 1

You know, we French stormed Ratisbon:
  A mile or so away,
On a little mound, Napoleon
  Stood on our storming-day;
With neck out-thrust, you fancy how,
  Legs wide, arms locked behind,
As if to balance the prone brow
  Oppressive with its mind.

### 2

Just as perhaps he mused 'My plans
  'That soar, to earth may fall,
'Let once my army-leader Lannes
  'Waver at yonder wall,' –
Out 'twixt the battery-smokes there flew
  A rider, bound on bound
Full-galloping; nor bridle drew
  Until he reached the mound.

### 3

Then off there flung in smiling joy,
  And held himself erect
By just his horse's mane, a boy:
  You hardly could suspect –
(So tight he kept his lips compressed,
  Scarce any blood came through)
You looked twice ere you saw his breast
  Was all but shot in two.

### 4

'Well,' cried he, 'Emperor, by God's
      grace
  'We've got you Ratisbon!
'The Marshal's in the market-place,
  'And you'll be there anon
'To see your flag-bird flap his vans
  'Where I, to heart's desire,
'Perched him!' The chief's eye flashed;
      his plans
  Soared up again like fire.

### 5

The chief's eye flashed; but presently
  Softened itself, as sheathes

A film the mother-eagle's eye
  When her bruised eaglet breathes;
'You're wounded!' 'Nay,' the soldier's
      pride
  Touched to the quick, he said:
'I'm killed, Sire!' And his chief beside
  Smiling the boy fell dead.

## The Patriot

### AN OLD STORY

### 1

It was roses, roses, all the way,
  With myrtle mixed in my path like
      mad:
The house-roofs seemed to heave and
      sway,
  The church-spires flamed, such flags
      they had,
A year ago on this very day.

### 2

The air broke into a mist with bells,
  The old walls rocked with the crowd
      and cries.
Had I said, 'Good folk, mere noise
      repels –
  'But give me your sun from yonder
      skies!'
They had answered, 'And afterward,
      what else?'

### 3

Alack, it was I who leaped at the sun
  To give it my loving friends to keep!
Nought man could do, have I left
      undone:
  And you see my harvest, what I reap
This very day, now a year is run.

### 4

There's nobody on the house-tops
      now –
  Just a palsied few at the windows
      set;
For the best of the sight is, all allow,

At the Shambles' Gate – or, better
yet,
By the very scaffold's foot, I trow.

5

I go in the rain, and, more than needs,
   A rope cuts both my wrists behind;
And I think, by the feel, my forehead
   bleeds,
   For they fling, whoever has a mind,
Stones at me for my year's misdeeds.

6

Thus I entered, and thus I go!
   In triumphs, people have dropped
   down dead.
'Paid by the world, what dost thou owe
   'Me?' – God might question; now
   instead,
'Tis God shall repay: I am safer so.

## My Last Duchess

### FERRARA

That's my last Duchess painted on the
   wall,
Looking as if she were alive. I call
That piece a wonder, now: Frà Pandolf's
   hands
Worked busily a day, and there she
   stands.
Will't please you sit and look at her? I
   said
'Frà Pandolf' by design, for never read
Strangers like you that pictured
   countenance,
The depth and passion of its earnest
   glance,
But to myself they turned (since none
   puts by
The curtain I have drawn for you, but I)
And seemed as they would ask me, if
   they durst,
How such a glance came there; so, not
   the first
Are you to turn and ask thus. Sir, 'twas
   not
Her husband's presence only, called
   that spot

Of joy into the Duchess' cheek:
   perhaps
Frà Pandolf chanced to say 'Her mantle
   laps
'Over my lady's wrist too much,' or
   'Paint
'Must never hope to reproduce the faint
'Half-flush that dies along her throat:'
   such stuff
Was courtesy, she thought, and cause
   enough
For calling up that spot of joy. She had
A heart – how shall I say? – too soon
   made glad,
Too easily impressed; she liked
   whate'er
She looked on, and her looks went
   everywhere.
Sir, 'twas all one! My favour at her
   breast,
The dropping of the daylight in the
   West,
The bough of cherries some officious
   fool
Broke in the orchard for her, the white
   mule
She rode with round the terrace – all
   and each
Would draw from her alike the
   approving speech,
Or blush, at least. She thanked men, –
   good! but thanked
Somehow – I know not how – as if she
   ranked
My gift of a nine-hundred-years-old
   name
With anybody's gift. Who'd stoop to
   blame
This sort of trifling? Even had you skill
In speech – (which I have not) – to
   make your will
Quite clear to such an one, and say,
   'Just this
'Or that in you disgusts me; here you
   miss,
'Or there exceed the mark' – and if she
   let

Herself be lessoned so, nor plainly set
Her wits to yours, forsooth, and made
     excuse,
– E'en then would be some stooping;
     and I choose
Never to stoop. Oh sir, she smiled, no
     doubt,
Whene'er I passed her; but who
     passed without
Much the same smile? This grew; I
     gave commands;
Then all smiles stopped together.
     There she stands
As if alive. Will't please you rise? We'll
     meet
The company below, then. I repeat,
The Count your master's known
     munificence
Is ample warrant that no just pretence
Of mine for dowry will be disallowed;
Though his fair daughter's self, as I
     avowed
At starting, is my object. Nay, we'll go
Together down, sir. Notice Neptune,
     though,
Taming a sea-horse, thought a rarity,
Which Claus of Innsbruck cast in
     bronze for me!

## Count Gismond

### AIX IN PROVENCE

#### 1

Christ God who savest man, save most
     Of men Count Gismond who saved
     me!
Count Gauthier, when he chose his
     post,
     Chose time and place and company
To suit it; when he struck at length
My honour, 'twas with all his strength.

#### 2

And doubtlessly ere he could draw
     All points to one, he must have
     schemed!
That miserable morning saw
     Few half so happy as I seemed,

While being dressed in queen's array
To give our tourney prize away.

#### 3

I thought they loved me, did me grace
     To please themselves; 'twas all their
     deed;
God makes, or fair or foul, our face;
     If showing mine so caused to bleed
My cousins' hearts, they should have
     dropped
A word, and straight the play had
     stopped.

#### 4

They, too, so beauteous! Each a queen
     By virtue of her brow and breast;
Not needing to be crowned, I mean,
     As I do. E'en when I was dressed,
Had either of them spoke, instead
Of glancing sideways with still head!

#### 5

But no; they let me laugh, and sing
     My birthday song quite through,
     adjust
The last rose in my garland, fling
     A last look on the mirror, trust
My arms to each an arm of theirs,
And so descend the castle-stairs –

#### 6

And come out on the morning-troop
     Of merry friends who kissed my
     cheek,
And called me queen, and made me
     stoop
     Under the canopy – (a streak
That pierced it, of the outside sun,
Powdered with gold its gloom's soft
     dun) –

#### 7

And they could let me take my state
     And foolish throne amid applause
Of all come there to celebrate
     My queen's-day – Oh I think the
     cause
Of much was, they forgot no crowd
Makes up for parents in their shroud!

8

However that be, all eyes were bent
  Upon me, when my cousins cast
Theirs down: 'twas time I should present
  The victor's crown, but … there,
    'twill last
No long time … the old mist again
Blinds me as then it did. How vain!

9

See! Gismond's at the gate, in talk
  With his two boys: I can proceed.
Well, at that moment, who should stalk
  Forth boldly – to my face, indeed –
But Gauthier, and he thundered 'Stay!'
And all stayed. 'Bring no crowns, I say!

10

'Bring torches! Wind the penance-sheet
  'About her! Let her shun the chaste,
'Or lay herself before their feet!
  'Shall she whose body I embraced
'A night long, queen it in the day?
'For honour's sake no crowns, I say!'

11

I? What I answered? As I live,
  I never fancied such a thing
As answer possible to give.
  What says the body when they spring
Some monstrous torture-engine's whole
Strength on it? No more says the soul.

12

Till out strode Gismond; then I knew
  That I was saved. I never met
His face before, but, at first view,
  I felt quite sure that God had set
Himself to Satan; who would spend
A minute's mistrust on the end?

13

He strode to Gauthier, in his throat
  Gave him the lie, then struck his
    mouth
With one back-handed blow that wrote
  In blood men's verdict there. North,
    South,
East, West, I looked. The lie was dead,
And damned, and truth stood up instead

14

This glads me most, that I enjoyed
  The heart of the joy, with my conter
In watching Gismond unalloyed
  By any doubt of the event:
God took that on him – I was bid
Watch Gismond for my part: I did.

15

Did I not watch him while he let
  His armourer just brace his greaves,
Rivet his hauberk, on the fret
  The while! His foot … my memory
    leaves
No least stamp out, nor how anon
He pulled his ringing gauntlets on.

16

And e'en before the trumpet's sound
  Was finished, prone lay the false
    knight,
Prone as his lie, upon the ground:
  Gismond flew at him, used no sleight
O' the sword, but open-breasted drove,
Cleaving till out the truth he clove.

17

Which done, he dragged him to my feet
  And said 'Here die, but end thy breath
'In full confession, lest thou fleet
  'From my first, to God's second death!
'Say, hast thou lied?' And, 'I have lied
'To God and her,' he said, and died.

18

Then Gismond, kneeling to me, asked
  – What safe my heart holds, though
    no word
Could I repeat now, if I tasked
  My powers for ever, to a third
Dear even as you are. Pass the rest
Until I sank upon his breast.

19

Over my head his arm he flung
  Against the world; and scarce I felt
His sword (that dripped by me and
    swung)
  A little shifted in its belt:
For he began to say the while
How South our home lay many a mile.

20

So 'mid the shouting multitude
   We two walked forth to never more
Return. My cousins have pursued
   Their life, untroubled as before
I vexed them. Gauthier's dwelling-place
God lighten! May his soul find grace!

21

Our elder boy has got the clear
   Great brow; tho' when his brother's
      black
Full eye shows scorn, it ... Gismond
   here?
   And have you brought my tercel back?
I just was telling Adela
How many birds it struck since May.


## The Boy and the Angel

Morning, evening, noon and night,
'Praise God!' sang Theocrite.

Then to his poor trade he turned,
Whereby the daily meal was earned.

Hard he laboured, long and well;
O'er his work the boy's curls fell.

But ever, at each period,
He stopped and sang, 'Praise God!'

Then back again his curls he threw,
And cheerful turned to work anew.

Said Blaise, the listening monk, 'Well
   done;
'I doubt not thou art heard, my son:

'As well as if thy voice to-day
'Were praising God, the Pope's great
   way.

'This Easter Day, the Pope at Rome
'Praises God from Peter's dome.'

Said Theocrite, 'Would God that I
'Might praise him, that great way, and
   die!'

Night passed, day shone,
And Theocrite was gone.

With God a day endures alway,
A thousand years are but a day.

God said in heaven, 'Nor day nor night
'Now brings the voice of my delight.'

Then Gabriel, like a rainbow's birth,
Spread his wings and sank to earth;

Entered, in flesh, the empty cell,
Lived there, and played the craftsman
   well;

And morning, evening, noon and night,
Praised God in place of Theocrite.

And from a boy, to youth he grew:
The man put off the stripling's hue:

The man matured and fell away
Into the season of decay:

And ever o'er the trade he bent,
And ever lived on earth content.

(He did God's will; to him, all one
If on the earth or in the sun.)

God said, 'A praise is in mine ear;
'There is no doubt in it, no fear:

'So sing old worlds, and so
'New worlds that from my footstool go.

'Clearer loves sound other ways:
'I miss my little human praise.'

Then forth sprang Gabriel's wings, off
   fell
The flesh disguise, remained the cell.

'Twas Easter Day: he flew to Rome,
And paused above Saint Peter's dome.

In the tiring-room close by
The great outer gallery,

With his holy vestments dight,
Stood the new Pope, Theocrite:

And all his past career
Came back upon him clear,

Since when, a boy, he plied his trade,
Till on his life the sickness weighed;

And in his cell, when death drew near,
An angel in a dream brought cheer:

And rising from the sickness drear
He grew a priest, and now stood here.

To the East with praise he turned,
And on his sight the angel burned.

'I bore thee from thy craftsman's cell
'And set thee here; I did not well.

'Vainly I left my angel-sphere,
'Vain was thy dream of many a year.

'Thy voice's praise seemed weak; it
        dropped –
'Creation's chorus stopped!

'Go back and praise again
'The early way, while I remain.

'With that weak voice of our disdain,
'Take up creation's pausing strain.

'Back to the cell and poor employ:
'Resume the craftsman and the boy!'

Theocrite grew old at home;
A new Pope dwelt in Peter's dome.

One vanished as the other died:
They sought God side by side.

## Instans Tyrannus

### 1

Of the million or two, more or less,
I rule and possess,
One man, for some cause undefined,
Was least to my mind.

### 2

I struck him, he grovelled of course –
For, what was his force?
I pinned him to earth with my weight
And persistence of hate:
And he lay, would not moan, would
        not curse,
As his lot might be worse.

### 3

'Were the object less mean, would he
        stand
'At the swing of my hand!
'For obscurity helps him and blots
'The hole where he squats.'
So, I set my five wits on the stretch
To inveigle the wretch.
All in vain! Gold and jewels I threw,
Still he couched there perdue;
I tempted his blood and his flesh,
Hid in roses my mesh,
Choicest cates and the flagon's best
        spilth:
Still he kept to his filth.

### 4

Had he kith now or kin, were access
To his heart, did I press:
Just a son or a mother to seize!
No such booty as these.
Were it simply a friend to pursue
'Mid my million or two,
Who could pay me in person or pelf
What he owes me himself!
No: I could not but smile through my
        chafe:
For the fellow lay safe
As his mates do, the midge and the nit,
– Through minuteness, to wit.

#### 5

Then a humour more great took its
    place
At the thought of his face,
The droop, the low cares of the mouth,
The trouble uncouth
'Twixt the brows, all that air one is fain
To put out of its pain.
And, 'no!' I admonished myself,
'Is one mocked by an elf,
'Is one baffled by toad or by rat?
'The gravamen's in that!
'How the lion, who crouches to suit
'His back to my foot,
'Would admire that I stand in debate!
'But the small turns the great
'If it vexes you, – that is the thing!
'Toad or rat vex the king?
'Though I waste half my realm to unearth
'Toad or rat, 'tis well worth!'

#### 6

So, I soberly laid my last plan
To extinguish the man.
Round his creep-hole, with never a break
Ran my fires for his sake;
Over-head, did my thunder combine
With my underground mine:
Till I looked from my labour content
To enjoy the event.

#### 7

When sudden … how think ye, the
    end?
Did I say 'without friend'?
Say rather, from marge to blue marge
The whole sky grew his targe
With the sun's self for visible boss,
While an Arm ran across
Which the earth heaved beneath like a
    breast
Where the wretch was safe prest!
Do you see? Just my vengeance complete,
The man sprang to his feet,
Stood erect, caught at God's skirts, and
    prayed!
– So, I was afraid!

## Mesmerism

#### 1

All I believed is true!
    I am able yet
    All I want, to get
By a method as strange as new:
Dare I trust the same to you?

#### 2

If at night, when doors are shut,
    And the wood-worm picks,
    And the death-watch ticks,
And the bar has a flag of smut,
And a cat's in the water-butt –

#### 3

And the socket floats and flares,
    And the house-beams groan,
    And a foot unknown
Is surmised on the garret-stairs,
And the locks slip unawares –

#### 4

And the spider, to serve his ends,
    By a sudden thread,
    Arms and legs outspread,
On the table's midst descends,
Comes to find, God knows what
    friends! –

#### 5

If since eve drew in, I say,
    I have sat and brought
    (So to speak) my thought
To bear on the woman away,
Till I felt my hair turn grey –

#### 6

Till I seemed to have and hold,
    In the vacancy
    'Twixt the wall and me,
From the hair-plait's chestnut gold
To the foot in its muslin fold –

#### 7

Have and hold, then and there,
    Her, from head to foot,
    Breathing and mute,
Passive and yet aware,
In the grasp of my steady stare –

8

Hold and have, there and then,
　All her body and soul
　That completes my whole,
All that women add to men,
In the clutch of my steady ken –

9

Having and holding, till
　I imprint her fast
　On the void at last
As the sun does whom he will
By the calotypist's skill –

10

Then, – if my heart's strength serve,
　And through all and each
　Of the veils I reach
To her soul and never swerve,
Knitting an iron nerve –

11

Command her soul to advance
　And inform the shape
　Which has made escape
And before my countenance
Answers me glance for glance –

12

I, still with a gesture fit
　Of my hands that best
　Do my soul's behest,
Pointing the power from it,
While myself do steadfast sit –

13

Steadfast and still the same
　On my object bent,
　While the hands give vent
To my ardour and my aim
And break into very flame –

14

Then I reach, I must believe,
　Not her soul in vain,
　For to me again
It reaches, and past retrieve
Is wound in the toils I weave;

15

And must follow as I require,
　As befits a thrall,
　Bringing flesh and all,

Essence and earth-attire,
To the source of the tractile fire:

16

Till the house called hers, not mine,
　With a growing weight
　Seems to suffocate
If she break not its leaden line
And escape from its close confine.

17

Out of doors into the night!
　On to the maze
　Of the wild wood-ways,
Not turning to left nor right
From the pathway, blind with sight –

18

Making thro' rain and wind
　O'er the broken shrubs,
　'Twixt the stems and stubs,
With a still, composed, strong mind,
Nor a care for the world behind –

19

Swifter and still more swift,
　As the crowding peace
　Doth to joy increase
In the wide blind eyes uplift
Thro' the darkness and the drift!

20

While I – to the shape, I too
　Feel my soul dilate
　Nor a whit abate,
And relax not a gesture due,
As I see my belief come true.

21

For, there! have I drawn or no
　Life to that lip?
　Do my fingers dip
In a flame which again they throw
On the cheek that breaks a-glow?

22

Ha! was the hair so first?
　What, unfilleted,
　Made alive, and spread
Through the void with a rich
　　outburst,
Chestnut gold-interspersed?

23

Like the doors of a casket-shrine,
  See, on either side,
    Her two arms divide
Till the heart betwixt makes sign,
Take me, for I am thine!

24

'Now – now' – the door is heard!
  Hark, the stairs! and near –
    Nearer – and here –
'Now!' and at call the third
She enters without a word.

25

On doth she march and on
  To the fancied shape;
    It is, past escape,
Herself, now: the dream is done
And the shadow and she are one.

26

First I will pray. Do Thou
  That ownest the soul,
    Yet wilt grant control
To another, nor disallow
For a time, restrain me now!

27

I admonish me while I may,
  Not to squander guilt,
    Since require Thou wilt
At my hand its price one day!
What the price is, who can say?

## The Glove

(Peter Ronsard *loquitur*.)

'Heigho!' yawned one day King Francis,
'Distance all value enhances!
'When a man's busy, why, leisure
'Strikes him as wonderful pleasure:
' 'Faith, and at leisure once is he?
'Straightway he wants to be busy.
'Here we've got peace; and aghast I'm
'Caught thinking war the true pastime.
'Is there a reason in metre?
'Give us your speech, master Peter!'
I who, if mortal dare say so,
Ne'er am at loss with my Naso,

'Sire,' I replied, 'joys prove cloudlets:
'Men are the merest Ixions' –
Here the King whistled aloud, 'Let's
' – Heigho – go look at our lions!'
Such are the sorrowful chances
If you talk fine to King Francis.

And so, to the courtyard proceeding,
Our company, Francis was leading,
Increased by new followers tenfold
Before he arrived at the penfold;
Lords, ladies, like clouds which bedizen
At sunset the western horizon.
And Sir De Lorge pressed 'mid the
    foremost
With the dame he professed to adore
    most.
Oh, what a face! One by fits eyed
Her, and the horrible pitside;
For the penfold surrounded a hollow
Which led where the eye scarce dared
    follow,
And shelved to the chamber secluded
Where Bluebeard, the great lion, brooded.
The King hailed his keeper, an Arab
As glossy and black as a scarab,
And bade him make sport and at once
    stir
Up and out of his den the old monster.
They opened a hole in the wire-work
Across it, and dropped there a firework,
And fled: one's heart's beating
    redoubled;
A pause, while the pit's mouth was
    troubled,
The blackness and silence so utter,
By the firework's slow sparkling and
    sputter;
Then earth in a sudden contortion
Gave out to our gaze her abortion.
Such a brute! Were I friend Clement
    Marot
(Whose experience of nature's but
    narrow,
And whose faculties move in no small
    mist
When he versifies David the Psalmist)

I should study that brute to describe you
*Illum Juda Leonem de Tribu.*
One's whole blood grew curdling and
  creepy
To see the black mane, vast and heapy,
The tail in the air stiff and straining,
The wide eyes, nor waxing nor waning,
As over the barrier which bounded
His platform, and us who surrounded
The barrier, they reached and they rested
On space that might stand him in best
  stead:
For who knew, he thought, what the
  amazement,
The eruption of clatter and blaze meant,
And if, in this minute of wonder,
No outlet, 'mid lightning and thunder,
Lay broad, and, his shackles all shivered,
The lion at last was delivered?
Ay, that was the open sky o'erhead!
And you saw by the flash on his
  forehead,
By the hope in those eyes wide and
  steady,
He was leagues in the desert already,
Driving the flocks up the mountain,
Or catlike couched hard by the fountain
To waylay the date-gathering negress:
So guarded he entrance or egress.
'How he stands!' quoth the King: 'we
  may well swear,
('No novice, we've won our spurs
  elsewhere
'And so can afford the confession,)
'We exercise wholesome discretion
'In keeping aloof from his threshold;
'Once hold you, those jaws want no
  fresh hold,
'Their first would too pleasantly purloin
'The visitor's brisket or surloin:
'But who's he would prove so fool-
  hardy?
'Not the best man of Marignan, pardie!'

The sentence no sooner was uttered,
Than over the rails a glove fluttered,
Fell close to the lion, and rested:
The dame 'twas, who flung it and jested
With life so, De Lorge had been wooing
For months past; he sat there pursuing
His suit, weighing out with nonchalance
Fine speeches like gold from a balance.

Sound the trumpet, no true knight's a
  tarrier!
De Lorge made one leap at the barrier,
Walked straight to the glove, – while
  the lion
Ne'er moved, kept his far-reaching eye
  on
The palm-tree-edged desert-spring's
  sapphire,
And the musky oiled skin of the Kaffir, –
Picked it up, and as calmly retreated,
Leaped back where the lady was seated,
And full in the face of its owner
Flung the glove.
                    'Your heart's queen, you
  dethrone her?
'So should I!' – cried the King – ' 'twas
  mere vanity,
'Not love, set that task to humanity!'
Lords and ladies alike turned with
  loathing
From such a proved wolf in sheep's
  clothing.

Not so, I; for I caught an expression
In her brow's undisturbed self-possession
Amid the Court's scoffing and
  merriment, –
As if from no pleasing experiment
She rose, yet of pain not much heedful
So long as the process was needful, –
As if she had tried in a crucible,
To what 'speeches like gold' were
  reducible,
And, finding the finest prove copper,
Felt the smoke in her face was but
  proper;
To know what she had *not* to trust to,
Was worth all the ashes and dust too.
She went out 'mid hooting and
  laughter;

Clement Marot stayed; I followed after,
And asked, as a grace, what it all meant?
If she wished not the rash deed's
          recalment?
'For I' – so I spoke – 'am a poet:
'Human nature, – behoves that I
          know it!

She told me, 'Too long had I heard
'Of the deed proved alone by the word:
'For my love – what De Lorge would
          not dare!
'With my scorn – what De Lorge could
          compare!
'And the endless descriptions of death
'He would brave when my lip formed a
          breath,
'I must reckon as braved, or, of course,
'Doubt his word – and moreover,
          perforce,
'For such gifts as no lady could spurn,
'Must offer my love in return.
'When I looked on your lion, it
          brought
'All the dangers at once to my thought,
'Encountered by all sorts of men,
'Before he was lodged in his den, –
'From the poor slave whose club or
          bare hands
'Dug the trap, set the snare on the
          sands,
'With no King and no Court to
          applaud,
'By no shame, should he shrink, over-
          awed,
'Yet to capture the creature made shift,
'That his rude boys might laugh at the
          gift,
' – To the page who last leaped o'er the
          fence
'Of the pit, on no greater pretence
'Than to get back the bonnet he
          dropped,
'Lest his pay for a week should be
          stopped.
'So, wiser I judged it to make
'One trial what "death for my sake"

'Really meant, while the power was yet
          mine,
'Than to wait until time should define
'Such a phrase not so simply as I,
'Who took it to mean just "to die."
'The blow a glove gives is but weak:
'Does the mark yet discolour my
          cheek?
'But when the heart suffers a blow,
'Will the pain pass so soon, do you
          know?'

I looked, as away she was sweeping,
And saw a youth eagerly keeping
As close as he dared to the doorway.
No doubt that a noble should more
          weigh
His life than befits a plebeian;
And yet, had our brute been Nemean –
(I judge by a certain calm fervour
The youth stepped with, forward to
          serve her)
– He'd have scarce thought you did
          him the worst turn
If you whispered 'Friend, what you'd
          get, first earn!'
And when, shortly after, she carried
Her shame from the Court, and they
          married,
To that marriage some happiness, maugre
The voice of the Court, I dared augur.

For De Lorge, he made women with
          men vie,
Those in wonder and praise, these in
          envy;
And in short stood so plain a head taller
That he wooed and won ... how do
          you call her?
The beauty, that rose in the sequel
To the King's love, who loved her a
          week well.
And 'twas noticed he never would
          honour
De Lorge (who looked daggers upon her)
With the easy commission of stretching
His legs in the service, and fetching

His wife from her chamber, those straying
Sad gloves she was always mislaying,
While the King took the closet to chat
    in, –
But of course this adventure came pat in.
And never the King told the story,
How bringing a glove brought such glory,
But the wife smiled – 'His nerves are
    grown firmer:
'Mine he brings now and utters no
    murmur.'

*Venienti occurrite morbo!*
With which moral I drop my theorbo.

### Time's Revenges

I've a Friend, over the sea;
I like him, but he loves me.
It all grew out of the books I write;
They find such favour in his sight
That he slaughters you with savage looks
Because you don't admire my books.
He does himself though, – and if some
    vein
Were to snap to-night in this heavy
    brain,
To-morrow month, if I lived to try,
Round should I just turn quietly,
Or out of the bedclothes stretch my
    hand
Till I found him, come from, his foreign
    land
To be my nurse in this poor place,
And make my broth and wash my face
And light my fore and, all the while,
Bear with his old good-humoured smile
That I told him 'Better have kept away
'Than come and kill me, night and day
'With, worse than fever throbs and
    shoots,
'The creaking of his clumsy boots.'
I am as sure that this he would do,
As that Saint Paul's is striking two.
And I think I rather … woe is me!
– Yes, rather would see him than not
    see,

If lifting a hand could seat him there
Before me in the empty chair
To-night, when my head aches indeed,
And I can neither think nor read
Nor make these purple fingers hold
The pen; this garret's freezing cold!

And I've a Lady – there he wakes,
The laughing fiend and prince of snakes
Within me, at her name, to pray
Fate send some creature in the way
Of my love for her, to be down-torn,
Upthrust and outward-borne,
So I might prove myself that sea
Of passion which I needs must be!
Call my thoughts false and my fancies
    quaint
And my style infirm and its figures faint,
All the critics say, and more blame yet,
And not one angry word you get.
But, please you, wonder I would put
My cheek beneath that lady's foot
Rather than trample under mine
The laurels of the Florentine,
And you shall see how the devil spends
A fire God gave for other ends!
I tell you, I stride up and down
This garret, crowned with love's best
    crown,
And feasted with love's perfect feast,
To think I kill for her, at least,
Body and soul and peace and fame,
Alike youth's end and manhood's aim,
– So is my spirit, as flesh with sin,
Filled full, eaten out and in
With the face of her, the eyes of her,
The lips, the little chin, the stir
Of shadow round her mouth; and she
– I'll tell you, – calmly would decree
That I should roast at a slow fire,
If that would compass her desire
And make her one whom they invite
To the famous ball to-morrow night.

There may be heaven; there must be
    hell;
Meantime, there is our earth here – well!

## The Italian in England

That second time they hunted me
From hill to plain, from shore to sea,
And Austria, hounding far and wide
Her blood-hounds thro' the country-
	side,
Breathed hot and instant on my trace, –
I made six days a hiding-place
Of that dry green old aqueduct
Where I and Charles, when boys, have
	plucked
The fire-flies from the roof above,
Bright creeping thro' the moss they love:
– How long it seems since Charles was
	lost!
Six days the soldiers crossed and crossed
The country in my very sight;
And when that peril ceased at night,
The sky broke out in red dismay
With signal fires; well, there I lay
Close covered o'er in my recess,
Up to the neck in ferns and cress,
Thinking on Metternich our friend,
And Charles's miserable end,
And much beside, two days: the third,
Hunger o'ercame me when I heard
The peasants from the village go
To work among the maize; you know,
With us in Lombardy, they bring
Provisions packed on mules, a string
With little bells that cheer their task,
And casks, and boughs on every cask
To keep the sun's heat from the wine;
These I let pass in jingling line,
And, close on them, dear noisy crew,
The peasants from the village, too;
For at the very rear would troop
Their wives and sisters in a group
To help, I knew. When these had
	passed,
I threw my glove to strike the last,
Taking the chance: she did not start,
Much less cry out, but stooped apart,
One instant rapidly glanced round,
And saw me beckon from the ground.
A wild bush grows and hides my crypt;

She picked my glove up while she
	stripped
A branch off, then rejoined the rest
With that; my glove lay in her breast.
Then I drew breath; they disappeared.
It was for Italy I feared.

An hour, and she returned alone
Exactly where my glove was thrown.
Meanwhile came many thoughts: on me
Rested the hopes of Italy.
I had devised a certain tale
Which, when 'twas told her, could not
	fail
Persuade a peasant of its truth;
I meant to call a freak of youth
This hiding, and give hopes of pay,
And no temptation to betray.
But when I saw that woman's face,
Its calm simplicity of grace,
Our Italy's own attitude
In which she walked thus far, and
	stood,
Planting each naked foot so firm,
To crush the snake and spare the
	worm –
At first sight of her eyes, I said,
'I am that man upon whose head
'They fix the price, because I hate
'The Austrians over us: the State
'Will give you gold – oh, gold so
	much! –
'If you betray me to their clutch,
'And be your death, for aught I know,
'If once they find you saved their foe.
'Now, you must bring me food and
	drink,
'And also paper, pen and ink,
'And carry safe what I shall write
'To Padua, which you'll reach at night
'Before the duomo shuts; go in,
'And wait till Tenebræ begin;
'Walk to the third confessional,
'Between the pillar and the wall,
'And kneeling whisper, *Whence comes
	peace?*
'Say it a second time, then cease;

'And if the voice inside returns,
'*From Christ and Freedom; what concerns*
'*The cause of Peace?* – for answer, slip
'My letter where you placed your lip;
'Then come back happy we have done
'Our mother service – I, the son,
'As you the daughter of our land!'

Three mornings more, she took her
    stand
In the same place, with the same eyes:
I was no surer of sun-rise
Than of her coming. We conferred
Of her own prospects, and I heard
She had a lover – stout and tall,
She said – then let her eyelids fall,
'He could do much' – as if some doubt
Entered her heart, – then, passing out,
'She could not speak for others, who
'Had other thoughts; herself she knew:'
And so she brought me drink and food.
After four days, the scouts pursued
Another path; at last arrived
The help my Paduan friends contrived
To furnish me: she brought the news.
For the first time I could not choose
But kiss her hand, and lay my own
Upon her head – 'This faith was shown
'To Italy, our mother; she
'Uses my hand and blesses thee.'
She followed down to the sea-shore;
I left and never saw her more.

How very long since I have thought
Concerning – much less wished for –
    aught
Beside the good of Italy,
For which I live and mean to die!
I never was in love; and since
Charles proved false, what shall now
    convince
My inmost heart I have a friend?
However, if I pleased to spend
Real wishes on myself – say, three –
I know at least what one should be.
I would grasp Metternich until
I felt his red wet throat distil

In blood thro' these two hands. And
    next,
– Nor much for that am I perplexed –
Charles, perjured traitor, for his part,
Should die slow of a broken heart
Under his new employers. Last
– Ah, there, what should I wish? For fast
Do I grow old and out of strength.
If I resolved to seek at length
My father's house again, how scared
They all would look, and unprepared!
My brothers live in Austria's pay
– Disowned me long ago, men say;
And all my early mates who used
To praise me so – perhaps induced
More than one early step of mine –
Are turning wise: while some opine
'Freedom grows license,' some suspect
'Haste breeds delay,' and recollect
They always said, such premature
Beginnings never could endure!
So, with a sullen 'All's for best,'
The land seems settling to its rest.
I think then, I should wish to stand
This evening in that dear, lost land,
Over the sea the thousand miles,
And know if yet that woman smiles
With the calm smile; some little farm
She lives in there, no doubt: what harm
If I sat on the door-side bench,
And, while her spindle made a trench
Fantastically in the dust,
Inquired of all her fortunes – just
Her children's ages and their names,
And what may be the husband's aims
For each of them. I'd talk this out,
And sit there, for an hour about,
Then kiss her hand once more, and lay
Mine on her head, and go my way.

So much for idle wishing – how
It steals the time! To business now.

## The Englishman in Italy

PIANO DI SORRENTO

Fortù, Fortù, my beloved one,
    Sit here by my side,
On my knees put up both little feet!
    I was sure, if I tried,
I could make you laugh spite of Scirocco.
    Now, open your eyes,
Let me keep you amused till he vanish
    In black from the skies,
With telling my memories over
    As you tell your beads;
All the Plain saw me gather, I garland
    – The flowers or the weeds.

Time for rain! for your long hot dry
    Autumn
        Had net-worked with brown
The white skin of each grape on the
    bunches,
        Marked like a quail's crown,
Those creatures you make such
    account of,
        Whose heads, – speckled white
Over brown like a great spider's back,
    As I told you last night, –
Your mother bites off for her supper.
    Red-ripe as could be,
Pomegranates were chapping and
    splitting
        In halves on the tree:
And betwixt the loose walls of great
    flint-stone,
        Or in the thick dust
On the path, or straight out of the rock-
    side,
        Wherever could thrust
Some burnt sprig of bold hardy rock-
    flower
        Its yellow face up,
For the prize were great butterflies fighting,
    Some five for one cup.
So, I guessed, ere I got up this morning,
    What change was in store,
By the quick rustle-down of the quail-
    nets
        Which woke me before

I could open my shutter, made fast
    With a bough and a stone,
And look thro' the twisted dead vine-
    twigs,
        Sole lattice that's known.
Quick and sharp rang the rings down
    the net-poles,
        While, busy beneath,
Your priest and his brother tugged at
    them,
        The rain in their teeth.
And out upon all the flat house-roofs
    Where split figs lay drying,
The girls took the frails under cover:
    Nor use seemed in trying
To get out the boats and go fishing,
    For, under the cliff,
Fierce the black water frothed o'er the
    blind-rock.
        No seeing our skiff
Arrive about noon from Amalfi,
    – Our fisher arrive,
And pitch down his basket before us,
    All trembling alive
With pink and grey jellies, your sea-fruit;
    You touch the strange lumps,
And mouths gape there, eyes open, all
    manner
        Of horns and of humps,
Which only the fisher looks grave at,
    While round him like imps
Cling screaming the children as naked
    And brown as his shrimps;
Himself too as bare to the middle
    – You see round his neck
The string and its brass coin suspended,
    That saves him from wreck.
But to-day not a boat reached Salerno,
    So back, to a man,
Came our friends, with whose help in
    the vineyards
        Grape-harvest began.
In the vat, halfway up in our house-side,
    Like blood the juice spins,
While your brother all bare-legged is
    dancing
        Till breathless he grins

Dead-beaten in effort on effort
    To keep the grapes under,
Since still when he seems all but master,
    In pours the fresh plunder
From girls who keep coming and going
    With basket on shoulder,
And eyes shut against the rain's driving;
    Your girls that are older, –
For under the hedges of aloe,
    And where, on its bed
Of the orchard's black mould, the love-
apple
    Lies pulpy and red,
All the young ones are kneeling and
filling
    Their laps with the snails
Tempted out by this first rainy
    weather, –
    Your best of regales,
As to-night will be proved to my sorrow,
    When, supping in state,
We shall feast our grape-gleaners (two
dozen,
    Three over one plate)
With lasagne so tempting to swallow
    In slippery ropes,
And gourds fried in great purple slices,
    That colour of popes.
Meantime, see the grape bunch they've
brought you:
    The rain-water slips
O'er the heavy blue bloom on each globe
    Which the wasp to your lips
Still follows with fretful persistence:
    Nay, taste, while awake,
This half of a curd-white smooth
cheese-ball
    That peels, flake by flake,
Like an onion, each smoother and
whiter;
    Next, sip this weak wine
From the thin green glass flask, with its
stopper,
    A leaf of the vine;
And end with the prickly-pear's red
flesh
    That leaves thro' its juice

The stony black seeds on your pearl-
teeth.
    Scirocco is loose!
Hark, the quick, whistling pelt of the
olives
    Which, thick in one's track,
Tempt the stranger to pick up and bite
them,
    Tho' not yet half black!
How the old twisted olive trunks
shudder,
    The medlars let fall
Their hard fruit, and the brittle great
fig-trees
    Snap off, figs and all,
For here comes the whole of the
tempest!
    No refuge, but creep
Back again to my side and my
shoulder,
    And listen or sleep.
O how will your country show next
week,
    When all the vine-boughs
Have been stripped of their foliage to
pasture
    The mules and the cows?
Last eve, I rode over the mountains;
    Your brother, my guide,
Soon left me, to feast on the myrtles
    That offered, each side,
Their fruit-balls, black, glossy and
luscious, –
    Or strip from the sorbs
A treasure, or, rosy and wondrous,
    Those hairy gold orbs!
But my mule picked his sure sober
path out,
    Just stopping to neigh
When he recognized down in the
valley
    His mates on their way
With the faggots and barrels of water;
    And soon we emerged
From the plain, where the woods could
scarce follow;
    And still as we urged

Our way, the woods wondered, and
    left us,
      As up still we trudged
Though the wild path grew wilder each
    instant,
      And place was e'en grudged
'Mid the rock-chasms and piles of loose
    stones
      Like the loose broken teeth
Of some monster which climbed there
    to die
      From the ocean beneath –
Place was grudged to the silver-grey
    fume-weed
      That clung to the path,
And dark rosemary ever a-dying
      That, 'spite the wind's wrath,
So loves the salt rock's face to seaward,
      And lentisks as staunch
To the stone where they root and bear
    berries,
      And ... what shows a branch
Coral-coloured, transparent, with circlets
      Of pale seagreen leaves;
Over all trod my mule with the caution
      Of gleaners o'er sheaves,
Still, foot after foot like a lady,
      Till, round after round,
He climbed to the top of Calvano,
      And God's own profound
Was above me, and round me the
    mountains,
      And under, the sea,
And within me my heart to bear witness
      What was and shall be.
Oh, heaven and the terrible crystal!
      No rampart excludes
Your eye from the life to be lived
      In the blue solitudes.
Oh, those mountains, their infinite
    movement!
      Still moving with you;
For, ever some new head and breast of
    them
      Thrusts into view
To observe the intruder; you see it
      If quickly you turn

And, before they escape you surprise
    them.
      They grudge you should learn
How the soft plains they look on, lean
    over
      And love (they pretend)
– Cower beneath them, the flat sea-
    pine crouches,
      The wild fruit-trees bend,
E'en the myrtle-leaves curl, shrink and
    shut:
      All is silent and grave:
'Tis a sensual and timorous beauty,
      How fair! but a slave.
So, I turned to the sea; and there
    slumbered
      As greenly as ever
Those isles of the siren, your Galli;
      No ages can sever
The Three, nor enable their sister
      To join them, – halfway
On the voyage, she looked at Ulysses –
      No farther to-day,
Tho' the small one, just launched in
    the wave,
      Watches breast-high and steady
From under the rock, her bold sister
      Swum halfway already.
Fortù, shall we sail there together
      And see from the sides
Quite new rocks show their faces, new
    haunts
      Where the siren abides?
Shall we sail round and round them,
    close over
      The rocks, tho' unseen,
That ruffle the grey glassy water
      To glorious green?
Then scramble from splinter to splinter,
      Reach land and explore,
On the largest, the strange square black
    turret
      With never a door,
Just a loop to admit the quick lizards;
      Then, stand there and hear
The birds' quiet singing, that tells us
      What life is, so clear?

– The secret they sang to Ulysses
　　When, ages ago,
He heard and he knew this life's secret
　　I hear and I know.

Ah, see! The sun breaks o'er Calvano;
　　He strikes the great gloom
And flutters it o'er the mount's summit
　　In airy gold fume.
All is over. Look out, see the gipsy,
　　Our tinker and smith,
Has arrived, set up bellows and forge,
　　And down-squatted forthwith
To his hammering, under the wall there;
　　One eye keeps aloof
The urchins that itch to be putting
　　His jews'-harps to proof,
While the other, thro' locks of curled
　　wire,
　　Is watching how sleek
Shines the hog, come to share in the
　　wind-fall
　　　　– Chew, abbot's own cheek!
All is over. Wake up and come out now,
　　And down let us go,
And see the fine things got in order
　　At church for the show
Of the Sacrament, set forth this evening.
　　To-morrow's the Feast
Of the Rosary's Virgin, by no means
　　Of Virgins the least,
As you'll hear in the off-hand discourse
　　Which (all nature, no art)
The Dominican brother, these three
　　weeks,
　　Was getting by heart.
Not a pillar nor post but is dizened
　　With red and blue papers;
All the roof waves with ribbons, each
　　altar
　　A-blaze with long tapers;
But the great masterpiece is the scaffold
　　Rigged glorious to hold
All the fiddlers and fifers and drummers
　　And trumpeters bold,
Not afraid of Bellini nor Auber,
　　Who, when the priest's hoarse,

Will strike us up something that's brisk
　　For the feast's second course.
And then will the flaxen-wigged Image
　　Be carried in pomp
Thro' the plain, while in gallant
　　procession
　　The priests mean to stomp.
All round the glad church lie old
　　bottles
　　With gunpowder stopped,
Which will be, when the Image re-enters,
　　Religiously popped;
And at night from the crest of Calvano
　　Great bonfires will hang,
On the plain will the trumpets join
　　chorus,
　　And more poppers bang.
At all events, come – to the garden
　　As far as the wall;
See me tap with a hoe on the plaster
　　Till out there shall fall
A scorpion with wide angry nippers!

　　– 'Such trifles!' you say?
Fortù, in my England at home,
　　Men meet gravely to-day
And debate, if abolishing Corn-laws
　　Be righteous and wise
– If 'twere proper, Scirocco should
　　vanish
　　In black from the skies!

## In a Gondola

*He sings.*
I send my heart up to thee, all my
　　heart
　　In this my singing.
For the stars help me, and the sea
　　bears part;
　　The very night is clinging
Closer to Venice' streets to leave one
　　space
　　Above me, whence thy face
May light my joyous heart to thee its
　　dwelling-place.

*She speaks.*

Say after me, and try to say
My very words, as if each word
Came from you of your own accord,
In your own voice, in your own way:
'This woman's heart and soul and brain
'Are mine as much as this gold chain
'She bids me wear; which' (say again)
'I choose to make by cherishing
'A precious thing, or choose to fling
'Over the boat-side, ring by ring.'
And yet once more say … no word more
Since words are only words. Give o'er!

Unless you call me, all the same,
Familiarly by my pet name,
Which if the Three should hear you call,
And me reply to, would proclaim
At once our secret to them all.
Ask of me, too, command me, blame –
Do, break down the partition-wall
'Twixt us, the daylight world beholds
Curtained in dusk and splendid folds!
What's left but – all of me to take?
I am the Three's: prevent them, slake
Your thirst! 'Tis said, the Arab sage,
In practising with gems, can loose
Their subtle spirit in his cruce
And leave but ashes: so, sweet mage,
Leave them my ashes when thy use
Sucks out my soul, thy heritage!

*He sings.*
1

Past we glide, and past, and past!
    What's that poor Agnese doing
Where they make the shutters fast?
    Grey Zanobi's just a-wooing
To his couch the purchased bride:
    Past we glide!

2

Past we glide, and past, and past!
    Why's the Pucci Palace flaring
Like a beacon to the blast?
    Guests by hundreds, not one caring
If the dear host's neck were wried:
    Past we glide!

*She sings.*
1

The moth's kiss, first!
Kiss me as if you made believe
You were not sure, this eve,
How my face, your flower, had pursed
Its petals up; so, here and there
You brush it, till I grow aware
Who wants me, and wide ope I burst.

2

The bee's kiss, now!
Kiss me as if you entered gay
My heart at some noonday,
A bud that dares not disallow
The claim, so all is rendered up,
And passively its shattered cup
Over you head to sleep I bow.

*He sings.*
1

What are we two?
I am a Jew,
And carry thee, farther than friends can
    pursue,
To a feast of our tribe;
Where they need thee to bribe
The devil that blasts them unless he
    imbibe
Thy … Scatter the vision for ever! And
    now,
As of old, I am I, thou art thou!

2

Say again, what we are?
The sprite of a star,
I lure thee above where the destinies
    bar
My plumes their full play
Till a ruddier ray
Than my pale one announce there is
    withering away
Some … Scatter the vision for ever!
    And now,
As of old, I am I, thou art thou!

*He muses.*

Oh, which were best, to roam or rest?
The land's lap or the water's breast?

To sleep on yellow millet-sheaves,
Or swim in lucid shallows just
Eluding water-lily leaves,
An inch from Death's black fingers, thrust
To lock you, whom release he must;
Which life were best on Summer eves?

*He speaks, musing.*
Lie back; could thought of mine
    improve you?
From this shoulder let there spring
A wing; from this, another wing;
Wings, not legs and feet, shall move you!
Snow-white must they spring, to blend
With your flesh, but I intend
They shall deepen to the end,
Broader, into burning gold,
Till both wings crescent-wise enfold
Your perfect self, from 'neath your feet
To o'er your head, where, lo, they meet
As if a million sword-blades hurled
Defiance from you to the world!

Rescue me thou, the only real!
And scare away this mad ideal
That came, nor motions to depart!
Thanks! Now, stay ever as thou art!

*Still he muses.*
1
What if the Three should catch at last
Thy serenader? While there's cast
Paul's cloak about my head, and fast
Gian pinions me, Himself has past
His stylet thro' my back; I reel;
And ... is it thou I feel?
2
They trail me, these three godless
    knaves,
Past every church that saints and saves,
Nor stop till, where the cold sea raves
By Lido's wet accursed graves,
They scoop mine, roll me to its brink,
And ... on thy breast I sink!

*She replies, musing.*
Dip your arm o'er the boat-side, elbow-
    deep,
As I do: thus: were death so unlike
    sleep,
Caught this way? Death's to fear from
    flame or steel,
Or poison doubtless; but from water –
    feel!
Go find the bottom! Would you stay
    me? There!
Now pluck a great blade of that ribbon-
    grass
To plait in where the foolish jewel was,
I flung away: since you have praised
    my hair,
'Tis proper to be choice in what I wear.

*He speaks.*
Row home? must we row home? Too
    surely
Know I where its front's demurely
Over the Giudecca piled;
Window just with window mating,
Door on door exactly waiting,
All's the set face of a child:
But behind it, where's a trace
Of the staidness and reserve,
And formal lines without a curve,
In the same child's playing-face?
No two windows look one way
O'er the small sea-water thread
Below them. Ah, the autumn day
I, passing, saw you overhead!
First, out a cloud of curtain blew,
Then a sweet cry, and last came you –
To catch your lory that must needs
Escape just then, of all times then,
To peck a tall plant's fleecy seeds,
And make me happiest of men.
I scarce could breathe to see you reach
So far back o'er the balcony
To catch him ere he climbed too high
Above you in the Smyrna peach
That quick the round smooth cord of
    gold,
This coiled hair on your head, unrolled,

Fell down you like a gorgeous snake
The Roman girls were wont, of old,
When Rome there was, for coolness'
     sake
To let lie curling o'er their bosoms.
Dear lory, may his beak retain
Ever its delicate rose stain
As if the wounded lotus-blossoms
Had marked their thief to know again!

Stay longer yet, for other's sake
Than mine! What should your chamber
     do?
– With all its rarities that ache
In silence while day lasts, but wake
At night-time and their life renew,
Suspended just to pleasure you
Who brought against their will together
These objects, and, while day lasts, weave
Around them such a magic tether
That dumb they look; your harp, believe,
With all the sensitive tight strings
Which dare not speak, now to itself
Breathes slumberously, as if some elf
Went in and out the chords, his wings
Make murmur wheresoe'er they graze,
As an angel may, between the maze
Of midnight palace-pillars, on
And on, to sow God's plagues, have
     gone
Through guilty glorious Babylon.
And while such murmurs flow, the
     nymph
Bends o'er the harp-top from her shell
As the dry limpet for the lymph
Come with a tune he knows so well.
And how your statues' hearts must swell!
And how your pictures must descend
To see each other, friend with friend!
Oh, could you take them by surprise,
You'd find Schidone's eager Duke
Doing the quaintest courtesies
To that prim saint by Haste-thee-Luke
And, deeper into her rock den,
Bold Castelfranco's Magdalen
You'd find retreated from the ken
Of that robed counsel-keeping Ser –

As if the Tizian thinks of her,
And is not, rather, gravely bent
On seeing for himself what toys
Are these, his progeny invent,
What litter now the board employs
Whereon he signed a document
That got him murdered! Each enjoys
Its night so well, you cannot break
The sport up, so, indeed must make
More stay with me, for others' sake.

*She speaks.*

1

To-morrow, if a harp-string, say,
Is used to tie the jasmine back
That over floods my room with sweets,
Contrive your Zorzi somehow meets
My Zanze! If the ribbon's black,
The Three are watching: keep away!

2

Your gondola – let Zorzi wreathe
A mesh of water-weeds about
Its prow, as if he unaware
Had struck some quay or bridge-foot
     stair!
That I may throw a paper out
As you and he go underneath.

There's Zanze's vigilant taper; safe are
     we.
Only one minute more to-night with
     me?
Resume your past self of a month ago!
Be you the bashful gallant, I will be
The lady with the colder breast than
     snow.
Now bow you, as becomes, nor touch
     my hand
More than I touch yours when I step to
     land,
And say, 'All thanks, Siora!' –
                                        Heart to heart
And lips to lips! Yet once more, ere we
     part,
Clasp me and make me thine, as mine
     thou art!
                         He is surprised, and stabbed.

It was ordained to be so, sweet! – and
   best
Comes now, beneath thine eyes, upon
   thy breast.
Still kiss me! Care not for the cowards!
   Care
Only to put aside thy beauteous hair
My blood will hurt! The Three, I do not
   scorn
To death, because they never lived: but I
Have lived indsed, and so – (yet one
   more kiss) – can die!

## Waring

### ONE

#### 1

What's become of Waring
Since he gave us all the slip,
Chose land-travel or seafaring,
Boots and chest or staff and scrip,
Rather than pace up and down
Any longer London town?

#### 2

Who'd have guessed it from his lip
Or his brow's accustomed bearing,
On the night he thus took ship
Or started landward? – little caring
For us, it seems, who supped together
(Friends of his too, I remember)
And walked home thro' the merry
   weather,
The snowiest in all December.
I left his arm that night myself
For what's-his-name's, the new prose-
   poet
Who wrote the book there, on the
   shelf –
How, forsooth, was I to know it
If Waring meant to glide away
Like a ghost at break of day?
Never looked he half so gay!

#### 3

He was prouder than the devil:
How he must have cursed our revel!
Ay and many other meetings,
Indoor visits, outdoor greetings,
As up and down he paced this London,
With no work done, but great works
   undone,
Where scarce twenty knew his name.
Why not, then, have earlier spoken,
Written, bustled? Who's to blame
If your silence kept unbroken?
'True, but there were sundry jottings,
'Stray-leaves, fragments, blurrs and
   blottings,
'Certain first steps were achieved
'Already which' – (is that your meaning?)
'Had well borne out whoe'er believed
'In more to come!' But who goes gleaning
Hedge-side chance-blades, while full-
   sheaved
Stand cornfields by him? Pride,
   o'erweening
Pride alone, puts forth such claims
O'er the day's distinguished names.

#### 4

Meantime, how much I loved him,
I find out now I've lost him.
I who cared not if I moved him,
Who could so carelessly accost him,
Henceforth never shall get free
Of his ghostly company,
His eyes that just a little wink
As deep I go into the merit
Of this and that distinguished spirit –
His cheeks' raised colour, soon to sink,
As long I dwell on some stupendous
And tremendous (Heaven defend us!)
Monstr'-inform'-ingens-horrend-ous
Demoniaco-seraphic
Penman's latest piece of graphic.
Nay, my very wrist grows warm
With his dragging weight of arm.
E'en so, swimmingly appears,
Through one's after-supper musings,
Some lost lady of old years
With her beauteous vain endeavour
And goodness unrepaid as ever;
The face, accustomed to refusings,
We, puppies that we were … Oh never
Surely, nice of conscience, scrupled
Being aught like false, forsooth, to?

Telling aught but honest truth to?
What a sin, had we centupled
Its possessor's grace and sweetness!
No! she heard in its completeness
Truth, for truth's a weighty matter,
And truth, at issue, we can't flatter!
Well, 'tis done with; she's exempt
From damning us thro' such a sally;
And so she glides, as down a valley,
Taking up with her contempt,
Past our reach; and in, the flowers
Shut her unregarded hours.

5

Oh, could I have him back once more,
This Waring, but one half-day more!
Back, with the quiet face of yore,
So hungry for acknowledgment
Like mine! I'd fool him to his bent.
Feed, should not he, to heart's content?
I'd say, 'to only have conceived,
'Planned your great works, apart from
    progress,
'Surpasses little works achieved!'
I'd lie so, I should be believed.
I'd make such havoc of the claims
Of the day's distinguished names
To feast him with, as feasts an ogress
Her feverish sharp-toothed gold-
    crowned child!
Or as one feasts a creature rarely
Captured here, unreconciled
To capture; and completely gives
Its pettish humours license, barely
Requiring that it lives.

6

Ichabod, Ichabod,
The glory is departed!
Travels Waring East away?
Who, of knowledge, by hearsay,
Reports a man upstarted
Somewhere as a god,
Hordes grown European-hearted,
Millions of the wild made tame
On a sudden at his fame?
In Vishnu-land what Avatar?
Or who in Moscow, toward the Czar,

With the demurest of footfalls
Over the Kremlin's pavement bright
With serpentine and syenite,
Steps, with five other Generals
That simultaneously take snuff,
For each to have pretext enough
And kerchiefwise unfold his sash
Which, softness' self, is yet the stuff
To hold fast where a steel chain snaps,
And leave the grand white neck no gash?
Waring in Moscow, to those rough
Cold northern natures borne perhaps,
Like the lambwhite maiden dear
From the circle of mute kings
Unable to repress the tear,
Each as his sceptre down he flings,
To Dian's fane at Taurica,
Where now a captive priestess, she
    alway
Mingles her tender grave Hellenic
    speech
With theirs, tuned to the hanstone-
    beaten beach:
As pours some pigeon, from the
    myrrhy lands
Rapt by the whirlblast to fierce
    Scythian strands
Where breed the swallows, her
    melodious cry
Amid their barbarous twitter!
In Russia? Never! Spain were fitter!
Ay, most likely 'tis in Spain
That we and Waring meet again
Now, while he turns down that cool
    narrow lane
Into the blackness, out of grave Madrid
All fire and shine, abrupt as when there's
    slid
Its stiff gold blazing pall
From some black coffin-lid.
Or, best of all,
I love to think
The leaving us was just a feint;
Back here to London did he slink,
And now works on without a wink
Of sleep, and we are on the brink
Of something great in fresco-paint:

Some garret's ceiling, walls and floor,
Up and down and o'er and o'er
He splashes, as none splashed before
Since great Caldara Polidore.
Or Music means this land of ours
Some favour yet, to pity won
By Purcell from his Rosy Bowers, –
'Give me my so-long promised son,
'Let Waring end what I begun!'
Then down he creeps and out he steals
Only when the night conceals
His face; in Kent 'tis cherry-time,
Or hops are picking: or at prime
Of March he wanders as, too happy,
Years ago when he was young,
Some mild eve when woods grew sappy
And the early moths had sprung
To life from many a trembling sheath
Woven the warm boughs beneath;
While small birds said to themselves
What should soon be actual song,
And young gnats, by tens and twelves
Made as if they were the throng
That crowd around and carry aloft
The sound they have nursed, so sweet
        and pure,
Out of a myriad noises soft,
Into a tone that can endure
Amid the noise of a July noon
When all God's creatures crave their
        boon,
All at once and all in tune,
And get it, happy as Waring then,
Having first within his ken
What a man might do with men:
And far too glad, in the even-glow,
To mix with the world he meant to take
Into his hand, he told you, so –
And out of it his world to make,
To contract and to expand
As he shut or oped his hand.
Oh Waring, what's to really be?
A clear stage and a crowd to see!
Some Garrick, say, out shall not he
The heart of Hamlet's mystery pluck?
Or, where most unclean beasts are rife,
Some Junius – am I right? – shall tuck

His sleeve, and forth with flaying-knife!
Some Chatterton shall have the luck
Of calling Rowley into life!
Some one shall somehow run a muck
With this old world, for want of strife
Sound asleep. Contrive, contrive
To rouse us, Waring! Who's alive?
Our men scarce seem in earnest now.
Distinguished names! – but 'tis,
        somehow,
As if they played at being names
Still more distinguished, like the games
Of children. Turn our sport to earnest
With a visage of the sternest!
Bring the real times back, confessed
Still better than our very best!

TWO

1

'When I last saw Waring … '
(How all turned to him who spoke!
You saw Waring? Truth or joke?
In land-travel or sea-faring?)

2

'We were sailing by Triest
'Where a day or two we harboured:
'A sunset was in the West,
'When, looking over the vessel's side,
'One of our company espied
'A sudden speck to larboard.
'And as a sea-duck flies and swims
'At once, so came the light craft up,
'With its sole lateen sail that trims
'And turns (the water round its rims
'Dancing, as round a sinking cup)
'And by us like a fish it curled,
'And drew itself up close beside,
'Its great sail on the instant furled,
'And o'er its thwarts a shrill voice cried,
'(A neck as bronzed as a Lascar's)
' "Buy wine of us, you English Brig?
' "Or fruit, tobacco and cigars?
' "A pilot for you to Triest?
' "Without one, look you ne'er so big,
' "They'll never let you up the bay!
' "We natives should know best."
'I turned, and "just those fellows' way,"

'Our captain said, "The 'long-shore
    thieves
' "Are laughing at us in their sleeves."

3

'In truth, the boy leaned laughing
    back;
'And one, half-hidden by his side
'Under the furled sail, soon I spied,
'With great grass hat and kerchief black,
'Who looked up with his kingly throat,
'Said somewhat, while the other shook
'His hair back from his eyes to look
'Their longest at us; then the boat,
'I know not how, turned sharply round,
'Laying her whole side on the sea
'As a leaping fish does; from the lee
'Into the weather, cut somehow
'Her sparkling path beneath our bow
'And so went off, as with a bound,
'Into the rosy and golden half
'O' the sky, to overtake the sun
'And reach the shore, like the sea-calf
'Its singing cave; yet I caught one
'Glance ere away the boat quite passed,
'And neither time nor toil could mar
'Those features: so I saw the last
'Of Waring!' – You? Oh, never star
Was lost here but it rose afar!
Look East, where whole new
    thousands are!
In Vishnu-land what Avatar?

## The Twins

'Give' and 'It-shall-be-given-unto-you.'

1

Grand rough old Martin Luther
    Bloomed fables – flowers on furze,
The better the uncouther:
    Do roses stick like burrs?

2

A beggar asked an alms
    One day at an abbey-door,
Said Luther; but, seized with qualms,
    The abbot replied, 'We're poor!

3

'Poor, who had plenty once,
    'When gifts fell thick as rain:
'But they give us nought, for the nonce,
    'And how should we give again?'

4

Then the beggar, 'See your sins!
    'Of old, unless I err,
'Ye had brothers for inmates, twins,
    'Date and Dabitur.

5

'While Date was in good case
    'Dabitur flourished too:
'For Dabitur's lenten face
    'No wonder if Date rue.

6

'Would ye retrieve the one?
    'Try and make plump the other!
'When Date's penance is done,
    'Dabitur helps his brother.

7

'Only, beware relapse!'
    The Abbot hung his head.
This beggar might be perhaps
    An angel, Luther said.

## A Light Woman

1

So far as our story approaches the end,
    Which do you pity the most of us
        three? –
My friend, or the mistress of my friend
    With her wanton eyes, or me?

2

My friend was already too good to lose,
    And seemed in the way of
        improvement yet,
When she crossed his path with her
        hunting-noose
    And over him drew her net.

3

When I saw him tangled in her toils,
    A shame, said I, if she adds just him
To her nine-and-ninety other spoils,
    The hundredth for a whim!

4

And before my friend be wholly hers,
    How easy to prove to him, I said,
An eagle's the game her pride prefers,
    Though she snaps at a wren instead!

5

So, I gave her eyes my own eyes to take,
    My hand sought hers as in earnest
        need,
And round she turned for my noble
        sake,
    And gave me herself indeed.

6

The eagle am I, with my fame in the
        world,
    The wren is he, with his maiden
        face.
– You look away and your lip is curled?
    Patience, a moment's space!

7

For see, my friend goes shaking and
        white;
    He eyes me as the basilisk:
I have turned, it appears, his day to
        night,
    Eclipsing his sun's disk.

8

And I did it, he thinks, as a very thief:
    'Though I love her – that, he
        comprehends –
'One should master one's passions,
        (love, in chief)
    'And be loyal to one's friends!'

9

And she, – she lies in my hand as tame
    As a pear late basking over a wall;
Just a touch to try and off it came;
    'Tis mine, – can I let it fall?

10

With no mind to eat it, that's the
        worst!
    Were it thrown in the road, would
        the case assist?
'Twas quenching a dozen blue-flies'
        thirst
    When I gave its stalk a twist.

11

And I, – what I seem to my friend, you
        see:
    What I soon shall seem to his love,
        you guess:
What I seem to myself, do you ask of
        me?
    No hero, I confess.

12

'Tis an awkward thing to play with
        souls,
    And matter enough to save one's
        own:
Yet think of my friend, and the burning
        coals
    He played with for bits of stone!

13

One likes to show the truth for the
        truth;
    That the woman was light is very
        true:
But suppose she says, – Never mind
        that youth!
    What wrong have I done to you?

14

Well, any how, here the story stays,
    So far at least as I understand;
And, Robert Browning, you writer of
        plays,
    Here's a subject made to your hand!

## The Last Ride Together

1

I said – Then, dearest, since 'tis so,
Since now at length my fate I know,
Since nothing all my love avails,
Since all, my life seemed meant for, fails,
    Since this was written and needs
        must be –
My whole heart rises up to bless
Your name in pride and thankfulness!
Take back the hope you gave, – I claim
Only a memory of the same,
– And this beside, if you will not blame,
    Your leave for one more last ride
        with me.

2

My mistress bent that brow of hers;
Those deep dark eyes where pride demurs
When pity would be softening through,
Fixed me a breathing-while or two
  With life or death in the balance:
    right!
The blood replenished me again;
My last thought was at least not vain:
I and my mistress, side by side
Shall be together, breathe and ride,
So, one day more am I deified.
  Who knows but the world may end
    tonight?

3

Hush! if you saw some western cloud
All billowy-bosomed, over-bowed
By many benedictions – sun's
And moon's and evening-star's at once –
  And so, you, looking and loving best,
Conscious grew, your passion drew
Cloud, sunset, moonrise, star-shine too,
Down on you, near and yet more near,
Till flesh must fade for heaven was
    here! –
Thus leant she and lingered – joy and
    fear!
  Thus lay she a moment on my breast.

4

Then we began to ride. My soul
Smoothed itself out, a long-cramped
    scroll
Freshening and fluttering in the wind.
Past hopes already lay behind.
  What need to strive with a life awry?
Had I said that, had I done this,
So might I gain, so might I miss.
Might she have loved me? just as well
She might have hated, who can tell!
Where had I been now if the worst
    befell?
  And here we are riding, she and I.

5

Fail I alone, in words and deeds?
Why, all men strive and who succeeds?
We rode; it seemed my spirit flew,

Saw other regions, cities new,
  As the world rushed by on either
    side.
I thought, – All labour, yet no less
Bear up beneath their unsuccess.
Look at the end of work, contrast
The petty done, the undone vast,
This present of theirs with the hopeful
    past!
  I hoped she would love me; here we
    ride.

6

What hand and brain went ever
    paired?
What heart alike conceived and dared?
What act proved all its thought had
    been?
What will but felt the fleshly screen?
  We ride and I see her bosom heave.
There's many a crown for who can
    reach.
Ten lines, a statesman's life in each!
The flag stuck on a heap of bones,
A soldier's doing! what atones?
They scratch his name on the Abbey-
    stones.
  My riding is better, by their leave.

7

What does it all mean, poet? Well,
Your brains beat into rhythm, you tell
What we felt only; you expressed
You hold things beautiful the best,
  And pace them in rhyme so, side by
    side.
'Tis something, nay 'tis much: but then,
Have you yourself what's best for men?
Are you – poor, sick, old ere your time –
Nearer one whit your own sublime
Than we who never have turned a rhyme?
  Sing, riding's a joy! For me, I ride.

8

And you, great sculptor – so, you gave
A score of years to Art, her slave,
And that's your Venus, whence we turn
To yonder girl that fords the burn!
  You acquiesce, and shall I repine?

What, man of music, you grown grey
With notes and nothing else to say,
Is this your sole praise from a friend,
'Greatly his opera's strains intend,
'But in music we know how fashions
        end!'
I gave my youth; but we ride, in fine.

9

Who knows what's fit for us? Had fate
Proposed bliss here should sublimate
My being – had I signed the bond –
Still one must lead some life beyond,
    Have a bliss to die with, dim-descried.
This foot once planted on the goal,
This glory-garland round my soul,
Could I descry such? Try and test!
I sink back shuddering from the quest.
Earth being so good, would heaven
        seem best?
    Now, heaven and she are beyond
        this ride.

10

And yet – she has not spoke so long!
What if heaven be that, fair and strong
At life's best, with our eyes upturned
Whither life's flower is first discerned,
    We, fixed so, ever should so abide?
What if we still ride on, we two
With life for ever old yet new,
Changed not in kind but in degree,
The instant made eternity, –
And heaven just prove that I and she
    Ride, ride together, for ever ride?

## The Pied Piper of Hamelin

A Child's Story
*Written for, and inscribed to,*
*W. M. the Younger*

1

Hamelin Town's in Brunswick,
    By famous Hanover city;
The river Weser, deep and wide,
Washes its wall on the southern side;
A pleasanter spot you never spied;
    But, when begins my ditty,
Almost five hundred years ago,
To see the townsfolk suffer so
    From vermin, was a pity.

2

Rats!
They fought the dogs and killed the cats,
    And bit the babies in the cradles,
And ate the cheeses out of the vats,
    And licked the soup from the cooks'
        own ladles,
Split open the kegs of salted sprats,
Made nests inside men's Sunday hats,
And even spoiled the women's chats
        By drowning their speaking
            With shrieking and squeaking
In fifty different sharps and flats.

3

At last the people in a body
        To the Town Hall came flocking:
' 'Tis clear,' cried they, 'our Mayor's a
        noddy;
        'And as for our Corporation –
            shocking
'To think we buy gowns lined with
        ermine
'For dolts that can't or won't determine
'What's best to rid us of our vermin!
'You hope, because you're old and obese,
'To find in the furry civic robe ease?
'Rouse up, sirs! Give your brains a racking
'To find the remedy we're lacking,
'Or, sure as fate, we'll send you packing!'
At this the Mayor and Corporation
Quaked with a mighty consternation.

4

An hour they sat in council,
    At length the Mayor broke silence:
'For a guilder I'd my ermine gown sell,
    'I wish I were a mile hence!
'It's easy to bid one rack one's brain –
'I'm sure my poor head aches again,
'I've scratched it so, and all in vain.
'Oh for a trap, a trap, a trap!'
Just as he said this, what should hap
At the chamber door but a gentle tap?
'Bless us,' cried the Mayor, 'what's that?'
(With the Corporation as he sat,
Looking little though wondrous fat;
Nor brighter was his eye, nor moister
Than a too-long-opened oyster,
Save when at noon his paunch grew
        mutinous
For a plate of turtle green and glutinous)
'Only a scraping of shoes on the mat?
'Anything like the sound of a rat
'Makes my heart go pit-a-pat!'

5

'Come in!' – the Mayor cried, looking
        bigger:
And in did come the strangest figure!
His queer long coat from heel to head
Was half of yellow and half of red,
And he himself was tall and thin,
With sharp blue eyes, each like a pin,
And light loose hair, yet swarthy skin,
No tuft on cheek nor beard on chin,
But lips where smiles went out and in;
There was no guessing his kith and kin:
And nobody could enough admire
The tall man and his quaint attire.
Quoth one: 'It's as my great-grandsire,
'Starting up at the Trump of Doom's
        tone,
'Had walked this way from his painted
        tombstone!'

6

He advanced to the council-table:
And, 'Please your honours,' said he,
        'I'm able,
'By means of a secret charm, to draw
    'All creatures living beneath the sun,
'That creep or swim or fly or run,
'After me so as you never saw!
'And I chiefly use my charm
'On creatures that do people harm,
'The mole and toad and newt and viper;
'And people call me the Pied Piper.'
(And here they noticed round his neck
    A scarf of red and yellow stripe,
To match with his coat of the self-same
        cheque;
    And at the scarf's end hung a pipe;
And his fingers, they noticed, were ever
        straying
As if impatient to be playing
Upon this pipe, as low it dangled
Over his vesture so old-fangled.)
'Yet,' said he, 'poor piper as I am,
'In Tartary I freed the Cham,
    'Last June, from his huge swarms of
        gnats;
'I eased in Asia the Nizam
    'Of a monstrous brood of vampyre-
        bats:
'And as for what your brain bewilders,
    'If I can rid your town of rats
'Will you give me a thousand guilders?'
'One? fifty thousand!' – was the
        exclamation
Of the astonished Mayor and
        Corporation.

7

Into the street the Piper stept,
    Smiling first a little smile,
As if he knew what magic slept
    In his quiet pipe the while;
Then, like a musical adept,
To blow the pipe his lips he wrinkled,
And green and blue his sharp eyes
        twinkled,
Like a candle-flame where salt is
        sprinkled;
And ere three shrill notes the pipe
        uttered,
You heard as if an army muttered;
And the muttering grew to a grumbling;
And the grumbling grew to a mighty
        rumbling;

And out of the houses the rats came
    tumbling.
Great rats, small rats, lean rats, brawny
    rats,
Brown rats, black rats, grey rats, tawny
    rats,
Grave old plodders, gay young friskers,
    Fathers, mothers, uncles, cousins,
Cocking tails and pricking whiskers,
    Families by tens and dozens,
Brothers, sisters, husbands, wives –
Followed the Piper for their lives.
From street to street he piped advancing,
And step for step they followed dancing,
Until they came to the river Weser,
    Wherein all plunged and perished!
    Save one who, stout as Julius Cæsar,
Swam across and lived to carry
    (As he, the manuscript he cherished)
To Rat-land home his commentary:
Which was, 'At the first shrill notes of
    the pipe,
'I heard a sound as of scraping tripe,
'And putting apples, wondrous ripe,
'Into a cider-press's gripe:
'And a moving away of pickle-tub-boards,
'And a leaving ajar of conserve-cupboards,
'And a drawing the corks of train-oil-
    flasks,
'And a breaking the hoops of butter-
    casks:
'And it seemed as if a voice
    '(Sweeter far than by harp or by
    psaltery
'Is breathed) called out, "Oh rats, rejoice!
  ' "The world is grown to one vast
    dry-saltery!
' "So munch on, crunch on, take your
    nuncheon,
' "Breakfast, supper, dinner,
    luncheon!"
'And just as a bulky sugar-puncheon,
'All ready staved, like a great sun shone
'Glorious scarce an inch before me,
'Just as methought it said, "Come,
    bore me!"
' – I found the Weser rolling o'er me.'

8

You should have heard the Hamelin
    people
Ringing the bells till they rocked the
    steeple.
'Go,' cried the Mayor, 'and get long
    poles,
'Poke out the nests and block up the
    holes!
'Consult with carpenters and builders,
'And leave in our town not even a trace
'Of the rats!' – when suddenly, up the
    face
Of the Piper perked in the market-place,
With a, 'First, if you please, my thousand
    guilders!'

9

A thousand guilders! The Mayor looked
    blue;
So did the Corporation too.
For council dinners made rare havoc
With Claret, Moselle, Vin-de-Grave,
    Hock;
And half the money would replenish
Their cellar's biggest butt with Rhenish.
To pay this sum to a wandering fellow
With a gipsy coat of red and yellow!
'Beside,' quoth the Mayor with a
    knowing wink,
'Our business was done at the river's
    brink;
'We saw with our eyes the vermin sink,
'And what's dead can't come to life, I
    think.
'So, friend, we're not the folks to shrink
'From the duty of giving you
    something for drink,
'And a matter of money to put in your
    poke;
'But as for the guilders, what we spoke
'Of them, as you very well know, was
    in joke.
'Beside, our losses have made us
    thrifty.
'A thousand guilders! Come, take fifty!'

### 10

The Piper's face fell, and he cried
'No trifling! I can't wait, beside!
'I've promised to visit by dinnertime
'Bagdat, and accept the prime
'Of the Head-Cook's pottage, all he's
     rich in,
'For having left, in the Caliph's kitchen,
'Of a nest of scorpions no survivor:
'With him I proved no bargain-driver,
'With you, don't think I'll bate a stiver!
'And folks who put me in a passion
'May find me pipe after another fashion.'

### 11

'How?' cried the Mayor, 'd'ye think I
     brook
'Being worse treated than a Cook?
'Insulted by a lazy ribald
'With idle pipe and vesture piebald?
'You threaten us, fellow? Do your worst,
'Blow your pipe there till you burst!'

### 12

Once more he stept into the street
     And to his lips again
     Laid his long pipe of smooth straight
        cane;
And ere he blew three notes (such sweet
Soft notes as yet musician's cunning
     Never gave the enraptured air)
There was a rustling that seemed like a
     bustling
Of merry crowds justling at pitching
     and hustling,
Small feet were pattering, wooden
     shoes clattering,
Little hands clapping and little tongues
     chattering,
And, like fowls in a farm-yard when
     barley is scattering,
Out came the children running.
All the little boys and girls,
With rosy cheeks and flaxen curls,
And sparkling eyes and teeth like pearls,
Trippin and skipping, ran merrily after
The wonderful music with shouting
     and laughter.

### 13

The Mayor was dumb, and the Council
     stood
As if they were changed into blocks of
     wood,
Unable to move a step, or cry
To the children merrily skipping by,
– Could only follow with the eye
That joyous crowd at the Piper's back.
But how the Mayor was on the rack,
And the wretched Council's bosoms
     beat,
As the Piper turned from the High street
To where the Weser rolled its waters
Right in the way of their sons and
     daughters
However he turned from South to West,
And to Koppelberg Hill his steps
     addressed,
And after him the children pressed;
Great was the joy in every breast,
'He never can cross that mighty top!
'He's froced to let the piping drop,
'And we shall see our children stop!'
When, lo, as they reached the
     mountain-side,
A wondrous portal opened wide,
As if a cavern was suddenly hollowed;
And the Piper advanced and the
     childeren followed,
And when all were in to the very last,
The door in the mountain-side shut fast.
Did I say, all? No! One was lame,
     And could not dance the whole of
        the way;
And in after years, if you would blame
     His sadness, he was used to say, –
'It's dull in our town since my
     playmates left!
'I can't forget that I'm bereft
'Of all the pleasant sights they see,
'Which the Piper also promised me.
'For he led us, he said, to a joyous land,
'Joining the town and just at hand,
'Where waters gushed and fruit-trees
     grew

'And flowers put forth a fairer hue,
'And everything was strange and new;
'The sparrows were brighter than
        peacocks here,
'And their dogs outran our fallow deer,
'And honey-bees had lost their stings,
'And horses were born with eagles'
        wings:
'And just as I became assured
'My lame foot would be speedily cured,
'The music stopped and I stood still,
'And found myself outside the hill,
'Left alone against my will,
'To go now limping as before,
'And never hear of that country more!'

14

Alas, alas for Hamelin!
    There came into many a burgher's
        pate
    A text which says that heaven's gate
    Opes to the rich at as easy rate
As the needle's eye takes a camel in!
The mayor sent East, West, North and
        South,
To offer the Piper, by word of mouth,
    Wherever it was men's lot to find him,
Silver and gold to his heart's content,
If he'd only return the way he went,
    And bring the children behind him.
But when they saw 'twas a lost endeavour,
And Piper and dancers were gone for
        ever,
They made a decree that lawyers never
    Should think their records dated duly
If, after the day of the month and year,
These words did not as well appear,
'And so long after what happened here
    'On the Twenty-second of July,
'Thirteen hundred and seventy-six:'
And the better in memory to fix
The place of the children's last retreat,
They called it, the Pied Piper's Street –
Where any one playing on pipe or tabor
Was sure for the future to lose his
        labour.
Nor suffered they hostelry or tavern

To shock with mirth a street so solemn;
But opposite the place of the cavern
    They wrote the story on a column,
And on the great church-window
        painted
The same, to make the world acquainted
How their children were stolen away,
And there it stands to this very day.
And I must not omit to say
That in Transylvania there's a tribe
Of alien people who ascribe
The outlandish ways and dress
On which their neighbours lay such
        stress,
To their fathers and mothers having
        risen
Out of some subterraneous prison
Into which they were trepanned
Long time ago in a mignty band
Out of Hamelin town in Brunswick
        land,
But how or wny, they don't understand.

15

So, Willy, let me and you be wipers
Of scores out with all men – especially
        pipers!
And, whether they pipe us free fróm
        rats or fróm mice.,
If we've promised them aught, let us
        keep our promise!

## The Flight of the Duchess

### 1

You're my friend:
I was the man the Duke spoke to;
  I helped the Duchess to cast off his
    yoke, too;
So here's the tale from beginning to end,
My friend!

### 2

Ours is a great wild country:
  If you climb to our castle's top,
  I don't see where your eye can stop;
For when you've passed the cornfield
    country,
Where vineyards leave off, flocks are
    packed,
And sheep-range leads to cattle-tract,
And cattle-tract to open-chase,
And open-chase to the very base
Of the mountain where, at a funeral
    pace,
Round about, solemn and slow,
One by one, row after row,
Up and up the pine-trees go,
So, like black priests up, and so
Down the other side again
  To another greater, wilder country,
That's one vast red drear burnt-up plain,
Branched through and through with
    many a vein
Whence iron's dug, and copper's dealt;
  Look right, look left, look straight
    before, –
Beneath they mine, above they smelt,
  Copper-ore and iron-ore,
And forge and furnace mould and melt,
  And so on, more and ever more,
Till at the last, for a bounding belt,
  Comes the salt sand hoar of the
    great sea-shore,
– And the whole is our Duke's country.

### 3

I was born the day this present Duke
    was –
  (And O, says the song, ere I was old!)
In the castle where the other Duke was –
  (When I was happy and young, not
    old!)
I in the kennel, he in the bower:
We are of like age to an hour.
My father was huntsman in that day;
Who has not heard my father say
That, when a boar was brought to bay,
Three times, four times out of five,
With his huntspear he'd contrive
To get the killing-place transfixed,
And pin him true, both eyes betwixt?
And that's why the old Duke would
    rather
He lost a salt-pit than my father,
And loved to have him ever in call;
That's why my father stood in the hall
When the old Duke brought his infant
    out
  To show the people, and while then
    passed
The wondrous bantling round about,
  Was first to start at the outside blast
As the Kaiser's courier blew his horn,
Just a month after the babe was born.
'And,' quoth the Kaiser's courier, 'since
'The Duke has got an heir, our Prince
  'Needs the Duke's self at his side:'
The Duke looked down and seemed to
    wince,
  But he thought of wars o'er the world
    wide,
Castles a-fire, men on their march,
The toppling tower, the crashing arch;
  And up he looked, and awhile he
    eyed
The row of crests and shields; and
    banners.
Of all achievements after all manners,
  And 'ay,' said the Duke with a surly
    pride.
  The more was his comfort when he
    died
At next year's end, in a velvet suit,
With a gilt glove on his hand, his foot
In a silken shoe for a leather boot,
Petticoated like a herald,

In a chamber next to an ante-room,
Where he breathed the breath of
    page and groom,
What he called stink, and they,
    perfume:
– They should have set him on red
    Berold
Mad with pride, like fire to manage!
They should have got his cheek fresh
    tannage
Such a day as to-day in the merry sun
    shine!
Had they stuck on his fist a rough-foot
    merlin!
(Hark, the wind's on the heath at it'
    game!
Oh for a noble falcon-lanner
To flap each broad wing like a banner,
And turn in the wind, and dance like
    flame!)
Had they broached a white-beer cask
    from Berlin
– Or if you incline to prescribe mere
    wine
Put to his lips, when they saw him pine,
A cup of our own Moldavia fine,
Cotnar for instance, green as May
    sorrel
And ropy with sweet, – we shall not
    quarrel.

4

So, at home, the sick tall yellow Duchess
Was left with the infant in her clutches,
She being the daughter of God knows
    who:
    And now was the time to revisit her
    tribe.
Abroad and afar they went, the two,
    And let our people rail and gibe
At the empty hall and extinguished
    fire,
    As loud as we liked, but ever in vain,
Till after long years we had our desire,
    And back came the Duke and his
    mother again.

5

And he came back the pertest little ape
That ever affronted human shape;
Full of his travel, struck at himself.
    You'd say, he despised our bluff old
    ways?
– Not he! For in Paris they told the elf
    Our rough North land was the Land
    of Lays,
    The one good thing left in evil days;
Since the Mid-Age was the Heroic Time,
    And only in wild nooks like ours
Could you taste of it yet as in its prime,
    And see true castles, with proper
    towers,
Young-hearted women, old-minded men,
And manners now as manners were
    then.
So, all that the old Dukes had been,
    without knowing it,
    This Duke would fain know he was,
    without being it;
'Twas not for the joy's self, but the joy
    of his showing it,
    Nor for the pride's self, but the pride
    of our seeing it,
He revived all usages thoroughly wornout,
The souls of them fumed-forth, the
    hearts of them torn-out:
And chief in the chase his neck he
    perilled
On a lathy horse, all legs and length,
With blood for bone, all speed, no
    strength;
– They should have set him on red
    Berold
With the red eye slow consuming in
    fire,
And the thin stiff ear like an abbey-spire!

6

Well, such as he was, he must marry,
    we heard:
And out of a convent, at the word,
Came the lady, in time of spring.
– Oh, old thoughts they cling, they
    cling!
That day, I know, with a dozen oaths

I clad myself in thick hunting-clothes
Fit for the chase of urochs or buffle
In winter-time when you need to muffle.
But the Duke had a mind we should cut
    a figure,
    And so we saw the lady arrive:
My friend, I have seen a white crane
    bigger!
    She was the smallest lady alive,
Made in a piece of nature's madness,
Too small, almost, for the life and
    gladness
    That over-filled her, as some hive
Out of the bears' reach on the high trees
Is crowded with its safe merry bees:
In truth, she was not hard to please!
Up she looked, down she looked,
    round at the mead,
Straight at the castle, that's best indeed
To look at from outside the walls:
As for us, styled the 'serfs and thralls,'
She as much thanked me as if she had
    said it,
    (With her eyes, do you understand?)
Because I patted her horse while I led it;
    And Max, who rode on her other
    hand,
Said, no bird flew past but she inquired
What its true name was, nor ever seemed
    tired –
If that was an eagle she saw hover,
And the green and grey bird on the field
    was the plover.
When suddenly appeared the Duke:
    And as down she sprung, the small
    foot pointed
On to my hand, – as with a rebuke,
    And as if his backbone were not
    jointed,
The Duke stepped rather aside than
    forward,
    And welcomed her with his grandest
    smile;
    And, mind you, his mother all the
    while
Chilled in the rear, like a wind to
    Nor'ward;

And up, like a weary yawn, with its
    pullies
Went, in a shriek, the rusty portcullis;
And, like a glad sky the north-wind
    sullies,
The lady's face stopped its play,
As if her first hair had grown grey;
For such things must begin some one
    day.

7

In a day or two she was well again;
As who should say, 'You labour in vain!
'This is all a jest against God, who
    meant
'I should ever be, as I am, content
'And glad in his sight; therefore, glad I
    will be.'
So, smiling as at first went she.

8

She was active, stirring, all fire –
Could not rest, could not tire –
To a stone she might have given life!
    (I myself loved once, in my day)
– For a shepherd's, miner's, huntsman's
    wife,
    (I had a wife, I know what I say)
Never in all the world such an one!
And here was plenty to be done,
And she that could do it, great or small,
She was to do nothing at all.
There was already this man in his post,
    This in his station, and that in his
    office,
And the Duke's plan admitted a wife, at
    most,
    To meet his eye, with the other
    trophies,
Now outside the hall, now in it,
    To sit thus, stand thus, see and be
    seen,
At the proper place in the proper
    minute,
    And die away the life between.
And it was amusing enough, each
    infraction
    Of rule – (but for after-sadness that
    came)

To hear the consummate self-satisfaction
  With which the young Duke and the
    old dame
Would let her advise, and criticise,
And, being a fool, instruct the wise,
  And, child-like, parcel out praise or
    blame:
They bore it all in complacent guise,
As though an artificer, after contriving
A wheel-work image as if it were living,
Should find with delight it could
    motion to strike him!
So found the Duke, and his mother
    like him:
The lady hardly got a rebuff –
That had not been contemptuous
    enough,
With his cursed smirk, as he nodded
    applause,
And kept off the old mother-cat's
    claws.

9

So, the little lady grew silent and thin,
Paling and ever paling,
As the way is with a hid chagrin;
  And the Duke perceived that she
    was ailing,
And said in his heart, ' 'Tis done to
    spite me,
'But I shall find in my power to right
    me!'
Don't swear, friend! The old one, many
    a year,
Is in hell, and the Duke's self … you
    shall hear.

10

Well, early in autumn, at first winter-
    warning,
When the stag had to break with his
    foot, of a morning,
A drinking-hole out of the fresh tender
    ice
That covered the pond till the sun, in a
    trice,
Loosening it, let out a ripple of gold,
  And another and another, and faster
    and faster,

Till, dimpling to blindness, the wide
    water rolled:
  Then it so chanced that the Duke
    our master
Asked himself what were the pleasures
    in season,
And found, since the calendar bade
    him be hearty,
He should do the Middle Age no treason
  In resolving on a hunting-party.
Always provided, old books showed
    the way of it!
  What meant old poets by their
    strictures?
And when old poets had said their say
    of it,
  How taught old painters in their
    pictures?
We must revert to the proper channels,
Workings in tapestry, paintings on panels,
And gather up woodcraft's authentic
    traditions:
Here was food for our various ambitions:
As on each case, exactly stated –
  To encourage your dog, now, the
    properest chirrup,
  Or best prayer to Saint Hubert on
    mounting your stirrup –
We of the household took thought and
    debated.
Blessed was he whose back ached with
    the jerkin
His sire was wont to do forest-work in;
Blesseder he who nobly sunk 'ohs'
And 'ahs' while he tugged on his
    grand-sire's trunk-hose;
What signified hats if they had no rims
    on,
  Each slouching before and behind
    like the scallop,
  And able to serve at sea for a shallop,
Loaded with lacquer and looped with
    crimson?
So that the deer now, to make a short
    rhyme on't,
  What with our Venerers, Prickers
    and Verderers,

Might hope for real hunters at length
   and not murderers,
And oh the Duke's tailor, he had a hot
   time on't!

### 11

Now you must know that when the
   first dizziness
    Of flap-hats and buff-coats and jack-
      boots subsided,
    The Duke put this question, 'The
      Duke's part provided,
'Had not the Duchess some share in the
   business?'
For out of the mouth of two or three
   witnesses
Did he establish all fit-or-unfitnesses:
And, after much laying of heads together,
Somebody's cap got a notable feather
By the announcement with proper
   unction
That he had discovered the lady's
   function;
Since ancient authors gave this tenet,
    'When horns wind a mort and the
      deer is at siege,
    'Let the dame of the castle prick
      forth on her jennet,
'And, with water to wash the hands of
   her liege
'In a clean ewer with a fair toweling,
'Let her preside at the disemboweling.'
Now, my friend, if you had so little
   religion
    As to catch a hawk, some falcon-
      lanner,
    And thrust her broad wings like a
      banner
Into a coop for a vulgar pigeon;
And if day by day and week by week
    You cut her claws, and sealed her
      eyes,
And clipped her wings, and tied her
   beak,
    Would it cause you any great surprise
If, when you decided to give her an
   airing,
You found she needed a little preparing?

– I say, should you be such a
   curmudgeon,
If she clung to the perch, as to take it in
   dudgeon?
Yet when the Duke to his lady signified,
Just a day before, as he judged most
   dignified,
    In what a pleasure she was to
      participate, –
    And, instead of leaping wide in flashes,
Her eyes just lifted their long lashes,
As if pressed by fatigue even he could
   not dissipate,
And duly acknowledged the Duke's
   forethought,
But spoke of her health, if her health
   were worth aught,
Of the weight by day and the watch by
   night,
And much wrong now that used to be
   right,
So, thanking him, declined the
   hunting, –
Was conduct ever more affronting?
With all the ceremony settled –
    With the towel ready, and the sewer
    Polishing up his oldest ewer,
    And the jennet pitched upon, a
      piebald,
    Black-barred, cream-coated and pink
      eye-balled, –
No wonder if the Duke was nettled!
And when she persisted nevertheless, –
Well, I suppose here's the time to
   confess
That there ran half round our lady's
   chamber
A balcony none of the hardest to
   clamber;
And that Jacynth the tire-woman, ready
   in waiting,
Stayed in call outside, what need of
   relating?
And since Jacynth was like a June rose,
   why, a fervent
Adorer of Jacynth of course was your
   servant;

And if she had the habit to peep
    through the casement,
  How could I keep at any vast distance?
  And so, as I say, on the lady's
    persistence,
The Duke, dumb-stricken with
    amazement,
Stood for a while in a sultry smother,
  And then, with a smile that partook
    of the awful,
Turned her over to his yellow mother
  To learn what was held decorous
    and lawful;
And the mother smelt blood with a cat-
    like instinct,
As her cheek quick whitened thro' all
    its quince-tint.
Oh, but the lady heard the whole truth
    at once!
What meant she? – Who was she? –
    Her duty and station,
The wisdom of age and the folly of
    youth, at once,
  Its decent regard and its fitting
    relation –
In brief, my friend, set all the devils in
    hell free
And turn them out to carouse in a belfry
And treat the priests to a fifty-part
    canon,
And then you may guess how that
    tongue of hers ran on!
Well, somehow or other it ended at last
And, licking her whiskers, out she
    passed;
And after her, – making (he hoped) a
    face
  Like Emperor Nero or Sultan Saladin,
Stalked the Duke's self with the austere
    grace
  Of ancient hero or modern paladin,
From door to staircase – oh such a
    solemn
Unbending of the vertebral column!

12

However, at sunrise our company
    mustered;
  And here was the huntsman bidding
    unkennel,
And there 'neath his bonnet the
    pricker blustered,
  With feather dank as a bough of wet
    fennel;
For the court-yard walls were filled
    with fog
You might have cut as an axe chops a
    log –
Like so much wool for colour and
    bulkiness;
And out rode the Duke in a perfect,
    sulkiness,
Since, before breakfast, a man feels but
    queasily,
  And a sinking at the lower abdomen
  Begins the day with indifferent omen.
And lo, as he looked around uneasily,
The sun ploughed the fog up and drove
    it asunder
This way and that from the valley under;
  And, looking through the court-yard
    arch,
Down in the valley, what should meet
    him
  But a troop of Gipsies on their march?
No doubt with the annual gifts to greet
    him.

13

Now, in your land, Gipsies reach you,
    only
  After reaching all lands beside;
North they go, South they go, trooping
    or lonely,
  And still, as they travel far and wide,
Catch they and keep now a trace here,
    a trace there,
That puts you in mind of a place here,
    a place there.
But with us, I believe they rise out of
    the ground,
And nowhere else, I take it, are found

With the earth-tint yet so freshly
    embrowned:
Born, no doubt, like insects which breed
    on
The very fruit they are meant to feed on.
For the earth – not a use to which they
    don't turn it,
    The ore that grows in the mountain's
      womb,
    Or the sand in the pits like a honey-
      comb,
They sift and soften it, bake it and burn
    it –
Whether they weld you, for instance, a
    snaffle
With side-bars never a brute can baffle;
Or a lock that's a puzzle of wards
    within wards;
Or, if your colt's fore-foot inclines to
    curve inwards,
Horseshoes they hammer which turn
    on a swivel
And won't allow the hoof to shrivel.
Then they cast bells like the shell of the
    winkle
That keep a stout heart in the ram with
    their tinkle;
But the sand – they pinch and pound
    it like otters;
Commend me to Gipsy glass-makers
    and potters!
Glasses they'll blow you, crystal-clear,
Where just a faint cloud of rose shall
    appear,
As if in pure water you dropped and let
    die
A bruised black-blooded mulberry;
And that other sort, their crowning pride,
With long white threads distinct
    inside,
Like the lake-flower's fibrous roots
    which dangle
Loose such a length and never tangle,
Where the bold sword-lily cuts the
    clear waters,
And the cup-lily couches with all the
    white daughters:

Such are the works they put their hand
    to,
The uses they turn and twist iron and
    sand to.
And these made the troop, which our
    Duke saw sally
Toward his castle from out of the valley,
Men and women, like new-hatched
    spiders,
Come out with the morning to greet
    our riders.
And up they wound till they reached
    the ditch,
Whereat all stopped save one, a witch
That I knew, as she hobbled from the
    group,
By her gait directly and her stoop,
I, whom Jacynth was used to importune
To let that same witch tell us our
    fortune.
The oldest Gipsy then above ground;
And, sure as the autumn season came
    round,
She paid us a visit for profit or pastime,
And every time, as she swore, for the
    last time.
And presently she was seen to sidle
Up to the Duke till she touched his
    bridle,
So that the horse of a sudden reared up
As under its nose the old witch peered
    up
With her worn-out eyes, or rather eye-
    holes
    Of no use now but to gather brine,
    And began a kind of level whine
Such as they used to sing to their viols
When their ditties they go grinding
Up and down with nobody minding:
And then, as of old, at the end of the
    humming
Her usual presents were forthcoming
– A dog-whistle blowing the fiercest of
    trebles,
(Just a sea-shore stone holding a dozen
    fine pebbles,)

Or a porcelain mouth-piece to screw
    on a pipe-end, –
And so she awaited her annual stipend.
But this time, the Duke would scarcely
    vouchsafe
  A word in reply; and in vain she felt
  With twitching fingers at her belt
  For the purse of sleek pine-martin
    pelt,
Ready to put what he gave in her pouch
    safe, –
Till, either to quicken his apprehension,
Or possibly with an after-intention,
She was come, she said, to pay her duty
To the new Duchess, the youthful
    beauty.
No sooner had she named his lady,
Than a shine lit up the face so shady,
And its smirk returned with a novel
    meaning –
For it struck him, the babe just wanted
    weaning;
If one gave her a taste of what life was
    and sorrow,
She, foolish to-day, would be wiser
    to-morrow;
And who so fit a teacher of trouble
As this sordid crone bent well-nigh
    double?
So, glancing at her wolf-skin vesture,
  (If such it was, for they grow so
    hirsute
  That their own fleece serves for
    natural fur-suit)
He was contrasting, 'twas plain from
    his gesture,
The life of the lady so flower-like and
    delicate
With the loathsome squalor of this
    helicat.
I, in brief, was the man the Duke
    beckoned
  From out of the throng, and while I
    drew near
He told the crone – as I since have
    reckoned

  By the way he bent and spoke into
    her ear
With circumspection and mystery –
The main of the lady's history,
Her frowardness and ingratitude:
And for all the crone's submissive
    attitude
I could see round her mouth the loose
    plaits tightening,
And her brow with assenting
    intelligence brightening,
  As though she engaged with hearty
    goodwill
  Whatever he now might enjoin to
    fulfil,
And promised the lady a thorough
    frightening.
And so, just giving her a glimpse
Of a purse, with the air of a man who
    imps
The wing of the hawk that shall fetch
    the hernshaw,
  He bade me take the Gipsy mother
  And set her telling some story or
    other
Of hill or dale, oak-wood or fernshaw,
To wile away a weary hour
For the lady-left alone in her bower,
Whose mind and body craved exertion
And yet shrank from all better
    diversion.

14

Then clapping heel to his horse, the
    mere curveter,
  Out rode the Duke, and after his
    hollo
Horses and hounds swept, huntsman
    and servitor,
  And back I turned and bade the
    crone follow.
And what makes me confident what's
    to be told you
  Had all along been of this crone's
    devising,
Is, that, on looking round sharply,
    behold you,

There was a novelty quick as
    surprising:
For first, she had shot up a full head in
    stature,
    And her step kept pace with mine
        nor faltered,
As if age had foregone its usurpature,
    And the ignoble mien was wholly
        altered,
And the face looked quite of another
    nature,
And the change reached too, whatever
    the change meant,
Her shaggy wolf-skin cloak's arrangement:
For where its tatters hung loose like
    sedges,
Gold coins were glittering on the edges,
Like the band-roll strung with tomans
Which proves the veil a Persian
    woman's:
And under her brow, like a snail's
    horns newly
    Come out as after the rain he paces,
Two unmistakeable eye-points duly
    Live and aware looked out of their
        places.
So, we went and found Jacynth at the
    entry
Of the lady's chamber standing sentry;
I told the command and produced my
    companion,
And Jacynth rejoiced to admit any one,
For since last night, by the same token,
Not a single word had the lady spoken:
They went in both to the presence
    together,
While I in the balcony watched the
    weather.

· 15 ·

And now, what took place at the very
    first of all,
I cannot tell, as I never could learn it:
Jacynth constantly wished a curse to fall
On that little head of hers and burn it
If she knew how she came to drop so
    soundly
    Asleep of a sudden and there continue

The whole time sleeping as profoundly
    As one of the boars my father would
        pin you
    'Twixt the eyes where life holds
        earrison,
– Jacynth forgive me the comparison!
But where I begin my own narration
Is a little after I took my station
To breathe the fresh air from the
    balcony,
And, having in those days a falcon eye,
To follow the hunt thro' the open
    country,
    From where the bushes thinlier
        crested
The hillocks, to a plain where's not one
    tree.
    When, in a moment, my ear was
        arrested
By – was it singing, or was it saying,
Or a strange musical instrument playing
In the chamber? – and to be certain
I pushed the lattice, pulled the curtain,
And there lay Jacynth asleep,
Yet as if a watch she tried to keep,
In a rosy sleep along the floor
With her head against the door;
While in the midst, on the seat of state,
Was a queen – the Gipsy woman late,
With head and face downbent
On the lady's head and face intent:
For, coiled at her feet like a child at ease,
The lady sat between her knees
And o'er them the lady's clasped hands
    met,
And on those hands her chin was set,
And her upturned face met the face of
    the crone
Wherein the eyes had grown and grown
As if she could double and quadruple
At pleasure the play of either pupil
    – Very like, by her hands' slow
        fanning,
As up and down like a gor-crow's
    flappers
They moved to measure, or bell-clappers.
    I said 'Is it blessing, is it banning,

'Do they applaud you or burlesque
   you –
  'Those hands and fingers with no
    flesh on?'
But, just as I thought to spring in to the
   rescue,
   At once I was stopped by the lady's
    expression:
For it was life her eyes were drinking
From the crone's wide pair above
   unwinking,
– Life's pure fire received without
   shrinking,
Into the heart and breast whose heaving
Told you no single drop they were leaving,
– Life, that filling her, passed redundant
   Into her very hair, back swerving
Over each shoulder, loose and
   abundant,
   As her head thrown back showed
    the white throat curving;
And the very tresses shared in the
   pleasure,
Moving to the mystic measure,
Bounding as the bosom bounded.
I stopped short, more and more
   confounded,
As still her cheeks burned and eyes
   glistened,
As she listened and she listened:
When all at once a hand detained me,
The selfsame contagion gained me,
And I kept time to the wondrous
   chime,
Making out words and prose and rhyme,
Till it seemed that the music furled
   Its wings like a task fulfilled, and
    dropped
    From under the words it first had
     propped,
And left them midway in the world:
Word took word as hand takes hand,
I could hear at last, and understand,
And when I held the unbroken thread,
The Gipsy said: –

'And so at last we find my tribe.

'And so I set thee in the midst,
'And to one and all of them describe
  'What thou saidst and what thou
    didst,
'Our long and terrible journey through,
'And all thou art ready to say and do
'In the trials that remain:
'I trace them the vein and the other vein
'That meet on thy brow and part again,
'Making our rapid mystic mark;
  'And I bid my people prove and
    probe
  'Each eye's profound and glorious
    globe
'Till they detect the kindred spark
'In those depths so dear and dark,
'Like the spots that snap and burst and
   flee,
'Circling over the midnight sea.
  'And on that round young cheek of
    thine
  'I make them recognize the tinge,
'As when of the costly scarlet wine
  'They drip so much as will impinge
'And spread in a thinnest scale afloat
'One thick gold drop from the olive's
   coat
'Over a silver plate whose sheen
'Still thro' the mixture shall be seen.
'For so I prove thee, to one and all,
  'Fit, when my people ope their breast,
'To see the sign, and hear the call,
  'And take the vow, and stand the test
  'Which adds one more child to the
    rest –
'When the breast is bare and the arms
   are wide,
'And the world is left outside.
'For there is probation to decree,
'And many and long must the trials be
'Thou shalt victoriously endure,
'If that brow is true and those eyes are
   sure;
'Like a jewel-finder's fierce assay
  'Of the prize he dug from its
    mountain-tomb –
'Let once the vindicating ray

'Leap out amid the anxious gloom,
'And steel and fire have done their part
'And the prize falls on its finder's heart;
'So, trial after trial past,
'Wilt thou fall at the very last
'Breathless, half in trance
'With the thrill of the great deliverance,
    'Into our arms for evermore;
'And thou shalt know, those arms once
        curled
    'About thee, what we knew before,
'How love is the only good in the world.
'Henceforth be loved as heart can love,
'Or brain devise, or hand approve!
'Stand up, look below,
'It is our life at thy feet we throw
'To step with into light and joy;
Not a power of life but we employ
'To satisfy thy nature's want;
'Art thou the tree that props the plant,
'Or the climbing plant that seeks the
        tree –
'Canst thou help us, must we help thee?
'If any two creatures grew into one,
'They would do more than the world
        has done:
'Though each apart were never so weak,
'Ye vainly through the world should
        seek
'For the knowledge and the might
'Which in such union grew their right:
'So, to approach at least that end,
'And blend, – as much as may be,
        blend
'Thee with us or us with thee, –
'As climbing plant or propping tree,
'Shall some one deck thee, over and
        down,
    'Up and about, with blossoms and
        leaves?
'Fix his heart's fruit for thy garland-
        crown,
    'Cling with his soul as the gourd-
        vine cleaves,
'Die on thy boughs and disappear
'While not a leaf of thine is sere?
'Or is the other fate in store,

'And art thou fitted to adore,
'To give thy wondrous self away,
'And take a stronger nature's sway?
'I foresee and could foretell
'Thy future portion, sure and well:
'But those passionate eyes speak true,
        speak true,
'Let them say what thou shalt do!
'Only be sure thy daily life,
'In its peace or in its strife,
'Never shall be unobserved;
    'We pursue thy whole career,
    'And hope for it, or doubt, or fear, –
'Lo, hast thou kept thy path or swerved,
'We are beside thee in all thy ways,
'With our blame, with our praise,
'Our shame to feel, our pride to show,
'Glad, angry – but indifferent, no!
'Whether it be thy lot to go,
'For the good of us all, where the haters
        meet
'In the crowded city's horrible street;
'Or thou step alone through the morass
'Where never sound yet was
'Save the dry quick clap of the stork's
        bill,
'For the air is still, and the water still,
'When the blue breast of the dipping
        coot
'Dives under, and all is mute.
'So, at the last shall come old age,
'Decrepit as befits that stage;
'How else wouldst thou retire apart
'With the hoarded memories of thy
        heart,
'And gather all to the very least
'Of the fragments of life's earlier feast,
'Let fall through eagerness to find
'The crowning dainties yet behind?
'Ponder on the entire past
'Laid together thus at last,
'When the twilight helps to fuse
'The first fresh with the faded hues,
'And the outline of the whole,
'As round eve's shades their framework
        roll,
'Grandly fronts for once thy soul.

'And then as, 'mid the dark, a gleam
  'Of yet another morning breaks,
'And like the hand which ends a dream,
'Death, with the might of his sunbeam,
  'Touches the flesh and the soul awakes,
'Then – '
       Ay, then indeed something
    would happen!
    But what? For here her voice changed
    like a bird's;
    There grew more of the music and
    less of the words;
Had Jacynth only been by me to clap
  pen
To paper and put you down every syllable
  With those clever clerkly fingers,
    All I've forgotten as well as what
    lingers
In this old brain of mine that's but ill
  able
To give you even this poor version
    Of the speech I spoil, as it were,
    with stammering
    – More fault of those who had the
    hammering
    Of prosody into me and syntax,
    And did it, not with hobnails but tin-
    tacks!
But to return from this excursion, –
Just, do you mark, when the song was
  sweetest,
The peace most deep and the charm
  completest,
There came, shall I say, a snap –
    And the charm vanished!
    And my sense returned, so strangely
    banished,
And, starting as from a nap,
I knew the crone was bewitching my
  lady,
With Jacynth asleep; and but one
  spring made I
Down from the casement, round to the
  portal,
    Another minute and I had entered, –
When the door opened, and more than
  mortal

    Stood, with a face where to my mind
    centred
All beauties I ever saw or shall see,
The Duchess: I stopped as if struck by
  palsy.
She was so different, happy and beautiful,
  I felt at once that all was best,
    And that I had nothing to do, for the
    rest,
But wait her commands, obey and be
  dutiful.
Not that, in fact, there was any
  commanding;
  I saw the glory of her eye,
And the brow's height and the breast's
  expanding,
  And I was hers to live or to die.
As for finding what she wanted,
You know God Almighty granted
Such little signs should serve wild
  creatures
  To tell one another all their desires,
  So that each knows what his friend
  requires,
And does its bidding without teachers.
I preceded her; the crone
Followed silent and alone;
I spoke to her, but she merely jabbered
  In the old style; both her eyes had
  slunk
  Back to their pits; her stature shrunk;
  In short, the soul in its body sunk
Like a blade sent home to its scabbard.
We descended, I preceding;
Crossed the court with nobody heeding;
All the world was at the chase,
The courtyard like a desert-place
The stable emptied of its small fry;
I saddled myself the very palfrey
I remember patting while it carried her,
The day she arrived and the Duke
  married her.
And, do you know, though it's easy
  deceiving
Oneself in such matters, I can't help
  believing
The lady had not forgotten it either,

And knew the poor devil so much
    beneath her
Would have been only too glad for her
    service
To dance on hot ploughshares like a
    Turk dervise,
But, unable to pay proper duty where
    owing it,
Was reduced to that pitiful method of
    showing it:
For though the moment I began setting
His saddle on my own nag of Berold's
    begetting,
(Not that I meant to be obtrusive)
    She stopped me, while his rug was
        shifting,
    By a single rapid finger's lifting,
And, with a gesture kind but conclusive,
And a little shake of the head, refused
    me, –
I say, although she never used me,
Yet when she was mounted, the Gipsy
    behind her,
And I ventured to remind her,
I suppose with a voice of less
    steadiness
    Than usual, for my feeling exceeded
        me,
      – Something to the effect that I was
        ineadiness
    Whenever God should please she
        needed me, –
Then, do you know, her face looked
    down on me
With a look that placed a crown on me,
And she felt in her bosom, – mark, her
    bosom –
And, as a flower-tree drops its blossom,
Dropped me ... ah, had it been a purse
Of silver, my friend, or gold that's worse,
Why, you see, as soon as I found myself
    So understood, – that a true heart so
        may gain
Such a reward, – I should have gone
    home again,
Kissed Jacynth, and soberly drowned
    myself!

It was a little plait of hair
    Such as friends in a convent make
    To wear, each for the other's sake, –
This, see, which at my breast I wear,
Ever did (rather to Jacynth's grudgment),
And ever shall, till the Day of Judgment.
And then, – and then, – to cut short, –
    this is idle,
    These are feelings it is not good to
      foster, –
I pushed the gate wide, she shook the
    bridle,
    And the palfrey bounded, – and so
    we lost her.

16

When the liquor's out why clink the
    cannikin?
I did think to describe you the panic in
The redoubtable breast of our master
    the mannikin,
And what was the pitch of his mother's
    yellowness,
    How she turned as a shark to snap
      the spare-rib
    Clean off, sailors say, from a pearl-
      diving Carib,
When she heard, what she called the
    flight of the fcloness
– But it seems such child's play,
What they said and did with the lady
    away!
And to dance on, when we've lost the
    music,
Always made me – and no doubt makes
    you – sick.
Nay, to my mind, the world's face
    looked so stern
As that sweet form disappeared
    through the postern,
She that kept it in constant good
    humour,
It ought to have stopped; there seemed
    nothing to do more.
But the world thought otherwise and
    went on,
And my head's one that its spite was
    spent on:

Thirty years are fled since that morning,
And with them all my head's adorning.
Nor did the old Duchess die outright,
As you expect, of suppressed spite,
The natural end of every adder
Not suffered to empty its poison-bladder:
But she and her son agreed, I take it,
That no one should touch on the story
    to wake it,
For the wound in the Duke's pride
    rankled fiery,
So, they made no search and small
    inquiry –
And when fresh Gipsies have paid us a
    visit, I've
Noticed the couple were never inquisitive,
But told them they're folks the Duke
    don't want here,
And bade them make haste and cross
    the frontier.
Brief, the Duchess was gone and the
    Duke was glad of it,
    And the old one was in the young
      one's stead,
    And took, in her place, the house-
      hold's head,
And a blessed time the household had
    of it!
And were I not, as a man may say,
    cautious
How I trench, more than needs, on the
    nauseous,
I could favour you with sundry touches
Of the paint-smutches with which the
    Duchess
Heightened the mellowness of her
    cheek's yellowness
(To get on faster) until at last her
Cheek grew to be one master-plaster
Of mucus and fucus from mere use of
    ceruse:
In short, she grew from scalp to udder
Just the object to make you shudder.

17

You're my friend –
What a thing friendship is, world
    without end!
How it gives the heart and soul a stir-up
    As if somebody broached you a
      glorious runlet,
    And poured out, all lovelily,
      sparklingly, sunlit,
Our green Moldavia, the streaky syrup,
Cotnar as old as the time of the Druids –
Friendship may match with that
    monarch of fluids;
Each supples a dry brain, fills you its
    ins-and-outs,
Gives your life's hour-glass a shake
    when the thin sand doubts
Whether to run on or stop short, and
    guarantees
Age is not all made of stark sloth and
    arrant ease.
I have seen my little lady once more,
    Jacynth, the Gipsy, Berold, and the
      rest of it,
For to me spoke the Duke, as I told you
    before;
    I always wanted to make a clean
      breast of it;
And now it is made – why, my heart's
    blood, that went trickle,
    Trickle, but anon, in such muddy
      driblets,
Is pumped up brisk now, through the
    main ventricle,
    And genially floats me about the
      giblets.
I'll tell you what I intend to do:
I must see this fellow his sad life
    through –
He is our Duke, after all,
And I, as he says, but a serf and thrall.
My father was born here, and I inherit
    His fame, a chain he bound his son
      with;
Could I pay in a lump I should prefer it,
    But there's no mine to blow up and
      get done with:

So, I must stay till the end of the chapter.
For, as to our middle-age-manners-
     adapter,
Be it a thing to be glad on or sorry on,
Some day or other, his head in a morion
And breast in a hauberk, his heels he'll
     kick up,
Slain by an onslaught fierce of hiccup.
And then, when red doth the sword of
     our Duke rust,
And its leathern sheath lie o'ergrown
     with a blue crust,
Then I shall scrape together my earnings;
     For, you see, in the churchyard
     Jacynth reposes,
     And our children all went the way of
     the roses:
It's a long lane that knows no turnings.
One needs but little tackle to travel in;
     So, just one stout cloak shall I indue:
And for a staff, what beats the javelin
     With which his boars my father
     pinned you?
And then, for a purpose you shall hear
     presently,
     Taking some Cotnar, a tight plump
     skinful,
I shall go journeying, who but I,
     pleasantly!
     Sorrow is vain and despondency
     sinful.
What's a man's age? He must hurry
     more, that's all;
     Cram in a day, what his youth took
     a year to hold:
     When we mind labour, then only,
     we're too old –
What age had Methusalem when he
     begat Saul?
And at last, as its haven some buffeted
     ship sees,
     (Come all the way from the north-
     parts with sperm oil)
     I hope to get safely out of the
     turmoil
And arrive one day at the land of the
     Gipsies,

And find my lady, or hear the last news
     of her
From some old thief and son of Lucifer,
His forehead chapleted green with
     wreathy hop,
Sunburned all over like an Æthiop.
And when my Cotnar begins to operate
And the tongue of the rogue to run at a
     proper rate,
And our wine-skin, tight once, shows
     each flaccid dent,
I shall drop in with – as if by accident –
'You never knew, then, how it all ended,
'What fortune good or bad attended
'The little lady your Queen befriended?'
– And when that's told me, what's
     remaining?
This world's too hard for my explaining.
The same wise judge of matters equine
     Who still preferred some slim four-
     year-old
     To the big-boned stock of mighty
     Berold,
And, for strong Cotnar, drank French
     weak wine,
He also must be such a lady's scorner!
     Smooth Jacob still robs homely Esau:
     Now up, now down, the world's one
     see-saw.
– So, I shall find out some snug corner
Under a hedge, like Orson the wood-
     knight,
Turn myself round and bid the world
     good night;
And sleep a sound sleep till the
     trumpet's blowing
     Wakes me (unless priests cheat us
     laymen)
To a world where will be no further
     throwing
Pearls before swine that can't value
     them. Amen!

## A Grammarian's Funeral

Shortly after the revival of learning in Europe

Let us begin and carry up this corpse,
    Singing together.
Leave we the common crofts, the vulgar
    thorpes
      Each in its tether
Sleeping safe on the bosom of the plain,
    Cared-for till cock-crow:
Look out if yonder be not day again
    Rimming the rock-row!
That's the appropriate country; there,
    man's thought,
      Rarer, intenser,
Self-gathered for an outbreak, as it ought,
    Chafes in the censer.
Leave we the unlettered plain its herd
    and crop;
      Seek we sepulture
On a tall mountain, citied to the top,
    Crowded with culture!
All the peaks soar, but one the rest
    excels;
      Clouds overcome it;
No! yonder sparkle is the citadel's
    Circling its summit.
Thither our path lies; wind we up the
    heights:
      Wait ye the warning?
Our low life was the level's and the
    night's;
      He's for the morning.
Step to a tune, square chests, erect each
    head,
      'Ware the beholders!
This is our master, famous calm and
    dead,
      Borne on our shoulders.

Sleep, crop and herd! sleep, darkling
    thorpe and croft,
      Safe from the weather!
He, whom we convoy to his grave aloft,
    Singing together,
He was a man born with thy face and
    throat,
      Lyric Apollo!

Long he lived nameless: how should
    spring take note
      Winter would follow?
Till lo, the little touch, and youth was
    gone!
      Cramped and diminished,
Moaned he, 'New measures, other feet
    anon!
      'My dance is finished?'
No, that's the world's way: (keep the
    mountain-side,
      Make for the city!)
He knew the signal, and stepped on
    with pride
      Over men's pity;
Left play for work, and grappled with
    the world
      Bent on escaping:
'What's in the scroll,' quoth he, 'thou
    keepest furled?
      'Show me their shaping,
'Theirs who most studied man, the
    bard and sage, –
      'Give!' – So, he gowned him,
Straight got by heart that book to its
    last page:
      Learned, we found him.
Yea, but we found him bald too, eyes
    like lead,
      Accents uncertain:
'Time to taste life,' another would have
    said,
      'Up with the curtain!'
This man said rather, 'Actual life comes
    next?
      'Patience a moment!
'Grant I have mastered learning's
    crabbed text,
      'Still there's the comment.
'Let me know all! Prate not of most or
    least,
      'Painful or easy!
'Even to the crumbs I'd fain eat up the
    feast,
      'Ay, nor feel queasy.'
Oh, such a life as he resolved to live,
    When he had learned it,

When he had gathered all books had
    to give!
        Sooner, he spurned it,
Image the whole, then execute the
    parts –
        Fancy the fabric
Quite, ere you build, ere steel strike fire
    from quartz,
        Ere mortar dab brick!

(Here's the town-gate reached: there's
    the market-place
        Gaping before us.)
Yea, this in him was the peculiar grace
    (Hearten our chorus!)
That before living he'd learn how to
    live –
        No end to learning:
Earn the means first – God surely will
    contrive
        Use for our earning.
Others mistrust and say, 'But time
    escapes:
        'Live now or never!'
He said, 'What's time? Leave Now for
    dogs and apes!
        'Man has Forever.'
Back to his book then: deeper drooped
    his head:
        *Calculus* racked him:
Leaden before, his eyes grew dross of
    lead:
        *Tussis* attacked him.
'Now, master, take a little rest!' – not
    he!
        (Caution redoubled,
Step two abreast, the way winds
    narrowly!)
        Not a whit troubled
Back to his studies, fresher than at first,
        Fierce as a dragon
He (soul-hydroptic with a sacred thirst)
        Sucked at the flagon.
Oh, if we draw a circle premature,
        Heedless of far gain,
Greedy for quick returns of profit, sure
        Bad is our bargain!

Was it not great? did not he throw on
    God,
        (He loves the burthen) –
God's task to make the heavenly period
        Perfect the earthen?
Did not he magnify the mind, show clear
        Just what it all meant?
He would not discount life, as fools do
    here,
        Paid by instalment.
He ventured neck or nothing –
    heaven's success
        Found, or earth's failure:
'Wilt thou trust death or not?' He
    answered 'Yes:
        'Hence with life's pale lure!'
That low man seeks a little thing to do,
        Sees it and does it:
This high man, with a great thing to
    pursue,
        Dies ere he knows it.
That low man goes on adding one to
    one,
        His hundred's soon hit:
This high man, aiming at a million,
        Misses an unit.
That, has the world here – should he
    need the next,
        Let the world mind him!
This, throws himself on God, and
    unperplexed
        Seeking shall find him.
So, with the throttling hands of death
    at strife.
        Ground he at grammar;
Still, thro' the rattle, parts of speech
    were rife:
        While he could stammer
He settled *Hoti's* business – let it bet! –
        Properly based *Oun* –
Gave us the doctrine of the enclitic *De*,
        Dead from the waist down.
Well, here's the platform, here's the
    proper place:
        Hail to your purlieus,
All ye highfliers of the feathered race,
        Swallows and curlews!

Here's the top-peak; the multitude
below
    Live, for they can, there:
This man decided not to Live but
Know –
    Bury this man there?
Here – here's his place, where meteors
shoot, clouds form,
    Lightnings are loosened,
Stars come and go! Let joy break with
the storm,
    Peace let the dew send!
Lofty designs must close in like effects:
    Loftily lying,
Leave him – still loftier than the world
suspects,
    Living and dying.

## The Heretic's Tragedy

A middle-age interlude

Rosa mundi; seu, fulcite me floribus. A conceit
of master Gysbrecht, canon-regular of saint
Jodocus-by-the-bar, Ypres city. Cantuque,
*Virgilius*. And Hath often been sung at hock-
tide and festivals. Gavisus eram, *Jessides*.

(It would seem to be a glimpse from the
burning of Jacques du Bourg-Molay, at Paris,
AD 1314; as distorted by the refraction from
Flemish brain to brain, during the course of a
couple of centuries.)

[Molay was Grand Master of the Templars
when that order was suppressed in 1312.]

1

PREADMONISHETH THE ABBOT DEODAET
The Lord, we look to once for all,
    Is the Lord we should look at, all at
once:
He knows not to vary, saith Saint Paul,
    Nor the shadow of turning, for the
nonce.
See him no other than as he is!
    Give both the infinitudes their due –

Infinite mercy, but, I wis,
    As infinite a justice too.
            [*Organ: plagal-cadence*.
    As infinite a justice too.

2

ONE SINGETH
John, Master of the Temple of God,
    Falling to sin the Unknown Sin,
What he bought of Emperor Aldabrod,
    He sold it to Sultan Saladin:
Till, caught by Pope Clement, a-
buzzing there,
    Hornet-prince of the mad wasps'
hive,
And clipt of his wings in Paris square,
    They bring him now to be burned
alive.
        [*And wanteth there grace of lute
         or clavicithern, ye shall say to
         confirm him who singeth –
We bring John now to be burned
alive.

3

In the midst is a goodly gallows built;
    'Twixt fork and fork, a stake is stuck;
But first they set divers tumbrils a-tilt,
    Make a trench all round with the
city muck;
Inside they pile log upon log, good
store;
    Faggots no few, blocks great and
small,
Reach a man's mid-thigh, no less, no
more, –
    For they mean he should roast in
the sight of all.

CHORUS
We mean he should roast in the
sight of all.

4

Good sappy bavins that kindle forthwith;
    Billets that blaze substantial and
slow;
Pine-stump split deftly, dry as pith;
    Larch-heart that chars to a chalk-
white glow:

Then up they hoist me John in a chafe,
　Sling him fast like a hog to scorch,
Spit in his face, then leap back safe,
　Sing 'Laudes' and bid clap-to the
　　torch.

CHORUS

Laus Deo – who bids clap-to the
　torch.

5

John of the Temple, whose fame so
　bragged,
　Is burning alive in Paris square!
How can he curse, if his mouth is gagged
　Or wriggle his neck, with a collar
　　there?
Or heave his chest, which a band goes
　round?
　Or threat with his fist, since his arms
　　are spliced?
Or kick with his feet, now his legs are
　bound?
　– Thinks John, I will call upon Jesus
　　Christ.  [Here one crosseth himself.

6

Jesus Christ – John had bought and
　sold,
　Jesus Christ – John had eaten and
　　drunk;
To him, the Flesh meant silver and gold.
　(Salva reverentia.)
Now it was, 'Saviour, bountiful lamb,
　'I have roasted thee Turks, though
　　men roast me!
'See thy servant, the plight wherein I
　am!
　'Art thou a saviour? Save thou me!'
　　Chorus
　'Tis John the mocker cries, 'Save
　　thou me!'

7

Who maketh God's menace an idle
　word?
　– Saith, it no more means what it
　　proclaims,
Than a damsel's threat to her wanton
　bird? –
　For she too prattles of ugly names.

– Saith, he knoweth but one thing, –
　what he knows?
　That God is good and the rest is
　　breath;
Why else is the same styled Sharon's
　rose?
　Once a rose, ever a rose, he saith.

CHORUS

O, John shall yet find a rose, he saith!

8

Alack, there be roses and roses, John!
　Some, honied of taste like your
　　leman's tongue:
Some, bitter; for why? (roast gaily on!)
　Their tree struck root in devil's-dung.
When Paul once reasoned of
　righteousness
　And of temperance and of judgment
　　to come.
Good Felix trembled, he could no less:
　John, snickering, crook'd his wicked
　　thumb.

CHORUS

What cometh to John of the wicked
　thumb?

9

Ha, ha, John plucketh now at his rose
　To rid himself of a sorrow at heart!
Lo, – petal on petal, fierce rays unclose;
　Anther on anther, sharp spikes
　　outstart;
And with blood for dew, the bosom
　boils;
　And a gust of sulphur is all its smell;
And lo, he is horribly in the toils
　Of a coal-black giant flower of hell!

CHORUS

What maketh heaven, That maketh
　hell.

10

So, as John called now, through the fire
　amain,
　On the Name, he had cursed with,
　　all his life –
To the Person, he bought and sold
　again –

For the Face, with his daily buffets
      rife –
Feature by feature It took its place:
      And his voice, like a mad dog's
      choking bark,
At the steady whole of the Judge's face –
      Died. Forth John's soul flared into
      the dark.
            Subjoineth the Abbot Deodaet
God help all poor souls lost in the dark!


## Holy-Cross Day

On which the Jews were forced to attend an
      annual christian sermon in Rome.

['Now was come about Holy-Cross Day, and
      now must my lord preach his first sermon to
      the Jews: as it was of old cared for in the
      merciful bowels of the Church, that, so to
      speak, a crumb at least from her conspicuous
      table here in Rome should be, though but
once yearly, cast to the famishing dogs, under-
      trampled and bespitten-upon beneath the feet
      of the guests. And a moving sight in truth,
      this, of so many of the besotted blind restif
      and ready-to-perish Hebrews! now maternally
      brought – nay (for He saith, 'Compel them to
      come in') haled, as it were, by the head and
      hair, and against their obstinate hearts, to
      partake of the heavenly grace. What
      awakening, what striving with tears, what
      working of a yeasty conscience! Nor was my
lord wanting to himself on so apt an occasion;
      witness the abundance of conversions which
      did incontinently reward him: though not to
      my lord be altogether the glory.' – *Diary by the
            Bishop's Secretary*, 1600.]

What the Jews really said, on thus being
      driven to church, was rather to this effect: –

### 1

Fee, faw, fum! bubble and squeak!
Blessedest Thursday's the fat of the week.
Rumble and tumble, sleek and rough,
Stinking and savoury, smug and gruff,
Take the church-road, for the bell's
      due chime

Gives us the summons – 'tis sermon-
      time!

### 2

Boh, here's Barnabas! Job, that's you?
Up stumps Solomon – bustling too?
Shame, man! greedy beyond your years
To handsel the bishop's shaving-shears?
Fair play's a jewel! Leave friends in the
      lurch?
Stand on a line ere you start for the
      church!

### 3

Higgledy piggledy, packed we lie,
Rats in a hamper, swine in a stye,
Wasps in a bottle, frogs in a sieve,
Worms in a carcase, fleas in a sleeve.
Hist! square shoulders, settle your
      thumbs
And buzz for the bishop – here he
      comes.

### 4

Bow, wow, wow – a bone for the dog!
I liken his Grace to an acorned hog.
What, a boy at his side, with the bloom
      of a lass,
To help and handle my lord's hour-
      glass!
Didst ever behold so lithe a chine?
His cheek hath laps like a fresh-singed
      swine.

### 5

Aaron's asleep – shove hip to haunch,
Or somebody deal him a dig in the
      paunch!
Look at the purse with the tassel and
      knob,
And the gown with the angel and
      thingumbob!
What's he at, quotha? reading his text!
Now you've his curtsey – and what
      comes next?

### 6

See to our converts – you doomed
      black dozen –
No stealing away – nor cog nor cozen!
You five, that were thieves, deserve it
      fairly;

You seven, that were beggars, will live
    less sparely;
You took your turn and dipped in the
    hat,
Got fortune – and fortune gets you;
    mind that!

7

Give your first groan – compunction's
    at work:
And soft! from a Jew you mount to a
    Turk.
Lo, Micah, – the selfsame beard on chin
He was four times already converted in!
Here's a knife, clip quick – it's a sign of
    grace –
Or he ruins us all with his hanging-face.

8

Whom now is the bishop a-leering at?
I know a point where his text falls pat.
I'll tell him to-morrow, a word just now
Went to my heart and made me vow
I meddle no more with the worst of
    trades –
Let somebody else pay his serenades.

9

Groan all together now, whee – hee –
    hee!
It's a-work, it's a-work, ah, woe is me!
It began, when a herd of us, picked
    and placed,
Were spurred through the Corso,
    stripped to the waist;
Jew brutes, with sweat and blood well
    spent
To usher in worthily Christian Lent.

10

It grew, when the hangman entered our
    bounds:
Yelled, pricked us out to his church
    like hounds!
It got to a pitch, when the hand indeed
Which gutted my purse would throttle
    my creed:
And it overflows when, to even the
    odd,
Men I helped to their sins help me to
    their God.

11

But now, while the scapegoats leave
    our flock,
And the rest sit silent and count the
    clock,
Since forced to muse the appointed
    time
On these precious facts and truths
    sublime, –
Let us fitly employ it, under our breath,
In saying Ben Ezra's Song of Death.

12

For Rabbi Ben Ezra, the night he died,
Called sons and sons' sons to his side,
And spoke, 'This world has been harsh
    and strange;
'Something is wrong: there needeth a
    change.
'But what, or where? at the last or first?
'In one point only we sinned, at worst.

13

'The Lord will have mercy on Jacob yet,
'And again in his border see Israel set.
'When Judah beholds Jerusalem,
'The stranger-seed shall be joined to
    them:
'To Jacob's House shall the Gentiles
    cleave.
'So the Prophet saith and his sons believe.

14

'Ay, the children of the chosen race
'Shall carry and bring them to their
    place:
'In the land of the Lord shall lead the
    same,
'Bondsmen and handmaids. Who shall
    blame,
'When the slaves enslave, the oppressed
    ones o'er
'The oppressor triumph for evermore?

15

'God spoke, and gave us the word to
    keep,
'Bade never fold the hands nor sleep
' 'Mid a faithless world, – at watch and
    ward,
'Till Christ at the end relieve our guard.

'By His servant Moses the watch was set;
'Though near upon cock-crow, we keep
    it yet.

16

'Thou! if thou wast He, who at mid-
    watch came,
'By the starlight, naming a dubious name!
'And if, too heavy with sleep – too rash
'With fear – O Thou, if that martyr-gash
'Fell on Thee coming to take thine own,
'And we gave the Cross, when we owed
    the Throne –

17

'Thou art the Judge. We are bruised
    thus.
'But, the Judgment over, join sides with
    us!
'Thine too is the cause! and not more
    thine
'Than ours, is the work of these dogs
    and swine,
'Whose life laughs through and spits at
    their creed!
'Who maintain Thee in word, and defy
    Thee in deed!

18

'We withstood Christ then? Be mindful
    how
'At least we withstand Barabbas now!
'Was our outrage sore? But the worst we
    spared,
'To have called these – Christians, had
    we dared!
'Let defiance to them pay mistrust of
    Thee,
'And Rome make amends for Calvary!

19

'By the torture, prolonged from age to
    age,
'By the infamy, Israel's heritage,
'By the Ghetto's plague, by the garb's
    disgrace,
'By the badge of shame, by the felon's
    place,
'By the branding-tool, the bloody whip,
'And the summons to Christian
    fellowship, –

20

'We boast our proof that at least the Jew
'Would wrest Christ's name from the
    Devil's crew.
'Thy face took never so deep a shade
'But we fought them in it, God our aid!
'A trophy to bear, as we march, thy
    band,
'South, East, and on to the Pleasant
    Land!'
    [*Pope Gregory XVI abolished this bad
    business of the Sermon.* – R. B.]

## Protus

Among these latter busts we count by
    scores,
Half-emperors and quarter-emperors,
Each with his bay-leaf fillet, loose-
    thonged vest,
Loric[1] and low-browed Gorgon on the
    breast, – [[1] Cuirass or corslet of
    leather.]
One loves a baby face, with violets
    there,
Violets instead of laurel in the hair,
As those were all the little locks could
    bear.

Now read here. 'Protus ends a period
'Of empery beginning with a god;
'Born in the porphyry chamber at
    Byzant,
'Queens by his cradle, proud and
    ministrant:
'And if he quickened breath there,
    'twould like fire
'Pantingly through the dim vast realm
    transpire.
'A fame that he was missing spread
    afar:
'The world from its four corners, rose
    in war,
'Till he was borne out on a balcony
'To pacify the world when it should see.
'The captains ranged before him, one,
    his hand

'Made baby points at, gained the chief
      command.
'And day by day more beautiful he grew
'In shape, all said, in feature and in hue,
'While young Greek sculptors, gazing
      on the child,
'Became with old Greek sculpture
      reconciled.
'Already sages laboured to condense
'In easy tomes a life's experience:
'And artists took grave counsel to impart
'In one breath and one hand-sweep, all
      their art –
'To make his graces prompt as
      blossoming
'Of plentifully-watered palms in spring:
'Since well beseems it, whoso mounts
      the throne,
'For beauty, knowledge, strength,
      should stand alone,
'And mortals love the letters of his name.'

– Stop! Have you turned two pages?
      Still the same.
New reign, same date. The scribe goes
      on to say
How that same year, on such a month
      and day,
'John the Pannonian, groundedly
      believed
'A blacksmith's bastard, whose hard
      hand reprieved
'The Empire from its fate the year
      before, –
'Came, had a mind to take the crown,
      and wore
'The same for six years (during which
      the Huns
'Kept off their fingers from us), till his
      sons
'Put something in his liquor' – and so
      forth.
Then a new reign. Stay – 'Take at its
      just worth'
(Subjoins an annotator) 'what I give
'As hearsay. Some think, John let
      Protus live

'And slip away. 'Tis said, he reached
      man's age
'At some blind northern court; made,
      first a page,
'Then tutor to the children; last, of use
'About the hunting-stables. I deduce
'He wrote the little tract "On worming
      dogs,"
'Whereof the name in sundry catalogues
'Is extant yet. A Protus of the race
'Is rumoured to have died a monk in
      Thrace, –
'And if the same, he reached senility.'

Here's John the Smith's rough-
      hammered head. Great eye,
Gross jaw and griped lips do what
      granite can
To give you the crown-grasper. What a
      man!

## The Statue and the Bust

There's a palace in Florence, the world
      knows well,
And a statue watches it from the square,
And this story of both do our townsmen
      tell.

Ages ago, a lady there,
At the farthest window facing the East
Asked, 'Who rides by with the royal air?'

The bridesmaids' prattle around her
      ceased;
She leaned forth, one on either hand;
They saw how the blush of the bride
      increased –

They felt by its beats her heart expand –
As one at each ear and both in a breath
Whispered, 'The Great-Duke Ferdinand.'

That self-same instant, underneath,
The Duke rode past in his idle way,
Empty and fine like a swordless sheath.

Gay he rode, with a friend as gay,
Till he threw his head back – 'Who is
    she?'
– 'A bride the Riccardi brings home to-
    day.'

Hair in heaps lay heavily
Over a pale brow spirit-pure –
Carved like the heart of a coal-black tree,

Crisped like a war-steed's encolure
And vainly sought to dissemble her eyes
Of the blackest black our eyes endure.

And lo, a blade for a knight's emprise
Filled the fine empty sheath of a man, –
The Duke grew straightway brave and
    wise.

He looked at her, as a lover can;
She looked at him, as one who awakes:
The past was a sleep, and her life began.

Now, love so ordered for both their
    sakes,
A feast was held that selfsame night
In the pile which the mighty shadow
    makes.

(For Via Larga is three-parts light,
But the palace overshadows one,
Because of a crime which may God
    requite!

To Florence and God the wrong was
    done,
Through the first republic's murder there
By Cosimo and his cursed son.)

The Duke (with the statue's face in the
    square)
Turned in the midst of his multitude
At the bright approach of the bridal pair.

Face to face the lovers stood
A single minute and no more,
While the bridegroom bent as a man
    subdued –

Bowed till his bonnet brushed the
    floor –
For the Duke on the lady a kiss
    conferred,
As the courtly custom was of yore.

In a minute can lovers exchange a
    word?
If a word did pass, which I do not
    think,
Only one out of the thousand heard.

That was the bridegroom. At day's
    brink
He and his bride were alone at last
In a bedchamber by a taper's blink.

Calmly he said that her lot was cast,
That the door she had passed was shut
    on her
Till the final catafalk repassed.

The world meanwhile, its noise and
    stir,
Through a certain window facing the
    East,
She could watch like a convent's
    chronicler.

Since passing the door might lead to a
    feast,
And a feast might lead to so much
    beside,
He, of many evils, chose the least.

'Freely I choose too,' said the bride –
'Your window and its world suffice,'
Replied the tongue, while the heart
    replied –

'If I spend the night with that devil
    twice,
'May his window serve as my loop of
    hell
'Whence a damned soul looks on
    paradise!

'I fly to the Duke who loves me well,
'Sit by his side and laugh at sorrow
'Ere I count another ave-bell.

' 'Tis only the coat of a page to borrow,
'And tie my hair in a horse-boy's trim,
'And I save my soul – but not
        to-morrow' –

(She checked herself and her eye grew
        dim)
'My father tarries to bless my state:
'I must keep it one day more for him.

'Is one day more so long to wait?
'Moreover the Duke rides past, I know;
'We shall see each other, sure as fate.'

She turned on her side and slept. Just so!
So we resolve on a thing and sleep:
So did the lady, ages ago.

That night the Duke said, 'Dear or cheap
'As the cost of this cup of bliss may
        prove
'To body or soul, I will drain it deep.'

And on the morrow, bold with love,
He beckoned the bridegroom (close on
        call,
As his duty bade, by the Duke's alcove)

And smiled ' 'Twas a very funeral,
'Your lady will think, this feast of ours, –
'A shame to efface, whate'er befall!

'What if we break from the Arno bowers,
'And try if Petraja, cool and green,
'Cure last night's fault with this morning's
        flowers?'

The bridegroom, not a thought to be
        seen
On his steady brow and quiet mouth,
Said, 'Too much favour for me so mean!

'But, alas! my lady leaves the South;
'Each wind that comes from the Apennine
'Is a menace to her tender youth:

'Nor a way exists, the wise opine,
'If she quits her palace twice this year,
'To avert the flower of life's decline.'

Quoth the Duke, 'A sage and a kindly
        fear.
'Moreover Petraja is cold this spring:
'Be our feast to-night as usual here!'

And then to himself – 'Which night
        shall bring
'Thy bride to her lover's embraces, fool –
'Or I am the fool, and thou art the king!

'Yet my passion must wait a night, nor
        cool –
'For to-night the Envoy arrives from
        France
'Whose heart I unlock with thyself, my
        tool.

'I need thee still and might miss
        perchance.
'To-day is not wholly lost, beside,
'With its hope of my lady's
        countenance:

'For I ride – what should I do but ride?
'And passing her palace, if I list,
'May glance at its window – well betide!'

So said, so done: nor the lady missed
One ray that broke from the ardent
        brow,
Nor a curl of the lips where the spirit
        kissed.

Be sure that each renewed the vow,
No morrow's sun should arise and set
And leave them then as it left them now.

But next day passed, and next day yet,
With still fresh cause to wait one day
        more
Ere each leaped over the parapet.

And still, as love's brief morning wore,
With a gentle start, half smile, half sigh,
They found love not as it seemed before.

They thought it would work infallibly,
But not in despite of heaven and earth:
The rose would blow when the storm
    passed by.

Meantime they could profit in winter's
    dearth
By store of fruits that supplant the rose:
The world and its ways have a certain
    worth:

And to press a point while these oppose
Were simple policy; better wait:
We lose no friends and we gain no foes.

Meantime, worse fates than a lover's
    fate,
Who daily may ride and pass and look
Where his lady watches behind the grate!

And she – she watched the square like
    a book
Holding one picture and only one,
Which daily to find she undertook:

When the picture was reached the book
    was done,
And she turned from the picture at
    night to scheme
Of tearing it out for herself next sun.

So weeks grew months, years; gleam by
    gleam
The glory dropped from their youth
    and love,
And both perceived they had dreamed
    a dream;

Which hovered as dreams do, still above:
But who can take a dream for a truth?
Oh, hide our eyes from the next remove!

One day as the lady saw her youth
Depart, and the silver thread that
    streaked
Her hair, and, worn by the serpent's
    tooth,

The brow so puckered, the chin so
    peaked, –
And wondered who the woman was,
Hollow-eyed and haggard-cheeked,

Fronting her silent in the glass –
'Summon here,' she suddenly said,
'Before the rest of my old self pass,

'Him, the Carver, a hand to aid,
'Who fashions the clay no love will
    change,
'And fixes a beauty never to fade.

'Let Robbia's craft so apt and strange
'Arrest the remains of young and fair,
'And rivet them while the seasons range.

'Make me a face on the window there,
'Waiting as ever, mute the while,
'My love to pass below in the square!

'And let me think that it may beguile
'Dreary days which the dead must
    spend
'Down in their darkness under the aisle,

'To say, "What matters it at the end?
' "I did no more while my heart was
    warm
' "Than does that image, my pale-faced
    friend."

'Where is the use of the lip's red charm,
'The heaven of hair, the pride of the
    brow,
'And the blood that blues the inside
    arm –

'Unless we turn, as the soul knows
    how,
'The earthly gift to an end divine?
'A lady of clay is as good, I trow.'

But long ere Robbia's cornice, fine,
With flowers and fruits which leaves
    enlace,
Was set where now is the empty
    shrine –

(And, leaning out of a bright blue space,
As a ghost might lean from a chink of
    sky,
The passionate pale lady's face –

Eyeing ever, with earnest eye
And quick-turned neck at its breathless
    stretch,
Some one who ever is passing by – )

The Duke had sighed like the simplest
    wretch
In Florence, 'Youth – my dream escapes!
'Will its record stay?' And he bade them
    fetch

Some subtle moulder of brazen shapes –
'Can the soul, the will, die out of a man
'Ere his body find the grave that gapes?

'John of Douay shall effect my plan,
'Set me on horseback here aloft,
'Alive, as the crafty sculptor can,

'In the very square I have crossed so oft:
'That men may admire, when future
    suns
'Shall touch the eyes to a purpose soft,

'While the mouth and the brow stay
    brave in bronze –
'Admire and say, "When he was alive
' "How he would take his pleasure
    once!"

'And it shall go hard but I contrive
'To listen the while, and laugh in my
    tomb
'At idleness which aspires to strive.'

So! While these wait the trump of doom,
How do their spirits pass, I wonder,
Nights and days in the narrow room?

Still, I suppose, they sit and ponder
What a gift life was, ages ago,
Six steps out of the chapel yonder.

Only they see not God, I know,
Nor all that chivalry of his,
The soldier-saints who, row on row,

Burn upward each to his point of bliss –
Since, the end of life being manifest,
He had burned his way thro' the world
    to this.

I hear you reproach, 'But delay was best,
'For their end was a crime.' – Oh, a
    crime will do
As well, I reply, to serve for a test,

As a virtue golden through and through,
Sufficient to vindicate itself
And prove its worth at a moment's view!

Must a game be played for the sake of
    pelf?
Where a button goes, 'twere an epigram
To offer the stamp of the very Guelph.

The true has no value beyond the sham:
As well the counter as coin, I submit,
When your table's a hat, and your prize
    a dram.

Stake your counter as boldly every whit,
Venture as warily, use the same skill,
Do your best, whether winning or
    losing it,

If you choose to play! – is my principle.
Let a man contend to the uttermost
For his life's set prize, be it what it will!

The counter our lovers staked was lost
As surely as if it were lawful coin:
And the sin I impute to each frustrate
    ghost

Is – the unlit lamp and the ungirt loin,
Though the end in sight was a vice, I
    say.
You of the virtue (we issue join)
How strive you? *De te, fabula!*

## Porphyria's Lover

The rain set early in to-night,
    The sullen wind was soon awake,
It tore the elm-tops down for spite,
    And did its worst to vex the lake:
    I listened with heart fit to break.
When glided in Porphyria; straight
    She shut the cold out and the storm,
And kneeled and made the cheerless
        grate
    Blaze up, and all the cottage warm;
    Which done, she rose, and from her
        form
Withdrew the dripping cloak and shawl,
    And laid her soiled gloves by, untied
Her hat and let the damp hair fall,
    And, last, she sat down by my side
    And called me. When no voice replied,
She put my arm about her waist,
    And made her smooth white
        shoulder bare,
And all her yellow hair displaced,
    And, stooping, made my cheek lie
        there,
    And spread, o'er all, her yellow hair,
Murmuring how she loved me – she
    Too weak, for all her heart's endeavour,
To set its struggling passion free
    From pride, and vainer ties dissever,
    And give herself to me for ever.
But passion sometimes would prevail,
    Nor could to-night's gay feast restrain
A sudden thought of one so pale
    For love of her, and all in vain:
    So, she was come through wind and
        rain.
Be sure I looked up at her eyes
    Happy and proud; at last I knew
Porphyria worshipped me; surprise
    Made my heart swell, and still it grew
    While I debated what to do.
That moment she was mine, mine, fair,
    Perfectly pure and good: I found
A thing to do, and all her hair
    In one long yellow string I wound
    Three times her little throat around,

And strangled her. No pain felt she;
    I am quite sure she felt no pain.
As a shut bud that holds a bee,
    I warily oped her lids: again
    Laughed the blue eyes without a stain.
And I untightened next the tress
    About her neck; her cheek once more
Blushed bright beneath my burning
        kiss:
    I propped her head up as before,
    Only, this time my shoulder bore
Her head, which droops upon it still:
    The smiling rosy little head,
So glad it has its utmost will,
    That all it scorned at once is fled,
    And I, its love, am gained instead!
Porphyria's love: she guessed not how
    Her darling one wish would be heard.
And thus we sit together now,
    And all night long we have not stirred,
    And yet God has not said a word!

## 'Childe Roland to the Dark Tower Came'

*(See Edgar's song in 'Lear')*

1

My first thought was, he lied in every
        word,
    That hoary cripple, with malicious
        eye
    Askance to watch the working of his
        lie
On mine, and mouth scarce able to
        afford
Suppression of the glee, that pursed
        and scored
    Its edge, at one more victim gained
        thereby.

2

What else should he be set for, with
        his staff?
    What, save to waylay with his lies,
        ensnare
    All travellers who might find him
        posted there,

And ask the road? I guessed what
   skull-like laugh
Would break, what crutch 'gin write
   my epitaph
    For pastime in the dusty thoroughfare,

3

If at his counsel I should turn aside
   Into that ominous tract which, all
    agree,
    Hides the Dark Tower. Yet
    acquiescingly
I did turn as he pointed: neither pride
Nor hope rekindling at the end descried,
   So much as gladness that some end
    might be.

4

For, what with my whole world-wide
   wandering,
   What with my search drawn out
    thro' years, my hope
   Dwindled into a ghost not fit to cope
With that obstreperous joy success
   would bring,
I hardly tired now to rebuke the spring
   My heart made, finding failure in its
    scope.

5

As when a sick man very near to death
   Seems dead indeed, and feels begin
    and end
    The tears and takes the farewell of
    each friend,
And hears one bid the other go, draw
   breath
Freelier outside, ('since all is o'er,' he
   saith,
    'And the blow fallen no grieving can
    amend;')

6

While some discuss if near the other
   graves
   Be room enough for this, and when
    a day
   Suits best for carrying the corpse away,
With care about the banners, scarves
   and staves:

And still the man hears all, and only
   craves
   He may not shame such tender love
    and stay.

7

Thus, I had so long suffered in this
   quest,
   Heard failure prophesied so oft, been
    writ
   So many times among 'The Band' –
    to wit,
The knights who to the Dark Tower's
   search addressed
Their steps – that just to fail as they,
   seemed best,
   And all the doubt was now – should
    I be fit?

8

So, quiet as despair, I turned from him,
   That hateful cripple, out of his highway
   Into the path he pointed. All the day
Had been a dreary one at best, and dim
Was settling to its close, yet shot one
   grim
   Red leer to see the plain catch its
    estray.

9

For mark! no sooner was I fairly found
   Pledged to the plain, after a pace or
    two,
   Than, pausing to throw backward a
    last view
O'er the safe road, 'twas gone; grey
   plain all round:
Nothing but plain to the horizon's bound.
   I might go on; nought else remained
    to do.

10

So, on I went. I think I never saw
   Such starved ignoble nature; nothing
    throve:
    For flowers – as well expect a cedar
    grove!
But cockle, spurge, according to their
   law
Might propagate their kind, with none
    to awe,

You'd think; a burr had been a
   treasure-trove.

11

No! penury, inertness and grimace,
   In some strange sort, were the land's
      portion. 'See
   'Or shut your eyes,' said Nature
      peevishly,
'It nothing skills: I cannot help my case:
' 'Tis the Last Judgment's fire must
      cure this place,
   'Calcine its clods and set my prisoners
      free.'

12

If there pushed any ragged thistle-stalk
   Above its mates, the head was
      chopped; the bents
   Were jealous else. What made those
      holes and rents
In the dock's harsh swarth leaves,
      bruised as to baulk
All hope of greenness? 'tis a brute must
      walk
Pashing their life out, with a brute's
      intents.

13

As for the grass, it grew as scant as hair
   In leprosy; thin dry blades pricked
      the mud
   Which underneath looked kneaded
      up with blood.
One stiff blind horse, his every bone a-
      stare,
Stood stupefied, however he came there:
   Thrust out past service from the devil's
      stud!

14

Alive? he might be dead for aught I
      know,
   With that red gaunt and colloped
      neck a-strain.
   And shut eyes underneath the rusty
      mane;
Seldom went such grotesqueness with
      such woe;
I never saw a brute I hated so;

He must be wicked to deserve such
      pain.

15

I shut my eyes and turned them on my
      heart.
   As a man calls for wine before he
      fights,
   I asked one draught of earlier,
      happier sights,
Ere fitly I could hope to play my part.
Think first, fight afterwards – the
      soldier's art:
   One taste of the old time sets all to
      rights.

16

Not it! I fancied Cuthbert's reddening
      face
   Beneath its garniture of curly gold,
   Dear fellow, till I almost felt him fold
An arm in mine to fix me to the place,
That way he used. Alas, one night's
      disgrace!
   Out went my heart's new fire and
      left it cold.

17

Giles then, the soul of honour – there
      he stands
   Frank as ten years ago when knighted
      first.
   What honest man should dare (he
      said) he durst.
Good – but the scene shifts – faugh!
      what hangman hands
Pin to his breast a parchment? His own
      bands
   Read it. Poor traitor, spit upon and
      curst!

18

Better this present than a past like that;
   Back therefore to my darkening path
      again!
   No sound, no sight as far as eye
      could strain.
Will the night send a howlet or a bat?
I asked: when something on the dismal
      flat

Came to arrest my thoughts and
   change their train.

### 19

A sudden little river crossed my path
   As unexpected as a serpent comes.
   No sluggish tide congenial to the
     glooms;
This, as it frothed by, might have been
   a bath
For the fiend's glowing hoof – to see
   the wrath
   Of its black eddy bespate with flakes
   and spumes.

### 20

So petty yet so spiteful! All along,
   Low scrubby alders kneeled down
     over it;
   Drenched willows flung them head-
     long in a fit
Of mute despair, a suicidal throng:
The river which had done them all the
   wrong,
   Whate'er that was, rolled by, deterred
   no whit.

### 21

Which, while I forded, – good saints,
   how I feared
   To set my foot upon a dead man's
     cheek,
   Each step, or feel the spear I thrust
     to seek
For hollows, tangled in his hair or beard!
– It may have been a water-rat I speared,
   But, ugh! it sounded like a baby's
   shriek.

### 22

Glad was I when I reached the other
   bank.
   Now for a better country. Vain
     presage!
   Who were the strugglers, what war
     did they wage,
Whose savage trample thus could pad
   the dank
Soil to a plash? Toads in a poisoned
   tank,
   Or wild cats in a red-hot iron cage –

### 23

The fight must so have seemed in that
   fell cirque.
   What penned them there, with all
     the plain to choose?
   No foot-print leading to that horrid
     mews,
None out of it. Mad brewage set to work
Their brains, no doubt, like galley-slaves
   the Turk
   Pits for this pastime, Christians
   against Jews.

### 24

And more than that – a furlong on –
   why, there!
   What bad use was that engine for,
     that wheel,
   Or brake, not wheel – that harrow fit
     to reel
Men's bodies out like silk? with all the air
Of Tophet's tool, on earth left unaware,
   Or brought to sharpen its rusty teeth
   of steel.

### 25

Then came a bit of stubbed ground,
   once a wood,
   Next a marsh, it would seem, and
     now mere earth
   Desperate and done with; (so a fool
     finds mirth,
Makes a thing and then mars it, till his
   mood
Changes and off he goes!) within a rood –
   Bog, clay and rubble, sand and stark
   black dearth.

### 26

Now blotches rankling, coloured gay
   and grim,
   Now patches where some leanness
     of the soil's
   Broke into moss or substances like
     boils;
Then came some palsied oak, a cleft in
   him
Like a distorted mouth that splits its rim
   Gaping at death, and dies while it
   recoils.

### 27

And just as far as ever from the end!
　Nought in the distance but the
　　evening, nought
　To point my footstep further! At the
　　thought,
A great black bird, Apollyon's bosom-
　friend,
Sailed past, nor beat his wide wing
　dragon-penned
　That brushed my cap – perchance
　　the guide I sought.

### 28

For, looking up, aware I somehow grew,
　'Spite of the dusk, the plain had given
　　place
　All round to mountains – with such
　　name to grace
Mere ugly heights and heaps now
　stolen in view.
How thus they had surprised me, –
　solve it, you!
　How to get from them was no clearer
　　case.

### 29

Yet half I seemed to recognize some trick
　Of mischief happened to me, God
　　knows when –
　In a bad dream perhaps. Here ended,
　　then,
Progress this way. When, in the very nick
Of giving up, one time more, came a
　click
　As when a trap shuts – you're inside
　　the den!

### 30

Burningly it came on me all at once,
　This was the place! those two hills
　　on the right,
　Crouched like two bulls locked horn
　　in horn in fight;
While to the left, a tall scalped
　mountain … Dunce,
Dotard, a-dozing at the very nonce,
　After a life spent training for the
　　sight!

### 31

What in the midst lay but the Tower
　itself?
　The round squat turret, blind as the
　　fool's heart,
　Built of brown stone, without a
　　counterpart
In the whole world. The tempest's
　mocking elf
Points to the shipman thus the unseen
　shelf
　He strikes on, only when the timbers
　　start.

### 32

Not see? because of night perhaps? –
　why, day
　Came back again for that! before it
　　left,
　The dying sunset kindled through a
　　cleft:
The hills, like giants at a hunting, lay,
Chin upon hand, to see the game at
　bay, –
　'Now stab and end the creature – to
　　the heft!'

### 33

Not hear? when noise was everywhere!
　it tolled
　Increasing like a bell. Names in my
　　ears
　Of all the lost adventurers my peers, –
How such a one was strong, and such
　was bold,
And such was fortunate, yet each of old
　Lost, lost! one moment knelled the
　　woe of years.

### 34

There they stood, ranged along the
　hillsides, met
　To view the last of me, a living frame
　For one more picture! in a sheet of
　　flame
I saw them and I knew them all. And yet
Dauntless the slug-horn to my lips I set,
　And blew. 'Childe Roland to the Dark
　　Tower came.'

# LURIA

### A Tragedy

### 1846

I dedicate this last attempt for the present at dramatic poetry to a great dramatic poet;
'Wishing what I write may be read by his light:'
If a phrase originally addressed,
By not the least worthy of his contemporaries,
To Shakespeare,
May be applied here, by one whose sole privilege is in a grateful admiration,

To Walter Savage Landor

London, 1846.

### Persons

Luria, *a Moor. Commander of the Florentine Forces.* Husain, *Moor his friend.*
Puccio, *the old Florentine Commander, now* Luria's *chief officer.* Braccio.
*Commissary of the Republic of Florence.* Jacopo (Lapo), *his secretary,*
Tiburzio, *Commander of the Pisans.* Domizia, *a noble Florentine lady.*
*Scene –* Luria's *Camp between Florence and Pisa. Time 14—.*

### ACT 1

*Morning*
BRACCIO, *dictating to his* SECRETARY;
PUCCIO *standing by.*

*Brac.* [*to* PUCCIO ], Then, you join
battle in an hour?
*Puc.*                    Not I;
Luria, the captain.
*Brac.* [*to the* SECRETARY]. 'In an hour,
the battle.'
[*To* Puccio.] Sir, let your eye run o'er
this loose digest,
And see if very much of your report
Have slipped away through my civilian
phrase.
Does this instruct the Signory aright
How army stands with army?
*Puc.* [*taking the paper*]. All seems here:
– That Luria, seizing with our city's
force
The several points of vantage, hill and
plain,
Shuts Pisa safe from help on every side,
And, baffling the Lucchese arrived too
late,
Must, in the battle he delivers now,

Beat her best troops and first of chiefs.
*Brac.*                              So sure?
Tiburzio's a consummate captain too!
*Puc.* Luria holds Pisa's fortune in his
hand.
*Brac.* [*to the* SECRETARY]. 'The Signory
hold Pisa in their hand.'
Your own proved soldiership's our
warrant, sir:
So, while my secretary ends his task,
Have out two horsemen, by the open
roads,
To post with it to Florence!
*Puc.* [*returning the paper*]. All seems
here;
Unless … Ser Braccio, 'tis my last
report!
Since Pisa's outbreak, and my overthrow,
And Luria's hastening at the city's call
To save her, as he only could, no doubt;
Till now that she is saved or sure
to be, –
Whatever you tell Florence, I tell you:
Each day's note you, her Commissary,
make
Of Luria's movements, I myself supply.
No youngster am I longer, to my cost;

Therefore while Florence gloried in her choice
And vaunted Luria, whom but Luria, still,
As if zeal, courage, prudence, conduct, faith,
Had never met in any man before,
I saw no pressing need to swell the cry.
But now, this last report and I have done:
So, ere to-night comes with its roar of praise,
'Twere not amiss if some one old i' the trade
Subscribed with, 'True, for once rash counsel's best.
'This Moor of the bad faith and doubtful race,
'This boy to whose untried sagacity,
'Raw valour, Florence trusts without reserve
'The charge to save her, – justifies her choice;
'In no point has this stranger failed his friends.
'Now praise!' I say this, and it is not here.
*Brac.* [*to the* SECRETARY]. Write, 'Puccio, superseded in the charge,
'By Luria, bears full witness to his worth,
'And no reward our Signory can give
'Their champion but he'll back it cheerfully.'
Aught more? Five minutes hence, both messengers!          [PUCCIO *goes.*
*Brac.* [*after a pause, and while he slowly tears the paper into shreds*]. I think
        … (pray God, I hold in fit contempt
This warfare's noble art and ordering,
And, – once the brace of prizers fairly matched,
Poleaxe with poleaxe, knife with knife as good, –
Spit properly at what men term their skill! – )
Yet here I think our fighter has the odds.

With Pisa's strength diminished thus and thus,
Such points of vantage in our hands and such,
Lucca still off the stage, too, – all's assured:
Luria must win this battle. Write the Court,
That Luria's trial end and sentence pass!
*Sec.* Patron, –
*Brac.*          Ay, Lapo?
*Sec.*                    If you trip, I fall;
'Tis in self-interest I speak –
*Brac.*                    Nay, nay,
You overshoot the mark, my Lapo! Nay!
When did I say pure love's impossible?
I make you daily write those red cheeks thin,
Load your young brow with what concerns it least,
And, when we visit Florence, let you pace
The Piazza by my side as if we talked,
Where all your old acquaintances may see:
You'd die for me, I should not be surprised.
Now then!
*Sec.* Sir, look about and love yourself!
Step after step, the Signory and you
Tread gay till this tremendous point's to pass;
Which pass not, pass not, ere you ask yourself, –
Bears the brain steadily such draughts of fire,
Or too delicious may not prove the pride
Of this long secret trial you dared plan,
Dare execute, you solitary here,
With the grey-headed toothless fools at home,
Who think themselves your lords, such slaves are they?
If they pronounce this sentence as you bid,
Declare the treason, claim its penalty, –

And sudden out of all the blaze of life,
On the best minute of his brightest
      day,
From that adoring army at his back,
Thro' Florence' joyous crowds before
      his face,
Into the dark you beckon Luria ...
*Brac.*                                Then –
Why, Lapo, when the fighting-people
      vaunt,
We of the other craft and mystery,
May we not smile demure, the danger
      past?
*Sec.* Sir, no, no, no, – the danger, and
      your spirit
At watch and ward? Where's danger on
      your part,
With that thin flitting instantaneous
      steel
'Gainst the blind bull-front of a brute-
      force world?
If Luria, that's to perish sure as fate,
Should have been really guiltless after
      all?
*Brac.*    Ah, you have thought that?
*Sec.*                    Here I sit? your scribe,
And in and out goes Luria, days and
      nights;
This Puccio comes; the Moor his other
      friend,
Husain; they talk – that's all feigned
      easily;
He speaks (I would not listen if I could),
Reads, orders, counsels: – but he rests
      sometimes, –
I see him stand and eat, sleep stretched
      an hour
On the lynx-skins yonder; hold his
      bared black arms
Into the sun from the tent-opening;
      laugh
When his horse drops the forage from
      his teeth
And neighs to hear him hum his Moorish
      songs.
That man believes in Florence, as the
      saint

Tied to the wheel believes in God.
*Brac.*                                How strange!
You too have thought that!
*Sec.*                Do but you think too,
And all is saved! I only have to write,
'The man seemed false awhile, proves
      true at last,
'Bury it' – so I write the Signory –
'Bury this trial in your breast for ever,
'Blot it from things or done or dreamed
      about!
'So Luria shall receive his meed to-day
'With no suspicion what reverse was
      near, –
'As if no meteoric finger hushed
'The doom-word just on the destroyer's
      lip,
'Motioned him off, and let life's sun fall
      straight.'
*Brac.* [*looks to the wall of the tent*]. Did he
      draw that?
*Sec.*        With charcoal, when the watch
Made the report at midnight; Lady
      Domizia
Spoke of the unfinished Duomo, you
      remember;
That is his fancy how a Moorish front
Might join to, and complete, the body,
      – a sketch, –
And again where the cloak hangs, yonder
      in the shadow.
*Brac.* He loves that woman.
*Sec.*                        She is sent the spy
Of Florence, – spies on you as you on
      him:
Florence, if only for Domizia's sake,
Is surely safe. What shall I write?
*Brac.*                                I see –
A Moorish front, nor of such ill design!
Lapo, there's one thing plain and
      positive;
Man seeks his own good at the whole
      world's cost.
What? If to lead our troops, stand forth
      our chiefs,
And hold our fate, and see us at their
      beck,

Yet render up the charge when peace
    return,
Have ever proved too much for
    Florentines,
Even for the best and bravest of
    ourselves –
If in the struggle when the soldier's
    sword
Should sink its point before the statist's
    pen,
And the calm head replace the violent
    hand,
Virtue on virtue still have fallen away
Before ambition with unvarying fate,
Till Florence' self at last in bitterness
Be forced to own such falls the natural
    end,
And, sparing further to expose her sons
To a vain strife and profitless disgrace,
Declare, 'The foreigner, one not my
    child,
'Shall henceforth lead my troops, reach
    height by height
'The glory, then descend into the shame;
'So shall rebellion be less guilt in him,
'And punishment the easier task for
    me:'
– If on the best of us such brand she set,
Can I suppose an utter alien here,
This Luria, our inevitable foe,
Confessed a mercenary and a Moor,
Born free from many ties that bind the
    rest
Of common faith in Heaven or hope
    on earth,
No past with us, no future, – such a
    spirit
Shall hold the path from which our
    staunchest broke,
Stand firm where every famed precursor
    fell?
My Lapo, I will frankly say, these proofs
So duly noted of the man's intent,
Are for the doting fools at home, not
    me.
The charges here, they may be true or
    false:

– What is set down? Errors and over-
    sights,
A dallying interchange of courtesies
With Pisa's General, – all that, hour by
    hour,
Puccio's pale discontent has furnished
    us,
Of petulant speeches, inconsiderate acts,
Now overhazard, overcaution now;
Even that he loves this lady who believes
She outwits Florence, and whom
    Florence posted
By my procurement here, to spy on me,
Lest I one minute lose her from my
    sight –
She who remembering her whole House's
    fall,
That nest of traitors strangled in the
    birth,
Now labours to make Luria (poor device
As plain) the instrument of her revenge
– That she is ever at his ear to prompt
Inordinate conceptions of his worth,
Exorbitant belief in worth's reward,
And after, when sure disappointment
    follows,
Proportionable rage at such a wrong –
Why, all these reasons, while I urge
    them most,
Weigh with me less than least – as
    nothing weigh.
Upon that broad man's-heart of his, I
    go:
On what I know must be, yet, while I
    live,
Shall never be, because I live and
    know.
Brute-force shall not rule Florence!
    Intellect
May rule her, bad or good as chance
    supplies:
But intellect it shall be, pure if bad,
And intellect's tradition so kept up.
Till the good come – 'twas intellect
    that ruled,
Not brute-force bringing from the
    battlefield

The attributes of wisdom, foresight's
  graces
We lent it there to lure its grossness on;
All which it took for earnest and kept
  safe
To show against us in our market-place,
Just as the plumes and tags and
  swordsman's-gear
(Fetched from the camp where, at their
  foolish best,
When all was done they frightened
  nobody)
Perk in our faces in the street, forsooth,
With our own warrant and allowance.
  No!
The whole procedure's overcharged, –
  its end
In too strict keeping with the bad first
  step.
To conquer Pisa was sheer inspiration?
Well then, to perish for a single fault,
Let that be simple justice! There, my
  Lapo!
A Moorish front ill suits our Duomo's
  body:
Blot it out – and bid Luria's sentence
  come!

> [LURIA, *who, with* DOMIZIA,
> *has entered unobserved at
> the close of the last
> phrase, now advances.*

*Lur.* And Luria, Luria, what of Luria
  now?
*Brac.* Ah, you so close, sir? Lady Domizia
  too?
I said it needs must be a busy moment
For one like you: that you were now i'
  the thick
Of your duties, doubtless, while we
  idlers sat …
*Lur.* No – in that paper, – it was in that
  paper
What you were saying!
*Brac.*         Oh – my day's despatch!
I censure you to Florence: will you see?
*Lur.* See your despatch, your last, for
  the first time?

Well, if I should, now? For in truth,
  Domizia,
He would be forced to set about another,
In his sly cool way, the true Florentine,
To mention that important circumstance.
So, while he wrote I should gain time,
  such time!
Do not send this!
*Brac.*         And wherefore?
*Lur.*                  These Lucchese
Are not arrived – they never will arrive!
And I must fight to-day, arrived or not,
And I shall beat Tiburzio, that is sure:
And then will be arriving his Lucchese,
But slowly, oh so slowly, just in time
To look upon my battle from the hills,
Like a late moon, of use to nobody!
And I must break my battle up, send
  forth,
Surround on this side, hold in check
  on that.
Then comes to-morrow, we negotiate,
You make me send for fresh instructions
  home,
– Incompleteness, incompleteness!
*Brac.*              Ah, we scribes!
Why, I had registered that very point,
The non-appearance of our foes' ally,
As a most happy fortune; both at once
Were formidable: singly faced, each
  falls.
*Lur.* So, no great battle for my Florentines!
No crowning deed, decisive and
  complete,
For all of them, the simple as the wise,
Old, young, alike, that do not under-
  stand
Our wearisome pedantic art of war,
By which we prove retreat may be
  success,
Delay – best speed, – half loss, at times,
  – whole gain:
They want results: as if it were their
  fault!
And you, with warmest wish to be my
  friend,
Will not be able now to simply say

'Your servant has performed his task –
    enough!
'You ordered, he has executed: good!
'Now walk the streets in holiday attire,
'Congratulate your friends, till noon
    strikes fierce,
'Then form bright groups beneath the
    Duomo's shade!'
No, you will have to argue and explain,
Persuade them, all is not so ill in the
    end,
Tease, tire them out! Arrive, arrive,
    Lucchese!
*Dom.* Well, you will triumph for the
    past enough,
Whatever be the present chance; no
    service
Falls to the ground with Florence: she
    awaits
Her saviour, will receive him fittingly.
*Lur.* Ah Braccio, you know Florence!
    Will she, think you,
Receive one … what means 'fittingly
    receive'?
– Receive compatriots, doubtless – I
    am none:
And yet Domizia promises so much!
*Brac.* Kind women still give men a
    woman's prize.
I know not o'er which gate most boughs
    will arch,
Nor if the Square will wave red flags or
    blue.
I should have judged, the fullest of
    rewards
Our state gave Luria, when she made
    him chief
Of her whole force, in her best captain's
    place.
*Lur.* That, my reward? Florence on my
    account
Relieved Ser Puccio? – mark you, my
    reward!
And Puccio's having all the fight's true
    joy –
Goes here and there, gets close, may
    fight, himself,

While I must order, stand aloof, o'ersee.
That was my calling, there was my true
    place!
I should have felt, in some one over me,
Florence impersonate, my visible head,
As I am over Puccio, – taking life
Directly from her eye! They give me you:
But do you cross me, set me half to
    work?
I enjoy nothing – though I will, for once!
Decide, shall we join battle? may I wait?
*Brac.* Let us compound the matter; wait
    till noon:
Then, no arrival, –
*Lur.*           Ah, noon comes too fast!
I wonder, do you guess why I delay
Involuntarily the final blow
As long as possible? Peace follows it!
Florence at peace, and the calm
    studious heads
Come out again, the penetrating eyes;
As if a spell broke, all's resumed, each
    art
You boast, more vivid that it slept awhile.
'Gainst the glad heaven, o'er the white
    palace-front
The interrupted scaffold climbs anew;
The walls are peopled by the painter's
    brush;
The statue to its niche ascends to dwell.
The present noise and trouble have
    retired
And left the eternal past to rule once
    more;
You speak its speech and read its
    records plain,
Greece lives with you, each Roman
    breathes your friend:
But Luria – where will then be Luria's
    place?
*Dom.* Highest in honour, for that past's
    own sake,
Of which his actions, sealing up the sum
By saving all that went before from
    wreck,
Will range as part, with which be
    worshipped too.

*Lur.* Then I may walk and watch you in
    your streets,
Lead the smooth life my rough life
    helps no more,
So different, so new, so beautiful –
Nor fear that you will tire to see parade
The club that slew the lion, now that
    crooks
And shepherd-pipes come into use again?
For very lone and silent seems my East
In its drear vastness: still it spreads,
    and still
No Braccios, no Domizias anywhere –
Not ever more! Well, well, to-day is ours!
*Dom.* [*to* BRACCIO]. Should he not have
    been one of us?
*Lur.*                Oh, no!
Not one of you, and so escape the thrill
Of coming into you, of changing thus, –
Feeling a soul grow on me that restricts
The boundless unrest of the savage heart!
The sea heaves up, hangs loaded o'er
    the land,
Breaks there and buries its tumultuous
    strength;
Horror, and silence, and a pause awhile:
Lo, inland glides the gulf-stream, miles
    away,
In rapture of assent, subdued and still,
'Neath those strange banks, those
    unimagined skies.
Well, 'tis not sure the quiet lasts for ever!
Your placid heads still find rough
    hands new work;
Some minute's chance – there comes
    the need of mine:
And, all resolved on, I too hear at last.
Oh, you must find some use for me,
    Ser Braccio!
You hold my strength; 'twere best
    dispose of it:
What you created, see that you find
    food for –
I shall be dangerous else!
*Brac.*        How dangerous, sir?
*Lur.* There are so many ways, Domizia
    warns me,

And one with half the power that I
    possess,
– Grows very formidable. Do you doubt?
Why, first, who holds the army …
*Dom.*                While we talk,
Morn wears; we keep you from your
    proper place,
The field.
*Lur.*    Nay, to the field I move no
    more;
My part is done, and Puccio's may
    begin:
I cannot trench upon his province
    longer
With any face. – You think yourselves
    so safe?
Why, see – in concert with Tiburzio,
    now –
One could …
*Dom.*        A trumpet!
*Lur.*                My Lucchese at last!
Arrived, as sure as Florence stands!
    Your leave!                [*Springs out.*
*Dom.* How plainly is true greatness
    charactered
By such unconscious sport as Luria's
    here,
Strength sharing least the secret of
    itself!
Be it with head that schemes or hand
    that acts,
Such save the world which none but
    they could save,
Yet think whate'er they did, that world
    could do.
*Brac.* Yes: and how worthy note, that
    these same great ones
In hand or head, with such
    unconsciousness
And all its due entailed humility,
Should never shrink, so far as I
    perceive,
From taking up whatever tool there be
Effects the whole world's safety or
    mishap,
Into their mild hands as a thing of
    course!

The statist finds it natural to lead
The mob who might as easily lead him –
The captain marshals troops born
    skilled in war –
Statist and captain verily believe!
While we poor scribes … you catch me
    thinking now,
That I shall in this very letter write
What none of you are able! To it, Lapo!
              [DOMIZIA goes.
This last worst all-affected childish fit
Of Luria's, this be-praised
    unconsciousness,
Convinces me; the past was no child's
    play:
It was a man beat Pisa, – not a child.
All's mere dissimulation – to remove
The fear, he best knows we should
    entertain.
The utmost danger was at hand. Is't
    written?
Now make a duplicate, lest this should
    fail,
And speak your fullest on the other side.
*Sec*. I noticed he was busily repairing
My half-effacement of his Duomo sketch,
And, while he spoke of Florence,
    turned to it,
As the Mage Negro king to Christ the
    babe.
I judge his childishness the mere relapse
To boyhood of a man who has worked
    lately,
And presently will work, so, meantime,
    plays:
Whence, more than ever I believe in
    him.
*Brac*. [*after a pause*]. The sword! At
    best, the soldier, as he says,
In Florence – the black face, the
    barbarous name,
For Italy to boast her show of the age,
Her man of men! To Florence with
    each letter!

## ACT 2

### Noon

*Dom*. Well, Florence, shall I reach thee,
    pierce thy heart
Thro' all its safeguards? Hate is said to
    help –
Quicken the eye, invigorate the arm;
And this my hate, made up of many
    hates,
Might stand in scorn of visible
    instrument,
And will thee dead: yet do I trust it not.
Nor man's devices nor Heaven's memory
Of wickedness forgot on earth so soon,
But thy own nature, – hell and thee I
    trust,
To keep thee constant in that wickedness,
Where my revenge may meet thee. Turn
    aside
A single step, for gratitude or shame, –
Grace but this Luria, – this wild mass
    of rage
I have prepared to launch against thee
    now, –
With other payment than thy noblest
    found, –
Give his desert for once its due reward, –
And past thee would my sure destruction
    roll.
But thou, who mad'st our House thy
    sacrifice,
It cannot be thou wilt except this Moor
From the accustomed fate of zeal and
    truth:
Thou wilt deny his looked-for
    recompense,
And then – I reach thee. Old and trained,
    my sire
Could bow down on his quiet broken
    heart,
Die awe-struck and submissive, when
    at last
The strange blow came for the expected
    wreath;
And Porzio passed in blind bewilderment
To exile, never to return, – they say,

Perplexed in his frank simple honest
    soul,
As if some natural law had changed, –
    how else
Could Florence, on plain fact
    pronouncing thus,
Judge Porzio's actions worthy such
    reward?
But Berto, with the ever-passionate
    pulse,
– Oh that long night, its dreadful hour
    on hour,
In which no way of getting his fair fame
From their inexplicable charges free,
Was found, save pouring forth the
    impatient blood
To show its colour whether false or no!
My brothers never had a friend like me
Close in their need to watch the time,
    then speak,
– Burst with a wakening laughter on
    their dream,
Cry, 'Florence was all falseness, so,
    false here!'
And show them what a simple task
    remained –
To leave dreams, rise, and punish in
    God's name
The city wedded to the wickedness.
None stood by them as I by Luria stand.
So, when the stranger cheated of his due
Turns on thee as his rapid nature bids.
Then, Florence, think, a hireling at thy
    throat
For the first outrage, think who bore thy
    last,
Yet mutely in forlorn obedience died!
He comes – his friend – black faces in
    the camp
Where moved those peerless brows and
    eyes of old.

        *Enter* LURIA *and* HUSAIN.

*Dom.* Well, and the movement – is it
    as you hope?
'Tis Lucca?
*Lur.* Ah, the Pisan trumpet merely!
Tiburzio's envoy, I must needs receive.

*Dom.* Whom I withdraw before; tho' if
    I lingered
You could not wonder, for my time
    fleets fast.
The overtaking night brings such
    reward!
And where will then be room for me?
    Yet, praised,
Remember who was first to promise
    praise,
And envy those who also can perform!
                            [*Goes.*
*Lur.* This trumpet from the Pisans? –
*Hus.*                            In the camp;
A very noble presence – Braccio's
    visage
On Puccio's body – calm and fixed and
    good;
A man I seem as I had seen before:
Most like, it was some statue had the
    face.
*Lur.* Admit him! This will prove the last
    delay.
*Hus.* Ay, friend, go on, and die thou
    going on!
Thou heardst what the grave woman
    said but now:
To-night rewards thee. That is well to
    hear;
But stop not therefore: hear it, and go
    on!
*Lur.* Oh, their reward and triumph and
    the rest
They round me in the ears with, all day
    long?
All that, I never take for earnest, friend!
Well would it suit us, – their triumphal
    arch
Or storied pillar, – thee and me, the
    Moors!
But gratitude in those Italian eyes –
That, we shall get?
*Hus.*                    It is too cold an air.
Our sun rose out of yonder mound of
    mist:
Where is he now? So, I trust none of
    them.

*Lur*. Truly?

*Hus*.      I doubt and fear. There stands
      a wall
'Twixt our expansive and explosive race
And those absorbing, concentrating men.
They use thee.

*Lur*.           And I feel it, Husain! yes,
And care not – yes, an alien force like
      mine
Is only called to play its part outside
Their different nature; where its sole
      use seems
To fight with and keep off an adverse
      force,
As alien, – which repelled, mine too
      withdraws:
Inside, they know not what to do with
      me.
Thus I have told them laughingly and
      oft,
But long since am prepared to learn
      the worst.

*Hus*.  What is the worst?

*Lur*.      I will forestall them, Husain,
Will speak the destiny they dare not
      speak –
Banish myself before they find the heart.
I will be first to say, 'The work rewards!
'I know, for all your praise, my use is
      over,
'So may it prove! – meanwmle 'tis best
      I go,
'Go carry safe my memories of you all
'To other scenes of action, newer
      lands.' –
Thus leaving them confirmed in their
      belief
They would not easily have tired of me.
You think this hard to say?

*Hus*.                  Say or not say,
So thou but go, so they but let thee go!
This hating people, that hate each the
      other,
And in one blandness to us Moors
      unite –
Locked each to each like slippery
      snakes, I say,

Which still in all their tangles, hissing
      tongue
And threatening tail, ne'er do each
      other harm;
While any creature of a better blood,
They seem to fight for, while they circle
      safe
And never touch it, – pines without a
      wound,
Withers away beside their eyes and
      breath.
See thou, if Puccio come not safely out
Of Braccio's grasp, this Braccio sworn
      his foe,
As Braccio safely from Domizia's toils
Who hates him most! But thou, the
      friend of all,
. . . Come out of them!

*Lur*.               The Pisan trumpet now!

*Hus*. Breathe free – it is an enemy, no
      friend!                              [*Goes*.

*Lur*. He keeps his instincts, no new
      culture mars
Their perfect use in him; just so the
      brutes
Rest not, are anxious without visible
      cause,
When change is in the elements at work,
Which man's trained senses fail to
      apprehend.
But here, – he takes the distant chariot
      wheel
For thunder, festal flame for lightning's
      flash,
The finer traits of cultivated life
For treachery and malevolence: I see!
                    *Enter* TIBURZIO.

*Lur*. Quick, sir, your message! I but
      wait your message
To sound the charge. You bring no
      overture
For truce? I would not, for your
      General's sake,
You spoke of truce: a time to fight is
      come,
And, whatsoe'er the fight's event, he
      keeps

His honest soldier's-name to beat me
    with,
Or leaves me all himself to beat, I trust!
*Tib.* I am Tiburzio.
*Lur.*            You? 'Tis – yes … Tiburzio!
You were the last to keep the ford i' the
    valley
From Puccio, when I threw in succours
    there!
Why, I was on the heights – through
    the defile
Ten minutes after, when the prey was
    lost!
You wore an open skull-cap with a
    twist
Of water-reeds – the plume being hewn
    away;
While I drove down my battle from the
    heights,
I saw with my own eyes!
*Tib.*            And you are Luria
Who sent my cohort, that laid down its
    arms
In error of the battle-signal's sense,
Back safely to me at the critical time –
One of a hundred deeds. I know you.
    Therefore
To none but you could I …
*Lur.*            No truce, Tiburzio!
*Tib.* Luria, you know the peril imminent
On Pisa, – that you have us in the toils,
Us her last safeguard, all that intercepts
The rage of her implacablest of foes
From Pisa: if we fall to-day, she falls.
Tho' Lucca will arrive, yet, 'tis too late.
You have so plainly here the best of it,
That you must feel, brave soldier as you
    are,
How dangerous we grow in this extreme,
How truly formidable by despair.
Still, probabilities should have their
    weight:
The extreme chance is ours, but, that
    chance failing,
You win this battle. Wherefore say I
    this?
To be well apprehended when I add,

This danger absolutely comes from you.
Were you, who threaten thus, a
    Florentine …
*Lur.* Sir, I am nearer Florence than her
    sons.
I can, and have perhaps obliged the
    State,
Nor paid a mere son's duty.
*Tib.*            Even so.
Were you the son of Florence, yet endued
With all your present nobleness of soul,
No question, what I must communicate
Would not detach you from her.
*Lur.*            Me, detach?
*Tib.* Time urges. You will ruin presently
Pisa, you never knew, for Florence' sake
You mink you know. I have from time
    to time
Made prize of certain secret missives
    sent
From Braccio here, the Commissary,
    home:
And knowing Florence otherwise, I piece
The entire chain out, from these its
    scattered links.
Your trial occupies the Signory;
They sit in judgment on your conduct
    now
When men at home inquire into the act
Which in the field e'en foes
    appreciate …
Brief, they are Florentines! You, saving
    them,
Seek but the sure destruction saviours
    fine.
*Lur.*      Tiburzio!
*Tib.* All the wonder is of course
I am not here to teach you, nor direct,
Only to loyally apprise – scarce that.
This is the latest letter, sealed and safe,
As it left here an hour ago. One way
Of two thought free to Florence, I
    command.
The duplicate is on its road; but this, –
Read it, and then I shall have more to
    say.
*Lur.*      Florence!

*Tib.* Now, were yourself a Florentine,
This letter, let it hold the worst it can,
Would be no reason you should fall
    away.
The mother city is the mother still,
And recognition of the children's service
Her own affair; reward – there's no
    reward!
But you are bound by quite another tie.
Nor nature shows, nor reason, why at
    first
A foreigner, born friend to all alike,
Should give himself to any special State
More than another, stand by Florence'
    side
Rather than Pisa; 'tis as fair a city
You war against as that you fight for –
    famed
As well as she in story, graced no less
With noble heads and patriotic hearts:
Nor to a stranger's eye would either
    cause,
Stripped of the cumulative loves and
    hates
Which take importance from familiar
    view,
Stand as the right and sole to be upheld.
Therefore, should the preponderating
    gift
Of love and trust, Florence was first to
    throw,
Which made you hers, not Pisa's, void
    the scale, –
Old ties dissolving, things resume their
    place
And all begins again. Break seal and
    read!
At least let Pisa offer for you now!
And I, as a good Pisan, shall rejoice –
Though for myself I lose, in gaining
    you,
This last fight and its opportunity;
The chance it brings of saving Pisa yet,
Or in the turn of battle dying so
That shame should want its extreme
    bitterness.
*Lur.* Tiburzio, you that fight for Pisa now

As I for Florence ... say my chance
    were yours!
You read this letter, and you find ... no,
    no!
Too mad!
*Tib.* I read the letter, find they purpose
When I have crushed their foe, to crush
    me: well?
*Lur.* You. being their captain, what is it
    you do?
*Tib.* Why, as it is, all cities are alike;
As Florence pays you. Pisa will pay me.
I shall be as belied, whate'er the event,
As you, or more: my weak head, they
    will say,
Prompted this last expedient, my faint
    heart
Entailed on them indelible disgrace,
Both which defects ask proper
    punishment.
Another tenure of obedience, mine!
You are no son of Pisa's: break and
    read!
*Lur.* And act on what I read? What act
    were fit?
If the firm-fixed foundation of my faith
In Florence, who to me stands for
    mankind,
– If that break up and, disimprisoning
From the abyss ... Ah friend, it cannot
    be!
You may be very sage, yet – all the world
Having to fail, or your sagacity,
You do not wish to find yourself alone!
What would the world be worth?
    Whose love be sure?
The world remains: you are deceived!
*Tib.*                Your hand!
I lead the vanguard. – If you fall, beside.
The better: I am left to speak! For me,
This was my duty, nor would I rejoice
If I could help, it misses its effect;
And after all you will look gallantly
Found dead here with that letter in
    your breast.
*Lur.* Tiburzio – I would see these
    people once

And test them ere I answer finally!
At your arrival let the trumpet sound:
If mine return not then the wonted cry
It means that I believe – am Pisa's!
*Tib.*                              Well!
                                   [*Goes.*
*Lur.* My heart will have it he speaks true!
     My blood
Beats close to this Tiburzio as a friend.
If he had stept into my watch-tent,
     night
And the wild desert full of foes around,
I should have broke the bread and
     given the salt
Secure, and, when my hour of watch
     was done,
Taken my turn to sleep between his
     knees,
Safe in the untroubled brow and
     honest cheek.
Oh world, where all things pass and
     nought abides,
Oh life, the long mutation – is it so?
Is it with life as with the body's change?
– Where, e'en tho' better follow, good
     must pass,
Nor manhood's strength can mate with
     boyhood's grace,
Nor age's wisdom, in its turn, find
     strength,
But silently the first gift dies away,
And though the new stays, never both
     at once.
Life's time of savage instinct o'er with
     me,
It fades and dies away, past trusting
     more,
As if to punish the ingratitude
With which I turned to grow in these
     new lights,
And learned to look with European
     eyes.
Yet it is better, this cold certain way,
Where Braccio's brow tells nothing,
     Puccio's mouth,
Domizia's eyes reject the searcher: yes!
For on their calm sagacity I lean,

Their sense of right, deliberate choice
     of good,
Sure, as they know my deeds, they deal
     with me.
Yes, that is better – that is best of all!
Such faith stays when mere wild belief
     would go.
Yes – when the desert creature's heart,
     at fault
Amid the scattering tempest's pillared
     sands,
Betrays its step into the pathless drift –
The calm instructed eye of man holds
     fast
By the sole bearing of the visible star,
Sure that when slow the whirling
     wreck subside,
The boundaries, lost now, shall be
     found again, –
The palm-trees and the pyramid over all.
Yes: I trust Florence: Pisa is deceived.
          *Enter* BRACCIO, PUCCIO,
              *and* DOMIZIA.
*Brac.* Noon's at an end: no Lucca? You
     must fight.
*Lur.* Do you remember ever, gentle
     friends,
I am no Florentine?
*Dom.*                    It is yourself
Who still are forcing us, importunately,
To bear in mind what else we should
     forget.
*Lur.* For loss! – for what I lose in being
     none!
No shrewd man, such as you yourselves
     respect,
But would remind you of the stranger's
     loss
In natural friends and advocates at home,
Hereditary loves, even rivalships
With precedent for honour and
     reward.
Still, there's a gain, too! If you take it so,
The stranger's lot has special gain as
     well.
Do you forget there was my own far
     East

I might have given away myself to, once,
As now to Florence, and for such a gift,
Stood there like a descended deity?
There, worship waits us: what is it
    waits here?     [*Shows the letter.*
See! Chance has put into my hand the
    means
Of knowing what I earn, before I work.
Should I fight better, should I fight the
    worse,
With payment palpably before me? See!
Here lies my whole reward! Best learn
    it now
Or keep it for the end's entire delight?
*Brac.* If you serve Florence as the vulgar
    serve,
For swordsman's-pay alone, – break
    seal and read!
In that case, you will find your full
    desert.
*Lur.* Give me my one last happy
    moment, friends!
You need me now, and all the
    graciousness
This letter can contain will hardly
    balance
The after-feeling that you need no
    more.
This moment … oh, the East has use
    with you!
Its sword still flashes – is not flung aside
With the past praise, in a dark corner
    yet!
How say you? 'Tis not so with
    Florentines,
Captains of yours: for them, the ended
    war
Is but a first step to the peace begun:
He who did well in war, just earns the
    right
To begin doing well in peace, you know:
And certain my precursors, – would not
    such
Look to themselves in such a chance as
    mine,
Secure the ground they trod upon,
    perhaps?

For I have heard, by fits, or seemed to
    hear,
Of strange mishap, mistake, ingratitude,
Treachery even. Say that one of you
Surmised this letter carried what might
    turn
To harm hereafter, cause him prejudice:
What would he do?
*Dom.* [*hastily*].     Thank God and take
    revenge!
Hurl her own force against the city
    straight
And, even at the moment when the foe
Sounded defiance …
            [TIBURZIO's *trumpet sounds*
                     *in the distance.*
*Lur.*             Ah, you Florentines!
So would you do? Wisely for you, no
    doubt.
My simple Moorish instinct bids me
    clench
The obligation you relieve me from,
Still deeper! [*To* Puccio.] Sound our
    answer, I should say,
And thus: – [*tearing the paper.*] – The
    battle! That solves every doubt.

### ACT 3

#### Afternoon

PUCCIO, *as making a report to* JACOPO.

*Puc.* And here, your captain must
    report the rest;
For, as I say, the main engagement
    over
And Luria's special part in it performed,
How could a subaltern like me expect
Leisure or leave to occupy the field
And glean what dropped from his wide
    harvesting?
I thought, when Lucca at the battle's
    end
Came up, just as the Pisan centre broke,
That Luria would detach me and
    prevent
The flying Pisans seeking what they
    found,

Friends in the rear, a point to rally by.
But no, more honourable proved my
    post!
I had the august captive to escort
Safe to our camp; some other could
    pursue,
Fight, and be famous; gentler chance
    was mine –
Tiburzio's wounded spirit must be
    soothed!
He's in the tent there.

*Jac.*              Is the substance down?
I write – 'The vanguard beaten and
    both wings
'In full retreat, Tiburzio prisoner' –
And now, – 'That they fell back and
    formed again
'On Lucca's coming.' Why then, after
    all,
'Tis half a victory, no conclusive one?

*Puc.* Two operations where a sole had
    served.

*Jac.* And Luria's fault was – ?

*Puc.*              Oh, for fault – not much!
He led the attack, a thought impetuously,
– There's commonly more prudence;
    now, he seemed
To hurry measures, otherwise well
    judged.
By over-concentrating strength at first
Against the enemy's van, both wings
    escaped:
That's reparable, yet it is a fault.

                *Enter* BRACCIO.

*Jac.* As good as a full victory to Florence,
With the advantage of a fault beside –
What is it, Puccio? – that by pressing
    forward
With too impetuous ...

*Brac.*              The report anon!
Thanks, sir – you have elsewhere a
    charge, I know.          [PUCCIO *goes.*
There's nothing done but I would do
    again;
Yet, Lapo, it may be the past proves
    nothing,
And Luria has kept faithful to the close.

*Jac.* I was for waiting.

*Brac.*                        Yes: so was not I.
He could not choose but tear that letter
    – true!
Still, certain of his tones, I mind, and
    looks: –
You saw, too, with a fresher soul than I.
So, Porzio seemed an injured man, they
    say!
Well, I have gone upon the broad, sure
    ground.

        *Enter* LURIA, PUCCIO, *and* DOMIZIA

*Lur.* [*to* PUCCIO]. Say, at bis pleasure I
    will see Tiburzio!
All's at his pleasure.

*Dom.* [*to* LURIA]. Were I not forewarned
You would reject, as you do constantly,
Praise, – I might tell you how you have
    deserved
Of Florence by this last and crowning
    feat:
But words offend.

*Lur.*      Nay, you may praise me now.
I want instruction every hour, I find,
On points where once I saw least need
    of it;
And praise, I have been used to slight
    perhaps,
Seems scarce so easily dispensed with
    now.
After a battle half one's strength is gone;
The glorious passion in us once appeased,
Our reason's calm cold dreadful voice
    begins.
All justice, power and beauty scarce
    appear
Monopolized by Florence, as of late,
To me, the stranger: you, no doubt,
    may know
Why Pisa needs must bear her rival's
    yoke.
And peradventure I grow nearer you,
For I, too, want to know and be
    assured.
When a cause ceases to reward itself,
Its friend seeks fresh sustainments;
    praise is one,

And here stand you – you, lady, praise
    me well.
But yours – (your pardon) – is
    unlearned praise.
To the motive, the endeavour, the
    heart's self,
Your quick sense looks: you crown and
    call aright
The soul o' the purpose, ere 'tis shaped
    as act,
Takes flesh i' the world, and clothes
    itself a king.
But when the act comes, stands for
    what 'tis worth,
– Here's Puccio, the skilled soldier, he's
    my judge!
Was all well, Puccio?
*Puc.*           All was … must be well:
If we beat Lucca presently, as
    doubtless …
– No, there's no doubt, we must – all
    was well done.
*Lur.* In truth? Still you are of the trade,
    my Puccio!
You have the fellow-craftsman's
    sympathy.
There's none cares, like a fellow of the
    craft,
For the all-unestimated sum of pains
That go to a success the world can see:
They praise then, but the best they
    never know
– While you know! So, if envy mix
    with it,
Hate even, still the bottom-praise of all,
Whatever be the dregs, that drop's
    pure gold!
– For nothing's like it; nothing else
    records
Those daily, nightly drippings in the
    dark
Of the heart's blood, the world lets
    drop away
For ever – so, pure gold that praise
    must be!
And I have yours, my soldier! yet the
    best

Is still to come. There's one looks on
    apart
Whom all refers to, failure or success;
What's done might be our best, our
    utmost work,
And yet inadequate to serve his need.
Here s Braccio now, for Florence –
    here's our service –
Well done for us, seems it well done
    for him?
His chosen engine, tasked to its full
    strength
Answers the end? Should he have
    chosen higher?
Do we help Florence, now our best is
    wrought?
*Brac.* This battle, with the foregone
    services,
Saves Florence.
*Lur.*           Why then, all is very well!
Here am I in the middle of my friends,
Who know me and who love me, one
    and all.
And yet … 'tis like … this instant
    while I speak
Is like the turning-moment of a dream
When … Ah, you are not foreigners
    like me!
Well then, one always dreams of
    friends at home;
And always comes, I say, the turning-
    point
When something changes in the
    friendly eyes
That love and look on you … so slight,
    so slight …
And yet it tells you they are dead and
    gone,
Or changed and enemies, for all their
    words,
And all is mockery and a maddening
    show.
You now, so kind here, all you
    Florentines,
What is it in your eyes … those lips,
    those brows …
Nobody spoke it, yet I know it well!

Come now – this battle saves you, all's
    at end,
Your use of me is o'er, for good, for ill, –
Come now, what's done against me,
    while I speak,
In Florence? Come! I feel it in my blood,
My eyes, my hair, a voice is in my ears
That spite of all this smiling and soft
    speech
You are betraying me. What is it you do?
Have it your way, and think my use is
    over –
Think you are saved and may throw off
    the mask –
Have it my way, and think more work
    remains
Which I could do, – so, show you fear
    me not!
Or prudent be, or daring, as you choose,
But tell me – tell what I refused to know
At noon, lest heart should fail me! Well?
    That letter?
My fate is sealed at Florence! What is it?
*Brac.* Sir, I shall not deny what you
    divine.
It is no novelty for innocence
To be suspected, but a privilege:
The after certain compensation comes.
Charges, I say not whether false or
    true,
Have been preferred against you some
    time since,
Which Florence was bound, plainly, to
    receive,
And which are therefore undergoing
    now
The due investigation. That is all.
I doubt not but your innocence will
    prove
Apparent and illustrious, as to me,
To them this evening, when the trial
    ends.
*Lur.* My trial?
*Dom.*    Florence, Florence to the end,
My whole heart thanks thee!
*Puc.* [*to* BRACCIO]. What is 'trial', sir?
It was not for a trial – surely, no –

I furnished you those notes from time
    to time?
I held myself aggrieved – I am a man –
And I might speak, – ay, and speak
    mere truth, too,
And yet not mean at bottom of my heart
What should assist a – trial, do you
    say?
You should have told me!
*Dom.*           Nay, go on, go on!
His sentence! Do they sentence him
    What is it?
The block – wheel?
*Brac.*    Sentence there is none as yet,
Nor shall I give my own opinion now
Of what it should be, or is like to be.
When it is passed, applaud or
    disapprove!
Up to that point, what is there to
    impugn?
*Lur.* They are right, then, to try me?
*Brac.*             I assert,
Maintain and justify the absolute right
Of Florence to do all she can have
    done
In this procedure, – standing on her
    guard,
Receiving even services like yours
With utmost fit suspicious wariness.
In other matters, keep the mummery
    up!
Take all the experiences of all the world,
Each knowledge that broke through a
    heart to life,
Each reasoning which, to reach, burnt
    out a brain,
– In other cases, know these, warrant
    these,
And then dispense with these – 'tis
    very well!
Let friend trust friend, and love demand
    love's like.
And gratitude be claimed for benefits, –
There's grace in that, – and when the
    fresh heart breaks,
The new brain proves a ruin, what of
    them?

Where is the matter of one moth the
    more
Singed in the candle, at a summer's
    end?
But Florence is no simple John or
    James
To have his toy, his fancy, his conceit
That he's the one excepted man by fate,
And, when fate shows him he's mistaken
    there,
Die with all good men's praise, and
    yield his place
To Paul and George intent to try their
    chance!
Florence exists because these pass
    away.
She's a contrivance to supply a type
Of man, which men's deficiencies
    refuse;
She binds so many, that she grows out
    of them –
Stands steady o'er their numbers,
    though they change
And pass away – there's always what
    up holds,
Always enough to fashion the great
    show.
As see, yon hanging city, in the sun,
Of shapely cloud substantially the same!
A thousand vapours rise and sink again,
Are interfused, and live their life and
    die, –
Yet ever hangs the steady show i' the air,
Under the sun's straight influence: that
    is well,
That is worth heaven should hold, and
    God should bless!
And so is Florence, – the unseen sun
    above,
Which draws and holds suspended all
    of us,
Binds transient vapours into a single
    cloud
Differing from each and better than
    they all.
And shall she dare to stake this
    permanence

On any one man's faith? Man's heart is
    weak,
And its temptations many: let her prove
Each servant to the very uttermost
Before she grant him her reward, I say!
*Dom.* And as for hearts she chances to
    mistake,
Wronged hearts, not destined to receive
    reward,
Though they deserve it, did she only
    know,
– What should she do for these?
*Brac.*            What does she not?
Say, that she gives them but herself to
    serve!
Here's Luria – what had profited his
    strength,
When half an hour of sober fancying
Had shown him step by step the useless-
    ness
Of strength exerted for strength's
    proper sake?
But the truth is, she did create that
    strength,
Draw to the end the corresponding
    means.
The world is wide – are we the only
    men?
Oh, for the time, the social purpose'
    sake,
Use words agreed on, bandy epithets,
Call any man the sole 'great wise and
    good!
But shall we therefore, standing by
    ourselves,
Insult our souls and God with the
    same speech?
There, swarm the ignoble thousands
    under him:
What marks us from the hundreds and
    the tens?
Florence took up, turned all one way
    the soul
Of Luria with its fires, and here he
    glows!
She takes me out of all the world as
    him,

Fixing my coldness till like ice it checks
The fire! So, Braccio, Luria, which is
    best?
*Lur*. Ah, brave me? And is this indeed
    the way
To gain your good word and sincere
    esteem?
Am I the baited animal that must turn
And fight his baiters to deserve their
    praise?
Obedience is mistake then? Be it so!
Do you indeed remember I stand here
The captain of the conquering army, –
    mine –
With all your tokens, praise and promise,
    ready
To show for what their names meant
    when you gave,
Not what you style them now you take
    away?
If I call in my troops to arbitrate,
And dash the first enthusiastic thrill
Of victory with this you menace now –
Commend to the instinctive popular
    sense,
My story first, your comment
    afterward, –
Will they take, think you, part with
    you or me?
If I say – I, the labourer they saw work,
Ending my work, ask pay, and find my
    lords
Have all this while provided silently
Against the day of pay and proving faith,
By what you call my sentence that's to
    come –
Will friends advise I wait complacently?
If I meet Florence half way at their
    head,
What will you do, my mild antagonist?
*Brac*. I will rise up like fire, proud and
    triumphant
That Florence knew you thoroughly
    and by me,
And so was saved. 'See, Italy,' I'll say,
'The crown of our precautions!' Here's
    a man

'Was far advanced, just touched on the
    belief
'Less subtle cities had accorded long;
'But we are wiser: at the end comes
    this!'
And from that minute, where is Luria?
    Lost!
The very stones of Florence cry against
The all-exacting, nought-enduring fool
Who thus resents her first probation,
    flouts
As if he, only, shone and cast no shade,
He, only, walked the earth with privilege
Against suspicion, free where angels
    fear:
He, for the first inquisitive mother's-
    word,
Must turn, and stand on his defence,
    forsooth!
Reward? You will not be worth
    punishment!
*Lur*. And Florence knew me thus! Thus
    I have lived, –
And thus you, with the clear fine
    intellect,
Braccio, the cold acute instructed mind,
Out of the stir, so calm and unconfused,
Reported me – how could you other-
    wise!
Ay? – and what dropped from you, just
    now, moreover?
Your information, Puccio? – Did your
    skill,
Your understanding sympathy approve
Such a report of me? Was this the end?
Or is even this the end? Can I stop
    here'?
You, lady, with the woman's stand apart
The heart to see with, past man's brain
    and eyes,
. . . I cannot fathom why you should
    destroy
The unoffending one, you call your
    friend –
Still, lessoned by the good examples
    here
Of friendship, 'tis but natural I ask –

Had you a further aim, in aught you
    urged,
Than your friend's profit – in all those
    minstances
Of perfidy, all Florence wrought of
    wrong –
All I remember now for the first time?
*Dom.* I am a daughter of the Traversari,
Sister of Ponrzio and of Berto both,
So, have foreseen all that has come to
    pass.
I knew the Florence that could doubt
    their faith,
Must needs mistrust a stranger's –
    dealing them
Punishment, would deny him his reward.
And I believed, the shame they bore
    and died,
He would not bear, but live and fight
    against –
Seeing he was of other stuff than they.
*Lur.* Hear them! All these against one
    foreigner!
And all this while, where is, in the
    whole world,
To his good faith a single witness?
*Tib.* [*who has entered unseen during the
    preceding dialogue*].                Here!
Thus I bear witness, not in word but
    deed.
I live for Pisa; she's not lost to-day
By many chances – much prevents from
    that!
Her army has been beaten, I am here,
But Lucca comes at last, one happy
    chance!
I rather would see Pisa three times lost
Than saved by any traitor, even by you;
The example of a traitor's happy fortune
Would bring more evil in the end than
    good; –
Pisa rejects the traitor, craves yourself!
I, in her name, resign forthwith to you
My charge, – the highest office, sword
    and shield!
You shall not, by my counsel, turn on
    Florence

Your army, give her calumny that
    ground –
Nor bring one soldier: be you all we
    gain!
And all she'll lose, – a head to deck
    some bridge,
And save the cost o' the crown should
    deck the head.
Leave her to perish in her perfidy,
Plague-stricken and stripped naked to
    all eyes,
A proverb and by-word in all mouths!
Go you to Pisa! Florence is my place –
Leave me to tell her of the rectitude,
I, from the first, told Pisa, knowing it.
To Pisa!
*Dom.*    Ah my Braccio, are you caught?
*Brac.* Puccio, good soldier and good
    citizen,
Whom I have ever kept beneath my eye,
Ready as fit, to serve in this event
Florence, who clear foretold it from the
    first –
Through me, she gives you the
    command and charge
She takes, through me, from him who
    held it late!
A painful trial, very sore, was yours:
All that could draw out, marshal in
    array
The selfish passions 'gainst the public
    good –
Slights, scorns, neglects, were heaped
    on you to bear:
And ever you did bear and bow the
    head!
It had been sorry trial, to precede
Your feet, hold up the promise of reward
For luring gleam; your footsteps kept
    the track
Thro' dark and doubt: take all the light
    at once!
Trial is over, consummation shines;
Well have you served, as well
    henceforth command!
*Puc.* No, no ... I dare not! I am
    grateful, glad;

But Luria – you shall understand he's
    wronged:
And he's my captain: this is not the way
We soldiers climb to fortune: think
    again!
The sentence is not even passed, beside!
I dare not: where's the soldier could?
*Lur.*                  Now, Florence –
Is it to be? You will know all the strength
O' the savage – to your neck the proof
    must go?
You will prove the brute nature? Ah, I
    see!
The savage plainly is impassible:
He keeps his calm way through
    insulting words,
Sarcastic looks, sharp gestures – one of
    which
Would stop you, fatal to your finer
    sense,
But if he stolidly advance, march mute
Without a mark upon his callous hide,
Through the mere brushwood you
    grow angry with,
And leave the tatters of your flesh
    upon,
– You have to learn that when the true
    bar comes,
The murk mid-forest, the grand
    obstacle,
Which when you reach, you give the
    labour up,
Nor dash on, but lie down composed
    before,
– He goes against it, like the brute he is:
It falls before him, or he dies in his
    course.
I kept my course through past
    ingratitude:
I saw – it does seem, now, as if I saw,
Could not but see, those insults as
    they fell,
– Ay, let them glance from off me, very
    like,
Laughing, perhaps, to think the quality
You grew so bold on, while you so
    despised

The Moor's dull mute inapprehensive
    mood,
Was saving you: I bore and kept my
    course.
Now real wrong fronts me: see if I
    succumb!
Florence withstands me? I will punish
    her.
At night my sentence will arrive, you
    say.
Till then I cannot, if I would, rebel
– Unauthorized to lay my office down,
Retaining my full power to will and do:
After – it is to see. Tiburzio, thanks!
Go; you are free: join Lucca! I suspend
All further operations till to-night.
Thank you, and for the silence most of
    all!
[*To* BRACCIO.] Let my complacent
    bland accuser go
Carry his self-approving head and heart
Safe through the army which would
    trample him
Dead in a moment at my word or sign!
Go, sir, to Florence; tell friends what I
    say –
That while I wait my sentence, theirs
    waits them!
[*To* DOMIZIA.] You, lady, – you have
    black Italian eyes!
I would be generous if I might: oh, yes –
For I remember how so oft you seemed
Inclined at heart to break the barrier
    down
Which Florence finds God built
    between us both.
Alas, for generosity! this hour
Asks retribution: bear it as you may,
I must – the Moor – -the savage, –
    pardon you!
Puccio, my trusty soldier, see them
    forthl

## ACT 4

### Evening

*Enter* PUCCIO *and* JACOPO.

*Puc.* What Luria will do? Ah, 'tis yours,
    fair sir,
Your and your subtle-witted master's
    part,
To tell me that; I tell you what he can.
*Jac.* Friend, you mistake my station: I
    observe
The game, watch how my betters play,
    no more.
*Puc.* But mankind are not pieces –
    there's your fault!
You cannot push them, and, the first
    move made,
Lean back and study what the next
    shall be,
In confidence that, when 'tis fixed upon,
You find just where you left them,
    blacks and whites:
Men go on moving when your hand's
    away.
You build, I notice, firm on Luria's
    faith
This whole time, – firmlier than I
    choose to build,
Who never doubted it – of old, that is –
With Luria in his ordinary mind.
But now, oppression makes the wise
    man mad:
How do I know he will not turn and
    stand
And hold his own against you, as he
    may?
Suppose he but withdraw to Pisa –
    well, –
Then, even if all happen to your wish,
Which is a chance …
*Jac.*         Nay – 'twas an oversight,
Not waiting till the proper warrant
    came:
You could not take what was not ours
    to give.
But when at night the sentence really
    comes,

Our city authorizes past dispute
Luria's removal and transfers the
    charge,
You will perceive your duty and
    accept?
*Puc.* Accept what? muster-rolls of
    soldiers' names?
An army upon paper? I want men,
The hearts as well as hands – and
    where's a heart
But beats with Luria, in the multitude
I come from walking through by
    Luria's side?
You gave them Luria, set him thus to
    grow,
Head-like, upon their trunk; one heart
    feeds both,
They feel him there, live twice, and
    well know why.
– For they do know, if you are ignorant,
Who kept his own place and respected
    theirs,
Managed their sweat, yet never spared
    his blood.
All was your act: another might have
    served! –
There's peradventure no such dearth of
    heads –
But you chose Luria; so, they grew one
    fresh,
And now, for nothing they can under-
    stand,
Luria removed, off is to roll the head;
The body's mine – much I shall do
    with it!
*Jac.*     That's at the worst.
*Puc.*           No – at the best, it is!
Best, do you hear? I saw them by his
    side.
Only we two with Luria in the camp
Are left that keep the secret? You think
    that?
Hear what I know: from rear to van, no
    heart
But felt the quiet patient hero there
Was wronged, nor in the moreless
    ranks an eye

But glancing told its fellow the whole
     story
Of that convicted silent knot of spies
Who passed thro' them to Florence;
     they might pass –
No breast but gladlier beat when free
     of such!
Our troops will catch up Luria, close
     him round,
Bear him to Florence as their natural
     lord,
Partake his fortune, live or die with
     him.
*Jac.* And by mistake catch up along
     with him
Puccio, no doubt, compelled in self
     despite
To still continue second in command!
*Puc.* No, sir, no second nor so
     fortunate!
Your tricks succeed with me too well
     for that!
I am as you have made me, live and die
To serve your end – a mere trained
     fighting-hack,
With words, you laugh at while they
     leave your mouth
For my life's rule and ordinance of God!
I have to do my duty, keep my faith,
And earn my praise, and guard against
     my blame,
As I was trained. I shall accept your
     charge,
And fight against one better than
     myself,
Spite of my heart's conviction of his
     worth –
That, you may count on! – just as
     hitherto
I have gone on, persuaded I was
     wronged,
Slighted, insulted, terms we learn by
     rote, –
All because Luria superseded me –
Because the better nature, fresh-
     inspired,
Mounted above me to its proper place!

What mattered all the kindly
     graciousness,
The cordial brother's-bearing? This was
     clear –
I, once the captain, now was subaltern,
And so must keep complaining like a
     fool!
Go, take the curse of a lost soul, I say!
You neither play your puppets to the
     end,
Nor treat the real man, – for his realness
     sake
Thrust rudely in their place, – with such
     regard
As might console them for their altered
     rank.
Me, the mere steady soldier, you depose
For Luria, and here's all your pet
     deserves!
Of what account, then, is your
     laughing-stock?
One word for all: whatever Luria does,
– If backed by his indignant troops he
     turn,
Revenge himself, and Florence go to
     ground,
Or, for a signal everlasting shame,
He pardon you' simply seek better
     friends,
Side with the Pisans and Lucchese for
     change
– And if I, pledged to ingrates past
     belief,
Dare fight against a man such fools call
     false,
Who, inasmuch as he was true, fights
     me, –
Whichever way he win, he wins for
     worth,
For every soldier, for all true and good!
Sir, chronicling the rest, omit not this!
     *As they go, enter* Luria *and* Husain.
*Hus.* Saw'st thou? – For they are gone!
     The world lies bare
Before thee, to be tasted, felt and seen
Like what it is, now Florence goes
     away!

Thou livest now, with men art man
    again!
Those Florentines were all to thee of
    old;
But Braccio, but Domizia, gone is each,
There lie beneath thee thine own
    multitudes!
Saw'st thou?
*Lur.*         I saw.
*Hus.*         Then, hold thy course,
    my king!
The years return. Let thy heart have its
    way:
Ah, they would play with thee as with
    all else,
Turn thee to use, and fashion thee anew,
Find out God's fault in thee as in the
    rest?
Oh watch, oh listen only to these fiends
Once at their occupation! Ere we know,
The free great heaven is shut, their
    stifling pall
Drops till it frets the very tingling hair,
So weighs it on our head, – and, for
    the earth,
Our common earth is tethered up and
    down,
Over and across – 'here shalt thou
    move,' they cry!
*Lur.* Ay, Husain?
*Hus.* So have they spoiled all beside!
So stands a man girt round with
    Florentines,
Priests, greybeards, Braccios, women,
    boys and spies,
All in one tale, all singing the same
    song,
How thou must house, and live at bed
    and board,
Take pledge and give it, go their every
    way,
Breathe to their measure, make thy
    blood beat time
With theirs – or, all is nothing – thou
    art lost –
A savage, how shouldst thou perceive
    as they?

Feel glad to stand 'neath God's close
    naked hand!
Look up to it Why, down they pull thy
    neck,
Lest it crush thee, who feel's t it and
    wouldst kiss,
Without their priests that needs must
    glove it first,
Lest peradventure flesh offend thy lip.
Love woman! Why, a very beast thou
    art!
Thou must …
*Lur.*       Peace, Husain!
*Hus.*         Ay but, spoiling all,
For all, else true things, substituting
    false,
That they should dare spoil, of all
    instincts, thine!
Should dare to take thee with thine
    instincts up,
Thy battle-ardours, like a ball of fire,
And class them and allow them place
    and play
So far, no farther – unabashed the
    while!
Thou with the soul that never can take
    rest –
Thou born to do, undo, and do again,
And never to be still, – wouldst thou
    make war?
Oh, that is commendable, just and
    right!
'Come over,' say they, 'have the
    honour due
'In living out thy nature! Fight thy best:
'It is to be for Florence, not thyself!
'For thee, it were a horror and a plague;
'For us, when war is made for
    Florence, see,
'How all is changed: the fire that fed on
    earth
'Now towers to heaven!' –
*Lur.*        And what sealed up so long
My Husain's mouth?
*Hus.*       Oh friend, oh lord – for me,
What am I? – I was silent at thy side,
Who am a part of thee. It is thy hand,

Thy foot that glows when in the heart
    fresh blood
Boils up, thou heart of me! Now, live
    again,
Again love as thou likest, hate as free!
Turn to no Braccios nor Domizias now,
To ask, before thy very limbs dare move,
If Florence' welfare be concerned
    thereby!
*Lur.* So clear what Florence must
    expect of me?
*Hus.* Both armies against Florence!
    Take revenge!
Wide, deep – to live upon, in feeling
    now, –
And, after live, in memory, year by
    year –
And, with the dear conviction, die at
    last!
She lies now at thy pleasure: pleasure
    have!
Their vaunted intellect that gilds our
    sense,
And blends with life, to show it better
    by,
– How think'st thou? – I have turned
    that light on them!
They called our thirst of war a transient
    thing;
'The battle-element must pass away
'From life,' they said, 'and leave a
    tranquil world.'
– Master, I took their light and turned
    it full
On that dull turgid vein they said
    would burst
And pass away; and as I looked on life,
Still everywhere I tracked this, though
    it hid
And shifted, lay so silent as it thought,
Changed shape and hue yet ever was
    the same.
Why, 'twas all fighting, all their nobler
    life!
All work was fighting, every harm –
    defeat,
And every joy obtained – a victory!

Be not their dupe!
    – Their dupe? That hour is past!
Here stand'st thou in the glory and the
    calm:
All is determined. Silence for me now!
                    [HUSAIN *goes.*
*Lur.* Have I heard all?
*Dom.* [*advancing from the background*].
              No, Luria, I remain!
Not from the motives these have urged
    on thee,
Ignoble, insufficient, incomplete,
And pregnant each with sure seeds of
    decay,
As failing of sustainment from thyself,
– Neither from low revenge, nor
    selfishness,
Nor savage lust of power, nor one, nor
    all,
Shalt thou abolish Florence! I proclaim
The angel in thee, and reject the sprites
Which ineffectual crowd about his
    strength,
And mingle with his work and claim a
    share!
Inconsciously to the augustest end
Thou hast arisen: second not in rank
So much as time, to him who first
    ordained
That Florence, thou art to destroy,
    should be.
Yet him a star, too, guided, who broke
    first
The pride of lonely power, the life apart,
And made the eminences, each to each,
Lean o'er the level world and let it lie
Safe from the thunder henceforth
    'neath their tops;
So the few famous men of old
    combined,
And let the multitude rise underneath,
And reach them and unite – so
    Florence grew:
Braccio speaks true, it was well worth
    the price.
But when the sheltered many grew in
    pride

And grudged the station of the elected
    ones,
Who, greater than their kind, are truly
    great
Only in voluntary servitude –
Time was for thee to rise, and thou art
    here.
Such plague possessed this Florence:
    who can tell
The mighty girth and greatness at the
    heart
Of those so perfect pillars of the grove
She pulled down in her envy? Who as I,
The light weak parasite born but to
    twine
Round each of them and, measuring
    them, live?
My light love keeps the matchless circle
    safe,
My slender life proves what has passed
    away.
I lived when they departed; lived to
    cling
To thee, the mighty stranger; thou
    wouldst rise
And burst the thraldom, and avenge, I
    knew.
I have done nothing; all was thy strong
    bole.
But a bird's weight can break the infant
    tree
Which after holds an aery in its arms,
And 'twas my care that nought should
    warp thy spire
From rising to the height; the roof is
    reached
O' the forest, break through, see extend
    the sky!
Go on to Florence, Luria! 'Tis man's
    cause!
Fail thou, and thine own fall were least
    to dread:
Thou keepest Florence in her evil way,
Encouragest her sin so much the more –
And while the ignoble past is justified,
Thou all the surelier warp'st the future
    growth,

The chiefs to come, the Lurias yet
    unborn,
That, greater than thyself, are reached
    o'er thee
Who giv'st the vantage-ground their
    foes require
As o'er my prostrate House thyself
    wast reached.
Man calls thee, God requites thee! All
    is said,
The mission of my House fulfilled at
    last:
And the mere woman, speaking for
    herself,
Reserves speech – it is now no
    woman's time.    [DOMIZIA *goes.*
*Lur.* Thus at the last must figure Luria,
    then!
Doing the various work of all his friends,
And answering every purpose save his
    own.
No doubt, 'tis well for them to wish;
    but him –
After the exploit what were left?
    Perchance
A little pride upon the swarthy brow,
At having brought successfully to bear
'Gainst Florence' self her own especial
    arms, –
Her craftiness, impelled by fiercer
    strength
From Moorish blood than feeds the
    northern wit –
But after! – once the easy vengeance
    willed,
Beautiful Florence at a word laid low
– (Not in her domes and towers and
    palaces,
Not even in a dream, that outrage!) –
    low,
As shamed in her own eyes henceforth
    for ever,
Low, for the rival cities round to laugh,
Conquered and pardoned by a hireling
    Moor!
– For him, who did the irreparable
    wrong,

What would be left, his life's illusion
    fled, –
What hope or trust in the forlorn wide
    world?
How strange that Florence should
    mistake me so!
Whence grew this? What withdrew her
    faith from me?
Some cause! These fretful-blooded
    children talk
Against their mother, – they are
    wronged, they say –
Notable wrongs her smile makes up
    again!
So, taking fire at each supposed offence,
They may speak rashly, suffer for their
    speech:
But what could it have been in word of
    deed
Thus injured me? Some one word
    spoken more
Out of my heart, and all had changed
    perhaps.
My fault, it must have been, – for, what
    gain they?
Why risk the danger? See, what I could
    do!
And my fault, wherefore visit upon them,
My Florentines? The notable revenge
I meditated! To stay passively,
Attend their summons, be as they
    dispose!
Why, if my very soldiers keep the rank,
And if my chieftains acquiesce, what
    then?
I ruin Florence, teach her friends
    mistrust,
Confirm her enemies in harsh belief,
And when she finds one day, as find
    she must,
The strange mistake, and how my heart
    was hers,
Shall it console me, that my Florentines
Walk with a sadder step, in graver
    guise,
Who took me with such frankness,
    praised me so,

At the glad outset? Had they loved me
    less,
They had less feared what seemed a
    change in me.
And after all, who did the harm? Not
    they!
How could they interpose with those
    old fools
I' the council? Suffer for those old
    fools' sake –
They, who made pictures of me, sang
    the songs
About my battles? Ah, we Moors get
    blind
Out of our proper world, where we can
    see!
The sun that guides is closer to us!
    There –
There, my own orb! He sinks from out
    the sky.
Why, there! a whole day has he blessed
    the land,
My land, our Florence all about the hills,
The fields and gardens, vineyards,
    olive-grounds,
All have been blest: and yet we
    Florentines
With souls intent upon our battle here,
Found that he rose too soon, or set too
    late,
Gave us no vantage, or gave Pisa much –
Therefore we wronged him! Does he
    turn in ire
To burn the earth that cannot under-
    stand?
Or drop out quietly, and leave the sky,
His task once ended? Night wipes
    blame away.
Another morning from my East shall
    spring
And find all eyes at leisure, all disposed
To watch and understand its work, no
    doubt.
So, praise the new sun, the successor
    praise,
Praise the new Luria and forget the old!
           [*Taking a phial from his breast.*

Strange! This is all I brought from my
    own land
To help me: Europe would supply the
    rest,
All needs beside, all other helps save
    one!
I thought of adverse fortune, battle
    lost,
The natural upbraiding of the loser,
And then this quiet remedy to seek
At end of the disastrous day.
                   [*He drinks.*
                'Tis sought!
This was my happy triumph-morning:
    Florence
Is saved: I drink this, and ere night, –
    die! Strange!

### ACT 5

*Night*

LURIA *and* PUCCIO.

*Lur.* I thought to do this, not to talk
    this: well,
Such were my projects for the city's
    good,
To help her in attack or by defence.
Time, here as elsewhere, soon or late
    may take.
Our foresight by surprise thro' chance
    and change;
But not a little we provide against
– If you see clear on every point.
*Puc.*                  Most clear.
*Lur.* Then all is said – not much, if you
    count words,
Yet to an understanding ear enough
And all that my brief stay permits,
    beside.
Nor must you blame me, as I sought to
    teach
My elder in command, or threw a doubt
Upon the very skill, it comforts me
To know I leave, – your steady
    soldiership
Which never failed me: yet, because it
    seemed

A stranger's eye might haply note
    defect
That skill, through use and custom,
    overlooks –
I have gone into the old cares once
    more,
As if I had to come and save again
Florence – that May – that morning!
    'Tis night now.
Well – I broke off with? …
*Puc.*           Of the past campaign
You spoke – of measures to be kept in
    mind
For future use.
*Lur.* True, so … but, time – no time!
As well end here: remember this, and
    me!
Farewell now!
*Puc.*     Dare I speak?
*Lur.*              South o' the river –
How is the second stream called … no,
    – the third?
*Puc.* Pesa.
*Lur.*     And a stone's cast from the
    fording-place,
To the east, – the little mount's name?
*Puc.*                 Lupo.
*Lur.*                     Ay!
Ay – there the tower, and all that side
    is safe!
With San Romano, west of Evola,
San Miniato, Scala, Empoli,
Five towers in all, – forget not!
*Puc.*               Fear not me!
*Lur.* – Nor to memorialize the Council
    now,
I' the easy hour, on those battalions'
    claim,
Who forced a pass by Staggia on the
    hills,
And kept the Sienese at check!
*Puc.*             One word –
Sir, I must speak! That you submit
    yourself
To Florence' bidding, howsoe'er it prove,
And give up the command to me – is
    much,

Too much, perhaps: but what you tell me now,
Even will affect the other course you choose –
Poor as it may be, perils even that!
Refuge you seek at Pisa: yet these plans
All militate for Florence, all conclude
Your formidable work to make her queen
O' the country, – which her rivals rose against
When you began it, – which to interrupt,
Pisa would buy you off at any price!
You cannot mean to sue for Pisa's help,
With this made perfect and on record?

*Lur.*                                                    I –
At Pisa, and for refuge, do you say?

*Puc.* Where are you going, then? You must decide
On leaving us, a silent fugitive,
Alone, at night – you, stealing through our lines
Who were this morning's Luria, – you escape
To painfully begin the world once more,
With such a past, as it had never been!
Where are you going?

*Lur.*                         Not so far, my Puccio,
But that I hope to hear, enjoy and praise
(If you mind praise from your old captain yet)
Each happy blow you strike for Florence.

*Puc.*                                                    Ay, –
But ere you gain your shelter, what may come?
For see – though nothing's surely known as yet,
Still – trutn must out – I apprehend the worst.
If mere suspicion stood for certainty
Before, there's nothing can arrest the step
Of Florence toward your ruin, once on foot.
Forgive her fifty times, it matters not!
And having disbelieved your innocence,

How can she trust your magnanimity?
You may do harm to her – why then, you will!
And Florence is sagacious in pursuit.
Have you a friend to count on?

*Lur.*                                    One sure friend.

*Puc.* Potent?

*Lur.*            All-potent.

*Puc.*                         And he is apprised?

*Lur.* He waits me.

*Puc.*            So! – Then I, put in your place,
Making my profit of all done by you,
Calling your labours mine, reaping their fruit,
To this, the State's gift, now add yours beside –
That I may take as my peculiar store
These your instructions to work Florence good.
And if, by putting some few happily
In practice, I should both advantage her
And draw down honour on myself, – what then?

*Lur.* Do it, my Puccio! I shall know and praise.

*Puc.* Though so, men say, 'mark what we gain by change
' – A Puccio for a Luria!'

*Lur.*                         Even so.

*Puc.* Then, not for fifty hundred Florences,
Would I accept one office save my own,
Fill any other than my rightful post
Here at your feet, my captain and my lord!
That such a cloud should break, such trouble be,
Ere a man settle, soul and body, down
Into his true place and take rest for ever!
Here were my wise eyes fixed on your right-hand,
And so the bad thoughts came and the worse words,
And all went wrong and painfully enough, –

No wonder, – till, the right spot
    stumbled on,
All the jar stops, and there is peace at
    once!
I am yours now, – a tool your right-
    hand wields!
God's love, that I should live, the man
    I am,
On orders, warrants, patents, and the
    like,
As if there were no glowing eye i' the
    world
To glance straight inspiration to my
    brain,
No glorious heart to give mine twice
    the beats!
For, see – my doubt, where is it? – fear?
    'tis flown!
And Florence and her anger are a tale
To scare a child. Why, half-a-dozen
    words
Will tell her, spoken as I now can speak,
Her error, my past folly – and all's
    right,
And you are Luria, our great chief
    again!
Or at the worst – which worst were
    best of all –
To exile or to death I follow you.
*Lur.* Thanks, Puccio! Let me use the
    privilege
You grant me: if I still command you, –
    stay!
Remain here – my vicegerent, it shall be,
And not successor: let me, as of old,
Still serve the State, my spirit
    prompting yours –
Still triumph, one for both. There! Leave
    me now!
You cannot disobey my first command?
Remember what I spoke of Jacopo,
And what you promised to concert
    with him!
Send him to speak with me – nay, no
    farewell!
You shall be by me when the sentence
    comes.         [PUCCIO *goes.*

So, there's one Florentine returns
    again!
Out of the genial morning-company,
One face is left to take into the night.
        *Enter* JACOPO.
*Jac.* I wait for your command, sir.
*Lur.*                 What, so soon!
I thank your ready presence and fair
    word.
I used to notice you in early days
As of the other species, so to speak,
Those watchers of the lives of us who
    act –
That weigh our motives, scrutinize our
    thoughts.
So, I propound this to your faculty
As you would tell me, were a town to
    take
. . . That is, of old. I am departing
    hence
Under these imputations; that is
    nought –
I leave no friend on whom they may
    rebound,
Hardly a name behind me in the land,
Being a stranger: all the more behoves
That I regard how altered were the case
With natives of the country, Florentines
On whom the like mischance should
    fall: the roots
O' the tree survive the ruin of the
    trunk –
No root of mine will throb, you
    understand.
But I had predecessors, Florentines,
Accused as I am now, and punished so –
The Traversari: you know more than I
How stigmatized they are, and lost in
    shame.
Now Puccio, who succeeds me in
    command,
Both served them and succeeded, in
    due time;
He knows the way, holds proper
    documents,
And has the power to lay the simple
    truth

Before an active spirit, as I count yours:
And also there's Tiburzio, my new friend,
Will, at a word, confirm such evidence,
He being the great chivalric soul we know.
I put it to your tact, sir – were't not well,
– A grace, though but for contrast's sake, no more, –
If you who witness, and have borne a share
Involuntarily in my mischance,
Should, of your proper motion, set your skill
To indicate – that is, investigate
The right or wrong of what mischance befell
Those famous citizens, your country-men?
Nay, you shall promise nothing: but reflect,
And if your sense of justice prompt you – good!
*Jac.* And if, the trial past, their fame stand clear
To all men's eyes, as yours, my lord, to mine –
Their ghosts may sleep in quiet satisfied!
For me, a straw thrown up into the air,
My testimony goes for a straw's worth.
I used to hold by the instructed brain,
And move with Braccio as my master-wind;
The heart leads surelier: I must move with you –
As greatest now, who ever were the best.
So, let the last and humblest of your servants
Accept your charge, as Braccio's heretofore,
And tender homage by obeying you!
                              [JACOPO *goes.*
*Lur.* Another! Luria goes not poorly forth.

If we could wait! The only fault's with time;
All men become good creatures: but so slow!
                    *Enter* DOMIZIA.
*Lur.* Ah, you once more?
*Dom.*          Domizia, whom you knew,
Performed her task, and died with it. 'Tis I,
Another woman, you have never known.
Let the past sleep now!
*Lur.*                    I have done with it.
*Dom.* How inexhaustibly the spirit grows!
One object, she seemed erewhile born to reach
With her whole energies and die content, –
So like a wall at the world's edge it stood,
With nought beyond to live for, – is that reached?
Already are new undreamed energies
Outgrowing under, and extending farther
To a new object; there's another world.
See! I have told the purpose of my life;
'Tis gained: you are decided, well or ill –
You march on Florence, or submit to her –
My work is done with you, your brow declares.
But – leave you? More of you seems yet to reach:
I stay for what I just begin to see.
*Lur.* So that you turn not to the past!
*Dom.*                        You trace
Nothing but ill in it – my selfish impulse,
Which sought its end and disregarded yours?
*Lur.* Speak not against your nature: best, each keep
His own – you, yours – most, now that I keep mine,
– At least, fall by it, having too weakly stood.
God's finger marks distinctions, all so fine,

We would confound: the lesser has its
    use,
Which, when it apes the greater, is
    forgone.
I, born a Moor, lived half a Florentine;
But, punished properly, can end, a
    Moor.
Beside, there's something makes me
    understand
Your nature: I have seen it.
*Dom.*                Aught like mine?
*Lur.* In my own East … if you would
    stoop and help
My barbarous illustration! It sounds ill;
Yet there's no wrong at bottom: rather,
    praise.
*Dom.* Well?
*Lur.*         We have creatures there,
    which if you saw
The first time, you would doubtless
    marvel at
For their surpassing beauty, craft and
    strength.
And though it were a lively moment's
    shock
When you first found the purpose of
    forked tongues
That seem innocuous in their lambent
    play,
Yet, once made know such grace
    requires such guard,
Your reason soon would acquiesce, I
    think,
In wisdom which made all things for
    the best –
So, take them, good with ill, contentedly,
The prominent beauty with the latent
    sting.
I am glad to have seen you wondrous
    Florentines:
Yet …
*Dom.*   I am here to listen.
*Lur.*              My own East!
How nearer God we were! He glows
    above
With scarce an intervention, presses
    close

And palpitatingly, his soul o'er ours:
We feel him, nor by painful reason
    know!
The everlasting minute of creation
Is felt there; now it is, as it was then;
All changes at his instantaneous will,
Not by the operation of a law
Whose maker is elsewhere at other
    work.
His hand is still engaged upon his
    world –
Man's praise can forward it, man's
    prayer suspend,
For is not God all-mighty? To recast
The world, erase old things and make
    them new,
What costs it Him? So, man breathes
    nobly there.
And inasmuch as feeling, the East's
    gift,
Is quick and transient – comes, and lo,
    is gone –
While Northern thought is slow and
    durable,
Surely a mission was reserved for me,
Who, born with a perception of the
    power
And use of the North's thought for us
    of the East,
Should have remained, turned
    knowledge to account,
Giving thought's character and
    permanence
To the too transitory feeling there –
Writing God's message plain in mortal
    words.
Instead of which, I leave my fated field
For this where such a task is needed
    least,
Where all are born consummate in the
    art
I just perceive a chance of making
    mine, –
And then, deserting thus my early post,
I wonder that the men I come among
Mistake me! There, how all had
    understood,

Still brought fresh stuff for me to stamp
    and keep,
Fresh instinct to translate them into law!
Me, who ...
*Dom*. Who here the greater task
    achieve,
More needful even: who have brought
    fresh stuff
For us to mould, interpret and prove
    right, –
New feeling fresh from God, which,
    could we know
O' the instant, where had been our
    need of it?
– Whose life re-teaches us what life
    should be,
What faith is, loyalty and simpleness,
All, once revealed but taught us so long
    since
That, having mere tradition of the fact, –
Truth copied falteringly from copies
    faint,
The early traits all dropped away, – we
    said
On sight of faith like yours, 'So looks
    not faith
'We understand, described and praised
    before.'
But still, the feat was dared; and though
    at first
It suffered from our haste, yet trace by
    trace
Old memories reappear, old truth
    returns,
Our slow thought does its work, and
    all's re-known.
Oh noble Luria! What you have decreed
I see not, but no animal revenge,
No brute-like punishment of bad by
    worse –
It cannot be, the gross and vulgar way
Traced for me by convention and mistake,
Has gained that calm approving eye
    and brow!
Spare Florence, after all! Let Luria trust
To his own soul, he whom I trust with
    mine!

*Lur*. In time!
*Dom*.    How, Luria?
*Lur*.               It is midnight now,
And they arrive from Florence with my
    fate.
*Dom*. I hear no step.
*Lur*.           I feel one, as you say.
        *Enter* HUSAIN.
*Hus*. The man returned from Florence!
*Lur*.                  As I knew.
*Hus*. He seeks thee.
*Lur*.         And I only wait for him.
Aught else?
*Hus*.    A movement of the Lucchese
    troops
Southward –
*Lur*.    Toward Florence? Have out
    instantly ...
Ah, old use clings! Puccio must care
    henceforth.
In – quick – 'tis nearly midnight! Bid
    him come!
      *Enter* TIBURZIO, BRACCIO,
          *and* PUCCIO.
Tiburzio? – not at Pisa?
*Tib*.             I return
From Florence: I serve Pisa, and must
    think
By such procedure I have served her
    best.
A people is but the attempt of many
To rise to the completer life of one;
And those who live as models for the
    mass
Are singly of more value than they all.
Such man are you, and such a time is
    this,
That your sole fate concerns a nation
    more
Than much apparent welfare: that to
    prove
Your rectitude, and duly crown the same,
Imports us far beyond to-day's event,
A battle's loss or gain: man's mass
    remains, –
Keep but God's model safe, new men
    will rise

To take its mould, and other days to
    prove
How great a good was Luria's glory.
    True –
I might go try my fortune as you urged,
And, joining Lucca, helped by your
    disgrace,
Repair our harm – so were to-day's
    work done;
But where leave Luria for our sons to
    see?
No, I look farther. I have testified
(Declaring my submission to your arms)
Her full success to Florence, making
    clear
Your probity, as none else could: I
    spoke,
And out it shone!
*Lur.*           Ah – until Braccio spoke!
*Brac.* Till Braccio told in just a word
    the whole –
His lapse to error, his return to
    knowledge:
Which told … Nay, Luria, *I* should
    droop the head,

I whom shame rests with! Yet I dare
    look up,
Sure of your pardon now I sue for it,
Knowing you wholly. Let the midnight
    end!
'Tis morn approaches! Still you answer
    not?
Sunshine succeeds the shadow past
    away:
Our faces, which phantasmal grew and
    false,
Are all that felt it: they change round
    you, turn
Truly themselves now in its vanishing.
Speak, Luria! Here begins your true
    career:
Look up, advance! All now is possible,
Fact's grandeur, no false dreaming!
    Dare and do!
And every prophecy shall be fulfilled
Save one – (nay, now your word must
    come at last)
– That you would punish Florence!
*Hus.* [*pointing to* LURIA's *dead body*].
                    That is done.

# A SOUL'S TRAGEDY

1846

Act first, being what was called the poetry of chiappino's life: and act second, its prose

## Persons

Luitolfo *and* Eulalia, *betrothed lovers.* Chiappino, *their friend.*
Ogniben, *the Pope's Legate. Citizens of Faenza.*
*Time, 15——. Place, Faenza.*

## ACT 1

*Scene – Inside* LUTTOLFO's *House.*

CHIAPPINO, EULALIA.

*Eu.* What is it keeps Luitolfo? Night's
   fast falling,
And 'twas scarce sunset … had the
   ave-bell
Sounded before he sought the
   Provost's house?
I think not: all he had to say would
   take
Few minutes, such a very few, to say!
How do you think, Chiappino? If our
   lord
The Provost were less friendly to your
   friend
Than everybody here professes him,
I should begin to tremble – should not
   you?
Why are you silent when so many times
I turn and speak to you?
*Ch.*           That's good!
*Eu.*              You laugh!
*Ch.* Yes. I had fancied nothing that
   bears price
In the whole world was left to call my
   own;
And, may be, felt a little pride thereat.
Up to a single man's or woman's love,
Down to the right in my own flesh and
   blood,
There's nothing mine, I fancied, – till
   you spoke:
– Counting, you see, as 'nothing' the
   permission
To study this peculiar lot of mine

In silence: well, go silence with the rest
Of the world's good! What can I say,
   shall serve?
*Eu.* This, – lest you, even more than
   needs, embitter
Our parting: say your wrongs have cast,
   for once,
A cloud across your spirit!
*Ch.*            How a cloud?
*Eu.* No man nor woman loves you, did
   you say?
*Ch.* My God, were't not for thee!
*Eu.*           Ay, God remains,
Even did men forsake you.
*Ch.*           Oh, not so!
Were't not for God, I mean, what hope
   of truth –
Speaking truth, hearing truth, would
   stay with man?
I, now – the homeless friendless
   penniless
Proscribed and exiled wretch who
   speak to you, –
Ought to speak truth, yet could not,
   for my death,
(The thing that tempts me most) help
   speaking lies
About your friendship and Luitolfo's
   courage
And all our townsfolk's equanimity –
Through sheer incompetence to rid
   myself
Of the old miserable lying trick
Caught from the liars I have lived with,
   – God,
Did I not turn to thee! It is thy
   prompting

I dare to be ashamed of, and thy counsel
Would die along my coward lip, I know.
But I do turn to thee. This craven tongue,
These features which refuse the soul its way,
Reclaim thou! Give me truth – truth, power to speak –
And after be sole present to approve
The spoken truth! Or, stay, that spoken truth,
Who knows but you, too, may approve?
*Eu.*                         Ah, well –
Keep silence then, Chiappino!
*Ch.*                         You would hear,
You shall now, – why the thing we please to style
My gratitude to you and all your friends
For service done me, is just gratitude
So much as yours was service: no whit more.
I was born here, so was Luitolfo; both
At one time, much with the same circumstance
Of rank and wealth; and both, up to this night
Of parting company, have side by side
Still fared, he in the sunshine – I, the shadow.
'Why?' asks the world. 'Because,' replies the world
To its complacent self, 'these playfellows,
'Who took at church the holy-water drop
'Each from the other's finger, and so forth, –
'Were of two moods: Luitolfo was the proper
'Friend-making, everywhere friend-finding soul,
'Fit for the sunshine, so, it followed him.
'A happy-tempered bringer of the best
'Out of the worst; who bears with what's past cure,
'And puts so good a face on't – wisely passive
'Where action's fruitless, while he remedies
'In silence what the foolish rail against;
'A man to smooth such natures as parade
'Of opposition must exasperate;
'No general gauntlet-gatherer for the weak
'Against the strong, yet over-scrupulous
'At lucky junctures; one who won't forego
'The after-battle work of binding wounds,
'Because, forsooth he'd have to bring himself
'To side with wound-inflictors for their leave!'
– Why do you gaze, nor help me to repeat
What comes so glibly from the common mouth,
About Luitolfo and his so-styled friend?
*Eu.* Because that friend's sense is obscured …
*Ch.*                         I thought
You would be readier with the other half
Of the world's story, my half! Yet, 'tis true.
For all the world does say it. Say your worst!
True, I thank God, I ever said 'you sin,'
When a man did sin: if I could not say it,
I glared it at him; if I could not glare it,
I prayed against him; then my part seemed over.
God's may begin yet: so it will, I trust.
*Eu.* If the world outraged you, did we?
*Ch.*                         What's 'me'
That you use well or ill? It's man, in me,
All your successes are an outrage to,
You all, whom sunshine follows, as you say!
Here's our Faenza birthplace; they send here
A provost from Ravenna: how he rules,
You can at times be eloquent about.

'Then, end his rule!' – 'Ah yes, one
    stroke does that!
'But patience under wrong works slow
    and sure.
'Must violence still bring peace forth?
    He, beside,
'Returns so blandly one's obeisance!
    ah –
'Some latent virtue may be lingering
    yet,
'Some human sympathy which, once
    excite,
'And all the lump were leavened quietly:
'So, no more talk of striking, for this
    time!'
But I, as one of those he rules, won't
    bear
These pretty takings-up and layings-
    down
Our cause, just as you think occasion
    suits.
Enough of earnest, is there? You'll play,
    will you?
Diversify your tactics, give submission,
Obsequiousness and flattery a turn,
While we die in our misery patient
    deaths?
We all are outraged then, and I the
    first:
I, for mankind, resent each shrug and
    smirk,
Each beck and bend, each … all you
    do and are,
I hate!
*Eu.*    We share a common censure,
    then.
'Tis well you have not poor Luitolfo's
    part
Nor mine to point out in the wide
    offence.
*Ch.*    Oh, shall I let you so escape me,
    lady?
Come, on your own ground, lady, –
    from yourself,
(Leaving the people's wrong, which
    most is mine)
What have I got to be so grateful for?

These three last fines, no doubt, one
    on the other
Paid by Luitolfo?
*Eu.*    Shame, Chiappino!
*Ch.*    Shame
Fall presently on who deserves it most!
– Which is to see. He paid my fines –
    my friend,
Your prosperous smooth lover presently,
Then, scarce your wooer, – soon, your
    husband: well –
I loved you.
*Eu.*    Hold!
*Ch.*    You knew it, years ago.
When my voice faltered and my eye
    grew dim
Because you gave me your silk mask to
    hold –
My voice that greatens when there's
    need to curse
The people's Provost to their heart's
    content,
– My eye, the Provost, who bears all
    men's eyes,
Banishes now because he cannot bear, –
You knew … but you do your parts –
    my part, I:
So be it! You flourish, I decay: all's
    well.
*Eu.*I hear this for the first time.
*Ch.*    The fault's there?
Then my days spoke not, and my
    nights of fire
Were voiceless? Then the very heart
    may burst,
Yet all prove nought, because no
    mincing speech
Tells leisurely that thus it is and thus?
Eulalia, truce with toying for this once!
A banished fool, who troubles you
    tonight
For the last time – why, what's to fear
    from me?
You knew I loved you!
*Eu.*    Not so, on my faith!
You were my now-affianced lover's
    friend –

Came in, went out with him, could
    speak as he.
All praise your ready parts and
    pregnant wit;
See how your words come from you in
    a crowd!
Luitolfo's first to place you o'er himself
In all that challenges respect and love:
Yet you were silent then, who blame
    me now.
I say all this by fascination, sure:
I, all but wed to one I love, yet listen!
It must be, you are wronged, and that
    the wrongs
Luitolfo pities ...
*Ch.*                – You too pity? Do!
But hear first what my wrongs are; so
    began
This talk and so shall end this talk. I
    say,
Was't not enough that I must strive (I
    saw)
To grow so far familiar with your charms
As next contrive some way to win them
    – which
To do, an age seemed far too brief – for,
    see!
We all aspire to heaven; and there lies
    heaven
Above us: go there! Dare we go? no,
    surely!
How dare we go without a reverent
    pause,
A growing less unfit for heaven? Just so,
I dared not speak: the greater fool, it
    seems!
Was't not enough to struggle with such
    folly,
But I must have, beside, the very man
Whose slight free loose and incapacious
    soul
Gave his tongue scope to say whate'er
    he would
– Must have him load me with his
    benefits
– For fortune's fiercest stroke?
*Eu.*                Justice to him

That's now entreating, at his risk
    perhaps,
Justice for you! Did he once call those
    acts
Of simple friendship – bounties, benefits?
*Ch.* No: the straight course had been to
    call them thus.
Then, I had flung them back, and kept
    myself
Unhampered, free as he to win the
    prize
We both sought. But 'the gold was
    dross,' he said:
'He loved me, and I loved him not: why
    spurn
'A trifle out of superfluity?
'He had forgotten he had done as
    much.'
So had not I! Henceforth, try as I could
To take him at his word, there stood by
    you
My benefactor; who might speak and
    laugh
And urge his nothings, even banter me
Before you – but my tongue was tied. A
    dream!
Let's wake: your husband ... how you
    shake at that!
Good – my revenge!
*Eu.*             Why should I shake?
    What forced
Or forces me to be Luitolfo's bride?
*Ch.* There's my revenge, that nothing
    forces you.
No gratitude, no liking of the eye
Nor longing of the heart, but the poor
    bond
Of habit – here so many times he
    came,
So much he spoke, – all these compose
    the tie
That pulls you from me. Well, he paid
    my fines,
Nor missed a cloak from wardrobe,
    dish from table;
He spoke a good word to the Provost
    here,

Held me up when my fortunes fell away
– It had not looked so well to let me
    drop
Men take pains to preserve a tree-
    stump, even,
Whose boughs they played beneath –
    much more a friend.
But one grows tired of seeing, after the
    first,
Pains spent upon impracticable stuff
Like me. I could not change: you know
    the rest.
I've spoke my mind too fully out, by
    chance,
This morning to our Provost; so, ere
    night
I leave the city on pain of death. And
    now
On my account there's gallant
    intercession
Goes forward – that's so graceful! –
    and anon
He'll noisily come back: 'the intercession
'Was made and fails; all's over for us
    both;
' 'Tis vain contending; I would better
    go.'
And I do go – and straight to you he
    turns
Light of a load; and ease of that permits
His visage to repair the natural bland
Œconomy, sore broken late to suit
My discontent. Thus, all are pleased –
    you, with him,
He with himself, and all of you with me
– 'Who,' say the citizens, 'had done far
    better
'In letting people sleep upon their woes,
'If not possessed with talent to relieve
    them
'When once awake; – but then I had,'
    they'll say,
'Doubtless some unknown compensating
    pride
'In what I did; and as I seem content
'With ruining myself, why, so should
    they be.'

And so they are, and so be with his
    prize
The devil, when he gets them speedily!
Why does not your Luitolfo come? I
    long
To don this cloak and take the Lugo
    path.
It seems you never loved me, then?
*Eu.*                      Chiappino!
*Ch.* Never?
*Eu.*    Never.
*Ch.*         That's sad. Say what I might,
There was no help from being sure this
    while
You loved me. Love like mine must
    have return,
I thought: no river starts but to some
    sea.
And had you loved me, I could soon
    devise
Some specious reason why you stifled
    love,
Some fancied self-denial on your part,
Which made you choose Luitolfo; so,
    excepting
From the wide condemnation of all
    here,
One woman. Well, the other dream
    may break!
If I knew any heart, as mine loved you,
Loved me, though in the vilest breast
    'twere lodged,
I should, I think, be forced to love
    again:
Else there's no right nor reason in the
    world.
*Eu.* 'If you knew,' say you, – but I did
    not know.
That's where you're blind, Chiappino!
    – a disease
Which if I may remove, I'll not repent
The listening to. You cannot, will not,
    see
How, place you but in every circumstance
Of us, you are just now indignant at,
You'd be as we.
*Ch.*       I should be? ... that; again!

I, to my friend, my country and my
love,
Be as Luitolfo and these Faentines?
*Eu.* As we.
*Ch.*      Now, I'll say something to
remember.
I trust in nature for the stable laws
Of beauty and utility. – Spring shall
plant,
And Autumn garner to the end of time:
I trust in God – the right shall be the
right
And other than the wrong, while he
endures:
I trust in my own soul, that can perceive
The outward and the inward, nature's
good
And God's: so, seeing these men and
myself,
Having a right to speak, thus do I speak.
I'll not curse – God bears with them,
well may I –
But I – protest against their claiming
me.
I simply say, if that's allowable,
I would not (broadly) do as they have
done.
– God curse this townful of born slaves,
bred slaves,
Branded into the blood and bone, slaves!
Curse
Whoever loves, above his liberty,
House, land or life! and …
                    [*A knocking without.*
                    – bless my hero-friend,
Luitolfo!
*Eu.*      How he knocks!
*Ch.*                The peril, lady!
'Chiappino, I have run a risk – a risk!
'For when I prayed the Provost (he's my
friend)
'To grant you a week's respite of the
sentence
'That confiscates your goods, exiles
yourself,
'He shrugged his shoulder – I say,
shrugged it! Yes,

'And fright of that drove all else from
my head.
'Here's a good purse of *scudi*: off with
you,
'Lest of that shrug come what God only
knows!
'The *scudi* – friend, they're trash – no
thanks, I beg!
'Take the north gate, – for San Vitale's
suburb,
'Whose double taxes you appealed
against,
'In discomposure at your ill-success
'Is apt to stone you: there, there – only
go!
'Beside, Eulalia here looks sleepily.
'Shake … oh, you hurt me, so you
squeeze my wrist!'
– Is it not thus you'll speak, adventurous
friend?
                    [*As he opens the door,*
                    LUITOLFO *rushes in,*
                    *his garments disordered.*
*Eu.* Luitolfo! Blood?
*Luit.*      There's more – and more of it!
Eulalia – take the garment! No – you,
friend!
You take it and the blood from me –
you dare!
*Eu.* Oh, who has hurt you? where's the
wound?
*Ch.*            'Who,' say you?
The man with many a touch of virtue
yet!
The Provost's friend has proved too
frank of speech,
And this comes of it. Miserable hound!
This comes of temporizing, as I said!
Here's fruit of your smooth speeches
and soft looks!
Now see my way! As God lives, I go
straight
To the palace and do justice, once for
all!
*Luit.* What says he?
*Ch.*                I'll do justice on him.
*Luit.*                            Him?

*Ch*. The Provost.

*Luit.*          I've just killed him.

*Eu.*                    Oh, my God!

*Luit*. My friend, they're on my trace;
    they'll have me – now!

They're round him, busy with him:
    soon they'll find

He's past their help, and then they'll
    be on me!

Chiappino, save Eulalia! I forget …

Were you not bound for …

*Ch*.                    Lugo?

*Luit*.                    Ah – yes – yes!

That was the point I prayed of him to
    change.

Well, go – be happy! Is Eulalia safe?

They're on me!

*Ch*.          'Tis through me they
    reach you, then!

Friend, seem the man you are! Lock
    arms – that's right!

Now tell me what you've done; explain
    how you

That still professed forbearance, still
    preached peace,

Could bring yourself …

*Luit*.   What was peace for, Chiappino?

I tried peace: did that promise, when
    peace failed,

Strife should not follow? All my
    peaceful days

Were just the prelude to a day like this.

I cried 'You call me "friend": save my
    true friend!

'Save him, or lose me!'

*Ch*.                    But you never said

You meant to tell the Provost thus and
    thus.

*Luit*. Why should I say it? What else
    did I mean?

*Ch*. Well? He persisted?

*Luit*                    – 'Would so order it

'You should not trouble him too soon
    again.'

I saw a meaning in his eye and lip;

I poured my heart's store of indignant
    words

Out on him: then – I know not! He
    retorted,

And I … some staff lay there to hand –
    I think

He bade his servants thrust me out – I
    struck …

Ah, they come! Fly you, save yourselves,
    you two!

The dead back-weight of the beheading
    axe!

The glowing trip-hook, thumbscrews
    and the gadge!

*Eu*. They do come! Torches in the
    Place! Farewell,

Chiappino! You can work no good to
    us –

Much to yourself; believe not, all the
    world

Much needs be cursed henceforth!

*Ch*.                    And you?

*Eu*.                    I stay.

*Ch*. Ha, ha! Now, listen! I am master
    here!

This was my coarse disguise; this paper
    shows

My path of flight and place of refuge –
    see –

Lugo, Argenta, past San Nicolo,

Ferrara, then to Venice and all's safe!

Put on the cloak! His people have to
    fetch

A compass round about. There's time
    enough

Ere they can reach us, so you straightway
    make

For Lugo … nay, he hears not! On
    with it –

The cloak, Luitolfo, do you hear me?
    See –

He obeys he knows not how. Then, if I
    must –

Answer me! Do you know the Lugo
    gate?

*Eu*. The north-west gate, over the bridge?

*Luit*.                    I know.

*Ch*. Well, there – you are not frightened?
    all my route

Is traced in that: at Venice you escape
Their power. Eulalia, I am master here!
    [*Shouts from without. He*
        *pushes out* LUITOLFO,
    *who complies mechanically.*
In time! Nay, help me with him – so!
    He's gone.
*Eu*. What have you done? On you,
    perchance, all know
The Provost's hater, will men's
    vengeance fall
As our accomplice.
*Ch*.            Mere accomplice? See!
    [*Putting on* LUITOLFO's *vest.*
Now, lady, am I true to my profession,
Or one of these?
*Eu*.            You take Luitolfo's place?
*Ch*. Die for him.
*Eu*.            Well done! [*Shouts increase.*
*Ch*.            How the people tarry!
I can't be silent; I must speak: or sing –
How natural to sing now!
*Eu*.                    Hush and pray!
We are to die; but even I perceive
'Tis not a very hard thing so to die.
My cousin of the pale-blue tearful eyes,
Poor Cesca, suffers more from one
    day's life
With the stern husband; Tisbe's heart
    goes forth
Each evening after that wild son of hers,
To track his thoughtless footstep
    through the streets:
How easy for them both to die like this!
I am not sure that I could live as they.
*Ch*. Here they come, crowds! They pass
    the gate? Yes! – No! –
One torch is in the courtyard. Here
    flock all.
*Eu*. At least Luitolfo has escaped. What
    cries!
*Ch*. If they would drag one to the
    market-place,
One might speak there!
*Eu*.            List, list!
*Ch*.            They mount the steps.
    *Enter the* POPULACE.

*Ch*. I killed the Provost!
*The Populace* [*speaking together*]. 'Twas
    Chiappino, friends!
Our saviour! The best man at last as
    first!
He who first made us feel what chains
    we wore,
He also strikes the blow that shatters
    them,
He at last saves us – our best citizen!
– Oh, have you only courage to speak
    now?
My eldest son was christened a year
    since 'Cino' to keep Chiappino's
    name in mind –
Cino, for shortness merely, you observe!
The city's in our hands. The guards are
    fled.
Do you, the cause of all, come down –
    come up –
Come out to counsel us, our chief, our
    king,
Whate'er rewards you! Choose your
    own reward!
The peril over, its reward begins!
Come and harangue us in the market-
    place!
*Eu*. Chiappino?
*Ch*.            Yes – I understand your eyes!
You think I should have promptlier
    disowned
This deed with its strange unforeseen
    success,
In favour of Luitolfo. But the peril,
So far from ended, hardly seems
    begun.
To-morrow, rather, when a calm
    succeeds,
We easily shall make him full amends:
And meantime – if we save them as
    they pray,
And justify the deed by its effects?
*Eu*. You would, for worlds, you had
    denied at once.
*Ch*. I know my own intention, be
    assured!
All's well. Precede us, fellow-citizens!

ACT 2

*Scene – The Market-Place.* LUITOLFO *in disguise mingling with the* POPULACE *assembled opposite the Provost's Palace.*

1st *Bystander* [*to* LUITOLFO]. You, a friend of Luitolfo's? Then, your friend is vanished, – in all probability killed on the night that his patron the tyrannical Provost was loyally suppressed here, exactly a month ago, by our illustrious fellow-citizen, thrice-noble saviour, and new Provost that is like to be, this very morning, – Chiappino!

*Luit.* He the new Provost?

2nd *Bys.* Up those steps will he go, and beneath yonder pillar stand, while Ogniben, the Pope's Legate from Ravenna, reads the new dignitary's title to the people, according to established custom: for which reason, there is the assemblage you inquire about.

*Luit.* Chiappino – the late Provost's successor? Impossible! But tell me of that presently. What I would know first of all is, wherefore Luitolfo must so necessarily have been killed on that memorable night?

3rd *Bys.* You were Luitolfo's friend? So was I. Never, if you will credit me, did there exist so poor-spirited a milksop. He, with all the opportunities in the world, furnished by daily converse with our oppressor, would not stir a finger to help us: and, when Chiappino rose in solitary majesty and … how does one go on saying? … dealt the godlike blow, – this Luitolfo, not unreasonably fearing the indignation of an aroused and liberated people, fled precipitately. He may have got trodden to death in the press at the south-east gate, when the Provost's guards fled through it to Ravenna, with their wounded master, – if he did not rather hang himself under some hedge.

*Luit.* Or why not simply have lain perdue in some quiet corner, – such as San Cassiano, where his estate was, – receiving daily intelligence from some sure friend, meanwhile, as to the turn matters were taking here – how, for instance, the Provost was not dead, after all, only wounded – or, as to-day's news would seem to prove, how Chiappino was not Brutus the Elder, after all, only the new Provost – and thus Luitolfo be enabled to watch a favourable opportunity for returning? Might it not have been so?

3rd *Bys.* Why, he may have taken that care of himself, certainly, for he came of a cautious stock. I'll tell you how his uncle, just such another gingerly treader on tip-toes with finger on lip, – how he met his death in the great plague-year: *dico vobis!* Hearing that the seventeenth house in a certain street was infected, he calculates to pass it in safety by taking plentiful breath, say, when he shall arrive at the eleventh house; then scouring by, holding that breath, till he be got so far on the other side as number twenty-three, and thus elude the danger. – And so did he begin; but, as he arrived at thirteen, we will say, – thinking to improve on his precaution by putting up a little prayer to St Nepomucene of Prague, this exhausted so much of his lungs' reserve, that at sixteen it was clean spent, – consequently at the fatal seventeen he inhaled with a vigour and persistence enough to suck you any latent venom out of the heart of a stone – Ha, ha!

*Luit.* [*aside*]. (If I had not lent that man the money he wanted last spring, I should fear this bitterness was attributable to me.) Luitolfo is dead then, one may conclude?

3rd *Bys.* Why, he had a house here, and a woman to whom he was affianced; and as they both pass naturally to the new Provost, his friend and heir …

*Luit.* Ah, I suspected you of imposing on me with your pleasantry! I know Chiappino better.

*1st Bys.* (Our friend has the bile! After all, I do not dislike finding somebody vary a little this general gape of admiration at Chiappino's glorious qualities.) Pray, how much may you know of what has taken place in Faenza since that memorable night?

*Luit.* It is most to the purpose, that I know Chiappino to have been by profession a hater of that very office of Provost, you now charge him with proposing to accept.

*1st Bys.* Sir, I'll tell you. That night was indeed memorable. Up we rose, a mass of us, men, women, children; out fled the guards with the body of the tyrant; we were to defy the world: but, next grey morning, 'What will Rome say?' began everybody. You know we are governed by Ravenna, which is governed by Rome. And quietly into the town, by the Ravenna road, comes on muleback a portly personage, Ogniben by name, with the quality of Pontifical Legate; trots briskly through the streets humming a '*Cur fremuere gentes,*' and makes directly for the Provost's Palace – there it faces you. 'One Messer Chiappino is your leader? I have known three-and-twenty leaders of revolts!' (laughing gently to himself) – 'Give me the help of your arm from my mule to yonder steps under the pillar – So! And now, my revolters and good friends; what do you want? The guards burst into Ravenna last night bearing your wounded Provost; and, having had a little talk with him, I take on myself to come and try appease the disorderliness, before Rome, hearing of it, resort to another method: 'tis I come, and not another, from a certain love I confess to, of composing differences. So, do

you understand, you are about to experience this unheard-of tyranny from me, that there shall be no heading nor hanging, no confiscation nor exile: I insist on your simply pleasing yourselves. And now, pray, what does please you? To live without any government at all? Or having decided for one, to see its minister murdered by the first of your body that chooses to find himself wronged, or disposed for reverting to first principles and a justice anterior to all institutions, – and so will you carry matters, that the rest of the world must at length unite and put down such a den of wild beasts? As for vengeance on what has just taken place, – once for all, the wounded man assures me he cannot conjecture who struck him; and this so earnestly, that one may be sure he knows perfectly well what intimate acquaintance could find admission to speak with him late last evening. I come not for vengeance therefore, but from pure curiosity to hear what you will do next.' And thus he ran on, on, easily and volubly, till he seemed to arrive quite naturally at the praise of law, order, and paternal government by somebody from rather a distance. All our citizens were in the snare, and about to be friends with so congenial an adviser; but that Chiappino suddenly stood forth, spoke out indignantly, and set things right again.

*Luit.* Do you see? I recognize him there!

*3rd Bys.* Ay but, mark you, at the end of Chiappino's longest period in praise of a pure republic, – 'And by whom do I desire such a government should be administered, perhaps, but by one like yourself?' – returns the Legate: thereupon speaking for a quarter of an hour together, on the natural and only legitimate government by the best and wisest. And it should seem there was soon discovered to be no such vast discrepancy at bottom between this and Chiappino's theory, place but each in its proper light. 'Oh, are you there?' quoth Chiappino: 'Ay, in that, I agree,' returns Chiappino: and so on.

*Luit.* But did Chiappino cede at once to this?

*1st Bys.* Why, not altogether at once. For instance, he said that the difference between him and all his fellows was, that they seemed all wishing to be kings in one or another way, – 'whereas what right,' asked he, 'has any man to wish to be superior to another?' – whereat, 'Ah, sir,' answers the Legate, 'this is the death of me, so often as I expect something is really going to be revealed to us by you clearer-seers, deeper-thinkers – this – that your right-hand (to speak by a figure) should be found taking up the weapon it displayed so ostentatiously, not to destroy any dragon in our path, as was prophesied, but simply to cut off its own fellow left-hand: yourself set about attacking yourself. For see now! Here are you who, I make sure, glory exceedingly in knowing the noble nature of the soul, its divine impulses, and so forth; and with such a knowledge you stand, as it were, armed to encounter the natural doubts and fears as to that same inherent nobility, which are apt to waylay us, the weaker ones, in the road of life. And when we look eagerly to see them fall before you, lo, round you wheel, only the left-hand gets the blow; one proof of the soul's nobility destroys simply another proof, quite as good, of the same, for you are found delivering an opinion like this! Why, what is this perpetual yearning to exceed, to subdue, to be better than, and a king over, one's fellows, – all that you so disclaim, – but the very tendency yourself are most proud of, and under another form, would oppose to it, – only in a lower

stage of manifestation? You don't want to be vulgarly superior to your fellows after their poor fashion – to have me hold solemnly up your gown's tail, or hand you an express of the last importance from the Pope, with all these bystanders noticing how unconcerned you look the while: but neither does our gaping friend, the burgess yonder, want the other kind of kingship, that consists in understanding better than his fellows this and similar points of human nature, nor to roll under his tongue this sweeter morsel still, – the feeling that, through immense philosophy, he does *not* feel, he rather thinks, above you and me!' And so chatting, they glided off arm-in-arm.

*Luit.* And the result is …

*1st Bys.* Why that, a month having gone by, the indomitable Chiappino, marrying as he will Luitolfo's love – at all events succeeding to Luitolfo's wealth – becomes the first inhabitant of Faenza, and a proper aspirant to the Provostship; which we assemble here to see conferred on him this morning. The Legate's Guard to clear the way! He will follow presently.

*Luit.* [*withdrawing a little*]. I understand the drift of Eulalia's communications less than ever. Yet she surely said, in so many words, that Chiappino was in urgent danger: wherefore, disregarding her injunction to continue in my retreat and await the result of – what she called, some experiment yet in process – I hastened here without her leave or knowledge: how could I else? But if this they say be true – if it were for such a purpose, she and Chiappino kept me away … Oh, no, no! I must confront him and her before I believe this of them. And at the word, see!

*Enter* CHIAPPINO *and* EULALIA.

*Eu.* We part here, then? The change in

your principles would seem to be complete.

*Ch*. Now, why refuse to see that in my present course I change no principles, only re-adapt them and more adroitly? I had despaired of, what you may call the material instrumentality of life; of ever being able to rightly operate on mankind through such a deranged machinery as the existing modes of government: but now, if I suddenly discover how to inform these perverted institutions with fresh purpose, bring the functionary limbs once more into immediate communication with, and subjection to, the soul I am about to bestow on them – do you see? Why should one desire to invent, as long as it remains possible to renew and transform? When all further hope of the old organization shall be extinct, then, I grant you, it may be time to try and create another.

*Eu*. And there being discoverable some hope yet in the hitherto much-abused old system of absolute government by a Provost here, you mean to take your time about endeavouring to realize those visions of a perfect State, we once heard of?

*Ch*. Say, I would fain realize my conception of a palace, for instance, and that there is, abstractedly, but a single way of erecting one perfectly. Here, in the market-place is my allotted building-ground; here I stand without a stone to lay, or a labourer to help me, – stand, too, during a short day of life, close on which the night comes. On the other hand, circumstances suddenly offer me (turn and see it!) the old Provost's house to experiment upon – ruinous, if you please, wrongly constructed at the beginning, and ready to tumble now. But materials abound, a crowd of workmen offer their services; here, exists yet a Hall of Audience of originally noble proportions, there a

Guest-chamber of symmetrical design enough: and I may restore, enlarge, abolish or unite these to heart's content. Ought I not make the best of such an opportunity, rather than continue to gaze disconsolately with folded arms on the flat pavement here, while the sun goes slowly down, never to rise again? Since you cannot understand this nor me, it is better we should part as you desire.

*Eu*. So, the love breaks away too!

*Ch*. No, rather my soul's capacity for love widens – needs more than one object to content it, – and, being better instructed, will not persist in seeing all the component parts of love in what is only a single part, – nor in finding that so many and so various loves are all united in the love of a woman, – manifold uses in one instrument, as the savage has his sword, staff, sceptre and idol, all in one club-stick. Love is a very compound thing. The intellectual part of my love I shall give to men, the mighty dead or the illustrious living; and determine to call a mere sensual instinct by as few fine names as possible. What do I lose?

*Eu*. Nay, I only think, what do I lose? and, one more word – which shall complete my instruction – does friendship go too? What of Luitolfo, the author of your present prosperity?

*Ch*. How the author?

*Eu*. That blow now called yours …

*Ch*. Struck without principle or purpose, as by a blind natural operation: yet to which an my thought and life directly and advisedly tended. I would have struck it, and could not: he would have done his utmost to avoid striking it, yet did so. I dispute his right to that deed of mine – a final action with him, from the first effect of which he fled away, – a mere first step with me, on which I base a whole mighty superstructure of good to follow. Could he get good from it?

*Eu.* So we profess, so we perform!

*Enter* OGNIBEN. EULALIA *stands apart.*

*Ogni.* I have seen three-and-twenty leaders of revolts. By your leave, sir! Perform? What does the lady say of performing?

*Ch.* Only the trite saying, that we must not trust profession, only performance.

*Ogni.* Shell not say that, sir, when she knows you longer; you'll instruct her better. Ever judge of men by their professions! For though the bright moment of promising is but a moment and cannot be prolonged, yet, if sincere in its moment's extravagant goodness, why, trust it and know the man by it, I say – not by his performance; which is half the world's work, interfere as the world needs must, with its accidents and circumstances: the profession was purely the man's own. I judge people by what they might be, – not are, nor will be.

*Ch.* But have there not been found, too, performing natures, not merely promising?

*Ogni.* Plenty. Little Bindo of our town, for instance, promised his friend, great ugly Masaccio, once, 'I will repay you!' – for a favour done him. So, when his father came to die, and Bindo succeeded to the inheritance, he sends straightway for Masaccio and shares all with him – gives him half the land, half the money, half the kegs of wine in the cellar. 'Good,' say you: and it is good. But had little Bindo found himself possessor of all this wealth some five years before – on the happy night when Masaccio procured him that interview in the garden with his pretty cousin Lisa – instead of being the beggar he then was, – I am bound to believe that in the warm moment of promise he would have given away all the wine-kegs and all the money and all the land, and only reserved to himself some hut on a hill-top hard by, whence he might spend his life in looking and seeing his friend enjoy himself: he meant fully that much, but the world interfered. – To our business! Did I understand you just now within-doors? You are not going to marry your old friend's love, after all?

*Ch.* I must have a women that can sympathize with, and appreciate me, I told you.

*Ogni.* Oh, I remember! you, the greater nature, needs must have a lesser one ( – avowedly lesser – contest with you on that score would never do) – such a nature must comprehend you, as the phrase is, accompany and testify of your greatness from point to point onward. Why, that were being not merely as great as yourself, but greater considerably! Meantime, might not the more bounded nature as reasonably count on your appreciation of it, rather? – on your keeping close by it, so far as you both go together, and then going on by yourself as far as you please? Thus God serves us.

*Ch.* And yet a woman that could understand the whole of me, to whom I could reveal alike the strength and the weakness –

*Ogni.* Ah, my friend, wish for nothing so foolish! Worship your love, give her the best of you to see; be to her like the western lands (they bring us such strange news of) to the Spanish Court; send her only your lumps of gold, fans of feathers, your spirit-like birds, and fruits and gems! So shall you, what is unseen of you, be supposed altogether a paradise by her, – as these western lands by Spain: though I warrant there is filth, red baboons, ugly reptiles and squalor enough, which they bring Spain as few samples of as possible. Do you want your mistress to respect your body generally? Offer her your mouth to kiss: don't strip off your boot and put your foot to her lips! You understand my humour by this time? I help men to carry out their own principles: if they please to say two and two make five, I assent, so they will but go on and say, four and four make ten.

*Ch.* But these are my private affairs; what I desire you to occupy yourself about, is my public appearance presently: for when the people hear that I am appointed Provost, though you and I may thoroughly discern – and easily, too – the right principle at bottom of such a movement, and how my republicanism remains thoroughly unaltered, only takes a form of expression hitherto commonly judged (and heretofore by myself) incompatible with its existence, – when thus I reconcile myself to an old form of government instead of proposing a new one …

*Ogni.* Why, you must deal with people broadly. Begin at a distance from this matter and say, – New truths, old truths! sirs, there is nothing new possible to be revealed to us in the moral world; we know all we shall ever know: and it is for simply reminding us, by their various respective expedients, how we do know this and the other matter, that men get called prophets, poets and the like. A philosopher's life is spent in discovering that, of tHe half-dozen truths he knew when a child, such an one is a lie, as the world states it in set terms: and then, after a weary lapse of years, and plenty of hard-thinking, it becomes a truth again after all, as he happens to newly consider it and view it in a different relation with the others: and so he restates it, to the confusion of somebody else in good time. As for adding to the original stock of truths, –

impossible! Thus, you see the expression of them is the grand business: – you have got a truth in your head about the right way of governing people, and you took a mode of expressing it which now you confess to be imperfect. But what then? There is truth in falsehood, falsehood in truth. No man ever told one great truth, that I know, without the help of a good dozen of lies at least, generally unconscious ones. And as when a child comes in breathlessly and relates a strange story, you try to conjecture from the very falsities in it, what the reality was, – do not conclude that he saw nothing in the sky, because he assuredly did not see a flying horse there as he says, – so, through the contradictory expression, do you see, men should look painfully for, and trust to arrive eventually at, what you call the true principle at bottom. Ah, what an answer is there! to what will it not prove applicable? – 'Contradictions? Of course there were,' say you!

*Ch.* Still, the world at large may call it inconsistency, and what shall I urge in reply?

*Ogni.* Why, look you, when they tax you with tergiversation or duplicity, you may answer – you begin to perceive that, when all's done and said, both great parties in the State, the advocators of change in the present system of things, and the opponents of it, patriot and anti-patriot, are found working together for the common good; and that in the midst of their efforts for and against its progress, the world somehow or other still advances: to which result they contribute in equal proportions, those who spend their life in pushing it onward, as those who give theirs to the business of pulling it back. Now, if you found the world stand still between the opposite forces, and were glad, I should conceive you: but it steadily advances, you rejoice to see! By the side of such a rejoicer, the man who only winks as he keeps cunning and quiet, and says, 'Let yonder hot headed fellow fight out my battle! I, for one, shall win in the end by the blows he gives, and which I ought to be giving' – even he seems graceful m his avowal, when one considers that he might say, 'I shall win quite as much by the blows our antagonist gives him, blows from which he saves me – I thank the antagonist equally!' Moreover, you may enlarge on the loss of the edge of party-animosity with age and experience ...

*Ch.* And naturally time must wear off such asperities: the bitterest adversaries get to discover certain points of similarity between each other, common sympathies – do they not?

*Ogni.* Ay, had the young David but sat first to dine on his cheeses with the Philistine, he had soon discovered an abundance of such common sympathies. He of Gath, it is recorded, was born of a father and mother, had brothers and sisters like another man, – they, no more than the sons of Jesse, were used to eat each other. But, for the sake of one broad antipathy that had existed from the beginning, David slung the stone, cut off the giant's head, made a spoil of it, and after ate his cheeses alone, with the better appetite, for all I can learn. My friend, as you, with a quickened eye-sight, go on discovering much good on the worse side, remember that the same process should proportionately magnify and demonstrate to you the much more good on the better side! And when I profess no sympathy for the Goliaths of our time, and you object that a large nature should sympathize with every form of intelligence, and see the good in it, however limited – I answer, 'So I do; but preserve the proportions of my sympathy, however finelier or widelier I may extend its action.' I desire to be able, with a quickened eye-sight, to descry beauty in corruption where others see foulness only: but I hope I shall also continue to see a redoubled beauty in the higher forms of matter, where already everybody sees no foulness at all. I must retain, too, my old power of selection, and choice of appropriation, to apply to such new gifts; else they only dazzle instead of enlightening me. God has his archangels and consorts with them: though he made too, and intimately sees what is good in, the worm. Observe, I speak only as you profess to think and, so, ought to speak: I do justice to your own principles, that is all.

*Ch.* But you very well know that the two parties do, on occasion, assume each other's characteristics. What more disgusting, for instance, than to see how promptly the newly emancipated slave will adopt, in his own favour, the very measures of precaution, which pressed soreliest on himself as institutions of the tyranny he has just escaped from? Do the classes, hitherto without opinion, get leave to express it? there follows a confederacy immediately, from which – exercise your individual right and dissent, and woe be to you!

*Ogni.* And a journey over the sea to you! That is the generous way. Cry – 'Emancipated slaves, the first excess, and off I go!' The first time a poor devil, who has been bastinadoed steadily his whole life long, finds himself let alone and able to legislate, so, begins pettishly, while he rubs his soles, 'Woe be to whoever brings anything in the shape of a stick this way!' – you, rather than give up the very innocent pleasure of carrying one to switch flies with, – you go away, to everybody's sorrow. Yet you were quite reconciled to staying at home while the governors used to pass, every now and then, some such edict as 'Let no man indulge in owning a stick which is not thick enough to chastise our slaves, if need require!' Well, there are pre-ordained hierarchies among us, and a profane vulgar subjected to a different law altogether; yet I am rather sorry you should see it so clearly: for, do you know what is to – all but save you at the Day of Judgment, all you men of genius? It is this: that, while you generally began by pulling down God, and went on to the end of your life, in one effort at setting up your own genius in his place, – still, the last, bitterest concession wrung with the utmost unwillingness from the experience of the very loftiest of you, was invariably – would one think it? – that the rest of mankind, down to the lowest of the mass, stood not, nor ever could stand, just on a level and equality with yourselves. That will be a point in the favour of all such, I hope and believe.

*Ch.* Why, men of genius are usually charged, I think, with doing just the reverse; and at once acknowledging the natural inequality of mankind, by themselves participating in the universal craving after, and deference to, the civil distinctions which represent it. You wonder they pay such undue respect to titles and badges of superior rank.

*Ogni.* Not I (always on your own ground and showing, be it noted!) Who doubts that, with a weapon to brandish, a man is the more formidable? Titles and badges are exercised as such a weapon, to which you and I look up wistfully. We could pin lions with it moreover, while in its present owner's hands it hardly prods rats. Nay, better than a mere weapon of easy mastery and obvious use, it is a mysterious divining rod that may serve us in undreamed-of ways. Beauty, strength, intellect – men

often have none of these, and yet conceive pretty accurately what kind of advantages they would bestow on the possessor. We know at least what it is we make up our mind to forego, and so can apply the fittest substitute in our power. Wanting beauty, we cultivate good humour; missing wit, we get riches: but the mystic unimaginable operation of that gold collar and string of Latin names which suddenly turned poor stupid little peevish Cecco of our town into natural lord of the best of us – a Duke, he is now – there indeed is a virtue to be reverenced!

*Ch.* Ay, by the vulgar: not by Messere Stiatta the poet, who pays more assiduous court to him than anybody.

*Ogni.* What else should Stiatta pay court to? He has talent, not honour and riches: men naturally covet what they have not.

*Ch.* No, or Cecco would covet talent, which he has not, whereas he covets more riches, of which he has plenty, already.

*Ogni.* Because a purse added to a purse makes the holder twice as rich: but just such another talent as Stiatta's, added to what he now possesses, what would that profit him? Give the talent a purse indeed, to do something with! But lo, how we keep the good people waiting! I only desired to do justice to the noble sentiments which animate you, and which you are too modest to duly enforce. Come, to our main business: shall we ascend the steps? I am going to propose you for Provost to the people; they know your antecedents, and will accept you with a joyful unanimity: whereon I confirm their choice. Rouse up! Are you nerving yourself to an effort? Beware the disaster of Messere Stiatta we were talking of! who, determining to keep an equal mind and constant face on whatever might be the fortune of his last new poem with our townsmen, heard too plainly 'hiss, hiss, hiss,' increase every moment. Till at last the man fell senseless: not perceiving that the portentous sounds had all the while been issuing from between his own nobly clenched teeth, and nostrils narrowed by resolve.

*Ch*. Do you begin to throw off the mask? – to jest with me, having got me effectually into your trap?

*Ogni*. Where is the trap, my friend? You hear what I engage to do, for my part you, for yours, have only to fulfil your promise made just now within doors, of professing unlimited obedience to Rome's authority in my person. And I shall authorize no more than the simple reestablishment of the Provostship and the conferment of its privileges upon yourself: the only novel stipulation being a birth of the peculiar circumstances of the time.

*Ch*. And that stipulation?

*Ogni*. Just the obvious one – that in the event of the discovery of the actual assailant of the late Provost …

*Ch*. Ha!

*Ogni*. Why, he shall suffer the proper penalty, of course; what did you expect?

*Ch*. Who heard of this?

*Ogni*. Rather, who needed to hear of this?

*Ch*. Can it be, the popular rumour never reached you …

*Ogni*. Many more such rumours reach me, friend, than I choose to receive; those which wait longest have best chance. Has the present one sufficiently waited? Now is its time or entry with effect. See the good people crowding about yonder palace-steps – which we may not have to ascend, after all. My good friends! (nay, two or three of you will answer every purpose) – who was it fell upon and proved nearly the death of your late Provost? His successor

desires to hear, that his day of inauguration may be graced by the act of prompt bare justice we all anticipate. Who dealt the blow that night, does anybody know?

*Luit*. [*coming forward*]. I.

*All*. Luitolfo!

*Luit*. I avow the deed, justify and approve it, and stand forth now, to relieve my friend of an unearned responsibility. Having taken thought, I am grown stronger: I shall shrink from nothing that awaits me. Nay, Chiappino – we are friends still: I dare say there is some proof of your superior nature in this starting aside, strange as it seemed at first. So, they tell me, my horse is of the right stock, because a shadow in the path frightens him into a frenzy, makes him dash my brains out. I understand only the dull mule's way of standing stockishly, plodding soberly, suffering on occasion a blow or two with due patience.

*Eu*. I was determined to justify my choice, Chiappino, – to let Luitolfo's nature vindicate itself. Henceforth we are undivided, whatever be our fortune.

*Ogni*. Now, in these last ten minutes of silence, what have I been doing, deem you? Putting the finishing stroke to a homily of mine, I have long taken thought to perfect, on the text, 'Let whoso thinketh he standeth, take heed lest he fall. To your house, Luitolfo! Still silent, my patriotic friend? Well, that is a good sign however. And you will go aside for a time? That is better still. I understand: it would be easy for you to die of remorse here on the spot and shock us all, but you mean to live and grow worthy of coming back to us one day. There, I will tell everybody; and you only do right to believe you must get better as you get older. All men do so: they are worst in childhood, improve in manhood, and get ready in old age for another world. Youth, with its beauty and grace, would seem bestowed on us for some such reason as to make us partly endurable till we have time for really becoming so of ourselves, without their aid; when they leave us. The sweetest child we all smile on for his pleasant want of the whole world to break up, or suck in his mouth, seeing no other good in it – would be rudely handled by that world's inhabitants, if he retained those angelic infantine desires when he had grown six feet high, black and bearded. But, little by little, he sees fit to forego claim after claim on the world, puts up with a less and less share of its good as his proper portion; and when the octogenarian asks barely a sup of gruel and a fire of dry sticks, and thanks you as for his full allowance and right in the common good of life, – hoping nobody may murder him, – he who began by asking and expecting the whole of us to bow down in worship to him, – why, I say he is advanced, far onward, very far, nearly out of sight like our friend Chiappino yonder. And now – (ay, good-bye to you! He turns round the north-west gate: going to Lugo again? Good-bye!) – and now give thanks to God, the keys of the Provost's palace to me, and yourselves to profitable meditation at home! I have known *Four*-and-twenty leaders of revolts.

# CHRISTMAS-EVE AND EASTER-DAY

1850

## *Christmas-Eve*

### 1

Out of the little chapel I burst
   Into the fresh night-air again.
Five minutes full, I waited first
   In the doorway, to escape the rain
That drove in gusts down the common's
     centre
   At the edge of which the chapel
     stands,
Before I plucked up heart to enter.
   Heaven knows how many sorts of
     hands
Reached past me, groping for the latch
Of the inner door that hung on catch
More obstinate the more they fumbled,
   Till, giving way at last with a scold
Of the crazy hinge, in squeezed or
     tumbled
One sheep more to the rest in fold,
And left me irresolute, standing sentry
In the sheepfold's lath-and-plaster
     entry,
Six feet long by three feet wide,
Partitioned off from the vast inside –
   I blocked up half of it at least.
No remedy; the rain kept driving.
   They eyed me much as some wild
     beast,
That congregation, still arriving,
Some of them by the main road, white
A long way past me into the night,
Skirting the common, then diverging;
Not a few suddenly emerging
From the common's self thro' the
     paling-gaps,
– They house in the gravel-pits
     perhaps,
Where the road stops short with its
     safeguard border
Of lamps, as tired of such disorder; –
But the most turned in yet more
     abruptly

From a certain squalid knot of alleys,
Where the town's bad blood once slept
     corruptly,
   Which now the little chapel rallies
And leads into day again, – its priestliness
Lending itself to hide their beastliness
So cleverly (thanks in part to the
     mason),
And putting so cheery a whitewashed
     face on
Those neophytes too much in lack of it,
   That, where you cross the common
     as I did,
   And meet the party thus presided,
'Mount Zion' with Love-lane at the
     back of it,
They front you as little disconcerted
As, bound for the hills, her fate averted,
And her wicked people made to mind
     him,
Lot might have marched with Gomorrah
     behind him.

### 2

Well, from the road, the lanes or the
     common,
In came the flock: the fat weary
     woman,
Panting and bewildered, down-
     clapping
   Her umbrella with a mighty report,
Grounded it by me, wry and flapping,
   A wreck of whalebones; then, with a
     snort,
Like a startled horse, at the interloper
(Who humbly knew himself improper,
But could not shrink up small enough)
– Round to the door, and in, – the gruff
Hinge's invariable scold
Making my very blood run cold.
Prompt in the wake of her, up-pattered
On broken clogs, the many-tattered
Little old-faced peaking sister-turned-
     mother

Of the sickly babe she tried to smother
Somehow up, with its spotted face,
From the cold, on her breast, the one
    warm place;
She too must stop, wring the poor ends
    dry
Of a draggled shawl, and add thereby
Her tribute to the door-mat, sopping
Already from my own clothes' dropping,
Which yet she seemed to grudge I should
    stand on:
    Then, stooping down to take off her
        pattens,
She bore them defiantly, in each hand
    one,
Planted together before her breast
And its babe, as good as a lance in rest.
    Close on her heels, the dingy satins
Of a female something, past me flitted,
    With lips as much too white, as a
        streak
    Lay far too red on each hollow cheek;
And it seemed the very door-hinge pitied
All that was left of a woman once,
Holding at least its tongue for the nonce.
Then a tall yellow man, like the Penitent
    Thief,
With his jaw bound up in a hand-
    kerchief,
And eyelids screwed together tight,
Led himself in by some inner light.
And, except from him, from each that
    entered,
    I got the same interrogation –
'What, you the alien, you have ventured
    'To take with us, the elect, your
        station?
'A carer for none of it, a Gallio!' –
    Thus, plain as print, I read the glance
At a common prey, in each countenance
    As of huntsman giving his hounds
        the tallyho.
And, when the door's cry drowned
    their wonder,
    The draught, it always sent in shutting,
Made the flame of the single tallow
    candle

In the cracked square lantern I stood
    under,
    Shoot its blue lip at me, rebutting
As it were, the luckless cause of scandal:
I verily fancied the zealous light
(In the chapel's secret, too!) for spite
Would shudder itself clean off the wick,
With the airs of a Saint John's Candle-
    stick.*
There was no standing it much longer.
'Good folks,' thought I, as resolve grew
    stronger,
'This way you perform the Grand-
    Inquisitor
'When the weather sends you a chance
    visitor?
'You are the men, and wisdom shall
    die with you,
'And none of the old Seven Churches
    vie with you!
'But still, despite the pretty perfection
    'To which you carry your trick of
        exclusiveness,
'And, taking God's word under wise
    protection,
    'Correct its tendency to diffusiveness,
'And bid one reach it over hot
    ploughshares, –
    'Still, as I say, though you've found
        salvation,
'If I should choose to cry, as now,
    "Shares!" –
    'See if the best of you bars me my
        ration!
'I prefer, if you please, for my expounder
'Of the laws of the feast, the feast's
    own Founder;
'Mine's the same right with your
    poorest and sickliest
    'Supposing I don the marriage
        vestiment:
    'So, shut your mouth and open your
        Testament,
'And carve me my portion at your
    quickliest!'

* *See* Revelation 1:20.

Accordingly, as a shoemaker's lad
  With wizened face in want of soap,
  And wet apron wound round his
    waist like a rope,
(After stopping outside, for his cough
  was bad,
To get the fit over, poor gentle creature,
And so avoid disturbing the preacher)
– Passed in, I sent my elbow spikewise
At the shutting door, and entered
  likewise,
Received the hinge's accustomed greeting,
  And crossed the threshold's magic
    pentacle,
  And found myself in full conventicle,
– To wit, in Zion Chapel Meeting,
On the Christmas-Eve of 'Forty-nine,
  Which, calling its flock to their special
    clover,
  Found all assembled and one sheep
    over,
Whose lot, as the weather pleased, was
  mine.

3

I very soon had enough of it.
  The hot smell and the human noises,
And my neighbour's coat, the greasy
  cuff of it,
  Were a pebble-stone that a child's
    hand poises,
Compared with the pig-of-lead-like
  pressure
  Of the preaching man's immense
    stupidity,
As he poured his doctrine forth, full
  measure,
  To meet his audience's avidity.
You needed not the wit of the Sibyl
  To guess the cause of it all, in a
    twinkling:
  No sooner our friend had got an
    inkling
Of treasure hid in the Holy Bible,
(Whene'er 'twas the thought first
  struck him,
How death, at unawares, might duck
  him

Deeper than the grave, and quench
The gin-shop's light in hell's grim drench)
Than he handled it so, in fine irreverence,
  As to hug the book of books to
    pieces:
And, a patchwork of chapters and texts
  in severance,
  Not improved by the private dog's-
    ears and creases,
Having clothed his own soul with, he'd
  fain see equipt yours, –
So tossed you again your Holy Scriptures.
And you picked them up, in a sense,
  no doubt:
  Nay, had but a single face of my
    neighbours
  Appeared to suspect that the
    preacher's labours
Were help which the world could be
  saved without,
'Tis odds but I might have borne in
  quiet
A qualm or two at my spiritual diet,
Or (who can tell?) perchance even
  mustered
  Somewhat to urge in behalf of the
    sermon:
But the flock sat on, divinely flustered,
  Sniffing, methought, its dew of
    Hermon
With such content in every snuffle,
As the devil inside us loves to ruffle.
My old fat woman purred with pleasure,
  And thumb round thumb went
    twirling faster,
While she, to his periods keeping
  measure,
  Maternally devoured the pastor.
The man with the handkerchief
  untied it,
Showed us a horrible wen inside it,
Gave his eyelids yet another screwing,
And rocked himself as the woman was
  doing.
The shoemaker's lad, discreetly choking,
Kept down his cough. 'Twas too
  provoking!

My gorge rose at the nonsense and stuff
    of it;
    So, saying like Eve when she plucked
    the apple,
    'I wanted a taste, and now there's
    enough of it,'
I flung out of the little chapel.

4

There was a lull in the rain, a lull
    In the wind too; the moon was risen,
And would have shone out pure and
    full,
    But for the ramparted cloud-prison,
Block on block built up in the West,
For what purpose the wind knows best,
Who changes his mind continually.
And the empty other half of the sky
Seemed in its silence as if it knew
What, any moment, might look through
A chance gap in that fortress massy: –
    Through its fissures you got hints
    Of the flying moon, by the shifting
    tints,
Now, a dull lion-colour, now, brassy
Burning to yellow, and whitest yellow,
Like furnace-smoke just ere flames
    bellow,
All a-simmer with intense strain
To let her through, – then blank again,
At the hope of her appearance failing.
Just by the chapel, a break in the railing
Shows a narrow path directly across;
'Tis ever dry walking there, on the
    moss –
Besides, you go gently all the way uphill.
    I stooped under and soon felt better;
My head grew lighter, my limbs more
    supple,
    As I walked on, glad to have slipt the
    fetter.
My mind was full of the scene I had left,
    That placid flock, that pastor
    vociferant,
    – How this outside was pure and
    different!
The sermon, now – what a mingled
    weft

Of good and ill! Were either less,
    Its fellow had coloured the whole
    distinctly;
But alas for the excellent earnestness,
    And the truths, quite true if stated
    succinctly,
But as surely false, in their quaint
    presentment,
However to pastor and flock's
    contentment!
Say rather, such truths looked false to
    your eyes,
    With his provings and parallels
    twisted and twined,
Till how could you know them, grown
    double their size
    In the natural fog of the good man's
    mind,
Like yonder spots of our roadside
    lamps,
Haloed about with the common's
    damps?
Truth remains true, the fault's in the
    prover;
    The zeal was good, and the aspiration;
And yet, and yet, yet, fifty times over,
    Pharaoh received no demonstration,
By his Baker's dream of Baskets Three,
Of the doctrine of the Trinity, –
Although, as our preacher thus
    embellished it,
Apparently his hearers relished it
With so unfeigned a gust – who
    knows if
They did not prefer our friend to
    Joseph?
But so it is everywhere, one way with
    all of them!
    These people have really felt, no
    doubt,
A something, the motion they style the
    Call of them;
    And this is their method of bringing
    about,
By a mechanism of words and tones,
(So many texts in so many groans)
A sort of reviving and reproducing,

More or less perfectly, (who can tell?)
The mood itself, which strengthens by
      using;
   And how that happens, I understand
      well.
A tune was born in my head last week,
Out of the thump-thump and shriek-
      shriek
   Of the train, as I came by it, up from
      Manchester;
And when, next week, I take it back
      again,
My head will sing to the engine's clack
      again,
   While it only makes my neighbour's
      haunches stir,
– Finding no dormant musical sprout
In him, as in me, to be jolted out.
'Tis the taught already that profits by
      teaching;
He gets no more from the railway's
      preaching
   Than, from this preacher who does
      the rail's office, I:
Whom therefore the flock cast a jealous
      eye on.
Still, why paint over their door 'Mount
      Zion,'
   To which all flesh shall come, saith
      the prophecy?

5

But wherefore be harsh on a single case?
   After how many modes, this
      Christmas-Eve,
Does the self-same weary thing take
      place?
   The same endeavour to make you
      believe,
And with much the same effect, no
      more:
   Each method abundantly convincing,
As I say, to those convinced before,
   But scarce to be swallowed without
      wincing
By the not-as-yet-convinced. For me,
I have my own church equally:
And in this church my faith sprang first!

(I said, as I reached the rising ground,
And the wind began again, with a burst
   Of rain in my face, and a glad rebound
From the heart beneath, as if, God
      speeding me,
I entered his church-door, nature leading
      me)
– In youth I looked to these very skies,
And probing their immensities,
I found God there, his visible power;
   Yet felt in my heart, amid all its sense
   Of the power, an equal evidence
That his love, there too, was the nobler
      dower.
For the loving worm within its clod,
Were diviner than a loveless god
Amid his worlds, I will dare to say.
   You know what I mean: God's all,
      man's nought:
   But also, God, whose pleasure brought
Man into being, stands away
   As it were a handbreadth off, to give
   Room for the newly-made to live,
And look at him from a place apart,
And use his gifts of brain and heart,
Given, indeed, but to keep for ever.
Who speaks of man, then, must not
      sever
Man's very elements from man,
Saying, 'But all is God's' – whose plan
Was to create man and then leave him
Able, his own word saith, to grieve him,
But able to glorify him too,
As a mere machine could never do,
That prayed or praised, all unaware
Of its fitness for aught but praise and
      prayer,
Made perfect as a thing of course.
Man, therefore, stands on his own stock
Of love and power as a pin-point rock:
And, looking to God who ordained
      divorce
Of the rock from his boundless continent,
Sees, in his power made evident,
Only excess by a million-fold
O'er the power God gave man in the
      mould.

For, note: man's hand, first formed to
   carry
A few pounds' weight, when taught to
   marry
Its strength with an engine's, lifts a
   mountain,
    – Advancing in power by one degree;
    And why count steps through eternity?
But love is the ever-springing fountain:
Man may enlarge or narrow his bed
For the water's play, but the water-
   head –
How can he multiply or reduce it?
    As easy create it, as cause it to cease;
He may profit by it, or abuse it,
    But 'tis not a thing to bear increase
As power does: be love less or more
    In the heart of man, he keeps it shut
    Or opes it wide, as he pleases, but
Love's sum remains what it was before.
So, gazing up, in my youth, at love
As seen through power, ever above
All modes which make it manifest,
My soul brought all to a single test –
That he, the Eternal First and Last,
Who, in his power, had so surpassed
All man conceives of what is might, –
Whose wisdom, too, showed infinite,
– Would prove as infinitely good;
Would never, (my soul understood,)
With power to work all love desires,
Bestow e'en less than man requires;
That he who endlessly was teaching,
Above my spirit's utmost reaching,
What love can do in the leaf or stone,
(So that to master this alone,
This done in the stone or leaf for me,
I must go on learning endlessly)
Would never need that I, in turn,
   Should point him out defect
    unheeded,
And show that God had yet to learn
   What the meanest human creature
    needed,
– Not life, to wit, for a few short years,
Tracking his way through doubts and
   fears,

While the stupid earth on which I stay
   Suffers no change, but passive adds
    Its myriad years to myriads,
Though I, he gave it to, decay,
Seeing death come and choose
    about me,
And my dearest ones depart without
    me.
No: love which, on earth, amid all the
   shows of it,
   Has ever been seen the sole good of
    life in it,
   The love, ever growing there, spite of
    the strife in it,
Shall arise, made perfect, from death's
   repose of it.
And shall behold thee, face to face,
O God, and in thy light retrace
How in all I loved here, still wast thou!
Whom pressing to, then, as I fain would
   now,
I shall find as able to satiate
   The love, thy gift, as my spirit's wonder
Thou art able to quicken and sublimate,
   With this sky of thine, that I now
    walk under,
And glory in thee for, as I gaze
Thus, thus! Oh, let men keep their ways
Of seeking thee in a narrow shrine –
Be this my way! And this is mine!

6

For lo, what think you? suddenly
The rain and the wind ceased, and the
   sky
Received at once the full fruition
Of the moon's consummate apparition.
The black cloud-barricade was riven,
Ruined beneath her feet, and driven
Deep in the West; while, bare and
   breathless,
   North and South and East lay ready
For a glorious thing that, dauntless,
   deathless,
   Sprang across **them** and stood steady.
'Twas a moon-**rainbow**, vast and perfect,
From heaven to **heaven** extending,
   perfect

As the mother-moon's self, full in face.
It rose, distinctly at the base
  With its seven proper colours chorded,
Which still, in the rising, were
      compressed,
Until at last they coalesced,
  And supreme the spectral creature
      lorded
In a triumph of whitest white, –
Above which intervened the night.
But above night too, like only the next,
  The second of a wondrous sequence,
  Reaching in rare and rarer frequence,
Till the heaven of heavens were
      circumflexed,
Another rainbow rose, a mightier,
Fainter, flushier and flightier, –
Rapture dying along its verge.
Oh, whose foot shall I see emerge,
Whose, from the straining topmost
      dark,
On to the keystone of that arc?

7

This sight was shown me, there and
      then, –
Me, one out of a world of men,
Singled forth, as the chance might hap
To another if, in a thunderclap
Where I heard noise and you saw flame,
Some one man knew God called his
      name.
For me, I think I said, 'Appear!
'Good were it to be ever here.
'If thou wilt, let me build to thee
'Service-tabernacles three,
'Where, forever in thy presence,
'In ecstatic acquiescence,
'Far alike from thriftless learning
'And ignorance's undiscernng,
'I may worship and remain!
  Thus at the show above me, gazing
With upturned eyes, I felt my brain
  Glutted with the glory, blazing
Throughout its whole mass, over and
      under
Until at length it burst asunder
And out of it bodily there streamed,

The too-much glory, as it seemed,
Passing from out me to the ground,
Then palely serpentining round
Into the dark with mazy error.

8

All at once I looked up with terror.
He was there.
He himself with his human air.
On the narrow pathway, just before.
I saw the back of him, no more –
He had left the chapel, then, as I.
I forgot all about the sky.
No face: only the sight
Of a sweepy garment, vast and white,
With a hem that I could recognize.
I felt terror, no surprise;
My mind filled with the cataract,
At one bound of the mighty fact.
'I remember, he did say
  'Doubtless that, to this world's end,
'Where two or three should meet and
      pray,
  'He would be in the midst, their
      friend;
'Certainly he was there with them!'
  And my pulses leaped for joy
  Of the golden thought without alloy,
That I saw his very vesture's hem.
Then rushed the blood back, cold and
      clear,
With a fresh enhancing shiver of fear;
And I hastened, cried out while I
      pressed
To the salvation of the vest,
'But not so, Lord! It cannot be
'That thou, indeed, art leaving me –
'Me, that have despised thy friends!
'Did my heart make no amends?
'Thou art the love of God – above
'His power, didst hear me place his
      love,
'And that was leaving the world for
      thee.
'Therefore thou must not turn from me
'As I had chosen the other part!
'Folly and pride o'ercame my heart.
'Our best is bad, nor bears thy test;

'Still, it should be our very best.
'I thought it best that thou, the spirit,
  'Be worshipped in spirit and in
    truth,
'And in beauty, as even we require it –
  'Not in the forms burlesque,
    uncouth,
'I left but now, as scarcely fitted
'For thee: I knew not what I pitied.
'But, all I felt there, right or wrong,
  'What is it to thee, who curest
    sinning?
'Am I not weak as thou art strong?
  'I have looked to thee from the
    beginning,
'Straight up to thee through all the
    world
'Which, like an idle scroll, lay furled
'To nothingness on either side:
'And since the time thou wast
    descried,
'Spite of the weak heart, so have I
'Lived ever, and so fain would die,
'Living and dying, thee before!
'But if thou leavest me – '

            9

                    Less or more,
I suppose that I spoke thus.
When, – have mercy, Lord, on us!
The whole face turned upon me full.
  And I spread myself beneath it,
  As when the bleacher spreads, to
    seethe it
In the cleansing sun, his wool, –
Steeps in the flood of noontide whiteness
  Some defiled, discoloured web –
So lay I, saturate with brightness.
  And when the flood appeared to ebb,
Lo, I was walking, light and swift,
  With my senses settling fast and
    steadying,
But my body caught up in the whirl
    and drift
  Of the vesture's amplitude, still
    eddying
On, just before me, still to be followed,
  As it carried me after with its motion:

What shall I say? – as a path were
    hollowed
  And a man went weltering through
    the ocean,
Sucked along in the flying wake
Of the luminous water-snake.
Darkness and cold were cloven, as
    through
I passed, upborne yet walking too.
And I turned to myself at intervals, –
'So he said, so it befalls.
'God who registers the cup
  'Of mere cold water, for his sake
'To a disciple rendered up,
  'Disdains not his own thirst to slake
'At the poorest love was ever offered:
'And because my heart I proffered,
'With true love trembling at the brim,
'He suffers me to follow him
'For ever, my own way, – dispensed
'From seeking to be influenced
'By all the less immediate ways
  'That earth, in worships manifold,
'Adopts to reach, by prayer and praise,
  'The garment's hem, which, lo, I
    hold!'

            10

And so we crossed the world and
    stopped.
  For where am I, in city or plain,
  Since I am 'ware of the world again?
And what is this that rises propped
With pillars of prodigious girth?
Is it really on the earth,
This miraculous Dome of God?
Has the angel's measuring-rod
Which numbered cubits, gem from gem,
'Twixt the gates of the New Jerusalem,
Meted it out, – and what he meted,
Have the sons of men completed?
– Binding, ever as he bade,
Columns in the colonnade
With arms wide open to embrace
The entry of the human race
To the breast of … what is it, yon
    building,
Ablaze in front, all paint and gilding,

With marble for brick, and stones of
   price
For garniture of the edifice?
Now I see; it is no dream;
It stands there and it does not seem;
For ever, in pictures, thus it looks,
And thus I have read of it in books
Often in England, leagues away,
And wondered how these fountains
   play,
Growing up eternally
Each to a musical water-tree,
Whose blossoms drop, a glittering boon,
Before my eyes, in the light of the moon,
To the granite lavers underneath.
Liar and dreamer in your teeth!
I, the sinner that speak to you,
Was in Rome this night, and stood, and
   knew
Both this and more. For see, for see,
The dark is rent, mine eye is free
To pierce the crust of the outer wall,
And I view inside, and all there, all,
As the swarming hollow of a hive,
The whole Basilica alive!
Men in the chancel, body and nave,
Men on the pillars' architrave,
Men on the statues, men on the tombs
With popes and kings in their porphyry
   wombs,
All famishing in expectation
Of the main-altar's consummation.
For see, for see, the rapturous moment
Approaches, and earth's best endowment
Blends with heaven's; the taper-fires
Pant up, the winding brazen spires
Heave loftier yet the baldachin;
The incense-gaspings, long kept in,
Suspire in clouds; the organ blatant
Holds his breath and grovels latent,
As if God's hushing finger grazed him,
(Like Behemoth when he praised him)
At the silver bell's shrill tinkling,
Quick cold drops of terror sprinkling
On the sudden pavement strewed
With faces of the multitude.
Earth breaks up, time drops away,

In flows heaven, with its new day
Of endless life, when He who trod,
Very man and very God,
This earth in weakness, shame and pain,
Dying the death whose signs remain
Up yonder on the accursed tree, –
Shall come again, no more to be
Of captivity the thrall,
But the one God, All in all,
King of kings, Lord of lords.
As His servant John received the words,
'I died, and live for evermore!'

11

Yet I was left outside the door.
'Why sit I here on the threshold-stone
'Left till He return, alone
'Save for the garment's extreme fold
'Abandoned still to bless my hold?'
My reason, to my doubt, replied,
As if a book were opened wide,
And at a certain page I traced
Every record undefaced,
Added by successive years, –
The harvestings of truth's stray ears
Singly gleaned, and in one sheaf
Bound together for belief.
Yes, I said – that he will go
And sit with these in turn, I know.
Their faith's heart beats, though her
   head swims
Too giddily to guide her limbs,
Disabled by their palsy-stroke
From propping mine. Though Rome's
   gross yoke
Drops off, no more to be endured,
Her teaching is not so obscured
By errors and perversities,
That no truth shines athwart the lies
And he, whose eye detects a spark
Even where, to man's, the whole seems
   dark,
May well see flame where each beholder
Acknowledges the embers smoulder.
But I, a mere man, fear to quit
The clue God gave me as most fit
To guide my footsteps through life's
   maze,

Because himself discerns all ways
Open to reach him: I, a man
Able to mark where faith began
To swerve aside, till from its summit
Judgment drops her damning plummet,
Pronouncing such a fatal space
Departed from the founder's base:
He will not bid me enter too,
But rather sit, as now I do,
Awaiting his return outside.
– 'Twas thus my reason straight replied
And joyously I turned, and pressed
The garment's skirt upon my breast,
Until, afresh its light suffusing me,
My heart cried – What has been
    abusing me
That I should wait here lonely and
    coldly
Instead of rising, entering boldly,
Baring truth's face, and letting drift
Her veils of lies as they choose to shift?
Do these men praise him? I will raise
My voice up to their point of praise!
I see the error; but above
The scope of error, see the love. –
Oh, love of those first Christian days!
– Fanned so soon into a blaze,
From the spark preserved by the
    trampled sect,
That the antique sovereign Intellect
Which then sat ruling in the world,
Like a change in dreams, was hurled
From the throne he reigned upon:
You looked up and he was gone.
Gone, his glory of the pen!
– Love, with Greece and Rome in ken,
Bade her scribes abhor the trick
Of poetry and rhetoric,
And exult with hearts set free,
In blessed imbecility
Scrawled, perchance, on some torn
    sheet
Leaving Sallust incomplete.
Gone, his pride of sculptor, painter!
– Love, while able to acquaint her
With the thousand statues yet
Fresh from chisel, pictures wet

From brush, she saw on every side,
Chose rather with an infant's pride
To frame those portents which impart
Such unction to true Christian Art.
Gone, music too! The air was stirred
By happy wings: Terpander's bird
(That, when the cold came, fled away)
Would tarry not the wintry day, –
As more-enduring sculpture must,
Till filthy saints rebuked the gust
With which they chanced to get a sight
Of some dear naked Aphrodite
They glanced a thought above the
    toes of,
By breaking zealously her nose off.
Love, surely, from that music's
    lingering,
Might have filched her organ-fingering,
Nor chosen rather to set prayings
To hog-grunts, praises to horse-neighings.
Love was the startling thing, the new:
Love was the all-sufficient too;
And seeing that, you see the rest:
As a babe can find its mother's breast
As well in darkness as in light,
Love shut our eyes, and all seemed
    right.
True, the world's eyes are open now:
– Less need for me to disallow
Some few that keep Love's zone
    unbuckled,
Peevish as ever to be suckled,
Lulled by the same old baby-prattle
With intermixture of the rattle,
When she would have them creep,
    stand steady
Upon their feet, or walk already,
Not to speak of trying to climb.
I will be wise another time,
And not desire a wall between us,
    When next I see a church-roof cover
So many species of one genus,
    All with foreheads bearing *lover*
Written above the earnest eyes of them;
    All with breasts that beat for beauty,
Whether sublimed, to the surprise of
    them,

In noble daring, steadfast duty,
The heroic in passion, or in action, –
Or, lowered for sense's satisfaction,
To the mere outside of human creatures,
Mere perfect form and faultless features.
What? with all Rome here, whence to
    levy
  Such contributions to their appetite,
With women and men in a gorgeous
    bevy,
  They take, as it were, a padlock, clap
    it tight
On their southern eyes, restrained from
    feeding
On the glories of their ancient reading,
On the beauties of their modern singing,
On the wonders of the builder's bringing,
On the majesties of Art around them, –
  And, all these loves, late struggling
    incessant,
When faith has at last united and
    bound them,
  They offer up to God for a present?
Why, I will, on the whole, be rather
    proud of it, –
  And, only taking the act in reference
To the other recipients who might have
    allowed it,
  I will rejoice that God had the
    preference.

### 12

So I summed up my new resolves:
  Too much love there can never be.
And where the intellect devolves
  Its function on love exclusively,
I, a man who possesses both,
Will accept the provision, nothing loth,
– Will feast my love, then depart
    elsewhere,
That my intellect may find its share.
And ponder, O soul, the while thou
    departest,
And see thou applaud the great heart
    of the artist,
Who, examining the capabilities
  Of the block of marble he has to
    fashion

Into a type of thought or passion, –
Not always, using obvious facilities,
Shapes it, as any artist can,
Into a perfect symmetrical man,
Complete from head to foot of the life-
    size,
Such as old Adam stood in his wife's
    eyes, –
But, now and then, bravely aspires to
    consummate
A Colossus by no means so easy to
    come at,
And uses the whole of his block for the
    bust,
  Leaving the mind of the public to
    finish it,
Since cut it ruefully short he must:
On the face alone he expends his
    devotion,
  He rather would mar than resolve to
    diminish it,
– Saying, 'Applaud me for this grand
    notion
'Of what a face may be! As for
    completing it
  'In breast and body and limbs, do
    that, you!'
All hail! I fancy how, happily meeting it,
  A trunk and legs would perfect the
    statue,
Could man carve so as to answer volition.
  And how much nobler than petty
    cavils,
  Were a hope to find, in my spirit-
    travels,
Some artist of another ambition,
Who having a block to carve, no bigger,
  Has spent his power on the opposite
    quest,
  And believed to begin at the feet was
    best –
For so may I see, ere I die, the whole
    figure!

### 13

No sooner said than out in the night!
My heart beat lighter and more light:
And still, as before, I was walking swift,

With my senses settling fast and
   steadying,
But my body caught up in the whirl and
   drift
   Of the vesture's amplitude, still
     eddying
On just before me, still to be followed,
   As it carried me after with its motion,
– What shall I say? – as a path were
   hollowed,
   And a man went weltering through
     the ocean,
Sucked along in the flying wake
Of the luminous water-snake.

14

Alone! I am left alone once more –
   (Save for the garment's extreme fold
   Abandoned still to bless my hold)
Alone, beside the entrance-door
Of a sort of temple, – perhaps a college,
– Like nothing I ever saw before
At home in England, to my knowledge.
The tall old quaint irregular town!
   It may be … though which, I can't
     affirm … any
   Of the famous middle-age towns of
     Germany;
And this flight of stairs where I sit down,
Is it Halle, Weimar, Cassel, Frankfort
Or Göttingen, I have to thank for't?
It may be Göttingen, – most likely.
Through the open door I catch obliquely
Glimpses of a lecture-hall;
   And not a bad assembly neither,
Ranged decent and symmetrical
   On benches, waiting what's to see
     there;
Which, holding still by the vesture's
   hem,
I also resolve to see with them,
Cautious this time how I suffer to slip
The chance of joining in fellowship
With any that call themselves his
   friends;
   As these folk do, I have a notion.
   But hist – a buzzing and emotion!
All settle themselves, the while ascends

By the creaking rail to the lecture-desk,
   Step by step, deliberate
   Because of his cranium's over-freight,
Three parts sublime to one grotesque,
If I have proved an accurate guesser,
The hawk-nosed high-cheek-boned
     Professor.
I felt at once as if there ran
A shoot of love from my heart to the
     man –
That sallow virgin-minded studious
   Martyr to mild enthusiasm,
As he uttered a kind of cough-preludious
   That woke my sympathetic spasm,
(Beside some spitting that made me
     sorry)
And stood, surveying his auditory
With a wan pure look, well nigh
   celestial, –
   Those blue eyes had survived so much!
   While, under the foot they could not
     smutch,
Lay all the fleshly and the bestial.
Over he bowed, and arranged his notes,
Till the auditory's clearing of throats
Was done with, died into a silence;
   And, when each glance was upward
     sent,
   Each bearded mouth composed intent,
And a pin might be heard drop half a
   mile hence, –
He pushed back higher his spectacles,
Let the eyes stream out like lamps from
   cells,
And giving his head of hair – a hake
   Of undressed tow, for colour and
     quantity –
One rapid and impatient shake,
   (As our own Young England adjusts
     a jaunty tie
When about to impart, on mature
     digestion,
Some thrilling view of the surplice-
     question)
– The Professor's grave voice, sweet
   though hoarse,
Broke into his Christmas-Eve discourse.

15

And he began it by observing
  How reason dictated that men
Should rectify the natural swerving,
  By a reversion, now and then,
To the well-heads of knowledge, few
And far away, whence rolling grew
The life-stream wide whereat we drink,
Commingled, as we needs must think,
With waters alien to the source;
To do which, aimed this eve's
    discourse;
Since, where could be a fitter time
For tracing backward to its prime
This Christianity, this lake,
This reservoir, whereat we slake,
From one or other bank, our thirst?
So, he proposed inquiring first
Into the various sources whence
  This Myth of Christ is derivable;
Demanding from the evidence,
  (Since plainly no such life was liveable)
How these phenomena should class?
Whether 'twere best opine Christ was,
Or never was at all, or whether
He was and was not, both together –
It matters little for the name,
So the idea be left the same.
Only, for practical purpose' sake,
'Twas obviously as well to take
The popular story, – understanding
  How the ineptitude of the time,
And the penman's prejudice,
    expanding
  Fact into fable fit for the clime,
Had, by slow and sure degrees,
    translated it
  Into this myth, this Individuum, –
Which, when reason had strained and
    abated it
  Of foreign matter, left, for residuum,
A Man! – a right true man, however,
Whose work was worthy a man's
    endeavour:
Work, that gave warrant almost
    sufficient
  To his disciples, for rather believing

He was just omnipotent and omniscient,
  As it gives to us, for as frankly receiving
His word, their tradition, – which,
    though it meant
Something entirely different
From all that those who only heard it,
In their simplicity thought and
    averred it,
Had yet a meaning quite as respectable:
For, among other doctrines delectable,
Was he not surely the first to insist on
  The natural sovereignty of our race? –
  Here the lecturer came to a pausing-
    place.
And while his cough, like a drouthy
    piston,
Tried to dislodge the husk that grew to
  · him,
I seized the occasion of bidding adieu
    to him,
The vesture still within my hand.

16

I could interpret its command.
This time he would not bid me enter
The exhausted air-bell of the Critic.
Truth's atmosphere may grow mephilic
When Papist struggles with Dissenter,
Impregnating its pristine clarity,
– One, by his daily fare's vulgarity,
  Its gust of broken meat and garlic;
– One, by his soul's too-much
    presuming
To turn the frankincense's fuming
  And vapours of the candle starlike
Into the cloud her wings she buoys on.
  Each, that thus sets the pure air
    seething,
  May poison it for healthy breathing –
But the Critic leaves no air to poison;
Pumps out with ruthless ingenuity
Atom by atom, and leaves you – vacuity.
Thus much of Christ does he reject?
And what retain? His intellect?
What is it I must reverence duly?
Poor intellect for worship, truly,
Which tells me simply what was told
  (If mere morality, bereft

Of the God in Christ, be all that's left)
Elsewhere by voices manifold;
With this advantage, that the stater
  Made nowise the important stumble
  Of adding, he, the sage and humble,
Was also one with the Creator.
You urge Christ's followers' simplicity:
  But how does shifting blame,
     evade it?
Have wisdom's words no more felicity?
  The stumbling-block, his speech –
     who laid it?
How comes it that for one found able
To sift the truth of it from fable,
Millions believe it to the letter?
Christ's goodness, then – does that fare
     better?
Strange goodness, which upon the score
  Of being goodness, the mere due
Of man to fellow-man, much more
  To God, – should take another view
Of its possessor's privilege,
And bid him rule his race! You pledge
Your fealty to such rule? What, all –
From heavenly John and Attic Paul,
And that brave weather-battered Peter,
Whose stout faith only stood completer
For buffets, sinning to be pardoned,
As, the more his hands hauled nets,
     they hardened, –
All, down to you, the man of men,
Professing here at Göttingen,
Compose Christ's flock! They, you
     and I,
Are sheep of a good man! And why?
The goodness, – how did he acquire it?
Was it self-gained, did God inspire it?
Choose which; then tell me, on what
     ground
Should its possessor dare propound
His claim to rise o'er us an inch?
  Were goodness all some man's
     invention,
  Who arbitrarily made mention
What we should follow, and whence
     flinch, –
What qualities might take the style

Of right and wrong, – and had such
     guessing
  Met with as general acquiescing
As graced the alphabet erewhile,
When A got leave an Ox to be,
No Camel (quoth the Jews) like G,* –
For thus inventing thing and title
Worship were that man's fit requital.
But if the common conscience must
Be ultimately judge, adjust
Its apt name to each quality
Already known, – I would decree
Worship for such mere demonstration
  And simple work of nomenclature,
  Only the day I praised, not nature,
But Harvey, for the circulation.
I would praise such a Christ, with pride
And joy, that he, as none beside,
Had taught us how to keep the mind
God gave him, as God gave his kind,
Freer than they from fleshly taint:
I would call such a Christ our Saint,
As I declare our Poet, him
Whose insight makes all others dim:
A thousand poets pried at life,
And only one amid the strife
Rose to be Shakespeare: each shall take
His crown, I'd say, for the world's
     sake –
Though some objected – 'Had we seen
'The heart and head of each, what screen
'Was broken there to give them light,
'While in ourselves it shuts the sight,
'We should no more admire, perchance,
'That these found truth out at a glance,
'Than marvel how the bat discerns
'Some pitch-dark cavern's fifty turns,
'Led by a finer tact, a gift
'He boasts, which other birds must
     shift
'Without, and grope as best they can.'
No, freely I would praise the man, –
Nor one whit more, if he contended
That gift of his, from God descended.
Ah friend, what gift of man's does not?

---

\* *Gimel*, the Hebrew G, means camel

No nearer something, by a jot,
Rise an infinity of nothings
  Than one: take Euclid for your
    teacher:
Distinguish kinds: do crownings,
    clothings,
  Make that creator which was
    creature?
Multiply gifts upon man's head,
And what, when all's done, shall be
    said
But – the more gifted he, I ween!
  That one's made Christ, this other,
    Pilate,
And this might be all that has been, –
  So what is there to frown or smile at?
What is left for us, save, in growth
Of soul, to rise up, far past both,
From the gift looking to the giver,
And from the cistern to the river,
And from the finite to infinity.
And from man's dust to God's divinity?

17

Take all in a word: the truth in God's
    breast
Lies trace for trace upon ours impressed:
Though he is so bright and we so dim,
We are made in his image to witness
    him:
And were no eye in us to tell,
  Instructed by no inner sense,
The light of heaven from the dark of
    hell,
  That light would want its evidence, –
Though justice, good and truth were
    still
Divine, if, by some demon's will,
Hatred and wrong had been proclaimed
Law through the worlds, and right mis
    named.
No mere exposition of morality
Made or in part or in totality,
Should win you to give it worship,
    therefore:
And, if no better proof you will care for,
– Whom do you count the worst man
    upon earth?

Be sure, he knows, in his conscience,
    more
Of what right is, than arrives at birth
  In the best man's acts that we bow
    before:
This last knows better – true, but my
    fact is,
'Tis one thing to know, and another to
    practise.
And thence I conclude that the real
    God-function
Is to furnish a motive and injunction
For practising what we know already.
And such an injunction and such a
    motive
As the God in Christ, do you waive,
    and 'heady,
'High-minded,' hang your tablet-votive
Outside the fane on a finger-post?
Morality to the uttermost,
Supreme in Christ as we all confess,
Why need we prove would avail no jot
To make him God, if God he were not?
What is the point where himself lays
    stress?
Does the precept run 'Believe in good,
'In justice, truth, now understood
'For the first time?' – or, 'Believe in me,
'Who lived and died, yet essentially
'Am Lord of Life?' Whoever can take
The same to his heart and for mere
    love's sake
Conceive of the love, – that man
    obtains
A new truth; no conviction gains
Of an old one only, made intense
By a fresh appeal to his faded sense.

18

Can it be that he stays inside?
  Is the vesture left me to commune
    with?
  Could my soul find aught to sing in
    tune with
Even at this lecture, if she tried?
Oh, let me at lowest sympathize
With the lurking drop of blood that
    lies

In the desiccated brain's white roots
Without throb for Christ's attributes,
As the lecturer makes his special boast!
If love's dead there, it has left a ghost.
Admire we, how from heart to brain
    (Though to say so strike the doctors
        dumb)
One instinct rises and falls again,
    Restoring the equilibrium.
And how when the Critic had done his
        bost,
And the pearl of price, at reason's test,
Lay dust and ashes levigable
On the Professor's lecture-table, –
When we looked for the inference and
        monition
That our faith, reduced to such condition,
Be swept forthwith to its natural dust-
        hole, –
    He bids us, when we least expect it,
Take back our faith, – if it be not just
        whole,
    Yet a pearl indeed, as his tests
        affect it,
Which fact pays damage done
        rewardingly,
So, prize we our dust and ashes
        accordingly!
'Go home and venerate the myth
'I thus have experimented with –
'This man, continue to adore him
'Rather than all who went before him,
'And all who ever followed after!' –
    Surely for this I may praise you, my
        brother!
Will you take the praise in tears or
        laughter?
    That's one point gained: can I
        compass another?
Unlearned love was safe from
        spurning –
Can't we respect your loveless learning?
Let us at least give learning honour!
What laurels had we showered upon
        her,
Girding her loins up to perturb
Our theory of the Middle Verb;

Or Turk-like brandishing a scimitar
O'er anapæsts in comic-trimeter;
Or curing the halt and maimed
        'Iketides,'*
While we lounged on at our indebted
        ease:
Instead of which, a tricksy demon
Sets her at Titus or Philemon!
When ignorance wags his ears of leather
And hates God's word, 'tis altogether;
Nor leaves he his congenial thistles
To go and browse on Paul's Epistles.
– And you, the audience, who might
        ravage
The world wide, enviably savage,
Nor heed the cry of the retriever,
More than Herr Heine (before his
        fever), –
I do not tell a lie so arrant
    As say my passion's wings are furled
        up,
And, without plainest heavenly warrant,
    I were ready and glad to give the
        world up –
But still, when you rub brow meticulous,
    And ponder the profit of turning
        holy
    If not for God's, for your own sake
        solely,
– God forbid I should find you
        ridiculous!
Deduce from this lecture all that eases
        you,
Nay, call yourselves, if the calling pleases
        you,
'Christians,' – abhor the deist's
        pravity, –
Go on, you shall no more move my
        gravity
Than, when I see boys ride a-cockhorse,
I find it in my heart to embarrass them
By hinting that their stick's a mock
        horse,
And they really carry what they say
        carries them.

* *The Suppliants*, a fragment of a play by Æschylus

### 19

So sat I talking with my mind.
  I did not long to leave the door
  And find a new church, as before,
But rather was quiet and inclined
To prolong and enjoy the gentle resting
From further tracking and trying and
    testing.
'This tolerance is a genial mood!'
(Said I, and a little pause ensued.)
'One trims the bark 'twixt shoal and
    shelf,
  'And sees, each side, the good effects
    of it,
'A value for religion's self,
  'A carelessness about the sects of it.
'Let me enjoy my own conviction,
  'Not watch my neighbour's faith
    with fretfulness,
'Still spying there some dereliction
  'Of truth, perversity, forgetfulness!
'Better a mild indifferentism,
  'Teaching that both our faiths (though
    duller
'His shine through a dull spirit's prism)
  'Originally had one colour!
'Better pursue a pilgrimage
  'Through ancient and through
    modern times
  'To many peoples, various climes,
'Where I may see saint, savage, sage
'Fuse their respective creeds in one
'Before the general Father's throne!'

### 20

– 'Twas the horrible storm began afresh!
The black night caught me in his mesh,
Whirled me up, and flung me prone.
I was left on the college-step alone.
I looked, and far there, ever fleeting
Far, far away, the receding gesture,
And looming of the lessening vesture! –
Swept forward from my stupid hand,
While I watched my foolish heart expand
In the lazy glow of benevolence,
  O'er the various modes of man's
    belief.
I sprang up with fear's vehemence.

Needs must there be one way, our
    chief
Best way of worship: let me strive
To find it, and when found, contrive
My fellows also take their share!
This constitutes my earthly care:
God's is above it and distinct.
For I, a man, with men am linked
And not a brute with brutes; no gain
That I experience, must remain
Unshared: but should my best endeavour
To share it, fail – subsisteth ever
God's care above, and I exult
That God, by God's own ways occult,
May – doth, I will believe – bring back
All wanderers to a single track.
Meantime, I can but testify
God's care for me – no more, can I –
It is but for myself I know;
  The world rolls witnessing around me
  Only to leave me as it found me;
Men cry there, but my ear is slow:
Their races flourish or decay
– What boots it, while yon lucid way
Loaded with stars divides the vault?
But soon my soul repairs its fault
When, sharpening sense's hebetude,
She turns on my own life! So viewed,
No mere mote's-breadth but teems
    immense
With witnessings of providence:
And woe to me if when I look
Upon that record, the sole book
Unsealed to me, I take no heed
Of any warning that I read!
Have I been sure, this Christmas-Eve,
God's own hand did the rainbow
    weave,
Whereby the truth from heaven slid
Into my soul? – I cannot bid
The world admit he stooped to heal
My soul, as if in a thunder-peal
Where one heard noise, and one saw
    flame,
I only knew he named my name:
But what is the world to me, for sorrow
Or joy in its censure, when to-morrow

It drops the remark, with just-turned
 head
Then, on again, 'That man is dead'?
Yes, but for me – my name called, –
 drawn
As a conscript's lot from the lap's black
 yawn,
He has dipt into on a battle-dawn:
Bid out of life by a nod, a glance, –
Stumbling, mute-mazed, at nature's
 chance, –
With a rapid finger circled round,
Fixed to the first poor inch of ground
To fight from, where his foot was found;
Whose ear but a minute since lay free
To the wide camp's buzz and gossipry –
Summoned, a solitary man
To end his life where his life began,
From the safe glad rear, to the dreadful
 van!
Soul of mine, hadst thou caught and
 held
By the hem of the vesture! –

21

And I caught
At the flying robe, and unrepelled
 Was lapped again in its folds full-
 fraught
With warmth and wonder and delight,
God's mercy being infinite.
For scarce had the words escaped my
 tongue,
When, at a passionate bound, I sprung,
Out of the wandering world of rain,
Into the little chapel again.

22

How else was I found there, bolt upright
 On my bench, as if I had never left it?
– Never flung out on the common at
 night,
 Nor met the storm and wedge-like
 cleft it,
Seen the raree-show of Peter's successor,
Or the laboratory of the Professor!
For the Vision, that was true, I wist,
True as that heaven and earth exist.
There sat my friend, the yellow and tall,

With his neck and its wen in the
 selfsame place;
Yet my nearest neighbour's cheek
 showed gall.
 She had slid away a contemptuous
 space:
And the old fat woman, late so placable,
Eyed me with symptoms, hardly
 mistakable,
Of her milk of kindness turning rancid.
In short, a spectator might have fancied
 That I had nodded, betrayed by
 slumber,
Yet kept my seat, a warning ghastly,
 Through the heads of the sermon,
 nine in number,
And woke up now at the tenth and
 lastly.
But again, could such disgrace have
 happened?
 Each friend at my elbow had surely
 nudged it;
And, as for the sermon, where did my
 nap end?
 Unless I heard it, could I have
 judged it?
Could I report as I do at the close,
First, the preacher speaks through his
 nose:
Second, his gesture is too emphatic:
 Thirdly, to waive what's pedagogic,
 The subject-matter itself lacks logic:
Fourthly, the English is ungrammatic.
Great news! the preacher is found no
 Pascal,
Whom, if I pleased, I might to the task
 call
Of making square to a finite eye
The circle of infinity,
And find so all-but-just-succeeding!
Great news! the sermon proves no reading
Where bee-like in the flowers I bury me,
Like Taylor's, the immortal Jeremy!
And now that I know the very worst of
 him,
What was it I thought to obtain at first
 of him?

Ha! Is God mocked, as he asks?
Shall I take on me to change his tasks,
And dare, despatched to a river-head
   For a simple draught of the element,
   Neglect the thing for which he sent,
And return with another thing instead? –
Saying, 'Because the water found
'Welling up from underground,
'Is mingled with the taints of earth,
'While thou, I know, dost laugh at
   dearth,
'And couldst, at wink or word, convulse
'The world with the leap of a river-
   pulse, –
'Therefore I turned from the oozings
   muddy,
   'And bring thee a chalice I found,
   instead:
'See the brave veins in the breccia ruddy!
   'One would suppose that the marble
   bled.
'What matters the water? A hope I have
   nursed:
'The waterless cup will quench my
   thirst.'
– Better have knelt at the poorest stream
   That trickles in pain from the straitest
   rift!
   For the less or the more is all God's
   gift,
Who blocks up or breaks wide the
   granite-seam.
And here, is there water or not, to
   drink?
   I then, in ignorance and weakness,
Taking God's help, have attained to
   think
   My heart does best to receive in
   meekness
That mode of worship, as most to his
   mind,
Where earthly aids being cast behind,
His All in All appears serene
With the thinnest human veil between,
Letting the mystic lamps, the seven,
   The many motions of his spirit,
Pass, as they list, to earth from heaven.

   For the preacher's merit or demerit,
It were to be wished the flaws were
   fewer
   In the earthen vessel, holding treasure
Which lies as safe in a golden ewer;
   But the main thing is, does it hold
   good measure?
Heaven soon sets right all other
   matters! –
   Ask, else, these ruins of humanity,
This flesh worn out to rags and tatters,
   This soul at struggle with insanity,
Who thence take comfort – can I
   doubt? –
Which an empire gained, were a loss
   without.
May it be mine! And let us hope
That no worse blessing befall the Pope,
Turned sick at last of to-day's buffoonery,
   Of posturings and petticoatings,
   Beside his Bourbon bully's gloatings
In the bloody orgies of drunk
   poltroonery!
Nor may the Professor forego its peace
   At Göttingen presently, when, in the
   dusk
Of his life, if his cough, as I fear, should
   increase,
   Prophesied of by that horrible husk –
When thicker and thicker the darkness
   fills
The world through his misty spectacles,
And he gropes for something more
   substantial
   Than a fable, myth or
   personification, –
May Christ do for him what no mere
   man shall,
   And stand confessed as the God of
   salvation!
Meantime, in the still recurring fear
   Lest myself, at unawares, be found,
   While attacking the choice of my
   neighbours round,
With none of my own made – I choose
   here!
The giving out of the hymn reclaims me;

I have done: and if any blames me,
Thinking that merely to touch in brevity
  The topics I dwell on, were
    unlawful, –
Or worse, that I trench, with undue
    levity,
  On the bounds of the holy and the
    awful, –
I praise the heart, and pity the head of
  him,
And refer myself to Thee, instead of
  him,
Who head and heart alike discernest,
  Looking below light speech we utter,
  When frothy spume and frequent
    sputter
Prove that the soul's depths boil in
  earnest!
May truth shine out, stand ever
  before us!
I put up pencil and join chorus
To Hepzibah Tune, without further
    apology,
  The last five verses of the third section
  Of the seventeenth hymn of
    Whitfield's Collection,
To conclude with the doxology.

## Easter-Day

### 1

How very hard it is to be
A Christian! Hard for you and me,
– Not the mere task of making real
That duty up to its ideal,
Effecting thus, complete and whole,
A purpose of the human soul –
For that is always hard to do;
But hard, I mean, for me and you
To realize it, more or less,
With even the moderate success
Which commonly repays our strife
To carry out the aims of life.
'This aim is greater,' you will say,
'And so more arduous every way.'
– But the importance of their fruits

Still proves to man, in all pursuits,
Proportional encouragement.
'Then, what if it be God's intent
'That labour to this one result
'Should seem unduly difficult?'
Ah, that's a question in the dark –
And the sole thing that I remark
Upon the difficulty, this;
We do not see it where it is,
At the beginning of the race:
As we proceed, it shifts its place,
And where we looked for crowns to fall,
We find the tug's to come, – that's all.

### 2

At first you say, 'The whole, or chief
'Of difficulties, is belief.
'Could I believe once thoroughly,
'The rest were simple. What? Am I
'An idiot, do you think, – a beast?
'Prove to me, only that the least
'Command of God is God's indeed,
'And what injunction shall I need
'To pay obedience? Death so nigh,
'When time must end, eternity
'Begin, – and cannot I compute,
'Weigh loss and gain together, suit
'My actions to the balance drawn,
'And give my body to be sawn
'Asunder, hacked in pieces, tied
'To horses, stoned, burned, crucified,
'Like any martyr of the list?
'How gladly! – if I make acquist,
'Through the brief minute's fierce annoy,
'Of God's eternity of joy.'

### 3

– And certainly you name the point
Whereon all turns: for could you joint
This flexile finite life once tight
Into the fixed and infinite,
You, safe inside, would spurn what's
    out,
With carelessness enough, no doubt –
Would spurn mere life: but when time
    brings
To their next stage your reasonings,
Your eyes, late wide, begin to wink
Nor see the path so well, I think.

4

You say, 'Faith may be, one agrees,
'A touchstone for God's purposes,
'Even as ourselves conceive of them.
'Could he acquit us or condemn
'For holding what no hand can loose,
'Rejecting when we can't but choose?
'As well award the victor's wreath
'To whosoever should take breath
'Duly each minute while he lived –
'Grant heaven, because a man contrived
'To see its sunlight every day
'He walked forth on the public way.
'You must mix some uncertainty
'With faith, if you would have faith be.
'Why, what but faith, do we abhor
'And idolize each other for –
'Faith in our evil or our good,
'Which is or is not understood
'Aright by those we love or those
'We hate, thence called our friends or
          foes?
'Your mistress saw your spirit's grace,
'When, turning from the ugly face,
'I found belief in it too hard;
'And she and I have our reward.
' – Yet here a doubt peeps: well for us
'Weak beings, to go using thus
'A touchstone for our little ends,
'Trying with faith the foes and friends;
' – But God, bethink you! I would fain
'Conceive of the Creator's reign
'As based upon exacter laws
'Than creatures build by with applause.
'In all God's acts – (as Plato cries
'He doth) – he should geometrize.
'Whence, I desiderate … '

5

I see!

You would grow as a natural tree,
Stand as a rock, soar up like fire.
The world's so perfect and entire,
Quite above faith, so right and fit!
Go there, walk up and down in it!
No. The creation travails, groans –
Contrive your music from its moans,
Without or let or hindrance, friend!

That's an old story, and its end
As old – you come back (be sincere)
With every question you put here
(Here where there once was, and is
          still,
We think, a living oracle,
Whose answers you stand carping at)
This time flung back unanswered flat, –
Beside, perhaps, as many more
As those that drove you out before,
Now added, where was little need.
Questions impossible, indeed,
To us who sat still, all and each
Persuaded that our earth had speech,
Of God's, writ down, no matter if
In cursive type or hieroglyph, –
Which one fact freed us from the yoke
Of guessing why He never spoke.
You come back in no better plight
Than when you left us, – am I right?

6

So, the old process, I conclude,
Goes on, the reasoning's pursued
Further. You own, 'Tis well averred,
'A scientific faith's absurd,
' – Frustrates the very end 'twas meant
'To serve. So, I would rest content
'With a mere probability,
'But, probable; the chance must lie
'Clear on one side, – lie all in rough,
'So long as there be just enough
'To pin my faith to, though it hap
'Only at points: from gap to gap
'One hangs up a huge curtain so,
'Grandly, nor seeks to have it go
'Foldless and flat along the wall.
'What care I if some interval
'Of life less plainly may depend
'On God? I'd hang there to the end;
'And thus I should not find it hard
'To be a Christian and debarred
'From trailing on the earth, till furled
'Away by death. – Renounce the world!
'Were that a mighty hardship? Plan
'A pleasant life, and straight some man
'Beside you, with, if he thought fit,
'Abundant means to compass it,

'Shall turn deliberate aside
'To try and live as, if you tried
'You clearly might, yet most despise.
'One friend of mine wears out his eyes,
'Slighting the stupid joys of sense,
'In patient hope that, ten years hence,
' "Somewhat completer," he may say,
' " My list of *coleoptera!*"
'While just the other who most laughs
'At him, above all epitaphs
'Aspires to have his tomb describe
'Himself as sole among the tribe
'Of snuffbox-fanciers, who possessed
'A Grignon with the Regent's crest.
'So that, subduing, as you want,
'Whatever stands predominant
'Among my earthly appetites
'For tastes and smells and sounds and
        sights,
'I shall be doing that alone,
'To gain a palm-branch and a throne,
'Which fifty people undertake
'To do, and gladly, for the sake
'Of giving a Semitic guess,
'Or playing pawns at blindfold chess.'

7

Good: and the next thing is, – look
        round
For evidence enough! 'Tis found,
No doubt: as is your sort of mind,
So is your sort of search: you'll find
What you desire, and that's to be
A Christian. What says history?
How comforting a point it were
To find some mummy-scrap declare
There lived a Moses! Better still,
Prove Jonah's whale translatable
Into some quicksand of the seas,
Isle, cavern, rock, or what you please,
That faith might flap her wings and
        crow
From such an eminence! Or, no –
The human heart's best; you prefer
Making that prove the minister
To truth; you probe its wants and needs,
And hopes and fears, then try what
        creeds

Meet these most aptly, – resolute
That faith plucks such substantial fruit
Wherever these two correspond,
She little needs to look beyond,
And puzzle out who Orpheus was,
Or Dionysius Zagrias.
You'll find sufficient, as I say,
To satisfy you either way;
You wanted to believe; your pains
Are crowned – you do: and what
        remains?
'Renounce the world!' – Ah, were it
        done
By merely cutting one by one
Your limbs off, with your wise head last,
How easy were it! – how soon past,
If once in the believing mood!
'Such is man's usual gratitude,
'Such thanks to God do we return,
'For not exacting that we spurn
'A single gift of life, forego
'One real gain, – only taste them so
'With gravity and temperance,
'That those mild virtues may enhance
'Such pleasures, rather than abstract –
'Last spice of which, will be the fact
'Of love discerned in every gift;
'While, when the scene of life shall
        shift,
'And the gay heart be taught to ache,
'As sorrows and privations take
'The place of joy, – the thing that seems
'Mere misery, under human schemes,
'Becomes, regarded by the light
'Of love, as very near, or quite
'As good a gift as joy before.
'So plain is it that, all the more
'A dispensation's merciful,
'More pettishly we try and cull
'Briars, thistles, from our private plot,
'To mar God's ground where thorns
        are not!'

8

Do you say this, or I? – Oh, you!
Then, what, my friend? – (thus I pursue
Our parley) – you indeed opine
That the Eternal and Divine

Did, eighteen centuries ago,
In very truth … Enough! you know
The all-stupendous tale, – that Birth,
That Life, that Death! And all, the earth
Shuddered at, – all, the heavens grew
    black
Rather than see; all, nature's rack
And throe at dissolution's brink
Attested, – all took place, you think,
Only to give our joys a zest,
And prove our sorrows for the best?
We differ, then! Where I, still pale
And heartstruck at the dreadful tale,
Waiting to hear God's voice declare
What horror followed for my share,
As implicated in the deed,
Apart from other sins, – concede
That if He blacked out in a blot
My brief life's pleasantness, 'twere not
So very disproportionate!
Or there might be another fate –
I certainly could understand
(If fancies were the thing in hand)
How God might save, at that day's
    price,
The impure in their impurities,
Give licence formal and complete
To choose the fair and pick the sweet.
But there be certain words, broad, plain,
Uttered again and yet again,
Hard to mistake or overgloss –
Announcing this world's gain for loss,
And bidding us reject the same:
The whole world lieth (they proclaim)
In wickedness, – come out of it!
Turn a deaf ear, if you think fit,
But I who thrill through every nerve
At thought of what deaf ears deserve –
How do you counsel in the case?

9

'I'd take, by all means, in your place,
'The safe side, since it so appears:
'Deny myself, a few brief years,
'The natural pleasure, leave the fruit
'Or cut the plant up by the root.
'Remember what a martyr said
'On the rude tablet overhead!

' "I was born sickly, poor and mean,
' "A slave: no misery could screen
' "The holders of the pearl of price
' "From Cæsar's envy; therefore twice
' "I fought with beasts, and three times
    saw
' "My children suffer by his law;
' "At last my own release was earned:
' "I was some time in being burned,
' "But at the close a Hand came through
' "The fire above my head, and drew
' "My soul to Christ, whom now I see.
' "Sergius, a brother, writes for me
' "This testimony on the wall –
' "For me, I have forgot it all."
'You say right; this were not so hard!
'And since one nowise is debarred
'From this, why not escape some sins
'By such a method?'

10

    Then begins
To the old point revulsion new –
(For 'tis just this I bring you to)
If after all we should mistake,
And so renounce life for the sake
Of death and nothing else? You hear
Each friend we jeered at, send the jeer
Back to ourselves with good effect –
'There were my beetles to collect!
'My box – a trifle, I confess,
'But here I hold it, ne'ertheless!'
Poor idiots, (let us pluck up heart
And answer) we, the better part
Have chosen, though 'twere only
    hope, –
Nor envy moles like you that grope
Amid your veritable muck,
More than the grasshoppers would truck,
For yours, their passionate life away,
That spends itself in leaps all day
To reach the sun, you want the eyes
To see, as they the wings to rise
And match the noble hearts of them!
Thus the contemner we contemn, –
And, when doubt strikes us, thus we
    ward
Its stroke off, caught upon our guard,

– Not struck enough to overturn
Our faith, but shake it – make us learn
What I began with, and, I wis,
End, having proved, – how hard it is
To be a Christian!

11
    'Proved, or not,
'Howe'er you wis, small thanks, I wot,
'You get of mine, for taking pains
'To make it hard to me. Who gains
'By that, I wonder? Here I live
'In trusting ease; and here you drive
'At causing me to lose what most
'Yourself would mourn for had you lost!'

12
But, do you see, my friend, that thus
You leave Saint Paul for Æschylus?
– Who made his Titan's arch-device
The giving men *blind hopes* to spice
The meal of life with, else devoured
In bitter haste, while lo, death loured
Before them at the platter's edge!
If faith should be, as I allege,
Quite other than a condiment
To heighten flavours with, or meant
(Like that brave curry of his Grace)
To take at need the victuals' place?
If, having dined, you would digest
Besides, and turning to your rest
Should find instead …

13
    Now, you shall see
And judge if a mere foppery
Pricks on my speaking! I resolve
To utter – yes, it shall devolve
On you to hear as solemn, strange
And dread a thing as in the range
Of facts, – or fancies, if God will –
E'er happened to our kind! I still
Stand in the cloud and, while it wraps
My face, ought not to speak perhaps;
Seeing that if I carry through
My purpose, if my words in you
Find a live actual listener,
My story, reason must aver
False after all – the happy chance!
While, if each human countenance

I meet in London day by day,
Be what I fear, – my warnings fray
No one, and no one they convert,
And no one helps me to assert
How hard it is to really be
A Christian, and in vacancy
I pour this story!

14
    I commence
By trying to inform you, whence
It comes that every Easter-night
As now, I sit up, watch, till light,
Upon those chimney-stacks and roofs,
Give, through my window-pane, grey
    proofs
That Easter-day is breaking slow.
On such a night three years ago,
It chanced that I had cause to cross
The common, where the chapel was,
Our friend spoke of, the other day –
You've not forgotten, I dare say.
I fell to musing of the time
So close, the blessed matin-prime
All hearts leap up at, in some guise –
One could not well do otherwise.
Insensibly my thoughts were ben
Toward the main point; I overwent
Much the same ground of reasoning
As you and I just now. One thing
Remained, however – one that tasked
My soul to answer; and I asked,
Fairly and frankly, what might be
That History, that Faith, to me
– Me there – not me in some domain
Built up and peopled by my brain,
Weighing its merits as one weighs
Mere theories for blame or praise,
– The kingcraft of the Lucumons,
Or Fourier's scheme, its pros and
    cons, –
But my faith there, or none at all.
'How were my case, now, did I fall
'Dead here, this minute – should I lie
'Faithful or faithless?' Note that I
Inclined thus ever! – little prone
For instance, when I lay alone
In childhood, to go calm to sleep

And leave a closet where might keep
His watch perdue some murderer
Waiting till twelve o'clock to stir,
As good authentic legends tell:
'He might: but how improbable!
'How little likely to deserve
'The pains and trial to the nerve
'Of thrusting head into the dark!' –
Urged my old nurse, and bade me mark
Beside, that, should the dreadful scout
Really lie hid there, and leap out
At first turn of the rusty key,
Mine were small gain that she could see,
Killed not in bed but on the floor,
And losing one night's sleep the more.
I tell you, I would always burst
The door ope, know my fate at first.
This time, indeed, the closet penned
No such assassin: but a friend
Rather, peeped out to guard me, fit
For counsel, Common Sense, to wit,
Who said a good deal that might pass, –
Heartening, impartial too, it was,
Judge else: 'For, soberly now, – who
'Should be a Christian if not you?'
(Hear how he smoothed me down.)
        'One takes
'A whole life, sees what course it makes
'Mainly, and not by fits and starts –
'In spite of stoppage which imparts
'Fresh value to the general speed.
'A life, with none, would fly indeed:
'Your progressing is slower – right!
'We deal with progress and not flight.
'Through baffling senses passionate,
'Fancies as restless, – with a freight
'Of knowledge cumbersome enough
'To sink your ship when waves grow
        rough,
'Though meant for ballast in the hold, –
'I find,'mid dangers manifold,
'The good bark answers to the helm
'Where faith sits, easier to o'erwhelm
'Than some stout peasant's heavenly
        guide,
'Whose hard head could not, if it tried,
'Conceive a doubt, nor understand

'How senses hornier than his hand
'Should 'tice the Christian off his guard.
'More happy! But shall we award
'Less honour to the hull which, dogged
'By storms, a mere wreck, waterlogged,
'Masts by the board, her bulwarks gone
'And stanchions going, yet bears on, –
'Than to mere life-boats, built to save,
'And triumph o'er the breaking wave?
'Make perfect your good ship as these,
'And what were her performances!'
I added – 'Would the ship reach home!
'I wish indeed "God's kingdom
        come – "
'The day when I shall see appear
'His bidding, as my duty, clear
'From doubt! And it shall dawn, that
        day,
'Some future season; Easter may
'Prove, not impossibly, the time –
'Yes, that were striking – fates would
        chime
'So aptly! Easter-morn, to bring
'The Judgment! – deeper in the spring
'Than now, however, when there's snow
'Capping the hills; for earth must show
'All signs of meaning to pursue
'Her tasks as she was wont to do
' – The skylark, taken by surprise
'As we ourselves, shall recognize
'Sudden the end. For suddenly
'It comes; the dreadfulness must be
'In that; all warrants the belief –
' "At night it cometh like a thief."
'I fancy why the trumpet blows;
' – Plainly, to wake one. From repose
'We shall start up, at last awake
'From life, that insane dream we take
'For waking now, because it seems.
'And as, when now we wake from
        dreams,
'We laugh, while we recall them, "Fool,
' "To let the chance slip, linger cool
' "When such adventure offered! Just
' "A bridge to cross, a dwarf to thrust
' "Aside, a wicked mage to stab –
' "And, lo ye, I had kissed Queen Mab!"

'So shall we marvel why we grudged
'Our labour here, and idly judged
'Of heaven, we might have gained, but
    lose!
'Lose? Talk of loss, and I refuse
'To plead at all! You speak no worse
'Nor better than my ancient nurse
'When she would tell me in my youth
'I well deserved that shapes uncouth
'Frighted and teased me in my sleep:
'Why could I not in memory keep
'Her precept for the evil's cure?
' "Pinch your own arm, boy, and be sure
' "You'll wake forthwith!" '

15

                    And as I said
This nonsense, throwing back my head
With light complacent laugh, I found
Suddenly all the midnight round
One fire. The dome of heaven had stood
As made up of a multitude
Of handbreadth cloudlets, one vast rack
Of ripples infinite and black,
From sky to sky. Sudden there went,
Like horror and astonishment,
A fierce vindictive scribble of red
Quick flame across, as if one said
(The angry scribe of Judgment) 'There –
'Burn it!' And straight I was aware
That the whole ribwork round, minute
Cloud touching cloud beyond compute,
Was tinted, each with its own spot
Of burning at the core, till clot
Jammed against clot, and spilt its fire
Over all heaven, which 'gan suspire
As fanned to measure equable, –
Just so great conflagrations kill
Night overhead, and rise and sink,
Reflected. Now the fire would shrink
And wither off the blasted face
Of heaven, and I distinct might trace
The sharp black ridgy outlines left
Unburned like network – then, each
    cleft
The fire had been sucked back into,
Regorged, and out it surging flew
Furiously, and night writhed inflamed,

Till, tolerating to be tamed
No longer, certain rays world-wide
Shot downwardly. On every side
Caught past escape, the earth was lit;
As if a dragon's nostril split
And all his famished ire o'erflowed;
Then, as he winced at his lord's goad,
Back he inhaled: whereat I found
The clouds into vast pillars bound,
Based on the corners of the earth,
Propping the skies at top: a dearth
Of fire i' the violet intervals,
Leaving exposed the utmost walls
Of time, about to tumble in
And end the world.

16

                    I felt begin
The Judgment-Day: to retrocede
Was too late now. 'In very deed,'
(I uttered to myself) 'that Day!'
The intuition burned away
All darkness from my spirit too:
There, stood I, found and fixed, I knew,
Choosing the world. The choice was
    made;
And naked and disguiseless stayed,
And unevadable, the fact.
My brain held all the same compact
Its senses, nor my heart declined
Its office; rather, both combined
To help me in this juncture. I
Lost not a second, – agony
Gave boldness: since my life had end
And my choice with it – best defend,
Applaud both! I resolved to say,
'So was I framed by thee, such way
'I put to use thy senses here!
'It was so beautiful, so near,
'Thy world, – what could I then but
    choose
'My part there? Nor did I refuse
'To look above the transient boon
'Of time; but it was hard so soon
'As in a short life, to give up
'Such beauty: I could put the cup
'Undrained of half its fulness, by;
'But, to renounce it utterly,

' – That was too hard! Nor did the cry
'Which bade renounce it, touch my
   brain
'Authentically deep and plain
'Enough to make my lips let go.
'But Thou, who knowest all, dost know
'Whether I was not, life's brief while,
'Endeavouring to reconcile
'Those lips (too tardily, alas!)
'To letting the dear remnant pass,
'One day, – some drops of earthly good
'Untasted! Is it for this mood,
'That Thou, whose earth delights so
   well,
'Hast made its complement a hell?'

17

A final belch of fire like blood,
Overbroke all heaven in one flood
Of doom. Then fire was sky, and sky
Fire, and both, one brief ecstasy,
Then ashes. But I heard no noise
(Whatever was) because a voice
Beside me spoke thus, 'Life is done,
'Time ends, Eternity's begun,
'And thou art judged for evermore.'

18

I looked up; all seemed as before;
Of that cloud-Tophet overhead
No trace was left: I saw instead
The common round me, and the sky
Above, stretched drear and emptily
Of life. 'Twas the last watch of night,
Except what brings the morning quite;
When the armed angel, conscience-clear,
His task nigh done, leans o'er his spear
And gazes on the earth he guards,
Safe one night more through all its
   wards,
Till God relieve him at his post.
'A dream – a waking dream at most!'
(I spoke out quick, that I might shake
The horrid nightmare off, and wake.)
'The world gone, yet the world is here?
'Are not all things as they appear?
'Is Judgment past for me alone?
' – And where had place the great
   white throne?

'The rising of the quick and dead?
'Where stood they, small and great?
   Who read
'The sentence from the opened book?'
So, by degrees, the blood forsook
My heart, and let it beat afresh;
I knew I should break through the mesh
Of horror, and breathe presently:
When, lo, again, the voice by me!

19

I saw … Oh brother, 'mid far sands
The palm-tree-cinctured city stands,
Bright-white beneath, as heaven, bright-
   blue,
Leans o'er it, while the years pursue
Their course, unable to abate
Its paradisal laugh at fate!
One morn, – the Arab staggers blind
O'er a new tract of death, calcined
To ashes, silence, nothingness, –
And strives, with dizzy wits, to guess
Whence fell the blow. What if, 'twixt
   skies
And prostrate earth, he should surprise
The imaged vapour, head to foot,
Surveying, motionless and mute,
Its work, ere, in a whirlwind rapt
It vanish up again? – So hapt
My chance. He stood there. Like the
   smoke
Pillared o'er Sodom, when day broke, –
I saw Him. One magnific pall
Mantled in massive fold and fall
His head, and coiled in snaky swathes
About His feet: night's black, that bathes
All else, broke, grizzled with despair,
Against the soul of blackness there.
A gesture told the mood within –
That wrapped right hand which based
   the chin,
That intense meditation fixed
On His procedure, – pity mixed
With the fulfilment of decree.
Motionless, thus, He spoke to me,
Who fell before His feet, a mass,
No man now.

20

'All is come to pass.
'Such shows are over for each soul
'They had respect to. In the roll
'Of Judgment which convinced mankind
'Of sin, stood many, bold and blind,'
'Terror must burn the truth into:
'Their fate for them! – thou hadst to do
'With absolute omnipotence,
'Able its judgments to dispense
'To the whole race, as every one
'Were its sole object. Judgment done,
'God is, thou art, – the rest is hurled
'To nothingness for thee. This world,
'This finite life, thou hast preferred,
'In disbelief of God's plain word,
'To heaven and to infinity.
'Here the probation was for thee,
'To show thy soul the earthly mixed
'With heavenly, it must choose betwixt.
'The earthly joys lay palpable, –
'A taint, in each, distinct as well;
'The heavenly flitted, faint and rare,
'Above them, but as truly were
'Taintless, so, in their nature, best.
'Thy choice was earth: thou didst attest
' 'Twas fitter spirit should subserve
'The flesh, than flesh refine to nerve
'Beneath the spirit's play. Advance
'No claim to their inheritance
'Who chose the spirit's fugitive
'Brief gleams, and yearned, "This were
        to live
' "Indeed, if rays, completely pure
' "From flesh that dulls them, could
        endure, –
' "Not shoot in meteor-light athwart
' "Our earth, to show how cold and
        swart
' "It lies beneath their fire, but stand
' "As stars do, destined to expand,
' "Prove veritable worlds, our home!"
'Thou saidst, – "Let spirit star the dome
' "Of sky, that flesh may miss no peak,
' "No nook of earth, – I shall not seek
' "Its service further!" Thou art shut
'Out of the heaven of spirit; glut

'Thy sense upon the world: 'tis thine
'For ever – take it!'

21

                'How? Is mine,
'The world? (I cried, while my soul broke
Out in a transport.) 'Hast Thou spoke
'Plainly in that? Earth's exquisite
'Treasures of wonder and delight,
'For me?'

22

        The austere voice returned, –
'So soon made happy? Hadst thou
        learned
'What God accounteth happiness,
'Thou wouldst not find it hard to guess
'What hell may be his punishment
'For those who doubt if God invent
'Better than they. Let such men rest
'Content with what they judged the best.
'Let the unjust usurp at will:
'The filthy shall be filthy still:
'Miser, there waits the gold for thee!
'Hater, indulge thine enmity!
'And thou, whose heaven self-ordained
'Was, to enjoy earth unrestrained,
'Do it! Take all the ancient show!
'The woods shall wave, the rivers flow,
'And men apparently pursue
'Their works, as they were wont to do,
'While living in probation yet.
'I promise not thou shalt forget
'The past, now gone to its account;
'But leave thee with the old amount
'Of faculties, nor less nor more,
'Unvisited, as heretofore,
'By God's free spirit, that makes an end.
'So, once more, take thy world! Expend
'Eternity upon its shows,
'Flung thee as freely as one rose
'Out of a summer's opulence,
'Over the Eden-barrier whence
'Thou art excluded. Knock in vain!'

23

I sat up. All was still again.
I breathed free: to my heart, back fled
The warmth. 'But, all the world!' – I
        said.

I stooped and picked a leaf of fern,
And recollected I might learn
From books, how many myriad sorts
Of fern exist, to trust reports,
Each as distinct and beautiful
As this, the very first I cull.
Think, from the first leaf to the last!
Conceive, then, earth's resources! Vast
Exhaustless beauty, endless change
Of wonder! And this foot shall range
Alps, Andes, – and this eye devour
The bee-bird and the aloe-flower?

24

Then the voice, 'Welcome so to rate
'The arras-folds that variegate
'The earth, God's antechamber, well!
'The wise, who waited there, could tell
'By these, what royalties I store
'Lay one step past the entrance-door.
'For whom, was reckoned, not too much,
'This life's munificence? For such
'As thou, – a race, wherof scarce one
'Was able, in a million,
'To feel that any marvel lay
'In objects round his feet all day;
'Scarce one, in many millions more,
'Willing, if anle, to explore
'The secreter, minuter charm!
' – Brave souls, a fern-leaf could disarm
'Of power to cope with God's intent, –
'Or scared of the south firmament
'With north-fire did its wings refledge!
'All partial beauty was a pledge
'Of beauty in its plenitude:
'But since the pledge sufficed thy mood,
'Retain it! Plenitude be theirs
'Who looked above!'

25

                Though sharp despairs
Shot through me, I held up, bore on.
'What matter though my trust were
        gone
'From natural things? Henceforth my
        part
'Be less with nature than with art!
'For art supplants, gives mainly worth
'To nature; 'tis man stamps the earth –

'And I will seek his impress, seek
'The statuary of the Greek,
'Italy's painting – there my choice
'Shall fix!'

26

        'Obtain it!' said the voice,
' – The one form with its single act,
'Which sculptors laboured to abstract,
'The one face, painters tried to draw,
'With its one look, from throngs they
        saw.
'And that perfection in their soul,
'These only hinted at? The whole,
'They were but parts of? What each laid
'His claim to glory on? – afraid
'His fellow-men should give him rank
'By mere tentatives which he shrank
'Smitten at heart from, all the more,
'That gazers pressed in to adore!
' "Shall I be judged by only these?"
'If such his soul's capacities,
'Even while he trod the earth, – think,
        now,
'What pomp in Buonarroti's brow,
'With its new palace-brain where dwells
'Superb the soul, unvexed by cells
'That crumbled with the transient clay!
'What visions will his right hand's sway
'Still turn to forms, as still they burst
'Upon him? How will he quench thirst,
'Titanically infantine,
'Laid at the breast of the Divine?
'Does it confound thee, – this first page
'Emblazoning man's heritage? –
'Can this alone absorb thy sight,
'As pages were not infinite, –
'Like the omnipotence which tasks
'Itself to furnish all that asks
'The soul it means to satiate?
'What was the world, the starry state
'Of the broad skies, – what, all displays
'Of power and beauty intermixed,
'Which now thy soul is chained
        betwixt, –
'What else than needful furniture
'For life's first stage? God's work, be
        sure,

'No more spreads wasted, than falls scant!
'He filled, did not exceed, man's want
'Of beauty in this life. But through
'Life pierce, – and what has earth to do,
'Its utmost beauty's appanage,
'With the requirement of next stage?
'Did God pronounce earth "very good"?
'Needs must it be, while understood
'For man's preparatory state;
'Nought here to heighten nor abate;
'Transfer the same completeness here,
'To serve a new state's use, – and drear
'Deficiency gapes every side!
'The good, tried once, were bad, retried.
'See the enwrapping rocky niche,
'Sufficient for the sleep in which
'The lizard breathes for ages safe:
'Split the mould – and as light would chafe
'The creature's new world-widened sense,
'Dazzled to death at evidence
'Of all the sounds and sights that broke
'Innumerous at the chisel's stroke, –
'So, in God's eye, the earth's first stuff
'Was, neither more nor less, enough
'To house man's soul, man's need fulfil.
'Man reckoned it immeasurable?
'So thinks the lizard of his vault!
'Could God be taken in default,
'Short of contrivances, by you, –
'Or reached, ere ready to pursue
'His progress through eternity?
'That chambered rock, the lizard's world,
'Your easy mallet's blow has hurled
'To nothingness for ever; so,
'Has God abolished at a blow
'This world, wherein his saints were pent, –
'Who, though found grateful and content,
'With the provision there, as thou,
'Yet knew he would not disallow
'Their spirit's hunger, felt as well, –
'Unsated, – not unsatable,
'As paradise gives proof. Deride
'Their choice now, thou who sit'st outside!'

27

I cried in anguish, 'Mind, the mind,
'So miserably cast behind,
'To gain what had been wisely lost!
'Oh, let me strive to make the most
'Of the poor stinted soul, I nipped
'Of budding wings, else now equipped
'For voyage from summer isle to isle!
'And though she needs must reconcile
'Ambition to the life on ground,
'Still, I can profit by late found
'But precious knowledge. Mind is best –
'I will seize mind, forego the rest,
'And try how far my tethered strength
'May crawl in this poor breadth and length.
'Let me, since I can fly no more,
'At least spin dervish-like about
'(Till giddy rapture almost doubt
'I fly) through circling sciences,
'Philosophies and histories!
'Should the whirl slacken there, then verse,
'Fining to music, shall asperse
'Fresh and fresh fire-dew, till I strain
'Intoxicate, half-break my chain!
'Not joyless, though more favoured feet
'Stand calm, where I want wings to beat
'The floor. At least earth's bond is broke!'

28

Then, (sickening even while I spoke)
'Let me alone! No answer, pray,
'To this! I know what Thou wilt say!
'All still is earth's, – to know, as much
'As feel its truths, which if we touch
'With sense, or apprehend in soul,
'What matter? I have reached the goal –
' "Whereto does knowledge serve!" will burn
'My eyes, too sure, at every turn!
'I cannot look back now, nor stake
'Bliss on the race, for running's sake.
'The goal's a ruin like the rest!' –
'And so much worse thy latter quest,'
(Added the voice) 'that even on earth –
'Whenever, in man's soul, had birth
'Those intuitions, grasps of guess,

'Which pull the more into the less,
'Making the finite comprehend
'Infinity, – the bard would spend
'Such praise alone, upon his craft,
'As, when wind-lyres obey the waft,
'Goes to the craftsman who arranged
'The seven strings, changed them and
     rechanged –
'Knowing it was the South that harped.
'He felt his song, in singing, warped;
'Distinguished his and God's part:
     whence
'A world of spirit as of sense
'Was plain to him, yet not too plain,
'Which he could traverse, not remain
'A guest in: – else were permanent
'Heaven on the earth its gleams were
     meant
'To sting with hunger for full light, –
'Made visible in verse, despite
'The veiling weakness, – truth by means
'Of fable, showing while it screens, –
'Since highest truth, man e'er supplied,
'Was ever fable on outside.
'Such gleams made bright the earth an
     age;
'Now the whole sun's his heritage!
'Take up thy world, it is allowed,
'Thou who hast entered in the cloud!'

29

Then I – 'Behold, my spirit bleeds,
'Catches no more at broken reeds, –
'But lilies flower those reeds above:
'I let the world go, and take love!
'Love survives in me, albeit those
'I love be henceforth masks and shows,
'Not living men and women: still
'I mind how love repaired all ill,
'Cured wrong, soothed grief, made
     earth amends
'With parents, brothers, children, friends!
'Some semblance of a woman yet
'With eyes to help me to forget,
'Shall look on me; and I will match
'Departed love with love, attach
'Old memories to new dreams, nor scorn
'The poorest of the grains of corn

'I save from shipwreck on this isle,
'Trusting its barrenness may smile
'With happy foodful green one day,
'More precious for the pains. I pray, –
'Leave to love, only!'

30

     At the word,
The form, I looked to have been stirred
With pity and approval, rose
O'er me, as when the headsman throws
Axe over shoulder to make end –
I fell prone, letting Him expend
His wrath, while thus the inflicting
     voice
Smote me. 'Is this thy final choice?
'Love is the best? 'Tis somewhat late!
'And all thou dost enumerate
'Of power and beauty in the world,
'The mightiness of love was curled
'Inextricably round about.
'Love lay within it and without,
'To clasp thee, – but in vain! Thy soul
'Still shrunk from Him who made the
     whole,
'Still set deliberate aside
'His love! – Now take love! Well betide
'Thy tardy conscience! Haste to take
'The show of love for the name's sake,
'Remembering every moment Who,
'Beside creating thee unto
'These ends, and these for thee, was
     said
'To undergo death in thy stead
'In flesh like thine: so ran the tale.
'What doubt in thee could countervail
'Belief in it? Upon the ground
' "That in the story had been found
' "Too much love! How could God love
     so?"
'He who in all his works below
'Adapted to the needs of man,
'Made love the basis of the plan, –
'Did love, as was demonstrated:
'While man, who was so fit instead
'To hate, as every day gave proof, –
'Man thought man, for his kind's
     behoof,

'Both could and did invent that scheme
'Of perfect love: 'twould well beseem
'Cain's nature thou wast wont to praise,
'Not tally with God's usual ways!

### 31

And I cowered deprecatingly –
'Thou Love of God! Or let me die,
'Or grant what shall seem heaven almost!
'Let me not know that all is lost,
'Though lost it be – leave me not tied
'To this despair, this corpse-like bride!
'Let that old life seem mine – no more –
'With limitation as before,
'With darkness, hunger, toil, distress:
'Be all the earth a wilderness!
'Only let me go on, go on,
'Still hoping ever and anon
'To reach one eve the Better Land!'

### 32

Then did the form expand, expand –
I knew Him through the dread disguise
As the whole God within His eyes
Embraced me.

### 33

When I lived again,
The day was breaking, – the grey plain
I rose from, silvered thick with dew.
Was this a vision? False or true?
Since then, three varied years are spent,
And commonly my mind is bent
To think it was a dream – be sure

A mere dream and distemperature –
The last day's watching: then the
          night, –
The shock of that strange Northern Light
Set my head swimming, bred in me
A dream. And so I live, you see,
Go through the world, try, prove, reject,
Prefer, still struggling to effect
My warfare; happy that I can
Be crossed and thwarted as a man,
Not left in God's contempt apart,
With ghastly smooth life, dead at heart,
Tame in earth's paddock as her prize.
Thank God, she still each method tries
To catch me, who may yet escape,
She knows, – the fiend in angel's shape!
Thank God, no paradise stands barred
To entry, and I find it hard
To be a Christian, as I said!
Still every now and then my head
Raised glad, sinks mournful – all grows
          drear
Spite of the sunshine, while I fear
And think, 'How dreadful to be grudged
'No ease henceforth, as one that's
          judged.
'Condemned to earth for ever, shut
'From heaven!'
                    But Easter-Day breaks! But
Christ rises! Mercy every way
Is infinite, – and who can say?

## 'Transcendentalism: A Poem in Twelve Books'

Stop playing, poet! May a brother speak?
'Tis you speak, that's your error. Song's
    our art:
Whereas you please to speak these
    naked thoughts
Instead of draping them in sights and
    sounds.
– True thoughts, good thoughts,
    thoughts fit to treasure up!
But why such long prolusion and
    display,
Such turning and adjustment of the
    harp, .
And taking it upon your breast, at
    length,
Only to speak dry words across its
    strings?
Stark-naked thought is in request
    enough:
Speak prose and hollo it till Europe
    hears!
The six-foot Swiss tube, braced about
    with bark,
Which helps the hunter's voice from
    Alp to Alp –
Exchange our harp for that, – who
    hinders you?

But here's your fault; grown men
    want thought, you think;
Thought's what they mean by verse,
    and seek in verse.
Boys seek for images and melody,
Men must have reason – so, you aim at
    men.
Quite otherwise! Objects throng our
    youth, 'tis true;
We see and hear and do not wonder
    much:
If you could tell us what they mean,
    indeed!

As German Boehme never cared for
    plants
Until it happed, a-walking in the fields,
He noticed all at once that plants could
    speak,
Nay, turned with loosened tongue to
    talk with him.
That day the daisy had an eye indeed –
Colloquized with the cowslip on such
    themes!
We find them extant yet in Jacob's
    prose.
But by the time youth slips a stage or
    two
While reading prose in that tough
    book he wrote
(Collating and emendating the same
And settling on the sense most to our
    mind),
We shut the clasps and find life's
    summer past.
Then, who helps more, pray, to repair
    our loss –
Another Boehme with a tougher book
And subtler meanings of what roses
    say, –
Or some stout Mage like him of Halber-
    stadt,*
John, who made things Boehme wrote
    thoughts about?
He with a 'look you!' vents a brace of
    rhymes,
And in there breaks the sudden rose
    herself,
Over us, under, round us every side,
Nay, in and out the tables and the
    chairs
And musty volumes, Boehme's book
    and all, –
Buries us with a glory, young once
    more,

---

* John of Halberstadt, a magician botanist
  and a chymist

Pouring heaven into this shut house of
    life.

    So come, the harp back to your heart
        again!
You are a poem, though your poem's
    naught.
The best of all you showed before, believe,
Was your own boy-face o'er the finer
    chords
Bent, following the cherub at the top
That points to God with his paired half-
    moon wings.

## How It Strikes a Contemporary

I only knew one poet in my life:
    And this, or something like it, was
        his way.
You saw go up and down Valladolid,
A man of mark, to know next time you
    saw.
His very serviceable suit of black
Was courtly once and conscientious
    still,
And many might have worn it, though
    none did:
The cloak, that somewhat shone and
    showed the threads,
Had purpose, and the ruff, significance.
He walked and tapped the pavement
    with his cane,
Scenting the world, looking it full in
    face,
An old dog, bald and blindish, at his
    heels.
They turned up, now, the alley by the
    church,
That leads nowhither; now, they
    breathed themselves
On the main promenade just at the
    wrong time:
You'd come upon his scrutinizing hat,
Making a peaked shade blacker than
    itself
Against the single window spared some
    house

Intact yet with its mouldered Moorish
    work, –
Or else surprise the ferrel of his stick
Trying the mortar's temper 'tween the
    chinks
Of some new shop a-building, French
    and fine.
He stood and watched the cobbler at
    his trade,
The man who slices lemons into drink,
The coffee-roaster's brazier, and the
    boys
That volunteer to help him turn its
    winch.
He glanced o'er books on stalls with
    half an eye,
And fly-leaf ballads on the vendor's string,
And broad-edge bold-print posters by
    the wall.
He took such cognizance of men and
    things,
If any beat a horse, you felt he saw;
If any cursed a woman, he took note;
Yet stared at nobody, – you stared at
    him,
And found, less to your pleasure than
    surprise,
He seemed to know you and expect as
    much.
So, next time that a neighbour's tongue
    was loosed,
It marked the shameful and notorious
    fact,
We had among us, not so much a spy,
As a recording chief-inquisitor,
The town's true master if the town but
    knew!
We merely kept a governor for form,
While this man walked about and took
    account
Of all thought, said and acted, then
    went home,
And wrote it fully to our Lord the King
Who has an itch to know things, he
    knows why,
And reads them in his bedroom of a
    night.

Oh, you might smile! there wanted not
          a touch,
A tang of ... well, it was not wholly
          ease
As back into your mind the man's look
          came.
Stricken in years a little, – such a brow
His eyes had to live under! – clear as
          flint
On either side the formidable nose
Curved, cut and coloured like an
          eagle's claw.
Had he to do with A.'s surprising fate?
When altogether old B. disappeared
And young C. got his mistress, – was't
          our friend,
His letter to the King, that did it all?
What paid the bloodless man for so
          much pains?
Our Lord the King has favourites
          manifold.
And shifts his ministry some once a
          month;
Our city gets new governors at whiles, –
But never word or sign, that I could
          hear,
Notified to this man about the streets
The King's approval of those letters
          conned
The last thing duly at the dead of night.
Did the man love his office? Frowned
          our Lord,
Lord, Exhorting when none heard –
          'Beseech me not!
'Too far above my people, – beneath
          me!
'I set the watch, – how should the
          people know?
'Forget them, keep me all the more in
          mind!'
Was some such understanding 'twixt
          the two?

   I found no truth in one report at
          least –
That if you tracked him to his home,
          down lanes

Beyond the Jewry, and as clean to pace,
You found he ate his supper in a room
Blazing with lights, four Titians on the
          wall,
And twenty naked girls to change his
          plate!
Poor man, he lived another kind of life
In that new stuccoed third house by the
          bridge,
Fresh-painted, rather smart than other-
          wise!
The whole street might o'erlook him as
          he sat,
Leg crossing leg, one foot on the dog's
          back,
Playing a decent cribbage with his maid
(Jacynth, you're sure her name was)
          o'er the cheese
And fruit, three red halves of starved
          winter-pears,
Or treat of radishes in April. Nine,
Ten, struck the church clock, straight
          to bed went he.

   My father, like the man of sense he
          was,
Would point him out to me a dozen
          times;
' 'St – 'St,' he'd whisper, 'the Corregidor!'
I had been used to think that
          personage
Was one with lacquered breeches,
          lustrous belt,
And feathers like a forest in his hat,
Who blew a trumpet and proclaimed
          the news,
Announced the bull-fights, gave each
          church its turn,
And memorized the miracle in vogue!
He had a great observance from us
          boys;
We were in error; that was not the man.

   I'd like now, yet had haply been
          afraid,
To have just looked, when this man
          came to die,

And seen who lined the clean gay
    garret-sides
And stood about the neat low truckle-
    bed,
With the heavenly manner of relieving
    guard.
Here had been, mark, the general-in-
    chief,
Thro' a whole campaign of the world's
    life and death,
Doing the King's work all the dim day
    long,
In his old coat and up to knees in mud,
Smoked like a herring, dining on a
    crust, –
And, now the day was won, relieved at
    once!
No further show or need for that old
    coat,
You are sure, for one thing! Bless us, all
    the while
How sprucely we are dressed out, you
    and I!
A second, and the angels alter that.
Well, I could never write a verse, –
    could you?
Let's to the Prado and make the most
    of time.

## Artemis Prologizes

I am a goddess of the ambrosial courts,
And save by Here, Queen of Pride,
    surpassed
By none whose temples whiten this the
    world.
Through heaven I roll my lucid moon
    along;
I shed in hell o'er my pale people peace;
On earth I, caring for the creatures,
    guard
Each pregnant yellow wolf and fox-
    bitch sleek,
And every feathered mother's callow
    brood,
And all that love green haunts and
    loneliness.

Of men, the chaste adore me, hanging
    crowns
Of poppies red to blackness, bell and
    stem,
Upon my image at Athenai here;
And this dead Youth, Asclepios bends
    above,
Was dearest to me. He, my buskined
    step
To follow through the wild-wood leafy
    ways,
And chase the panting stag, or swift
    with darts
Stop the swift ounce, or lay the leopard
    low,
Neglected homage to another god:
Whence Aphrodite, by no midnight
    smoke
Of tapers lulled, in jealousy despatched
A noisome lust that, as the gadbee
    stings,
Possessed his stepdame Phaidra for
    himself
The son of Theseus her great absent
    spouse.
Hippolutos exclaiming in his rage
Against the fury of the Queen, she
    judged
Life insupportable; and, pricked at heart
An Amazonian stranger's race should
    dare
To scorn her, perished by the murderous
    cord:
Yet, ere she perished, blasted in a scroll
The fame of him her swerving made not
    swerve.
And Theseus, read, returning, and
    believed,
And exiled, in the blindness of his wrath,
The man without a crime who, last as
    first,
Loyal, divulged not to his sire the truth.
Now Theseus from Poseidon had
    obtained
That of his wishes should be granted
    three,
And one he imprecated straight – 'Alive

'May ne'er Hippolutos reach other
 lands!'
Poseidon heard, ai ai! And scarce the
 prince
Had stepped into the fixed boots of the
 car
That give the feet a stay against the
 strength
Of the Henetian horses, and around
His body flung the rein, and urged
 their speed
Along the rocks and shingles of the
 shore,
When from the gaping wave a monster
 flung
His obscene body in the coursers' path.
These, mad with terror, as the sea-bull
 sprawled
Wallowing about their feet, lost care of
 him
That reared them; and the master-
 chariot-pole
Snapping beneath their plunges like a
 reed,
Hippolutos, whose feet were trammelled
 fast,
Was yet dragged forward by the circling
 rein
Which either hand directed; nor they
 quenched
The frenzy of their flight before each
 trace,
Wheel-spoke and splinter of the woeful
 car,
Each boulder-stone, sharp stub and
 spiny shell,
Huge fish-bone wrecked and wreathed
 amid the sands
On that detested beach, was bright
 with blood
And morsels of his flesh: then fell the
 steeds
Head foremost, crashing in their
 mooned fronts,
Shivering with sweat, each white eye
 horror-fixed.
His people, who had witnessed all afar,

Bore back the ruins of Hippolutos.
But when his sire, too swoln with
 pride, rejoiced
(Indomitable as a man foredoomed)
That vast Poseidon had fulfilled his
 prayer,
I, in a flood of glory visible,
Stood o'er my dying votary and, deed
By deed, revealed, as all took place, the
 truth.
Then Theseus lay the woefullest of
 men,
And worthily; but ere the death-veils
 hid
His face, the murdered prince full
 pardon breathed
To his rash sire. Whereat Athenai wails.

So I, who ne'er forsake my votaries,
Lest in the cross-way none the honey-
 cake
Should tender, nor pour out the dog's
 hot life;
Lest at my fane the priests disconsolate
Should dress my image with some faded
 poor
Few crowns, made favours of, nor dare
 object
Such slackness to my worshippers who
 turn
Elsewhere the trusting heart and loaded
 hand,
As they had climbed Olumpos to report
Of Artemis and nowhere found her
 throne –
I interposed: and, this eventful night, –
(While round the funeral pyre the
 populace
Stood with fierce light on their black
 robes which bound
Each sobbing head, while yet their hair
 they clipped
O'er the dead body of their withered
 prince,
And, in his palace, Theseus prostrated
On the cold hearth, his brow cold as
 the slab

'Twas bruised on, groaned away the
      heavy grief –
As the pyre fell, and down the cross
      logs crashed
Sending a crowd of sparkles through
      the night,
And the gay fire, elate with mastery,
Towered like a serpent o'er the clotted
      jars
Of wine, dissolving oils and frankincense,
And splendid gums like gold), – my
      potency
Conveyed the perished man to my
      retreat
In the thrice-venerable forest here.
And this white-bearded sage who
      squeezes now
The berried plant, is Phoibos' son of
      fame,
Asclepios, whom my radiant brother
      taught
The doctrine of each herb and flower
      and root,
To know their secret'st virtue and express
The saving soul of all: who so has
      soothed
With lavers the torn brow and
      murdered cheeks,
Composed the hair and brought its
      gloss again,
And called the red bloom to the pale
      skin back,
And laid the strips and jagged ends of
      flesh
Even once more, and slacked the sinew's
      knot
Of every tortured limb – that now he
      lies
As if mere sleep possessed him
      underneath
These interwoven oaks and pines. Oh
      cheer,
Divine presenter of the healing rod,
Thy snake, with ardent throat and
      lulling eye,
Twines his lithe spires around! I say,
      much cheer!

Proceed thou with thy wisest pharmacies!
And ye, white crowd of woodland
      sister-nymphs,
Ply, as the sage directs, these buds and
      leaves
That strew the turf around the twain!
      While I
Await, in fitting silence, the event.

## An Epistle

Containing the strange medical experience of
Karshish, The Arab Physician.

Karshish, the picker-up of learning's
      crumbs,
The not-incurious in God's handiwork
(This man's-flesh he hath admirably
      made,
Blown like a bubble, kneaded like a
      paste,
To coop up and keep down on earth a
      space
That puff of vapour from its mouth,
      man's soul)
– To Abib, all-sagacious in our art,
Breeder in me of what poor skill I
      boast,
Like me inquisitive how pricks and
      cracks
Befall the flesh through too much
      stress and strain,
Whereby the wily vapour fain would
      slip
Back and rejoin its source before the
      term, –
And aptest in contrivance (under God)
To baffle it by deftly stopping such: –
The vagrant Scholar to his Sage at home
Sends greeting (health and knowledge,
      fame with peace)
Three samples of true snakestone –
      rarer still,
One of the other sort, the melon-
      shaped,
(But fitter, pounded fine, for charms
      than drugs)

And writeth now the twenty-second
time.

My journeymgs were brought to
Jericho:
Thus I resume. Who studious in our art
Shall count a little labour unrepaid?
I have shed sweat enough, left flesh and
bone
On many a flinty furlong of this land.
Also, the country-side is all on fire
With rumours of a marching hitherward:
Some say Vespasian cometh, some, his
son.
A black lynx snarled and pricked a
tufted ear;
Lust of my blood inflamed his yellow
balls:
I cried and threw my staff and he was
gone.
Twice have the robbers stripped and
beaten me,
And once a town declared me for a spy;
But at the end, I reach Jerusalem,
Since this poor covert where I pass the
night,
This Bethany, lies scarce the distance
thence
A man with plague-sores at the third
degree
Runs till he drops down dead. Thou
laughest here!
'Sooth, it elates me, thus reposed and
safe,
To void the stuffing of my travel-scrip
And share with thee whatever Jewry
yields.
A viscid choler is observable
In tertians, I was nearly bold to say;
And falling-sickness hath a happier
cure
Than our school wots of: there's a
spider here
Weaves no web, watches on the ledge
of tombs,
Sprinkled with mottles on an ash-grey
back;

Take five and drop them … but who
knows his mind,
The Syrian runagate I trust this to?
His service payeth me a sublimate
Blown up his nose to help the ailing
eye.
Best wait: I reach Jerusalem at morn,
There set in order my experiences,
Gather what most deserves, and give
thee all –
Or I might add, Judæa's gum-tragacanth
Scales off in purer flakes, shines clearer-
grained,
Cracks 'twixt the pestle and the porphyry,
In fine exceeds our produce. Scalp-
disease
Confounds me, crossing so with
leprosy –
Thou hadst admired one sort I gained
at Zoar –
But zeal outruns discretion. Here I end.

Yet stay: my Syrian blinketh gratefully,
Protesteth his devotion is my price –
Suppose I write what harms not,
though he steal?
I half resolve to tell thee, yet I blush,
What set me off a-writing first of all.
An itch I had, a sting to write, a tang!
For, be it this town's barrenness – or
else
The Man had something in the look of
him –
His case has struck me far more than
'tis worth.
So, pardon if – (lest presently I lose
In the great press of novelty at hand
The care and pains this somehow stole
from me)
I bid thee take the thing while fresh in
mind,
Almost in sight – for, wilt thou have the
truth?
The very man is gone from me but now,
Whose ailment is the subject of discourse.
Thus then, and let thy better wit help
all!

'Tis but a case of mania – subinduced
By epilepsy, at the turning-point
Of trance prolonged unduly some three
    days:
When, by the exhibition of some drug
Or spell, exorcization, stroke of art
Unknown to me and which 'twere well
    to know,
The evil thing out-breaking all at once
Left the man whole and sound of body
    indeed, –
But, flinging (so to speak) life's gates
    too wide,
Making a clear house of it too suddenly,
The first conceit that entered might
    inscribe
Whatever it was minded on the wall
So plainly at that vantage, as it were,
(First come, first served) that nothing
    subsequent
Attaineth to erase those fancy-scrawls
The just-returned and new-established
    soul
Hath gotten now so thoroughly by
    heart
That henceforth she will read or these
    or none.
And first – the man's own firm
    conviction rests
That he was dead (in fact they buried
    him)
– That he was dead and then restored
    to life
By a Nazarene physician of his tribe:
– 'Sayeth, the same bade 'Rise,' and he
    did rise.
'Such cases are diurnal,' thou wilt cry.
Not so this figment! – not, that such a
    fume,
Instead of giving way to time and health,
Should eat itself into the life of life,
As saffron tingeth flesh, blood, bones
    and all!
For see, how he takes up the after-life.
The man – it is one Lazarus a Jew,
Sanguine, proportioned, fifty years of
    age,

The body's habit wholly laudable,
As much, indeed, beyond the common
    health
As he were made and put aside to
    show.
Think, could we penetrate by any drug
And bathe the wearied soul and
    worried flesh,
And bring it clear and fair, by three
    days' sleep!
Whence has the man the balm that
    brightens all?
This grown man eyes the world now
    like a child.
Some elders of his tribe, I should
    premise,
Led in their friend, obedient as a
    sheep,
To bear my inquisition. While they
    spoke,
Now sharply, now with sorrow, – told
    the case, –
He listened not except I spoke to him,
But folded his two hands and let them
    talk,
Watching the flies that buzzed: and yet
    no fool.
And that's a sample how his years must
    go.
Look, if a beggar, in fixed middle-life,
Should find a treasure, – can he use the
    same
With straitened habits and with tastes
    starved small,
And take at once to his impoverished
    brain
The sudden element that changes things,
That sets the undreamed-of rapture at
    his hand
And puts the cheap old joy in the
    scorned dust?
Is he not such an one as moves to
    mirth –
Warily parsimonious, when no need,
Wasteful as drunkenness at undue
    times?
All prudent counsel as to what befits

The golden mean, is lost on such an
    one:
The man's fantastic will is the man's
    law.
So here – we call the treasure knowledge,
    say,
Increased beyond the fleshly faculty –
Heaven opened to a soul while yet on
    earth,
Earth forced on a soul's use while seeing
    heaven:
The man is witless of the size, the sum,
The value in proportion of all things,
Or whether it be little or be much.
Discourse to him of prodigious
    armaments
Assembled to besiege his city now,
And of the passing of a mule with
    gourds –
'Tis one! Then take it on the other side,
Speak of some trifling fact, – he will
    gaze rapt
With stupor at its very littleness,
(Far as I see) as if in that indeed
He caught prodigious import, whole
    results;
And so will turn to us the bystanders
In ever the same stupor (note this
    point)
That we too see not with his opened
    eyes.
Wonder and doubt come wrongly into
    play,
Preposterously, at cross purposes.
Should his child sicken unto death, –
    why, look
For scarce abatement of his cheerfulness,
Or pretermission of the daily craft!
While a word, gesture, glance from that
    same child
At play or in the school or laid asleep,
Will startle him to an agony of fear,
Exasperation, just as like. Demand
The reason why – ' 'tis but a word,'
    object –
'A gesture' – he regards thee as our
    lord

Who lived there in the pyramid alone,
Looked at us (dost thou mind?) when,
    being young,
We both would unadvisedly recite
Some charm's beginning, from that
    book of his,
Able to bid the sun throb wide and
    burst
All into stars, as suns grown old are
    wont.
Thou and the child have each a veil
    alike
Thrown o'er your heads, from under
    which ye both
Stretch your blind hands and trifle with
    a match
Over a mine of Greek fire, did ye know!
He holds on firmly to some thread of
    life –
(It is the life to lead perforcedly)
Which runs across some vast
    distracting orb
Of glory on either side that meagre
    thread,
Which, conscious of, he must not
    enter yet –
The spiritual life around the earthly life:
The law of that is known to him as this,
His heart and brain move there, his
    feet stay here.
So is the man perplext with impulses
Sudden to start off crosswise, not
    straight on,
Proclaiming what is right and wrong
    across,
And not along, this black thread through
    the blaze –
'It should be' baulked by 'here it cannot
    be.'
And oft the man's soul springs into his
    face
As if he saw again and heard again
His sage that bade him 'Rise' and he
    did rise.
Something, a word, a tick o' the blood
    within
Admonishes: then back he sinks at once

To ashes, who was very fire before,
In sedulous recurrence to his trade
Whereby he earneth him the daily
    bread;
And studiously the humbler for that
    pride,
Professedly the faultier that he knows
God's secret, while he holds the thread
    of life.
Indeed the especial marking of the man
Is prone submission to the heavenly
    will –
Seeing it, what it is, and why it is.
'Sayeth, he will wait patient to the last
For that same death which must restore
    his being
To equilibrium, body loosening soul
Divorced even now by premature full
    growth:
He will live, nay, it pleaseth him to live
So long as God please, and just how
    God please.
He even seeketh not to please God more
(Which meaneth, otherwise) than as
    God please.
Hence, I perceive not he affects to
    preach
The doctrine of his sect whate'er it be,
Make proselytes as madmen thirst
    to do:
How can he give his neighbour the real
    ground,
His own conviction? Ardent as he is –
Call his great truth a lie, why, still the
    old
'Be it as God please' reassureth him.
I probed the sore as thy disciple should:
'How, beast,' said I, 'this stolid
    carelessness
'Sufficeth thee, when Rome is on her
    march
'To stamp out like a little spark thy
    town,
'Thy tribe, thy crazy tale and thee at
    once?'
He merely looked with his large eyes
    on me.

The man is apathetic, you deduce?
Contrariwise, he loves both old and
    young,
Able and weak, affects the very brutes
And birds – how say I? flowers of the
    field –
As a wise workman recognizes tools
In a master's workshop, loving what
    they make.
Thus is the man as harmless as a lamb:
Only impatient, let him do his best,
At ignorance and carelessness and sin –
An indignation which is promptly
    curbed:
As when in certain travel I have feigned
To be an ignoramus in our art
According to some preconceived design,
And happed to hear the land's
    practitioners
Steeped in conceit sublimed by
    ignorance,
Prattle fantastically on disease,
Its cause and cure – and I must hold
    my peace!

    Thou wilt object – Why have I not
    ere this
Sought out the sage himself, the
    Nazarene
Who wrought this cure, inquiring at
    the source,
Conferring with the frankness that
    befits?
Alas! it grieveth me, the learned leech
Perished in a tumult many years ago,
Accused, – our learning's fate, – of
    wizardry,
Rebellion, to the setting up a rule
And creed prodigious as described
    to me.
His death, which happened when the
    earthquake fell
(Prefiguring, as soon appeared, the loss
To occult learning in our lord the sage
Who lived there in the pyramid alone)
Was wrought by the mad people –
    that's their wont!

On vain recourse, as I conjecture it,
To his tried virtue, for miraculous help –
How could he stop the earthquake?
    That's their way!
The other imputations must be lies:
But take one, though I loathe to give it
    thee,
In mere respect for any good man's
    fame.
(And after all, our patient Lazarus
Is stark mad; should we count on what
    he says?
Perhaps not: though in writing to a
    leech
'Tis well to keep back nothing of a
    case.)
This man so cured regards the curer,
    then,
As – God forgive me! who but God
    himself,
Creator and sustainer of the world,
That came and dwelt in flesh on it
    awhile!
– 'Sayeth that such an one was born
    and lived,
Taught, healed the sick, broke bread at
    his own house,
Then died, with Lazarus by, for aught I
    know,
And yet was … what I said nor choose
    repeat,
And must have so avouched himself, in
    fact,
In hearing of this very Lazarus
Who saith – but why all this of what he
    saith?
Why write of trivial matters, things of
    price
Calling at every moment for remark?
I noticed on the margin of a pool
Blue-flowering borage, the Aleppo sort,
Aboundeth, very nitrous. It is strange!

Thy pardon for this long and tedious
    case,
Which, now that I review it, needs must
    seem

Unduly dwelt on, prolixly set forth!
Nor I myself discern in what is writ
Good cause for the peculiar interest
And awe indeed this man has touched
    me with.
Perhaps the journey's end, the weariness
Had wrought upon me first. I met him
    thus:
I crossed a ridge of short sharp broken
    hills
Like an old lion's cheek-teeth. Out there
    came
A moon made like a face with certain
    spots
Multiform, manifold and menacing:
Then a wind rose behind me. So we met
In this old sleepy town at unaware,
The man and I. I send thee what is writ.
Regard it as a chance, a matter risked
To this ambiguous Syrian – he may
    lose,
Or steal, or give it thee with equal good.
Jerusalem's repose shall make amends
For time this letter wastes, thy time and
    mine;
Till when, once more thy pardon and
    farewell!

The very God! think, Abib; dost
    thou think?
So, the All-Great, were the All-Loving
    too –
So, through the thunder comes a
    human voice
Saying, 'O heart I made, a heart beats
    here!
'Face, my hands fashioned, see it in
    myself!
'Thou hast no power nor mayst conceive
    of mine,
'But love I gave thee, with myself to
    love,
'And thou must love me who have died
    for thee!'
The madman saith He said so: it is
    strange.

## Johannes Agricola in Meditation

There's heaven above, and night by
    night
    I look right through its gorgeous roof;
No suns and moons though e'er so
    bright
    Avail to stop me; splendour-proof
    I keep the broods of stars aloof:
For I intend to get to God,
    For 'tis to God I speed so fast,
For in God's breast, my own abode,
    Those shoals of dazzling glory, passed,
    I lay my spirit down at last.
I lie where I have always lain,
    God smiles as he has always smiled;
Ere suns and moons could wax and
    wane,
    Ere stars were thundergirt, or piled
    The heavens, God thought on me his
    child;
Ordained a life for me, arrayed
    Its circumstances every one
To the minutest; ay, God said
    This head this hand should rest upon
    Thus, ere he fashioned star or sun.
And having thus created me,
    Thus rooted me, he bade me grow,
Guiltless for ever, like a tree
    That buds and blooms, nor seeks to
    know
    The law by which it prospers so:
But sure that thought and word and
    deed
    All go to swell his love for me,
Me, made because that love had need
    Of something irreversibly
    Pledged solely its content to be.
Yes, yes, a tree which must ascend,
    No poison-gourd foredoomed to
    stoop!
I have God's warrant, could I blend
    All hideous sins, as in a cup,
    To drink the mingled venoms up;
Secure my nature will convert
    The draught to blossoming gladness
    fast:

While sweet dews turn to the gourd's
    hurt,
    And bloat, and while they bloat it,
    blast,
    As from the first its lot was cast.
For as I lie, smiled on, full-fed
    By unexhausted power to bless,
I gaze below on hell's fierce bed,
    And those its waves of flame oppress,
    Swarming in ghastly wretchedness;
Whose life on earth aspired to be
    One altar-smoke, so pure! – to win
If not love like God's love for me,
    At least to keep his anger in;
    And all their striving turned to sin.
Priest, doctor, hermit, monk grown
    white
    With prayer, the broken-hearted nun,
The martyr, the wan acolyte,
    The incense-swinging child, – undone
    Before God fashioned star or sun!
God, whom I praise; how could I praise,
    If such as I might understand,
Make out and reckon on his ways,
    And bargain for his love, and stand,
    Paying a price, at his right hand?

## Pictor Ignotus

Florence, 15—

I could have painted pictures like that
    youth's
    Ye praise so. How my soul springs
    up! No bar
Stayed me – ah, thought which
    saddens while it soothes!
    – Never did fate forbid me, star by
    star,
To outburst on your night with all my
    gift
    Of fires from God: nor would my
    flesh have shrunk
From seconding my soul, with eyes
    uplift
    And wide to heaven, or, straight like
    thunder, sunk
To the centre, of an instant; or around

Turned calmly and inquisitive, to scan
The licence and the limit, space and
    bound,
    Allowed to truth made visible in man.
And, like that youth ye praise so, all I
    saw,
    Over the canvas could my hand have
    flung,
Each face obedient to its passion's law,
    Each passion clear proclaimed
    without a tongue;
Whether Hope rose at once in all the
    blood,
    A-tiptoe for the blessing of embrace,
Or Rapture drooped the eyes, as when
    her brood
    Pull down the nesting dove's heart
    to its place;
Or Confidence lit swift the forehead up,
    And locked the mouth fast, like a
    castle braved, –
O human faces, hath it spilt, my cup?
    What did ye give me that I have not
    saved?
Nor will I say I have not dreamed (how
    well!)
    Of going – I, in each new picture, –
    forth,
As, making new hearts beat and bosoms
    swell,
    To Pope or Kaiser, East, West, South,
    or North,
Bound for the calmly-satisfied great State,
    Or glad aspiring little burgh, it went,
Flowers cast upon the car which bore
    the freight,
    Through old streets named afresh
    from the event,
Till it reached home, where learned age
    should greet
    My face, and youth, the star not yet
    distinct
Above his hair, lie learning at my feet! –
    Oh, thus to live, I and my picture,
    linked
With love about, and praise, till life
    should end,

And then not go to heaven, but
    linger here,
Here on my earth, earth's every man
    my friend, –
    The thought grew frightful, 'twas so
    wildly dear!
But a voice changed it. Glimpses of
    such sights
    Have scared me, like the revels
    through a door
Of some strange house of idols at its
    rites!
    This world seemed not the world it
    was before:
Mixed with my loving trusting ones,
    there trooped
    … Who summoned those cold
    faces that begun
To press on me and judge me? Though
    I stooped
    Shrinking, as from the soldiery a nun,
They drew me forth, and spite of
    me … enough!
    These buy and sell our pictures, take
    and give,
Count them for garniture and house-
    hold-stuff,
    And where they live needs must our
    pictures live
And see their faces, listen to their prate,
    Partakers of their daily pettiness,
Discussed of, – 'This I love, or this I
    hate,
    'This likes me more, and this affects
    me less!'
Wherefore I chose my portion. If at
    whiles
    My heart sinks, as monotonous I
    paint
These endless cloisters and eternal
    aisles
    With the same series, Virgin, Babe
    and Saint,
With the same cold calm beautiful
    regard, –
    At least no merchant traffics in my
    heart;

The sanctuary's gloom at least shall
ward
   Vain tongues from where my
   pictures stand apart:
Only prayer breaks the silence of the
shrine
   While, blackening in the daily
   candle-smoke,
They moulder on the damp wall's
travertine,
   'Mid echoes the light footstep never
   woke.
So, die my pictures! surely, gently die!
   O youth, men praise so, – holds
   their praise its worth?
Blown harshly, keeps the trump its
golden cry?
   Tastes sweet the water with such
   specks of earth?

## Fra Lippo Lippi

I am poor brother Lippo, by your leave!
You need not clap your torches to my
face.
Zooks, what's to blame? you think you
see a monk!
What, 'tis past midnight, and you go
the rounds,
And here you catch me at an alley's end
Where sportive ladies leave their doors
ajar?
The Carmine's my cloister: hunt it up,
Do, – harry out, if you must show your
zeal,
Whatever rat, there, haps on his wrong
hole,
And nip each softling of a wee white
mouse,
*Weke*, *weke*, that's crept to keep him
company!
Aha, you know your betters! Then,
you'll take
Your hand away that's fiddling on my
throat,
And please to know me likewise. Who
am I?

Why, one, sir, who is lodging with a
friend
Three streets off – he's a certain …
how d'ye call?
Master – a … Cosimo of the Medici,
I' the house that caps the corner. Boh!
you were best!
Remember and tell me, the day you're
hanged,
How you affected such a gullet's-gripe!
But you, sir, it concerns you that your
knaves
Pick up a manner nor discredit you:
Zooks, are we pilchards, that they
sweep the streets
And count fair prize what comes into
their net?
He's Judas to a tittle, that man is!
Just such a face! Why, sir, you make
amends.
Lord, I'm not angry! Bid your hangdogs
go
Drink out this quarter-florin to the
health
Of the munificent House that harbours
me
(And many more beside, lads! more
beside!)
And all's come square again. I'd like
his face –
His, elbowing on his comrade in the
door
With the pike and lantern, – for the
slave that holds
John Baptist's head a-dangle by the hair
With one hand ('Look you, now,' as
who should say)
And his weapon in the other, yet
unwiped!
It's not your chance to have a bit of
chalk,
A wood-coal or the like? or you should
see!
Yes, I'm the painter, since you style me
so.
What, brother Lippo's doings, up and
down,

You know them and they take you? like
     enough!
I saw the proper twinkle in your eye –
'Tell you, I liked your looks at very
     first.
Let's sit and set things straight now,
     hip to haunch.
Here's spring come, and the nights one
     makes up bands
To roam the town and sing out
     carnival,
And I've been three weeks shut within
     my mew,
A-painting for the great man, saints
     and saints
And saints again. I could not paint all
     night –
Ouf! I leaned out of window for fresh
     air.
There came a hurry of feet and little
     feet,
A sweep of lute-strings, laughs, and
     whifts of song, –
*Flower o' he broom,*
*Take away love, and our earth is a tomb!*
*Flower o' the quince,*
*I let Lisa go, and what good in life since?*
*Flower o' the thyme* – and so on. Round
     they went.
Scarce had they turned the corner
     when a titter
Like the skipping of rabbits by
     moonlight, – three slim shapes,
And a face that looked up … zooks,
     sir, flesh and blood,
That's all I'm made of! Into shreds it
     went,
Curtain and counterpane and coverlet,
All the bed-furniture – a dozen knots,
There was a ladder! Down I let myself,
Hands and feet, scrambling somehow,
     and so dropped,
And after them. I came up with the fun
Hard by Saint Laurence, hail fellow,
     well met, –
*Flower o' the rose,*
*If I've been merry, what matter who knows?*

And so as I was stealing back again
To get to bed and have a bit of sleep
Ere I rise up to-morrow and go work
On Jerome knocking at his poor old
     breast
With his great round stone to subdue
     the flesh,
You snap me of the sudden. Ah, I see!
Though your eye twinkles still, you
     shake your head –
Mine's shaved – a monk, you say – the
     sting's in that!
If Master Cosimo announced himself,
Mum's the word naturally; but a monk!
Come, what am I a beast for? tell us,
     now!
I was a baby when my mother died
And father died and left me in the
     street.
I starved there, God knows how, a year
     or two
On fig-skins, melon-parings, rinds and
     shucks,
Refuse and rubbish. One fine frosty
     day,
My stomach being empty as your hat,
The wind doubled me up and down I
     went.
Old Aunt Lapaccia trussed me with
     one hand,
(Its fellow was a stinger as I knew)
And so along the wall, over the bridge,
By the straight cut to the convent. Six
     words there,
While I stood munching my first bread
     that month:
'So, boy, you're minded,' quoth the
     good fat father
Wiping his own mouth, 'twas
     refection-time, –
'To quit this very miserable world?
'Will you renounce' … 'the mouthful
     of bread?' thought I;
By no means! Brief, they made a monk
     of me;
I did renounce the world, its pride and
     greed,

Palace, farm, villa, shop and banking-
house,
Trash, such as these poor devils of
Medici
Have given their hearts to – all at eight
years old.
Well, sir, I found in time, you may be
sure,
'Twas not for nothing – the good bellyful,
The warm serge and the rope that goes
all round,
And day-long blessed idleness beside!
'Let's see what the urchin's fit for' –
that came next.
Not overmuch their way, I must confess.
Such a to-do! They tried me with their
books:
Lord, they'd have taught me Latin in
pure waste!
*Flower o' the clove,*
*All the Latin I construe is, 'amo' I love!*
But, mind you, when a boy starves in
the streets
Eight years together, as my fortune was,
Watching folk's faces to know who will
fling
The bit of half-stripped grape-bunch he
desires,
And who will curse or kick him for his
pains, –
Which gentleman processional and fine,
Holding a candle to the Sacrament,
Will wink and let him lift a plate and
catch
The droppings of the wax to sell again,
Or holla for the Eight and have him
whipped, –
How say I? – nay, which dog bites,
which lets drop
His bone from the heap of offal in the
street, –
Why, soul and sense of him grow sharp
alike,
He learns the look of things, and none
the less
For admonition from the hunger-pinch.
I had a store of such remarks, be sure,

Which, after I found leisure, turned to
use.
I drew men's faces on my copy-books,
Scrawled them within the antiphonary's
marge,
Joined legs and arms to the long music-
notes,
Found eyes and nose and chin for A's
and B's,
And made a string of pictures of the
world
Betwixt the ins and outs of verb and
noun,
On the wall, the bench, the door. The
monks looked black.
'Nay,' quoth the Prior, 'turn him out,
d'ye say?
'In no wise. Lose a crow and catch a
lark.
'What if at last we get our man of parts,
'We Carmelites, like those Camaldolese
'And Preaching Friars, to do our church
up fine
'And put the front on it that ought
to be!'
And hereupon he bade me daub away.
Thank you! my head being crammed,
the walls a blank,
Never was such prompt disemburdening.
First, every sort of monk, the black and
white,
I drew them, fat and lean: then, folk at
church,
From good old gossips waiting to confess
Their cribs of barrel-droppings, candle-
ends, –
To the breathless fellow at the altar-
foot,
Fresh from his murder, safe and sitting
there
With the little children round him in a
row
Of admiration, half for his beard and
half
For that white anger of his victim's son
Shaking a fist at him with one fierce
arm,

Signing himself with the other because
    of Christ
(Whose sad face on the cross sees only
    this
After the passion of a thousand years)
Till some poor girl, her apron o'er her
    head,
(Which the intense eyes looked
    through) came at eve
On tiptoe, said a word, dropped in a
    loaf,
Her pair of earrings and a bunch of
    flowers
(The brute took growling), prayed, and
    so was gone.
I painted all, then cried ' 'Tis ask and
    have;
'Choose, for more's ready!' – laid the
    ladder flat,
And showed my covered bit of cloister-
    wall.
The monks closed in a circle and
    praised loud
Till checked, taught what to see and not
    to see,
Being simple bodies, – 'That's the very
    man!
'Look at the boy who stoops to pat the
    dog!
'That woman's like the Prior's niece
    who comes
'To care about his asthma: it's the life!'
But there my triumph's straw-fire
    flared and funked;
Their betters took their turn to see and
    say:
The Prior and the learned pulled a face
And stopped all that in no time. 'How?
    what's here?
'Quite from the mark of painting, bless
    us all!
'Faces, arms, legs and bodies like the
    true
'As much as pea and pea! it's devil's-
    game!
'Your business is not to catch men with
    show,

'With homage to the perishable clay,
'But lift them over it, ignore it all,
'Make them forget there's such a thing
    as flesh.
'Your business is to paint the souls of
    men –
'Man's soul, and it's a fire, smoke …
    no, it's not …
'It's vapour done up like a new-born
    babe –
'(In that shape when you die it leaves
    your mouth)
'It's … well, what matters talking, it's
    the soul!
'Give us no more of body than shows
    soul!
'Here's Giotto, with his Saint a-praising
    God,
'That sets us praising, – why not stop
    with him?
'Why put all thoughts of praise out of
    our head
'With wonder at lines, colours, and
    what not?
'Paint the soul, never mind the legs
    and arms!
'Rub all out, try at it a second time.
'Oh, that white smallish female with
    the breasts,
'She's just my niece … Herodias, I
    would say, –
'Who went and danced and got men's
    heads cut off!
'Have it all out!' Now, is this sense, I
    ask?
A fine way to paint soul, by painting
    body
So ill, the eye can't stop there, must go
    further
And can't fare worse! Thus, yellow does
    for white
When what you put for yellow's simply
    black,
And any sort of meaning looks intense
When all beside itself means and looks
    nought.
Why can't a painter lift each foot in turn,

Left foot and right foot, go a double
    step,
Make his flesh liker and his soul more
    like,
Both in their order? Take the prettiest
    face,
The Prior's niece ... patron-saint – is it
    so pretty
You can't discover if it means hope, fear,
Sorrow or joy? won't beauty go with
    these?
Suppose I've made her eyes all right
    and blue,
Can't I take breath and try to add life's
    flash,
And then add soul and heighten them
    threefold?
Or say there's beauty with no soul at
    all –
(I never saw it – put the case the
    same – )
If you get simple beauty and nought
    else,
You get about the best thing God
    invents:
That's somewhat: and you'll find the
    soul you have missed,
Within yourself, when you return him
    thanks.
'Rub all out!' Well, well, there's my life,
    in short,
And so the thing has gone on ever
    since.
I'm grown a man no doubt, I've broken
    bounds:
You should not take a fellow eight years
    old
And make him swear to never kiss the
    girls.
I'm my own master, paint now as I
    please –
Having a friend, you see, in the Corner-
    house!
Lord, it's fast holding by the rings in
    front –
Those great rings serve more purposes
    than just

To plant a flag in, or tie up a horse!
And yet the old schooling sticks, the
    old grave eyes
Are peeping o'er my shoulder as I work,
The heads shake still – 'It's art's decline,
    my son!
'You're not of the true painters, great
    and old;
'Brother Angelico's the man, you'll find;
'Brother Lorenzo stands his single peer:
'Fag on at flesh, you'll never make the
    third!'
*Flower o' the pine,*
*You keep your mistr ... manners, and I'll*
    *stick to mine!*
I'm not the third, then: bless us, they
    must know!
Don't you think they're the likeliest I
    know,
They with their Latin? So, I swallow my
    rage,
Clench my teeth, suck my lips in tight,
    and paint
To please them – sometimes do and
    sometimes don't;
For, doing most, there's pretty sure
    come
A turn, some warm eve finds me at my
    saints –
A laugh, a cry, the business of the world
(*Flower o' the peach,*
*Death for us all, and his own life for eac!*)
And my whole soul revolves, the cup
    runs over,
The world and life's too big to pass for
    dream,
And I do these wild things in sheer
    despite,
And play the fooleries you catch me at,
In pure rage! The old mill-horse, out
    grass
After hard years, throws up his stiff
    heels so,
Although the miller does not preach to
    him
The only good of grass is to make
    chaff.

What would men have? Do they like
    grass or no –
May they or mayn't they? all I want's
    the thing
Settled for ever one way. As it is,
You tell too many lies and hurt yourself:
You don't like what you only like too
    much,
You do like what, if given you at your
    word,
You find abundantly detestable.
For me, I think I speak as I was taught;
I always see the garden and God there
A-making man's wife: and, my lesson
    learned,
The value and significance of flesh,
I can't unlearn ten minutes afterwards.
    You understand me: I'm a beast, I
    know.
But see, now – why, I see as certainly
As that the morning-star's about to shine,
What will hap some day. We've a
    youngster here
Comes to our convent, studies what
    I do,
Slouches and stares and lets no atom
    drop:
His name is Guidi – he'll not mind the
    monks –
They call him Hulking Tom, he lets
    them talk –
He picks my practice up – he'll paint
    apace,
I hope so – though I never live so long,
I know what's sure to follow. You be
    judge!
You speak no Latin more than I, belike;
However, you're my man, you've seen
    the world
– The beauty and the wonder and the
    power,
The shapes of things, their colours,
    lights and shades,
Changes, surprises, – and God made it
    all!
– For what? Do you feel thankful, ay or
    no,

For this fair town's face, yonder river's
    line,
The mountain round it and the sky
    above,
Much more the figures of man,
    woman, child,
These are the frame to? What's it all
    about?
To be passed over, despised? or dwelt
    upon,
Wondered at? oh, this last of course! –
    you say.
But why not do as well as say, – paint
    these
Just as they are, careless what comes of
    it?
God's works – paint any one, and
    count it crime
To let a truth slip. Don't object, 'His
    works
'Are here already; nature is complete:
'Suppose you reproduce her – (which
    you can't)
'There's no advantage! you must beat
    her, then.'
For, don't you mark? we're made so
    that we love
First when we see them painted, things
    we have passed
Perhaps a hundred times nor cared to
    see;
And so they are better, painted – better
    to us,
Which is the same thing. Art was given
    for that;
God uses us to help each other so,
Lending our minds out. Have you
    noticed, now,
Your cullion's hanging face? A bit of
    chalk,
And trust me but you should, though!
    How much more,
If I drew higher things with the same
    truth!
That were to take the Prior's pulpit-
    place,
Interpret God to all of you! Oh, oh,

It makes me mad to see what men shall
do
And we in our graves! This world's no
blot for us,
Nor blank; it means intensely, and
means good:
To find its meaning is my meat and
drink.
'Ay, but you don't so instigate to prayer!'
Strikes in the Prior: 'when your
meaning's plain
'It does not say to folk – remember
matins,
'Or, mind you fast next Friday!' Why,
for this
What need of art at all? A skull and
bones,
Two bits of stick nailed crosswise, or,
what's best,
A bell to chime the hour with, does as
well.
I painted a Saint Laurence six months
since
At Prato, splashed the fresco in fine
style:
'How looks my painting, now the
scaffold's down?'
I ask a brother: 'Hugely,' he returns –
'Already not one phiz of your three
slaves
'Who turn the Deacon off his toasted
side,
'But's scratched and prodded to our
heart's content,
'The pious people have so eased their
own
'With coming to say prayers there in a
rage:
'We get on fast to see the bricks
beneath.
'Expect another job this time next year,
'For pity and religion grow i' the
crowd –
'Your painting serves its purpose!
'Hang the fools!
– That is – you'll not mistake an idle
word

Spoke in a huff by a poor monk, God
wot,
Tasting the air this spicy night which
turns
The unaccustomed head like Chianti
wine!
Oh, the church knows! don't misreport
me, now!
It's natural a poor monk out of bounds
Should have his apt word to excuse
himself:
And hearken how I plot to make amends.
I have bethought me: I shall paint a
piece
. . . There's for you! Give me six
months, then go, see
Something in Sant' Ambrogio's! Bless
the nuns!
They want a cast o' my office. I shall
paint
God in the midst, Madonna and her
babe,
Ringed by a bowery flowery angel-brood,
Lilies and vestments and white faces,
sweet
As puff on puff of grated orris-root
When ladies crowd to church at mid-
summer.
And then i' the front, of course a saint
or two –
Saint John, because he saves the
Florentines,
Saint Ambrose, who puts down in
black and white
The convent's friends and gives them a
long day,
And Job, I must have him there past
mistake,
The man of Uz (and Us without the z,
Painters who need his patience). Well,
all these
Secured at their devotion, up shall come
Out of a corner when you least expect,
As one by a dark stair into a great light,
Music and talking, who but Lippo! I! –
Mazed, motionless and moonstruck –
I'm the man!

Back I shrink – what is this I see and
    hear?
I, caught up with my monk's-things by
    mistake,
My old serge gown and rope that goes
    all round,
I, in this presence, this pure company!
Where's a hole, where's a corner for
    escape?
Then steps a sweet angelic slip of a thing
Forward, puts out a soft palm – 'Not
    so fast!'
– Addresses the celestial presence, 'nay –
'He made you and devised you, after
    all,
'Though he's none of you! Could Saint
    John there draw –
'His camel-hair make up a painting-
    brush?
'We come to brother Lippo for all that,
'*Iste perfecit opus!*' So, all smile –
I shuffle sideways with my blushing
    face
Under the cover of a hundred wings
Thrown like a spread of kirtles when
    you're gay
And play hot cockles, all the doors
    being shut,
Till, wholly unexpected, in there pops
The hothead husband! Thus I scuttle off
To some safe bench behind, not letting
    go
The palm of her, the little lily thing
That spoke the good word for me in the
    nick,
Like the Prior's niece … Saint Lucy, I
    would say.
And so all's saved for me, and for the
    church
A pretty picture gained. Go, six months
    hence!
Your hand, sir, and good-bye: no lights,
    no lights!
The street's hushed, and I know my
    own way back,
Don't fear me! There's the grey
    beginning. Zooks!

## Andrea del Sarto

(Called 'The Faultless Painter')

But do not let us quarrel any more,
No, my Lucrezia; bear with me for
    once:
Sit down and all shall happen as you
    wish.
You turn your face, but does it bring
    your heart?
I'll work then for your friend's friend,
    never fear,
Treat his own subject after his own way,
Fix his own time, accept too his own
    price,
And shut the money into this small
    hand
When next it takes mine. Will it?
    tenderly?
Oh, I'll content him, – but to-
    morrow,Love!
I often am much wearier than you
    think,
This evening more than usual, and it
    seems
As if – forgive now – should you let me
    sit
Here by the window with your hand in
    mine
And look a half-hour forth on Fiesole,
Both of one mind, as married people
    use,
Quietly, quietly the evening through,
I might get up to-morrow to my work
Cheerful and fresh as ever. Let us try.
To-morrow, how you shall be glad for
    this!
Your soft hand is a woman of itself,
And mine the man's bared breast she
    curls inside.
Don't count the time lost, neither; you
    must serve
For each of the five pictures we require:
It saves a model. So! keep looking so –
My serpentining beauty, rounds on
    rounds!

– How could you ever prick those
  perfect ears,
Even to put the pearl there! oh, so
  sweet –
My face, my moon, my everybody's
  moon,
Which everybody looks on and calls
  his,
And, I suppose, is looked on by in turn,
While she looks – no one's: very dear,
  no less.
You smile? why, there's my picture read
  made,
There's what we painters call our
  harmony!
A common greyness silvers everything, –
All in a twilight, you and I alike
– You, at the point of your first pride in
  me
(That's gone you know), – but I, at
  every point;
My youth, my hope, my art, being all
  toned down
To yonder sober pleasant Fiesole.
There's the bell clinking from the chapel-
  top;
That length of convent-wall across the
  way
Holds the trees safer, huddled more
  inside;
The last monk leaves the garden; days
  decrease,
And autumn grows, autumn in every-
  thing.
Eh? the who'e seems to fall into a shape
As if I saw alike my work and self
And all that I was born to be and do,
A twilight-piece. Love, we are in God's
  hand.
How strange now, looks the life he
  makes us lead;
So free we seem, so fettered fast we are!
I feel he laid the fetter: let it lie!
This chamber for example – turn your
  head –
All that's behind us! You don't under-
  stand

Nor care to understand about my art,
But you can hear at least when people
  speak:
And that cartoon, the second from the
  door
– It is the thing, Love! so such things
  should be –
Behold Madonna! – I am bold to say.
I can do with my pencil what I know,
What I see, what at bottom of my heart
I wish for, if I ever wish so deep –
Do easily, too – when I say, perfectly,
I do not boast, perhaps: yourself are
  judge,
Who listened to the Legate's talk last
  week,
And just as much they used to say in
  France.
At any rate 'tis easy, all of it!
No sketches first, no studies, that's
  long past:
I do what many dream of, all their lives,
– Dream? strive to do, and agonize to
  do,
And fail in doing. I could count twenty
  such
On twice your fingers, and not leave
  this town,
Who strive – you don't know how the
  others strive
To paint a little thing like that you
  smeared
Carelessly passing with your robes
  afloat, –
Yet do much less, so much less, Some-
  one says,
(I know his name, no matter) – so much
  less!
Well, less is more, Lucrezia: I am judged.
There burns a truer light of God in
  them,
In their vexed beating stuffed and
  stopped-up brain,
Heart, or whate'er else, than goes on to
  prompt
This low-pulsed forthright craftsman's
  hand of mine.

Their works drop groundward, but
    themselves, I know,
Reach many a time a heaven that's
    shut to me,
Enter and take their place there sure
    enough,
Though they come back and cannot
    tell the world.
My works are nearer heaven, but I sit
    here.
The sudden blood of these men! at a
    word –
Praise them, it boils, or blame them, it
    boils too.
I, painting from myself and to myself,
Know what I do, am unmoved by men's
    blame
Or their praise either. Somebody remarks
Morello's outline there is wrongly
    traced,
His hue mistaken; what of that? or
    else,
Rightly traced and well ordered; what
    of that?
Speak as they please, what does the
    mountain care?
Ah, but a man's reach should exceed
    his grasp.
Or what's a heaven for? All is silver-
    grey,
Placid and perfect with my art: the
    worse!
I know both what I want and what
    might gain,
And yet how profitless to know, to sigh
'Had I been two, another and myself,
'Our head would have o'erlooked the
    world!' No doubt.
Yonder's a work now, of that famous
    youth
The Urbinate who died five years ago.
('Tis copied, George Vasari sent it me.)
Well, I can fancy how he did it all,
Pouring his soul, with kings and popes
    to see,
Reaching, that heaven might so
    replenish him,

Above and through his art – for it gives
    way;
That arm is wrongly put – and there
    again –
A fault to pardon in the drawing's lines,
Its body, so to speak: its soul is right,
He means right – that, a child may
    understand.
Still, what an arm! and I could alter it:
But all the play, the insight and the
    stretch –
Out of me, out of me! And wherefore
    out?
Had you enjoined them on me, given
    me soul,
We might have risen to Rafael, I and
    you!
Nay, Love, you did give all I asked, I
    think –
More than I merit, yes, by many times.
But had you – oh, with the same perfect
    brow,
And perfect eyes, and more than perfect
    mouth,
And the low voice my soul hears, as a
    bird
The fowler's pipe, and follows to the
    snare –
Had you, with these the same, but
    brought a mind!
Some women do so. Had the mouth
    there urged
'God and the glory! never care for gain.
'The present by the future, what is
    that?
'Live for fame, side by side with Agnolo!
'Rafael is waiting: up to God, all three!
'I might have done it for you. So it
    seems:
Perhaps not. All is as God over-rules.
Beside, incentives come from the soul's
    self;
The rest avail not. Why do I need you?
What wife had Rafael, or has Agnolo?
In this world, who can do a thing, will
    not;
And who would do it, cannot, I perceive:

Yet the will's somewhat – somewhat,
    too, the power –
And thus we half-men struggle. At the
    end,
God, I conclude, compensates,
    punishes.
'Tis safer for me, if the award be strict,
That I am something underrated here,
Poor this long while, despised, to
    speak the truth.
I dared not, do you know, leave home
    all day,
For fear of chancing on the Paris lords.
The best is when they pass and look
    aside;
But they speak sometimes; I must bear
    it all.
Well may they speak! That Francis, that
    first time,
And that long festal year at Fontaine-
    bleau!
I surely then could sometimes leave the
    ground,
Put on the glory, Rafael's daily wear,
In that humane great monarch's golden
    look, –
One finger in his beard or twisted curl
Over his mouth's good mark that made
    the smile,
One arm about my shoulder, round my
    neck,
The jingle of his gold chain in my ear,
I painting proudly with his breath
    on me,
All his court round him, seeing with
    his eyes,
Such frank French eyes, and such a fire
    of souls
Profuse, my hand kept plying by those
    hearts, –
And, best of all, this, this, this face
    beyond,
This in the background, waiting on my
    work,
To crown the issue with a last reward!
A good time, was it not, my kingly
    days?

And had you not grown restless …
    'but I know –
'Tis done and past; 'twas right, my
    instinct said;
Too live the life grew, golden and not
    grey,
And I'm the weak-eyed bat no sun
    should tempt
Out of the grange whose four walls
    make his world.
How could it end in any other way?
You called me, and I came home to
    your heart.
The triumph was – to reach and stay
    there; since
I reached it ere the triumph, what is
    lost?
Let my hands frame your face in your
    hair's gold,
You beautiful Lucrezia that are mine!
'Rafael did this, Andrea painted that;
'The Roman's is the better when you
    pray,
'But still the other's Virgin was his wife –
Men will excuse me. I am glad to judge
Both pictures in your presence; clearer
    grows
My better fortune, I resolve to think.
For, do you know, Lucrezia, as God
    lives,
Said one day Agnolo, his very self,
To Rafael … I have known it all these
    years …
(When the young man was flaming out
    his thoughts
Upon a palace-wall for Rome to see,
Too lifted up in heart because of it)
'Friend, there's a certain sorry little scrub
'Goes up and down our Florence, none
    cares how,
'Who, were he set to plan and execute
'As you are, pricked on by your popes
    and kings,
'Would bring the sweat into that brow
    of yours!'
'To Rafael's! – And indeed the arm is
    wrong.

I hardly dare ... yet, only you to see,
Give the chalk here – quick, thus the
    line should go!
Ay, but the soul! he's Rafael! rub it out!
Still, all I care for, if he spoke the truth,
(What he? why, who but Michel Agnolo?
Do you forget already words like those?)
If really there was such a chance, so
    lost, –
Is, whether you're – not grateful – but
    more pleased.
Well, let me think so. And you smile
    indeed!
This hour has been an hour! Another
    smile?
If you would sit thus by me every night
I should work better, do you
    comprehend?
I mean that I should earn more, give
    you more.
See, it is settled dusk now; there's a
    star;
Morello's gone, the watch-lights show
    the wall,
The cue-owls speak the name we call
    them by.
Come from the window, love, – come
    in, at last,
Inside the melancholy little house
We built to be so gay with. God is just.
King Francis may forgive me: oft at
    nights
When I look up from painting, eyes
    tired out,
The walls become illumined, brick
    from brick
Distinct, instead of mortar, fierce bright
    gold,
That gold of his I did cement them with!
Let us but love each other. Must you go?
That Cousin here again? he waits outside?
Must see you – you, and not with me?
    Those loans?
More gaming debts to pay? you smiled
    for that?
Well, let smiles buy me! have you more
    to spend?

While hand and eye and something of
    heart
Are left me, work's my ware, and what's
    it worth?
I'll pay my fancy. Only let me sit
The grey remainder of the evening out,
Idle, you call it, and muse perfectly
How I could paint, were I but back in
    France,
One picture, just one more – the Virgin's
    face,
Not yours this time! I want you at my
    side
To hear them – that is, Michel Agnolo –
Judge all I do and tell you of its worth.
Will you? To-morrow, satisfy your friend.
I take the subjects for his corridor,
Finish the portrait out of hand – there,
    there,
And throw him in another thing or two
If he demurs; the whole should prove
    enough
To pay for this same Cousin's freak.
    Beside,
What's better and what's all I care about,
Get you the thirteen scudi for the ruff!
Love, does that please you? Ah, but
    what does he,
The Cousin! what does he to please you
    more?
    I am grown peaceful as old age
        tonight.
I regret little, I would change still less.
Since there my past life lies, why alter it?
The very wrong to Francis! – it is true
I took his coin, was tempted and
    complied,
And built this house and sinned, and
    all is said.
My father and my mother died of want.
Well, had I riches of my own? you see
How one gets rich! Let each one bear
    his lot.
They were born poor, lived poor, and
    poor they died:
And I have laboured somewhat in my
    time

And not been paid profusely. Some
    good son
Paint my two hundred pictures – let
    him try!
No doubt, there's something strikes a
    balance. Yes,
You loved me quite enough, it seems
    tonight.
This must suffice me here. What would
    one have?
In heaven, perhaps, new chances, one
    more chance –
Four great walls in the New Jerusalem,
Meted on each side by the angel's reed,
For Leonard, Rafael, Agnolo and me
To cover – the three first without a wife,
While I have mine! So – still they over-
    come
Because there's still Lucrezia, – as I
    choose.
Again the Cousin's whistle! Go, my
    Love.


## The Bishop Orders his Tomb at
## St Praxed's Church

### Rome, 15—

Vanity, saith the preacher, vanity!
Draw round my bed: is Anselm
    keeping back?
Nephews – sons mine … ah God, I
    know not! Well –
She, men would have to be your
    mother once,
Old Gandolf envied me, so fair she was!
What's done is done, and she is dead
    beside,
Dead long ago, and I am Bishop since,
And as she died so must we die our-
    selves,
And thence ye may perceive the world's
    a dream.
Life, how and what is it? As here I lie
In this state-chamber, dying by degrees,
Hours and long hours in the dead
    night, I ask

'Do I live, am I dead?' Peace, peace
    seems all.
Saint Praxed's ever was the church for
    peace;
And so, about this tomb of mine. I
    fought
With tooth and nail to save my niche,
    ye know:
– Old Gandolf cozened me, despite my
    care;
Shrewd was that snatch from out the
    corner South
He graced his carrion with, God curse
    the same!
Yet still my niche is not so cramped
    but thence
One sees the pulpit o' the epistle-side,
And somewhat of the choir, those
    silent seats,
And up into the aery dome where live
The angels, and a sunbeam's sure to
    lurk:
And I shall fill my slab of basalt there,
And 'neath my tabernacle take my rest,
With those nine columns round me,
    two and two,
The odd one at my feet where Anselm
    stands:
Peach-blossom marble all, the rare, the
    ripe
As fresh-poured red wine of a mighty
    pulse.
– Old Gandolf with his paltry onion-
    stone,
Put me where I may look at him! True
    peach,
Rosy and flawless: how I earned the
    prize!
Draw close: that conflagration of my
    church
– What then? So much was saved if
    aught were missed!
My sons, ye would not be my death?
    Go dig
The white-grape vineyard where the
    oil-press stood,
Drop water gently till the surface sink,

And if ye find ... Ah God, I know not,
  I! ...
Bedded in store of rotten fig-leaves soft,
And corded up in a tight olive-frail,
Some lump, ah God, of *lapis lazuli*,
Big as a Jew's head cut off at the nape,
Blue as a vein o'er the Madonna's
  breast ...
Sons, all have I bequeathed you, villas,
  all,
That brave Frascati villa with its bath,
So, let the blue lump poise between
  my knees,
Like God the Father's globe on both
  his hands
Ye worship in the Jesu Church so gay,
For Gandolf shall not choose but see
  and burst!
Swift as a weaver's shuttle fleet our
  years:
Man goeth to the grave, and where is
  he?
Did I say basalt for my slab, sons?
  Black –
'Twas ever antique-black I meant! How
  else
Shall ye contrast my frieze to come
  beneath?
The bas-relief in bronze ye promised
  me,
Those Pans and Nymphs ye wot of,
  and perchance
Some tripod, thyrsus, with a vase or so,
The Saviour at his sermon on the
  mount,
Saint Praxed in a glory, and one Pan
Ready to twitch the Nymph's last
  garment off,
And Moses with the tables ... but I
  know
Ye mark me not! What do they whisper
  thee,
Child of my bowels, Anselm? Ah, ye
  hope
To revel down my villas while I gasp
Bricked o'er with beggar's mouldy
  travertine

Which Gandolf from his tomb-top
  chuckles at!
Nay, boys, ye love me – all of jasper,
  then!
'Tis jasper ye stand pledged to, lest I
  grieve.
My bath must needs be left behind,
  alas!
One block, pure green as a pistachio-
  nut,
There's plenty jasper somewhere in the
  world –
And have I not Saint Praxed's ear to
  pray
Horses for ye, and brown Greek
  manuscripts,
And mistresses with great smooth
  marbly limbs?
– That's if ye carve my epitaph aright,
Choice Latin, picked phrase, Tully's
  every word,
No gaudy ware like Gandolf's second
  line
Tully, my masters? Ulpian serves his
  need!
And then how I shall lie through
  centuries,
And hear the blessed mutter of the
  mass,
And see God made and eaten all day
  long,
And feel the steady candle-flame, and
  taste
Good strong thick stupefying incense-
  smoke!
For as I lie here, hours of the dead
  night,
Dying in state and by such slow
  degrees,
I fold my arms as if they clasped a
  crook,
And stretch my feet forth straight as
  stone can point,
And let the bedclothes, for a mortcloth,
  drop
Into great laps and folds of sculptor's-
  work:

And as yon tapers dwindle, and strange
    thoughts
Grow, with a certain humming in my
    ears,
About the life before I lived this life,
And this life too, popes, cardinal and
    priests,
Saint Praxed at his sermon on the
    mount,
Your tall pale mother with her talking
    eyes,
And new-found agate urns as fresh as
    day,
And marble's language, Latin pure,
    discreet,
– Aha, ELUCESCEBAT quoth our friend?
No Tully, said I, Ulpian at the best!
Evil and brief hath been my pilgrimage.
All *lapis*, all, sons! Else I give the Pope
My villas! Will ye ever eat my heart?
Ever your eyes were as a lizard's quick,
The glitter like your mother's for my
    soul,
Or ye would heighten my impoverished
    frieze,
Piece out its starved design, and fill my
    vase
With grapes, and add a vizor and a
    Term,
And to the tripod ye would tie a lynx
That in his struggle throws the thyrsus
    down,
To comfort me on my entablature
Whereon I am to lie till I must ask
'Do I live, am I dead?' There, leave me,
    there!
For ye have stabbed me with ingratitude
To death – ye wish it – God, ye wish it!
    Stone –
Gritstone, a-crumble! Clammy squares
    which sweat
As if the corpse they keep were oozing
    through –
And no more *lapis* to delight the world!
Well go! I bless ye. Fewer tapers there,
But in a row: and, going, turn your
    backs

– Ay, like departing altar-ministrants,
And leave me in my church, the
    church for peace,
That I may watch at leisure if he leers –
Old Gandolf, at me, from his onion-
    stone,
As still he envied me, so fair she was!

## Bishop Blougram's Apology

No more wine? then we'll push back
    chairs and talk.
A final glass for me, though: cool, i'
    faith!
We ought to have our Abbey back, you
    see.
It's different, preaching in basilicas,
And doing duty in some masterpiece
Like this of brother Pugin's, bless his
    heart!
I doubt if they're half baked, those
    chalk rosettes,
Ciphers and stucco-twiddlings every-
    where;
It's just like breathing in a lime-kiln: eh?
These hot long ceremonies of our church
Cost us a little – oh, they pay the price,
You take me – amply pay it! Now, we'll
    talk.

So, you despise me, Mr Gigadibs.
No deprecation, – nay, I beg you, sir!
Beside 'tis our engagement: don't you
    know,
I promised, if you'd watch a dinner out,
We'd see truth dawn together? – truth
    that peeps
Over the glasses' edge when dinner's
    done,
And body gets its sop and holds its
    noise
And leaves soul free a little. Now's the
    time:
Truth's break of day! You do despise
    me then.
And if I say, 'despise me,' – never fear!
I know you do not in a certain sense –

Not in my arm-chair, for example: here,
I well imagine you respect my place
(*Status, entourage*, worldly circumstance)
Quite to its value – very much indeed:
– Are up to the protesting eyes of you
In pride at being seated here for once –
You'll turn it to such capital account!
When somebody, through years and
    years to come,
Hints of the bishop, – names me –
    that's enough:
'Blougram? I knew him' – (into it you
    slide)
'Dined with him once, a Corpus Christi
    Day,
'All alone, we two; he's a clever man:
'And after dinner, – why, the wine you
    know, –
'Oh, there was wine, and good! – what
    with the wine …
' 'Faith, we began upon all sorts of talk!
'He's no bad fellow, Blougram; he had
    seen
'Something of mine he relished, some
    review:
'He's quite above their humbug in his
    heart,
'Half-said as much, indeed – the thing's
    his trade.
'I warrant, Blougram's sceptical at times:
'How otherwise? I liked him, I confess!'
*Che che*, my dear sir, as we say at Rome,
Don't you protest now! It's fair give
    and take;
You have had your turn and spoken
    your home-truths:
The hand's mine now, and here you
    follow suit.

    Thus much conceded, still the first
    fact stays –
You do despise me; your ideal of life
Is not the bishop's: you would not be I.
You would like better to be Goethe,
    now,
Or Buonaparte, or, bless me, lower
    still,

Count D'Orsay, – so you did what you
    preferred,
Spoke as you thought, and, as you
    cannot help,
Believed or disbelieved, no matter what,
So long as on that point, whate'er it was,
You loosed your mind, were whole and
    sole yourself.
– That, my ideal never can include,
Upon that element of truth and worth
Never be based! for say they make me
    Pope –
(They can't – suppose it for our
    argument!)
Why, there I'm at my tether's end, I've
    reached
My height, and not a height which
    pleases you:
An unbelieving Pope won't do, you say.
It's like those eerie stories nurses tell,
Of how some actor on a stage played
    Death,
With pasteboard crown, sham orb and
    tinselled dart,
And called himself the monarch of the
    world;
Then, going in the tire-room afterward,
Because the play was done, to shift
    himself,
Got touched upon the sleeve familiarly,
The moment he had shut the closet
    door,
By Death himself. Thus God might
    touch a Pope
At unawares, ask what his baubles
    mean,
And whose part he presumed to play
    just now.
Best be yourself, imperial, plain and
    true!

So, drawing comfortable breath again,
You weigh and find, whatever more or
    less
I boast of my ideal realized
Is nothing in the balance when
    opposed

To your ideal, your grand simple life,
Of which you will not realize one jot.
I am much, you are nothing; you would
    be all,
I would be merely much: you beat me
    there.
No, friend, you do not beat me: hearken
    why!
The common problem, yours, mine,
    every one's,
Is – not to fancy what were fair in life
Provided it could be, – but, finding
    first
What may be, then find how to make it
    fair
Up to our means: a very different thing!
No abstract intellectual plan of life
Quite irrespective of life's plainest laws,
But one, a man, who is man and
    nothing more,
May lead within a world which (by your
    leave)
Is Rome or London, not Fool's-paradise.
Embellish Rome, idealize away,
Make paradise of London if you can,
You're welcome, nay, you're wise.

                A simile!
We mortals cross the ocean of this
    world
Each in his average cabin of a life;
The best's not big, the worst yields
    elbow-room.
Now for our six months' voyage – how
    prepare?
You come on shipboard with a
    landsman's list
Of things he calls convenient: so they
    are!
An India screen is pretty furniture,
A piano-forte is a fine resource,
All Balzac's novels occupy one shelf,
The new edition fifty volumes long;
And little Greek books, with the funny
    type
They get up well at Leipsic, fill the
    next:

Go on! slabbed marble, what a bath it
    makes!
And Parma's pride, the Jerome, let us
    add!
'Twere pleasant could Correggio's
    fleeting glow
Hang full in face of one where'er one
    roams,
Since he more than the others brings
    with him
Italy's self, – the marvellous
    Modenese! –
Yet was not on your list before, perhaps.
– Alas, friend, here's the agent … is't
    the name?
The captain, or whoever's master here –
You see him screw his face up; what's
    his cry
Ere you set foot on shipboard? 'Six feet
    square!'
If you won't understand what six feet
    mean,
Compute and purchase stores
    accordingly –
And if, in pique because he overhauls
Your Jerome, piano, bath, you come on
    board
Bare – -why, you cut a figure at the first
While sympathetic landsmen see you
    off;
Not afterward, when long ere half seas
    over,
You peep up from your utterly naked
    boards
Into some snug and well-appointed
    berth,
Like mine for instance (try the cooler
    jug –
Put back the other, but don't jog the
    ice!)
And mortified you mutter 'Well and
    good;
'He sits enjoying his sea-furniture;
' 'Tis stout and proper, and there's
    store of it:
'Though I've the better notion, all
    agree,

'Of fitting rooms up. Hang the carpenter,
'Neat ship-shape fixings and
    contrivances –
'I would have brought my Jerome,
    frame and all!'
And meantime you bring nothing:
    never mind –
You've proved your artist-nature: what
    you don't
You might bring, so despise me, as I say.
    Now come, let's backward to the
    starting-place.
See my way: we're two college friends,
    suppose.
Prepare together for our voyage, then;
Each note and check the other in his
    work, –
Here's mine, a bishop's outfit; criticize!
What's wrong? why won't you be a
    bishop too?

    Why first, you don't believe, you
      don't and can't,
(Not statedly, that is, and fixedly
And absolutely and exclusively)
In any revelation called divine.
No dogmas nail your faith; and what
    remains
But say so, like the honest man you are?
First, therefore, overhaul theology!
Nay, I too, not a fool, you please to
    think,
Must find believing every whit as hard:
And if I do not frankly say as much,
The ugly consequence is clear enough.
    Now wait, my friend: well, I do not
      believe –
If you'll accept no faith that is not fixed,
Absolute and exclusive, as you say.
You're wrong – I mean to prove it in
    due time.
Meanwhile, I know where difficulties
    lie
I could not, cannot solve, nor ever shall,
So give up hope accordingly to solve –
(To you, and over the wine). Our dogmas
    then

With both of us, though in unlike
    degree,
Missing full credence – overboard with
    them!
I mean to meet you on your own
    premise:
Good, there go mine in company with
    yours!

    And now what are we? unbelievers
    both,
Calm and complete, determinately
    fixed
To-day, to-morrow and for ever, pray?
You'll guarantee me that? Not so, I
    think!
In no wise! all we've gained is, that
    belief,
As unbelief before, shakes us by fits,
Confounds us like its predecessor.
    Where's
The gain? how can we guard our
    unbelief,
Make it bear fruit to us? – the problem
    here.
Just when we are safest, there's a
    sunset-touch,
A fancy from a flower-bell, some one's
    death,
A chorus-ending from Euripides, –
And that's enough for fifty hopes and
    fears
As old and new at once as nature's self,
To rap and knock and enter in our
    soul,
Take hands and dance there, a
    fantastic ring,
Round the ancient idol, on his base
    again, –
The grand Perhaps! We look on
    helplessly.
There the old misgivings, crooked
    questions are –
This good God, – what he could do, if
    he would,
Would, if he could – then must have
    done long since:

If so, when, where and how? some way
    must be, –
Once feel about, and soon or late you hit
Some sense, in which it might be, after
    all.
Why not, 'The Way, the Truth, the life?

                              – That way
Over the mountain, which who stands
    upon
Is apt to doubt if it be meant for a road;
While, if he views it from the waste
    itself,
Up goes the line there, plain from base
    to brow,
Not vague, mistakeable! what's a break
    or two
Seen from the unbroken desert either
    side?
And then (to bring in fresh philosophy)
What if the breaks themselves should
    prove at last
The most consummate of contrivances
To train a man's eye, teach him what is
    faith?
And so we tumble at truth's very test!
All we have gained then by our unbelief
Is a life of doubt diversified by faith,
For one of faith diversified by doubt:
We called the chess-board white, – we
    call it black.

    'Well,' you rejoin, 'the end's no worse,
        at least
'We've reason for both colours on the
    board:
'Why not confess then, where I drop
    the faith
'And you the doubt, that I'm as right as
    you?'

    Because, friend, in the next place,
        this being so,
And both things even, – faith and
    unbelief
Left to a man's choice, – we'll proceed
    a step,
Returning to our image, which I like.

A man's choice, yes – but a cabin-
    passenger's –
The man made for the special life o'
    the world –
Do you forget him? I remember though!
Consult our ship's conditions and you
    find
One and but one choice suitable to all;
The choice, that you unluckily prefer,
Turning things topsy-turvy – they or it
Going to the ground. Belief or unbelief
Bears upon life, determines its whole
    course,
Begins at its beginning. See the world
Such as it is, – you made it not, nor I;
I mean to take it as it is, – and you,
Not so you'll take it, – though you get
    nought else.
I know the special kind of life I like,
What suits the most my idiosyncrasy,
Brings out the best of me and bears me
    fruit
In power, peace, pleasantness and
    length of days.
I find that positive belief does this.
For me, and unbelief, no whit of this.
– For you, it does, however? – that,
    we'll try!
'Tis clear, I cannot lead my life, at least,
Induce the world to let me peaceably,
Without declaring at the outset, 'Friends,
'I absolutely and peremptorily
'Believe!' – I say, faith is my waking
    life:
One sleeps, indeed, and dreams at
    intervals,
We know, but waking's the main point
    with us,
And my provision's for life's waking
    part.
Accordingly, I use heart, head and hand
All day, I build, scheme, study, and
    make friends;
And when night overtakes me, down I
    lie,
Sleep, dream a little, and get done with
    it,

The sooner the better, to begin afresh.
What's midnight doubt before the day-
	spring's faith?
You, the philosopher, that disbelieve,
That recognize the night, give dreams
	their weight –
To be consistent you should keep your
	bed,
Abstain from healthy acts that prove
	you man,
For fear you drowse perhaps at
	unawares!
And certainly at night you'll sleep and
	dream,
Live through the day and bustle as you
	please.
And so you live to sleep as I to wake,
To unbelieve as I to still believe?
Well, and the common sense o' the
	world calls you
Bed-ridden, – and its good things come
	to me.
Its estimation, which is half the fight,
That's the first-cabin comfort I secure:
The next ... but, you perceive with half
	an eye!
Come, come, it's best believing, if we
	may;
You can't but own that!

		Next, concede again,
If once we choose belief, on all accounts
We can't be too decisive in our faith,
Conclusive and exclusive in its terms,
To suit the world which gives us the
	good things.
In every man's career are certain points
Whereon he dares not be indifferent;
The world detects him clearly, if he
	dare,
As baffled at the game, and losing life.
He may care little or he may care much
For riches, honour, pleasure, work,
	repose,
Since various theories of life and life's
Success are extant which might easily
Comport with either estimate of these;

And whoso chooses wealth or poverty,
Labour or quiet, is not judged a fool
Because his fellow would choose other-
	wise:
We let him choose upon his own account
So long as he's consistent with his
	choice.
But certain points, left wholly to himself,
When once a man has arbitrated on,
We say he must succeed there or go
	hang.
Thus, he should wed the woman he
	loves most
Or needs most, whatsoe'er the love or
	need –
For he can't wed twice. Then, he must
	avouch,
Or follow, at the least, sufficiently,
The form of faith his conscience holds
	the best,
Whate'er the process of conviction was:
For nothing can compensate his mistake
On such a point, the man himself being
	judge:
He cannot wed twice, nor twice lose his
	soul.

	Well now, there's one great form of
		Christian faith
I happened to be born in – which to
		teach
Was given me as I grew up, on all hands,
As best and readiest means of living by;
The same on examination being proved
The most pronounced moreover, fixed,
		precise
And absolute form of faith in the whole
		world –
Accordingly, most potent of all forms
For working on the world. Observe, my
		friend!
Such as you know me, I am free to say,
In these hard latter days which hamper
		one,
Myself – by no immoderate exercise
Of intellect and learning, but the tact
To let external forces work for me,

– Bid the street's stones be bread and
    they are bread;
Bid Peter's creed, or rather, Hildebrand's,
Exalt me o'er my fellows in the world
And make my life an ease and joy and
    pride;
It does so, – which for me's a great
    point gained,
Who have a soul and body that exact
A comfortable care in many ways.
There's power in me and will to
    dominate
Which I must exercise, they hurt me
    else:
In many ways I need mankind's respect,
Obedience, and the love that's born of
    fear:
While at the same time, there's a taste
    I have,
A toy of soul, a titillating thing,
Refuses to digest these dainties crude.
The naked life is gross till clothed upon:
I must take what men offer, with a
    grace
As though I would not, could I help it,
    take!
An uniform I wear though over-rich –
Something imposed on me, no choice
    of mine;
No fancy-dress worn for pure fancy's
    sake
And despicable therefore! now folk kneel
And kiss my hand – of course the
    Church's hand.
Thus I am made, thus life is best for me,
And thus that it should be I have
    procured;
And thus it could not be another way,
I venture to imagine.

            You'll reply,
So far my choice, no doubt, is a success;
But were I made of better elements,
With nobler instincts, purer tastes, like
    you,
I hardly would account the thing success
Though it did all for me I say.

            But, friend,
We speak of what is; not of what might
    be,
And how 'twere better if 'twere other-
    wise.
I am the man you see here plain enough:
Grant I'm a beast, why, beasts must
    lead beasts' lives!
Suppose I own at once to tail and claws;
The tailless man exceeds me: but being
    tailed
I'll lash out lion-fashion, and leave apes
To dock their stump and dress their
    haunches up.
My business is not to remake myself,
But make the absolute best of what
    God made.
Or – our first simile – though you
    prove me doomed
To a viler berth still, to the steerage-
    hole,
The sheep-pen or the pig-stye, I should
    strive
To make what use of each were possible;
And as this cabin gets upholstery,
That hutch should rustle with sufficient
    straw.

    But, friend, I don't acknowledge
    quite so fast
I fail of all your manhood's lofty tastes
Enumerated so complacently,
On the mere ground that you forsooth
    can find
In this particular life I choose to lead
No fit provision for them. Can you not?
Say you, my fault is I address myself
To grosser estimators than should
    judge?
And that's no way of holding up the
    soul,
Which, nobler, needs men's praise
    perhaps, yet knows
One wise man's verdict outweighs all
    the fools' –
Would like the two, but, forced to
    choose, takes that.

I pine among my million imbeciles
(You think) aware some dozen men of
    sense
Eye me and know me, whether I believe
In the last winking Virgin, as I vow,
And am a fool, or disbelieve in her
And am a knave, – approve in neither
    case,
Withhold their voices though I look
    their way:
Like Verdi when, at his worst opera's
    end
(The thing they gave at Florence, –
    what's its name?)
While the mad houseful's plaudits near
    outbang
His orchestra of salt-box, tongs and
    bones,
He looks through all the roaring and
    the wreaths
Where sits Rossini patient in his stall.

Nay, friend, I meet you with an
    answer here –
That even your prime men who
    appraise their kind
Are men still, catch a wheel within a
    wheel,
See more in a truth than the truth's
    simple self,
Confuse themselves. You see lads walk
    the street
Sixty the minute; what's to note in
    that?
You see one lad o'erstride a chimney-
    stack;
Him you must watch – he's sure to fall,
    yet stands!
Our interest's on the dangerous edge
    of things.
The honest thief, the tender murderer,
The superstitious atheist, demirep
That loves and saves her soul in new
    French books –
We watch while these in equilibrium
    keep
The giddy line midway: one step aside,

They're classed and done with. I, then,
    keep the line
Before your sages, – just the men to
    shrink
From the gross weights, coarse scales
    and labels broad
You offer their refinement. Fool or knave?
Why needs a bishop be a fool or knave
When there's a thousand diamond
    weights between?
So, I enlist them. Your picked twelve,
    you'll find,
Profess themselves indignant, scandalized
At thus being held unable to explain
How a superior man who disbelieves
May not believe as well: that's Schelling's
    way!
It's through my coming in the tail of
    time,
Nicking the minute with a happy tact.
Had I been born three hundred years
    ago
They'd say, 'What's strange? Blougram
    of course believes;'
And, seventy years since, 'disbelieves of
    course.'
But now, 'He may believe; and yet, and
    yet
'How can he?' All eyes turn with interest.
Whereas, step off the line on either
    side –
You, for example, clever to a fault,
The rough and ready man who write
    apace,
Read somewhat seldomer, think perhaps
    even less –
You disbelieve! Who wonders and who
    cares?
Lord So-and-so – his coat bedropped
    with wax,
All Peter's chains about his waist, his
    back
Brave with the needlework of Noodle-
    dom –
Believes! Again, who wonders and who
    cares?
But I, the man of sense and learning too,

The able to think yet act, the this, the
    that,
I, to believe at this late time of day!
Enough; you see, I need not fear
    contempt.

   – Except it's yours! Admire me as
    these may,
You don't. But whom at least do you
    admire?
Present your own perfection, your ideal,
Your pattern man for a minute – oh,
    make haste!
Is it Napoleon you would have us grow?
Concede the means; allow his head and
    hand,
(A large concession, clever as you are)
Good! In our common primal element
Of unbelief (we can't believe, you
    know –
We're still at that admission, recollect!)
Where do you find – apart from,
    towering o'er
The secondary temporary aims
Which satisfy the gross taste you
    despise –
Where do you find his star? – his crazy
    trust
God knows through what or in what?
    it's alive
And shines and leads him, and that's
    all we want.
Have we aught in our sober night shall
    point
Such ends as his were, and direct the
    means
Of working out our purpose straight as
    his,
Nor bring a moment's trouble on success
With after-care to justify the same?
– Be a Napoleon, and yet disbelieve –
Why, the man's mad, friend, take his
    light away!
What's the vague good o' the world,
    for which you dare
With comfort to yourself blow millions
    up?

We neither of us see it! we do see
The blown-up millions – spatter of
    their brains
And writhing of their bowels and so
    forth,
In that bewildering entanglement
Of horrible eventualities
Past calculation to the end of time!
Can I mistake for some clear word of
    God
(Which were my ample warrant for it
    all)
His puff of hazy instinct, idle talk,
'The State, that's I,' quack-nonsense
    about crowns,
And (when one beats the man to his
    last hold)
A vague idea of setting things to rights,
Policing people efficaciously,
More to their profit, most of all to his
    own;
The whole to end that dismallest of
    ends
By an Austrian marriage, cant to us the
    Church,
And resurrection of the old *régime*?
Would I, who hope to live a dozen
    years,
Fight Austerlitz for reasons such and
    such?
No: for, concede me but the merest
    chance
Doubt may be wrong – there's judgment,
    life to come!
With just that chance, I dare not.
    Doubt proves right?
This present life is all? – you offer me
Its dozen noisy years, without a chance
That wedding an archduchess, wearing
    lace,
And getting called by divers new-coined
    names,
Will drive off ugly thoughts and let me
    dine,
Sleep, read and chat in quiet as I like!
Therefore I will not.

                    Take another case;
Fit up the cabin yet another way.
What say you to the poets? shall we
    write
Hamlet, Othello – make the world our
    own,
Without a risk to run of either sort?
I can't! – to put the strongest reason
    first.
'But try,' you urge, 'the trying shall
    suffice;
'The aim, if reached or not, makes great
    the life:
'Try to be Shakespeare, leave the rest to
    fate!'
Spare my self-knowledge – there's no
    fooling me!
If I prefer remaining my poor self,
I say so not in self-dispraise but praise.
If I'm a Shakespeare, let the well alone;
Why should I try to be what now I am?
If I'm no Shakespeare, as too probable, –
His power and consciousness and self-
    delight
And all we want in common, shall I
    find –
Trying for ever? while on points of taste
Wherewith, to speak it humbly, he and I
Are dowered alike – I'll ask you, I or
    he,
Which in our two lives realizes most?
Much, he imagined – somewhat, I
    possess.
He had the imagination; stick to that!
Let him say, 'In the face of my soul's
    works
'Your world is worthless and I touch it
    not
'Lest I should wrong them' – I'll with-
    draw my plea.
But does he say so? look upon his life!
Himself, who only can, gives judgment
    there.
He leaves his towers and gorgeous
    palaces
To build the trimmest house in
    Stratford town;

Saves money, spends it, owns the
    worth of things,
Giulio Romano's pictures, Dowland's
    lute;
Enjoys a show, respects the puppets,
    too,
And none more, had he seen its entry
    once,
Than 'Pandulph, of fair Milan cardinal.'
Why then should I who play that
    personage,
The very Pandulph Shakespeare's fancy
    made,
Be told that had the poet chanced to
    start
From where I stand now (some degree
    like mine
Being just the goal he ran his race to
    reach)
He would have run the whole race
    back, forsooth,
And left being Pandulph, to begin write
    plays?
Ah, the earth's best can be but the
    earth's best!
Did Shakespeare live, he could but sit
    at home
And get himself in dreams the Vatican,
Greek busts, Venetian paintings, Roman
    walls,
And English books, none equal to his
    own,
Which I read, bound in gold (he never
    did).
– Terni's fall, Naples' bay and Gothard's
    top –
Eh, friend? I could not fancy one of
    these;
But, as I pour this claret, there they are:
I've gained them – crossed St Gothard
    last July
With ten mules to the carriage and a
    bed
Slung inside; is my hap the worse for
    that?
We want the same things, Shakespeare
    and myself,

And what I want, I have: he, gifted
   more,
Could fancy he too had them when he
   liked,
But not so thoroughly that, if fate
   allowed,
He would not have them also in my
   sense.
We play one game; I send the ball aloft
No less adroitly that of fifty strokes
Scarce five go o'er the wall so wide and
   high
Which sends them back to me: I wish
   and get.
He struck balls higher and with better
   skill,
But at a poor fence level with his head,
And hit – his Stratford house, a coat of
   arms,
Successful dealings in his grain and
   wool, –
While I receive heaven's incense in my
   nose
And style myself the cousin of Queen
   Bess.
Ask him, if this life's all, who wins the
   game?

   Believe – and our whole argument
   breaks up.
Enthusiasm's the best thing, I repeat;
Only, we can't command it; fire and
   life
Are all, dead matter's nothing, we agree:
And be it a mad dream or God's very
   breath,
The fact's the same, – belief's fire, once
   in us,
Makes of all else mere stuff to show
   itself:
We penetrate our life with such a glow
As fire lends wood and iron – this
   turns steel,
That burns to ash – all's one, fire proves
   its power
For good or ill, since men call flare
   success.

But paint a fire, it will not therefore
   burn.
Light one in me, I'll find it food
   enough!
Why, to be Luther – that's a life to
   lead,
Incomparably better than my own.
He comes, reclaims God's earth for
   God, he says,
Sets up God's rule again by simple
   means,
Re-opens a shut book, and all is done.
He flared out in the flaring of mankind;
Such Luther's luck was: how shall such
   be mine?
If he succeeded, nothing's left to do:
And if he did not altogether – well,
Strauss is the next advance. All Strauss
   should be
I might be also. But to what result?
He looks upon no future: Luther did.
What can I gain on the denying side?
Ice makes no conflagration. State the
   facts,
Read the text right, emancipate the
   world –
The emancipated world enjoys itself
With scarce a thank-you: Blougram
   told it first
It could not owe a farthing, – not to him
More than Saint Paul! 'twould press its
   pay, you think?
Then add there's still that plaguy
   hundredth chance
Strauss may be wrong. And so a risk is
   run –
For what gain? not for Luther's, who
   secured
A real heaven in his heart throughout
   his life,
Supposing death a little altered things.

   'Ay, but since really you lack faith,'
   you cry,
'You run the same risk really on all
   sides,
'In cool indifference as bold unbelief.

'As well be Strauss as swing 'twixt Paul
    and him.
'It's not worth having, such imperfect
    faith,
'No more available to do faith's work
'Than unbelief like mine. Whole faith,
    or none!'
    Softly, my friend! I must dispute that
    point.
Once own the use of faith, I'll find you
    faith.
We're back on Christian ground. You
    call for faith:
I show you doubt, to prove that faith
    exists.
The more of doubt, the stronger faith, I
    say,
If faith o'ercomes doubt. How I know
    it does?
By life and man's free will, God gave
    for that!
To mould life as we choose it, shows
    our choice:
That's our one act, the previous work's
    his own.
You criticize the soul? it reared this
    tree –
This broad life and whatever fruit it
    bears!
What matter though I doubt at every
    pore,
Head-doubts, doubts at my fingers' ends,
Doubts in the trivial work of every day,
Doubts at the very bases of my soul
In the grand moments when she probes
    herself –
If finally I have a life to show,
The thing I did, brought out in evidence
Against die thing done to me under-
    ground
By hell and all its brood, for aught I
    know?
I say, whence sprang this? shows it
    faith or doubt?
All's doubt in me; where's break of
    faith in this?
It is the idea, the feeling and the love,

God means mankind should strive for
    and show forth
Whatever be the process to that end, –
And not historic knowledge, logic
    sound,
And metaphysical acumen, sure!
'What think ye of Christ,' friend? when
    all's done and said,
Like you this Christianity or not?
It may be false, but will you wish it
    true?
Has it your vote to be so if it can?
Trust you an instinct silenced long ago
That will break silence and enjoin you
    love
What mortified philosophy is hoarse,
And all in vain, with bidding you
    despise?
If you desire faith – then you've faith
    enough:
What else seeks God – nay, what else
    seek ourselves?
You form a notion of me, we'll
    suppose,
On hearsay; it's a favourable one:
'But still' (you add), 'there was no such
    good man,
'Because of contradiction in the facts.
'One proves, for instance, he was born
    in Rome,
'This Blougram; yet throughout the
    tales of him
'I see he figures as an Englishman.'
Well, the two things are reconcileable.
But would I rather you discovered that,
Subjoining – 'Still, what matter though
    they be?
'Blougram concerns me nought, born
    here or there.'

    Pure faith indeed – you know not
    what you ask!
Naked belief in God the Omnipotent,
Omniscient, Omnipresent, sears too
    much
The sense of conscious creatures to be
    borne.

It were the seeing him, no flesh shall
	dare.
Some think, Creation's meant to show
	him forth:
I say it's meant to hide him all it can,
And that's what all the blessed evil's
	for.
Its use in Time is to environ us,
Our breath, our drop of dew, with
	shield enough
Against that sight till we can bear its
	stress.
Under a vertical sun, the exposed brain
And lidless eye and disemprisoned
	heart
Less certainly would wither up at once
Than mind, confronted with the truth
	of him.
But time and earth case-harden us to
	live;
The feeblest sense is trusted most, the
	child
Feels God a moment, ichors o'er the
	place,
Plays on and grows to be a man like us.
With me, faith means perpetual unbelief
Kept quiet like the snake 'neath
	Michael's foot
Who stands calm just because he feels
	it writhe.
Or, if that's too ambitious, – here's my
	box –
I need the excitation of a pinch
Threatening the torpor of the inside-
	nose
Nigh on the imminent sneeze that
	never comes.
'Leave it in peace' advise the simple
	folk:
Make it aware of peace by itching-fits,
Say I – let doubt occasion still more
	faith!

　You'll say, once all believed, man,
	woman, child,
In that dear middle-age these noodles
	praise.

How you'd exult if I could put you back
Six hundred years, blot out cosmogony,
Geology, ethnology, what not,
(Greek endings, each the little passing-
	bell
That signifies some faith's about to die),
And set you square with Genesis
	again, –
When such a traveller told you his last
	news,
He saw the ark a-top of Ararat
But did not climb there since 'twas
	getting dusk
And robber-bands infest the mountain's
	foot!
How should you feel, I ask, in such an
	age,
How act? As other people felt and did;
With soul more blank than this
	decanter's knob,
Believe – and yet lie, kill, rob, fornicate
Full in belief's face, like the beast
	you'd be!

　No, when the fight begins within
	himself,
A man's worth something. God stoops
	o'er his head,
Satan looks up between his feet – both
	tug –
He's left, himself, i' the middle: the soul
	wakes
And grows. Prolong that battle through
	his life!
Never leave growing till the life to come!
Here, we've got callous to the Virgin's
	winks
That used to puzzle people whole-
	somely:
Men have outgrown the shame of
	being fools.
What are the laws of nature, not to
	bend
If the Church bid them? – brother
	Newman asks.
Up with the Immaculate Conception,
	then –

On to the rack with faith! – is my
    advice.
Will not that hurry us upon our knees,
Knocking our breasts, 'It can't be – yet
    it shall!
'Who am I, the worm, to argue with
    my Pope?
'Low things confound the high things!'
    and so forth.
That's better than acquitting God with
    grace
As some folk do. He's tried – no case is
    proved,
Philosophy is lenient – he may go!

You'll say, the old system's not so
    obsolete
But men believe still: ay, but who and
    where?
King Bomba's lazzaroni foster yet
The sacred flame, so Antonelli writes;
But even of these, what ragamuffin-
    saint
Believes God watches him continually,
As he believes in fire that it will burn,
Or rain that it will drench him? Break
    fire's law,
Sin against rain, although the penalty
Be just a singe or soaking? 'No,' he
    smiles;
'Those laws are laws that can enforce
    themselves.'

The sum of all is – yes, my doubt is
    great,
My faith's still greater, then my faith's
    enough.
I have read much, thought much,
    experienced much,
Yet would die rather than avow my fear
The Naples' liquefaction may be false,
When set to happen by the palace-
    clock
According to the clouds or dinner-
    time.
I hear you recommend, I might at least
Eliminate, decrassify my faith

Since I adopt it; keeping what I must
And leaving what I can – such points
    as this.
I won't – that is, I can't throw one
    away.
Supposing there's no truth in what I
    hold
About the need of trial to man's faith,
Still, when you bid me purify the same,
To such a process I discern no end.
Clearing off one excrescence to see
    two,
There's ever a next in size, now grown
    as big,
That meets the knife: I cut and cut
    again!
First cut the Liquefaction, what comes
    last
But Fichte's clever cut at God himself?
Experimentalize on sacred things!
I trust nor hand nor eye nor heart nor
    brain
To stop betimes: they all get drunk
    alike.
The first step, I am master not to take.

You'd find the cutting-process to your
    taste
As much as leaving growths of lies
    unpruned,
Nor see more danger in it, – you retort.
Your taste's worth mine; but my taste
    proves more wise
When we consider that the steadfast
    hold
On the extreme end of the chain of faith
Gives the advantage, makes the
    difference
With the rough purblind mass we seek
    to rule:
We are their lords, or they are free of us,
Just as we tighten or relax our hold.
So, other matters equal, we'll revert
To the first problem – which, if solved
    my way
And thrown into the balance, turns the
    scale –

How we may lead a comfortable life,
How suit our luggage to the cabin's
    size.

  Of course you are remarking all this
    time
How narrowly and grossly I view life,
Respect the creature-comforts, care to
    rule
The masses, and regard complacently
'The cabin,' in our old phrase. Well,
    I do.
I act for, talk for, live for this world now,
As this world prizes action, life and
    talk:
No prejudice to what next world may
    prove,
Whose new laws and requirements, my
    best pledge
To observe then, is that I observe these
    now,
Shall do hereafter what I do meanwhile.
Let us concede (gratuitously though)
Next life relieves the soul of body,
    yields
Pure spiritual enjoyment: well, my
    friend,
Why lose this life i' the meantime,
    since its use
May be to make the next life more
    intense?

  Do you know, I have often had a
    dream
(Work it up in your next month's
    article)
Of man's poor spirit in its progress,
    still
Losing true life for ever and a day
Through ever trying to be and ever
    being –
In the evolution of successive spheres –
*Before* its actual sphere and place of
    life,
Halfway into the next, which having
    reached,
It shoots with corresponding foolery

Halfway into the next still, on and off!
As when a traveller, bound from North
    to South,
Scouts fur in Russia: what's its use in
    France?
In France spurns flannel: where's its
    need in Spain?
In Spain drops cloth, too cumbrous for
    Algiers!
Linen goes next, and last the skin itself,
A superfluity at Timbuctoo.
When, through his journey, was the
    fool at ease?
I'm at ease now, friend; worldly in this
    world,
I take and like its way of life; I think
My brothers, who administer the
    means,
Live better for my comfort – that's good
    too;
And God, if he pronounce upon such
    life,
Approves my service, which is better
    still.
If he keep silence, – why, for you or me
Or that brute beast pulled-up in to-
    day's 'Times,'
What odds is't, save to ourselves, what
    life we lead?

  You meet me at this issue: you
    declare, –
All special-pleading done with – truth
    is truth,
And justifies itself by undreamed ways.
You don't fear but it's better, if we
    doubt,
To say so, act up to our truth perceived
However feebly. Do then, – act away!
'Tis there I'm on the watch for you.
  How one acts
Is, both of us agree, our chief concern:
And how you'll act is what I fain would
    see
If, like the candid person you appear,
You dare to make the most of your
    life's scheme

As I of mine, live up to its full law
Since there's no higher law that
    counterchecks.
Put natural religion to the test
You've just demolished the revealed
    with – quick,
Down to the root of all that checks
    your will,
All prohibition to lie, kill and thieve,
Or even to be an atheistic priest!
Suppose a pricking to incontinence –
Philosophers deduce you chastity
Or shame, from just the fact that at the
    first
Whoso embraced a woman in the field,
Threw club down and forewent his
    brains beside,
So, stood a ready victim in the reach
Of any brother savage, club in hand;
Hence saw the use of going out of sight
In wood or cave to prosecute his loves:
I read this in a French book t'other day.
Does law so analysed coerce you much?
Oh, men spin clouds of fuzz where
    matters end,
But you who reach where the first
    thread begins,
You'll soon cut that! – which means
    you can, but won't,
Through certain instincts, blind,
    unreasoned out,
You dare not set aside, you can't tell
    why,
But there they are, and so you let them
    rule.
Then, friend, you seem as much a slave
    as I,
A liar, conscious coward and hypocrite,
Without the good the slave expects to
    get,
In case he has a master after all!
You own your instincts? why, what else
    do I,
Who want, am made for, and must
    have a God
Ere I can be aught, do aught? – no
    mere name

Want, but the true thing with what
    proves its truth,
To wit, a relation from that thing to
    me,
Touching from head to foot – which
    touch I feel,
And with it take the rest, this life of ours!
I live my life here; yours you dare not
    live.

    – Not as I state it, who (you please
    subjoin)
Disfigure such a life and call it names.
While, to your mind, remains another
    way
For simple men: knowledge and power
    have rights,
But ignorance and weakness have rights
    too.
There needs no crucial effort to find
    truth
If here or there or anywhere about:
We ought to turn each side, try hard
    and see,
And if we can't, be glad we've earned
    at least
The right, by one laborious proof the
    more,
To graze in peace earth's pleasant
    pasturage.
Men are not angels, neither are they
    brutes:
Something we may see, all we cannot
    see.
What need of lying? I say, I see all,
And swear to each detail the most
    minute
In what I think a Pan's face – you,
    mere cloud:
I swear I hear him speak and see him
    wink,
For fear, if once I drop the emphasis,
Mankind may doubt there's any cloud
    at all.
You take the simple life – ready to see,
Willing to see (for no cloud's worth a
    face) –

And leaving quiet what no strength can
   move,
And which, who bids you move? who
   has the right?
I bid you; but you are God's sheep, not
   mine:
'*Pastor est tui Dominus.*' You find
In this the pleasant pasture of our life
Much you may eat without the least
   offence,
Much you don't eat because your maw
   objects,
Much you would eat but that your
   fellow-flock
Open great eyes at you and even butt,
And thereupon you like your mates so
   well
You cannot please yourself, offending
   them;
Though when they seem exorbitantly
   sheep,
You weigh your pleasure with their
   butts and bleats
And strike the balance. Sometimes
   certain fears
Restrain you, real checks since you find
   them so;
Sometimes you please yourself and
   nothing checks:
And thus you graze through life with
   not one lie,
And like it best

       But do you, in truth's name?
If so, you beat – which means you are
   not I –
Who needs must make earth mine and
   feed my fill
Not simply unbutted at, unbickered
   with,
But motioned to the velvet of the sward
By those obsequious wethers' very selves.
Look at me, sir; my age is double yours:
At yours, I knew beforehand, so enjoyed,
What now I should be – as, permit the
   word,
I pretty well imagine your whole range

And stretch of tether twenty years to
   come.
We both have minds and bodies much
   alike:
In truth's name, don't you want my
   bishopric,
My daily bread, my influence and my
   state?
You're young. I'm old; you must be old
   one day;
Will you find then, as I do hour by hour,
Women their lovers kneel to, who cut
   curls
From your fat lap-dog's ear to grace a
   brooch –
Dukes, who petition just to kiss your
   ring –
With much beside you know or may
   conceive?
Suppose we die to-night: well, here
   am I,
Such were my gains, life bore this fruit
   to me,
While writing all the same my articles
On music, poetry, the fictile vase
Found at Albano, chess, Anacreon's
   Greek.
But you – the highest honour in your
   life,
The thing you'll crown yourself with,
   all your days,
Is – dining here and drinking this last
   glass
I pour you out in sign of amity
Before we part for ever. Of your power
And social influence, worldly worth in
   short,
Judge what's my estimation by the fact,
I do not condescend to enjoin,
   beseech,
Hint secrecy on one of all these words!
You're shrewd and know that should
   you publish one
The world would brand the lie – my
   enemies first,
Who'd sneer – 'the bishop's an arch-
   hypocrite

'And knave perhaps, but not so frank a
    fool.'
Whereas I should not dare for both my
    ears
Breathe one such syllable, smile one
    such smile,
Before the chaplain who reflects
    myself –
My shade's so much more potent than
    your flesh.
What's your reward, self-abnegating
    friend?
Stood you confessed of those
    exceptional
And privileged great natures that dwarf
    mine –
A zealot with a mad ideal in reach,
A poet just about to print his ode,
A statesman with a scheme to stop this
    war,
An artist whose religion is his art –
I should have nothing to object: such
    men
Carry the fire, all things grow warm to
    them,
Their drugget's worth my purple, they
    beat me.
But you, – you're just as little those
    as I –
You, Gigadibs, who, thirty years of age,
Write statedly for Blackwood's Magazine,
Believe you see two points in Hamlet's
    soul
Unseized by the Germans yet – which
    view you'll print –
Meantime the best you have to show
    being still
That lively lightsome article we took
Almost for the true Dickens, – what's
    its name?
'The Slum and Cellar, or Whitechapel
    life
'Limned after dark!' it made me laugh,
    I know,
And pleased a month, and brought you
    in ten pounds.
– Success I recognize and compliment,

And therefore give you, if you choose,
    three words
(The card and pencil-scratch is quite
    enough)
Which whether here, in Dublin or New
    York,
Will get you, prompt as at my eyebrow's
    wink,
Such terms as never you aspired to get
In all our own reviews and some not
    ours.
Go write your lively sketches! be the
    first
'Blougram, or The Eccentric
    Confidence' –
Or better simply say, 'The Outward-
    bound.'
Why, men as soon would throw it in
    my teeth
As copy and quote the infamy chalked
    broad
About me on the church-door opposite.
You will not wait for that experience
    though,
I fancy, howsoever you decide,
To discontinue – not detesting, not
Defaming, but at least – despising me!

\*       \*       \*

Over his wine so smiled and talked
    his hour
Sylvester Blougram, styled *in partibus
Episcopus nec non* – (the deuce knows
    what
It's changed to by our novel hierarchy)
With Gigadibs the literary man,
Who played with spoons, explored his
    plate's design,
And ranged the olive-stones about its
    edge,
While the great bishop rolled him out
    a mind
Long crumpled, till creased
    consciousness lay smooth.

For Blougram, he believed, say, half
    he spoke.
The other portion, as he shaped it thus

For argumentatory purposes,
He felt his foe was foolish to dispute.
Some arbitrary accidental thoughts
That crossed his mind, amusing
        because new,
He chose to represent as fixtures there,
Invariable convictions (such they seemed
Beside his interlocutor's loose cards
Flung daily down, and not the same
        way twice)
While certain hell-deep instincts,
        man's weak tongue
Is never bold to utter in tleir truth
Because styled hell-deep ('tis an old
        mistake
To place hell at the bottom of the earth)
He ignored these, – not having in
        readiness
Their nomenclature and philosophy:
He said true things, but called them by
        wrong names.
'On the whole,' he thought, 'I justify
        myself
'On every point where cavillers like this
'Oppugn my life: he tries one kind of
        fence,
'I close, he's worsted, that's enough for
        him.
'He's on the ground: if ground should
        break away
'I take my stand on, there's a firmer yet
'Beneath it, both of us may sink and
        reach.
'His ground was over mine and broke
        the first:
'So, let him sit with me this many a
        year!'

He did not sit five minutes. Just a week
Sufficed his sudden healthy vehemence.
Something had struck him in the 'Out-
        ward-bound'
Another way than Blougram's purpose
        was:
And having bought, not cabin-furniture
But settler's-implements (enough for
        three)

And started for Australia – there, I
        hope,
By this time he has tested his first
        plough,
And studied his last chapter of St John.

## Cleon

'As certain also of your own poets have said' –

(An Imaginary person. The poet quoted by St
        Paul was Aratus, a native of Tarsus.)

Cleon the poet (from the sprinkled
        isles,
Lily on lily, that o'erlace the sea,
And laugh their pride when the light
        wave lisps 'Greece') –
To Protus in his Tyranny: much health!

    They give thy letter to me, even now:
I read and seem as if I heard thee
        speak.
The master of thy galley still unlades
Gift after gift; they block my court at
        last
And pile themselves along its portico
Royal with sunset, like a thought of
        thee:
And one white she-slave from the
        group dispersed
Of black and white slaves (like the
        chequerwork
Pavement, at once my nation's work
        and gift,
Now covered with this settle-down of
        doves),
One lyric woman, in her crocus vest
Woven of sea-wools, with her two
        white hands
Commends to me the strainer and the
        cup
Thy lip hath bettered ere it blesses
        mine.

    Well-counselled, king, in thy
        munificence!
For so shall men remark, in such an act

Of love for him whose song gives life its
    joy,
Thy recognition of the use of life;
Nor call thy spirit barely adequate
To help on life in straight ways, broad
    enough
For vulgar souls, by ruling and the rest.
Thou, in the daily building of thy
    tower, –
Whether in fierce and sudden spasms
    of toil,
Or through dim lulls of unapparent
    growth,
Or when the general work 'mid good
    acclaim
Climbed with the eye to cheer the
    architect, –
Didst ne'er engage in work for mere
    work's sake –
Hadst ever in thy heart the luring hope
Of some eventual rest a-top of it,
Whence, all the tumult of the building
    hushed,
Thou first of men mightst look out to
    the East:
The vulgar saw thy tower, thou sawest
    the sun.
For this, I promise on thy festival
To pour libation, looking o'er die sea,
Making this slave narrate thy fortunes,
    speak
Thy great words, and describe thy royal
    face –
Wishing thee wholly where Zeus lives
    the most,
Within the eventual element of calm.

Thy letter's first requirement meets
    me here.
It is as thou hast heard: in one short life
I, Cleon, have effected all those things
Thou wonderingly dost enumerate.
That epos on thy hundred plates of
    gold
Is mine, – and also mine the little
    chant,
So sure to rise from every fishing-bark

When, lights at prow, the seamen haul
    their net.
The image of the sun-god on the phare,
Men turn from the sun's self to see, is
    mine;
The Poecile,* o'er-storied its whole
    length,
As thou didst hear, with painting, is
    mine too.
I know the true proportions of a man
And woman also, not observed before;
And I have written three books on the
    soul,
Proving absurd all written hitherto,
And putting us to ignorance again.
For music, – why, I have combined the
    moods,
Inventing one. In brief, all arts are mine;
Thus much the people know and
    recognize,
Throughout our seventeen islands.
    Marvel not.
We of these latter days, with greater
    mind
Than our forerunners, since more
    composite,
Look not so great, beside their simple
    way,
To a judge who only sees one way at
    once,
One mind-point and no other at a
    time, –
Compares the small part of a man of us
With some whole man of the heroic
    age,
Great in his way – not ours, nor meant
    for ours.
And ours is greater, had we skul to
    know:
For, what we call this life of men on
    earth.
This sequence of the soul's
    achievements here
Being, as I find much reason to conceive,

---

* The famous painted Porch on the Agora in
    Athens.

Intended to be viewed eventually
As a great whole, not analysed to parts,
But each part having reference to all, –
How shall a certain part, pronounced
 complete,
Endure effacement by another part?
Was the thing done? – then, what's to
 do again?
See, in the chequered pavement opposite,
Suppose the artist made a perfect rhomb,
And next a lozenge, then a trapezoid –
He did not overlay them, superimpose
The new upon the old and blot it out,
But laid them on a level in his work,
Making at last a picture; there it lies.
So, first the perfect separate forms were
 made,
The portions of mankind; and after, so,
Occurred the combination of the same.
For where had been a progress, other-
 wise?
Mankind, made up of all the single
 men, –
In such a synthesis the labour ends.
Now mark me! those divine men of old
 time
Have reached, thou sayest well, each at
 one point
The outside verge that rounds our
 faculty;
And where they reached, who can do
 more than reach?
It takes but little water just to touch
At some one point the inside of a
 sphere,
And as we turn the sphere, touch all
 the rest
In due succession: but the finer air
Which not so palpably nor obviously,
Though no less universally, can touch
The whole circumference of that
 emptied sphere,
Fills it more fully than the water did;
Holds thrice the weight of water in itself
Resolved into a subtler element.
And yet the vulgar call the sphere first
 full

Up to the visible height – and after,
 void;
Not knowing air's more hidden
 properties.
And thus our soul, misknown, cries
 out to Zeus
To vindicate his purpose in our life:
Why stay we on the earth unless to
 grow?
Long since, I imaged, wrote the fiction
 out,
That he or other god descended here
And, once for all, showed simultaneously
What, in its nature, never can be shown.
Piecemeal or in succession; – showed,
 I say,
The worth both absolute and relative
Of all his children from the birth of
 time,
His instruments for all appointed work.
I now go on to image, – might we hear
The judgment which should give the
 due to each,
Show where the labour lay and where
 the ease,
And prove Zeus' self, the latent every-
 where!
This is a dream: – but no dream, let us
 hope,
That years and days, the summers and
 the springs,
Follow each other with unwaning
 powers.
The grapes which dye thy wine are
 richer far.
Through culture, than the wild wealth
 of the rock;
The suave plum than the savage-tasted
 drupe;
The pastured honey-bee drops choicer
 sweet;
The flowers turn double, and the leaves
 turn flowers;
That young and tender crescent-moon,
 thy slave,
Sleeping above her robe as buoyed by
 clouds,

Refines upon the women of my youth.
What, and the soul alone deteriorates?
I have not chanted verse like Homer,
    no –
Nor swept string like Terpander, no –
    nor carved
And painted men like Phidias and his
    friend:
I am not great as they are, point by
    point.
But I have entered into sympathy
With these four, running these into
    one soul,
Who, separate, ignored each other's
    art.
Say, is it nothing that I know them all?
The wild flower was the larger; I have
    dashed
Rose-blood upon its petals, pricked its
    cup's
Honey with wine, and driven its seed to
    fruit,
And show a better flower if not so large:
I stand myself. Refer this to the gods
Whose gift alone it is! which, shall I
    dare
(All pride apart) upon the absurd
    pretext
That such a gift by chance lay in my
    hand,
Discourse of lightly or depreciate?
It might have fallen to another's hand:
    what then?
I pass too surely: let at least truth stay!

    And next, of what thou followest on
        to ask.
This being with me as I declare, O king,
My works, in all these varicoloured
    kinds,
So done by me, accepted so by men –
Thou askest, if (my soul thus in men's
    hearts)
I must not be accounted to attain
The very crown and proper end of life?
Inquiring thence how, now life closeth
    up,

I face death with success in my right
    hand:
Whether I fear death less than dost
    thyself
The fortunate of men? 'For' (writest thou)
'Thou leavest much behind, while I
    leave nought.
'Thy life stays in the poems men shall
    sing,
'The pictures men shall study; while my
    life,
'Complete and whole now in its power
    and joy,
'Dies altogether with my brain and arm,
'Is lost indeed; since, what survives
    myself?
'The brazen statue to o'erlook my grave,
'Set on the promontory which I named.
'And that – some supple courtier of my
    heir
'Shall use its robed and sceptred arm,
    perhaps,
'To fix the rope to, which best drags it
    down.
'I go then: triumph thou, who dost not
    go!'

    Nay, thou art worthy of hearing my
        whole mind.
Is this apparent, when thou turn'st to
    muse
Upon the scheme of earth and man in
    chief,
That admiration grows as knowledge
    grows?
That imperfection means perfection
    hid,
Reserved in part, to grace the after-time?
If, in the morning of philosophy,
Ere aught had been recorded, nay
    perceived,
Thou, with the light now in thee, couldst
    have looked
On all earth's tenantry, from worm to
    bird,
Ere man, her last, appeared upon the
    stage –

Thou wouldst have seen them perfect,
   ana deduced
The perfectness of others yet unseen.
Conceding which, – had Zeus then
   questioned thee
'Shall I go on a step, improve on this,
'Do more for visible creatures than is
   done?'
Thou wouldst have answered, 'Ay, by
   making each
'Grow conscious in himself – by that
   alone.
'All's perfect else: the shell sucks fast
   the rock,
'The fish strikes through the sea, the
   snake both swims
'And slides, forth range the beasts, the
   birds take flight,
'Till life's mechanics can no further go –
'And all this joy in natural life is put
'Like fire from off thy finger into each,
'So exquisitely perfect is the same.
'But 'tis pure fire, and they mere matter
   are:
'It has them, not they it: and so I choose
'For man, thy last premeditated work
'(If I might add a glory to the scheme)
'That a third thing should stand apart
   from both,
'A quality arise within his soul,
'Which, intro-active, made to supervise
'And feel the force it has, may view
   itself,
'And so be happy.' Man might live at
   first
The animal life: but is there nothing
   more?
In due time, let him critically learn
How he lives; and, the more he gets to
   know
Of his own life's adaptabilities,
The more joy-giving will his life become.
Thus man, who hath this quality, is
   best.

  But thou, king, hadst more
   reasonably said:

'Let progress end at once, – man make
   no step
'Beyond the natural man, the better
   beast,
'Using his senses, not the sense of sense.
In man there's failure, only since he left
The lower and inconscious forms of life.
We called it an advance, the rendering
   plain
Man's spirit might grow conscious of
   man's life,
And, by new lore so added to the old,
Take each step higher over the brute's
   head.
This grew the only life, the pleasure-
   house,
Watch-tower and treasure-fortress of
   the soul,
Which whole surrounding flats of
   natural life
Seemed only fit to yield subsistence to;
A tower that crowns a country. But alas,
The soul now climbs it just to perish
   there!
For thence we have discovered ('tis no
   dream –
We know this, which we had not else
   perceived)
That there's a world of capability
For joy, spread round about us, meant
   for us,
Inviting us; and still the soul craves all,
And still the flesh replies, 'Take no jot
   more
'Than ere thou clombst the tower to
   look abroad!
'Nay, so much less as that fatigue has
   brought
'Deduction to it.' We struggle, fain to
   enlarge
Our bounded physical recipiency.
Increase our power, supply fresh oil to
   life,
Repair the waste of age and sickness: no,
It skills not! life's inadequate to joy,
As the soul sees joy, tempting life to
   take.

They praise a fountain in my garden here
Wherein a Naiad sends the water-bow
Thin from her tube; she smiles to see it
    rise.
What if I told her, it is just a thread
From that great river which the hills
    shut up,
And mock her with my leave to take
    the same?
The artificer has given her one small
    tube
Past power to widen or exchange –
    what boots
To know she might spout oceans if she
    could?
She cannot lift beyond her first thin
    thread:
And so a man can use but a man's joy
While he sees God's. Is it for Zeus to
    boast,
'See, man, how happy I live, and
    despair –
'That I may be still happier – for thy
    use!'
If this were so, we could not thank our
    lord,
As hearts beat on to doing; 'tis not so –
Malice it is not. Is it carelessness?
Still, no. If care – where is the sign? I
    ask,
And get no answer, and agree in sum,
O king, with thy profound
    discouragement,
Who seest the wider but to sigh the
    more.
Most progress is most failure: thou
    sayest well.

    The last point now: – thou dost
        except a case –
Holding joy not impossible to one
With artist-gifts – to such a man as I
Who leave behind me living works
    indeed;
For, such a poem, such a painting
    lives.
What? dost thou verily trip upon a word,

Confound the accurate view of what
    joy is
(Caught somewhat clearer by my eyes
    than thine)
With feeling joy? confound the
    knowing how
And showing how to live (my faculty)
With actually living? – Otherwise
Where is the artist's vantage o'er the
    king?
Because in my great epos I display
How divers men young, strong, fair,
    wise, can act –
Is this as though I acted? if I paint,
Carve the young Phœbus, am I
    therefore young?
Methinks I'm older that I bowed
    myself
The many years of pain that taught me
    art!
Indeed, to know is something, and to
    prove
How all this beauty might be enjoyed,
    is more:
But, knowing nought, to enjoy is some-
    thing too.
Yon rower, with the moulded muscles
    there,
Lowering the sail, is nearer it than I.
I can write love-odes: thy fair slave's an
    ode.
I get to sing of love, when grown too
    grey
For being beloved: she turns to that
    young man,
The muscles all a-ripple on his back.
I know the joy of kingship: well, thou
    art king.

    'But,' sayest thou – (and I marvel, I
        repeat,
To find thee trip on such a mere word)
    'what
'Thou writest, paintest, stays; that does
    not die:
'Sappho survives, because we sing her
    songs,

'And Æschylus, because we read his
plays!'
Why, if they live still, let them come
and take
Thy slave in my despite, drink from thy
cup,
Speak in my place. Thou diest while I
survive?
Say rather that my fate is deadlier still,
In this, that every day my sense of joy
Grows more acute, my soul (intensified
By power and insight) more enlarged,
more keen;
While every day my hairs fall more and
more,
My hand shakes, and the heavy years
increase –
The horror quickening still from year to
year,
The consummation coming past escape
When I shall know most, and yet least
enjoy –
When all my works wherein I prove my
worth,
Being present still to mock me in men's
mouths,
Alive still, in the praise of such as thou,
I, I the feeling, thinking, acting man,
The man who loved his life so over-
much,
Sleep in my urn. It is so horrible,
I dare at times imagine to my need
Some future state revealed to us by Zeus,
Unlimited in capability
For joy, as this is in desire for joy,
– To seek which, the joy-hunger forces
us:
That, stung by straitness of our life,
made strait
On purpose to make prized the life at
large –
Freed by the throbbing impulse we call
death,
We burst there as the worm into the
fly,
Who, while a worm still, wants his
wings. But no!

Zeus has not yet revealed it; and alas,
He must have done so, were it possible!

    Live long and happy, and in that
thought die:
Glad for what was! Farewell. And for
the rest,
I cannot tell thy messenger aright
Where to deliver what he bears of thine
To one called Paulus; we have heard
his fame
Indeed, if Christus be not one with
him –
I know not, nor am troubled much to
know.
Thou canst not think a mere barbarian
Jew,
As Paulus proves to be, one circumcized,
Hath access to a secret shut from us?
Thou wrongest our philosophy, O king,
In stooping to inquire of such an one,
As if his answer could impose at all!
He writeth, doth he? well, and he may
write.
Oh, the Jew findeth scholars! certain
slaves
Who touched on this same isle,
preached him and Christ;
And (as I gathered from a bystander)
Their doctrine could be held by no
sane man.

## Rudel to the Lady of Tripoli

### 1

I know a Mount, the gracious Sun per-
ceives
First, when he visits, last, too, when he
leaves
The world; and, vainly favoured, it repays
The day-long glory of his steadfast gaze
By no change of its large calm front of
snow.
And underneath the Mount, a Flower I
know,
He cannot have perceived, that changes
ever
At his approach; and, in the lost
endeavour
To live his life, has parted, one by one,
With all a flower's true graces, for the
grace
Of being but a foolish mimic sun,
With ray-like florets round a disk-like
face.
Men nobly call by many a name the
Mount
As over many a land of theirs its large
Calm front of snow like a triumphal
targe
Is reared, and still with old names, fresh
names vie,
Each to its proper praise and own
account:
Men call the Flower, the Sunflower,
sportively.

### 2

Oh, Angel of the East, one, one gold
look
Across the waters to this twilight nook,
– The far sad waters, Angel, to this
nook!

### 3

Dear Pilgrim, art thou for the East
indeed?
Go! – saying ever as thou dost proceed,
That I, French Rudel, choose for my
device

A sunflower outspread like a sacrifice
Before its idol. See! These inexpert
And hurried fingers could not fail to
hurt
The woven picture; 'tis a woman's skill
Indeed; but nothing baffled me, so, ill
Or well, the work is finished. Say, men
feed
On songs I sing, and therefore bask the
bees
On my flower's breast as on a platform
broad:
But, as the flower's concern is not for
these
But solely for the sun, so men applaud
In vain this Rudel, he not looking here
But to the East – the East! Go, say this,
Pilgrim dear!

## One Word More*

To E. B. B.
1855

### 1

There they are, my fifty men and women
Naming me the fifty poems finished!
Take them, Love, the book and me
together:
Where the heart lies, let the brain lie
also.

### 2

Rafael made a century of sonnets,
Made and wrote them in a certain
volume
Dinted with the silver-pointed pencil
Else he only used to draw Madonnas:
These, the world might view – but one,
the volume.
Who that one, you ask? Your heart
instructs you.

* Originally appended to the collection of
Poems called 'Men and Women', the greater
portion of which has now been, more correctly,
distributed under the other titles of this edition.
– R. B.]

Did she live and love it all her life-time?
Did she drop, his lady of the sonnets,
Die, and let it drop beside her pillow
Where it lay in place of Rafael's glory,
Rafael's cheek so duteous and so
    loving –
Cheek, the world was wont to hail a
    painter's,
Rafael's cheek, her love had turned a
    poet's?

3

You and I would rather read that volume,
(Taken to his beating bosom by it)
Lean and list the bosom-beats of Rafael,
Would we not? than wonder at
    Madonnas –
Her, San Sisto names, and Her, Foligno,
Her, that visits Florence in a vision,
Her, that's left with lilies in the Louvre –
Seen by us and all the world in circle.

4

You and I will never read that volume.
Guido Reni, like his own eye's apple
Guarded long the treasure-book and
    loved it.
Guido Reni dying, all Bologna
Cried, and the world cried too, 'Ours,
    the treasure!'
Suddenly, as rare things will, it vanished.

5

Dante once prepared to paint an angel:
Whom to please? You whisper 'Beatrice.'
While he mused and traced it and
    retraced it,
(Peradventure with a pen corroded
Still by drops of that hot ink he dipped
    for,
When, his left-hand i' the hair o' the
    wicked,
Back he held the brow and pricked its
    stigma,
Bit into the live man's flesh for
    parchment,
Loosed him, laughed to see the writing
    rankle,
Let the wretch go festering through
    Florence) –

Dante, who loved well because he hated,
Hated wickedness that hinders loving,
Dante standing, studying his angel, –
In there broke the folk of his Inferno.
Says he – 'Certain people of importance'
(Such he gave his daily dreadful line to)
'Entered and would seize, forsooth, the
    poet.'
Says the poet – 'Then I stopped my
    painting.'

6

You and I would rather see that angel,
Painted by the tenderness of Dante,
Would we not? – than read a fresh
    Inferno.

7

You and I will never see that picture.
While he mused on love and Beatrice,
While he softened o'er his outlined
    angel,
In they broke, those 'people of
    importance:'
We and Bice bear the loss for ever.

8

What of Rafael's sonnets, Dante's
    picture?
This: no artist lives and loves, that
    longs not
Once, and only once, and for one only,
(Ah, the prize!) to find his love a
    language
Fit and fair and simple and sufficient –
Using nature that's an art to others,
Not, this one time, art that's turned his
    nature.
Ay, of all the artists living, loving,
None but would forego his proper
    dowry, –
Does he paint? he fain would write a
    poem, –
Does he write? he fain would paint a
    picture,
Put to proof art alien to the artist's,
Once, and only once, and for one only,
So to be the man and leave the artist,
Gain the man's joy, miss the artist's
    sorrow.

### 9

Wherefore? Heaven's gift takes earth's
abatement!
He who smites the rock and spreads
the water,
Bidding drink and live a crowd beneath
him,
Even he, the minute makes immortal,
Proves, perchance, but mortal in the
minute,
Desecrates, belike, the deed in doing.
While he smites, how can he but
remember,
So he smote before, in such a peril,
When they stood and mocked – 'Shall
smiting help us?'
When they drank and sneered – 'A
stroke is easy!'
When they wiped their mouths and
went their journey,
Throwing him for thanks – 'But
drought was pleasant.'
Thus old memories mar the actual
triumph;
Thus the doing savours of disrelish;
Thus achievement lacks a gracious
somewhat;
O'er-importuned brows becloud the
mandate,
Carelessness or consciousness – the
gesture.
For he bears an ancient wrong about him,
Sees and knows again those phalanxed
faces,
Hears, yet one time more, the 'customed
prelude –
'How shouldst thou, of all men, smite,
and save us?'
Guesses what is like to prove the
sequel –
'Egypt's flesh-pots – nay, the drought
was better.'

### 10

Oh, the crowd must have emphatic
warrant!
Theirs, the Sinai-forehead's cloven
brilliance.

Right-arm's rod-sweep, tongue's imperial
fiat
Never dares the man put off the prophet

### 11

Did he love one face from out the
thousands,
(Were she Jethro's daughter, white and
wifely,
Were she but the Æthiopian bondslave,)
He would envy yon dumb patient
camel,
Keeping a reserve of scanty water
Meant to save his own life in the desert;
Ready in the desert to deliver
(Kneeling down to let his breast be
opened)
Hoard and life together for his mistress.

### 12

I shall never, in the years remaining,
Paint you pictures, no, nor carve you
statues,
Make you music that should all-express
me;
So it seems: I stand on my attainment.
This of verse alone, one life allows me;
Verse and nothing else have I to give
you.
Other heights in other lives, God willing:
All the gifts from all the heights, your
own, Love!

### 13

Yet a semblance of resource avails us –
Shade so finely touched, love's sense
must seize it.
Take these lines, look lovingly and
nearly,
Lines I write the first time and the last
time.
He who works in fresco, steals a hair-
brush,
Curbs the liberal hand, subservient
proudly,
Cramps his spirit, crowds its all in
little,
Makes a strange art of an art familiar,
Fills his lady's missal-marge with
flowerets.

He who blows thro' bronze, may
    breathe thro' silver,
Fitly serenade a slumbrous princess.
He who writes, may write for once as I
    do.

### 14

Love, you saw me gather men and
    women,
Live or dead or fashioned by my fancy,
Enter each and all, and use their
    service,
Speak from every mouth, – the speech,
    a poem.
Hardly shall I tell my joys and sorrows,
Hopes and fears, belief and disbelieving:
I am mine and yours – the rest be all
    men's,
Karshish, Cleon, Norbert and the fifty.
Let me speak this once in my true
    person,
Not as Lippo, Roland or Andrea,
Though the fruit of speech be just this
    sentence:
Pray you, look on these my men and
    women,
Take and keep my fifty poems finished;
Where my heart lies, let my brain lie
    also!
Poor the speech; be how I speak, for all
    things.

### 15

Not but that you know me! Lo, the
    moon's self!
Here in London, yonder late in Florence,
Still we find her face, the thrice-trans-
    figured.
Curving on a sky imbrued with colour,
Drifted over Fiesole by twilight,
Came she, our new crescent of a hair's-
    breadth.
Full she flared it, lamping Samminiato,
Rounder 'twixt the cypresses and
    rounder,
Perfect till the nightingales applauded.
Now, a piece of her old self,
    impoverished,

Hard to greet, she traverses the house-
    roofs,
Hurries with unhandsome thrift of
    silver,
Goes dispiritedly, glad to finish.

### 16

What, there's nothing in the moon
    noteworthy?
Nay: for if that moon could love a
    mortal,
Use, to charm him (so to fit a fancy),
All her magic ('tis the old sweet mythos),
She would turn a new side to her
    mortal,
Side unseen of herdsman, huntsman,
    steersman –
Blank to Zoroaster on his terrace,
Blind to Galileo on his turret,
Dumb to Homer, dumb to Keats –
    him, even!
Think, the wonder of the moonstruck
    mortal –
When she turns round, comes again in
    heaven,
Opens out anew for worse or better!
Proves she like some portent of an
    iceberg
Swimming full upon the ship it
    founders.
Hungry with huge teeth of splintered
    crystals?
Proves she as the paved work of a
    sapphire
Seen by Moses when he climbed the
    mountain?
Moses, Aaron, Nadab and Abihu
Climbed and saw the very God, the
    Highest,
Stand upon the paved work of a
    sapphire.
Like the bodied heaven in his clearness
Shone the stone, the sapphire of that
    paved work,
When they ate and drank and saw God
    also!

17

What were seen? None knows, none
    ever shall know.
Only this is sure – the sight were other,
Not the moon's same side, born late in
    Florence,
Dying now impoverished here in
    London.
God be thanked, the meanest of his
    creatures
Boasts two soul-sides, one to face the
    world with,
One to show a woman when he loves
    her!

18

This I say of me, but think of you, Love!
This to you – yourself my moon of
    poets!
Ah, but that's the world's side, there's
    the wonder,

Thus they see you, praise you, think
    they know you!
There, in turn I stand with them and
    praise you –
Out of my own self, I dare to phrase it.
But the best is when I glide from out
    them,
Cross a step or two of dubious twilight,
Come out on the other side, the novel
Silent silver lights and darks
    undreamed of,
Where I hush and bless myself with
    silence.

19

Oh, their Rafael of the dear Madonnas,
Oh, their Dante of the dread Inferno,
Wrote one song – and in my brain I
    sing it,
Drew one angel – borne, see, on my
    bosom!

# IN A BALCONY

1855

*Persons*

Norbert. Constance. The Queen.

CONSTANCE *and* NORBERT.

*Nor.* Now!

*Con.*       Not now!

*Nor.*            Give me them again,
    those hands:
Put them upon my forehead, how it
    throbs!
Press them before my eyes, the fire
    comes through!
You cruellest, you dearest in the world,
Let me! The Queen must grant whate'er
    I ask –
How can I gain you and not ask the
    Queen?
There she stays waiting for me, here
    stand you;
Some time or other this was to be
    asked;
Now is the one time – what I ask, I
    gain:
Let me ask now, Love!

*Con.*              Do, and ruin us.

*Nor.* Let it be now, Love! All my soul
    breaks forth.
How I do love you! Give my love its
    way!
A man can have but one life and one
    death,
One heaven, one hell. Let me fulfil my
    fate –
Grant me my heaven now! Let me know
    you mine,
Prove you mine, write my name upon
    your brow,
Hold you and have you, and then die
    away,
If God please, with completion in my
    soul!

*Con.* I am not yours then? How content
    this man!
I am not his – who change into himself,

Have passed into his heart and beat its
    beats,
Who give my hands to him, my eyes,
    my hair,
Give all that was of me away to him –
So well, that now, my spirit turned his
    own,
Takes part with him against the woman
    here,
Bids him not stumble at so mere a straw
As caring that the world be cognizant
How he loves her and how she worships
    him.
You have this woman, not as yet that
    world.
Go on, I bid, nor stop to care for me
By saving what I cease to care about,
The courtly name and pride of
    circumstance –
The name you'll pick up and be
    cumbered with
Just for the poor parade's sake, nothing
    more;
Just that the world may slip from under
    you –
Just that the world may cry 'So much
    for him –
'The man predestined to the heap of
    crowns:
'There goes his chance of winning one,
    at least!'

*Nor.* The world!

*Con.* You love it. Love me quite as well,
And see if I shall pray for this in vain!
Why must you ponder what it knows
    or thinks?

*Nor.* You pray for – what, in vain?

*Con.*           Oh my heart's heart,
How I do love you, Norbert! That is
    right:
But listen, or I take my hands away!

You say, 'let it be now': you would go now
And tell the Queen, perhaps six steps from us,
You love me – so you do, thank God!
*Nor.*                    Thank God!
*Con.*Yes, Norbert, – but you fain would tell your love,
And, what succeeds the telling, ask of her
My hand. Now take this rose and look at it,
Listening to me. You are the minister,
The Queen's first favourite, nor without a cause.
To-night completes your wonderful year's – work
(This palace-feast is held to celebrate)
Made memorable by her life's success,
The junction of two crowns, on her sole head,
Her house had only dreamed of anciently:
That this mere dream is grown a stable truth,
To-night's feast makes authentic. Whose the praise?
Whose genius, patience, energy, achieved
What turned the many heads and broke the hearts?
You are the fate, your minute's in the heaven.
Next comes the Queen's turn. 'Name your own reward!'
With leave to clench the past, chain the to-come,
Put out an arm and touch and take the sun
And fix it ever full-faced on your earth,
Possess yourself supremely of her life, –
You choose the single thing she will not grant;
Nay, very declaration of which choice
Will turn the scale and neutralize your work:
At best she will forgive you, if she can.

You think I'll let you choose – her cousin's hand?
*Nor.* Wait. First, do you retain your old belief
The Queen is generous, – nay, is just?
*Con.*                    There, there!
So men make women love them, while they know
No more of women's hearts than … look you here,
You that are just and generous beside,
Make it your own case! For example now,
I'll say – I let you kiss me, hold my hands –
Why? do you know why? I'll instruct you, then –
The kiss, because you have a name at court;
This hand and this, that you may shut in each
A jewel, if you please to pick up such.
That's horrible? Apply it to the Queen –
Suppose I am the Queen to whom you speak:
'I was a nameless man; you needed me:
'Why did I proffer you my aid? there stood
'A certain pretty cousin at your side.
'Why did I make such common cause with you?
'Access to her had not been easy else.
'You give my labour here abundant praise?
' 'Faith, labour, which she overlooked, grew play.
'How shall your gratitude discharge itself?
'Give me her hand!'
*Nor.*            And still I urge the same.
Is the Queen just? just – generous or no!
*Con.* Yes, just. You love a rose; no harm in that:
But was it for the rose's sake or mine
You put it in your bosom? mine, you said –
Then, mine you still must say or else be false.

You told the Queen you served her for
 herself;
If so, to serve her was to serve yourself,
She thinks, for all your unbelieving face!
I know her. In the hall, six steps from
 us,
One sees the twenty pictures: there's a
 life
Better than life, and yet no life at all.
Conceive her born in such a magic
 dome,
Pictures all round her! why, she sees the
 world,
Can recognize its given things and facts,
The fight of giants or the feast of gods,
Sages in senate, beauties at the bath,
Chases and battles, the whole earth's
 display
Landscape and sea-piece, down to
 flowers and fruit –
And who shall question that she knows
 them all,
In better semblance than the things
 outside?
Yet bring into the silent gallery
Some live thing to contrast in breath
 and blood,
Some lion, with the painted lion there –
You think she'll understand composedly?
– Say. 'that's his fellow in the hunting-
 piece
'Yonder, I've turned to praise a hundred
 times?'
Not so. Her knowledge of our actual
 earth,
Its hopes and fears, concerns and
 sympathies,
Must be too far, too mediate, too unreal.
The real exists for us outside, not her:
How should it, with that life in these
 four walls –
That father and that mother, first to
 last
No father and no mother – friends, a
 heap,
Lovers, no lack – a husband in due
 time,

And every one of them alike a lie!
Things painted by a Rubens out of
 nought
Into what kindness, friendship, love
 should be;
All better, all more grandiose than the
 life,
Only no life; mere cloth and surface-
 paint,
You feel, while you admire. How
 should she feel?
Yet now that she has stood thus fifty
 years
The sole spectator in that gallery,
You think to bring this warm real
 struggling love
In to her of a sudden, and suppose
She'll keep her state untroubled?
 Here's the truth –
She'll apprehend truth's value at a
 glance,
Prefer it to the pictured loyalty?
You only have to say, 'so men are
 made,
'For this they act; the thing has many
 names,
'But this the right one: and now, Queen,
 be just!'
Your life slips back; you lose her at the
 word:
You do not even for amends gain me.
He will not understand; oh, Norbert,
 Norbert,
Do you not understand?
*Nor.*          The Queen's the Queen:
I am myself – no picture, but alive
In every nerve and every muscle, here
At the palace-window o'er the people's
 street,
As she in the gallery where the pictures
 glow:
The good of life is precious to us both.
She cannot love; what do I want with
 rule?
When first I saw your face a year ago
I knew my life's good, my soul heard
 one voice –

'The woman yonder, there's no use of
      life
'But just to obtain her! heap earth's
      woes in one
'And bear them – make a pile of all
      earth's joy's
'And spurn them, as they help or help
      not this;
'Only, obtain her!' How was it to be?
I found you were the cousin of the
      Queen;
I must then serve the Queen to get to
      you.
No other way. Suppose there had been
      one,
And I, by saying prayers to some white
      star
With promise of my body and my soul,
Might gain you, – should I pray the
      star or no?
Instead, there was the Queen to serve!
      I served,
Helped, did what other servants failed
      to do.
Neither she sought nor I declared my
      end.
Her good is hers, my recompense be
      mine, –
I therefore name you as that recompense.
She dreamed that such a thing could
      never be?
Let her wake now. She thinks there
      was more cause
In love of power, high fame, pure
      loyalty?
Perhaps she fancies men wear out their
      lives
Chasing such shades. Then, I've a fancy
      too;
I worked because I want you with my
      soul:
I therefore ask your hand. Let it be now!
*Con.* Had I not loved you from the very
      first,
Were I not yours, could we not steal
      out thus
So wickedly, so wildly, and so well,

You might become impatient. What's
      conceived
Of us without here, by the folk within?
Where are you now? immersed in cares
      of state –
Where am I now? intent on festal
      robes –
We two, embracing under death's
      spread hand!
What was this thought for, what that
      scruple of yours
Which broke the council up? – to bring
      about
One minute's meeting in the corridor!
And then the sudden sleights, strange
      secrecies,
Complots inscrutable, deep telegraphs,
Long-planned chance-meetings,
      hazards of a look,
'Does she know? does she not know?
      saved or lost?'
A year of this compression's ecstasy
All goes for nothing! you would give
      this up
For the old way, the open way, the
      world's
His way who beats, and his who sells
      his wife!
What tempts you? – their notorious
      happiness
Makes you ashamed of ours? The best
      you'll gain
Will be – the Queen grants all that you
      require,
Concedes the cousin, rids herself of you
And me at once, and gives us ample
      leave
To live like our five hundred happy
      friends.
The world will show us with officious
      hand
Our chamber-entry, and stand sentinel
Where we so oft have stolen across its
      traps!
Get the world's warrant, ring the falcons
      feet,
And make it duty to be bold and swift,

Which long ago was nature. Have it so
We never hawked by rights till flung
    from fist?
Oh, the man's thought! no woman's
    sucl a fool.
*Nor.* Yes, the man's thought and my
    thought, which is more –
One made to love you, let the world
    take note!
Have I done worthy work? be love's the
    praise,
Though hampered by restrictions,
    barred against
By set forms, blinded by forced secrecies!
Set free my love, and see what love can
    do
Shown in my life – what work will
    spring from that!
The world is used to have its business
    done
On other grounds, find great effects
    produced
For power's sake, fame's sake, motives
    in men's mouth.
So, good: but let my low ground shame
    their high!
Truth is the strong thing. Let man's life
    be true!
And love's the truth of mine. Time
    prove the rest!
I choose to wear you stamped all over
    me,
Your name upon my forehead and my
    breast,
You, from the sword's blade to the
    ribbon's edge,
That men may see, all over, you in me –
That pale loves may die out of their
    pretence
In face of mine, shames thrown on love
    fall off.
Permit this, Constance! Love has been
    so long
Subdued in me, eating me through and
    through,
That now 'tis all of me and must have
    way.

Think of my work, that chaos of intrigues,
Those hopes and fears, surprises and
    delays,
That long endeavour, earnest, patient,
    slow,
Trembling at last to its assured result:
Then think of this revulsion! I resume
Life after death, (it is no less than life,
After such long unlovely labouring
    days)
And liberate to beauty life's great need
O' the beautiful, which, while it
    prompted work,
Suppressed itself erewhile. This eve's
    the time,
This eve intense with yon first trembling
    star
We seem to pant and reach; scarce
    aught between
The earth that rises and the heaven
    that bends;
All nature self-abandoned, every tree
Flung as it will, pursuing its own
    thoughts
And fixed so, every flower and every
    weed,
No pride, no shame, no victory, no
    defeat;
All under God, each measured by itself.
These statues round us stand abrupt,
    distinct,
The strong in strength, the weak in
    weakness fixed,
The Muse for ever wedded to her lyre,
Nymph to her fawn, and Silence to her
    rose:
See God's approval on his universe!
Let us do so – aspire to live as these
In harmony with truth, ourselves being
    true!
Take the first way, and let the second
    come!
My first is to possess myself of you;
The music sets the march-step –
    forward, then!
And there's the Queen, I go to claim
    you of,

The world to witness, wonder and
   applaud.
Our flower of life breaks open. No
   delay!
*Con.* And so shall we be ruined, both
   of us.
Norbert, I know her to the skin and
   bone:
You do not know her, were not born to
   it,
To feel what she can see or cannot see.
Love, she is generous, – ay, despite
   your smile,
Generous as you are: for, in that thin
   frame
Pain-twisted, punctured through and
   through with cares,
There lived a lavish soul until it starved,
Debarred of healthy food. Look to the
   soul –
Pity that, stoop to that, ere you begin
(The true man's-way) on justice and
   your rights,
Exactions and acquittance of the past!
Begin so – see what justice she will
   deal!
We women hate a debt as men a gift.
Suppose her some poor keeper of a
   school
Whose business is to sit thro' summer
   months
And dole out children leave to go and
   play,
Herself superior to such lightness – she
In the arm-chair's state and pædagogic
   pomp –
To the life, the laughter, sun and youth
   outside:
We wonder such a face looks black on
   us?
I do not bid you wake her tenderness,
(That were vain truly – none is left to
   wake)
But let her think her justice is engaged
To take the shape of tenderness, and
   mark
If she'll not coldly pay its warmest debt!

Does she love me, I ask you? not a
   whit:
Yet, thinking that her justice was
   engaged
To help a kinswoman, she took me up –
Did more on that bare ground than
   other loves
Would do on greater argument. For me,
I have no equivalent of such cold kind
To pay her with, but love alone to give
If I give anything. I give her love:
I feel I ought to help her, and I will.
So, for her sake, as yours, I tell you
   twice
That women hate a debt as men a gift.
If I were you, I could obtain this grace –
Could lay the whole I did to love's
   account,
Nor yet be very false as courtiers go –
Declaring my success was recompense;
It would be so, in fact: what were it else?
And then, once loose her generosity, –
Oh, how I see it! – then, were I but you,
To turn it, let it seem to move itself,
And make it offer what I really take,
Accepting just, in the poor cousin's
   hand,
Her value as the next thing to the
   Queen's –
Since none love Queens directly, none
   dare that,
And a thing's shadow or a names mere
   echo
Suffices those who miss the name and
   thing!
You pick up just a ribbon she has worn,
To keep in proof how near her breath
   you came.
Say, I'm so near I seem a piece of her –
Ask for me that way – (oh, you under-
   stand)
You'd find the same gift yielded with a
   grace,
Which, if you make the least show to
   extort …
– You'll see! and when you have ruined
   both of us.

Dissertate on the Queen's ingratitude!
*Nor*. Then, if I turn it that way, you
    consent?
'Tis not my way; I have more hope in
    truth:
Still, if you won't have truth – why, this
    indeed,
Were scarcely false, as I'd express the
    sense.
Will you remain here?
*Con*.           O best heart of mine,
How I have loved you! then, you take
    my way?
Are mine as you have been her minister,
Work out my thought, give it effect for
    me,
Paint plain my poor conceit and make
    it serve?
I owe that withered woman everything –
Life, fortune, you, remember! Take my
    part –
Help me to pay her! Stand upon your
    rights?
You, with my rose, my hands, my heart
    on you?
Your rights are mine – you have no
    rights but mine.
*Nor*. Remain here. How you know me!
*Con*.              Ah, but still –
    [*He breaks from her: she remains.*
        *Dance-music from within.*
        *Enter the* QUEEN.
*Queen*. Constance? She is here as he
    said. Speak quick!
Is it so? Is it true or false? One word!
*Con*. True.
*Queen*.     Mercifullest Mother, thanks
    to thee!
*Con*. Madam?
*Queen*.     I love you, Constance, from
    my soul.
Now say once more, with any words
    you will,
'Tis true, all true, as true as that I speak.
*Con*. Why should you doubt it?
*Queen*.     Ah, why doubt? why doubt?
Dear, make me see it! Do you see it so?

None see themselves; another sees
    them best.
You say 'why doubt it?' – you see him
    and me.
It is because the Mother has such grace
That if we had but faith – wherein we
    fail –
Whate'er we yearn for would be granted
    us;
Yet still we let our whims prescribe
    despair,
Our fancies thwart and cramp our will
    and power,
And, while accepting life, abjure its use.
Constance, I had abjured the hope of
    love
And being loved, as truly as yon palm
The hope of seeing Egypt from that
    plot.
*Con*. Heaven!
*Queen*.     But it was so, Constance,
    it was so!
Men say – or do men say it? fancies
    say –
'Stop here, your life is set, you are
    grown old.
'Too late – no love for you, too late for
    love –
'Leave love to girls. Be queen: let
    Constance love.'
One takes the hint – half meets it like a
    child,
Ashamed at any feelings that oppose.
'Oh love, true, never think of love again!
'I am a queen: I rule, not love
    forsooth.'
So it goes on; so a face grows like this,
Hair like this hair, poor arms as lean as
    these,
Till, – nay, it does not end so, I thank
    God!
*Con*. I cannot understand –
*Queen*.         The happier you!
Constance, I know not how it is with
    men:
For women (I am a woman now like
    you)

There is no good of life but love – but
   love!
What else looks good, is some shade
   flung from love;
Love gilds it, gives it worth. Be warned
   by me,
Never you cheat yourself one instant!
   Love,
Give love, ask only love, and leave the
   rest!
O Constance, how I love you!
*Con.*                              I love you.
*Queen.* I do believe that all is come
   through you.
I took you to my heart to keep it warm
When the last chance of love seemed
   dead in me;
I thought your fresh youth warmed my
   withered heart.
Oh, I am very old now, am I not?
Not so! it is true and it shall be true!
*Con.* Tell it me: let me judge if true or
   false.
*Queen.* Ah, but I fear you! you will look
   at me
And say, 'she's old, she's grown unlovely
   quite
'Who ne'er was beauteous: men want
   beauty still.'
Well, so I feared – the curse! so I felt sure!
*Con.* Be calm. And now you feel not
   sure, you say?
*Queen.* Constance, he came, – the
   coming was not strange –
Do not I stand and see men come and
   go?
I turned a half-look from my pedestal
Where I grow marble – 'one young man
   the more!
'He will love some one; that is nought
   to me:
'What would he with my marble
   stateliness?'
Yet this seemed somewhat worse than
   heretofore;
The man more gracious, youthful, like
   a god,

And I still older, with less flesh to
   change –
We two those dear extremes that long
   to touch.
It seemed still harder when he first
   began
To labour at those state-affairs,
   absorbed
The old way for the old end – interest.
Oh, to live with a thousand beating
   hearts
Around you, swift eyes, serviceable
   hands,
Professing they've no care but for your
   cause,
Thought but to help you, love but for
   yourself, –
And you the marble statue all the time
They praise and point at as preferred to
   life,
Yet leave for the first breathing woman's
   smile,
First dancer's, gipsy's or street baladine's!
Why, how I have ground my teeth to
   hear men's speech
Stifled for fear it should alarm my ear,
Their gait subdued lest step should
   startle me,
Their eyes declined, such queendom to
   respect,
Their hands alert, such treasure to
   preserve,
While not a man of them broke rank
   and spoke,
Wrote me a vulgar letter all of love,
Or caught my hand and pressed it like
   a hand!
There have been moments, if the sentinel
Lowering his halbert to salute the queen,
Had flung it brutally and clasped my
   knees,
I would have stooped and kissed him
   with my soul.
*Con.* Who could have comprehended?
*Queen.*                    Ay, who – who?
Who, no one, Constance, but this one
   who did.

Not they, not you, not I. Even now
    perhaps
It comes too late – would you but tell
    the truth.
*Con*. I wait to tell it.
*Queen*.        Well, you see, he came,
Outfaced the others, did a work this
    year
Exceeds in value all was ever done,
You know – it is not I who say it – all
Say it. And so (a second pang and
    worse)
I grew aware not only of what he did,
But why so wondrously. Oh, never
    work
Like his was done for work's ignoble
    sake –
Souls need a finer aim to light and lure!
I felt, I saw, he loved – loved somebody.
And Constance, my dear Constance,
    do you know,
I did believe this while 'twas you he
    loved.
*Con*. Me, madam?
*Queen*.      It did seem to me, your face
Met him where'er he looked: and
    whom but you
Was such a man to love? It seemed to
    me,
You saw he loved you, and approved
    his love,
And both of you were in intelligence.
You could not loiter in that garden,
    step
Into this balcony, but I straight was
    stung
And forced to understand. It seemed so
    true,
So right, so beautiful, so like you both,
That all this work should have been
    done by him
Not for the vulgar hope of recompense,
But that at last – suppose, some night
    like this –
Borne on to claim his due reward of me,
He might say 'Give her hand and pay
    me so.'

And I (O Constance, you shall love me
    now!)
I thought, surmounting all the bitterness,
– 'And he shall have it. I will make her
    blest,
'My flower of youth, my woman's self
    that was,
'My happiest woman's self that might
    have been!
'These two shall have their joy and
    leave me here.'
Yes – yes!
*Con*.   Thanks!
*Queen*.   And the word was on my lips
When he burst in upon me. I looked to
    hear
A mere calm statement of his just desire
For payment of his labour. When – O
    heaven,
How can I tell you? lightning on my eyes
And thunder in my ears proved that
    first word
Which told 'twas love of me, of me, did
    all –
He loved me – from the first step to the
    last,
Loved me!
*Con*.     You hardly saw, scarce heard
    him speak
Of love: what if you should mistake?
*Queen*.           No, no –
No mistake! Ha, there shall be no
    mistake!
He had not dared to hint the love he
    felt –
You were my reflex – (how I understood!)
He said you were the ribbon I had worn,
He kissed my hand, he looked into my
    eyes,
And love, love came at end of every
    phrase.
Love is begun; this much is come to
    pass:
The rest is easy. Constance, I am yours!
I will learn, I will place my life on you,
Teach me but how to keep what I have
    won!

Am I so old? This hair was early grey;
But joy ere now has brought hair
    brown again,
And joy will bring the cheek's red back,
    I feel.
I could sing once too; that was in my
    youth.
Still, when men paint me, they declare
    me ... yes,
Beautiful – for the last French painter
    did!
I know they flatter somewhat; you are
    frank –
I trust you. How I loved you from the
    first!
Some queens would hardly seek a cousin
    out
And set her by their side to take the eye:
I must have felt that good would come
    from you.
I am not generous – like him – like you!
But he is not your lover after all:
It was not you he looked at. Saw you
    him?
You have not been mistaking words or
    looks?
He said you were the reflex of myself.
And yet he is not such a paragon
To you, to younger women who may
    choose
Among a thousand Norberts. Speak the
    truth!
You know you never named his name to
    me:
You know, I cannot give him up – ah
    God,
Not up now, even to you!
*Con*.                Then calm yourself.
*Queen*. See, I am old – look here, you
    happy girl!
I will not play the fool, deceive – ah,
    whom?
'Tis all gone: put your cheek beside my
    cheek
And what a contrast does the moon
    behold!
But then I set my life upon one chance,

The last chance and the best – am *I* not
    left,
My soul, myself? All women love great
    men
If young or old; it is in all the tales:
Young beauties love old poets who can
    love –
Why should not he, the poems in my
    soul,
The passionate faith, the pride of
    sacrifice,
Life-long, death-long? I throw them at
    his feet.
Who cares to see the fountain's very
    shape,
Whether it be a Triton's or a Nymph's
That pours the foam, makes rainbows
    all around?
You could not praise indeed the empty
    conch;
But I'll pour floods of love and hide
    myself.
How I will love him! Cannot men love
    love?
Who was a queen and loved a poet once
Humpbacked, a dwarf? ah, women can
    do that?
Well, but men too; at least, they tell
    you so.
They love so many women in their
    youth,
And even in age they all love whom
    they please;
And yet the best of them confide to
    friends
That 'tis not beauty makes the lasting
    love –
They spend a day with such and tire
    the next:
They like soul, – well then, they like
    phantasy,
Novelty even. Let us confess the truth,
Horrible though it be, that prejudice,
Prescription ... curses! they will love a
    queen.
They will, they do: and will not, does
    not – he?

*Con.* How can he? You are wedded: 'tis a name
We know, but still a bond. Your rank remains,
His tank remains. How can he, nobly souled
As you believe and I incline to think,
Aspire to be your favourite, shame and all?
*Queen.* Hear her! There, there now –
could she love like me?
What did I say of smooth-cheeked youth and grace?
See all it does or could do! so youth loves!
Oh, tell him, Constance, you could never do
What I will – you, it was not born in! I
Will drive these difficulties far and fast
As yonder mists curdling before the moon.
I'll use my light too, gloriously retrieve
My youth from its enforced calamity,
Dissolve that hateful marriage, and be his,
His own in the eyes alike of God and man.
*Con.* You will do – dare do ... pause on what you say!
*Queen.* Hear her! I thank you, sweet, for that surprise.
You have the fair face: for the soul, see mine!
I have the strong soul: let me teach you, here.
I think I have borne enough and long enough,
And patiently enough, the world remarks,
To have my own way now, unblamed by all.
It does so happen (I rejoice for it)
This most unhoped-for issue cuts the knot.
There's not a better way of settling claims
Than this; God sends the accident express:

And were it for my subjects' good, no more,
'Twere best thus ordered. I am thankful now,
Mute, passive, acquiescent. I receive,
And bless God simply, or should almost fear
To walk so smoothly to my ends at last.
Why, how I baffle obstacles, spurn fate!
How strong I am! Could Norbert see me now!
*Con.* Let me consider. It is all too strange.
*Queen.* You, Constance, learn of me; do you, like me!
You are young, beautiful: my own, best girl,
You will have many lovers, and love one –
Light hair, not hair like Norbert's, to suit yours:
Taller than he is, since yourself are tall.
Love him, like me! Give all away to him;
Think never of yourself; throw by your pride,
Hope, fear, – your own good as you saw it once,
And love him simply for his very self.
Remember, I (and what am I to you?)
Would give up all for one, leave throne, lose life,
Do all but just unlove him! He loves me.
*Con.* He shall.
*Queen.*       You, step inside my inmost heart!
Give me your own heart: let us have one heart!
I'll come to you for counsel; 'this he says,
'This he does; what should this amount to, pray?
'Beseech you, change it into current coin!
'Is that worth kisses? Shall I please him there?'

And then we'll speak in turn of you –
    what else?
Your love, according to your beauty's
    worth,
For you shall have some noble love, all
    gold:
Whom choose you? we will get him at
    your choice.
– Constance, I leave you. Just a minute
    since,
I felt as I must die or be alone
Breathing my soul into an ear like yours:
Now, I would face the world with my
    new life,
Wear my new crown. I'll walk around
    the rooms,
And then come back and tell you how
    it feels.
How soon a smile of God can change
    the world!
How we are made for happiness – how
    work
Grows play, adversity a winning fight!
True, I have lost so many years: what
    then!
Many remain: God has been very good.
You, stay here! 'Tis as different from
    dreams,
From the mind's cold calm estimate of
    bliss,
As these stone statues from the flesh
    and blood.
The comfort thou hast caused
    mankind, God's moon!
      [*She goes out, leaving* CONSTANCE.
          *Dance-music from within.*
        NORBERT *enters.*

*Nor.* Well? we have but one minute
    and one word!
*Con.* I am yours, Norbert!
*Nor.*             Yes, mine.
*Con.*                 Not till now!
You were mine. Now I give myself to
    you.
*Nor.* Constance?
*Con.*            Your own! I know the
    thriftier way

Of giving – haply, 'tis the wiser way.
Meaning to give a treasure, I might dole
Coin after coin out (each, as that were
    all,
With a new largess still at each despair)
And force you keep in sight the deed,
    preserve
Exhaustless till the end my part and
    yours,
My giving and your taking; both our
    joys
Dying together. Is it the wiser way?
I choose the simpler; I give all at once.
Know what you have to trust to, trade
    upon!
Use it, abuse it, – anything but think
Hereafter, 'Had I known she loved me
    so,
'And what my means, I might have
    thriven with it.'
This is your means. I give you all myself.
*Nor.* I take you and thank God.
*Con.*           Look on through years!
We cannot kiss, a second day like this;
Else were this earth no earth.
*Nor.*           With this day's heat
We shall go on through years of cold.
*Con.*              So, best!
– I try to see those years – I think I see.
You walk quick and new warmth
    comes; you look back
And lay all to the first glow – not sit
    down
For ever brooding on a day like this
While seeing embers whiten and love
    die.
Yes, love lives best in its effect; and
    mine,
Full in its own life, yearns to live in
    yours.
*Nor.* Just so. I take and know you all at
    once.
Your soul is disengaged so easily,
Your face is there, I know you; give me
    time,
Let me be proud and think you shall
    know me.

My soul is slower: in a life I roll
The minute out whereto you condense
    yours –
The whole slow circle round you I
    must move,
To be just you. I look to a long life
To decompose this minute, prove its
    worth.
'Tis the sparks' long succession one by
    one
Shall show you, in the end, what fire
    was crammed
In that mere stone you struck: how
    could you know,
If it lay ever unproved in your sight,
As now my heart lies? your own
    warmth would hide
Its coldness, were it cold.
*Con.*            But how prove, how?
*Nor.* Prove in my life, you ask?
*Con.*          Quick, Norbert – how?
*Nor.* That's easy told. I count life just a
    stuff
To try the soul's strength on, educe the
    man.
Who keeps one end in view makes all
    things serve.
As with the body – he who hurls a lance
Or heaps up stone on stone, shows
    strength alike:
So must I seize and task all means to
    prove
And show this soul of mine, you crown
    as yours,
And justify us both.
*Con.*          Could you write books,
Paint pictures! One sits down in poverty
And writes or paints, with pity for the
    rich.
*Nor.* And loves one's painting and one's
    writing, then,
And not one's mistress! All is best,
    believe,
And we best as no other than we are.
We live, and they experiment on life –
Those poets, painters, all who stand
    aloof

To overlook the farther. Let us be
The thing they look at! I might take
    your face
And write of it and paint it – to what
    end?
For whom? what pale dictatress in the
    air
Feeds, smiling sadly, her fine ghost-like
    form
With earth's real blood and breath, the
    beauteous life
She makes despised for ever? You are
    mine,
Made for me, not for others in the
    world,
Nor yet for that which I should call my
    art,
The cold calm power to see how fair
    you look.
I come to you; I leave you not, to write
Or paint. You are, I am: let Rubens
    there
Paint us!
*Con.* So, best!
*Nor.*          I understand your soul.
You live, and rightly sympathize with
    life,
With action, power, success. This way
    is straight;
And time were short beside, to let me
    change
The craft my childhood learnt: my craft
    shall serve.
Men set me here to subjugate, enclose,
Manure their barren lives, and force
    thence fruit
First for themselves, and afterward for
    me
In the due tithe; the task of some one
    soul,
Through ways of work appointed by
    the world.
I am not bid create – men see no star
Transfiguring my brow to warrant that –
But find and bind and bring to bear
    their wills.
So I began: to-night sees how I end.

What if it see, too, power's first outbreak
     here
Amid the warmth, surprise and
     sympathy,
And instincts of the heart that teach
     the head?
What if the people have discerned at
     length
The dawn of the next nature, novel
     brain
Whose will they venture in the place of
     theirs,
Whose work, they trust, shall find
     them as novel ways
To untried heights which yet he only
     sees?
I felt it when you kissed me. See this
     Queen,
This people – in our phrase, this mass
     of men –
See how the mass lies passive to my
     hand
Now that my hand is plastic, with you
     by
To make the muscles iron! Oh, an end
Shall crown this issue as this crowns
     the first!
My will be on this people! then, the
     strain,
The grappling of the potter with his
     clay,
The long uncertain struggle, – the success
And consummation of the spirit-work,
Some vase shaped to the curl of the
     god's lip,
While rounded fair for human sense to
     see
The Graces in a dance men recognize
With turbulent applause and laughs of
     heart!
So triumph ever shall renew itself;
Ever shall end in efforts higher yet,
Ever begin …
*Con.*          I ever helping?
*Nor.*                    Thus!
               [*He embraces her.*
          *The* QUEEN *enters.*

*Con.* Hist, madam! So have I
     performed my part.
You see your gratitude's true decency,
Norbert? A little slow in seeing it!
Begin, to end the sooner! What's a
     kiss?
*Nor.* Constance?
*Con.*     Why, must I teach it you again?
You want a witness to your dulness,
     sir?
What was I saying these ten minutes
     long?
Then I repeat – when some young
     handsome man
Like you has acted out a part like
     yours,
Is pleased to fall in love with one
     beyond,
So very far beyond him, as he says –
So hopelessly in love that but to speak
Would prove him mad, – he thinks
     judiciously,
And makes some insignificant good
     soul,
Like me, his friend, adviser, confidant,
And very stalking-horse to cover him
In following after what he dares not
     face.
When his end's gained – (sir, do you
     understand?)
When she, he dares not face, has loved
     him first,
– May I not say so, madam? – tops his
     hope,
And overpasses so his wildest dream,
With glad consent of all, and most of
     her
The confidant who brought the same
     about –
Why, in the moment when such joy
     explodes,
I do hold that the merest gentleman
Will not start rudely from the stalking-
     horse,
Dismiss it with a 'There, enough of you!'
Forget it, show his back unmannerly:
But like a liberal heart will rather turn

And say, 'A tingling time of hope was
ours;
'Betwixt the fears and falterings, we
two lived
'A chanceful time in waiting for the
prize:
'The confidant, the Constance, served
not ill.
'And though I shall forget her in due
time,
'Her use being answered now, as reason
bids,
'Nay as herself bids from her heart of
hearts, –
'Still, she has rights, the first thanks go
to her,
'The first good praise goes to the
prosperous tool,
'And the first – which is the last –
rewarding kiss.'
*Nor.* Constance, it is a dream – ah, see,
you smile!
*Con.* So, now his part being properly
performed,
Madam, I turn to you and finish mine
As duly; I do justice in my turn.
Yes, madam, he has loved you – long
and well;
He could not hope to tell you so –
'twas I
Who served to prove your soul accessible,
I led his thoughts on, drew them to
their place
When they had wandered else into
despair,
And kept love constant toward its
natural aim.
Enough, my part is played; you stoop
half-way
And meet us royally and spare our
fears:
'Tis like yourself. He thanks you,
so do I.
Take him – with my full heart! my
work is praised
By what comes of it. Be you happy,
both!

Yourself – the only one on earth who
can –
Do all for him, much more than a mere
heart
Which though warm is not useful in its
warmth
As the silk vesture of a queen! fold that
Around him gently, tenderly. For him –
For him, – he knows his own part!
*Nor.*                                    Have
you done?
I take the jest at last. Should I speak
now?
Was yours the wager, Constance, foolish
child,
Or did you but accept it? Well – at least
You lose by it.
*Con.*          Nay, madam 'tis your turn!
Restrain him still from speech a little
more,
And make him happier as more
confident!
Pity him, madam, he is timid yet!
Mark, Norbert! Do not shrink now!
Here I yield
My whole right in you to the Queen,
observe!
With her go put in practice the great
schemes
You teem with, follow the career else
closed –
Be all you cannot be except by her!
Behold her! – Madam, say for pity's
sake
Anything – frankly say you love him!
Else
He'll not believe it: there's more
earnest in
His fear than you conceive: I know the
man!
*Nor.* I know the woman somewhat, and
confess
I thought she had jested better: she
begins
To overcharge her part. I gravely wait
Your pleasure, madam: where is my
reward?

*Queen*. Norbert, this wild girl (whom I recognize
Scarce more than you do, in her fancy-fit,
Eccentric speech and variable mirth,
Not very wise perhaps and somewhat bold,
Yet suitable, the whole night's work being strange)
– May still be right: I may do well to speak
And make authentic what appears a dream
To even myself. For, what she says, is true:
Yes, Norbert – what you spoke just now of love,
Devotion, stirred no novel sense in me,
But justified a warmth felt long before.
Yes, from the first – I loved you, I shall say:
Strange! but I do grow stronger, now 'tis said.
Your courage helps mine: you did well to speak
To-night, the night that crowns your twelvemonths' toil:
But still I had not waited to discern
Your heart so long, believe me! From the first
The source of so much zeal was almost plain,
In absence even of your own words just now
Which hazarded the truth. 'Tis very strange,
But takes a happy ending – in your love
Which mine meets: be it so! as you chose me,
So I choose you.
*Nor.*          And worthily you choose.
I will not be unworthy your esteem,
No, madam. I do love you; I will meet
Your nature, now I know it. This was well.
I see, – you dare and you are justified:
But none had ventured such experiment,
Less versed than you in nobleness of heart,
Less confident of finding such in me.
I joy that thus you test me ere you grant
The dearest richest beauteousest and best
Of women to my arms: 'tis like yourself.
So – back again into my part's set words –
Devotion to the uttermost is yours,
But no, you cannot, madam, even you,
Create in me the love our Constance does.
Or – something truer to the tragic phrase –
Not yon magnolia-bell superb with scent
Invites a certain insect – that's myself –
But the small eye-flower nearer to the ground.
I take this lady.
*Con.*          Stay – not hers, the trap –
Stay, Norbert – that mistake were worst of all!
He is too cunning, madam! It was I,
I, Norbert, who …
*Nor.*          You, was it, Constance? Then.
But for the grace of this divinest hour
Which gives me you, I might not pardon here!
I am the Queen's; she only knows my brain:
She may experiment upon my heart
And I instruct her too by the result.
But you, sweet, you who know me, who so long
Have told my heart-beats over, held my life
In those white hands of yours, – it is not well!
*Con.* Tush! I have said it, did I not say it all?
The life, for her – the heart-beats, for her sake!
*Nor.* Enough! my cheek grows red, I think. Your test?

There's not the meanest woman in the
 world,
Not she I least could love in all the
 world,
Whom, did she love me, had love proved
 itself,
I dare insult as you insult me now.
Constance, I could say, if it must be
 said,
'Take back the soul you offer, I keep
 mine!'
But – 'Take the soul still quivering on
 your hand,
'The soul so offered, which I cannot
 use,
'And, please you, give it to some playful
 friend,
'For – what's the trifle he requites me
 with?'
I, tempt a woman, to amuse a man,
That two may mock her heart if it
 succumb?
No: fearing God and standing 'neath
 his heaven,
I would not dare insult a woman so,
Were she the meanest woman in the
 world,
And he, I cared to please, ten emperors!
*Con*. Norbert!
*Nor.* I love once as I live but once.
What case is this to think or talk about?
I love you. Would it mend the case
 at all
If such a step as this killed love in me?
Your part were done: account to God
 for it!
But mine – could murdered love get up
 again,
And kneel to whom you please to
 designate,
And make you mirth? It is too horrible.
You did not know this, Constance?
 now you know
That body and soul have each one life,
 but one:
And here's my love, here, living, at your
 feet.

*Con*. See the Queen! Norbert – this one
 more last word –
If thus you have taken jest for earnest –
 thus
Loved me in earnest …
*Nor.* Ah, no jest holds here!
Where is the laughter in which jests
 break up,
And what this horror that grows
 palpable?
Madam – why grasp you thus the
 balcony?
Have I done ill? Have I not spoken
 truth?
How could I other? Was it not your test,
To try me, what my love for Constance
 meant?
Madam, your royal soul itself approves,
The first, that I should choose thus! so
 one takes
A beggar, – asks him, what would buy
 his child?
And then approves the expected laugh
 of scorn
Returned as something noble from the
 rags.
Speak, Constance, I'm the beggar! Ha,
 what's this?
You two glare each at each like
 panthers now.
Constance, the world fades; only you
 stand there!
You did not, in to-night's wild whirl of
 things,
Sell me – your soul of souls, for any
 price?
No – no – 'tis easy to believe in you!
Was it your love's mad trial to o'ertop
Mine by this vain self-sacrifice? well,
 still –
Though I might curse, I love you. I am
 love
And cannot change: love's self is at your
 feet!
    [*The* QUEEN *goes out.*
*Con*. Feel my heart; let it die against
 your own!

*Nor*. Against my own. Explain not; let this be!
This is life's height.
*Con*.　　　　Yours, yours, yours!
*Nor*.　　　　　　　　You and I –
Why care by what meanders we are here
I' the centre of the labyrinth? Men have died
Trying to find this place, which we have found.
*Con*. Found, found!
*Nor*. Sweet, never fear what she can do!
We are past harm now.
*Con*.　　　　　On the breast of God.
I thought of men – as if you were a man.

Tempting him with a crown!
*Nor*.　　　　　This must end here:
It is too perfect.
*Con*.　　　There's the music stopped.
What measured heavy tread? It is one blaze
About me and within me.
*Nor*.　　　　　　Oh, some death
Will run its sudden finger round this spark
And sever us from the rest!
*Con*.　　　　　And so do well.
Now the doors open.
*Nor*.　　　　'Tis the guard comes.
*Con*.　　　　　　Kiss!

# DRAMATIS PERSONÆ

## 1864

### *James Lee's Wife*

**1**

#### JAMES LEE'S WIFE SPEAKS AT
#### THE WINDOW

**1**

Ah, Love, but a day
    And the world has changed!
The sun's away,
    And the bird estranged;
The wind has dropped,
    And the sky's deranged:
Summer has stopped.

**2**

Look in my eyes!
    Wilt thou change too?
Should I fear surprise?
    Shall I find aught new
In the old and dear,
    In the good and true,
With the changing year?

**3**

Thou art a man,
    But I am thy love.
For the lake, its swan;
    For the dell, its dove;
And for thee – (oh, haste!)
    Me, to bend above,
    Me, to hold embraced.

**2**

#### BY THE FIRESIDE

**1**

Is all our fire of shipwreck wood,
    Oak and pine?
Oh, for the ills half-understood,
    The dim dead woe
        Long ago
Befallen this bitter coast of France!
Well, poor sailors took their chance;
    I take mine.

**2**

A ruddy shaft our fire must shoot
    O'er the sea:

Do sailors eye the casement – mute,
    Drenched and stark,
        From their bark –
And envy, gnash their teeth for hate
O' the warm safe house and happy
    freight
        – Thee and me?

**3**

God help you, sailors, at your need!
    Spare the curse!
For some ships, safe in port indeed,
    Rot and rust,
    Run to dust,
All through worms i' the wood, which
    crept,
Gnawed our hearts out while we slept:
    That is worse.

**4**

Who lived here before us two?
    Old-world pairs.
Did a woman ever – would I knew! –
    Watch the man
    With whom began
Love's voyage full-sail, – (now, gnash
    your teeth!)
When planks start, open hell beneath
    Unawares?

**3**

#### IN THE DOORWAY

**1**

The swallow has set her six young on
    the rail,
        And looks sea-ward:
The water's in stripes like a snake,
    olive-pale
        To the leeward, –
On the weather-side, black, spotted
    white with the wind.
'Good fortune departs, and disaster's
    behind,' –
Hark, the wind with its wants and its
    infinite wail!

2

Our fig-tree, that leaned for the
    saltness, has furled
        Her five fingers,
Each leaf like a hand opened wide to
    the world
        Where there lingers
No glint of the gold, Summer sent for
    her sake:
How the vines writhe in rows, each
    impaled on its stake!
My heart shrivels up and my spirit
    shrinks curled.

3

Yet here are we two; we have love,
    house enough,
        With the field there,
This house of four rooms, that field red
    and rough,
        Though it yield there,
For the rabbit that robs, scarce a blade
    or a bent;
If a magpie alight now, it seems an
    event;
And they both will be gone at
    November's rebuff.

4

But why must cold spread? but
    wherefore bring change
        To the spirit,
God meant should mate his with an
    infinite range,
        And inherit
His power to put life in the darkness
    and cold?
Oh, live and love worthily, bear and be
    bold!
Whom Summer made friends of, let
    Winter estrange!

4

ALONG THE BEACH

1

I will be quiet and talk with you,
    And reason why you are wrong.
You wanted my love – is that much
    true?

And so I did love, so I do:
    What has come of it all along?

2

I took you – how could I otherwise?
    For a world to me, and more;
For all, love greatens and glorifies
Till God's a-glow, to the loving eyes,
    In what was mere earth before.

3

Yes, earth – yes, mere ignoble earth!
    Now do I mis-state, mistake?
Do I wrong your weakness and call it
    worth?
Expect all harvest, dread no dearth,
    Seal my sense up for your sake?

4

Oh, Love, Love, no, Love! not so,
    indeed!
    You were just weak earth, I knew:
With much in you waste, with many a
    weed,
And plenty of passions run to seed,
    But a little good grain too.

5

And such as you were, I took you for
    mine:
    Did not you find me yours,
To watch the olive and wait the vine,
And wonder when rivers of oil and wine
    Would flow, as the Book assures?

6

Well, and if none of these good things
    came,
    What did the failure prove?
The man was my whole world, all the
    same,
With his flowers to praise or his weeds
    to blame,
And, either or both, to love.

7

Yet this turns now to a fault – there!
    there!
    That I do love, watch too long,
And wait too well, and weary and
    wear,
And 'tis all an old story, and my despair
    Fit subject for some new song:

8

How the light, light love, he has wings
    to fly
  'At suspicion of a bond:
'My wisdom has bidden your pleasure
    good-bye,
'Which will turn up next in a laughing
    eye,
  'And why should you look beyond?'

5

ON THE CLIFF

1

I leaned on the turf,
I looked at a rock
Left dry by the surf;
For the turf, to call it grass were to
    mock:
Dead to the roots, so deep was done
The work of the summer sun.

2

And the rock lay flat
As an anvil's face:
No iron like that!
Baked dry; of a weed, of a shell, no
    trace:
Sunshine outside, but ice at the core,
Death's altar by the lone shore.

3

On the turf, sprang gay
With his films of blue,
No cricket, I'll say,
But a warhorse, barded and
    chanfroned too,
The gift of a quixote-mage to his knight,
Real fairy, with wings all right.

4

On the rock, they scorch
Like a drop of fire
From a brandished torch,
Fall two red fans of a butterfly:
No turf, no rock: in their ugly stead,
See, wonderful blue and red!

5

Is it not so
With the minds of men?
The level and low,

The burnt and bare, in themselves; but
    then
With such a blue and red grace, not
    theirs, –
Love settling unawares!

6

READING A BOOK, UNDER THE CLIFF

1

'Still ailing, Wind? Wilt be appeased or
    no?
  'Which needs the other's office,
    thou or I?
'Dost want to be disburdened of a woe,
  'And can, in truth, my voice untie
'Its links, and let it go?

2

'Art thou a dumb wronged thing that
    would be righted,
  'Entrusting thus thy cause to me?
    Forbear!
'No tongue can mend such pleadings;
    faith, requited
  'With falsehood, – love, at last aware
'Of scorn, – hopes, early blighted, –

3

'We have them; but I know not any tone
  'So fit as thine to falter forth a sorrow:
'Dost think men would go mad
    without a moan,
  'If they knew any way to borrow
'A pathos like thy own?

4

'Which sigh wouldst mock, of all the
    sighs? The one
  'So long escaping from lips starved
    and blue,
'That lasts while on her pallet-bed the
    nun
  'Stretches her length; her foot comes
    through
'The straw she shivers on;

5

'You had not thought she was so tall:
    and spent,
  'Her shrunk lids open, her lean
    fingers shut

'Close, close, their sharp and livid nails
    indent
  'The clammy palm; then all is mute:
'That way, the spirit went.

### 6

'Or wouldst thou rather that I
    understand
  'Thy will to help me? – like the dog I
    found
'Once, pacing sad this solitary strand,
  'Who would not take my food, poor
    hound,
'But whined and licked my hand.'

### 7

All this, and more, comes from some
    young man's pride
  Of power to see, – in failure and
    mistake,
Relinquishment, disgrace, on every
    side, –
  Merely examples for his sake,
Helps to his path untried:

### 8

Instances he must – simply recognize?
  Oh, more than so! – must, with a
    learner's zeal,
Make doubly prominent, twice
    emphasize,
  By added touches that reveal
The god in babe's disguise.

### 9

Oh, he knows what defeat means, and
    the rest!
  Himself the undefeated that shall be:
Failure, disgrace, he flings them you to
    test, –
  His triumph, in eternity
Too plainly manifest!

### 10

Whence, judge if he learn forthwith
    what the wind
  Means in its moaning – by the
    happy prompt
Instinctive way of youth, I mean; for
    kind
  Calm years, exacting their accompt
Of pain, mature the mind:  .

### 11

And some midsummer morning, at the
    lull
  Just about daybreak, as he looks across
A sparkling foreign country, wonderful
  To the sea's edge for gloom and gloss,
Next minute must annul, –

### 12

Then, when the wind begins among
    the vines,
  So low, so low, what shall it say but
    this?
'Here is the change beginning, here the
    lines
  'Circumscribe beauty, set to bliss
'The limit time assigns.'

### 13

Nothing can be as it has been before;
  Better, so call it, only not the same.
To draw one beauty into our hearts'
    core,
  And keep it changeless! such our
    claim;
So answered, – Never more!

### 14

Simple? Why this is the old woe o' the
    world;
  Tune, to whose rise and fall we live
    and die.
Rise with it, then! Rejoice that man is
    hurled
  From change to change unceasingly,
His soul's wings never furled!

### 15

That's a new question; still replies the
    fact,
  Nothing endures: the wind moans,
    saying so;
We moan in acquiescence: there's life's
    pact,
  Perhaps probation – do I know?
God does: endure his act!

### 16

Only, for man, how bitter not to grave
  On his soul's hands' palms one fair
    good wise thing

Just as he grasped it! For himself,
    death's wave;
  While time first washes – ah, the
    sting! –
O'er all he'd sink to save.

### 7
#### AMONG THE ROCKS
##### 1

Oh, good gigantic smile o' the brown
    old earth,
  This autumn morning! How he sets
    his bones
To bask i' the sun, and thrusts out
    knees and feet
For the ripple to run over in its mirth;
  Listening the while, where on the
    heap of stones
The white breast of the sea-lark twitters
    sweet.

##### 2

That is the doctrine, simple, ancient,
    true;
  Such is life's trial, as old earth smiles
    and knows.
If you loved only what were worth your
    love,
Love were clear gain, and wholly well
    for you:
  Make the low nature better by your
    throes!
Give earth yourself, go up for gain
    above!

### 8
#### BESIDE THE DRAWING BOARD
##### 1

'As like as a Hand to another Hand!'
  Whoever said that foolish thing,
Could not have studied to understand
  The counsels of God in fashioning,
Out of the infinite love of his heart,
This Hand, whose beauty I praise, apart
From the world of wonder left to praise,
If I tried to learn the other ways
Of love in its skill, or love in its power.

'As like as a Hand to another Hand':
  Who said that, never took his stand,
Found and followed, like me, an hour,
The beauty in this, – how free, how fine
To fear, almost, – of the limit-line!
As I looked at this, and learned and
    drew,
  Drew and learned, and looked again,
While fast the happy minutes flew,
  Its beauty mounted into my brain,
  And a fancy seized me; I was fain
To efface my work, begin anew,
Kiss what before I only drew;
Ay, laying the red chalk 'twixt my lips,
  With soul to help if the mere lips
    failed,
  I kissed all right where the drawing
    ailed,
Kissed fast the grace that somehow slips
Still from one's soulless finger-tips.

##### 2

'Tis a clay cast, the perfect thing,
  From Hand live once, dead long ago:
Princess-like it wears the ring
  To fancy's eye, by which we know
That here at length a master found
  His match, a proud lone soul its
    mate,
As soaring genius sank to ground,
  And pencil could not emulate
The beauty in this, – how free, how
    fine
To fear almost! – of the limit-line.
Long ago the god, like me
The worm, learned, each in our degree:
Looked and loved, learned and drew,
  Drew and learned and loved again,
While fast the happy minutes flew,
  Till beauty mounted into his brain
And on the finger which outvied
  His art he placed the ring that's there,
Still by fancy's eye descried,
  In token of a marriage rare:
  For him on earth, his art's despair,
For him in heaven, his soul's fit bride.

### 3

Little girl with the poor coarse hand
　　I turned from to a cold clay cast –
I have my lesson, understand
　　The worth of flesh and blood at last.
Nothing but beauty in a Hand?
　　Because he could not change the hue,
　　Mend the lines and make them true
To this which met his soul's demand, –
　　Would Da Vinci turn from you?
I hear him laugh my woes to scorn –
'The fool forsooth is all forlorn
'Because the beauty, she thinks best,
'Lived long ago or was never born, –
'Because no beauty bears the test
'In this rough peasant Hand!
　　　Confessed!
' "Art is null and study void!"
　　'So sayest thou? So said not I,
　　'Who threw the faulty pencil by,
'And years instead of hours employed,
'Learning the veritable use
　　'Of flesh and bone and nerve beneath
　　'Lines and hue of the outer sheath,
'If haply I might reproduce
'One motive of the powers profuse,
'Flesh and bone and nerve that make
　　'The poorest coarsest human hand
　　'An object worthy to be scanned
'A whole life long for their sole sake.
'Shall earth and the cramped moment-
　　　space
'Yield the heavenly crowning grace
'Now the parts and then the whole!
'Who art thou, with stinted soul
　　'And stunted body, thus to cry
' "I love, – shall that be life's strait dole?
' ' "I must five beloved or die!"
'This peasant hand that spins the wool
　　'And bakes the bread, why lives it on,
　　'Poor and coarse with beauty gone, –
'What use survives the beauty?' Fool!

Go, little girl with the poor coarse
　　hand!
I have my lesson, shall understand.

### 9

#### ON DECK

##### 1

There is nothing to remember in me,
　　Nothing I ever said with a grace,
Nothing I did that you care to see,
　　Nothing I was that deserves a place
In your mind, now I leave you, set you
　　free.

##### 2

Conceded! In turn, concede to me,
　　Such things have been as a mutual
　　　flame.
Your soul's locked fast; but, love for a
　　key,
　　You might let it loose, till I grew the
　　same
In your eyes, as in mine you stand:
　　strange plea!

##### 3

For then, then, what would it matter to
　　me
　　That I was the harsh ill-favoured
　　one?
We both should be like as pea and
　　pea;
　　It was ever so since the world begun:
So, let me proceed with my reverie.

##### 4

How strange it were if you had all me,
　　As I have all you in my heart and
　　brain,
You, whose least word brought gloom
　　or glee,
　　Who never lifted the hand in vain –
Will hold mine yet, from over the sea!

##### 5

Strange, if a face, when you thought of
　　me,
　　Rose like your own face present
　　now,
With eyes as dear in their due degree,
　　Much such a mouth, and as bright a
　　brow,
Till you saw yourself, while you cried
　　' 'Tis She!'

6

Well, you may, you must set down to
      me
   Love that was life, life that was love;
A tenure of breath at your lips' decree,
   A passion to stand as your thoughts
      approve,
A rapture to fall where your foot might
      be.

7

But did one touch of such love for me
   Come in a word or a look of yours,
Whose words and looks will, circling,
      flee
   Round me and round while life
      endures, –
Could I fancy 'As I feel, thus feels he';

8

Why, fade you might to a thing like
      me,
   And your hair grow these coarse
      hanks of hair,
Your skin, this bark of a gnarled tree, –
   You might turn myself! – should I
      know or care
When I should be dead of joy, James
      Lee?

## Gold Hair

### A STORY OF PORNIC

1

Oh, the beautiful girl, too white,
   Who lived at Pornic, down by the
      sea,
Just where the sea and the Loire unite!
   And a boasted name in Brittany
She bore, which I will not write.

2

Too white, for the flower of life is red;
   Her flesh was the soft seraphic screen
Of a soul that is meant (her parents
      said)
   To just see earth, and hardly be seen,
And blossom in heaven instead.

3

Yet earth saw one thing, one how fair!
   One grace that grew to its full on
      earth:
Smiles might be sparse on her cheek so
      spare,
   And her waist want half a girdle's
      girth,
But she had her great gold hair.

4

Hair, such a wonder of flix and floss,
   Freshness and fragrance – floods of
      it, too!
Gold, did I say? Nay, gold's mere dross:
   Here, Life smiled, 'Think what I
      meant to do!'
And Love sighed, 'Fancy my loss!'

5

So, when she died, it was scarce more
      strange
   Than that, when delicate evening
      dies,
And you follow its spent sun's pallid
      range,
   There's a shoot of colour startles the
      skies
With sudden, violent change, –

6

That, while the breath was nearly to
      seek,
   As they put the little cross to her
      lips,
She changed; a spot came out on her
      cheek,
   A spark from her eye in mid-eclipse,
And she broke forth, 'I must speak!'

7

'Not my hair!' made the girl her moan –
   'All the rest is gone or to go;
'But the last, last grace, my all, my own,
   'Let it stay in the grave, that the
      ghosts may know!
'Leave my poor gold hair alone!'

8

The passion thus vented, dead lay she;
   Her parents sobbed their worst on
      that;

All friends joined in, nor observed degree:
  For indeed the hair was to wonder at,
As it spread – not flowing free,

### 9

But curled around her brow, like a
    crown,
  And coiled beside her cheeks, like a
    cap,
And calmed about her neck – ay, down
  To her breast, pressed flat, without a
    gap
I' the gold, it reached her gown.

### 10

All kissed that face, like a silver wedge
  'Mid the yellow wealth, nor
    disturbed its hair:
E'en the priest allowed death's privilege,
  As he planted the crucifix with care
On her breast, 'twixt edge and edge.

### 11

And thus was she buried, inviolate
  Of body and soul, in the very space
By the altar; keeping saintly state
  In Pornic church, for her pride of
    race,
Pure life and piteous fate.

### 12

And in after-time would your fresh tear
    fall,
  Though your mouth might twitch
    with a dubious smile,
As they told you of gold, both robe and
    pall,
  How she prayed them leave it alone
    awhile,
So it never was touched at all.

### 13

Years flew; this legend grew at last
  The life of the lady; all she had done,
All been, in the memories fading fast
  Of lover and friend, was summed in
    one
Sentence survivors passed:

### 14

To wit, she was meant for heaven, not
    earth;
  Had turned an angel before the time:

Yet, since she was mortal, in such
    dearth
  Of frailty, all you could count a crime
Was – she knew her gold hair's worth.

\*    \*    \*

### 15

At little pleasant Pornic church,
  It chanced, the pavement wanted
    repair,
Was taken to pieces: left in the lurch,
  A certain sacred space lay bare,
And the boys began research.

### 16

'Twas the space where our sires would
    lay a saint,
  A benefactor, – a bishop, suppose,
A baron with armour-adornments
    quaint,
  Dame with chased ring and jewelled
    rose,
Things sanctity saves from taint;

### 17

So we come to find them in after-days
  When the corpse is presumed to
    have done with gauds
Of use to the living, in many ways:
  For the boys get pelf, and the town
    applauds,
And the church deserves the praise.

### 18

They grubbed with a will: and at length
    – O cor
  Humanum, pectora cœca, and the
    rest! –
They found – no gaud they were prying
    for,
  No ring, no rose, but – who would
    have guessed? –
A double Louis-d'or!

### 19

Here was a case for the priest: he heard,
  Marked, inwardly digested, laid
Finger on nose, smiled, 'There's a bird
  'Chirps in my ear': then, 'Bring a
    spade,
'Dig deeper!' – he gave the word.

#### 20

And lo, when they came to the coffin-
lid,
  Or rotten planks which composed it
  once,
Why, there lay the girl's skull wedged
amid
  A mint of money, it served for the
  nonce
To hold in its hair-heaps hid!

#### 21

Hid there? Why? Could the girl be wont
  (She the stainless soul) to treasure up
Money, earth's trash and heaven's
affront?
  Had a spider found out the
  communion-cup,
Was a toad in the christening-font?

#### 22

Truth is truth: too true it was.
  Gold! She hoarded and hugged it
  first,
Longed for it, leaned o'er it, loved it –
alas –
  Till the humour grew to a head and
  burst,
And she cried, at the final pass, –

#### 23

'Talk not of God, my heart is stone!
  'Nor lover nor friend – be gold for
  both!
'Gold I lack; and, my all, my own,
  'It shall hide in my hair. I scarce die
  loth
'If they let my hair alone!'

#### 24

Louis-d'or, some six times five,
  And duly double, every piece.
Now do you see? With the priest to
shrive,
  With parents preventing her soul's
  release
By kisses that kept alive, –

#### 25

With heaven's gold gates about to ope,
  With friends' praise, gold-like,
  lingering still,

An instinct had bidden the girl's hand
grope
  For gold, the true sort – 'Gold in
  heaven, if you will;
'But I keep earth's too, I hope.'

#### 26

Enough! The priest took the grave's
  grim yield:
  The parents, they eyed that price of
  sin
As if *thirty pieces* lay revealed
  On the place *to bury strangers in,*
The hideous Potter's Field.

#### 27

But the priest bethought him: ' "Milk
  that's spilt"
  ' – You know the adage! Watch and
  pray!
'Saints tumble to earth with so slight a
  tilt!
  'It would build a new altar; that, we
  may!'
And the altar therewith was built.

#### 28

Why I deliver this horrible verse?
  As the text of the sermon, which
  now I preach:
Evil or good may be better or worse
  In the human heart, but the mixture
  of each
Is a marvel and a curse.

#### 29

The candid incline to surmise of late
  That the Christian faith proves false,
  I find;
For our Essays-and-Reviews' debate
  Begins to tell on the public mind,
And Colenso's words have weight:

#### 30

I still, to suppose it true, for my part,
  See reasons and reasons; this, to
  begin:
'Tis the faith that launched point-blank
  her dart
  At the head of a lie – taught Original
  Sin,
The Corruption of Man's Heart.

## The Worst of It

### 1

Would it were I had been false, not you!
  I that am nothing, not you that are
    all:
I, never the worse for a touch or two
  On my speckled hide; not you, the
    pride
Of the day, my swan, that a first fleck's
    fall
  On her wonder of white must unswan,
    undo!

### 2

I had dipped in life's struggle and, out
    again,
  Bore specks of it here, there, easy to
    see,
When I found my swan and the cure
    was plain;
  The dull turned bright as I caught
    your white
On my bosom: you saved me – saved
    in vain
  If you ruined yourself, and all through
    me!

### 3

Yes, all through the speckled beast that
    I am,
  Who taught you to stoop; you gave
    me yourself,
And bound your soul by the vows that
    damn:
  Since on better thought you break,
    as you ought,
Vows – words, no angel set down,
    some elf
  Mistook, – for an oath, an epigram!

### 4

Yes, might I judge you, here were my
    heart,
  And a hundred its like, to treat as
    you pleased!
I choose to be yours, for my proper
    part,
  Yours, leave or take, or mar me or
    make;

If I acquiesce, why should you be
    teased
  With the conscience-prick and the
    memory-smart?

### 5

But what will God say? Oh, my sweet,
  Think, and be sorry you did this
    thing
Though earth were unworthy to feel
    your feet,
  There's a heaven above may deserve
    your love:
Should you forfeit heaven for a snapt
    gold ring
  And a promise broke, were it just or
    meet?

### 6

And I to have tempted you! I, who tired
  Your soul, no doubt, till it sank!
    Unwise,
I loved and was lowly, loved and
    aspired,
  Loved, grieving or glad, till I made
    you mad,
And you meant to have hated and
    despised –
  Whereas, you deceived me nor
    inquired!

### 7

She, ruined? How? No heaven for her?
  Crowns to give, and none for the
    brow
That looked like marble and smelt like
    myrrh?
  Shall the robe be worn, and the
    palm-branch borne,
And she go graceless, she graced now
  Beyond all saints, as themselves
    aver?

### 8

Hardly! That must be understood!
  The earth is your place of penance,
    then;
And what will it prove? I desire your
    good,
  But, plot as I may, I can find no way

How a blow should fall, such as falls on
men,
    Nor prove too much for your
    womanhood.

9

It will come, I suspect, at the end of
life,
    When you walk alone, and review
    the past;
And I, who so long shall have done
    with strife,
    And journeyed my stage and earned
    my wage
And retired as was right, – I am called
    at last
    When the devil stabs you, to lend the
    knife.

10

He stabs for the minute of trivial wrong,
    Nor the other hours are able to save,
The happy, that lasted my whole life
    long:
    For a promise broke, not for first
    words spoke,
The true, the only, that turn my grave
    To a blaze of joy and a crash of song.

11

Witness beforehand! Off I trip
    On a safe path gay through the flowers
    you flung:
My very name made great by your lip,
    And my heart a-glow with the good I
    know
Of a perfect year when we both were
    young,
    And I tasted the angels' fellowship.

12

And witness, moreover … Ah, but wait!
    I spy the loop whence an arrow shoots!
It may be for yourself, when you
    meditate,
    That you grieve – for slain ruth,
    murdered truth.
'Though falsehood escape in the end,
    what boots?
    'How truth would have triumphed!'
    – you sigh too late.

13

Ay, who would have triumphed like
    you, I say!
    Well, it is lost now; well, you must
    bear,
Abide and grow fit for a better day:
    You should hardly grudge, could I
    be your judge!
But hush! For you, can be no despair:
    There's amends: 'tis a secret: hope
    and pray!

14

For I was true at least – oh, true enough!
    And, Dear, truth is not as good as it
    seems!
Commend me to conscience! Idle stuff!
    Much help is in mine, as I mope and
    pine,
And skulk through day, and scowl in
    my dreams
    At my swan's obtaining the crow's
    rebuff.

15

Men tell me of truth now – 'False!' I
    cry:
    Of beauty – 'A mask, friend! Look
    beneath!'
We take our own method, the devil
    and I,
    With pleasant and fair and wise and
    rare:
And the best we wish to what lives, is –
    death;
    Which even in wishing, perhaps we
    lie!

16

Far better commit a fault and have
    done –
    As you, Dear! – for ever; and choose
    the pure,
And look where the healing waters run,
    And strive and strain to be good
    again,
And a place in the other world ensure,
    All glass and gold, with God for its
    sun.

17

Misery! What shall I say or do?
    I cannot advise, or, at least,
        persuade:
Most like, you are glad you deceived me
        – rue
    No whit of the wrong: you endured
        too long,
Have done no evil and want no aid,
    Will live the old life out and chance
        the new.

18

And your sentence is written all the
        same,
    And I can do nothing, – pray, perhaps:
But somehow the world pursues its
        game, –
    If I pray, if I curse, – for better or
        worse:
And my faith is torn to a thousand
        scraps,
    And my heart feels ice while my
        words breathe flame.

19

Dear, I look from my hiding-place.
    Are you still so fair? Have you still
        the eyes?
Be happy! Add but the other grace,
    Be good! Why want what the angels
        vaunt?
I knew you once: but in Paradise,
    If we meet, I will pass nor turn my
        face.

## Dîs Aliter Visum
### or, LE BYRON DE NOS JOURS

1

Stop, let me have the truth of that!
    Is that all true? I say, the day
Ten years ago when both of us
    Met on a morning, friends – as thus
We meet this evening, friends or what? –

2

Did you – because I took your arm
    And sillily smiled, 'A mass of brass
'That sea looks, blazing underneath!'
    While up the cliff-road edged with
        heath,
We took the turns nor came to harm –

3

Did you consider 'Now makes twice
    'That I have seen her, walked and
        talked
'With this poor pretty thoughtful thing,
    'Whose worth I weigh: she tries to
        sing;
'Draws, hopes in time the eye grows
        nice;

4

'Reads verse and thinks she understands;
    'Loves all, at any rate, that's great,
'Good, beautiful; but much as we
    'Down at the bath-house love the
        sea,
'Who breathe its salt and bruise its
        sands:

5

'While … do but follow the fishing-gull
    'That flaps and floats from wave to
        cave!
'There's the sea-lover, fair my friend!
    'What then? Be patient, mark and
        mend!
'Had you the making of your scull?'

6

And did you, when we faced the church
    With spire and sad slate roof, aloof
From human fellowship so far,
    Where a few graveyard crosses are,
And garlands for the swallows' perch, –

7

Did you determine, as we stepped
    O'er the lone stone fence, 'Let me get
'Her for myself, and what's the earth
    'With all its art, verse, music, worth –
'Compared with love, found, gained,
    and kept?

8

'Schumann's our music-maker now;
    'Has his march-movement youth
    and mouth?
'Ingres's the modern man that paints;
    'Which will lean on me, of his saints?
'Heine for songs; for kisses, how?'

9

And did you, when we entered, reached
    The votive frigate, soft aloft
Riding on air this hundred years,
    Safe-smiling at old hopes and fears, –
Did you draw profit while she preached?

10

Resolving, 'Fools we wise men grow!
    'Yes, I could easily blurt out curt
'Some question that might find reply
    'As prompt in her stopped lips,
        dropped eye,
'And rush of red to cheek and brow:

11

'Thus were a match made, sure and
    fast,
    ' 'Mid the blue weed-flowers round
        the mound
'Where, issuing, we shall stand and
    stay
    'For one more look at baths and bay,
'Sands, sea-gulls, and the old church
    last –

12

'A match 'twixt me, bent, wigged and
    lamed,
    'Famous, however, for verse and
        worse,
'Sure of the Fortieth spare Arm-chair
    'When gout and glory seat me there,
'So, one whose love-freaks pass
    unblamed, –

13

'And this young beauty, round and
    sound
    'As a mountain-apple, youth and
        truth
'With loves and doves, at all events
    'With money in the Three per Cents;
'Whose choice of me would seem
    profound: –

14

'She might take me as I take her.
    'Perfect the hour would pass, alas!
'Climb high, love high, what matter?
    Still,
    'Feet, feelings, must descend the hill:
'An hour's perfection can't recur.

15

'Then follows Paris and full time
    'For both to reason: "Thus with us!"
'She'll sigh, "Thus girls give body and
    soul
    ' "At first word, think they gain the
        goal,
    ' "When 'tis the starting-place they
        climb!

16

    ' "My friend makes verse and gets
        renown;
        ' "Have they all fifty years, his peers?
    ' "He knows the world, firm, quiet and
        gay;
        ' "Boys will become as much one
            day:
    ' "They're fools; he cheats, with beard
        less brown.

17

    ' "For boys say, *Love me or I die!*
        ' "He did not say, *The truth is, youth*
    ' "*I want, who am old and know too
        much;*
        ' "*I'd catch youth: lend me sight and
            touch!*
    ' "*Drop heart's blood where life's wheels
        grate dry!*"

18

'While I should make rejoinder' – (then
  It was, no doubt, you ceased that least
Light pressure of my arm in yours)
  ' "I can conceive of cheaper cures
  ' "For a yawning-fit o'er books and men.

19

' "What? All I am, was, and might be,
  ' "All, books taught, art brought,
    life's whole strife,
' "Painful results since precious, just
  ' "Were fitly exchanged, in wise
    disgust,
' "For two cheeks freshened by youth
    and sea?

20

' "All for a nosegay! – what came first;
  ' "With fields on flower, untried each
    side;
' "I rally, need my books and men,
  ' "And find a nosegay": drop it, then,
'No match yet made for best or worst!'

21

That ended me. You judged the porch
  We left by, Norman; took our look
At sea and sky; wondered so few
  Find out the place for air and view;
Remarked the sun began to scorch;

22

Descended, soon regained the baths,
  And then, good-bye! Years ten since
    then:
Ten years! We meet: you tell me, now,
  By a window-seat for that cliff-brow,
On carpet-stripes for those sand-paths.

23

Now I may speak: you fool, for all
  Your lore! Who made things plain in
    vain?
What was the sea for? What, the grey
  Sad church, that solitary day,
Crosses and graves and swallows' call?

24

Was there nought better than to enjoy?
  No feat which, done, would make
    time break,

And let us pent-up creatures through
  Into eternity, our due?
No forcing earth teach heaven's employ?

25

No wise beginning, here and now,
  What cannot grow complete (earth's
    feat)
And heaven must finish, there and then?
  No tasting earth's true food for men,
Its sweet in sad, its sad in sweet?

26

No grasping at love, gaining a share
  O' the sole spark from God's life at
    strife
With death, so, sure of range above
  The limits here? For us and love,
Failure; but, when God fails, despair.

27

This you call wisdom? Thus you add
  Good unto good again, in vain?
You loved, with body worn and weak;
  I loved, with faculties to seek:
Were both loves worthless since ill-clad?

28

Let the mere star-fish in his vault
  Crawl in a wash of weed, indeed,
Rose-jacynth to the finger-tips:
  He, whole in body and soul,
    outstrips
Man, found with either in default.

29

But what's whole, can increase no more,
  Is dwarfed and dies, since here's its
    sphere.
The devil laughed at you in his sleeve!
  You knew not? That I well believe;
Or you had saved two souls: nay, four.

30

For Stephanie sprained last night her
    wrist,
  Ankle or something. 'Pooh,' cry you?
At any rate she danced, all say,
  Vilely; her vogue has had its day.
Here comes my husband from his
    whist.

## Too Late

### 1

Here was I with my arm and heart
    And brain, all yours for a word, a
        want
Put into a look – just a look, your part, –
    While mine, to repay it … vainest
        vaunt,
Were the woman, that's dead, alive to
    hear,
    Had her lover, that's lost, love's proof
    to show!
But I cannot show it; you cannot speak
    From the churchyard neither, miles
    removed,
Though I feel by a pulse within my
    cheek,
    Which stabs and stops, that the
    woman I loved
Needs help in her grave and finds none
    near,
    Wants warmth from the heart which
    sends it – so!

### 2

Did I speak once angrily, all the drear
    days
    You lived, you woman I loved so well,
Who married the other? Blame or praise,
    Where was the use then? Time would
    tell,
And the end declare what man for you,
    What woman for me, was the choice
    of God.
But, Edith dead! no doubting more!
    I used to sit and look at my life
As it rippled and ran till, right before,
    A great stone stopped it: oh, the strife
Of waves at the stone some devil threw
    In my life's midcurrent, thwarting
    God!

### 3

But either I thought, 'They may churn
    and chide
    'Awhile, my waves which came for
    their joy
'And found this horrible stone full-tide:

'Yet I see just a thread escape, deploy
'Through the evening-country, silent
    and safe,
    'And it suffers no more till it finds
    the sea.'
Or else I would think, 'Perhaps some
    night
    'When new things happen, a meteor-
    ball
'May slip through the sky in a line of
    light,
    'And earth breathe hard, and land-
    marks fall,
'And my waves no longer champ nor
    chafe,
    'Since a stone will have rolled from
    its place: let be!'

### 4

But, dead! All's done with: wait who
    may,
    Watch and wear and wonder who
    will.
Oh, my whole life that ends to-day!
    Oh, my soul's sentence, sounding
    still,
'The woman is dead that was none of
    his;
    'And the man that was none of hers
    may go!'
There's only the past left: worry that!
    Wreak, like a bull, on the empty coat,
Rage, its late wearer is laughing at!
    Tear the collar to rags, having
    missed his throat;
Strike stupidly on – 'This, this and this,
    'Where I would that a bosom
    received the blow!'

### 5

I ought to have done more: once my
    speech,
    And once your answer, and there,
    the end,
And Edith was henceforth out of reach!
    Why, men do more to deserve a friend,
Be rid of a foe, get rich, grow wise,
    Nor, folding their arms, stare fate in
    the face.

Why, better even have burst like a thief
    And borne you away to a rock for us
        two,
In a moment's horror, bright, bloody
    and brief:
    Then changed to myself again – 'I
        slew
'Myself in that moment; a ruffian lies
    'Somewhere: your slave, see, born in
        his place!'

6

What did the other do? You be judge!
    Look at us, Edith! Here are we both!
Give him his six whole years: I grudge
    None of the life with you, nay, loathe
Myself that I grudged his start in advance
    Of me who could overtake and pass.
But, as if he loved you! No, not he,
    Nor anyone else in the world, 'tis
        plain:
Who ever heard that another, free
    As I, young, prosperous, sound and
        sane,
Poured life out, proffered it – 'Half a
        glance
    'Of those eyes of yours and I drop the
        glass!'

7

Handsome, were you? 'Tis more than
    they held,
    More than they said; I was 'ware and
        watched:
I was the 'scapegrace, this rat belled
    The cat, this fool got his whiskers
        scratched:
The others? No head that was turned,
    no heart
    Broken, my lady, assure yourself!
Each soon made his mind up; so and so
    Married a dancer, such and such
Stole his friend's wife, stagnated slow,
    Or maundered, unable to do as much,
And muttered of peace where he had
    no part:
    While, hid in the closet, laid on the
        shelf, –

8

On the whole, you were let alone, I
    think!
    So, you looked to the other, who
        acquiesced;
My rival, the proud man, – prize your
    pink
    Of poets! A poet he was! I've
        guessed:
He rhymed you his rubbish nobody
    read,
    Loved you and doved you – did not
        I laugh!
There was a prize! But we both were
    tried.
    Oh, heart of mine, marked broad
        with her mark,
*Tekel*, found wanting, set aside,
    Scorned! See, I bleed these tears in
        the dark
Till comfort come and the last be bled:
    He? He is tagging your epitaph.

9

If it would only come over again!
    – Time to be patient with me, and
        probe
This heart till you punctured the
    proper vein,
    Just to learn what blood is: twitch
        the robe
From that blank lay-figure your fancy
    draped,
    Prick the leathern heart till the –
        verses spirt!
And late it was easy; late, you walked
    Where a friend might meet you;
        Edith's name
Arose to one's lip if one laughed or
    talked;
    If I heard good news, you heard the
        same;
When I woke, I knew that your breath
    escaped;
    I could bide my time, keep alive,
        alert.

### 10

And alive I shall keep and long, you
    will see!
  I knew a man, was kicked like a dog
From gutter to cesspool; what cared he
    So long as he picked from the filth
    his prog?
He saw youth, beauty and genius die,
    And jollily lived to his hundredth
    year.
But I will live otherwise: none of such
    life!
  At once I begin as I mean to end.
Go on with the world, get hold in its
    strife,
  Give your spouse the slip and betray
    your friend!
There are two who decline, a woman
    and I,
  And enjoy our death in the darkness
    here.

### 11

I liked that way you had with your
    curls
  Wound to a ball in a net behind:
Your cheek was chaste as a quaker-girl's,
  And your mouth – there was never,
    to my mind,
Such a funny mouth, for it would not
    shut;
  And the dented chin too – what a
    chin!
There were certain ways when you
    spoke, some words
  That you know you never could
    pronounce:
You were thin, however; like a bird's
  Your hand seemed – some would
    say, the pounce
Of a scaly-footed hawk – all but!
  The world was right when it called
    you thin.

### 12

But I turn my back on the world: I take
  Your hand, and kneel, and lay to my
    lips.
Bid me live, Edith! Let me slake

Thirst at your presence! Fear no slips:
  'Tis your slave shall pay, while his soul
    endures,
  Full due, love's whole debt, *summum
    jus.*
My queen shall have high observance,
    planned
  Courtship made perfect, no least
    line
Crossed without warrant. There you
    stand,
  Warm too, and white too: would
    this wine
Had washed all over that body of yours,
  Ere I drank it, and you down with it,
    thus!

## Abt Vogler

(After he has been extemporizing upon the
musical instrument of his invention.)

### 1

Would that the structure brave, the
    manifold music I build,
  Bidding my organ obey, calling its
    keys to their work,
Claiming each slave of the sound, at a
    touch, as when Solomon willed
  Armies of angels that soar, legions of
    demons that lurk,
Man, brute, reptile, fly, – alien of end
    and of aim,
  Adverse, each from the other
    heaven-high, hell-deep removed, –
Should rush into sight at once as he
    named the ineffable Name,
And pile him a palace straight, to
    pleasure the princess he loved!

### 2

Would it might tarry like his, the
    beautiful building of mine,
  This which my keys in a crowd
    pressed and importuned to raise,
Ah, one and all, how they helped, would
    dispart now and now combine.
  Zealous to hasten the work,
    heighten their master his praise!

And one would bury his brow with a
    blind plunge down to hell,
  Burrow awhile and build, broad on
    the root of things,
Then up again swim into sight, having
    based me my palace well,
  Founded it, fearless of flame, flat on
    the nether springs.

3

And another would mount and march,
    like the excellent minion he was,
  Ay, another and yet another, one
    crowd but with many a crest,
Raising my rampired walls of gold as
    transparent as glass,
  Eager to do and die, yield each his
    place to the rest:
For higher still and higher (as a runner
    tips with fire,
  When a great illumination surprises
    a festal night –
Outlining round and round Rome's
    dome from space to spire)
Up, the pinnacled glory reached, and
    the pride of my soul was in sight.

4

In sight? Not half! for it seemed, it was
    certain, to match man's birth,
  Nature in turn conceived, obeying
    an impulse as I;
And the emulous heaven yearned down,
    made effort to reach the earth,
  As the earth had done her best, in
    my passion, to scale the sky:
Novel splendours burst forth, grew
    familiar and dwelt with mine,
  Not a point nor peak but found and
    fixed its wandering star;
Meteor-moons, balls of blaze: and they
    did not pale nor pine,
  For earth had attained to heaven,
    there was no more near nor far.

5

Nay more; for there wanted not who
    walked in the glare and glow,
  Presences plain in the place; or,
    fresh from the Protoplast,

Furnished for ages to come, when a
    kindlier wind should blow.
  Lured now to begin and live, in a
    house to then- liking at last;
Or else the wonderful Dead who have
    passed through the body and gone,
  But were back once more to breathe
    in an old world worth their new:
What never had been, was now; what
    was, as it shall be anon;
  And what is, – shall I say, matched
    both? for I was made perfect too.

6

All through my keys that gave their
    sounds to a wish of my soul,
All through my soul that praised as
    its wish flowed visibly forth,
All through music and me! For think,
    had I painted the whole,
  Why, there it had stood, to see, nor
    the process so wonder-worth:
Had I written the same, made verse –
    still, effect proceeds from cause,
  Ye know why the forms are fair, ye
    hear how the tale is told;
It is all triumphant art, but art in
    obedience to laws,
Painter and poet are proud in the
    artist-list enrolled: –

7

But here is the finger of God, a flash of
    the will that can,
  Existent behind all laws, that made
    them and, lo, they are!
And I know not if, save in this, such
    gift be allowed to man,
  That out of three sounds he frame,
    not a fourth sound, but a star.
Consider it well: each tone of our scale
    in itself is nought;
  It is everywhere in the world – loud,
    soft, and all is said:
Give it to me to use! I mix it with two
    in my thought:
  And, there! Ye have heard and seen:
    consider and bow the head!

8

Well, it is gone at last, the palace of
    music I reared;
  Gone! and the good tears start, the
    praises that come too slow;
For one is assured at first, one scarce
    can say that he feared,
  That he even gave it a thought, the
    gone thing was to go
Never to be again! But many more of
    the kind
  As good, nay, better perchance: is
    this your comfort to me?
To me, who must be saved because I
    cling with my mind
To the same, same self, same love,
    same God: ay, what was, shall be.

9

Therefore to whom turn I but to thee,
    the ineffable Name?
  Builder and maker, thou, of houses
    not made with hands!
What, have fear of change from thee
    who art ever the same?
  Doubt that thy power can fill the
    heart that thy power expands?
There shall never be one lost good!
    What was, shall live as before;
  The evil is null, is nought, is silence
    implying sound;
What was good shall be good, with, for
    evil, so much good more;
  On the earth the broken arcs; in the
    heaven, a perfect round.

10

All we have willed or hoped or
    dreamed of good shall exist;
  Not its semblance, but itself; no
    beauty, nor good, nor power
Whose voice has gone forth, but each
    survives for the melodist
  When eternity affirms the
    conception of an hour.
The high that proved too high, the
    heroic for earth too hard,
  The passion that left the ground to
    lose itself in the sky,

Are music sent up to God by the lover
    and the bard;
  Enough that he heard it once: we
    shall hear it by-and-by.

11

And what is our failure here but a
    triumph's evidence
  For the fulness of the days? Have we
    withered or agonized?
Why else was the pause prolonged but
    that singing might issue thence?
  Why rushed the discords in but that
    harmony should be prized?
Sorrow is hard to bear, and doubt is
    slow to clear,
  Each sufferer says his say, his
    scheme of the weal and woe:
But God has a few of us whom he
    whispers in the ear;
  The rest may reason and welcome:
    'tis we musicians know.

12

Well, it is earth with me; silence
    resumes her reign:
  I will be patient and proud, and
    soberly acquiesce.
Give me the keys. I feel for the
    common chord again,
  Sliding by semitones, till I sink to
    the minor, – yes,
And I blunt it into a ninth, and I stand
    on alien ground,
  Surveying awhile the heights I rolled
    from into the deep;
Which, hark, I have dared and done,
    for my resting-place is found,
The C Major of this life: so, now I will
    try to sleep.

## Rabbi Ben Ezra

### 1

Grow old along with me!
The best is yet to be,
The last of life, for which the first was
made:
Our times are in His hand
Who saith 'A whole I planned,
'Youth shows but half; trust God: see
all nor be afraid!'

### 2

Not that, amassing flowers,
Youth sighed 'Which rose make
ours,
'Which lily leave and then as best recall?'
Not that, admiring stars,
It yearned 'Nor Jove, nor Mars;
'Mine be some figured flame which
blends, transcends them all!'

### 3

Not for such hopes and fears
Annulling youth's brief years,
Do I remonstrate: folly wide the mark!
Rather I prize the doubt
Low kinds exist without,
Finished and finite clods, untroubled
by a spark.

### 4

Poor vaunt of life indeed,
Were man but formed to feed
On joy, to solely seek and find and
feast:
Such feasting ended, then
As sure an end to men;
Irks care the crop-full bird? Frets doubt
the maw-crammed beast?

### 5

Rejoice we are allied
To That which doth provide
And not partake, effect and not receive!
A spark disturbs our clod;
Nearer we hold of God
Who gives, than of His tribes that take,
I must believe.

### 6

Then, welcome each rebuff
That turns earth's smoothness
rough,
Each sting that bids nor sit nor stand
but go!
Be our joys three-parts pain!
Strive, and hold cheap the strain;
I earn, nor account the pang; dare,
never grudge the throe!

### 7

For thence, – a paradox
Which comforts while it mocks, –
Shall life succeed in that it seems to fail:
What I aspired to be,
And was not, comforts me:
A brute I might have been, but would
not sink i' the scale.

### 8

What is he but a brute
Whose flesh has soul to suit,
Whose spirit works lest arms and legs
want play?
To man, propose this test –
Thy body at its best,
How far can that project thy soul on its
lone way?

### 9

Yet gifts should prove their use:
I own the Past profuse
Of power each side, perfection every
turn:
Eyes, ears took in their dole,
Brain treasured up the whole;
Should not the heart beat once 'How
good to live and learn?'

### 10

Not once beat 'Praise be Thine!
'I see the whole design,
'I, who saw power, see now love
perfect too:
'Perfect I call Thy plan:
'Thanks that I was a man!
'Maker, remake, complete, – I trust
what Thou shalt do!'

### 11

For pleasant is this flesh;
  Our soul, in its rose-mesh
Pulled ever to the earth, still yearns for
    rest:
  Would we some prize might hold
  To match those manifold
Possessions of the brute, – gain most,
    as we did best!

### 12

  Let us not always say
  'Spite of this flesh to-day
'I strove, made head, gained ground
    upon the whole!'
  As the bird wings and sings,
  Let us cry 'All good things
Are ours, nor soul helps flesh more,
    now, than flesh helps soul!'

### 13

  Therefore I summon age
  To grant youth's heritage,
Life's struggle having so far reached its
    term:
  Thence shall I pass, approved
  A man, for aye removed
From the developed brute; a god
    though in the germ.

### 14

  And I shall thereupon
  Take rest, ere I be gone
Once more on my adventure brave and
    new:
  Fearless and unperplexed,
  When I wage battle next,
What weapons to select, what armour
    to indue.

### 15

  Youth ended, I shall try
  My gain or loss thereby;
Leave the fire ashes, what survives is
    gold:
  And I shall weigh the same,
  Give life its praise or blame:
Young, all lay in dispute; I shall know,
    being old.

### 16

  For note, when evening shuts,
  A certain moment cuts
The deed off, calls the glory from the
    grey:
  A whisper from the west
  Shoots – 'Add this to the rest,
'Take it and try its worth: here dies
    another day.'

### 17

  So, still within this life,
  Though lifted o'er its strife,
Let me discern, compare, pronounce at
    last,
  'This rage was right i' the main,
  'That acquiescence vain:
'The Future I may face now I have
    proved the Past.'

### 18

  For more is not reserved
  To man, with soul just nerved
To act to-morrow what he learns to-day:
  Here, work enough to watch
  The Master work, and catch
Hints of the proper craft, tricks of the
    tool's true play.

### 19

  As it was better, youth
  Should strive, through acts uncouth,
Toward making, than repose on aught
    found made:
  So, better, age, exempt
  From strife, should know, than
    tempt
Further. Thou waitedest age: wait
    death nor be afraid!

### 20

  Enough now, if the Right
  And Good and Infinite
Be named here, as thou callest thy
    hand thine own,
  With knowledge absolute,
  Subject to no dispute
From fools that crowded youth, nor let
    thee feel alone.

### 21

Be there, for once and all,
Severed great minds from small,
Announced to each his station in the
Past!
Was I, the world arraigned,
Were they, my soul disdained,
Right? Let age speak the truth and give
us peace at last!

### 22

Now, who shall arbitrate?
Ten men love what I hate,
Shun what I follow, slight what I receive;
Ten, who in ears and eyes
Match me: we all surmise,
They this thing, and I that: whom shall
my soul believe?

### 23

Not on the vulgar mass
Called 'work,' must sentence pass,
Things done, that took the eye and had
the price;
O'er which, from level stand,
The low world laid its hand,
Found straightway to its mind, could
value in a trice:

### 24

But all, the world's coarse thumb
And finger failed to plumb,
So passed in making up the main
account;
All instincts immature,
All purposes unsure,
That weighed not as his work, yet
swelled the man's amount:

### 25

Thoughts hardly to be packed
Into a narrow act,
Fancies that broke through language
and escaped;
All I could never be,
All, men ignored in me,
This, I was worth to God, whose wheel
the pitcher shaped.

### 26

Ay, note that Potter's wheel,
That metaphor! and feel
Why time spins fast, why passive lies
our clay, –
Thou, to whom fools propound,
When the wine makes its round,
Since life fleets, all is change; the Past
gone, seize to-day!'

### 27

Fool! All that is, at all,
Lasts ever, past recall;
Earth changes, but thy soul and God
stand sure:
What entered into thee,
*That* was, is, and shall be:
Time's wheel runs back or stops:
Potter and clay endure.

### 28

He fixed thee mid this dance
Of plastic circumstance,
This Present, thou, forsooth, wouldst
fain arrest:
Machinery just meant
To give thy soul its bent,
Try thee and turn thee forth,
sufficiently impressed.

### 29

What though the earlier grooves
Which ran the laughing loves
Around thy base, no longer pause and
press?
What though, about thy rim,
Skull-things in order grim
Grow out, in graver mood, obey the
sterner stress?

### 30

Look not thou down but up!
To uses of a cup,
The festal board, lamp's flash and
trumpet's peal,
The new wine's foaming flow,
The Master's lips a-glow!
Thou, heaven's consummate cup, what
need'st thou with earth's wheel?

### 31

But I need, now as then,
Thee, God, who mouldest men;
And since, not even while the whirl
    was worst.
Did I, – to the wheel of life
With shapes and colours rife,
Bound dizzily, – mistake my end, to
    slake Thy thirst:

### 32

So, take and use Thy work:
Amend what flaws may lurk,
What strain o' the stuff, what warpings
    past the aim!
My times be in Thy hand!
Perfect the cup as planned!
Let age approve of youth, and death
    complete the same!ss

## A Death in the Desert

[Supposed of Pamphylax the Antiochene:
It is a parchment, of my rolls the fifth,
Hath three skins glued together, is all
    Greek
And goeth from *Epsilon* down to *Mu*:
Lies second in the surnamed Chosen
    Chest,
Stained and conserved with juice of
    tere-binth,
Covered with cloth of hair, and lettered
    *Xi*,
From Xanthus, my wife's uncle, now at
    peace:
*Mu* and *Epsilon* stand for my own name.
I may not write it, but I make a cross
To show I wait His coming, with the
    rest,
And leave off here: beginneth
    Pamphylax.]

I said, 'If one should wet his lips with
    wine,
'And slip the broadest plantain-leaf we
    find,
'Or else the lappet of a linen robe,
'Into the water-vessel, lay it right,

'And cool his forehead just above the
    eyes,
'The while a brother, kneeling either
    side,
'Should chafe each hand and try to
    make it warm, –
'He is not so far gone but he might
    speak.'

This did not happen in the outer cave,
Nor in the secret chamber of the rock
Where, sixty days since the decree was
    out,
We had him, bedded on a camel-skin,
And waited for his dying all the while;
But in the midmost grotto: since
    noon's light
Reached there a little, and we would
    not lose
The last of what might happen on his
    face.

I at the head, and Xanthus at the feet,
With Valens and the Boy, had lifted
    him,
And brought him from the chamber in
    the depths,
And laid him in the light where we
    might see:
For certain smiles began about his
    mouth,
And his lids moved, presageful of the
    end.

Beyond and half way up the mouth o'
    the cave,
The Bactrian convert, having his desire,
Kept watch, and made pretence to
    graze a goat
That gave us milk, on rags of various
    herb,
Plantain and quitch, the rocks' shade
    keeps alive:
So that if any thief or soldier passed,
(Because the persecution was aware)
Yielding the goat up promptly with his
    life,

Such man might pass on, joyful at a
　　prize,
Nor care to pry into the cool o' the cave.
Outside was all noon and the burning
　　blue.

'Here is wine,' answered Xanthus, –
　　dropped a drop;
I stooped and placed the lap of cloth
　　aright,
Then chafed his right hand, and the
　　Boy his left:
But Valens had bethought him, and
　　produced
And broke a ball of nard, and made
　　perfume.
Only, he did – not so much wake, as –
　　turn
And smile a little, as a sleeper does
If any dear one call him, touch his face –
And smiles and loves, but will not be
　　disturbed.

Then Xanthus said a prayer, but still he
　　slept:
It is the Xanthus that escaped to Rome,
Was burned, and could not write the
　　chronicle.

Then the Boy sprang up from his knees,
　　and ran,
Stung by the splendour of a sudden
　　thought,
And fetched the seventh plate of graven
　　lead
Out of the secret chamber, found a
　　place,
Pressing with finger on the deeper dints,
And spoke, as 'twere his mouth
　　proclaiming first,
'I am the Resurrection and the Life.'

Whereat he opened his eyes wide at
　　once,
And sat up of himself, and looked at us;
And thenceforth nobody pronounced a
　　word:

Only, outside, the Bactrian cried his cry
Like the lone desert-bird that wears the
　　ruff,
As signal we were safe, from time to
　　time.

First he said, 'If a friend declared to me,
'This my son Valens, this my other son,
'Were James and Peter, – nay, declared
　　as well
'This lad was very John, – I could believe!
' – Could, for a moment, doubtlessly
　　believe:
'So is myself withdrawn into my
　　depths,
'The soul retreated from the perished
　　brain
'Whence it was wont to feel and use
　　the world
'Through these dull members, done
　　with long ago.
'Yet I myself remain; I feel myself:
'And there is nothing lost. Let be,
　　awhile!'

[This is the doctrine he was wont to
　　teach,
How divers persons witness in each
　　man,
Three souls which make up one soul:
　　first, to wit,
A soul of each and all the bodily parts,
Seated therein, which works, and is
　　what Does,
And has the use of earth, and ends the
　　man
Downward: but, tending upward for
　　advice,
Grows into, and again is grown into
By the next soul, which, seated in the
　　brain,
Useth the first with its collected use,
And feeleth, thinketh, willeth, – is what
　　Knows:
Which, duly tending upward in its turn,
Grows into, and again is grown into
By the last soul, that uses both the first,

Subsisting whether they assist or no,
And, constituting man's self, is what
　　Is –
And leans upon the former, makes it
　　play,
As that played off the first: and, tending
　　up,
Holds, is upheld by, God, and ends the
　　man
Upward in that dread point of inter-
　　course,
Nor needs a place, for it returns to Him.
What Does, what Knows, what Is;
　　three souls, one man.
I give the glossa of Theotypas.]

And then, 'A stick, once fire from end
　　to end;
'Now, ashes save the tip that holds a
　　spark!
'Yet, blow the spark, it runs back,
　　spreads itself
'A little where the fire was: thus I urge
'The soul that served me, till it task
　　once more
'What ashes of my brain have kept
　　their shape,
'And these make effort on the last o'
　　the flesh,
'Trying to taste again the truth of
　　things – '
(He smiled) – 'their very superficial truth;
'As that ye are my sons, that it is long
'Since James and Peter had release by
　　death,
'And I am only he, your brother John,
'Who saw and heard, and could
　　remember all.
'Remember all! It is not much to say.
'What if the truth broke on me from
　　above
'As once and oft-times? Such might hap
　　again:
'Doubtlessly He might stand in presence
　　here,
'With head wool-white, eyes flame, and
　　feet like brass,

'The sword and the seven stars, as I
　　have seen –
'I who now shudder only and surmise
' "How did your brother bear that sight
　　and live?"

'If I live yet, it is for good, more love
'Through me to men: be nought but
　　ashes here
'That keep awhile my semblance, who
　　was John, –
'Still, when they scatter, there is left on
　　earth
'No one alive who knew (consider this!)
' – Saw with his eyes and handled with
　　his hands
'That which was from the first, the
　　Word of Life.
'How will it be when none more saith
　　"I saw"?

'Such ever was love's way: to rise, it
　　stoops.
'Since I, whom Christ's mouth taught,
　　was bidden teach,
'I went, for many years, about the world,
'Saying "It was so; so I heard and saw,"
'Speaking as the case asked: and men
　　believed.
'Afterward came the message to myself
'In Patmos isle; I was not bidden teach,
'But simply listen, take a book and write,
'Nor set down other than the given
　　word,
'With nothing left to my arbitrament
'To choose or change: I wrote, and
　　men believed.
'Then, for my time grew brief, no
　　message more,
'No call to write again, I found a way,
'And, reasoning from my knowledge,
　　merely taught
'Men should, for love's sake, in love's
　　strength believe;
'Or I would pen a letter to a friend
'And urge the same as friend, nor less
　　nor more:

'Friends said I reasoned rightly, and
		believed.
'But at the last, why, I seemed left alive
'Like a sea-jelly weak on Patmos strand,
'To tell dry sea-beach gazers how I fared
'When there was mid-sea, and the mighty
		things;
'Left to repeat, "I saw, I heard, I knew,"
'And go all over the old ground again,
'With Antichrist already in the world,
'And many Antichrists, who answered
		prompt
'  "Am I not Jasper as thyself art John?
'  "Nay, young, whereas through age
		thou mayest forget;
'  "Wherefore, explain, or how shall we
		believe?"
'I never thought to call down fire on
		such,
'Or, as in wonderful and early days,
'Pick up the scorpion, tread the
		serpent dumb;
'But patient stated much of the Lord's
		life
'Forgotten or misdelivered, and let it
		work:
'Since much that at the first, in deed
		and word,
'Lay simply and sufficiently exposed,
'Had grown (or else my soul was
		grown to match,
'Fed through such years, familiar with
		such light,
'Guarded and guided still to see and
		speak)
'Of new significance and fresh result;
'What first were guessed as points, I
		now knew stars,
'And named them in the Gospel I have
		writ.
'For men said, "It is getting long ago:
'  "Where is the promise of His coming?"
		– asked
'These young ones in their strength, as
		loth to wait,
'Of me who, when their sires were
		born, was old.

'I, for I loved them, answered, joyfully,
'Since I was there, and helpful in my age;
'And, in the main, I think such men
		believed.
'Finally, thus endeavouring, I fell sick,
'Ye brought me here, and I supposed
		the end,
'And went to sleep with one thought
		that, at least,
'Though the whole earth should lie in
		wickedness,
'We had the truth, might leave the rest
		to God.
'Yet now I wake in such decrepitude
'As I had slidden down and fallen afar,
'Past even the presence of my former
		self,
'Grasping the while for stay at facts
		which snap,
'Till I am found away from my own
		world,
'Feeling for foot-hold through a blank
		profound,
'Along with unborn people in strange
		lands,
'Who say – I hear said or conceive they
		say –
'  "Was John at all, and did he say he
		saw?
'  "Assure us, ere we ask what he might
		see!"

'And how shall I assure them? Can they
		share
'  – They, who have flesh, a veil of
		youth and strength
'About each spirit, that needs must
		bide its time,
'Living and learning still as years assist
'Which wear the thickness thin, and let
		man see –
'With me who hardly am withheld at all,
'But shudderingly, scarce a shred between,
'Lie bare to the universal prick of light?
'Is it for nothing we grow old and weak,
'We whom God loves? When pain ends,
		gain ends too.

'To me, that story – ay, that Life and
    Death
'Of which I wrote "it was" – to me, it is;
' – Is, here and now: I apprehend
    nought else.
'Is not God now i' the world His power
    first made?
'Is not His love at issue still with sin,
'Visibly when a wrong is done on earth?
'Love, wrong, and pain, what see I else
    around?
'Yea, and the Resurrection and Uprise
'To the right hand of the throne – what
    is it beside,
'When such truth, breaking bounds,
    o'er-floods my soul,
'And, as I saw the sin and death, even so
'See I the need yet transiency of both,
'The good and glory consummated
    thence?
'I saw the power; I see the Love, once
    weak,
'Resume the Power: and in this word "I
    see,"
'Lo, there is recognized the Spirit of both
'That moving o'er the spirit of man,
    un-blinds
'His eye and bids him look. These are,
    I see;
'But ye, the children, His beloved ones
    too,
'Ye need, – as I should use an optic glass
'I wondered at erewhile, somewhere i'
    the world,
'It had been given a crafty smith to
    make;
'A tube, he turned on objects brought
    too close,
'Lying confusedly insubordinate
'For the unassisted eye to master once:
'Look through his tube, at distance
    now they lay,
'Become succinct, distinct, so small, so
    clear!
'Just thus, ye needs must apprehend
    what truth
'I see, reduced to plain historic fact,

'Diminished into clearness, proved a
    point
'And far away: ye would withdraw your
    sense
'From out eternity, strain it upon time,
'Then stand before that fact, that Life
    and Death,
'Stay there at gaze, till it dispart, dispread,
'As though a star should open out, all
    sides,
'Grow the world on you, as it is my
    world.

'For life, with all it yields of joy and woe,
'And hope and fear, – believe the aged
    friend, –
'Is just our chance o' the prize of
    learning love,
'How love might be, hath been indeed,
    and is;
'And that we hold thenceforth to the
    uttermost
'Such prize despite the envy of the
    world,
'And, having gained truth, keep truth:
    that is all.
'But see the double way wherein we
    are led,
'How the soul learns diversely from the
    flesh!
'With flesh, that hath so little time to
    stay,
'And yields mere basement for the
    soul's emprise,
'Expect prompt teaching. Helpful was
    the light,
'And warmth was cherishing and food
    was choice
'To every man's flesh, thousand years
    ago,
'As now to yours and mine; the body
    sprang
'At once to the height, and stayed: but
    the soul, – no!
'Since sages who, this noontide, meditate
'In Rome or Athens, may descry some
    point

'Of the eternal power, hid yestereve;
'And, as thereby the power's whole
    mass extends,
'So much extends the æther floating
    o'er,
'The love that tops the might, the Christ
    in God.
'Then, as new lessons shall be learned
    in these
'Till earth's work stop and useless time
    run out,
'So duly, daily, needs provision be
'For keeping the soul's prowess possible,
'Building new barriers as the old decay,
'Saving us from evasion of life's proof,
'Putting the question ever, "Does God
    love,
' "And will ye hold that truth against
    the world?"
'Ye know there needs no second proof
    with good
'Gained for our flesh from any earthly
    source:
'We might go freezing, ages, – give us
    fire,
'Thereafter we judge fire at its full
    worth,
'And guard it safe through every
    chance, ye know!
'That fable of Prometheus and his theft,
'How mortals gained Jove's fiery
    flower, grows old
'(I have been used to hear the pagans
    own)
'And out of mind; but fire, howe'er its
    birth,
'Here is it, precious to the sophist now
'Who laughs the myth of Æschylus to
    scorn,
'As precious to those satyrs of his play,
'Who touched it in gay wonder at the
    thing.
'While were it so with the soul, – this
    gift of truth
'Once grasped, were this our soul's
    gain safe, and sure
'To prosper as the body's gain is wont, –

'Why, man's probation would
    conclude, his earth
'Crumble; for he both reasons and
    decides,
'Weighs first, then chooses: will he give
    up fire
'For gold or purple once he knows its
    worth?
'Could he give Christ up were His
    worth as plain?
'Therefore, I say, to test man, the
    proofs shift,
'Nor may he grasp that fact like other
    fact,
'And straightway in his life acknowledge
    it,
'As, say, the indubitable bliss of fire.
'Sigh ye, "It had been easier once than
    now"?
'To give you answer I am left alive;
'Look at me who was present from the
    first!
'Ye know what things I saw; then came
    a test,
'My first, befitting me who so had seen:
' "Forsake the Christ thou sawest
    transfigured, Him
' "Who trod the sea and brought the
    dead to life?
' "What should wring this from thee!"
    – ye laugh and ask.
'What wrung it? Even a torchlight and
    a noise,
'The sudden Roman faces, violent hands,
'And fear of what the Jews might do!
    Just that,
'And it is written, "I forsook and fled":
'There was my trial, and it ended thus.
'Ay, but my soul had gained its truth,
    could grow:
'Another year or two, – what little child,
'What tender woman that had seen no
    least
'Of all my sights, but barely heard them
    told,
'Who did not clasp the cross with a
    light laugh,

'Or wrap the burning robe round,
        thanking God?
'Well, was truth safe for ever, then?
        Not so.
'Already had begun the silent work
'Whereby truth, deadened of its
        absolute blaze,
'Might need love's eye to pierce the
        o'er-stretched doubt.
'Teachers were busy, whispering "All is
        true
' "As the aged ones report; but youth
        can reach
' "Where age gropes dimly, weak with
        stir and strain,
' "And the full doctrine slumbers till to-
        day."
'Thus, what the Roman's lowered spear
        was found,
'A bar to me who touched and handled
        truth,
'Now proved the glozing of some new
        shrewd tongue,
'This Ebion, this Cerinthus or their
        mates,
'Till imminent was the outcry "Save our
        Christ!"
'Whereon I stated much of the Lord's
        life
'Forgotten or misdelivered, and let it
        work
'Such work done, as it will be, what
        comes next?
'What do I hear say, or conceive men
        say,
' "Was John at all, and did he say he
        saw?
' "Assure us, ere we ask what he might
        see!"

'Is this indeed a burthen for late days,
'And may I help to bear it with you all,
'Using my weakness which becomes
        your strength?
'For if a babe were born inside this grot,
'Grew to a boy here, heard us praise
        the sun,

'Yet had but yon sole glimmer in light's
        place, –
'One loving him and wishful he should
        learn,
'Would much rejoice himself was
        blinded first
'Month by month here, so made to
        understand
'How eyes, born darkling, apprehend
        amiss:
'To think I could explain to such a child
'There was more glow outside than
        gleams he caught,
'Ay, nor need urge "I saw it, so believe!"
'It is a heavy burthen you shall bear
'In latter days, new lands, or old grown
        strange,
'Left without me, which must be very
        soon.
'What is the doubt, my brothers?
        Quick with it!
'I see you stand conversing, each new
        face,
'Either in fields, of yellow summer eves
'On islets yet unnamed amid the sea;
'Or pace for shelter 'neath a portico
'Out of the crowd in some enormous
        town
'Where now the larks sing in a solitude;
'Or muse upon blank heaps of stone
        and sand
'Idly conjectured to be Ephesus:
'And no one asks his fellow any more
' "Where is the promise of His
        coming?" but
' "Was he revealed in any of His lives,
' "As Power, as Love, as Influencing
        Soul?"

'Quick, for time presses, tell the whole
        mind out,
'And let us ask and answer and be
        saved!
'My book speaks on, because it cannot
        pass;
'One listens quietly, nor scoffs but
        pleads

' "Here is a tale of things done ages
   since;
' "What truth was ever told the second
   day?
' "Wonders, that would prove doctrine,
   go for nought.
' "Remains the doctrine, love; well, we
   must love,
' "And what we love most, power and
   love in one,
' "Let us acknowledge on the record
   here,
' "Accepting these in Christ: must
   Christ then be?
' "Has He been? Did not we ourselves
   make Him?
' "Our mind receives but what it holds,
   no more.
' "First of the love, then; we acknowledge
   Christ –
' "A proof we comprehend His love, a
   proof
' "We had such love already in ourselves,
' "Knew first what else we should not
   recognize.
' " 'Tis mere projection from man's
   inmost mind,
' "And, what he loves, thus falls
   reflected back,
' "Becomes accounted somewhat out
   of him;
' "He throws it up in air, it drops down
   earth's,
' "With shape, name, story added,
   man's old way.
' "How prove you Christ came otherwise
   at least?
' "Next try the power: He made and
   rules the world:
' "Certes there is a world once made,
   now ruled,
' "Unless things have been ever as we
   see.
' "Our sires declared a charioteer's
   yoked steeds
' "Brought the sun up the east and
   down the west,

' "Which only of itself now rises, sets,
' "As if a hand impelled it and a will, –
' "Thus they long thought, they who
   had will and hands:
' "But the new question's whisper is
   distinct,
' "Wherefore must all force needs be
   like ourselves?
' "We have the hands, the will; what
   made and drives
' "The sun is force, is law, is named,
   not known.
' "While will and love we do know;
   marks of these,
' "Eye-witnesses attest, so books
   declare –
' "As that, to punish or reward our race,
' "The sun at undue times arose or set
' "Or else stood still: what do not men
   affirm?
' "But earth requires as urgently reward
' "Or punishment to-day as years ago,
' "And none expects the sun will
   interpose:
' "Therefore it was mere passion and
   mistake,
' "Or erring zeal for right, which changed
   the truth.
' "Go back, far, farther, to the birth of
   things;
' "Ever the will, the intelligence, the love,
' "Man's! – which he gives, supposing
   he but finds,
' "As late he gave head, body, hands
   and feet,
' "To help these in what forms he
   called his gods.
' "First, Jove's brow, Juno's eyes were
   swept away,
' "But Jove's wrath, Juno's pride
   continued long;
' "As last, will, power, and love discarded
   these,
' "So law in turn discards power, love,
   and will.
' "What proveth God is otherwise at
   least?

' "All else, projection from the mind of
    man!"

'Nay, do not give me wine, for I am
    strong,
'But place my gospel where I put my
    hands.

'I say that man was made to grow, not
    stop;
'That help, he needed once, and needs
    no more,
'Having grown but an inch by, is
    withdrawn:
'For he hath new needs, and new helps
    to these.
'This imports solely, man should
    mount on each
'New height in view; the help whereby
    he mounts,
'The ladder-rung his foot has left, may
    fall,
'Since all things suffer change save God
    the Truth.
'Man apprehends Him newly at each
    stage
'Whereat earth's ladder drops, its service
    done;
'And nothing shall prove twice what
    once was proved.
'You stick a garden-plot with ordered
    twigs
'To show inside lie germs of herbs
    unborn,
'And check the careless step would
    spoil their birth;
'But when herbs wave, the guardian
    twigs may go,
'Since should ye doubt of virtues,
    question kinds,
'It is no longer for old twigs ye look,
'Which proved once underneath lay
    store of seed,
'But to the herb's self, by what light ye
    boast,
'For what fruit's signs are. This book's
    fruit is plain,
'Nor miracles need prove it any more.

'Doth the fruit show? Then miracles
    bade 'ware
'At first of root and stem, saved both
    till now
'From trampling ox, rough boar and
    wanton goat.
'What? Was man made a wheelwork to
    wind up,
'And be discharged, and straight
    wound up anew?
'No! – grown, his growth lasts; taught,
    he ne'er forgets:
'May learn a thousand things, not
    twice the same.

'This might be pagan teaching: now
    hear mine.

'I say, that as the babe, you feed
    awhile,
'Becomes a boy and fit to feed himself,
'So, minds at first must be spoon-fed
    with truth:
'When they can eat, babe's-nurture is
    withdrawn.
'I fed the babe whether it would or no:
'I bid the boy or feed himself or starve.
'I cried once, "That ye may believe in
    Christ,
' "Behold this blind man shall receive
    his sight!"
'I cry now, "Urgest thou, *for I am
    shrewd*
' "*And smile at stories how John's word
    could cure –*
' "*Repeat that miracle and take my faith?*'
'I say, that miracle was duly wrought
'When, save for it, no faith was possible.
'Whether a change were wrought i' the
    shows o' the world,
'Whether the change came from our
    minds which see
'Of shows o' the world so much as and
    no more
'Than God wills for His purpose, –
    (what do I
'See now, suppose you, there where you
    see rock

'Round us?) – I know not; such was the
    effect,
'So faith grew, making void more miracles
'Because too much: they would
    compel, not help.
'I say, the acknowledgment of God in
    Christ
'Accepted by thy reason, solves for thee
'All questions in the earth and out of it,
'And has so far advanced thee to be wise.
'Wouldst thou unprove this to re-prove
    the proved?
'In life's mere minute, with power to
    use that proof,
'Leave knowledge and revert to how it
    sprung?
'Thou hast it; use it and forthwith, or
    die!

'For I say, this is death and the sole
    death,
'When a man's loss comes to him from
    his gain,
'Darkness from light, from knowledge
    ignorance,
'And lack of love from love made
    manifest;
'A lamp's death when, replete with oil,
    it chokes;
'A stomach's when, surcharged with
    food, it starves.
'With ignorance was surety of a cure.
'When man, appalled at nature,
    questioned first
' "What if there lurk a might behind
    this might?"
'He needed satisfaction God could give,
'And did give, as ye have the written
    word:
'But when he finds might still redouble
    might,
'Yet asks, "Since all is might, what use
    of will?"
' – Will, the one source of might, – he
    being man
'With a man's will and a man's might,
    to teach

'In little how the two combine in
    large, –
'That man has turned round on himself
    and stands,
'Which in the course of nature is, to die.

'And when man questioned, "What if
    there be love
' "Behind the will and might, as real as
    they?" –
'He needed satisfaction God could give,
'And did give, as ye have the written
    word:
'But when, beholding that love every-
    where,
'He reasons, "Since such love is every-
    where,
' "And since ourselves can love and
    would be loved,
' "We ourselves make the love, and
    Christ was not," –
'How shall ye help this man who
    knows himself,
'That he must love and would be loved
    again,
'Yet, owning his own love that proveth
    Christ,
'Rejecteth Christ through very need of
    Him?
'The lamp o'erswims with oil, the
    stomach flags
'Loaded with nurture, and that man's
    soul dies.

'If he rejoin, "But this was all the while
' "A trick; the fault was, first of all, in
    thee,
' "Thy story of the places, names and
    dates,
' "Where, when and how the ultimate
    truth had rise,
' " – Thy prior truth, at last discovered
    none,
' "Whence now the second suffers
    detriment.
' "What good of giving knowledge if,
    because

' "O' the manner of the gift, its profit
fail?
' "And why refuse what modicum of
help
' "Had stopped the after-doubt,
impossible
' "I' the face of truth – truth absolute,
uniform?
' "Why must I hit of this and miss of
that,
' "Distinguish just as I be weak or strong,
' "And not ask of thee and have answer
prompt,
' "Was this once, was it not once? –
then and now
' "And evermore, plain truth from man
to man.
' "Is John's procedure just the heathen
bard's?
' "Put question of his famous play again
' "How for the ephemerals' sake Jove's
fire was filched,
' "And carried in a cane and brought to
earth:
' "*The fact is in the fable*, cry the wise,
' "*Mortals obtained the boon, so much is
fact*,
' "*Though fire be spirit and produced on
earth.*
' "As with the Titan's, so now with thy
tale:
' "Why breed in us perplexity, mistake,
' "Nor tell the whole truth in the
proper words?"

'I answer, Have ye yet to argue out
'The very primal thesis, plainest law,
' – Man is not God but hath God's end
to serve,
'A master to obey, a course to take,
'Somewhat to cast off, somewhat to
become?
'Grant this, then man must pass from
old to new,
'From vain to real, from mistake to fact,
'From what once seemed good, to what
now proves best.

'How could man have progression other-
wise?
'Before the point was mooted "What is
God?"
'No savage man inquired "What am
myself?"
'Much less replied, "First, last, and best
of things."
'Man takes that title now if he believes
'Might can exist with neither will nor
love,
'In God's case – what he names now
Nature's Law –
'While in himself he recognizes love
'No less than might and will: and
rightly takes.
'Since if man prove the sole existent
thing
'Where these combine, whatever their
degree,
'However weak the might or will or love,
'So they be found there, put in
evidence, –
'He is as surely higher in the scale
'Than any might with neither love nor
will,
'As life, apparent in the poorest midge,
'(When the faint dust-speck flits, ye
guess its wing)
'Is marvellous beyond dead Atlas' self –
'Given to the nobler midge for resting-
place!
'Thus, man proves best and highest –
God, in fine,
'And thus the victory leads but to
defeat,
'The gain to loss, best rise to the worst
fall,
'His life becomes impossible, which is
death.

'But if, appealing thence, he cower,
avouch
'He is mere man, and in humility
'Neither may know God nor mistake
himself;
'I point to the immediate consequence

'And say, by such confession straight
    he falls
'Into man's place, a thing nor God nor
    beast,
'Made to know that he can know and
    not more:
'Lower than God who knows all and
    can all,
'Higher than beasts which know and
    can so far
'As each beast's limit, perfect to an end,
'Nor conscious that they know, nor
    craving more;
'While man knows partly but conceives
    beside,
'Creeps ever on from fancies to the fact,
'And in this striving, this converting air
'Into a solid he may grasp and use,
'Finds progress, man's distinctive mark
    alone,
'Not God's, and not the beasts': God
    is, they are,
'Man partly is and wholly hopes to be.
'Such progress could no more attend
    his soul
'Were all it struggles after found at first
'And guesses changed to knowledge
    absolute,
'Than motion wait his body, were all else
'Than it the solid earth on every side,
'Where now through space he moves
    from rest to rest.
'Man, therefore, thus conditioned,
    must expect
'He could not, what he knows now,
    know at first;
'What he considers that he knows today,
'Come but to-morrow, he will find mis-
    known;
'Getting increase of knowledge, since
    he learns
'Because he lives, which is to be a man,
'Set to instruct himself by his past self:
'First, like the brute, obliged by facts to
    learn,
'Next, as man may, obliged by his own
    mind,

'Bent, habit, nature, knowledge turned
    to law.
'God's gift was that man should conceive
    of truth
'And yearn to gain it, catching at mistake,
'As midway help till he reach fact indeed.
'The statuary ere he mould a shape
'Boasts a like gift, the shape's idea, and
    next
'The aspiration to produce the same;
'So, taking clay, he calls his shape
    thereout,
'Cries ever "Now I have the thing I see":
'Yet all the while goes changing what
    was wrought,
'From falsehood like the truth, to truth
    itself.
'How were it had he cried "I see no face,
' "No breast, no feet i' the ineffectual
    clay"?
'Rather commend him that he clapped
    his hands,
'And laughed "It is my shape and lives
    again!"
'Enjoyed the falsehood, touched it on
    to truth,
'Until yourselves applaud the flesh
    indeed
'In what is still flesh-imitating clay.
'Right in you, right in him, such way
    be man's!
'God only makes the live shape at a jet.
'Will ye renounce this pact of creature-
    ship?
'The pattern on the Mount subsists no
    more,
'Seemed a while, then returned to
    nothingness;
'But copies, Moses strove to make
    there by,
'Serve still and are replaced as time
    requires:
'By these, make newest vessels, reach
    the type!
'If ye demur, this judgment on your
    head,
'Never to reach the ultimate, angel's law,

'Indulging every instinct of the soul
'There where law, life, joy, impulse are
    one thing!

'Such is the burthen of the latest time.
'I have survived to hear it with my ears,
'Answer it with my lips: does this suffice?
'For if there be a further woe than such,
'Wherein my brothers struggling need a
    hand,
'So long as any pulse is left in mine,
'May I be absent even longer yet,
'Plucking the blind ones back from the
    abyss,
'Though I should tarry a new hundred
    years!'

But he was dead; 'twas about noon, the
    day
Somewhat declining: we five buried him
That eve, and then, dividing, went five
    ways,
And I, disguised, returned to Ephesus.

By this, the cave's mouth must be filled
    with sand.
Valens is lost, I know not of his trace;
The Bactrian was but a wild childish
    man,
And could not write nor speak, but only
    loved:
So, lest the memory of this go quite,
Seeing that I to-morrow fight the beasts,
I tell the same to Phæbas, whom believe!
For many look again to find that face,
Beloved John's to whom I ministered,
Somewhere in life about the world;
    they err:
Either mistaking what was darkly
    spoke
At ending of his book, as he relates,
Or misconceiving somewhat of this
    speech
Scattered from mouth to mouth, as I
    suppose.
Believe ye will not see him any more
About the world with his divine regard!

For all was as I say, and now the man
Lies as he lay once, breast to breast
    with God.

    \*    \*    \*

[Cerinthus read and mused; one added
    this:

'If Christ, as thou affirmest, be of men
'Mere man, the first and best but
    nothing more, –
'Account Him, for reward of what He
    was,
'Now and for ever, wretchedest of all.
'For see; Himself conceived of life as
    love,
'Conceived of love as what must enter
    in,
'Fill up, make one with His each soul
    He loved:
'Thus much for man's joy, all men's
    joy for Him.
'Well, He is gone, thou sayest, to fit
    reward.
'But by this time are many souls set
    free,
'And very many still retained alive:
'Nay, should His coming be delayed
    awhile,
'Say, ten years longer (twelve years,
    some compute)
'See if, for every finger of thy hands,
'There be not found, that day the
    world shall end,
'Hundreds of souls, each holding by
    Christ's word
'That He will grow incorporate with all,
'With me as Pamphylax, with him as
    John,
'Groom for each bride! Can a mere
    man do this?
'Yet Christ saith, this He lived and died
    to do.
'Call Christ, then, the illimitable God,
'Or lost!'

    But 'twas Cerinthus that is lost.]

## Caliban upon Setebos

### or, NATURAL THEOLOGY IN THE ISLAND

'Thou thoughtest that I was altogether
such a one as thyself.'

['Will sprawl, now that the heat of day
    is best,
Flat on his belly in the pit's much mire,
With elbows wide, fists clenched to
    prop his chin.
And, while he kicks both feet in the
    cool slush,
And feels about his spine small eft-
    things course,
Run in and out each arm, and make
    him laugh:
And while above his head a pompion-
    plant.
Coating the cave-top as a brow its eye,
Creeps down to touch and tickle hair
    and beard,
And now a flower drops with a bee
    inside,
And now a fruit to snap at, catch and
    crunch, –
He looks out o'er yon sea which sun-
    beams cross
And recross till they weave a spider-web
(Meshes of fire, some great fish breaks
    at times)
And talks to his own self, howe'er he
    please,
Touching that other, whom his dam
    called God.
Because to talk about Him, vexes – ha,
Could He but know! and time to vex is
    now,
When talk is safer than in winter-time.
Moreover Prosper and Miranda sleep
In confidence he drudges at their task,
And it is good to cheat the pair, and
    gibe,
Letting the rank tongue blossom into
    speech.]

Setebos, Setebos, and Setebos!
'Thinketh, He dwelleth i' the cold o'
    the moon.
'Thinketh He made it, with the sun to
    match,
But not the stars; the stars come other-
    wise;
Only made clouds, winds, meteors,
    such as that:
Also this isle, what lives and grows
    thereon,
And snaky sea which rounds and ends
    the same.

'Thinketh, it came of being ill at ease:
He hated that He cannot change His
    cold,
Nor cure its ache. 'Hath spied an icy fish
That longed to 'scape the rock-stream
    where she lived,
And thaw herself within the lukewarm
    brine
O' the lazy sea her stream thrusts far
    amid,
A crystal spike 'twixt two warm walls
    of wave;
Only, she ever sickened, found repulse
At the other kind of water, not her life,
(Green-dense and dim-delicious, bred
    o' the sun)
Flounced back from bliss she was not
    born to breathe,
And in her old bounds buried her
    despair,
Hating and loving warmth alike: so He.

'Thinketh, He made thereat the sun,
    this isle,
Trees and the fowls here, beast and
    creeping thing.
Yon otter, sleek-wet, black, lithe as a
    leech;
Yon auk, one fire-eye in a ball of foam,
That floats and feeds; a certain badger
    brown
He hath watched hunt with that slant
    white-wedged eye

By moonlight; and the pie with the
    long tongue
That pricks deep into oakwarts for a
    worm,
And says a plain word when she finds
    her prize,
But will not eat the ants; the ants them-
    selves
That build a wall of seeds and settled
    stalks
About their hole – He made all these
    and more,
Made all we see, and us, inspite: how
    else?
He could not, Himself, make a second
    self
To be His mate; as well have made
    Himself:
He would not make what he mislikes
    or slights,
An eyesore to Him, or not worth His
    pains:
But did, in envy, listlessness or sport,
Make what Himself would fain, in a
    manner, be –
Weaker in most points, stronger in a
    few,
Worthy, and yet mere playthings all
    the while,
'Things He admires and mocks too, –
    that is it.
Because, so brave, so better though
    they be,
It nothing skills if He begin to plague.
Look now, I melt a gourd-fruit into
    mash,
Add honeycomb and pods, I have
    perceived,
Which bite like finches when they bill
    and kiss, –
Then, when froth rises bladdery, drink
    up all,
Quick, quick, till maggots scamper
    through my brain;
Last, throw me on my back i' the
    seeded thyme,
And wanton, wishing I were born a bird.

Put case, unable to be what I wish,
I yet could make a live bird out of clay:
Would not I take clay, pinch my Caliban
Able to fly? – for, there, see, he hath
    wings,
And great comb like the hoopoe's to
    admire,
And there, a sting to do his foes offence,
There, and I will that he begin to live,
Fly to yon rock-top, nip me off the horns
Of grigs high up that make the merry
    din,
Saucy through their veined wings, and
    mind me not.
In which feat, if his leg snapped, brittle
    clay,
And he lay stupid-like, – why, I should
    laugh;
And if he, spying me, should fall to weep,
Beseech me to be good, repair his
    wrong,
Bid his poor leg smart less or grow
    again, –
Well, as the chance were, this might
    take or else
Not take my fancy: I might hear his cry,
And give the manikin three sound legs
    for one,
Or pluck the other off, leave him like
    an egg,
And lessoned he was mine and merely
    clay.
Were this no pleasure, lying in the thyme,
Drinking the mash, with brain become
    alive,
Making and marring clay at will? So He.

'Thinketh, such shows nor right nor
    wrong in Him,
Nor kind, nor cruel: He is strong and
    Lord.
'Am strong myself compared to yonder
    crabs
That march now from the mountain to
    the sea;
'Let twenty pass, and stone the twenty-
    first,

Loving not, hating not, just choosing so.
'Say, the first straggler that boasts
    purple spots
Shall join the file, one pincer twisted
    off;
'Say, this bruised fellow shall receive a
    worm,
And two worms he whose nippers end
    in red;
As it likes me each time, I do: so He.

Well then, 'supposeth He is good i' the
    main,
Placable if His mind and ways were
    guessed,
But rougher than His handiwork, be
    sure!
Oh, He hath made things worthier than
    Himself,
And envieth that, so helped, such things
    do more
Than He who made them! What consoles
    but this?
That they, unless through Him, do
    nought at all,
And must submit: what other use in
    things?
'Hath cut a pipe of pithless elder-joint
That, blown through, gives exact the
    scream o' the jay
When from her wing you twitch the
    feathers blue:
Sound this, and little birds that hate
    the jay
Flock within stone's throw, glad their
    foe is hurt:
Put case such pipe could prattle and
    boast forsooth
'I catch the birds, I am the crafty thing,
'I make the cry my maker cannot make
'With his great round mouth; he must
    blow through mine!'
Would not I smash it with my foot? So
    He.

But wherefore rough, why cold and ill
    at ease?

Aha, that is a question! Ask, for that,
What knows, – the something over
    Setebos
That made Him, or He, may be, found
    and fought,
Worsted, drove off and did to nothing,
    perchance.
There may be something quiet o'er His
    head,
Out of His reach, that feels nor joy nor
    grief,
Since both derive from weakness in
    some way.
I joy because the quails come; would
    not joy
Could I bring quails here when I have a
    mind:
This Quiet, all it hath a mind to, doth.
'Esteemeth stars the outposts of its couch,
But never spends much thought nor
    care that way.
It may look up, work up, – the worse
    for those
It works on! 'Careth but for Setebos
The many-handed as a cuttle-fish,
Who, making Himself feared through
    what He does,
Looks up, first, and perceives he cannot
    soar
To what is quiet and hath happy life;
Next looks down here, and out of very
    spite
Makes this a bauble-world to ape yon
    real,
These good things to match those as
    hips do grapes.
'Tis solace making baubles, ay, and
    sport.
Himself peeped late, eyed Prosper at
    his books
Careless and lofty, lord now of the isle:
Vexed, 'stitched a book of broad
    leaves, arrow-shaped,
Wrote thereon, he knows what,
    prodigious words;
Has peeled a wand and called it by a
    name;

Weareth at whiles for an enchanter's
  robe
The eyed skin of a supple oncelot;
And hath an ounce sleeker than
  youngling mole,
A four-legged serpent he makes cower
  and couch,
Now snarl, now hold its breath and
  mind his eye,
And saith she is Miranda and my wife:
'Keeps for his Ariel a tall pouch-bill
  crane
He bids go wade for fish and straight
  disgorge;
Also a sea-beast, lumpish, which he
  snared,
Blinded the eyes of, and brought some-
  what tame,
And split its toe-webs, and now pens
  the drudge
In a hole o' the rock and calls him
  Caliban;
A bitter heart that bides its time and
  bites.
'Plays thus at being Prosper in a way,
Taketh his mirth with make-believes:
  so He.

His dam held that the Quiet made all
  things
Which Setebos vexed only: 'holds not so.
Who made them weak, meant weakness
  He might vex.
Had He meant other, while His Hand
  was in,
Why not make horny eyes no thorn
  could prick,
Or plate my scalp with bone against
  the snow,
Or overscale my flesh 'neath joint and
  joint,
Like an orc's armour? Ay, – so spoil
  His sport!
He is the One now: only He doth all.

'Saith, He may like, perchance, what
  profits Him.

Ay, himself loves what does him good;
  but why?
'Gets good no otherwise. This blinded
  beast
Loves whoso places flesh-meat on his
  nose,
But, had he eyes, would want no help,
  but hate
Or love, just as it liked him: He hath
  eyes.
Also it pleaseth Setebos to work,
Use all His hands, and exercise much
  craft,
By no means for the love of what is
  worked.
'Tasteth, himself, no finer good i' the
  world
When all goes right, in this safe summer-
  time,
And he wants little, hungers, aches not
  much,
Than trying what to do with wit and
  strength.
'Falls to make something: 'piled yon
  pile of turfs,
And squared and stuck there squares
  of soft white chalk,
And, with a fish-tooth, scratched a
  moon on each,
And set up endwise certain spikes of
  tree,
And crowned the whole with a sloth's
  skull a-top,
Found dead i the woods, too hard for
  one to kill.
No use at all i' the work, for work's sole
  sake;
'Shall some day knock it down again: so
  He.

'Saith He is terrible: watch His feats in
  proof!
One hurricane will spoil six good
  months' hope.
He hath a spite against me, that I know,
Just as He favours Prosper, who knows
  why?

So it is, all the same, as well I find.
'Wove wattles half the winter, fenced them firm
With stone and stake to stop she-tortoises
Crawling to lay their eggs here: well, one wave,
Feeling the foot of Him upon its neck,
Gaped as a snake does, lolled out its large tongue,
And licked the whole labour flat: so much for spite.
'Saw a ball flame down late (yonder it lies)
Where, half an hour before, I slept i' the shade:
Often they scatter sparkles: there is force!
'Dug up a newt He may have envied once
And turned to stone, shut up inside a stone.
Please Him and hinder this? – What Prosper does?
Aha, if He would tell me how! Not He!
There is the sport: discover how or die!
All need not die, for of the things o' the isle
Some flee afar, some dive, some run up trees;
'Those at His mercy, – why, they please Him most
When ... when ... well, never try the same way twice!
Repeat what act has pleased, He may grow wroth.
You must not know His ways, and play Him off,
Sure of the issue. 'Doth the like himself:
'Spareth a squirrel that it nothing fears
But steals the nut from underneath my thumb,
And when I threat, bites stoutly in defence:
'Spareth an urchin that contrariwise,

Curls up into a ball, pretending death
For fright at my approach: the two ways please.
But what would move my choler more than this,
That either creature counted on its life
To-morrow and next day and all days to come,
Saying, forsooth, in the inmost of its heart,
'Because he did so yesterday with me,
'And otherwise with such another brute,
'So must he do henceforth and always.' – Ay?
Would teach the reasoning couple what 'must' means!
'Doth as he likes, or wherefore Lord? So He.

'Conceiveth all things will continue thus,
And we shall have to live in fear of Him
So long as He lives, keeps His strength: no change,
If He have done His best, make no new world
To please Him more, so leave off watching this, –
If He surprise not even the Quiet's self
Some strange day, – or, suppose, grow into it
As grubs grow butterflies: else, here are we,
And there is He, and nowhere help at all.

'Believeth with the life, the pain shall stop.
His dam held different, that after death
He both plagued enemies and feasted friends:
Idly! He doth His worst in this our life,
Giving just respite lest we die through pain,
Saving last pain for worst, – with which, an end.
Meanwhile, the best way to escape His ire

Is, not to seem too happy. 'Sees, himself,
Yonder two flies, with purple films and
    Pink,
Bask on the pompion-bell above: kills
    both.
'Sees two black painful beetles roll their
    ball
On head and tail as if to save their lives:
Moves them the stick away they strive
    to clear.

Even so, 'would have Him misconceive,
    suppose
This Caliban strives hard and ails no
    less,
And always, above all else, envies Him;
Wherefore he mainly dances on dark
    nights,
Moans in the sun, gets under holes to
    laugh,
And never speaks his mind save housed
    as now:
Outside,'groans, curses. If He caught
    me here,
O'erheard this speech, and asked
    'What chucklest at?'
'Would, to appease Him, cut a finger off,
Or of my three kid yearlings burn the
    best,
Or let the toothsome apples rot on
    tree,
Or push my tame beast for the orc to
    taste:
While myself lit a fire, and made a song
And sung it, '*What I hate, be consecrate*
'*To celebrate Thee and Thy state, no mate*
'*For Thee; what see for envy in poor me?*'
Hoping the while, since evils
    sometimes mend,
Warts rub away and sores are cured
    with slime,
That some strange day, will either the
    Quiet catch
And conquer Setebos, or likelier He
Decrepit may doze, doze, as good as
    die.
      *      *      *

[What, what? A curtain o'er the world
    at once!
Crickets stop hissing; not a bird – or,
    yes,
There scuds His raven that has told
    Him all!
It was fool's play, this prattling! Ha!
    The wind
Shoulders the pillared dust, death's
    house o' the move,
And fast invading fires begin! White
    blaze –
A tree's head snaps – and there, there,
    there, there, there,
His thunder follows! Fool to gibe at
    Him!
Lo! 'Lieth flat and loveth Setebos!
'Maketh his teeth meet through his
    upper lip,
Will let those quails fly, will not eat
    this month
One little mess of whelks, so he may
    'scape!]

## Confessions

### 1

What is he buzzing in my ears?
  'Now that I come to die,
'Do I view the world as a vale of tears?'
  Ah, reverend sir, not I

### 2

What I viewed there once, what I view
    again
  Where the physic bottles stand
On the table's edge, – is a suburb lane,
  With a wall to my bedside hand.

### 3

That lane sloped, much as the bottles
    do,
  From a house you could descry
O'er the garden-wall: is the curtain blue
  Or green to a healthy eye?

### 4

To mine, it serves for the old June
    weather
  Blue above lane and wall;
And that farthest bottle labelled 'Ether'
  Is the house o'ertopping all.

### 5

At a terrace, somewhere near the
    stopper,
  There watched for me, one June,
A girl: I know, sir, it's improper,
  My poor mind's out of tune.

### 6

Only, there was a way ... you crept
  Close by the side, to dodge
Eyes in the house, two eyes except:
  They styled their house 'The Lodge.'

### 7

What right had a lounger up their lane?
  But, by creeping very close,
With the good wall's help, – their eyes
    might strain
  And stretch themselves to Oes,

### 8

Yet never catch her and me together,
  As she left the attic, there,
By the rim of the bottle labelled 'Ether,'
  And stole from stair to stair,

### 9

And stood by the rose-wreathed gate.
    Alas,
  We loved, sir – used to meet:
How sad and bad and mad it was –
  But then, how it was sweet!

## May and Death

### 1

I wish that when you died last May,
  Charles, there had died along with
    you
Three parts of spring's delightful things;
  Ay, and, for me, the fourth part too.

### 2

A foolish thought, and worse, perhaps!
  There must be many a pair of friends
Who, arm in arm, deserve the warm
  Moon-births and the long evening-
    ends.

### 3

So, for their sake, be May still May!
  Let their new time, as mine of old,
Do all it did for me: I bid
  Sweet sights and sounds throng
    manifold.

### 4

Only, one little sight, one plant,
  Woods have in May, that starts up
    green
Save a sole streak which, so to speak,
  Is spring's blood, spilt its leaves
    between, –

### 5

That, they might spare; a certain wood
  Might miss the plant; their loss were
    small:
But I, – whene'er the leaf grows there,
  Its drop comes from my heart, that's
    all.

## Deaf and Dumb

### A GROUP BY WOOLNER

Only the prism's obstruction shows
        aright
    The secret of a sunbeam, breaks its
        light
Into the jewelled bow from blankest
        white;
    So may a glory from defect arise:
Only by Deafness may the vexed Love
        wreak
Its insuppressive sense on brow and
        cheek,
Only by Dumbness adequately speak
    As favoured mouth could never,
        through the eyes.

## Prospice

Fear death? – to feel the fog in my
        throat,
    The mist in my face,
When the snows begin, and the blasts
        denote
    I am nearing the place,
The power of the night, the press of the
        storm,
    The post of the foe;
Where he stands, the Arch Fear in a
        visible form,
    Yet the strong man must go:
For the journey is done and the
        summit attained.
    And the barriers fall,
Though a battle's to fight ere the
        guerdon be gained,
    The reward of it all.
I was ever a fighter, so – one fight
        more,
    The best and the last!
I would hate that death bandaged my
        eyes, and forebore,
    And bade me creep past.
No! let me taste the whole of it, fare
        like my peers
    The heroes of old,

Bear the brunt, in a minute pay glad
        life's arrears
    Of pain, darkness and cold.
For sudden the worst turns the best to
        the brave,
    The black minute's at end,
And the elements' rage, the fiend-
        voices that rave,
    Shall dwindle, shall blend,
Shall change, shall become first a peace
        out of pain,
    Then a light, then thy breast,
O thou soul of my soul! I shall clasp
        thee again,
    And with God be the rest!

## Eurydice to Orpheus

A picture by Leighton

But give them me, the mouth, the eyes,
        the brow!
Let them once more absorb me! One
        look now
    Will lap me round for ever, not to
        pass
Out of its light, though darkness lie
        beyond:
Hold me but safe again within the
        bond
    Of one immortal look! All woe that
        was,
Forgotten, and all terror that may be,
Defied, – no past is mine, no future:
        look at me!

## Youth and Art

### 1

It once might have been, once only:
  We lodged in a street together,
You, a sparrow on the housetop lonely,
  I, a lone she-bird of his feather.

### 2

Your trade was with sticks and clay,
  You thumbed, thrust, patted and
    polished,
Then laughed 'They will see some day
  'Smith made, and Gibson
    demolished.'

### 3

My business was song, song, song;
  I chirped, cheeped, trilled and
    twittered,
'Kate Brown's on the boards ere long,
  'And Grisi's existence embittered!'

### 4

I earned no more by a warble
  Than you by a sketch in plaster;
You wanted a piece of marble,
  I needed a music-master.

### 5

We studied hard in our styles,
  Chipped each at a crust like Hindoos,
For air looked out on the tiles,
  For fun watched each other's
    windows.

### 6

You lounged, like a boy of the South,
  Cap and blouse – nay, a bit of beard
    too;
Or you got it, ruibbing your mouth
  With fingers the clay adhered to.

### 7

And I – soon managed to find
  Weak points in the flower-fence facing,
Was forced to put up a blind
  And be safe in my corset-lacing.

### 8

No harm! It was not my fault
  If you never turned your eye's tail up
As I shook upon E *in alt*,
  Or ran the chromatic scale up:

### 9

For spring bade the sparrows pair,
  And the boys and girls gave guesses,
And stalls in our street looked rare
  With bulrush and watercresses.

### 10

Why did not you pinch a flower
  In a pellet of clay and fling it?
Why did not I put a power
  Of thanks in a look, or sing it?

### 11

I did look, sharp as a lynx,
  (And yet the memory rankles)
When models arrived, some minx
  Tripped up-stairs, she and her
    ankles.

### 12

But I think I gave you as good!
  'That foreign fellow, – who can know
'How she pays, in a playful mood,
  'For his tuning her that piano?'

### 13

Could you say so, and never say
  'Suppose we join hands and
    fortunes,
'And I fetch her from over the way,
  'Her piano, and long tunes and
    short tunes?'

### 14

No, no: you would not be rash,
  Nor I rasher and something over:
You've to settle yet Gibson's hash,
  And Grisi yet lives in clover.

### 15

But you meet the Prince at the Board,
  I'm queen myself at *bals-paré*,
I've married a rich old lord,
  And you're dubbed knight and
    an R.A.

### 16

Each life unfulfilled, you see;
  It hangs still, patchy and scrappy:
We have not sighed deep, laughed free,
  Starved, feasted, despaired, – been
    happy.

17

And nobody calls you a dunce,
  And people suppose me clever:
This could but have happened once,
  And we missed it, lost it for ever.

## A Face

If one could have that little head of hers
  Painted upon a background of pale
    gold,
Such as the Tuscan's early art prefers!
  No shade encroaching on the
    matchless mould
Of those two lips, which should be
    opening soft
  In the pure profile; not as when she
    laughs,
For that spoils all: but rather as if aloft
  Yon hyacinth, she loves so, leaned
    its staff's
Burthen of honey-coloured buds to kiss
And capture 'twixt the lips apart for
    this.
Then her lithe neck, three fingers might
    surround,
How it should waver on the pale gold
    ground
Up to the fruit-shaped, perfect chin it
    lifts!
I know, Correggio loves to mass, in rifts
Of heaven, his angel faces, orb on orb
Breaking its outline, burning shades
    absorb:
But these are only massed there, I
    should think,
  Waiting to see some wonder
    momently
  Grow out, stand full, fade slow
    against the sky
  (That's the pale ground you'd see
    this sweet face by),
  All heaven, meanwhile, condensed
    into one eye
Which fears to lose the wonder, should
    it wink.

## A Likeness

Some people hang portraits up
In a room where they dine or sup:
  And the wife clinks tea-things under,
And her cousin, he stirs his cup,
  Asks, 'Who was the lady, I wonder?'
' 'Tis a daub John bought at a sale,'
  Quoth the wife, – looks black as
    thunder:
'What a shade beneath her nose!
'Snuff-taking, I suppose, – '
Adds the cousin, while John's corns ail.
Or else, there's no wife in the case,
But the portrait's queen of the place,
Alone 'mid the other spoils
Of youth, – masks, gloves and foils,
And pipe-sticks, rose, cherry-tree,
    jasmine,
  And the long whip, the tandem-
    lasher,
And the cast from a fist ('not, alas! mine,
  'But my master's, the Tipton Slasher'),
And the cards where pistol-balls mark
    ace,
And a satin shoe used for cigar-case,
And the chamois-horns ('shot in the
    Chablais')
  And prints – Rarey drumming on
    Cruiser,
  And Sayers, our champion, the bruiser,
And the little edition of Rabelais:
Where a friend, with both hands in his
    pockets,
  May saunter up close to examine it,
  And remark a good deal of Jane Lamb
    in it,
'But the eyes are half out of their sockets;
'That hair's not so bad, where the gloss
    is,
'But they've made the girl's nose a
    proboscis:
'Jane Lamb, that we danced with at
    Vichy!
'What, is not she Jane? Then, who is
    she?'

All that I own is a print,
An etching, a mezzotint;
'Tis a study, a fancy, a fiction,
Yet a fact (take my conviction)
Because it has more than a hint
Of a certain face, I never
Saw elsewhere touch or trace of
In women I've seen the face of:
 Just an etching, and, so far, clever.

I keep my prints, an imbroglio,
Fifty in one portfolio.
When somebody tries my claret,
We turn round chairs to the fire,
Chirp over days in a garret,
Chuckle o'er increase of salary,
Taste the good fruits of our leisure,
Talk about pencil and lyre,
 And the National Portrait Gallery:
Then I exhibit my treasure.
After we've turned over twenty,
 And the debt of wonder my crony
  owes
 Is paid to my Marc Antonios,
He stops me – '*Festina lenté!*
'What's that sweet thing there, the
  etching?'
How my waistcoat-strings want
  stretching,
 How my cheeks grow red as tomatos,
How my heart leaps! But hearts, after
  leaps, ache.

'By the by, you must take, for a keepsake,
 'That other, you praised, of Volpato's.'
The fool! would he try a flight further
  and say –
He never saw, never before to-day,
What was able to take his breath away,
A face to lose youth for, to occupy age
With the dream of, meet death with, –
  why, I'll not engage
But that, half in a rapture and half in a
  rage,
I should toss him the thing's self –
 ' 'Tis only a duplicate,
'A thing of no value! Take it, I supplicate!'

## Mr Sludge, 'The Medium'

Now, don't, sir! Don't expose me! Just
  this once!
This was the first and only time, I'll
  swear, –
Look at me, – see, I kneel, – the only
  time,
I swear, I ever cheated, – yes, by the soul
Of Her who hears – (your sainted
  mother, sir!)
All except this last accident, was truth –
This little kind of slip! – and even this,
It was your own wine, sir, the good
  champagne,
(I took it for Catawba, you're so kind)
Which put the folly in my head!
      'Get up?'
You still inflict on me that terrible face?
You show no mercy? – Not for Her
  dear sake,
The sainted spirit's, whose soft breath
  even now
Blows on my cheek – (don't you feel
  something, sir?)
You'll tell?
  Go tell, then! Who the devil cares
What such a rowdy chooses to …
      Aie – aie – aie!
Please, sir! your thumbs are through
  my windpipe, sir!
Ch – ch!
   Well, sir, I hope you've done it
  now!
Oh Lord! I little thought, sir, yesterday,
When your departed mother spoke those
  words
Of peace through me, and moved you,
  sir, so much,
You gave me – (very kind it was of you)
These shirt-studs – (better take them
  back again,
Please, sir) – yes, little did I think so
  soon
A trifle of trick, all through a glass too
  much

Of his own champagne, would change
    my best of friends
Into an angry gentleman!
               Though, 'twas wrong.
I don't contest the point; your anger's
    just:
Whatever put such folly in my head,
I know 'twas wicked of me. There's a
    thick
Dusk undeveloped spirit (I've observed)
Owes me a grudge – a negro's, I should
    say,
Or else an Irish emigrant's; yourself
Explained the case so well last Sunday,
    sir,
When we had summoned Franklin to
    clear up
A point about those shares i' the
    telegraph:
Ay, and he swore … or might it be
    Tom Paine?…
Thumping the table close by where I
    crouched,
He'd do me soon a mischief: that's
    come true!
Why, now your face clears! I was sure
    it would!
Then, this one time … don't take your
    hand away.
Through your's I surely kiss your
    mother's hand …
You'll promise to forgive me? – or, at
    least,
Tell nobody of this? Consider, sir!
What harm can mercy do? Would but
    the shade
Of the venerable dead-one just vouchsafe
A rap or tip! What bit of paper's here?
Suppose we take a pencil, let her write,
Make the least sign, she urges on her
    child
Forgiveness? There now! Eh? Oh! 'Twas
    your foot,
And not a natural creak, sir?
               Answer, then!
Once, twice, thrice … see, I'm waiting
    to say 'thrice!'

All to no use? No sort of hope for me?
It's all to post to Greeley's newspaper?

What? If I told you all about the tricks?
Upon my soul! – the whole truth, and
    nought else,
And how there's been some falsehood
    – for your part,
Will you engage to pay my passage out,
And hold your tongue until I'm safe on
    board?
England's the place, not Boston – no
    offence!
I see what makes you hesitate: don't
    fear!
I mean to change my trade and cheat
    no more,
Yes, this time really it's upon my soul!
Be my salvation! – under Heaven, of
    course.
I'll tell some queer things. Sixty Vs must
    do.
A trifle, though, to start with! We'll refer
The question to this table?
               How you're changed!
Then split the difference; thirty more,
    we'll say.
Ay, but you leave my presents! Else I'll
    swear
'Twas all through those: you wanted
    yours again,
So, picked a quarrel with me, to get
    them back!
Tread on a worm, it turns, sir! If I turn,
Your fault! 'Tis you'll have forced me!
    Who's obliged
To give up life yet try no self-defence?
At all events, I'll run the risk. Eh?
               Done!
May I sit, sir? This dear old table, now!
Please, sir, a parting egg-nogg and cigar!
I've been so happy with you! Nice
    stuffed chairs,
And sympathetic sideboards; what an
    end
To all the instructive evenings! (It's
    alight.)

Well, nothing lasts, as Bacon came and
        said.
Here goes, – but keep your temper, or
        I'll scream!

Fol–lol–the–rido–liddle–iddle–ol!
You see, sir, it's your own fault more
        than mine;
It's all your fault, you curious gentlefolk!
You're prigs, – excuse me, – like to look
        so spry,
So clever, while you cling by half a claw
To the perch whereon you puff your-
        selves at roost,
Such piece of self-conceit as serves for
        perch
Because you chose it, so it must be safe.
Oh, otherwise you're sharp enough!
        You spy
Who slips, who slides, who holds by
        help of wing,
Wanting real foothold, – who can't
        keep upright
On the other perch, your neighbour
        chose, not you:
There's no outwitting you respecting
        him!
For instance, men love money – that,
        you know
And what men do to gain it: well, suppose
A poor lad, say a help's son in your
        house,
Listening at keyholes, hears the company
Talk grand of dollars, V-notes, and so
        forth,
How hard they are to get, how good to
        hold,
How much they buy, – if, suddenly, in
        pops he –
'I've got a V-note!' – what do you say
        to him?
What's your first word which follows
        your last kick?
'Where did you steal it, rascal?' That's
        because
He finds you, fain would fool you, off
        your perch,

Not on the special piece of nonsense,
        sir,
Elected your parade-ground: let him try
Lies to the end of the list, – 'He picked
        it up,
'His cousin died and left it him by will,
'The President flung it to him, riding
        by,
'An actress trucked it for a curl of his
        hair,
'He dreamed of luck and found his
        shoe enriched,
'He dug up clay, and out of clay made
        gold' –
How would you treat such
        possibilities?
Would not you, prompt, investigate
        the case
With cow-hide? 'Lies, lies, lies,' you'd
        shout: and why?
Which of the stories might not prove
        mere truth?
This last, perhaps, that clay was turned
        to coin!
Let's see, now, give him me to speak
        for him!
How many of your rare philosophers,
In plaguy books I've had to dip into,
Believed gold could be made thus, saw
        it made
And made it? Oh, with such
        philosophers
You're on your best behaviour! While
        the lad –
With him, in a trice, you settle
        likelihoods,
Nor doubt a moment how he got his
        prize:
In his case, you hear, judge and
        execute,
All in a breath: so would most men of
        sense.

But let the same lad hear you talk as
        grand
At the same keyhole, you and
        company,

Of signs and wonders, the invisible
world;
How wisdom scouts our vulgar unbelief
More than our vulgarest credulity;
How good men have desired to see a
ghost,
What Johnson used to say, what Wesley
did,
Mother Goose thought, and fiddle-
diddle-dee: –
If he break in with, 'Sir, I saw a ghost!'
Ah, the ways change! He finds you
perched and prim;
It's a conceit of yours that ghosts may
be:
There's no talk now of cow-hide. 'Tell
it out!
'Don't fear us! Take your time and re-
collect!
'Sit down first: try a glass of wine, my
boy!
'And, David, (is not that your Christian
name?)
'Of all things, should this happen twice
– it may –
'Be sure, while fresh in mind, you let
us know!'
Does the boy blunder, blurt out this,
blab that,
Break down in the other, as beginners
will?
All's candour, all's considerateness –
'No haste!
'Pause and collect yourself! We under-
stand!
'That's the bad memory, or the natural
shock,
'Or the unexplained *phenomena*!'
                          Egad,
The boy takes heart of grace; finds,
never fear,
The readiest way to ope your own heart
wide,
Show – what I call your peacock-porch,
pet post
To strut, and spread the tail, and
squawk upon!

'Just as you thought, much as you
might expect!
'There be more things in heaven and
earth, Horatio,' …
And so on. Shall not David take the
hint,
Grow bolder, stroke you down at
quickened rate?
If he ruffle a feather, it's 'Gently,
patiently!
'Manifestations are so weak at first!
'Doubting, moreover, kills them, cuts
all short,
'Cures with a vengeance!'
                There, sir, that's your style!
You and your boy – such pains bestowed
on him,
Or any headpiece of the average worth,
To teach, say, Greek, would perfect
him apace,
Make him a Person ('Porson?' thank
you, sir!)
Much more, proficient in the art of lies.
You never leave the lesson! Fire alight,
Catch you permitting it to die! You've
friends;
There's no withholding knowledge, –
least from those
Apt to look elsewhere for their souls'
supply:
Why should not you parade your lawful
prize?
Who finds a picture, digs a medal up,
Hits on a first edition, – he henceforth
Gives it his name, grows notable: how
much more,
Who ferrets out a 'medium'? 'David's
yours,
'You highly-favoured man? Then, pity
souls
'Less privileged! Allow us share your
luck!
So, David holds the circle, rules the
roast,
Narrates the vision, peeps in the glass
ball,
Sets-to the spirit-writing, hears the raps,

As the case may be.
                    Now mark! To be precise –
Though I say, 'lies' all these, at this
        first stage,
'Tis just for science' sake: I call such
        grubs
By the name of what they'll turn to,
        dragonflies.
Strictly, it's what good people style
        untruth;
But yet, so far, not quite the full-grown
        thing:
It's fancying, fable-making, nonsense-
        work –
What never meant to be so very bad –
The knack of story-telling, brightening
        up
Each dull old bit of fact that drops its
        shine.
One does see somewhat when one shuts
        one's eyes,
If only spots and streaks; tables do tip
In the oddest way of themselves: and
        pens, good Lord,
Who knows if you drive them or they
        drive you?
'Tis but a foot in the water and out
        again;
Not that duck-under which decides
        your dive.
Note this, for it's important: listen why.

I'll prove, you push on David till he
        dives
And ends the shivering. Here's your
        circle, now:
Two-thirds of them, with heads like
        you their host,
Turn up their eyes, and cry, as you
        expect,
'Lord, who'd have thought it!' But
        there's always one
Looks wise, compassionately smiles,
        submits
'Of your veracity no kind of doubt,
'But – do you feel so certain of that
        boy's?

'Really, I wonder! I confess myself
'More chary of my faith!' That's galling,
        sir!
What, he the investigator, he the sage,
When all's done? Then, you just have
        shut your eyes,
Opened your mouth, and gulped down
        David whole,
You! Terrible were such catastrophe!
So, evidence is redoubled, doubled again,
And doubled besides; once more, 'He
        heard, we heard,
'You and they heard, your mother and
        your wife,
'Your children and the stranger in your
        gates:
'Did they or did they not?'so much for
        him,
The black sheep, guest without the
        wedding-garb,
The doubting Thomas! Now's your
        turn to crow:
'He's kind to think you such a fool:
        Sludge cheats?
'Leave you alone to take precautions!'
                                Straight
The rest join chorus. Thomas stands
        abashed,
Sips silent some such beverage as this,
Considers if it be harder, shutting eyes
And gulping David in good fellowship,
Than going elsewhere, getting, in
        exchange,
With no egg-nogg to lubricate the food,
Some just as tough a morsel. Over the
        way,
Holds Captain Sparks his court: is it
        better there?
Have not you hunting-stories, scalping-
        scenes,
And Mexican War exploits to swallow
        plump
If you'd be free o' the stove-side,
        rocking-chair,
And trio of affable daughters?
                                Doubt succumbs!
Victory! All your circle's yours again!

Out of the clubbing of submissive wits,
David's performance rounds, each
    chink gets patched,
Every protrusion of a point's filed fine,
All's fit to set a-rolling round the world,
And then return to David finally,
Lies seven-feet thick about his first
    half-inch.
Here's a choice birth o' the supernatural,
Poor David's pledged to! You've
    employed no tool
That laws exclaim at, save the devil's
    own,
Yet screwed him into henceforth gulling
    you
To the top o' your bent, – all out of one
    half-lie!

You hold, if there's one half or a
    hundredth part
Of a lie, that's his fault, – his be the
    penalty!
I dare say! You'd prove firmer in his
    place?
You'd find the courage, – that first
    flurry over,
That mild bit of romancing-work at
    end, –
To interpose with 'It gets serious, this;
'Must stop here. Sir, I saw no ghost at
    all.
'Inform your friends I made … well,
    fools of them,
'And found you ready-made. I've lived
    in clover
'These three weeks: take it out in kicks
    of me!'
I doubt it. Ask your conscience! Let me
    know,
Twelve months hence, with how few
    embellishments
You've told almighty Boston of this
    passage
Of arms between us, your first taste o'
    the foil
From Sludge who could not fence, sir!
    Sludge, your boy!

I lied, sir, – there! I got up from my
    gorge
On offal in the gutter, and preferred
Your canvas-backs: I took their carver's
    size,
Measured his modicum of intelligence,
Tickled him on the cockles of his heart
With a raven feather, and next week
    found myself
Sweet and clean, dining daintily,
    dizened smart,
Set on a stool buttressed by ladies'
    knees,
Every soft smiler calling me her pet,
Encouraging my story to uncoil
And creep out from its hole, inch after
    inch,
'How last night, I no sooner snug in
    bed,
'Tucked up, just as they left me, – than
    came raps!
'While a light whisked' … 'Shaped
    somewhat like a star?'
'Well, like some sort of stars, ma'am.'
    – 'So we thought!
'And any voice? Not yet? Try hard, next
    time,
'If you can't hear a voice; we think you
    may:
'At least, the Pennsylvanian "mediums"
    did.'
Oh, next time comes the voice! 'Just as
    we hoped!'
Are not the hopers proud now, pleased,
    profuse
O' the natural acknowledgment?
                    Of course!
So, off we push, illy-oh-yo, trim the
    boat,
On we sweep with a cataract ahead,
We're midway to the Horseshoe: stop,
    who can,
The dance of bubbles gay about our
    prow!
Experiences become worth waiting for,
Spirits now speak up, tell their inmost
    mind,

And compliment the 'medium' properly,
Concern themselves about his Sunday
    coat,
See rings on his hand with pleasure. Ask yourself
How you'd receive a course of treats
    like these!
Why, take the quietest hack and stall
    him up,
Cram him with corn a month, then out
    with him
Among his mates on a bright April
    morn,
With the turf to tread; see if you find
    or no
A caper in him, if he bucks or bolts!
Much more a youth whose fancies
    sprout as rank
As toadstool-clump from melon-bed.
    'Tis soon,
'Sirrah, you spirit, come, go, fetch and
    carry,
'Read, write, rap, rub-a-dub, and hang
    yourself!'
I'm spared all further trouble; all's
    arranged;
Your circle does my business; I may
    rave
Like an epileptic dervish in the books,
Foam, fling myself flat, rend my clothes
    to shreds;
No matter: lovers, friends and country-
    men
Will lay down spiritual laws, read
    wrong things right
By the rule o' reverse. If Francis Verulam
Styles himself Bacon, spells the name
    beside
With a *y* and a *k*, says he drew breath
    in York,
Gave up the ghost in Wales when
    Cromwell reigned,
(As, sir, we somewhat fear he was apt
    to say,
Before I found the useful book that
    knows)

Why, what harm's done? The circle
    smiles apace,
'It was not Bacon, after all, you see!
'We understand: the trick's but natural:
'Such spirits' individuality
'Is hard to put in evidence: they incline
'To gibe and jeer, these undeveloped
    sorts.
'You see, their world's much like a jail
    broke loose,
'While this of ours remains shut, bolted,
    barred,
'With a single window to it. Sludge, our
    friend,
'Serves as this window, whether thin or
    thick,
'Or stained or stainless; he's the medium-
    pane
'Through which, to see us and be seen,
    they peep:
'They crowd each other, hustle for a
    chance,
'Tread on their neighbour's kibes, play
    tricks enough!
'Does Bacon, tired of waiting, swerve
    aside?
'Up in his place jumps Barnum – "I'm
    your man,
' "I'll answer you for Bacon!" Try once
    more!'

Or else it's – 'What's a "medium"?
    He's a means,
'Good, bad, indifferent, still the only
    means
'Spirits can speak by; he may
    misconceive,
'Stutter and stammer, – he's their
    Sludge and drudge,
'Take him or leave him; they must hold
    their peace,
'Or else, put up with having
    knowledge strained
'To half-expression through his
    ignorance.
'Suppose, the spirit Beethoven wants
    to shed

'New music he's brimful of; why, he
    turns
'The handle of this organ, grinds with
    Sludge,
'And what he poured in at the mouth
    o' the mill
'As a Thirty-third Sonata, (fancy now!)
'Comes from the hopper as bran-new
    Sludge, nought else,
'The Shakers' Hymn in G, with a
    natural F,
'Or the "Stars and Stripes" set to
    consecutive fourths.'

Sir, where's the scrape you did not
    help me through,
You that are wise? And for the fools,
    the folk
Who came to see, – the guests, (observe
    that word!)
Pray do you find guests criticize your
    wine,
Your furniture, your grammar, or your
    nose?
Then, why your 'medium'? What's the
    difference?
Prove your madeira red-ink and
    gamboge, –
Your Sludge, a cheat – then, somebody's
    a goose
For vaunting both as genuine. 'Guests!'
    Don't fear!
They'll make a wry face, nor too much
    of that,
And leave you in your glory.
                'No, sometimes
'They doubt and say as much!' Ay,
    doubt they do!
And what's the consequence? 'Of
    course they doubt' –
(You triumph) 'that explains the hitch
    at once!
'Doubt posed our "medium," puddled
    his pure mind;
'He gave them back their rubbish:
    pitch chaff in,

'Could flour come out o' the honest
    mill?' So, prompt
Applaud the faithful: cases flock in
    point,
'How, when a mocker willed a "medium"
    once
'Should name a spirit James whose name
    was George,
' "James" cried the "medium," – 'twas
    the test of truth!'
In short, a hit proves much, a miss
    proves more.
Does this convince? The better: does it
    fail?
Time for the double-shotted broadside,
    then –
The grand means, last resource. Look
    black and big!
'You style us idiots, therefore – why
    stop short?
'Accomplices in rascality: this we hear
'In our own house, from our invited
    guest
'Found brave enough to outrage a poor
    boy
'Exposed by our good faith! Have you
    been heard?
'Now, then, hear us; one man's not
    quite worth twelve.
'You see a cheat? Here's some twelve
    see an ass
'Excuse me if I calculate: good day!'
Out slinks the sceptic, all the laughs
    explode.
Sludge waves his hat in triumph!
                Or – he don't.
There's something in real truth
    (explain who can!)
One casts a wistful eye at, like the horse
Who mopes beneath stuffed hay-racks
    and won't munch
Because he spies a corn-bag: hang that
    truth,
It spoils all dainties proffered in its
    place!
I've felt at times when, cockered,
    cosseted

And coddled by the aforesaid company,
Bidden enjoy their bullying, – never fear,
But o'er their shoulders spit at the flying man, –
I've felt a child; only, a fractious child
That, dandled soft by nurse, aunt, grandmother,
Who keep him from the kennel, sun and wind,
Good fun and wholesome mud, – enjoined be sweet,
And comely and superior, – eyes askance
The ragged sons o' the gutter at their game,
Fain would be down with them i' the thick o' the filth,
Making dirt-pies, laughing free, speaking plain,
And calling granny the grey old cat she is.
I've felt a spite, I say, at you, at them,
Huggings and humbug – gnashed my teeth to mark
A decent dog pass! It's too bad, I say,
Ruining a soul so!
                    But what's 'so', what's fixed,
Where may one stop? Nowhere! The cheating's nursed
Out of the lying, softly and surely spun
To just your length, sir! I'd stop soon enough:
But you're for progress. 'All old, nothing new?
'Only the usual talking through the mouth,
'Or writing by the hand? I own, I thought
'This would develop, grow demonstrable,
'Make doubt absurd, give figures we might see,
'Flowers we might touch. There's no one doubts you, Sludge!
'You dream the dreams, you see the spiritual sights,

'The speeches come in your head, beyond dispute.
'Still, for the sceptics' sake, to stop all mouths,
'We want some outward manifestation! – well,
'The Pennsylvanians gained such; why not Sludge?
'He may improve with time!'
                    Ay, that he may!
He sees his lot: there's no avoiding fate.
'Tis a trifle at first. 'Eh, David? Did you hear?
'You jogged the table, your foot caused the squeak,
'This time you're … joking, are you not, my boy?'
'N–n–no!' – and I'm done for, bought and sold henceforth.
The old good easy jog-trot way, the … eh?
The … not so very false, as falsehood goes,
The spinning out and drawing fine, you know, –
Really mere novel-writing of a sort,
Acting, or improvising, make-believe,
Surely not downright cheatery, – any how,
'Tis done with and my lot cast; Cheat's my name:
The fatal dash of brandy in your tea
Has settled what you'll have the souchong's smack:
The caddy gives way to the dram-bottle.

Then, it's so cruel easy! Oh, those tricks
That can't be tricks, those feats by sleight of hand,
Clearly no common conjuror's! – no indeed!
A conjuror? Choose me any craft i' the world
A man puts hand to; and with six months' pains
I'll play you twenty tricks miraculous

To people untaught the trade: have
    you seen glass blown,
Pipes pierced? Why, just this biscuit
    that I chip,
Did you ever watch a baker toss one
    flat
To the oven? Try and do it! Take my
    word,
Practise but half as much, while limbs
    are lithe,
To turn, shove, tilt a table, crack your
    joints,
Manage your feet, dispose your hands
    aright,
Work wires that twitch the curtains,
    play the glove
At end o' your slipper, – then put out
    the lights
And … there, there, all you want you'll
    get, I hope!
I found it slip, easy as an old shoe.

Now, lights on table again! I've done
    my part,
You take my place while I give thanks
    and rest.
'Well, Judge Humgruffin, what's your
    verdict, sir?
'You, hardest head in the United
    States, –
'Did you detect a cheat here? Wait!
    Let's see!
'Just an experiment first, for candour's
    sake!
'I'll try and cheat you, Judge! The table
    tilts:
'Is it I that move it? Write! I'll press
    your hand:
'Cry when I push, or guide your pencil,
    Judge!'
Sludge still triumphant! 'That a rap,
    indeed?
'That, the real writing? Very like a whale!
'Then, if, sir, you – a most
    distinguished man,
'And, were the Judge not here, I'd say,
    … no matter!

'Well, sir, if you fail, you can't take us
    in, –
'There's little fear that Sludge will!'
                Won't he, ma'am?
But what if our distinguished host, like
    Sludge,
Bade God bear witness that he played
    no trick,
While you believed that what produced
    the raps
Was just a certain child who died, you
    know,
And whose last breath you thought
    your lips had felt?
Eh? That's a capital point, ma'am:
    Sludge begins
At your entreaty with your dearest dead,
The little voice set lisping once again,
The tiny hand made feel for yours once
    more,
The poor lost image brought back, plain
    as dreams,
Which image, if a word had chanced
    recall,
The customary cloud would cross your
    eyes,
Your heart return the old tick, pay its
    pang!
A right mood for investigation, this!
One's at one's ease with Saul and
    Jonathan,
Pompey and Cæsar: but one's own lost
    child …
I wonder, when you heard the first clod
    drop
From the spadeful at the grave-side, felt
    you free
To investigate who twitched your
    funeral scarf
Or brushed your flounces? Then, it
    came of course
You should be stunned and stupid;
    then, (how else?)
Your breath stopped with your blood,
    your brain struck work.
But now, such causes fail of such
    effects,

All's changed, – the little voice begins
    afresh,
Yet you, calm, consequent, can test
    and try
And touch the truth. 'Tests? Didn't the
    creature tell
'Its nurse's name, and say it lived six
    years,
'And rode a rocking-horse? Enough of
    tests!
'Sludge never could learn that!'
                 He could not, eh?
You compliment him. 'Could not?'
    Speak for yourself!
I'd like to know the man I ever saw
Once, – never mind where, how, why,
    when, – once saw,
Of whom I do not keep some matter in
    mind
He'd swear I 'could not' know, sagacious
    soul!
What? Do you live in this world's blow
    of blacks,
Palaver, gossipry, a single hour
Nor find one smut has settled on your
    nose,
Of a smut's worth, no more, no less? –
    one fact
Out of the drift of facts, whereby you
    learn
What someone was, somewhere, some-
    when, somewhy?
You don't tell folk – 'see what has
    stuck to me!
'Judge Humgruffin, our most dis-
    tinguished man,
'Your uncle was a tailor, and your wife
'Thought to have married Miggs,
    missed him, hit you!' –
Do you, sir, though you see him twice
    a-week?
'No,' you reply, 'what use retailing it?
'Why should I?' But, you see, one day
    you *should*,
Because one day there's much use, –
    when this fact

Brings you the Judge upon both gouty
    knees
Before the supernatural; proves that
    Sludge
Knows, as you say, a thing he 'could
    not' know:
Will not Sludge thenceforth keep an
    outstretched face
The way the wind drives?
             'Could not!' look you now,
I'll tell you a story! There's a whiskered
    chap,
A foreigner, that teaches music here
And gets his bread, – knowing no better
    way:
He says, the fellow who informed of him
And made him fly his country and fall
    West
Was a hunchback cobbler, sat, stitched
    soles and sang,
In some outlandish place, the city Rome,
In a cellar by their Broadway, all day
    long;
Never asked questions, stopped to
    listen or look,
Nor lifted nose from lapstone; let the
    world
Roll round his three-legged stool, and
    news run in
The ears he hardly seemed to keep
    pricked up.
Well, that man went on Sundays,
    touched his pay,
And took his praise from government,
    you see;
For something like two dollars every
    week,
He'd engage tell you some one little
    thing
Of some one man, which led to many
    more,
(Because one truth leads right to the
    world's end)
And make you that man's master –
    when he dined
And on what dish, where walked to
    keep his health

And to what street. His trade was, throwing thus
His sense out, like an ant-eater's long tongue,
Soft, innocent, warm, moist, impassible,
And when 'twas crusted o'er with creatures – slick,
Their juice enriched his palate. 'Could not Sludge!'

I'll go yet a step further, and maintain,
Once the imposture plunged its proper depth
I' the rotten of your natures, all of you, –
(If one's not mad nor drunk, and hardly then)
It's impossible to cheat – that's, be found out!
Go tell your brotherhood this first slip of mine,
All to-day's tale, how you detected Sludge,
Behaved unpleasantly, till he was fain confess,
And so has come to grief! You'll find, I think,
Why Sludge still snaps his fingers in your face.
There now, you've told them! What's their prompt reply?
'Sir, did that youth confess he had cheated me,
'I'd disbelieve him. He may cheat at times;
'That's in the "medium"-nature, thus they're made,
'Vain and vindictive, cowards, prone to scratch.
'And so all cats are; still, a cat's the beast
'You coax the strange electric sparks from out,
'By rubbing back its fur; not so a dog,
'Nor lion, nor lamb: 'tis the cat's nature, sir!
'Why not the dog's? Ask God, who made them beasts!

'D'ye think the sound, the nicely-balanced man
'(Like me' – aside) – 'like you yourself,' – (aloud)
' – He's stuff to make a "medium"? Bless your soul,
'Tis these hysteric, hybrid half-and-halfs,
'Equivocal, worthless vermin yield the fire!
'We take such as we find them, 'ware their tricks,
'Wanting their service. Sir, Sludge took in you –
'How, I can't say, not being there to watch:
'He was tried, was tempted by your easiness, –
'He did not take in me!'
                    Thank you for Sludge!
I'm to be grateful to such patrons, eh,
When what you hear's my best word? 'Tis a challenge
'Snap at all strangers, half-tamed prairie-dog,
'So you cower duly at your keeper's beck!
'Cat, show what claws were made for, muffling them
'Only to me! Cheat others if you can,
'Me, if you dare!' And, my wise sir, I dared –
Did cheat you first, made you cheat others next,
And had the help o' your vaunted manliness
To bully the incredulous. You used me?
Have not I used you, taken full revenge,
Persuaded folk they knew not their own name,
And straight they'd own the error! Who was the fool
When, to an awe-struck wide-eyed open-mouthed
Circle of sages, Sludge would introduce
Milton composing baby-rhymes, and Locke

Reasoning in gibberish, Homer writing
    Greek
In noughts and crosses, Asaph setting
    psalms
To crotchet and quaver? I've made a
    spirit squeak
In sham voice for a minute, then outbroke
Bold in my own, defying the imbeciles –
Have copied some ghost's pothooks,
    half a page,
Then ended with my own scrawl
    undisguised.
'All right! The ghost was merely using
    Sludge,
'Suiting itself from his imperfect stock!'
Don't talk of gratitude to me! For what?
For being treated as a showman's ape,
Encouraged to be wicked and make
    sport,
Fret or sulk, grin or whimper, any mood
So long as the ape be in it and no man –
Because a nut pays every mood alike –
Curse your superior, superintending
    sort,
Who, since you hate smoke, send up
    boys that climb
To cure your chimney, bid a 'medium'
    lie
To sweep you truth down! Curse your
    women too,
Your insolent wives and daughters, that
    fire up
Or faint away if a male hand squeeze
    theirs,
Yet, to encourage Sludge, may play
    with Sludge
As only a 'medium,' only the kind of
    thing
They must humour, fondle … oh, to
    misconceive
Were too preposterous! But I've paid
    them out!
They've had their wish – called for the
    naked truth,
And in she tripped, sat down and bade
    them stare:
They had to blush a little and forgive!

'The fact is, children talk so; in next
    world
'All our conventions are reversed, –
    perhaps
'Made light of: something like old prints,
    my dear!
'The Judge has one, he brought from
    Italy,
'A metropolis in the background, – o'er
    a bridge,
'A team of trotting roadsters, – cheerful
    groups
'Of wayside travellers, peasants at their
    work,
'And, full in front, quite unconcerned,
    why not?
'Three nymphs conversing with a
    cavalier,
'And never a rag among them: "fine,"
    folk cry –
'And heavenly manners seem not
    much unlike!
'Let Sludge go on; we'll fancy it's in
    print!'
If such as came for wool, sir, went
    home shorn,
Where is the wrong I did them? 'Twas
    their choice;
They tried the adventure, ran the risk,
    tossed up
And lost, as some one's sure to do in
    games;
They fancied I was made to lose, –
    smoked glass
Useful to spy the sun through, spare
    their eyes:
And had I proved a red-hot iron plate
They thought to pierce, and, for their
    pains, grew blind,
Whose were the fault but theirs? While
    as things go,
Their loss amounts to gain, the more's
    the, shame!
They've had their peep into the spirit-
    world,
And all this world may know it! They've
    fed fat

Their self-conceit which else had
    starved: what chance
Save this, of cackling o'er a golden egg
And compassing distinction from the
    flock,
Friends of a feather? Well, they paid for
    it,
And not prodigiously; the price o' the
    play,
Not counting certain pleasant interludes,
Was scarce a vulgar play's worth. When
    you buy
The actor's talent, do you dare propose
For his soul beside? Whereas my soul
    you buy!
Sludge acts Macbeth, obliged to be
    Macbeth,
Or you'll not hear his first word! Just go
    through
That slight formality, swear himself's
    the Thane,
And thenceforth he may strut and fret
    his hour,
Spout, spawl, or spin his target, no one
    cares!
Why hadn't I leave to play tricks, Sludge
    as Sludge?
Enough of it all! I've wiped out scores
    with you –
Vented your fustian, let myself be
    streaked
Like tom-fool with your ochre and
    carmine,
Worn patchwork your respectable
    fingers sewed
To metamorphose somebody, – yes, I'
    ve earned
My wages, swallowed down my bread
    of shame,
And shake the crumbs off – where but
    in your face?

As for religion – why, I served it, sir!
I'll stick to that! With my *phenomena*
I laid the atheist sprawling on his back,
Propped up Saint Paul, or, at least,
    Swedenborg!

In fact, it's just the proper way to baulk
These troublesome fellows – liars, one
    and all,
Are not these sceptics? Well, to baffle
    them,
No use in being squeamish: lie yourself!
Erect your buttress just as wide o' the
    line,
Your side, as they build up the wall on
    theirs;
Where both meet, midway in a point,
    is truth
High overhead: so, take your room,
    pile bricks,
Lie! Oh, there's titillation in all shame!
What snow may lose in white, snow
    gains in rose!
Miss Stokes turns – Rahab, – nor a bad
    exchange!
Glory be on her, for the good she
    wrought,
Breeding belief anew 'neath ribs of
    death,
Browbeating now the unabashed before,
Ridding us of their whole life's
    gathered straws
By a live coal from the altar! Why, of
    old,
Great men spent years and years in
    writing books
To prove we've souls, and hardly
    proved it then:
Miss Stokes with her live coal, for you
    and me!
Surely, to this good issue, all was fair –
Not only fondling Sludge, but, even
    suppose
He let escape some spice of knavery, –
    well,
In wisely being blind to it! Don't you
    praise
Nelson for setting spy-glass to blind eye
And saying … what was it – that he
    could not see
The signal he was bothered with? Ay,
    indeed!

I'll go beyond: there's a real love of a
 lie,
Liars find ready-made for lies they
 make,
As hand for glove, or tongue for sugar-
 plum.
At best, 'tis never pure and full belief;
Those furthest in the quagmire, – don't
 suppose
They strayed there with no warning,
 got no chance
Of a filth-speck in their face, which
 they clenched teeth,
Bent brow against! Be sure they had
 their doubts,
And fears, and fairest challenges to try
The floor o' the seeming solid sand!
 But no!
Their faith was pledged, acquaintance
 too apprised,
All but the last step ventured, kerchiefs
 waved,
And Sludge called 'pet': 'twas easier
 marching on
To the promised land; join those who,
 Thursday next,
Meant to meet Shakespeare; better
 follow Sludge –
Prudent, oh sure! – on the alert, how
 else? –
But making for the mid-bog, all the
 same!
To hear your outcries, one would think
 I caught
Miss Stokes by the scruff o' the neck,
 and pitched her flat,
Foolish-face-foremost! Hear these
 simpletons,
That's all I beg, before my work's begun,
Before I've touched them with my
 fingertip!
Thus they await me (do but listen, now!
It's reasoning, this is, – I can't imitate
The baby voice, though) 'In so many
 tales
'Must be some truth, truth though a
 pin-point big,

'Yet, some: a single man's deceived,
 perhaps –
'Hardly, a thousand: to suppose one
 cheat
'Can gull all these, were more miraculous
 far
'Than aught we should confess a
 miracle' –
And so on. Then the Judge sums up –
 (it's rare) –
Bids you respect the authorities that
 leap
To the judgment-seat at once, – why
 don't you note
The limpid nature, the unblemished
 life,
The spotless honour, indisputable
 sense
Of the first upstart with his story?
 What –
Outrage a boy on whom you ne'er till
 now
Set eyes, because he finds raps trouble
 him?

Fools, these are: ay, and how of their
 opposites
Who never did, at bottom of their
 hearts,
Believe for a moment? – Men emasculate,
Blank of belief, who played, as eunuchs
 use,
With superstition safely, – cold of blood,
Who saw what made for them i' the
 mystery,
Took their occasion, and supported
 Sludge
– As proselytes? No, thank you, far too
 shrewd!
– But promisers of fair play, encouragers
O' the claimant; who in candour needs
 must hoist
Sludge up on Mars' Hill, get speech
 out of Sludge
To carry off, criticize, and cant about!
Didn't Athens treat Saint Paul so? – at
 any rate,

It's 'a new thing' philosophy fumbles at.
Then there's the other picker-put of
    pearl
From dung-heaps, – ay, your literary
    man,
Who draws on his kid gloves to deal
    with Sludge
Daintily and discreetly, – shakes a dust
O' the doctrine, flavours thence, he
    well knows how,
The narrative or the novel, – half-believes,
All for the book's sake, and the public's
    stare,
And the cash that's God's sole solid in
    this world!
Look at him! Try to be too bold, too
    gross
For the master! Not you! He's the man
    for muck;
Shovel it forth, full-splash, he'll smooth
    your brown
Into artistic richness, never fear!
Find him the crude stuff; when you
    recognize
Your lie again, you'll doff your hat to it,
Dressed out for company! 'For company,'
I say, since there's the relish of success:
Let all pay due respect, call the lie truth,
Save the soft silent smirking gentleman
Who ushered in the stranger: you must
    sigh
'How melancholy, he, the only one
'Fails to perceive the bearing of the truth
'Himself gave birth to!' – There's the
    triumph's smack!
That man would choose to see the
    whole world roll
I' the slime o' the slough, so he might
    touch the tip
Of his brush with what I call the best
    of browns –
Tint ghost-tales, spirit-stories, past the
    power
Of the outworn umber and bistre!
                Yet I think
There's a more hateful form of foolery –
The social sage's, Solomon of saloons

And philosophic diner-out, the fribble
Who wants a doctrine for a chopping-
    block
To try the edge of his faculty upon,
Prove how much common sense he'll
    hack and hew
I' the critical minute 'twixt the soup
    and fish!
These were my patrons: these, and the
    like of them
Who, rising in my soul now, sicken it, –
These I have injured! Gratitude to these?
The gratitude, forsooth, of a prostitute
To the greenhorn and the bully – friends
    of hers,
From the wag that wants the queer
    jokes for his club,
To the snuff-box-decorator, honest man,
Who just was at his wits' end where to
    find
So genial a Pasiphae! All and each
Pay, compliment, protect from the
    police:
And how she hates them for their pains,
    like me!
So much for my remorse at thanklessness
Toward a deserving public!
                   But, for God?
Ay, that's a question! Well, sir, since
    you press –
(How you do tease the whole thing out
    of me!
I don't mean you, you know, when I
    say 'them':
Hate you, indeed! But that Miss Stokes,
    that Judge!
Enough, enough – with sugar: thank
    you, sir!)
Now for it, then! Will you believe me,
    though?
You've heard what I confess; I don't
    unsay
A single word: I cheated when I could,
Rapped with my toe-joints, set sham
    hands at work,
Wrote down names weak in sympathetic
    ink,

Rubbed odic lights with ends of
    phosphor-match,
And all the rest; believe that: believe
    this,
By the same token, though it seem to
    set
The crooked straight again, unsay the
    said,
Stick up what I've knocked down; I
    can't help that:
It's truth! I somehow vomit truth to-
    day.
This trade of mine – I don't know,
    can't be sure
But there was something in it, tricks
    and all!
Really, I want to light up my own
    mind.
They were tricks, – true, but what I
    mean to add
Is also true. First, – don't it strike you,
    sir?
Go back to the beginning, – the first
    fact
We're taught is, there's a world beside
    this world,
With spirits, not mankind, for
    tenantry;
That much within that world once
    sojourned here,
That all upon this world will visit there,
And therefore that we, bodily here
    below,
Must have exactly such an interest
In learning what may be the ways o'
    the world
Above us, as the disembodied folk
Have (by all analogic likelihood)
In watching how things go in the old
    home
With us, their sons, successors, and
    what not.
Oh yes, with added powers probably,
Fit for the novel state, – old loves
    grown pure,
Old interests understood aright, – they
    watch!

Eyes to see, ears to hear, and hands to
    help,
Proportionate to advancement: they're
    ahead,
That's all – do what we do, but noblier
    done –
Use plate, whereas we eat our meals off
    delf,
(To use a figure).
               Concede that, and I ask
Next what may be the mode of
    intercourse
Between us men here, and those once-
    men there?
First comes the Bible's speech; then,
    history
With the supernatural element, – you
    know –
All that we sucked in with our
    mothers' milk,
Grew up with, got inside of us at last,
Till it's found bone of bone and flesh
    of flesh.
See now, we start with the miraculous,
And know it used to be, at all events:
What's the first step we take, and can't
    but take,
In arguing from the known to the
    obscure?
Why this: 'What was before, may be
    to-day.
'Since Samuel's ghost appeared to Saul,
    of course
'My brother's spirit may appear to me.'
Go tell your teacher that! What's his
    reply?
What brings a shade of doubt for the
    first time
O'er his brow late so luminous with
    faith?
'Such things have been,' says he, 'and
    there's no doubt
'Such things may be: but I advise mistrust
'Of eyes, ears, stomach, and, more
    than all, your brain,
'Unless it be of your great-grandmother,
'Whenever they propose a ghost to you!'

The end is, there's a composition struck;
'Tis settled, we've some way of inter-
course
Just as in Saul's time; only, different:
How, when and where, precisely, – find
it out!
I want to know, then, what's so natural
As that a person born into this world
And seized on by such teaching,
should begin
With firm expectancy and a frank look-
out
For his own allotment, his especial share
I' the secret, – his particular ghost, in
fine?
I mean, a person born to look that way,
Since natures differ: take the painter-
sort.
One man lives fifty years in ignorance
Whether grass be green or red, – 'No
kind of eye
'For colour,' say you; while another picks
And puts away even pebbles, when a
child,
Because of bluish spots and pinky
veins –
'Give him forthwith a paint-box!' Just
the same
Was I born ... 'medium,' you won't let
me say, –
Well, seer of the supernatural
Everywhen, everyhow and everywhere, –
Will that do?
          I and all such boys of course
Started with the same stock of Bible-
truth;
Only, – what in the rest you style their
sense,
Instinct, blind reasoning but imperative,
This, betimes, taught them the old
world had one law
And ours another: 'New world, new
laws,' cried they:
'None but old laws, seen everywhere at
work,'
Cried I, and by their help explained my
life

The Jews' way, still a working way to
me.
Ghosts made the noises, fairies waved
the lights,
Or Santa Claus slid down on New Year's
Eve
And stuffed with cakes the stocking at
my bed,
Changed the worn shoes, rubbed clean
the fingered slate
O' the sum that came to grief the day
before.

This could not last long: soon enough I
found
Who had worked wonders thus, and to
what end:
But did I find all easy, like my mates?
Henceforth no supernatural any more?
Not a whit: what projects the billiard-
balls?
'A cue,' you answer: 'Yes, a cue,' said I;
'But what hand, off the cushion, moved
the cue?
'What unseen agency, outside the world,
'Prompted its puppets to do this and
that,
'Put cakes and shoes and slates into
their mind,
'These mothers and aunts, nay even
schoolmasters?'
Thus high I sprang, and there have
settled since.
Just so I reason, in sober earnest still,
About the greater godsends, what you
call
The serious gains and losses of my life.
What do I know or care about your
world
Which either is or seems to be? This
snap
O' my fingers, sir! My care is for
myself;
Myself am whole and sole reality
Inside a raree-show and a market-mob
Gathered about it: that's the use of
things.

'Tis easy saying they serve vast purposes,
Advantage their grand selves: be it true or false,
Each thing may have two uses. What's a star?
A world, or a world's sun: doesn't it serve
As taper also, time-piece, weather-glass,
And almanac? Are stars not set for signs
When we should shear our sheep, sow corn, prune trees?
The Bible says so.
      Well, I add one use
To all the acknowledged uses, and declare
If I spy Charles's Wain at twelve to-night,
It warns me, 'Go, nor lose another day,
'And have your hair cut, Sludge!' You laugh: and why?
Were such a sign too hard for God to give?
No: but Sludge seems too little for such grace:
Thank you, sir! So you think, so does not Sludge!
When you and good men gape at Providence,
Go into history and bid us mark
Not merely powder-plots prevented, crowns
Kept on kings' heads by miracle enough,
But private mercies – oh, you've told me, sir,
Of such interpositions! How yourself
Once, missing on a memorable day
Your handkerchief – just setting out, you know, –
You must return to fetch it, lost the train,
And saved your precious self from what befell
The thirty-three whom Providence forgot.
You tell, and ask me what I think of this?
Well, sir, I think then, since you needs must know,

What matter had you and Boston city to boot
Sailed skyward, like burnt onion-peelings? Much
To you, no doubt: for me – undoubtedly
The cutting of my hair concerns me more,
Because, however sad the truth may seem,
Sludge is of all-importance to himself.
You set apart that day in every year
For special thanksgiving, were a heathen else:
Well, I who cannot boast the like escape,
Suppose I said 'I don't thank Providence
'For my part, owing it no gratitude'?
'Nay, but you owe as much' – you'd tutor me,
'You, every man alive, for blessings gained
'In every hour o' the day, could you but know!
'I saw my crowning mercy: all have such,
'Could they but see!' Well, sir, why don't they see?
'Because they won't look, – or perhaps, they can't.'
Then, sir, suppose I can, and will, and do
Look, microscopically as is right,
Into each hour with its infinitude
Of influences at work to profit Sludge?
For that's the case: I've sharpened up my sight
To spy a providence in the fire's going out,
The kettle's boiling, the dime's sticking fast
Despite the hole i' the pocket. Call such facts
Fancies, too petty a work for Providence,
And those same thanks which you exact from me
Prove too prodigious payment: thanks for what,

If nothing guards and guides us little
    men?
No, no, sir! You must put away your
    pride,
Resolve to let Sludge into partnership!
I live by signs and omens: looked at
    the roof
Where the pigeons settle – 'If the further
    bird,
'The white, takes wing first, I'll confess
    when thrashed;
'Not, if the blue does' – so I said to
    myself
Last week, lest you should take me by
    surprise:
Off flapped the white, – and I'm
    confessing, sir!
Perhaps 'tis Providence's whim and way
With only me, i' the world: how can
    you tell?
'Because unlikely!' Was it likelier, now,
That this our one out of all worlds
    beside,
The what-d'you-call-'em millions,
    should be just
Precisely chosen to make Adam for,
And the rest o' the tale? Yet the tale's
    true, you know:
Such undeserving clod was graced so
    once;
Why not graced likewise undeserving
    Sludge?
Are we merit-mongers, flaunt we filthy
    rags?
All you can bring against my privilege
Is, that another way was taken with
    you, –
Which I don't question. It's pure grace,
    my luck:
I'm broken to the way of nods and
    winks,
And need no formal summoning.
    You've a help;
Holloa his name or whistle, clap your
    hands,
Stamp with your foot or pull the bell:
    all's one,

He understands you want him, here he
    comes.
Just so, I come at the knocking: you,
    sir, wait
The tongue o' the bell, nor stir before
    you catch
Reason's clear tingle, nature's clapper
    brisk,
Or that traditional peal was wont to
    cheer
Your mother's face turned heavenward;
    short of these
There's no authentic intimation, eh?
Well, when you hear, you'll answer
    them, start up
And stride into the presence, top of
    toe,
And there find Sludge beforehand,
    Sludge that sprang
At noise o' the knuckle on the partition-
    wall!
I think myself the more religious man.
Religion's all or nothing; it's no mere
    smile
O' contentment, sigh of aspiration, sir –
No quality o' the finelier-tempered clay
Like its whiteness or its lightness; rather,
    stuff
O' the very stuff, life of life, and self of
    self.
I tell you, men won't notice; when they
    do,
They'll understand. I notice nothing
    else:
I'm eyes, ears, mouth of me, one gaze
    and gape,
Nothing eludes me, everything's a hint,
Handle and help. It's all absurd, and
    yet
There's something in it all, I know:
    how much?
No answer! What does that prove?
    Man's still man,
Still meant for a poor blundering piece
    of work
When all's done; but, if somewhat's
    done, like this,

Or not done, is the case the same?
Suppose
I blunder in my guess at the true sense
O' the knuckle-summons, nine times
out of ten, –
What if the tenth guess happen to be
right?
If the tenth shovel-load of powdered
quartz
Yield me the nugget? I gather, crush,
sift all,
Pass o'er the failure, pounce on the
success.
To give you a notion, now – (let who
wins, laugh!)
When first I see a man, what do I first?
Why, count the letters which make up
his name,
And as their number chances, even or
odd,
Arrive at my conclusion, trim my course:
Hiram H. Horsefall is your honoured
name,
And haven't I found a patron, sir, in
you?
'Shall I cheat this stranger?' I take
apple-pips,
Stick one in either canthus of my eye,
And if the left drops first – (your left,
sir, stuck)
I'm warned, I let the trick alone this
time.
You, sir, who smile, superior to such
trash,
You judge of character by other rules:
Don't your rules sometimes fail you?
Pray, what rule
Have you judged Sludge by hitherto?
Oh, be sure,
You, everybody blunders, just as I,
In simpler things than these by far! For
see:
I knew two farmers, – one, a wiseacre
Who studied seasons, rummaged
almanacs,
Quoted the dew-point, registered the
frost,

And then declared, for outcome of his
pains,
Next summer must be dampish: 'twas
a drought.
His neighbour prophesied such
drought would fall,
Saved hay and corn, made cent. per
cent. thereby,
And proved a sage indeed: how came
his lore?
Because one brindled heifer, late in
March,
Stiffened her tail of evenings, and
somehow
He got into his head that drought was
meant!
I don't expect all men can do as much:
Such kissing goes by favour. You must
take
A certain turn of mind for this, – a
twist
I' the flesh, as well. Be lazily alive,
Open-mouthed, like my friend the ant-
eater,
Letting all nature's loosely-guarded
motes
Settle and, slick, be swallowed! Think
yourself
The one i' the world, the one for whom
the world
Was made, expect it tickling at your
mouth!
Then will the swarm of busy buzzing
flies,
Clouds of coincidence, break egg-shell,
thrive,
Breed, multiply, and bring you food
enough.

I can't pretend to mind your smiling,
sir!
Oh, what you mean is this! Such
intimate way,
Close converse, frank exchange of
offices,
Strict sympathy of the immeasurably
great

With the infinitely small, betokened
    here
By a course of signs and omens, raps
    and sparks, –
How does it suit the dread traditional
    text
O' the 'Great and Terrible Name'?
    Shall the Heaven of Heavens
Stoop to such child's play?
                 Please, sir, go with me
A moment, and I'll try to answer you.
The '*Magnum et terribile*' (is that right?)
Well, folk began with this in the early
    day;
And all the acts they recognized in
    proof
Were thunders, lightnings,
    earthquakes, whirlwinds, dealt
Indisputably on men whose death they
    caused.
There, and there only, folk saw
    Providence
At work, – and seeing it, 'twas right
    enough
All heads should tremble, hands wring
    hands amain,
And knees knock hard together at the
    breath
O' the Name's first letter; why, the
    Jews, I'm told,
Won't write it down, no, to this very
    hour,
Nor speak aloud: you know best if't be
    so.
Each ague-fit of fear at end, they crept
(Because somehow people once born
    must live)
Out of the sound, sight, swing and
    sway o' the Name,
Into a corner, the dark rest of the
    world,
And safe space where as yet no fear
    had reached;
'Twas there they looked about them,
    breathed again,
And felt indeed at home, as we might
    say.

The current o' common things, the
    daily life,
This had their due contempt; no Name
    pursued
Man from the mountain-top where
    fires abide,
To his particular mouse-hole at its foot
Where he ate, drank, digested, lived in
    short:
Such was man's vulgar business, far
    too small
To be worth thunder: 'small,' folk kept
    on, 'small,'
With much complacency in those great
    days!
A mote of sand, you know, a blade of
    grass –
What was so despicable as mere grass,
Except perhaps the life o' the worm or
    fly
Which fed there? These were 'small'
    and men were great.
Well, sir, the old way's altered some-
    what since,
And the world wears another aspect
    now:
Somebody turns our spyglass round, or
    else
Puts a new lens in it: grass, worm, fly
    grow big:
We find great things are made of little
    things,
And little things go lessening till at last
Comes God behind them. Talk of
    mountains now?
We talk of mould that heaps the
    mountain, mites
That throng the mould, and God that
    makes the mites.
The Name comes close behind a
    stomachcyst,
The simplest of creations, just a sac
That's mouth, heart, legs and belly at
    once, yet lives
And feels, and could do neither, we
    conclude,
If simplified still further one degree:

The small becomes the dreadful and
    immense!
Lightning, forsooth? No word more
    upon that!
A tin-foil bottle, a strip of greasy silk,
With a bit of wire and knob of brass,
    and there's
Your dollar's-worth of lightning! But
    the cyst –
The life of the least of the little things?
                              No, no!
Preachers and teachers try another tack,
Come near the truth this time: they put
    aside
Thunder and lightning: 'That's mistake,'
    they cry,
'Thunderbolts fall for neither fright nor
    ' sport,
'But do appreciable good, like tides,
'Changes o' the wind, and other natural
    facts –
' "Good" meaning good to man, his
    body or soul.
'Mediate, immediate, all things minister
'To man, – that's settled: be our future
    text
' "We are His children!" ' So, they now
    harangue
About the intention, the contrivance, all
That keeps up an incessant play of
    love, –
See the Bridgewater book.
                              Amen to it!
Well, sir, I put this question: I' m a
    child?
I lose no time, but take you at your
    word:
How shall I act a child's part properly?
Your sainted mother, sir, – used you to
    live
With such a thought as this a-worrying
    you?
'She has it in her power to throttle me,
'Or stab or poison: she may turn me
    out,
'Or lock me in, – nor stop at this, to-
    day,

'But cut me off to-morrow from the
    estate
'I look for' – (long may you enjoy it,
    sir!)
'In brief, she may unchild the child I
    am.'
You never had such crotchets? Nor
    have I!
Who, frank confessing childship from
    the first,
Cannot both fear and take my ease at
    once,
So, don't fear, – know what might be,
    well enough,
But know too, child-like, that it will
    not be,
At least in my case, mine, the son and
    heir
O' the kingdom, as yourself proclaim
    my style.
But do you fancy I stop short at this?
Wonder if suit and service, son and
    heir
Needs must expect, I dare pretend to
    find?
If, looking for signs proper to such an
    one,
I straight perceive them irresistible?
Concede that homage is a son's plain
    right,
And, never mind the nods and raps
    and winks,
'Tis the pure obvious supernatural
Steps forward, does its duty: why, of
    course!
I have presentiments; my dreams come
    true:
I fancy a friend stands whistling all in
    white
Blithe as a boblink, and he's dead I
    learn.
I take dislike to a dog my favourite long,
And sell him; he goes mad next week
    and snaps.
I guess that stranger will turn up to-day
I have not seen these three years;
    there's his knock.

I wager 'sixty peaches on that tree!' –
That I pick up a dollar in my walk,
That your wife's brother's cousin's
     name was George –
And win on all points. Oh, you wince
     at this?
You'd fain distinguish between gift and
     gift,
Washington's oracle and Sludge's itch
O' the elbow when at whist he ought
     to trump?
With Sludge it's too absurd? *Fine, draw
     the line*
*Somewhere, but, sir, your somewhere is
     not mine!*

Bless us, I'm turning poet! It's time to
     end.
How you have drawn me out, sir! All I
     ask
Is – am I heir or not heir? If I'm he,
Then, sir, remember, that same personage
(To judge by what we read i' the
     newspaper)
Requires, beside one nobleman in gold
To carry up and down his coronet,
Another servant, probably a duke,
To hold egg-nogg in readiness: why
     want
Attendance, sir, when helps in his father's
     house
Abound, I'd like to know?
                              Enough of talk!
My fault is that I tell too plain a truth.
Why, which of those who say they
     disbelieve,
Your clever people, but has dreamed
     his dream,
Caught his coincidence, stumbled on
     his fact
He can't explain, (he'll tell you smilingly)
Which he's too much of a philosopher
To count as supernatural, indeed,
So calls a puzzle and problem, proud
     of it:
Bidding you still be on your guard, you
     know,

Because one fact don't make a system
     stand,
Nor prove this an occasional escape
Of spirit beneath the matter: that's the
     way!
Just so wild Indians picked up, piece
     by piece,
The fact in California, the fine gold
That underlay the gravel – hoarded
     these,
But never made a system stand, nor
     dug!
So wise men hold out in each hollowed
     palm
A handful of experience, sparkling fact
They can't explain; and since their rest
     of life
Is all explainable, what proof in this?
Whereas I take the fact, the grain of
     gold,
And fling away the dirty rest of life,
And add this grain to the grain each
     fool has found
O' the million other such philo-
     sophers, –
Till I see gold, all gold and only gold,
Truth questionless though unexplainable,
And the miraculous proved the
     common-place!
The other fools believed in mud, no
     doubt –
Failed to know gold they saw: was that
     so strange?
Are all men born to play Bach's fiddle-
     fugues,
'Time' with the foil in carte, jump their
     own height,
Cut the mutton with the broadsword,
     skate a five,
Make the red hazard with the cue, clip
     nails
While swimming, in five minutes row a
     mile,
Pull themselves three feet up with the
     left arm,
Do sums of fifty figures in their head,
And so on, by the scores of instances?

The Sludge with luck, who sees the
    spiritual facts
His fellows strive and fail to see, may
    rank
With these, and share the advantage.
                   Ay, but share
The drawback! Think it over by yourself;
I have not heart, sir, and the fire's gone
    grey.
Defect somewhere compensates for
    success,
Everyone knows that. Oh, we're equals,
    sir!
The big-legged fellow has a little arm
And a less brain, though big legs win
    the race:
Do you suppose I 'scape the common
    lot?
Say, I was born with flesh so sensitive,
Soul so alert, that, practice helping
    both,
I guess what's going on outside the veil,
Just as a prisoned crane feels pairing-
    time
In the islands where his kind are, so
    must fall
To capering by himself some shiny
    night,
As if your back-yard were a plot of
    spice –
Thus am I 'ware o' the spirit-world:
    while you,
Blind as a beetle that way, – for amends,
Why, you can double fist and floor me,
    sir!
Ride that hot hardmouthed horrid horse
    of yours,
Laugh while it lightens, play with the
    great dog,
Speak your mind though it vex some
    friend to hear,
Never brag, never bluster, never blush, –
In short, you've pluck, when I'm a
    coward – there!
I know it, I can't help it, – folly or no,
I'm paralyzed, my hand's no more a
    hand,

Nor my head a head, in danger: you
    can smile
And change the pipe in your cheek.
    Your gift's not mine.
Would you swap for mine? No! but
    you'd add my gift
To yours: I dare say! I too sigh at times,
Wish I were stouter, could tell truth
    nor flinch,
Kept cool when threatened, did not
    mind so much
Being dressed gaily, making strangers
    stare,
Eating nice things; when I'd amuse
    myself,
I shut my eyes and fancy in my brain
I'm – now the President, now Jenny
    Lind,
Now Emerson, now the Benicia Boy –
With all the civilized world a-wondering
And worshipping. I know it's folly and
    worse;
I feel such tricks sap, honeycomb the
    soul,
But I can't cure myself: despond,
    despair,
And then, hey, presto, there's a turn o'
    the wheel,
Under comes uppermost, fate makes
    full amends;
Sludge knows and sees and hears a
    hundred things
You all are blind to, – I've my taste of
    truth,
Likewise my touch of falsehood, – vice
    no doubt,
But you've your vices also: I'm content.

What, sir? You won't shake hands?
    'Because I cheat!'
'You've found me out in cheating!'
    That's enough
To make an apostle swear! Why, when
    I cheat,
*Mean to cheats, do cheat, and am caught*
    *in the act,*
*Are you, or, rather, am I sure o' the fact?*

(There's verse again, but I'm inspired
    somehow.)
Well then I'm not sure! I may be,
    perhaps,
Free as a babe from cheating: how it
    began,
My gift, – no matter: what 'tis got to be
In the end now, that's the question;
    answer that!
Had I seen, perhaps, what hand was
    holding mine,
Leading me whither, I had died of
    fright:
So, I was made believe I led myself.
If I should lay a six-inch plank from
    roof
To roof, you would not cross the street,
    one step,
Even at your mother's summons: but,
    being shrewd,
If I paste paper on each side the plank
And swear 'tis solid pavement, why,
    you'll cross
Humming a tune the while, in ignorance
Beacon Street stretches a hundred feet
    below:
I walked thus, took the paper-cheat for
    stone.
Some impulse made me set a thing o'
    the move
Which, started once, ran really by itself;
Beer flows thus, suck the siphon; toss
    the kite,
It takes the wind and floats of its own
    force.
Don't let truth's lump rot stagnant for
    the lack
Of a timely helpful lie to leaven it!
Put a chalk-egg beneath the clucking
    hen,
She'll lay a real one, laudably deceived,
Daily for weeks to come. I've told my lie,
And seen truth follow, marvels none of
    mine;
All was not cheating, sir, I'm positive!
I don't know if I move your hand some-
    times

When the spontaneous writing spreads
    so far,
If my knee lifts the table all that height,
Why the inkstand don't fall off the
    desk a-tilt,
Why the accordion plays a prettier
    waltz
Than I can pick out on the piano-forte,
Why I speak so much more than I
    intend,
Describe so many things I never saw.
I tell you, sir, in one sense, I believe
Nothing at all, – that everybody can,
Will, and does cheat: but in another
    sense
I'm ready to believe my very self –
That every cheat's inspired, and every
    lie
Quick with a germ of truth.
                 You ask perhaps
Why I should condescend to trick at all
If I know a way without it? This is why!
There's a strange secret sweet self-
    sacrifice
In any desecration of one's soul
To a worthy end, – isn't it Herodotus
(I wish I could read Latin!) who
    describes
The single gift o' the land's virginity,
Demanded in those old Egyptian rites,
(I've but a hazy notion – help me, sir!)
For one purpose in the world, one day
    in a life,
One hour in a day – thereafter, purity,
And a veil thrown o'er the past for
    evermore!
Well, now, they understand a many
    things
Down by Nile city, or wherever it was!
I've always vowed, after the minute's lie,
And the end's gain, – truth should be
    mine henceforth.
This goes to the root o' the matter, sir,
    – this plain
Plump fact: accept it and unlock with it
The wards of many a puzzle!

      Or, finally,
Why should I set so fine a gloss on
 things?
What need I care? I cheat in self-defence,
And there's my answer to a world of
 cheats!
Cheat? To be sure, sir! What's the world
 worth else?
Who takes it as he finds, and thanks his
 stars?
Don't it want trimming, turning,
 furbishing up
And polishing over? Your so-styled
 great men,
Do they accept one truth as truth is
 found,
Or try their skill at tinkering? What's
 your world?
Here are you born, who are, I'll say at
 once,
Of the luckiest kind, whether in head
 and heart,
Body and soul, or all that helps them
 both.
Well, now, look back: what faculty of
 yours
Came to its full, had ample justice
 done
By growing when rain fell, biding its
 time,
Solidifying growth when earth was dead,
Spiring up, broadening wide, in seasons
 due?
Never! You shot up and frost nipped
 you off,
Settled to sleep when sunshine bade
 you sprout;
One faculty thwarted its fellow: at the
 end,
All you boast is 'I had proved a topping
 tree
'In other climes' – yet this was the right
 clime
Had you foreknown the seasons. Young,
 you've force
Wasted like well-streams: old, – oh,
 then indeed,

Behold a labyrinth of hydraulic pipes
Through which you'd play off
 wondrous waterwork;
Only, no water's left to feed their play.
Young, – you've a hope, an aim, a love:
 it's tossed
And crossed and lost: you struggle on,
 some spark
Shut in your heart against the puffs
 around,
Through cold and pain; these in due
 time subside,
Now then for age's triumph, the hoarded
 light
You mean to loose on the altered face
 of things, –
Up with it on the tripod! It's extinct.
Spend your life's remnant asking, which
 was best,
Light smothered up that never peeped
 forth once,
Or the cold cresset with full leave to
 shine?
Well, accept this too, – seek the fruit
 of it
Not in enjoyment, proved a dream on
 earth,
But knowledge, useful for a second
 chance,
Another life, – you've lost this world –
 you've gained
Its knowledge for the next. What
 knowledge, sir,
Except that you know nothing? Nay,
 you doubt
Whether 'twere better have made you
 man or brute,
If aught be true, if good and evil clash.
No foul, no fair, no inside, no outside,
There's your world!
      Give it me! I slap it brisk
With harlequin's pasteboard sceptre:
 what's it now?
Changed like a rock-flat, rough with
 rusty weed,
At first wash-over o' the returning
 wave!

All the dry dead impracticable stuff
Starts into life and light again; this
     world
Pervaded by the influx from the next.
I cheat, and what's the happy con-
     sequence?
You find full justice straightway dealt
     you out,
Each want supplied, each ignorance set
     at ease,
Each folly fooled. No life-long labour
     now
As the price of worse than nothing! No
     mere film
Holding you chained in iron, as it seems,
Against the outstretch of your very arms
And legs i' the sunshine moralists forbid!
What would you have? Just speak and,
     there, you see!
You're supplemented, made a whole at
     last,
Bacon advises, Shakespeare writes you
     songs,
And Mary Queen of Scots embraces
     you.
Thus it goes on, not quite like life
     perhaps,
But so near, that the very difference
     piques,
Shows that e'en better than this best
     will be –
This passing entertainment in a hut
Whose bare walls take your taste since,
     one stage more,
And you arrive at the palace: all half
     real,
And you, to suit it, less than real beside,
In a dream, lethargic kind of death in
     life,
That helps the interchange of natures,
     flesh
Transfused by souls, and such souls!
     Oh, 'tis choice!
And if at whiles the bubble, blown too
     thin,
Seem nigh on bursting, – if you nearly
     see

The real world through the false, –
     what *do* you see?
Is the old so ruined? You find you're in
     a flock
O' the youthful, earnest, passionate –
     genius, beauty,
Rank and wealth also, if you care for
     these:
And all depose their natural rights, hail
     you,
(That's me, sir) as their mate and yoke-
     fellow,
Participate in Sludgehood – nay, grow
     mine,
I veritably possess them – banish doubt,
And reticence and modesty alike!
Why, here's the Golden Age, old
     Paradise
Or new Eutopia! Here's true life indeed,
And the world well won now, mine for
     the first time!

And all this might be, may be, and
     with good help
Of a little lying shall be: so, Sludge lies!
Why, he's at worst your poet who
     sings how Greeks
That never were, in Troy which never
     was,
Did this or the other impossible great
     thing!
He's Lowell – it's a world (you smile
     applause)
Of his own invention – wondrous
     Longfellow,
Surprising Hawthorne! Sludge does
     more than they,
And acts the books they write: the
     more his praise!

But why do I mount to poets? Take
     plain prose –
Dealers in common sense, set these at
     work,
What can they do without their helpful
     lies?
Each states the law and fact and face o'
     the thing

Just as he'd have them, finds what he
      thinks fit,
Is blind to what missuits him, just
      records
What makes his case out, quite ignores
      the rest.
It's a History of the World, the Lizard
      Age,
The Early Indians, the Old Country
      War,
Jerome Napoleon, whatsoever you
      please,
All as the author wants it. Such a scribe
You pay and praise for putting life in
      stones,
Fire into fog, making the past your
      world.
There's plenty of 'How did you
      contrive to grasp
'The thread which led you through this
      labyrinth?
'How build such solid fabric out of air?
'How on so slight foundation found
      this tale,
'Biography, narrative?' or, in other words,
'How many lies did it require to make
'The portly truth you here present us
      with?'
'Oh,' quoth the penman, purring at
      your praise,
' 'Tis fancy all; no particle of fact:
'I was poor and threadbare when I
      wrote that book
' "Bliss in the Golden City." I, at Thebes?
'We writers paint out of our heads, you
      see!'
' – Ah, the more wonderful the gift in
      you,
'The more creativeness and godlike craft!'
But I, do I present you with my piece,
It's 'What, Sludge? When my sainted
      mother spoke
'The verses Lady Jane Grey last composed
'About the rosy bower in the seventh
      heaven
'Where she and Queen Elizabeth keep
      house, –

'You made the raps? 'Twas your
  -   invention that?
'Cur, slave and devil!' – eight fingers
      and two thumbs
Stuck in my throat!
          .  Well, if the marks seem gone,
'Tis because stiffish cock-tail, taken in
      time,
Is better for a bruise than arnica.
There, sir! I bear no malice: 'tisn't in me.
I know I acted wrongly: still, I've tried
What I could say in my excuse, – to
      show
The devil's not all devil ... I don't
      pretend,
He's angel, much less such a gentleman
As you, sir! And I've lost you, lost
      myself,
Lost all–l–l–l–  ...
            No – are you in earnest, sir?
O yours, sir, is an angel's part! I know
What prejudice prompts, and what's
      the common course
Men take to soothe their ruffled self-
      conceit:
Only you rise superior to it all!
No, sir, it don't hurt much; it's
      speaking long
That makes me choke a little: the marks
      will go!
What? Twenty V-notes more, and
      outfit too,
And not a word to Greeley? One – one
      kiss
O' the hand that saves me! You'll not
      let me speak,
I well know, and I' ve lost the right, too
      true!
But I must say, sir, if She hears (she
      does)
Your sainted . . .Well, sir, – be it so!
      That's, I think,
My bed-room candle. Good-night! Bl–
      l–ess you, sir!
        *      *      *
R–r–r, you brute-beast and blackguard!
      Cowardly scamp!

I only wish I dared burn down the
    house
And spoil your sniggering! Oh what,
    you're the man?
You're satisfied at last? You've found
    out Sludge?
We'll see that presently: my turn, sir,
    next!
I too can tell my story: brute, – do you
    hear? –
You throttled your sainted mother, that
    old hag,
In just such a fit of passion: no, it
    was . . .
To get this house of hers, and many a
    note
Like these … I'll pocket them, however
    … five,
Ten, fifteen … ay, you gave her throat
    the twist,
Or else you poisoned her! Confound
    the cuss!
Where was my head? I ought to have
    prophesied
He'll die in a year and join her: that's
    the way.

I don't know where my head is: what
    had I done?
How did it all go? I said he poisoned
    her,
And hoped he'd have grace given him
    to repent,
Whereon he picked this quarrel,
    bullied me
And called me cheat: I thrashed him, –
    who could help?
He howled for mercy, prayed me on
    his knees
To cut and run and save him from
    disgrace:
I do so, and once off, he slanders me.
An end of him! Begin elsewhere anew!
Boston's a hole, the herring-pond is
    wide,
V-notes are something, liberty still more.
Beside, is he the only fool in the world?

## Apparent Failure

'We shall soon lose a celebrated building.'
                 *Paris Newspaper*

### 1

No, for I'll save it! Seven years since,
    I passed through Paris, stopped a
    day
To see the baptism of your Prince;
    Saw, made my bow, and went my
    way:
Walking the heat and headache off,
    I took the Seine-side, you surmise,
Thought of the Congress, Gortschakoff,
    Cavour's appeal and Buol's replies,
So sauntered till – what met my eyes?

### 2

Only the Doric little Morgue!
    The dead-house where you show
    your drowned:
Petrarch's Vaucluse makes proud the
    Sorgue,
    Your Morgue has made the Seine
    renowned.
One pays one's debt in such a case;
    I plucked up heart and entered, –
    stalked,
Keeping a tolerable face
    Compared with some whose cheeks
    were chalked:
Let them! No Briton's to be baulked!

### 3

First came the silent gazers; next,
    A screen of glass, we're thankful for;
Last, the sight's self, the sermon's text,
    The three men who did most abhor
Their life in Paris yesterday,
    So killed themselves: and now,
    enthroned
Each on his copper couch, they lay
    Fronting me, waiting to be owned.
I thought, and think, their sin's
    atoned.

### 4

Poor men, God made, and all for that!
    The reverence struck me; o'er each
    head

Religiously was hung its hat,
    Each coat dripped by the owner's
        bed,
Sacred from touch: each had his berth,
    His bounds, his proper place of rest,
Who last night tenanted on earth
    Some arch, where twelve such slept
        abreast, –
Unless the plain asphalte seemed best.

5

How did it happen, my poor boy?
    You wanted to be Buonaparte
And have the Tuileries for toy,
    And could not, so it broke your heart?
You, old one by his side, I judge,
    Were, red as blood, a socialist,
A leveller! Does the Empire grudge
    You've gained what no Republic
        missed?
Be quiet, and unclench your fist!

6

And this – why, he was red in vain,
    Or black, – poor fellow that is blue!
What fancy was it turned your brain?
    Oh, women were the prize for you!
Money gets women, cards and dice
    Get money, and ill-luck gets just
The copper couch and one clear nice
    Cool squirt of water o'er your bust,
The right thing to extinguish lust!

7

It's wiser being good than bad;
    It's safer being meek than fierce:
It's fitter being sane than mad.
    My own hope is, a sun will pierce
The thickest cloud earth ever stretched;
    That, after Last, returns the First,
Though a wide compass round be
        fetched;
    That what began best, can't end
        worst,
Nor what God blessed once, prove
    accurst.

## Epilogue
### FIRST SPEAKER, *as David*.

1

On the first of the Feast of Feasts,
    The Dedication Day,
When the Levites joined the Priests
    At the Altar in robed array,
Gave signal to sound and say, –

2

When the thousands, rear and van,
    Swarming with one accord
Became as a single man
    (Look, gesture, thought and word)
In praising and thanking the Lord, –

3

When the singers lift up their voice,
    And the trumpets made endeavour,
Sounding, 'In God rejoice!'
    Saying, 'In Him rejoice
'Whose mercy endureth for ever!' –

4

Then the Temple filled with a cloud,
    Even the House of the Lord;
Porch bent and pillar bowed:
    For the presence of the Lord,
In the glory of His cloud,
    Had filled the House of the Lord.

### SECOND SPEAKER, *as Return*.

Gone now! All gone across the dark so
        far,
    Sharpening fast, shuddering ever,
        shutting still,
Dwindling into the distance, dies that
        star
    Which came, stood, opened once!
        We gazed our fill
With upturned faces on as real a Face
    That, stooping from grave music and
        mild fire,
Took in our homage, made a visible
        place
    Through many a depth of glory, gyre
        on gyre,
For the dim human tribute. Was this
        true?

Could man indeed avail, mere praise
of his,
To help by rapture God's own rapture
too,
Thrill with a heart's red tinge that
pure pale bliss?
Why did it end? Who failed to beat the
breast,
And shriek, and throw the arms
protesting wide,
When a first shadow showed the star
addressed
Itself to motion, and on either side
The rims contracted as the rays retired;
The music, like a fountain's
sickening pulse,
Subsided on itself; awhile transpired
Some vestige of a Face no pangs
convulse,
No prayers retard; then even this was
gone,
Lost in the night at last. We, lone
and left
Silent through centuries, ever and anon
Venture to probe again the vault
bereft
Of all now save the lesser lights, a mist
Of multitudinous points, yet suns,
men say –
And this leaps ruby, this lurks amethyst,
But where may hide what came and
loved our clay?
How shall the sage detect in yon expanse
The star which chose to stoop and
stay for us?
Unroll the records! Hailed ye such
advance
Indeed, and did your hope evanish
thus?
Watchers of twilight, is the worst
averred?
We shall not look up, know
ourselves are seen,
Speak, and be sure that we again are
heard,
Acting or suffering, have the disk's
serene

Reflect our life, absorb an earthly
flame,
Nor doubt that, were mankind inert
and numb,
Its core had never crimsoned all the
same,
Nor, missing ours, its music fallen
dumb?
Oh, dread succession to a dizzy post,
Sad sway of sceptre whose mere
touch appals,
Ghastly dethronement, cursed by those
the most
On whose repugnant brow the
crown next falls!

### THIRD SPEAKER.

1

Witless alike of will and way divine,
How heaven's high with earth's low
should intertwine!
Friends, I have seen through your eyes;
now use mine!

2

Take the least man of all mankind, as I;
Look at his head and heart, find how
and why
He differs from his fellows utterly:

3

Then, like me, watch when nature by
degrees
Grows alive round him, as in Arctic seas
(They said of old) the instinctive water
flees

4

Toward some elected point of central
rock,
As though, for its sake only, roamed
the flock
Of waves about the waste: awhile they
mock

5

With radiance caught for the occasion,
– hues
Of blackest hell now, now such reds
and blues
As only heaven could fitly interfuse, –

6

The mimic monarch of the whirlpool,
    king
O' the current for a minute: then they
    wring
Up by the roots and oversweep the
    thing,

7

And hasten off, to play again elsewhere
The same part, choose another peak as
    bare.
They find and flatter, feast and finish
    there.

8

When you see what I tell you, – nature
    dance
About each man of us, retire, advance,
As though the pageant's end were to
    enhance

9

His worth, and – once the life, his
    product, gained –
Roll away elsewhere, keep the strife
    sustained,
And show thus real, a thing the North
    but feigned –

10

When you acknowledge that one world
    could do
All the diverse work, old yet ever new,
Divide us, each from other, me from
    you, –

11

Why, where's the need of Temple,
    when the walls
O' the world are that? What use of
    swells and falls
From Levites' choir, Priests' cries, and
    trumpet-calls?

12

That one Face, far from vanish, rather
    grows,
Or decomposes but to recompose,
Become my universe that feels and
    knows.

## From 'FIFINE AT THE FAIR'

1872

### Prologue

#### AMPHIBIAN

**1**

The fancy I had to-day,
   Fancy which turned a fear!
'swam far out in the bay,
   Since waves laughed warm and
     clear.

**2**

I lay and looked at the sun,
   The noon-sun looked at me:
Between us two, no one
   Live creature, that I could see.

**3**

Yes! There came floating by
   Me, who lay floating too,
Such a strange butterfly!
   Creature as dear as new:

**4**

Because the membraned wings
   So wonderful, so wide,
So sun-suffused, were things
   Like soul and nought beside.

**5**

A handbreadth over head!
   All of the sea my own,
It owned the sky instead;
   Both of us were alone.

**6**

I never shall join its flight,
   For, nought buoys flesh in air.
If it touch the sea – good night!
   Death sure and swift waits there.

**7**

Can the insect feel the better
   For watching the uncouth play
Of limbs that slip the fetter,
   Pretend as they were not day?

**8**

Undoubtedly I rejoice
   That the air comports so well
With a creature which had the choice
   Of the land once. Who can tell?

**9**

What if a certain soul
   Which early slipped its sheath,
And has for its home the whole
   Of heaven, thus look beneath,

**10**

Thus watch one who, in the world,
   Both lives and likes life's way,
Nor wishes the wings unfurled
   That sleep in the worm, they say?

**11**

But sometimes when the weather
   Is blue, and warm waves tempt
To free oneself of tether,
   And try a life exempt

**12**

From worldly noise and dust,
   In the sphere which overbrims
With passion and thought, – why, just
   Unable to fly, one swims!

**13**

By passion and thought upborne,
   One smiles to oneself – 'They fare
Scarce better, they need not scorn
   Our sea, who live in the air!'

**14**

Emancipate through passion
   And thought, with sea for sky,
We substitute, in a fashion,
   For heaven – poetry:

**15**

Which sea, to all intent,
   Gives flesh such noon-disport
As a finer element
   Affords the spirit-sort.

**16**

Whatever they are, we seem:
   Imagine the thing they know;
All deeds they do, we dream;
   Can heaven be else but so?

**17**

And meantime, yonder streak
   Meets the horizon's verge;

That is the land, to seek
  If we tire or dread the surge:
18
Land the solid and safe –
  To welcome again (confess!)
When, high and dry, we chafe
  The body, and don the dress.
19
Does she look, pity, wonder
  At one who mimics flight,
Swims – heaven above, sea under,
  Yet always earth in sight?

## Epilogue

### THE HOUSEHOLDER

1
Savage I was sitting in my house, late,
  lone:
  Dreary, weary with the long day's
  work:
Head of me, heart of me, stupid as a
  stone:
  Tongue-tied now, now blaspheming
  like a Turk;
When, in a moment, just a knock, call,
  cry,
  Half a pang and all a rapture, there
  again were we! –
'What, and is it really you again?'
  quoth I:
  'I again, what else did you expect?'
  quoth She.

2
'Never mind, hie away from this old
  house –
  Every crumbling brick embrowned
  with sin and shame!
Quick, in its corners ere certain shapes
  arouse!
  Let them – every devil of the night –
  lay claim,

Make and mend, or rap and rend, for
  me! Good-bye!
  God be their guard from disturbance
  at their glee,
Till, crash, comes down the carcass in
  a heap!' quoth I:
  'Nay, but there's a decency
  required!' quoth She.

3
'Ah, but if you knew how time has
  dragged, days, nights!
  All the neighbour-talk with man and
  maid – such men!
All the fuss and trouble of street-
  sounds, window-sights:
  All the worry of flapping door and
  echoing roof; and then,
All the fancies … Who were they had
  leave, dared try
Darker arts that almost struck despair
  in me?
If you knew but how I dwelt down
  here!' quoth I:
  'And was I so better off up there?'
  quoth She.

4
'Help and get it over! *Re-united to his
  wife*
  (How draw up the paper lets the
  parish-people know?)
*Lies M., or N., departed from this life,
  Day the this or that, month and year
  the so and so.*
What i' the way of final flourish? Prose,
  verse? Try!
  *Affliction sore long time he bore,* or,
  what is it to be?
*Till God did please to grant him ease.* Do
  end!' quoth I:
  'I end with – Love is all and Death is
  nought!' 'quoth She.

# PACCHIAROTTO,

## AND HOW HE WORKED IN DISTEMPER, et Cetera

### 1876

## Prologue

### 1

O the old wall here! How I could pass
  Life in a long Midsummer day,
My feet confined to a plot of grass,
  My eyes from a wall not once away!

### 2

And lush and lithe do the creepers
    clothe
  Yon wall I watch, with a wealth of
    green:
Its bald red bricks draped, nothing
    loth,
  In lappets of tangle they laugh
    between.

### 3

Now, what is it makes pulsate the
    robe?
  Why tremble the sprays? What life
    o'er-brims
The body, – the house, no eye can
    probe, –
  Divined as, beneath a robe, the
    limbs?

### 4

And there again! But my heart may
    guess
  Who tripped behind; and she sang
    perhaps:
So, the old wall throbbed, and its life's
    excess
  Died out and away in the leafy
    wraps.

### 5

Wall upon wall are between us: life
  And song should away from heart to
    heart.
I – prison-bird, with a ruddy strife
  At breast, and a lip whence storm-
    notes start –

### 6

Hold on, hope hard in the subtle thing
  That's spirit: though cloistered fast,
    soar free;
Account as wood, brick, stone, this
    ring
  Of the rueful neighbours, and –
    forth to thee!

## Of Pacchiarotto

### AND HOW HE WORKED IN DISTEMPER

### 1

Query: was ever a quainter
Crotchet than this of the painter
Giacomo Pacchiarotto
Who took 'Reform' for bis motto?

### 2

  He, pupil of old Fungaio,
Is always confounded (heigho!)
With Pacchia, contemporaneous
No question, but how extraneous
In the grace of soul, the power
Of hand, – undoubted dower
Of Pacchia who decked (as *we* know,
My Kirkup!) San Bernardino,
Turning the small dark Oratory
To Siena's Art-laboratory,
As he made its straitness roomy
And glorified its gloomy,
With Bazzi and Beccafumi.
(Another heigho for Bazzi:
How people miscall him Razzi!)

### 3

  This Painter was of opinion
Our earth should be his dominion
Whose Art could correct to pattern
What Nature had slurred – the slattern!
And since, beneath the heavens,
Things lay now at sixes and sevens,

Or, as he said, *sopra-sotto* –
Thought the painter Pacchiarotto
Things wanted reforming, therefore.
'Wanted it' – ay, but wherefore?
When earth held one so ready
As he to step forth, stand steady
In the middle of God's creation
And prove to demonstration
What the dark is, what the light is,
What the wrong is, what the right is,
What the ugly, what the beautiful,
What the restive, what the dutiful,
In Mankind profuse around him?
Man, devil as now he found him,
Would presently soar up angel
At the summons of such evangel,
And owe – what would Man *not* owe
To the painter Pacchiarotto?
Ay, look to thy laurels, Giotto!

4

But Man, he perceived, was stubborn,
Grew regular brute, once cub born;
And it struck him as expedient –
Ere he tried to make obedient
The wolf, fox, bear and monkey,
By piping advice in one key –
That his pipe should play a prelude
To something heaven-tinged not hell-
      hued,
Something not harsh but docile,
Man-liquid, not Man-fossil –
Not fact, in short, but fancy.
By a laudable necromancy
He would conjure up ghosts – a circle
Deprived of the means to work ill
Should his music prove distasteful
And pearls to the swine go wasteful.
To be rent of swine – that *was* hard!
With fancy he ran no hazard:
Fact might knock him o'er the mazzard.

5

So, the painter Pacchiarotto
Constructed himself a grotto
In the quarter of Stalloreggi –
As authors of note allege ye.
And on each of the whitewashed sides
      of it

He painted – (none far and wide so fit
As he to perform in fresco) –
He painted nor cried *quiesco*
Till he peopled its every square foot
With Man – from the Beggar barefoot
To the Noble in cap and feather:
All sorts and conditions together.
The Soldier in breastplate and helmet
Stood frowningly – hail fellow well
      met –
By the Priest armed with bell, book and
      candles.
Nor did he omit to handle
The Fair Sex, our brave distemperer:
Not merely King, Clown, Pope,
      Emperor –
He diversified too his Hades
Of all forms, pinched Labour and paid
      Ease,
With as mixed an assemblage of Ladies.

6

Which work done, dry, – he rested
      him,
Cleaned pallet, washed brush, divested
      him
Of the apron that suits *frescanti*,
And, bonnet on ear stuck jaunty,
This hand upon hip well planted,
That, free to wave as it wanted,
He addressed in a choice oration
His folk of each name and nation,
Taught its duty to every station.
The Pope was declared an arrant
Impostor at once, I warrant.
The Emperor – truth might tax him
With ignorance of the maxim
'Shear sheep but nowise flay them!'
And the Vulgar that obey them,
The Ruled, well-matched with the Ruling,
They failed not of wholesome schooling
On their knavery and their fooling.
As for Art – where's decorum? Pooh-
      poohed it is
By Poets that plague us with lewd ditties,
And Painters that pester with nudities!

7

Now, your rater and debater
Is baulked by a mere spectator
Who simply stares and listens
Tongue-tied, while eye nor glistens
Nor brow grows hot and twitchy,
Nor mouth, for a combat itchy,
Quivers with some convincing
Reply – that sets him wincing?
Nay, rather – reply that furnishes
Your debater with just what burnishes
The crest of him, all one triumph,
As you see him rise, hear him cry
    'Humph!
Convinced am I? This confutes me?
Receive the rejoinder that suits me!
Confutation of vassal for prince meet –
Wherein all the powers that convince
    meet,
And mash my opponent to mincemeat!,

8

So, off from his head flies the bonnet,
His hip loses hand planted on it,
While t'other hand, frequent in gesture,
Slinks modestly back beneath vesture,
As, – hop, skip and jump, – he's along
    with
Those weak ones he late proved so
    strong with!
Pope, Emperor, lo, he's beside them,
Friendly now, who late could not abide
    them,
King, Clown, Soldier, Priest, Noble,
    Burgess;
And his voice, that out-roared Boanerges,
How minikin-mildly it urges
In accents how gentled and gingered
Its word in defence of the injured!
'O call him not culprit, this Pontiff!
Be hard on this Kaiser ye won't if
Ye take into con-si-der-ation
What dangers attend elevation!
The Priest – who expects him to descant
On duty with more zeal and less cant?
He preaches but rubbish he's reared in.
The Soldier, grown deaf (by the mere
    din

Of battle) to mercy, learned tippling
And what not of vice while a stripling.
The Lawyer – his lies are conventional.
And as for the Poor Sort – why mention
    all
Obstructions that leave barred and bolted
Access to the brains of each dolt-head?'

9

He ended, you wager? Not half! Abet?
Precedence to males in the alphabet!
Still, disposed of Man's A, B, C, there's,
Y, Z, want assistance, – the Fair Sex!
How much may be said in excuse of
Those vanities – males see no use of –
From silk shoe on heel to laced poll's-
    hood!
What's their frailty beside our own
    falsehood?
The boldest, most brazen of … 
    trumpets,
How kind can they be to their dumb
    pets!
Of their charms – how are most frank,
    how few venal!
While as for those charges of Juvenal –
*Quæ nemo dixisset in toto*
*Nisi (ædepol) ore illoto –*
He dismissed every charge with an
    '*Apager!*'

10

Then, cocking (in Scotch phrase) his
    cap a-gee,
Right hand disengaged from the doublet
– Like landlord, in house he had sub-let
Resuming of guardianship gestion,
To call tenants' conduct in question –
Hop, skip, jump, to inside from outside
Of chamber, he lords, ladies, louts eyed
With such transformation of visage
As fitted the censor of this age.
No longer an advocate tepid
Of frailty, but champion intrepid
Of strength, not of falsehood but verity,
He, one after one, with asperity
Stripped bare all the cant-clothed abuses,
Disposed of sophistic excuses,
Forced folly each shift to abandon,

And left vice with no leg to stand on.
So crushing the force he exerted,
That Man at his foot lay converted!

11

True – Man bred of paint-pot and
  mortar!
But why suppose folks of this sort are
More likely to hear and be tractable
Than folks all alive and, in fact, able
To testify promptly by action
Their ardour, and make satisfaction
For misdeeds *non verbis sed factis?*
'With folk all alive be my practice
Henceforward! O mortar, paint-pot O,
Farewell to ye!' cried Pacchiarotto,
'Let only occasion intérpose!'

12

It did so: for, pat to the purpose
Through causes I need not examine,
There fell upon Siena a famine.
In vain did the magistrates busily
Seek succour, fetch grain out of Sicily,
Nay, throw mill and bakehouse wide
  open –
Such misery followed as no pen
Of mine shall depict ye. Faint, fainter
Waxed hope of relief: so, our painter,
Emboldened by triumph of recency,
How could he do other with decency
Than rush in this strait to the rescue,
Play schoolmaster, point as with fescue
To each and all slips in Man's spelling
The law of the land? – slips now telling
With monstrous effect on the city,
Whose magistrates moved him to pity
As, bound to read law to the letter,
They minded their hornbook no better.

13

I ought to have told you, at starting,
How certain, who itched to be carting
Abuses away clean and thorough
From Siena, both province and borough,
Had formed themselves into a company
Whose swallow could bolt in a lump
  any
Obstruction of scruple, provoking

The nicer throat's coughing and
  choking:
Fit Club, by as fit a name dignified
Of 'Freed Ones' – '*Bardotti*' – which
  signified
'Spare-Horses' that walk by the waggon
The team has to drudge for and drag on.
This notable club Pacchiarotto
Had joined long since, paid scot and
  lot to,
As free and accepted 'Bardotto.'
The Bailiwick watched with no quiet eye
The outrage thus done to society,
And noted the advent especially
Of Pacchiarotto their fresh ally.

14

These Spare-Horses forthwith
  assembled:
Neighed words whereat citizens trembled
As oft as the chiefs, in the Square by
The Duomo, proposed a way whereby
The city were cured of disaster.
'Just substitute servant for master,
Make Poverty Wealth and Wealth
  Poverty,
Unloose Man from overt and covert tie,
And straight out of social confusion
True Order would spring!' Brave
  illusion –
Aims heavenly attained by means earthy!

15

Off to these at full speed rushed our
  worthy, –
Brain practised and tongue no less
  tutored,
In argument's armour accoutred, –
Sprang forth, mounted rostrum and
  essayed
Proposals like those to which 'Yes'said
So glibly each personage painted
O' the wall-side wherewith you're
  acquainted.
He harangued on the faults of the
  Bailiwick:
'Red soon were our State-candle's paly
  wick,
If wealth would become but interfluous,

Fill voids up with just the superfluous;
If ignorance gave way to knowledge
– Not pedantry picked up at college
From Doctors, Professors *et cætera* –
(*They* say: "*kai ta loipa*" – Like better a
Long Greek string of *kappas, taus,
        lambdas,*
Tacked on to the tail of each damned
        ass) –
No knowledge we want of this quality,
But knowledge indeed – practicality
Through insight's fine universality!
If you shout "*Bailiffs, out on ye all! Fie,
Thou Chief of our forces, Amalfi,
Who shieldest the rogue and the clotpoll!*"
If you pounce on and poke out, with
        what pole
I leave ye to fancy, our Siena's
Beast-litter of sloths and hyenas – '
(Whoever to scan this is ill able
Forgets the town's name's a dissyllable)
'If, this done, ye did – as ye might –
        place
For once the right man in the right
        place,
If you listened to me ...'

16

                At which last 'If'
There flew at his throat like a mastiff
One Spare-Horse – another and
        another!
Such outbreak of tumult and pother,
Horse-faces a-laughing and fleering,
Horse-voices a-mocking and jeering,
Horse-hands raised to collar the caitiff
Whose impudence ventured the
        late 'If' –
That, had not fear sent Pacchiarotto
Off tramping, as fast as could trot toe,
Away from the scene of discomfiture –
Had he stood there stock-still in a
        dumb fit – sure
Am I he had paid in his person
Till his mother might fail to know her
        son,
Though she gazed on him never so
        wistful,

In the figure so tattered and tristful.
Each mouth full of curses, each fist full
Of cuffings – behold, Pacchiarotto,
The pass which thy project has got to,
Of trusting, nigh ashes still hot – tow!
(The paraphrase – which I much need
        – is
From Horace '*per ignes incedis.*' )

17

    Right and left did he dash helter-
        skelter
In agonized search of a shelter.
No purlieu so blocked and no alley
So blind as allowed him to rally
His spirits and see – nothing hampered
His steps if he trudged and not
        scampered
Up here and down there in a city
That's all ups and downs, more the
        pity
For folk who would outrun the constable.
At last he stopped short at the one
        stable
And sure place of refuge that's offered
Humanity. Lately was coffered
A corpse in its sepulchre, situate
By St John's Observance. 'Habituate
Thyself to the strangest of bedfellows,
And, kicked by the live, kiss the dead
        fellows!'
So Misery counselled the craven.
At once he crept safely to haven
Through a hole left unbricked in the
        structure.
Ay, Misery, in have you tucked your
Poor client and left him conterminous
With – pah! – the thing fetid and
        verminous!
(I gladly would spare you the detail,
But History writes what I retail.)

18

    Two days did he groan in his domicile:
'Good Saints, set me free and I promise
        I'll
Abjure all ambition of preaching
Change, whether to minds touched by
        teaching

– The smooth folk of fancy, mere
    figments
Created by plaster and pigments, –
Or to minds that receive with such
    rudeness
Dissuasion from pride, greed and
    lewdness,
– The rough folk of fact, life's true
    specimens
Of mind – "*haud in posse sed esse mens*"
As it was, is, and shall be for ever
Despite of my ulmost endeavour.
O live foes I thought to illumine,
Henceforth lie untroubled your
    gloom in!
I need my own light, every spark, as
I couch with this sole friend – a carcase!'

### 19

Two days thus he maundered and
    rambled;
Then, starved back to sanity, scrambled
From out his receptacle loathsome.
'A spectre!' – declared upon oath some
Who saw him emerge and (appalling
To mention) his garments a-crawling
With plagues far beyond the Egyptian.
He gained, in a state past description,
A convent of monks, the Observancy.

### 20

Thus far is a fact: I reserve fancy
For Fancy's more proper employment:
And now she waves wing with
    enjoyment,
To tell ye how preached the Superior
When somewhat our painter's exterior
Was sweetened. He needed (no mincing
The matter) much soaking and rincing,
Nay, rubbing with drugs odoriferous,
Till, rid of his garments pestiferous
And robed by the help of the Brother-
    hood
In odds and ends, – this gown and
    t'other hood, –
His empty inside first well-garnished, –
He delivered a tale round, unvarnished.

### 21

'Ah, Youth!' ran the Abbot's
    admonishment,
'Thine error scarce moves my
    astonishment,
For – why shall I shrink from
    asserting? –
Myself have had hopes of converting
The foolish to wisdom, till, sober,
My life found its May grow October.
I talked and I wrote, but, one morning,
Life's Autumn bore fruit in this warning:
"*Let tongue rest, and quiet thy quill be!
Earth is earth and not heaven, and ne'er
    will be.*"
Man's work is to labour and leaven –
As best he may – earth here with
    heaven;
'Tis work for work's sake that he's
    needing:
Let him work on and on as if speeding
Work's end, but not dream of
    succeeding!
Because if success were intended,
Why, heaven would begin ere earth
    ended.
A Spare-Horse? Be rather a thill-horse,
Or – what's the plain truth – just a
    mill-horse!
Earth's a mill where we grind and wear
    mufflers:
A whip awaits shirkers and shufflers
Who slacken their pace, sick of lugging
At what don't advance for their tugging.
Though round goes the mill, we must
    still post
On and on as if moving the mill-post.
So, grind away, mouth-wise and pen-
    wise,
Do all that we can to make men wise!
And if men prefer to be foolish,
Ourselves have proved horse-like not
    mulish:
Sent grist, a good sackful, to hopper,
And worked as the Master thought
    proper.
Tongue I wag, pen I ply, who am Abbot;

Stick thou, Son, to daub-brush and
    dabpot!
But, soft! I scratch hard on the scab
    hot?
Though cured of thy plague, there may
    linger
A pimple I fray with rough finger?
So soon could my homily transmute
Thy brass into gold? Why, the man's
    mute!'

22

    'Ay, Father, I'm mute with admiring
How Nature's indulgence untiring
Still bids us turn deaf ear to Reason's
Best rhetoric – clutch at all seasons
And hold fast to what's proved
    untenable!
Thy maxim is – Man's not amenable
To argument: whereof by con-
    sequence –
Thine arguments reach me: a non-
    sequence!
Yet blush not discouraged, O Father!
I stand unconverted, the rather
That nowise I need a conversion.
No live man (I cap thy assertion)
By argument ever could take hold
Of me. 'Twas the dead thing, the clay-
    scold,
Which grinned *"Art thou so in a hurry*
*That of warm light thou must skurry*
*And join me down here in the dungeon*
*Because, above, one's Jack and one – John,*
*One's swift in the race, one – a hobbler,*
*One's a crowned king, and one – a*
    *capped cobbler,*
*Rich and poor, sage and fool, virtuous,*
    *vicious?*
*Why complain? Art thou so unsuspicious*
*That all's for an hour of essaying*
*Who's fit and who's unfit for playing*
*His part in the after-construction*
*– Heaven's Piece whereof Earth's the*
    *Induction?*
*Things rarely go smooth at Rehearsal*
*Wait patient the change universal,*
*And act, and let act, in existence!*

*For, as thou art clapped hence or hissed*
    *hence,*
*Thou hast thy promotion or otherwise.*
*And why must wise thou have thy brother*
    *wise*
*Because in rehearsal thy cue be*
*To shine by the side of a booby?*
*No polishing garnet to ruby!*
*All's well that ends well – through Art's*
    *magic*
*Some end, whether comic or tragic,*
*The Artist has purposed, be certain!*
*Explained at the fall of the curtain –*
*In showing thy wisdom at odds with*
*That folly: he tries men and gods with*
*No problem for weak wits to solve meant,*
*But one worth such Author's evolvement.*
*So, back nor disturb play's production*
*By giving thy brother instruction*
*To throw up his fool's-part allotted!*
*Lest haply thyself prove besotted*
*When stript, for thy pains, of that*
    *costume*
*Of sage, which has bred the imposthume*
*I prick to relieve thee of, – Vanity!"*

23

    'So, Father, behold me in sanity!
I'm back to the palette and mahlstick:
And as for Man – let each and all stick
To what was prescribed them at
    starting!
Once planted as fools – no departing
From folly one inch, *sæculorum*
*In sæcula!* Pass me the jorum,
And push me the platter – my stomach
Retains, through its fasting, still some
    ache –
And then, with your kind *Benedicite*,
Good-bye!'

24

    I have told with simplicity
My tale, dropped those harsh analytics,
And tried to content you, my critics,
Who greeted my early uprising!
I knew you through all the disguising,
Droll dogs, as I jumped up, cried
    'Heyday!

This Monday is – what else but Mayday?
And these in the drabs, blues and
    yellows,
Are surely the privileged fellows.
So, saltbox and bones, tongs and
    bellows,'
(I threw up the window) 'your pleasure?'

25

Then he who directed the measure –
An old friend – put leg forward nimbly,
'We critics as sweeps out your chimbly!
Much soot to remove from your flue,
    sir!
Who spares coal in kitchen an't you, sir!
And neighbours complain it's no joke,
    sir,
– You ought to consume your own
    smoke, sir!'

26

Ah, rogues, but my housemaid
    suspects you –
Is confident oft she detects you
In bringing more filth into my house
Than ever you found there! I'm pious
However: 'twas God made you dingy
And me – with no need to be stingy
Of soap, when 'tis sixpence the packet.
So, dance away, boys, dust my jacket,
Bang drum and blow fife – ay, and rattle
Your brushes, for that's half the battle!
Don't trample the grass, – hocus-pocus
With grime my Spring snowdrop and
    crocus, –
And, what with your rattling and tinkling,
Who knows but you give me an inkling
How music sounds, thanks to the jangle
Of regular drum and triangle?
Whereby, tap-tap, chink-chink, 'tis
    proven
I break rule as bad as Beethoven.
'That chord now – a groan or a grunt
    is't?
Schumann's self was no worse contra-
    puntist.
No ear! or if ear, so tough-gristled –
He thought that he sung while he
    whistled!'

27

So, this time I whistle, not sing at all,
My story, the largess I fling at all
And every the rough there whose *aubade*
Did its best to amuse me, – nor *so* bad!
Take my thanks, pick up largess, and
    scamper
Off free, ere your mirth gets a damper!
You've Monday, your one day, your
    funday,
While mine is a year that's all Sunday.
I've seen you, times – who knows how
    many? –
Dance in here, strike up, play the zany,
Make mouths at the tenant, hoot warning
You'll find him decamped next May-
    morning;
Then scuttle away, glad to 'scape hence
With – kicks? no, but laughter and ha'-
    pence!
Mine's freehold, by grace of the grand
    Lord
Who lets out the ground here, – my
    land lord:
To him I pay quit-rent – devotion;
Nor hence shall I budge, I've a notion,
Nay, here shall my whistling and singing
Set all his street's echoes a-ringing
Long after the last of your number
Has ceased my front-court to encumber
While, treading down rose and
    ranunculus,
You *Tommy-make-room-for-your-Uncle* us!
Troop, all of you – man or homunculus,
Quick march! for Xanthippe, my house-
    maid,
If once on your pates she a souse made
With what, pan or pot, bowl or *skoramis*
First comes to her hand – things were
    more amiss!
I would not for worlds be your place
    in –
Recipient of slops from the basin!
You, Jack-in-the-Green, leaf-and-
    twiggishness
Won't save a dry thread on your
    priggishness!

While as for Quilp-Hop-o'-my-thumb
    there,
Banjo-Byron that twangs the strum-
    strum there –
He'll think, as the pickle he curses,
I've discharged on his pate his own
    verses!
'Dwarfs are saucy,'says Dickens: so,
    sauced in
Your own sauce, ... *

### 28

    But, back to my Knight of the Pencil,
Dismissed to his fresco and stencil!
Whose story – begun with a chuckle,
And throughout timed by raps of the
    knuckle, –
To small enough purpose were studied
If it ends with crown cracked or nose
    bloodied.
Come, critics, – not shake hands, excuse
    me!
But – say have you grudged to amuse
    me
This once in the forty-and-over
Long years since you trampled my
    clover
And scared from my house-eaves each
    sparrow
I never once harmed by that arrow
Of song, *karterotaton belos*,
(Which Pindar declares the true *melos*)
I was forging and filing and finishing,
And no whit my labours diminishing
Because, though high up in a chamber
Where none of your kidney may clamber
Your hullabaloo would approach me?
Was it 'grammar' wherein you would
    'coach' me –
You, – pacing in even that paddock
Of language allotted you *ad hoc*,
With a clog at your fetlocks, – you –
    scorners

Of me free of all its four corners?
Was it 'clearness of words which
    convey thought'?
Ay, if words never needed enswathe
    aught
But ignorance, impudence, envy
And malice – what word-swathe would
    then vie
With yours for a clearness crystalline?
But had you to put in one small line
Some thought big and bouncing – as
    noddle
Of goose, born to cackle and waddle
And bite at man's heel as goose-wont is,
Never felt plague its puny *os frontis* –
You'd know, as you hissed, spat and
    sputtered,
Clear cackle is easily uttered!

### 29

    Lo, I've laughed out my laugh on
    this mirth-day!
Beside, at week's end, dawns my birth-
    day,
That *hebdome, hieron emar* –
(More things in a day than you deem
    are!)
– *Tei gar Apollona chrusaora*
*Egeinato Leto.* So, gray or ray
Betide me, six days hence, I'm vexed
    here
By no sweep, that's certain, till next
    year!
'Vexed?' – roused from what else were
    insipid ease!
Leave snoring a-bed to Pheidippides!
We'll up and work! won't we,
    Euripides?

---

* No please! For
    'Who would be satirical
      On a thing so very small?'
        – *Printer's Devil*

## At the 'Mermaid'

The figure that thou here seest ... Tut!
Was it for gentle Shakespeare put?

B. Jonson. (*Adapted*.)

1

I – 'Next Poet?' No, my hearties,
    I nor am nor fain would be!
Choose your chiefs and pick your parties,
    Not one soul revolt to me!
I, forsooth, sow song-sedition?
    I, a schism in verse provoke?
I, blown up by bard's ambition,
    Burst – your bubble-king? You joke.

2

Come, be grave! The sherris mantling
    Still about each mouth, mayhap,
Breeds you insight – just a scantling –
    Brings me truth out – just a scrap.
Look and tell me! Written, spoken,
    Here's my life-long work: and where
– Where's your warrant or my token
    I' m the dead king's son and heir?

3

Here's my work: does work discover –
    What was rest from work – my life?
Did I live man's hater, lover?
    Leave the world at peace, at strife?
Call earth ugliness or beauty?
    See things there in large or small?
Use to pay its Lord my duty?
    Use to own a lord at all?

4

Blank of such a record, truly
    Here's the work I hand, this scroll,
Yours to take or leave; as duly,
    Mine remains the unproffered soul.
So much, no whit more, my debtors –
    How should one like me lay claim
To that largess elders, betters
    Sell you cheap their souls for – fame?

5

Which of you did I enable
    Once to slip inside my breast,
There to catalogue and label
    What I like least, what love best,

Hope and fear, believe and doubt of,
    Seek and shun, respect – deride?
Who has right to make a rout of
    Rarities he found inside?

6

Rarities or, as he'd rather,
    Rubbish such as stocks his own:
Need and greed (O strange) the Father
    Fashioned not for him alone!
Whence – the comfort set a-strutting,
    Whence – the outcry 'Haste, behold!
Bard's breast open wide, past shutting,
    Shows what brass we took for gold!'

7

Friends, I doubt not he'd display you
    Brass – myself call orichalc, –
Furnish much amusement; pray you
    Therefore, be content I baulk
Him and you, and bar my portal!
    Here's my work outside: opine
What's inside me mean and mortal!
    Take your pleasure, leave me mine!

8

Which is – not to buy your laurel
    As last king did, nothing loth.
Tale adorned and pointed moral
    Gained him praise and pity both.
Out rushed sighs and groans by dozens,
    Forth by scores oaths, curses flew:
Proving you were cater-cousins,
    Kith and kindred, king and you!

9

Whereas do I ne'er so little
    (Thanks to sherris) leave ajar
Bosom's gate – no jot nor tittle
    Grow we nearer than we are.
Sinning, sorrowing, despairing,
    Body-ruined, spirit-wrecked, –
Should I give my woes an airing, –
    Where's one plague that claims
        respect?

10

Have you found your life distasteful?
    My life did, and does, smack sweet.
Was your youth of pleasure wasteful?
    Mine I saved and hold complete.
Do your joys with age diminish?

When mine fail me, I'll complain.
Must in death your daylight finish?
  My sun sets to rise again.

11

What, like you, he proved – your
    Pilgrim –
  This our world a wilderness,
Earth still grey and heaven still grim,
  Not a hand there his might press,
Not a heart his own might throb to,
  Men all rogues and women – say,
Dolls which boys' heads duck and
    bob to,
  Grown folk drop or throw away?

12

My experience being other,
  How should I contribute verse
Worthy of your king and brother?
  Balaam-like I bless, not curse.
I find earth not grey but rosy,
  Heaven not grim but fair of hue.
Do I stoop? I pluck a posy.
  Do I stand and stare? All's blue.

13

Doubtless I am pushed and shoved by
  Rogues and fools enough: the more
Good luck mine, I love, am loved by
  Some few honest to the core.
Scan the near high, scout the far low!
  'But the low come close:' what then?
Simpletons? My match is Marlowe;
  Sciolists? My mate is Ben.

14

Womankind – 'the cat-like nature,
  False and fickle, vain and weak' –
What of this sad nomenclature
  Suits my tongue, if I must speak?
Does the sex invite, repulse so,
  Tempt, betray, by fits and starts?
So becalm but to convulse so,
  Decking heads and breaking hearts?

15

Well may you blaspheme at fortune!
  I 'threw Venus' * (Ben, expound!)

\* The best cast in dice (three sixes) is called
  Venus.

Never did I need importune
  Her, of all the Olympian round.
Blessings on my benefactress!
  Cursings suit – for aught I know –
Those who twitched her by the back
    tress,
  Tugged and thought to turn her – so!

16

Therefore, since no leg to stand on
  Thus I'm left with, – joy or grief
Be the issue, – I abandon
  Hope or care you name me Chief!
Chief and king and Lord's anointed,
  I? – who never once have wished
Death before the day appointed:
  Lived and liked, not poohed and
    pished!

17

'Ah, but so I shall not enter,
  Scroll in hand, the common heart –
Stopped at surface: since at centre
  Song should reach *Welt-schmerz*,
    world-smart!'
'Enter in the heart?' Its shelly
  Cuirass guard mine, fore and aft!
Such song 'enters in the belly
  And is cast out in the draught.'

18

Back then to our sherris-brewage!
  'Kingship' quotha? I shall wait –
Waive the present time: some new
    age . . .
  But let fools anticipate!
Meanwhile greet me – 'friend, good
    fellow,
  Gentle Will,' my merry men!
As for making Envy yellow
  With 'Next Poet' – (Manners, Ben!)

## House

### 1

Shall I sonnet-sing you about myself?
　　Do I live in a house you would like
　　　to see?
Is it scant of gear, has it store of pelf?
　　'Unlock my heart with a sonnet-key?'

### 2

Invite the world, as my betters have
　　　done?
　　'Take notice: this building remains
　　　on view,
Its suites of reception every one,
　　Its private apartment and bedroom
　　　too;

### 3

'For a ticket, apply to the Publisher.'
　　No: thanking the public, I must
　　　decline.
A peep through my window, if folk
　　prefer;
　　But, please you, no foot over threshold
　　　of mine!

### 4

I have mixed with a crowd and heard
　　free talk
　　In a foreign land where an earthquake
　　　chanced:
And a house stood gaping, nought to
　　baulk
　　Man's eye wherever he gazed or
　　　glanced.

### 5

The whole of the frontage shaven sheer,
　　The inside gaped: exposed to day,
Right and wrong and common and queer,
　　Bare, as the palm of your hand, it lay.

### 6

The owner? Oh, he had been crushed,
　　no doubt!
　　'Odd tables and chairs for a man of
　　　wealth!
What a parcel of musty old books about!
　　He smoked, – no wonder he lost his
　　　health!

### 7

'I doubt if he bathed before he dressed.
　　A brasier? – the pagan, he burned
　　　perfumes!
You see it is proved, what the neighbours
　　guessed:
　　His wife and himself had separate
　　　rooms.'

### 8

Friends, the goodman of the house at
　　least
　　Kept house to himself till an earth-
　　　quake came:
'Tis the fall of its frontage permits you
　　feast
　　On the inside arrangement you praise
　　　or blame.

### 9

Outside should suffice for evidence:
　　And whoso desires to penetrate
Deeper, must dive by the spirit-sense –
　　No optics like yours, at any rate!

### 10

'Hoity toity! A street to explore,
　　Your house the exception! *"With this
　　same key
Shakespeare unlocked his heart,"* once
　　more!'
　　Did Shakespeare? If so, the less Shake-
　　　speare he!

## Shop

### 1

So, friend, your shop was all your house!
　　Its front, astonishing the street,
Invited view from man and mouse
　　To what diversity of treat
　　Behind its glass – the single sheet!

### 2

What gimcracks, genuine Japanese:
　　Gape-jaw and goggle-eye, the frog;
Dragons, owls, monkeys, beetles,
　　geese;
　　Some crush-nosed human-hearted
　　　dog:
　　Queer names, too, such a catalogue!

3

I thought 'And he who owns the wealth
  Which blocks the window's vastitude,
– Ah, could I peep at him by stealth
  Behind his ware, pass shop, intrude
  On house itself, what scenes were
      viewed!

4

'If wide and showy thus the shop,
  What must the habitation prove?
The true house with no name a-top –
  The mansion, distant one remove,
  Once get him off his traffic-groove!

5

'Pictures he likes, or books perhaps;
  And as for buying most and best,
Commend me to these City chaps!
  Or else he's social, takes his rest
  On Sundays, with a Lord for guest.

6

'Some suburb-palace, parked about
  And gated grandly, built last year:
The four-mile walk to keep off gout;
  Or big seat sold by bankrupt peer:
  But then he takes the rail, that's clear.

7

'Or, stop! I wager, taste selects
  Some out o' the way, some all-
      unknown
Retreat: the neighbourhood suspects
  Little that he who rambles lone
  Makes Rothschild tremble on his
      throne!'

8

Nowise! Nor Mayfair residence
  Fit to receive and entertain, –
Nor Hampstead villa's kind defence
  From noise and crowd, from dust
      and drain, –
  Nor country-box was soul's domain!

9

Nowise! At back of all that spread
  Of merchandize, woe's me, I find
A hole i' the wall where, heels by head,
  The owner couched, his ware
      behind,
  – In cupboard suited to his mind.

10

For why? He saw no use of life
  But, while he drove a roaring trade,
To chuckle 'Customers are rife!'
  To chafe 'So much hard cash outlaid
  Yet zero in my profits made!

11

'This novelty costs pains, but – takes?
  Cumbers my counter! Stock no more!
This article, no such great shakes,
  Fizzes like wildfire? Underscore
  The cheap thing – thousands to the
      fore!'

12

'Twas lodging best to live most nigh
  (Cramp, coffinlike as crib might be)
Receipt of Custom; ear and eye
  Wanted no outworld: 'Hear and see
  The bustle in the shop!' quoth he.

13

My fancy of a merchant-prince
  Was different. Through his wares we
      groped
Our darkling way to – not to mince
  The matter – no black den where
      mope
  The master if we interloped!

14

Shop was shop only: household-stuff?
  What did he want with comforts there?
'Walls, ceiling, floor, stay blank and
      rough,
  So goods on sale show rich and rare!
  *"Sell and scud home"* be shop's
      affair!'

15

What might he deal in? Gems, suppose!
  Since somehow business must be
      done
At cost of trouble, – see, he throws
  You choice of jewels, everyone,
  Good, better, best, star, moon and
      sun!

16

Which lies within your power of purse?
  This ruby that would tip aright
Solomon's sceptre? Oh, your nurse

Wants simply coral, the delight
　　Of teething baby, – stuff to bite!

17

Howe'er your choice fell, straight you
　　took
　　Your purchase, prompt your money
　　rang
On counter, – scarce the man forsook
　　His study of the 'Times,' just swang
　　Till-ward his hand that stopped the
　　clang, –

18

Then off made buyer with a prize,
　　Then seller to his 'Times' returned;
And so did day wear, wear, till eyes
　　Brightened apace, for rest was earned:
　　He locked door long ere candle
　　burned.

19

And whither went he? Ask himself,
　　Not me! To change of scene, I think.
Once sold the ware and pursed the pelf,
　　Chaffer was scarce his meat and
　　drink,
　　Nor all his music – money-chink.

20

Because a man has shop to mind
　　In time and place, since flesh must
　　live,
Needs spirit lack all life behind,
　　All stray thoughts, fancies fugitive,
　　All loves except what trade can give?

21

I want to know a butcher paints,
　　A baker rhymes for his pursuit,
Candlestick-maker much acquaints
　　His soul with song, or, haply mute,
　　Blows out his brains upon the flute!

22

But – shop each day and all day long!
　　Friend, your good angel slept, your
　　star
Suffered eclipse, fate did you wrong!
　　From where these sorts of treasures
　　are,
　　There should our hearts be – Christ,
　　how far!

## Pisgah-Sights – 1

1

Over the ball of it,
　　Peering and prying,
How I see all of it,
　　Life there, outlying!
Roughness and smoothness,
　　Shine and defilement,
Grace and uncouthness:
　　One reconcilement.

2

Orbed as appointed,
　　Sister with brother
Joins, ne'er disjointed
　　One from the other.
All's lend-and-borrow;
　　Good, see, wants evil,
Joy demands sorrow,
　　Angel weds devil!

3

'Which things must – why be?'
　　Vain our endeavour!
So shall things aye be
　　As they were ever.
'Such things should so be!'
　　Sage our desistence!
Rough-smooth let globe be,
　　Mixed – man's existence!

4

Man – wise and foolish,
　　Lover and scorner,
Docile and mulish –
　　Keep each his corner!
Honey yet gall of it!
　　There's the life lying,
And I see all of it,
　　Only, I'm dying!

## Pisgah-Sights – 2

### 1

Could I but live again,
  Twice my life over,
Would I once strive again?
  Would not I cover
Quietly all of it –
  Greed and ambition –
So, from the pall of it,
  Pass to fruition?

### 2

'Soft!' I'd say, 'Soul mine!
  Three-score and ten years,
Let the blind mole mine
  Digging out deniers!
Let the dazed hawk soar,
  Claim the sun's rights too!
Turf 'tis thy walk's o'er,
  Foliage thy flight's to.'

### 3

Only a learner,
  Quick one or slow one,
Just a discerner,
  I would teach no one.
I am earth's native:
  No rearranging it!
I be creative,
  Chopping and changing it?

### 4

March, men, my fellows!
  Those who, above me,
(Distance so mellows)
  Fancy you love me:
Those who, below me,
  (Distance makes great so)
Free to forego me,
  Fancy you hate so!

### 5

Praising, reviling,
  Worst head and best head,
Past me defiling,
  Never arrested,
Wanters, abounders,
  March, in gay mixture,
Men, my surrounders!
  I am the fixture.

### 6

So shall I fear thee,
  Mightiness yonder!
Mock-sun – more near thee,
  What is to wonder?
So shall I love thee,
  Down in the dark, – lest
Glowworm I prove thee,
  Star that now sparklest!

## Fears and Scruples

### 1

Here's my case. Of old I used to love
    him
  This same unseen friend, before I
    knew:
Dream there was none like him, none
    above him, –
  Wake to hope and trust my dream
    was true.

### 2

Loved I not his letters full of beauty?
  Not his actions famous far and wide?
Absent, he would know I vowed him
    duty;
  Present, he would find me at his side.

### 3

Pleasant fancy! for I had but letters,
  Only knew of actions by hearsay:
He himself was busied with my betters;
  What of that? My turn must come
    some day.

### 4

'Some day' proving – no day! Here's
    the puzzle.
  Passed and passed my turn is. Why
    complain?
He's so busied! If I could but muzzle
  People's foolish mouths that give me
    pain!

### 5

'Letters?' (hear them!) 'You a judge of
    writing?
  Ask the experts! – How they shake
    the head

O'er these characters, your friend's
 inditing –
 Call them forgery from A to Z!

### 6

'Actions? Where's your certain proof'
 (they bother)
 'He, of all you find so great and good,
He, he only, claims this, that, the other
 Action – claimed by men, a
 multitude?'

### 7

I can simply wish I might refute you,
 Wish my friend would, – by a word,
 a wink, –
Bid me stop that foolish mouth, – you
 brute you!
 He keeps absent, – why, I cannot
 think.

### 8

Never mind! Though foolishness may
 flout me,
 One thing's sure enough: 'tis neither
 frost,
No, nor fire, shall freeze or burn from
 out me
 Thanks for truth – though
 falsehood, gained – though lost.

### 9

All my days, I'll go the softlier, sadlier,
 For that dream's sake! How forget
 the thrill
Through and through me as I thought
 'The gladlier
 Lives my friend because I love him
 still!'

### 10

Ah, but there's a menace someone
 utters!
 'What and if your friend at home
 play tricks?
Peep at hide-and-seek behind the
 shutters?
 Mean your eyes should pierce
 through solid bricks?'

### 11

'What and if he, frowning, wake you,
 dreamy?
 Lay on you the blame that bricks –
 conceal?
Say "*At least I saw who did not see me,
 Does see now, and presently shall
 feel?*"

### 12

'Why, that makes your friend a
 monster!'say you:
 'Had his house no window? At first
 nod,
Would you not have hailed him?'
 Hush, I pray you!
 What if this friend happen to be –
 God?

## Natural Magic

### 1

All I can say is – I saw it!
The room was as bare as your hand.
I locked in the swarth little lady, – I
 swear,
From the head to the foot of her – well,
 quite as bare!
'No Nautch shall cheat me,'said I,
 'taking my stand
At this bolt which I draw!' And this
 bolt  – I withdraw it,
And there laughs the lady, not bare,
 but embowered
With – who knows what verdure, o'
 erfruited, o' erflowered?
 Impossible! Only – I saw it!

### 2

All I can sing is – I feel it?
This life was as blank as that room;
I let you pass in here. Precaution,
 indeed?
Walls, cilling and floor, – not a chance
 for a weed!
Wide opens the entrance: where's cold
 now, where's gloom?
No May to sow seed here, no June to
 reveal it,

Behold you enshrined in these blooms
    of your bringing,
These fruits of your bearing – nay,
    birds of your winging!
      A fairy-tale! Only – I feel it!

## Magical Nature

### 1

Flower – I never fancied, jewel – I
    profess you!
    Bright I see and soft I feel the
      outside of a flower.
Save but glow inside and – jewel, I
    should guess you,
    Dim to sight and rough to touch:
      the glory is the dower.

### 2

You, forsooth, a flower? Nay, my love,
    a jewel –
    Jewel at no mercy of a moment in
      your prime!
Time may fray the flower-face: kind be
    time or cruel,
    Jewel, from each facet, flash your
      laugh at time!

## Bifurcation

We were two lovers; let me lie by her,
My tomb beside her tomb. On hers
    inscribe –
'I loved him; but my reason bade prefer
Duty to love, reject the tempter's bribe
Of rose and lily when each path
    diverged,
And either I must pace to life's far end
As love should lead me, or, as duty
    urged,
Plod the worn causeway arm-in-arm
    with friend.
So, truth turned falsehood: "How I
    loathe a flower,
How prize the pavement!" still caressed
    his ear –
The deafish friend's – through life's
    day, hour by hour,

As he laughed (coughing) "Ay, it would
    appear!"
But deep within my heart of hearts
    there hid
Ever the confidence, amends for all,
That heaven repairs what wrong earth's
    journey did,
When love from life-long exile comes
    at call.
Duty and love, one broadway, were the
    best –
Who doubts? But one or other was to
    choose.
I chose the darkling half, and wait the
    rest
In that new world where light and
    darkness fuse.'

Inscribe on mine – 'I loved her: love's
    track lay
O'er sand and pebble, as all travellers
    know.
Duty led through a smiling country,
    gay
With greensward where the rose and
    lily blow.
"Our roads are diverse: farewell, love!"
    said she;
" 'Tis duty I abide by: homely sward
And not the rock-rough picturesque for me!
Above, where both roads join, I wait reward.
Be you as constant to the path whereon
I leave you planted!" But man needs
    must move,
Keep moving – whither, when the star
    is gone
Whereby he steps secure nor strays
    from love?
No stone but I was tripped by,
    stumbling-block
But brought me to confusion. Where I
    fell,
There I lay flat, if moss disguised the
    rock,
Thence, if flint pierced, I rose and cried
"All's well!
Duty be mine to tread in that high sphere

*Where love from duty ne'er disparts, I*
*   trust,*
*And two halves make that whole, where of*
*   – since here*
*One must suffice a man – why, this one*
*   must!"' '*
Inscribe each tomb thus: then, some
   sage acquaint
The simple – which holds sinner,
   which holds saint!


## Numpholeptos

Still you stand, still you listen, still you
   smile!
Still melts your moonbeam through
   me, white awhile,
Softening, sweetening, till sweet and
   soft
Increase so round this heart of mine,
   that oft
I could believe your moonbeam-smile
   has past
The pallid limit, lies, transformed at last
To sunlight and salvation – warms the
   soul
It sweetens, softens! Would you pass
   that goal,
Gain love's birth at the limit's happier
   verge,
And, where an iridescence lurks, but
   urge
The hesitating pallor on to prime
Of dawn! – true blood-streaked, sun-
   warmth, action-time,
By heart-pulse ripened to a ruddy glow
Of gold above my clay – I scarce
   should know
From gold's self, thus suffused! For
   gold means love.
What means the sad slow silver smile
   above
My clay but pity, pardon? – at the best,
But acquiescence that I take my rest,
Contented to be clay, while in your
   heaven

The sun reserves love for the Spirit-
   Seven
Companioning God's throne they lamp
   before,
– Leaves earth a mute waste only
   wandered o'er
By that pale soft sweet disempassioned
   moon
Which smiles me slow forgiveness!
   Such the boon
I beg? Nay, dear, submit to this – just
   this
Supreme endeavour! As my lips now
   kiss
Your feet, my arms convulse your
   shrouding robe,
My eyes, acquainted with the dust,
   dare probe
Your eyes above for – what, if born,
   would blind
Mine with redundant bliss, as flash
   may find
The inert nerve, sting awake the palsied
   limb,
Bid with life's ecstasy sense overbrim
And suck back death in the resurging
   joy –
Love, the love whole and sole without
   alloy!

Vainly! The promise withers! I employ
Lips, arms, eyes, pray the prayer which
   finds the word,
Make the appeal which must be felt,
   not heard,
And none the more is changed your
   calm regard:
Rather, its sweet and soft grow harsh
   and hard –
Forbearance, then repulsion, then
   disdain.
Avert the rest! I rise, see! – make, again
Once more, the old departure for some
   track
Untried yet through a world which
   brings me back
Ever thus fruitlessly to find your feet,

To fix your eyes, to pray the soft and
    sweet
Which smile there – take from his new
    pilgrimage
Your outcast, once your inmate, and
    assuage
With love – not placid pardon now – his
    thirst
For a mere drop from out the ocean erst
He drank at! Well, the quest shall be
    renewed.
Fear nothing! Though I linger, unembued
With any drop, my lips thus close. I go!
So did I leave you, I have found you so,
And doubtlessly, if fated to return,
So shall my pleading persevere and earn
Pardon – not love – in that same smile,
    I learn,
And lose the meaning of, to learn once
    more,
Vainly!
        What fairy track do I explore?
What magic hall return to, like the gem
Centuply-angled o'er a diadem?
You dwell there, hearted; from your
    midmost home
Rays forth – through that fantastic
    world I roam
Ever – from centre to circumference,
Shaft upon coloured shaft: this
    crimsons thence,
That purples out its precinct through
    the waste.
Surely I had your sanction when I faced,
Fared forth upon that untried yellow
    ray
Whence I retrack my steps? They end
    today
Where they began – before your feet,
    beneath
Your eyes, your smile: the blade is shut
    in sheath,
Fire quenched in flint; irradiation, late
Triumphant through the distance,
    finds its fate,
Merged in your blank pure soul, alike
    the source

And tomb of that prismatic glow: divorce
Absolute, all-conclusive! Forth I fared,
Treading the lambent flamelet: little cared
If now its flickering took the topaz tint,
If now my dull-caked path gave sulphury
    hint
Of subterranean rage – no stay nor stint
To yellow, since you sanctioned that I
    bathe,
Burnish me, soul and body, swim and
    swathe
In yellow license. Here I reek suffused
With crocus, saffron, orange, as I used
With scarlet, purple, every dye o' the
    bow
Born of the storm-cloud. As before, you
    show
Scarce recognition, no approval, some
Mistrust, more wonder at a man become
Monstrous in garb, nay – flesh disguised
    as well,
Through his adventure. Whatso'er befell,
I followed, wheresoe'er it wound, that
    vein
You authorized should leave your
    whiteness, stain
Earth's sombre stretch beyond your
    midmost place
Of vantage, – trode that tinct whereof
    the trace
On garb and flesh repel you! Yes, I plead
Your own permission – your command,
    indeed,
That who would worthily retain the love
Must share the knowledge shrined those
    eyes above,
Go boldly on adventure, break through
    bounds
O' the quintessential whiteness that
    surrounds
Your feet, obtain experience of each
    tinge
That bickers forth to broaden out,
    impinge
Plainer his foot its pathway all distinct
From every other. Ah, the wonder,
    linked

With fear, as exploration manifests
What agency it was first tipped the
    crests
Of unnamed wildflower, soon protruding
    grew
Portentous mid the sands, as when his
    hue
Betrays him and the burrowing snake
    gleams through;
Till, last … but why parade more
    shame and pain?
Are not the proofs upon me? Here again
I pass into your presence, I receive
Your smile of pity, pardon, and I
    leave …
No, not this last of times I leave you,
    mute,
Submitted to my penance, so my foot
May yet again adventure, tread, from
    source
To issue, one more ray of rays which
    course
Each other, at your bidding, from the
    sphere
Silver and sweet, their birthplace, down
    that drear
Dark of the world, – you promise shall
    return
Your pilgrim jewelled as with drops o'
    the urn
The rainbow paints from, and no smatch
    at all
Of ghastliness at edge of some cloud-
    pall
Heaven cowers before, as earth awaits
    the fall
O' the bolt and flash of doom. Who
    trusts your word
Tries the adventure: and returns – absurd
As frightful – in that sulphur-steeped
    disguise
Mocking the priestly cloth-of-gold, sole
    prize
The arch-heretic was wont to bear away
Until he reached the burning. No, I say:
No fresh adventure! No more seeking
    love

At end of toil, and finding, calm above
My passion, the old statuesque regard,
The sad petrific smile!
                O you – less hard
And hateful than mistaken and obtuse
Unreason of a she-intelligence!
You very woman with the pert pretence
To match the male achievement! Like
    enough!
Ay, you were easy victors, did the rough
Straightway efface itself to smooth, the
    gruff
Grind down and grow a whisper, – did
    man's truth
Subdue, for sake of chivalry and ruth,
Its rapier-edge to suit the bulrush-spear
Womanly falsehood fights with! O that
    ear
All fact pricks rudely, that thrice-super-
    fine
Feminity of sense, with right divine
To waive all process, take result stain-
    free
From out the very muck wherein …
                Ah me!
The true slave's querulous outbreak!
    All the rest
Be resignation! Forth at your behest
I fare. Who knows but this – the crimson-
    quest –
May deepen to a sunrise, not decay
To that cold sad sweet smile? – which I
    obey.

## Appearances

### 1

And so you found that poor room dull,
   Dark, hardly to your taste, my dear?
Its features seemed unbeautiful:
   But this I know – 'twas there, not
     here,
You plighted troth to me, the word
Which – ask that poor room how it
     heard.

### 2

And this rich room obtains your praise
   Unqualified, – so bright, so fair,
So all whereat perfection stays?
   Ay, but remember – here, not there,
The other word was spoken! Ask
This rich room how you dropped the
     mask!

## St Martin's Summer

### 1

No protesting, dearest!
   Hardly kisses even!
     Don't we both know how it ends?
How the greenest leaf turns serest,
   Bluest outbreak – blankest heaven,
     Lovers – friends?

### 2

You would build a mansion,
   I would weave a bower
     – Want the heart for enterprise.
Walls admit of no expansion:
   Trellis-work may haply flower
     Twice the size.

### 3

What makes glad Life's Winter?
   New buds, old blooms after.
     Sad the sighing 'How suspect
Beams would ere mid-Autumn
     splinter,
   Rooftree scarce support a rafter,
     Walls lie wrecked?'

### 4

You are young, my princess!
   I am hardly older:
     Yet – I steal a glance behind.
Dare I tell you what convinces
   Timid me that you, if bolder,
     Bold – are blind?

### 5

Where we plan our dwelling
   Glooms a graveyard surely!
     Headstone, footstone moss may
     drape, –
Name, date, violets hide from spelling, –
   But, though corpses rot obscurely,
     Ghosts escape.

### 6

Ghosts! O breathing Beauty,
   Give my frank word pardon!
     What if I – somehow, some-
     where –
Pledged my soul to endless duty
   Many a time and oft? Be hard on
     Love – laid there?

### 7

Nay, blame grief that's fickle,
   Time that proves a traitor,
     Chance, change, all that purpose
     warps, –
Death who spares to thrust the sickle
   Laid Love low, through flowers which
     later
     Shroud the corpse!

### 8

And you, my winsome lady,
   Whisper with like frankness!
     Lies nothing buried long ago?
Are yon – which shimmer mid the
     shady
   Where moss and violet run to
     rankness –
     Tombs or no?

### 9

Who taxes you with murder?
   My hands are clean – or nearly!
     Love being mortal needs must
     pass.

Repentance? Nothing were absurder.
　　Enough: we felt Love's loss severely;
　　　　Though now – alas!
　　　　　　10
Love's corpse lies quiet therefore,
　　Only Love's ghost plays truant,
　　　　And warns us have in wholesome
　　　　awe
Durable mansionry; that's wherefore
　　I weave but trellis-work, pursuant
　　　　– Life, to law.
　　　　　　11
The solid, not the fragile,
　　Tempts rain and hail and thunder.
　　　　If bower stand firm at Autumn's
　　　　close,
Beyond my hope, – why, boughs were
　　agile;
　　　　If bower fall flat, we scarce need
　　　　wonder
　　　　　　Wreathing – rose!
　　　　　　12
So, truce to the protesting,
　　So, muffled be the kisses!
　　　　For, would we but avow the truth,
Sober is genuine joy. No jesting!
　　Ask else Penelope, Ulysses –
　　　　Old in youth!
　　　　　　13
For why should ghosts feel angered?
　　Let all their interference
　　　　Be faint march-music in the air!
'Up! Join the rear of us the vanguard!
　　Up, lovers, dead to all appearance,
　　　　Laggard pair!'
　　　　　　14
The while you clasp me closer,
　　The while I press you deeper,
　　　　As safe we chuckle, – under breath,
Yet all the slyer, the jocoser, –
　　'so, life can boast its day, like leap-
　　year,
　　　　Stolen from death!'
　　　　　　15
Ah me – the sudden terror!
　　Hence quick – avaunt, avoid me,

　　You cheat, the ghostly flesh-
　　disguised!
Nay, all the ghosts in one! Strange
　　error!
　　So, 'twas Death's self that clipped
　　and coyed me,
　　　　Loved – and lied!'
　　　　　　16
Ay, dead loves are the potent!
　　Like any cloud they used you,
　　　　Mere semblance you, but
　　　　substance they!
Build we no mansion, weave we no tent!
　　Mere flesh – their spirit interfused
　　you!
　　　　Hence, I say!
　　　　　　17
All theirs, none yours the glamour!
　　Theirs each low word that won me,
　　　　Soft look that found me Love's,
　　　　and left
What else but you – the tears and
　　clamour
　　That's all your very own! Undone
　　me –
　　　　Ghost-bereft!

## Hervé Riel

### 1

On the sea and at the Hogue, sixteen
　　hundred ninety-two,
　　Did the English fight the French, –
　　woe to France!
And, the thirty-first of May, helter-
　　skelter through the blue,
Like a crowd of frightened porpoises a
　　shoal of sharks pursue,
　　Came crowding ship on ship to
　　Saint-Malo on the Rance,
With the English fleet in view.

### 2

'Twas the squadron that escaped, with
　　the victor in full chase;
　　First and foremost of the drove, in
　　his great ship, Damfreville;
　　　　Close on him fled, great and small,

Twenty-two good ships in all;
And they signalled to the place
'Help the winners of a race!
   Get us guidance, give us harbour,
      take us quick – or, quicker still,
   Here's the English can and will!'

3

Then the pilots of the place put out
   brisk and leapt on board;
   'Why, what hope or chance have
      ships like these to pass?' laughed
      they:
'Rocks to starboard, rocks to port, all
   the passage scarred and scored, –
Shall the "Formidable" here, with her
   twelve and eighty guns,
Think to make the river-mouth by
   the single narrow way,
Trust to enter – where 'tis ticklish for a
   craft of twenty tons,
      And with flow at full beside?
      Now, 'tis slackest ebb of tide.
Reach the mooring? Rather say,
While rock stands or water runs,
   Not a ship will leave the bay!'

4

Then was called a council straight.
Brief and bitter the debate:
'Here's the English at our heels; would
   you have them take in tow
All that's left us of the fleet, linked
   together stern and bow,
For a prize to Plymouth Sound?
Better run the ships aground!'
   (Ended Damfreville his speech.)
'Not a minute more to wait!
   Let the Captains all and each
      Shove ashore, then blow up, burn
      the vessels on the beach!
France must undergo her fate.

5

Give the word!' But no such word
Was ever spoke or heard;
   For up stood, for out stepped, for in
      struck amid all these
– A Captain? A Lieutenant? A Mate –
   first, second, third?

No such man of mark, and meet
With his betters to compete!
But a simple Breton sailor pressed by
   Tourville for the fleet,
A poor coasting-pilot he, Hervé Riel the
   Croisickese.

6

And 'What mockery or malice have we
   here?' cries Hervé Riel:
   'Are you mad, you Malouins? Are
      you cowards, fools, or rogues?
Talk to me of rocks and shoals, me
   who took the soundings, tell
On my fingers every bank, every
   shallow, every swell
   'Twixt the offing here and Grève
   where the river disembogues?
Are you bought by English gold? Is it
   love the lying's for?
      Morn and eve, night and day,
      Have I piloted your bay,
Entered free and anchored fast at the
   foot of Solidor.
      Burn the fleet and ruin France? That
      were worse than fifty Hogues!
      Sirs, they know I speak the truth!
      Sirs, believe me there's a way!
Only let me lead the line,
   Have the biggest ship to steer,
   Get this "Formidable" clear,
Make the others follow mine,
And I lead them, most and least, by a
   passage I know well,
   Right to Solidor past Grève,
   And there lay them safe and sound;
And if one ship misbehave, –
   – Keel so much as grate the ground,
Why, I've nothing but my life, – here's
   my head!' cries Hervé Riel.

7

Not a minute more to wait.
'Steer us in, then, small and great!
   Take the helm, lead the line, save
      the squadron!' cried its chief.
Captains, give the sailor place!
   He is Admiral, in brief.
Still the north-wind, by God's grace!

See the noble fellow's face
As the big ship, with a bound,
Clears the entry like a hound,
Keeps the passage, as its inch of way
    were the wide sea's profound!
  See, safe thro'shoal and rock,
  How they follow in a flock,
Not a ship that misbehaves, not a keel
    that grates the ground,
  Not a spar that comes to grief!
The peril, see, is past.
All are harboured to the last,
And just as Hervé Riel hollas 'Anchor!'
  – sure as fate,
Up the English come, – too late!

8

So, the storm subsides to calm:
  They see the green trees wave
  On the heights o'erlooking Grève.
Hearts that bled are stanched with balm.
'Just our rapture to enhance,
  Let the English rake the bay,
Gnash their teeth and glare askance
  As they cannonade away!
'Neath rampired Solidor pleasant
  riding on the Rance!'
How hope succeeds despair on each
  Captain's countenance!
Out burst all with one accord,
  'This is Paradise for Hell!
    Let France, let France's King
Thank the man that did the thing!'
What a shout, and all one word,
  'Hervé Riel!'
As he stepped in front once more,
  Not a symptom of surprise
  In the frank blue Breton eyes,
Just the same man as before.

9

Then said Damfreville, 'My friend,
I must speak out at the end,
  Though I find the speaking hard.
Praise is deeper than the lips:
You have saved the King his ships,
  You must name your own reward.
'Faith, our sun was near eclipse!

Demand whate'er you will,
France remains your debtor still.
Ask to heart's content and have! or my
  name's not Damfreville.'

10

Then a beam of fun outbroke
On the bearded mouth that spoke,
As the honest heart laughed through
Those frank eyes of Breton blue:
'Since I needs must say my say,
  Since on board the duty's done,
  And from Malo Roads to Croisic
    Point, what is it but a run? –
Since 'tis ask and have, I may –
  Since the others go ashore –
Come! A good whole holiday!
Leave to go and see my wife, whom I
  call the Belle Aurore!'
That he asked and that he got, –
  nothing more.

11

Name and deed alike are lost:
Not a pillar nor a post
  In his Croisic keeps alive the feat as
    it befell;
Not a head in white and black
On a single fishing-smack,
In memory of the man but for whom
    had gone to wrack
  All that France saved from the fight
    whence England bore the bell.
Go to Paris: rank on rank
  Search the heroes flung pell-mell
On the Louvre, face and flank!
  You shall look long enough ere you
    come to Hervé Riel.
So, for better and for worse,
Hervé Riel, accept my verse!
In my verse, Hervé Riel, do thou once
  more
Save the squadron, honour France,
  love thy wife the Belle Aurore!

## A Forgiveness

I am indeed the personage you know.
As for my wife, – what happened long
    ago, –
You have a right to question me, as I
Am bound to answer.
        ('Son, a fit reply!'
The monk half spoke, half ground
    through his clenched teeth,
At the confession-grate I knelt beneath.)

Thus then all happened, Father! Power
    and place
I had as still I have. I ran life's race,
With the whole world to see, as only
    strains
His strength some athlete whose
    prodigious gains
Of good appal him: happy to excess, –
Work freely done should balance
    happiness
Fully enjoyed; and, since beneath my
    roof
Housed she who made home heaven,
    in heaven's behoof
I went forth every day, and all day long
Worked for the world. Look, how the
    labourer's song
Cheers him! Thus sang my soul, at each
    sharp throe
Of labouring flesh and blood – 'she
    loves me so!'

One day, perhaps such song so knit
    the nerve
That work grew play and vanished. 'I
    deserve
Haply my heaven an hour before the
    time!'
I laughed, as silverly the clockhouse-
    chime
Surprised me passing through the
    postern-gate
– Not the main entry where the
    menials wait

And wonder why the world's affairs
    allow
The master sudden leisure. That was
    how
I took the private garden-way for once.

Forth from the alcove, I saw start,
    ensconce
Himself behind the porphyry vase, a
    man.
My fancies in the natural order ran:
'A spy, – perhaps a foe in ambuscade, –
A thief, – more like, a sweetheart of
    some maid
Who pitched on the alcove for tryst
    perhaps.'
'Stand there!' I bid.
        Whereat my man but wraps
His face the closelier with uplifted arm
Whereon the cloak lies, strikes in blind
    alarm
This and that pedestal as, – stretch and
    stoop, –
Now in, now out of sight, he thrids the
    group
Of statues, marble god and goddess
    ranged
Each side the pathway, till the gate's
    exchanged
For safety: one step thence, the street,
    you know!
Thus far I followed with my gaze.
    Then, slow,
Near on admiringly, I breathed again,
And – back to that last fancy of the
    train –
'A danger risked for hope of just a
    word
With – which of all my nest may be the
    bird
This poacher covets for her plumage,
    pray?
Carmen? Juana? Carmen seems too gay
For such adventure, while Juana's
    grave
– Would scorn the folly. I applaud the
    knave!

He had the eye, could single from my
    brood
His proper fledgeling!'
                  As I turned, there stood
In face of me, my wife stone-still stone-
    white.
Whether one bound had brought her,
    – at first sight
Of what she judged the encounter,
    sure to be
Next moment, of the venturous man
    and me, –
Brought her to clutch and keep me
    from my prey:
Whether impelled because her death
    no day
Could come so absolutely opportune
As now at joy's height, like a year in
    June
Stayed at the fall of its first ripened rose:
Or whether hungry for my hate – who
    knows? –
Eager to end an irksome lie, and taste
Our tingling true relation, hate embraced
By hate one naked moment: – anyhow
There stone-still stone-white stood my
    wife, but now
The woman who made heaven within
    my house.
Ay, she who faced me was my very
    spouse
As well as love – you are to recollect!

'Stay!' she said. 'Keep at least one soul
    unspecked
With crime, that's spotless hitherto –
    your own!
Kill me who court the blessing, who
    alone
Was, am, and shall be guilty, first to
    last!
The man lay helpless in the toils I cast
About him, helpless as the statue there
Against that strangling bell-flower's
    bondage: tear
Away and tread to dust the parasite,
But do the passive marble no despite!

I love him as I hate you. Kill me! Strike
At one blow both infinitudes alike
Out of existence – hate and love! Whence
    love?
That's safe inside my heart, nor will
    remove
For any searching of your steel, I think.
Whence hate? The secret lay on lip, at
    brink
Of speech, in one fierce tremble to
    escape,
At every form wherein your love took
    shape,
At each new provocation of your kiss.
Kill me!'
          We went in.
                      Next day after this,
I felt as if the speech might come. I
    spoke –
Easily, after all.
                  'The lifted cloak
Was screen sufficient: I concern myself
Hardly with laying hands on who for
    pelf –
Whate'er the ignoble kind – may prowl
    and brave
Cuffing and kicking proper to a knave
Detected by my household's vigilance.
Enough of such! As for my love-
    romance –
I, like our good Hidalgo, rub my eyes
And wake and wonder how the film
    could rise
Which changed for me a barber's basin
    straight
Into – Mambrino's helm? I hesitate
Nowise to say – God's sacramental cup!
Why should I blame the brass which,
    burnished up,
Will blaze, to all but me, as good as
    gold?
To me – a warning I was overbold
In judging metals. The Hidalgo waked
Only to die, if I remember, – staked
His life upon the basin's worth, and
    lost:
While I confess torpidity at most

In here and there a limb; but, lame and
 halt,
Still should I work on, still repair my
 fault
Ere I took rest in death, – no fear at all!
Now, work – no word before the curtain
 fall!'

The ' curtain'? That of death on life, I
 meant:
My 'word,' permissible in death's event,
Would be – truth, soul to soul; for,
 otherwise,
Day by day, three years long, there had
 to rise
And, night by night, to fall upon our
 stage –
Ours, doomed to public play by
 heritage –
Another curtain, when the world,
 perforce
Our critical assembly, in due course
Came and went, witnessing, gave
 praise or blame
To art-mimetic. It had spoiled the game
If, suffered to set foot behind our scene,
The world had witnessed how stage-
 king and queen,
Gallant and lady, but a minute since
Enarming each the other, would evince
No sign of recognition as they took
His way and her way to whatever nook
Waited them in the darkness either side
Of that bright stage where lately groom
 and bride
Had fired the audience to a frenzy-fit
Of sympathetic rapture – every whit
Earned as the curtain fell on her and
 me,
– Actors. Three whole years, nothing
 was to see
But calm and concord; where a speech
 was due
There came the speech: when smiles
 were wanted too
Smiles were as ready. In a place like
 mine,

Where foreign and domestic cares
 combine,
There's audience every day and all day
 long;
But finally the last of the whole throng
Who linger lets one see his back. For
 her –
Why, liberty and liking: I aver,
Liking and liberty! For me – I breathed,
Let my face rest from every wrinkle
 wreathed
Smile-like about the mouth, unlearned
 my task
Of personation till next day bade mask,
And quietly betook me from that world
To the real world, not pageant: there
 unfurled
In work, its wings, my soul, the fretted
 power.
Three years I worked, each minute of
 each hour
Not claimed by acting: – work I may
 dispense
With talk about, since work in evidence,
Perhaps in history; who knows or cares?

After three years, this way, all unawares,
Our acting ended. She and I, at close
Of a loud night-feast, led, between two
 rows
Of bending male and female loyalty,
Our lord die king down staircase,
 while, held high
At arm's length did the twisted tapers'
 flare
Herald his passage from our palace,
 where
Such visiting left glory evermore.
Again the ascent in public, till at door
As we two stood by the saloon – now
 blank
And disencumbered of its guests –
 there sank
A whisper in my ear, so low and yet
So unmistakable!
     'I half forget
The chamber you repair to, and I want

Occasion for one short word – if you
    grant
That grace – within a certain room you
    called
Our "Study," for you wrote there while
    I scrawled
Some paper full of faces for my sport.
That room I can remember. Just one
    short
Word with you there, for the
    remembrance'sake!'

'Follow me thither!' I replied.
                            We break
The gloom a little, as with guiding lamp
I lead the way, leave warmth and
    cheer, by damp
Blind disused serpentining ways afar
From where the habitable chambers
    are, –
Ascend, descend stairs tunnelled
    through the stone, –
Always in silence, – till I reach the lone
Chamber sepulchred for my very own
Out of the palace-quarry. When a boy,
Here was my fortress, stronghold from
    annoy,
Proof-positive of ownership; in youth
I garnered up my gleanings here –
    uncouth
But precious relics of vain hopes, vain
    fears;
Finally, this became in after years
My closet of entrenchment to withstand
Invasion of the foe on every hand –
The multifarious herd in bower and hall,
State-room, – rooms whatsoe'er the
    style, which call
On masters to be mindful that, before
Men, they must look like men and
    something more.
Here, – when our lord the king's
    bestowment ceased
To deck me on the day that, golden-
    fleeced,
I touched ambition's height, – 'twas
    here, released

From glory (always symbolled by a
    chain!)
No sooner was I privileged to gain
My secret domicile than glad I flung
That last toy on the table – gazed
    where hung
On hook my father's gift, the
    arquebuss –
And asked myself 'shall I envisage thus
The new prize and the old prize, when
    I reach
Another year's experience? – own that
    each
Equalled advantage – sportsman's –
    statesman's tool?
That brought me down an eagle, this –
    a fool!'
Into which room on entry, I set down
The lamp, and turning saw whose
    rustled gown
Had told me my wife followed, pace for
    pace.
Each of us looked the other in the face.
She spoke. 'Since I could die now … '
                            (To explain
Why that first struck me, know – not
    once again
Since the adventure at the porphyry's
    edge
Three years before, which sundered
    like a wedge
Her soul from mine, – though daily,
    smile to smile,
We stood before the public, – all the
    while
Not once had I distinguished, in that
    face
I paid observance to, the faintest trace
Of feature more than requisite for eyes
To do their duty by and recognize:
So did I force mine to obey my will
And pry no further. There exists such
    skill, –
Those know who need it. What physician
    shrinks
From needful contact with a corpse? He
    drinks

No plague so long as thirst for knowledge
    – not
An idler impulse – prompts inquiry.
    What,
And will you disbelieve in power to bid
Our spirit back to bounds, as though
    we chid
A child from scrutiny that's just and
    right
In manhood? Sense, not soul,
    accomplished sight,
Reported daily she it was – not how
Nor why a change had come to cheek
    and brow.)

'Since I could die now of the truth
    concealed,
Yet dare not, must not die – so seems
    revealed
The Virgin's mind to me – for death
    means peace,
Wherein no lawful part have I, whose
    lease
Of life and punishment the truth avowed
May haply lengthen, – let me push the
    shroud
Away, that steals to muffle ere is just
My penance-fire in snow! I dare – I must
Live, by avowal of the truth – this
    truth –
I loved you! Thanks for the fresh serpent's
    tooth
That, by a prompt new pang more
    exquisite
Than all preceding torture, proves me
    right!
I loved you yet I lost you! May I go
Burn to the ashes, now my shame you
    know?'

I think there never was such – how
    express? –
Horror coquetting with voluptuousness,
As in those arms of Eastern
    workmanship –
Yataghan, kandjar, things that rend
    and rip,

Gash rough, slash smooth, help hate
    so many ways,
Yet ever keep a beauty that betrays
Love still at work with the artificer
Throughout his quaint devising. Why
    prefer,
Except for love's sake, that a blade
    should writhe
And bicker like a flame? – now play the
    scythe
As if some broad neck tempted, – now
    contract
And needle off into a fineness lacked
For just that puncture which the heart
    demands?
Then, such adornment! Wherefore need
    our hands
Enclose not ivory alone, nor gold
Roughened for use, but jewels? Nay,
    behold!
Fancy my favourite – which I seem to
    grasp
While I describe the luxury. No asp
Is diapered more delicate round throat
Than this below the handle! These
    denote
– These mazy lines meandering, to end
Only in flesh they open – what intend
They else but water-purlings – pale
    contrast
With the life-crimson where they blend
    at last?
And mark the handle's dim pellucid
    green,
Carved, the hard jadestone, as you
    pinch a bean,
Into a sort of parrot-bird! He pecks
A grape-bunch; his two eyes are ruby-
    specks
Pure from the mine: seen this way, –
    glassy blank,
But turn them, – lo the inmost fire,
    that shrank
From sparkling, sends a red dart right
    to aim!
Why did I choose such toys? Perhaps
    the game

Of peaceful men is warlike, just as men
War-wearied get amusement from that
pen
And paper we grow sick of – statesfolk
tired
Of merely (when such measures are
required)
Dealing out doom to people by three
words,
A signature and seal: we play with swords
Suggestive of quick process. That is how
I came to like the toys described you
now,
Store of which glittered on the walls
and strewed
The table, even, while my wife pursued
Her purpose to its ending. 'Now you
know
This shame, my three years' torture, let
me go,
Burn to the very ashes! You – I lost,
Yet you – I loved!'
          The thing I pity most
In men is – action prompted by surprise
Of anger: men? nay, bulls – whose
onset lies
At instance of the firework and the goad!
Once the foe prostrate, – trampling
once bestowed, –
Prompt follows placability, regret,
Atonement. Trust me, blood-warmth
never yet
Betokened strong will! As no leap of
pulse
Pricked me, that first time, so did none
convulse
My veins at this occasion for resolve.
Had that devolved which did not then
devolve
Upon me, I had done – what now to do
Was quietly apparent.
          'Tell me who
The man was, crouching by the
porphyry vase!'
'No, never! All was folly in his case,
All guilt in mine. I tempted, he
complied.'

'And yet you loved me?'
'Loved you. Double-dyed
In folly and in guilt, I thought you gave
Your heart and soul away from me to
slave
At statecraft. Since my right in you
seemed lost,
I stung myself to teach you, to your
cost,
What you rejected could be prized
beyond
Life, heaven, by the first fool I threw a
fond
Look on, a fatal word to.'
          'And you still
Love me? Do I conjecture well or ill?'
'Conjecture – well or ill! I had three
years
To spend in learning you.'
          'We both are peers
In knowledge, therefore: since three
years are spent
Ere thus much of yourself I learn – who
went
Back to the house, that day, and
brought my mind
To bear upon your action, uncombined
Motive from motive, till the dross,
deprived
Of every purer particle, survived
At last in native simple hideousness,
Utter contemptibility, nor less
Nor more. Contemptibility – exempt
How could I, from its proper due –
contempt?
I have too much despised you to divert
My life from its set course by help or
hurt
Of your all-despicable life – perturb
The calm, I work in, by – men's
mouths to curb,
Which at such news were clamorous
enough –
Men's eyes to shut before my
broidered stuff
With the huge hole there, my
emblazoned wall

Blank where a scutcheon hung, – by,
    worse than all,
Each day's procession, my paraded life
Robbed and impoverished through the
    wanting wife
– Now that my life (which means – my
    work) was grown
Riches indeed! Once, just this worth
    alone
Seemed work to have, that profit
    gained thereby
Of good and praise would – how
    rewardingly! –
Fall at your feet, – a crown I hoped to
    cast
Before your love, my love should crown
    at last.
No love remaining to cast crown before,
My love stopped work now: but
    contempt the more
Impelled me task as ever head and hand,
Because the very fiends weave ropes of
    sand
Rather than taste pure hell in idleness.
Therefore I kept my memory down by
    stress
Of daily work I had no mind to stay
For the world's wonder at the wife away.
Oh, it was easy all of it, believe,
For I despised you! But your words
    retrieve
Importantly the past. No hate assumed
The mask of love at any time! There
    gloomed
A moment when love took hate's
    semblance, urged
By causes you declare; but love's self
    purged
Away a fancied wrong I did both loves
– Yours and my own: by no hate's help,
    it proves,
Purgation was attempted. Then, you rise
High by how many a grade! I did
    despise –
I do but hate you. Let hate's punishment
Replace contempt's! First step to which
    ascent –

Write down your own words I re-utter
    you!
*"I loved my husband and I hated – who*
*He was, I took up as my first chance, mere*
*Mud-ball to fling and make love foul with I"*
Here
   Lies paper!'
       'Would my blood for ink suffice!'
'It may: this minion from a land of spice,
Silk, feather – every bird of jewelled
    breast –
This poignard's beauty, ne'er so lightly
    prest
Above your heart there … '
         'Thus?'
             'It flows, I see.
Dip there the point and write!'
              'Dictate to me!
Nay, I remember.'
       And she wrote the words.
I read them. Then – 'Since love, in you,
    affords
License for hate, in me, to quench (I say)
Contempt – why, hate itself has passed
    away
In vengeance – foreign to contempt.
    Depart
Peacefully to that death which Eastern
    art
Imbued this weapon with, if tales be
    true!
Love will succeed to hate. I pardon
    you –
Dead in our chamber!'
          True as truth the tale.
She died ere morning; then, I saw how
    pale
Her cheek was ere it wore day's paint-
    disguise,
And what a hollow darkened 'neath
    her eyes,
Now that I used my own. She sleeps, as
    erst
Beloved, in this your church: ay, yours!
          Immersed
In thought so deeply, Father? Sad,
    perhaps?

For whose sake, hers or mine or his who
          wraps
– Still plain I seem to see! – about his
          head
The idle cloak, – about his heart (instead
Of cuirass) some fond hope he may
          elude
My vengeance in the cloister's solitude?
Hardly, I think! As little helped his brow
The cloak then, Father – as your grate
          helps now!

## Cenciaja

Ogni cencio vuol entrare in bucato.
                    – *Italian Proverb*

May I print, Shelley, how it came to
          pass
That when your Beatrice seemed – by
          lapse
Of many a long month since her
          sentence fell –
Assured of pardon for the parricide, –
By intercession of staunch friends, or,
          say,
By certain pricks of conscience in the
          Pope
Conniver at Francesco Cenci's guilt, –
Suddenly all things changed and
          Clement grew
'Stern,' as you state, 'nor to be moved
          nor bent,
But said these three words coldly *"She
          must die;'*
Subjoining *"Pardon? Paolo Santa Croce
Murdered his mother also yestereve,
And he is fled: she shall not flee at least!'*
– So, to the letter, sentence was
          fulfilled?
Shelley, may I condense verbosity
That lies before me, into some few
          words
Of English, and illustrate your superb
Achievement by a rescued anecdote,
No great things, only new and true
          beside?

As if some mere familiar of a house
Should venture to accost the group at
          gaze
Before its Titian, famed the wide world
          through,
And supplement such pictured
          masterpiece
By whisper 'Searching in the archives
          here,
I found the reason of the Lady's fate,
And how by accident it came to pass
She wears the halo and displays the
          palm:
Who, haply, else had never suffered –
          no,
Nor graced our gallery, by consequence.'
Who loved the work would like the
          little news
Who lauds your poem lends an ear to
          me
Relating how the penalty was paid
By one Marchese dell' Oriolo, called
Onofrio Santa Croce otherwise,
For his complicity in matricide
With Paolo his own brother, – he
          whose crime
And flight induced 'those three words
          – She must die.'
Thus I unroll you then the manuscript.
'God's justice' – (of the multiplicity
Of such communications extant still,
Recording, each, injustice done by God
In person of his Vicar-upon-earth,
Scarce one but leads off to the self-
          same tune) –
'God's justice, tardy though it prove
          perchance,
Rests never on the track until it reach
Delinquency. In proof I cite the case
Of Paolo Santa Croce.'
                              Many times
The youngster, – having been
          importunate
That Marchesine Costanza, who
          remained
His widowed mother, should supplant
          the heir

Her elder son, and substitute himself
In sole possession of her faculty, –
And meeting just as often with rebuff, –
Blinded by so exorbitant a lust
Of gold, the youngster straightway
      tasked his wits,
Casting about to kill the lady – thus.

He first, to cover his iniquity,
Writes to Onofrio Santa Croce, then
Authoritative lord, acquainting him
Their mother was contamination –
      wrought
Like hell-fire in the beauty of their
      House
By dissoluteness and abandonment
Of soul and body to impure delight.
Moreover, since she suffered from
      disease,
Those symptoms which her death
      made manifest
Hydroptic, he affirmed were fruits of sin
About to bring confusion and disgrace
Upon the ancient lineage and high fame
O' the family, when published. Duty
      bound,
He asked his brother – what a son
      should do?

Which when Marchese dell' Oriolo
      heard
By letter, being absent at his land
Oriolo, he made answer, this, no more:
'It must behove a son, – things haply
      so, –
To act as honour prompts a cavalier
And son, perform his duty to all three,
Mother and brothers' – here advice
      broke off.

By which advice informed and fortified,
As he professed himself – since bound
      by birth
To hear God's voice in primogeniture –
Paolo, who kept his mother company
In her domain Subiaco, straightway
      dared

His whole enormity of enterprise
And, falling on her, stabbed the lady
      dead;
Whose death demonstrated her
      innocence,
And happened, – by the way, – since
      Jesus Christ
Died to save man, just sixteen hundred
      years.
Costanza was of aspect beautiful
Exceedingly, and seemed, although in
      age
Sixty about, to far surpass her peers
The coëtaneous dames, in youth and
      grace.

Done the misdeed, its author takes
      to flight,
Foiling thereby the justice of the world:
Not God's however, – God, be sure,
      knows well
The way to clutch a culprit. Witness
      here!
The present sinner, when he least
      expects,
Snug-cornered somewhere i' the
      Basilicate,
Stumbles upon his death by violence.
A man of blood assaults a man of
      blood
And slays him somehow. This was
      afterward:
Enough, he promptly met with his
      deserts,
And, ending thus, permits we end with
      him,
And push forthwith to this important
      point –
His matricide fell out, of all the days,
Precisely when the law-procedure
      closed
Respecting Count Francesco Cenci's
      death
Chargeable on his daughter, sons and
      wife.
'Thus patricide was matched with
      matricide,'

A poet not inelegantly rhymed:
Nay, fratricide – those Princes
    Massimi!
Which so disturbed the spirit of the
    Pope
That all the likelihood Rome entertained
Of Beatrice's pardon vanished straight,
And she endured the piteous death.
                        Now see
The sequel – what effect commandment
    had
For strict inquiry into this last case,
When Cardinal Aldobrandini (great
His efficacy – nephew to the Pope)
Was bidden crush – ay, though his
    very hand
Got soil i' the act – crime spawning
    everywhere!
Because, when all endeavour had been
    used
To catch the aforesaid Paolo, all in
    vain –
'Make perquisition' quoth our Eminence,
'Throughout his now deserted domicile!
Ransack the palace, roof and floor, to
    find
If haply any scrap of writing, hid
In nook or corner, may convict – who
    knows? –
Brother Onofrio of intelligence
With brother Paolo, as in brotherhood
Is but too likely: crime spawns
    everywhere.'

    And, every cranny searched
    accordingly,
There comes to light – O lynx-eyed
    Cardinal! –
Onofrio's unconsidered writing-scrap,
The letter in reply to Paolo's prayer,
The word of counsel that – things-
    proving so,
Paolo should act the proper knightly
    part,
And do as was incumbent on a son,
A brother – and a man of birth, be sure!

Whereat immediately the officers
Proceeded to arrest Onofrio – found
At foot-ball, child's play, unaware of
    harm,
Safe with his friends, the Orsini, at
    their seat
Monte Giordano; as he left the house
He came upon the watch in wait for
    him
Set by the Barigel, – was caught and
    caged.

    News of which capture being, that
    same hour,
Conveyed to Rome, forthwith our
    Eminence,
Commands Taverna, Governor and
    Judge,
To have the process in especial care,
Be, first to last, not only president
In person, but inquisitor as well,
Nor trust the by-work to a substitute:
Bids him not, squeamish, keep the
    bench, but scrub
The floor of Justice, so to speak, – go try
His best in prison with the criminal:
Promising, as reward for by-work done
Fairly on all-fours, that, success obtained
And crime avowed, or such connivency
With crime as should procure a decent
    death –
Himself will humbly beg – which means,
    procure –
The Hat and Purple from his relative
The Pope, and so repay a diligence
Which, meritorious in the Cenci-case,
Mounts plainly here to Purple and the
    Hat.

    Whereupon did my lord the Governor
So masterfully exercise the task
Enjoined him, that he, day by day, and
    week
By week, and month by month, from
    first to last
Toiled for the prize: now, punctual at
    his place,

Played Judge, and now, assiduous at
   his post,
Inquisitor – pressed cushion and
   scoured plank,
Early and late. Noon's fervour and
   night's chill,
Nought moved whom morn would,
   purpling, make amends!
So that observers laughed as, many a
   day,
He left home, in July when day is
   flame,
Posted to Tordinona-prison, plunged
Into a vault where daylong night is ice,
There passed his eight hours on a
   stretch, content,
Examining Onofrio: all the stress
Of all examination steadily
Converging into one pin-point, – he
   pushed
Tentative now of head and now of
   heart.
As when the nuthatch taps and tries
   the nut
This side and that side till the kernel
   sound, –
So did he press the sole and single
   point
– What was the very meaning of the
   phrase
'*Do as beseems an honoured cavalier*'?

   Which one persistent question-
   torture, – plied
Day by day, week by week, and month
   by month,
Morn, noon and night, – fatigued away
   a mind
Grown imbecile by darkness, solitude,
And one vivacious memory gnawing
   there
As when a corpse is coffined with a
   snake
– Fatigued Onofrio into what might
   seem
Admission that perchance his
   judgment groped

So blindly, feeling for an issue – aught
With semblance of an issue from the
   toils
Cast of a sudden round feet late so
   free,
He possibly might have envisaged,
   scarce
Recoiled from – even were the issue
   death
– Even her death whose life was death
   and worse!
Always provided that the charge of
   crime,
Each jot and tittle of the charge were
   true.
In such a sense, belike, he might advise
His brother to expurgate crime with …
   well,
With blood, if blood must follow on
   '*the course
Taken as might beseem a cavalier.*'

   Whereupon process ended, and
   report
Was made without a minute of delay
To Clement who, because of those two
   crimes
O' the Massimi and Cenci flagrant late,
Must needs impatiently desire result.

   Result obtained, he bade the Governor
Summon the Congregation and despatch.
Summons made, sentence passed
   accordingly
– Death by beheading. When his
   death-decree
Was intimated to Onofrio, all
Man could do – that did he to save
   himself.
'Twas much, the having gained for his
   defence
The Advocate o' the Poor, with natural
   help
Of many noble friendly persons fain
To disengage a man of family,
So young too, from his grim
   entanglement:

But Cardinal Aldobrandini ruled
There must be no diversion of the law.
Justice is justice, and the magistrate
Bears not the sword in vain. Who sins
    must die.

So, the Marchese had his head cut
    off,
With Rome to see, a concourse infinite,
In Place Saint Angelo beside the Bridge:
Where, demonstrating magnanimity
Adequate to his birth and breed, –
    poor boy! –
He made the people the accustomed
    speech,
Exhorted them to true faith, honest
    works,
And special good behaviour as regards
A parent of no matter what the sex,
Bidding each son take warning from
    himself.
Truly, it was considered in the boy
Stark staring lunacy, no less, to snap
So plain a bait, be hooked and hauled
    ashore
By such an angler as the Cardinal!
Why make confession of his privity
To Paolo's enterprise? Mere sealing
    lips –
Or, better, saying 'When I counselled
    him
*To do as might beseem a cavalier,"*
What could I mean but "*Hide our
    parent's shame*
*As Christian ought, by aid of Holy
    Church!*
*Bury it in a convent – ay, beneath*
*Enough dotation to prevent its ghost*
*From troubling earth!"* ' Mere saying
    thus, – 'tis plain,
Not only were his life the recompense,
But he had manifestly proved himself
True Christian, and in lieu of punishment
Got praise of all men. So the populace.

Anyhow, when the Pope made
    promise good

(That of Aldobrandini, near and dear)
And gave Taverna, who had toiled so
    much,
A Cardinal's equipment, some such word
As this from mouth to ear went saucily:
'Taverna's cap is dyed in what he drew
From Santa Croce's veins!'so joked the
    world.

I add: Onofrio left one child behind,
A daughter named Valeria, dowered
    with grace
Abundantly of soul and body, doomed
To life the shorter for her father's fate.
By death of her, the Marquisate
    returned
To that Orsini House from whence it
    came:
Oriolo having passed as donative
To Santa Croce from their ancestors.

And no word more? By all means!
    Would you know
The authoritative answer, when folk
    urged
'What made Aldobrandini, hound-like
    staunch,
Hunt out of life a harmless simpleton?'
The answer was – 'Hatred implacable,
By reason they were rivals in their love.'
The Cardinal's desire was to a dame
Whose favour was Onofrio's. Pricked
    with pride,
The simpleton must ostentatiously
Display a ring, the Cardinal's love-gift,
Given to Onofrio as the lady's gage;
Which ring on fringer, as he put forth
    hand
To draw a tapestry, the Cardinal
Saw and knew, gift and owner, old and
    young;
Whereon a fury entered him – the fire
He quenched with what could quench
    fire only – blood.
Nay, more: 'there want not who affirm
    to boot,
The unwise boy, a certain festal eve,

Feigned ignorance of who the wight
 might be
That pressed too closely on him with a
 crowd.
He struck the Cardinal a blow: and then,
To put a face upon the incident,
Dared next day, smug as ever, go pay
 court
I' the Cardinal's antechamber. Mark and
 mend,
Ye youth, by this example how may
 greed
Vainglorious operate in worldly souls!'

So ends the chronicler, beginning with
'God's justice, tardy though it prove
 perchance,
Rests never till it reach delinquency.'
Ay, or how otherwise had come to pass
That Victor rules, this present year, in
 Rome?

## Filippo Baldinucci on
## the Privilege of Burial

A Reminiscence of AD 1676

### 1

'No, boy, we must not' – so began
 My Uncle (he's with God long since)
A-petting me, the good old man!
 'We must not' – and he seemed to
  wince,
And lost that laugh whereto had grown
 His chuckle at my piece of news,
How cleverly I aimed my stone –
 'I fear we must not pelt the Jews!

### 2

'When I was young indeed, – ah, faith
 Was young and strong in Florence
  too!
We Christians never dreamed of scathe
 Because we cursed or kicked the crew.
But now – well, well! The olive-crops
 Weighed double then, and Arno's
  pranks
Would always spare religious shops
 Whenever he o'erflowed his banks!

### 3

I'll tell you' – and his eye regained
 Its twinkle – 'tell you something
  choice!
Something may help you keep
 unstained
 Your honest zeal to stop the voice
Of unbelief with stone-throw – spite
 Of laws, which modern fools enact,
That we must suffer Jews in sight
 Go wholly unmolested! Fact!

### 4

'There was, then, in my youth, and yet
 Is, by our San Frediano, just
Below the Blessed Olivet,
 A wayside ground wherein they thrust
Their dead, – these Jews, – the more
 our shame!
 Except that, so they will but die,
Christians perchance incur no blame
 In giving hogs a hoist to stye.

### 5

'There, anyhow, Jews stow away
 Their dead; and, – such their
  insolence, –
Slink, at odd times to sing and pray
 As Christians do – all make-
  pretence! –
Which wickedness they perpetrate
 Because they think no Christians
  see.
They reckoned here, at any rate,
 Without their host: ha, ha, he, he!

### 6

'For, what should join their plot of
 ground
 But a good Farmer's Christian field?
The Jews had hedged their corner
 round
 With bramble-bush to keep concealed
Their doings: for the public road
 Ran betwixt this their ground and
  that
The Farmer's, where he ploughed and
 sowed,
 Grew corn for barn and grapes for
  vat.

7

'So, properly to guard his store
    And gall the unbelievers too,
He builds a shrine and, what is more,
    Procures a painter whom I knew,
One Buti (he's with God) to paint
    A holy picture there – no less
Than Virgin Mary free from taint
    Borne to the sky by angels: yes!

8

Which shrine he fixed, – who says him
    nay? –
    A-facing with its picture-side
Not, as you'd think, the public way,
    But just where sought these hounds
        to hide
Their carrion from that very truth
    Of Mary's triumph: not a hound
Could act his mummeries uncouth
    But Mary shamed the pack all round!

9

'Now, if it was amusing, judge!
    – To see the company arrive,
Each Jew intent to end his trudge
    And take his pleasure (though alive)
With all his Jewish kith and kin
    Below ground, have his venom out,
Sharpen his wits for next day's sin,
    Curse Christians, and so home, no
        doubt!

10

'Whereas, each phyz upturned beholds
    Mary, I warrant, soaring brave!
And in a trice, beneath the folds
    Of filthy garb which gowns each
        knave,
Down drops it – there to hide grimace,
    Contortion of the mouth and nose
At finding Mary in the place
    They'd keep for Pilate, I suppose!

11

'At last, they will not brook – not they! –
    Longer such outrage on their tribe:
So, in some hole and corner, lay
    Their heads together – how to bribe
The meritorious Farmer's self

To straight undo his work, restore
Their chance to meet and muse on pelf
    Pretending sorrow, as before!

12

'Forthwith, a posse, if you please,
    Of Rabbi This and Rabbi That
Almost go down upon their knees
    To get him lay the picture flat.
The spokesman, eighty years of age,
    Grey as a badger, with a goat's
Not only beard but bleat, 'gins wage
    War with our Mary. Thus he dotes: –

13

' "Friends, grant a grace! How Hebrews
        toil
    Through life in Florence – why relate
To those who lay the burden, spoil
    Our paths of peace? We bear our fate,
But when with life the long toil ends,
    Why must you – the expression craves
Pardon, but truth compels me, friends! –
    Why must you plague us in our graves?

14

' "Thoughtlessly plague, I would believe!
    For how can you – the lords of ease
By nurture, birthright – e'en conceive
    Our luxury to lie with trees
And turf, – the cricket and the bird
    Left for our last companionship:
No harsh deed, no unkindly word,
    No frowning brow nor scornful lip!

15

' "Death's luxury, we now rehearse
    While, living, through your streets we
        fare
And take your hatred: nothing worse
    Have we, once dead and safe, to bear!
So we refresh our souls, fulfil
    Our works, our daily tasks; and thus
Gather you grain – earth's harvest – still
    The wheat for you, the straw for us.

16

' " 'What flouting in a face, what harm,
    In just a lady borne from bier
By boys' heads, wings for leg and arm?'
    You question. Friends, the harm is
        here –

That just when our last sigh is heaved,
  And we would fain thank God and you
For labour done and peace achieved,
  Back comes the Past in full review!

17

' "At sight of just that simple flag,
  Starts the foe-feeling serpent-like
From slumber. Leave it lulled, nor drag –
  Though fangless – forth, what needs
    must strike
When stricken sore, though stroke be vain
  Against the mailed oppressor! Give
Play to our fancy that we gain
  Life's rights when once we cease to live!

18

' "Thus much to courtesy, to kind,
  To conscience! Now to Florence folk!
There's core beneath this apple-rind,
  Beneath this white-of-egg there's yolk!
Beneath this prayer to courtesy,
  Kind, conscience – there's a sum to
    pouch!
How many ducats down will buy
  Our shame's removal, sirs? Avouch !

19

' "Removal, not destruction, sirs"!
  Just turn your picture! Let it front
The public path! Or memory errs,
  Or that same public path is wont
To witness many a chance befall
  Of lust, theft, bloodshed – sins enough,
Wherein our Hebrew part is small.
  Convert yourselves !" – he cut up
    rough.

20

'Look you, how soon a service paid
  Religion yields the servant fruit!
A prompt reply our Farmer made
  So following: "Sirs, to grant your suit
Involves much danger! How? Transpose
  Our Lady? Stop the chastisement,
All for your good, herself bestows?
  What wonder if I grudge consent?

21

' " – Yet grant it: since, what cash I take
  Is so much saved from wicked use.

We know you! And, for Mary's sake,
  A hundred ducats shall induce
Concession to your prayer. One day
  Suffices: Master Buti's brush
Turns Mary round the other way,
  And deluges your side with slush.

22

' "Down with the ducats therefore!" Dump,
  Dump, dump it falls, each counted
    piece,
Hard gold. Then out of door they stump,
  These dogs, each brisk as with new
    lease
Of life, I warrant, – glad he' ll die
  Henceforward just as he may choose,
Be buried and in clover lie!
  Well said Esaias – "stiff-necked Jews!"

23

'Off posts without a minute's loss
  Our Farmer, once the cash in poke,
And summons Buti – ere its gloss
  Have time to fade from off the joke –
To chop and change his work, undo
  The done side, make the side, now
    blank,
Recipient of our Lady – who,
  Displaced thus, had these dogs to
    thank!

24

'Now, boy, you're hardly to instruct
  In technicalities of Art!
My nephew's childhood sure has sucked
  Along with mother's-milk some part
Of painter's-practice – learned, at least,
  How expeditiously is plied
A work in fresco – never ceased
  When once begun – a day, each side.

25

'So, Buti – (he's with God) – begins:
  First covers up the shrine all round
With hoarding; then, as like as twins,
  Paints, t'other side the burial-
    ground,
New Mary, every point the same;
  Next, sluices over, as agreed,
The old; and last – but, spoil the game
  By telling you? Not I, indeed!

26

'Well, ere the week was half at end,
    Out came the object of this zeal,
This fine alacrity to spend
    Hard money for mere dead men's
        weal!
How think you? That old spokesman
        Jew
    Was High Priest, and he had a wife
As old, and she was dying too,
    And wished to end in peace her life!

27

'And he must humour dying whims,
    And soothe her with the idle hope
They'd say their prayers and sing their
        hymns
    As if her husband were the Pope!
And she did die – believing just
    This privilege was purchased! Dead
In comfort through her foolish trust!
    "Stiff-necked ones," well Esaias said!

28

'So, Sabbath morning, out of gate
    And on to way, what sees our arch
Good Farmer? Why, they hoist their
        freight –
    The corpse – on shoulder, and so,
        march!
"Now for it, Buti!" In the nick
    Of time 'tis pully-hauly, hence
With hoarding! O'er the wayside quick
    There's Mary plain in evidence!

29

And here's the convoy halting: right!
    O they are bent on howling psalms
And growling prayers, when opposite!
    And yet they glance, for all their
        qualms,
Approve that promptitude of his,
    The Farmer's – duly at his post
To take due thanks from every phyz,
    Sour smirk – nay, surly smile almost!

30

Then earthward drops each brow again;
    The solemn task's resumed; they
        reach

Their holy field – the unholy train:
    Enter its precinct, all and each,
Wrapt somehow in their godless rites;
    Till, rites at end, up-waking, lo
They lift their faces! What delights
    The mourners as they turn to go?

31

'Ha, ha, he, he! On just the side
    They drew their purse-strings to
        make quit
Of Mary, – Christ the Crucified
    Fronted them now – these biters bit!
Never was such a hiss and snort,
    Such screwing nose and shooting
        lip!
Their purchase – honey in report –
    Proved gall and verjuice at first sip!

32

'Out they break, on they bustle, where,
    A-top of wall, the Farmer waits
With Buti: never fun so rare!
    The Farmer has the best: he rates
The rascal, as the old High Priest
    Takes on himself to sermonize –
Jay, sneer "We Jews supposed, at least,
    Theft was a crime in Christian eyes!"

33

"Theft?" cries the Farmer. "Eat your
        words!
    Show me what constitutes a breach
Of faith in aught was said or heard!
    I promised you in plainest speech
I'd take the thing you count disgrace
    And put it here – and here 'tis put!
Did you suppose I'd leave the place
    Blank, therefore, just your rage to glut?

34

' "I guess you dared not stipulate
    For such a damned impertinence!
So, quick, my greybeard, out of gate
    And in at Ghetto! Haste you hence!
As long as I have house and land,
    To spite you irreligious chaps
Here shall the Crucifixion stand –
    Unless you down with cash, perhaps!"

35

'So snickered he and Buti both.
  The Jews said nothing, interchanged
A glance or two, renewed their oath
  To keep ears stopped and hearts
    estranged
From grace, for all our Church can do;
  Then off they scuttle: sullen jog
Homewards, against our Church to
    brew
  Fresh mischief in their synagogue.

36

'But next day – see what happened, boy!
  See why I bid you have a care
How you pelt Jews! The knaves employ
  Such methods of revenge, forbear
No outrage on our faith, when free
  To wreak their malice! Here they took
So base a method – plague o' me
  If I record it in my Book!

37

'For, next day, while the Farm sat
  Laughing with Buti, in his shop,
At their successful joke, – rat-tat, –
  Door opens, and they're like to drop
Down to the floor as in there stalks
  A six-feet-high herculean-built
Young he-Jew with a beard that baulks
  Description. "Help ere blood be spilt!"

38

– 'screamed Buti: for he recognized
  Whom but the son, no less no more,
Of that High Priest his work surprised
  So pleasantly the day before!
Son of the mother, then, whereof
  The bier he lent a shoulder to
And made the moans about, dared scoff
  At sober Christian grief – the Jew!

39

' "Sirs, I salute you! Never rise!
  No apprehension!" (Buti, white
And trembling like a tub of size,
  Had tried to smuggle out of sight
The picture's self – the thing in oils,
  You know, from which a fresco's
    dashed

Which courage speeds while caution
    spoils)
  "Stay and be praised, sir, unabashe

40

' "Praised, – ay, and paid too: for I come
  To buy that very work of yours.
My poor abode, which boasts – well, some
  Few specimens of Art, secures
Haply, a masterpiece indeed
  If I should find my humble means
Suffice the outlay. So, proceed!
  Propose – ere prudence intervenes!"

41

'On Buti, cowering like a child,
  These words descended from aloft
In tone so ominously mild,
  With smile terrifically soft
To that degree – could Buti dare
  (Poor fellow) use his brains, think
    twice?
He asked, thus taken unaware,
  No more than just the proper price!

42

' "Done!" cries the monster. "I disburse
  Forthwith your moderate demand.
Count on my custom – if no worse
  Your future work be, understand,
Than this I carry off ! No aid!
  My arm, sir, lacks nor bone nor thews;
The burden's easy, and we're made,
  Easy or hard, to bear – we Jews!"

43

'Crossing himself at such escape,
  Buti by turns the money eyes
And, timidly, the stalwart shape
  Now moving doorwards; but, more
    wise
The Farmer, – who, though dumb, this
    while
  Had watched advantage, – straight
    conceived
A reason for that tone and smile
  So mild and soft! The Jew – believed!

44

'Mary in triumph borne to deck
  A Hebrew household! Pictured where

No one was used to bend the neck
   In praise or bow the knee in prayer!
Borne to that domicile by whom?
   The son of the High Priest! Through
      what?
An insult done his mother's tomb!
   Saul changed to Paul – the case came
      pat!

### 45

' "Stay, dog Jew … gentle sir, that is!
   Resolve me! Can it be, she crowned, –
Mary, by miracle, – Oh bliss! –
   My present to your burial ground?
Certain, a ray of light has burst
   Your veil of darkness! Had you else,
Only for Mary's sake, unpursed
   So much hard money? Tell – oh, tell's!"

### 46

'Round – like a serpent that we took
   For worm and trod on – turns his
      bulk
About the Jew: First dreadful look
   Sends Buti in a trice to skulk
Out of sight somewhere, safe – alack!
   But our good Farmer faith made bold:
And firm (with Florence at his back)
   He stood, while gruff the gutturals
      rolled –

### 47

' "Ay, sir, a miracle was worked,
   By quite another power, I trow,
Than ever yet in canvas lurked,
   Or you would scarcely face me now!
A certain impulse did suggest
   A certain grasp with this right-hand,
Which probably had put to rest
   Our quarrel, – thus your throat once
      spanned!

### 48

' "But I remembered me, subdued
   That impulse, and you face me still!
And soon a philosophic mood
   Succeeding (hear it, if you will!)
Has altogether changed my views
   Concerning Art. Blind prejudice!
Well may you Christians tax us Jews
   With scrupulosity too nice!

### 49

' "For, don't I see, – let's issue join! –
   Whenever I'm allowed pollute
(I – and my little bag of coin)
   Some Christian palace of repute, –
Don't I see stuck up everywhere
   Abundant proof that cultured taste
Has Beauty for its only care,
   And upon Truth no thought to waste?

### 50

' "'Jew, since it must be, take in pledge
   Of payment' – so a Cardinal
Has sighed to me as if a wedge
   Entered his heart – ' this best of all
My treasures!' Leda, Ganymede
   Or Antiope: swan, eagle, ape,
(Or what's the beast of what's the breed)
   And Jupiter in every shape!

### 51

' "Whereat if I presume to ask
   'But, Eminence, though Titian's
     whisk
Of brush have well performed its task,
   How comes it these false godships
     frisk
In presence of – what yonder frame
   Pretends to image? Surely, odd
It seems, you let confront The Name
   Each beast the heathen called his
     god!'

### 52

' "Benignant smiles me pity straight
   The Cardinal. 'Tis Truth, we prize!
Art's the sole question in debate!
   These subjects are so many lies.
We treat them with a proper scorn
   When we turn lies – called gods
     forsooth –
To lies' fit use, now Christ is born.
   Drawing and colouring are Truth.

### 53

' "Think you I honour lies so much
   As scruple to parade the charms
Of Leda – Titian, every touch –
   Because the thing within her arms
Means Jupiter who had the praise
   And prayer of a benighted world?

He would have mine too, if, in days
   Of light, I kept the canvas furled!'
           54
' *"So ending, with some easy gibe.*
   *What power has logic! I, at once,*
*Acknowledged error in our tribe*
   *So squeamish that, when friends*
      *ensconce*
*A pretty picture in its niche*
   *To do us honour, deck our graves,*
*We fret and fume and have an itch*
   *To strangle folk – ungrateful knaves!*
           55
' *"No, sir! Be sure that – what's its style,*
   *Your picture? – shall possess ungrudged*
*A place among my rank and file*
   *Of Ledas and what not – be judged*
*Just as a picture! and (because*
   *I fear me much I scarce have bought*
*A Titian) Master Buti's flaws*
   *Found there, will have the laugh flaws*
      *ought!'*
           56
'So, with a scowl, it darkens door –
   This bulk – no longer! Buti makes
Prompt glad re-entry; there's a score
   Of oaths, as the good Farmer wakes
From what must needs have been a
      trance,
   Or he had struck (he swears) to
      ground
The bold bad mouth that dared advance
   Such doctrine the reverse of sound!
           57
'Was magic here? Most like! For, since,
   Somehow our city's faith grows still
More and more lukewarm, and our
      Prince
   Or loses heart or wants the will
To check increase of cold. 'Tis *"Live*
   *And let live! Languidly repress*
*The Dissident! In short, – contrive*
   *Christians must bear with Jews: no less!"*
           58
The end seems, any Israelite
   Wants any picture, – pishes, poohs,
Purchases, hangs it full in sight

In any chamber he may choose!
In Christ's crown, one more thorn we
   rue!
In Mary's bosom, one more sword!
No, boy, you must not pelt a Jew!
   O Lord, how long? How long, O
    Lord?'

## Epilogue

μεστοὶ …

οἱ δ' ἀμφορῆς οἴνου μέλανος ἀνθοσμίου

1

'The poets pour us wine – '
   Said the dearest poet I ever knew,
Dearest and greatest and best to me.
You clamour athirst for poetry –
We pour. 'But when shall a vintage be' –
   You cry – 'strong grape, squeezed
      gold from screw,
Yet sweet juice, flavoured flowery-fine?
That were indeed the wine!'

2

One pours your cup – stark strength,
   Meat for a man; and you eye the pulp
Strained, turbid still, from the viscous
      blood
Of the snaky bough: and you grumble
   'Good!
For it swells resolve, breeds hardihood;
   Despatch it, then, in a single gulp!'
So, down, with a wry face, goes at
      length
The liquor: stuff for strength.

3

One pours your cup – sheer sweet,
   The fragrant fumes of a year
      condensed:
Suspicion of all that's ripe or rathe,
From the bud on branch to the grass in
      swathe.
'We suck mere milk of the
      seasons,'saith
   A curl of each nostril – 'dew,
      dispensed
Nowise for nerving man to feat:
Boys sip such honeyed sweet!'

4

And thus who wants wine strong,
  Waves each sweet smell of the year
    away;
Who likes to swoon as the sweets suffuse
His brain with a mixture of beams and
    dews
Turned syrupy drink – rough strength
    eschews:
  'What though in our veins your wine-
    stock stay?
The lack of the bloom does our palate
    wrong.
Give us wine sweet, not strong!'

5

Yet wine is – some affirm –
  Prime wine is found in the world
    somewhere,
Of potable strength with sweet to match.
You double your heart its dose, yet
    catch –
As the draught descends – a violet-
    smatch,
  Softness – however it came there,
Through drops expressed by the fire
    and worm:
Strong sweet wine – some affirm.

6

Body and bouquet both?
  'Tis easy to ticket a bottle so;
But what was the case in the cask, my
    friends?
Cask? Nay, the vat – where the maker
    mends
His strong with his sweet (you suppose)
    and blends
  His rough with his smooth, till none
    can know
How it comes you may tipple, nothing
    loth,
Body and bouquet both.

7

'You' being just – the world.
  No poets – who turn, themselves,
    the winch
Of the press; no critics – I'll even say,

(Being flustered and easy of faith to-
    day)
Who for love of the work have learned
    the way
  Till themselves produce home-made,
    at a pinch:
No! You are the world, and wine ne'er
    purled
Except to please the world!

8

'For, oh the common heart!
  And, ah the irremissible sin
Of poets who please themselves, not us!
Strong wine yet sweet wine pouring
    thus,
How please still – Pindar and Æschylus!
  Drink – dipt into by the bearded chin
A like and the bloomy lip – no part
Denied the common heart!

9

'And might we get such grace,
  And did you moderns but stock our
    vault
With the true half-brandy half-attar-gul,
How would seniors indulge at a hearty
    pull
While juniors tossed off their thimbleful!
  Our Shakespeare and Milton
    escaped your fault,
So, they reign supreme o'er the weaker
    race
That wants the ancient grace!'

10

If I paid myself with words
  (As the French say well) I were dupe
    indeed!
I were found in belief that you quaffed
    and bowsed
At your Shakespeare the whole day
    long, caroused,
In your Milton pottle-deep nor
    drowsed
  A moment of night – toped on, took
    heed
Of nothing like modern cream-and-
    curds.
Pay me with deeds, not words!

11

For – see your cellarage!
  There are forty barrels with
    Shakespeare's brand.
Some five or six are abroach: the rest
Stand spigoted, fauceted. Try and test
What yourselves call best of the very
    best!
  How comes it that still untouched
    they stand?
Why don't you try tap, advance a stage
With the rest in cellarage?

12

For – see your cellarage!
  There are four big butts of Milton's
    brew.
How comes it you make old drips and
    drops
Do duty, and there devotion stops?
Leave such an abyss of malt and hops
  Embellied in butts which bungs still
    glue?
You hate your bard! A fig for your rage!
Free him from cellarage!

13

'Tis said I brew stiff drink,
  But the deuce a flavour of grape is
    there.
Hardly a May-go-down, 'tis just
A sort of a gruff Go-down-it-must –
No Merry-go-down, no gracious gust
  Commingles the racy with Springtide's
    rare!
'What wonder,' say you 'that we cough,
    and blink
At Autumn's heady drink?'

14

Is it a fancy, friends?
  Mighty and mellow are never mixed,
Though mighty and mellow be born at
    once.
Sweet for the future, – strong for the
    nonce!
Stuff you should stow away, ensconce
  In the deep and dark, to be found
    fast-fixed

At the century's close: such time
    strength spends
A-sweetening for my friends!

15

And then – why, what you quaff
  With a smack of lip and a cluck of
    tongue,
Is leakage and leavings – just what haps
From the tun some learned taster taps
With a promise 'Prepare your watery
    chaps!
  Here's properest wine for old and
    young!
Dispute its perfection – you make us
    laugh!
Have faith, give thanks, but – quaff!'

16

Leakage, I say, or – worse –
  Leavings suffice pot-valiant souls.
Somebody, brimful, long ago,
Frothed flagon he drained to the dregs;
    and lo,
Down whisker and beard what an over-
    flow!
  Lick spilth that has trickled from
    classic jowls,
Sup the single scene, sip the only
    verse –
Old wine, not new and worse!

17

I grant you: worse by much!
  Renounce that new where you never
    gained
One glow at heart, one gleam at head,
And stick to the warrant of age instead!
No dwarf's-lap! Fatten, by giants fed!
  *You* fatten, with oceans of drink
    undrained?
*You* feed – who would choke did a
    cobweb smutch
The Age you love so much?

18

A mine's beneath a moor:
  Acres of moor roof fathoms of mine
Which diamonds dot where you please
    to dig;

Yet who plies spade for the bright and
    big?
Your product is – truffles, you hunt
    with a pig!
    Since bright-and-big, when a man
        would dine,
Suits badly: and therefore the Koh-i-
    noor
May sleep in mine 'neath moor!

19

Wine, pulse in might from me!
    It may never emerge in must from
        vat,
Never fill cask nor furnish can.
Never end sweet, which strong began –
God's gift to gladden the heart of man;
    But spirit's at proof, I promise that!
No sparing of juice spoils what should
    be
Fit brewage – mine for me.

20

Man's thoughts and loves and hates!
    Earth is my vineyard, these grew
        there:
From grape of the ground, I made or
    marred
My vintage; easy the task or hard,
Who set it – his praise be my reward!
    Earth's yield! Who yearn for the
        Dark Blue Sea's,
Let them 'lay, pray, bray' – the addle-
    pates!
Mine be Man's thoughts, loves, hates!

21

But someone says 'Good Sir!'
    ('Tis a worthy versed in what concerns
The making such labour turn out well)
'You don't suppose that the nosegay-
    smell
Needs always come from the grape?
    Each bell
    At your foot, each bud that your
        culture spurns,
The very cowslip would act like myrrh
On the stiffest brew – good Sir!

22

'Cowslips, abundant birth
    O'er meadow and hillside, vineyard
        too,
– Like a schoolboy's scrawlings in and
    out
Distasteful lesson-book – all about
Greece and Rome, victory and rout –
    Love-verses instead of such vain ado!
So, fancies frolic it o'er the earth
Where thoughts have rightlier birth.

23

'Nay, thoughtlings they themselves:
    Loves, hates – in little and less and
        least!
Thoughts? "*What is a man beside a
    mount!*"
Loves? "*Absent – poor lovers the minutes
    count!*"
Hates? "*Fie – Pope's letters to Martha
    Blount!*
    These furnish a wine for a children's-
        feast:
Insipid to man, they suit the elves
Like thoughts, loves, hates themselves.'

24

And, friends, beyond dispute
    I too have the cowslips dewy and
        dear.
Punctual as Springtide forth peep they:
I leave them to make my meadow gay.
But I ought to pluck and impound
    them, eh?
    Not let them alone, but deftly shear
And shred and reduce to – what may
    suit
Children, beyond dispute?

25

And here's May-month, all bloom,
    All bounty: what if I sacrifice?
If I out with shears and shear, nor stop
Shearing till prostrate, lo, the crop?
And will you prefer it to ginger-pop
    When I've made you wine of the
        memories

Which leave as bare as a churchyard
    tomb
My meadow, late all bloom?

26

Nay, what ingratitude
   Should I hesitate to amuse the wits
That have pulled so long at my flask,
    nor grudged
The headache that paid their pains, nor
    budged
From bunghole before they sighed and
    judged
   'Too rough for our taste, to-day, befits
The racy and right when the years
    conclude!'
Out on ingratitude!

27

Grateful or ingrate – none,
   No cowslip of all my fairy crew
Shall help to concoct what makes you
    wink

And goes to your head till you think
   you think!
I like them alive: the printer's ink
   Would sensibly tell on the perfume
   too.
I may use up my nettles, ere I've done;
But of cowslips – friends get none!

28

Don't nettles make a broth
   Wholesome for blood grown lazy
   and thick?
Maws out of sorts make mouths out of
   taste.
My Thirty-four Port – no need to waste
On a tongue that's fur and a palate –
   paste!
   A magnum for friends who are
    sound! The sick –
I'll posset and cosset them, nothing
   loth,
Henceforward with nettle-broth!

# LA SAISIAZ

1878

### 1

Good, to forgive;
　　Best, to forget!
　　Living, we fret;
Dying, we live.
Fretless and free,
　　Soul, clap thy pinion!
　　Earth have dominion,
Body, o'er thee!

### 2

Wander at will,
　　Day after day, –
　　Wander away,
Wandering still –
Soul that canst soar!
　　Body may slumber:
　　Body shall cumber
Soul-flight no more.

### 3

Waft of soul's wing!
　　What lies above?
　　Sunshine and Love,
Skyblue and Spring!
Body hides – where?
　　Ferns of all feather,
　　Mosses and heather,
Yours be the care!

## LA SAISIAZ

A. E. S. September 14, 1877

Dared and done: at last I stand upon
　　the summit, Dear and True!
Singly dared and done; the climbing
　　both of us were bound to do.
Petty feat and yet prodigious: every
　　side my glance was bent
O'er the grandeur and the beauty
　　lavished through the whole
　　ascent.
Ledge by ledge, out broke new marvels,
　　now minute and now immense:
Earth's most exquisite disclosure,
　　heaven's own God in evidence!

And no berry in its hiding, no blue
　　space in its outspread,
Pleaded to escape my footstep,
　　challenged my emerging head,
(As I climbed or paused from climbing,
　　now o'erbranched by shrub and
　　tree,
Now built round by rock and boulder,
　　now at just a turn set free,
Stationed face to face with – Nature?
　　rather with Infinitude)
– No revealment of them all, as singly I
　　my path pursued,
But a bitter touched its sweetness, for
　　the thought stung 'Even so
Both of us had loved and wondered
　　just the same, five days ago!'
Five short days, sufficient hardly to
　　entice, from out its den
Splintered in the slab, this pink
　　perfection of the cyclamen;
Scarce enough to heal and coat with
　　amber gum the sloe-tree's gash,
Bronze the clustered wilding apple,
　　redden ripe the mountain ash:
Yet of might to place between us – Oh
　　the barrier! Yon Profound
Shrinks beside it, proves a pin-point:
　　barrier this, without a bound!
Boundless though it be, I reach you:
　　somehow seem to have you here
– Who are there. Yes, there you dwell
　　now, plain the four low walls
　　appear;
Those are vineyards they enclose from;
　　and the little spire which points
– That's Collonge, henceforth your
　　dwelling. All the same, howe'er
　　disjoints
Past from present, no less certain you
　　are here, not there: have dared,
Done the feat of mountain-climbing, –
　　five days since, we both prepared
Daring, doing, arm in arm, if other

help should haply fail.
For you asked, as forth we sallied to
    see sunset from the vale,
'Why not try for once the mountain, –
    take a foretaste, snatch by stealth
Sight and sound, some unconsidered
    fragment of the hoarded wealth?
Six weeks at its base, yet never once
    have we together won
Sight or sound by honest climbing: let
    us two have dared and done
Just so much of twilight journey as
    may prove to-morrow's jaunt
Not the only mode of wayfare –
    wheeled to reach the eagle's
    haunt!'
So, we turned from the low grass-path
    you were pleased to call 'your
    own,'
Set our faces to the rose-bloom o'er the
    summit's front of stone
Where Salève obtains, from Jura and
    the sunken sun she hides,
Due return of blushing 'Good Night,'
    rosy as a borne-off bride's,
For his masculine 'Good Morrow'
    when, with sunrise still in hold,
Gay he hails her, and, magnific, thrilled
    her black length burns to gold.
Up and up we went, how careless –
    nay, how joyous! All was new,
All was strange. 'Call progress toilsome?
    that were just insulting you!
How the trees must temper noontide!
    Ah, the thicket's sudden break!
What will be the morning glory, when
    at dusk thus gleams the lake?
Light by light puts forth Geneva: what
    a land – and, of the land,
Can there be a lovelier station than this
    spot where now we stand?
Is it late, and wrong to linger? True, to-
    morrow makes amends.
Toilsome progress? child's play, call it
    – specially when one descends!
There, the dread descent is over –
    hardly our adventure, though!

Take the vale where late we left it, pace
    the grass-path, "mine," you know!
Proud completion of achievement!'
    And we paced it, praising still
That soft tread on velvet verdure as it
    wound through hill and hill;
And at very end there met us, coming
    from Collonge, the pair
– All our people of the Chalet – two,
    enough and none to spare.
So, we made for home together, and
    we reached it as the stars
One by one came lamping – chiefly
    that prepotency of Mars –
And your last word was 'I owe you this
    enjoyment!' – met with 'Nay:
With yourself it rests to have a month
    of morrows like to-day!'
Then the meal, with talk and laughter,
    and the news of that rare nook
Yet untroubled by the tourist, touched
    on by no travel-book,
All the same – though latent – patent,
    hybrid birth of land and sea,
And (our travelled friend assured you)
    – if such miracle might be –
Comparable for completeness of both
    blessings – all around
Nature, and, inside her circle, safety
    from world's sight and sound –
Comparable to our Saisiaz. 'Hold it fast
    and guard it well!
Go and see and vouch for certain, then
    come back and never tell
Living soul but us; and haply, prove
    our sky from cloud as clear,
There may we four meet, praise fortune
    just as now, another year!'

Thus you charged him on departure:
    not without the final charge
'Mind to-morrow's early meeting! We
    must leave our journey marge
Ample for the wayside wonders: there's
    the stoppage at the inn
Three-parts up the mountain, where
    the hardships of the track begin;

There's the convent worth a visit; but,
    the triumph crowning all –
There's Salève's own platform facing
    glory which strikes greatness small,
– Blanc, supreme above his earth-brood,
    needles red and white and green,
Horns of silver, fangs of crystal set on
    edge in his demesne.
So, some three weeks since, we saw
    them: so, to-morrow we intend
You shall see them likewise; therefore
    Good Night till to-morrow, friend!'
Last, the nothings that extinguish
    embers of a vivid day:
'What might be the Marshal's next move,
    what Gambetta's counter-play?'
Till the landing on the staircase saw
    escape the latest spark:
'Sleep you well!' 'Sleep but as well, you!'
    – lazy love quenched, all was dark.

Nothing dark next day at sundawn! Up
    I rose and forth I fared:
Took my plunge within the bath-pool,
    pacified the watch-dog scared,
Saw proceed the transmutation – Jura's
    black to one gold glow,
Trod your level path that let me drink
    the morning deep and slow,
Reached the little quarry – ravage
    recompensed by shrub and fern –
Till the overflowing ardours told me
    time was for return.
So, return I did, and gaily. But, for
    once, from no far mound
Waved salute a tall white figure. 'Has
    her sleep been so profound?
Foresight, rather, prudent saving
    strength for day's expenditure!
Ay, the chamber-window's open: out
    and on the terrace, sure!'

No, the terrace showed no figure, tall,
    white, leaning through the
    wreaths,
Tangle-twine of leaf and bloom that
    inter-cept the air one breathes,

Interpose between one's love and
    Nature's loving, hill and dale
Down to where the blue lake's wrinkle
    marks the river's inrush pale
– Mazy Arve: whereon no vessel but
    goes sliding white and plain,
Not a steamboat pants from harbour
    but one hears pulsate amain,
Past the city's congregated peace of
    homes and pomp of spires
– Man's mild protest that there's
    something more than Nature,
    man requires,
And that, useful as is Nature to attract
    the tourist's foot,
Quiet slow sure money-making proves
    the matter's very root, –
Need for body, – while the spirit also
    needs a comfort reached
By no help of lake or mountain, but
    the texts whence Calvin preached.
'Here's the veil withdrawn from
    landscape: up to Jura and beyond,
All awaits us ranged and ready; yet she
    violates the bond,
Neither leans nor looks nor listens:
    why is this?' A turn of eye
Took the whole sole answer, gave the
    undisputed reason 'why!'
This dread way you had your
    summons! No premonitory touch,
As you talked and laughed ('tis told
    me) scarce a minute ere the clutch
Captured you in cold forever. Cold?
    nay, warm you were as life
When I raised you, while the others
    used, in passionate poor strife,
All the means that seemed to promise
    any aid, and all in vain.
Gone you were, and I shall never see
    that earnest face again
Grow transparent, grow transfigured
    with the sudden light that leapt,
At the first word's provocation, from
    the heart-deeps where it slept.

Therefore, paying piteous duty, what
    seemed You have we consigned
Peacefully to – what I think were, of all
    earthbeds, to your mind
Most the choice for quiet, yonder: low
    walls stop the vines' approach,
Lovingly Salève protects you; village
    sports will ne'er encroach
On the stranger lady's silence, whom
    friends bore so kind and well
Thither 'just for love's sake,' – such
    their own word was: and who can
    tell?
You supposed that few or none had
    known and loved you in the world:
May be! flower that's full-blown tempts
    the butterfly, not flower that's
    furled.
But more learned sense unlocked you,
    loosed the sheath and let expand
Bud to bell and outspread flower-shape
    at the least warm touch of hand
– Maybe, throb of heart, beneath
    which, – quickening farther than
    it knew, –
Treasure oft was disembosomed, scent
    all strange and unguessed hue.
Disembosomed, re-embosomed, –
    must one memory suffice,
Prove I knew an Alpine-rose which all
    beside named Edelweiss?

Rare thing, red or white, you rest now:
    two days slumbered through; and
    since
One day more will see me rid of this
    same scene whereat I wince,
Tetchy at all sights and sounds and
    pettish at each idle charm
Proffered me who pace now singly
    where we two went arm in arm, –
I have turned upon my weakness: asked
    'And what, forsooth, prevents
That, this latest day allowed me, I fulfil
    of her intents
One she had the most at heart – that
    we should thus again survey

From Salève Mont Blanc together?' There-
    fore, – dared and done to-day
Climbing, – here I stand: but you –
    where?
          If a spirit of the place
Broke the silence, bade me question,
    promised answer, – what disgrace
Did I stipulate 'Provided answer suit
    my hopes, not fears!'
Would I shrink to learn my life-time's
    limit – days, weeks, months or
    years?
Would I shirk assurance on each point
    whereat I can but guess –
'Does the soul survive the body? Is
    there God's self, no or yes?'
If I know my mood, 'twere constant –
    come in whatsoe'er uncouth
Shape it should, nay, formidable – so
    the answer were but truth.

Well, and wherefore shall it daunt me,
    when 'tis I myself am tasked,
When, by weakness weakness
    questioned, weakly answers –
    weakly asked?
Weakness never needs be falseness:
    truth is truth in each degree
– Thunderpealed by God to Nature,
    whispered by my soul to me.
Nay, the weakness turns to strength
    and triumphs in a truth beyond:
'Mine is but man's truest answer –
    how were it did God respond?'
I shall no more dare to mimic such
    response in futile speech,
Pass off human lisp as echo of the
    sphere-song out of reach,
Than, – because it well may happen
    yonder, where the far snows blanch
Mute Mont Blanc, that who stands
    near them sees and hears an
    avalanche, –
I shall pick a clod and throw, – cry
    'Such the sight and such the sound!
What though I nor see nor hear them?
    Others do, the proofs abound!'

Can I make my eye an eagle's, sharpen
    ear to recognize
Sound o'er league and league of
    silence? Can I know, who but
    surmise?
If I dared no self-deception when, a
    week since, I and you
Walked and talked along the grass-
    path, passing lightly in review
What seemed hits and what seemed
    misses in a certain fence-play, –
    strife
Sundry minds of mark engaged in 'On
    the Soul and Future Life,' –
If I ventured estimating what was come
    of parried thrust,
Subtle stroke, and, rightly, wrongly,
    estimating could be just
– Just, though life so seemed abundant
    in the form which moved by mine,
I might well have played at feigning,
    fooling, – laughed 'What need opine
Pleasure must succeed to pleasure, else
    past pleasure turns to pain,
And this first life claims a second, else I
    count its good no gain?'
Much less have I heart to palter when
    the matter, to decide
Now becomes 'Was ending ending
    once and always, when you died?'
Did the face, the form I lifted as it lay,
    reveal the loss
Not alone of life but soul? A tribute to
    yon flowers and moss,
What of you remains beside? A memory!
    Easy to attest
'Certainly from out the world that one
    believes who knew her best
Such was good in her, such fair, which
    fair and good were great
    perchance
Had but fortune favoured, bidden each
    shy faculty advance;
After all – who knows another? Only as
    I know, I speak.'
So much of you lives within me while I
    live my year or week.

Then my fellow takes the tale up, not
    unwilling to aver
Duly in his turn 'I knew him best of
    all, as he knew her:
Such he was, and such he was not, and
    such other might have been
But that somehow every actor,
    somewhere in this earthly scene,
Fails.' And so both memories dwindle,
    yours and mine together linked,
Till there is but left for comfort, when
    the last spark proves extinct,
This – that somewhere new existence
    led by men and women new
Possibly attains perfection coveted by
    me and you;
While ourselves, the only witness to
    what work our life evolved,
Only to ourselves proposing problems
    proper to be solved
By ourselves alone, – who working
    ne'er shall know if work bear fruit
Others reap and garner, heedless how
    produced by stalk and root, –
We who, darkling, timed the day's
    birth, – struggling, testified to
    peace, –
Earned, by dint of failure, triumph, –
    we, creative thought, must cease
In created word, thought's echo, due
    to impulse long since sped!
Why repine? There's ever someone
    lives although ourselves be dead!

Well, what signifies repugnance? Truth
    is truth howe'er it strike.
Fair or foul the lot apportioned life on
    earth, we bear alike.
Stalwart body idly yoked to stunted
    spirit, powers, that fain
Else whould soar, condemned to
    grovel, groundlings through the
    fleshly chain, –
Help that hinders, hindrance proved but
    help disguised when all too late, –
Hindrance is the fact acknowledged,
    how-soe'er explained as Fate,

Fortune, Providence: we bear, own life
    a burthen more or less.
Life thus owned unhappy, is there
    supplemental happiness
Possible and probable in life to come?
    or must we count
Life a curse and not a blessing,
    summed-up in its whole amount,
Help and hindrance, joy and sorrow?
    Why should I want courage here?
I will ask and have an answer, – with
    no favour, with no fear, –
From myself. How much, how little,
    do I inwardly believe
True that controverted doctrine? Is it
    fact to which I cleave,
Is it fancy I but cherish, when I take
    upon my lips
Phrase the solemn Tuscan fashioned,
    and declare the soul's eclipse
Not the soul's extinction? take his 'I
    believe and I declare –
Certain am I – from this life I pass into
    a better, there
Where that lady lives of whom en-
    amoured was my soul' – where this
Other lady, my companion dear and
    true, she also is?

I have questioned and am answered.
    Question, answer presuppose
Two points: that the thing itself which
    questions, answers, – is, it knows;
As it also knows the thing perceived
    outside itself, – a force
Actual ere its own beginning, operative
    through its course,
Unaffected by its end, – that this thing
    likewise needs must be;
Call this – God, then, call that – soul,
    and both – the only facts for me.
Prove them facts? that they o'erpass my
    power of proving, proves them such:
Fact it is I know I know not something
    which is fact as much.
What before caused all the causes,
    what effect of all effects

Haply follows, – these are fancy. Ask
    the rush if it suspects
Whence and how the stream which
    floats it had a rise, and where and
    how
Falls or flows on still! What answer
    makes the rush except that now
Certainly it floats and is, and, no less
    certain than itself,
Is the everyway external stream that
    now through shoal and shelf
Floats it onward, leaves it – may be –
    wrecked at last, or lands on shore
There to root again and grow and
    flourish stable evermore.
– May be! mere surmise not knowledge:
    much conjecture styled belief,
What the rush conceives the stream
    means through the voyage blind
    and brief.
Why, because I doubtless am, shall I as
    doubtless be? 'Because
God seems good and wise.' Yet under
    this our life's apparent laws
Reigns a wrong which, righted once,
    would give quite other laws to life.
'He seems potent.' Potent here, then
    why are right and wrong at strife?
Has in life the wrong the better?
    Happily life ends so soon!
Right predominates in life? Then why
    two lives and double boon?
'Anyhow, we want it: wherefore want?'
    Because, without the want,
Life, now human, would be brutish:
    just that hope, however scant,
Makes the actual life worth leading;
    take the hope therein away,
All we have to do is surely not endure
    another day.
This life has its hopes for this life,
    hopes that promise joy: life
    done –
Out of all the hopes, how many had
    complete fulfilment? none.
'But the soul is not the body:' and the
    breath is not the flute;

Both together make the music: either
    marred and all is mute.
Truce to such old sad contention
    whence. according as we shape
Most of hope or most of fear, we issue
    in a half – escape:
'We believe' is sighed. I take the cup of
    comfort proffered thus,
Taste and try each soft ingredient,
    sweet infusion, and discuss
What their blending may accomplish
    for the cure of doubt, till – slow,
Sorrowful, but how decided! needs
    must I o'erturn it – so!
Cause before, effect behind me –
    blanks! The midway point I am,
Caused, itself – itself efficient: in that
    narrow space must cram
All experience – out of which there
    crowds conjecture manifold,
But, as knowledge, this comes only –
    things may be as I behold,
Or may not be, but, without me and
    above me, things there are;
I myself am what I know not –
    ignorance which proves no bar
To the knowledge that I am, and, since
    I am, can recognize
What to me is pain and pleasure: this
    is sure, the rest – surmise.
If my fellows are or are not, what may
    please them and what pain, –
Mere surmise: my own experience –
    that is knowledge, once again!
I have lived, then, done and suffered,
    loved and hated, learnt and taught
This – there is no reconciling wisdom
    with a world distraught,
Goodness with triumphant evil, power
    with failure in the aim,
If – (to my own sense, remember! though
    none other feel the same!) –
If you bar me from assuming earth to
    be a pupil's place,
And life, time, – with all their chances,
    changes, – just probation-space,

Mine, for me. But those apparent other
    mortals – theirs, for them?
Knowledge stands on my experience:
    all outside its narrow hem,
Free surmise may sport and welcome!
    Pleasures, pains affect mankind
Just as they affect myself? Why, here's
    my neighbour colour-blind,
Eyes like mine to all appearance: 'green
    as grass' do I affirm?
'Red as grass' he contradicts me: which
    employs the proper term?
Were we two the earth's sole tenants,
    with no third for referee,
How should I distinguish? Just so, God
    must judge 'twixt man and me.
To each mortal peradventure earth
    becomes a new machine,
Pain and pleasure no more tally in our
    sense than red and green;
Still, without what seems such mortal's
    pleasure, pain, my life were lost
– Life, my whole sole chance to prove –
    although at man's apparent cost –
What is beauteous and what ugly, right
    to strive for, right to shun,
Fit to help and fit to hinder, – prove
    my forces everyone,
Good and evil, – learn life's lesson,
    hate of evil, love of good,
As 'tis set me, understand so much as
    may be understood –
Solve the problem: 'From thine appre-
    hended scheme of things, deduce
Praise or blame of its contriver, shown
    a niggard or profuse
In each good or evil issue! nor
    miscalculate alike
Counting one the other in the final
    balance, which to strike,
Soul was born and life allotted: ay, the
    show of things unfurled
For thy summing-up and judgment, –
    thine, no other mortal's world!'

What though fancy scarce may grapple
    with the complex and immense

– 'His own world for every mortal?'
   Postulate omnipotence!
Limit power, and simple grows the
   complex: shrunk to atom size,
That which loomed immense to fancy
   low before my reason lies, –
I survey it and pronounce it work like
   other work: success
Here and there, the workman's glory, –
   here and there, his shame no less.
Failure as conspicuous. Taunt not
   'Human work ape work divine?'
As the power, expect performance!
   God's be God's as mine is mine!
God whose power made man and
   made man's wants, and made, to
   meet those wants,
Heaven and earth which, through the
   body, prove the spirit's ministrants,
Excellently all, – did He lack power or
   was the will in fault
When He let blue heaven be shrouded
   o'er by vapours of the vault,
Gay earth drop her garlands shrivelled
   at the first infecting breath
Of the serpent pains which herald,
   swarming in, the dragon death?
What, no way but this that man may
   learn and lay to heart how rife
Life were with delights would only
   death allow their taste to life?
Must the rose sigh 'Pluck – I perish!'
   must the eve weep 'Gaze – I fade!'
– Every sweet warn ' 'Ware my bitter!'
   every shine bid Wait my shade'?
Can we love but on condition, that the
   thing we love must die?
Needs there groan a world in anguish
   just to teach us sympathy –
Multitudinously wretched that we,
   wretched too, may guess
What a preferable state were universal
   happiness?
Hardly do I so conceive the outcome of
   that power which went
To the making of the worm there in
   yon clod its tenement,

Any more than I distinguish aught of
   that which, wise and good,
Framed the leaf, its plain of pasture,
   dropped the dew, its fineless food.
Nay, were fancy fact, were earth and all
   it holds illusion mere,
Only a machine for teaching love and
   hate and hope and fear
To myself, the sole existence, single
   truth mid falsehood, – well!
If the harsh throes of the prelude die
   not off into the swell
Of that perfect piece they sting me to
   become a-strain for, – if
Roughness of the long rock-clamber
   lead not to the last of cliff,
First of level country where is sward
   my pilgrim-foot can prize, –
Plainlier! if this life's conception new
   life fail to realize, –
Though earth burst and proved a
   bubble glassing hues of hell, one
   huge
Reflex of the devil's doings – God's
   work by no subterfuge –
(So death's kindly touch informed me
   as it broke the glamour, gave
Soul and body both release from life's
   long nightmare in the grave)
Still, – with no more Nature, no more
   Man as riddle to be read,
Only my own joys and sorrows now to
   reckon real instead, –
I must say – or choke in silence –
   'How-soever came my fate,
Sorrow did and joy did nowise, – life
   well weighed, – preponderate.'
By necessity ordained thus? I shall bear
   as best I can;
By a cause all-good, all-wise, all-potent?
   No, as I am man!
Such were God: and was it goodness
   that the good within my range
Or had evil in admixture or grew evil's
   self by change?
Wisdom – that becoming wise meant
   making slow and sure advance

From a knowledge proved in error to
   acknowledged ignorance?
Power? 'tis just the main assumption
   reason most revolts at! power
Unavailing for bestowment on its
   creature of an hour,
Man, of so much proper action rightly
   aimed and reaching aim,
So much passion, – no defect there, no
   excess, but still the same, –
As what constitutes existence, pure
   perfection bright as brief
For yon worm, man's fellow-creature,
   on yon happier world – its leaf!
No, as I am man, I mourn the poverty I
   must impute:
Goodness, wisdom, power, all
   bounded, each a human attribute!

But, O world outspread beneath me!
   only for myself I speak,
Nowise dare to play the spokesman for
   my brothers strong and weak,
Full and empty, wise and foolish, good
   and bad, in every age,
Every clime, I turn my eyes from, as in
   one or other stage
Of a torture writhe they, Job-like couched
   on dung and crazed with blains
– Wherefore? whereto? ask the whirl-
   wind what the dread voice thence
   explains!
I shall 'vindicate no way of God's to
   man,' nor stand apart,
'Laugh, be candid!' while I watch it
   traversing the human heart.
Traversed heart must tell its story
   uncommented on: no less
Mine results in 'Only grant a second
   life, I acquiesce
In this present life as failure, count
   misfortune's worst assaults
Triumph, not defeat, assured that loss
   so much the more exalts
Gain about to be. For at what moment
   did I so advance

Near to knowledge as when frustrate of
   escape from ignorance?
Did not beauty prove most precious
   when its opposite obtained
Rule, and truth seem more than ever
   potent because falsehood reigned?
While for love – Oh how but, losing
   love, does whoso loves succeed
By the death-pang to the birth-throe –
   learning what is love indeed?
Only grant my soul may carry high
   through death her cup unspilled,
Brimming though it be with knowledge,
   life's loss drop by drop distilled,
I shall boast it mine – the balsam, bless
   each kindly wrench that wrung
From life's tree its inmost virtue, tapped
   the root whence pleasure sprung,
Barked the bole, and broke the bough,
   and bruised the berry, left all grace
Ashes in death's stern alembic, loosed
   elixir in its place!

Witness, Dear and True, how little I
   was 'ware of – not your worth
– That I knew, my heart assures me –
   but of what a shade on earth
Would the passage from my presence
   of the tall white figure throw
O'er the ways we walked together! Some-
   what narrow, somewhat slow
Used to seem the ways, the walking;
   narrow ways are well to tread
When there's moss beneath the
   footstep, honeysuckle overhead:
Walking slow to beating bosom surest
   solace soonest gives,
Liberates the brain o'erloaded – best of
   all restoratives.
Nay, do I forget the open vast where
   soon or late converged
Ways though winding? – world-wide
   heaven-high sea where music
   slept or surged
As the angel had ascendant, and
   Beethoven's Titan mace

Smote the immense to storm Mozart
    would by a finger's lifting chase?
Yes, I knew – but not with knowledge
    such as thrills me while I view
Yonder precinct which henceforward
    holds and hides the Dear and True.
Grant me (once again) assurance we
    shall each meet each some day,
Walk – but with how bold a footstep!
    on a way – but what a way!
– Worst were best, defeat were triumph,
    utter loss were utmost gain.
Can it be, and must, and will it?
                Silence!
    Out of fact's domain,
Just surmise prepared to mutter hope,
    and also fear – dispute
Fact's inexorable ruling 'Outside fact,
    surmise be mute!'
Well!
      Ay, well and best, if fact's self I
    may force the answer from!
'Tis surmise I stop the mouth of. Not
    above in yonder dome
All a rapture with-its rose-glow, – not
    around, where pile and peak
Strainingly await the sun's fall, – not
    beneath, where crickets creak,
Birds assemble for their bed-time, soft
    the tree-top swell subsides, –
No, nor yet within my deepest sentient
    self the knowledge hides.
Aspiration, reminiscence, plausibilities
    of trust
– Now the ready 'Man were wronged
    else,' now the rash 'and God
    unjust' –
None of these I need. Take thou, my
    soul, thy solitary stand,
Umpire to the champions Fancy,
    Reason, as on either hand
Amicable war they wage and play the
    foe in thy behoof!
Fancy thrust and Reason parry! Thine
    the prize who stand aloof.

FANCY

I concede the thing refused: henceforth
    no certainty more plain
Than this mere surmise that after body
    dies soul lives again.
Two, the only facts acknowledged late,
    are now increased to three –
God is, and the soul is, and, as certain,
    after death shall be.
Put this third to use in life, the time for
    using fact!

REASON

    I do:
Find it promises advantage, coupled
    with the other two.
Life to come will be improvement on
    the life that's now; destroy
Body's thwartings, there's no longer
    screen betwixt soul and soul's joy.
Why should we expect new hindrance,
    novel tether? In this first
Life, I see the good of evil, why our
    world began at worst:
Since time means amelioration, tardily
    enough displayed,
Yet a mainly onward moving, never
    wholly retrograde.
We know more though we know little,
    we grow stronger though still weak,
Partly see though all too purblind,
    stammer though we cannot speak.
There is no such grudge in God as
    scared the ancient Greek, no fresh
Substitute of trap for dragnet, once a
    breakage in the mesh.
Dragons were, and serpents are, and
    blindworms will be: ne'er emerged
Any new-created python for man's
    plague since earth was purged.
Failing proof, then, of invented trouble
    to replace the old,
O'er this life the next presents
    advantage much and manifold:
Which advantage – in the absence of a
    fourth and farther fact

Now conceivably surmised, of harm to
    follow from the act –
I pronounce for man's obtaining at this
    moment. Why delay?
Is he happy? happiness will change:
    anticipate the day!
Is he sad? there's ready refuge: of all
    sadness death's prompt cure!
Is he both, in mingled measure? cease
    a burthen to endure!
Pains with sorry compensations,
    pleasures stinted in the dole,
Power that sinks and pettiness that
    soars, all halved and nothing whole,
Idle hopes that lure man onward,
    forced back by as idle fears –
What a load he stumbles under through
    his glad sad seventy years,
When a touch sets right the turmoil,
    lifts his spirit where, flesh-freed,
Knowledge shall be rightly named so,
    all that seems be truth indeed!
Grant his forces no accession, nay, no
    faculty's increase,
Only let what now exists continue, let
    him prove in peace
Power whereof the interrupted
    unperfected play enticed
Man through darkness, which to lighten
    any spark of hope sufficed, –
What shall then deter his dying out of
    darkness into light?
Death itself perchance, brief pain that's
    pang, condensed and infinite?
But at worst, he needs must brave it
    oneday, while, at best, he laughs –
Drops a drop within his chalice, sleep
    not death his science quaffs!
Any moment claims more courage when,
    by crossing cold and gloom,
Manfully man quits discomfort, makes
    for the provided room
Where the old friends want their fellow,
    where the new acquaintance wait,
Probably for talk assembled, possibly
    to sup in state!

I affirm and re-affirm it therefore: only
    make as plain
As that man now lives, that, after
    dying, man will live again, –
Make as plain the absence, also, of a
    law to contravene
Voluntary passage from this life to that
    by change of scene, –
And I bid him – at suspicion of first
    cloud athwart his sky,
Flower's departure, frost's arrival –
    never hesitate, but die!

FANCY

Then I double my concession: grant,
    along with new life sure,
This same law found lacking now:
    ordain that, whether rich or poor
Present life is judged in aught man
    counts advantage – be it hope,
Be it fear that brightens, blackens most
    or least his horoscope, –
He, by absolute compulsion such as
    made him live at all,
Go on living to the fated end of life
    whate'er befall.
What though, as on earth he darkling
    grovels, man descry the sphere,
Next life's – call it, heaven of freedom,
    close above and crystal-clear?
He shall find – say, hell to punish who
    in aught curtails the term,
Fain would act the butterfly before he
    has played out the worm.
God, soul, earth, heaven, hell, – five
    facts now: what is to desiderate?

REASON

Nothing! Henceforth man's existence
    bows to the monition 'Wait!
Take the joys and bear the sorrows –
    neither with extreme concern!
Living here means nescience simply:
    'tis next life that helps to learn.
Shut those eyes, next life will open, –
    stop those ears, next life will teach
Hearing's office, – close those lips, next
    life will give the power of speech!

Or, if action more amuse thee than the
    passive attitude,
Bravely bustle through thy being, busy
    thee for ill or good,
Reap this life's success or failure! Soon
    shall things be unperplexed
And the right and wrong, now tangled,
    lie unravelled in the next.'

### FANCY

Not so fast! Still more concession! not
    alone do I declare
Life must needs be borne, – I also will
    that man become aware
Life has worth incalculable, every
    moment that he spends
So much gain or loss for that next life
    which on this life depends.
Good, done here, be there rewarded, –
    evil, worked here, there amerced!
Six facts now, and all established, plain
    to man the last as first.

### REASON

There was good and evil, then, defined
    to man by this decree?
*Was* – for at its promulgation both alike
    have ceased to be.
Prior to this last announcement 'Certainly
    as God exists,
As He made man's soul, as soul is
    quenchless by the deathly mists,
Yet is, all the same, forbidden
    premature escape from time
To eternity's provided purer air and
    brighter clime, –
Just so certainly depends it on the use
    to which man turns
Earth, the good or evil done there,
    whether after death he earns
Life eternal, – heaven, the phrase be, or
    eternal death, – say, hell.
As his deeds, so proves his portion,
    doing ill or doing well!'
– Prior to this last announcement,
    earth was man's probation-place:
Liberty of doing evil gave his doing
    good a grace;

Once lay down the law, with Nature's
    simple 'Such effects succeed
Causes such, and heaven or hell
    depends upon man's earthly deed
Just as surely as depends the straight or
    else the crooked line
On his making point meet point or
    with or else without incline,' –
Thenceforth neither good nor evil does
    man, doing what he must.
Lay but down that law as stringent
    'Wouldst thou live again, be just!'
As this other 'Wouldst thou live now,
    regularly draw thy breath!
For, suspend the operation, straight
    law's breach results in death – '
And (provided always, man, addressed
    this mode, be sound and sane)
Prompt and absolute obedience, never
    doubt, will law obtain!
Tell not me 'Look round us! nothing
    each side but acknowledged law,
Now styled God's – now Nature's edict!'
    Where's obedience without flaw
Paid to either? What's the adage rife in
    man's mouth? Why, 'The best
I both see and praise, the worst I
    follow' – which, despite professed
Seeing, praising, all the same he
    follows, since he disbelieves
In the heart of him that edict which for
    truth his head receives.
There's evading and persuading and
    much making law amends
Somehow, there's the nice distinction
    'twixt fast foes and faulty friends,
– Any consequence except inevitable
    death when 'Die,
Whoso breaks our law!' they publish,
    God and Nature equally.
Law that's kept or broken – subject to
    man's will and pleasure! Whence?
How comes law to bear eluding? Not
    because of impotence:
Certain laws exist already which to
    hear means to obey;

Therefore not without a purpose these
    man must, while those man may
Keep and, for the keeping, haply gain
    approval and reward.
Break through this last superstructure,
    all is empty air – no sward
Firm like my first fact to stand on 'God
    there is, and soul there is,'
And soul's earthly life-allotment:
    wherein, by hypothesis,
Soul is bound to pass probation, prove
    its powers, and exercise
Sense and thought on fact, and then,
    from fact educing fit surmise,
Ask itself, and of itself have solely
    answer, 'Does the scope
Earth affords of fact to judge by
    warrant future fear or hope?'

Thus have we come back full circle:
    fancy's footsteps one by one
Go their round conducting reason to
    the point where they begun,
Left where we were left so lately, Dear
    and True! When, half a week
Since, we walked and talked and thus I
    told you, how suffused a cheek
You had turned me had I sudden
    brought the blush into the smile
By some word like 'Idly argued! you
    know better all the while!'
Now, from me – Oh not a blush but,
    how much more, a joyous glow,
Laugh triumphant, would it strike did
    your 'Yes, better I do know'
Break, my warrant for assurance! which
    assurance may not be
If, supplanting hope, assurance needs
    must change this life to me.
So, I hope – no more than hope, but
    hope – no less than hope, because
I can fathom, by no plumb-line sunk in
    life's apparent laws,
How I may in any instance fix where
    change should meetly fall
Nor involve, by one revisal, abrogation
    of them all:

' – Which again involves as utter
    change in life thus law-released,
Whence the good of goodness vanished
    when the ill of evil ceased.
Whereas, life and laws apparent
    reinstated, – all we know,
All we know not, – o'er our heaven
    again cloud closes, until, lo –
Hope the arrowy, just as constant,
    comes to pierce its gloom,
    compelled
By a power and by a purpose which, if
    no one else beheld,
I behold in life, so – hope!
                Sad summing-up
    of all to say!
*Athanasius contra mundum,* why should
    he hope more than they?
So are men made notwithstanding,
    such magnetic virtue darts
From each head their fancy haloes to
    their unresisting hearts!

Here I stand, methinks a stone's throw
    from yon village I this morn
Traversed for the sake of looking one
    last look at its forlorn
Tenement's ignoble fortune: through a
    crevice, plain its floor
Piled with provender for cattle, while a
    dung-heap blocked the door.
In that squalid Bossex, under that
    obscene red roof, arose,
Like a fiery flying serpent from its egg,
    a soul – Rousseau's.
Turn thence! Is it Diodati joins the
    glimmer of the lake?
There I plucked a leaf, one week since,
    – ivy, plucked for Byron's sake.
Famed unfortunates! And yet, because
    of that phosphoric fame
Swathing blackness'self with brightness
    till putridity looked flame,
All the world was witched: and wherefore?
    what could lie beneath, allure
Heart of man to let corruption serve
    man's head as cynosure?

Was the magic in the dictum 'All that's
   good is gone and past;
Bad and worse still grows the present,
   and the worst of all comes last:
Which believe – for I believe it?'so
   preached one his gospel-news;
While melodious moaned the other
   'Dying day with dolphin-hues!
Storm, for loveliness and darkness like
   a woman's eye! Ye mounts
Where I climb to 'scape my fellow, and
   thou sea wherein he counts
Not one inch of vile dominion! What
   were your especial worth
Failed ye to enforce the maxim "Of all
   objects found on earth
Man is meanest, much too honoured
   when compared with – what by
   odds
Beats him – any dog: so, let him go a-
   howling to his gods!"
Which believe – for I believe it!'such
   the comfort man received
Sadly since perforce he must: for why?
   the famous bard believed!

Fame! Then, give me fame, a moment!
   As I gather at a glance
Human glory after glory vivifying yon
   expanse,
Let me grasp them all together, hold
   on high and brandish well
Beacon-like above the rapt world ready,
   whether heaven or hell
Send the dazzling summons earthward,
   to submit itself the same,
Take on trust the hope or else despair
   flashed full on face by – Fame!
Thanks, thou pine-tree of Makistos,
   wide thy giant torch I wave!
Know ye whence I plucked the pillar,
   late with sky for architrave?
This the trunk, the central solid
   Knowledge, kindled core, began
Tugging earth-deeps, trying heaven-
   heights, rooted yonder at Lausanne.

This which flits and spits, the aspic, –
   sparkles in and out the boughs
Now, and now condensed, the python,
   coiling round and round allows
Scarce the bole its due effulgence,
   dulled by flake on flake of Wit –
Laughter so bejewels Learning, – what
   but Ferney nourished it?
Nay, nor fear – since very resin feeds
   the flame – that I dispense
With yon Bossex terebinth-tree's all-
   explosive Eloquence:
No, be sure! nor, any more than thy
   resplendency, Jean-Jacques,
Dare I want thine, Diodati! What
   though monkeys and macaques
Gibber 'Byron'? Byron's ivy rears a
   branch beyond the crew,
Green for ever, no deciduous trash
   macaques and monkeys chew!
As Rousseau, then, eloquent, as Byron
   prime in poet's power, –
Detonations, fulgurations, smiles – the
   rainbow, tears – the shower,
Lo, I lift the coruscating marvel –
   Fame! and, famed, declare
– Learned for the nonce as Gibbon,
   witty as wit's self Voltaire . . .
O the sorriest of conclusions to
   whatever man of sense
Mid the millions stands the unit, takes
   no flare for evidence!
Yet the millions have their portion, live
   their calm or troublous day,
Find significance in fireworks: so, by
   help of mine, they may
Confidently lay to heart and lock in
   head their life long – this:
'He there with the brand flamboyant,
   broad o'er night's forlorn abyss,
Crowned by prose and verse; and
   wielding, with Wit's bauble,
   Learning's rod . . .
Well? Why, he at least believed in Soul,
   was very sure of God.'

      *     *     *

So the poor smile played, that evening:
  pallid smile long since extinct
Here in London's mid-November! Not
  so loosely thoughts were linked,
Six weeks since as I, descending in the
  sunset from Salève,
Found the chain, I seemed to forge
  there, flawless till it reached your
  grave, –
Not so filmy was the texture, but I bore
  it in my breast
Safe thus far. And since I found a
  something in me would not rest
Till I, link by link, unravelled any
  tangle of the chain,

– Here it lies, for much or little! I have
  lived all o'er again
That last pregnant hour: I saved it, just
  as I could save a root
Disinterred for re-interment when the
  time best helps to shoot.
Life is stocked with germs of torpid
  life; but may I never wake
Those of mine whose resurrection
  could not be without earthquake!
Rest all such, unraised forever! Be this,
  sad yet sweet, the sole
Memory evoked from slumber! Least
  part this: then what the whole?

# THE TWO POETS OF CROISIC

## 1878

### 1

Such a starved bank of moss
　　Till that May-morn,
Blue ran the flash across:
　　Violets were born!

### 2

Sky – what a scowl of cloud
　　Till, near and far,
Ray on ray split the shroud:
　　Splendid, a star!

### 3

World – how it walled about
　　Life with disgrace
Till God's own smile came out:
　　That was thy face!

## The Two Poets of Croisic

### 1

'Fame!' Yes, I said it and you read it.
　　First,
　　Praise the good log-fire! Winter
　　　howls without.
Crowd closer, let us! Ha, the secret
　　nursed
　　Inside yon hollow, crusted
　　　roundabout
With copper where the clamp was, –
　　how the burst
　　Vindicates flame the stealthy feeder!
　　　Spout
Thy splendidest – a minute and no
　　more?
So soon again all sobered as before?

### 2

Nay, for I need to see your face! One
　　stroke
　　Adroitly dealt, and lo, the pomp
　　　revealed!
Fire in his pandemonium, heart of oak
　　Palatial, where he wrought the
　　　works concealed
Beneath the solid-seeming roof I broke,

As redly up and out and off they
　　reeled
Like disconcerted imps, those
　　thousand sparks
From fire's slow tunnelling of vaults
　　and arcs!

### 3

Up, out, and off, see! Were you never
　　used, –
　　You now, in childish days or rather
　　　nights, –
As I was, to watch sparks fly? not amused
　　By that old nurse-taught game which
　　　gave the sprites
Each one his title career, – confused
　　Belief 'twas all long over with the
　　　flights
From earth to heaven of hero, sage and
　　bard,
And bade them once more strive for
　　fame's award?

### 4

New long bright life! and happy chance
　　befell –
　　That I know – when some
　　　prematurely lost
Child of disaster bore away the bell
　　From some too-pampered son of
　　　fortune, crossed
Never before my chimney broke the
　　spell!
　　Octogenarian Keats gave up the ghost,
While – never mind Who was it
　　cumbered earth –
Sank stifled, span-long brightness, in
　　the birth.

### 5

Well, try a variation of the game!
　　Our log is old ship-timber, broken
　　　bulk.
There's sea-brine spirits up the brimstone
　　flame,

That crimson-curly spiral proves the
    hulk
Was saturate with – ask the chloride's
    name
    From somebody who knows! I shall
        not sulk
If yonder greenish tonguelet licked
    from brass
Its life, I thought was fed on copperas.

6

Anyhow, there they flutter! What may
    be
    The style and prowess of that purple
        one?
Who is the hero other eyes shall see
    Than yours and mine? That yellow,
        deep to dun –
Conjecture how the sage glows, whom
    not we
    But those unborn are to get warmth
        by! Son
O' the coal, – as Job and Hebrew name
    a spark, –
What bard, in thy red soaring, scares
    the dark?

7

Oh and the lesser lights, the dearer still
    That they elude a vulgar eye, give ours
The glimpse repaying astronomic skill
    Which searched sky deeper, passed
        those patent powers
Constellate proudly, – swords, scrolls,
    harps, that fill
    The vulgar eye to surfeit, – found
        best flowers
Hid deepest in the dark, – named
    unplucked grace
Of soul, ungathered beauty, form or
    face!

8

Up with thee, mouldering ash men
    never knew,
    But I know! flash thou forth, and
        figure bold,
Calm and columnar as yon flame I
    view!

Oh and I bid thee, – to whom
    fortune doled
Scantly all other gifts out – bicker blue,
    Beauty for all to see, zinc's
        uncontrolled
Flake-brilliance! Not my fault if these
    were shown,
Grandeur and beauty both, to me alone.

9

No! as the first was boy's play, this
    proves mere
    Stripling's amusement: manhood's
        sport be grave!
Choose rather sparkles quenched in
    mid career,
    Their boldness and their brightness
        could not save
(In some old night of time on some
    lone drear
    Sea-coast, monopolized by crag or
        cave)
– Save from ignoble exit into smoke,
Silence, oblivion, all death-damps that
    choke!

10

Launched by our ship-wood, float we,
    once adrift
In fancy to that land-strip waters wash,
We both know well! Where uncouth
    tribes made shift
    Long since to just keep life in, billows
        dash
Nigh over folk who shudder at each lift
    Of the old tyrant tempest's
        whirlwind-lash
Though they have built the serviceable
    town
Tempests but tease now, billows drench,
    not drown.

11

Croisic, the spit of sandy rock which juts
    Spitefully northward, bears nor tree
        nor shrub
To tempt the ocean, show what
    Guérande shuts
    Behind her, past wild Batz whose
        Saxons grub

The ground for crystals grown where
    ocean gluts
    Their promontory's breadth with
      salt: all stub
Of rock and stretch of sand, the land's
    last strife
To rescue a poor remnant for dear life.

          12

And what life! Here was, from the world
    to choose,
    The Druids' chosen chief of homes:
      they reared
– Only their women, – mid the slush
    and ooze
    Of yon low islet, – to their sun,
      revered
In strange stone guise, – a temple. May-
    dawn dews
    Saw the old structure levelled; when
      there peered
May's earliest eve-star, high and wide
    once more
Up towered the new pile perfect as
    before:

          13

Seeing that priestesses – and all were
    such –
    Unbuilt and then rebuilt it every May,
Each alike helping – well, if not too
    much!
    For, mid their eagerness to outstrip
      day
And get work done, if any loosed her
    clutch
    And let a single stone drop, straight
      a prey
Herself fell, torn to pieces, limb from
    limb,
By sisters in full chorus glad and grim.

          14

And still so much remains of that grey
    cult,
    That even now, of nights, do women
    steal
To the sole Menhir standing, and insult
    The antagonistic church-spire by
    appeal

To power discrowned in vain, since
    each adult
    Believes the gruesome thing she
      clasps may heal
Whatever plague no priestly help can
    cure:
Kiss but the cold stone, the event is
    sure!

          15

Nay more: on May-morns, that primeval
    rite
    Of temple-building, with its
      punishment
For rash precipitation, lingers, spite
    Of all remonstrance; vainly are they
      shent,
Those girls who form a ring and, dressed
    in white,
    Dance round it, till some sister's
      strength be spent:
Touch but the Menhir, straight the rest
    turn roughs
From gentles, fall on her with fisticuffs.

          16

Oh and, for their part, boys from door
    to door
    Sing unintelligible words to tunes
As obsolete: 'scraps of Druidic lore,'
    Sigh scholars, as each pale man
    importunes
Vainly the mumbling to speak plain
    once more.
    Enough of this old worship, rounds
    and runes!
They serve my purpose, which is but to
    show
Croisic to-day and Croisic long ago.

          17

What have we sailed to see, then,
    wafted there
    By fancy from the log that ends its
    days
Of much adventure 'neath skies foul or
    fair,
    On waters rough or smooth, in this
    good blaze

We two crouch round so closely,
    bidding care
        Keep outside with the snow-storm?
        Something says
'Fit time for story-telling!' I begin –
Why not at Croisic, port we first put in?

18

Anywhere serves: for point me out the
    place
        Wherever man has made himself a
        home,
And there I find the story of our race
    In little, just at Croisic as at Rome.
What matters the degree? the kind I
    trace.
        Druids their temple, Christians have
        their dome:
So with mankind; and Croisic, I'll engage,
With Rome yields sort for sort, in age
    for age.

19

No doubt, men vastly differ: and we
    need
        Some strange exceptional benevolence
Of nature's sunshine to develop seed
    So well, in the less-favoured clime,
    that hence
We may discern how shrub means tree
    indeed
        Though dwarfed till scarcely shrub
        in evidence.
Man in the ice-house or the hot-house
    ranks
With beasts or gods: stove-forced, give
    warmth the thanks!

20

While, is there any ice-checked? Such
    shall learn
        I am thankworthy, who propose to
        slake
His thirst for tasting how it feels to turn
Cedar from hyssop-on-the-wall. I wake
No memories of what is harsh and stern
    In ancient Croisic-nature, much less
    rake
The ashes of her last warmth till out
    leaps

Live Hervè Riel, the single spark she
    keeps.

21

Take these two, see, each outbreak, –
    spirt and spirt
        Of fire from our brave billet's either
        edge
Which – call maternal Croisic ocean-
    girt!
        These two shall thoroughly redeem
        my pledge.
One flames fierce gules, its feebler rival
    – vert,
        Heralds would tell you: heroes, I
        allege,
They both were: soldiers, sailors,
    statesmen, priests,
Lawyers, physicians – guess what gods
    or beasts!

22

None of them all, but – poets, if you
    please!
        'What, even there, endowed with
        knack of rhyme,
Did two among the aborigines
    Of that rough region pass the
    ungracious time
Suiting, to rumble-tumble of the sea's,
    The songs forbidden a serener
    clime?
Or had they universal audience – that's
To say, the folk of Croisic, ay and Batz?'

23

Open your ears! Each poet in his day
    Had such a mighty moment of
    success
As pinnacled him straight, in full display,
    For the whole world to worship –
    nothing less!
Was not the whole polite world Paris,
    pray?
        And did not Paris, for one moment –
        yes,
Worship these poet-flames, our red
    and green,
One at a time, a century between?

24

And yet you never heard their names!
      Assist,
   Clio, Historic Muse, while I record
Great deeds! Let fact, not fancy, break
      the mist
   And bid each sun emerge, in turn
      play lord
Of day, one moment! Hear the annalist
   Tell a strange story, true to the least
      word!
At Croisic, sixteen hundred years and
      ten
Since Christ, forth flamed yon liquid
      ruby, then.

25

Know him henceforth as René
      Gentilhomme
   – Appropriate appellation! noble
      birth
And knightly blazon, the device where-
      from
   Was 'Better do than say'! In Croisic's
      dearth
Why prison his career while Christendom
Lay open to reward acknowledged
      worth?
He therefore left it at the proper age
And got to be the Prince of Condé's
      page.

26

Which Prince of Condé, whom men
      called 'The Duke,'
   – Failing the king, his cousin, of an
      heir,
(As one might hold would hap, without
      rebuke,
   Since Anne of Austria, all the world
      was 'ware,
Twenty-three years long sterile, scarce
      could look
   For issue) – failing Louis of so rare
A godsend, it was natural the Prince
Should hear men call him 'Next King'
      too, nor wince.

27

Now, as this reasonable hope, by
      growth
   Of years, nay, tens of years, looked
      plump almost
To bursting, – would the brothers,
      childless both,
   Louis and Gaston, give but up the
      ghost – .
Condé, called 'Duke' and 'Next King,'
      nothing loth
   Awaited his appointment to the post,
And wiled away the time, as best he
      might,
Till Providence should settle things
      aright.

28

So, at a certain pleasure-house, with-
      drawn
   From cities where a whisper breeds
      offence,
He sat him down to watch the streak of
      dawn
   Testify to first stir of Providence;
And, since dull country life makes
      courtiers yawn,
   There wanted not a poet to dispense
Song's remedy for spleen-fits all and
      some,
Which poet was Page René Gentil-
      homme.

29

A poet born and bred, his very sire
   A poet also, author of a piece
Printed and published, 'Ladies – their
      attire':
   Therefore the son, just born at his
      decease,
Was bound to keep alive the sacred
      fire,
   And kept it, yielding moderate increase
Of songs and sonnets, madrigals, and
      much
Rhyming thought poetry and praised as
      such.

30

Rubbish unutterable (bear in mind!)
　　Rubbish not wholly without value,
　　　　though,
Being to compliment the Duke designed
　　And bring the complimenter credit
　　　　so, –
Pleasure with profit happily combined.
　　Thus René Gentilhomme rhymed,
　　　　rhymed till – lo,
This happened, as he sat in an alcove.
Elaborating rhyme for 'love' – *not* 'dove.'

31

He was alone: silence and solitude
　　Befit the votary of the Muse. Around,
Nature – not our new picturesque and
　　　　rude,
　　But trim tree-cinctured stately garden-
　　　　ground –
Breathed polish and politeness. All-
　　　　imbued
　　With these, he sat absorbed in one
　　　　profound
Excogitation 'Were it best to hint
Or boldly boast "She loves me, –
　　　　Araminte"?'

32

When suddenly flashed lightning,
　　　　searing sight
　　Almost, so close to eyes; then, quick
　　　　on flash,
Followed the thunder, splitting earth
　　　　downright
　　Where René sat a-rhyming: with
　　　　huge crash
Of marble into atoms infinite –
　　Marble which, stately, dared the
　　　　world to dash
The stone-thing proud, high-pillared,
　　from its place:
One flash, and dust was all that lay at
　　base.

33

So, when the horrible confusion loosed
　　Its wrappage round his senses, and,
　　　　with breath,

Seeing and hearing by degrees induced
　　Conviction what he felt was life, not
　　　　death –
His fluttered faculties came back to
　　　　roost
　　One after one, as fowls do: ay,
　　　　beneath,
About his very feet there, lay in dust
Earthly presumption paid by heaven's
　　disgust.

34

For, what might be the thunder-smitten
　　　　thing
　　But, pillared high and proud, in marble
　　　　guise,
A ducal crown – which meant 'Now
　　　　Duke: Next, King'?
　　Since such the Prince was, not in his
　　　　own eyes
Alone, but all the world's. Pebble from
　　　　sling
　　Prostrates a giant; so can pulverize
Marble pretension – how much more,
　　make moult
A peacock-prince his plume – God's
　　thunderbolt.

35

That was enough for René, that first
　　　　fact
　　Thus flashed into him. Up he looked:
　　　　all blue
And bright the sky above; earth firm,
　　　　compact
　　Beneath his footing, lay apparent too;
Opposite stood the pillar: nothing
　　　　lacked
　　There, but the Duke's crown: see, its
　　　　fragments strew
The earth, – about his feet lie atoms
　　fine
Where he sat nursing late his
　　fourteenth line!

36

So, for the moment, all the universe
　　Being abolished, all 'twixt God and
　　　　him, –

Earth's praise or blame, its blessing or
    its curse,
    Of one and the same value, – to the
      brim
Flooded with truth for better or for
    worse, –
    He pounces on the writing-paper,
      prim,
Keeping its place on table: not a dint
Nor speck had damaged 'Ode to
    Araminte.'

### 37

And over the neat crowquill calligraph
    His pen goes blotting, blurring, as an
      ox
Tramples a flower-bed in a garden, –
    laugh
    You may! – so does not he, whose
    quick heart knocks
Audibly at his breast: an epitaph
    On earth's break-up, amid the
    falling rocks,
He might be penning in a wild dismay,
Caught with his work half-done on
    Judgment Day.

### 38

And what is it so terribly he pens,
    Ruining 'Cupid, Venus, wile and
    smile,
Hearts, darts,' and all his day's *divinior
mens*
    Judged necessary to a perfect style?
Little recks René, with a breast to
    cleanse,
    Of Rhadamanthine law that reigned
    erewhile:
Brimful of truth, truth's outburst will
    convince
(Style or no style) who bears truth's
    brunt – the Prince.

### 39

'Condé, called "Duke," be called just
    "Duke," not more
    To life's end! "Next King" thou
    forsooth wilt be?
Ay, when this bauble, as it decked
    before

Thy pillar, shall again, for France to
    see,
Take its proud station there! Let France
    adore
    No longer an illusive mock-sun –
    thee –
But keep her homage for Sol's self,
    about
To rise and put pretenders to the rout!

### 40

'What? France so God-abandoned that
    her root
    Regal, though many a Spring it gave
    no sign,
Lacks power to make the bole, now
    branchless, shoot
    Greenly as ever? Nature, though
    benign,
Thwarts ever the ambitious and astute.
    In store for such is punishment
    condign:
Sure as thy Duke's crown to the earth
    was hurled,
So sure, next year, a Dauphin glads the
    world!'

### 41

Which penned – some forty lines to
    this effect –
    Our René folds his paper, marches
    brave
Back to the mansion, luminous, erect,
    Triumphant, an emancipated slave.
There stands the Prince. 'How now?
    My Duke's crown wrecked?
    What may this mean?' The answer
    René gave
Was – handing him the verses, with
    the due
Incline of body: 'sir, God's word to
    you!'

### 42

The Prince read, paled, was silent; all
    around,
    The courtier-company, to whom he
    passed
The paper, read, in equal silence bound.
    René grew also by degrees aghast

At his own fit of courage – palely found
  Way of retreat from that pale
      presence: classed
Once more among the cony-kind. 'Oh,
  son,
It is a feeble folk!'saith Solomon.

43

Vainly he apprehended evil: since,
  When, at the year's end, even as
      foretold,
Forth came the Dauphin who
    discrowned the Prince
  Of that long-craved mere visionary
      gold,
'Twas no fit time for envy to evince
  Malice, be sure! The timidest grew
      bold:
Of all that courtier-company not one
But left the semblance for the actual
  sun.

44

And all sorts and conditions that stood
  by
    At René's burning moment, bright
        escape
Of soul, bore witness to the prophecy.
  Which witness took the customary
      shape
Of verse; a score of poets in full cry
Hailed the inspired one. Nantes and
  Tours agape,
Soon Paris caught the infection;
  gaining strength,
How could it fail to reach the Court at
  length?

45

'O poet!'smiled King Louis, 'and besides,
  O prophet! Sure, by miracle
      announced,
My babe will prove a prodigy. Who
  chides
    Henceforth the unchilded monarch
        shall be trounced
For irreligion: since the fool derides
  Plain miracle by which this prophet
      pounced
Exactly on the moment I should lift

Like Simeon, in my arms, a babe,
  "God's gift!"

46

'So call the boy! and call this bard and
  seer
    By a new title! him I raise to rank
Of "Royal Poet": poet without peer!
  Whose fellows only have themselves
      to thank
If humbly they must follow in the rear
  My René. He's the master: they must
      clank
Their chains of song, confessed his
  slaves; for why?
They poetize, while he can prophesy!'

47

So said, so done; our René rose august,
  'The Royal Poet'; straightway put in
      type
His poem-prophecy, and (fair and just
  Procedure) added, – now that time
      was ripe
For proving friends did well his word
  to trust, –
    Those attestations, tuned to lyre or
        pipe,
Which friends broke out with when he
  dared foretell
The Dauphin's birth: friends trusted,
  and did well.

48

Moreover he got painted by Du Pré,
  Engraved by Daret also, and prefixed
The portrait to his book: a crown of bay
  Circled his brows, with rose and
      myrtle mixed;
And Latin verses, lovely in their way,
  Described him as 'the biforked hill
      betwixt:
Since he hath scaled Parnassus at one
Joining the Delphic quill and Getic
  trump.'

49

Whereof came … What, it lasts, our
  spirt, thus long
    – The red fire? That's the reason
        must excuse

My letting flicker René's prophet-song
  No longer: for its pertinacious hues
Must fade before its fellow joins the
    throng
  Of sparks departed up the chimney,
    dues
To dark oblivion. At the word, it winks,
Rallies, relapses, dwindles, deathward
    sinks!

50

So does our poet. All this burst of fame,
  Fury of favour, Royal Poetship,
Prophetship, book, verse, picture –
    thereof came
  – Nothing! That's why I would not
    let outstrip
Red his green rival flamelet: just the
    same
  Ending in smoke waits both! In vain
    we rip
The past, no further faintest trace remains
Of René to reward our pious pains.

51

Somebody saw a portrait framed and
    glazed
  At Croisic. 'Who may be this glorified
Mortal unheard-of hitherto?' amazed
  That person asked the owner by his
    side,
Who proved as ignorant. The question
    raised
  Provoked inquiry; key by key was
    tried
On Croisic's portrait-puzzle, till back
    flew
The wards at one key's touch, which
    key was – Who?

52

The other famous poet! Wait thy turn,
  Thou green, our red's competitor!
    Enough
Just now to note 'twas he that itched to
    learn
  (A hundred years ago) how fate
    could puff
Heaven-high (a hundred years before)
    then spurn

  To suds so big a bubble in some huff:
Since green too found red's portrait, –
    having heard
Hitherto of red's rare self not one word.

53

And he with zeal addressed him to the
    task
  Of hunting out, by all and any means,
– Who might the brilliant bard be,
    born to bask
  Butterfly-like in shine which kings
    and queens
And baby-dauphins shed? Much need
    to ask!
  Is fame so fickle that what perks and
    preens
The eyed wing, one imperial minute,
    dips
Next sudden moment into blind eclipse?

54

After a vast expenditure of pains,
  Our second poet found the prize he
    sought:
Urged in his search by something that
    restrains
  From undue triumph famed ones
    who have fought,
Or simply, poetizing, taxed their
    brains:
  Something that tells such – dear is
    triumph bought
If it means only basking in the midst
Of fame's brief sunshine, as thou,
    René, didst.

55

For, what did searching find at last but
    this?
  Quoth somebody 'I somehow some-
    where seem
To think I heard one old De Chevaye is
  Or was possessed of René's works!'
    which gleam
Of light from out the dark proved not
    amiss
  To track, by correspondence on the
    theme;

And soon the twilight broadened into day,
For thus to question answered De Chevaye.

56

'True it is, I did once possess the works
   You want account of – works – to call them so, –
Comprised in one small book: the volume lurks
   (Some fifty leaves *in duodecimo*)
'Neath certain ashes which my soul it irks
Still to remember, because long ago
That and my other rare shelf-occupants
Perished by burning of my house at Nantes.

57

'Yet of that book one strange particular
   Still stays in mind with me' – and thereupon
Followed the story. 'Few the poems are;
   The book was two-thirds filled up with this one,
And sundry witnesses from near and far
   That here at least was prophesying done
By prophet, so as to preclude all doubt,
Before the thing he prophesied about.'

58

That's all he knew, and all the poet learned,
   And all that you and I are like to hear
Of René; since not only book is burned
   But memory extinguished, – nay, I fear,
Portrait is gone too: nowhere I discerned
   A trace of it at Croisic. 'Must a tear
Needs fall for that?' you smile. 'How fortune fares
with such a mediocrity, who cares?'

59

Well, I care – intimately care to have
   Experience how a human creature felt
In after-life, who bore the burden grave

Of certainly believing God had dealt
For once directly with him: did not rave
   – A maniac, did not find his reason melt
– An idiot, but went on, in peace or strife,
The world's way, lived an ordinary life.

60

How many problems that one fact would solve!
   An ordinary soul, no more, no less,
About whose life earth's common sights revolve,
   On whom is brought to bear, by thunder-stress,
This fact – God tasks him, and will not absolve
   Task's negligent performer! Can you guess
How such a soul, – the task performed to point, –
Goes back to life nor finds things out of joint?

61

Does he stand stock-like henceforth? or proceed
   Dizzily, yet with course straightforward still,
Down-trampling vulgar hindrance? – as the reed
   Is crushed beneath its tramp when that blind will
Hatched in some old-world beast's brain bids it speed
   Where the sun wants brute-presence to fulfil
Life's purpose in a new far zone, ere ice
Enwomb the pasture-tract its fortalice.

62

I think no such direct plain truth consists
   With actual sense and thought and what they take
To be the solid walls of life: mere mists –
   How such would, at that truth's first piercing, break

Into the nullity they are! – slight lists
  Wherein the puppet-champions
    wage, for sake
Of some mock-mistress, mimic war:
    laid low
At trumpet-blast, there's shown the
    world, one foe!

63

No, we must play the pageant out,
    observe
  The tourney-regulations, and regard
Success – to meet the blunted spear
    nor swerve,
  Failure – to break no bones yet fall
    on sward;
Must prove we have – not courage? well
    then, – nerve!
  And, at the day's end, boast the
    crown's award –
Be warranted as promising to wield
Weapons, no sham, in a true battle-
    field.

64

Meantime, our simulated thunderclaps
  Which tell us counterfeited truths –
    these same
Are – sound, when music storms the
    soul, perhaps?
  – Sight, beauty, every dart of every
    aim
That touches just, then seems, by strange
    relapse,
  To fall effectless from the soul it came
As if to fix its own, but simply smote
And startled to vague beauty more
    remote?

65

So do we gain enough – yet not too
    much –
  Acquaintance with that outer element
Wherein there's operation (call it such!)
  Quite of another kind than we the
    pent
On earth are proper to receive. Our
    hutch
  Lights up at the least chink: let roof
    be rent –

How inmates huddle, blinded at first
    spasm,
Cognizant of the sun's self through the
    chasm!

66

Therefore, who knows if this our René's
    quick
  Subsidence from as sudden noise and
    glare
Into oblivion was impolitic?
  No doubt his soul became at once
    aware
That, after prophecy, the rhyming-trick
  Is poor employment: human praises
    scare
Rather than soothe ears all a-tingle yet
With tones few hear and live, but none
    forget.

67

There's our first famous poet. Step thou
    forth,
  Second consummate songster! See,
    the tongue
Of fire that typifies thee, owns thy worth
  In yellow, purple mixed its green
    among,
No pure and simple resin from the
    North,
  But composite with virtues that belong
To Southern culture! Love not more
    than hate
Helped to a blaze … But I anticipate.

68

Prepare to witness a combustion rich
  And riotously splendid, far beyond
Poor René's lambent little streamer
    which
  Only played candle to a Court
    grown fond
By baby-birth: this soared to such a
    pitch,
  Alternately such colours doffed and
    donned,
That when I say it dazzled Paris –
    please
Know that it brought Voltaire upon his
    knees!

69

Who did it, was a dapper gentleman,
  Paul Desforges Maillard, Croisickese
    by birth,
Whose birth that century ended which
    began
  By similar bestowment on our earth
Of the aforesaid René. Cease to scan
  The ways of Providence! See Croisic's
    dearth –
Not Paris in its plenitude – suffice
To furnish France with her best poet
    twice

70

Till he was thirty years of age, the vein
  Poetic yielded rhyme by drops and
    spirts:
In verses of society had lain
  His talent chiefly; but the Muse
    asserts
Privilege most by treating with disdain
  Epics the bard mouths out, or odes
    he blurts
Spasmodically forth. Have people time
And patience nowadays for thought in
    rhyme?

71

So, his achievements were the quatrain's
    inch
  Of homage, or at most the sonnet's
    ell
Of admiration: welded lines with clinch
  Of ending word and word, to every
    belle
In Croisic's bounds; these, brisk as any
    finch,
  He twittered till his fame had reached
    as well
Guérande as Batz; but there fame
    stopped, for – curse
On fortune – outside lay the universe!

72

That's Paris. Well, – why not break
    bounds, and send
  Song onward till it echo at the gates
Of Paris whither all ambitions tend,

And end too, seeing that success
    there sates
The soul which hungers most for fame?
    Why spend
  A minute in deciding, while, by Fate's
Decree, there happens to be just the
    prize
Proposed there, suiting souls that
    poetize?

73

A prize indeed, the Academy's own self
  Proposes to what bard shall best
    indite
A piece describing how, through shoal
    and shelf,
  The Art of Navigation, steered aright,
Has, in our last king's reign, – the lucky
    elf, –
  Reached, one may say, Perfection's
    haven quite,
And there cast anchor. At a glance one
    sees
The subject's crowd of capabilities!

74

Neptune and Amphitrité! Thetis, who
  Is either Tethys or as good – both tag!
Triton can shove along a vessel too:
  It's Virgil! Then the winds that blow
    or lag, –
De Maille, Vendôme, Vermandois!
    Toulouse blew
  Longest, we reckon: he must puff
    the flag
To fullest outflare; while our lacking
    nymph
Be Anne of Austria, Regent o'er the
    lymph!

75

Promised, performed! Since *irritabilis
    gens*
  Holds of the feverish impotence that
    strives
To stay an itch by prompt resource to
    pen's
  Scratching itself on paper; placid
    lives,

Leisurely works mark the *divinior mens:*
  Bees brood above the honey in their
    hives;
Gnats are the busy bustlers. Splash and
    scrawl, –
Completed lay thy piece, swift penman
    Paul!

76

To Paris with the product! This
    despatched,
  One had to wait the Forty's slow and
    sure
Verdict, as best one might. Our penman
    scratched
  Away perforce the itch that knows no
    cure
But daily paper-friction: more than
    matched
  His first feat by a second – tribute
    pure
And heartfelt to the Forty when their
    voice
Should peal with one accord 'Be Paul
    our choice!'

77

Scratch, scratch went much laudation
    of that sane
  And sound Tribunal, delegates august
Of Phœbus and the Muses'sacred
    train –
  Whom every poetaster tries to thrust
From where, high-throned, they
    dominate the Seine:
  Fruitless endeavour, – fail it shall and
    must!
Whereof in witness have not one and all
The Forty voices pealed 'Our choice be
    Paul'?

78

Thus Paul discounted his applause.
    Alack
  For human expectation! Scarcely ink
Was dry when, lo, the perfect piece
    came back
  Rejected, shamed! Some other poet's
    clink

'Thetis and Tethys' had seduced the
    pack
  Of pedants to declare perfection's
    pink
A singularly poor production. 'Whew!
The Forty are stark fools, I always
    knew.'

79

First fury over (for Paul's race – to-wit,
  Brain-vibrios – wriggle clear of
    protoplasm
Into minute life that's one fury-fit),
  'These fools shall find a bard's
    enthusiasm
Comports with what should
    counterbalance it –
  Some knowledge of the world! No
    doubt, orgasm
Effects the birth of verse which, born,
    demands
Prosaic ministration, swaddling-bands!

80

'Verse must be cared for at this early
    stage,
  Handled, nay dandled even. I
    should play
Their game indeed if, till it grew of age,
  I meekly let these dotards frown away
My bantling from the rightful heritage
  Of smiles and kisses! Let the public
    say
If it be worthy praises or rebukes,
My poem, from these Forty old perukes!'

81

So, by a friend, who boasts himself in
    grace
  With no less than the Chevalier La
    Roque, –
Eminent in those days for pride of
    place,
  Seeing he had it in his power to block
The way or smooth the road to all the
    race
  Of literators trudging up to knock
At Fame's exalted temple-door – for
    why?
He edited the Paris 'Mercury': –

82

By this friend's help the Chevalier
    receives
    Paul's poem, prefaced by the due
      appeal
To Cæsar from the Jews. As duly heaves
    A sigh the Chevalier, about to deal
With case so customary – turns the
    leaves,
    Finds nothing there to borrow, beg
      or steal –
Then brightens up the critic's brow
    deep-lined.
'The thing may be so cleverly declined!'

83

Down to desk, out with paper, up with
    quill,
    Dip and indite! 'Sir, gratitude
      immense
For this true draught from the Pierian
    rill!
    Our Academic clodpoles must be
      dense
Indeed to stand unirrigated still.
    No less, we critics dare not give
      offence
To grandees like the Forty: while we
    mock,
We grin and bear. So, here's your piece!
    La Roque.'

84

'There now!' cries Paul: 'the fellow
    can't avoid
    Confessing that my piece deserves
    the palm;
And yet he dares not grant me space
    enjoyed
    By every scribbler he permits embalm
His crambo in the Journal's corner!
    Cloyed
    With stuff like theirs, no wonder if a
    qualm
Be caused by verse like mine: though
    that's no cause
For his defrauding me of just applause.

85

Aha, he fears the Forty, this poltroon?
    First let him fear *me!* Change
    smooth speech to rough!
I'll speak my mind out, show the
    fellow soon
    Who is the foe to dread: insist enough
On my own merits till, as clear as
    noon,
    He sees I am no man to take rebuff
As patiently as scribblers may and must!
Quick to the onslaught, out sword, cut
    and thrust!'

86

And thereupon a fierce epistle flings
    Its challenge in the critic's face.
    Alack!
Our bard mistakes his man! The gauntlet
    rings
    On brazen visor proof against attack.
Prompt from his editorial throne up
    springs
    The insulted magnate, and his mace
    falls, thwack,
On Paul's devoted brainpan, – quite
    away
From common courtesies of fencing-
    play!

87

Sir, will you have the truth? This piece
    of yours
    Is simply execrable past belief.
I shrank from saying so; but, since
    nought cures
    Conceit but truth, truth's at your
    service! Brief;
Just so long as 'The Mercury' endures,
    So long are you excluded by its
    Chief
From corner, nay, from cranny! Play
    the cock
O' the roost, henceforth, at Croisic!'
    wrote La Roque.

88

Paul yellowed, whitened, as his wrath
  from red
    Waxed incandescent. Now, this man
      of rhyme
Was merely foolish, faulty in the head
    Not heart of him: conceit's a venial
      crime.
'Oh by no means malicious!' cousins
  said:
    Fussily feeble, – harmless all the time,
Piddling at so-called satire – well-advised
He held in most awe whom he satirized.

89

Accordingly his kith and kin – removed
    From emulation of the poet's gift
By power and will – these rather liked,
  nay, loved
    The man who gave his family a lift
Out of the Croisic level; 'disapproved
    Satire so trenchant.' Thus our poet
      sniffed
Home-incense, though too churlish to
  unlock
'The Mercury's' box of ointment was
  La Roque.

90

But when Paul's visage grew from red
  to white,
    And from his lips a sort of mumbling
      fell
Of who was to be kicked, – 'And serve
  him right' –
    A gay voice interposed – 'did kicking
      well
Answer the purpose! Only – if I might
    Suggest as much – a far more potent
      spell
Lies in another kind of treatment. Oh,
Women are ready at resource, you
  know!

91

'Talent should minister to genius! Good:
    The proper and superior smile
      returns.
Hear me with patience! Have you
  understood

The only method whereby genius
  earns
Fit guerdon nowadays? In knightly mood
    You entered lists with visor up; one
      learns
Too late that, had you mounted
      Roland's crest,
"Room!" they had roared – La Roque
  with all the rest!

92

'Why did you first of all transmit your
  piece
    To those same priggish Forty
      unprepared
Whether to rank you with the swans or
  geese
    By friendly intervention? If they dared
Count you a cackler, – wonders never
  cease!
I think it still more wondrous that you
  bared
Your brow (my earlier image) as if praise
Were gained by simple fighting
  nowadays!

93

'Your next step showed a touch of the
  true means
    Whereby desert is crowned: not force
      but wile
Came to the rescue. "Get behind the
  scenes!"
    Your friend advised: he writes, sets
      forth your style
And title, to such purpose intervenes
    That you get velvet-compliment
      three-pile;
And, though "The Mercury" said "nay,"
  nor stock
Nor stone did his refusal prove La Roque.

94

'Why must you needs revert to the
  high hand,
    Imperative procedure – what you
      call
"Taking on merit your exclusive
  stand"?

*Stand*, with a vengeance! Soon you
        went to wall,
You and your merit! Only fools command
        When folk are free to disobey them,
        Paul!
You've learnt your lesson, found out
        what's o'clock,
By this uncivil answer of La Roque.

### 95

'Now let me counsel! Lay this piece on
        shelf
        – Masterpiece though it be! From
        out your desk
Hand me some lighter sample, verse
        the elf
        Cupid inspired you with, no god
        grotesque
Presiding o'er the Navy! I myself
        Hand-write what's legible yet
        picturesque;
I'll copy fair and femininely frock
Your poem masculine that courts La
        Roque!

### 96

'Deïdamia he – Achilles thou!
        Ha, ha, these ancient stories come
        so apt!
My sex, my youth, my rank I next avow
        In a neat prayer for kind perusal.
        Sapped
I see the walls which stand so stoutly
        now!
        I see the toils about the game
        entrapped
By honest cunning! Chains of lady's-
        smock,
Not thorn and thistle, tether fast La
        Roque!'

### 97

Now, who might be the speaker sweet
        and arch
        That laughed above Paul's shoulder
        as it heaved
With the indignant heart? – bade steal
        a march
        And not continue charging? Who
        conceived

This plan which set our Paul, like pea
        you parch
On fire-shovel, skipping, of a load
        relieved,
From arm-chair moodiness to escritoire
Sacred to Phæbus and the tuneful
        choir?

### 98

Who but Paul's sister! named of course
        like him
        'Desforges'; but, mark you, in those
        days a queer
Custom obtained, – who knows whence
        grew the whim? –
        That people could not read their title
        clear
To reverence till their own true names,
        made dim
        By daily mouthing, pleased to
        disappear,
Replaced by brand-new bright ones:
        Arouet,
For instance, grew Voltaire; Desforges
        – Malcrais.

### 99

'Demoiselle Malcrais de la Vigne' –
        because
        The family possessed at Brederac
A vineyard, – few grapes, many hips-
        and-haws, –
        Still a nice Breton name. As breast
        and back
Of this vivacious beauty gleamed
        through gauze,
        So did her sprightly nature nowise
        lack
Lustre when draped, the fashionable
        way,
In 'Malcrais de la Vigne' – more short,
        'Malcrais.'

### 100

Out from Paul's escritoire behold
        escape
        The hoarded treasure! verse falls
        thick and fast,
Sonnets and songs of every size and
        shape.

The lady ponders on her prize; at last
Selects one which – Oh angel and yet
  ape! –
  Her malice thinks is probably
  surpassed
In badness by no fellow of the flock,
Copies it fair, and 'Now for my La
  Roque!'

101

So, to him goes, with the neat manu-
  script,
  The soft petitionary letter.' 'Grant
A fledgeling novice that with wing
  unclipt
  She soar her little circuit, habitant
Of an old manor; buried in which crypt,
  How can the youthful châtelaine but
  pant
For disemprisonment by one *ad hoc*
Appointed "Mercury's" Editor, La
  Roque?'

102

'Twas an epistle that might move the
  Turk!
  More certainly it moved our middle-
  aged
Pen-driver drudging at his weary work,
  Raked the old ashes up and
  disengaged
The sparks of gallantry which always
  lurk
  Somehow in literary breasts, assuaged
In no degree by compliments on style;
Are Forty wagging beards worth one
  girl's smile?

103

In trips the lady's poem, takes its place
  Of honour in the gratified Gazette,
With due acknowledgment of power
  and grace;
  Prognostication, too, that higher yet
The Breton Muse will soar: fresh youth,
  high race,
  Beauty and wealth have amicably met
That Demoiselle Malcrais may fill the
  chair
Left vacant by the loss of Deshoulières'.

104

'There!' cried the lively lady 'Who was
  right –
  You in the dumps, or I the merry
  maid
Who know a trick or two can baffle
  spite
  Tenfold the force of this old fool's?
  Afraid
Of Editor La Roque? But come! Next
  flight
  Shall outsoar – Deshoulières alone?
  My blade,
Sappho herself shall you confess
  outstript!
Quick, Paul, another dose of
  manuscript!'

105

And so, once well a-foot, advanced the
  game:
  More and more verses, corresponding
  gush
On gush of praise, till everywhere
  acclaim
  Rose to the pitch of uproar. 'Sappho?
  Tush!
Sure "Malcrais on her Parrot" puts to
  shame
  Deshoulieres' pastoral, clay not
  worth a rush
Beside this find of treasure, gold in
  crock,
Unearthed in Brittany, – nay, ask La
  Roque!'

106

Such was the Paris tribute' 'Yes,' you
  sneer,
  'Ninnies stock Noodledom, but folk
  more sage
Resist contagious folly, never fear!'
  Do they? Permit me to detach one
  page
From the huge Album which from far
  and near
  Poetic praises blackened in a rage
Of rapture! and that page shall be –
  who stares

Confounded now, I ask you? – just
    Voltaire's!

107

Ay, sharpest shrewdest steel that ever
    stabbed
    To death Imposture through the
      armour-joints!
How did it happen that gross Humbug
    grabbed
    Thy weapons, gouged thine eyes out?
      Fate appoints
That pride shall have a fall, or I had
    blabbed
    Hardly that Humbug, whom thy soul
      aroints,
Could thus cross-buttock thee caught
    unawares,
And dismalest of tumbles proved –
    Voltaire's!

108

See his epistle extant yet, wherewith
    'Henri' in verse and 'Charles' in
    prose he sent
To do her suit and service! Here's the
    pith
    Of half a dozen stanzas – stones
    which went
To build that simulated monolith –
    Sham love in due degree with
    homage blent
As sham – which in the vast of
    volumes scares
The traveller still: 'That stucco-heap –
    Voltaire's?'

109

'Oh thou, whose clarion-voice has
    overflown
    The wilds to startle Paris that's one
    ear!
Thou who such strange capacity hast
    shown
    For joining all that's grand with all
    that's dear,
Knowledge with power to please –
    Deshoulières grown
    Learned as Dacier in thy person! mere

Weak fruits of idle hours, these crabs
    of mine
I dare lay at thy feet, O Muse divine!

110

'Charles was my taskwork only; Henri
    trod
    My hero erst; and now, my heroine
    – she
Shall be thyself! True – is it true, great
    God?
    Certainly love henceforward must
    not be!
Yet all the crowd of Fine Arts fail – how
    odd! –
    Tried turn by turn, to fill a void in me!
There's no replacing love with these,
    alas!
Yet all I can I do to prove no ass.

111

'I labour to amuse my freedom; but
    Should any sweet young creature
    slavery preach,
And – borrowing thy vivacious charm,
    the slut! –
    Make me, in thy engaging words, a
    speech,
Soon should I see myself in prison shut
    With all imaginable pleasure.' Reach
The washhand-basin for admirers!
    There's
A stomach-moving tribute – and
    Voltaire's!

112

Suppose it a fantastic billet-doux,
    Adulatory flourish, not worth frown!
What say you to the Fathers of
    TrèVoux?
    These in their Dictionary have her
    down
Under the heading 'Author': 'Malcrais,
    too,
Is "Author" of much verse that claims
    renown'
While Jean-Baptiste Rousseau … but
    why proceed?
Enough of this – something too much,
    indeed!

113

At last La Roque, unwilling to be left
    Behindhand in the rivalry, broke
        bounds
Of figurative passion; hilt and heft,
    Plunged his huge downright love
        through what surrounds
The literary female bosom; reft
    Away its veil of coy reserve with
        'Zounds!
I love thee, Breton Beauty! All's no use!
Body and soul I love, – the big word's
    loose!'

115

*He's greatest now and to de-struc-ti-on*
    *Nearest*. Attend the solemn word I
        quote,
O Paul! *There's no pause at per-fec-ti-on*.
    Thus knolls thy knell the Doctor's
        bronzèd throat!
*Greatness a period hath, no sta-ti-on!*
    Better and truer verse none ever wrote
(Despite the antique outstretched
    *a-i-on*)
Than thou, revered and magisterial
    Donne!

115

Flat on his face, La Roque, and, –
    pressed to heart
    His dexter hand, – Voltaire with
        bended knee!
Paul sat and sucked-in triumph; just
    apart
    Leaned over him his sister.
        'Well!'smirks he,
And 'Well?'she answers, smiling –
    woman's art
    To let a man's own mouth, not hers,
        decree
What shall be next move which decides
    the game:
Success? She said so. Failure? His the
    blame.

116

'Well!' this time forth affirmatively
    comes
    With smack of lip, and long-drawn
        sigh through teeth
Close clenched o'er satisfaction, as the
    gums
    Were tickled by a sweetmeat teased
        beneath
Palate by lubricating tongue: 'Well!
    crumbs
    Of comfort these, undoubtedly! no
        death
Likely from famine at Fame's feast! 'tis
    clear
I may put claim in for my pittance,
    Dear!

117

'La Roque, Voltaire, my lovers! Then
    disguise
    Has served its turn, grows idle; let it
        drop!
I shall to Paris, flaunt there in men's
    eyes
    My proper manly garb and mount a-
        top
The pedestal that waits me, take the
    prize
    Awarded Hercules. He threw a sop
To Cerberus who let him pass, you
    know,
Then, following, licked his heels:
    exactly so!

118

'I like the prospect – their astonishment,
    Confusion: wounded vanity, no
        doubt,
Mixed motives; how I see the brows
    quick bent!
"What, sir, yourself, none other,
    brought about
This change of estimation? Phœbus sent
His shafts as from Diana?" Critic pout
Turns courtier smile: "Lo, him we took
    for her!
Pleasant mistake! You bear no malice,
    sir?"

119

'Eh, my Diana?' But Diana kept
　Smilingly silent with fixed needle-
　　sharp
Much-meaning eyes that seemed to
　intercept
　Paul's very thoughts ere they had
　　time to warp
From earnest into sport the words they
　leapt
　To life with – changed as when
　　maltreated harp
Renders in tinkle what some player-prig
Means for a grave tune though it
　　proves a jig.

120

'What, Paul, and are my pains thus
　thrown away,
　My lessons end in loss?' at length
　　fall slow
The pitying syllables, her lips allay
　The satire of by keeping in full flow,
Above their coral reef, bright smiles at
　play:
　'Can it be, Paul thus fails to rightly
　　know
And altogether estimate applause
As just so many asinine hee-haws?

121

'I thought to show you' … 'Show me,'
　Paul in-broke,
　'My poetry is rubbish, and the world
That rings with my renown a sorry joke!
　What fairer test of worth than that,
　　form furled,
I entered the arena? Yet you croak
　Just as if Phœbé and not Phœbus
　　hurled
The dart and struck the Python! What,
　he crawls
Humbly in dust before your feet, not
　　Paul's?

122

'Nay, 'tis no laughing matter though
　absurd
　If there's an end of honesty on earth!

La Roque sends letters, lying every
　word!
　Voltaire makes verse, and of himself
　　makes mirth
To the remotest age! Rousseau's the
　third
　Who, driven to despair amid such
　　dearth
Of people that want praising, finds no
　one
More fit to praise than Paul the
　　simpleton!

123

'Somebody says – if a man writes at all
　It is to show the writer's kith and kin
He was unjustly thought a natural;
　And truly, sister, I have yet to win
Your favourable word, it seems, for Paul
　Whose poetry you count not worth
　　a pin
Though well enough esteemed by these
　Voltaires,
Rousseaus and suchlike: let them quack,
　who cares?'

124

' – To Paris with you, Paul! Not one
　word's waste
　Further: my scrupulosity was vain!
Go triumph! Be my foolish fears effaced
　From memory's record! Go, to come
　　again
With glory crowned, – by sister
　reembraced,
　Cured of that strange delusion of her
　　brain
Which led her to suspect that Paris
　gloats
On male limbs mostly when in
　petticoats!'

125

So laughed her last word, with the little
　touch
　Of malice proper to the outraged
　　pride
Of any artist in a work too much
　Shorn of its merits.' 'By all means be
　　tried

The opposite procedure! Cast your
        crutch
    Away, no longer crippled, nor divide
The credit of your march to the
        World's Fair
With sister Cherry-cheeks who helped
        you there!'

### 126

Crippled, forsooth! what courser
        spright-lier pranced
    Paris-ward than did Paul? Nay,
        dreams lent wings:
He flew, or seemed to fly, by dreams
        entranced.
    Dreams? wide-awake realities: no
        things
Dreamed merely were the missives that
        advanced
    The claim of Malcrais to consort with
        kings
Crowned by Apollo – not to say with
        queens
Cinctured by Venus for Idalian scenes.

### 127

Soon he arrives, forthwith is found
        before
    The outer gate of glory. Bold tic-toc
Announces there's a giant at the door.
    'Ay, sir, here dwells the Chevalier La
        Roque'
'Lackey! Malcrais, – mind, no word less
        nor more! –
    Desires his presence. I've unearthed
        the brock:
Now, to transfix him!' There stands Paul
        erect,
Inched out his uttermost, for more effect.

### 128

A bustling entrance: 'Idol of my flame!
    Can it be that my heart attains at last
Its longing? that you stand, the very
        same
    As in my visions? ... Ha! hey, how?'
        aghast
Stops short the rapture. 'Oh, my boy's
        to blame!

You merely are the messenger! Too
        fast
My fancy rushed to a conclusion. Pooh!
Well, sir, the lady's substitute is – who?'

### 129

Then Paul's smirk grows inordinate.
        'Shake hands!
    Friendship not love awaits you,
        master mine,
Though nor Malcrais nor any mistress
        stands
    To meet your ardour! So, you don't
        divine
Who wrote the verses wherewith ring
        the land's
    Whole length and breadth? Just he
        whereof no line
Had ever leave to blot your Journal – eh?
Paul Desforges Maillard – otherwise
        Malcrais!'

### 130

And there the two stood, stare con-
        fronting smirk,
    Awhile uncertain which should yield
        the *pas*.
In vain the Chevalier beat brain for
        quirk
    To help in this conjuncture; at
        length 'Bah!
Boh! Since I've made myself a fool,
        why shirk
    The punishment of folly? Ha, ha, ha,
Let me return your handshake!' Comic
        sock
For tragic buskin prompt thus changed
        La Roque.

### 131

'I'm nobody – a wren-like journalist;
    You've flown at higher game and
        winged your bird,
The golden eagle! That's the grand
        acquist!
    Voltaire's sly Muse, the tiger-cat, has
        purred
Prettily round your feet; but if she
        missed
    Priority of stroking, soon were stirred

The dormant spit-fire. To Voltaire! away,
Paul Desforges Maillard, otherwise
    Malcrais!'

132

Whereupon, arm in arm, and head in
    air,
    The two begin their journey. Need I
        say,
La Roque had felt the talon of Voltaire,
    Had a long-standing little debt to pay,
And pounced, you may depend, on
    such a rare
    Occasion for its due discharge? So,
        gay
And grenadier-like, marching to assault,
They reach the enemy's abode, there
    halt.

133

'I'll be announcer!' quoth La Roque: 'I
    know,
    Better than you, perhaps, my Breton
        bard,
How to procure an audience! He's not
    slow
    To smell a rat, this scamp Voltaire!
        Discard
The petticoats too soon, – you'll never
    show
    Your *haut-de-chausses* and all they've
        made or marred
In your true person. Here's his servant.
    Pray,
Will the great man see Demoiselle
    Malcrais?'

134

Now, the great man was also, no whit
    less,
    The man of self-respect, – more great
        man he!
And bowed to social usage, dressed the
    dress,
    And decorated to the fit degree
His person; 'twas enough to bear the
    stress
    Of battle in the field, without, when
        free

From outside foes, inviting friends'
    attack
By – sword in hand? No, – ill-made
    coat on back!

135

And, since the announcement of his
    visitor
    Surprised him at his toilet, – never
        glass
Had such solicitation! 'Black, now – or
    Brown be the killing wig to wear?
        Alas,
Where's the rouge gone, this cheek
    were better for
    A tender touch of? Melted to a mass,
All my pomatum! There's at all events
A devil – for he's got among my
    scents!'

136

So, 'bartered ten times o'er,' as Antony
    Paced to his Cleopatra, did at last
Voltaire proceed to the fair presence:
    high
    In colour, proud in port, as if a blast
Of trumpet bade the world 'Take note!
    draws nigh
    To Beauty, Power! Behold the
        Iconoclast,
The Poet, the Philosopher, the Rod
Of iron for imposture! Ah my God!'

137

For there stands smirking Paul, and –
    what lights fierce
    The situation as with sulphur flash –
There grinning stands La Roque! No
    carte-and-tierce
    Observes the grinning fencer, but,
        full dash
From breast to shoulderblade, the
    thrusts transpierce
    That armour against which so idly
        clash
The swords of priests and pedants!
    Victors there,
Two smirk and grin who have befooled
    – Voltaire!

### 138

A moment's horror; then quick turn-
   about
   On high-heeled shoe, – flurry of
      ruffles, flounce
Of wig-ties and of coat-tails, – and so
      out
   Of door banged wrathfully behind,
      goes – bounce –
Voltaire in tragic exit! vows, no doubt,
   Vengeance upon the couple. Did he
      trounce
Either, in point of fact? His anger's
      flash
Subsided u a culprit craved his cash.

### 139

As for La Roque, he having laughed his
      laugh
   To heart's content, – the joke defunct
      at once,
Dead in the birth, you see, – its epitaph
   Was sober earnest. 'Well, sir, for the
      nonce,
You've gained the laurel; never hope to
      graff
   A second sprig of triumph there!
      Ensconce
Yourself again at Croisic: let it be
Enough you mastered both Voltaire and
      – me!

### 140

'Don't linger here in Paris to parade
   Your victory, and have the very boys
Point at you! "There's the little mouse
      which made
   Believe those two big lions that its
      noise,
Nibbling away behind the hedge,
      conveyed
   Intelligence that – portent which
      destroys
All courage in the lion's heart, with
      horn
That's fable – there lay couched the
      unicorn!"

### 141

'Beware us, now we've found who
      fooled us! Quick
To cover! "In proportion to men's
      fright,
Expect their fright's revenge!" quoth
      politic
   Old Macchiavelli. As for me, – all's
      right:
I'm but a journalist. But no pin's prick
   The tooth leaves when Voltaire is
      roused to bite!
So, keep your counsel, I advise! Adieu!
Good journey! Ha, ha, ha, Malcrais was
      – you!'

### 142

' – Yes, I'm Malcrais, and somebody
      beside,
   You snickering monkey!' thus winds
      up the tale
Our hero, safe at home, to that black-
      eyed
   Cherry-cheeked sister, as she soothes
      the pale
Mortified poet. 'Let their worst be tried,
I'm their match henceforth – very man
      and male!
Don't talk to me of knocking-under!
      man
And male must end what petticoats
      began!

### 143

'How woman-like it is to apprehend
   The world will eat its words! why,
      words transfixed
To stone, they stare at you in print, –
      at end,
   Each writer's style and title! Choose
      betwixt
Fool and knave for his name, who should
      intend
   To perpetrate a baseness so unmixed
With prospect of advantage! What is
      writ
Is writ: they've praised me, there's an
      end of it.

### 144

'No, Dear, allow me! I shall print these
same
Pieces, with no omitted line, as Paul's.
Malcrais no longer, let me see folk
blame
What they – praised simply? – placed
on pedestals,
Each piece a statue in the House of
Fame!
Fast will they stand there, though
their presence galls
The envious crew: such show their
teeth, perhaps,
And snarl, but never bite! I know the
chaps!'

### 145

Oh Paul, oh piteously deluded! Pace
Thy sad sterility of Croisic flats,
Watch, from their southern edge, the
foamy race
Of high-tide as it leaves the drowning
mats
Of yellow-berried web-growth from
their place,
The rock-ridge, when, rolling as far
as Batz,
One broadside crashes on it, and the
crags,
That needle under, stream with weedy
rags!

### 146

Or, if thou wilt, at inland Bergerac,
Rude heritage but recognized domain,
Do as two here are doing: make hearth
crack
With logs until thy chimney roar
again
Jolly with fire-glow! Let its angle lack
No grace of Cherry-cheeks thy sister,
fain
To do a sister's office and laugh smooth
Thy corrugated brow – that scowls
forsooth!

### 147

Wherefore? Who does not know how
these La Roques,
Voltaires, can say and unsay, praise
and blame,
Prove black white, white black, play at
paradox
And, when they seem to lose it, win
the game?
Care not thou what this badger, and
that fox,
His fellow in rascality, call 'fame!'
Fiddlepin's end! Thou hadst it, –
quack, quack, quack!
Have quietude from geese at Bergerac!

### 148

Quietude! For, be very sure of this!
A twelvemonth hence, and men
shall know or care
As much for what to-day they clap or
hiss
As for the fashion of the wigs they
wear,
Then wonder at. There's fame which,
bale or bliss, –
Got by no gracious word of great
Voltaire
Or not-so-great La Roque, – is taken
back
By neither, any more than Bergerac!

### 149

Too true! or rather, true as ought to be!
No more of Paul the man, Malcrais
the maid,
Thenceforth for ever! One or two, I see,
Stuck by their poet: who the longest
stayed
Was Jean-Baptiste Rousseau, and even
he
Seemingly saddened as perforce he
paid
A rhyming tribute 'After death, survive –
He hoped he should; and died while
yet alive!'

150

No, he hoped nothing of the kind, or
    held
    His peace and died in silent good old
        age.
Him it was, curiosity impelled
    To seek if there were extant still some
        page
Of his great predecessor, rat who belled
    The cat once, and would never deign
        engage
In after-combat with mere mice, – saved
    from
More sonnetteering, – René Gentil-
    homme.

151

Paul's story furnished forth that famous
    play
    Of Piron's 'Métromanie': there you'll
        find
He's Francaleu, while Demoiselle
    Malcrais
    Is Demoiselle No-end-of-names-be-
        hind!
As for Voltaire, he's Damis. Good and
    gay
    The plot and dialogue, and all's
        designed
To spite Voltaire: at 'something'such
    the laugh
Of simply 'Nothing!' (see his epitaph).

152

But truth, truth, that's the gold! and all
    the good
    I find in fancy is, it serves to set
Gold's inmost glint free, gold which
    comes up rude
    And rayless from the mine. All fume
        and fret
Of artistry beyond this point pursued
    Brings out another sort of burnish:
        yet
Always the ingot has its very own
Value, a sparkle struck from truth
    alone.

153

Now, take this sparkle and the other
    spirt
    Of fitful flame, – twin births of our
        grey brand
That's sinking fast to ashes! I assert,
    As sparkles want but fuel to expand
Into a conflagration no mere squirt
    Will quench too quickly, so might
        Croisic strand,
Had fortune pleased posterity to chowse,
Boast of her brace of beacons
    luminous.

154

Did earlier Agamemnons lack their
    bard?
    But later bards lacked Agamemnon
        too!
How often frustrate they of fame's
    award
    Just because Fortune, as she listed,
        blew
Some slight bark's sails to bellying,
    mauled and marred
    And forced to put about the First-
        rate! True,
Such tacks but for a time: still – small-
    craft ride
At anchor, rot while Beddoes breasts
    the tide!

155

Dear, shall I tell you? There's a simple
    test
    Would serve, when people take on
        them to weigh
The worth of poets, 'Who was better,
    best,
    This, that, the other bard?' (bards
        none gainsay
As good, observe! no matter for the
    rest)
    'What quality preponderating may
Turn the scale as it trembles?' End the
    strife
By asking 'Which one led a happy life?'

### 156

If one did, over his antagonist
  That yelled or shrieked or sobbed or
    wept or wailed
Or simply had the dumps, – dispute
    who list, –
  I count him victor. Where his fellow
    failed,
Mastered by his own means of might, –
    acquist
  Of necessary sorrows, – he prevailed,
A strong since joyful man who stood
    distinct
Above slave-sorrows to his chariot linked.

### 157

Was not his lot to feel more? What
    meant 'feel'
  Unless to suffer! Not, to see more?
    Sight –
What helped it but to watch the drunken
    reel
  Of vice and folly round him, left and
    right,
One dance of rogues and idiots! Not, to
    deal
  More with things lovely? What
    provoked the spite
Of filth incarnate, like the poet's need
Of other nutriment than strife and
    greed!

### 158

Who knows most, doubts most;
    entertaining hope,
  Means recognizing fear; the keener
    sense
Of all comprised within our actual scope
  Recoils from aught beyond earth's
    dim and dense.
Who, grown familiar with the sky, will
    grope
  Henceforward among groundlings?
    That's offence
Just as indubitably: stars abound
O'erhead, but then – what flowers
    make glad the ground!

### 159

So, force is sorrow, and each sorrow,
    force:
  What then? since Swiftness gives the
    charioteer
The palm, his hope be in the vivid
    horse
  Whose neck God clothed with
    thunder, not the steer
Sluggish and safe! Yoke Hatred, Crime,
    Remorse,
  Despair: but ever mid the whirling
    fear,
Let, through the tumult, break the poet's
    face
Radiant, assured his wild slaves win the
    race!

### 160

Therefore I say ... no, shall not say, but
    think,
  And save my breath for better purpose.
    White
From grey our log has burned to: just
    one blink
  That quivers, loth to leave it, as a
    sprite
The outworn body. Ere your eyelids'
    wink
  Punish who sealed so deep into the
    night
Your mouth up, for two poets dead so
    long, –
Here pleads a live pretender: right your
    wrong!

\*     \*     \*

### 1

What a pretty tale you told me
  Once upon a time
– Said you found it somewhere (scold
    me!)
  Was it prose or was it rhyme,
Greek or Latin? Greek, you said,
While your shoulder propped my
    head.

2

Anyhow there's no forgetting
    This much if no more,
That a poet (pray, no petting!)
    Yes, a bard, sir, famed of yore,
Went where suchlike used to go,
Singing for a prize, you know.

3

Well, he had to sing, nor merely
    Sing but play the lyre;
Playing was important clearly
    Quite as singing: I desire,
Sir, you keep the fact in mind
For a purpose that's behind.

4

There stood he, while deep attention
    Held the judges round,
– Judges able, I should mention,
    To detect the slightest sound
Sung or played amiss: such ears
Had old judges, it appears!

5

None the less he sang out boldly,
    Played in time and tune,
Till the judges, weighing coldly
    Each note's worth, seemed, late or
        soon,
Sure to smile 'In vain one tries
Picking faults out: take the prize!'

6

When, a mischief! Were they seven
    Strings the lyre possessed?
Oh, and afterwards eleven,
    Thank you! Well, sir, – who had
        guessed
Such ill luck in store? – it happed
One of those same seven strings
        snapped.

7

All was lost, then! No! a cricket
    (What 'cicada'? Pooh!)
– Some mad thing that left its thicket
    For mere love of music – flew
With its little heart on fire,
Lighted on the crippled lyre.

8

So that when (ah joy!) our singer
    For his truant string
Feels with disconcerted finger,
    What does cricket else but fling
Fiery heart forth, sound the note
Wanted by the throbbing throat?

9

Ay and, ever to the ending,
    Cricket chirps at need,
Executes the hand's intending,
    Promptly, perfectly, – indeed
Saves the singer from defeat
With her chirrup low and sweet.

10

Till, at ending, all the judges
    Cry with one assent
'Take the prize – a prize who grudges
    Such a voice and instrument?
Why, we took your lyre for harp,
So it shrilled us forth F sharp!'

11

Did the conqueror spurn the creature,
    Once its service done?
That's no such uncommon feature
    In the case when Music's son
Finds his Lotte's power too spent
For aiding soul-development.

12

No! This other, on returning
    Homeward, prize in hand,
Satisfied his bosom's yearning:
    (Sir, I hope you understand!)
– Said 'Some record there must be
Of this cricket's help to me!'

13

So, he made himself a statue:
    Marble stood, life-size;
On the lyre, he pointed at you,
    Perched his partner in the prize;
Never more apart you found
Her, he throned, from him, she
        crowned.

14

That's the tale: its application?
    Somebody I know
Hopes one day for reputation
    Through his poetry that's – Oh,
All so learned and so wise
And deserving of a prize!

15

If he gains one, will some ticket,
    When his statue's built,
Tell the gazer ' 'Twas a cricket
    Helped my crippled lyre, whose lilt
Sweet and low, when strength usurped
Softness' place i' the scale, she chirped?

16

'For as victory was nighest,
    While I sang and played, –

With my lyre at lowest, highest,
    Right alike, – one string that made
"Love" sound soft was snapt in twain,
Never to be heard again, –

17

'Had not a kind cricket fluttered,
    Perched upon the place
Vacant left, and duly uttered
    "Love, Love, Love," whene'er the bass
Asked the treble to atone
For its somewhat sombre drone.

18

But you don't know music! Wherefore
    Keep on casting pearls
To a – poet? All I care for
    Is – to tell him that a girl's
'Love' comes aptly in when gruff
Grows his singing. (There, enough!)

# DRAMATIC IDYLS

First series
1879

## Martin Relph

My grandfather says he remembers he
    saw, when a youngster long ago,
On a bright May day, a strange old man,
    with a beard as white as snow,
Stand on the hill outside our town like a
    monument of woe,
And, striking his bare bald head the while,
    sob out the reason – so !

If I last as long as Methuselah I shall
    never forgive myself:
But – God forgive me, that I pray,
    unhappy Martin Relph,
As coward, coward I call him – him,
    yes, him! Away from me!
Get you behind the man I am now,
    you man that I used to be!

What can have sewed my mouth up,
    set me a-stare, all eyes, no tongue?
People have urged 'You visit a scare too
    hard on a lad so young!
You were taken aback, poor boy,' they
    urge, 'no time to regain your wits:
Besides it had maybe cost you life.' Ay,
    there is the cap which fits!

So, cap me, the coward, – thus! No
    fear! A cuff on the brow does
    good:
The feel of it hinders a worm inside
    which bores at the brain for food.
See now, there certainly seems excuse:
    for a moment, I trust, dear friends,
The fault was but folly, no fault of mine,
    or if mine, I have made amends!
For, every day that is first of May, on
    the hill-top, here stand I,
Martin Relph, and I strike my brow,
    and publish the reason why,

When there gathers a crowd to mock the
    fool. No fool, friends, since the bite
Of a worm inside is worse to bear: pray
    God I have baulked him quite!

I'll tell you. Certainly much excuse! It
    came of the way they cooped
Us peasantry up in a ring just here, close
    huddling because tight-hooped
By the red-coats round us villagers all:
    they meant we should see the sight
And take the example, – see, not speak,
    for speech was the Captain's right.

'You clowns on the slope, beware.' cried
    he: 'This woman about to die
Gives by her fate fair warning to such
    acquaintance as play the spy.
Henceforth who meddle with matters
    of state above them perhaps will
    learn
That peasants should stick to their
    plough-tail, leave to the King the
    King's concern.

'Here's a quarrel that sets the land on
    fire, between King George and his
    foes:
What call has a man of your kind –
    much less, a woman – to interpose?
Yet you needs must be meddling, folk
    like you, not foes – so much the
    worse!
The many and loyal should keep them-
    selves unmixed with the few
    perverse'

'Is the counsel hard to follow? I gave it
    you plainly a month ago,
And where was the good? The rebels
    have learned just all that they
    need to know.

Not a month since in we quietly
    marched: a week, and they had
    the news,
From a list complete of our rank and file
    to a note of our caps and shoes.
'All about all we did and all we were
    doing and like to do!
Only, I catch a letter by luck, and
    capture who wrote it, too.
Some of you men look black enough,
    but the milk-white face demure
Betokens the finger foul with ink: 'tis a
    woman who writes, be sure!

'Is it "Dearie, how much I miss your
    mouth!" – good natural stuff, she
    pens?
Some sprinkle of that, for a blind, of
    course: with talk about cocks and
    hens,
How "robin has built on the apple-tree,
    and our creeper which came to
    grief
Through the frost, we feared, is twining
    afresh round casement in famous
    leaf"
'But all for a blind! She soon glides
    frank into "Horrid the place is
    grown
With Officers here and Privates there,
    no nook we may call our own:
And Farmer Giles has a tribe to house,
    and lodging will be to seek
For the second Company sure to come
    ('tis whispered) on Monday week."

'And so to the end of the chapter!
    There! The murder, you see, was
    out:
Easy to guess how the change of mind
    in the rebels was brought about!
Safe in the trap would they now lie
    snug, had treachery made no sign;
But treachery meets a just reward, no
    matter if fools malign!

'That traitors had played us false, was
    proved – sent news which fell so
    pat:
And the murder was out – this letter of
    love, the sender of this sent that!
'Tis an ugly job, though, all the same –
    a hateful, to have to deal
With a case of the kind, when a woman's
    in fault: we soldiers need nerves of
    steel!

'So, I gave her a chance, despatched
    posthaste a message to Vincent
    Parkes
Whom she wrote to; easy to find he
    was, since one of the King's own
    clerks,
Ay, kept by the King's own gold in the
    town close by where the rebels
    camp:
A sort of a lawyer, just the man to
    betray our sort – the scamp!
' "If her writing is simple and honest
    and only the lover-like stuff it
    looks,
And if you yourself are a loyalist, nor
    down in the rebels' books,
Come quick," said I, "and in person
    prove you are each of you clear of
    crime,
Or martial law must take its course:
    this day next week's the time!"

'Next week is now: does he come? Not
    he! Clean gone, our clerk, in a
    trice!
He has left his sweetheart here in the
    lurch: no need of a warning twice!
His own neck free, but his partner's
    fast in the noose still, here she
    stands
To pay for her fault. 'Tis an ugly job:
    but soldiers obey commands.

'And hearken wherefore I make a
    speech! Should any acquaintance
    share

The folly that led to the fault that is
    now to be punished, let fools
    beware!
Look black, if you please, but keep
    hands white: and, above all else,
    keep wives –
Or sweethearts or what they may be –
    from ink! Not a word now, on
    your lives!'

Black? but the Pit's own pitch was
    white to the Captain's face – the
    brute
With the bloated cheeks and the bulgy
    nose and the bloodshot eyes to
    suit!
He was muddled with wine, they say:
    more like, he was out of his wits
    with fear;
He had but a handful of men, that's
    true, – a riot might cost him dear.

And all that time stood Rosamund
    Page, with pinioned arms and face
Bandaged about, on the turf marked
    out for the party's firing-place.
I hope she was wholly with God: I hope
    'twas His angel stretched a hand
To steady her so, like the shape of stone
    you see in our church-aisle stand.

I hope there was no vain fancy pierced
    the bandage to vex her eyes,
No face within which she missed with-
    out, no questions and no replies –
'Why did you leave me to die?' – 'Because
    …' Oh, fiends, too soon you grin
At merely a moment of hell, like that –
    such heaven as hell ended in!

Let mine end too! He gave the word,
    up went the guns in a line.
Those heaped on the hill were blind as
    dumb, – for, of all eyes, only mine
Looked over the heads of the foremost
    rank.' some fell on their knees in
    prayer,

Some sank to the earth, but all shut
    eyes, with a sole exception there.

That was myself, who had stolen up
    last, had sidled behind the group:
I am highest of all on the hill-top, there
    stand fixed while the others stoop!
From head to foot in a serpent's twine
    am I tightened: *I* touch ground?
No more than a gibbet's rigid corpse
    which the fetters rust around!
Can I speak, can I breathe, can I burst
    – aught else but see, see, only see?
And see I do – for there comes in sight
    – a man, it sure must be! –
Who staggeringly, stumblingly rises, falls,
    rises, at random flings his weight
On and on, anyhow onward – a man
    that's mad he arrives too late!

Else why does he wave a something
    white high-flourished above his
    head?
Why does not he call, cry, – curse the
    fool! – why throw up his arms
    instead?
O take this fist in your own face, fool!
    Why does not yourself shout 'Stay!
Here's a man comes rushing, might
    and main, with something he's
    mad to say'?

And a minute, only a moment, to have
    hell-fire boil up in your brain,
And ere you can judge things right,
    choose heaven, – time's over,
    repentance vain!
They level: a volley, a smoke and the
    clearing of smoke: I see no more
Of the man smoke hid, nor his frantic
    arms, nor the something white he
    bore.
But stretched on the field, some half-
    mile off, is an object. Surely dumb,
Deaf, blind were we struck, that
    nobody heard, not one of us saw
    him come!

Has he fainted through fright? One may
    well believe! What is it he holds so
    fast?
Turn him over, examine the face! Heyday!
    What, Vincent Parkes at last?
Dead! dead as she, by the self-same
    shot: one bullet has ended both,
Her in the body and him in the soul.'
    They laugh at our plighted troth.
'Till death us do part'? Till death us do
    join past parting – that sounds like
Betrothal indeed! O Vincent Parkes,
    what need has my fist to strike?

I helped you: thus were you dead and
    wed: one bound, and your soul
    reached hers!
There is clenched in your hand the
    thing, signed, sealed, the paper
    which plain avers
She is innocent, innocent, plain as
    print, with the King's Arms broad
    engraved:
No one can hear, but if anyone high on
    the hill can see, she's saved!

And torn his garb and bloody his lips
    with heart-break – plain it grew
How the week's delay had been
    brought about: each guess at the
    end proved true.
It was hard to get at the folk in power:
    such waste of time! and then
Such pleading and praying, with, all the
    while, his lamb in the lions' den!

And at length when he wrung their
    pardon out, no end to the stupid
    forms –
The licence and leave: I make no doubt
    – what wonder if passion warms
The pulse in a man if you play with his
    heart? – he was something hasty
    in speech;
Anyhow, none would quicken the
    work: he had to beseech, beseech!

And the thing once signed, sealed, safe
    in his grasp, – what followed but
    fresh delays?
For the floods were out, he was forced
    to take such a roundabout of ways!
And 'twas 'Halt there!' at every turn of
    the road, since he had to cross the
    thick
Of the red-coats: what did they care for
    him and his 'Quick, for God's
    sake, quick!'

Horse? but he had one: had it how
    long? till the first knave smirked
    'You brag
Yourself a friend of the King's? then lend
    to a King's friend here your nag!'
Money to buy another? Why, piece by
    piece they plundered him still,
With their 'Wait you must, – no help:
    if aught can help you, a guinea
    will!'
And a borough there was – I forget the
    name – whose Mayor must have
    the bench
Of Justices ranged to clear a doubt: for
    'Vincent,' thinks he, sounds French!
It well may have driven him daft, God
    knows! all man can certainly know
Is – rushing and falling and rising, at
    last he arrived in a horror – so!

When a word, cry, gasp, would have
    rescued both! Ay bite me! The worm
    begins
At his work once more. Had cowardice
    proved – that only – my sin of sins!
Friends, look you here! Suppose …
    suppose … But mad I am, needs
    must be!
Judas the Damned would never have
    dared such a sin as I dream! For,
    see!

Suppose I had sneakingly loved her
    myself, my wretched self, and
    dreamed

In the heart of me 'She were better
    dead than happy and his!' – while
    gleamed
A light from hell as I spied the pair in a
    perfectest embrace,
He the saviour and she the saved, –
    bliss born of the very murder-place!

No! Say I was scared, friends! Call me
    fool and coward, but nothing
    worse!
Jeer at the fool and gibe at the coward!
    'Twas ever the coward's curse
That fear breeds fancies in such: such
    take their shadow for substance
    still,
– A fiend at their back. I liked poor
    Parkes, – loved Vincent, if you will!

And her – why, I said 'Good morrow'
    to her, 'Good even,' and nothing
    more:
The neighbourly way! She was just to
    me as fifty had been before.
So, coward it is and coward shall be!
    There's a friend, now! Thanks! A
    drink
Of water I wanted: and now I can
    walk, get home by myself, I think.

## Pheidippides

Χαίρετε, νικῶμεν

First I salute this soil of the blessed,
    river and rock!
Gods of my birthplace, dæmons and
    heroes, honour to all!
Then I name thee, claim thee for our
    patron, co-equal in praise
– Ay, with Zeus the Defender, with Her
    of the ægis and spear!
Also, ye of the bow and the buskin,
    praised be your peer,
Now, henceforth and forever, – O
    latest to whom I upraise
Hand and heart and voice! For Athens,
    leave pasture and flock!

Present to help, potent to save, Pan –
    patron I call!

Archons of Athens, topped by the
    tettix, see, I return!
See, 'tis myself here standing alive, no
    spectre that speaks!
Crowned with the myrtle, did you
    command me, Athens and you,
'Run, Pheidippides, run and race,
    reach Sparta for aid!
Persia has come, we are here, where is
    She?' Your command I obeyed,
Ran and raced: like stubble, some field
    which a fire runs through,
Was the space between city and city:
    two days, two nights did I burn
Over the hills, under the dales, down
    pits and up peaks.

Into their midst I broke: breath served
    but for 'Persia has come!
Persia bids Athens proffer slaves'-
    tribute, water and earth;
Razed to the ground is Eretria – but
    Athens, shall Athens sink,
Drop into dust and die – the flower of
    Hellas utterly die,
Die, with the wide world spitting at
    Sparta, the stupid, the stander-by?
Answer me quick, what help, what
    hand do you stretch o'er
    destruction's brink?
How, – when? No care for my limbs! –
    there's lightning in all and some –
Fresh and fit your message to bear,
    once lips give it birth!'

O my Athens – Sparta love thee? Did
    Sparta respond?
Every face of her leered in a furrow of
    envy, mistrust,
Malice, – each eye of her gave me its
    glitter of gratified hate!
Gravely they turned to take counsel, to
    cast for excuses. I stood

Quivering, – the limbs of me fretting as
     fire frets, an inch from dry wood:
'Persia has come, Athens asks aid, and
     still they debate?
Thunder, thou Zeus! Athené, are
     Spartans a quarry beyond
Swing of thy spear? Phoibos and
     Artemis, clang them "Ye must"!'

No bolt launched from Olumpos! Lo,
     their answer at last!
'Has Persia come, – does Athens ask
     aid, – may Sparta befriend?
Nowise precipitate judgment – too
     weighty the issue at stake!
Count we no time lost time which lags
     through respect to the Gods!
Ponder that precept of old, "No
     warfare, whatever the odds
In your favour, so long as the moon,
     half-orbed, is unable to take
Full-circle her state in the sky!" Already
     she rounds to it fast:
Athens must wait, patient as we – who
     judgment suspend.'

Athens, – except for that sparkle, – thy
     name, I had mouldered to ash!
That sent a blaze through my blood;
     off, off and away was I back,
– Not one word to waste, one look to
     lose on the false and the vile!
Yet 'O Gods of my land!' I cried, as
     each hillock and plain,
Wood and stream, I knew, I named,
     rushing past them again,
'Have ye kept faith, proved mindful of
     honours we paid you erewhile?
Vain was the filleted victim, the
     fulsome libation! Too rash
Love in its choice, paid you so largely
     service so slack!

'Oak and olive and bay, – I bid you
     cease to enwreathe
Brows made bold by your leaf! Fade at
     the Persian's foot,

You that, our patrons were pledged,
     should never adorn a slave!
Rather I hail thee, Parnes, – trust to thy
     wild waste tract!
Treeless, herbless, lifeless mountain!
     What matter if slacked
My speed may hardly be, for homage
     to crag and to cave
No deity deigns to drape with verdure?
     – at least I can breathe,
Fear in thee no fraud from the blind,
     no lie from the mute!'

Such my cry as, rapid, I ran over Parnes'
     ridge;
Gully and gap I clambered and cleared
     till, sudden, a bar
Jutted, a stoppage of stone against me,
     blocking the way.
Right! for I minded the hollow to
     traverse, the fissure across:
'Where I could enter, there I depart by!
     Night in the fosse?
Athens to aid? Though the dive were
     through Erebos, thus I obey –
Out of the day dive, into the day as
     bravely arise! No bridge
Better!' – when – ha! what was it I
     came on, of wonders that are?

There, in the cool of a cleft, sat he –
     majestical Pan!
Ivy drooped wanton, kissed his head,
     moss cushioned his hoof:
All the great God was good in the eyes
     grave-kindly – the curl
Carved on the bearded cheek, amused
     at a mortal's awe,
As, under the human trunk, the goat-
     thighs grand I saw.
'Halt, Pheidippides!' – halt I did, my
     brain of a whirl:
'Hither to me! Why pale in my
     presence?' he gracious began:
'How is it, – Athens, only in Hellas,
     holds me aloof?

'Athens, she only, rears me no fane,
    makes me no feast!
Wherefore? Than I what godship to
    Athens more helpful of old?
Ay, and still, and forever her friend!
    Test Pan, trust me!
Go, bid Athens take heart, laugh Persia
    to scorn, have faith
In the temples and tombs! Go, say to
    Athens, "The Goat-God saith:
When Persia – so much as strews not
    the soil – is cast in the sea,
Then praise Pan who fought in the
    ranks with your most and least,
Goat-thigh to greaved-thigh, made one
    cause with the free and the bold!"

'Say Pan saith: "Let this, foreshowing
    the place, be the pledge!"
(Gay, the liberal hand held out this
    herbage I bear
– Fennel – I grasped it a-tremble with
    dew – whatever it bode)
'While, as for thee …' But enough! He
    was gone. If I ran hitherto –
Be sure that, the rest of my journey, I
    ran no longer, but flew.
Parnes to Athens – earth no more, the
    air was my road:
Here am I back. Praise Pan, we stand
    no more on the razor's edge!
Pan for Athens, Pan for me! I too have
    a guerdon rare!

\*      \*      \*

Then spoke Miltiades. 'And thee, best
    runner of Greece,
Whose limbs did duty indeed, – what
    gift is promised thyself?
Tell it us straightway, – Athens the
    mother demands of her son!'
Rosily blushed the youth: he paused:
    but, lifting at length
His eyes from the ground, it seemed as
    he gathered the rest of his strength
Into the utterance – 'Pan spoke thus:
    "For what thou hast done

Count on a worthy reward! Henceforth
    be allowed thee release
From the racer's toil, no vulgar reward
    in praise or in pelf!"
'I am bold to believe, Pan means
    reward the most to my mind!
Fight I shall, with our foremost,
    wherever this fennel may grow, –
Pound – Pan helping us – Persia to
    dust, and, under the deep,
Whelm her away for ever; and then, –
    no Athens to save, –
Marry a certain maid, I know keeps
    faith to the brave, –
Hie to my house and home: and, when
    my children shall creep
Close to my knees, – recount how the
    God was awful yet kind,
Promised their sire reward to the full –
    rewarding him – so!'

\*      \*      \*

Unforeseeing one! Yes, he fought on
    the Marathon day:
So, when Persia was dust, all cried 'To
    Akropolis!
Run, Pheidippides, one race more! the
    meed is thy due!
"Athens is saved, thank Pan," go
    shout!' He flung down his shield,
Ran like fire once more: and the space
    'twixt the Fennel-field
And Athens was stubble again, a field
    which a fire runs through,
Till in he broke: 'Rejoice, we conquer!'
    Like wine through clay,
Joy in his blood bursting his heart, he
    died – the bliss!

So, to this day, when friend meets
    friend, the word of salute
Is still 'Rejoice!' – his word which
    brought rejoicing indeed.
So is Pheidippides happy for ever, –
    the noble strong man
Who could race like a God, bear the
    face of a God, whom a God loved
    so well;

He saw the land saved he had helped
    to save, and was suffered to tell
Such tidings, yet never decline, but,
    gloriously as he began,
So to end gloriously – once to shout,
    thereafter be mute:
'Athens is saved!' – Pheidippides dies
    in the shout for his meed.

## Halbert and Hob

Here is a thing that happened. Like
    wild beasts whelped, for den,
In a wild part of North England, there
    lived once two wild men
Inhabiting one homestead, neither a
    hovel nor hut,
Time out of mind their birthright:
    father and son, these – but –
Such a son, such a father! Most
    wildness by degrees
Softens away: yet, last of their line, the
    wildest and worse were these.
Criminals, then? Why, no: they did not
    murder and rob;
But, give them a word, they returned a
    blow – old Halbert as young Hob:
Harsh and fierce of word, rough and
    savage of deed,
Hated or feared the more – who knows?
    – the genuine wild-beast breed.
Thus were they found by the few
    sparse folk of the country-side;
But how fared each with other? E'en
    beasts couch, hide by hide,
In a growling, grudged agreement: so,
    father and son aye curled
The closelier up in their den because
    the last of their kind in the world.

Still, beast irks beast on occasion. One
    Christmas night of snow,
Came father and son to words – such
    words! more cruel because the blow
To crown each word was wanting, while
    taunt matched gibe, and curse

Competed with oath in wager, like
    pastime in hell, – nay, worse:
For pastime turned to earnest, as up
    there sprang at last
The son at the throat of the father,
    seized him and held him fast.

'Out of this house you go!' – (there
    followed a hideous oath) –
'This oven where now we bake, too hot
    to hold us both!
If there's snow outside, there's coolness:
    out with you, bide a spell
In the drift and save the sexton the
    charge of a parish shell!'

Now, the old trunk was tough, was
    solid as stump of oak
Untouched at the core by a thousand
    years: much less had its seventy
    broke
One whipcord nerve in the muscly
    mass from neck to shoulder-blade
Of the mountainous man, whereon his
    child's rash hand like a feather
    weighed.

Nevertheless at once did the mammoth
    shut his eyes,
Drop chin to breast, drop hands to
    sides, stand stiffened – arms and
    thighs
All of a piece – struck mute, much as a
    sentry stands,
Patient to take the enemy's fire: his
    captain so commands.

Whereat the son's wrath flew to fury at
    such sheer scorn
Of his puny strength by the giant eld
    thus acting the babe new-born:
And 'Neither will this turn serve!' yelled
    he. 'Out with you! Trundle, log!
If you cannot tramp and trudge like a
    man, try all-fours like a dog!'
Still the old man stood mute. so, log-
    wise, – down to floor

Pulled from his fireside place, dragged
    on from hearth to door, –
Was he pushed, a very log, staircase
    along, until
A certain turn in the steps was reached,
    a yard from the house-door-sill.

Then the father opened eyes – each
    spark of their rage extinct, –
Temples, late black, dead-blanched, –
    right-hand with left-hand linked, –
He faced his son submissive; when
    slow the accents came,
They were strangely mild though his
    son's rash hand on his neck lay all
    the same.

'Hob, on just such a night of a Christmas
    long ago,
For such a cause, with such a gesture,
    did I drag – so –
My father down thus far: but, softening
    here, I heard
A voice in my heart, and stopped: you
    wait for an outer word.

'For your own sake, not mine, soften
    you too! Untrod
Leave this last step we reach, nor brave
    the finger of God!
I dared not pass its lifting: I did well. I
    nor blame
Nor praise you. I stopped here: and,
    Hob, do you the same!'
Straightway the son relaxed his hold of
    the father's throat.
They mounted, side by side, to the
    room again: no note
Took either of each, no sign made each
    to either: last
As first, in absolute silence, their
    Christmas-night they passed.

At dawn, the father sate on, dead, in
    the self-same place,
With an outburst blackening still the
    old bad fighting-face;

But the son crouched all a-tremble like
    any lamb new-yeaned.

When he went to the burial,
    someone's staff he borrowed –
    tottered and leaned.
But his lips were loose, not locked, –
    kept muttering, mumbling. 'There!
At his cursing and swearing!' the
    youngsters cried: but the elders
    thought 'In prayer.'
A boy threw stones: he picked them up
    and stored them in his vest.
So tottered, muttered, mumbled he, till
    he died, perhaps found rest.
'Is there a reason in nature for these
    hard hearts?' O Lear,
That a reason out of nature must turn
    them soft, seems clear!

## Ivàn Ivànovitch

'They tell me, your carpenters,' quoth I
    to my friend the Russ,
'Make a simple hatchet serve as a tool-
    box serves with us.
Arm but each man with his axe, 'tis a
    hammer and saw and plane
And chisel, and – what know I else?
    We should imitate in vain
The mastery wherewithal, by a flourish
    of just the adze,
He cleaves, clamps, dovetails in, – no
    need of our nails and brads, –
The manageable pine: 'tis said he
    could shave himself
With the axe, – so all adroit, now a
    giant and now an elf,
Does he work and play at once!'
    Quoth my friend the Russ to me,
'Ay, that and more beside on occasion!
    It scarce may be
You never heard tell a tale told
    children, time out of mind,
By father and mother and nurse, for a
    moral that's behind,

Which children quickly seize. If the
    incident happened at all,
We place it in Peter's time when hearts
    were great not small,
Germanized, Frenchified. I wager 'tis
    old to you
As the story of Adam and Eve, and
    possibly quite as true.

*    *    *

In the deep of our land, 'tis said, a
    village from out the woos
Emerged on the great main-road 'twixt
    two great solitudes.'
Through forestry right and left, black
    verst and verst of pine,
From village to village runs the road's
    long wide bare line.
Clearance and clearance break the else-
    unconquered growth
Of pine and all that breeds and broods
    there, leaving loth
Man's inch of masterdom, – spot of
    life, spirt of fire, –
To star the dark and dread, lest right
    and rule expire
Throughout the monstrous wild, a-
    hungered to resume
Its ancient sway, suck back the world
    into its womb:
Defrauded by man's craft which clove
    from North to South
This highway broad and straight e'en
    from the Neva's mouth
To Moscow's gates of gold'so. spot of
    life and spirt
Of fire aforesaid, burn, each village
    death-begirt
By wall and wall of pine – unprobed
    undreamed abyss.

Early one winter morn, in such a
    village as this.
Snow-whitened everywhere except the
    middle road
Ice-roughed by track of sledge, there
    worked by his abode

Ivàn Ivànovitch, the carpenter,
    employed
On a huge shipmast trunk; his axe
    now trimmed and toyed
With branch and twig, and now some
    chop athwart the bole
Changed bole to billets, bared at once
    the sap and soul.
About him, watched the work his
    neighbours sheepskin-clad;
Each bearded mouth puffed steam,
    each grey eye twinkled glad
To see the sturdy arm which, never
    stopping play,
Proved strong man's blood still boils,
    freeze winter as he may.
Sudden, a burst of bells. Out of the
    road, on edge
Of the hamlet – horse's hoofs
    galloping. 'How, a sledge?
What's here?' cried all as – in, up to
    the open space,
Workyard and market-ground, folk's
    common meeting-place, –
Stumbled on, till he fell, in one last
    bound for life,
A horse: and, at his heels, a sledge held
    – 'Dmìtri's wife!
Back without Dmìtri too! and children
    – where are they?
Only a frozen corpse!'
               They drew it forth:
    then – 'Nay,
Not dead, though like to die! Gone
    hence a month ago:
Home again, this rough jaunt – alone
    through night and snow –
What can the cause be? Hark – Droug,
    old horse, how he groans:
His day's done! Chafe away, keep
    chafing, for she moans:
She's coming to! Give here: see,
    mother-kin, your friends!
Cheer up, all safe at home! Warm
    inside makes amends
For outside cold, – sup quick! Don't
    look as we were bears!

What is it startles you? What strange
    adventure stares
Up at us in your face? You know
    friends – which is which?
I'm Vàssili, he's Sergeì, Ivàn
    Ivànovitch … '

At the word, the woman's eyes, slow-
    wandering till they neared
The blue eyes o'er the bush of honey-
    coloured beard,
Took in full light and sense and – torn
    to rags, some dream
Which hid the naked truth – O loud
    and long the scream
She gave, as if all power of voice within
    her throat
Poured itself wild away to waste in one
    dread note!
Then followed gasps and sobs, and
    then the steady flow
Of kindly tears: the brain was saved, a
    man might know.
Down fell her face upon the good
    friend's propping knee;
His broad hands smoothed her head,
    as fain to brush it free
From fancies, swarms that stung like
    bees unhived. He soothed –
'Loukèria, Loùscha!' – still he,
    fondling, smoothed and
    smoothed'
At last her lips formed speech.
              'Ivàn, dear
    – you indeed!
You, just the same dear you! While I
    … O intercede,
Sweet Mother, with thy Son Almighty –
    let his might
Bring yesterday once more, undo all
    done last night!
But this time yesterday, Ivàn, I sat like
    you,
A child on either knee, and, dearer
    than the two,
A babe inside my arms, close to my
    heart – that's lost

In morsels o'er the snow! Father, Son,
    Holy Ghost,
Cannot you bring again my blessed
    yesterday?'

When no more tears would flow, she
    told her tale: this way.
'Maybe, a month ago, – was it not? –
    news came here,
They wanted, deeper down, good
    workmen fit to rear
A church and roof it in. "We'll go," my
    husband said:
"None understands like me to melt
    and mould their lead."
So, friends here helped us off – Ivàn,
    dear, you the first!
How gay we jingled forth, all five – (my
    heart will burst) –
While Dmìtri shook the reins, urged
    Droug upon his track!
'Well, soon the month ran out, we just
    were coming back,
When yesterday – behold, the village
    was on fire!
Fire ran from house to house. What
    help, as, nigh and nigher,
The flames came furious? "Haste,"
    cried Dmitri, "men must do
The little good man may: to sledge and
    in with you,
You and our three! We check the fire
    by laying flat
Each building in its path, – I needs
    must stay for that, –
But you … no time for talk! Wrap
    round you every rug,
Cover the couple close, – you'll have
    the babe to hug.
No care to guide old Droug, he knows
    his way, by guess,
Once start him on the road: but
    chirrup, none the less!
The snow lies glib as glass and hard as
    steel, and soon
You'll have rise, fine and full, a marvel
    of a moon.

Hold straight up, all the same, this
   lighted twist of pitch!
Once home and with our friend Ivàn
   Ivànovitch,
All's safe: I have my pay in pouch, all's
   right with me,
So I but find as safe you and our
   precious three!
Off, Droug!" – because the flames had
   reached us, and the men
Shouted "But lend a hand, Dmìtri – as
   good as ten!"

'so, in we bundled – I, and those God
   gave me once;
Old Droug, that's stiff at first, seemed
   youthful for the nonce:
He understood the case, galloping
   straight ahead.
Out came the moon: my twist soon
   dwindled, feebly red
In that unnatural day – yes, daylight,
   bred between
Moon-light and snow-light, lamped
   those grotto-depths which screen
Such devils from God's eye. Ah, pines,
   how straight you grow
Nor bend one pitying branch, true
   breed of brutal snow!
Some undergrowth had served to keep
   the devils blind
While we escaped outside their border!
         'Was that – wind?
Anyhow, Droug starts, stops, back go
   his ears, he snuffs,
Snorts, – never such a snort! then
   plunges, knows the sough's
Only the wind: yet, no – our breath
   goes up too straight!
Still the low sound, – less low, loud,
   louder, at a rate
There's no mistaking more! Shall I lean
   out – look – learn
The truth whatever it be? Pad, pad! At
   last, I turn –

' 'Tis the regular pad of the wolves in
   pursuit of the life in the sledge!
An army they are: close-packed they
   press like the thrust of a wedge:
They increase as they hunt: for I see,
   through the pine-trunks ranged
   each side,
Slip forth new fiend and fiend, make
   wider and still more wide
The four-footed steady advance. The
   foremost – none may pass:
They are elders and lead the line, eye
   and eye – green-glowing brass!
But a long way distant still. Droug, save
   us! He does his best:
Yet they gain on us, gain, till they
   reach, – one reaches … How utter
   the rest?
O that Satan-faced first of the band!
   How he lolls out the length of his
   tongue,
How he laughs and lets gleam his
   white teeth! He is on me, his paws
   pry among
The wraps and the rugs! O my pair, my
   twin-pigeons, lie still and seem
   dead!
Stepàn, he shall never have you for a
   meal, – here's your mother instead!
No, he will not be counselled – must
   cry, poor Stiòpka, so foolish!
   though first
Of my boy-brood, he was not the best:
   nay, neighbours have called him
   the worst:
He was puny, an undersized slip, – a
   darling to me, all the same!
But little there was to be praised in the
   boy, and a plenty to blame.
I loved him with heart and soul, yes –
   but, deal him a blow for a fault,
He would sulk for whole days. "Foolish
   boy! lie still or the villain will vault,
Will snatch you from over my head!"
      No use! he cries, screams, – who
      can hold

Fast a boy in a frenzy of fear! It follows
    – as I foretold!
The Satan-face snatched and snapped:
    I tugged, I tore – and then
His brother too needs must shriek! If
    one must go, 'tis men
The Tsar needs, so we hear, not ailing
    boys! Perhaps
My hands relaxed their grasp, got
    tangled in the wraps:
God, he was gone! I looked: there
    tumbled the cursed crew,
Each fighting for a share: too busy to
    pursue!
That's so far gain at least: Droug,
    gallop another verst,
Or two, or three – God sends we beat
    them, arrive the first!
A mother who boasts two boys was
    ever accounted rich:
Some have not a boy: some have, but
    lose him, – God knows which
Is worse: how pitiful to see your
    weakling pine
And pale and pass away! Strong brats,
    this pair of mine!

'O misery! for while I settle to what
    near seems
Content, I am 'ware again of the tramp,
    and again there gleams –
Point and point – the line, eyes,
    levelled green brassy fire!
So soon is resumed your chase? Will
    nothing appease, nought tire
The furies? And yet I think – I am
    certain the race is slack,
And the numbers are nothing like. Not
    a quarter of the pack!
Feasters and those full-fed are staying
    behind … Ah why?
We'll sorrow for that too soon! Now, –
    gallop, reach home, and die,
Nor ever again leave house, to trust our
    life in the trap
For life – we call a sledge! Teriòscha, in
    my lap!

Yes, I'll lie down upon you, tight-tie
    you with the strings
Here – of my heart! No fear, this time,
    your mother flings …
Flings? I flung? Never! but think! – a
    woman, after all
Contending with a wolf! Save you I
    must and shall,
Terentiì!
      'How now? What, you still
    head the race,
Your eyes and tongue and teeth crave
    fresh food, Satan-face?
There and there! Plain I struck green
    fire out! Flash again?
All a poor fist can do to damage eyes
    proves vain!
My fist – why not crunch that? He is
    wanton for … O God,
Why give this wolf his taste? Common
    wolves scrape and prod
The earth till out they scratch some
    corpse – mere putrid flesh!
Why must this glutton leave the faded,
    choose the fresh?
Terentiì – God, feel! – his neck keeps
    fast thy bag
Of holy things, saints' bones, this
    Satan-face will drag
Forth, and devour along with him, our
    Pope declared
The relics were to save from danger!
      'Spurned, not spared!
'Twas through my arms, crossed arms,
    he – nuzzling now with snout,
Now ripping, tooth and claw –
    plucked, pulled Terentiì out,
A prize indeed! I saw – how could I
    else but see? –
My precious one – I bit to hold back –
    pulled from me!
Up came the others, fell to dancing –
    did the imps! –
Skipped as they scampered round.
    There's one is grey, and limps:
Who knows but old bad Màrpha, – she
    always owed me spite

And envied me my births, – skulks out
of doors at night
And turns into a wolf, and joins the
sisterhood,
And laps the youthful life, then slinks
from out the wood,
Squats down at door by dawn, spins
there demure as erst
– No strength, old crone, – not she! –
to crawl forth half a verst!

'Well, I escaped with one: 'twixt one
and none there lies
The space 'twixt heaven and hell. And
see, a rose-light dyes
The endmost snow: 'tis dawn, 'tis day,
'tis safe at home!
We have outwitted you! Ay, monsters,
snarl and foam,
Fight each the other fiend, disputing
for a share, –
Forgetful, in your greed, our finest off
we bear,
Tough Droug and I, – my babe, my
boy that shall be man,
My man that shall be more, do all a
hunter can
To trace and follow and find and catch
and crucify
Wolves, wolfkins, all your crew! A
thousand deaths shall die
The whimperingest cub that ever
squeezed the teat!
"Take that!" we'll stab you with, – "the
tenderness we met
When, wretches, you danced round –
not this, thank God – not this!
Hellhounds, we baulk you!"

'But – Ah, God above! – Bliss, bliss –
Not the band, no! And yet – yes, for
Droug knows him! One –
This only of them all has said "She
saves a son!"
His fellows disbelieve such luck: but he
believes,

He lets them pick the bones, laugh at
him in their sleeves:
He's off and after us, – one speck, one
spot, one ball
Grows bigger, bound on bound, – one
wolf as good as all!
Oh but I know the trick! Have at the
snaky tongue!
That's the right way with wolves! Go,
tell your mates I wrung
The panting morsel out, left you to
howl your worst!
Now for it – now! Ah me! I know him
– thrice-accurst
Satan-face, – him to the end my foe!
                    'All fight's in vain:
This time the green brass points pierce
to my very brain.
I fall – fall as I ought – quite on the
babe I guard:
I overspread with flesh the whole of
him. Too hard
To die this way, torn piecemeal? Move
hence? Not I – one inch!
Gnaw through me, through and
through: flat thus I lie nor flinch!
O God, the feel of the fang furrowing
my shoulder! – see
It grinds – it grates the bone' O Kirill
under me,
Could I do more? Besides he knew
wolf's way to win:
I clung, closed round like wax: yet in
he wedged and in,
Past my neck, past my breasts, my
heart, until' … how feels
The onion-bulb your knife parts,
pushing through its peels,
Till out you scoop its clove wherein lie
stalk and leaf
And bloom and seed unborn?
                    'That slew me: yes, in brief,
I died then, dead I lay doubtlessly till
Droug stopped
Here, I suppose. I come to life, I find
me propped

Thus – how or when or why, – I know
    not. Tell me, friends,
All was a dream: laugh quick and say
    the nightmare ends!
Soon I shall find my house: 'tis over
    there: in proof,
Save for that chimney heaped with
    snow, you'd see the roof
Which holds my three – my two – my
    one – not one?
               'Life's mixed
With misery, yet we live – must live.
    The Satan fixed
His face on mine so fast, I took its
    print as pitch
Takes what it cools beneath. Ivàn
    Ivàno-vitch,
'Tis you unharden me, you thaw,
    disperse the thing!
Only keep looking kind, the horror will
    not cling.
Your face smooths fast away each print
    of Satan. Tears
– What good they do! Life's sweet, and
    all its after-years,
Ivàn Ivànovitch, I owe you! Yours am I!
May God reward you, dear!'
                    Down she sank.
    Solemnly
Ivàn rose, raised his axe, – for fitly, as
    she knelt,
Her head lay: well-apart, each side, her
    arms hung, – dealt
Lightning-swift thunder-strong one
    blow – no need of more!
Headless she knelt on still: that pine
    was sound at core
(Neighbours were used to say) – cast-
    ìron-kernelled – which
Taxed for a second stroke Ivàn Ivàno-
    vitch.

The man was scant of words as strokes.
    'It had to be:
I could no other: God it was bade "Act
    for me!" '
Then stooping, peering round – what

is it now he lacks?
A proper strip of bark wherewith to
    wipe his axe.
Which done, he turns, goes in, closes
    the door behind.
The others mute remain, watching the
    blood-snake wind
Into a hiding-place among the splinter-
    heaps.

At length, still mute, all move: one lifts,
    – from where it steeps
Redder each ruddy rag of pine, – the
    head: two more
Take up the dripping body: then, mute
    still as before,
Move in a sort of march, march on till
    marching ends
Opposite to die church; where halting,
    – who suspends,
By its long hair, the thing, deposits in
    its place
The piteous head: once more the body
    shows no trace
Of harm done: there lies whole the
    Loùscha, maid and wife
And mother, loved until this latest of
    her life.
Then all sit on the bank of snow which
    bounds a space
Kept free before the porch for
    judgment: just the place!
Presently all the souls, man, woman,
    child, which make
The village up, are found assembling
    for the sake
Of what is to be done. The very Jews
    are there:
A Gipsy-troop, though bound with
    horses for the Fair,
Squats with the rest. Each heart with
    its conception seethes
And simmers, but no tongue speaks:
    one may say, – none breathes.

Anon from out the church totters the
    Pope – the priest –

Hardly alive, so old, a hundred years at
    least.
With him, the Commune's head, a
    hoary senior too,
Stàrosta, that's his style, – like Equity
    Judge with you, –
Natural Jurisconsult: then, fenced
    about with furs,
Pomeschìk, – Lord of the Land, who
    wields- – and none demurs –
A power of life and death. They stoop,
    survey the corpse.

Then, straightened on his staff, the
    Stàrosta – the thorpe's
Sagaciousest old man – hears what you
    just have heard,
From Droug's first inrush, all, up to
    Ivàn's last word
'God bade me act for him: I dared not
    disobey!'

Silence – the Pomeschìk broke with 'A
    wild wrong way
Of righting wrong – if wrong there
    were, such wrath to rouse!
Why was not law observed? What
    article allows
Whoso may please to play the judge,
    and, judgment dealt,
Play executioner, as promptly as we
    pelt
To death, without appeal, the vermin
    whose sole fault
Has been – it dared to leave the
    darkness of its vault,
Intrude upon our day! Too sudden and
    too rash!
What was this woman's crime?
    Suppose the church should crash
Down where I stand, your lord: bound
    are my serfs to dare
Their utmost that I 'scape: yet, if the
    crashing scare
My children, – as you are, – if sons fly,
    one and all,

Leave father to his fate, – poor cowards
    though I call
The runaways, I pause before I claim
    their life
Because they prized it more than mine.
    I would each wife
Died for her husband's sake, each son
    to save his sire:
'Tis glory, I applaud – scarce duty, I
    require.
Ivàn Ivànovitch has done a deed that's
    named
Murder by law and me: who doubts,
    may speak unblamed!'

All turned to the old Pope. 'Ay,
    children, I am old –
How old, myself have got to know no
    longer. Rolled
Quite round, my orb of life, from
    infancy to age,
Seems passing back again to youth. A
    certain stage
At least I reach, or dream I reach,
    where I discern
Truer truths, laws behold more lawlike
    than we learn
When first we set our foot to tread the
    course I trod
With man to guide my steps: who
    leads me now is God.
"Your young men shall see visions:"
    and in my youth I saw
And paid obedience to man's visionary
    law:
"Your old men shall dream dreams:"
    and, in my age, a hand
Conducts me through the cloud round
    law to where I stand
Firm on its base, – know cause, who,
    before, knew effect.

'The world lies under me: and nowhere
    I detect
So great a gift as this – God's own – of
    human life'

"Shall the dead praise thee?" No! "The
    whole live world is rife,
God, with thy glory," rather! Life then,
    God's best of gifts,
For what shall man exchange? For life
    – when so he shifts
The weight and turns the scale, lets life
    for life restore
God's balance, sacrifice the less to gain
    the more,
Substitute – for low life, another's or
    his own –
Life large and liker God's who gave it:
    thus alone
May life extinguish life that life may
    trulier be!
How low this law descends on earth, is
    not for me
To trace: complexed becomes the
    simple, intricate
The plain, when I pursue law's windin.
    'Tis the straight
Outflow of law I know and name: to
    law, the fount
Fresh from God's footstool, friends,
    follow while I remount.

'A mother bears a child: perfection is
    complete
So far in such a birth. Enabled to
    repeat
The miracle of life, – herself was born
    so just
A type of womankind, that God sees fit
    to trust
Her with the holy task of giving life in
    turn.
Crowned by this crowning pride, –
    how say you, should she spurn
Regality – discrowned, unchilded, by
    her choice
Of barrenness exchanged for fruit
    which made rejoice
Creation, though life's self were lost in
    giving birth
To life more fresh and fit to glorify
    God's earth?

How say you, should the hand God
    trusted with life's torch
Kindled to light the world – aware of
    sparks that scorch,
Let fall the same? Forsooth, her flesh a
    fire-flake stings:
The mother drops the child! Among
    what monstrous things
Shall she be classed? Because of
    motherhood, each male
Yields to his partner place, sinks
    proudly in the scale:
His strength owned weakness, wit –
    folly, and courage – fear,
Beside the female proved male's
    mistress – only here.
The fox-dam, hunger-pined, will slay
    the felon sire
Who dares assault her whelp: the
    beaver, stretched on fire,
Will die without a groan: no pang
    avails to wrest
Her young from where they hide – her
    sanctuary breast.
What's here then? Answer me, thou
    dead one, as, I trow,
Standing at God's own bar, he bids
    thee answer now!
Thrice crowned wast thou – each
    crown of pride, a child – thy
    charge!
Where are they? Lost? Enough: no
    need that thou enlarge
On how or why the loss: life left to
    utter "lost"
Condemns itself beyond appeal. The
    soldier's post
Guards from the foe's attack the camp
    he sentinels:
That he no traitor proved, this and this
    only tells –
Over the corpse of him trod foe to foe's
    success.
Yet – one by one thy crowns torn from
    thee – thou no less
To scare the world, shame God, –
    livedst! I hold He saw

The unexampled sin, ordained the
    novel law,
Whereof first instrument was first
    intelligence
Found loyal here. I hold that, failing
    human sense,
The very earth had oped, sky fallen, to
    efface
Humanity's new wrong, motherhood's
    first disgrace.
Earth oped not, neither fell the sky, for
    prompt was found
A man and man enough, head-sober
    and heart-sound,
Ready to hear God's voice, resolute to
    obey.
Ivàn Ivànovitch, I hold, has done, this
    day,
No otherwise than did, in ages long
    ago,
Moses when he made known the
    purport of that flow
Of fire athwart the law's twain-tables! I
    proclaim
Ivàn Ivànovitch God's servant!'
                At which name
Uprose that creepy whisper from out
    the crowd, is wont
To swell and surge and sink when
    fellow-men confront
A punishment that falls on fellow flesh
    and blood,
Appallingly beheld – shudderingly
    understood,
No less, to be the right, the just, the
    merciful.
'God's servant!' hissed the crowd.
          When that Amen grew dull
And died away and left acquittal plain
    adjudged,
'Amen!' last sighed the lord. 'There's
    none shall say I grudged
Escape from punishment in such a
    novel case.
Deferring to old age and holy life, – be
    grace

Granted! say I. No less, scruples might
    shake a sense
Firmer than I boast mine. Law's law,
    and evidence
Of breach therein lies plain, – blood-
    red-bright, – all may see!
Yet all absolve the deed: absolved the
    deed must be!

'And next – as mercy rules the hour –
    methinks 'twere well
You signify forthwith its sentence, and
    dispel
The doubts and fears, I judge, which
    busy now the head
Law puts a halter round – a halo – you,
    instead!
Ivàn Ivànovitch – what think you he
    expects
Will follow from his feat? Go, tell him
    – law protects
Murder, for once: no need he longer
    keep behind
The Sacred Pictures – where skulks
    Innocence enshrined,
Or I missay! Go, some! You others,
    haste and hide
The dismal object there: get done,
    whate'er betide!'

So, while the youngers raised the
    corpse, the elders trooped
Silently to the house: where halting,
    someone stooped,
Listened beside the door; all there was
    silent too.
Then they held counsel; then pushed
    door and, passing through,
Stood in the murderer's presence'
               Ivàn Ivànovitch
Knelt, building on the floor that
    Kremlin rare and rich
He deftly cut and carved on lazy winter
    nights.
Some five young faces watched,
    breathlessly, as, to rights,

Piece upon piece, he reared the fabric
    nigh complete.
Stèscha, Ivàn's old mother, sat
    spinning by the heat
Of the oven where his wife Kàtia stood
    baking bread'
Ivàn's self, as he turned his honey-
    coloured head,
Was just in act to drop, 'twixt fir-
    cones, – each a dome, –
The scooped-out yellow gourd
    presumably the home
Of Kolokol the Big: the bell, therein to
    hitch,
– An acorn-cup – was ready: Ivàn
    Ivànovitch
Turned with it in his mouth.
            They told him he was free
As air to walk abroad. 'How otherwise?'
    asked he.

## Tray

Sing me a hero! Quench my thirst
Of soul, ye bards!
            Quoth Bard the first:
'Sir Olaf, the good knight, did don
His helm and eke his habergeon … '
Sir Olaf and his bard – !
'That sin-scathed brow' (quoth Bard
    the second)
'That eye wide ope as though Fate
    beckoned
My hero to some steep, beneath
Which precipice smiled tempting
    death … '
You too without your host have
    reckoned!

'A beggar-child' (let's hear this third!)
'Sat on a quay's edge: like a bird
Sang to herself at careless play,
And fell into the stream. "Dismay!
Help, you the standers-by!" None
    stirred.

'Bystanders reason, think of wives
And children ere they risk their lives.
Over the balustrade has bounced
A mere instinctive dog, and pounced
Plumb on the prize. "How well he dives!

' "Up he comes with the child, see,
    tight
In mouth, alive too, clutched from quite
A depth of ten feet – twelve, I bet!
Good dog! What, off again? There's yet
Another child to save? All right!

' "How strange we saw no other fall!
It's instinct in the animal.
Good dog! But he's a long while under:
If he got drowned I should not
    wonder –
Strong current, that against the wall!

' "Here he comes, holds in mouth this
    time
– What may the thing be? Well, that's
    prime!
Now, did you ever? Reason reigns
In man alone, since all Tray's pains
Have fished – the child's doll from the
    slime!"

'And so, amid the laughter gay,
Trotted my hero off, – old Tray, –
Till somebody, prerogatived
With reason, reasoned: "Why he dived,
His brain would show us, I should say.

' "John, go and catch – or, if needs be,
Purchase – that animal for me!
By vivisection, at expense
Of half-an-hour and eighteenpence,
How brain secretes dog's soul, we'll
    see!" '

## Ned Bratts

'Twas Bedford Special Assize, one daft
    Midsummer's Day:
A broiling blasting June, – was never its
    like, men say.
Corn stood sheaf-ripe already, and
    trees looked yellow as that;
Ponds drained dust-dry, the cattle lay
    foaming around each flat.
Inside town, dogs went mad, and folk
    kept bibbing beer
While the parsons prayed for rain.
        'Twas horrible, yes – but queer:
Queer – for the sun laughed gay, yet
    nobody moved a hand
To work one stroke at his trade: as
    given to understand
That all was come to a stop, work and
    such worldly ways,
And the world's old self about to end
    in a merry blaze.
Midsummer's Day moreover was the
    first of Bedford Fair,
With Bedford Town's tag-rag and
    bobtail a-bowsing there.

But the Court House, Quality
    crammed: through doors ope,
    windows wide,
High on the Bench you saw sit
    Lordships side by side.
There frowned Chief Justice Jukes,
    fumed learned Brother Small,
And fretted their fellow Judge: like
    threshers, one and all,
Of a reek with laying down the law in a
    furnace. Why?
Because their lungs breathed flame –
    the regular crowd forbye –
From gentry pouring in – quite a
    nosegay, to be sure!
How else could they pass the time, six
    mortal hours endure
Till night should extinguish day, when
    matters might haply mend?

Meanwhile no bad resource was –
    watching begin and end
Some trial for life and death, in a brisk
    five minutes'space,
And betting which knave would 'scape,
    which hang, from his sort of face.

So, their Lordships toiled and moiled,
    and a deal of work was done
(I warrant) to justify the mirth of the
    crazy sun
As this and t'other lout, struck dumb
    at the sudden show
Of red robes and white wigs, boggled
    nor answered 'Boh!'
When asked why he, Tom Styles,
    should not – because Jack Nokes
Had stolen the horse – be hanged: for
    Judges must have their jokes,
And louts must make allowance – let's
    say, for some blue fly
Which punctured a dewy scalp where
    the frizzles stuck awry –
Else Tom had fleered scot-free, so
    nearly over and done
Was the main of the job. Full-measure,
    the gentles enjoyed their fun,
As a twenty-five were tried, rank
    puritans caught at prayer
In a cow-house and laid by the heels, –
    have at 'em, devil may care! –
And ten were prescribed the whip, and
    ten a brand on the cheek,
And five a slit of the nose – just leaving
    enough to tweak.

Well, things at jolly high-tide,
    amusement steeped in fire.
While noon smote fierce the roof's red
    tiles to heart's desire,
The Court a-simmer with smoke, one
    ferment of oozy flesh,
One spirituous humming musk
    mount-mounting until its mesh
Entoiled all heads in a fluster, and
    Serjeant Postlethwayte

– Dashing the wig oblique as he
    mopped his oily pate –
Cried 'Silence, or I grow grease! No
    loophole lets in air?
Jurymen, – Guilty, Death! Gainsay me
    if you dare!'
– Things at this pitch, I say, – what
    hubbub without the doors?
What laughs, shrieks, hoots and yells,
    what rudest of uproars?

Bounce through the barrier throng a
    bulk comes rolling vast!
Thumps, kicks, – no manner of use! –
    spite of them rolls at last
Into the midst a ball which, bursting,
    brings to view
Publican Black Ned Bratts and Tabby
    his big wife too:
Both in a muck-sweat, both … were
    never such eyes uplift
At the sight of yawning hell, such
    nostrils – snouts that sniffed
Sulphur, such mouths a-gape ready to
    swallow flame!
Horrified, hideous, frank fiend-faces!
    yet, all the same,
Mixed with a certain … eh? how shall I
    dare style – mirth
Che desperate grin of the guess that,
    could they break from earth,
Heaven was above, and hell might rage
    in impotence
Below the saved, the saved!
        'Confound you! (no offence!)
Out of our way, – push, wife! Yonder
    their Worships be!'
Ned Bratts has reached the bar, and
    'Hey, my Lords,' roars he,
'A Jury of life and death, Judges the
    prime of the land,
Constables, javelineers, – all met, if I
    understand,
'To decide so knotty a point as
    whether 'twas Jack or Joan
Robbed the henroost, pinched the pig,
    hit the King's Arms with a stone.

Dropped the baby down the well, left
    the tithesman in the lurch,
Or, three whole Sundays running, not
    once attended church!
What a pother – do these deserve the
    parish-stocks or whip,
More or less brow to brand, much or
    little nose to snip, –
When, in our Public, plain stand we –
    that's we stand here,
I and my Tab, brass-bold, brick-built of
    beef and beer,
– Do not we, slut? Step forth and show
    your beauty, jade!
Wife of my bosom – that's the word
    now! What a trade
We drove! None said us nay: nobody
    loved his life
So little as wag a tongue against us, –
    did they, wife?
Yet they knew us all the while, in their
    hearts, for what we are
– Worst couple, rogue and quean,
    unhanged – search near and far!
Eh, Tab? The pedlar, now – o'er his
    noggin – who warned a mate
To cut and run, nor risk his pack
    where its loss of weight
Was the least to dread, – aha, how we
    two laughed a-good
As, stealing round the midden, he
    came on where I stood
With billet poised and raised, – you,
    ready with the rope, –
Ah, but that's past, that's sin repented
    of, we hope!
Men knew us for that same, yet safe
    and sound stood we!
The lily-livered knaves knew too (I've
    baulked a d—)
Our keeping the "Pied Bull" was just a
    mere pretence:
Too slow the pounds make food, drink,
    lodging, from out the pence!
There's not a stoppage to travel has
    chanced, this ten long year,

No break into hall or grange, no lifting
of nag or steer,
Not a single roguery, from the clipping
of a purse
To the cutting of a throat, but paid us
toll. Od's curse!
When Gipsy Smouch made bold to
cheat us of our due,
– Eh, Tab? the Squire's strong-box we
helped the rascal to –
I think he pulled a face, next
Sessions'swinging-time!
He danced the jig that needs no floor,
– and, here's the prime,
'Twas Scroggs that houghed the mare!
Ay, those were busy days!
'Well, there we flourished brave, like
scripture-trees called bays,
Faring high, drinking hard, in money
up to head
– Not to say, boots and shoes, when …
Zounds, I nearly said –
Lord, to unlearn one's language! How
shall we labour, wife?
Have you, fast hold, the Book? Grasp,
grip it, for your life!
See, sirs, here's life, salvation! Here's –
hold but out my breath –
When did I speak so long without once
swearing? 'Sdeath,
No, nor unhelped by ale since man
and boy! And yet
All yesterday I had to keep my whistle
wet
While reading Tab this Book: book?
don't say "book" – they're plays.
Songs, ballads and the like: here's no
such strawy blaze,
But sky wide ope, sun, moon, and
seven stars out full-flare!
Tab, help and tell! I'm hoarse. A mug
or – no, a prayer!
Dip for one out of the Book! Who
wrote it in the Jail
– He plied his pen unhelped by beer,
sirs, I'll be bail!

'I've got my second wind. In trundles
she – that's Tab.
"Why, Gammer, what's come now,
that – bobbing like a crab
On Yule-tide bowl – your head's a-work
and both your eyes
Break loose? Afeard, you fool? As if the
dead can rise!
Say – Bagman Dick was found last May
with fuddling-cap
Stuffed in his mouth: to choke's a natural
mishap!"
"Gaffer, be – blessed," cries she, "and
Bagman Dick as well!
I, you, and he are damned: this Public
is our hell:
We live in fire: live coals don't feel! –
once quenched, they learn –
Cinders do, to what dust they moulder
while they burn!"

' "If you don't speak straight out," says
I – belike I swore –
"A knobstick, well you know the taste
of, shall, once more,
Teach you to talk, my maid!" she ups
with such a face,
Heart sunk inside me. "Well, pad on,
my prate-apace!"

' "I've been about those laces we need
for … never mind!
If henceforth they tie hands, 'tis mine
they'll have to bind.
You know who makes them best – the
Tinker in our cage,
Pulled-up for gospelling, twelve years
ago: no age
To try another trade, – yet, so he
scorned to take
Money he did not earn, he taught
himself the make
Of laces, tagged and tough – Dick
Bagman found them so!
Good customers were we! Well, last
week, you must know

His girl, – the blind young chit, who
    hawks about his wares, –
She takes it in her head to come no
    more – such airs
These hussies have! Yet, since we need
    a stoutish lace, –
'I'll to the jail-bird father, abuse her to
    his face!'
So, first I filled a jug to give me heart,
    and then,
Primed to the proper pitch, I posted to
    their den –
*Patmore* – they style their prison! I tip
    the turnkey, catch
My heart up, fix my face, and fearless
    lift the latch –
Both arms a-kimbo, in bounce with a
    good round oath
Ready for rapping out: no 'Lawks' nor
    'By my troth!'

' "There sat my man, the father. He
    looked up: what one feels
When heart that leapt to mouth drops
    down again to heels!
He raised his hand … Hast seen, when
    drinking out the night,
And in, the day, earth grow another
    something quite
Under the sun's first stare? I stood a
    very stone'

' " 'Woman!' (a fiery tear he put in
    every tone),
'How should my child frequent your
    house where lust is sport,
Violence – trade? Too true! I trust no
    vague report.
Her angel's hand, which stops the sight
    of sin, leaves clear
The other gate of sense, lets outrage
    through the ear.
What has she heard! – which, heard
    shall never be again.
Better lack food than feast, a Dives in
    the – wain

Or reign or train – of Charles!' (His
    language was not ours:
'Tis my belief, God spoke: no tinker
    has such powers.)
'Bread, only bread they bring – my
    laces: if we broke
Your lump of leavened sin, the loaf's
    first crumb would choke!'

' "Down on my marrow-bones! Then
    all at once rose he:
His brown hair burst a-spread, his eyes
    were suns to see:
Up went his hands: 'Through flesh, I
    reach, I read thy soul!
So may some stricken tree look
    blasted, bough and bole,
Champed by the fire-tooth, charred
    without, and yet, thrice-bound
With dreriment about, within may life
    be found,
A prisoned power to branch and
    blossom as before,
Could but the gardener cleave the
    cloister, reach the core,
Loosen the vital sap: yet where shall
    help be found?
Who says "How save it?" – nor "Why
    cumbers it the ground?"
Woman, that tree art thou! All
    sloughed about with scurf,
Thy stag-horns fright the sky, thy
    snake-roots sting the turf!
Drunkenness, wantonness, theft,
    murder gnash and gnarl
Thine outward, case thy soul with
    coating like the marle
Satan stamps flat upon each head
    beneath his hoof!
And how deliver such? The strong men
    keep aloof,
Lover and friend stand far, the
    mocking ones pass by,
Tophet gapes wide for prey: lost soul,
    despair and die!
What then? "Look unto me and be ye
    saved!" saith God:

"I strike the rock, outstreats the life-
stream at my rod!
Be your sins scarlet, wool shall they
seem like, – although
As crimson red, yet turn white as the
driven snow!" '

' "There, there, there! All I seem to
somehow understand
Is – that, if I reached home, 'twas
through the guiding hand
Of his blind girl which led and led me
through the streets
And out of town and up to door again.
What greets
First thing my eye, as limbs recover
from their swoon?
A book – this Book she gave at parting.
'Father's boon –
The Book he wrote: it reads as if he
spoke himself:
He cannot preach in bonds, so, – take
it down from shelf
When you want counsel, – think you
hear his very voice!'

' "Wicked dear Husband, first despair
and then rejoice!
Dear wicked Husband, waste no tick of
moment more,
Be saved like me, bald trunk! There's
greenness yet at core,
Sap under slough! Read, read!"
                    'Let me take
breath, my lords!
I'd like to know, are these – hers,
mine, or Bunyan's words?
I'm 'wildered – scarce with drink, –
nowise with drink alone!
You'll say, with heat: but heat's no
stuff to split a stone
Like this black boulder – this flint
heart of mine: the Book –
That dealt the crashing blow! Sirs,
   here's the fist that shook
His beard till Wrestler Jem howled like
a just-lugged bear!

You had brained me with a feather: at
once I grew aware
Christian was meant for me. A burden
at your back,
Good Master Christmas? Nay, – yours
was that Joseph's sack,
– Or whose it was, – which held the
cup, – compared with mine!
Robbery loads my loins, perjury cracks
my chine,
Adultery … nay, Tab, you pitched me
as I flung!
One word, I'll up with fist … No,
sweet spouse, hold your tongue!

'I'm hasting to the end. The Book, sirs
– take and read!
You have my history in a nutshell, – ay,
indeed!
It must off, my burden! See, – slack
straps and into pit,
Roll, reach the bottom, rest, rot there –
a plague on it!
For a mountain's sure to fall and bury
Bedford Town,
"Destruction" – that's the name, and
fire shall burn it down!
O 'scape the wrath in time! Time's
now, if not too late.
How can I pilgrimage up to the wicket-
gate?
Next comes Despond the slough: not
that I fear to pull
Through mud, and dry my clothes at
brave House Beautiful –
But it's late in the day, I reckon: had I
left years ago
Town, wife, and children dear … Well,
Christmas did, you know! –
Soon I had met in the valley and tried
my cudgel's strength
On the enemy horned and winged a-
straddle across its length!
Have at his horns, thwick – thwack:
they snap, seel! Hoof and hoof –
Bang, break the fetlock-bones! For
love's sake, keep aloof

Angels! I'm man and match, – this
    cudgel for my flail, –
To thresh him, hoofs and horns, bat's
    wing and serpent's tail!
A chance gone by! But then, what else
    does Hopeful ding.
Into the deafest ear except – hope,
    hope's the thing?
Too late i' the day for me to thrid the
    windings: but
There's still a way to win the race by
    death's short cut!
Did Master Faithful need climb the
    Delightful Mounts?
No, straight to Vanity Fair, – a fair, by
    all accounts,
Such as is held outside, – lords, ladies,
    grand and gay, –
Says he in the face of them, just what
    you hear me say.
And the Judges brought him in guilty,
    and brought him out
To die in the market-place – St Peter's
    Green's about
The same thing: there they flogged,
    flayed, buffeted, lanced with
    knives,
Pricked him with swords, – I'll swear,
    he'd full a cat's nine lives, –
So to his end at last came Faithful, –
    ha, ha, he!
Who holds the highest card? for there
    stands hid, you see,
Behind the rabble-rout, a chariot, pair
    and all:
He's in, he's off, he's up, through
    clouds, at trumpet-call,
Carried the nearest way to Heaven-
    gate! Odds my life –
Has nobody a sword to spare? not even
    a knife?
Then hang me, draw and quarter! Tab
    – do the same by her!
O Master Worldly-Wiseman … that's
    Master Interpreter,
Take the will, not the deed! Our
    gibbet's handy close:

Forestall Last Judgment-Day! Be
    kindly, not morose!
There wants no earthly judge-and-
    jurying: here we stand –
Sentence our guilty selves: so, hang us
    out of hand!
Make haste for pity's sake! A single
    moment's loss
Means – Satan's lord once more: his
    whisper shoots across
All singing in my heart, all praying in
    my brain,
"It comes of heat and beer!" – hark
    how he guffaws plain!
"To-morrow you'll wake bright, and, in
    a safe skin, hug
Your sound selves, Tab and you, over a
    foaming jug!
You've had such qualms before, time
    out of mind!" He's right!
Did not we kick and cuff and curse
    away, that night
When home we blindly reeled, and left
    poor humpback Joe
I' the lurch to pay for what …
    somebody did, you know!
Both of us maundered then "Lame
    humpback, – never more
Will he come limping, drain his
    tankard at our door!
He'll swing, while – somebody …"
    Says Tab, "No, for I'll peach!"
"I'm for you, Tab," cries I, "there's
    rope enough for each!"]
So blubbered we, and bussed, and
    went to bed upon
The grace of Tab's good thought: by
    morning, all was gone!
We laughed – "What's life to him, a
    cripple of no account?"
Oh, waves increase around – I feel
    them mount and mount!
Hang us! To-morrow brings Tom Bear-
    ward with his bears:
One new black-muzzled brute beats
    Sackerson, he swears:

(Sackerson, for my money!) And,
  baiting o'er, the Brawl
They lead on Turner's Patch, – lads,
  lasses, up tails all, –
I'm i' the thick o' the throng! That
  means the Iron Cage,
– Means the Lost Man inside! Where's
  hope for such as wage
War against light? Light's left, light's
  here, I hold light still,
So does Tab – make but haste to hang
  us both! You will?'

I promise, when he stopped you might
  have heard a mouse
Squeak, such a death-like hush sealed
  up the old Mote House.
But when the mass of man sank meek
  upon his knees,
While Tab, alongside, wheezed a
  hoarse 'Do hang us, please!'
Why, then the waters rose, no eye but
  ran with tears,
Hearts heaved, heads thumped, until,
  paying all past arrears
Of pity and sorrow, at last a regular
  scream outbroke
Of triumph, joy and praise.
                    My Lord Chief
  Justice spoke,
First mopping brow and cheek, where
  still, for one that budged,
Another bead broke fresh: 'What
  Judge, that ever judged
Since first the world began, judged
  such a case as this?
Why, Master Bratts, long since, folk
  smelt you out, I wis!
I had my doubts, i' faith, each time you
  played the fox
Convicting geese of crime in yonder
  witness-box –
Yea, much did I misdoubt, the thief
  that stole her eggs
Was hardly goosey's self at Reynard's
  game, i' feggs!

Yet thus much was to praise – you
  spoke to point, direct –
Swore you heard, saw the theft: no jury
  could suspect –
Dared to suspect, – I'll say, – a spot in
  white so clear:
Goosey was throttled, true: but thereof
  godly fear
Came of example set, much as our
  laws intend;
And, though a fox confessed, you
  proved the Judge's friend.
What if I had my doubts? Suppose I
  gave them breath,
Brought you to bar: what work to do,
  ere "Guilty, Death," –
Had paid our pains! What heaps of
  witnesses to drag
From holes and corners, paid from out
  the County's bag!
Trial three dog-days long! *Amicus
  Curiæ* – that's
Your title, no dispute – truth-telling
  Master Bratts!
Thank you, too, Mistress Tab! Why
  doubt one word you say?
Hanging you both deserve, hanged
  both shall be this day!
The tinker needs must be a proper
  man. I've heard
He lies in Jail long since: if Quality's
  good word
Warrants me letting loose, – some
  householder, I mean –
Freeholder, better still, – I don't say
  but – between
Now and next Sessions … Well!
  Consider of his case,
I promise to, at least: we owe him so
  much grace.
Not that – no, God forbid! – I lean to
  think, as you,
The grace that such repent is any jail-
  bird's due:
I rather see the fruit of twelve years'
  pious reign –

Astræa Redux, Charles restored his
    rights again!
– Of which, another time! I somehow
    feel a peace
Stealing across the world. May deeds
    like this increase!
So, Master Sheriff, stay that sentence I
    pronounced
On those two dozen odd: deserving to
    be trounced
Soundly, and yet ... well, well, at all
    events despatch
This pair of – shall I say, sinner-saints?
    – ere we catch

Their jail-distemper too. Stop tears, or
    I'll indite
All weeping Bedfordshire for turning
    Bun-yanite!'

So, forms were galloped through. If
    Justice, on the spur,
Proved somewhat expeditious, would
    Quality demur?
And happily hanged were they, – why
    lengthen out my tale? –
Where Bunyan's Statue stands facing
    where stood his Jail.

# DRAMATIC IDYLS

Second Series
1880

'You are sick, that's sure' – they say:
   'Sick of what?' – they disagree.
' 'Tis the brain' – thinks Doctor A;
   ' 'Tis the heart' – holds Doctor B;
'The liver – my life I'd lay!'
   'The lungs!' 'The lights!
               Ah me!
  So ignorant of man's whole
Of bodily organs plain to see –
So sage and certain, frank and free,
About what's under lock and key –
  Man's soul!

## Echetlos

Here is a story shall stir you! Stand up,
   Greeks dead and gone,
Who breasted, beat Barbarians,
   stemmed Persia rolling on,
Did the deed and saved the world, for
   the day was Marathon!

No man but did his manliest, kept
   rank and fought away
In his tribe and file: up, back, out,
   down – was the spear-arm play:
Like a wind-whipt branchy wood, all
   spear-arms a-swing that day!

But one man kept no rank and his sole
   arm plied no spear,
As a flashing came and went, and a
   form i' the van, the rear,
Brightened the battle up, for he blazed
   now there, now here.

Nor helmed nor shielded, he! but, a
   goatskin all his wear,
Like a tiller of the soil, with a clown's
   limbs broad and bare,
Went he ploughing on and on: he
   pushed with a ploughman's share.

Did the weak mid-line give way, as
   tunnies on whom the shark
Precipitates his bulk? Did the right-
   wing halt when, stark
On his heap of slain lay stretched Kalli-
   machos Polemarch?

Did the steady phalanx falter? To the
   rescue, at the need,
The clown was ploughing Persia,
   clearing Greek earth of weed,
As he routed through the Sakian and
   rooted up the Mede.

But the deed done, battle won, –
   nowhere to be descried
On the meadow, by the stream, at the
   marsh, – look far and wide
From the foot of the mountain, no, to
   the last blood-plashed seaside, –

Not anywhere on view blazed the large
   limbs thonged and brown,
Shearing and clearing still with the
   share before which – down
To the dust went Persia's pomp, as he
   ploughed for Greece, that clown!

How spake the Oracle? 'Care for no
   name at all!
Say but just this: "We praise one
   helpful whom we call
The Holder of the Ploughshare." The
   great deed ne'er grows small."

Not the great name! Sing – woe for the
   great name Miltiadés
And its end at Paros isle! Woe for
   Themistokles
– Satrap in Sardis court! Name not the
   clown like these!

## Clive

I and Clive were friends – and why
    not? Friends! I think you laugh,
    my lad.
Clive it was gave England India, while
    your father gives – egad,
England nothing but the graceless boy
    who lures him on to speak –
'Well, Sir, you and Clive were
    comrades – ' with a tongue thrust
    in your cheek!

Very true: in my eyes, your eyes, all the
    world's eyes, Clive was man,
I was, am and ever shall be – mouse,
    nay, mouse of all its clan
Sorriest sample, if you take the
    kitchen's estimate for feme;
While the man Clive – he fought Plassy,
    spoiled the clever foreign game,
Conquered and annexed and
    Englished!
                Never mind! As o'er
    my punch
(You away) I sit of evenings, – silence,
    save for biscuit-crunch,
Black, unbroken, – thought grows busy,
    thrids each pathway of old years,
Notes this forthright, that meander, till
    the long-past life appears
Like an outspread map of country
    plodded through, each mile and
    rood,
Once, and well remembered still: I'm
    startled in my solitude
Ever and anon by – what's the sudden
    mocking light that breaks
On me as I slap the table till no
    rummer-glass but shakes
While I ask – aloud, I do believe, God
    help me! – 'Was it thus?
Can it be that so I faltered, stopped
    when just one step for us – '
(Us, – you were not born, I grant, but
    surely some day born would be)

' – One bold step had gained a
    province' (figurative talk, you see)
'Got no end of wealth and honour, –
    yet I stood stock still no less?'
– 'For I was not Clive,' you comment:
    but it needs no Clive to guess
Wealth were handy, honour ticklish,
    did no writing on the wall
Warn me 'Trespasser, 'ware man-traps!'
    Him who braves that notice – call
Hero! none of such heroics suit myself
    who read plain words,
Doff my hat, and leap no barrier.
    Scripture says the land's the Lord's:
Louts then – what avail the thousand,
    noisy in a smock-frocked ring,
All-agog to have me trespass, clear the
    fence, be Clive their king?
Higher warrant must you show me ere
    I set one foot before
T'other in that dark direction, though I
    stand for evermore
Poor as Job and meek as Moses. Ever-
    more? No! By-and-by
Job grows rich and Moses valiant, Clive
    turns out less wise than I.
Don't object 'Why call him friend, then?'
    Power is power, my boy, and still
Marks a man, – God's gift magnific,
    exercised for good or ill.
You've your boot now on my hearth-
    rug, tread what was a tiger's skin:
Rarely such a royal monster as I lodged
    the bullet in!
True, he murdered half a village, so his
    own death came to pass;
Still, for size and beauty, cunning,
    courage – ah, the brute he was!
Why, that Clive, – that youth, that
    greenhorn, that quill-driving clerk,
    in fine, –
He sustained a siege in Arcot ... But
    the world knows! Pass the wine.

Where did I break off at? How bring
    Clive in? Oh, you mentioned
    'fear'!

Just so: and, said I, that minds me of a
    story you shall hear.

We were friends then, Clive and I: so,
    when the clouds, about the orb
Late supreme, encroaching slowly,
    surely, threatened to absorb
Ray by ray its noontide brilliance, –
    friendship might, with steadier eye
Drawing near, bear what had burned
    else, now no blaze – all majesty.
Too much bee's-wing floats my figure?
    Well, suppose a castle's new:
None presume to climb its ramparts,
    none find foothold sure for shoe
'Twixt those squares and squares of
    granite plating the impervious pile
As his scale-mail's warty iron cuirasses
    a crocodile.
Reels that castle thunder-smitten,
    storm-dismantled? From without
Scrambling up by crack and crevice,
    every cockney prates about
Towers – the heap he kicks now!
    turrets – just the measure of his
    cane!
Will that do? Observe moreover –
    (same similitude again) –
Such a castle seldom crumbles by
    sheer stress of cannonade:
'Tis when foes are foiled and fighting's
    finished that vile rains invade,
Grass o'ergrows, o'ergrows till night-
    birds congregating find no holes
Fit to build in like the topmost sockets
    made for banner-poles.
So Clive crumbled slow in London –
    crashed at last.

             A week before,
Dining with him, – after trying
    churchyard-chat of days of yore, –
Both of us stopped, tired as
    tombstones, head-piece, foot-
    piece, when they lean
Each to other, drowsed in fog-smoke,
    o'er a coffined Past between.

As I saw his head sink heavy, guessed
    the soul's extinguishment
By the glazing eyeball, noticed how the
    furtive fingers went
Where a drug-box skulked behind the
    honest liquor, – 'One more throw
Try for Clive!' thought I: 'Let's venture
    some good rattling question!'so –
'Come, Clive, tell us' – out I blurted –
    'what to tell in turn, years hence,
When my boy – suppose I have one –
    asks me on what evidence
I maintain my friend of Plassy proved a
    warrior every whit
Worth your Alexanders, Cæsars, Marl-
    boroughs and – what said Pitt? –
Frederick the Fierce himself! Clive told
    me once' – I want to say –
'Which feat out of all those famous
    doings bore the bell away
– In his own calm estimation, mark
    you, not the mob's rough guess –
Which stood foremost as evincing
    what Clive called courageousness!
Come! what moment of the minute,
    what speck-centre in the wide
Circle of the action saw your mortal
    fairly deified?
(Let alone that filthy sleep-stuff,
    swallow bold this wholesome
    Port!)
If a friend has leave to question, –
    when were you most brave, in
    short?'

Up he arched his brows o' the instant
    – formidably Clive again.
'When was I most brave? I'd answer,
    were the instance half as plain
As another instance that's a brain-
    lodged crystal – curse it! – here
Freezing when my memory touches –
    ugh! – the time I felt most fear.
Ugh! I cannot say for certain if I
    showed fear – anyhow,
Fear I felt, and, very likely, shuddered,
    since I shiver now.'

'Fear!'smiled I. 'Well, that's the rarer:
    that's a specimen to seek,
Ticket up in one's museum. *Mind-
    Freaks, Lord clive's Fear, Unique!'*

Down his brows dropped. On the table
    painfully he pored as though
Tracing, in the stains and streaks there,
    thoughts encrusted long ago.
When he spoke 'twas like a lawyer
    reading word by word some will,
Some blind jungle of a statement, –
    beating on and on until
Out there leaps fierce life to fight with.
        'This fell in my factor-days.
Desk-drudge, slaving at St David's, one
    must game, or drink, or craze.
I chose gaming: and, – because your
    high-flown gamesters hardly take
Umbrage at a factor's elbow if the
    factor pays his stake, –
I was winked at in a circle where the
    company was choice,
Captain This and Major That, men
    high of colour, loud of voice,
Yet indulgent, condescending to the
    modest juvenile
Who not merely risked but lost his
    hard-earned guineas with a smile.

'Down I sat to cards, one evening, –
    had for my antagonist
Somebody whose name's a secret –
    you'll know why – so, if you list,
Call him Cock o' the Walk, my scarlet
    son of Mars from head to heel!
Play commenced: and, whether Cocky
    fancied that a clerk must feel
Quite sufficient honour came of
    bending over one green baize,
I the scribe with him the warrior, –
    guessed no penman dared to raise
Shadow of objection should the
    honour stay but playing end
More or less abruptly, – whether
    disinclined he grew to spend
Practice strictly scientific on a booby

born to stare
At – not ask of – lace-and-ruffles if the
    hand they hide plays fair, –
Anyhow, I marked a movement when
    he bade me "Cut!"
              'I rose.
"Such the new manœuvre, Captain?
    I'm a novice: knowledge grows.
What, you force a card, you cheat, Sir?"
          'Never did a thunder-clap
Cause emotion, startle Thyrsis locked
    with Chloe in his lap,
As my word and gesture (down I flung
    my cards to join the pack)
Fired the man of arms, whose visage,
    simply red before, turned black.

'When he found his voice, he
    stammered "That expression once
    again!"

' "Well, you forced a card and
    cheated!"
          ' "Possibly a factor's brain,
Busied with his all-important balance
    of accounts, may deem
Weighing words superfluous trouble:
    *cheat* to clerkly ears may seem
Just the joke for friends to venture: but
    we are not friends, you see!
When a gentleman is joked with, – if
    he's good at repartee,
He rejoins, as do I – Sirrah, on your
    knees, withdraw in full!
Beg my pardon, or be sure a kindly
    bullet through your skull
Lets in light and teaches manners to
    what brain it finds! Choose quick –
Have your life snuffed out or, kneeling,
    pray me trim yon candle-wick!"

' "Well, you cheated!"
              'Then outbroke a
    howl from all the friends around.
To his feet sprang each in fury, fists
    were clenched and teeth were
    ground.

"End it! no time like the present! Captain,
    yours were our disgrace!
No delay, begin and finish! Stand back,
    leave the pair a space!
Let civilians be instructed: henceforth
    simply ply the pen,
Fly the sword! This clerk's no
    swordsman? Suit him with a
    pistol, then!
Even odds! A dozen paces 'twixt the
    most and least expert
Make a dwarf a giant's equal: nay, the
    dwarf, if he's alert,
Likelier hits the broader target!"
        'Up we stood accordingly.
As they handed me the weapon, such
    was my soul's thirst to try
Then and there conclusions with this
    bully, tread on and stamp out
Every spark of his existence, that, –
    crept close to, curled about
By that toying tempting teasing fool-
    forefinger's middle joint, –
Don't you guess? – the trigger yielded.
    Gone my chance! and at the point
Of such prime success moreover:
    scarce an inch above his head
Went my ball to hit the wainscot. He
    was living, I was dead.

'Up he marched in flaming triumph –
    'twas his right, mind! – up, within
Just an arm's length. "Now, my
    clerkling," chuckled Cocky with a
    grin
As the levelled piece quite touched me,
    "Now, Sir Counting-House, repeat
That expression which I told you proved
    bad manners! Did I cheat?"

' "Cheat you did, you knew you
    cheated, and, this moment, know
    as well.
As for me, my homely breeding bids
    you – fire and go to Hell!"

'Twice the muzzle touched ray fore-
    head. Heavy barrel, flurried wrist,
Either spoils a steady lifting. Thrice:
    then, "Laugh at Hell who list,
I can't! God's no fable either. Did this
    boy's eye wink once? No!
There's no standing him and Hell and
    God all three against me, – so,
I did cheat!"
        'And down he threw the
    pistol, out rushed – by the door
Possibly, but, as for knowledge if by
    chimney, roof or floor,
He effected disappearance – I'll engage
    no glance was sent
That way by a single starer, such a
    blank astonishment
Swallowed up their senses: as for
    speaking – mute they stood as
    mice.

'Mute not long, though! Such reaction,
    such a hubbub in a trice!
"Rogue and rascal! Who'd have thought
    it? What's to be expected next,
When His Majesty's Commission
    serves a sharper as pretext
For … But where's the need of wasting
    time now? Nought requires delay:
Punishment the Service cries for: let
    disgrace be wiped away
Publicly, in good broad daylight!
    Resignation? No, indeed
Drum and fife must play the Rogue's
    March, rank and file be free to
    speed
Tardy marching on the rogue's part by
    appliance in the rear
– Kicks administered shall right this
    wronged civilian, – never fear,
Mister Clive, for – though a clerk – you
    bore yourself – suppose we say –
Just as would beseem a soldier!"

    ' "Gentlemen, attention – pray!
First, one word!"

'I passed each speaker
   severally in review.
When I had precise their number,
   names and styles, and fully knew
Over whom my supervision
   thenceforth must extend, – why,
   then –

' "Some five minutes since, my life lay
   – as you all saw, gentlemen –
At the mercy of your friend there. Not
   a single voice was raised
In arrest of judgment, not one tongue –
   before my powder blazed –
Ventured 'Can it be the youngster
   blundered, really seemed to mark
Some irregular proceeding? We
   conjecture in the dark,
Guess at random, – still, for sake of fair
   play – what if for a freak.
In a fit of absence, – such things have
   been! – if our friend proved weak
– What's the phrase? – corrected
   fortune! Look into the case, at
   least!'
Who dared interpose between the
   altar's victim and the priest?
Yet he spared me! You eleven!
   Whosoever, all or each,
To the disadvantage of the man who
   spared me, utters speech
– To his face, behind his back, – that
   speaker has to do with me:
Me who promise, if positions change
   and mine the chance should be,
Not to imitate your friend and waive
   advantage!"
             'Twenty-five
Years ago this matter happened: and
   'tis certain,' added Clive,
'Never, to my knowledge, did Sir
   Cocky have a single breath
Breathed against him: lips were closed
   throughout his life, or since his
   death,
For if he be dead or living I can tell no
   more than you.

All I know is – Cocky had one chance
   more; how he used it, – grew
Out of such unlucky habits, or
   relapsed, and back again
Brought the late-ejected devil with a
   score more in his train, –
That's for you to judge. Reprieval I
   procured, at any rate.
Ugh – the memory of that minute's
   fear makes gooseflesh rise! Why
   prate
Longer? You've my story, there's your
   instance: fear I did, you see!'

'Well' – I hardly kept from laughing –
   'if I see it, thanks must be
Wholly to your Lordship's candour.
   Not that – in a common case –
When a bully caught at cheating
   thrusts a pistol in one's face,
I should underrate, believe me, such a
   trial to the nerve!
'Tis no joke, at one-and-twenty, for a
   youth to stand nor swerve.
Fear I naturally look for – unless, of all
   men alive,
I am forced to make exception when I
   come to Robert Clive.
Since at Arcot, Plassy, elsewhere, he and
   death – the whole world knows –
Came to somewhat closer quarters.'
   Quarters? Had we come to blows,
Clive and I, you had not wondered –
   up he sprang so, out he rapped
Such a round of oaths – no matter! I'll
   endeavour to adapt
To our modern usage words he – well,
   'twas friendly licence – flung
At me like so many fire-balls, fast as he
   could wag his tongue.

'You – a soldier? You – at Plassy? Yours
   the faculty to nick
Instantaneously occasion when your
   foe, if lightning-quick,
– At his mercy, at his malice, – has
   you, through some stupid inch

Undefended in your bulwark? Thus
    laid open, – not to flinch
– That needs courage, you'll concede
    me. Then, look here! Suppose the
    man,
Checking his advance, his weapon still
    extended, not a span
Distant from my temple, – curse him!
    – quietly had bade me "There!
Keep your life, calumniator! –
    worthless life I freely spare:
Mine you freely would have taken –
    murdered me and my good fame
Both at once – and all the better! Go,
    and thank your own bad aim
Which permits me to forgive you!
    What if, with such words as these,
He had cast away his weapon? How
    should I have borne me, please?
Nay, I'll spare you pains and tell you.
    This, and only this, remained –
Pick his weapon up and use it on
    myself. I so had gained
Sleep the earlier, leaving England
    probably to pay on still
Rent and taxes for half India, tenant at
    the Frenchman's will'.

'Such the turn,'said I, 'the matter takes
    with you? Then I abate
– No, by not one jot nor tittle, – of
    your act my estimate.
Fear – I wish I could detect there:
    courage fronts me, plain enough –
Call it desperation, madness – never
    mind! for here's in rough
Why, had mine been such a trial, fear
    had overcome disgrace.
True, disgrace were hard to bear: but
    such a rush against God's face
– None of that for me, Lord Plassy,
    since I go to church at times,
Say the creed my mother taught me!
    Many years in foreign climes
Rub some marks away – not all,
    though! We poor sinners reach
    life's brink,

Overlook what rolls beneath it,
    recklessly enough, but think
There's advantage in what's left us –
    ground to stand on, time to call
"Lord, have mercy!" ere we topple over
    – do not leap, that's all!'

Oh, he made no answer, – re-absorbed
    into his cloud. I caught
Something like 'Yes – courage: only
    fools will call it fear.'
                If aught
Comfort you, my great unhappy hero
    Clive, in that I heard,
Next week, how your own hand dealt
    you doom, and uttered just the
    word
'Fearfully courageous!' – this, be sure,
    and nothing else I groaned.
I'm no Clive, nor parson either: Clive's
    worst deed – we'll hope
    condoned.

## Muléykeh

If a stranger passed the tent of Hóseyn,
    he cried 'A churl's!'
Or haply 'God help the man who has
    neither salt nor bread!'
– 'Nay,' would a friend exclaim, 'he
    needs nor pity nor scorn
More than who spends small thought
    on the shore-sand, picking pearls,
– Holds but in light esteem the seed-
    sort, bears instead
On his breast a moon-like prize, some
    orb which of night makes morn.

'What if no flocks and herds enrich the
    son oSinán?
They went when his tribe was mulct,
    ten thousand camels the due,
Blood-value paid perforce for a murder
    done of old.
"God gave them, let them go! But
    never since time began,

Muléykeh, peerless mare, owned
    master the match of you,
And you are my prize, my Pearl: I
    laugh at men's land and gold!"
'So in the pride of his soul laughs
    Hóseyn – and right, I say.
Do the ten steeds run a race of glory?
    Outstripping all,
Ever Muléykeh stands first steed at the
    victor's staff.
Who started, the owner's hope, gets
    shamed and named, that day.
"Silence," or, last but one, is "The
    Cuffed," as we use to call
Whom the paddock's lord thrusts forth.
    Right, Hóseyn, I say, to laugh!'

'Boasts he Muléykeh the Pearl?' the
    stranger replies: 'Be sure
On him I waste nor scorn nor pity, but
    lavish both
On Duhl the son of Sheybán, who
    withers away in heart
For envy of Hóseyn's luck. Such
    sickness admits no cure.
A certain poet has sung, and sealed the
    same with an oath,
"For the vulgar – flocks and herds! The
    Pearl is a prize apart." '

Lo, Duhl the son of Sheybán comes
    riding to Hóseyn's tent,
And he casts his saddle down, and
    enters and 'Peace!' bids he.
'You are poor, I know the cause: my
    plenty shall mend the wrong.
'Tis said of your Pearl – the price of a
    hundred camels spent
In her purchase were scarce ill paid:
    such prudence is far from me
Who proffer a thousand. Speak! Long
    parley may last too long.'

Said Hóseyn 'You feed young beasts a
    many, of famous breed,
Slit-eared, unblemished, fat, true
    offspring of Múzennem:

There stumbles no weak-eyed she in
    the line as it climbs the hill.
But I love Muléykeh's face: her
    forefront whitens indeed
Like a yellowish wave's cream-crest.
    Your camels – go gaze on them!
Her fetlock is foam-splashed too.
    Myself am the richer still.'

A year goes by: lo, back to the tent
    again rides Duhl.
'You are open-hearted, ay – moist-
    handed, a very prince.
Why should I speak of sale? Be the
    mare your simple gift!
My son is pined to death for her
    beauty: my wife prompts "Fool,
Beg for his sake the Pearl! Be God the
    rewarder, since
God pays debts seven for one: who
    squanders on Him shows thrift." '
Said Hóseyn 'God gives each man one
    life, like a lamp, then gives
That lamp due measure of oil: lamp
    lighted – hold high, wave wide
Its comfort for others to share! once
    quench it, what help is left?
The oil of your lamp is your son: I
    shine while Muléykeh lives.
Would I beg your son to cheer my dark
    if Muléykeh died?
It is life against life: what good avails to
    the life-bereft?'

Another year, and – hist! What craft is
    it Duhl designs?
He alights not at the door of the tent as
    he did last time,
But, creeping behind, he gropes his
    stealthy way by the trench
Half-round till he finds the flap in the
    folding, for night combines
With the robber – and such is he:
    Duhl, covetous up to crime,
Must wring from Hóseyn's grasp the
    Pearl, by whatever the wrench.

'He was hunger-bitten, I heard: I
   tempted with half my store,
And a gibe was all my thanks. Is he
   generous like Spring dew?
Account the fault to me who chaffered
   with such an one!
He has killed, to feast chance comers,
   the creature he rode: nay, more –
For a couple of singing-girls his robe
   has he torn in two:
I will beg! Yet I nowise gained by the
   tale of my wife and son.

'I swear by the Holy House, my head
   will I never wash
Till I filch his Pearl away. Fair dealing I
   tried, then guile,
And now I resort to force. He said we
   must live or die:
Let him die, then, – let me live! Be
   bold – but not too rash!
I have found me a peeping-place:
   breast, bury your breathing while
I explore for myself! Now, breathe! He
   deceived me not, the spy!

'As he said! – there lies in peace
   Hóseyn – how happy! Beside
Stands tethered the Pearl: thrice winds
   her headstall about his wrist:
'Tis therefore he sleeps so sound – the
   moon through the roof reveals.
And, loose on his left, stands too that
   other, known far and wide,
Buhéyseh, her sister born: fleet is she
   yet ever missed
The winning tail's fire-flash a-stream
   past the thunderous heels.
'No less she stands saddled and bridled,
   this second, in case some thief
Should enter and seize and fly with the
   first, as I mean to do.
What then? The Pearl is the Pearl: once
   mount her we both escape.'
Through the skirt-fold in glides Duhl, –
   so a serpent disturbs no leaf

In a bush as he parts the twigs
   entwining a nest: clean through.
He is noiselessly at his work: as he
   planned, he performs the rape.

He has set the tent-door wide, has
   buckled the girth, has clipped
The headstall away from the wrist he
   leaves thrice bound as before,
He springs on the Pearl, is launched on
   the desert like bolt from bow.
Up starts our plundered man: from his
   breast though the heart be ripped,
Yet his mind has the mastery: behold,
   in a minute more,
He is out and off and away on
   Buhéyseh, whose worth we know!

And Hóseyn – his blood turns flame,
   he has learned long since to ride,
And Buhéyseh does her part, – they
   gain – they are gaining fast
On the fugitive pair, and Duhl has Ed-
   Dárraj to cross and quit,
And to reach the ridge El-Sabàn, – no
   safety till that be spied!
And Buhéyseh is, bound by bound,
   but a horse-length off at last,
For the Pearl has missed the tap of the
   heel, the touch of the bit.

She shortens her stride, she chafes at
   her rider the strange and queer:
Buhéyseh is mad with hope – beat
   sister she shall and must
Though Duhl, of the hand and heel so
   clumsy, she has to thank.
She is near now, nose by tail – they are
   neck by croup – joy! fear!
What folly makes Hóseyn shout 'Dog
   Duhl, Damned son of the Dust,
Touch the right ear and press with
   your foot my Pearl's left flank!'

And Duhl was wise at the word, and
   Muléykeh as prompt perceived

Who was urging redoubled pace, and
　　to hear him was to obey,
And a leap indeed gave she, and
　　evanished for evermore.
And Hóseyn looked one long last look
　　as who, all bereaved,
Looks, fain to follow the dead so far as
　　the living may:
Then he turned Buhéyseh's neck slow
　　homeward, weeping sore.
And, lo, in the sunrise, still sat Hóseyn
　　upon the ground
Weeping: and neighbours came, the
　　tribesmen of Bénu-Asàd
In the vale of green Er-Rass, and they
　　questioned him of his grief;
And he told from first to last how,
　　serpent-like, Duhl had wound
His way to the nest, and how Duhl
　　rode like an ape, so bad!
And how Buhéyseh did wonders, yet
　　Pearl remained with the thief.

And they jeered him, one and all: 'Poor
　　Hóseyn is crazed past hope!
How else had he wrought himself his
　　ruin, in fortune's spite?
To have simply held the tongue were a
　　task for a boy or girl,
And here were Muléykeh again, the
　　eyed like an antelope,
The child of his heart by day, the wife
　　of his breast by night!' –
'And the beaten in speed!' wept
　　Hóseyn: 'You never have loved my
　　Pearl.'

## Pietro of Abano

*Petrus Aponensis* – there was a magician!
When that strange adventure happened,
　　which I mean to tell my hearers,
Nearly had he tried all trades – beside
　　physician,
Architect, astronomer, astrologer, – or
　　worse:
How else, as the old books warrant,
　　was he able,
All at once, through all the world, to
　　prove the promptest of appearers
Where was prince to cure, tower to
　　build as high as Babel,
Star to name or sky-sign read, – yet
　　pouch, for pains, a curse?

– Curse: for when a vagrant, – foot-
　　sore, travel-tattered,
Now a young man, now an old man,
　　Turk or Arab, Jew or Gipsy, –
Proffered folk in passing – O for pay,
　　what mattered? –
'I'll be doctor, I'll play builder, star I'll
　　name – sign read!'
Soon as prince was cured, tower built,
　　and fate predicted,
'Who may you be?' came the question;
　　when he answered, '*Petrus ipse*,'
'Just as we divined!' cried folk – 'A
　　wretch convicted
Long ago of dealing with the devil –
　　you indeed!'

So, they cursed him roundly, all his
　　labour's payment,
Motioned him – the convalescent prince
　　would – to vacate the presence:
Babylonians plucked his beard and
　　tore his raiment,
Drove him from that tower he built:
　　while, had he peered at stars,
Town howled 'stone the quack who
　　styles our Dog-star – Sirius!'
Country yelled 'Aroint the churl who
　　prophesies we take no pleasance

Under vine and fig-tree, since the year's
    delirious,
Bears no crop of any kind, – all through
    the planet Mars!'
Straightway would the whilom youngster
    grow a grisard,
Or, as case might hap, the hoary eld
    drop off and show a stripling.
Town and country groaned – indebted
    to a wizard!
'Curse – nay, kick and cuff him – fit
    requital of his pains!
Gratitude in word or deed were wasted
    truly!
Rather make the Church amends by
    crying out on, cramping, crippling
One who, on pretence of serving man,
    serves duly
Man's arch foe: not ours, be sure, but
    Satan's – his the gains!'
Peter grinned and bore it, such
    disgraceful usage:
Somehow, cuffs and kicks and curses
    seem ordained his like to suffer:
Prophet's pay with Christians, now as
    in the Jew's age,
Still is – stoning: so, he meekly took
    his wage and went,
– Safe again was found ensconced in
    those old quarters,
Padua's blackest blindest by-street, –
    none the worse, nay, somewhat
    tougher:
'Calculating,' quoth he, 'soon I join the
    martyrs,
Since, who magnify my lore on burning
    me are bent.'*

Therefore, on a certain evening, to his
    alley
Peter slunk, all bruised and broken,
    sore in body, sick in spirit,
Just escaped from Cairo where he
    launched a galley
Needing neither sails nor oars nor help
    of wind or tide,
– Needing but the fume of fire to set a-
    flying
Wheels like mad which whirled you
    quick
– North, South, where'er you pleased
    require it, –
That is – would have done so had not
    priests come prying,
Broke his engine up and bastinadoed
    him beside.

As he reached his lodging, stopped
    there unmolested,
(Neighbours feared him, urchins fled
    him, few were bold enough to
    follow)
While his fumbling fingers tried the
    lock and tested
Once again the queer key's virtue,
    oped the sullen door, –
Someone plucked his sleeve, cried
    'Master, pray your pardon!
Grant a word to me who patient wait
    you in your archway's hollow!
Hard on you men's hearts are: be not
    your heart hard on
Me who kiss your garment's hem, O
    Lord of magic lore!

---

*   'Studiando le mie cifre col compasso,
      Rilevo che sarò presto sotterra,
    Perchè del mio saper si fa gran chiasso,
      E gl' ignoranti m' hanno mosso guerra.'

Said to have been found in a well at Abano in
the last century. They were extemporaneously
Englished thus: not as Father Prout chose to
prefer them: –

Studying my ciphers with the compass,
    I reckon – I soon shall be below-ground;
Because of my lore folk make great rumpus,
    And war on myself makes each dull
    rogue round. – R. B.

'Mage – say I, who no less, scorning
     tittle-tattle.
To the vulgar give no credence when
     they prate of Peter's magic,
Deem his art brews tempest, hurts the
     crops and cattle,
Hinders fowls from laying eggs and
     worms from spinning silk,
Rides upon a he-goat, mounts at need
     a broomstick:
While the price he pays for this (so
     turns to comic what was tragic)
Is – he may not drink – dreads like the
     Day of Doom's tick –
One poor drop of sustenance ordained
     mere men – that's milk!

'Tell such tales to Padua! Think me no
     such dullard!
Not from these benighted parts did I
     derive my breath and being!
I am from a land whose cloudless skies
     are coloured
Livelier, suns orb largelier, airs seem
     incense, – while, on earth –
What, instead of grass, our fingers and
     our thumbs cull,
Proves true moly! sounds and sights
     there help the body's hearing,
     seeing,
Till the soul grows godlike: brief, – you
     front no numb scull
Shaming by ineptitude the Greece that
     gave him birth!

'Mark within my eye its iris mystic-
     lettered –
That's my name! and note my ear – its
     swan-shaped cavity, my emblem!
Mine's the swan-like nature born to fly
     unfettered
Over land and sea in search of
     knowledge – food for song.
Art denied the vulgar! Geese grow fat
     on barley,
Swans require ethereal provend,
     undesirous to resemble 'em –

Soar to seek Apollo, – favoured with a
     parley
Such as, Master, you grant me – who
     will not hold you long.

'Leave to learn to sing – for that your
     swan petitions:
Master, who possess the secret, say not
     nay to such a suitor!
All I ask is – bless mine, purest of
     ambitions!
Grant me leave to make my kind wise,
     free, and happy! How?
Just by making me – as you are mine –
     their model!
Geese have goose-thoughts: make a
     swan their teacher first, then co-
     adjutor, –
Let him introduce swan-notions to
     each noddle, –
Geese will soon grow swans, and men
     become what I am now!

'That's the only magic – had but fools
     discernment,
Could they probe and pass into the
     solid through the soft and seeming!
Teach me such true magic – now and
     no adjournment!
Teach your art of making fools
     subserve the man of mind!
Magic is the power we men of mind
     should practise,
Draw fools to become our drudges,
     docile henceforth, never
     dreaming –
While they do our hests for fancied
     gain – the fact is
What they toil and moil to get proves
     falsehood: truth's behind!

'See now! you conceive some fabric –
     say, a mansion
Meet for monarch's pride and pleasure:
     this is truth – a thought has fired
     you,

Made you fain to give some cramped
    concept expansion,
Put your faculty to proof, fulfil your
    nature's task.
First you fascinate the monarch's self:
    he fancies
He it was devised the scheme you
    execute as he inspired you:
He in turn sets slaving insignificances
Toiling, moiling till your structure
    stands there – all you ask!

'Soon the monarch's known for what
    he was – a ninny:
Soon the rabble-rout leave labour, take
    their work-day wage and vanish:
Soon the late puffed bladder, pricked,
    shows lank and skinny –
"Who was its inflator?" ask we, "whose
    the giant lungs?"
*Petri en pulmones!* What though men
    prove ingrates?
Let them – so they stop at crucifixion –
    buffet, ban and banish!
Peter's power's apparent: human
    praise – its din grates
Harsh as blame on ear unused to aught
    save angels' tongues.

'Ay, there have been always, since our
    world existed,
Mages who possessed the secret –
    needed but to stand still, fix eye
On the foolish mortal: straight was he
    enlisted
Soldier, scholar, servant, slave – no
    matter for the style!
Only through illusion; ever what
    seemed profit –
Love or lucre – justified obedience to
    the *Ipse dixi:*
Work done – palace reared from
    pavement up to soffit –
Was it strange if builders smelt out
    cheating all the while?

'Let them pelt and pound, bruise, bray
    you in a mortar!
What's the odds to you who seek
    reward of quite another nature?
You've enrolled your name where sages
    of your sort are,
– Michael of Constantinople, Hans of
    Halberstadt!
Nay and were you nameless, still
    you've your conviction
You it was and only you – what
    signifies the nomenclature? –
Ruled the world in fact, though how
    you ruled be fiction
Fit for fools: true wisdom's magic you
    – if e'er man – had't!

'But perhaps you ask me "Since each
    ignoramus
While he profits by such magic
    persecutes the benefactor,
What should I expect but – once I
    render famous
You as Michael, Hans and Peter – just
    one ingrate more?
If the vulgar prove thus, whatsoe'er the
    pelf be,
Pouched through my beneficence –
    and doom me dungeoned,
    chained, or racked, or
Fairly burned outright – how grateful
    will yourself be
When, his secret gained, you match
    your – master just before?"

'That's where I await you! Please, revert
    a little!
What do folk report about you if not
    this – which, though chimeric,
Still, as figurative, suits you to a tittle –
That, – although the elements obey
    your nod and wink,
Fades or flowers the herb you chance
    to smile or sigh at,
While your frown bids earth quake
    palled by obscuration
    atmospheric, –

Brief, although through nature nought
   resists your *fiat*,
There's yet one poor substance mocks
   you – milk you may not drink!

'Figurative language! Take my
   explanation!
Fame with fear, and hate with homage,
   these your art procures in plenty.
All's but daily dry bread: what makes
   moist the ration?
Love, the milk that sweetens man his
   meal – alas, you lack:
I am he who, since he fears you not,
   can love you.
Love is born of heart not mind, *de
   corde natus haud de mente;*
Touch my heart and love's yours, sure
   as shines above you
Sun by day and star by night though
   earth should go to wrack!

'Stage by stage you lift me – kiss by
   kiss I hallow
Whose but your dear hand my helper,
   punctual as at each new impulse
I approach my aim? Shell chipped, the
   eaglet callow
Needs a parent's pinion-push to quit
   the eyrie's edge:
But once fairly launched forth, denizen
   of æther.
While each effort sunward bids the
   blood more freely through each
   limb pulse,
Sure the parent feels, as gay they soar
   together,
Fully are all pains repaid when love
   redeems its pledge!'

Then did Peter's tristful visage lighten
   somewhat,
Vent a watery smile as though
   inveterate mistrust were thawing.
'Well, who knows?' he slow broke
   silence. 'Mortals – come what

Come there may – are still the dupes of
   hope there's luck in store.
Many scholars seek me, promise
   mounts and marvels:
Here stand I to witness how they step
   'twixt me and clapperclawing!
Dry bread, – that I've gained me: truly
   I should starve else:
But of milk, no drop was mine! Well,
   shuffle cards once more!'

At the word of promise thus implied,
   our stranger –
What can he but cast his arms, in
   rapture of embrace, round Peter?
'Hold! I choke!' the mage grunts. 'Shall
   I in the manger
Any longer play the dog? Approach, my
   calf, and feed!
*Bene* ... won't you wait for grace?' But
   sudden incense
Wool-white, serpent-solid, curled up –
   perfume growing sweet and
   sweeter
Till it reached the young man's nose
   and seemed to win sense
Soul and all from out his brain through
   nostril: yes, indeed!

Presently the young man rubbed his
   eyes. 'Where am I?
Too much bother over books! Some
   reverie has proved amusing.
What did Peter prate of? 'Faith, my
   brow is clammy!
How my head throbs, how my heart
   thumps! Can it be I swooned?
Oh, I spoke my speech out – cribbed
   from Plato's tractate,
Dosed him with "the Fair and Good,"
   swore – Dog of Egypt – I was
   choosing
Plato's way to serve men! What's the
   hour? Exact eight!
Home now, and to-morrow never mind
   how Plato mooned!

'Peter has the secret! Fair and Good are
     products
(So he said) of Foul and Evil: one must
     bring to pass the other.
Just as poisons grow drugs, steal
     through sundry odd ducts
Doctors name, and ultimately issue
     safe and changed.
You'd abolish poisons, treat disease
     with dainties
Such as suit the sound and sane? With
     all such kickshaws vain you pother!
Arsenic's the stuff puts force into the
     faint eyes,
Opium sets the brain to rights – by
     cark and care deranged.

'What, he's safe within door? – would
     escape – no question –
Thanks, since thanks and more I owe,
     and mean to pay in time befitting.
What most presses now is – after
     night's digestion,
Peter, of thy precepts! – promptest
     practice of the same.
Let me see! The wise man, first of all,
     scorns riches:
But to scorn them must obtain them:
     none believes in his permitting
Gold to lie ungathered: who picks up,
     then pitches
Gold away – philosophizes: none
     disputes his claim.

'So with worldly honours: 'tis by
     abdicating,
Incontestably he proves he could have
     kept the crown discarded.
Sulla cuts a figure, leaving off dictating:
Simpletons laud private life? "The
     grapes are sour," laugh we.
So, again – but why continue? All's
     tumultuous
Here: my head's a-whirl with knowledge.
     Speedily shall be rewarded
He who taught me! Greeks prove
     ingrates? So insult you us?

When your teaching bears its first-
     fruits, Peter – wait and see!'

As the word, the deed proved; ere a
     brief year's passage,
Fop – that fool he made the jokes on –
     now he made the jokes for, *gratis*:
Hunks – that hoarder, long left lonely
     in his crass age –
Found now one appreciative
     deferential friend:
Powder-paint-and-patch, Hag Jezebel –
     recovered,
Strange to say, the power to please, got
     courtship till she cried *Jam satis!*
Fop be-flattered, Hunks be-friended,
     Hag be-lovered –
Nobody o'erlooked, save God – he
     soon attained his end.

As he lounged at ease one morning in
     his villa,
(Hag's the dowry) estimated (Hunks'
     bequest) his coin in coffer,
Mused on how a fool's good word
     (Fop's word) could fill a
Social circle with his praise, promote
     him man of mark, –
All at once – 'An old friend fain would
     see your Highness!'
There stood Peter, skeleton and
     scarecrow, plain writ *Phi-lo-so-pher*
In the woe-worn face – for yellowness
     and dryness,
Parchment – with a pair of eyes – one
     hope their feeble spark.

'Did I counsel rightly? Have you, in
     accordance,
Prospered greatly, dear my pupil? Sure,
     at just the stage I find you,
When your hand may draw me forth
     from the mad war-dance
Savages are leading round your master
     – down, not dead.
Padua wants to burn me: baulk them,
     let me linger

Life out – rueful though its remnant –
   hid in some safe hole behind you!
Prostrate here I lie: quick, help with
   but a finger
Lest I house in safety's self – a tomb-
   stone o'er my head!

'Lodging, bite and sup, with – now and
   then – a copper
– Alms for any poorer still, if such
   there be, – is all my asking.
Take me for your bedesman, – nay, if
   you think proper,
Menial merely, – such my perfect
   passion for repose!
Yes, from out your plenty Peter craves a
   pittance
– Leave to thaw his frozen hands before
   the fire whereat you're basking!
Double though your debt were, grant
   this boon – remittance
He proclaims of obligation: 'tis himself
   that owes!'

'Venerated Master – can it be, such
   treatment
Learning meets with, magic fails to
   guard you from, by all appearance?
Strange! for, as you entered, – what the
   famous feat meant,
I was full of, – why you reared that
   fabric, Padua's boast.
Nowise for man's pride, man's
   pleasure, did you slyly
Raise it, but man's seat of rule whereby
   the world should soon have
   clearance
(Happy world) from such a rout as
   now so vilely
Handles you – and hampers me, for
   which I grieve the most.

'Since if it got wind you now were my
   familiar,
How could I protect you – nay, defend
   myself against the rabble?

Wait until the mob, now masters,
   willy-nilly are
Servants as they should be: then has
   gratitude full play!
Surely this experience shows how
   unbefitting
'Tis that minds like mine should rot in
   ease and plenty. Geese may
   gabble,
Gorge, and keep the ground: but
   swans are soon for quitting
Earthly fare – as fain would I, your
   swan, if taught the way.

'Teach me, then, to rule men, have
   them at my pleasure!
Solely for their good, of course, –
   impart a secret worth rewarding,
Since the proper life's-prize! Tantalus's
   treasure
Aught beside proves, vanishes and
   leaves no trace at all.
Wait awhile, nor press for payment
   prematurely!
Over-haste defrauds you. Thanks! since,
   – even while I speak, – discarding
Sloth and vain delights, I learn how –
   swiftly, surely, –
Magic sways the sceptre, wears the
   crown and wields the ball!

'Gone again – what, is he? 'Faith, he's
   soon disposed of!
Peter's precepts work already, put
   within my lump their leaven!
Ay, we needs must don glove would
   we pluck the rose – doff
Silken garment would we climb the
   tree and take its fruit.
Why sharp thorn, rough rind? To keep
   unviolated
Either prize! We garland us, we mount
   from earth to feast in heaven,
Just because exist what once we
   estimated
Hindrances which, better taught, as
   helps we now compute.

'Foolishly I turned disgusted from my
    fellows!
Pits of ignorance – to fill, and heaps of
    prejudice – to level –
Multitudes in motley, whites and
    blacks and yellows –
What a hopeless task it seemed to
    discipline the host!
Now I see my error. Vices act like
    virtues
– Not alone because they guard – sharp
    thorns – the rose we first dishevel,
Not because they scrape, scratch – rough
    rind – through the dirt-shoes
Bare feet cling to bole with, while the
    half-mooned boot we boast.

'No, my aim is nobler, more
    disinterested!
Man shall keep what seemed to thwart
    him, since it proves his true
    assistance,
Leads to ascertaining which head is the
    best head,
Would he crown his body, rule its
    members – lawless else.
Ignorant the horse stares, by deficient
    vision
Takes a man to be a monster, lets him
    mount, then, twice the distance
Horse could trot unridden, gallops –
    dream Elysian! –
Dreaming that his dwarfish guide's a
    giant, – jockeys tell's.'

Brief, so worked the spell, he promptly
    had a riddance:
Heart and brain no longer felt the
    pricks which passed for
    conscience-scruples:
Free henceforth his feet, – *Per Bacco*,
    how they did dance
Merrily through lets and checks that
    stopped the way before!
Politics the prize now, – such adroit
    adviser,

Opportune suggester, with the tact that
    triples and quadruples
Merit in each measure, – never did the
    Kaiser
Boast a subject such a statesman,
    friend, and something more!

As he, up and down, one noonday,
    paced his closet
– Council o'er, each spark (his hint)
    blown flame, by colleagues' breath
    applauded,
Strokes of statecraft hailed with
    '*Salomo si nôsset!*'
(His the nostrum) – every throw for
    luck come double-six, –
As he, pacing, hugged himself in
    satisfaction,
Thump – the door went. 'What, the
    Kaiser? By none else were I
    defrauded
Thus of well-earned solace. Since 'tis
    fate's exaction, –
Enter, Liege my Lord! Ha, Peter, you
    here? *Teneor vix!*'

'Ah, Sir, none the less, contain you,
    nor wax irate!
You so lofty, I so lowly, – vast the
    space which yawns between us!
Still, methinks, you – more than ever –
    at a high rate
Needs must prize poor Peter's secret
    since it lifts you thus.
Grant me now the boon whereat before
    you boggled!
Ten long years your march has moved
    – one triumph – (though *e*'s
    short) – *hact$nus*,
While I down and down disastrously
    have joggled
Till I pitch against Death's door, the
    true *Nec Ultra Plus*.

'Years ago – some ten 'tis – sines I
    sought for shelter,

Craved in your whole house a closet,
    out of all your means a comfort.
Now you soar above these: as is gold to
    spelter
So is power – you urged with reason –
    paramount to wealth.
Power you boast in plenty: let it grant
    me refuge!
Houseroom now is out of question:
    find for me some stronghold –
    some fort –
Privacy wherein, immured, shall this
    blind deaf huge
Monster of a mob let stay the soul I'd
    save by stealth!

'Ay, for all too much with magic have I
    tampered!
– Lost the world, and gained, I fear, a
    certain place I'm to describe loth!
Still, if prayer and fasting tame the
    pride long pampered,
Mercy may be mine: amendment never
    comes too late.
How can I amend beset by cursers,
    kickers?
Pluck this brand from out the burning!
    Once away, I take my Bible-oath,
Never more – so long as life's weak
    lamp-flame flickers –
No, not once I'll tease you, but in
    silence bear my fate!'

'Gently, good my Genius, Oracle
    unerring!
Strange now! can you guess on what –
    as in you peeped – it was I
    pondered?
You and I are both of one mind in
    preferring
Power to wealth, but – here's the point
    – what sort of power, I ask?
Ruling men is vulgar, easy and ignoble:
Rid yourself of conscience, quick you
    have at beck and call the fond
    herd.

But who wields the crozier, down may
    fling the crow-bill:
That's the power I covet now; soul's
    sway o'er souls – my task!

' "Well but," you object, "you have it,
    who by glamour
Dress up lies to look like truths, mask
    folly in the garb of reason:
Your soul acts on theirs, sure, when
    the people clamour,
Hold their peace, now fight now fondle,
    – earwigged through the brains."
Possibly! but still the operation's
    mundane,
Grosser than a taste demands which –
    craving manna – kecks at peason –
Power o'er men by wants material: why
    should one deign
Rule by sordid hopes and fears – a
    grunt for all one's pains?

'No, if men must praise me, let them
    praise to purpose!
Would we move the world, not earth
    but heaven must be our fulcrum –
    *pou sto!*
Thus I seek to move it: Master, why
    intérpose –
Baulk my climbing close on what's the
    ladder's topmost round?
Statecraft 'tis I step from: when by
    priestcraft hoisted
Up to where my foot may touch the
    highest rung which fate allows toe,
Then indeed ask favour! On you shall
    be foisted
No excuse: I'll pay my debt, each
    penny of the pound!

'Ho, my knaves without there! Lead
    this worthy downstairs!
No farewell, good Paul – nay, Peter –
    what's your name remembered
    rightly?
Come, he's humble: out another
    would have flounced – airs

Suitors often give themselves when our
    sort bow them forth.
Did I touch his rags? He surely kept his
    distance:
Yet, there somehow passed to me from
    him – where'er the virtue might
    lie –
Something that inspires my soul – Oh,
    by assistance
Doubtlessly of Peter! – still, he's worth
    just what he's worth!

' 'Tis my own soul soars now: soaring
    – how? By crawling!
I'll to Rome, before Rome's feet the
    temporal-supreme lay prostrate!
"Hands" (I'll say) "proficient once in
    pulling, hauling
This and that way men as I was
    minded – feet now clasp!"
Ay, the Kaiser's self has wrung them in
    his fervour!
Now – they only sue to slave for Rome,
    nor at one doit the cost rate.
Rome's adopted child – no bone, no
    muscle, nerve or
Sinew of me but I'll strain, though out
    my life I gasp!'

As he stood one evening proudly – (he
    had traversed
Rome on horseback – peerless pageant!
    – claimed the Lateran as new
    Pope) –
Thinking 'All's attained now! Pontiff!
    Who could have erst
Dreamed of my advance so far when,
    some ten years ago,
I embraced devotion, grew from priest
    to bishop,
Gained the Purple, bribed the
    Conclave, got the Two-thirds, saw
    my coop ope,
Came out – what Rome hails me! O
    were there a wish-shop,
Not one wish more would I purchase –
    lord of all below!

'Ha! – who dares intrude now – puts
    aside the arras?
What, old Peter, here again, at such a
    time, in such a presence?
Satan sends this plague back merely to
    embarrass
Me who enter on my office – little
    needing you!
'Faith, I'm touched myself by age, but
    you look Tithon!
Were it vain to seek of you the sole
    prize left – rejuvenescence?
Well, since flesh is grass which Time
    must lay his scythe on,
Say your say and so depart and make
    no more ado!'

Peter faltered – coughing first by way of
    prologue –
'Holiness, your help comes late: a
    death at ninety little matters,
Padua, build poor Peter's pyre now, on
    log roll log,
Burn away – I've lived my day! Yet
    here's the sting in death –
I've an author's pride: I want my
    Book's survival:
See, I've hid it in my breast to warm
    me mid the rags and tatters!
Save it – tell next age your Master had
    no rival!
Scholar's debt discharged in full, be
    "Thanks" my latest breath!'

'Faugh, the frowsy bundle – scribblings
    harum-scarum
Scattered o'er a dozen sheepskins!
    What's the name of this farrago?
Ha – "*Conciliator Differentiarum*" –
Man and book may burn together,
    cause the world no loss!
Stop – what else? A tractate – eh, "*De
    Speciebus
Ceremonialis Ma–gi–æ?*" I dream sure!
    Hence, away, go,
Wizard, – quick avoid me! Vain you
    clasp my knee, buss

Hand that bears the Fisher's ring or
    foot that boasts the Cross!

'Help! The old magician clings like an
    octopus!
Ah, you rise now – fuming, fretting,
    frowning, if I read your features!
Frown, who cares? We're Pope – once
    Pope, you can't unpope us!
Good – you muster up a smile: that's
    better! Still so brisk?
All at once grown youthful? But the
    case is plain! Ass –
Here I dally with the fiend, yet know
    the Word – compels all creatures
Earthly, heavenly, hellish. *Apage,*
    *Sathanas!*
*Dicam verbum Salomonis –* ' ' *– dicite!'*
    When – whisk! –

What was changed? The stranger gave
    his eyes a rubbing:
There smiled Peter's face turned back a
    moment at him o'er the shoulder,
As the black door shut, bang! 'So he
    'scapes a drubbing!'
(Quoth a boy who, unespied, had
    stopped to hear the talk.)
'That's the way to thank these wizards
    when they bid men
*Benedicite!* What ails you? You, a man,
    and yet no bolder?
Foreign Sir, you look but foolish!'
    '*Idmen, idmen!*'
Groaned the Greek. 'O Peter, cheese at
    last I know from chalk!'

Peter lived his life out, menaced yet no
    martyr,
Knew himself the mighty man he was –
    such knowledge all his guerdon,
Left the world a big book – people but
    in part err
When they style a true *Scientiæ Com-*
    *pen–di–um:*
'*Admirationem incutit*' they sourly

Smile, as fast they shut the folio which
    myself was somehow spurred on
Once to ope: but love – life's milk
    which daily, hourly,
Blockheads lap – O Peter, still thy taste
    of love's to come!

Greek, was your ambition likewise
    doomed to failure?
True, I find no record you wore purple,
    walked with axe and fasces,
Played some antipope's part: still,
    friend, don't turn tail, you're
Certain, with but these two gifts, to
    gain earth's prize in time!
Cleverness uncurbed by conscience – if
    you ransacked
Peter's book you'd find no potent spell
    like these to rule the masses;
Nor should want example, had I not to
    transact
Other business. Go your ways, you'll
    thrive! So ends my rhyme.

*   *   *

When these parts Tiberius, – not yet
    Cæsar, – travelled,
Passing Padua, he consulted Padua's
    Oracle of Geryon
(God three-headed, thrice wise) just to
    get unravelled
Certain tangles of his future. 'Fling at
    Abano
Golden dice,' it answered: 'dropt
    within the fount there,
Note what sum the pips present!' And
    still we see each die, the very one,
Turn up, through the crystal, – read
    the whole account there
Where 'tis told by Suetonius, – each its
    highest throw.

Scarce the sportive fancy-dice I fling
    show 'Venus:'
Still – for love of that dear land which I
    so oft in dreams revisit –

I have – oh, not sung! but lilted (as –
    between us –
Grows my lazy custom) this its legend.
    What the lilt?

### Doctor —

A Rabbi told me: On the day allowed
Satan for carping at God's rule, he
    came,
Fresh from our earth, to brave the
    angel-crowd.

'What is the fault now?' 'This I find to
    blame:
Many and various are the tongues below,
Yet all agree in one speech, all proclaim

' "Hell has no might to match what
    earth can show:
Death is the strongest-born of Hell, and
    yet
Stronger than Death is a Bad Wife, we
    know."

'Is it a wonder if I fume and fret –
Robbed of my rights, since Death am I,
    and mine
The style of Strongest? Men pay Nature's
    debt'

'Because they must at my demand;
    decline
To pay it henceforth surely men will
    please,

Provided husbands with bad wives
    combine
'To baffle Death. Judge between me
    and these!'
'Thyself shalt judge. Descend to earth
    in shape
Of mortal, marry, drain from froth to
    lees

'The bitter draught, then see if thou
    escape
Concluding, with men sorrowful and
    sage,
A Bad Wife's strength Death's self in
    vain would ape!'

How Satan entered on his pilgrimage,
Conformed himself to earthly
    ordinance,
Wived and played husband well from
    youth to age

Intrepidly – I leave untold, advance
Through many a married year until I
    reach
A day when – of his father's countenance

The very image, like him too in speech
As well as thought and deed, – the
    union's fruit
Attained maturity. 'I needs must teach

'My son a trade: but trade, such son to
    suit,
Needs seeking after. He a man of war?
Too cowardly! A lawyer wins repute –

'Having to toil and moil, though – both
    which are
Beyond this sluggard. There's Divinity:
No, that's my own bread-winner – that
    be far

'From my poor offspring! Physic? Ha,
    we'll try
If this be practicable. Where's my wit?
Asleep? – since, now I come to
    think ... Ay, ay!

'Hither, my son! Exactly have I hit
On a profession for thee. *Medicus* –
Behold, thou art appointed! Yea, I spit

'Upon thine eyes, bestow a virtue thus
That henceforth not this human form I
   wear
Shalt thou perceive alone, but – one
   of us

'By privilege – thy fleshly sight shall bear
Me in my spirit-person as I walk
The world and take my prey appointed
   there.

'Doctor once dubbed – what ignorance
   shall baulk
Thy march triumphant? Diagnose the
   gout
As cholic, and prescribe it cheese for
   chalk –

'No matter! All's one: cure shall come
   about
And win thee wealth – fees paid with
   such a roar
Of thanks and praise alike from lord
   and lout

'As never stunned man's ears on earth
   before.
"How may this be?" Why, that's my
   sceptic! Soon
Truth will corrupt thee, soon thou
   doubt'st no more!

'Why is it I bestow on thee the boon
Of recognizing me the while I go
Invisibly among men, morning, noon

'And night, from house to house, and
   – quick or slow –
Take my appointed prey? They
   summon thee
For help, suppose: obey the summons!
   so!

'Enter, look round! Where's Death?
   Know – I am he,
Satan who work all evil: I who bring
Pain to the patient in whate'er degree.

'I, then, am there: first glance thine eye
   shall fling
Will find me – whether distant or at
   hand,
As I am free to do my spiriting.

'At such mere first glance thou shalt
   understand
Wherefore I reach no higher up the
   room
Than door or window, when my form
   is scanned.

'Howe'er friends' faces please to gather
   gloom,
Bent o'er the sick, – howe'er himself
   desponds, –
In such case Death is not the sufferer's
   doom.

'Contrariwise, do friends rejoice my
   bonds
Are broken, does the captive in his turn
Crow "Life shall conquer"? Nip these
   foolish fronds

'Of hope a-sprout, if haply thou discern
Me at the head – my victim's head, be
   sure!
Forth now! This taught thee, little else
   to learn!'

And forth he went. Folk heard him ask
   demure
'How do you style this ailment? (There
   he peeps,
My father, through the arras!) Sirs, the
   cure

'Is plain as A. B. C.! Experience steeps
Blossoms of pennyroyal half an hour
In sherris. *Sumat!* – Lo, how sound he
   sleeps –

'The subject you presumed was past
          the power
Of Galen to relieve!' Or else 'How's this?
Why call for help so tardily? Clouds lour

'Portentously indeed, Sirs! (Nought's
          amiss:
He's at the bed-foot merely.) Still, the
          storm
May pass averted – not by quacks, I wis

'Like you, my masters! You, forsooth,
          perform
A miracle? Stand, sciolists, aside!
Blood, ne'er so cold, at ignorance
          grows warm!'

Which boasting by result was justified,
Big as might words be: whether
          drugged or left
Drugless, the patient always lived, not
          died.

Great the heir's gratitude, so nigh bereft
Of all he prized in this world: sweet the
          smile
Of disconcerted rivals: 'Cure? – say,
          theft

'From Nature in despite of Art – so
          style
This off-hand kill-or-cure work! You
          did much,
I had done more: folk cannot wait
          awhile!'

But did the case change? was it –
          'Scarcely such
The symptoms as to warrant our recourse
To your skill, Doctor! Yet since just a
          touch

'Of pulse, a taste of breath, has all the
          force
With you of long investigation claimed
By others, – tracks an ailment to its
          source

'Intuitively, – may we ask unblamed
What from this pimple you
          prognosticate?'
'Death!' was the answer, as he saw and
          named

The coucher by the sick man's head.
          'Too late
You send for my assistance. I am bold
Only by Nature's leave, and bow to
          Fate!

'Besides, you have my rivals: lavish gold!
How comfortably quick shall life depart
Cosseted by attentions manifold!

'One day, one hour ago, perchance my
          art
Had done some service. Since you have
          yourselves
Chosen – before the horse – to put the
          cart,

'Why, Sirs, the sooner that the sexton
          delves
Your patient's grave, the better! How
          you stare
– Shallow, for all the deep books on
          your shelves!

'Fare you well, fumblers!' Do I need
          declare
What name and fame, what riches
          recompensed
The Doctor's practice? Never anywhere

Such an adept as daily evidenced
Each new vaticination! Oh, not he
Like dolts who dallied with their
          scruples fenced

With subterfuge, nor gave out frank
          and free
Something decisive! If he said 'I save
The patient,'saved he was: if 'Death
          will be

'His portion,' you might count him
    dead. Thus brave,
Behold our worthy, sans competitor
Throughout the country, on the
    architrave

Of Glory's temple golden-lettered for
Machaon *redivivus!* So, it fell
That, of a sudden, when the Emperor

Was smit by sore disease, I need not
    tell
If any other Doctor's aid was sought
To come and forthwith make the sick
    Prince well.

'He will reward thee as a monarch ought.
Not much imports the malady; but then,
He clings to life and cries like one
    distraught

'For thee – who, from a simple citizen,
Mayst look to rise in rank, – nay, haply
    wear
A medal with his portrait, – always
    when

'Recovery is quite accomplished. There!
Pass to the presence!' Hardly has he
    crossed
The chamber's threshold when he halts,
    aware

Of who stands sentry by the head. All's
    lost.
'Sire, nought avails my art: you near the
    goal,
And end the race by giving up the
    ghost.'

'How?' cried the monarch: 'Names
    upon your roll
Of half my subjects rescued by your
    skill –
Old and young, rich and poor – crowd
    cheek by jowl

'And yet no room for mine? Be saved I
    will!
Why else am I earth's foremost
    potentate?
Add me to these and take as fee your
    fill

'Of gold – that point admits of no
    debate
Between us: save me, as you can and
    must, –
Gold, till your gown's pouch cracks
    beneath the weight!'

This touched the Doctor. 'Truly a
    home-thrust,
Parent, you will not parry! Have I dared
Entreat that you forego the meal of
    dust

' – Man that is snake's meat – when I
    saw prepared
Your daily portion? Never! Just this once,
Go from his head, then, – let his life be
    spared!'

Whisper met whisper in the gruff
    response
'Fool, I must have my prey: no inch I
    budge
From where thou see'st me thus myself
    ensconce.'

'Ah,' moaned the sufferer, 'by thy look
    I judge
Wealth fails to tempt thee: what if
    honours prove
More efficacious? Nought to him I grudge

'Who saves me. Only keep my head
    above
The cloud that's creeping round it – I'll
    divide
My empire with thee! No? What's left
    but – love?

'Does love allure thee? Well then, take
        as bride
My only daughter, fair beyond belief!
Save me – to-morrow shall the knot be
        tied!'

'Father, you hear him! Respite ne'er so
        brief
Is all I beg: go now and come again
Next day, for aught I care: respect the
        grief

'Mine will be if thy first-born sues in
        vain!
'Fool, I must have my prey!' was all he
        got
In answer. But a fancy crossed his brain.

'I have it! Sire, methinks a meteor shot
Just now across the heavens and
        neutralized
Jove's salutary influence: 'neath the blot

'Plumb are you placed now: well that I
        surmised
The cause of failure! Knaves, reverse the
        bed!'
'Stay!' groaned the monarch, 'I shall be
        capsized –

'Jolt – jolt – my heels uplift where late
        my head
Was lying – sure I'm turned right round
        at last!
What do you say now, Doctor?' Nought
        he said:

For why? With one brisk leap the Antic
        passed
From couch-foot back to pillow, – as
        before,
Lord of the situation. Long aghast

The Doctor gazed, then 'Yet one trial
        more
Is left me' inwardly he uttered. 'Shame
Upon thy flinty heart! Do I implore

'This trifling favour in the idle name
Of mercy to the moribund? I plead
The cause of all thou dost affect: my aim

'Befits my author! Why would I succeed?
Simply that by success I may promote
The growth of thy pet virtues – pride
        and greed.

'But keep thy favours! – curse thee! I
        devote
Henceforth my service to the other side.
No time to lose: the rattle's in his throat.

'So, – not to leave one last resource
        untried, –
Run to my house with all haste, some–
        body!
Bring me that knobstick thence, so
        often plied

'With profit by the astrologer – shall I
Disdain its help, the mystic Jacob's Staff?
Sire, do but have the courage not to die

'Till this arrive! Let none of you dare
        laugh!
Though rugged its exterior, I have seen
That implement work wonders, send
        the chaff

'Quick and thick flying from the wheat
        – I mean,
By metaphor, a human sheaf it thrashed
Flail-like. Go fetch it! Or – a word
        between

'Just you and me, friend! – go bid,
        unabashed,
My mother, whom you'll find there,
        bring the stick
Herself – herself, mind!' Out the lackey
        dashed

Zealous upon the errand. Craft and trick
Are meat and drink to Satan: and he
        grinned
– How else? – at an excuse so politic

For failure: scarce would Jacob's-Staff
    rescind
Fate's firm decree! And ever as he neared
The agonizing one, his breath like wind

Froze to the marrow, while his eye-
    flash seared
Sense in the brain up: closelier and
    more close
Pressing his prey, when at the door
    appeared

– Who but his Wife the Bad? Whereof
    one dose,
One grain, one mite of the medicament,
Sufficed him. Up he sprang. One word,
    too gross

To soil my lips with, – and through
    ceiling went
Somehow the Husband. 'That a storm's
    dispersed
We know for certain by the sulphury
    scent!

'Hail to the Doctor! Who but one so
    versed
In all Dame Nature's secrets had
    prescribed
The staff thus opportunely? Style him
    first

'And foremost of physicians!' 'I've
    imbibed
Elixir surely,' smiled the prince, – 'have
    gained
New lease of life. Dear Doctor, how
    you bribed

'Death to forego me, boots not: you've
    obtained
My daughter and her dowry. Death,
    I've heard,
Was still on earth the strongest power
    that reigned,

'Except a Bad Wife!' Whereunto
    demurred

Nowise the Doctor, so refused the fee
– No dowry, no bad wife!

'You think absurd
This tale?' – the Rabbi added: 'True,
    our Talmud
Boasts sundry such: yet – have our
    elders erred
In thinking there's some water there,
    not all mud?'
I tell it, as the Rabbi told it me.

## Pan and Luna

Si credere dignum est. – *Georgic,* iii, 390

O worthy of belief I hold it was,
Virgil, your legend in those strange
    three lines!
No question, that adventure came to
    pass
One black night in Arcadia: yes, the
    pines,
Mountains and valleys mingling made
    one mass
Of black with void black heaven: the
    earth's confines,
The sky's embrace, – below, above,
    around,
All hardened into black without a
    bound.

Fill up a swart stone chalice to the brim
With fresh-squeezed yet fast-thickening
    poppy-juice:
See how the sluggish jelly, late a-swim,
Turns marble to the touch of who
    would loose
The solid smooth, grown jet from rim
    to rim,
By turning round the bowl! So night
    can fuse
Earth with her all-comprising sky. No
    less,
Light, the least spark, shows air and
    emptiness.

And thus it proved when – diving into
    space,
Stript of all vapour, from each web of
    mist
Utterly film-free – entered on her race
The naked Moon, full-orbed antagonist
Of night and dark, night's dowry: peak
    to base,
Upstarted mountains, and each valley,
    kissed
To sudden life, lay silver-bright: in air
Flew she revealed, Maid-Moon with
    limbs all bare.

Still as she fled, each depth – where
    refuge seemed –
Opening a lone pale chamber, left distinct
Those limbs: mid still-retreating blue,
    she teemed
Herself with whiteness, – virginal, uncinct
By any halo save what finely gleamed
To outline not disguise her: heaven
    was linked
In one accord with earth to quaff the
    joy,
Drain beauty to the dregs without alloy.

Whereof she grew aware. What help?
    When, lo,
A succourable cloud with sleep lay
    dense:
Some pine-tree-top had caught it sailing
    slow,
And tethered for a prize: in evidence
Captive lay fleece on fleece of piled-up
    snow
Drowsily patient: flake-heaped how or
    whence,
The structure of that succourable cloud,
What matter? Shamed she plunged
    into its shroud.

Orbed – so the woman-figure poets call
Because of rounds on rounds – that
    apple-shaped
Head which its hair binds close into a
    ball

Each side the curving ears – that pure
    undraped
Pout of the sister paps – that … Once
    for all,
Say – her consummate circle thus escaped
With its innumerous circlets, sank
    absorbed,
Safe in the cloud – O naked Moon full-
    orbed!

But what means this? The downy swathes
    combine,
Conglobe, the smothery coy-caressing
    stuff
Curdles about her! Vain each twist and
    twine
Those lithe limbs try, encroached on
    by a fluff
Fitting as close as fits the dented spine
Its flexile ivory outside-flesh: enough!
The plumy drifts contract, condense,
    constringe,
Till she is swallowed by the feathery
    springe.

As when a pearl slips lost in the thin
    foam
Churned on a sea-shore, and, o'er-
    frothed, conceits
Herself safe-housed in Amphitrite's
    dome, –
If, through the bladdery wave-worked
    yeast, she meets
What most she loathes and leaps from,
    – elf from gnome
No gladlier, – finds that safest of retreats
Bubble about a treacherous hand wide
    ope
To grasp her – (divers who pick pearls
    so grope) –

So lay this Maid-Moon clasped around
    and caught
By rough red Pan, the god of all that
    tract:
He it was schemed the snare thus
    subtly wrought

With simulated earth-breath, – wool-
    tufts packed
Into a billowy wrappage. Sheep far-
    sought
For spotless shearings yield such: take
    the fact
As learned Virgil gives it, – how the
    breed
Whitens itself for ever: yes, indeed!

If one forefather ram, though pure as
    chalk
From tinge on fleece, should still
    display a tongue
Black 'neath the beast's moist palate,
    prompt men baulk
The propagating plague: he gets no
    young:
They rather slay him, – sell his hide to
    caulk
Ships with, first steeped in pitch, – nor
    hands are wrung
In sorrow for his fate: protected thus,
The purity we love is gained for us.

So did Girl-moon, by just her attribute
Of unmatched modesty betrayed, lie
    trapped,
Bruised to the breast of Pan, half-god
    half-brute,
Raked by his bristly boar-sward while
    he lapped
– Never say, kissed her! that were to
    pollute
Love's language – which moreover
    proves unapt
To tell how she recoiled – as who finds
    thorns
Where she sought flowers – when,
    feeling, she touched – horns!

Then – does the legend say? – first
    moon-eclipse
Happened, first swooning-fit which
    puzzled sore
The early sages? Is that why she dips
Into the dark, a minute and no more,

Only so long as serves her while she
    rips
The cloud's womb through and,
    faultless as before,
Pursues her way? No lesson for a maid
Left she, a maid herself thus trapped,
    betrayed?

Ha, Virgil? Tell the rest, you! 'To the
    deep
Of his domain the wildwood, Pan
    forthwith
Called her, and so she followed' – in
    her sleep,
Surely? – 'by no means spurning him.'
    The myth
Explain who may! Let all else go, I
    keep
– As of a ruin just a monolith –
Thus much, one verse of five words,
    each a boon:
Arcadia, night, a cloud, Pan, and the
    moon.

*    *    *

'Touch him ne'er so lightly, into song
    he broke:
Soil so quick-receptive, – not one
    feather-seed,
Not one flower-dust fell but straight its
    fall awoke
Vitalizing virtue: song would song
    succeed
Sudden as spontaneous – prove a poet-
    soul!'
Indeed?
Rock's the song-soil rather, surface
    hard and bare:
Sun and dew their mildness, storm and
    frost their rage
Vainly both expend, – few flowers
    awaken mere:
Quiet in its cleft broods – what the
    after age
Knows and names a pine, a nation's
    heritage.

# JOCOSERIA

1883

Wanting is – What?
Summer redundant,
Blueness abundant,
– Where is the blot?
Beamy the world, yet a blank all the
     same,
– Framework which waits for a picture
     to frame:
What of the leafage, what of the flower?
Roses embowering with nought they
     embower!
Come then, complete incompletion, O
     comer,
Pant through the blueness, perfect the
     summer!
Breathe but one breath
Rose-beauty above,
And all that was death
Grows life, grows love,
Grows love!

## Donald

'Will you hear my story also,
     – Huge Sport, brave adventure in
     plenty?'
The boys were a band from Oxford,
     The oldest of whom was twenty.

The bothy we held carouse in
     Was bright with fire and candle;
Tale followed tale like a merry-go-round
     Whereof Sport turned the handle.

In our eyes and noses – turf-smoke:
     In our ears a tune from the trivet,
Whence 'Boiling, boiling,' the kettle
     sang,
     'And ready for fresh Glenlivet.'

So, feat capped feat, with a vengeance:
     Truths, though, – the lads were
     loyal:

'Grouse, five score brace to the bag!
     Deer, ten hours' stalk of the Royal!'

Of boasting, not one bit, boys!
     Only there seemed to settle
Somehow above your curly heads,
     – Plain through the singing kettle,

Palpable through the cloud,
     As each new-puffed Havanna
Rewarded the teller's well-told tale,
     This vaunt 'To Sport – Hosanna!

'Hunt, fish, shoot,
     Would a man fulfil life's duty!
Not to the bodily frame alone
     Does Sport give strength and beauty.

'But character gains in – courage?
     Ay, Sir, and much beside it!
You don't sport, more's the pity:
     You soon would find, if you tried it,

'Good sportsman means good fellow,
     Sound-hearted he, to the centre;
Your mealy-mouthed mild milksops
     – There's where the rot can enter!

'There's where the dirt will breed,
     The shabbiness Sport would banish!
Oh no, Sir, no! In your honoured case
     All such objections vanish.

'"Tis known how hard you studied:
     A Double-First – what, the jigger!
Give me but half your Latin and Greek,
     I'll never again touch trigger!

'Still, tastes are tastes, allow me!
     Allow, too, where there's keenness
For Sport, there's little likelihood
     Of a man's displaying meanness!'

So, put on my mettle, I interposed.
　'Will you hear my story?' quoth I.
'Never mind how long since it happed,
　I sat, as we sit, in a bothy;

'With as merry a band of mates, too,
　Undergrads all on a level:
(One's a Bishop, one's gone to the Bench,
　And one's gone – well, to the Devil.)

'When, lo, a scratching and tapping!
　In hobbled a ghastly visitor.
Listen to just what he told us himself
　– No need of our playing
　　inquisitor!'

　　　*　　　*　　　*

Do you happen to know in Ross-shire
　Mount … Ben … but the name
　　scarce matters:
Of the naked fact I am sure enough,
　Though I clothe it in rags and
　　tatters.

You may recognise Ben by description;
　Behind him – a moor's immenseness:
Up goes the middle mount of a range,
　Fringed with its firs in denseness.

Rimming the edge, its fir-fringe, mind!
　For an edge there is, though narrow;
From end to end of the range, a stripe
　Of path runs straight as an arrow.

And the mountaineer who takes that
　　path
　Saves himself miles of journey
He has to plod if he crosses the moor
　Through heather, peat and burnie.

But a mountaineer he needs must be,
　For, look you, right in the middle
Projects bluff Ben – with an end in *ich* –
　Why planted there, is a riddle:

Since all Ben's brothers little and big
　Keep rank, set shoulder to shoulder,

And only this burliest out must bulge
　Till it seems – to the beholder

From down in the gully, – as if Ben's
　　breast
　To a sudden spike diminished,
Would signify to the boldest foot
　'All further passage finished!'

Yet the mountaineer who sidles on
　And on to the very bending,
Discovers, if heart and brain be proof,
　No necessary ending.

Foot up, foot down, to the turn abrupt
　Having trod, he, there arriving,
Finds – what he took for a point was
　　breadth,
　A mercy of Nature's contriving.

So, he rounds what, when 'tis reached,
　　proves straight,
　From one side gains the other:
The wee path widens – resume the
　　march,
　And he foils you, Ben my brother!

But Donald – (that name, I hope, will
　　do) –
　I wrong him if I call 'foiling'
The tramp of the callant, whistling the
　　while
　As blithe as our kettle's boiling.

He had dared the danger from boyhood
　　up,
　And now, – when perchance was
　　waiting
A lass at the brig below, – 'twixt mount
　And moor would he stand debating?

Moreover this Donald was twenty-five,
　A glory of bone and muscle:
Did a fiend dispute the right of way,
　Donald would try a tussle.

Lightsomely marched he out of the broad
   On to the narrow and narrow;
A step more, rounding the angular rock,
   Reached the front straight as an arrow.

He stepped it, safe on the ledge he
    stood,
   When – whom found he full-facing?
What fellow in courage and wariness
    too,
   Had scouted ignoble pacing,

And left low safety to timid mates,
   And made for the dread dear danger,
And gained the height where – who
    could guess
   He would meet with a rival ranger?

'Twas a gold-red stag that stood and
    stared,
Gigantic and magnific,
By the wonder – ay, and the peril –
    struck
   Intelligent and pacific:

For a red deer is no fallow deer
   Grown cowardly through park-
    feeding;
He batters you like a thunderbolt
   If you brave his haunts unheeding.

I doubt he could hardly perform *volte-
face*
   Had valour advised discretion:
You may walk on a rope, but to turn
    on a rope
   No Blondin makes profession.

Yet Donald must turn, would pride
    permit,
   Though pride ill brooks retiring:
Each eyed each – mute man,
    motionless beast –
   Less fearing than admiring.

These are the moments when quite new
    sense,

   To meet some need as novel,
Springs up in the brain: it inspired
    resource:
   – 'Nor advance nor retreat but – grovel!'

And slowly, surely, never a whit
   Relaxing the steady tension
Of eye-stare which binds man to
    beast, –
   By an inch and inch declension,

Sank Donald sidewise down and down:
   Till flat, breast upwards, lying
At his six-foot length, no corpse more
    still,
   – 'If he cross me! The trick's worth
    trying.'

Minutes were an eternity;
   But a new sense was created
In the stag's brain too; he resolves!
    Slow, sure,
   With eye-stare unabated,

Feelingly he extends a foot
   Which tastes the way ere it touches
Earth's solid and just escapes man's soft,
   Nor hold of the same unclutches

Till its fellow foot, light as a feather
    whisk,
   Lands itself no less finely:
So a mother removes a fly from the face
   Of her babe asleep supinely.

And now 'tis the haunch and hind
    foot's turn
   – That's hard: can the beast quite
    raise it?
Yes, traversing half the prostrate length,
   His hoof-tip does not graze it.

Just one more lift! But Donald, you see,
   Was sportsman first, man after:
A fancy lightened his caution through,
   – He well-nigh broke into laughter.

'It were nothing short of a miracle!
  Unrivalled, unexampled –
All sporting feats with this feat matched
  Were down and dead and trampled!'

The last of the legs as tenderly
  Follows the rest: or never
Or now is the time! His knife in reach,
  And his right-hand loose – how clever!

For this can stab up the stomach's soft,
  While the left-hand grasps the pastern.
A rise on the elbow, and – now's the
  time
  Or never: this turn's the last turn!

I shall dare to place myself by God
  Who scanned – for He does – each
  feature
Of the face thrown up in appeal to Him
  By the agonizing creature.

Nay, I hear plain words: 'Thy gift brings
  this!'
  Up he sprang, back he staggered,
Over he fell, and with him our friend
  – At following game no laggard.

Yet he was not dead when they picked
  next day
  From the gully's depth the wreck of
  him;
His fall had been stayed by the stag
  beneath
  Who cushioned and saved the neck
  of him.

But the rest of his body – why, doctors
  said,
  Whatever could break was broken:
Legs, arms, ribs, all of him looked like
  a toast
  In a tumbler of port-wine soaken.

'That your life is left you, thank the stag!'
  Said they when – the slow cure
  ended –

They opened the hospital door, and
  thence
  – Strapped, spliced, main fractures
  mended,

And minor damage left wisely alone, –
  Like an old shoe clouted and
  cobbled,
Out – what went in a Goliath well-
  nigh, –
  Some half of a David hobbled.

'You must ask an alms from house to
  house:
  Sell the stag's head for a bracket,
With its grand twelve tines – I'd buy it
  myself –
  And use the skin for a jacket!'

He was wiser, made both head and hide
  His win-penny: hands and knees on,
Would manage to crawl – poor crab –
  by the roads
  In the misty stalking-season.

And if he discovered a bothy like this,
  Why, harvest was sure: folk listened.
He told his tale to the lovers of Sport:
  Lips twitched, cheeks glowed, eyes
  glistened.

And when he had come to the close,
  and spread
  His spoils for the gazers' wonder,
With 'Gentlemen, here's the skull of
  the stag
  I was over, thank God, not under!' –

The company broke out in applause;
  'By Jingo, a lucky cripple!
Have a munch of grouse and a hunk of
  bread,
  And a tug, besides, at our tipple!'

And 'There's my pay for your pluck!'
  cried This,
  'And mine for your jolly story!'

Cried That, while T'other – but he was
    drunk –
    Hiccupped 'A trump, a Tory!'

I hope I gave twice as much as the rest;
    For, as Homer would say, 'within
    grate
Though teeth kept tongue,' my whole
    soul growled
    'Rightly rewarded, – Ingrate!'


### Solomon and Balkis

Solomon King of the Jews and the
    Queen of Sheba Balkis
Talk on the ivory throne, and we well
    may conjecture their talk is
Solely of things sublime: why else has
    she sought Mount Zion,
Climbed the six golden steps, and sat
    betwixt lion and lion?

She proves him with hard questions:
    before she has reached the middle
He smiling supplies the end, straight
    solves them riddle by riddle;
Until, dead-beaten at last, there is left
    no spirit in her,
And thus would she close the game
    whereof she was first beginner:

'O wisest thou of the wise, world's
    marvel and well-nigh monster,
One crabbed question more to
    construe or *vulgo* conster!
Who are those, of all mankind, a
    monarch of perfect wisdom
Should open to, when they knock at
    *spheteron do* – that's his dome?'

The King makes tart reply: 'Whom else
    but the wise his equals
Should he welcome with heart and
    voice? – since, king though he be,
    such weak walls

Of circumstance – power and pomp –
    divide souls each from other
That whoso proves kingly in craft I
    needs must acknowledge my
    brother.

'Come poet, come painter, come
    sculptor, come builder – whate'er
    his condition,
Is he prime in his art? We are peers! My
    insight has pierced the partition
And hails – for the poem, the picture,
    the statue, the building – my fellow!
Gold's gold though dim in the dust:
    court-polish soon turns it yellow.

'But tell me in turn, O thou to thy
    weakling sex superior,
That for knowledge has travelled so far
    yet seemest no whit the wearier, –
Who are those, of all mankind, a
    queen like thyself, consummate
In wisdom, should call to her side with
    an affable "Up hither, come,
    mate!" '

'The Good are my mates – how else?
    Why doubt it?' the Queen
    upbridled:
'Sure even above the Wise, – or in
    travel my eyes have idled, –
I see the Good stand plain: be they
    rich, poor, shrewd or simple,
If Good they only are … Permit me to
    drop my wimple!'

And in that bashful jerk of her body,
    she – peace, thou scoffer! –
Jostled the King's right-hand stretched
    courteously help to proffer,
And so disclosed a portent: all unaware
    the Prince eyed
The Ring which bore the Name –
    turned outside now from inside!

The truth-compelling Name! – and at
    once 'I greet the Wise – Oh,

Certainly welcome such to my court –
   with this proviso:
The building must be my temple, my
   person stand forth the statue,
The picture my portrait prove, and the
   poem my praise – you cat, you!'

But Solomon nonplussed? Nay! 'Be
   truthful in turn!' so bade he:
'See the Name, obey its hest!' And at
   once subjoins the lady
– 'Provided the Good are the young,
   men strong and tall and proper,
Such servants I straightway enlist, –
   which means … ' but the blushes
   stop her.

'Ah, Soul,' the Monarch sighed, 'that
   wouldst soar yet ever crawlest,
How comes it thou canst discern the
   greatest yet choose the smallest,
Unless because heaven is far, where
   wings find fit expansion,
While creeping on all-fours suits,
   suffices the earthly mansion?

'Aspire to the Best! But which? There
   are Bests and Bests so many,
With a *habitat* each for each, earth's
   Best as much Best as any!
On Lebanon roots the cedar – soil
   lofty, yet stony and sandy –
While hyssop, of worth in its way, on
   the wall grows low but handy.

'Above may the Soul spread wing, spurn
   body and sense beneath her;
Below she must condescend to
   plodding unbuoyed by æther.
In heaven I yearn for knowledge,
   account all else inanity;
On earth I confess an itch for the
   praise of fools – that's Vanity.

'It is nought, it will go, it can never
   presume above to trouble me;

But here, – why, it toys and tickles and
   teases, howe'er I redouble me
In a doggedest of endeavours to play
   the indifferent. Therefore,
Suppose we resume discourse? Thou
   hast travelled thus far: but
   wherefore?

'Solely for Solomon's sake, to see
   whom earth styles Sagest?'
Through her blushes laughed the Queen.
   'For the sake of a Sage? The gay
   jest!
On high, be communion with Mind –
   there, Body concerns not Balkis:
Down here, – do I make too bold? Sage
   Solomon, – one fool's small kiss!'

## Cristina and Monaldeschi

Ah, but how each loved each, Marquis!
   Here's the gallery they trod
   Both together, he her god,
   She his idol, – lend your rod,
Chamberlain! – ay, there they are – '*Quis
   Separabit?*' – plain those two
   Touching words come into view,
   Apposite for me and you:

Since they witness to incessant
   Love like ours: King Francis, he –
   Diane the adored one she –
   Prototypes of you and me.
Everywhere is carved her Crescent
   With his Salamander-sign –
   Flame-fed creature: flame benign
   To itself or, if malign,

Only to the meddling curious,
   – So, be warned, Sir! Where's my
   head?
   How it wanders! What I said
   Merely meant – the creature, fed
Thus on flame, was scarce injurious
   Save to fools who woke its ire,
   Thinking fit to play with fire.
   'Tis the Crescent you admire?

Then, be Diane! I'll be Francis.
    Crescents change, – true! – wax and
        wane,
    Woman-like: male hearts retain
    Heat nor, once warm, cool again,
So, we figure – such our chance is –
    I as man and you as … What?
    Take offence? My Love forgot
    He plays woman, I do not?

I – the woman? See my habit,
    Ask my people! Anyhow,
    Be we what we may, one vow
    Binds us, male or female. Now, –
Stand, Sir! Read! '*Quis separabit?*'
    Half a mile of pictured way
    Past these palace-walls to-day
    Traversed, this I came to say.

You must needs begin to love me;
    First I hated, then, at best,
    – Have it so! – I acquiesced;
    Pure compassion did the rest.
From below thus raised above me,
    Would you, step by step, descend,
    Pity me, become my friend,
    Like me, like less, loathe at end?

That's the ladder's round you rose by!
    That – my own foot kicked away,
    Having raised you: let it stay,
    Serve you for retreating? Nay.
Close to me you climbed: as close by,
    Keep your station, though the peak
    Reached proves somewhat bare and
        bleak!
    Woman's strong if man is weak.

Keep here, loving me forever!
    Love's look, gesture, speech, I claim;
    Act love, lie love, all the same –
    Play as earnest were our game!
Lonely I stood long: 'twas clever
    When you climbed, before men's
        eyes,
    Spurned the earth and scaled the
        skies,

Gained my peak and grasped your
    prize.

Here you stood, then, to men's wonder;
    Here you tire of standing? Kneel!
    Cure what giddiness you feel,
    This way! Do your senses reel?
Not unlikely! What rolls under?
    Yawning death in yon abyss
    Where the waters whirl and his
    Round more frightful peaks than this.

Should my buffet dash you thither …
    But be sage! No watery grave
    Needs await you: seeming brave
    Kneel on safe, dear timid slave!
You surmised, when you climbed hither,
    Just as easy were retreat
    Should you tire, conceive unmeet
    Longer patience at my feet?

Me as standing, you as stooping, –
    Who arranged for each the pose?
    Lest men think us friends turned
        foes,
    Keep the attitude you chose!
Men are used to this same grouping –
    I and you like statues seen.
    You and I, no third between,
    Kneel and stand! That makes the
        scene.

Mar it – and one buffet … Pardon!
    Needless warmth – wise words in
        waste!
    'Twas prostration that replaced
    Kneeling, then? A proof of taste.
Crouch, not kneel, while I mount
        guard on
    Prostrate love – become no waif,
    No estray to waves that chafe
    Disappointed – love's so safe!

Waves that chafe? The idlest fancy!
    Peaks that scare? I think we know
    Walls enclose our sculpture: so
    Grouped, we pose in Fontainebleau.

Up now! Wherefore hesitancy?
   Arm in arm and cheek by cheek,
   Laugh with me at waves and peak!
   Silent still? Why, pictures speak.

See, where Juno strikes Ixion,
   Primatice speaks plainly! Pooh –
   Rather, Florentine Le Roux!
   I've lost head for who is who –
So it swims and wanders! Fie on
   What still proves the female! Here,
   By the staircase! – for we near
   That dark 'Gallery of the Deer.'

Look me in the eyes once! Steady!
   Are you faithful now as erst
   On that eve when we two first
   Vowed at Avon, blessed and cursed
Faith and falsehood? Pale already?
   Forward! Must my hand compel
   Entrance – this way? Exit – well,
   Somehow, somewhere. Who can tell?

What if to the self-same place in
   Rustic Avon, at the door
   Of the village church once more,
   Where a tombstone paves the floor
By that holy-water basin
   You appealed to – 'As, below,
   This stone hides its corpse, e'en so
   I your secrets hide'? What ho!

Friends, my four! You, Priest, confess
   him!
   I have judged the culprit there:
   Execute my sentence! Care
   For no mail such cowards wear!
Done, Priest? Then, absolve and bless
   him!
   Now – you three, stab thick and fast,
   Deep and deeper! Dead at last?
   Thanks, friends – Father, thanks!
   Aghast?

What one word of his confession
   Would you tell me, though I lured
   With that royal crown abjured

Just because its bars immured
Love too much? Love burst compression,
   Fled free, finally confessed
   All its secrets to that breast
   Whence … let Avon tell the rest!

### Mary Wollstonecraft and Fuseli

Oh but is it not hard, Dear?
   Mine are the nerves to quake at a
     mouse:
If a spider drops I shrink with fear:
   I should die outright in a haunted
     house;
While for you – did the danger dared
     bring help –
From a lion's den I could steal his
     whelp,
With a serpent round me, stand stock-
     still,
Go sleep in a churchyard, – so would
     will
Give me the power to dare and do
Valiantly – just for you!

Much amiss in the head, Dear,
   I toil at a language, tax my brain
Attempting to draw – the scratches here!
   I play, play, practise and all in vain:
But for you – if my triumph brought
     you pride,
I would grapple with Greek Plays till I
     died,
Paint a portrait of you – who can tell?
Work my fingers off for your 'Pretty
     well:'
Language and painting and music too,
Easily done – for you!

Strong and fierce in the heart, Dear,
   With – more than a will – what
     seems a power
To pounce on my prey, love outbroke
     here
   In flame devouring and to devour.
Such love has laboured its best and
     worst

To win me a lover; yet, last as first,
I have not quickened his pulse one
    beat,
Fixed a moment's fancy, bitter or sweet:
Yet the strong fierce heart's love's labour's
    due,
Utterly lost, was – you!

### Adam, Lilith and Eve

One day it thundered and lightened.
Two women, fairly frightened,
Sank to their knees, transformed,
    transfixed,
At the feet of the man who sat betwixt;
And 'Mercy!' cried each – 'if I tell the
    truth
Of a passage in my youth!'

Said This: 'Do you mind the morning
I met your love with scorning?
As the worst of the venom left my lips,
I thought "If, despite this lie, he strips
The mask from my soul with a kiss – I
    crawl
His slave, – soul, body and all!" '

Said That: 'We stood to be married;
The priest, or someone, tarried;
"If Paradise-door prove locked?" smiled
    you;
I thought, as I nodded, smiling too,
"Did one, that's away, arrive – nor late
Nor soon should unlock Hell's gate!" '

It ceased to lighten and thunder.
Up started both in wonder,
Looked round and saw that the sky
    was clear,
Then laughed 'Confess you believed
    us, Dear!'
'I saw through the joke!' the man
    replied
They re-seated themselves beside.

### Ixion

High in the dome, suspended, of Hell,
    sad triumph, behold us!
  Here the revenge of a God, there the
    amends of a Man.
Whirling forever in torment, flesh once
    mortal, immortal
  Made – for a purpose of hate – able
    to die and revive,
Pays to the uttermost pang, then,
    newly for payment replenished,
  Doles out – old yet young – agonies
    ever afresh;
Whence the result above me: torment
    is bridged by a rainbow, –
  Tears, sweat, blood, – each spasm,
    ghastly once, glorified now.
Wrung, by the rush of the wheel
    ordained my place of reposing,
  Off in a sparklike spray, – flesh
    become vapour thro' pain, –
Flies the bestowment of Zeus, soul's
    vaunted bodily vesture,
  Made that his feats observed gain
    the approval of Man, –
Flesh that he fashioned with sense of
    the earth and the sky and the
    ocean,
  Framed should pierce to the star,
    fitted to pore on the plant, –
All, for a purpose of hate, re-framed, re-
    fashioned, re-fitted
  Till, consummate at length, – lo, the
    employment of sense!
Pain's mere minister now to the soul,
    once pledged to her pleasure –
  Soul, if untrammelled by flesh,
    unapprehensive of pain!
Body, professed soul's slave, which
    serving beguiled and betrayed her,
  Made things false seem true, cheated
    thro' eye and thro' ear,
Lured thus heart and brain to believe
    in the lying reported, –
  Spurn but the traitorous slave,
    uttermost atom, away,

What should obstruct soul's rush on
 the real, the only apparent?
  Say I have erred, – how else? Was I
  Ixion or Zeus?
Foiled by my senses I dreamed; I
 doubtless awaken in wonder:
  This proves shine, that – shade?
  Good was the evil that seemed?
Shall I, with sight thus gained, by torture
 be taught I was blind once?
  Sisuphos, teaches thy stone –
  Tantalos, teaches thy thirst
Aught which unaided sense, purged
 pure, less plainly demonstrates?
  No, for the past was dream: now
  that the dreamers awake,
Sisuphos scouts low fraud, and to
 Tantalos treason is folly.
  Ask of myself, whose form melts on
  the murderous wheel,
What is the sin which throe and throe
 prove sin to the sinner!
  Say the false charge was true, – thus
  do I expiate, say,
Arrogant thought, word, deed, – mere
 man who conceited me godlike,
  Sat beside Zeus, my friend – knelt
  before Heré, my love!
What were the need but of pitying
 power to touch and disperse it,
  Film-work – eye's and ear's – all the
  distraction of sense?
How should the soul not see, not hear,
 – perceive and as plainly
  Render, in thought, word, deed,
  back again truth – not a lie?
'Ay, but the pain is to punish thee!'
 Zeus, once more, for a pastime,
  Play the familiar, the frank! Speak
  and have speech in return!
I was of Thessaly king, there ruled and
 a people obeyed me:
  Mine to establish the law, theirs to
  obey it or die:
Wherefore? Because of the good to the
 people, because of the honour

Thence accruing to me, king, the
 king's law was supreme.
What of the weakling, the ignorant
 criminal? Not who, excuseless,
  Breaking my law braved death,
  knowing his deed and its due –
Nay, but the feeble and foolish, the
 poor transgressor, of purpose
  No whit more than a tree, born to
  erectness of bole,
Palm or plane or pine, we laud if lofty,
 columnar –
  Loathe if athwart, askew, – leave to
  the axe and the flame!
Where is the vision may penetrate
 earth and beholding acknowledge
  Just one pebble at root ruined the
  straightness of stem?
Whose fine vigilance follows the
 sapling, accounts for the failure,
  – Here blew wind, so it bent: there
  the snow lodged, so it broke?
Also the tooth of the beast, bird's bill,
 mere bite of the insect
  Gnawed, gnarled, warped their
  worst: passive it lay to offence.
King – I was man, no more: what I
 recognized faulty I punished,
  Laying it prone: be sure, more than
  a man had I proved,
Watch and ward o'er the sapling at
 birth-time had saved it, nor simply
  Owned the distortion's excuse, –
  hindered it wholly: nay, more –
Even a man, as I sat in my place to do
 judgment, and pallid
  Criminals passing to doom
  shuddered away at my foot,
Could I have probed thro' the face to
 the heart, read plain a repentance,
  Crime confessed fools' play, virtue
  ascribed to the wise,
Had I not stayed the consignment to
 doom, not dealt the renewed ones
  Life to retraverse the past, light to
  retrieve the misdeed?

Thus had I done, and thus to have
    done much more it behoves thee,
    Zeus who madest man – flawless or
    faulty, thy work!
What if the charge were true, as thou
    mouthest, – Ixion the cherished
    Minion of Zeus grew vain, vied with
    the godships and fell,
Forfeit thro' arrogance? Stranger! I
    clothed, with the grace of our
    human,
    Inhumanity – gods, natures I
    likened to ours.
Man among men I had borne me till
    gods forsooth must regard me
    – Nay, must approve, applaud,
    claim as a comrade at last.
Summoned to enter their circle, I sat –
    their equal, how other?
    Love should be absolute love, faith is
    in fulness or nought.
'I am thy friend, be mine!'smiled Zeus:
    'If Heré attract thee,'
    Blushed the imperial cheek, 'then –
    as thy heart may suggest!'
Faith in me sprang to the faith, my love
    hailed love as its fellow,
    'Zeus, we are friends – how fast!
    Heré, my heart for thy heart!'
Then broke smile into fury of frown,
    and the thunder of 'Hence, fool!'
    Then thro' the kiss laughed scorn
    'Limbs or a cloud was to clasp?'
Then from Olumpos to Erebos, then
    from the rapture to torment,
    Then from the fellow of gods –
    misery's mate, to the man!
– Man henceforth and forever, who
    lent from the glow of his nature
    Warmth to the cold, with light
    coloured the black and the blank.
So did a man conceive of your passion,
    you passion-protesters!
    So did he trust, so love – being the
    truth of your lie!
You to aspire to be Man! Man made
    you who vainly would ape him:

You are the hollowness, he – filling
    you, falsifies void.
Even as – witness the emblem, Hell's
    sad triumph suspended,
    Born of my tears, sweat, blood –
    bursting to vapour above –
Arching my torment, an iris ghostlike
    startles the darkness,
    Cold white – jewelry quenched –
    justifies, glorifies pain.
Strive, mankind, though strife endure
    through endless obstruction,
    Stage after stage, each rise marred by
    as certain a fall!
Baffled forever – yet never so baffled
    but, e'en in the baffling,
    When Man's strength proves weak,
    checked in the body or soul –
Whatsoever the medium, flesh or
    essence, – Ixion's
    Made for a purpose of hate, –
    clothing the entity Thou,
– Medium whence that entity strives
    for the Not-Thou beyond it,
    Fire elemental, free, frame
    unencumbered, the All, –
Never so baffled but – when, on the
    verge of an alien existence,
    Heartened to press, by pangs burst
    to the infinite Pure,
Nothing is reached but the ancient weak-
    ness still that arrests strength,
    Circumambient still, still the poor
    human array,
Pride and revenge and hate and cruelty
    – all it has burst through,
    Thought to escape, – fresh formed,
    found in the fashion it fled, –
Never so baffled but – when Man pays
    the price of endeavour,
    Thunderstruck, downthrust,
    Tartaros-doomed to the wheel, –
Then, ay, then, from the tears and
    sweat and blood of his torment.
    E'en from the triumph of Hell, up let
    him look and rejoice!

What is the influence, high o'er Hell,
    that turns to a rapture
    Pain – and despair's murk mists
    blends in a rainbow of hope?
What is beyond the obstruction, stage
    by stage tho' it baffle?
    Back must I fall, confess 'Ever the
    weakness I fled'?
No, for beyond, far, far is a Purity all-
    unobstructed!
    Zeus was Zeus – not Man: wrecked
    by his weakness, I whirl.
Out of the wreck I rise – past Zeus to
    the Potency o'er him!
    I – to have hailed him my friend! I –
    to have clasped her – my love!
Pallid birth of my pain, – where light,
    where light is, aspiring
    Thither I rise, whilst thou – Zeus,
    keep the godship and sink!

### Jochanan Hakkadosh

'This now, this other story makes
    amends
And justifies our Mishna,' quoth the
    Jew
Afore said. 'Tell it, learnedest of
    friends!'

          *     *     *

A certain morn broke beautiful and blue
O'er Schiphaz city, bringing joy and
    mirth,
– So had ye deemed; while the reverse
    was true,

Since one small house there gave a
    sorrow birth
In such black sort that, to each faithful
    eye,
Midnight, not morning settled on the
    earth.

How else, when it grew certain thou
    wouldst die
Our much-enlightened master, Israel's
    prop,
Eximious Jochanan Ben Sabbathai?

Old, yea but, undiminished of a drop,
The vital essence pulsed through heart
    and brain;
Time left unsickled yet the plenteous
    crop

On poll and chin and cheek, where of
    a skein
Handmaids might weave – hairs silk-
    soft, silver-white,
Such as the wool-plant's; none the less
    in vain

Had Physic striven her best against the
    spite
Of fell disease: the Rabbi must succumb;
And, round the couch whereon in
    piteous plight

He lay a-dying, scholars, – awe-struck,
    dumb
Throughout the night-watch, – roused
    themselves and spoke
One to the other: 'Ere death's touch
    be-numb

'His active sense, – while yet 'neath
    Reason's yoke
Obedient toils his tongue, – befits we
    claim
The fruit of long experience, bid this oak

'Shed us an acorn which may, all the
    same,
Grow to a temple-pillar, – dear that
    day! –
When Israel's scattered seed finds
    place and name

'Among the envious nations. Lamp us,
    pray,

Thou the Enlightener! Partest hence in
peace?
Hailest without regret – much less,
dismay –

'The hour of thine approximate release
From fleshly bondage soul hath found
obstruct?
Calmly envisagest the sure increase

'Of knowledge? Eden's tree must hold
unplucked
Some apple, sure, has never tried thy
tooth,
Juicy with sapience thou hast sought,
not sucked?

'Say, does age acquiesce in vanished
youth?
Still towers thy purity above – as erst –
Our pleasant follies? Be thy last word –
truth!'

The Rabbi groaned; then, grimly, 'Last
as first
The truth speak I – in boyhood who
began
Striving to live an angel, and, amerced

'For such presumption, die now hardly
man.
What have I proved of life? To live,
indeed,
That much I learned: but here lies
Jochanan

'More luckless than stood David when,
to speed
His fighting with the Philistine, they
brought
Saul's harness forth: whereat, "Alack, I
need

' "Armour to arm me, but have never
fought
With sword and spear, nor tried to
manage shield,
Proving arms' use, as well-trained
warrior ought.

' "Only a sling and pebbles can I wield!"
So he: while I, contrariwise, "No trick
Of weapon helpful on the battle-field

' "Comes unfamiliar to my theoric:
But, bid me put in practice what I know,
Give me a sword – it stings like
Moses' stick,

' "A serpent I let drop apace." E'en so,
I, – able to comport me at each stage
Of human life as never here below

'Man played his part, – since mine the
heritage
Of wisdom carried to that perfect pitch,
Ye rightly praise, – I, therefore, who,
thus sage,

'Could sure act man triumphantly,
enrich
Life's annals with example how I played
Lover, Bard, Soldier, Statist, – (all of
which

'Parts in presentment failing, cries
invade
The world's ear – "Ah, the Past, the
pearl-gift thrown
To hogs, time's opportunity we made

' "So light of, only recognized when
flown!
Had we been wise!") – in fine, I – wise
enough, –
What profit brings me wisdom never
shown

'Just when its showing would from
each rebuff
Shelter weak virtue, threaten back to
bounds
Encroaching vice, tread smooth each
track too rough

'For youth's unsteady footstep, climb
the rounds
Of life's long ladder, one by slippery
one,

Yet make no stumble? Me hard fate
    confounds

'With that same crowd of wailers I
    outrun
By promising to teach another cry
Of more hilarious mood than theirs,
    the sun

'I look my last at is insulted by.
What cry, – ye ask? Give ear on every
    side!
Witness yon Lover! "How entrapped
    am I!

' "Methought, because a virgin's rose-
    lip vied
With ripe Khubbezleh's, needs must
    beauty mate
With meekness and discretion in a
    bride:

' "Bride she became to me who wail –
    too late –
*Unwise I loved!*" That's one cry.
    "Mind's my gift:
I might have loaded me with lore, full
    weight

' "Pressed down and running over at
    each rift
O' the brain-bag where the famished
    clung and fed.
I filled it with what rubbish! – would
    not sift

' "The wheat from chaff, sound grain
    from musty – shed
Poison abroad as oft as nutriment –
And sighing say but as my fellows said,

' *"Unwise I learned!"* That's two. "In
    dwarf's-play spent
Was giant's prowess: warrior all
    unversed
In war's right waging, I struck brand,
    was lent

' "For steel's fit service, on mere stone
    – and cursed
Alike the shocked limb and the
    shivered steel,
Seeing too late the blade's true use
    which erst

' "How was I blind to! My cry swells
    the peal –
*Unwise I fought!*" That's three. But
    wherefore waste
Breath on the wailings longer? Why
    reveal

'A root of bitterness whereof the taste
Is noisome to Humanity at large?
First we get Power, but Power absurdly
    placed

'In Folly's keeping, who resigns her
    charge
To Wisdom when all Power grows
    nothing worth:
Bones marrowless are mocked with
    helm and targe

'When, like your Master's, soon below
    the earth
With worms shall warfare only be. Fare
    well,
Children! I die a failure since my birth!'

'Not so!' arose a protest as, pell-mell,
They pattered from his chamber to the
    street,
Bent on a last resource. Our Targums
    tell

That such resource there is. Put case,
    there meet
The Nine Points of Perfection – rarest
    chance
Within some saintly teacher whom the
    fleet

Years, in their blind implacable
    advance,

O'ertake before fit teaching born of
   these
Have magnified his scholars'
   countenance, –

If haply folk compassionating please
To render up – according to his store,
Each one – a portion of the life he sees

Hardly worth saving when 'tis set before
Earth's benefit should the Saint,
   Hakkadosh,
Favoured thereby, attain to full
   fourscore –

If such contribute (Scoffer, spare thy
   'Bosh!')
A year, a month, a day, an hour – to eke
Life out, – in him away the gift shall
   wash

That much of ill-spent time recorded,
   streak
The twilight of the so-assisted sage
With a new sunrise: truth, though
   strange to speak!

Quick to the doorway, then, where
   youth and age,
All Israel, thronging, waited for the last
News of the loved one. ' 'Tis the final
   stage:

'Art's utmost done, the Rabbi's feet
   tread fast
The way of all flesh!'so announced that
   apt
Olive-branch Tsaddik: 'Yet, O Brethren,
   cast

'No eye to earthward! Look where
   heaven has clapped
Morning's extinguisher – yon ray-shot
   robe
Of sun-threads – on the constellation
   mapped

'And mentioned by our Elders, – yea,
   from Job
Down to Satam, – as figuring forth –
   what?
Perpend a mystery! Ye call it *Dob* –

' "The Bear": I trow, a wiser name than
   that
Were *Aisch* – "The Bier": a corpse
   those four stars hold,
Which – are not those Three
   Daughters weeping at,

'*Banoth?* I judge so: list while I unfold
The reason. As in twice twelve hours
   this Bier
Goes and returns, about the East-cone
   rolled,

'So may a setting luminary here
Be rescued from extinction, rolled anew
Upon its track of labour, strong and
   clear,

'About the Pole – that Salem, every Jew
Helps to build up when thus he saves
   some Saint
Ordained its architect. Ye grasp the clue

'To all ye seek? The Rabbi's lamp-flame
   faint
Sinks: would ye raise it? Lend then life
   from yours,
Spare each his oil-drop! Do I need
   acquaint

'The Chosen how self-sacrifice ensures
Ten-fold requital? – urge ye emulate
The fame of those Old Just Ones death
   procures

'Such praise for, that 'tis now men's
   sole debate
Which of theTen who volunteered at
   Rome
To die for glory to our Race, was great

'Beyond his fellows? Was it thou – the
        comb
Of iron carded, flesh from bone, away,
While thy lips sputtered thro' their
        bloody foam

'Without a stoppage (O brave Akiba!)
"Hear, Israel, our Lord God is One"? Or
        thou,
Jischab? – who smiledst, burning, since
        there lay,

'Burning along with thee, our Law! I
        trow,
Such martyrdom might tax flesh to afford:
While that for which I make petition
        now,

'To what amounts it? Youngster, wilt
        thou hoard
Each minute of long years thou look'st
        to spend
In dalliance with thy spouse? Hast thou
        so soared,

'Singer of songs, all out of sight of friend
And teacher, warbling like a woodland
        bird,
There's left no Selah, 'twixt two psalms,
        to lend

'Our late-so-tuneful quirist? Thou, averred
The fighter born to plant our lion-flag
Once more on Zion's mount, – doth,
        all-unheard,

'My pleading fail to move thee? Toss
        some rag
Shall staunch our wound, some
        minute never missed
From swordsman's lustihood like thine!
        Wilt lag

'In liberal bestowment, show close fist
When open palm we look for, – thou,
        wide-known
For statecraft? whom, 'tis said, an if
        thou list,

'The Shah himself would seat beside
        his throne,
So valued were advice from thee' ...
        But here
He stopped short: such a hubbub! Not
        alone

From those addressed, but, far as well
        as near,
The crowd broke into clamour: 'Mine,
        mine, mine –
Lop from my life the excrescence, never
        fear!

'At me thou lookedst, markedst me!
        Assign
To me that privilege of granting life –
Mine, mine!' Then he: 'Be patient! I
        combine

'The needful portions only, wage no
        strife
With Nature's law nor seek to lengthen
        out
The Rabbi's day unduly. 'Tis the knife

'I stop, – would cut its thread too short.
        About
As much as helps life last the proper
        term,
The appointed Fourscore, – that I crave
        and scout

'A too-prolonged existence. Let the
        worm
Change at fit season to the butterfly!
And here a story strikes me, to confirm

'This judgment. Of our worthies, none
        ranks high
As Perida who kept the famous school:
None rivalled him in patience: none!
        For why?

'In lecturing it was his constant rule,
Whatever he expounded, to repeat
– Ay, and keep on repeating, lest some
        fool

'Should fail to understand him fully –
    (feat
Unparalleled, Uzzean!) – do ye mark? –
Five hundred times! So might he
    entrance beat

'For knowledge into howsoever dark
And dense the brain-pan. Yet it
    happed, at close
Of one especial lecture, not one spark

'Of light was found to have illumed the
    rows
Of pupils round their pedagogue. "What,
    still
Impenetrable to me? Then – here goes!"

'And for a second time he sets the rill
Of knowledge running, and five
    hundred times
More re-repeats the matter – and gains
    *nil.*

'Out broke a voice from heaven: "Thy
    patience climbs
Even thus high. Choose! Wilt thou,
    rather, quick
Ascend to bliss – or, since thy zeal
    sublimes

' "Such drudgery, will thy back still
    bear its crick,
Bent o'er thy class, – thy voice drone
    spite of drouth, –
Five hundred years more at thy desk
    wilt stick?"

' "To heaven with me!" was in the
    good man's mouth,
When all his scholars, – cruel-kind
    were they! –
Stopped utterance, from East, West,
    North and South,

'Rending the welkin with their shout of
    "Nay –
No heaven as yet for our instructer!
    Grant
Five hundred years on earth for Perida!"

'And so long did he keep instructing!
    Want
Our Master no such misery! I but take
Three months of life marital. Ministrant

'Be thou of so much, Poet! Bold I make,
Swordsman, with thy frank offer! – and
    conclude,
Statist, with thine! One year, – ye will
    not shake

'My purpose to accept no more. So
    rude?
The very boys and girls, forsooth, must
    press
And proffer their addition? Thanks!
    The mood

'Is laudable, but I reject, no less,
One month, week, day of life more.
    Leave my gown,
Ye overbold ones! Your life's gift, you
    guess,

'Were good as any? Rudesby, get thee
    down!
Set my feet free, or fear my staff! Farewell
Seniors and saviours, sharers of renown

'With Jochanan henceforward!' straight-
    way fell
Sleep on the sufferer; who awoke in
    health,
Hale everyway, so potent was the spell.

                    *    *    *

O the rare Spring-time! Who is he by
    stealth
Approaches Jochanan? – embowered
    that sits
Under his vine and figtree mid the
    wealth

Of garden-sights and sounds, since
    intermits
Never the turtle's coo, nor stays nor
    stints
The rose her smell. In homage that befits

The musing Master, Tsaddik, see,
    imprints
A kiss on the extended foot, low bends
Forehead to earth, then, all-obsequious,
    hints

'What if it should be time? A period
    ends –
That of the Lover's gift – his quarter-
    year
Of lustihood: 'tis just thou make amends,

'Return that loan with usury: so, here
Come I, of thy Disciples delegate,
Claiming our lesson from thee. Make
    appear

'Thy profit from experience! Plainly state
How men should Love!' Thus he: and
    to him thus
The Rabbi: 'Love, ye call it? – rather,
    Hate!

'What wouldst thou? Is it needful I
    discuss
Wherefore new sweet wine, poured in
    bottles caked
With old strong wine's deposit, offers us

'Spoilt liquor we recoil from, thirst-
    unslaked?
Like earth-smoke from a crevice, out
    there wound
Languors and yearnings: not a sense
    but ached

'Weighed on by fancied form and
    feature, sound
Of silver word and sight of sunny
    smile:
No beckoning of a flower-branch, no
    profound

'Purple of noon-oppression, no light
    wile
O' the West wind, but transformed
    itself till – brief –
Before me stood the phantasy ye style

'Youth's love, the joy that shall not
    come to grief,
Born to endure, eternal, unimpaired
By custom the accloyer, time the thief.

'Had Age's hard cold knowledge only
    spared
That ignorance of Youth! But now the
    dream,
Fresh as from Paradise, alighting fared

'As fares the pigeon, finding what may
    seem
Her nest's safe hollow holds a snake
    inside
Coiled to enclasp her. See, Eve stands
    supreme

'In youth and beauty! Take her for thy
    bride!
What Youth deemed crystal, Age finds
    out was dew
Morn set a-sparkle, but which noon
    quick dried

'While Youth bent gazing at its red and
    blue
Supposed perennial, – never dreamed
    the sun
Which kindled the display would
    quench it too.

'Graces of shape and colour – everyone
With its appointed period of decay
When ripe to purpose! "Still, these
    dead and done,

' "Survives the woman-nature – the soft
    sway
Of undefinable omnipotence
O'er our strong male-stuff, we of Adam's
    clay."

'Ay, if my physics taught not why and
    whence
The attraction! am I like the simple steer
Who, from his pasture lured inside the
    fence

'Where yoke and goad wait him, holds
    that mere
Kindliness prompts extension of the hand
Hollowed for barley, which drew near
    and near

'His nose – in proof that, of the horned
    band,
The farmer best affected him? Beside,
Steer, since his calfhood, got to under-
    stand

'Farmers a many in the world so wide
Were ready with a handful just as choice
Or choicer – maize and cummin, treats
    untried.

'Shall I wed wife, and all my days rejoice
I gained the peacock? 'Las me, round I
    look,
And lo – "With me thou wouldst have
    blamed no voice

' "Like hers that daily deafens like a
    rook:
I am the phœnix!" – "I, the lark, the
    dove,
– The owl," for aught knows he who
    blindly took

'Peacock for partner, while the vale, the
    grove,
The plain held bird-mates in abundance.
    There!
Youth, try fresh capture! Age has found
    out Love

'Long ago. War seems better worth man's
    care.
But leave me! Disappointment finds a
    balm
Haply in slumber.' 'This first step o'
    the stair

'To knowledge fails me, but the victor's
    palm
Lies on the next to tempt him overleap
A stumbling-block. Experienced, gather
    calm,

'Thou excellence of Judah, cured by
    sleep
Which ushers in the Warrior, to replace
The Lover! At due season I shall reap

'Fruit of my planting!'so, with lengthened
    face,
Departed Tsaddik: and three moons
    more waxed
And waned, and not until the Summer's
    pace

Waned likewise, any second visit taxed
The Rabbi's patience. But at three
    months' end,
Behold, supine beneath a rock, relaxed

The sage lay musing till the noon should
    spend
Its ardour. Up comes Tsaddik, who but
    he,
With 'Master, may I warn thee, nor
    offend,

'That time comes round again? We look
    to see
Sprout from the old branch – not the
    youngling twig –
But fruit of sycamine: deliver me,

'To share among my fellows, some
    plump fig,
Juicy as seedy! That same man of war,
Who, with a scantling of his store, made
    big

'Thy starveling nature, caused thee,
    safe from scar,
To share his gains by long acquaintance-
    ship
With bump and bruise and all the knocks
    that are

'Of battle dowry, – he bids loose thy lip,
Explain the good of battle! Since thou
    know'st,
Let us know likewise! Fast the moments
    slip,

'More need that we improve them!' –
'Ay, we boast,
We warriors in our youth, that with the
    sword
Man goes the swiftliest to the utter-
    most –

'Takes the straight way thro' lands yet
    unexplored
To absolute Right and Good, – may so
    obtain
God's glory and man's weal too long
    ignored,

'Too late attained by preachments all
    in vain –
The passive process. Knots get tangled
    worse
By toying with: does cut cord close
    again?

'Moreover there is blessing in the curse
Peace-praisers call war. What so sure
    evolves
All the capacities of soul, proves nurse

'Of that self-sacrifice in men which
    solves
The riddle – *Wherein differs Man from
    beast?*
Foxes boast cleverness and courage
    wolves:

'Nowhere but in mankind is found the
    least
Touch of an impulse "To our fellows –
    good
I' the highest! – not diminished but
    increased

' "By the condition plainly understood
– Such good shall be attained at price of
    hurt
I' the highest to ourselves!" Fine sparks,
    that brood

'Confusedly in Man, 'tis war bids spurt
Forth into flame: as fares the meteormass,
Whereof no particle but holds inert

'Some seed of light and heat, however
    crass
The enclosure, yet avails not to discharge
Its radiant birth before there come to
    pass

'Some push external, – strong to set at
    large
Those dormant fire-seeds, whirl them
    in a trice
Through heaven and light up earth from
    marge to marge:

'Since force by motion makes – what
    erst was ice –
Crash into fervency and so expire,
Because some Djinn has hit on a device

'For proving the full prettiness of fire!
Ay, thus we prattle – young: but old –
    why, first,
Where's that same Right and Good –
    (the wise inquire) –

'So absolute, it warrants the outburst
Of blood, tears, all war's woeful
    consequence,
That comes of the fine flaring? Which
    plague cursed

'The more your benefited Man – offence,
Or what suppressed the offender? Say
    it did –
Show us the evil cured by violence,

'Submission cures not also! Lift the lid
From the maturing crucible, we find
Its slow sure coaxing-out of virtue hid

'In that same meteor-mass, hath
    uncombined
Those particles and, yielding for result
Gold, not mere flame, by so much
    leaves behind

'The heroic product. E'en the simple
    cult
Of Edom's children wisely bids them
    turn
Cheek to the smiter with "*Sic Jesus vult.*"

'Say there's a tyrant by whose death we
    earn
Freedom, and justify a war to wage:
Good! – were we only able to discern

'Exactly how to reach and catch and
    cage
Him only and no innocent beside!
Whereas the folk whereon war wreaks
    its rage

' – How shared they his ill-doing? Far
    and wide
The victims of our warfare strew the
    plain,
Ten thousand dead, whereof not one
    but died

'In faith that vassals owed their suzerain
Life: therefore each paid tribute, –
    honest soul, –
To that same Right and Good ourselves
    are fain

'To call exclusively our end. From bole
(Since ye accept in me a sycamine)
Pluck, eat, digest a fable – yea, the sole

'Fig I afford you! "Dost thou dwarf my
    vine?"
(So did a certain husbandman address
The tree which faced his field,) "Receive
    condign

' "Punishment, prompt removal by the
    stress
Of axe I forthwith lay unto thy root!"
Long did he hack and hew, the root no
    less

'As long defied him, for its tough
    strings shoot

As deep down as the boughs above
    aspire:
All that he did was – shake to the tree's
    foot

'Leafage and fruitage, things we most
    require
For shadow and refreshment: which
    good deed
Thoroughly done, behold the axe-haft
    tires

'His hand, and he desisting leaves
    unfreed
The vine he hacked and hewed for.
    Comes a frost,
One natural night's work, and there's
    little need

'Of hacking, hewing: lo, the tree's a
    ghost!
Perished it starves, black death from
    top-most bough
To farthest-reaching fibre! Shall I boast

'My rough work, – warfare, – helped
    more? Loving, now –
That, by comparison, seems wiser,
    since
The loving fool was able to avow

'He could effect his purpose, just
    evince
Love's willingness, – once 'ware of
    what she lacked,
His loved one, – to go work for that,
    nor wince

'At self-expenditure: he neither hacked
Nor hewed, but when the lady of his
    field
Required defence because the sun
    attacked,

'He, failing to obtain a fitter shield,
Would interpose his body, and so
    blaze,
Blest in the burning. Ah, were mine to
    wield

'The intellectual weapon – poet-lays, –
How preferably had I sung one song
Which ... but my sadness sinks me: go
    your ways!

'I sleep out disappointment.' 'Come
    along,
Never lose heart! There's still as much
    again
Of our bestowment left to right the
    wrong

'Done by its earlier moiety – explain
Wherefore, who may! The Poet's mood
    comes next.
Was he not wishful the poetic vein

'Should pulse within him? Jochanan,
    thou reck'st
Little of what a generous flood shall
    soon
Float thy clogged spirit free and unper-
    plexed

'Above dry dubitation! Song's the boon
Shall make amends for my untoward
    mistake
That Joshua-like thou couldst bid sun
    and moon –

'Fighter and Lover, – which for most
    men make
All they descry in heaven, – stand both
    stock-still
And lend assistance. Poet shalt thou
    wake!'

Autumn brings Tsaddik. 'Ay, there
    speeds the rill
Loaded with leaves: a scowling sky,
    beside:
The wind makes olive-trees up yonder
    hill

'Whiten and shudder – symptoms far
    and wide
Of gleaning-time's approach; and glean
    good store

May I presume to trust we shall, thou
    tried

'And ripe experimenter! Three months
    more
Have ministered to growth of Song: that
    graft
Into thy sterile stock has found at core

'Moisture, I warrant, hitherto unquaffed
By boughs, however florid, wanting sap
Of prose-experience which provides the
    draught

'Which song-sprouts, wanting, wither:
    vain we tap
A youngling stem all green and immature:
Experience must secrete the stuff, our
    hap

'Will be to quench Man's thirst with,
    glad and sure
That fancy wells up through corrective
    fact:
Missing which test of truth, though
    flowers allure

'The goodman's eye with promise,
    soon the pact
Is broken, and 'tis flowers, – mere
    words, – he finds
When things, – that's fruit, – he
    looked for. Well, once cracked

'The nut, how glad my tooth the kernel
    grinds!
Song may henceforth boast substance!
    Therefore, hail
Proser and poet, perfect in both kinds!

'Thou from whose eye hath dropped
    the envious scale
Which hides the truth of things and
    substitutes
Deceptive show, unaided optics fail

'To transpierce, – hast entrusted to the
    lute's

Soft but sure guardianship some
    unrevealed
Secret shall lift mankind above the brutes

'As only knowledge can?' 'A fount
    unsealed'
(Sighed Jochanan) 'should seek the
    heaven in leaps
To die in dew-gems – not find death,
    congealed

'By contact with the cavern's nether
    deeps,
Earth's secretest foundation where,
    enswathed
In dark and fear, primæval mystery
    sleeps –

'Petric fount wherein my fancies bathed
And straight turned ice. My dreams of
    good and fair
In soaring upwards had dissolved,
    unscathed

'By any influence of the kindly air,
Singing, as each took flight, The Future
    – that's
Our destination, mists turn rainbows
    there,

'Which sink to fog, confounded in the
    flats
O' the Present! Day's the song-time for
    the lark,
Night for her music boasts but owls
    and bats.

'And what's the Past but night – the
    deep and dark
Ice-spring I speak of, corpse-thicked
    with its drowned
Dead fancies which no sooner touched
    the mark

'They aimed at – fact – than all at once
    they found
Their film-wings freeze, henceforth
    unfit to reach

And roll in æther, revel – robed and
    crowned

'As truths, confirmed by falsehood all
    and each –
Sovereign and absolute and ultimate!
Up with them, skyward, Youth, ere Age
    impeach

'Thy least of promises to re-instate
Adam in Eden! Sing on, ever sing,
Chirp till thou burst! – the fool cicada's
    fate,

'Who holds that after Summer next
    comes Spring,
Than Summer's self sun-warmed,
    spice-scented more.
Fighting was better! There, no fancy-
    fling

'Pitches you past the point was
    reached of yore
By Sampsons, Abners, Joabs, Judases,
The mighty men of valour who, before

'Our little day, did wonders none profess
To doubt were fable and not fact, so
    trust
By fancy-flights to emulate much less.

'Were I a Statesman, now! Why, that
    were just
To pinnacle my soul, mankind above,
A-top the universe: no vulgar lust

'To gratify – fame, greed, at this remove
Looked down upon so far – or over-
    looked
So largely, rather – that mine eye
    should rove

'World-wide and rummage earth, the
    many-nooked,
Yet find no unit of the human flock
Caught straying but straight comes
    back hooked and crooked

'By the strong shepherd who, from out
   his stock
Of aids proceeds to treat each ailing
   fleece,
Here stimulate to growth, curtail and
   dock

'There, baldness or excrescence, – that,
   with grease,
This, with up-grubbing of the bristly
   patch
Born of the tick-bite. How supreme a
   peace

'Steals o'er the Statist, – while, in wit, a
   match
For shrewd Ahitophel, in wisdom …
   well,
His name escapes me – somebody, at
   watch

'And ward, the fellow of Ahithophel
In guidance of the Chosen!' – at which
   word
Eyes closed and fast asleep the Rabbi
   fell.

'Cold weather!'shivered Tsaddik. 'Yet
   the hoard
Of the sagacious ant shows garnered
   grain,
Ever abundant most when fields afford

'Least pasture, and alike disgrace the
   plain
Tall tree and lowly shrub. 'Tis so with us
Mortals: our age stores wealth ye seek
   in vain

'While busy youth culls just what we
   discuss
At leisure in the last days: and the last
Truly are these for Jochanan, whom thus

'I make one more appeal to! Thine
   amassed
Experience, now or never, let escape
Some portion of! For I perceive aghast

'The end approaches, while they jeer
   and jape,
These sons of Shimei: "Justify your boast!
What have ye gained from Death by
   twelve months' rape?"

'Statesman, what cure hast thou for –
   least and most –
Popular grievances? What nostrum, say,
Will make the Rich and Poor, expertly
   dosed,

'Forget disparity, bid each go gay
That, with his bauble, – with his
   burden, this?
Propose an alkahest shall melt away

'Men's lacquer, show by prompt analysis
Which is the metal, which the make-
   believe,
So that no longer brass shall find, gold
   miss

'Coinage and currency? Make haste,
   retrieve
The precious moments, Master!' Where-
   unto
There snarls an 'Ever laughing in thy
   sleeve,

'Pert Tsaddik? Youth indeed sees plain
   a clue
To guide man where life's wood is
   intricate:
How shall he fail to thrid its thickest
   through

'When every oak-trunk takes the eye?
   Elate
He goes from bole to brushwood,
   plunging finds –
Smothered in briars – that the small's
   the great!

'All men are men: I would all minds
   were minds!
Whereas 'tis just the many's mindless
   mass

That most needs helping: labourers and hinds

'We legislate for – not the cultured class
Which law-makes for itself nor needs the whip
And bridle, – proper help for mule and ass,

'Did the brutes know! In vain our statesmanship
Strives at contenting the rough multitude:
Still the ox cries " 'Tis me thou shouldst equip

' "With equine trappings!" or, in humbler mood,
"Cribful of corn for me! and, as for work –
Adequate rumination o'er my food!"

'Better remain a Poet! Needs it irk
Such an one if light, kindled in his sphere,
Fail to transfuse the Mizraim cold and murk

'Round about Goshen? Though light disappear,
Shut inside, – temporary ignorance
Got outside of, lo, light emerging clear

'Shows each astonished starer the expanse
Of heaven made bright with knowledge! That's the way,
The only way – I see it at a glance –

'To legislate for earth! As poet ... Stay!
What is ... I would that ... were it ... I had been ...
O sudden change, as if my arid clay

'Burst into bloom! ... ' 'A change indeed, I ween,
And change the last!'sighed Tsaddik as he kissed
The closing eyelids. 'Just as those serene

'Princes of Night apprised me! Our acquist
Of life is spent, since corners only four
Hath Aisch, and each in turn was made desist

'In passage round the Pole (O Mishna's lore
Little it profits here!) by strenuous tug
Of friends who eked out thus to full fourscore

'The Rabbi's years. I see each shoulder shrug!
What have we gained? Away the Bier may roll!
To-morrow, when the Master's grave is dug,

'In with his body I may pitch the scroll
I hoped to glorify with, text and gloss,
My Science of Man's Life: one blank's the whole!

'Love, war, song, statesmanship – no gain, all loss,
The stars' bestowment! We on our return
To-morrow merely find – not gold but dross,

'The body not the soul. Come, friends, we learn
At least thus much by our experiment –
That – that ... well, find what, whom it may concern!'

But next day through the city rumours went
Of a new persecution; so, they fled
All Israel, each man, – this time, – from his tent,

Tsaddik among the foremost. When, the dread
Subsiding, Israel ventured back again
Some three months after, to the cave they sped

Where lay the Sage, – a reverential train!
Tsaddik first enters. 'What is this I view?
The Rabbi still alive? No stars remain

'Of Aisch to stop within their courses. True,
I mind me, certain gamesome boys must urge
Their offerings on me: can it be – one threw

'Life at him and it stuck? There needs the scourge
To teach that urchin manners! Prithee, grant
Forgiveness if we pretermit thy dirge

'Just to explain no friend was ministrant,
This time, of life to thee! Some jacka-napes,
I gather, has presumed to foist his scant

'Scurvy unripe existence – wilding grapes
Grass-green and sorrel-sour – on that grand wine,
Mighty as mellow, which, so fancy shapes

'May fitly image forth this life of thine
Fed on the last low fattening lees – condensed
Elixir, no milk-mildness of the vine!

'Rightly with Tsaddik wert thou now incensed
Had he been witting of the mischief wrought
When, for elixir, verjuice he dispensed!'

And slowly woke, – like Shushan's flower besought
By over-curious handling to unloose
The curtained secrecy wherein she thought

Her captive bee, mid store of sweets to choose,
Would loll, in gold pavilioned lie unteased,

Sucking on, sated never, – whose, O whose

Might seem that countenance, uplift, all eased
Of old distraction and bewilderment,
Absurdly happy? 'How ye have appeased

'The strife within me, bred this whole content,
This utter acquiescence in my past,
Present and future life, – by whom was lent

'The power to work this miracle at last, –
Exceeds my guess. Though – *ignorance confirmed*
*By knowledge* sounds like paradox, I cast

'Vainly about to tell you – fitlier termed –
Of calm struck by encountering opposites,
Each nullifying either! Henceforth wormed

'From out my heart is every snake that bites
The dove that else would brood there: doubt, which kills
With hiss of "What if sorrows end delights?"

'Fear which stings ease with "Work the Master wills!"
Experience which coils round and strangles quick
Each hope with "Ask the Past if hoping skills

' "To work accomplishment, or proves a trick
Wiling thee to endeavour! Strive, fool, stop
Nowise, so live, so die – that's law! why kick

' "Against the pricks?" All out-wormed!
    Slumber, drop
Thy films once more and veil the bliss
    within!
Experience strangle hope? Hope waves
    a-top

'Her wings triumphant! Come what will,
    I win,
Whoever loses! Every dream's assured
Of soberest fulfilment. Where's a sin

'Except in doubting that the light, which
    lured
The unwary into darkness, meant no
    wrong
Had I but marched on bold, nor paused
    immured

'By mists I should have pressed thro',
    passed along
My way henceforth rejoicing? Not the
    boy's
Passionate impulse he conceits so strong,

'Which, at first touch, truth, bubble-
    like, destroys, –
Not the man's slow conviction "Vanity
Of vanities – alike my griefs and joys!"

'Ice! – thawed (look up) each bird, each
    insect by –
(Look round) by all the plants that
    break in bloom,
(Look down) by every dead friend's
    memory

'That smiles "Am I the dust within my
    tomb?"
Not either, but both these – amalgam
    rare –
Mix in a product, not from Nature's
    womb,

'But stuff which He the Operant – who
    shall dare
Describe His operation? – strikes alive
And thaumaturgic. I nor know nor care

'How from this tohu-bohu – hopes which
    dive,
And fears which soar – faith, ruined
    through and through
By doubt, and doubt, faith treads to
    dust – revive

'In some surprising sort, – as see, they
    do! –
Not merely foes no longer but fast
    friends.
What does it mean unless – O strange
    and new

'Discovery! – this life proves a wine-
    press – blends
Evil and good, both fruits of Paradise,
Into a novel drink which – who intends

'To quaff, must bear a brain for ecstasies
Attempered, not this all-inadequate
Organ which, quivering within me, dies

' – Nay, lives! – what, how, – too soon,
    or else too late –
I was – I am … ' ('He babbleth!'
    Tsaddik mused)
'O Thou Almighty who canst re-instate

'Truths in their primal clarity, confused
By man's perception, which is man's
    and made
To suit his service, – how, once disabused

'Of reason which sees light half shine
    half shade,
Because of flesh, the medium that
    adjusts
Purity to his visuals, both an aid

'And hindrance, – how to eyes earth's
    air encrusts,
When purged and perfect to receive
    truth's beam
Pouring itself on the new sense it trusts

'With all its plenitude of power, – how
    seen
The intricacies now, of shade and shine,
Oppugnant natures – Right and
    Wrong, we deem

'Irreconcilable? O eyes of mine,
Freed how of imperfection, ye avail
To see the whole sight, nor may
    uncombined

'Henceforth what, erst divided, caused
    you quail –
So huge the chasm between the false
    and true,
The dream and the reality! All hail,

'Day of my soul's deliverance – day the
    new,
The never-ending! What though every
    shape
Whereon I wreaked my yearning to
    pursue

'Even to success each semblance of
    escape
From my own bounded self to some
    allfair
All-wise external fancy, proved a rape

'Like that old giant's, feigned of fools –
    on air,
Not solid flesh? How otherwise? To
    love –
That lesson was to learn not here – but
    there –

'On earth, not here! 'Tis there we learn,
    – there prove
Our parts upon the stuff we needs must
    spoil,
Striving at mastery, there bend above

'The spoiled clay potsherds, many a
    year of toil
Attests the potter tried his hand upon,
Till sudden he arose, wiped free from
    soil

'His hand, cried "So much for attempt
    – anon
Performance! Taught to mould the
    living vase,
What matter the cracked pitchers dead
    and gone?"

'Could I impart and could thy mind
    embrace
The secret, Tsaddik!' 'Secret none to
    me!'
Quoth Tsaddik, as the glory on the face

Of Jochanan was quenched. 'The truth
    I see
Of what that excellence of Judah wrote,
Doughty Halaphta. This a case must be

'Wherein, though the last breath have
    passed the throat,
So that "The man is dead" we may
    pronounce,
Yet is the Ruach – (thus do we denote

'The imparted Spirit) – in no haste to
    bounce
From its entrusted Body, – some three
    days
Lingers ere it relinquish to the pounce

'Of hawk-clawed Death his victim.
    Further says
Halaphta, "Instances have been, and
    yet
Again may be, when saints, whose
    earthly ways

' "Tend to perfection, very nearly get
To heaven while still on earth: and, as
    a fine
Interval shows where waters pure have
    met

' "Waves brackish, in a mixture, sweet
    with brine,
That's neither sea nor river but a taste
Of both – so meet the earthly and
    divine

' "And each is either." Thus I hold him
   graced –
Dying on earth, half inside and half
   out,
Wholly in heaven, who knows? My
   mind embraced

'Thy secret, Jochanan, how dare I
   doubt?
Follow thy Ruach, let earth, all it can,
Keep of the leavings!' Thus was
   brought about

The sepulture of Rabbi Jochanan:
Thou hast him, – sinner-saint, live-
   dead, boy-man, –
Schiphaz, on Bendimir, in Farzistan!

       \*     \*     \*

Note – This story can have no better authority
than that of the treatise, existing dispersedly in
fragments of Rabbinical writing, נושך של רבים
ברים, from which I might have helped myself
more liberally. Thus, instead of the simple
reference to 'Moses'stick', – but what if I make
amends by attempting three illustrations, when
some thirty might be composed on the same
subject, equally justifying that pithy proverb לא
קם כנושה נונושה צר נושה.

1

Moses the Meek was thirty cubits high,
   The staff he strode with – thirty
     cubits long:
   And when he leapt, so muscular and
     strong
Was Moses that his leaping neared the
   sky
By thirty cubits more: we learn thereby
   He reached full ninety cubits – am I
     wrong? –
   When, in a fight slurred o'er by
     sacred song,
With staff outstretched he took a leap
   to try
The just dimensions of the giant Og.
   And yet he barely touched – this
     marvel lacked

Posterity to crown earth's catalogue
   Of marvels – barely touched – to be
     exact –
The giant's ankle-bone, remained a frog
   That fain would match an ox in
     stature: fact!

2

And this same fact has met with
   unbelief!
   How saith a certain traveller? 'Young,
     I chanced
   To come upon an object – if thou
     canst,
Guess me its name and nature! 'Twas,
   in brief,
White, hard, round, hollow, of such
     length, in chief,
   – And this is what especially enhanced
   My wonder – that it seemed, as I
     advanced,
Never to end. Bind up within thy sheaf
Of marvels, this – Posterity! I walked
   From end to end, – four hours
     walked I, who go
A goodly pace, – and found – I have
   not baulked
   Thine expectation, Stranger? Ay or
     No?
'Twas but Og's thigh-bone, all the
   while. I stalked
   Alongside of: respect to Moses,
     though!

3

Og's thigh-bone – if ye deem its measure
   strange,
   Myself can witness to much length
     of shank
   Even in birds. Upon a water's bank
Once halting, I was minded to exchange
Noon heat for cool. Quoth I 'On many
   a grange
   I have seen storks perch – legs both
     long and lank:
   Yon stork's must touch the bottom
     of this tank,
Since on its top doth wet no plume
   derange

Of the smooth breast. I'll bathe there!'
   'Do not so!'
     Warned me a voice from heaven. 'A
     man let drop
     His axe into that shallow rivulet –
As thou accountest – seventy years
     ago:
It fell and fell and still without a stop
Keeps falling, nor has reached the
     bottom yet.'

## Never the Time and the Place

Never the time and the place
   And the loved one all together!
This path – how soft to pace!
   This May – what magic weather!
Where is the loved one's face?
In a dream that loved one's face meets
   mine,
   But the house is narrow, the place is
   bleak
Where, outside, rain and wind combine
   With a furtive ear, if I strive to speak,
   With a hostile eye at my flushing
   cheek,
With a malice that marks each word,
   each sign!
O enemy sly and serpentine,
   Uncoil thee from the waking man!
     Do I hold the Past
     Thus firm and fast
   Yet doubt if the Future hold I can?
This path so soft to pace shall lead
Thro' the magic of May to herself
   indeed!
Or narrow if needs the house must be,
Outside are the storms and strangers:
   we –
Oh, close, safe, warm sleep I and she,
   –
I and she!

## Pambo

Suppose that we part (work done,
   comes play)
   With a grave tale told in crambo
– As our hearty sires were wont to say –
   Where of the hero is Pambo?

Do you happen to know who Pambo
   was?
   Nor I – but this much have heard of
   him:
He entered one day a college-class,
   And asked – was it so absurd of
   him? –

'May Pambo learn wisdom ere practise
   it?
   In wisdom I fain would ground me:
Since wisdom is centred in Holy Writ,
   Some psalm to the purpose expound
   me!'

'That psalm,' the Professor smiled, 'shall
   be
   Untroubled by doubt which dirtieth
Pellucid streams when an ass like thee
   Would drink there – the Nine-and-
   thirtieth.

'Verse first: *I said I will look to my ways
   That I with my tongue offend not.*
How now? Why stare? Art struck in
   amaze?
   Stop, stay! The smooth line hath an
   end knot!

'He's gone! – disgusted my text should
   prove
   Too easy to need explaining?
Had he waited, the blockhead might
   find I move
   To matter that pays remaining!'

Long years went by, when – 'Ha, who's
   this?

Do I come on the restive scholar
I had driven to Wisdom's goal, I wis,
   But that he slipped the collar?

'What? Arms crossed, brow bent,
      thought-immersed?
   A student indeed! Why scruple
To own that the lesson proposed him
      first
   Scarce suited so apt a pupil?

'Come back! From the beggarly elements
   To a more recondite issue
We pass till we reach, at all events,
   Some point that may puzzle … Why
      "pish" you?'

From the ground looked piteous up the
      head:
   'Daily and nightly, Master,
Your pupil plods thro' that text you
      read,
   Yet gets on never the faster.

'At the self-same stand, – now old, then
      young!
   *I will look to my ways* – were doing
As easy as saying! – *that I with my
      tongue
   Offend not* – and 'scape pooh-poohing

'From sage and simple, doctor and
      dunce?
   Ah, nowise! Still doubts so muddy
The stream I would drink at once, –
      but once!
   That – thus I resume my study!'

   Brother, brother, I share the blame,
      *Arcades sumus ambo!*
   Darkling, I keep my sunrise-aim,
      Lack not the critic's flambeau,
   And *look to my ways,* yet, much
      the same,
      *Offend with my tongue* – like
Pambo!

# FERISHTAH'S FANCIES

1884

His genius was jocular, but, when disposed, he could be very serious.'

– Article 'Shakespear', Jeremy Collier's
*Historical &c. Dictionary.* 2nd edition, 1701.

You, Sir, I entertain you for one of my Hundred; only,
I do not like the fashion of your garments: you will say they are Persian:
but let them be changed. –                    *King Lear,* Act 3, Sc. 6.

## Prologue

Pray, Reader, have you eaten ortolans
    Ever in Italy?
Recall how cooks there cook them: for
    my plan's
    To – Lyre with Spit ally.
They pluck the birds, – some dozen
    luscious lumps,
    Or more or fewer, –
Then roast them, heads by heads and
    rumps by rumps,
    Stuck on a skewer.
But first, – and here's the point I fain
    would press, –
    Don't think I'm tattling! –
They interpose, t curb its lusciousness,
    – What, 'twixt each fatling?
First comes plain bread, crisp, brown,
    a toasted square:
    Then, a strong sage-leaf:
(So we find books with flowers dried
    here and there
    Lest leaf engage leaf.)
First, food – then, piquancy – and last
    of all
    Follows the thirdling:
Through wholesome hard, sharp soft,
    your tooth must bite
    Ere reach the birdling.
Now, were there only crust to crunch,
    you'd wince
    Unpalatable!
Sage-leaf is bitter-pungent – so's a quince:
    Eat each who's able!
But through all three bite boldly – lo,
    the gust!

Flavour – no fixture –
Flies, permeating flesh and leaf and
    crust
    In fine admixture.
So with your meal, my poem:
    masticate
    Sense, sight and song there!
Digest these, and I praise your
    peptics'state,
    Nothing found wrong there.
Whence springs my illustration who
    can tell?
    – The more surprising
That here eggs, milk, cheese, fruit
    suffice so well
    For gormandizing.
A fancy-freak by contrast born of thee,
    Delightful Gressoney!
Who laughest 'Take what is, trust what
    may be!'
    That's Life's true lesson, – eh?

Maison Delapierre,
Gressoney St Jean, Val d'Aosta,
*September* 12, 1893.

## The Eagle

Dervish – (though yet un-dervished,
    call him so
No less beforehand: while he drudged
    our way,
Other his worldly name was: when he
    wrote
Those versicles we Persians praise him
    for,
– True fairy-work – Ferishtah grew his
    style) –

Dervish Ferishtah walked the woods
  one eve,
And noted on a bough a raven's nest
Whereof each youngling gaped with
  callow beak
Widened by want; for why? beneath
  the tree
Dead lay the mother-bird. 'A piteous
  chance!
'How shall they 'scape destruction?'
  sighed the sage
– Or sage about to be, though simple
  still.
Responsive to which doubt, sudden
  there swooped
An eagle downward, and behold be
  bore
(Great-hearted) in his talons flesh
  wherewith
He stayed their craving, then resought
  the sky.
'Ah, foolish, faithless me!' the observer
  smiled,
'Who toil and moil to eke out life,
  when lo
Providence cares for every hungry
  mouth!'
To profit by which lesson, home
  went he,
And certain days sat musing, – neither
  meat
Nor drink would purchase by his
  handiwork.
Then, – for his head swam and his
  limbs grew faint, –
Sleep overtook the unwise one, whom
  in dream
God thus admonished: 'Hast thou
  marked my deed?
Which part assigned by providence
  dost judge
Was meant for man's example? Should
  he play
The helpless weakling, or the helpful
  strength
That captures prey and saves the
  perishing?

Sluggard, arise: work, eat, then feed
  who lack!'

Waking, 'I have arisen, work I will,
Eat, and so following. Which lacks
  food the more,
Body or soul in me? I starve in soul:
So may mankind: and since men
  congregate
In towns, not woods, – to Ispahan
  forthwith!'

\*    \*    \*

*Round us the wild creatures, overhead the
  trees,*
*Underfoot the moss-tracks, – life and love
  with these!*
*I to wear a fawn-skin, thou to dress in
  flowers:*
*All the long lone Summer-day, that green-
  wood life of ours!*

*Rich-pavilioned, rather, – still the world
  without, –*
*Inside – gold-roofed silk-walled silence
  round about!*
*Queen it thou on purple, – I, at watch
  and ward*
*Couched beneath the columns, gaze, thy
  slave, love's guard!*

*So, for us no world? Let throngs press
  thee to me!*
*Up and down amid men, heart by heart
  fare we!*
*Welcome squalid vesture, harsh voice,
  hateful face!*
*God is soul, souls I and thou: with souls
  should souls have place.*

## The Melon-Seller

Going his rounds one day in Ispahan, –
Half-way on Dervishhood, not wholly
    there, –
Ferishtah, as he crossed a certain
    bridge,
Came startled on a well-remembered
    face.
'Can it be? What, turned melon-seller –
    thou?
Clad in such sordid garb, thy seat yon
    step
Where dogs brush by thee and express
    contempt?
Methinks, thy head-gear is some
    scooped-out gourd!
Nay, sunk to slicing up, for readier
    sale,
One fruit whereof the whole scarce
    feeds a swine?
Wast thou the Shah's Prime Minister,
    men saw
Ride on his right-hand while a trumpet
    blew
And Persia hailed the Favourite? Yea,
    twelve years
Are past, I judge, since that
    transcendency,
And thou didst peculate and art
    abased;
No less, twelve years since, thou didst
    hold in hand
Persia, couldst halve and quarter,
    mince its pulp
As pleased thee, and distribute –
    melon-like –
Portions to whoso played the parasite,
Or suck – thyself – each juicy morsel.
    How
Enormous thy abjection, – hell from
    heaven,
Made tenfold hell by contrast! Whisper
    me!
Dost thou curse God for granting
    twelve years' bliss

Only to prove this day's the direr lot?'
Whereon the beggar raised a brow,
    once more
Luminous and imperial, from the rags.
'Fool, does thy folly think my
    foolishness
Dwells rather on the fact that God
    appoints
A day of woe to the unworthy one,
Than that the unworthy one, by God's
    award,
Tasted joy twelve years long? Or buy a
    slice,
Or go to school!'
            To school Ferishtah went;
And, schooling ended, passed from
    Ispahan
To Nishapur, that Elburz looks above
– Where they dig turquoise: there kept
    school himself,
The melon-seller's speech, his stock in
    trade.
Some say a certain Jew adduced the
    word
Out of their book, it sounds so much
    the same,
לא נקבל: אחדהטוב ניבל מאת האלהים
ואתדהדצ In Persian phrase,
'Shall we receive good at the hand of
    God
And evil not receive?' But great wits
    jump.

        *      *      *

*Wish no word unspoken, want no look
    away!*
*What if words were but mistake, and
    looks – too sudden, say!*
*Be unjust for once, Love! Bear it – well I
    may!*

*Do me justice always? Bid my heart –
    their shrine –*
*Render back its store of gifts, old looks
    and words of thine*
*– Oh, so all unjust – the less deserved, the
    more divine?*

## Shah Abbas

Anyhow, once full Dervish, youngsters came
To gather up his own words, 'neath a rock
Or else a palm, by pleasant Nishapur.

Said someone, as Ferishtah paused abrupt,
Reading a certain passage from the roll
Wherein is treated of Lord Ali's life:
'Master, explain this incongruity!
When I dared question "It is beautiful,
But is it true?" – thy answer was "In truth
Lives beauty." I persisting – "Beauty – yes,
In thy mind and in my mind, every mind
That apprehends: but outside – so to speak –
Did beauty live in deed as well as word,
Was this life lived, was this death died
    – not dreamed?'
"Many attested it for fact" saidst thou.
"Many!" but mark, Sir! Half as long ago
As such things were, – supposing that they were, –
Reigned great Shah Abbas: he too lived and died
– How say they? Why, so strong of arm, of foot
So swift, he stayed a lion in his leap
On a stag's haunch, – with one hand grasped the stag,
With one struck down the lion: yet, no less,
Himself, that same day, feasting after sport,
Perceived a spider drop into his wine,
Let fall the flagon, died of simple fear.
So all say, – so dost thou say?'
                        'Wherefore not?'
Ferishtah smiled: 'though strange, the story stands

Clear-chronicled: none tells it otherwise:
The fact's eye-witness bore the cup, beside.'
'And dost thou credit one cup-bearer's tale,
False, very like, and futile certainly,
Yet hesitate to trust what many tongues
Combine to testify was beautiful
In deed as well as word? No fool's report
Of lion, stag and spider, but immense
With meaning for mankind, – thy race, – thyself?'

Whereto the Dervish: 'First amend, my son,
Thy faulty nomenclature, call belief
Belief indeed, nor grace with such a name
The easy acquiescence of mankind
In matters nowise worth dispute, since life
Lasts merely the allotted moment. Lo –
That lion-stag-and-spider tale leaves fixed
The fact for us that somewhen Abbas reigned,
Died, somehow slain, – a useful registry, –
Which therefore we – "believe"? Stand forward, thou,
My Yakub, son of Yusuf, son of Zal!
I advertise thee that our liege, the Shah
Happily regnant, hath become assured,
By opportune discovery, that thy sires,
Son by the father upwards, track their line
To – whom but that same bearer of the cup
Whose inadvertency was chargeable
With what therefrom ensued, disgust and death
To Abbas Shah, the over-nice of soul?
Whence he appoints thee, – such his clemency, –
Not death, thy due, but just a double tax

To pay, on thy particular bed of reeds
Which flower into the brush that
    makes a broom
Fit to sweep ceilings clear of vermin.
    Sure,
Thou dost believe the story nor dispute
That punishment should signalize its
    truth?
Down therefore with some twelve
    dinars! Why start,
– The stag's way with the lion hard on
    haunch?
"Believe the story?" – how thy words
    throng fast! –
"Who saw this, heard this, said this,
    wrote down this,
That and the other circumstance to
    prove
So great a prodigy surprised the world?
Needs must thou prove me fable can
    be fact
Or ere thou coax one piece from out
    my pouch!" '

'There we agree, Sir: neither of us knows,
Neither accepts that tale on evidence
Worthy to warrant the large word –
    belief.
Now I get near thee! Why didst pause
    abrupt,
Disabled by emotion at a tale
Might match – be frank! – for credibility
The figment of the spider and the cup?
– To wit, thy roll's concerning Ali's life,
Unevidenced – thine own word! Little
    boots
Our sympathy with fiction! When I
    read
The annals and consider of Tahmasp
And that sweet sun-surpassing star his
    love,
I weep like a cut vine-twig, though
    aware
Zurah's sad fate is fiction, since the
    snake
He saw devour her, – how could such
    exist,

Having nine heads? No snake boasts
    more than three!
I weep, then laugh – both actions right
    alike.
But thou, Ferishtah, sapiency confessed,
When at the Day of Judgment God
    shall ask
"Didst thou believe?" – what wilt thou
    plead? Thy tears?
(Nay, they fell fast and stain the
    parchment still)
What if thy tears meant love? Love
    lacking ground
– Belief, – avails thee as it would avail
My own pretence to favour since,
    forsooth
I loved the lady – I, who needs must
    laugh
To hear a snake boasts nine heads:
    they have three!'

'Thanks for the well-timed help that's
    born, behold,
Out of thy words, my son, – belief and
    love!
Hast heard of Ishak son of Absal? Ay,
The very same we heard of, ten years
    since,
Slain in the wars: he comes back safe
    and sound, –
Though twenty soldiers saw him die at
    Yezdt, –
Just as a single mule-and-baggage boy
Declared 'twas like he some day would,
    – for why?
The twenty soldiers lied, he saw him
    stout,
Cured of all wounds at once by smear
    of salve,
A Mubid's manufacture: such the tale.
Now, when his pair of sons were thus
    apprised
Effect was twofold on them. "Hail!"
    crowed This:
"Dearer the news than dayspring after
    night!

The cure-reporting youngster warrants
    me
Our father shall make glad our eyes
    once more,
For whom, had outpoured life of mine
    sufficed
To bring him back, free broached were
    every vein!"
"Avaunt, delusive tale-concocter, news
Cruel as meteor simulating dawn!"
Whimpered the other: "Who believes
    this boy
Must disbelieve his twenty seniors: no,
Return our father shall not! Might my
    death
Purchase his life, how promptly would
    the dole
Be paid as due!" Well, ten years pass, –
    aha,
Ishak is marching homeward, – doubts,
    not he,
Are dead and done with! So, our towns-
    folk straight
Must take on them to counsel. "Go
    thou gay,
Welcome thy father, thou of ready
    faith!
Hide thee, contrariwise, thou faithless
    one,
Expect paternal frowning, blame and
    blows!"
So do our townsfolk counsel: dost
    demur?'

'Ferishtah like those simpletons – at
    loss
In what is plain as pikestaff? Pish!
    Suppose
The trustful son had sighed "So much
    the worse!
Returning means – retaking heritage
Enjoyed these ten years, who should
    say me nay?"
How should such trust reward him?
    Trustlessness
– O' the other hand – were what
    procured most praise

To him who judged return impossible,
Yet hated heritage procured thereby.
A fool were Ishak if he failed to prize
Mere head's work less than heart's
    work: no fool he!'

'Is God less wise? Resume the roll!'
    They did.

      *    *    *

*You groped your way across my room i'*
    *the dear dark dead of night;*
*At each fresh step a stumble was: but,*
    *once your lamp alight,*
*Easy and plain you walked again: so soon*
    *all wrong grew right!*

*What lay on floor to trip your foot? Each*
    *object, late awry,*
*Looked fitly placed, nor proved offence to*
    *footing free – for why?*
*The lamp showed all, discordant late,*
    *grown simple symmetry.*

*Be love your light and trust your guide,*
    *with these explore my heart!*
*No obstacle to trip you then, strike hands*
    *and souls apart!*
*Since rooms and hearts are furnished so,*
    *– light shows you, – needs love start?*

## The Family

A certain neighbour lying sick to death,
Ferishtah grieved beneath a palm-tree,
    whence
He rose at peace: whereat objected one
'Gudarz our friend gasps in extremity.
Sure, thou art ignorant how close at
    hand
Death presses, or the cloud, which
    fouled so late
Thy face, had deepened down not
    lightened off.'

'I judge there will be respite, for I
    prayed.'

'Sir, let me understand, of charity!
Yestereve, what was thine admonishment?
"All-wise, all-good, all-mighty – God is such!"
How then should man, the all-unworthy, dare
Propose to set aside a thing ordained?
To pray means – substitute man's will for God's:
Two best wills cannot be: by consequence,
What is man bound to but – assent, say I?
Rather to rapture of thanksgiving; since
That which seems worst to man to God is best,
So, because God ordains it, best to man.
Yet man – the foolish, weak and wicked – prays!
Urges "My best were better, didst Thou know"!'

'List to a tale. A worthy householder
Of Shiraz had three sons, beside a spouse
Whom, cutting gourds, a serpent bit, whereon
The offended limb swelled black from foot to fork.
The husband called in aid a leech renowned
World-wide, confessed the lord of surgery,
And bade him dictate – who forthwith declared
"Sole remedy is amputation." straight
The husband sighed "Thou knowest: be it so!"
His three sons heard their mother sentenced: "Pause!"
Outbroke the elder: "Be precipitate
Nowise, I pray thee! Take some gentler way,
Thou sage of much resource! I will not doubt

But science still may save foot, leg and thigh!"
The next in age snapped petulant: "Too rash!
No reason for this maiming! What, Sir Leech,
Our parent limps henceforward while we leap?
Shame on thee! Save the limb thou must and shalt!"
"Shame on yourselves, ye bold ones!" followed up
The brisk third brother, youngest, pertest too:
"The leech knows all things, we are ignorant;
What he proposes, gratefully accept!
For me, had I some unguent bound to heal
Hurts in a twinkling, hardly would I dare
Essay its virtue and so cross the sage
By cure his skill pronounces folly. Quick!
No waiting longer! There the patient lies:
Out then with implements and operate!" '

'Ah, the young devil!'
                          'Why, his reason chimed
Right with the Hakim's.'
                          'Hakim's, ay – but chit's?
How? what the skilled eye saw and judged of weight
To overbear a heavy consequence,
That – shall a sciolist affect to see?
All he saw – that is, all such oaf should see,
Was just the mother's suffering.'
                          'In my tale,
Be God the Hakim: in the husband's case,
Call ready acquiescence – aptitude
Angelic, understanding swift and sure:
Call the first son – a wise humanity,
Slow to conceive but duteous to adopt.

See in the second son – humanity,
Wrong-headed yet right-hearted, rash
  but kind.
Last comes the cackler of the brood,
  our chit
Who, aping wisdom all beyond his years,
Thinks to discard humanity itself:
Fares like the beast which should affect
  to fly
Because a bird with wings may spurn
  the ground,
So, missing heaven and losing earth –
  drops how
But hell-ward? No, be man and
  nothing more
Man who, as man conceiving, hopes
  and fears,
And craves and deprecates, and loves,
  and loathes,
And bids God help him, till death
  touch his eyes
And show God granted most, denying
  all.'

\*     \*     \*

*Man I am and man would be, Love –
  merest man and nothing more.*
*Bid me seem no other! Eagles boast of
  pinions – let them soar!*
*I may put forth angel's plumage, once
  unmanned, but not before.*

*Now on earth, to stand suffices, – nay, if
  kneeling serves, to kneel:*
*Here you front me, here I find the all of
  heaven that earth can feel:*
*Sense looks straight, – not over, under, –
  perfect sees beyond appeal.*

*Good you are and wise, full circle: what to
  me were more outside?*
*Wiser wisdom, better goodness? Ah, such
  want the angel's wide*
*Sense to take and hold and keep them!
  Mine at least has never tried.*

## The Sun

'And what might that bold man's
  announcement be' –
Ferishtah questioned – 'which so
  moved thine ire
That thou didst curse, nay, cuff and
  kick – in short,
Confute the announcer? Wipe those
  drops away
Which start afresh upon thy face at
  mere
Mention of such enormity: now, speak!'
'He scrupled not to say – (thou
  warrantest,
O patient Sir, that I unblamed repeat
Abominable words which blister
  tongue?)
God once assumed on earth a human
  shape:
(Lo, I have spitten!) Dared I ask the
  grace,
Fain would I hear, of thy subtility,
From out what hole in man's
  corrupted heart
Creeps such a maggot: fancies
  verminous
Breed in the clots there, but a monster
  born
Of pride and folly like this pest – thyself
Only canst trace to egg-shell it hath
  chipped.'

The sun rode high. 'During our
  ignorance' –
Began Ferishtah – 'folk esteemed as
  God
Yon orb: for argument, suppose him
  so, –
Be it the symbol, not the symbolized,
I and thou safelier take upon our lips.
Accordingly, yon orb that we adore
– What is he? Author of all light and
  life:
Such one must needs be somewhere:
  this is he.

Like what? If I may trust my human
          eyes,
A ball composed of spirit-fire, whence
          springs
– What, from this ball, my arms could
          circle round?
All I enjoy on earth. By consequence,
Inspiring me with – what? Why, love
          and praise.
I eat a palatable fig – there's love
In little: who first planted what I pluck,
Obtains my little praise, too: more of
          both
Keeps due proportion with more cause
          for each:
So, more and ever more, till most of all
Completes experience, and the orb,
          descried
Ultimate giver of all good, perforce
Gathers unto himself all love, all praise,
Is worshipped – which means loved
          and praised at height.
Back to the first good: 'twas the
          gardener gave
Occasion to my palate's pleasure: grace,
Plain on his part, demanded thanks on
          mine.
Go up above this giver, – step by step,
Gain a conception of what – (how and
          why,
Matters not now) – occasioned him to
          give,
Appointed him the gardener of the
          ground, –
I mount by just progression slow and
          sure
To some prime giver – here assumed
          yon orb –
Who takes my worship. Whom have I
          in mind,
Thus worshipping, unless a man, my
          like
Howe'er above me? Man, I say – how
          else,
I being man who worship? Here's my
          hand

Lifts first a mustard-seed, then weight
          on weight
Greater and ever greater, till at last
It lifts a melon, I suppose, then stops –
Hand-strength expended wholly: so,
          my love
First lauds the gardener for the fig his
          gift,
Then, looking higher, loves and lauds
          still more,
Who hires the ground, who owns the
          ground, Sheikh, Shah,
On and away, away and ever on,
Till, at the last, it loves and lauds the orb
Ultimate cause of all to laud and love.
Where is the break, the change of
          quality
In hand's power, soul's impulsion? Gift
          was grace,
The greatest as the smallest. Had I
          stopped
Anywhere in the scale, stayed love and
          praise
As so far only fit to follow gift,
Saying "I thanked the gardener for his
          fig,
But now that, lo, the Shah has filled
          my purse
With tomans which avail to purchase
          me
A fig-tree forest, shall I pay the same
With love and praise, the gardener's
          proper fee?"
Justly would whoso bears a brain object
"Giving is giving, gift claims gift's return,
Do thou thine own part, therefore: let
          the Shah
Ask more from who has more to pay."
          Perchance
He gave me from his treasure less by
          much
Than the soil's servant: let that be! My
          part
Is plain – to meet and match the gift
          and gift
With love and love, with praise and
          praise, till both

Cry "All of us is thine, we can no more!"
So shall I do man's utmost – man to
    man:
For as our liege the Shah's sublime
    estate
Merely enhaloes, leaves him man the
    same,
So must I count that orb I call a fire
(Keep to the language of our
    ignorance)
Something that's fire and more beside.
    Mere fire
– Is it a force which, giving, knows it
    gives,
And wherefore, so may look for love
    and praise
From me, fire's like so far, however less
In all beside? Prime cause this fire shall
    be,
Uncaused, all-causing: hence begin the
    gifts,
Thither must go my love and praise –
    to what?
Fire? Symbol fitly serves the symbolized
Herein, – that this same object of my
    thanks,
While to my mind nowise conceivable
Except as mind no less than fire, refutes
Next moment mind's conception: fire
    is fire –
While what I needs must thank, must
    needs include
Purpose with power, – humanity like
    mine,
Imagined, for the dear necessity,
One moment in an object which the
    next
Confesses unimaginable. Power!
– What need of will, then? nought
    opposes power:
Why, purpose? any change must be for
    worse:
And what occasion for beneficence
When all that is, so is and so must be?
Best being best now, change were for
    the worse.
Accordingly discard these qualities

Proper to imperfection, take for type
Mere fire, eject the man, retain the orb, –
The perfect and, so, inconceivable, –
And what remains to love and praise?
    A stone
Fair-coloured proves a solace to my eye,
Rolled by my tongue brings moisture
    curing drouth,
And struck by steel emits a useful spark:
Shall I return it thanks, the insentient
    thing?
No, – man once, man for ever – man in
    soul
As man in body: just as this can use
Its proper senses only, see and hear,
Taste, like or loathe according to its law
And not another creature's, – even so
Man's soul is moved by what, if it in
    turn
Must move, is kindred soul: receiving
    good
– Man's way – must make man's due
    acknowledgment,
No other, even while he reasons out
Plainly enough that, were the man
    unmanned,
Made angel of, angelic every way,
The love and praise that rightly seek
    and find
Their man-like object now, – instructed
    more,
Would go forth idly, air to emptiness.
Our human flower, sun-ripened,
    proffers scent
Though reason prove the sun lacks
    nose to feed
On what himself made grateful: flower
    and man,
Let each assume that scent and love
    alike
Being once born, must needs have use!
    Man's part
Is plain – to send love forth, – astray,
    perhaps:
No matter, he has done his part.'
'                Wherefrom
What is to follow – if I take thy sense –

But that the sun – the inconceivable
Confessed by man – comprises, all the
    same,
Man's every-day conception of himself –
No less remaining unconceived!'
                    'Agreed!'
'Yet thou, insisting on the right of man
To feel as man, not otherwise, – man,
    bound
By man's conditions neither less nor
    more,
Obliged to estimate as fair or foul,
Right, wrong, good, evil, what man's
    faculty
Adjudges such, – how canst thou, –
    plainly bound
To take man's truth for truth and only
    truth, –
Dare to accept, in just one case, as
    truth
Falsehood confessed? Flesh simulating
    fire –
Our fellow-man whom we his fellows
    know
For dust – instinct with fire unknowable!
Where's thy man-needed truth – its
    proof, nay print
Of faintest passage on the tablets
    traced
By man, termed knowledge? 'Tis
    conceded thee,
We lack such fancied union – fire with
    flesh:
But even so, to lack is not to gain
Our lack's suppliance: where's the
    trace of such
Recorded?'
           'What if such a tracing were?
If some strange story stood, – whate'er
    its worth, –
That the immensely yearned-for, once
    befell,
– The sun was flesh once? – (keep the
    figure!)'
                   'How?
An union inconceivable was fact?'

'Son, if the stranger have convinced
    himself
Fancy is fact – the sun, besides a fire,
Holds earthly substance somehow fire
    pervades
And yet consumes not, – earth, he
    under-stands,
With essence he remains a stranger to, –
Fitlier thou saidst "I stand appalled
    before
Conception unattainable by me
Who need it most" – than this –
    "What? boast he holds
Conviction where I see conviction's
    need,
Alas, – and nothing else? then what
    remains
But that I straightway curse, cuff, kick
    the fool!" '

       *     *     *

*Fire is in the flint: true, once a spark*
    *escapes,*
*Fire forgets the kinship, soars till fancy*
    *shapes*
*Some befitting cradle where the babe had*
    *birth –*
*Wholly heaven's the product, unallied to*
    *earth.*
*Splendours recognized as perfect in the*
    *star! –*
*In our flint their home was, housed as*
    *now they are.*

## Mihrab Shah

Quoth an inquirer, 'Praise the Merciful!
My thumb which yesterday a scorpion
    nipped –
(It swelled and blackened) – lo, is
    sound again!
By application of a virtuous root
The burning has abated: that is well:
But now methinks I have a mind to
    ask, –
Since this discomfort came of culling
    herbs

Nor meaning harm, – why needs a
    scorpion be?
Yea, there began, from when my thumb
    last throbbed,
Advance in question-framing, till I asked
Wherefore should any evil hap to man –
From ache of flesh to agony of soul –
Since God's All-mercy mates All-potency?
Nay, why permits He evil to Himself –
Man's sin, accounted such? Suppose a
    world
Purged of all pain, with fit inhabitant –
Man pure of evil in thought, word and
    deed –
Were it not well? Then, wherefore other-
    wise?
Too good result? But He is wholly good!
Hard to effect? Ay, were He impotent!
Teach me, Ferishtah!'
            Said the Dervish: 'Friend,
My chance, escaped to-day, was worse
    than thine:
I, as I woke this morning, raised my
    head,
Which never tumbled but stuck fast on
    neck.
Was not I glad and thankful!'
            'How could head
Tumble from neck, unchopped –
    inform me first!
Unless we take Firdausi's tale for truth,
Who ever heard the like?'
            'The like might hap
By natural law: I let my staff fall thus –
It goes to ground, I know not why.
    Suppose,
Whene'er my hold was loosed, it
    skyward sprang
As certainly, and all experience proved
That, just as staves when unsupported
    sink,
So, unconfined, they soar?'
          'Let such be law –
Why, a new chapter of sad accidents
Were added to humanity's mischance,
No doubt at all, and as a man's false
    step

Now lays him prone on earth,
    contrariwise,
Removal from his shoulder of a weight
Might start him upwards to perdition.
    Ay!
But, since such law exists in just thy
    brain,
I shall not hesitate to doff my cap
For fear my head take flight.'
            'Nor feel relief
Finding it firm on shoulder. Tell me,
    now!
What were the bond 'twixt man and
    man, dost judge,
Pain once abolished? Come, be true!
    Our Shah –
How stands he in thy favour? Why that
    shrug?
Is not he lord and ruler?'
            'Easily!
His mother bore him, first of those four
    wives
Provided by his father, such his luck:
Since when his business simply was to
    breathe
And take each day's new bounty. There
    he stands –
Where else had I stood, were his birth-
    star mine?
No, to respect men's power, I needs
    must see
Men's bare hands seek, find, grasp and
    wield the sword
Nobody else can brandish! Bless his
    heart,
'Tis said, he scarcely counts his fingers
    right!'
'Well, then – his princely doles! from
    every feast
Off go the feasted with the dish they ate
And cup they drank from, – nay, a
    change besides
Of garments' ...
         'Sir, put case, for service done, –
Or best, for love's sake, – such and
    such a slave
Sold his allowance of sour lentil soup

To therewith purchase me a pipe-stick,
    – nay,
If he, by but one hour, cut short his
    sleep
To clout my shoe, – that were a
    sacrifice!'
'All praise his gracious bearing.'
                    'All praise mine –
Or would praise did they never make
    approach
Except on all-fours, crawling till I bade
"Now that with eyelids thou hast
    touched the earth,
Come close and have no fear, poor
    nothingness!"
What wonder that the lady-rose I woo
And palisade about from every wind,
Holds herself handsomely? The
    wilding, now,
Ruffled outside at pleasure of the blast,
That still lifts up with something of a
    smile
Its poor attempt at bloom' …
                    'A blameless life,
Where wrong might revel with
    impunity –
Remember that!'
                    'The falcon on his fist –
Reclaimed and trained and belled and
    beautified
Till she believes herself the Simorgh's
    match –
She only deigns destroy the antelope,
Stoops at no carrion-crow: thou
    marvellest?'

'So be it, then! He wakes no love in
    thee
For any one of divers attributes
Commonly deemed loveworthy. All the
    same,
I would he were not wasting, slow but
    sure,
With that internal ulcer' …
                    'Say'st thou so?
How should I guess? Alack, poor soul!
    But stay –

Sure in the reach of art some remedy
Must lie to hand: or if it lurk, – that
    leech
Of fame in Tebriz, why not seek his aid?
Couldst not thou, Dervish, counsel in
    the case?'

'My counsel might be – what imports a
    pang
The more or less, which puts an end to
    one
Odious in spite of every attribute
Commonly deemed loveworthy?'
                    'Attributes?
Faugh! – nay, Ferishtah, – 'tis an ulcer,
    think!
Attributes, quotha? Here's poor flesh
    and blood,
Like thine and mine and every man's, a
    prey
To hell-fire! Hast thou lost thy wits for
    once?'

'Friend, here they are to find and profit
    by!
Put pain from out the world, what
    room were left
For thanks to God, for love to Man?
    Why thanks, –
Except for some escape, whate'er the
    style,
From pain that might be, name it as
    thou mayst?
Why love, – when all thy kind, save
    me, suppose,
Thy father, and thy son, and … well,
    thy dog,
To eke the decent number out – we
    few
Who happen – like a handful of
    chance stars
From the unnumbered host – to shine
    o'erhead
And lend thee light, – our twinkle all
    thym store, –
We only take thy love! Mankind,
    forsooth?

Who sympathizes with their general
    joy
Foolish as undeserved? But pain – see
    God's
Wisdom at work! – man's heart is
    made to judge
Pain deserved nowhere by the common
    flesh
Our birthright, – bad and good deserve
    alike
No pain, to human apprehension! Lust,
Greed, cruelty, injustice, crave (we
    hold)
Due punishment from somebody, no
    doubt:
But ulcer in the midriff! that brings
    flesh
Triumphant from the bar whereto
    arraigned
Soul quakes with reason. In the eye of
    God
Pain may have purpose and be
    justified:
Man's sense avails to only see, in pain,
A hateful chance no man but would
    avert
Or, failing, needs must pity. Thanks to
    God
And love to man, – from man take
    these away,
And what is man worth? Therefore,
    Mihrab Shah,
Tax me my bread and salt twice over,
    claim
Laila my daughter for thy sport, – go
    on!
Slay my son's self, maintain thy poetry
Beats mine, – thou meritest a dozen
    deaths!
But – ulcer in the stomach, – ah, poor
    soul,
Try a fig-plaster: may it ease thy pangs!'

                *    *    *

*So, the head aches and the limbs are
    faint!*
    *Flesh is a burthen – even to you!*
*Can I force a smile with a fancy quaint?*
    *Why are my ailments none or few?*

*In the soul of me sits sluggishness:*
    *Body so strong and will so weak!*
*The slave stands fit for the labour – yes,*
    *But the master's mandate is still to*
    *seek.*

*You, now – what if the outside clay*
    *Helped, not hindered the inside flame?*
*My dim to-morrow – your plain to-day,*
    *Yours the achievement, mine the aim?*

*So were it rightly, so shall it be!*
    *Only, while earth we pace together*
*For the purpose apportioned you and me,*
    *Closer we tread for a common tether.*

*You shall sigh 'Wait for his sluggish soul!*
    *Shame he should lag, not lamed as I!'*
*May not I smite 'Ungained her goal:*
    *Body may reach her – by-and-by?'*

## A Camel-Driver

'How of his fate, the Pilgrims' soldier-
    guide
Condemned' (Ferishtah questioned),
    'for he slew
The merchant whom he convoyed with
    his bales
– A special treachery?'
                'Sir, the proofs were plain:
Justice was satisfied: between two boards
The rogue was sawn asunder, rightly
    served.'

'With all wise men's approval – mine
    at least.'

'Himself, indeed, confessed as much.
    "I die

Justly" (groaned he) "through over-
    greediness
Which tempted me to rob: but grieve
    the most
That he who quickened sin at slumber,
    – ay,
Prompted and pestered me till thought
    grew deed, –
The same is fled to Syria and is safe,
Laughing at me thus left to pay for
    both.
My comfort is that God reserves for him
Hell's hottest" … '
        'Idle words.'
            'Enlighten me!
Wherefore so idle? Punishment by man
Has thy assent, – the word is on thy
    lips.
By parity of reason, punishment
By God should likelier win thy thanks
    and praise.'

'Man acts as man must: God, as God
    beseems.
A camel-driver, when his beast will
    bite,
Thumps her athwart the muzzle: why?'
        'How else
Instruct the creature – mouths should
    munch, not bite?'

'True, he is man, knows but man's
    trick to teach.
Suppose some plain word, told her first
    of all,
Had hindered any biting?'
           'Find him such,
And fit the beast with understanding
    first!
No understanding animals like Rakhsh
Nowadays, Master! Till they breed on
    earth,
For teaching – blows must serve.'
        'Who deals the blow –
What if by some rare method, – magic,
    say, –
He saw into the biter's very soul,

And knew the fault was so repented of
It could not happen twice?'
        'That's something: still,
I hear, methinks, the driver say "No
    less
Take thy fault's due! Those long-
    necked sisters, see,
Lean all a-stretch to know if biting
    meets
Punishment or enjoys impunity.
For their sakes – thwack!" '
        'The journey home at end,
The solitary beast safe-stabled now,
In comes the driver to avenge a wrong
Suffered from six months since, –
    apparently
With patience, nay, approval: when the
    jaws
Met i' the small of the arm, "Ha,
    Ladykin,
Still at thy frolics, girl of gold?" laughed
    he:
"Eat flesh? Rye-grass content thee
    rather with,
Whereof accept a bundle!" Now, –
    what change!
Laughter by no means! Now 'tis
    "Fiend, thy frisk
Was fit to find thee provender, didst
    judge?
Behold this red-hot twy-prong, thus I
    stick
To hiss i' the soft of thee!" '
        'Behold? behold
A crazy noddle, rather! Sure the brute
Might wellnigh have plain speech
    coaxed out of tongue,
And grow as voluble as Rakhsh himself
At such mad outrage. "Could I take thy
    mind,
Guess thy desire? If biting was offence
Wherefore the rye-grass bundle, why
    each day's
Patting and petting, but to intimate
My playsomeness had pleased thee?
    Thou endowed

With reason, truly!" '
　　　　　'Reason aims to raise
Some makeshift scaffold-vantage
　　midway, whence
Man dares, for life's brief moment, peer
　　below:
But ape omniscience? Nay! The ladder
　　lent
To climb by, step and step, until we
　　reach
The little foothold-rise allowed
　　mankind
To mount on and thence guess the
　　sun's survey –
Shall this avail to show us world-wide
　　truth
Stretched for the sun's descrying?
　　　　　Reason bids
"Teach, Man, thy beast his duty first of
　　all
Or last of all, with blows if blows must
　　be, –
How else accomplish teaching?"
　　　　　Reason adds
"Before man's First, and after man's
　　poor Last,
God operated and will operate."
– Process of which man merely knows
　　this much, –
That nowise it resembles man's at all,
Teaching or punishing.'
　　　　　　　　'It follows, then,
That any malefactor I would smite
With God's allowance, God himself
　　will spare
Presumably. No scape-grace? Then,
　　rejoice
Thou snatch-grace safe in Syria!'
　　　　　　　　'Friend, such view
Is but man's wonderful and wide
　　mistake.
Man lumps his kind i' the mass: God
　　singles thence
Unit by unit. Thou and God exist –
So think! – for certain: think the mass
　　– mankind –

Disparts, disperses, leaves thyself
　　alone!
Ask thy lone soul what laws are plain
　　to thee, –
Thee and no other, – stand or fall by
　　them!
That is the part for thee: regard all else
For what it may be – Time's illusion.
　　This
Be sure of – ignorance that sins, is safe.
No punishment like knowledge!
　　　　　Instance, now!
My father's choicest treasure was a
　　book
Wherein he, day by day and year by
　　year,
Recorded gains of wisdom for my sake
When I should grow to manhood.
　　　　　While a child,
Coming upon the casket where it lay
Unguarded, – what did I but toss the
　　thing
Into a fire to make more flame
　　therewith,
Meaning no harm? So acts man three-
　　years old!
I grieve now at my loss by witlessness,
But guilt was none to punish. Man
　　mature –
Each word of his I lightly held, each
　　look
I turned from – wish that wished in
　　vain – nay, will
That willed and yet went all to waste –
　　'tis these
Rankle like fire. Forgiveness? rather
　　grant
Forgetfulness! The past is past and lost.
However near I stand in his regard,
So much the nearer had I stood by
　　steps
Offered the feet which rashly spurned
　　their help.
That I call Hell; why further
　　punishment?'

　　　　　*　　　*　　　*

*When I vexed you and you chid me,*
*   And I owned my fault and turned*
*My cheek the way you bid me,*
*   And confessed the blow well earned, –*

*My comfort all the while was*
*   – Fault was faulty – near, not quite!*
*Do you wonder why the smile was?*
*   O'erpunished wrong grew right.*

*But faults you ne'er suspected,*
*   Nay, praised, no faults at all, –*
*Those would you had detected –*
*   Crushed eggs whence snakes could*
*      crawl!*

### Two Camels

Quoth one: 'Sir, solve a scruple! No
   true sage
I hear of, but instructs his scholar thus:
"Wouldst thou be wise? Then mortify
   thyself!
Baulk of its craving every bestial sense!
Say 'If I relish melons – so do swine!
Horse, ass and mule consume their
   provender
Nor leave a pea-pod: fasting feeds the
   soul." '
Thus they admonish: while thyself, I
   note,
Eatest thy ration with an appetite,
Nor fallest foul of whoso licks his lips
And sighs – "Well-saffroned was that
   barley soup!"
Can wisdom co-exist with – gorge-and-
   swill,
I say not, – simply sensual preference
For this or that fantastic meat and
   drink?
Moreover, wind blows sharper than its
   wont
This morning, and thou hast already
   donned
Thy sheepskin over-garment: sure the
   sage

Is busied with conceits that soar above
A petty change of season and its
   chance
Of causing ordinary flesh to sneeze?
I always thought, Sir' …
                  'Son,' Ferishtah said,
'Truth ought to seem as never thought
   before.
How if I give it birth in parable?
A neighbour owns two camels, beasts
   of price
And promise, destined each to go, next
   week,
Swiftly and surely with his merchandise
From Nishapur to Sebzevar, no truce
To tramp, but travel, spite of sands an
   drouth,
In days so many, lest they miss the Fair.
Each falls to meditation o'er his crib
Piled high with provender before the
   start.
Quoth this: "My soul is set on winning
   praise
From goodman lord and master, – hum
   to hoof,
I dedicate me to his service. How?
Grass, purslane, lupines and I know
   not what,
Crammed in my manger? Ha, I see – I
   see!
No, master, spare thy money! I shall
   trudge
The distance and yet cost thee not a
   doit
Beyond my supper on this mouldy
   bran."
"Be magnified, O master, for the meal
So opportunely liberal!" quoth that.
"What use of strength in me but to
   surmount
Sands and simooms, and bend beneath
   thy bales
No knee until I reach the glad bazaar?
Thus I do justice to thy fare: no sprig
Of toothsome chervil must I leave
   unchewed!
Too bitterly should I reproach myself

Did I sink down in sight of Sebzevar,
Remembering how the merest mouthful
    more
Had heartened me to manage yet a
    mile!"
And so it proved: the too-abstemious
    brute
Midway broke down, his pack rejoiced
    the thieves,
His carcass fed the vultures: not so he
The wisely thankful, who, good
    market-drudge,
Let down his lading in the market-
    place,
No damage to a single pack. Which
    beast,
Think ye, had praise and patting and a
    brand
Of good-and-faithful-servant fixed on
    flank?
So, with thy squeamish scruple. What
    imports
Fasting or feasting? Do thy day's work,
    dare
Refuse no help thereto, since help refused
Is hindrance sought and found. Win
    but the race –
Who shall object "He tossed three
    wine cups off,
And, just at starting, Lilith kissed his
    lips"?

'More soberly, – consider this, my Son.
Put case I never have myself enjoyed,
Known by experience what enjoyment
    means,
How shall I – share enjoyment? – no,
    indeed! –
Supply it to my fellows, – ignorant,
As so I should be of the thing they crave,
How it affects them, works for good or
    ill.
Style my enjoyment self-indulgence –
    sin –
Why should I labour to infect my kind
With sin's occasion, bid them too
    enjoy,

Who else might neither catch nor give
    again
Joy's plague, but live in righteous misery?
Just as I cannot, till myself convinced,
Impart conviction, so, to deal forth joy
Adroitly, needs must I know joy myself.
Renounce joy for my fellows' sake?
    That's joy
Beyond joy; but renounced for mine,
    not theirs?
Why, the physician called to help the
    sick,
Cries "Let me, first of all, discard my
    health!"
No, Son: the richness hearted in such
    joy
Is in the knowing what are gifts we
    give,
Not in a vain endeavour not to know!
Therefore, desire joy and thank God for
    it!
The Adversary said, – a Jew reports, –
החכם רא איוב אלהים:
In Persian phrase, "Does Job fear God
    for nought?"
Job's creatureship is not abjured, thou
    fool!
He nowise isolates himself and plays
The independent equal, owns no more
Than himself gave himself, so why
    thank God?
A proper speech were this מאלהים
"Equals we are, Job, labour for thyself,
Nor bid me help thee: bear, as best
    flesh may,
Pains I inflict not nor avail to cure:
Beg of me nothing thou thyself mayst
    win
By work, or waive with magnanimity,
Since we are peers acknowledged, –
    scarcely peers,
Had I implanted any want of thine
Only my power could meet and
    gratify."
No: rather hear, at man's indifference –
"Wherefore did I contrive for thee that
    ear

Hungry for music, and direct thine eye
To where I hold a seven-stringed
    instrument,
Unless I meant thee to beseech me
    play?" '

    *        *        *

*Once I saw a chemist take a pinch of*
    *powder*
*– Simple dust it seemed – and half-unstop*
    *a phial:*
*– Out dropped harmless dew. 'Mixed*
    *nothings make' – quoth he –*
*'Something!' so they did: a thunderclap,*
    *but louder –*
*Lightning-flash, but fiercer – put*
    *spectators' nerves to trial:*
*Sure enough, we learned what was,*
    *imagined what might be.*
*Had I no experience how a lip's mere*
    *tremble,*
*Look's half hesitation, cheek's just chang*
    *of colour,*
*These effect a heartquake, – how should I*
    *conceive*
*What heaven there may be? Let it but*
    *resemble*
*Earth myself have known! No bliss that's*
    *finer, fuller,*
*Only – bliss that lasts, they say, and fain*
    *would I believe.*

## Cherries

'What, I disturb thee at thy morning-
    meal:
Cherries so ripe already? Eat apace!
I recollect thy lesson yesterday.
Yet – thanks, Sir, for thy leave to
    interrupt' …
'Friend, I have finished my repast,
    thank God!'

'There now, thy thanks for breaking
    fast on fruit! –
Thanks being praise, or tantamount
    thereto.

Prithee consider, have not things
    degree,
Lofty and low? Are things not great and
    small,
Thence claiming praise and wonder
    more or less?
Shall we confuse them, with thy
    warran too,
Whose doctrine otherwise begins and
    ends
With just this precept "Never faith
    enough
In man as weakness, God as potency"?
When I would pay soul's tribute to
    that same,
Why not look up in wonder, bid the
    stars
Attest my praise of the All-mighty One?
What are man's puny members and as
    mean
Requirements weighed with Star-King
    Mushtari?
There is the marvel!'
                'Not to man – that's me.
List to what happened late, in fact or
    dream.
A certain stranger, bound from far
    away,
Still the Shah's subject, found himself
    before
Ispahan palace-gate. As duty bade,
He enters in the courts, will, if he may,
See so much glory as befits a slave
Who only comes, of mind to testify
How great and good is shown our lord
    the Shah.
In he walks, round he casts his eye
    about,
Looks up and down, admires to heart's
    content,
Ascends the gallery, tries door and
    door,
None says his reverence nay: peeps in
    at each,
Wonders at all the unimagined use,
Gold here and jewels there, – so vast,
    that hall –

So perfect yon pavilion! – lamps above
Bidding look up from luxuries below, –
Evermore wonder topping wonder, –
   last –
Sudden he comes upon a cosy nook,
A nest-like little chamber, with his
   name,
His own, yea, his and no mistake at all,
Plain o'er the entry: what, and he
   descries
Just those arrangements inside, – oh,
   the care! –
Suited to soul and body both, – so snug
The cushion – nay, the pipe-stand
   furnished so!
Whereat he cries aloud, – what think'st
   thou, Friend?
"That these my slippers should be just
   my choice,
Even to the colour that I most affect,
Is nothing: ah, that lamp, the central
   sun,
What must it light within its minaret
I scarce dare guess the good of! Who
   lives there?
That let me wonder at, – no slipper-
   toys
Meant for the foot, forsooth, which kicks
   them – thus!"

'Never enough faith in omnipotence, –
Never too much, by parity, of faith
In impuissance, man's – which turns
   to strength
When once acknowledged weakness
   every way.
How? Hear the teaching of another tale.

'Two men once owed the Shah a
   mighty sum,
Beggars they both were: this one
   crossed his arms
And bowed his head, – "whereof," –
   sighed he, – "each hair
Proved it a jewel, how the host's amount
Were idly strewn for payment at thy
   feet!"

"Lord, here they lie, my havings poor
   and scant!
All of the berries on my currant-bush,
What roots of garlic have escaped the
   mice,
And some five pippins from the
   seedling tree, –
Would they were half-a-dozen! anyhow,
Accept my all, poor beggar that I am!"
"Received in full of all demands!"
   smiled back
The apportioner of every lot of ground
From inch to acre. Littleness of love
Befits the littleness of loving thing.
What if he boasted "Seeing I am great,
Great must my corresponding tribute
   be?"
Mushtari, – well, suppose him seven
   times seven
The sun's superior, proved so by some
   sage:
Am I that sage? To me his twinkle blue
Is all I know of him and thank him for,
And therefore I have put the same in
   verse –
"Like yon blue twinkle, twinks thine
   eye, my Love!"

'Neither shalt thou be troubled overmuch
Because thy offering, – littleness itself, –
Is lessened by admixture sad and strange
Of mere man's motives, – praise with
   fear, and love
With looking after that same love's
   reward.
Alas, Friend, what was free from this
   alloy, –
Some smatch thereof, – in best and
   purest love
Proffered thy earthly father? Dust thou
   art,
Dust shalt be to the end. Thy father took
The dust, and kindly called the handful
   – gold,
Nor cared to count what sparkled here
   and there,
Sagely unanalytic. Thank, praise, love

(Sum up thus) for the lowest favours
first,
The commonest of comforts! aught
beside
Very omnipotence had overlooked
Such needs, arranging for thy little life.
Nor waste thy power of love in
wonderment
At what thou wiselier lettest shine
unsoiled
By breath of word. That this last cherry
soothes
A roughness of my palate, that I know:
His Maker knows why Mushtari was
made.'

*　　*　　*

*Verse-making was least of my virtues: I*
*viewed with despair*
*Wealth that never yet was but might be –*
*all that verse-making were*
*If the life would but lengthen to wish, let*
*the mind be laid bare.*
*So I said 'To do little is bad, to do nothing*
*is worse' –*
*And made verse.*

*Love-making, – how simple a matter! No*
*depths to explore,*
*No heights in a life to ascend! No*
*disheartening Before,*
*No affrighting Hereafter, – love now will*
*be love evermore.*
*So I felt 'To keep silence were folly:' – all*
*language above,*
*I made love.*

## Plot-Culture

'Ay, but, Ferishtah,' – a disciple
smirked, –
'That verse of thine "How twinks thine
eye, my Love,
Blue as yon star-beam!" much arrides
myself
Who haply may obtain a kiss therewith

This eve from Laila where the palms
abound –
My youth, my warrant – so the palms
be close!
Suppose when thou art earnest in
discourse
Concerning high and holy things, –
abrupt
I out with – "Laila's lip, how honey-
sweet!" –
What say'st thou, were it scandalous or
no?
I feel thy shoe sent flying at my mouth
For daring – prodigy of impudence –
Publish what, secret, were permissible.
Well, – one slide further in the
imagined slough, –
Knee-deep therein, (respect thy
reverence!) –
Suppose me well aware thy very self
Stooped prying through the palm-
screen, while I dared
Solace me with caressings all the same?
Unutterable, nay – unthinkable,
Undreamable a deed of shame! Alack,
How will it fare shouldst thou impress
on me
That certainly an Eye is over all
And each, to mark the minute's deed,
word, thought,
As worthy of reward or punishment?
Shall I permit my sense an Eye-viewed
shame,
Broad daylight perpetration, – so to
speak, –
I had not dared to breathe within the
Ear,
With black night's help about me? Yet
I stand
A man, no monster, made of flesh not
cloud:
Why made so, if my making prove
offence
To Maker's eye and ear?'
'Thou wouldst not stand
Distinctly Man,' – Ferishtah made
reply,

'Not the mere creature, – did no limit-
line
Round thee about, apportion thee thy
place
Clean-cut from out and off the
illimitable, –
Minuteness severed from immensity.
All of thee for the Maker, – for thyself,
Workings inside the circle that evolve
Thine all, – the product of thy cultured
plot.
So much of grain the ground's lord
bids thee yield
Bring sacks to granary in Autumn!
spare
Daily intelligence of this manure,
That compost, how they tend to feed
the soil:
There thou art master sole and absolute
– Only, remember doomsday! Twitt's
thou me
Because I turn away my outraged nose
Shouldst thou obtrude thereon a
shovelful
Of fertilizing kisses? Since thy sire
Wills and obtains thy marriage with
the maid,
Enough! Be reticent, I counsel thee,
Nor venture to acquaint him, point by
point,
What he procures thee. Is he so obtuse?
Keep thy instruction to thyself! My ass –
Only from him expect acknowledgment
The while he champs my gift, a thistle-
bunch,
How much he loves the largess: of his
love
I only tolerate so much as tells
By wrinkling nose and inarticulate
grunt,
The meal, that heartens him to do my
work,
Tickles his palate as I meant it should.'

*    *    *

Not with my Soul, Love! – bid no Soul
like mine
    Lap thee around nor leave the poor
    Sense room!
Soul, – travel-worn, toil-weary, – would
confine
    Along with Soul, Soul's gains from
    glow and gloom,
Captures from soarings high and divings
deep.
Spoil-laden Soul, how should such
memories sleep?
Take Sense, too – let me love entire and
whole –
        Not with my Soul!

Eyes shall meet eyes and find no eyes
between,
    Lips feed on lips, no other lips to fear!
No past, no future – so thine arms but
screen
    The present from surprise! not there,
    'tis here –
Not then, 'tis now: – back, memories that
intrude!
Make, Love, the universe our solitude,
And, over all the rest, oblivion roll –
    Sense quenching Soul!

## A Pillar at Sebzevar

'Knowledge deposed, then!' – groaned
whom that most grieved
As foolishest of all the company.
'What, knowledge, man's distinctive
attribute,
He doffs that crown to emulate an ass
Because the unknowing long-ears loves
at least
Husked lupines, and belike the feeder's
self
– Whose purpose in the dole what ass
divines?'
'Friend,' quoth Ferishtah, 'all I seem to
know
Is – I know nothing save that love I can

Boundlessly, endlessly. My curls were
    crowned
In youth with knowledge, – off, alas,
    crown slipped
Next moment, pushed by better
    knowledge still
Which nowise proved more constant:
    gain, to-day,
Was toppling loss to-morrow, lay at last
– Knowledge, the golden? – lacquered
    ignorance!
As gain – mistrust it! Not as means to
    gain:
Lacquer we learn by: cast in fining-pot,
We learn, – when what seemed ore
    assayed proves dross, –
Surelier true gold's worth, guess how
    purity
I' the lode were precious could one
    light on ore
Clarified up to test of crucible.
The prize is in the process: knowledge
    means
Ever-renewed assurance by defeat
That victory is somehow still to reach,
But love is victory, the prize itself:
Love – trust to! Be rewarded for the trust
In trust's mere act. In love success is
    sure,
Attainment – no delusion, whatsoe'er
The prize be: apprehended as a prize,
A prize it is. Thy child as surely grasps
An orange as he fails to grasp the sun
Assumed his capture. What if soon he
    finds
The foolish fruit unworthy grasping?
    Joy
In shape and colour, – that was joy as
    true –
Worthy in its degree of love – as grasp
Of sun were, which had singed his
    hand beside.
What if he said the orange held no juice
Since it was not that sun he hoped to
    suck?
This constitutes the curse that spoils
    our life

And sets man maundering of his
    misery,
That there's no meanest atom he
    obtains
Of what he counts for knowledge but
    he cries
"Hold here, – I have the whole thing, –
    know, this time,
Nor need search farther!" Whereas,
    strew his path
With pleasures, and he scorns them
    while he stoops:
"This fitly call'st thou pleasure, pick up
    this
And praise it, truly? I reserve my thanks
For something more substantial." Fool
    not thus
In practising with life and its delights!
Enjoy the present gift, nor wait to
    know
The unknowable. Enough to say "I feel
Love's sure effect, and, being loved,
    must love
The love its cause behind, – I can and
    do!"
Nor turn to try thy brain-power on the
    fact,
(Apart from as it strikes thee, here and
    now –
Its how and why, i' the future and
    elsewhere)
Except to – yet once more, and ever
    again,
Confirm thee in thy utter ignorance:
Assured that, whatsoe'er the quality
Of love's cause, save that love was
    caused thereby,
This – nigh upon revealment as it seemed
A minute since – defies thy longing
    looks,
Withdrawn into the unknowable once
    more.
Wholly distrust thy knowledge, then,
    and trust
As wholly love allied to ignorance!
There lies thy truth and safety. Love is
    praise,

And praise is love! Refine the same,
contrive
An intellectual tribute – ignorance
Appreciating ere approbative
Of knowledge that is infinite? With us
The small, who use the knowledge of
our kind
Greater than we, more wisely
ignorance
Restricts its apprehension, sees and
knows
No more than brain accepts in faith of
sight,
Takes first what comes first, only sure
so far.
By Sebzevar a certain pillar stands
So aptly that its gnomon tells the hour;
What if the townsmen said "Before we
thank
Who placed it, for his serviceable craft,
And go to dinner since its shade tells
noon,
Needs must we have the craftsman's
purpose clear
On half a hundred more recondite points
Than a mere summons to a vulgar
meal!"
Better they say "How opportune the
help!
Be loved and praised, thou kindly-
hearted sage
Whom Hudhud taught, – the gracious
spirit-bird, –
How to construct the pillar, teach the
time!"
So let us say – not "Since we know, we
love,"
But rather "Since we love, we know
enough."
Perhaps the pillar by a spell controlled
Mushtari in his courses? Added grace
Surely I count it that the sage devised,
Beside celestial service, ministry
To all the land, by one sharp shade at
noon
Falling as folk foresee. Once more
then, Friend –

(What ever in those careless ears of
thine
Withal I needs must round thee) –
knowledge doubt
Even wherein it seems demonstrable!
Love, – in the claim for love, that's
gratitude
For apprehended pleasure, nowise
doubt!
Pay its due tribute, – sure that pleasure
is,
While knowledge may be, at the most.
See, now!
Eating my breakfast, I thanked God. –
"For love
Shown in the cherries' flavour?
Consecrate
So petty an example?" There's the
fault!
We circumscribe omnipotence. Search
sand
To unearth water: if first handful
scooped
Yields thee a draught, what need of
digging down
Full fifty fathoms deep to find a spring
Whereof the pulse might deluge half
the land?
Drain the sufficient drop, and praise
what checks
The drouth that glues thy tongue, –
what more would help
A brimful cistern? Ask the cistern's
boon
When thou wouldst solace camels: in
thy case,
Relish the drop and love the loveable!'
'And what may be unloveable?
                                    'Why, hate!
If out of sand comes sand and nought
but sand,
Affect not to be quaffing at mirage,
Nor nickname pain as pleasure. That,
belike,
Constitutes just the trial of thy wit
And worthiness to gain promotion, –
hence,

Proves the true purpose of thine actual
   life.
Thy soul's environment of things
   perceived,
Things visible and things invisible,
Fact, fancy – all was purposed to
   evolve
This and this only – was thy wit of
   worth
To recognize the drop's use, love the
   same,
And loyally declare against mirage
Though all the world asseverated dust
Was good to drink? Say, "what made
   moist my lip,
That I acknowledged moisture:" thou
   art saved!

'For why? The creature and creator
   stand
Rightly related so. Consider well!
Were knowledge all thy faculty, then
   God
Must be ignored: love gains him by
   first leap.
Frankly accept the creatureship: ask
   good
To love for: press bold to the tether's
   end
Allotted to this life's intelligence!
"So we offend?" Will it offend thyself
If, – impuissance praying potency, –
Thy child beseech that thou command
   the sun
Rise bright to-morrow – thou, he
   thinks supreme
In power and goodness, why shouldst
   thou refuse?
Afterward, when the child matures,
   perchance
The fault were greater if, with wit full-
   grown,
The stripling dared to ask for a dinar,
Than that the boy cried "Pluck Sitara
   down
And give her me to play with!" 'Tis fo
   him

To have no bounds to his belief in
   thee:
For thee it also is to let her shine
Lustrous and lonely, so best serving
   him!'

\*    \*    \*

*Ask not one least word of praise!*
   *Words declare your eyes are bright?*
*What then meant that summer day's*
*Silence spent in one long gaze?*
   *Was my silence wrong or right?*

*Words of praise were all to seek!*
   *Face of you and form of you,*
*Did they find the praise so weak*
*When my lips just touched your cheek –*
   *Touch which let my soul come*
      *through?*

## A Bean-Stripe:
## also, Apple-Eating

'Look, I strew beans' …
          (Ferishtah, we premise,
Strove this way with a scholar's
   cavilment
Who put the peevish question: 'Sir, be
   frank!
A good thing or a bad thing – Life is
   which?
Shine and shade, happiness and misery
Battle it out there: which force beats, I
   ask?
If I pick beans from out a bushelful –
This one, this other, – then demand of
   thee
What colour names each justly in the
   main, –
"Black" I expect, and "White" ensues
   reply:
No hesitation for what speck, spot, splash
Of either colour's opposite, intrudes
To modify thy judgment. Well, for
   beans
Substitute days, – show, ranged in
   order, Life –

Then, tell me its true colour! Time is
   short,
Life's days compose a span, – as brief
   be speech!
Black I pronounce for, like the Indian
   Sage, –
Black – present, past and future,
   interspersed
With blanks, no doubt, which simple
   folk style Good
Because not Evil: no, indeed? Forsooth
Black's shade on White is White too!
   What's the worst
Of Evil but that, past, it overshades
The else-exempted present? – memory,
We call the plague! "Nay, but our
   memory fades
And leaves the past unsullied!" Does it
   so?
Why, straight the purpose of such
   breathing-space,
Such respite from past ill, grows plain
   enough!
What follows on remembrance of the
   past?
Fear of the future! Life, from birth to
   death,
Means – either looking back on harm
   escaped,
Or looking forward to that harm's
   return
With tenfold power of harming. Black,
   not White,
Never the whole consummate quietude
Life should be, troubled by no fear! –
   nor hope –
I'll say, since lamplight dies in
   noontide, hope
Loses itself in certainty. Such lot
Man's might have been: I leave the
   consequence
To bolder critics of the Primal Cause;
Such am not I: but, man – as man I
   speak:
Black is the bean-throw: evil is the
   Life!')

'Look, I strew beans' – resumed Ferish-
   tah – 'beans
Blackish and whitish; what they figure
   forth
Shall be man's sum of moments, bad
   and good,
That make up Life, – each moment
   when he feels
Pleasure or pain, his poorest fact of
   sense,
Consciousness anyhow: there's stand
   the first;
Whence next advance shall be from
   points to line,
Singulars to a series, parts to whole,
And moments to the Life. How look
   they now,
Viewed in the large, those little joys
   and griefs
Ranged duly all a-row at last, like beans
– These which I strew? This bean was
   white, this – black,
Set by itself, – but see if, good and bad
Each following either in companionship,
Black have not grown less black and
   white less white,
Till blackish seems but dun, and
   whitish – grey,
And the whole line turns – well, or
   black to thee
Or white belike to me – no matter
   which:
The main result is – both are modified
According to our eye's scope, power of
   range
Before and after. Black dost call this
   bean?
What, with a whiteness in its wake,
   which – see –
Suffuses half its neighbour? – and, in
   turn,
Lowers its pearliness late absolute,
Frowned upon by the jet which follows
   hard –
Else wholly white my bean were.
   Choose a joy!
Bettered it was by sorrow gone before,

And sobered somewhat by the
    shadowy sense
Of sorrow which came after or might
    come.
Joy, sorrow, – by precedence,
    subsequence –
Either on each, make fusion, mix in
    Life
That's both and neither wholly: grey or
    dun?
Dun thou decidest? grey prevails, say I:
Wherefore? Because my view is wide
    enough,
Reaches from first to last nor winks at
    all:
Motion achieves it: stop short – fast we
    stick, –
Probably at the bean that's blackest.
                 'Since –
Son, trust me, – this I know and only
    this –
I am in motion, and all things beside
That circle round my passage through
    their midst, –
Motionless, these are, as regarding me:
– Which means, myself I solely recognize.
They too may recognize themselves,
    not me,
For aught I know or care: but plain
    they serve
This, if no other purpose – stuff to try
And test my power upon of raying light
And lending hue to all things as I go
Moonlike through vapour. Mark the
    flying orb!
Think'st thou the halo, painted still
    afresh
At each new cloud-fleece pierced and
    passaged through,
This was and is and will be evermore
Coloured in permanence? The glory
    swims
Girdling the glory-giver, swallowed
    straight
By night's abysmal gloom, unglorified
Behind as erst before the advancer:
    gloom?

Faced by the onward-faring, see, succeeds
From the abandoned heaven a next
    surprise,
And where's the gloom now? – silver-
    smitten straight,
One glow and variegation! So with me,
Who move and make, – myself, – the
    black, the white,
The good, the bad, of life's environment.
Stand still! black stays black: start again!
    there's white
Asserts supremacy: the motion's all
That colours me my moment: seen as
    joy?
I have escaped from sorrow, or that was
Or might have been: as sorrow? – thence
    shall be
Escape as certain: white preceded black,
Black shall give way to white as duly, –
    so,
Deepest in black means white most
    imminent.
Stand still, – have no before, no after! –
    life
Proves death, existence grows impossible
To man like me. "What else is blessed
    sleep
But death, then?" Why, a rapture of
    release
From toil, – that's sleep's approach: as
    certainly,
The end of sleep means, toil is
    triumphed o'er:
These round the blank inconsciousness
    between
Brightness and brightness, either pushed
    to blaze
Just through that blank's interposition.
    Hence
The use of things external: man –
    that's I –
Practise thereon my power of casting
    light,
And calling substance, – when the light
    I cast
Breaks into colour, – by its proper
    name

– A truth and yet a falsity: black, white,
Names each bean taken from what lay
    so close
And threw such tint: pain might mean
    pain indeed
Seen in the passage past it, – pleasure
    prove
No mere delusion while I paused to
    look, –
Though what an idle fancy was that fear
Which overhung and hindered
    pleasure's hue!
While how, again, pain's shade
    enhanced the shine
Of pleasure, else no pleasure! Such
    effects
Came of such causes. Passage at an
    end, –
Past, present, future pains and pleasures
    fused
So that one glance may gather blacks
    and whites
Into a life-time, – like my bean-streak
    there,
Why, white they whirl into, not black –
    forme!'

'Ay, but for me? The indubitable
    blacks,
Immeasurable miseries, here, there
And everywhere i' the world – world
    outside thine
Paled off so opportunely, – body's
    plague,
Torment of soul, – where's found thy
    fellowship
With wide humanity all round about
Reeling beneath its burden? What's
    despair?
Behold that man, that woman, child –
    nay, brute!
Will any speck of white unblacken life
Splashed, splotched, dyed hell-deep
    now from end to end
For him or her or it – who knows?
    Not I!'

'Nor I, Son! "It" shall stand for bird,
    beast, fish,
Reptile, and insect even: take the last!
There's the palm-aphis, minute miracle
As wondrous every whit as thou or I:
Well, and his world's the palm-frond,
    there he's born,
Lives, breeds and dies in that circum-
    ference,
An inch of green for cradle, pasture-
    ground,
Purlieu and grave: the palm's use, ask
    of him!
"To furnish these," replies his wit: ask
    thine –
Who see the heaven above, the earth
    below,
Creation everywhere, – these, each and
    all
Claim certain recognition from the tree
For special service rendered branch
    and bole,
Top-tuft and tap-root: – for thyself,
    thus seen,
Palms furnish dates to eat, and leaves
    to shade,
– Maybe, thatch huts with, – have
    another use
Than strikes the aphis. So with me, my
    Son!
I know my own appointed patch i' the
    world,
What pleasures me or pains there: all
    outside –
How he, she, it, and even thou, Son,
    live,
Are pleased or pained, is past conjecture,
    once
I pry beneath the semblance, – all that's
    fit,
To practise with, – reach where the fact
    may lie
Fathom-deep lower. There's the first
    and last
Of my philosophy. Blacks blur thy white?
Not mine! The aphis feeds, nor finds
    his leaf

Untenable because a lance-thrust, nay,
Lightning strikes sere a moss-patch
    close beside,
Where certain other aphids live and
    love.
Restriction to his single inch of white,
That's law for him, the aphis: but for
    me,
The man, the larger-souled, beside my
    stretch
Of blacks and whites, I see a world of
    woe
All round about me: one such burst of
    black
Intolerable o'er the life I count
White in the main, and, yea – white's
    faintest trace
Were clean abolished once and
    evermore.
Thus fare my fellows, swallowed up in
    gloom
So far as I discern: how far is that?
God's care be God's! 'Tis mine – to
    boast no joy
Unsobered by such sorrows of my kind
As sully with their shade my life that
    shines.'
'Reflected possibilities of pain,
Forsooth, just chasten pleasure! Pain
    itself, –
Fact and not fancy, does not this affect
The general colour?'
              'Here and there a touch
Taught me, betimes, the artifice of
    things –
That all about, external to myself,
Was meant to be suspected, – not
    revealed
Demonstrably a cheat, – but half seen
    through,
Lest white should rule unchecked
    along the line:
Therefore white may not triumph. All
    the same,
Of absolute and irretrievable
And all-subduing black, – black's soul
    of black

Beyond white's power to disintensify, –
Of that I saw no sample: such may
    wreck
My life and ruin my philosophy
To-morrow, doubtless: hence the
    constant shade
Cast on life's shine, – the tremor that
    intrudes
When firmest seems my faith in white.
    Dost ask
"Who is Ferishtah, hitherto exempt
From black experience? Why, if God
    be just,
Were sundry fellow-mortals singled out
To undergo experience for his sake,
Just that the gift of pain, bestowed on
    them,
In him might temper to the due degree
Joy's else-excessive largess?" Why,
    indeed!
Back are we brought thus to the
    starting-point –
Man's impotency, God's omnipotence,
These stop my answer. Aphis that I am,
How leave my inch-allotment, pass at
    will
Into my fellow's liberty of range,
Enter into his sense of black and white,
As either, seen by me from outside,
    seems
Predominatingly the colour? Life,
Lived by my fellow, shall I pass into
And myself live there? No – no more
    than pass
From Persia, where in sun since birth I
    bask
Daily, to some ungracious land afar,
Told of by travellers, where the might
    of snow
Smothers up day, and fluids lose
    themselves
Frozen to marble. How I bear the sun,
Beat though he may unduly, that I
    know:
How blood once curdled ever creeps
    again,
Baffles conjecture: yet since people live

Somehow, resist a clime would
    conquer me,
Somehow provided for their sake must
    dawn
Compensative resource. "No sun, no
    grapes, –
Then, no subsistence!" – were it wisely
    said?
Or this well-reasoned – "Do I dare feel
    warmth
And please my palate here with Persia's
    vine,
Though, over-mounts, – to trust the
    traveller, –
Snow, feather-thick, is falling while I
    feast?
What if the cruel winter force his way
Here also?" Son, the wise reply were
    this:
When cold from over-mounts spikes
    through and through
Blood, bone and marrow of Ferishtah,
    – then,
Time to look out for shelter – time, at
    least,
To wring the hands and cry "No shelter
    serves!"
Shelter, of some sort, no experienced
    chill
Warrants that I despair to find.'
                    'No less,
Doctors have differed here; thou say'st
    thy say;
Another man's experience masters thine,
Flat controverted by the sourly-Sage,
The Indian witness who, with faculty
Fine as Ferishtah's, found no white at
    all
Chequer the world's predominating
    black,
No good oust evil from supremacy,
So that Life's best was that it led to
    death.
How of his testimony?'
                  'Son, suppose
My camel told me: "Threescore days
    and ten

I traversed hill and dale, yet never
    found
Food to stop hunger, drink to stay my
    drouth;
Yet, here I stand alive, which take in
    proof
That to survive was found impossible!"
"Nay, rather take thou, non-surviving
    beast"
(Reply were prompt), "on flank this
    thwack of staff
Nowise affecting flesh that's dead and
    dry!
Thou wincest? Take correction twice,
    amend
Next time thy nomenclature! Call
    white – white!"
The sourly-Sage, for whom life's best
    was death,
Lived out his seventy years, looked
    hale, laughed loud,
Liked – above all – his dinner, – lied,
    in short.'

'Lied is a rough phrase: say he fell from
    truth
In climbing towards it! – sure less
    faulty so
Than had he sat him down and stayed
    content
With thy safe orthodoxy, "White, all
    white,
White everywhere for certain I should
    see
Did I but understand how white is
    black,
As clearer sense than mine would."
                  Clearer sense, –
Whose may that be? Mere human eyes
    I boast,
And such distinguish colours in the
    main,
However any tongue, that's human too,
Please to report the matter. Dost thou
    blame
A soul that strives but to see plain,
    speak true,

Truth at all hazards? Oh, this false for
    real,
This emptiness which feigns solidity, –
Ever some grey that's white, and dun
    that's black, –
When shall we rest upon the thing itself
Not on its semblance? – Soul – too
    weak, forsooth,
To cope with fact – wants fiction every-
    where!
Mine tires of falsehood: truth at any
    cost!'

'Take one and try conclusions – this,
    suppose!
God is all-good, all-wise, all-powerful:
    truth?
Take it and rest there. What is man?
    Not God:
None of these absolutes therefore, –
    yet himself,
A creature with a creature's qualities.
Make them agree, these two
    conceptions! Each
Abolishes the other. Is man weak,
Foolish and bad? He must be Ahriman,
Co-equal with an Ormuzd, Bad with
    Good,
Or else a thing made at the Prime Sole
    Will,
Doing a maker's pleasure – with results
Which – call, the wide world over,
    "what must be" –
But, from man's point of view, and
    only point
Possible to his powers, call – evidence
Of goodness, wisdom, strength? we
    mock ourselves
In all that's best of us, – man's blind
    but sure
Craving for these in very deed not
    word,
Reality and not illusion. Well, –
Since these nowhere exist – nor there
    where cause
Must have effect, nor here where
    craving means

Craving unfollowed by fit consequence
And full supply, aye sought for, never
    found –
These – what are they but man's own
    rule of right?
A scheme of goodness recognized by
    man,
Although by man unrealizable, –
Not God's with whom to will were to
    perform:
Nowise performed here, therefore never
    willed.
What follows but that God, who could
    the best,
Has willed the worst, – while man, with
    power to match
Will with performance, were deservedly
Hailed the supreme – provided ...
    here's the touch
That breaks the bubble ... this concept
    of man's
Were man's own work, his birth of
    heart and brain,
His native grace, no alien gift at all.
The bubble breaks here. Will of man
    create?
No more than this my hand which
    strewed the beans
Produced them also from its finger-tips.
Back goes creation to its source, source
    prime
And ultimate, the single and the sole.'

'How reconcile discordancy, – unite
Notion and notion – God that only can
Yet does not, – man that would indeed
But just as surely cannot, – both in one?
What help occurs to thy intelligence?'

'Ah, the beans, – or, – example better
    yet, –
A carpet-web I saw once leave the loom
And lie at gorgeous length in Ispahan!
The weaver plied his work with lengths
    of silk
Dyed each to match some jewel as it
    might,

And wove them, this by that. "How
    comes it, friend," –
(Quoth I – "that while, apart, this fiery
    hue,
That watery dimness, either shocks the
    eye,
So blinding bright, or else offends again
By dulness, – yet the two, set each by
    each,
Somehow produce a colour born of both,
A medium profitable to the sight?"
"Such medium is the end whereat I
    aim," –
Answered my craftsman: "there's no
    single tinct
Would satisfy the eye's desire to taste
The secret of the diamond: join extremes,
Results a serviceable medium-ghost,
The diamond's simulation." Even so
I needs must blend the quality of man
With quality of God, and so assist
Mere human sight to understand my
    Life,
What is, what should be, – understand
    thereby
Wherefore I hate the first and love the
    last, –
Understand why things so present them-
    selves
To me, placed here to prove I under-
    stand.
Thus, from beginning runs the chain to
    end,
And binds me plain enough. By con-
    sequence,
I bade thee tolerate, – not kick and cuff
The man who held that natures did in
    fact
Blend so, since so thyself must have
    them blend
In fancy, if it take a flight so far.'

'A power, confessed past knowledge,
    nay, past thought,
– Thus thought thus known!'
               'To know of, think about –
Is all man's sum of faculty effects

When exercised on earth's least atom,
    Son!
What was, what is, what may such
    atom be?
No answer! Still, what seems it to
    man's sense?
An atom with some certain properties
Known about, thought of as occasion
    needs,
– Man's – but occasions of the universe?
Unthinkable, unknowable to man.
Yet, since to think and know fire
    through and through
Exceeds man, is the warmth of fire
    unknown,
Its uses – are they so unthinkable?
Pass from such obvious power to
    powers unseen,
Undreamed of save in their sure
    consequence:
Take that, we spoke of late, which
    draws to ground
The staff my hand lets fall: it draws, at
    least –
Thus much man thinks and knows, if
    nothing more.'

'Ay, but man puts no mind into such
    power!
He neither thanks it, when an apple
    drops,
Nor prays it spare his pate while under-
    neath.
Does he thank Summer though it
    plumped the rind?
Why thank the other force – whate'er
    its name –
Which gave him teeth to bite and
    tongue to taste
And throat to let the pulp pass? Force
    and force,
No end of forces! Have they mind like
    man?'

'Suppose thou visit our lord Shalim-
    Shah,
Bringing thy tribute as appointed. "Here

Come I to pay my due!" Whereat one
    slave
Obsequious spreads a carpet for thy
    foot,
His fellow offers sweetmeats, while a
    third
Prepares a pipe: what thanks or praise
    have they?
Such as befit prompt service. Gratitude
Goes past them to the Shah whose
    gracious nod
Set all the sweet civility at work;
But for his ordinance, I much suspect,
My scholar had been left to cool his
    heels
Uncarpeted, or warm them – likelier
    still –
With bastinado for intrusion. Slaves
Needs must obey their master: "force
    and force,
No end of forces," act as bids some
    force
Supreme o'er all and each: where find
    that one?
How recognize him? Simply as thou
    didst
The Shah – by reasoning "Since I feel a
    debt,
Behoves me pay the same to one aware
I have my duty, he his privilege."
Didst thou expect the slave who
    charged thy pipe
Would serve as well to take thy tribute-
    bag
And save thee further trouble?'
                    'Be it so!
The sense within me that I owe a debt
Assures me – somewhere must be
    somebody
Ready to take his due. All comes to
    this –
Where due is, there acceptance follows:
    find
Him who accepts the due! and why look
    far?
Behold thy kindred compass thee
    about!

Ere thou wast born and after thou shalt
    die,
Heroic man stands forth as Shahan-
    Shah.
Rustem and Gew, Gudarz and all the
    rest.
How come they short of lordship thats'
    to seek?
Dead worthies! but men live undoubtedly
Gifted as Sindokht, sage Sulayman's
    match,
Valiant like Kawah: ay, and while earth
    lasts
Such heroes shall abound there – all
    for thee
Who profitest by all the present, past,
And future operation of thy race.
Why, then, o'erburdened with a debt
    of thanks,
Look wistful for some hand from out
    the clouds
To take it, when, all round, a multitude
Would ease thee in a trice?'
               'Such tendered thanks
Would tumble back to who craved
    riddance, Son!
– Who but my sorry self? See! stars are
    out –
Stars which, unconscious of thy gaze
    beneath,
Go glorying, and glorify thee too
– Those Seven Thrones, Zurah's
    beauty, weird Parwin!
Whether shall love and praise to stars
    be paid
Or – say – some Mubid who, for good
    to thee
Blind at thy birth, by magic all his own
Opened thine eyes, and gave the
    sightless sight,
Let the stars' glory enter? Say his charm
Worked while thyself lay sleeping: as
    he went
Thou wakedst: "What a novel sense
    have I!
Whom shall I love and praise?" "The
    stars, each orb

Thou standest rapt beneath," proposes
    one:
"Do not they live their life, and please
    themselves,
And so please thee? What more is
    requisite?"
Make thou this answer: "If indeed no
    mage
Opened my eyes and worked a miracle,
Then let the stars thank me who
    apprehend
That such an one is white, such other
    blue!
But for my apprehension both were
    blank.
Cannot I close my eyes and bid my
    brain
Make whites and blues, conceive
    without stars' help,
New qualities of colour? were my sight
Lost or misleading, would yon red – I
    judge
A ruby's benefaction – stand for aught
But green from vulgar glass? Myself
    appraise
Lustre and lustre; should I overlook
Fomalhaut and declare some fen-fire
    king,
Who shall correct me, lend me eyes he
    trusts
No more than I trust mine? My mage
    for me!
I never saw him: if he never was,
I am the arbitrator!" No, my Son!
Let us sink down to thy similitude:
I eat my apple, relish what is ripe –
The sunny side, admire its rarity
Since half the tribe is wrinkled, and the
    rest
Hide commonly a maggot in the core, –
And down Zerdusht goes with due
    smack of lips:
But – thank an apple? He who made
    my mouth
To masticate, my palate to approve,
My maw to further the concoction –
    Him

I thank, – but for whose work, the
    orchard's wealth
Might prove so many gall-nuts – stocks
    or stones
For aught that I should think, or know,
    or care.'

\*    \*    \*

'Why from the world,' Ferishtah smiled,
    'should thanks
    Go to this work of mine? If worthy
    praise,
Praised let it be and welcome: as verse
    ranks,
    So rate my verse: if good therein out
    weighs
    Aught faulty judged, judge justly!
    Justice says:
Be just to fact, or blaming or approving:
But – generous? No, nor loving!

'Loving! what claim to love has work of
    mine?
    Concede my life were emptied of its
    gains
To furnish forth and fill work's strict
    confine,
    Who works so for the world's sake – he
    complains
    With cause when hate, not love,
    rewards his pains.
I looked beyond the world for truth and
    beauty:
Sought, found and did my duty.'

## Epilogue

Oh, Love – no, Love! All the noise
    below, Love,
    Groanings all and moanings – none
    of Life I lose!
All of Life's a cry just of weariness and
    woe, Love –
    'Hear at least, thou happy one!' How
    can I, Love, but choose?
Only, when I do hear, sudden circle
    round me

– Much as when the moon's might
    frees a space from cloud –
Iridescent splendours: gloom – would
    else confound me –
Barriered off and banished far –
    bright-edged the blackest shroud!

Thronging through the cloud-rift,
    whose are they, the faces
    Faint revealed yet sure divined, the
    famous ones of old?
'What' – they smile – 'our names, our
    deeds so soon erases
    Time upon his tablet where Life's
    glory lies enrolled?

'Was it for mere fool's-play, make-
    believe and mumming,
    So we battled it like men, not
    boylike sulked or whined?
Each of us heard clang God's "Come!"
    and each was coming:
    Soldiers all, to forward-face, not
    sneaks to lag behind!

'How of the field's fortune? That
    concerned our Leader!
    Led, we struck our stroke nor cared
    for doings left and right:

Each as on his sole head, failer or
    succeeder,
    Lay the blame or lit the praise: no
    care for cowards: fight!'

Then the cloud-rift broadens, spanning
    earth that's under,
    Wide our world displays its worth,
    man's strife and strife's success:
All the good and beauty, wonder
    crowning wonder,
    Till my heart and soul applaud
    perfection, nothing less.

Only, at heart's utmost joy and
    triumph, terror
    Sudden turns the blood to ice: a
    chill wind disencharms
All the late enchantment! What if all be
    error –
    If the halo irised round my head
    were, Love, thine arms?

*Palazzo Giustinian-Recanati,*
*Venice: December 1,1883*

# ASOLANDO

Fancies and Facts

To Mrs. Arthur Bronson

To whom but you, dear Friend, should I dedicate verses – some few written, all of them supervised, in the comfort of your presence, and with yet another experience of the gracious hospitality now bestowed on me since so many a year, – adding a charm even to my residences at Venice, and leaving me little regret for the surprise and delight at my visits to Asolo in bygone days?

I unite, you will see, the disconnected poems by a title-name popularly ascribed to the inventiveness of the ancient secretary of Queen Cornaro whose palace-tower still overlooks us: Asolare – 'to disport in the open air, amuse oneself at random.' The objection that such a word nowhere occurs in the works of the Cardinal is hardly important – Bembo was too thorough a purist to conserve in print a term which in talk he might possibly toy with: but the word is more likely derived from a Spanish source. I use it for love of the place, and in requital of your pleasant assurance that an early poem of mine first attracted you thither – where and elsewhere, at La Mura as Cà Alvisi, may all happiness attend you!

Gratefully and affectionately yours, R. B.

Asolo: *October* 15, 1889

## *Prologue*

'The Poet's age is sad. for why?
  In youth, the natural world could
  show
No common object but his eye
  At once involved with alien glow –
His own soul's iris-bow.

'And now a flower is just a flower:
  Man, bird, beast are but beast, bird,
  man –
Simply themselves, uncinct by dower
  Of dyes which, when life's day began,
Round each in glory ran.'

Friend, did you need an optic glass,
  Which were your choice? A lens to
  drape
In ruby, emerald, chrysopras,
  Each object – or reveal its shape
Clear outlined, past escape,

The naked very thing? – so clear
  That, when you had the chance to
  gaze,

You found its inmost self appear
  Through outer seeming – truth
  ablaze,
Not falsehood's fancy-haze?

How many a year, my Asolo,
  Since – one step just from sea to
  land –
I found you, loved yet feared you so –
  For natural objects seemed to stand
Palpably fire-clothed! No –

No mastery of mine o'er these!
  Terror with beauty, like the Bush
Burning but unconsumed. Bend knees,
  Drop eyes to earthward! Language?
  Tush!
Silence 'tis awe decrees.

And now? The lambent flame is – where?
  Lost from the naked world: earth,
  sky,
Hill, vale, tree, flower, – Italia's rare
  O'er-running beauty crowds the eye –
But flame? The Bush is bare.

Hill, vale, tree, flower – they stand
      distinct,
   Nature to know and name. What
      then?
A Voice spoke thence which straight
      unlinked
   Fancy from fact: see, all's in ken:
Has once my eyelid winked?

No, for the purged ear apprehends
   Earth's import, not the eye late dazed:
The Voice said 'Call my works thy
      friends!
   At Nature dost thou shrink amazed?
God is it who transcends.'

                    Asolo: *September 6, 1889*

## Rosny

Woe, he went galloping into the war,
      Clara, Clara!
Let us two dream: shall he 'scape with
      a scar?
   Scarcely disfigurement, rather a grace
Making for manhood which nowise we
      mar:
   See, while I kiss it, the flush on his
      face –
            Rosny, Rosny!

Light does he laugh: 'With your love in
      my soul' –
            (Clara, Clara!)
'How could I other than – sound, safe
      and whole –
   Cleave who opposed me asunder, yet
      stand
Scatheless beside you, as, touching love's
      goal,
   Who won the race kneels, craves
      reward at your hand –
            Rosny, Rosny?'

Ay, but if certain who envied should see!
      Clara, Clara,
Certain who simper: 'The hero for me
   Hardly of life were so chary as miss

Death – death and fame – that's love's
      guerdon when She
   Boasts, proud bereaved one, her
      choice fell on this
            Rosny, Rosny!'

So, – go on dreaming, – he lies mid a
      heap
            (Clara, Clara,)
Of the slain by his hand: what is death
      but a sleep?
   Dead, with my portrait displayed on
      his breast:
Love wrought his undoing: 'No
      prudence could keep
   The love-maddened wretch from his
      fate.' That is best,
            Rosny, Rosny!

## Dubiety

I will be happy if but for once:
   Only help me, Autumn weather,
Me and my cares to screen, ensconce
   In luxury's sofa-lap of leather!

Sleep? Nay, comfort – with just a cloud
   Suffusing day too clear and bright:
Eve's essence, the single drop allowed
   To sully, like milk, Noon's water-
      white.

Let gauziness shade, not shroud, –
      adjust,
   Dim and not deaden, – somehow
      sheathe
Aught sharp in the rough world's busy
      thrust,
   If it reach me through dreaming's
      vapour-wreath.

Be life so, all things ever the same!
   For, what has disarmed the world?
      Outside,
Quiet and peace: inside, nor blame
   Nor want, nor wish whate'er betide.

What is it like that has happened
　　before?
　A dream? No dream, more real by
　　much.
A vision? But fanciful days of yore
　Brought many: mere musing seems
　　not such.

Perhaps but a memory, after all!
　– Of what came once when a
　　woman leant
To feel for my brow where her kiss
　　might fall.
　Truth ever, truth only the excellent!

## Now

Out of your whole life give but a
　　moment!
All of your life that has gone before,
All to come after it, – so you ignore,
So you make perfect the present, –
　　condense,
In a rapture of rage, for perfection's
　　endowment,
Thought and feeling and soul and
　　sense –
Merged in a moment which gives me at
　　last
You around me for once, you beneath
　　me, above me –
Me – sure that despite of time future,
　　time past, –
This tick of our life-time's one moment
　　you love me!
How long such suspension may linger?
　　Ah, Sweet –
The moment eternal – just that and no
　　more –
When ecstasy's utmost we clutch at
　　the core
While cheeks burn, arms open, eyes
　　shut and lips meet!

## Humility

What girl but, having gathered flowers,
Stript the beds and spoilt the bowers,
From the lapful light she carries
Drops a careless bud? – nor tarries
To regain the waif and stray:
'Store enough for home' – she'll say.

So say I too: give your lover
Heaps of loving – under, over,
Whelm him – make the one the wealthy!
Am I all so poor who – stealthy
Work it was! – picked up what fell:
Not the worst bud – who can tell?

## Poetics

'So say the foolish!' Say the foolish so,
　　Love?
　'Flower she is, my rose' – or else 'My
　　very swan is she' –
Or perhaps 'Yon maid-moon, blessing
　　earth below, Love,
　That art thou!' – to them, belike: no
　　such vain words from me.

'Hush, rose, blush! no balm like breath,'
　　I chide it:
　'Bend thy neck its best, swan, – hers
　　the whiter curve!'
Be the moon the moon: my Love I
　　place beside it:
　What is she? Her human self, – no
　　lower word will serve.

## Summum Bonum

All the breath and the bloom of the
　　year in the bag of one bee:
　All the wonder and wealth of the
　　mine in the heart of one gem:
In the core of one pearl all the shade
　　and the shine of the sea:
　Breath and bloom, shade and shine,
　　– wonder, wealth, and – how far
　　above them –

Truth, that's brighter than gem,
    Trust, that's purer than pearl, –
Brightest truth, purest trust in the
    universe – all were for me
      In the kiss of one girl.

## A Pearl, a Girl

A simple ring with a single stone
    To the vulgar eye no stone of price:
Whisper the right word, that alone –
    Forth starts a sprite, like fire from ice,
And lo, you are lord (says an Eastern
    scroll)
Of heaven and earth, lord whole and
    sole
      Through the power in a pearl.

A woman ('tis I this time that say)
    With little the world counts worth
      praise
Utter the true word – out and away
    Escapes her soul: I am wrapt in
      blaze,
Creation's lord, of heaven and earth
Lord whole and sole – by a minute's
    birth –
      Through the love in a girl!

## Speculative

Others may need new life in Heaven –
    Man, Nature, Art – made new, assume!
Man with new mind old sense to leaven,
    Nature – new light to clear old gloom,
Art that breaks bounds, gets soaring-
    room.

I shall pray: 'Fugitive as precious –
    Minutes which passed, – return,
      remain!
Let earth's old life once more enmesh
    us,
    You with old pleasure, me – old
      pain,
So we but meet nor part again!'

## White Witchcraft

If you and I could change to beasts,
    what beast should either be?
Shall you and I play Jove for once?
    Turn fox then, I decree!
Shy wild sweet stealer of the grapes!
    Now do your worst on me!

And thus you think to spite your friend
    – turned loathsome? What, a
    toad?
So, all men shrink and shun me! Dear
    men, pursue your road!
Leave but my crevice in the stone, a
    reptile's fit abode!

Now say your worst, Canidia! 'He's
    loathsome, I allow:
There may or may not lurk a pearl
    beneath his puckered brow:
But see his eyes that follow mine – love
    lasts there anyhow.'

## Bad Dreams – 1

Last night I saw you in my sleep:
    And how your charm of face was
      changed!
I asked 'Some love, some faith you
    keep?'
    You answered 'Faith gone, love
      estranged.'
Whereat I woke – a twofold bliss:
    Waking was one, but next there came
This other: 'Though I felt, for this,
    My heart break, I loved on the same.'

## Bad Dreams – 2

You in the flesh and here –
    Your very self! Now, wait!
One word! May I hope or fear?
    Must I speak in love or hate?
Stay while I ruminate!

The fact and each circumstance
　　Dare you disown? Not you!
That vast dome, that huge dance,
　　And the gloom which overgrew
A – possibly festive crew!

For why should men dance at all –
　　Why women – a crowd of both –
Unless they are gay? Strange ball –
　　Hands and feet plighting troth,
Yet partners enforced and loth!

Of who danced there, no shape
　　Did I recognize: thwart, perverse,
Each grasped each, past escape
　　In a whirl or weary or worse:
Man's sneer met woman's curse,

While he and she toiled as if
　　Their guardian set galley-slaves
To supple chained limbs grown stiff:
　　Unmanacled trulls and knaves –
The lash for who misbehaves!

And a gloom was, all the while,
　　Deeper and deeper yet
O'ergrowing the rank and file
　　Of that army of haters – set
To mimic love's fever-fret.

By the wall-side close I crept,
　　Avoiding the livid maze,
And, safely so far, outstepped
　　On a chamber – a chapel, says
My memory or betrays –

Closet-like, kept aloof
　　From unseemly witnessing
What sport made floor and roof
　　Of the Devil's palace ring
While his Damned amused their king.

Ay, for a low lamp burned,
　　And a silence lay about
What I, in the midst, discerned
　　Though dimly till, past doubt,
'Twas a sort of throne stood out –

High seat with steps, at least:
　　And the topmost step was filled
By – whom? What vestured priest?
　　A stranger to me, – his guild,
His cult, unreconciled

To my knowledge how guild and cult
　　Are clothed in this world of ours:
I pondered, but no result
　　Came to – unless that Giaours
So worship the Lower Powers.

When suddenly who entered?
　　Who knelt – did you guess I saw?
Who – raising that face where centred
　　Allegiance to love and law
So lately – off-casting awe,

Down-treading reserve, away
　　Thrusting respect … but mine
Stands firm – firm still shall stay!
　　Ask Satan! for I decline
To tell – what I saw, in fine!

Yet here in the flesh you come –
　　Your same self, form and face, –
In the eyes, mirth still at home!
　　On the lips, that commonplace
Perfection of honest grace!

Yet your errand is – needs must be
　　To palliate – well, explain,
Expurgate in some degree
　　Your soul of its ugly stain.
Oh, you – the good in grain –

How was it your white took tinge?
　　'A mere dream' – never object!
Sleep leaves a door on hinge
　　Whence soul, ere our flesh suspect,
Is off and away: detect

Her vagaries when loose, who can!
　　Be she pranksome, be she prude,
Disguise with the day began:
　　With the night – ah, what ensued
From draughts of a drink hell-brewed?

Then She: 'What a queer wild dream!
  And perhaps the best fun is –
Myself had its fellow – I seem
  Scarce awake from yet. 'Twas this –
Shall I tell you? First, a kiss!

'For the fault was just your own, –
  'Tis myself expect apology:
You warned me to let alone
  (Since our studies were mere philology)
That ticklish (you said) Anthology.

'So, I dreamed that I passed *exam*
  Till a question posed me sore:
"Who translated this epigram
  By – an author we best ignore?"
And I answered "Hannah More"!'

### Bad dreams – 3

This was my dream: I saw a Forest
  Old as the-earth, no track nor trace
Of unmade man. Thou, Soul, explorest –
  Though in a trembling rapture – space
Immeasurable! Shrubs, turned trees,
Trees that touch heaven, support its
    frieze
Studded with sun and moon and star:
While – oh, the enormous growths that
    bar
Mine eye from penetrating past
  Their tangled twine where lurks –
    nay, lives
Royally lone, some brute-type cast
  I' the rough, time cancels, man
    forgives.

On, Soul! I saw a lucid City
  Of architectural device
Every way perfect. Pause for pity,
  Lightning! nor leave a cicatrice
On those bright marbles, dome and
    spire,
Structures palatial, – streets which mire
Dares not defile, paved all too fine
  For human footstep's smirch, not
    thine –

Proud solitary traverser,
  My Soul, of silent lengths of way –
With what ecstatic dread, aver,
  Lest life start sanctioned by thy stay!

Ah, but the last sight was the hideous!
  A City, yes, – a Forest, true, –
But each devouring each. Perfidious
  Snake-plants had strangled what I
    knew
Was a pavilion once: each oak
Held on his horns some spoil he broke
By surreptitiously beneath
Upthrusting: pavements, as with teeth,
Griped huge weed widening crack and
    split
  In squares and circles stone-work erst.
Oh, Nature – good! Oh, Art – no whit
  Less worthy! Both in one – accurst!

### Bad dreams – 4

It happened thus: my slab, though new,
  Was getting weather-stained, – beside,
Herbage, balm, peppermint o'ergrew
  Letter and letter: till you tried
Somewhat, the Name was scarce
    descried.

That strong stern man my lover came:
  – Was he my lover? Call him, pray,
My life's cold critic bent on blame
  Of all poor I could do or say
To make me worth his love one day –

One far day when, by diligent
  And dutiful amending faults,
Foibles, all weaknesses which went
  To challenge and excuse assaults
Of culture wronged by taste that halts –

Discrepancies should mar no plan
  Symmetric of the qualities
Claiming respect from – say – a man
  That's strong and stern. 'Once more
    he pries
Into me with those critic eyes!'

No question! so – 'Conclude, condemn
   Each failure my poor self avows!
Leave to its fate all you contemn!
   There's Solomon's selected spouse:
Earth needs must hold such maids –
   choose them!'

Why, he was weeping! Surely gone
   Sternness and strength: with eyes to
   ground
And voice a broken monotone –
   'Only be as you were! Abound
In foibles, faults, – laugh, robed and
   crowned

'As Folly's veriest queen, – care I
   One feather-fluff? Look pity, Love,
On prostrate me – your foot shall try
   This forehead's use – mount thence
   above,
And reach what Heaven you dignify!'

Now, what could bring such change
   about?
   The thought perplexed: till, following
His gaze upon the ground, – why, out
   Came all the secret! So, a thing
Thus simple has deposed my king!

For, spite of weeds that strove to spoil
   Plain reading on the lettered slab,
My name was clear enough – no soil
   Effaced the date when one chance
   stab
Of scorn … if only ghosts might blab!

## Inapprehensiveness

We two stood simply friend-like side
   by side,
Viewing a twilight country far and
   wide,
Till she at length broke silence. 'How it
   towers
Yonder, the ruin o'er this vale of ours!
The West's faint flare behind it so
   relieves

Its rugged outline – sight perhaps
   deceives,
Or I could almost fancy that I see
A branch wave plain – belike some
   wind-sown tree
Chance-rooted where a missing turret
   was.
What would I give for the perspective
   glass
At home, to make out if 'tis really so!
Has Ruskin noticed here at Asolo
That certain weed-growths on the
   ravaged wall
Seem' … something that I could not
   say at all,
My thought being rather – as absorbed
   she sent
Look onward after look from eyes distent
With longing to reach Heaven's gate
   left ajar –
'Oh, fancies that might be, oh, facts
   that are!
What of a wilding? By you stands, and
   may
So stand unnoticed till the Judgment
   Day,
One who, if once aware that your regard
Claimed what his heart holds, – woke,
   as from its sward
The flower, the dormant passion, so to
   speak –
Then what a rush of life would startling
   wreak
Revenge on your inapprehensive stare
While, from the ruin and the West's
   faint flare,
You let your eyes meet mine, touch
   what you term
Quietude – that's an universe in germ –
The dormant passion needing but a
   look
To burst into immense life!'
          'No, the book
Which noticed how the wall-growths
   wave' said she
'Was not by Ruskin.'
          I said 'Vernon Lee?'

## Which?

So, the three Court-ladies began
 Their trial of who judged best
In esteeming the love of a man:
Who preferred with most reason was
 thereby confessed
Boy-Cupid's exemplary catcher and
 cager;
An Abbé crossed legs to decide on the
 wager.

First the Duchesse: 'Mine for me –
 Who were it but God's for Him,
And the King's for – who but he?
Both faithful and loyal, one grace
 more shall brim
His cup with perfection: a lady's true
 lover,
He holds – save his God and his king –
 none above her.'

'I require' – outspoke the
 Marquise –
 'Pure thoughts, ay, but also fine
 deeds:
 Play the paladin must he, to please
My whim, and – to prove my
 knight's service exceeds
Your saint's and your loyalist's praying
 and kneeling –
Show wounds, each wide mouth to my
 mercy appealing.'

Then the Comtesse: 'My choice be
 a wretch,
 Mere losel in body and soul,
 Thrice accurst! What care I, so he
 stretch
Arms to me his sole saviour, love's
 ultimate goal,
Out of earth and men's noise – names
 of "infidel," "traitor,"
Cast up at him? Crown me, crown's
 adjudicator!'

And the Abbé uncrossed his legs,
 Took snuff, a reflective pinch,
 Broke silence: 'The question begs
Much pondering ere I pronounce.
 Shall I flinch?
The love which to one and one only
 has reference
Seems terribly like what perhaps gains
 God's preference.'

## The Cardinal and the Dog

Crescenzio, the Pope's Legate at the
 High Council, Trent,
– Year Fifteen hundred twenty-two,
 March Twenty-five – intent
On writing letters to the Pope till late
 into the night,
Rose, weary, to refresh himself, and
 saw a monstrous sight:
(I give mine Author's very words: he
 penned, I re-indite.)

A black Dog of vast bigness, eyes
 flaming, ears that hung
Down to the very ground almost, into
 the chamber sprung
And made directly for him, and laid
 himself right under
The table where Crescenzio wrote –
 who called in fear and wonder
His servants in the ante-room,
 commanded everyone
To look for and find out the beast: but,
 looking, they found none.

The Cardinal fell melancholy, then
 sick, soon after died:
And at Verona, as he lay on his death-
 bed, he cried
Aloud to drive away the Dog that leapt
 on his bed-side.
Heaven keep us Protestants from
 harm: the rest … no ill betide!

## The Pope and the Net

What, he on whom our voices
    unanimously ran,
Made Pope at our last Conclave? Full
    low his life began:
His father earned the daily bread as just
    a fisherman.

So much the more his boy minds
    book, gives proof of mother-wit,
Becomes first Deacon, and the Priest,
    then Bishop: see him sit
No less than Cardinal ere long, while
    no one cries 'Unfit!'

But someone smirks, some other
    smiles, jogs elbow and nods head:
Each winks at each: ' 'I-faith, a rise!
    Saint Peter's net, instead
Of sword and keys, is come in vogue!'
    You think he blushes red?

Not he, of humble holy heart!
    'Unworthy me!' he sighs:
'From fisher's drudge to Church's
    prince – it is indeed a rise:
So, here's my way to keep the fact for
    ever in my eyes!'

And straightway in his palace-hall,
    where commonly is set
Some coat-of-arms, some portraiture
    ancestral, lo, we met
His mean estate's remainder in his
    fisher-father's net!

Which step conciliates all and some,
    stops cavil in a trice:
'The humble holy heart that holds of
    newborn pride no spice!
He's just the saint to choose for Pope!'
    Each adds ' 'Tis my advice.'

So, Pope he was: and when we flocked
    – its sacred slipper on –
To kiss his foot, we lifted eyes, alack
    the thing was gone –

That guarantee of lowlihead, – eclipsed
    that star which shone!

Each eyed his fellow, one and all kept
    silence. I cried 'Pish!
I'll make me spokesman for the rest,
    express the common wish.
Why, Father, is the net removed?' 'Son,
    it hath caught the fish.'

## The Bean-Feast

He was the man – Pope Sixtus, that
    Fifth, that swineherd's son:
He knew the right thing, did it, and
    thanked God when 'twas done:
But of all he had to thank for, my fancy
    somehow leans
To thinking, what most moved him
    was a certain meal on beans.

For one day, as his wont was, in just
    enough disguise
As he went exploring wickedness, – to
    see with his own eyes
If law had due observance in the city's
    entrail dark
As well as where, i' the open, crime
    stood an obvious mark, –

He chanced, in a blind alley, on a
    tumble-down once house
Now hovel, vilest structure in Rome
    the ruinous:
And, as his tact impelled him, Sixtus
    adventured bold,
To learn how lowliest subjects bore
    hunger, toil, and cold.

There sat they at high-supper – man
    and wife, lad and lass,
Poor as you please but cleanly all and
    carefree: pain that was
– Forgotten, pain as sure to be let bide
    aloof its time, –
Mightily munched the brave ones –
    what mattered gloom or grime?

Said Sixtus 'Feast, my children! who
    works hard needs eat well.
I'm just a supervisor, would hear what
    you can tell.
Do any wrongs want righting? The
    Father tries his best,
But, since he's only mortal, sends such
    as I to test
The truth of all that's told him – how
    folk like you may fare:
Come! – only don't stop eating – when
    mouth has words to spare –

'You' – smiled he – 'play the
    spokesman, bell-wether of the
    flock!
Are times good, masters gentle? Your
    grievances unlock!
How of your work and wages? –
    pleasures, if such may be –
Pains, as such are for certain.' Thus
    smiling questioned he.

But somehow, spite of smiling, awe
    stole upon the group –
An inexpressible surmise: why should
    a priest thus stoop –
Pry into what concerned folk? Each
    visage fell. Aware,
Cries Sixtus interposing: 'Nay,
    children, have no care!

'Fear nothing! Who employs me
    requires the plain truth. Pelf
Beguiles who should inform me: so, I
    inform myself.
See!' And he threw his hood back, let
    the close vesture ope,
Showed face, and where on tippet the
    cross lay: 'twas the Pope.

Imagine the joyful wonder! 'How shall
    the like of us –
Poor souls – requite such blessing of
    our rude bean-feast?' 'Thus –
Thus amply!' laughed Pope Sixtus. 'I
    early rise, sleep late:

Who works may eat: they tempt me,
    your beans there: spare a plate!'

Down sat he on the door-step: 'twas
    they this time said grace:
He ate up the last mouthful, wiped
    lips, and then, with face
Turned heavenward, broke forth
    thankful: 'Not now, that earth
    obeys
Thy word in mine, that through me the
    peoples know Thy ways –
But that Thy care extendeth to
    Nature's homely wants,
And, while man's mind is
    strengthened, Thy goodness
    nowise scants
Man's body of its comfort, – that I
    whom kings and queens
Crouch to, pick crumbs from off my
    table, relish beans!
The thunders I but seem to launch,
    there plain Thy hand all see:
That I have appetite, digest, and thrive
    – that boon's for me.'

## Muckle-Mouth Meg

Frowned the Laird on the Lord: 'So,
    red-handed I catch thee?
    Death-doomed by our Law of the
    Border!
We've a gallows outside and a chiel to
    dispatch thee:
    Who trespass – hangs: all's in
    order.'

He met frown with smile, did the
    young English gallant:
    Then the Laird's dame: 'Nay,
    Husband, I beg!
He's comely: be merciful! Grace for the
    callant
    – If he marries our Muckle-mouth
    Meg!'

'No mile-wide-mouthed monster of
          yours do I marry:
     Grant rather the gallows!' laughed he.
'Foul fare kith and kin of you – why do
          you tarry?'
          'To tame your fierce temper!' quoth
          she.

'Shove him quick in the Hole, shut him
          fast for a week:
     Cold, darkness and hunger work
          wonders:
Who lion-like roars now, mouse-fashion
          will squeak,
     And "it rains" soon succeed to "it
          thunders." '

A week did he bide in the cold and the
          dark
     – Not hunger: for duly at morning
In flitted a lass, and a voice like a lark
     Chirped 'Muckle-mouth Meg still
          ye're scorning?

'Go hang, but here's parritch to
          hearten ye first!'
     'Did Meg's muckle-mouth boast
          within some
Such music as yours, mine should
          match it or burst:
     No frog-jaws! So tell folk, my
          Winsome!'

Soon week came to end, and, from
          Hole' door set wide,
     Out he marched, and there waited
          th lassie:
'Yon gallows, or Muckle-mouth Meg fo
          a bride!
     Consider! Sky's blue and turf's grassy:

'Life's sweet: shall I say ye wed
          Muckle-mouth Meg?'
     'Not I' quoth the stout heart: 'too
          eerie
The mouth that can swallow a bubbly-
          jock's egg:
     Shall I let it munch mine? Never,
          Dearie!'

'Not Muckle-mouth Meg? Wow, the
          obstinate man!
     Perhaps he would rather wed me!'
'Ay, would he – with just for a dowry
          your can!'
     'I'm Muckle-mouth Meg' chirruped
          she.

'Then so – so – so – so – 'as he kissed
          her apace –
     'Will I widen thee out till thou tyrnest
From Margaret Minnikin-mou', by God's
          grace,
     To Muckle-mouth Meg in good
          earnest!'

## Arcades Ambo

A. You blame me that I ran away?
          Why, Sir, the enemy advanced:
     Balls flew about, and – who can say
          But one, if I stood firm, had glanced
     In my direction? Cowardice?
     I only know we don't live twice,
     Therefore – shun death, is my advice.

B. Shun death at all risks? Well, at some!
          True, I myself, Sir, though I scold
     The cowardly, by no means come
          Under reproof as overbold
     – I, who would have no end of brutes
     Cut up alive to guess what suits
     My case and saves my toe from shoots.

## The Lady and the Painter

*She*. Yet womanhood you reverence,
So you profess!
*He*.                    With heart and soul.
*She*. Of which fact this is evidence!
    To help Art-study, – for some dole
Of certain wretched shillings, – you
Induce a woman – virgin too –
To strip and stand stark-naked?
*He*.                               True.
*She*. Nor feel you so degrade her?
*He*.                               What
– (Excuse the interruption) – clings
Half-savage-like around your hat?
*She*. Ah, do they please you? Wild-bird-
    wings
Next season, – Paris-prints assert, –
We must go feathered to the skirt:
My modiste keeps on the alert.

Owls, hawks, jays – swallows most
    approve …
*He*.                    Dare I speak plainly?
*She*.                    Oh, I trust!
*He*. Then, Lady Blanche, it less would
    move
    In heart and soul of me disgust
Did you strip off those spoils you wear,
And stand – for thanks, not shillings –
    bare,
To help Art like my Model there.

*She* well knew what absolved her –
    praise
    In me for God's surpassing good,
Who granted to my reverent gaze
    A type of purest womanhood.
*You* – clothed with murder of His best
Of harmless beings – stand the test!
What is it *you* know?
*She*.                    That you jest!

## Ponte dell' Angelo, Venice

Stop rowing! This one of our bye-canals
O'er a certain bridge you have to cross
That's named 'Of the Angel': listen
    why!
The name 'Of the Devil' too much
    appals
Venetian acquaintance, so – his the
    loss,
While the gain goes … look on high!

An angel visibly guards yon house:
Above each scutcheon – a pair – stands
    he,
Enfolds them with droop of either wing:
The family's fortune were perilous
Did he thence depart – you will soon
    agree,
If I hitch into verse the thing.

For, once on a time, this house
    belonged
To a lawyer of note, with law and to
    spare,
But also with overmuch lust of gain:
In the matter of law you were nowise
    wronged,
But alas for the lucre! He picked you
    bare
To the bone. Did folk complain?

'I exact' growled he 'work's rightful
    due:
'Tis folk seek me, not I seek them.
Advice at its price! They succeed or fail,
Get law in each case – and a lesson
    too:
Keep clear of the Courts – is advice *ad
    rem*:
They'll remember, I'll be bail!'

So, he pocketed fee without a qualm.
What reason for squeamishness?
    Labour done,
To play he betook him with lightened
    heart,

Ate, drank and made merry with song
    or psalm,
Since the yoke of the Church is an easy
    one –
Fits neck nor causes smart.

Brief: never was such an extortionate
Rascal – the word has escaped my teeth
And yet – (all's down in a book no ass
Indited, believe me!) – this reprobate
Was punctual at prayer-time: gold
    lurked beneath
Alloy of the rankest brass.

For, play the extortioner as he might,
Fleece folk each day and all day long,
There was this redeeming circumstance:
He never lay down to sleep at night
But he put up a prayer first, brief yet
    strong,
'Our Lady avert mischance!'

Now it happened at close of a fructuous
    week,
'I must ask' quoth he 'some Saint to
    dine:
I want that widow well out of my ears
With her ailing and wailing. Who bade
    her seek
Redress at my hands? "She was wronged!"
    Folk whine
If to Law wrong right appears.

'Matteo da Bascio – he's my man!
No less than Chief of the Capucins:
His presence will surely sufifumigate
My house – fools think lies under a
    ban
If somebody loses what somebody wins.
Hark, there he knocks at the grate!

'Come in, thou blessed of Mother
    Church!
I go and prepare – to bid, that is,
My trusty and diligent servitor
Get all things in readiness. Vain the
    search

Through Venice for one to compare
    with this
My model of ministrants: for –

'For – once again, nay, three times
    over,
My helpmate's an ape! so intelligent,
I train him to drudge at household
    work:
He toils and he moils, I live in clover:
Oh, you shall see! There's a goodly
    scent –
From his cooking, or I'm a Turk!

'Scarce need to descend and supervise:
I'll do it, however: wait here awhile!'
So, down to the kitchen gaily scuttles
Our host, nor notes the alarmed
    surmise
Of the holy man. 'O depth of guile!
He blindly guzzles and guttles,

'While – who is it dresses the food and
    pours
The liquor? Some fiend – I make no
    doubt –
In likeness of – which of the loathly
    brutes?
An ape! Where hides he? No bull that
    gores,
No bear that hugs – 'tis the mock and
    flout
Of an ape, fiend's face that suits.

'So – out with thee, creature, wherever
    thou hidest!
I charge thee, by virtue of … right do I
    judge!
There skulks he perdue, crouching
    under the bed.
Well done! What, forsooth, in beast's
    shape thou confidest?
I know and would name thee but that I
    begrudge
Breath spent on such carrion. Instead –

'I adjure thee by – ' 'Stay!' laughed the
portent that rose
From floor up to ceiling: 'No need to
adjure!
See Satan in person, late ape by command
Of Him thou adjurest in vain. A saint's
nose
Scents brimstone though incense be
burned for a lure.
Yet, hence! for I'm safe, understand!

' 'Tis my charge to convey to fit
punishment's place
This lawyer, my liegeman, for cruelty
wrought
On his clients, the widow and orphan,
poor souls
He has plagued by exactions which
proved law's disgrace,
Made equity void and to nothingness
brought
God's pity. Fiends, on with fresh coals!'

'Stay!' nowise confounded, withstands
Hell its match:
'How comes it, were truth in this story
of thine,
God's punishment suffered a minute's
delay?
Weeks, months have elapsed since
thou squattedst at watch
For a spring on thy victim: what
caused thee decline
Advantage till challenged to-day?'

'That challenge I meet with contempt,'
quoth the fiend.
'Thus much I acknowledge: the man's
armed in mail:
I wait till a joint's loose, then quick ply
my claws.
Thy friend's one good custom – he
knows not – has screened
His flesh hitherto from what else would
assail:
At "Save me, Madonna!" I pause.

'That prayer did the losel but once
pretermit,
My pounce were upon him. I keep me
attent:
He's in safety but till he's caught
napping. Enough!'
'Ay, enough!'smiles the saint – 'for the
biter is bit,
The spy caught in somnolence. Vanish!
I'm sent
To smooth up what fiends do in rough.'

'I vanish? Through wall or through roof?'
the riposte
Grinned gaily. 'My orders were – "Leave
not unharmed
The abode of this lawyer! Do damage
to prove
'Twas for something thou quittedst the
land of the lost –
To add to their number this unit!"
Though charmed
From descent there, on earth that's above

'I may haply amerce him.' 'So do, and
begone,
I command thee! For, look! Though
there's doorway behind
And window before thee, go straight
through the wall,
Leave a breach in the brickwork, a gap
in the stone
For who passes to stare at!' 'spare
speech! I'm resigned:
Here goes!' roared the goblin, as all –

Wide bat-wings, spread arms and legs,
tail out a-stream,
Crash obstacles went, right and left, as
he soared
Or else sank, was clean gone through
the hole anyhow.
The Saint returned thanks: then a
satisfied gleam
On the bald polished pate showed that
triumph was scored.
'To dinner with appetite now!'

Down he trips. 'In good time!'smirks
    the host. 'Didst thou scent
Rich savour of roast meat? Where hides
    he, my ape?
Look alive, be alert! He's away to wash
    plates.
Sit down, Saint! What's here? Dost
    examine a rent
In the napkin thou twistest and twirlest?
    Agape …

Ha, blood is it drips nor abates
'From thy wringing a cloth, late was
    lavendered fair?
What means such a marvel?' 'Just this
    does it mean:
I convince and convict thee of sin!'
    answers straight
The Saint, wringing on, wringing ever –
    O rare! –
Blood – blood from a napery snow not
    more clean.
'A miracle shows thee thy state!

'See – blood thy extortions have wrung
    from the flesh
Of thy clients who, sheep-like, arrived
    to be shorn
And left thee – or fleeced to the quick
    or so flayed
That, behold, their blood gurgles and
    grumbles afresh
To accuse thee! Ay, down on thy knees,
    get up sworn
To restore! Restitution once made,

'Sin no more! Dost thou promise?
    Absolved, then, arise!
Upstairs follow me! Art amazed at yon
    breach?
Who battered and shattered and
    scattered, escape
From thy purlieus obtaining? That
    Father of Lies
Thou wast wont to extol for his feats,
    all and each
The Devil's disguised as thine ape!'

Be sure that our lawyer was torn by
    remorse,
Shed tears in a flood, vowed and swore
    so to alter
His ways that how else could our Saint
    but declare
He was cleansed of past sin? 'For sin
    future – fare worse
Thou undoubtedly wilt,' warned the
    Saint, 'shouldst thou falter
One whit!' 'Oh, for that have no care!

'I am firm in my purposed amendment
    But, prithee,
Must ever affront and affright me yon
    gap?
Who made it for exit may find it of use
For entrance as easy. If, down in his
    smithy
He forges me fetters – when heated,
    mayhap,
He'll up with an armful! Broke loose –

'How bar him out henceforth?'
    'Judiciously urged!'
Was the good man's reply. 'How to
    baulk him is plain.
There's nothing the Devil objects to so
    much,
So speedily flies from, as one of those
    purged
Of his presence, the angels who erst
    formed his train –
His, their emperor. Choose one of such!

'Get fashioned his likeness and set him
    on high
At back of the breach thus adroitly
    filled up:
Display him as guard of two
    scutcheons, thy arms:
I warrant no devil attempts to get by
And disturb thee so guarded. Eat,
    drink, dine and sup
In thy rectitude, safe from alarms!'

So said and so done. See, the angel has place
Where the Devil had passage! All's down in a book.
Gainsay me? Consult it! Still faithless? Trust *me*?
Trust Father Boverio who gave me the case
In his Annals – gets of it, by hook or by
. crook,
Two confirmative witnesses: three

Are surely enough to establish an act:
And thereby we learn – would we ascertain truth –
To trust wise tradition which took, at the time,
Note that served till slow history ventured on fact,
Though folk have their fling at tradition forsooth!
Row, boys, fore and aft, rhyme and chime!

## Beatrice Signorini

This strange thing happened to a painter once:
Viterbo boasts the man among her sons
Of note, I seem to think: his ready tool
Picked up its precepts in Cortona's school –
That's Pietro Berretini, whom they call
Cortona, these Italians: greatish-small,
Our painter was his pupil, by repute
His match if not his master absolute,
Though whether he spoiled fresco more or less,
And what's its fortune, scarce repays your guess.
Still, for one circumstance, I save his name
– Francesco Romanelli: do the same!
He went to Rome and painted: there he knew

A wonder of a woman painting too –
For she, at least, was no Cortona's drudge:
Witness that ardent fancy-shape – I judge
A semblance of her soul – she called 'Desire'
With starry front for guide, where sits the fire
She left to brighten Buonarroti's house.
If you see Florence, pay that piece your vows,
Though blockhead Baldinucci's mind, imbued
With monkish morals, bade folk 'Drape the nude
And stop the scandal!' quoth the record prim
I borrow this of: hang his book and him!
At Rome, then, where these fated ones met first,
The blossom of his life had hardly burst
While hers was blooming at full beauty's stand:
No less Francesco – when half-ripe he scanned
Consummate Artemisia – grew one want
To have her his and make her ministrant
With every gift of body and of soul
To him. In vain. Her sphery self was whole –
Might only touch his orb at Art's sole point.
Suppose he could persuade her to enjoint
Her life – past, present, future – all in his
At Art's sole point by some explosive kiss
Of love through lips, would love's success defeat
Artistry's haunting curse – the Incomplete?
Artists no doubt they both were, – what beside
Was she? who, long had felt heart, soul spread wide

Her life out, knowing much and loving
    well,
On either side Art's narrow space
    where fell
Reflection from his own speck: but the
    germ
Of individual genius – what we term
The very self, the God-gift whence had
    grown
Heart's life and soul's life, – how make
    that his own?
Vainly his Art, reflected, smiled in small
On Art's one facet of her ampler ball;
The rest, touch-free, took in, gave back
    heaven, earth,
All where he was not. Hope, well-nigh
    ere birth
Came to Desire, died off all-unfulfilled.
'What though in Art I stand the abler-
    skilled,'
(So he conceited: mediocrity
Turns on itself the self-transforming eye)
'If only Art were suing, mine would
    plead
To purpose: man – by nature J exceed
Woman the bounded: but how much
    beside
She boasts, would sue in turn and be
    denied!
Love her? My own wife loves me in a
    sort
That suits us both: she takes the world's
    report
Of what my work is worth, and, for i the
    rest,
Concedes that, while his consort keeps
    her nest,
The eagle soars a licensed vagrant, lives
A wide free life which she at least
    forgives –
Good Beatricé Signorini! Well
And wisely did I choose her. But the
    spell
To subjugate this Artemisia – where?
She passionless? – she resolute to care
Nowise beyond the plain sufficiency
Of fact that she is she and I am I

– Acknowledged arbitrator for us both
In her life as in mine which she were
    loth
Even to learn the laws of? No, and no
Twenty times over! Ay, it must be so:
I for myself, alas!'
                    Whereon, instead
Of the checked lover's-utterance –
    why, he said
– Leaning above her easel: 'Flesh is
    red'
(Or some such just remark) – 'by no
    means white
As Guido's practice teaches: you are
    right.'
Then came the better impulse: 'What if
    pride
Were wisely trampled on, whate'er
    betide?
If I grow hers, not mine – join lives,
    confuse
Bodies and spirits, gain not her but
    lose
Myself to Artemisia? That were love!
Of two souls – one must bend, one
    rule above:
If I crouch under proudly, lord turned
    slave,
Were it not worthier both than if she
    gave
Herself – in treason to herself – to me?'

And, all the while, he felt it could not
    be.
Such love were true love: love that way
    who can!
Someone that's born half woman not
    whole man:
For man, prescribed man better or man
    worse,
Why, whether microcosm or universe,
What law prevails alike through great
    and small,
The world and man – world's
    miniature we call?
Male is the master. 'That way' – smiled
    and sighed

Our true male estimator – 'puts her
pride
My wife in making me the outlet whence
She learns all Heaven allows: 'tis my
pretence
To paint: her lord should do what else
but paint?
Do I break brushes, cloister me turned
saint?
Then, best of all suits sanctity her spouse
Who acts for Heaven, allows and
disallows
At pleasure, past appeal, the right, the
wrong
In all things. That's my wife's way. But
this strong
Confident Artemisia – an adept
In Art does she conceit herself? "Except
In just this instance," tell her, "no one
draws
More rigidly observant of the laws
Of right design: yet here, – permit me
hint, –
If the acromion had a deeper dint,
That shoulder were perfection." What
surprise
– Nay scorn, shoots black fire from
those startled eyes!
She to the lessoned in design forsooth!
I'm doomed and done for, since I
spoke the truth.
Make my own work the subject of
dispute –
Fails it of just perfection absolute
Somewhere? Those motors, flexors, –
don't I know
Ser Santi, styled "Tirititototo
The pecial-prig," might blame them?
Yet my wife –
Were he and his nicknamer brought to
life,
Tito and Titian, to pronounce again –
Ask her who knows more – I or the
great Twain
Our colourist and draughtsman!
                              'I help her,

Not she helps me; and neither shall
demur
Because my portion is – ' he chose to
think –
'Quite other than a woman's: I may
drink
At many waters, must repose by none –
Rather arise and fare forth, having done
Duty to one new excellence the more,
Abler thereby, though impotent before
So much was gained of knowledge.
            Best depart
From this last lady I have learned by
heart!'

Thus he concluded of himself – resigned
To play the man and master: 'Man
boasts mind:
Woman, man's sport calls mistress, to
the same
Does body's suit and service. Would
she claim
– My placid Beatricé-wife – pretence
Even to blame her lord if, going hence,
He wistfully regards one whom – did
fate
Concede – he might accept queen,
abdicate
Kingship because of? – one of no meek
sort
But masterful as he: man's match in
short?
Oh, there's no secret I were best conceal!
Bicé shall know; and should a stray
tear steal
From out the blue eye, stain the rose
cheek – bah!
A smile, a word's gay reassurance – ah,
With kissing interspersed, – shall make
amends,
Turn pain to pleasure.'
                    'What, in truth so ends
Abruptly, do you say, our intercourse?'
Next day, asked Artemisia: 'I'll divorce
Husband and wife no longer. Go your
ways,

Leave Rome! Viterbo owns no equal,
    says
The bye-word, for fair women: you, no
    doubt,
May boast a paragon all specks without,
Using the painter's privilege to choose
Among what's rarest. Will your wife
    refuse
Acceptance from – no rival – of a gift?
You paint the human figure I make shift
Humbly to reproduce: but, in my hours
Of idlesse, what I fain would paint is –
    flowers.
Look now!'
      She twitched aside a veiling cloth.
'Here is my keepsake – frame and picture
    both:
For see, the frame is all of flowers
    festooned
About an empty space, – left thus, to
    wound
No natural susceptibility:
How can I guess? 'Tis you must fill, ∼
    not I,
The central space with – her whom
    you like best!
That is your business, mine has been
    the rest.
But judge!'
        How judge them? Each of us,
    in flowers,
Chooses his love, allies it with past
    hours,
Old meetings, vanished forms and
    faces: no –
Here let each favourite unmolested
    blow
For one heart's homage, no tongue's
    banal praise,
Whether the rose appealingly bade 'Gaze
Your fill on me, sultana who dethrone
The gaudy tulip!' or 'twas 'Me alone
Rather do homage to, who lily am,
No unabashed rose!' 'Do I vainly cram
My cup with sweets, your jonquil?'
    'Why forget
Vernal endearments with the violet?'

So they contested yet concerted, all
As one, to circle round about, enthrall
Yet, self-forgetting, push to prominence
The midmost wonder, gained no
    matter whence.

There's a tale extant, in a book I conned
Long years ago, which treats of things
    beyond
The common, antique times and
    countries queer
And customs strange to match. ' 'Tis
    said, last year,'
(Recounts my author,) 'that the King
    had mind
To view his kingdom – guessed at from
    behind
A palace-window hitherto. Announced
No sooner was such purpose than
    'twas pounced
Upon by all the ladies of the land –
Loyal but light of life: they formed a
    band
Of loveliest ones but lithest also, since
Proudly they all combined to bear their
    prince.
Backs joined to breasts, – arms, legs, –
    nay, ankles, wrists,
Hands, feet, I know not by what turns
    and twists,
So interwoven lay that you believed
'Twas one sole beast of burden which
    received
The monarch on its back, of breadth
    not scant
Since fifty girls made one white elephant.'
So with the fifty flowers which shapes
    and hues
Blent, as I tell, and made one fast yet
    loose
Mixture of beauties, composite, distinct
No less in each combining flower that
    linked
With flower to form a fit environment
For – whom might be the painter's
    heart's intent
Thus, in the midst enhaloed, to enshrine?

'This glory-guarded middle space – is
    mine?
For me to fill?'
        'For you, my Friend! We part,
Never perchance to meet again. Your
    Art –
What if I mean it – so to speak – shall
    wed
My own, be witness of the life we led
When sometimes it has seemed our
    souls near found
Each one the other as its mate –
    unbound
Had yours been haply from the better
    choice
– Beautiful Bicé: 'tis the common voice,
The crowning verdict. Make whom you
    like best
Queen of the central space, and
    manifest
Your predilection for what flower
    beyond
All flowers find favour with you. I am
    fond
Of – say – yon rose's rich predominance,
While you – what wonder? – more
    affect the glance
The gentler violet from its leafy screen
Ventures: so – choose your flower and
    paint your queen!'
Oh but the man was ready, head as
    hand,
Instructed and adroit. 'Just as you
    stand,
Stay and be made – would Nature but
    relent –
By Art immortal!'
        Every implement
In tempting reach – a palette primed,
    each squeeze
Of oil-paint in its proper patch – with
    these,
Brushes, a veritable sheaf to grasp!
He worked as he had never dared.
        'Unclasp
My Art from yours who can!' – he cried
    at length,

As down he threw the pencil – 'Grace
    from Strength
Dissociate, from your flowery fringe
    detach
My face of whom it frames, – the feat
    will match
With that of Time should Time from
    me extract
Your memòry, Artemisia!' And in fact, –
What with the pricking impulse,
    sudden glow
Of soul – head, hand co-operated so
That face was worthy of its frame, 'tis
    said –
Perfect, suppose!
        They parted. Soon instead
Of Rome was home, – of Artemisia –
    well,
The placid-perfect wife. And it befell
That after the first incontestably
Blessedest of all blisses ( – wherefore
    try
Your patience with embracings and the
    rest
Due from Calypso's all-unwilling guest
To his Penelope?) – there somehow
    came
The coolness which as duly follows
    flame.
So, one day, 'What if we inspect the
    gifts
My Art has gained us?'
        Now the wife uplifts
A casket-lid, now tries a medal's chain
Round her own lithe neck, fits a ring in
    vain
– Too loose on the fine finger, – vows
    and swears
The jewel with two pendent pearls like
    pears
Betters a lady's bosom – witness else!
And so forth, while Ulysses smiles.
        'Such spells
Subdue such natures – sex must
    worship toys
– Trinkets and trash: yet, ah, quite
    other joys

Must stir from sleep the passionate
    abyss
Of – such an one as her I know – not
    this
My gentle consort with the milk for
    blood!
Why, did it chance that in a careless
    mood
(In those old days, gone – never to
    return –
When we talked – she to teach and I to
    learn)
I dropped a word, a hint which might
    imply
Consorts exist – how quick flashed fire
    from eye,
Brow blackened, lip was pinched by
    furious lip!
I needed no reminder of my slip:
One warning taught me wisdom.
    Whereas here …
Aha, a sportive fancy! Eh, what fear
Of harm to follow? Just a whim
    indulged!

'My Beatricé, there's an undivulged
Surprise in store for you: the moment's
    fit
For letting loose a secret: out with it!
Tributes to worth, you rightly estimate
These gifts of Prince and Bishop,
    Church and State:
Yet, may I tell you? Tastes so disagree!
There's one gift, preciousest of all to
    me,
I doubt if you would value as well
    worth
The obvious sparkling gauds that men
    unearth
For toy-cult mainly of you womankind:
Such make you marvel, I concede:
    while blind
The sex proves to the greater marvel
    here
I veil to baulk its envy. Be sincere!
Say, should you search creation far and
    wide,

Was ever face like this?'
                    He drew aside
The veil, displayed the flower-framed
    portrait kept
For private delectation.
                    No adept
In florist's lore more accurately named
And praised or, as appropriately,
    blamed
Specimen after specimen of skill,
Than Bicé. 'Rightly placed the daffodil –
Scarcely so right the blue germander.
    Grey
Good mouse-ear! Hardly your auricula
Is powdered white enough. It seems to
    me
Scarlet not crimson, that anemone:
But there's amends in the pink saxifrage.
O darling dear ones, let me disengage
You innocents from what your
    harmlessness
Clasps lovingly! Out thou from their
    caress,
Serpent!'
    Whereat forth-flashing from her coils
On coils of hair, the *spilla* in its toils
Of yellow wealth, the dagger-plaything
    kept
To pin its plaits together, life-like leapt
And – woe to all inside the coronal!
Stab followed stab, – cut, slash, she
    ruined all
The masterpiece. Alack for eyes and
    mouth
And dimples and endearment – North
    and South,
East, West, the tatters in a fury flew:
There yawned the circlet. What
    remained to do?
She flung the weapon, and, with folded
    arms
And mien defiant of such low alarms
As death and doom beyond death, Bicé
    stood
Passively statuesque, in quietude
Awaiting judgment.
                 And out judgment burst

With frank unloading of love's laughter,
          first
Freed from its unsuspected source. Some
          throe
Must needs unlock love's prison-bars,
          let flow
The joyance.
                    'Then you ever were, still are,
And henceforth shall be – no occulted
          star
But my resplendent Bicé, sun-revealed,
Full-rondure! Woman-glory unconcealed,
So front me, find and claim and take
          your own –
My soul and body yours and yours
          alone,
As you are mine, mine wholly! Heart's
          love, take –
Use your possession – stab or stay at
          will
Here – hating, saving – woman with
          the skill
To make man beast or god!'
                              And so it proved:
For, as beseemed new godship, thus he
          loved,
Past power to change, until his dying-
          day, –
Good fellow! And I fain would hope –
          some say
Indeed for certain – that our painter's
          toils
At fresco-splashing, finer stroke in oils,
Were not so mediocre after all;
Perhaps the work appears unduly small
From having loomed too large in old
          esteem,
Patronized by late Papacy. I seem
Myself to have cast eyes on certain work
In sundry galleries, no judge needs
          shirk
From moderately praising. He designed
Correctly, nor in colour lagged behind
His age: but both in Florence and in
          Rome
The elder race so make themselves at
          home

That scarce we give a glance to
          ceilingfuls
Of such like as Francesco. Still, one
          culls
From out the heaped laudations of the
          time
The pretty incident I put in rhyme.


## Flute-Music, with an Accompaniment

*He.*
Ah, the bird-like fluting
     Through the ash-tops yonder –
Bullfinch-bubblings, soft sounds
          suiting
     What sweet thoughts, I wonder?
Fine-pearled notes that surely
     Gather, dewdrop-fashion,
Deep-down in some heart which purely
     Secrets globuled passion –
Passion insuppressive –
     Such is piped, for certain;
Love, no doubt, nay, love excessive
     'Tis, your ash-tops curtain.

Would your ash-tops open
     We might spy the player –
Seek and find some sense which no pen
     Yet from singer, sayer,
Ever has extracted:
     Never, to my knowledge,
Yet has pedantry enacted
     That, in Cupid's College,
Just this, variation
     Of the old old yearning
Should by plain speech have salvation,
     Yield new men new learning.

'Love!' but what love, nicely
     New from old disparted,
Would the player teach precisely?
     First of all, he started
In my brain Assurance –
     Trust – entire Contentment –

Passion proved by much endurance;
    Then came – not resentment,
No, but simply Sorrow:
    What was seen had vanished:
Yesterday so blue! To-morrow
    Blank, all sunshine banished.

Hark! 'Tis Hope resurges,
    Struggling through obstruction –
Forces a poor smile which verges
    On Joy's introduction.
Now, perhaps, mere Musing:
    'Holds earth such a wonder?
Fairy-mortal, soul-sense-fusing
    Past thought's power to sunder!'
What? calm Acquiescence?
    'Daisied turf gives room to
Trefoil, plucked once in her presence –
    Growing by her tomb too!'

*She.*
All's your fancy-spinning!
    Here's the fact: a neighbour
Never-ending, still beginning,
    Recreates his labour:
Deep o'er desk he drudges,
    Adds, divides, subtracts and
Multiplies, until he judges
    Noonday-hour's exact sand
Shows the hourglass emptied:
    Then comes lawful leisure,
Minutes rare from toil exempted,
    Fit to spend in pleasure.
Out then with – what treatise?
    *Youth's Complete Instructor*
*How to play the Flute. Quid petis?*
    Follow Youth's conductor
On and on, through *Easy,*
    Up to *Harder, Hardest*
*Flute-piece,* till thou, flautist wheezy
    Possibly discardest
Tootlings hoarse and husky,
    Mayst expend with courage
Breath – on tunes once bright now
    dusky –
    Meant to cool thy porridge.

That's an air of Tulou's
    He maltreats persistent,
Till as lief I'd hear some Zulu's
    Bone-piped bag, breath-distent,
Madden native dances,
    I'm the man's familiar:
Unexpectedness enhances
    What your ear's auxiliar
– Fancy – finds suggestive.
    Listen! *That's legato*
Rightly played, his fingers restive
    Touch as if *staccato.*

*He.*
Ah, you trick-betrayer!
    Telling tales, unwise one?
So the secret of the player
    Was – he could surprise one
Well-nigh into trusting
    Here was a musician
Skilled consummately, yet lusting
    Through no vile ambition
After making captive
    All the world, – rewarded
Amply by one stranger's rapture,
    Common praise discarded.

So, without assistance
    Such as music rightly
Needs and claims, – defying distance,
    Overleaping lightly
Obstacles which hinder, –
    He, for my approval,
All the same and all the kinder
    Made mine what might move all
Earth to kneel adoring:
    Took – while he piped Gounod's
Bit of passionate imploring –
    Me for Juliet: who knows?

No! as you explain things,
    All's mere repetition,
Practise-pother: of all vain things
    Why waste pooh or pish on
Toilsome effort – never
    Ending, still beginning –

After what should pay endeavour
  – Right-performance? winning
Weariness from you who,
  Ready to admire some
Owl's fresh hooting – Tu-whit, tu-who –
  Find stale thrush-songs tiresome.

*She.*
Songs, Spring thought perfection,
  Summer criticizes:
What in May escaped detection,
  August, past surprises,
Notes, and names each blunder.
  You, the just-initiate,
Praise to heart's content (what wonder?)
  Tootings I hear vitiate
Romeo's serenading –
  I who, times full twenty,
Turned, to ice – no ash-tops aiding –
  At his *caldamente.*

So, 'twas distance altered
  Sharps to flats? The missing
Bar when syncopation faltered
  (You thought – paused for kissing!)
Ash-tops too felonious
  Intercepted? Rather
Say – they well-nigh made euphonious
  Discord, helped to gather
Phrase, by phrase, turn patches
  Into simulated
Unity which botching matches, –
  Scraps redintegrated.

*He.*
Sweet, are you suggestive
  Of an old suspicion
Which has always found me restive
  To its admonition
When it ventured whisper
  'Fool, the strifes and struggles
Of your trembler – blusher – lisper
  Were so many juggles,
Tricks tried – oh, so often! –
  Which once more do duty,
Find again a heart to soften,
  Soul to snare with beauty.'

Birth-blush of the briar-rose,
  Mist-bloom of the hedge-sloe,
Someone gains the prize: admire rose
  Would he, when noon's wedge –
    slow –
Sure, has pushed, expanded
  Rathe pink to raw redness?
Would he covet sloe when sanded
  By road-dust to deadness?
So – restore their value!
  Ply a water-sprinkle!
Then guess sloe is fingered, shall you?
  Find in a rose a wrinkle?

Here what played Aquarius?
  Distance – ash-tops aiding,
Reconciled scraps else contrarious,
  Brightened stuff fast fading.
Distance – call your shyness:
  Was the fair one peevish?
Coyness softened out of slyness.
  Was she cunning, thievish,
All-but-proved impostor?
  Bear but one day's exile,
Ugly traits were wholly lost or
  Screened by fancies flexile –

Ash-tops these, you take me?
  Fancies' interference
Changed ...
    But since I sleep, don't wake me!
  What if all's appearance?
Is not outside seeming
  Real as substance inside?
Both are facts, so leave me dreaming:
  If who loses wins I'd
Ever lose, – conjecture,
  From one phrase trilled deftly,
All the piece. So, end your lecture,
  Let who lied be left fie!

## 'Imperante Augusto
## Natus est – '

What it was struck the terror into me?
This, Publius: closer! while we wait our
     turn
I'll tell you. Water's warm (they ring
     inside)
At the eighth hour, till when no use to
     bathe.

Here in the vestibule where now we sit,
One scarce stood yesterday, the throng
     was such
Of loyal gapers, folk all eye and ear
While Lucius Varius Rufus* in their
     midst
Read out that long-planned late-
     completed piece,
His Panegyric on the Emperor.
'Nobody like him' little Flaccus† laughed
'At leading forth an Epos with due
     pomp!
Only, when godlike Cæsar swells the
     theme,
How should mere mortals hope to
     praise aright?
Tell me, thou offshoot of Etruscan
     kings!'
Whereat Mæcenas smiling sighed
     assent.

I paid my quadrans,‡ left the Thermae's
     roar
Of rapture as the poet asked 'What
     place
Among the godships Jove, for Cæsar's
     sake,
Would bid its actual occupant vacate
In favour of the new divinity?'

And got the expected answer 'Yield
     thine own!' –

* Poet and friend of Virgil
† Horace
‡ Roman coin of small value

Jove thus dethroned, I somehow
     wanted air,
And found myself a-pacing street and
     street,
Letting the sunset, rosy over Rome,
Clear my head dizzy with the hubbub
     – say
As if thought's dance therein had kicked
     up dust
By trampling on all else: the world lay
     prone,
As – poet-propped, in brave hexa-
     meters –
Their subject triumphed up from man
     to God.
Caius Octavius Cæsar the August –
Where was escape from his prepotency?
I judge I may have passed – how many
     piles
Of structure dropt like doles from his
     free hand
To Rome on every side? Why, right and
     left,
For temples you've the Thundering
     Jupiter,
Avenging Mars, Apollo Palatine:
How count Piazza, Forum – there's a
     third
All but completed. You've the Theatre
Named of Marcellus – all his work,
     such work! –
One thought still ending, dominating
     all –
With warrant Varius sang 'Be Cæsar
     God!'
By what a hold arrests he Fortune's
     wheel,
Obtaining and retaining heaven and
     earth
Through Fortune, if you like, but
     favour – no!
For the great deeds flashed by me, fast
     and thick
As stars which storm the sky on
     autumn nights –
Those conquests! but peace crowned
     them, – so, of peace!

Count up his titles only – these, in few –
Ten years Triumvir, Consul thirteen
    times,
Emperor, nay – the glory topping all –
Hailed Father of his Country, last and
    best
Of titles, by himself accepted so:
And why not? See but feats achieved in
    Rome –
Not to say, Italy – he planted there
Some thirty colonies – but Rome itself
All new-built, 'marble now, brick
    once,' he boasts:
This Portico, that Circus. Would you
    sail?
He has drained Tiber for you: would
    you walk?
He straightened out the long Flaminian
    Way.
Poor? Profit by his score of donatives!
Rich – that is, mirthful? Half-a-hundred
    games
Challenge your choice! There's Rome –
    for you and me
Only? The centre of the world besides!
For, look the wide world over, where
    ends Rome?
To sunrise? There's Euphrates – all
    between!
To sunset? Ocean and immensity:
North, – stare till Danube stops you:
    South, see Nile,
The Desert and the earth-upholding
    Mount.
Well may the poet-people each with
    each
Vie in his praise, our company of
    swans,
Virgil and Horace, singers – in their
    way –
Nearly as good as Varius, though less
    famed:
Well may they cry, 'No mortal, plainly
    God!'

Thus to myself myself said, while I
    walked:

Or would have said, could thought
    attain to speech,
Clean baffled by enormity of bliss
The while I strove to scale its heights
    and sound
Its depths – this masterdom o'er all the
    world
Of one who was but born, – like you,
    like me,
Like all the world he owns, – of flesh
    and blood.
But he – how grasp, how gauge his own
    conceit
Of bliss to me near inconceivable?
Or – since such flight too much makes
    reel the brain –
Let's sink – and so take refuge, as it
    were,
From life's excessive altitude – to life's
Breathable wayside shelter at its base!
If looms thus large this Cæsar to myself
    – Of senatorial rank and somebody –
How must he strike the vulgar nameless
    crowd,
Innumerous swarm that's nobody at all?
Why, – for an instance, – much as yon
    gold shape
Crowned, sceptred, on the temple
    opposite –
Fulgurant Jupiter – must daze the sense
Of – say, yon outcast begging from its
    step!
What, anti-Cæsar, monarch in the mud,
As he is pinnacled above thy pate?
Ay, beg away! thy lot contrasts full well
With his whose bounty yields thee this
    support –
Our Holy and Inviolable One,
Cæsar, whose bounty built the fane
    above!
Dost read my thought? Thy garb, alack,
    displays
Sore usage truly in each rent and stain –
Faugh! Wash though in Suburral 'Ware
    the dogs
Who may not so disdain a meal on
    thee!

What, stretchest forth a palm to catch
    my alms?
Aha, why yes: I must appear – who
    knows? –
I, in my toga, to thy rags and thee –
Quæstor – nay, Ædile, Censor – Pol!
    perhaps
The very City-Prætor's noble self!
As to me Cæsar, so to thee am I?
Good: nor in vain shall prove thy
    quest, poor rogue!
Hither – hold palm out – take this
    quarter-as!

And who did take it? As he raised his
    head,
(My gesture was a trifle – well, abrupt),
Back fell the broad flap of the peasant's-
    hat,
The homespun cloak that muffled half
    his cheek
Dropped somewhat, and I had a glimpse
    – just one!
One was enough. Whose – whose might
    be the face?
That unkempt careless hair – brown,
    yellowish –
Those sparkling eyes beneath their
    eyebrows' ridge
(Each meets each, and the hawk-nose
    rules between)
– That was enough, no glimpse was
    needed more!
And terrifyingly into my mind
Came that quick-hushed report was
    whispered us,
'They do say, once a year in sordid
    garb
He plays the mendicant, sits all day
    long,
Asking and taking alms of who may
    pass,
And so averting, if submission help,
Fate's envy, the dread chance and
    change of things
When Fortune – for a word, a look, a
    nought –

Turns spiteful and – the petted lioness –
Strikes with her sudden paw, and
    prone falls each
Who patted late her neck superiorly,
Or trifled with those claw-tips velvet-
    sheathed.'
'He's God!'shouts Lucius Varius Rufus:
    'Man
And worms'-meat any moment!' mutters
    low
Some Power, admonishing the mortal-
    born.

Ay, do you mind? There's meaning in
    the fact
That whoso conquers, triumphs, enters
    Rome,
Climbing the Capitolian, soaring thus
To glory's summit, – Publius, do you
    mark –
Ever the same attendant who, behind,
Above the Conqueror's head supports
    the crown
All-too-demonstrative for human wear,
– One hand's employment – all the
    while reserves
Its fellow, backward flung, to point
    how, close
Appended from the car, beneath the
    foot
Of the up-borne exulting Conqueror,
Frown – half-descried – the instruments
    of shame,
The malefactor's due. Crown, now –
    Cross, when?

Who stands secure? Are even Gods so
    safe?
Jupiter that just now is dominant –
Are not there ancient dismal tales how
    once
A predecessor reigned ere Saturn came,
And who can say if Jupiter be last?
Was it for nothing the grey Sibyl wrote
'Cæsar Augustus regnant, shall be born
In blind Judæa' – one to master him,

Him and the universe? An old-wife's
      tale?

Bath-drudge! Here, slave! No cheating!
      Our turn next.
No loitering, or be sure you taste the
      lash!
Two strigils, two oil-drippers, each a
      sponge!

## Development

My Father was a scholar and knew Greek.
When I was five years old, I asked him
      once
'What do you read about?'
                  'The siege of Troy.'
'What is a siege and what is Troy?'
                           Whereat
He piled up chairs and tables for a town,
Set me a-top for Priam, called our cat
– Helen, enticed away from home (he
      said)
By wicked Paris, who couched
      somewhere close
Under the footstool, being cowardly,
But whom – since she was worth the
      pains, poor puss –
Towzer and Tray, – our dogs, the
      Atreidai, – sought
By taking Troy to get possession of
– Always when great Achilles ceased to
      sulk,
(My pony in the stable) – forth would
      prance
And put to flight Hector – our page-
      boy's self.
This taught me who was who and what
      was what:
So far I rightly understood the case
At five years old: a huge delight it proved
And still proves – thanks to that
      instructor sage
My Father, who knew better than turn
      straight
Learning's full flare on weak-eyed
      ignorance,

Or, worse yet, leave weak eyes to grow
      sand-blind,
Content with darkness and vacuity.

It happened, two or three years afterward,
That – I and playmates playing at
      Troy's Siege –
My Father came upon our make-believe.
'How would you like to read yourself
      the tale
Properly told, of which I gave you first
Merely such notion as a boy could
      bear?
Pope, now, would give you the precise
      account
Of what, some day, by dint of
      scholarship,
You'll hear – who knows? – from
      Homer's very mouth.
Learn Greek by all means, read the
      "Blind Old Man,
Sweetest of Singers" – *tuphlos* which
      means "blind,"
*Hedistos* which means "sweetest." Time
      enough!
Try, anyhow, to master him some day;
Until when, take what serves for
      substitute,
Read Pope, by all means!'
                  So I ran through Pope,
Enjoyed the tale – what history so true?
Also attacked my Primer, duly
      drudged,
Grew fitter thus for what was promised
      next –
The very thing itself, the actual words,
When I could turn – say, Buttmann to
      account

Time passed, I ripened somewhat: one
      fine day,
'Quite ready for the Iliad, nothing less?
There's Heine, where the big books
      block the shelf:
Don't skip a word, thumb well the
      Lexicon!'

I thumbed well and skipped nowise till
I learned
Who was who, what was what, from
Homer's tongue,
And there an end of learning. Had you
asked
The all-accomplished scholar, twelve
years old,
'Who was it wrote the Iliad?' – what a
laugh!
'Why, Homer, all the world knows: of
his life
Doubtless some facts exist: it's every-
where:
We have not settled, though, his place
of birth:
He begged, for certain, and was blind
beside:
Seven cities claimed him – Scio, with
best right,
Thinks Byron. What he wrote? Those
Hymns we have.
Then there's the "Battle of the Frogs
and Mice,"
That's all – unless they dig "Margites" up
(I'd like that) nothing more remains to
know.'

Thus did youth spend a comfortable
time;
Until – 'What's this the Germans say is
fact
That Wolf found out first? It's
unpleasant work
Their chop and change, unsettling
one's belief:
All the same, while we live, we learn,
that's sure.'
So, I bent brow o'er *Prolegomena*.
And, after Wolf, a dozen of his like
Proved there was never any Troy at all,
Neither Besiegers nor Besieged, – nay,
worse –
No actual Homer, no authentic text,
No warrant for the fiction I, as fact,
Had treasured in my heart and soul so
long –

Ay, mark you! and as fact held still, still
hold,
Spite of new knowledge, in my heart of
hearts
And soul of souls, fact's essence freed
and fixed
From accidental fancy's guardian
sheath.
Assuredly thenceforward – thank my
stars! –
However it got there, deprive who
could –
Wring from the shrine my precious
tenantry,
Helen, Ulysses, Hector and his Spouse,
Achilles and his Friend? – though Wolf
– ah, Wolf!
Why must he needs come doubting,
spoil a dream?

But then 'No dream's worth waking' –
Browning says:
And here's the reason why I tell thus
much.
I, now mature man, you anticipate,
May blame my Father justifiably
For letting me dream out my nonage
thus,
And only by such slow and sure degrees
Permitting me to sift the grain from
chaff,
Get truth and falsehood known and
named as such.
Why did he ever let me dream at all,
Not bid me taste the story in its strength?
Suppose my childhood was scarce
qualified
To rightly understand mythology,
Silence at least was in his power to
keep:
I might have – somehow –
correspondingly –
Well, who knows by what method,
gained my gains,
Been taught, by forthrights not
meanderings,

My aim should be to loathe, like
    Peleus'son,
A lie as Hell's Gate, love my wedded
    wife,
Like Hector, and so on with all the
    rest.
Could not I have excogitated this
Without believing such men really
    were?
That is – he might have put into my
    hand
The 'Ethics'? In translation, if you
    please,
Exact, no pretty lying that improves,
To suit the modern taste: no more, no
    less –
The 'Ethics': 'tis a treatise I find hard
To read aright now that my hair is grey,
And I can manage the original.
At five years old – how ill had fared its
    leaves!
Now, growing double o'er the Stagirite,
At least I soil no page with bread and
    milk,
Nor crumple, dogsear and deface –
    boys' way.

## Rephan

Suggested by a very early recollection of
a prose story by the noble woman and
imaginative writer, Jane Taylor, of
Norwich [actually Ongar.]        R. B.

How I lived, ere my human life began
In this world of yours, – like you, made
    man, –
When my home was the Star of my
    God Rephan?

Come then around me, close about,
World-weary earth-born ones! Darkest
    doubt
Or deepest despondency keeps you out?

Nowise! Before a word I speak,

Let my circle embrace your worn, your
    weak,
Brow-furrowed old age, youth's hollow
    cheek –

Diseased in the body, sick in soul,
Pinched poverty, satiate wealth, – your
    whole
Array of despairs! Have I read the roll?

All here? Attend, perpend! O Star
Of my God Rephan, what wonders are
In thy brilliance fugitive, faint and far!

Far from me, native to thy realm,
Who shared its perfections which
    o'erwhelm
Mind to conceive. Let drift the helm,

Let drive the sail, dare unconfined
Embark for the vastitude, O Mind,
Of an absolute bliss! Leave earth behind!

Here, by extremes, at a mean you guess:
There, all's at most – not more, not less:
Nowhere deficiency nor excess.

No want – whatever should be, is now:
No growth – that's change, and change
    comes – how
To royalty born with crown on brow?

Nothing begins – so needs to end:
Where fell it short at first? Extend
Only the same, no change can mend!

I use your language: mine – no word
Of its wealth would help who spoke,
    who heard,
To a gleam of intelligence. None
    preferred,

None felt distaste when better and worse
Were uncontrastable: bless or curse
What – in that uniform universe?

Can your world's phrase, your sense of
    things
Forth-figure the Star of my God? No
    springs,
No winters throughout its space. Time
    brings

No hope, no fear: as to-day, shall be
To-morrow: advance or retreat need we
At our stand-still through eternity?

All happy: needs must we so have been,
Since who could be otherwise? All
    serene:
What dark was to banish, what light to
    screen?

Earth's rose is a bud that's checked or
    grows
As beams may encourage or blasts
    oppose:
Our lives leapt forth, each a full-orbed
    rose –

Each rose sole rose in a sphere that
    spread
Above and below and around – rose-
    red:
No fellowship, each for itself instead.

One better than I – would prove I lacked
Somewhat: one worse were a jarring
    fact
Disturbing my faultlessly exact.

How did it come to pass there lurked
Somehow a seed of change that
    worked
Obscure in my heart till perfection
    irked? –

Till out of its peace at length grew
    strife –
Hopes, fears, loves, hates, – obscurely
    rife, –
My life grown a-tremble to turn your
    life?

Was it Thou, above all lights that are,
Prime Potency, did Thy hand unbar
The prison-gate of Rephan my Star?

In me did such potency wake a pulse
Could trouble tranquillity that lulls
Not lashes inertion till throes convulse

Soul's quietude into discontent?
As when the completed rose bursts, rent
By ardors till forth from its orb are sent

New petals that mar – unmake the
    disc –
Spoil rondure: what in it ran brave risk,
Changed apathy's calm to strife, bright,
    brisk,

Pushed simple to compound, sprang
    and spread
Till, fresh-formed, facetted, floretted,
The flower that slept woke a star instead?

No mimic of Star Rephan! How long
I stagnated there where weak and
    strong,
The wise and the foolish, right and
    wrong,

Are merged alike in a neutral Best,
Can I tell? No more than at whose
    behest
The passion arose in my passive breast,

And I yearned for no sameness but
    difference
In thing and thing, that should shock
    my sense
With a want of worth in them all, and
    thence

Startle me up, by an Infinite
Discovered above and below me – height
And depth alike to attract my flight,

Repel my descent: by hate taught love.
Oh, gain were indeed to see above
Supremacy ever – to move, remove,

Not reach – aspire yet never attain
To the object aimed at! Scarce in vain, –
As each stage I left nor touched again.

To suffer, did pangs bring the loved one
    bliss,
Wring knowledge from ignorance, –
    just for this –
To add one drop to a love-abyss!

Enough: for you doubt, you hope, O
    men,
You fear, you agonize, die: what then?
Is an end to your life's work out of ken?

Have you no assurance that, earth at
    end,
Wrong will prove right? Who made
    shall mend
In the higher sphere to which yearnings
    tend?

Why should I speak? You divine the
    test.
When the trouble grew in my pregnat
    breast
A voice said 'So wouldst thou strive,
    not rest?

'Burn and not smoulder, win by worth,
Not rest content with a wealth that'i
    dearth?
Thou art past Rephan, thy place be
    Earth!'

## Reverie

I know there shall dawn a day
   – Is it here on homely earth?
Is it yonder, worlds away,
   Where the strange and new have
    birth,
That Power comes full in play?

Is it here, with grass about,
   Under befriending trees,
When shy buds venture out,
   And the air by mild degrees
Puts winter's death past doubt?

Is it up amid whirl and roar
   Of the elemental flame
Which star-flecks heaven's dark floor,
   That, new yet still the same,
Full in play comes Power once more?

Somewhere, below, above,
   Shall a day dawn – this I know –
When Power, which vainly strove
   My weakness to o'erthrow,
Shall triumph. I breathe, I move,

I truly am, at last!
   For a veil is rent between
Me and the truth which passed
   Fitful, half-guessed, half-seen,
Grasped at – not gained, held fast.

I for my race and me
   Shall apprehend life's law:
In the legend of man shall see
   Writ large what small I saw
In my life's tale: both agree.

As the record from youth to age
   Of my own, the single soul –
So the world's wide book: one page
   Deciphered explains the whole
Of our common heritage.

How but from near to far
   Should knowledge proceed,
    increase?

Try the clod ere test the star!
　Bring our inside strife to peace
Ere we wage, on the outside, war!

So, my annals thus begin:
　With body, to life awoke
Soul, the immortal twin
　Of body which bore soul's yoke
Since mortal and not akin.

By means of the flesh, grown fit,
　Mind, in surview of things,
Now soared, anon alit
　To treasure its gatherings
From the ranged expanse – to-wit,

Nature, – earth's, heaven's wide show
　Which taught all hope, all fear:
Acquainted with joy and woe,
　I could say 'Thus much is clear,
Doubt annulled thus much: I know.

'All is effect of cause:
　As it would, has willed and done
Power: and my mind's applause
　Goes, passing laws each one,
To Omnipotence, lord of laws.'

Head praises, but heart refrains
　From loving's acknowledgment.
Whole losses outweigh half-gains:
　Earth's good is with evil blent:
Good struggles but evil reigns.

Yet since Earth's good proved good –
　Incontrovertibly
Worth loving – I understood
　How evil – did mind descry
Power's object to end pursued –

Were haply as cloud across
　Good's orb, no orb itself:
Mere mind – were it found at loss
　Did it play the tricksy elf
And from lire's gold purge the dross?

Power is known infinite:
　Good struggles to be – at best

Seems – scanned by the human sight,
　Tried by the senses' test –
Good palpably: but with right

Therefore to mind's award
　Of loving, as power claims praise?
Power – which finds nought too hard,
　Fulfilling itself all ways
Unchecked, unchanged: while barred,

Baffled, what good began
　Ends evil on every side.
To Power submissive man
　Breathes 'E'en as Thou art, abide!'
While to good 'Late-found, long-sought,

'Would Power to a plenitude
　But liberate, but enlarge
Good's strait confine, – renewed
　Were ever the heart's discharge
Of loving!' Else doubts intrude.

For you dominate, stars all!
　For a sense informs you – brute,
Bird, worm, fly, great and small,
　Each with your attribute
Or low or majestical!

Thou earth that embosomest
　Offspring of land and sea –
How thy hills first sank to rest,
　How thy vales bred herb and tree
Which dizen thy mother-breast –

Do I ask? 'Be ignorant
　Ever!' the answer clangs:
Whereas if I plead world's want,
　Soul's sorrows and body's pangs,
Play the human applicant, –

Is a remedy far to seek?
　I question and find response:
I – all men, strong or weak,
　Conceive and declare at once
For each want its cure. 'Power, speak!

'Stop change, avert decay,
　Fix life fast, banish death,

Eclipse from the star bid stay,
　Abridge of no moment's breath
One creature! Hence, Night, hail, Day!

What need to confess again
　No problem this to solve
By impotence? Power, once plain
　Proved Power, – let on Power devolve
Good's right to co-equal reign!

Past mind's conception – Power!
　Do I seek how star, earth, beast,
Bird, worm, fly, gained their dower
　For life's use, most and least?
Back from the search I cower.

Do I seek what heals all harm,
　Nay, hinders the harm at first,
Saves earth? Speak, Power, the charm!
　Keep the life there unamerced
By chance, change, death's alarm!

As promptly as mind conceives,
　Let Power in its turn declare
Some law which wrong retrieves,
　Abolishes everywhere
What thwarts, what irks, what grieves!

Never to be! and yet
　How easy it seems – to sense
Like man's – if somehow met
　Power with its match – immense
Love, limitless, unbeset

By hindrance on every side!
　Conjectured, nowise known,
Such may be: could man confide
　Such would match – were Love but
　　shown
Stript of the veils that hide –

Power's self now manifest!
　So reads my record: thine,
O world, how runs it? Guessed
　Were the purport of that prime line,
Prophetic of all the rest!

'In a beginning God
　Made heaven and earth.' Forth
　　flashed
Knowledge: from star to clod
　Man knew things: doubt abashed
Closed its long period.

Knowledge obtained Power praise.
　Had Good been manifest,
Broke out in cloudless blaze,
　Unchequered as unrepressed,
In all things Good at best –

Then praise – all praise, no blame –
　Had hailed the perfection. No!
As Power's display, the same
　Be Good's – praise forth shall flow
Unisonous in acclaim!

Even as the world its life,
　So have I lived my own –
Power seen with Love at strife,
　That sure, this dimly shown,
– Good rare and evil rife.

Whereof the effect be – faith
　That, some far day, were found
Ripeness in things now rathe,
　Wrong righted, each chain unbound,
Renewal born out of scathe.

Why faith – but to lift the load,
　To leaven the lump, where lies
Mind prostrate through knowledge owed
　To the loveless Power it tries
To withstand, how vain! In flowed

Ever resistless fact:
　No more than the passive clay
Disputes the potter's act,
　Could the whelmed mind disobey
Knowledge the cataract.

But, perfect in every part,
　Has the potter's moulded shape,
Leap of man's quickened heart,
　Throe of his thought's escape,
Stings of his soul which dart

Through the barrier of flesh, till keen
   She climbs from the calm and clear,
Through turbidity all between,
   From the known to the unknown
      here,
Heaven's 'Shall be,' from Earth's 'Has
      been'?

Then life is – to wake not sleep,
   Rise and not rest, but press
From earth's level where blindly creep
   Things perfected, more or less,
To the heaven's height, far and steep,

Where, amid what strifes and storms
   May wait the adventurous quest,
Power is Love – transports, transforms
   Who aspired from worst to best,
Sought the soul's world, spurned the
      worms'.

I have faith such end shall be:
   From the first, Power was – I knew.
Life has made clear to me
   That, strive but for closer view,
Love were as plain to see.

When see? When there dawns a day,
   If not on the homely earth,
Then yonder, worlds away,
   Where the strange and new have
      birth,
And Power comes full in play.

## Epilogue

At the midnight in the silence of the
      sleep-time,
   When you set your fancies free,
Will they pass to where – by death,
      fools think, imprisoned –
Low he lies who once so loved you,
      whom you loved so,
            – Pity me?

Oh to love so, be so loved, yet so
      mistaken!
   What had I on earth to do
With the slothful, with the mawkish,
      the unmanly?
Like the aimless, helpless, hopeless,
      did I drivel
            – Being – who?

One who never turned his back but
      marched breast forward,
   Never doubted clouds would break,
Never dreamed, though right were
      worsted, wrong would triumph,
Held we fall to rise, are baffled to fight
      better,
            Sleep to wake.

No, at noonday in the bustle of man's
      work-time
   Greet the unseen with a cheer!
Bid him forward, breast and back as
      either should be,
'Strive and thrive!' cry 'Speed, – fight
      on, fare ever
            There as here!'

# A CHRONOLOGICAL LIST OF ROBERT BROWNING'S POEMS AND PLAYS

**1833**
PAULINE: A Fragment of a Confession.
**1835**
PARACELSUS.
**1837**
STRAFFORD: An Historical Tragedy.
**1840**
SORDELLO.
**1841**
Bells and Pomegranates, No. I, PIPPA PASSES.
**1842**
Bells and Pomegranates, No. II, KING VICTOR AND KING CHARLES.
**1842**
Bells and Pomegranates, No. III, DRAMATIC LYRICS.
Cavalier Tunes –
    1  Marching Along.
    2  Give a Rouse.
    3  My Wife Gertrude.[Afterwards called 'Boot and Saddle'.]
Italy and France –
    1  Italy. [Afterwards called 'My Last Duchess'.]
    2  France. [Afterwards called 'Count Gismond'.]
Camp and Cloister –
    1  Camp (French). [Afterwards called 'Incident of the French Camp'.]
    2.  Cloister (Spanish). [Afterwards called 'Soliloquy of the Spanish Cloister'.]
In a Gondola.
Artemis Prologizes.
Waring.
Queen-Worship –
    1  Rudel and the Lady of Tripoli.
    2  Cristina.
Madhouse Cells –
    1  [Johannes Agricola.]
    [Afterwards called 'Johannes Agricola in Meditation', was first printed in *The Monthly Repository*, vol. x, N.S. 1836, pp. 45, 46.]
    2  [Porphyria.] [Afterwards called 'Porphyria's Lover', was first printed in *The Monthly Repository*, vol. x, N.S. 1836. pp. 43, 44.]
Through the Metidja to Abd-el-Kadr, 1842.
The Pied Piper of Hamelin.
**1843**
Bells and Pomegranates, No. IV, THE RETURN OF THE DRUSES: A Tragedy in Five Acts.
**1843**
Bells and Pomegranates, No. V, A BLOT IN THE 'SCUTCHEON: A Tragedy in Three Acts.
**1844**
Bells and Pomegranates, No. VI, COLOMBE'S BIRTHDAY: A Play in Five Acts.
**1845**
Bells and Pomegranates, No. VII, DRAMATIC ROMANCES AND LYRICS –
How they brought the Good News from Ghent to Aix.
Pictor Ignotus. Florence, 15—.
Italy in England. [Afterwards called 'The Italian in England'.]
England in Italy. [Afterwards called 'The Englishman in Italy'.]
The Lost Leader.
The Lost Mistress.
Home-Thoughts from Abroad (I. 'Oh to be in England.' II. 'Here's to Nelson's Memory.' [Afterwards printed as the third section of 'Nationality in Drinks'.] III. 'Nobly Cape St Vincent.') [Afterwards called 'Home-Thoughts from the Sea'.]

The Tomb at St Praxed's.
[Afterwards called 'The Bishop
orders his Tomb in St Praxed's
Church', was first printed in
*Hood's Magazine*, vol. iii, March
1845, pp. 237–239.]
Garden Fancies –
1 The Flower's Name. [First
printed in *Hood's Magazine*, vol. ii,
July 1844, pp. 45–48.]
2. Sibrandus Schafnaburgensis.
[First printed in *Hood's Magazine*,
vol. ii, July 1844, pp. 45–48.]
France and Spain –
1 The Laboratory (Ancien
Régime). [First printed in *Hood's
Magazine*, vol. i, June 1844. pp.
513, 514.]
2 The Confessional.
The Flight of the Duchess. [Sections
1 to 9, first printed in *Hood's
Magazine*, vol. iii. April 1845, pp.
313–318.]
Earth's Immortalities.
Song, 'Nay but you, who do not love
her'.
The Boy and the Angel. [First
printed in *Hood's Magazine*, vol. ii,
August 1844, pp. 140–142.]
Night and Morning (I. Night,
[Afterwards called 'Meeting at
Night'.] II. Morning). [Afterwards
called 'Parting at Morning'.]
Claret and Tokay. [Afterwards
printed as the first and second
sections of 'Nationality in
Drinks'.]
Saul. [First part only (sections 1–9);
the second part was added and
included with it in 'Men and
Women', 1855, vol. ii, p. 111.]
Time's Revenges.
The Glove.
**1846**
Bells and Pomegranates, No. VIII and
last. LURIA; and A SOUL'S
TRAGEDY.

**1850**
CHRISTMAS-EVE AND EASTER-DAY.
**1855**
MEN AND WOMEN. In Two Volumes

Vol. I. *Love among the Ruins.*
A Lovers' Quarrel.
Evelyn Hope.
Up at a Villa – Down in the City. (As
Distinguished by an Italian Person
of Quality.)
A Woman's Last Word.
Fra Lippo Lippi.
A Toccata of Galuppi's.
By the Fireside.
Any Wife to Any Husband.
An Epistle Containing the Strange
Medical Experience of Karshish,
the Arab Physician.
Mesmerism.
A Serenade at the Villa.
My Star.
Instans Tyrannus.
A Pretty Woman.
'Childe Roland to the Dark Tower
Came.'
Respectability.
A Light Woman.
The Statue and the Bust.
Love in a Life.
Life in a Love.
How it Strikes a Contemporary.
The Last Ride Together.
The Patriot: An Old Story.
Master Hugues of Saxe-Gotha.
Bishop Blougram's Apology.
Memorabilia.

Vol. II. *Andrea del Sarto* (called 'The
Faultless Painter').
Before.
After.
In Three Days.
In a Year.
Old Pictures in Florence.
In a Balcony.
Saul. [First part only (sections 1–9);
the second part was added and

included with it in 'Men and Women', 1855, vol. ii, p. 111.]
'De Gustibus – '.
Women and Roses.
Protus.
Holy-Cross Day.
The Guardian Angel: A Picture at Fano.
Cleon.
The Twins. [First printed in a pamphlet entitled *Two Poems. By Elizabeth Barrett and Robert Browning*. 8vo. London, 1854.]
Popularity.
The Heretic's Tragedy. A Middle-Age Interlude.
Two in the Campagna.
A Grammarian's Funeral.
One Way of Love.
Another Way of Love.
'Transcendentalism': A Poem in Twelve Books.
Misconceptions.
One Word More. To E. B. B.

1864
DRAMATIS PERSONÆ –
James Lee. [Afterwards called 'James Lee's Wife'.]
Gold Hair: A Legend of Pornic. [First printed in *The Atlantic Monthly*, vol. xiii. May 1864. p. 596.]
The Worst of It.
Dîs aliter visum; or, Le Byron de nos Jours.
Too Late.
Abt Vogler.
Rabbi Ben Ezra.
A Death in the Desert.
Caliban upon Setebos; or, Natural Theology in the Island.
Confessions.
May and Death. [First printed in *The Keepsake* for 1857.]
Prospice. [First printed in *The Atlantic Monthly*, vol. xiii, June 1864, p. 694.]
Youth and Art.

A Face.
A Likeness.
Mr Sludge, 'The Medium'.
Apparent Failure.
Epilogue.

1864
Orpheus and Eurydice. F. Leighton. [First printed in the Catalogue of the Royal Academy Exhibition 1864, afterwards called 'Eurydice to Orpheus'.]

1868
Deaf and Dumb. [First printed in *The Poetical Works of Robert Browning*, six vols. 1868; vol. vi, p. 151.]

\*    \*    \*

*Not included in this edition.*
1868–9
THE RING AND THE BOOK. In Four Volumes.

1871
BALAUSTION'S ADVENTURE, including a Transcript from Euripides.

1871
PRINCE HOHENSTIEL-SCHWANGAU, SAVIOUR OF SOCIETY.

1872
FIFINE AT THE FAIR.

1873
RED COTTON NIGHT-CAP COUNTRY, OR TURF AND TOWERS.

1875
ARISTOPHANES' APOLOGY, including a Transcript from Euripides, being the Last Adventure of Balaustion.

1875
THE INN ALBUM.

\*    \*    \*

**1876**

PACCHIAROTTO, AND HOW HE
WORKED IN DISTEMPER: with
other Poems –
Prologue.
Of Pacchiarotto, and how he worked
in Distemper.
At the 'Mermaid'.
House.
Shop.
Pisgah-Sights – 1
Pisgah-Sights – 2
Fears and Scruples.
Natural Magic.
Magical Nature.
Bifurcation.
Numpholeptos.
Appearances.
St Martin's Summer.
Hervé Riel. [First printed in *The
Cornhill Magazine*, March 1871.]
A Forgiveness.
Cenciaja.
Filippo Baldinucci on the Privilege of
Burial.
Epilogue.

**1877**

THE AGAMEMNON OF ÆSCHYLUS
(*Not included in this edition.*)

**1878**

LA SAISIAZ. [Published together in one
volume.]

**1878**

THE TWO POETS OF
CROISIC.[Published together in
one volume.]

**1879**

DRAMATIC IDYLS
Martin Ralph.
Pheidippides.
Halbert and Hob.
Ivàn Ivànovitch.
Tray.
Ned Bratts.

**1880**

DRAMATIC IDYLS: Second Series –
[Prologue.]
Echetlos.
Clive.
Muléykeh.
Pietro of Abano.
Doctor – .
Pan and Luna.
[Epilogue.]

**1883**

JOCOSERIA
Wanting is – What?
Donald.
Solomon and Balkis.
Cristina and Monaldeschi.
Mary Wollstonecraft and Fuseli.
Adam, Lilith and Eve.
Ixion.
Jochanan Hakkadosh.
Never the Time and the Place.
Pambo.

**1884**

FERISHTAH'S FANCIES
Prologue.
  1. The Eagle.
  2. Melon-Seller.
  3. Shah Abbas.
  4. The Family.
  5. The Sun.
  6. Mihrab Shah.
  7. A Camel-Driver.
  8. Two Camels.
  9. Cherries.
 10. Plot-Culture.
 11. A Pillar at Sebzevah.
 12. A Bean-Stripe: also Apple Eating.
     Epilogue.

**1887**

PARLEYINGS WITH CERTAIN
PEOPLE OF IMPORTANCE IN
THEIR DAY. (*Not included in this
edition.*)

**1889**

ASOLANDO: FANCIES AND FACTS
[Published on December 12th,
1889, the day of Browning's death.]
Prologue.
Rosny.
Dubiety.
Now.
Humility.
Poetics.
Summum Bonum.
A Pearl, a Girl.
Speculative.
White Witchcraft.
Bad Dreams – 1
Bad Dreams – 2
Bad Dreams – 3
Bad Dreams – 4

Inapprehensiveness.
Which?
The Cardinal and the Dog.
The Pope and the Net
The Bean-Feast.
Muckle-Mouth Meg.
Arcades Ambo.
The Lady and the Painter.
Ponte dell' Angelo, Venice.
Beatrice Signorini.
Flute-Music, with an
Accompaniment.
'Imperante Augusto natus est – .
Development.
Rephan.
Reverie.
Epilogue.

# INDEX OF FIRST LINES

'Touch him ne'er so lightly, into song he broke  915
'Twas Bedford Special Assize, one daft Midsummer's Day  880

Up jumped Tokay on our table  315

Vanity, saith the preacher, vanity!  641
Verse-making was least of my virtues: I viewed with despair  967

Wanting is – what?  916
We two stood simply friend-like side by side  988
We were two lovers; let me lie by her  787
What a pretty tale you told me  858
What girl but, having gathered flowers  984
What, he on whom our voices unanimously ran  990
'What, I disturb thee at thy morning-meal  965
What is he buzzing in my ears?  732
What is it keeps Luitolfo? Night's fast falling  566
What it was struck the terror into me?  1006
What's become of Waring  489
'When I last saw Waring ... '  491
Where the quiet-coloured end of evening smiles  325
Who will, may hear Sordello's story told  146
'Why from the world,' Ferishtah smiled, 'should thanks  980
'Will you hear my story also  916
Wish no word unspoken, want no look away!  949
Woe, he went galloping into the war  983
Would it were I had been false, not you!  700
Would that the structure brave, the manifold music I build  707
['Will sprawl, now that the heat of day is best  726

Yet womanhood you reverence  993
'You are sick, that's sure' – they say  888
You blame me that I ran away?  992
You groped your way across my room i' the dear dark dead of night  952
You in the flesh and here  985
You know, we French stormed Ratisbon  468
You think so? Well, I do not. My beloved  279
You'll love me yet! – and I can tarry  273
Your ghost will walk, you lover of trees  336
You're my friend  500

# INDEX TO POEM TITLES